Gildersleeve's Latin Grammar

Gildersleeve's Latin Grammar

BY

B. L. Gildersleeve

AND

G. Lodge

FOREWORD BY

Ward W. Briggs, Jr.

COMPREHENSIVE BIBLIOGRAPHY BY

William E. Wycislo

Bolchazy-Carducci Publishers, Inc.

Mundelein, Illinois USA

Front Cover Illustration: Reconstruction of the west end of the Forum.
© 1989 John T. Davis, found in *Monumenta Romana Nostra*
Bolchazy-Carducci Publishers, Inc., 1989.

Back Cover Illustration: B. L. Gildersleeve portrait, courtesy of
Ward W. Briggs, Jr.

Gildersleeve's Latin Grammar
Author Reprint of the 1895, third edition, Macmillan & Co. Ltd.

Foreword by: Ward W. Briggs

Bibliography: © 1997 William E. Wycislo

Bolchazy-Carducci Publishers, Inc.
1570 Baskin Road
Mundelein, Illinois 60060
www.bolchazy.com

Printed in the United States of America
2020
by Kingery Printing

Hardbound: ISBN 978-0-86516-477-2
Paperback: ISBN 978-0-86516-353-9

Library of Congress Cataloging-in-Publication Data

Gildersleeve, Basil L. (Basil Lanneau), 1831–1924
[Latin grammar]
Gildersleeve's Latin grammar / by B.L. Gildersleeve and G. Lodge ; foreword by Ward W. Briggs, Jr. : comprehensive bibliography by William E. Wycislo. -- 3rd. ed.
p. cm.
Originally published: New York : Macmillan & Co., 1895.
Includes bibliographical references and indexes.
ISBN 0-86516-477-0 (alk. paper)
ISBN 0-86516-353-7 (pbk. : alk. paper)
1. Latin language--Grammar. I. Lodge, Gonzalez, 1863–1942.
II. Title
PA2087.G5 1997 97-17220
478.2'421--DC21 CIP

PREFACE

THE first edition of this LATIN GRAMMAR appeared in 1867, the second in 1872; the third edition, carefully revised and very much enlarged, is herewith presented to the public. In the preparation of this third edition the office of the senior collaborator has been chiefly advisory, except in the Syntax. In the syntax nearly everything that pertains to the history of usage has been brought together by Professor LODGE; but for all deviations from the theory of former editions we bear a joint responsibility.

A manual that has held its place, however modest, for more than a quarter of a century, hardly needs an elaborate exposition of the methods followed; but as the new grammar embraces a multitude of details that were not taken up in the old grammar, it has been thought fit that Professor LODGE should indicate the sources of the notes with which he has enriched the original work.

B. L. GILDERSLEEVE
GONZALEZ LODGE

August 1, 1895

THE following supplementary note may serve to embody a partial bibliography of the more important works used in this revision, and some necessary explanations of the method:

Fairly complete bibliographies of works on Latin Etymology and Syntax may be found in REISIG'S *Vorlesungen über lateinische Sprachwissenschaft* (new edition, by HAGEN, SCHMALZ, and LANDGRAF, 1881–1888), and in the *Lateinische Grammatik* of STOLZ and SCHMALZ (in MÜLLER'S *Handbuch der klassischen Altertumswissenschaft;* 2d edition, 1890). Important also are the Grammars of KÜHNER (1877, 1878) * and ROBY (1881, 1882); though many statements in both, but especially in the former, must be corrected in the light of more recent study. Some indications of more modern theories may be found in

* A new Historical Grammar, by STOLZ, SCHMALZ, LANDGRAF, and WAGENER, was announced by TEUBNER in 1891

the *Erläuterungen zur lateinischen Grammatik* of DEECKE (1893). Many matters of importance both in Etymology and Syntax are treated in the *Archiv für lateinische Lexicographie*, and the constructions with individual words are often well discussed in KREBS' *Antibarbarus der lateinischen Sprache* (6th edition, by SCHMALZ, 1886).

For the accentuation and pronunciation of Latin we have also CORSSEN'S *Aussprache, Vocalismus und Betonung der lateinischen Sprache* (1868, 1870), and SEELMANN'S *Die Aussprache des Latein* (1885).

For the Etymology we must refer to BÜCHELER'S *Grundriss der lateinischen Declination* (2d edition, by WINDEKILDE, 1879) and to SCHWEIZER-SIDLER'S *Lateinische Grammatik* (1888); also to many articles in various journals, most of which are given by STOLZ. Indispensable is NEUE'S *Formenlehre der lateinischen Sprache*, of which the second volume of the third edition has already appeared (1892) and the first parts of the third volume (1894), under the careful revision of WAGENER; also GEORGES' *Lexikon der lateinischen Wortformen* (1890).

For the Formation of Words and the relation of Latin forms to those of the related languages we have HENRY'S *Précis de Grammaire Comparée* and BRUGMANN'S *Grundriss der vergleichenden Grammatik*, both now accessible in translations. On these, in connection with SCHWEIZER-SIDLER, the chapter on the Formation of Words has been based.

In the historical treatment of the Syntax we must still rely in large measure on DRAEGER'S *Historische Syntax der lateinischen Sprache* (2d edition, 1878, 1881), faulty and inaccurate though it often is: many of the false statements have been corrected on the basis of more recent individual studies by SCHMALZ; but even SCHMALZ is not always correct, and many statements of his treatise have been silently emended in the present book. For the theoretical study of some problems of Latin Syntax HAASE'S *Vorlesungen über lateinische Sprachwissenschaft* (1880) should not be overlooked. Since the appearance of the second edition of SCHMALZ, in 1890, considerable progress has been made in the various journals and other publications, as may be seen from DEECKE'S summary in BURSIAN'S *Jahresbericht* for 1893. Every effort has been made to incorporate in this grammar the main results of these studies as far as practicable. We may also draw attention to the following important articles, among others, some of which are mentioned in the books above referred to:

WÖLFFLIN'S numerous articles in the *Archiv*; THIELMANN'S articles in the *Archiv* on **habēre** with Perfect Participle Passive, and on the Reciprocal Relation; LANDGRAF'S articles on the *Figura Etymologica*, in the second volume of the *Acta Seminarii Erlangensis*, and on the Future Participle and the Final Dative, in the *Archiv*; HALE'S treatise on *The* **Cum** *Constructions*, attacking the theories of HOFFMANN (*Lateinische Zeitpartikeln*, 1874) and LÜBBERT (*Die Syntax von* **Quom**, 1869);

HOFFMANN's reply to HALE (1891), and WETZEL's *Der Streit zwischen* HOFFMANN *und* HALE (1892); DAHL's *Die lateinische Partikel* **ut** (1882), with GUTJAHR–PROBST's *Der Gebrauch von* **ut** *bei Terenz* (1888); ZIMMERMANN's article on **quod** *und* **quia** *im älteren Latein* (1880); SCHERER's article on **quando,** in *Studemund's Studien;* MORRIS's articles on the *Sentence Question in Plautus and Terence* in the A.J.P. (vols. x. and xi.); HALE's articles on the *Sequence of Tenses* in the A.J.P. (vols. viii. and ix.), containing a discussion of the earlier Literature; ELMER's articles on *the Latin Prohibitive* in A.J.P. (vol. xv.)

A bibliography of the treatises on Prosody and Versification may be found in GLEDITSCH's treatise in the second volume of MÜLLER's *Handbuch;* this, with PLESSIS' *Métrique Grecque et Latine* (1889), has been made the basis of the chapter on Prosody; but in the treatment of early metres, regard has been had to KLOTZ (*Altrömische Metrik,* 1890), and to LINDSAY's recent papers on the Saturnian in the A.J.P. (vol. xiv.). In the matter of the order of words we have followed WEIL's treatise on the Order of Words, translated by SUPER (1887).

The question of the correct measurement of hidden quantities is still an unsettled one in Latin; for the sake of consistency the usage of MARX, *Hülfsbüchlein für die Aussprache der lateinischen Vokale in positionslangen Silben* (2d edition, 1889) has been followed.

The quotations have been made throughout from the Teubner Text editions except as follows: *Plautus* is cited from the Triumvirate edition of RITSCHL; *Vergil* from the Editio Maior of RIBBECK; *Ovid* and *Terence* from the Tauchnitz Texts; *Horace* from the Editio Minor of KELLER and HOLDER; *Lucretius* from the edition of MUNRO; *Ennius* and *Lucilius* from the editions of L. MÜLLER; fragmentary Scenic Poets from the edition of RIBBECK. Special care has been taken to make the quotations exact both in spelling and wording; and any variation in the spelling of individual words is therefore due to the texts from which the examples are drawn.

Where it has been necessary to modify the quotations in order to make them suitable for citation, we have enclosed within square brackets words occurring in different form in the text, and in parentheses words that have been inserted; where the passage would not yield to such treatment, *Cf.* has been inserted before the reference. We have not thought it necessary to add the references in the Prosody except in the case of some of the citations from early Latin.

In the spelling of Latin words used out of quotation, as a rule **u** and **v** have been followed by **o** rather than by **u**; but here the requirements of clearness and the period of the language have often been allowed to weigh. Otherwise we have followed in the main BRAMBACH's *Hülfsbuchlein für lateinische Rechtschreibung* (translation by McCABE, 1877). G. L.

CONTENTS

ETYMOLOGY

SECTION

Conjugation, 127; Deponents, 128; Periphrastic, 129; Notes, 130, 131. Formation of the Stems, 132–135; Change in Conjugation, 136; List of Verbs, 137–167. Irregular Verbs, 168–174; **īre**, 169, 2; **quīre, nequīre**, 170; **ferre**, 171; **edere**, 172; **fierī**, 173; **velle, nōlle, mālle**, 174; Defective Verbs, 175.

Formation of Words 176–200

Simple Words, 179–192; Substantives, 180, 181; Adjectives, 182; Substantives without Suffixes, 183; Suffixes, 184–189; Verbs, 190–192; Compound Words, 193–200; Substantives, 194–198; Verbs, 199, 200.

SYNTAX

Simple Sentence 202–471

Subject, 203, 204; Predicate, 205–209; Concord, 210, 211; Voices, 212–221. Tenses, 222–252; Present, 227–230; Imperfect, 231–234; Perfect, 235–240; Pluperfect, 241; Future, 242, 243; Future Perfect, 244, 245; Periphrastic, 246–251; Tenses in Letters, 252. Moods, 253–283; Indicative, 254; Subjunctive, 255–265; Imperative, 266–275; Tenses in Moods and Verbal Substantives, 276–283.

Simple Sentence Expanded 284–471

Multiplication of the Subject 285–287

Qualification of the Subject 288–325

Adjectives, 289–303; Numerals, 292–295; Comparatives and Superlatives, 296–303; Pronouns, 304–319; Personal, 304; Demonstrative, 305–307; Determinative and Reflexive, 308–311; Possessive, 312; Indefinite, 313–319; Apposition, 320–325; Predicative Attribution and Apposition, 325.

Multiplication of Predicate 326

Qualification of Predicate 327–449

The Cases 328–418

Accusative, 328–343; Dative, 344–359; Genitive, 360–383; Ablative, 384–410; Locative, 411; Prepositions, 412–418; with Accusative, 416; with Ablative, 417; with Accusative and Ablative, 418.

Infinitive 419–424

Subject, 422; Object, 423; Predicate, 424.

PROSODY

FOREWORD TO GILDERSLEEVE'S LATIN GRAMMAR

> Grammar, as has often been noticed, has a special fascination for Americans. . . . and it has been ill-naturedly said that, not unlike the Romans, we had a grammar before we had a literature. Rightly interpreted, grammar is the culmination of philological study, and not its rudiment; and as one whose chief philological work has lain in one domain of grammar, I am not disposed to underrate its importance. No study of literature can yield its highest result without the close study of language, and consequently the close study of grammar. The lyric glorification of a misunderstood text does not commend itself to a sober mind; and it often happens that those who sneer at the deadness of the mere grammarian mistake disdain of the interpreter of the beautiful for indifference to the beautiful itself. There are doubtless those who turn the strings of the poet's lyre into clotheslines for airing grammatical notions, but there are others who thrill to the antique music with an exquisite delight that the uninitiated can never know. In fact, those who frankly resort to translation—and translation is becoming more and more an art—are far more congenial to true scholars than those whose only object in dealing with the classics is to show their own mastery of phrase, which too many mistake for mastery of theme.
>
> "Classical Studies in America," *Selected Classical Papers of Basil Lanneau Gildersleeve*, edited by Ward W. Briggs, Jr. [Atlanta: Scholars Press, 1992] 147.

Gildersleeve's Latin Grammar arose out of the Civil War and the perception by Southerners that Northern textbooks exercised excessive control over their education. As early as 1828 the Charlestonian editor and proponent of the classics Hugh Swinton Legaré (1797–1843) wrote of Columbia University's Charles Anthon (1797–1867), producer of the most extensive and popular series of classical texts of his day, "Who can estimate the injury done to classical learning by the use of Anthon's editions? Their inevitable effect is to make superficial scholars." (Michael O'Brien, *A Character of Hugh Legaré* [Knoxville: U. of Tennessee Press, 1985] 311). Before the war, the South lacked the great publishing houses, its scholars were disinclined to publish, and great libraries were scarce; during the war, the blockade of Southern ports, the shortage of paper, and the general disruption of life during the war made the production of any books, let alone textbooks, difficult, if not impossible. Nevertheless, in 1863 a new group called the Educational Association of the Confederate States of America met in Columbia, South Carolina, to address the concerns of Southerners obliged to use foreign or (worse) Northern textbooks. Writing after the war, Gildersleeve put the situation thus:

> For your true teacher should himself be an inquirer; and if he writes a book on the department that he teaches, he will find in his own spirit an increasing tendency to dogmatism, which is fossildom. And hence it is rather an advantage to our Professors that they have not devoted themselves as a body to book-making; it is an honor to them that they have not devoted themselves to such book-making as disgraces the literary market of the country. To Davies, to Anthon, to Owens, to Bullions, the North is welcome—oh! how heartily welcome; and the time is coming when the vast bulk of such manufactures must be kept at home, for want of a foreign market. True scholarship knows no parallels of latitude, no degrees of longitude; but the combination of sectional spirit with pretentious sciolism which characterizes so many of the Northern textbooks, has roused the Southern mind to greater vigilance and more severe criticism, so that even the better class of school-books of Northern parentage must undergo a more rigid scrutiny than heretofore, and encounter a livelier competition with foreign works and with productions of Southern growth. . . . we do not intend to permit the control of our educational interests to be wrested from our hands without a struggle and without an appeal.
>
> "Our Southern Colleges," *New Eclectic Magazine* 5 (Aug. 1869): 214–9

The first work of American classical scholarship to be taken seriously by Europeans was *Syntax of the Moods and Tenses of the Greek Verb* (1860) by Gildersleeve's classmate in Germany, William Watson Goodwin (1831–1912), Eliot Professor of Greek at Harvard. In the South, there were no Greek books of any consequence and during the war, only two Latin grammars were published, both in North Carolina: one, by Leonhard Schmitz, was imported from Scotland and published in Wilmington; the other, by William

Bingham (1835–1873), was published in Chapel Hill. Neither author had the background of Basil Lanneau Gildersleeve (1831–1924), professor of Greek at the University of Virginia.

Born in Charleston, South Carolina, Gildersleeve had graduated third in his class at Princeton in 1849 and been one of the first Americans to receive a Ph.D. from Göttingen (1853) in that feverish decade before the war. His classmates Goodwin and George M. Lane (1823–1897) of Harvard also took doctorates from Göttingen in this period and both wrote important works on grammar. Gildersleeve left the heady Olympus populated by August Böckh, Friedrich Ritschl, F.W. Schneidewin, and Karl Friedrich Hermann to find no prospects for employment in his provincial native land, save that of a private tutor to a family in the low country of South Carolina.

The appointment to the University of Virginia came in 1856 and Gildersleeve immediately set about inculcating the lessons of German philology into the minds of young Southerners. He began to write a Greek syntax developing his own system of categories fleshed out with his own examples. But the War deranged his plans, and a bullet wound suffered in battle during the fall of 1864 laid him up for nearly a year before he could return to his teaching and writing. In 1866 he found himself with a wife, intending to start a family in a state whose economy and manpower had been ravaged by the war. He needed an income-producing book and Greek was nowhere nearly as popular as Latin. As we have seen, he also believed firmly in Southerners producing textbooks for their own region.

In the year after the war, the New York publisher Charles B. Richardson took up the idea of a Southern textbook series. He contracted for and advertized a number of forthcoming textbooks by prominent Southern military and academic men. As Gildersleeve tells it:

> Among the Southern men there were those who had been trained in the best Northern schools, in the best European schools. . . . they set to work to create a Southern literature, to make textbooks for the rising generation. It was, as we look at it now, a pitiful business. We were a breed of politicians and fighters. A Northern business man who had published an *Army and Navy Journal,* or something of the sort, during the war, when he found his occupation gone, tried to exploit the local patriotism of the South by getting up a series of Southern textbooks, with results that will not be forgotten

> by those who invested their money or their time in the venture. . . . We indited scathing reviews of bad Northern textbooks. We should have been better employed in improving our own.
>
> "The Hazards of Reviewing," *Nation* 101 (1915): 49

In 1867 Richardson published Gildersleeve's *Latin Grammar* in 1867 and Matthew Fontaine Maury's (1806–1873) *Physical Geography*. Unfortunately, this edition "was so wretchedly printed and in every way so immature that I did not venture to submit it to the inspection of German scholars." (*The Letters of Basil Lanneau Gildersleeve*, ed. Ward Briggs [Baltimore: Johns Hopkins University Press, 1987] 43). He must have been relieved when in 1868 Richardson sold his operation to the University Publishing Company, founded in New York in that year with support from Horace Greeley and August Belmont of New York as well as Johns Hopkins of Baltimore, and others. The director and longtime vice-president was Gen. John B. Gordon (1832–1904), under whom Gildersleeve was serving when he was wounded in 1864. Jefferson Davis was an early stockholder.

In 1871, Gildersleeve found himself with two small children and more in need of a supplement to his salary than ever. Over the next few years he developed for the University Publishing Co. the Gildersleeve Latin Series, which began with *A Latin Exercise-Book* (1871) followed by a revision of his *Latin Grammar* (1872), *A Latin Reader* (1875), and *A Latin Primer* (1875). The series was the anchor of the firm's Latin offerings (it never offered Greek texts). In 1892 the company was reorganized by C.L. Patton and in 1895 the third edition of the *Grammar* appeared, revised and enlarged by Gonzalez Lodge (1863–1942) (Gildersleeve described his role as "chiefly advisory.").

As early as 1854, Gildersleeve had acknowledged not only the need for Southern textbooks, but also the Southerner's innate affinity for grammatical study: "The host of school-books published at the North, go for nothing in the philological account. We must wake to higher efforts, for which we are well adapted by the quick conception, love of classic form and instinctive rejection of extravagance, which are our birthright" ("Necessity of the Classics" *Selected Papers*, 17). His first love and chief fame was always Greek grammar, not Latin, but in this early stage of his career, he abandoned his Greek syntax "for good and sufficient reasons." (*A Syntax of Classical Greek from Homer to Demosthenes* Second Part, with Charles William Emil Miller [New York: American Book Co., 1911] iii). He would, of course, achieve his greatest fame in Europe as a distinctively American Hellenist, called by one German reviewer "the Mark Twain of Greek syntax" and noted by a French reviewer for his "humor Yankee." He nervously sent a copy of the 1872 edition to a German friend with this caveat: "I am not by any means easy about it. The fact is, for the last seventeen years I have devoted nearly all my time to the study of Greek and in my Latin Grammar I have done little more than apply my Greek categories to the little I know about Latin" (*Letters*, 43).

Characteristically, he saw his Latin series as unsuccessful: "My own elementary books have been decided failures," he wrote, and "My school books have yielded me little except labor and sorrow." (*Letters*, 225 and 242, n. 2). Reviewers thought otherwise. "Compare his work with any other treatise hitherto in use," said the *Southern Review*, "and its superiority will be manifest." The *Southern Magazine* in 1872 noted the clarity and fullness of the treatment of moods and *oratio obliqua* by the author, who "stands in the very first rank of classical scholars in the country." By 1906 the *Athenaeum* of London would say "Probably the nearest approach of late years to a standard Latin grammar has been the book by Profs. Gildersleeve and Lodge." The surest proof of the enduring quality of his *Latin Grammar* is the fact that you hold it now in your hands, as have members of every generation since its first publication, while his contemporary Albert Harkness's (1822–1907) *Latin Grammar for Schools and Colleges* (New York, 1864, rev. 1898) and his German classmate George M. Lane's *Latin Grammar for Schools and Colleges* (New York, 1898) are long forgotten.

Too often we are presented with a dichotomy: we study grammar or we read literature. There was no such mutual exclusivity for Gildersleeve the teacher or for Gildersleeve the man, since he believed that the intensive study of grammar yielded a broadened experience of culture: "Side by side, unless I err, side by side with the retrenchment of the grammatical element in the school runs a tendency to widen the range of reading, and even the post-classic periods of Greek and Roman literature are receiving more and more attention from year to year. The study of literature gains, the study of humanity gains, and grammar need not lose." ("Classical Studies in America," *Selected Papers*, 148).

Ward Briggs
Columbia, South Carolina
9 January 1997

LATIN GRAMMAR.

ETYMOLOGY.

Alphabet.

1. THE Latin alphabet has twenty-three letters :

A B C D E F G H I K L M N O P Q R S T V X Y Z

REMARKS.—1. The sounds represented by C and K were originally distinct, C having the sound of G, but they gradually approximated each other, until C supplanted K except in a few words, such as **Kalendae, Kaesō,** which were usually abbreviated, *Kal.*, *K.* The original force of C is retained only in **C.** (for **Gāius**) and **Cn.** (for **Gnaeus**).

2. J, the consonantal form of I, dates from the middle ages. V represented also the vowel **u** in the Latin alphabet ; and its resolution into two letters—V for the consonant, and U for the vowel—also dates from the middle ages. For convenience, V and U are still distinguished in this grammar.

3. Y and Z were introduced in the time of Cicero to transliterate Greek **υ** and **ζ**. In early Latin **υ** was represented by **u** (occasionally by **i** or **oi**), and **ζ** by **ss** or **s**. Z had occurred in the earliest times, but had been lost, and its place in the alphabet taken by G, which was introduced after C acquired the sound of K.

NOTE.—The Latin names for the letters were : **a, be, ce, de, e, ef, ge, ha, i, ka, el, em, en, o, pe, qu** (= **cu**), **er, es, te, u, ex** (**ix**), to be pronounced according to the rules given in 3, 7. For Y the sound was used, for Z the Greek name (zēta).

Vowels.

2. The vowels are **a, e, i, o, u, (y)** ; and are divided :

1. According to their *quality* (*i. e.*, the position of the organs used in pronunciation), into

guttural (or *back*), **a, o, u** ; *palatal* (or *front*), **e, i, (y)**.

2. According to their *quantity* or *prolongation* (*i. e.*, the time required for pronunciation), into

long, (—) ; *short*, (⏑).

REMARK.—Vowels whose quantity shifts in poetry are called *common* (see 13), and are distinguished thus :

⏑̄, by preference *short;* ⏑̄, by preference *long.*

3. Sounds of the Vowels.

ā	=	**a**	in *fa*ther.	ō	=	**o**	in b*o*ne.
ē	=	**e**	in pr*e*y.	ū	=	**oo**	in m*oo*n.
ī	=	**i**	in capr*i*ce.	ȳ	=	**u**	in sûr (French), German **ü**.

REMARK.—The short sounds are only less prolonged in pronunciation than the long sounds, and have no exact English equivalents.

Diphthongs.

4. There are but few *diphthongs* or *double sounds* in Latin. The theory of the diphthong requires that both elements be heard in a slur. The tendency in Latin was to reduce diphthongs to simple sounds ; for example, in the last century of the republic **ae** was gliding into **ē**, which took its place completely in the third century A. D. Hence arose frequent variations in spelling : as **glaeba** and **glēba**, *sod ;* so **oboedīre** and **obēdīre**, *obey ;* **faenum** (**foenum**) and **fēnum**, *hay.*

ae	=	**aye** (ăh-eh).	ei	=	**ei** in f*ei*nt (drawled).
oe	=	**oy** in b*oy*.	eu	=	**eu** in Spanish d*eu*da (**ĕh-oo**).
au	=	**ou** in *ou*r.	(ui	=	**we**, almost).

NOTE.—Before the time of the Gracchi we find **ai** and **oi** instead of **ae** and **oe.**

5. The sign ·· (*Diærĕsis*—Greek=*separation*) over the second vowel shows that each sound is to be pronounced separately : **āër**, *air ;* **Oenomaüs**, **aloë.**

Consonants.

6. Consonants are divided :

1. According to the principal *organs* by which they are pronounced, into

Labials	(lip-sounds):	**b, p,**	(**ph**), **f, v, m.**
Dentals	(tooth-sounds):	**d, t,**	(**th**), **l, n, r, s.**
Gutturals	(throat-sounds):	**g, c, k, qu,**	(**ch**), **h, n** (see 7).

NOTE.—Instead of *dental* and *guttural*, the terms *lingual* and *palatal* are often used.

2. According to their *prolongation*, into

A. *Semi-vowels :* of which

l, m, n, r, are *liquids* (**m** and **n** being *nasals*).
h is a *breathing.*
s is a *sibilant.*

B. *Mutes:* to which belong

P-mutes,	**p,**	**b,**	**(ph),**	**f,**	*labials.*
T-mutes,	**t,**	**d,**	**(th),**		*dentals.*
K-mutes,	**k, c, qu,**	**g,**	**(ch),**		*gutturals.*

Those on the same line are said to be of the *same organ.*

Mutes are further divided into

Tenuēs	(thin, smooth):	**p, t, k, c, qu,**	*hard* (surd).
Mediae	(middle):	**b, d, g,**	*soft* (sonant).
[**Aspīrātae**	(aspirate, rough):	**ph, th, ch,**]	*aspirate.*

Those on the same line are said to be of the *same order.*

The aspirates were introduced in the latter part of the second century B. C. in the transliteration of Greek words, and thence extended to some pure Latin words ; as, **pulcher, Gracchus.**

3. *Double consonants* are : **z** = **dz** in a*dz*e ; **x** = **cs** (**ks**), **gs** ; **i** and **u** between two vowels are double sounds, half vowel, half consonant.

Sounds of the Consonants.

7. The consonants are sounded as in English, with the following exceptions :

C is hard throughout = **k.**

Ch is not a genuine Latin combination (6, 2). In Latin words it is a **k** ; in Greek words a **kh,** commonly pronounced as **ch** in German.

G is hard throughout, as in *get, give.*

H at the beginning of a word is but slightly pronounced ; in the middle of a word it is almost imperceptible.

I *consonant* (**J**) has the sound of a broad **y**; nearly like **y** in *y*ule.

N has a guttural nasal sound before **c, g, q,** as in a*n*chor, a*n*guish.

Qu = **kw** (nearly) ; before **o, qu** = **c.** In early Latin **qu** was not followed by **u.** Later, when **o** was weakened to **u, qu** was replaced by **c**; thus **quom** became **cum.** Still later **qu** replaced **c,** yielding **quum.**

R is trilled.

S and **X** are always hard, as in hi*ss*, a*x*e.

T is hard throughout; never like **t** in na*t*ion.

U *consonant* (**V**) is pronounced like the vowel, but with a slur. In the third century A. D. it had nearly the sound of our **w.** In Greek it was frequently transliterated by **Οὐ**; so **Οὐαλέριος** = **Valerius.**

Phonetic Variations in Vowels and Consonants.

8. *Vowels.*

1. *Weakening.*—In the formation of words from roots or stems short vowels show a tendency to weaken ; that is, **a** tends to become **e**

and then **i**, or **o** and then **u**, while **o** tends towards **e** or **i**, and **u** towards **i**. This occurs most frequently in compound words, to a less degree in words formed by suffixes. Diphthongs are less frequently weakened and long vowels very rarely. The principal rules for these changes are as follows, but it must be remembered that to all there are more or less frequent exceptions :

A.—1. In the second part of compound words, and in reduplicated words, the root-vowel **ă** is weakened to **ĕ**, which usually passes over into **ĭ** in open syllables (11, R.), and often to **ŭ** before **l** and labial mutes : **cōn-scendō** (**scandō**); **con-cidō** (**cadō**); **dē-sultō** (**saltō**); **fefellī** (**fallō**). 2. As final vowel of the stem **ă** is weakened in the first part of a compound word, usually to **ĭ**, rarely to **ŏ** or **ŭ**: **aquili-fer** (**aquila-**); **causi-dicus** (**causa-**). 3. In or before suffixes, **ă** becomes **ĭ**: **domi-tus** (**doma-**).

NOTE.—**A** frequently resists change, especially in verbs of the First and Second Conjugations : as, **sē-parāre** (**parāre**); **circum-iacēre** (**iacēre**); so **satis-facere** (**facere**) and others.

E.—1. In the second part of compound words, root vowel **ĕ** is usually retained in a close (11, R.) syllable, and weakened to **ĭ** in an open syllable ; but it is invariably retained before **r** : **īn-flectō** (**flectō**); **ob-tineō** (**teneō**); **ad-vertō** (**vertō**). 2. In or before suffixes, and in the final syllable of a word, it also becomes **ĭ** : **geni-tor** (**gene-**); **ūn-decim** (**decem**).

I.—At the end of a word **ĭ** is changed to **ĕ** : **mare** (**mari**).

O.—1. In composition final stem-vowel **ŏ** is usually weakened to **ĭ** ; before labials sometimes to **ŭ** : **agri-cola** (**agro-**); **auru-fex** (usually **auri-fex**). 2. In suffixes, and in final syllables, it is weakened to **ĭ** : **amīci-tia** (**amīco-**); **gracili-s** (also **gracilu-s**).

U.—In composition final stem-vowel **ŭ** is usually weakened to **ĭ**; the same weakening occurs sometimes within a word or before a suffix : **mani-fēstus** (also **manu-fēstus**); **lacrima** (early **lacruma**).

AE, AU.—In the second part of a compound word root-diphthong **ae** is usually weakened to **ī**, but often there is no change ; **au** is occasionally changed to **ū** : **ex-quīrō** (**quaerō**); **con-clūdō** (**claudō**).

2. *Omission.*—Vowels are frequently omitted both in simple and compound words, either within the word (*syncope*) or at the end (*apocope*) : **dextera** and **dextra** ; **prīnceps** (for **prīmceps**, from **prīmiceps**) ; **pergō** (for **perregō**); **ut** (**utī**); **neu** (**nēve**).

3. *Epenthesis.*—Vowels are sometimes inserted to ease the pronunciation, but usually before liquids or in foreign words : **ager** (**agro-**) see 31 ; **Daphinē** (= **Daphnē**); **drachuma** (= **drachma**).

4. *Assimilation.*—Two vowels in adjoining syllables tend to become like each other; this assimilation is usually *regressive* (*i. e.*, of the first to the second), especially when **l** separates them ; it is rarely *progressive*. Compare **facilis** with **facul**, **familia** with **famulus**, **bene** with **bonus**.

5. A vowel before a liquid tends to become ŭ, less often **o** or **e**: **adulēscēns** and **adolēscēns**; **vulgus** and **volgus**; **decumus** (**decem**); compare **tempus** with **temporis**; **peperī** (from **pariō**), *etc.*

9. *Consonants.*

1. *Assimilation.*—When two consonants come together in Latin, they tend to assimilate one to the other. This assimilation is usually *regressive;* sometimes it is *progressive.* It is either *complete,* that is, the two consonants become the same; or *partial,* that is, the one is made of the *same order* or *same organ* as the other. These changes occur both in inflection and in composition, but they are especially noteworthy in the last consonant of prepositions in composition.

Scrīp-tum for **scrīb-tum** (regressive partial); **ac-cēdere** for **ad-cēdere** (regressive complete); **cur-sum** for **cur-tum** (progressive partial); **celerrimus** for **celer-simus** (progressive complete).

2. *Partial Assimilation.*—(*a*) The sonants **g** and **b**, before the surd **t**, or the sibilant **s**, often become surds (**c**, **p**); the surds **p**, **c**, **t** before liquids sometimes become sonants (**b**, **g**, **d**); the labials **p**, **b** before **n** become **m**; the labial **m** before the gutturals **c**, **q**, **g**, **h**, **i** (**j**), the dentals **t**, **d**, **s**, and the labials **f**, **v**, becomes **n**; the dental **n** before labials **p**, **b**, **m**, becomes **m**; **rēc-tum** (for **rēg-tum**); **scrīp-sī** (for **scrīb-sī**); **seg-mentum** (for **sec-mentum**); **som-nus** (for **sop-nus**); **prīn-ceps** (for **prīm-ceps**).

NOTE.—Similar is the change of **q** (**qu**) to **c** before **t** or **s**: **coc-tum** (for **coqu-tum**).

(*b*) After **l** and **r**, **t** of the suffixes **tor**, **tus**, **tum**, becomes **s** by *progressive assimilation:* **cur-sum** (for **cur-tum**).

3. *Complete Assimilation.*—There are many varieties, but the most important principle is that a mute or a liquid tends to assimilate to a liquid and to a sibilant: **puella** (**puer**); **cur-rere** (for **cur-sere**); **cēs-sī** (for **cēd-sī**); **corōlla** (**corōna**), *etc.*

4. *Prepositions.*—**Ab** takes the form **ā** before **m** or **v**, and in **ā-fuī**; appears as **au** in **au-ferō**, **au-fugiō**; as **abs** before **c**, **t**; as **as** before **p**. **Ad** is assimilated before **c**, **g**, **l**, **p**, **r**, **s**, **t**, with more or less regularity; before **gn**, **sp**, **sc**, **st**, it often appears as **ā**. **Ante** appears rarely as **anti**. **Cum** appears as **com** before **b**, **m**, **p**; **con** before **c**, **d**, **f**, **g**, **i**, **q**, **s**, **v**; **cō** before **gn**, **n**; assimilated sometimes before **l** and **r**. **Ex** becomes **ē** before **b**, **d**, **g**, **i** (**j**), **l**, **m**, **n**, **r**, **v**; **ef** or **ec**, before **f**. **In** usually becomes **im** before **b**, **m**, **p**; before **l**, **r** it is occasionally assimilated; the same holds good of the negative prefix **in**. **Ob** is usually assimilated before **c**, **f**, **g**, **p**; appears as **o** in **o-mittō**, **o-periō**, **obs** in **obs-olēscō**, and **os** in **ostendō**. **Sub** is assimilated before **c**, **f**, **g**, **p**, **r**; appears as **sus** in a few words, as **sus-cipiō**; occasionally **sū** before **s**, as **sū-spiciō**. **Trāns** sometimes becomes **trā** before **d**, **i** (**j**), **n**; **trān** before **s**. **Amb-** (inseparable) loses **b** before a consonant, and **am** is sometimes assimilated. **Circum** sometimes drops **m** before **i**. **Dis** becomes **dif** before **f**; **dir** before **a**

vowel ; **dī** before consonants, except **c, p, q, t, s,** followed by a vowel, when it is usually unchanged. The **d** of **red** and **sēd** is usually dropped before consonants.

NOTE.—In early Latin assimilation is much less common than in the classical period.

5. *Dissimilation.*—To avoid the harshness of sound when two syllables begin with the same letter, the initial letter of the one is often changed; this is true especially of liquids, but occasionally of other letters: **singu-lā-ris** (for **singu-lā-lis**); **merī-diē** (for **medī-diē**).

NOTE.—This principle often regulates the use of **-brum** or **-bulum**, and of **-crum** or **-culum** in word formation (181, 6): compare **perīculum** with **simulācrum.**

6. *Omission.*—(*a*) When a word closes with a doubled consonant or a group of consonants, the final consonant is regularly dropped in Latin ; sometimes after the preceding consonant has been assimilated to it. In the middle of a word, after a long syllable, **ss** and **ll** are simplified ; **ll** is sometimes simplified after a short vowel, which is then lengthened if the syllable is accented (*compensatory lengthening*) ; but if the syllable is unaccented, such lengthening need not take place. In this case other doubled consonants may also be simplified.

fel (for **fell**); **lac** (for **lact**); **vigil** (for **vigils**); **lapis** (for **lapid-s, lapiss**); **mīsī** (for **mīs-si**); **vīlla** and **vīlicus**; but **currus** and **cūrūlis.**

NOTE.—**X** is retained, even after **l** and **r,** as in **calx, arx**; also **ps, bs,** as in **stirps, urbs**; **ms** is found in **hiems** only.

(*b*) In the tendency to easier pronunciation consonants are often dropped both at the beginning and in the middle of a word: **stimulus** (for **stigmulus**); **pāstor** (for **pāsctor**); **āiō** (for **āhiō**); **nātus** (for **gnātus,** retained in early Latin, rarely later); **lātus** (for **tlātus**), *etc.*

7. *Epenthesis.*—Between **m** and **l, m** and **s, m** and **t,** a **p** is generated: **ex-em-p-lum** (**ex-imō**); **cōm-p-sī** (**cōmō**); **ēm-p-tus** (**emō**).

8. *Metathesis* or *transposition* of consonants occurs sometimes in Latin, especially in Perfect and Supine forms: **cernō**; Pf. **crē-vī,** *etc.*

Syllables.

10. The syllable is the unit of pronunciation ; it consists of a vowel, or a vowel and one or more consonants.

A word has as many syllables as it contains separate vowels and diphthongs.

In dividing a word into syllables, a consonant, between two vowels, belongs to the second : **a-mō,** *I love ;* **li-xa,** *a sutler.*

Any combination of consonants that can begin a word (including **mn,** under Greek influence) belongs to the following vowel; in other combinations the first consonant belongs to the preceding vowel: **a-sper,** *rough;* **fau-stus,** *lucky;* **li-brī,** *books;* **a-mnis,** *river.*

REMARKS.—1. The combinations incapable of beginning a word are (*a*) doubled consonants: **sic-cus,** *dry;* (*b*) a liquid and a consonant: **al-mus,** *fostering;* **am-bō,** *both;* **an-guis,** *snake;* **ar-bor,** *tree.*

2. Compounds are treated by the best grammarians as if their parts were separate words: **ab-igō,** *I drive off;* **rēs-pūblica,** *commonwealth.*

11. The last syllable of a word is called the *ultimate* (**ūltima,** *last*); the next to the last the *penult* (**paene,** *almost,* and **ūltima**); the one before the penult, the *antepenult* (**ante,** *before,* and **paenūltima**).

REMARK.—A syllable is said to be *open* when it ends with a vowel; *close,* when it ends with a consonant.

Quantity.

12. 1. A syllable is said to be long *by nature,* when it contains a long vowel or diphthong: **mōs,** *custom;* **caelum,** *heaven.*

REMARKS.—1. A vowel before **nf, ns, gm, gn,** is long *by nature:* **īnfēlīx,** *unlucky;* **mēnsa,** *table;* **āgmen,** *train;* **āgnus,** *lamb.* In many cases, however, the **n** has disappeared from the written word; so in some substantival terminations: **ōs** (Acc. Pl., 2d decl.), **ūs** (Acc. Pl., 4th decl.); in adjectives in **ōsus** (**fōrmōsus,** *shapely,* for **fōrmōnsus**); in the numerical termination **ēsimus** (= **ēnsimus**). See 95, N. 5.

2. Before **i** *consonant* (**j**) a vowel is long *by nature:* **Pompēius,** *Pompey;* except in compounds of **iugum,** *yoke* (**bĭ-iugus,** *two-horse*), and in a few other words.

NOTE.—From about 134 to about 74 B. C. **ā, ē, ū,** were often represented by **aa, ee, uu; ī** by **ei.** From the time of Augustus to the second century **ī** was indicated by a lengthened I. From Sulla's time until the third century long vowels (rarely, however, **ī**) were indicated by an Apex (′).

2. A syllable is said to be long *by position,* when a short vowel is followed by two or more consonants, or a double consonant: **ărs,** *art;* **cŏllum,** *neck;* **ăbrumpō,** *I break off;* **pĕr mare,** *through the sea;* **nĕx,** *murder.*

3. A syllable is said to be *short* when it contains a short vowel, which is not followed by two or more consonants: **lŏcus**, *place;* **tăbŭla**, *picture.*

Remark.—A vowel is short *by nature* when followed by another vowel, or by **nt**, **nd**: **dĕus**, *God;* **innocĕntia**, *innocence;* **amăndus**, *to be loved.*

13. A syllable ending in a short vowel, followed by a mute with **l** or **r**, is said to be *common* (**anceps**, *doubtful*) : **tenĕ-brae**, *darkness.*

Remark.—In prose such syllables are always short. In poetry they were short in early times, common in the Augustan period.

14. Every diphthong, and every vowel derived from a diphthong, or contracted from other vowels, is *long:* **saevus**, *cruel;* **conclūdō**, *I shut up* (from **claudō**, *I shut*); **cōgō** (from **co agō**), *I drive together.*

Accentuation.

15. 1. Dissyllabic words have the accent or stress on the penult: **équŏs** (= **equus**), *horse.*

2. Polysyllabic words have the accent on the penult, when the penult is long; on the antepenult, when the penult is short or common: **mandāre**, *to commit;* **mándĕre**, *to chew;* **íntēgrum**, *entire;* **circúmdare**, *to surround;* **supérstitēs**, *survivors.*

Remarks.—1. The little appendages (**enclitics**), **que**, **ve**, **ne**, add an accent to the ultimate of words accented on the antepenult: **lū́mináque**, *and lights;* **flū́mináve**, *or rivers;* **vṓmeréne?** *from a ploughshare?* Dissyllables and words accented on the penult are said to shift their accent to the final syllable before an enclitic: **egómet**, *I indeed;* **amāréve**, *or to love;* but it is more likely that the ordinary rule of accentuation was followed.

2. Compounds (not prepositional) of **facere** and **dare** retain the accent on the verbal form: **calefácit**, **vēnumdáre.**

3. Vocatives and genitives of substantives in **ius** of the second declension, as well as genitives of substantives in **ium**, retain the accent on the same syllable as the nominative: **Vergílī.**

Note.—Other exceptions will be noted as they occur. In the older language the accent was not bounded by the antepenult: **áccipiō** (**accípiō**), **cóncutiō** (**concútiō**).

Parts of Speech.

16. The Parts of Speech are the Noun (Substantive and Adjective), the Pronoun, the Verb, and the Particles (Adverb, Preposition, and Conjunction), defined as follows:

1. The *Substantive* gives a name: **vir,** *a man;* **Cocles,** *Cocles;* **dōnum,** *a gift.*

2. The *Adjective* adds a quality to the Substantive: **bonus vir,** *a* good *man.*

3. The *Pronoun* points out without describing: **hīc,** *this;* **ille,** *that;* **ego,** *I.*

4. The *Verb* expresses a complete thought, whether assertion, wish, or command; **amat,** *he loves;* **amet,** *may he love;* **amā,** *love thou!*

5. The *Adverb* shows *circumstances.*

6. The *Preposition* shows *local relation.*

7. The *Conjunction* shows *connection.*

REMARKS.—1. Substantive is short for noun-substantive, and adjective for noun-adjective. Substantives are often loosely called nouns.

2. The *Interjection* is either a mere cry of feeling: **āh**! *ah!* and does not belong to language, or falls under one of the above-mentioned classes.

3. The Particles are mainly mutilated forms of the noun and pronoun.

NOTES.—1. The difference between substantive and adjective is largely a difference of mobility; that is, the substantive is fixed in its application and the adjective is general.

2. Noun and pronoun have essentially the same inflection; but they are commonly separated, partly on account of the difference in signification, partly on account of certain peculiarities of the pronominal forms.

Inflection.

17. *Inflection* (**īnflexiō,** *bending*) is that *change* in the form of a word (chiefly in the end) which shows a change in the relations of that word. The noun, pronoun, and verb are inflected; the particles are not capable of further inflection.

The inflection of nouns and pronouns is called *declension,* and nouns and pronouns are said to be *declined.*

The inflection of verbs is called *conjugation,* and verbs are said to be *conjugated.*

The Substantive.

18. A Substantive is either *concrete* or *abstract*; *concrete* when it gives the name of a person or thing; *abstract* when it gives the name of a quality; as **amīcitia,** *friendship*.

Concrete substantives are either *proper* or *common*:

Proper when they are proper, or peculiar, to certain persons, places, or things: **Horātius,** *Horace;* **Neāpolis,** *Naples;* **Padus,** *Po.*

Common when they are common to a whole class: **dominus,** *a lord;* **urbs,** *a city;* **amnis,** *a river.*

Gender of Substantives.

19. For the names of animate beings, the gender is determined by the signification; for things and qualities, by the termination.

Names of males are masculine; names of females, feminine. Masculine: **Rōmulus; Iūppiter; vir,** *man;* **equus,** *horse.* Feminine: **Cornēlia; Iūnō; fēmina,** *woman;* **equa,** *mare.*

20. Some classes of words, without natural gender, have their gender determined by the signification:

I. All names of *months* and *winds,* most names of *rivers,* and many names of *mountains* are *masculine;* as: **Aprīlis,** *April, the opening month;* **Aquilo,** *the north wind;* **Albis,** *the River Elbe;* **Athōs,** *Mount Athos.*

Remarks.—1. Names of months, winds, and rivers were looked upon as adjectives in agreement with masculine substantives understood (**mēnsis,** *month;* **ventus,** *wind;* **fluvius, amnis,** *river*).

2. Of the rivers, **Allia, Lēthē, Matrona, Sagra, Styx** are feminine; **Albula, Acherōn, Garumna** vary, being sometimes masculine, sometimes feminine.

3. Of the mountains, **Alpēs,** *the Alps,* is feminine; so, too, sundry (Greek) names in **a** (G. **ae**), **ē** (G. **ēs**): **Aetna** (usually), **Calpē, Cyllēnē, Hybla, Īda, Ossa** (usually), **Oeta** (usually), **Rhodopē, Pholoē, Pȳrēnē,** and **Carambis, Pelōris. Pēlion** and **Sōracte** (usually), and names of mountains in **a** (G. **ōrum**), as **Maenala** (G. **Maenalōrum**), are neuter.

II. Names of *countries* (**terrae,** *fem.*), *islands* (**īnsulae,** *fem.*), *cities* (**urbēs,** *fem.*), *plants* (**plantae,** *fem.*), and *trees*

(arborēs, *fem.*), are *feminine:* **Aegyptus,** *Egypt;* **Rhodus,** *Rhodes;* **pirus,** *a pear-tree;* **abiēs,** *a fir-tree.*

REMARKS.—1. Names of countries and islands in **us** (**os**) (G. **i**) are masculine, except **Aegyptus, Chius, Chersonēsus, Cyprus, Dēlos, Ēpīrus, Lēmnos, Lesbos, Peloponnēsus, Rhodus, Samos, Bosporus** (the country).

2. Many Greek names of cities follow the termination. Towards the end of the republic many feminine names change the ending **-us** to **-um** and become neuter: **Abȳdus** and **Abȳdum, Saguntus** and **Saguntum.**

3. Most names of trees with stems in **-tro** (N. **-ter**) are masculine: **oleaster,** *wild olive;* **pīnaster,** *wild pine.* So also most shrubs: **dūmus,** *bramble-bush;* **rhūs,** *sumach.* Neuter are **acer,** *maple;* **lāser,** a plant; **papāver,** *poppy* (also masc. in early Latin); **rōbur,** *oak;* **sīler,** *willow;* **siser,** *skirret* (occasionally masc.); **sūber,** *cork-tree;* **tūber,** *mushroom.*

III. All indeclinable substantives, and all words and phrases treated as indeclinable substantives, are *neuter:* **fās,** *right;* **ā longum,** *ā long;* **scīre tuum,** *thy knowing;* **trīste valē,** *a sad "farewell."*

21. 1. Substantives which have but one form for masculine and feminine are said to be of *common* gender: **cīvis,** *citizen* (male or female); **comes,** *companion;* **iūdex,** *judge.*

2. **Substantīva mōbilia** are words of the same origin, whose different terminations designate difference of gender: **magister,** *master, teacher;* **magistra,** *mistress;* **servus, serva,** *slave* (masc. and fem.); **victor, victrīx,** *conqueror* (masc. and fem.).

3. If the male and female of animals have but one designation, **mās,** *male,* and **fēmina,** *female,* are added, when it is necessary to be exact: **pāvō mās (masculus),** *peacock;* **pāvō fēmina,** *peahen.* These substantives are called *epicene* (**ἐπίκοινα,** *utrīque generī commūnia,* common to each gender).

Number.

22. In Latin there are two numbers: the *Singular,* denoting *one;* the *Plural,* denoting *more than one.*

REMARK.—The *Dual,* denoting *two,* occurs in Latin only in two words (**duo,** *two;* **ambō,** *both*), in the nominative and vocative of the masculine and neuter.

Cases.

23. In Latin there are six cases:

1. Nominative (Case of the Subject).
   Answers: *who? what?*
2. Genitive (Case of the Complement).
   Answers: *whose? whereof?*
3. Dative (Case of Indirect Object or Personal Interest).
   Answers: *to whom? for whom?*
4. Accusative (Case of Direct Object).
   Answers: *whom? what?*
5. Vocative (Case of Direct Address).
6. Ablative (Case of Adverbial Relation).
   Answers: *where? whence? wherewith?*

NOTE.—These six cases are the remains of a larger number. The Locative (answers: *where?*), is akin to the Dative, and coincident with it in the 1st and 3d Declensions; in the 2d Declension it is lost in the Genitive; it is *often* blended with the Ablative in *form*, *regularly* in *syntax*. The Instrumental (answers: *wherewith?*), which is found in other members of the family, is likewise merged in the Ablative.

24. 1. According to their *form*, the cases are divided into *strong* and *weak*: The strong cases are Nominative, Accusative, and Vocative. The weak cases are Genitive, Dative, and Ablative.

2. According to their *syntactical use*, the cases are divided into **Cāsūs Rēctī**, or Independent Cases, and **Cāsūs Oblīquī**, or Dependent Cases. Nominative and Vocative are **Cāsūs Rēctī**, the rest **Cāsūs Oblīquī**.

25. The case-forms arise from the combination of the *case-endings* with the *stem*.

1. The stem is that which is common to a class of formations.

NOTES.—1. The stem is often so much altered by contact with the case-ending, and the case-ending so much altered by the wearing away of vowels and consonants, that they can be determined only by scientific analysis. So in the paradigm **mēnsa,** the stem is not **mēns**, but **mēnsā**, the final **ā** having been absorbed by the ending in the Dative and Ablative Plural **mēnsīs.** So **-d,** the ending of the Ablative Singular, has nearly disappeared, and the locative ending has undergone many changes (**ē, ēī, ī, ĕ**). The "crude form" it is often impossible to ascertain.

2. The root is an ultimate stem, and the determination of the root belongs to com-

parative etymology. The stem may be of any length, the root was probably a monosyllable. In **penna** the stem is **pennā-**; in **pennula, pennulā-**; in **pennātulus, pennātulo-**; the root is PET (**petna, pesna, penna**), and is found in **pet-ere,** *to fall upon, to fly at;* Greek, πέτ-ομαι, πτερόν; English, *feather*.

2. The case-endings are as follows, early forms being printed in parenthesis:

SG.—N.V.	Wanting or m. f. **-s**; n. **-m**.	PL.—N.V.	**-es** (eis, īs); **-ī**; n. **-a**.
G.	**-is** (-os, -us, -es); **-ī**.	G.	**-um** (om); **-rum** (som).
D.	**-ī** (-ē, -ei).	D.	**-bus**; **-is**.
Ac.	**-m, -em.**	Ac.	**-s** (for **-ns**); n. **-a**.
Ab.	Wanting (or **-d**); **-e**.	Ab.	**-bus**; **-is**.

Declensions.

26. There are five declensions in Latin, which are characterised by the final letter of their respective stems (*stem-characteristic*).

For practical purposes and regularly in lexicons they are also improperly distinguished by the ending of the Genitive Singular.

	STEM CHARACTERISTIC.	GENITIVE SINGULAR.
I.	**ă** (**ā**).	**ae.**
II.	**ŏ.**	**ī.**
III.	**ĭ, ŭ,** a consonant.	**ĭs.**
IV.	**ŭ.**	**ūs.**
V.	**ē.**	**ēī.**

REMARK.—The First, Second, and Fifth Declensions are called Vowel Declensions; the Third and Fourth, which really form but one, the Consonant Declension, **i** and **u** being semi-consonants.

27. The case-endings in combination with the stem-characteristics give rise to the following systems of terminations:

SINGULAR.

	I.	II.	III.
N.	**a.**	**us** (os); wanting; **um** (om).	**s**; wanting.
G.	**ae** (ās, **āī**, ai).	**ī** (eī).	**is** (us, es).
D.	**ae** (āī).	**ō** (oi).	**ī** (ēī, i).
Ac.	**am.**	**um** (om).	**em, im.**
V.	**a.**	**e**; wanting; **um** (om).	**s.**
Ab.	**ā** (**ād**).	**ō** (ōd).	**e, ī** (ēd, īd).

	IV.	V.
N. V.	**us ; ū.**	**ēs.**
G.	**ūs** (uos, uis).	**ĕī, ē** (es).
D.	**uī, ū** (uēī).	**ĕī, ē.**
Ac.	**um ; ū.**	**em.**
Ab.	**ū.**	**ē.**

PLURAL.

	I.	II.	III.
N. V.	**ae.**	**ī** (oe, ē, ēī) ; **ă.**	**ēs** (ēīs, īs) ; **a, ia.**
G.	**ārum.**	**um** (om), **ōrum.**	**um, ium.**
D. A.	**īs** (ēīs) ; **ābus.**	**īs** (ēīs), **ibus.**	**ibus.**
Ac.	**ās.**	**ōs ; ă.**	**īs, ēs ; a, ia.**

	IV.	V.
N. V.	**ūs** (ues, uus) ; **ua.**	**ēs.**
G.	**uum.**	**ērum.**
D. A.	**ubus, ibus.**	**ēbus.**
Ac.	**ūs ; ua.**	**ēs.**

NOTE.—Final -s and -m are frequently omitted in early inscriptions.

28. *General Rules of Declension.*

I. For the strong cases :

Neuter substantives have the Nominative and the Vocative like the Accusative ; in the Plural the strong cases always end in **ă.**

In the Third, Fourth, and Fifth Declensions the strong cases are alike in the Plural.

The Vocative is like the Nominative, except in the Singular of the Second Declension when the Nominative ends in **-us.**

II. For the weak cases :

The Dative and the Ablative Plural have a common form.

FIRST DECLENSION.

29. The stem ends in **ă,** which is weakened from an original **ā.** The Nominative has no ending.

SG.—N.	**mēnsa** (f.),	*the table,*	*a table.*
G.	**mēnsae,**	*of the table,*	*of a table.*
D.	**mēnsae,**	*to, for the table,*	*to, for a table.*
Ac.	**mēnsam,**	*the table,*	*a table.*
V.	**mēnsa,**	*O table !*	*table !*
Ab.	**mēnsā,**	*from, with, by, the table,*	*from, with, by, a table.*

Pl.—N.	**mēnsae,**	*the tables,*	*tables.*
G.	**mēnsārum,**	*of the tables,*	*of tables.*
D.	**mēnsīs,**	*to, for the tables,*	*to, for tables.*
Ac.	**mēnsās,**	*the tables,*	*tables.*
V.	**mēnsae,**	*O tables!*	*tables!*
Ab.	**mēnsīs,**	*from, with, by, the tables,*	*from, with, by, tables.*

Remarks.—1. The early ending of the Gen., **ās,** found in a few cases in early poets, is retained in the classical period (but not in Caesar or Livy) only in the form **familiās,** *of a family,* in combination with **pater,** *father,* **māter,** *mother,* **fīlius,** *son,* **fīlia,** *daughter,* viz.: **paterfamiliās, māterfamiliās, fīlius familiās, fīlia familiās.**

2. The Loc. Sing. is like the Genitive: **Rōmae,** *at Rome;* **mīlitiae,** *abroad.*

3. The Gen. Pl. sometimes takes the form **-um** instead of **-ārum;** this occurs chiefly in the Greek words **amphora** (*amphora, measure of tonnage*), and **drachma,** *franc*—(*Greek coin*). The poets make frequent use of this form in Greek patronymics in **-da, -dās,** and compounds of **-cola** (from **colō,** *I inhabit*) and **-gena** (from root **gen,** *beget*).

4. The ending **-ābus** is found (along with the regular ending) in the Dat. and Abl. Pl. of **dea,** *goddess,* and **fīlia,** *daughter.* In late Latin the use of this termination becomes more extended.

Notes.—1. A very few masc. substantives show Nom. Sing. in **ās** in early Latin.

2. A form of the Gen. Sing. in **āī,** subsequent to that in **ās,** is found in early inscriptions, and not unfrequently in early poets, but only here and there in classical poetry (Verg., *A.*, 3, 354, *etc.*) and never in classical prose.

3. The early ending of the Dat. **āī** (sometimes contracted into **ā**), is found occasionally in inscriptions throughout the whole period of the language.

4. The older ending of the Abl., **ād,** belongs exclusively to early Latin. Inscriptions show **ēis** for **īs** in Dat. and Abl. Pl., and once **ās** in the Dat. Plural.

30. *Rule of Gender.*—Substantives of the First Declension are feminine, except when males are meant.

Hadria, *the Adriatic,* is masculine.

SECOND DECLENSION.

31. The stem ends in **ŏ,** which in the classical period is weakened to **ŭ,** except after **ŭ** (vowel or consonant), where **ŏ** is retained until the first century A.D. In combination with the case-endings it merges into **ō** or disappears altogether. In the Vocative (except in neuters) it is weakened to **ĕ.**

The Nominative ends in **s** (m. and f.) and **m** (n.). But many masculine stems in which the final vowel, **ŏ,** is preceded by **r,** drop the (**os**) **us** and **e** of the Nominative and Vocative, and insert **ĕ** before the **r** if it was preceded by a consonant.

32. 1. Stems in **-ro**. The following stems in **-ro** do not drop the **(os) us** and **e** of the Nom. and Voc.: **erus**, *master;* **hesperus**, *evening star;* **icterus**, *jaundice;* **iūniperus**, *juniper;* **mōrus**, *mulberry;* **numerus**, *number;* **taurus**, *bull;* **vīrus**, *venom;* **umerus**, *shoulder;* **uterus**, *womb.*

NOTE.—**Socerus** is found in early Latin. Plautus uses **uterum** (n.) once.

2. In the following words the *stem* ends in **-ero** and the **e** is therefore retained throughout: **adulter**, *adulterer;* **gener**, *son-in-law;* **Līber**, *god of wine;* **puer**, *boy;* **socer**, *father-in-law;* **vesper**, *evening;* and in words ending in **-fer** and **-ger**, from **ferō**, *I bear*, and **gerō**, *I carry*, as, **sīgnifer**, *standard-bearer*, **armiger**, *armor-bearer*.

Also **Ibĕr** and **Celtibĕr** (names of nations) have in the Plural **Ibĕrī** and **Celtibĕrī.**

33. Hortus (m.), *garden;* **puer** (m.), *boy;* **ager** (m.), *field;* **bellum** (n.), *war;* are thus declined:

SG.—	N.	**hortus,**	**puer,**	**ager,**	**bellum,**
	G.	**hortī,**	**puerī,**	**agrī,**	**bellī,**
	D.	**hortō,**	**puerō,**	**agrō,**	**bellō,**
	Ac.	**hortum,**	**puerum,**	**agrum,**	**bellum,**
	V.	**horte,**	**puer,**	**ager,**	**bellum,**
	Ab.	**hortō.**	**puerō.**	**agrō.**	**bellō.**
PL.—	N.	**hortī,**	**puerī,**	**agrī,**	**bella,**
	G.	**hortōrum,**	**puerōrum,**	**agrōrum,**	**bellōrum,**
	D.	**hortīs,**	**puerīs,**	**agrīs,**	**bellīs,**
	Ac.	**hortōs,**	**puerōs,**	**agrōs,**	**bella,**
	V.	**hortī,**	**puerī,**	**agrī,**	**bella,**
	Ab.	**hortīs.**	**puerīs.**	**agrīs.**	**bellīs.**

REMARKS.—1. Stems in **-io** have Gen. Sing. for the most part in **ī** until the first century A. D., without change of accent: **ingénī** (N. **ingenium**), *of genius,* **Vergílī**, *of Vergil.* See 15, R. 3.

2. Proper names in **-ius** (stems in **-io**) have Voc. in **ī**, without change of accent: **Antōnī, Tullī, Gāī, Vergílī. Fīlius**, *son*, and **genius**, *genius*, form their Voc. in like manner: **fīlī, genī.** In solemn discourse **-us** of the Nom. is employed also for the Vocative. (See LIV. I. 24, 7.) So regularly **deus**, *God!*

3. The Loc. Sing. ends in **ī** (apparent Genitive), as **Rhodī**, *at Rhodes*, **Tarentī**, *at Tarentum.*

4. In the Gen. Pl. **-um** instead of **-ōrum** is found in words denoting coins and measures; as, **nummum**, *of moneys* (also **-ōrum**) = **sēstertium**, *of sesterces;* **dēnārium** (occasionally **-ōrum**); **talentum** (occasionally **-ōrum**); **tetrachmum**; **modium** (also **-ōrum**), *of measures;* **iūgerum**; **medimnum**; **stadium** (also **-ōrum**). Likewise in some names of persons: **deum** (also

-ōrum); **fabrum** (in technical expressions; as **praefectus fabrum,** otherwise **-ōrum**); **līberum** (also **-ōrum**); **virum** (poetical, except in technical expressions, as **triumvirum**); **socium** (also **-ōrum**). Some other examples are poetical, rare or late.

5. The Loc. Pl. is identical with the Dative: **Delphīs,** *at Delphi.*

6. **Deus,** *God,* is irregular. In addition to the forms already mentioned, it has in Nom. Pl. **deī, diī, dī**; in Dat. and Abl. Pl. **deīs, diīs, dīs.**

NOTES.—1. The ending **-ēī** for **-ī** in the Gen. Sing. is found only in inscriptions subsequent to the third Punic War.

2. **Puer,** *boy,* forms Voc. **puere** in early Latin.

3. The original Abl. ending **-d** belongs to early inscriptions.

4. In early inscriptions the Nom. Pl. ends occasionally in **ēs, ēīs, īs**: **magistrēs** (for **magistrī**) **virēīs** (for **virī**). The rare endings **oe** and **ē** (**ploirumē** for **plūrimī**) and the not uncommon ending **ēī** belong to the same period.

5. Inscriptions often show **ēīs** for **īs** in Dat. and Abl. Plural.

34. *Rule of Gender.*—Substantives in **-us** are masculine; in **-um** neuter.

EXCEPTIONS.—Feminine are: 1st. Cities and islands, as, **Corinthus, Samus.** 2d. Most trees, as, **fāgus,** *beech;* **pirus,** *pear-tree.* 3d. Many Greek nouns, as, **atomus,** *atom;* **dialectus,** *dialect;* **methodus,** *method;* **paragraphus,** *paragraph;* **periodus,** *period.* 4th. **Alvus,** *belly* (m. in PLAUT.); **colus** (61, N. 5), *distaff* (also m.); **humus,** *ground;* **vannus,** *wheat-fan.*

Neuters are: **pelagus,** *sea;* **vīrus,** *venom;* **vulgus,** *the rabble* (sometimes masculine).

THIRD DECLENSION.

35. 1. The stem ends in a consonant, or in the close vowels **i** and **u.**

2. The stems are divided according to their last letter, called the stem-characteristic, following the subdivisions of the letters of the alphabet:

I.—*Consonant Stems.*		II.—*Vowel Stems.*
A. Liquid stems, ending in **l, m, n, r.**		1. Ending in **i.**
B. Sibilant stems, ending in **s.**		2. Ending in **u,**
C. Mute stems,	1. Ending in a P-mute, **b, p.**	(Compare the Fourth
	2. Ending in a K-mute, **g, c.**	Declension.)
	3. Ending in a T-mute, **d, t.**	

36. 1. The Nominative Singular, masculine and feminine, ends in **s,** which, however, is dropped after **l, n, r, s,** and combines with a K-mute to form **x.** The final vowel of the stem undergoes various changes.

The Vocative is like the Nominative.

In the other cases, the endings are added to the unchanged stem.

2. Neuters always form :

The Nominative without the case-ending **s**.

The Accusative and Vocative cases in both numbers like the Nominative.

The Nominative Plural in **ă**.

Notes on the Cases.

37. *Singular.*

1. Genitive.—In old Latin we find on inscriptions the endings **-us** (Gr. -ος) and **-es.**

2. Dative.—The early endings of the Dat. are **-ēī** and **-ē.** These were succeeded by **ī** after the second century B. C., **ē** being retained in formulas like **iūrē dīcundō** (Liv., 42, 28, 6), in addition to the usual form.

3. Accusative.—The original termination **-im,** in stems of the vowel declension, loses ground, and stems of this class form their Acc. more and more in **-em,** after the analogy of consonant stems. For the classical usage see 57, r. 1.

4. Ablative.—In inscriptions of the second and first centuries B. C. we find **-ēī, -ī,** and **-e.** But **-ēī** soon disappears, leaving **e** and **ī.** In general **e** is the ending for the consonant stems and **ī** for the vowel. But as in the Acc., so in the Abl., the **e** makes inroads on the **i,** though never to the same extent. (See 57, r. 2.) On the other hand, some apparently consonant stems assume the ending **ī.** Thus some in **-ās, -ātis: hērēditātī** (200 B. C.), **aetātī** (rare); **lītī** (rare), **supellēctilī** (classical; early **e**); also the liquid stems which syncopate in the Gen., as **imber.** The ending **-d** is rare and confined to early inscriptions.

5. Locative.—Originally coincident in form with the Dat., the Loc. of the Third Declension was finally blended with Abl., both in form and in syntax. In the following proper names the old form is frequently retained: **Karthāginī,** *at Carthage*, **Sulmōnī,** *at Sulmo*, **Lacedaemonī,** *at Lacedaemon*, **Sicyōnī, Troezēnī, Anxurī, Tīburī.** Also **Acheruntī.** In the case of all except **Anxur, Tībur, Acherūns,** the regular form is more common.

The following Loc. forms of common nouns are found: **herī, lūcī, noctū** (principally in early Latin), **orbī** (Cic.), **peregrī** (early Latin), **praefiscinī** (early Latin), **rūrī, temperī** (the usual form in early Latin), **vesperī.** In all cases the Abl. form in **e** is also found.

38. *Plural.*

1. Nominative.—Early Latin shows **-ēīs, -īs** in the masc. and feminine. The latter was usually confined to vowel stems, but also occurs occasionally in consonant stems (**ioudicīs**). Later the ending was **-ēs** for all kinds of stems.

2. Genitive.—The ending **-um,** uniting with the vowel in vowel stems, gives **-ium.** But many apparently consonant stems show their original vowel form by taking **-ium**: (1) Many fem. stems in **-tāt-** (N. **tās**) with **-ium** as well as **-um.** (2) Monosyllabic and polysyllabic stems in **-t, -c,** with preceding consonant. (3) Monosyllables in **-p** and **-b,** sometimes with, sometimes without, a preceding consonant. (4) Stems in **-ss-**; see 48, r.

3. Accusative.—Old Latin shows also **-ēīs.** The classical form is **-ēs** for consonant and **-īs** for vowel stems. But **-ēs** begins to drive out **-īs** in some vowel stems and wholly supplants it in the early Empire. On the other hand, some apparently original consonant stems show **-īs** in early Latin, but the cases are not always certain.

I.—CONSONANT STEMS.

A.—Liquid Stems.

1. Liquid Stems in l.

39. Form the Nominative without s and fall into two divisions*:

A. Those in which the stem characteristic is preceded by a vowel:

1. ***-al, -alis:*** **sāl** (with compensatory lengthening), *salt;* Punic proper names like **Adherbal, Hannibal.**

2. ***-il, -ilis:*** **mūgil** (**mūgilis** is late), *mullet;* **pugil** (**pugilis** in Varro), *boxer;* **vigil**, *watchman.* ***-īl, -īlis:*** **sīl**, *ochre;* **Tanaquil** (with shortened vowel), a proper name.

3 ***-ōl, -ōlis:*** **sōl**, *sun.*

4. ***-ul, -ulis:*** **cōnsul**, *consul;* **exsul**, *exile;* **praesul**, *dancer.*

B. Two neuter substantives with stems in -ll, one of which is lost in the Nominative: **mel, mellis**, *honey;* **fel, fellis**, *gall.*

Sg.—N.	**cōnsul**, *consul* (m.).	Pl.—N.	**cōnsulēs**, *the consuls.*
G.	**cōnsulis,**	G.	**cōnsulum,**
D.	**cōnsulī,**	D.	**cōnsulibus,**
Ac.	**cōnsulem,**	Ac.	**cōnsulēs,**
V.	**cōnsul,**	V.	**cōnsulēs,**
Ab.	**cōnsule.**	Ab.	**cōnsulibus.**

Rules of Gender.—1. Stems in -l are masculine.

Exceptions: Sīl, *ochre,* **and sāl,** *salt* **(occasionally, but principally in the Sing.), are neuter.**

2. Stems in -ll are neuter

2. Liquid Stems in m.

40. Nominative with s. One example only: **hiem(p)s,** *winter* (f.); Gen., **hiem-is,** Dat., **hiem-ī,** *etc*

3. Liquid Stems in n.

41. *Most masculine* and *feminine* stems form the Nominative Singular by dropping the stem-characteristic and changing a preceding vowel to **o.**

---

* In the following enumerations of stem-varieties, Greek substantives are as a rule omitted.

Some masculine and *most neuter* stems retain the stem-characteristic in the Nominative and change a preceding **i** to **e**.

The following varieties appear :

1. ***-ēn, -ēnis :*** the masculine substantives **liēn, splēn,** *spleen ;* **rēnēs** (pl.), *kidneys.*

2. ***-ŏ, -inis :*** **homŏ,** *man ;* **nēmŏ,** *no one ;* **turbŏ,** *whirlwind ;* **Apollŏ,** *Apollo.* Also substantives in **-dō** (except **praedō,** G. **-ōnis,** *robber*) ; and in **-gō** (except **harpagō,** G. **-ōnis,** *grappling-hook ;* **ligō,** G. **-ōnis,** *mattock*) ; as, **grandō,** *hail ;* **virgō,** *virgin.* ***-en, inis :*** the masc. substantives **flāmen,** *priest ;* **ōscen** (also f.), *divining bird ;* **pecten,** *comb ;* musical performers, **cornicen, fidicen, liticen, tībīcen, tubicen.** Also many neuters : as **nōmen,** *name.*

3. ***-o*** (in early Latin **ō**, in classical period weakened), ***-ōnis :*** **leŏ,** *lion ;* and about seventy others. ***-o, -onis :*** **Saxo,** *Saxon* (late).

4. Irregular formations : **carŏ,** G. **carnis,** *flesh ;* **Aniŏ,** G. **Aniēnis,** a river ; **Nēriŏ,** G. **Nēriēnis,** a proper name. **Sanguis,** *blood,* and **pollis,** *flour,* drop the stem characteristic and add **s** to form nominative ; G. **sanguinis, pollinis.**

42.

		MASCULINE.	FEMININE.	NEUTER.
SG.—	N.	**leŏ,** *lion* (m.).	**imāgō,** *likeness* **(f.).**	**nōmen,** *name* **(n.).**
	G.	**leōnis,**	**imāginis,**	**nōminis,**
	D.	**leōnī,**	**imāginī,**	**nōminī,**
	Ac.	**leōnem,**	**imāginem,**	**nōmen,**
	V.	**leŏ,**	**imāgō,**	**nōmen,**
	Ab.	**leōne,**	**imāgine,**	**nōmine,**
PL.—	N.	**leōnēs,**	**imāginēs,**	**nōmina,**
	G.	**leōnum,**	**imāginum,**	**nōminum,**
	D.	**leōnibus,**	**imāginibus,**	**nōminibus,**
	Ac.	**leōnēs,**	**imāginēs,**	**nōmina,**
	V.	**leōnēs,**	**imāginēs,**	**nōmina,**
	Ab.	**leōnibus.**	**imāginibus.**	**nōminibus.**

NOTE.—Early Latin shows **homōnem,** *etc.*, occasionally.

43. *Rules of Gender.*—1. Substantives in **-ŏ** are masculine, except **carŏ,** *flesh,* and those in **-dō, -gō,** and **-iō.**

EXCEPTIONS.—Masculine are **cardō,** *hinge ;* **ōrdō,** *rank ;* **harpagō,** *grappling-hook ;* **ligō,** *mattock ;* **margō,** *border* (occasionally fem. in late Latin) ; and concrete nouns like **pūgiō,** *dagger,* **titiō,** *firebrand,* **vespertīliō,** *bat.*

2. Substantives in **-en (-men)** are neuter. See exceptions, 41, 1, 2.

4. Liquid Stems in r.

44. Form Nominative without **s**.

Stems fall into the following classes :

1. ***-ar, -aris:*** **salar**, *trout;* proper names like **Caesar, Hamilcar;** the neuters **baccar**, a plant ; **iubar**, *radiance;* **nectar**, *nectar.* ***-ār, -ăris:*** **Lār**, a deity. ***-ār, āris:*** **Nār** (Enn., Verg.), a river. ***-ār, arris:*** **fār** (n.) *spelt.*

2. ***-er, -eris:*** **acipēnser**, a fish ; **agger**, *mound;* **ānser**, *goose;* **asser**, *pole;* **aster**, a plant ; **cancer**, the disease ; **carcer**, *prison;* **later**, *brick;* **mulier** (f.), *woman;* **passer**, *sparrow;* **tūber** (m. and f.), *apple;* **vesper**, *evening* (68, 10) ; **vōmer**, *ploughshare* (47, 2). The neuters **acer**, *maple;* **cadāver**, *dead body;* **cicer**, *pea;* **lāser**, a plant ; **laver**, a plant ; **papāver**, *poppy;* **piper**, *pepper;* **sīler**, *willow;* **siser**, *skirret;* **sūber**, *cork;* **tūber**, *tumor;* **ūber**, *teat;* [**verber**], *thong.* ***-er, -ris:*** four words, **accipiter**, *hawk;* **frāter**, *brother;* **māter**, *mother;* **pater**, *father.* Also some proper names, as **Diēspiter, Falacer**, and the names of the months, **September, Octōber, November, December.** Also, **imber**, *shower*, **linter**, *skiff*, **ūter**, *bag*, **venter**, *belly*, which were probably vowel stems originally (see 45, R. 1). ***-ēr, -eris:*** **āēr**, *air;* **aethēr**, *ether.* ***-ēr, -ēris:*** **vēr**, *spring.*

3. ***-or, -oris:*** **arbor** (f.), *tree* (stem originally in **-os**) ; some Greek words in **-tor**, as **rhētor**, *rhetorician;* slave names in **-por**, as **Mārcipor**; the neuters : **ador**, *spelt;* **aequor**, *sea;* **marmor**, *marble.* ***-or, -ōris:*** very many abstract words, as **amor**, *love;* **color**, *colour;* **clāmor**, *outcry;* **soror**, *sister;* **uxor**, *wife;* these may come from stems in **ōs** (see 47, 4) ; also verbals in **-tor**, as **victor.**

4. ***-ur, -uris:*** **augur**, *augur;* **furfur**, *bran;* **turtur**, *dove;* **vultur**, *vulture;* **lemurēs** (pl.), *ghosts*, and a few proper names ; also the neuters **fulgur**, *lightning;* **guttur**, *throat;* **murmur**, *murmur;* **sulfur**, **sulphur.** ***-ūr, -ūris;*** **fūr**, *thief.*

5. Four neuters, **ebur**, *ivory;* **femur**, *thigh;* **iecur**, *liver;* **rōbur**, *oak*, show Gen. in **-oris**; two of these, **femur, iecur**, have also the irregular forms **feminis** and **iecineris, iecinoris, iocinoris.** **Iter**, *way*, has G. **itineris;** and **supellēx**, *furniture*, has G. **supellēctilis.**

45.

	SINGULAR.	PLURAL.	SINGULAR.	PLURAL.
N.	**labor**, *toil* (m.),	**labōrēs**,	**pater**, *father* (m.),	**patrēs**,
G.	**labōris**,	**labōrum**,	**patris**,	**patrum**,
D.	**labōrī**,	**labōribus**,	**patrī**,	**patribus**,
Ac.	**labōrem**,	**labōrēs**,	**patrem**,	**patrēs**,
V.	**labor**,	**labōrēs**,	**pater**,	**patrēs**,
Ab.	**labōre.**	**labōribus.**	**patre.**	**patribus.**

REMARKS.—1. **Imber**, *shower*, **linter**, *skiff*, **ūter**, *bag*, **venter**, *belly*, show the vowel nature of their stems by having Gen. Pl. in **-ium**. **Imber** has also sometimes Abl. Sing. in **ī**. (See 37, 4.)

2. **Rōbur**, *strength*, also forms a Nom. **rōbus** (47, 4), and **vōmer**, *ploughshare*, **vōmis** (47, 2).

NOTE.—**Arbor**, and many stems in **-ōr**, were originally stems in **-s**; the **s** became **r** (47) between two vowels in the oblique cases, and then reacted upon the Nominative. But many Nominatives in **-ōs** are still found in early Latin; and some are still retained in the classical times: **arbōs** (regularly in VERG., frequently in LUCR., HOR., OV.), **honōs** (regularly in VERG., commonly in CIC., LIVY), and others.

46. *Rules of Gender.*—1. Substantives in **-er** and **-or** are masculine. 2. Substantives in **-ar** and **-ur** are neuter.

EXCEPTIONS.—Masculine are **salar**, *trout*, and proper names in **-ar**; **augur**, *augur*; **furfur**, *bran*; names of animals in **-ur** and a few proper names in **-ur**.

Feminine are **arbor**, *tree*; **mulier**, *woman*; **soror**, *sister*; **uxor**, *wife*. Neuter are **acer**, *maple*; **ador**, *spelt*; **aequor**, *sea*; **cadāver**, *dead body*; **cicer**, *pea*; **iter**, *way*; **lāser**, a plant; **laver**, a plant; **marmor**, *marble*; **papāver**, *poppy*; **piper**, *pepper*; **sīler**, *willow*; **siser**, *skirret*; **sūber**, *cork*; **tūber**, *tumor*; **ūber**, *teat*; **vēr**, *spring*; [**verber**], *thong*.

B.—Sibilant Stems.

47. The Nominative has no additional **s**, and changes in masculines **e** to **i**, and in neuters **e** or **o** to **u** before **s**.

In the oblique cases, the **s** of the stem usually passes over, between two vowels, into **r** (*rhotacism*).

There are the following varieties of stems:

1. ***-ās, -aris:*** **mās**, *male*. ***-ās, -āsis:*** **vās** (n.), *vessel*. ***-ās, -assis:*** **ās** (m.), *a copper* (vowel long in Nom. by compensatory lengthening), and some of its compounds (with change of vowel), as **bes, semis**.

2. ***-ēs, -eris:*** **Cerēs**, *Ceres*. ***-is, -eris:*** **cinis**, *ashes*; **cucumis**, *cucumber* (see 57, R. 1), **pulvis** (occasionally **pulvīs**), *dust*; **vōmis**, *ploughshare* (see 45, R. 2). ***-us, -eris:*** **Venus**, and occasionally **pīgnus**, *pledge* (see 4).

3. ***-īs, -īris:*** **glīs**, *dormouse*.

4. ***-ōs, -ōsis:*** old Latin **ianitōs, labōs, clāmōs** (see 45, N.). ***-os, -ossis:*** **os** (n.), *bone*. ***-ōs, -ōris:*** **flōs**, *flower*; **glōs**, *sister-in-law*; **lepōs**, *charm*; **mōs** (m.), *custom*; **-ōs** (n.), *mouth*; **rōs**, *dew*. ***-us, -oris:*** **corpus**, *body*; **decus**, *grace*; **pīgnus**, *pledge*, and twelve others; on **rōbus** (see 45, R. 2).

5. ***-us, -uris:*** **Ligus**, *Ligurian*. ***-ūs, -ūris:*** **tellūs** (f.), *earth*; **mūs** (m.), *mouse*; the neuters: **crūs**, *leg*; **iūs**, *right*; **pūs**, *pus*; **rūs**, *country*; **tūs**, *incense*.

6. ***aes, aeris,*** *brass*.

48.	SINGULAR.	PLURAL.	SINGULAR.	PLURAL.
N. A. V.	**genus**, *kind* (n.),	**genera**,	**corpus**, *body* (n.),	**corpora**,
G.	**generis**,	**generum**,	**corporis**,	**corporum**,
D.	**generī**,	**generibus**,	**corporī**,	**corporibus**,
Ab.	**genere.**	**generibus.**	**corpore.**	**corporibus.**

REMARK.—**Ās**, *a copper*, and **os**, *bone*, form the Gen. Pl. in **-ium**, after the usage of vowel stems (see 38, 2). So also **mūs**, *mouse.*

49. *Rule of Gender.*—Masculine are substantives in **-is** (**-eris**), and **-ōs**, **-ōris**: except **ōs**, *mouth* (G. **ōris**), which is neuter.

Neuter are substantives in **-us** (G. **-eris**, **-oris**), and in **-ūs** (G. **-ūris**); except **tellūs**, *earth* (G. **tellūris**), which is feminine; and the masculines, **lepus**, *hare* (G. **leporis**); **mūs**, *mouse* (G. **mūris**).

C.—Mute Stems.

50. All masculines and feminines of mute stems have **s** in the Nominative. Before **s** a P-mute is retained, a K-mute combines with it to form **x**, a T-mute is dropped.

Most polysyllabic mute stems change their final vowel **i** into **e** in the Nominative.

The stems show variations as follows:

51. Stems in a P-mute.

1. ***-abs, -abis:*** **trabs**, *beam;* **Arabs.** ***-aps, -apis:*** [**daps**], *feast.*
2. ***-ēbs, ēbis:*** **plēbs**, *commons.*
3. ***-eps, -ipis:*** **prīnceps**, *chief*, and fourteen others. ***-ips, -ipis:*** **stips**, *dole.*
4. ***-ops, -opis:*** [**ops**], *power.*
5. ***-eps, upis:*** **auceps**, *fowler*, and the old Latin **manceps**, *contractor.*
6. ***-rbs, -rbis:*** **urbs**, *city.*
7. ***-rps, -rpis:*** **stirps**, *stock.*

SG.—N.	**prīnceps**, *chief* (m.),	PL.—**prīncipēs**,
G.	**prīncipis**,	**prīncipum**,
D.	**prīncipī**,	**prīncipibus**,
Ac.	**prīncipem**,	**prīncipēs**,
V.	**prīnceps**,	**prīncipēs**,
Ab.	**prīncipe.**	**prīncipibus.**

52. Stems in a K-mute.

1. ***-ax, -acis:*** **fax**, *torch*, and many Greek words in **-ax**, **Atax**, proper name. ***-āx, -ācis:*** **fornāx**, *furnace;* **līmāx**, *snail;* **pāx**, *peace;* and Greek **cordāx**, **thōrāx.**

2. ***-ex, -ecis*** : **faenisex**, *mower* ; **nex**, *murder* ; [**prex**], *prayer* ; [**resex**], *stump*. ***-ēx, -ēcis*** : **āllēx** (also **āllēc**), *brine* ; **vervēx**, *wether*. ***-ex, -egis*** : **grex**, *herd* ; **aquilex**, *water-inspector*. ***-ēx, -ēgis*** : **interrēx** ; **lēx**, *law* ; **rēx**, *king*.

3. ***-ex, -icis*** : **auspex**, *soothsayer*, and about forty others. ***-ex, -igis*** : **rēmex**, *rower*. ***-īx, īcis*** : **cervīx**, *neck*, and about thirty others ; verbals in **-īx**, as **victrīx**. ***-ix, -icis*** : **appendix**, *appendix*, and ten others. ***-ix, -igis*** : **strix**, *screech-owl* ; also many foreign proper names, as **Dumnorix**, which may, however, be forms in **-īx, -īgis**.

4. ***-ōx, -ōcis*** : **celōx**, *cutter* ; **vōx**, *voice*. ***-ox, -ocis*** : **Cappadox**, *Cappadocian*. ***-ox, -ogis*** : **Allobrox**, *Allobrogian*.

5. ***-ux, -ucis*** : **crux**, *cross* ; **dux**, *leader* ; **nux**, *nut*. ***-ūx, -ūcis*** : **lūx**, *light* ; **ballūx**, *gold-dust* ; **Pollūx**. ***-ux, -ugis*** : **cōniux** (**-unx**), *spouse*. ***-ūx, -ūgis*** : **frūx**, *fruit*.

6. ***-rx, -rcis*** : **arx**, *citadel* ; **merx**, *wares*. ***-lx, -lcis*** : **falx**, *sickle* ; **calx**, *heel, lime*. ***-nx, -ncis*** : **lanx**, *dish* ; compounds of **-unx**, as **quīncunx**, and a few names of animals ; **phalanx** has G. **phalangis**.

7. Unclassified : **nix** (G. **nivis**), *snow* ; **bōs** (G. **bovis** ; see 71), *ox* ; [**faux**] (G. **faucis**), *throat* ; **faex** (G. **faecis**), *dregs*.

Sg.—N.	**rēx**,	*king* (m.).	Pl.—	**rēgēs**,
G.	**rēgis**,			**rēgum**,
D.	**rēgī**,			**rēgibus**,
Ac.	**rēgem**,			**rēgēs**,
V.	**rēx**,			**rēgēs**,
Ab.	**rēge**,			**rēgibus**.

53. Stems in a T-mute

1. ***-ās, -ātis*** : many feminine abstracts, as **aetās**, *age* ; some proper names, as **Maecēnās**. ***-as, -atis*** : **anas**, *duck*. ***-as, -adis*** : **vas**, *bail* ; **lampas**, *torch*.

2. ***-es, -etis*** : **indiges**, *patron deity* ; **interpres**, *interpreter* ; **praepes**, *bird* ; **seges**, *crop* ; **teges**, *mat*. ***-ēs, -etis*** : **abiēs**, *fir* ; **ariēs**, *ram* ; **pariēs**, *wall*. ***-ēs, -ētis*** : **quiēs**, *quiet* ; **requiēs**, *rest*. ***-ēs, -edis*** : **pēs**, *foot*, and its compounds. ***-ēs, -ēdis*** : **hērēs**, *heir* ; **mercēs**, *hire*.

3. ***-es, -itis*** : **antistes**, *overseer* ; **caespes**, *sod*, and some fifteen others. ***-es, -idis*** : **obses**, *hostage* ; **praeses**, *protector*. ***-īs, -ītis*** : **līs**, *suit*. ***-is, -idis*** : **capis**, *bowl* ; **cassis**, *helmet*, and nearly forty others, mostly Greek.

4. ***-ōs, -ōtis*** : **cōs**, *whetstone* ; **dōs**, *dowry* ; **nepōs**, *grandson* ; **sacerdōs**, *priest*. ***-ōs, -ōdis*** : **cūstōs**, *guard*.

5. ***-ūs, -ūtis*** : **glūs**, *glue*, and some abstracts : **iuventūs**, *youth* ; **salūs**, *safety* ; **senectūs**, *old age* ; **servitūs**, *servitude* ; **virtūs**, *manliness*. ***-us, -udis*** : **pecus**, *sheep*. ***-ūs, -ūdis*** : **incūs**, *anvil* ; **palūs**, *marsh* ; **subscūs**, *tenon*.

6. ***-aes, -aedis :*** **praes**, *surety.* ***-aus, -audis :*** **laus**, *praise;* **fraus**, *fraud.*

7. ***-ls, -ltis :*** **puls**, *porridge.* ***-ns, -ntis :*** **īnfāns**, *infant;* **dēns**, *tooth;* **fōns**, *fountain;* **mōns**, *mountain;* **frōns**, *brow;* **pōns**, *bridge;* **gēns**, *tribe;* **lēns**, *lentil;* **mēns**, *mind;* **rudēns**, *rope;* **torrēns**, *torrent.* ***-s, -ntis :*** latinised Greek words like **gigās**, *giant.* ***-rs, -rtis :*** **ars**, *art;* **cohors**, *cohort;* **fors**, *chance;* **Mārs**; **mors**, *death;* **sors**, *lot.*

8. Unclassified : **cor** (G. **cordis**), *heart;* **nox** (G. **noctis**), *night;* **caput** (G. **capitis**), *head;* **lac** (G. **lactis**), *milk.*

Sg.—N.	**aetās**, *age* (f.).	Pl.—**aetātēs**,	Sg.—**pēs**, *foot* (m.).	Pl.—**pedēs**,
G.	**aetātis**,	**aetātum**,	**pedis**,	**pedum**,
D.	**aetātī**,	**aetātibus**,	**pedī**,	**pedibus**,
Ac.	**aetātem**,	**aetātēs**,	**pedem**,	**pedēs**,
V.	**aetās**,	**aetātēs**,	**pēs**,	**pedēs**,
Ab.	**aetāte**,	**aetātibus**.	**pede**,	**pedibus**.

54. Many substantives of this class were originally vowel stems (see 56), and show their origin by having the termination **-ium** in the Gen. Pl. and **-ī** in the Abl. Singular. Some not originally vowel stems do the same. (See 38, 2.)

Monosyllabic mute stems, with the characteristic preceded by a consonant, have the Gen. Pl. in **-ium**: **urbium**, *of cities;* **arcium**, *of citadels;* **montium**, *of mountains;* **partium**, *of parts;* **noctium**, *of the nights.* But **-um** is also found in **gentum** (Attius), **partum** (Ennius); so always **opum.**

Monosyllabic mute stems, with characteristic preceded by a long vowel or diphthong, vary : **dōt-ium**, **līt-ium**, **fauc-ium**, **fraud-um** (**-ium**), **laud-um** (**-ium**). But **praed-um**, **vōcum.**

Monosyllabic mute stems with characteristic preceded by a short vowel have **-um**; but **fac-ium**, **nuc-um** (**-ium**), **niv-ium** (**-um**).

The polysyllabic stems in **-nt** and **-rt** have more frequently **-ium**, as **clientium** (**-um**), *of clients;* **cohortium** (**-um**), *of companies.* So **adulēscentium** (**-um**), **amantium** (**-um**), **īnfantium** (**-um**), **parentum** (**-ium**), **serpentium** (**-um**), **torrentium** (**-um**); **rudentum** (**-ium**); but only **quadrantum.**

Of other polysyllabic stems feminine stems in **-āt** have frequently both **-um** and **-ium**, as **aetātum** and **aetātium**, **cīvitātum** and **cīvitātium**, *etc.;* the rest have usually **-um** : but **artifex**, **(h)aruspex**, **extispex**, **iūdex**, **supplex**, **cōniux**, **rēmex**, and usually **fornāx** have **-ium.** **Forceps**, **manceps**, **mūniceps**, **prīnceps** have **-um.** **Palūs** has usually **palūdium.**

Notes.—1. The accusative **lentim** from [**lēns**] is occasionally found, and **partim** from **pars**, as an adverb.

2. Sporadic ablatives in **-ī** occur as follows : **animantī** (Cic.), **bidentī** (Lucr.), **tridentī** (Sil., Verg.), **capitī**, **cōnsonantī** (gram.), **hērēdī** (inscr.), **lēgī** (inscr.), **lentī** (Titin., Col.), **lūcī** (early), **mentī** (Col.), **occipitī** (Pers., Aus.), **pācī** (Varro), **partī**, **rudentī** (Vitr.), **sortī**, **torrentī** (Sen.).

55. *Rule of Gender.*—Mute stems, with Nominative **in s**, are feminine.

1. *Exceptions in a* **k**-*mute.*

Masculines are substantives in **-ex**, **-ēx**, **-ix**, and **-unx**; except **cortex**, *bark*, **forfex**, *shears*, **frutex**, *shrub*, **imbrex**, *tile*, **latex**, *fluid*, **ōbex**, *bolt*, **silex**, *flint*, **varix**, *varicose vein*, which are sometimes masculine, sometimes feminine; and **faex**, *dregs*, **forpex**, *tongs*, **lēx**, *law*, **nex**, *slaughter*, **vībēx**, *weal*, and forms of [**prex**], *prayer*, which are feminine. **Calx**, *heel*, and **calx**, *chalk*, are sometimes masculine, sometimes feminine.

2. *Exceptions in a* **t**-*mute.*

Masculine are substantives in **-es**, **-itis**, except **merges** (f.), *sheaf;* also **pēs**, *foot*, and its compounds; **pariēs**, *wall;* **lapis**, *stone.*

Masculines in **-ns** are: **dēns**, *tooth*, and its compounds; **fōns**, *spring;* **mōns**, *mountain;* **pōns**, *bridge;* **rudēns**, *rope;* **torrēns**, *torrent;* also some substantivised adjectives and participles.

Neuters are only: **cor**, *heart*, **lac**, *milk*, and **caput**, *head.*

II.—VOWEL STEMS.

1.—Vowel Stems in i.

56. Masculines and feminines form their Nominative in **s**.

Some feminines change, in the Nominative, the stem-vowel **i** into **e**.

Neuters change, in the Nominative, the stem-vowel **i** into **e**. This **e** is generally dropped by polysyllabic neuters after **l** and **r**.

Stems in **i** have Genitive Plural in **-ium**.

Neuter stems in **i** have the Ablative Singular in **ī**, and Nominative Plural in **-ia**.

The varieties of stems are:

1. ***-is, -is:*** nearly one hundred substantives, like **cīvis**, *citizen.*

2. ***-ēs, -is:*** thirty-five, like **vulpēs**, *fox.* Some of these have also variant nominatives in **-is** in good usage.

3. ***-e, -is:*** some twenty neuters, as **mare**, *sea.*

4. ***—, -is:*** twenty-four neuters, which form Nominative by dropping the stem characteristic and shortening the preceding vowel: **animal**, **-ālis**, *animal;* **calcar** (G. **calcāris**), *spur.*

5. For substantives in ***-er, -ris,*** see 44, 2. Irregular is **senex**, (G. **senis**; see 57, R. 3), *old man.*

	M.	F.	F.	N.	N.
SG.—N.	**collis,** *hill.*	**turris,** *tower.*	**vulpēs,** *fox.*	**mare,** *sea.*	**animal,** *living being.*
G.	**collis,**	**turris,**	**vulpis,**	**maris,**	**animālis,**
D.	**collī,**	**turrī,**	**vulpī,**	**marī,**	**animālī,**
Ac.	**collem,**	**turrim(em),**	**vulpem,**	**mare,**	**animal,**
V.	**collis,**	**turris,**	**vulpēs,**	**mare,**	**animal,**
Ab.	**colle,**	**turrī(e),**	**vulpe,**	**marī,**	**animālī,**
PL.—N.	**collēs,**	**turrēs,**	**vulpēs,**	**maria,**	**animālia,**
G.	**collium,**	**turri-um,**	**vulpium,**	**marum,**	**animālium,**
D.	**collibus,**	**turri-bus,**	**vulpibus,**	**maribus,**	**animālibus,**
Ac.	**collīs(ēs),**	**turrīs(ēs),**	**vulpīs(ēs),**	**maria,**	**animālia,**
V.	**collēs,**	**turrēs,**	**vulpēs,**	**maria,**	**animālia,**
Ab.	**collibus.**	**turri-bus.**	**vulpibus.**	**maribus.**	**animālibus.**

57. REMARKS.—1. The proper ending of the Acc. Sing. **-im,** is retained *always* in **amussis, būris, cucumis** (see 47, 2), **fūtis, mephītis, rāvis, rūmis, sitis, tussis, vīs**; and in names of towns and rivers in **-is,** as **Neāpolis, Tiberis**; *usually* in **febris, puppis, pelvis, restis, secūris, turris**; *occasionally* in **bipennis, clāvis, crātis, cutis, len(ti)s** (see 54, N. 1), **messis, nāvis, neptis, praesaepis, sēmentis, strigilis.**

2. The Abl. in **-ī** is found in substantives that regularly have **-im** in Acc. (except perhaps **restis**): also not unfrequently in **amnis, avis, bipennis, canālis, cīvis, clāssis, fīnis** (in formulæ), **fūstis, īgnis** (in phrases), **orbis, sēmentis, strigilis, unguis**; occasionally in **anguis, bīlis, clāvis, collis, convallis, corbis, messis, neptis**; regularly in neuters in **e, al,** and **ar,** except in **rēte,** and in the towns **Caere, Praeneste.**

NOTE.—So also the adjectives of this class, when used as substantives by ellipsis: **annālis** (sc. **liber,** *book*), *chronicle*; **nātālis** (sc. **diēs,** *day*), *birthday*; **Aprīlis** (sc. **mēnsis,** *month*), and all the other months of the Third Declension: Abl., **annālī, nātālī, Aprīlī, Septembrī,** *etc.* But **iuvenis,** *young man*; and **aedīlis,** *aedile,* have Abl., **iuvene, aedīle**; adjectives used as proper nouns have generally Abl. in **-e,** as, **Iuvenālis, Iuvenāle.**

3. In the Gen. Pl., instead of the ending **-ium, -um** is found *always* in **canis,** *dog,* **iuvenis,** *young man,* **pānis,** *bread,* **senex,** *old,* **struēs,** *heap,* **volucris,** *bird*; *usually* in **apis,** *bee,* **sēdēs,** *seat,* **vātēs,** *bard*; *frequently* in **mēnsis,** *month.* On **imber,** *etc.*, see 45, R. 1. Post-classical and rare are **ambāgum, caedum, clādum, veprum,** and a few others; **marum** (the only form found) occurs once.

4. In the Nom. Pl. **-ēis** and **-īs** are found in early Latin. So occasionally in consonant stems (see 38, 1), but in classical times such usage is doubtful.

5. The proper ending of the Acc. Pl., **-īs** (archaic, **-ēis**), is found frequently in the classical period along with the later termination **-ēs,** which supplants **-īs** wholly in the early empire. On the other hand, **-īs** for **-ēs** in consonant stems is confined to a few doubtful cases in early Latin.

58. *Rule of Gender.*—1. Vowel stems, with Nominative in **-ēs** are feminine ; those with Nominative in **-is** are partly masculine, partly feminine.

Masculine are: **amnis,** *river* (f., early); **antēs** (pl.), *rows;* **axis,** *axle;* **būris,** *plough-tail;* **cassēs** (pl.), *toils;* **caulis,** *stalk;* **collis,** *hill;* **crīnis,** *hair;* **ēnsis,** *glaive;* **fascis,** *fagot;* **follis,** *bellows;* **fūnis,** *rope* (f., Lucr.); **fūstis,** *cudgel;* **īgnis,** *fire;* **mānēs** (pl.), *Manes;* **mēnsis,** *month;* **mūgil(is),** *mullet;* **orbis,** *circle;* **pānis,** *bread;* **postis,** *door-post;* **torris,** *fire-brand;* **unguis,** *nail;* **vectis,** *lever;* **vermis,** *worm.*

Common are: **callis,** *footpath;* **canālis,** *canal;* **clūnis,** *haunch;* **corbis,** *basket;* **fīnis,** *end;* **rētis,** *net* (also **rēte,** n.); **sentis** (usually pl.), *bramble;* **scrobis,** *ditch;* **torquis (es),** *necklace;* **tōlēs** (pl.), *goitre;* **veprēs** (pl.), *bramble.*

Remark.—Of the names of animals in **-is,** some are masculine ; **tigris,** *tiger* (fem. in poetry) ; **canis,** *dog* (also fem.) ; **piscis,** *fish;* others feminine : **apis,** *bee;* **avis,** *bird;* **ovis,** *sheep;* **fēlis,** *cat* (usually **fēlēs**).

2. Vowel stems, with Nominative in **-e, -al, -ar,** are neuter.

2. Vowel Stems in u.

59. Of stems in **u,** the *monosyllabic* stems, two in number, belong to the Third Declension.

Sg.—N.	**grūs,** *crane* (f.)	Pl.—**gruēs**
G.	**gruis**	**gruum**
D.	**gruī**	**gruibus**
Ac.	**gruem**	**gruēs**
V.	**grūs**	**gruēs**
Ab.	**grue**	**gruibus.**

Sūs, *swine* (commonly f.), usually **subus,** in Dat. and Abl. Plural.

Table of Nominative and Genitive Endings of the Third Declension.

The * before the ending denotes that it occurs only in the one word cited.

60. A. NOMINATIVES ENDING WITH A LIQUID.

Nom.	Gen.			Nom.	Gen.		
-al	**-āli-s**	**animal,**	*animal.*	**-ār**	***-arr-is**	**fār,**	*spelt.*
	-ăl-is	**Hannibal,**	proper name.	**-er**	**-er-is**	**ānser,**	*goose.*
-āl	***-ăl-is**	**sāl,**	*salt.*		**-r-is**	**pater,**	*father.*
-el	**-ell-is**	**mel,**	*honey.*		***-iner-is**	**iter,**	*journey.*
-il	**-il-is**	**pugil,**	*boxer.*	**-ēr**	***-ēr-is**	**vēr,**	*spring.*
	-īl-is	**Tanaquil,**	proper name.	**-or**	**-ōr-is**	**color,**	*colour.*
-ōl	***-ōl-is**	**sōl,**	*the sun.*		**-or-is**	**aequor,**	*expanse.*
-ul	**-ul-is**	**cōnsul,**	*consul.*		***-ord-is**	**cor,**	*heart.*
-ēn	**-ēn-is**	**rēnēs** (pl.),	*kidneys.*	**-ur**	**-ur-is**	**fulgur,**	*lightning*
-en	**-in-is**	**nōmen,**	*name.*		**-or-is**	**rōbur,**	*oak.*
-ar	**-āri-s**	**calcar,**	*spur.*	**-ūr**	**-ūr-is**	**fūr,**	*thief*
	-ari-s	**nectar,**	*nectar.*				

B. NOMINATIVES ENDING WITH **s**, OR **x** (cs, gs).

Nom.	Gen.			Nom.	Gen.		
-ās	*-ās-is	**vās,**	*dish.*	**-ls**	*-lt-is	**puls,**	*porridge.*
	*-ar-is	**mās,**	*male.*	**-m(p)s**	*-m-is	**hiems,**	*winter.*
	*ass-is	**ās,**	*a copper.*	**-ns**	-nd-is	**frōns,**	*leafy branch.*
	-āt-is	**aetās.**	*age.*		-nt-is	**frōns,**	*forehead.*
-as	*-ad-is	**vas,**	*surety.*	**-rs**	-rd-is	**concors,**	*concordant.*
	*-at-is	**anas.**	*duck.*		-rt-is	**pars,**	*part.*
-aes	*-aed-is	**praes,**	*surety.*	**-bs**	-b-is	**urbs,**	*city.*
	*aer-is	**aes,**	*brass.*	**-ps**	-p-is	**stirps,**	*stalk.*
-aus	-aud-is	**fraus,**	*cheatery.*	**-eps**	-ip-is	**prīnceps,**	*chief.*
-ēs	-is	**nūbēs,**	*cloud.*		*-up-is	**auceps,**	*fowler.*
	-ed-is	**pēs,**	*foot.*	**-āx**	-āc-is	**pāx,**	*peace.*
	*-er-is	**Cerēs,**	*Ceres.*	**-ax**	*-ac-is	**fax,**	*torch.*
	-et-is	**abiēs,**	*fir.*	**-aex**	-aec-is	**faex,**	*dregs.*
	-ēt-is	**quiēs,**	*rest.*	**-aux**	-auc-is	**[faux,]**	*throat.*
-es	-et-is	**seges,**	*crop.*	**-ex**	-ec-is	**nex,**	*death.*
	-id-is	**obses,**	*hostage.*		-ic-is	**iūdex,**	*judge.*
	-it-is	**mīles,**	*soldier.*		-eg-is	**grex,**	*flock.*
-is	-is	**amnis,**	*river.*		*-ig-is	**rēmex,**	*rower.*
	-id-is	**lapis,**	*stone.*	**-ēx**	*-ēc-is	**āllēx,**	*pickle.*
	-in-is	**sanguis,**	*blood.*		*-īc-is	**vībēx(īx),**	*weal.*
	-er-is	**cinis,**	*ashes.*		-ēg-is	**rēx,**	*king.*
-īs	*-īt-is	**līs,**	*suit at law.*	**-īx**	-īc-is	**cervīx,**	*neck.*
	*-īr-is	**glīs,**	*dormouse.*	**-ix**	-ic-is	**calix,**	*cup.*
-ōs	*-ōd-is	**cūstōs,**	*keeper.*		*-ig-is	**strix,**	*screech-owl.*
	-ōr-is	**flōs,**	*flower.*		*-iv-is	**nix,**	*snow.*
	-ōt-is	**cōs,**	*whetstone.*	**-ōx**	-ōc-is	**vōx,**	*voice.*
	*-ov-is	**bōs,**	*ox.*	**-ox**	*-oc-is	**praecox,**	*early-ripe.*
-os	*oss-is	**os,**	*bone.*		*-og-is	**Allobrox,**	*Allobrogian.*
-us	*-ud-is	**pecus,**	*cattle, sheep.*		*-oct-is	**nox,**	*night.*
	*-ur-is	**Ligus,**	*a Ligurian.*	**-ux**	-c-is	**crux,**	*cross.*
	-or-is	**corpus,**	*body.*		-ug-is	**cōniux,**	*spouse.*
	-er-is	**scelus,**	*crime.*	**-ūx**	-ūc-is	**lūx,**	*light.*
-ūs	-u-is	**sūs,**	*swine.*		-ūg-is	**[frūx,]**	*fruit.*
	-ūd-is	**incūs,**	*anvil.*	**-lx**	-lc-is	**falx,**	*sickle.*
	-ūr-is	**iūs,**	*right.*	**-nx**	-nc-is	**lanx,**	*dish.*
	-ūt-is	**salūs,**	*weal.*	**-rx**	-rc-is	**arx,**	*citadel.*

C. NOMINATIVES ENDING WITH A MUTE.

-ac	***-act-is**	**lac,**	*milk.*	**-ut**	***-it-is**	**caput,**	*head.*
-ēc	***-ēc-is**	**āllēc,**	*pickle* (68, 12).				

D. NOMINATIVES ENDING WITH A VOWEL.

-e	**-i-s**	**mare,** *sea.*
-o	**-on-is**	**Saxo,** *Saxon.*
-ō	**-ōn-is**	**pāvō,** *peacock.*
	-in-is	**homō,** *man.*
	***-n-is**	**carō,** *flesh.*

FOURTH DECLENSION.

61. The Fourth Declension embraces only dissyllabic and polysyllabic stems in **u.**

The endings are those of the Third Declension.

In the Genitive and Ablative Singular, and in the Nominative, Accusative, and Vocative Plural (sometimes, too, in the Dative Singular), the **u** of the stem absorbs the vowel of the ending, and becomes long. In the Dative and Ablative Plural it is weakened to **i** before the ending **-bus.**

The Accusative Singular, as always in vowel stems, has the ending **-m,** without a connecting vowel (compare the Accusative in **-i-m** of the stems in **i**), hence **-u-m.**

	MASCULINE.		NEUTER.	
Sg.—N.	**frūctus,** *fruit.*	Pl.—**frūctūs,**	Sg.—**cornū,** *horn.*	Pl.—**cornua,**
G.	**frūctūs,**	**frūctuum,**	**cornūs,**	**cornuum,**
D.	**frūctuī (fructū),**	**frūctibus,**	**cornū,**	**cornibus,**
Ac.	**frūctum,**	**frūctūs,**	**cornū,**	**cornua,**
V.	**frūctus,**	**frūctūs,**	**cornū,**	**cornua,**
Ab.	**frūctū.**	**frūctibus.**	**cornū.**	**cornibus.**

Remarks.—1. *Dat. Abl.* The original form **-u-bus** is retained always in **acus, arcus, quercus, tribus,** and in classical times in **partus.** But **artus, genu, lacus, portus, specus, tonitrū, verū,** have both forms.

2. **Domus,** *house,* is declined : G. domu-os (archaic), domu-is and domī (early), domu-us (late), **domūs.** D. domō (early), **domuī.** Ac. **domum.** V. **domus.** Ab. dom-ū (sporadic), **domō.** Loc. **domī.** Pl. N. **domūs.** G. **domōrum** (Lucr. always, Verg., Flor.), domuum (late). D. Ab. **domibus.** Ac. **domōs, domūs.** Classical forms are those in black-faced type. A classical variant for **domī** (Loc.) is **domuī.**

Notes.—1. *Singular: Genitive.* In early inscriptions we find the ending **-os,** as **senātuos**; and in early authors not unfrequently **-is,** along with the contraction **-ūs** (**-uis**), which becomes the regular form in classical times. In inscriptions under the empire **-us** is occasionally found, as **exercituus.** The termination **-ī,** after the analogy of the Second Declension, is common in early Latin, and is still retained in some words even into the classical period ; as **senātī** (Cic., Sall., Livy), **tumultī** (Sall.).

2. *Dative.* In the early time **-uēī** is found very rarely for **-uī.** Also **ū,** as **senātū, frūctū,** which became the only form for neuters. In classical times **-ū** in masc. and fem. is poetical only (Caesar uses, however, **cāsū, exercitū, magistrātū, senātū, quaestū**), but extends to prose in the Augustan age and later.

3. *Plural: Nom., Acc., Voc.* In imperial inscriptions **-uus** occurs.

4. *Genitive.* The poets frequently contract **-uum** into **-um** for metrical reasons, and this usage was sometimes extended to prose (not by Cicero) in common words ; as **passūm** for **passuum.**

5. **Colus,** *distaff,* belongs properly to the Second Declension, but has variants : **G. colūs,** Ab. **colū,** Pl., N., Ac., **colūs,** from the Fourth.

62. *Rule of Gender.*—Substantives in **-us** are masculine; those in **-ū** are neuter.

Exceptions.—*Feminines* are **acus**, *needle* (usually), **domus**, *house*, **īdūs** (pl.), *the Ides*, **manus**, *hand*, **penus**, *victuals* (also m.), **porticus**, *piazza*, **quīnquātrūs** (pl.), *festival of Minerva*, **tribus**, *tribe*. Early and late Latin show some further variations.

FIFTH DECLENSION.

63. The stem ends in **-ē**; Nominative in **s**.

In the Genitive and Dative Singular **-ē** has been shortened after a consonant.

In the Accusative Singular we find always **ĕ**.

The ending in the Genitive Singular is that of the Second Declension, **-ī**; the other endings are those of the Third.

	MASCULINE.		FEMININE.	
Sg.—N.	**diēs**, *day*.	Pl.—**diēs**,	Sg.—**rēs**, *thing*.	Pl.—**rēs**,
G.	**diēī**,	**diērum**,	**reī**,	**rērum**,
D.	**diēī**,	**diēbus**,	**reī**,	**rēbus**,
Ac.	**diem**,	**diēs**,	**rem**,	**rēs**,
V.	**diēs**,	**diēs**,	**rēs**,	**rēs**,
Ab.	**diē**.	**diēbus**.	**rē**.	**rēbus**.

Remarks.—1. *Plural: Gen., Dat., Abl.* Common in but two substantives, **diēs**, **rēs**. Late Latin shows also **speciēbus**, and very rarely **spēbus** and **aciēbus**.

2. Many words of the Fifth Declension have a parallel form, which follows the First Declension, as **mollitiēs**, *softness*, and **mollitia**. Where this is the case, forms of the Fifth Declension are usually found only in the Nom., Acc., and Abl. Singular.

Notes.—1. *Singular: Genitive.* The older ending **-ē-s** is found sporadically in early Latin, but usually the ending **-ē-ī**, which became later **-ĕ-ī** after consonants, though early poets show numerous examples of **rēī**, **spēī**, **fidēī**. **ēī** was occasionally scanned as one syllable, whence arose the contraction **ē**, which is retained not unfrequently in the classical period; so **aciē** (Caes., Sall.), **diē** (Pl., Caes., Sall., Livy, later), **fidē** (Pl., Hor., Ov., late Prose), and other less certain cases; **ī** occurs very rarely, principally in early Latin (but **diī**, Verg., **perniciī**, Cic.). **Plēbēs**, in combination with **tribūnus**, **aedīlis**, **scītum**, often shows a Gen. **plēbī** (**plēbeī**).

2. *Dative.* The contraction **-ē** is found, but less often than in the Gen.; **aciē** (Sall.); **diē**, **faciē** (early Latin); **fidē** (early Latin, Caes., Sall., Livy), **perniciē** (Livy), and a few other forms. The Dat. in **-ī** is found very rarely in early Latin.

64. *Rule of Gender.*—Substantives of the Fifth Declension are feminine except **diēs** (which in the Sing. is common, and in the Pl. masculine), and **merīdiēs** (m.), *midday*.

Declension of Greek Substantives.

65. Greek substantives, especially proper names, are commonly Latinised, and declined regularly according to their stem-characteristic. Many substantives, however, either retain their Greek form exclusively, or have the Greek and Latin forms side by side. These variations occur principally in the Singular, in the Plural the declension is usually regular.

Singular Forms of Greek Substantives.

First Declension.

N.	**Pēnelopē,**	**Leōnidās,**	**Anchīsēs,**
G.	**Pēnelopēs,**	**Leōnidae,**	**Anchīsae,**
D.	**Pēnelopae,**	**Leōnidae,**	**Anchīsae,**
Ac.	**Pēnelopēn,**	**Leōnidam, ān,**	**Anchīsēn, am,**
V.	**Pēnelopē,**	**Leōnidā,**	**Anchīsē, ā, ă,**
Ab.	**Pēnelopā.**	**Leōnidā.**	**Anchīsā.**

Second Declension.

N.	**Dēlos, us,**	**Īlion, um,**	**Panthūs,**	**Androgeōs, us,**
G.	**Dēlī,**	**Īliī,**	**Panthī,**	**Androgeī,**
D.	**Dēlō,**	**Īliō,**	**Panthō,**	**Androgeō,**
Ac.	**Dēlon, um,**	**Īlion, um,**	**Panthūn,**	**Androgeōn, ō, ōna.**
V.	**Dēle,**	**Īlion, um,**	**Panthū,**	**Androgeōs,**
Ab.	**Dēlō.**	**Īliō.**	**Panthō.**	**Androgeō.**

Third Declension.

N.	**Solōn, Solo,**	**āēr,** *air.*	**Xenophōn,**	**Atlās,**
G.	**Solōnis,**	**āeris,**	**Xenophōntis,**	**Atlantis,**
D.	**Solōnī,**	**āerī,**	**Xenophōntī,**	**Atlantī,**
Ac.	**Solōna, em,**	**āera, em,**	**Xenophōnta, em,**	**Atlanta,**
V.	**Solōn,**	**āēr,**	**Xenophōn,**	**Atlā,**
Ab.	**Solōne.**	**āere.**	**Xenophōnte.**	**Atlante.**

N.	**Thalēs,**	**Paris,**	**hērōs,** *hero,*
G.	**Thal-ētis, -is,**	**Paridis, os,**	**hērōis,**
D.	**Thal-ētī, -ī,**	**Paridī, ĭ,**	**hērōī,**
Ac.	**Thal-ēta, -ēn, -em,**	**Par-ida, -im, -in,**	**hērōa, em,**
V.	**Thalē,**	**Pari, Paris,**	**hērōs,**
Ab.	**Thalē.**	**Paride.**	**hērōe.**

Mixed Declensions.

	II. III.	II. III.	II. III.
N.	**Orpheūs,**	**Athōs,**	**Oedipŭs,**
G.	**Orpheī, ĕī,**	**Athō, ōnis,**	**Oedip-odis, -ī,**
D.	**Orpheō,**	**Athō,**	**Oedipodī,**
Ac.	**Orpheum, ea,**	**Athō, ōn, ōnem,**	**Oedip-um, -oda,**
V.	**Orpheū,**	**Athōs,**	**Oedipe,**
Ab.	**Orpheō.**	**Athōne.**	**Oedip-ode, -ō.**

	II. III.	II. III.	III. IV.
N.	**Achillēs, eus,**	**Sōcratēs,**	**Dīdō,**
G.	**Achillis, eī, ī, eōs,**	**Sōcratis, ī,**	**Dīdūs, ōnis,**
D.	**Achillī,**	**Sōcratī,**	**Dīdō, ōnī,**
Ac.	**Achillem, ea, ēn,**	**Sōcratēn, em,**	**Dīdō, ōnem,**
V.	**Achillēs, ē, eū, e,**	**Sōcratē, es,**	**Dīdō,**
Ab.	**Achille, ē, ī.**	**Sōcrate.**	**Dīdō, ōne.**

REMARKS.—1. In the Gen. Pl. **-ōn** and **-eōn** are found in the titles of books ; as, **Geōrgicōn, Metamorphōseōn.**

2. Many Greek names, of the Third Declension in Latin, pass over into the First Declension in the Plural ; as, **Thūcȳdidās, Hyperīdae,** and many names in **-cratēs** ; as **Sōcratēs** ; Pl., **Sōcratae** (also **Sōcratēs**).

3. In transferring Greek words into Latin, the Accusative Singular was sometimes taken as the stem:

So **κρατήρ**, Acc. **κρατῆρα**, (*punch*) *bowl.*
crātēr, crātēris (masc.), and **crātēra** (**crēterra**) **crātērae** (fem.).
Σαλαμίς, Acc. **Σαλαμῖνα**, *Salamis.*
Salamīs, Salamīnis, and **Salamīna, ae.**

66. NOTES.—1. *Singular: Genitive.* The Greek termination **oeo** (οιο) appears rarely in early Latin, but **ū** (ου) is more frequent, especially in geographical names, *etc.* The termination **-os** (ος) is rare except in feminine patronymics in **-is, -as,** (G. **-idos, -ados**).

2. *Dative.* The ending **-ĭ** is very rare ; and rarer still is the Dat. in **-ō** from feminines in **-ō,** and Dat. in **-ȳ** from Nominatives in **-ys.**

3. *Accusative.* **-a** is the most common termination in the Third Declension, and is found regularly in some words otherwise Latinised ; as **āera, aethera.** Stems in **-ō** usually have **-ō,** very rarely **-ōn.**

4. *Plural.* In the Second Declension **oe** is found occasionally in the Nom., in early Latin ; as, **adelphoe.** The Third Declension shows frequently **ĕs** in the Nom. and **ăs** in the Accusative ; also occasionally **ē** in the Nom. and Acc. of neuters, and **-si** (but only in the poets) in the Dative.

5. For other peculiarities, not observable in the paradigms, the dictionaries should be consulted. Sometimes the forms are merely transliterations of Greek cases.

IRREGULAR SUBSTANTIVES.

1. Redundant Substantives. (Abundantia.)

67. A. *Heterogeneous* Substantives, or those whose gender varies :

1. The variation occurs in several cases in either number or in both.

abrotonum,	**-us,**	a plant (rare),	**clipeus,**	**-um,**	*shield,*
aevom (um),	**-us,**	*age,*	**collum,**	**-us,**	*neck,*
baculum,	**-us,**	*staff,*	**costum,**	**-us,**	a plant (rare),
balteus,	**-um,**	*girdle,*	**forum,**	**-us,**	*market,*
buxus,	**-um,**	*box-wood* (rare),	**gladius,**	**-um,**	*sword,*
[calamister],	**-um,**	*curling-iron* (rare),	**intibus,**	**-um,**	*succory* (rare),
cāseus,	**-um,**	*cheese,*	**iugulum,**	**-us,**	*collar-bone,*
cavom (um),	**-us,**	*cavity,*	**nardum,**	**-us,**	*nard* (rare),
cingulum,	**-us,**	*belt,*	**nāsus,**	**-um,**	*nose,*

palātum,	**-us,**	*palate.*	**thēsaurus,**	**-um,**	*treasure,*
pīleus,	**-um,**	*cap,*	**uterus,**	**-um,**	*womb,*
sagum,	**-us,**	*cloak,*	**vāllus,**	**-um,**	*palisade,*
tergum,	**-us,**	*back,*	and many others.		

2. The gender varies in Singular and Plural. *a.* The Plural has **-a** sometimes, while the Singular ends in **-us** (or **-er**) : **clīvus,** *hill,* **iocus,** *jest,* **locus** (**loca,** *localities ;* **locī,** usually *passages in books, topics*), and many others, especially names of places.

b. The Plural has **-ī,** while the Singular ends in **-um** : **fīlum,** *thread,* **frēnum,** *bit,* **rāstrum,** *hoe,* and many others.

68. B. *Heteroclites,* or substantives which show different stems with the same Nominative ; *Metaplasts,* or those which have certain forms from another than the Nominative stem.

1. **1st, 2d.** **esseda,** **-um,** *chariot,* **margarīta,** **-um,** *pearl,* **ostrea,** **-um,** *oyster,*

2. **1st, 5th.** **dūritia,** **-ēs,** *hardness,* **māteria,** **-ēs,** *matter,* and many others. See 63, R. 2.

3. **2d, 1st.** **mendum,** **-a,** *fault,* **sertum,** **-a,** *wreath.*

The following form their Plural according to the First Declension only : **balneum,** *bath,* **dēlicium,** *pleasure,* **epulum,** *banquet,* **fulmentum,** *prop.*

4. **2d, 3d.** **sequester,** *trustee,* **Mulciber,** *Vulcan.*

5. **2d, 4th.** Many names of trees of the Second Declension have certain cases according to the Fourth ; never, however, the Gen. and Dat. Pl., and very rarely the Dat. Sing. ; as **cornus, cupressus, fāgus, fīcus, laurus, myrtus, pīnus,** and a few others.

Also **angiportus,** *alley,* **colus,** *distaff,* **domus,** *house,* and a large number of substantives of the Fourth Declension which have one or two cases of the Second ; so **arcus** has G. **arcī ; cōnātus** (**-um**), **iūssus** (**-um**), **vultus** have Nom. Pl. in **a ; senātus** has Gen. Sing. **senātī.** See 61, RR, NN.

Finally, some substantives of the Second Declension form individual cases according to the Fourth : **fāstī** (Ac. Pl. **fāstūs**), **fretum** (N. **fretus,** Ab. **fretū**), **lectus** (G. **lēctūs**), **tribūtum** (N. **tribūtus**), and others.

6. **2d, 5th.** **dīluvium, -ēs,** *flood.*

7. **3d. 2d.** **Vās,** *vessel,* and **vāsum ; palumbes,** *pigeon,* and **palumbus ;** [**iūger**], *acre,* and **iūgerum ;** all Greek nouns in **-a** (G. **atis**), as **poēma,** *poem* (G. **poēmatis**), but Pl. Gen. **poēmatōrum,** Dat. Abl. **poēmatīs.**

8. **3d, 5th.** **Fames,** *hunger,* **tābes,** *corruption,* have Abl. **famé, tābē ; requiēs,** *quiet* (G. **-ētis**) has Acc. **requiem,** Abl. **requiē ; satiās** (G. **ātis**) is early and late for **satietās,** *sufficiency,* and a form **satiēs** is cited from late authors ; **plēbs** (G. **plēbis**), *commons,* and **plēbēs** (G. **plēbeī**).

9. **4th, 3d.** **Specus,** *cave,* has occasionally forms of the Third Declension.

10. **2d, 3d, 1st.** **Vesper,** *evening,* has Acc. **vesperum ;** Dat. Abl. **vesperō ;** Pl. Nom. **vespera** of the Second Declension ; Acc. **vesperam ;** Abl. **vesperā** of the First ; Gen. **vesperis ;** Abl. **vespere ;** Loc. **vespere, vesperī** of the Third.

11. **4th, 2d, 3d.** **Penus,** *food,* (G. **ūs**). Forms of the Second Declension are rare ; of the Third early and late.

12. Variations in the same Declension : **femur** (G. **femoris, feminis,** *etc.*) ; **iecur** (G. **iecoris, iecinoris,** *etc.*) ; **pecus,** early, also **pecu** (G. **pecoris, pecudis,** *etc.*).

Also **āllēc** and **āllēx, baccar** and **baccaris, cassis** and **cassida, lac** and **lacte** (early), **pānis** and **pāne** (early), **rēte** and **rētis, satiās** and **satietās.**

II. Defective Substantives.

I. SUBSTANTIVES DEFECTIVE IN NUMBER.

69. A. Substantives used in Singular only : **Singulāria tantum.**

Most abstract substantives, and names of materials ; such as **iūstitia,** *justice,* **aurum,** *gold.*

B. Substantives used in Plural only : **Plūrālia tantum.**

altāria, ium,	*altar* (sing. late).
ambāgēs,	*round about.*
angustiae,	*straits.*
antae,	*door-posts.*
antēs,	*rows (of vines).*
arma, ōrum,	*arms.*
armāmenta, ōrum,	*tackle.*
bellāria, ōrum,	*dessert.*
bīgae, quadrīgae,	*two-horse, four-horse chariot* (sing. late).
cancellī,	*lattice.*
cassēs,	*toils (snare).*
caulae,	*opening.*
cervīcēs,	*neck* (sing. early, late, and poet.).
cibāria,	*victuals.*
claustrum,	*lock* (sing. late).
clītellae,	*pack-saddle.*
cōdicillī,	*a short note.*
compedēs,	*fetters.*
crepundia, ōrum,	*rattle.*
cūnae,	*cradle.*
dīvitiae,	*riches.*
dūmēta, ōrum,	*thorn-bush.*
epulae (epulum),	*banquet.*
excubiae,	*watching.*
exsequiae,	*funeral procession.*
exta, ōrum.	*the internal organs.*
exuviae,	*equipments.*
facētiae,	*witticism* (sing. early and late).
fāstī (fāstūs),	*calendar.*
faucēs,	*gullet.*
fēriae,	*holidays.*
flābra,	*breezes.*
forēs,	*door* (sing. early, late and poet.).
frāga, ōrum,	*strawberries.*
grātēs,	*thanks.*
hīberna,	*winter quarters.*
Īdūs, Kalendae, Nōnae,	*Ides, Calends, Nones.*
incūnābula,	*swaddling-clothes.*
indūtiae,	*truce.*
īnferiae,	*sacrifices for the dead.*
īnsidiae,	*ambuscade.*
lactēs,	*intestines.*
lāmenta,	*lamentations.*
lautomiae,	*stone-quarries.*
līberī,	*children.*
mānēs,	*shades of the dead.*
manubiae,	*spoils.*
minae,	*threats.*
moenia, ium,	*town-wall.*
nūndinae (-num),	*market.*
nūptiae,	*wedding.*
palpebrae,	*eyelids* (sing. late).
parentālia,	*festival for dead relations.*
parietinae,	*ruins.*
penātēs,	*the Penates.*
phalerae,	*trappings.*
praecordia, ōrum,	*diaphragm.*
praestrīgiae,	*jugglers' tricks.*
precēs, -um,	*prayer.*
prīmitiae,	*first-fruits.*
quisquiliae,	*rubbish.*
reliquiae,	*remains.*
rēnēs,	*kidneys.*
salīnae,	*salt-pits.*
scālae,	*stairway.*
sentēs,	*brambles.*
spolia, ōrum,	*spoils* (sing. late, and poet.).
spōnsālia, ium,	*betrothal.*
suppetiae,	*succor* (early and late).
tālāria, ium,	*winged sandals.*
tenebrae,	*darkness.*
thermae,	*warm baths.*
tōnsillae,	*tonsils.*
tormina,	*colic.*
trīcae,	*tricks.*
ūtēnsilia, ium,	*necessaries.*
valvae,	*folding-doors.*
verbera, um,	*scourging* (sing. poet. and late).
vindiciae,	*a legal claim.*
virgulta, ōrum,	*shrubbery.*
vīscera,	*entrails* (sing. poet. and late).

NOTES.—1. Four of these have the Abl. Sing. in **-e**: **ambāge, compede, fauce, prece.**

2. Names of persons or towns, and collectives and the like, may be either **singulāria tantum,** as **Iūppiter; Rōma; capillus,** *hair;* or **plūrālia tantum,** as **māiōrēs,** *ancestors;* **Quirītēs; līberī,** *children;* **pulmōnēs,** *lungs.* Many of these are not included in the above list, which is meant to contain only the principal forms.

Akin to **plūrālia tantum** are:

C. Substantives used in Plural with a special sense: **Heterologa.**

aedēs, is,	*temple* (better **aedis**),	**aedēs,**	*house, palace.*
aqua,	*water,*	**aquae,**	*mineral springs.*
auxilium,	*help,*	**auxilia,**	*auxiliaries, reinforcements.*
carcer,	*prison,*	**carcerēs,**	*barriers.*
castrum,	*fort,*	**castra,**	*camp.*
cēra,	*wax,*	**cērae,**	*waxen tablets.*
comitium,	*place of assemblage,*	**comitia,**	*assemblage for voting.*
cōpia,	*abundance,*	**cōpiae,**	*forces, troops.*
dēlicium,	*pleasure,*	**dēliciae,**	*pet.*
facultās,	*capability,*	**facultātēs,**	*goods.*
fīnis,	*end, limit,*	**fīnēs,**	*territory, borders.*
fortūna,	*fortune,*	**fortūnae,**	*possessions.*
habēna,	*strap,*	**habēnae,**	*reins.*
impedīmentum,	*hindrance,*	**impedīmenta,**	*baggage.*
līttera,	*letter* (of the alphabet),	**lītterae,**	*epistle, literature.*
lūdus,	*game, school,*	**lūdī,**	*public games.*
opera,	*work,*	**operae,**	*workmen.*
pars,	*part,*	**partēs,**	also *role.*
rōstrum,	*beak,*	**rōstra,**	*the tribunal at Rome.*
sors,	*lot,*	**sortēs,**	also *oracle.*
tabula,	*board, tablet,*	**tabulae,**	also *accounts.*
vigilia,	*a night-watch,*	**vigiliae,**	*pickets.*

2. SUBSTANTIVES DEFECTIVE IN CASE.

70. A. Substantives occurring in only one case: Gen. **dicis,** *form;* Acc. **īnfitiās (īre),** (to) *lie;* **pessum (īre),** (to) *perish;* Abl. **pondō,** *in weight;* **sponte,** *of free will;* **tābō,** *corruption* (Gen. late); and many verbals in **ū,** as **accītū, admonitū, arcessītū, coāctū, compressū, concēssū, domitū, inductū, interpositū, invītātū, iūssū** (other forms late), **iniūssū, mandātū, missū, nātū, permissū, prōmptū, rogātū.** A few others occur occasionally in ante-classical and post-classical Latin.

B. Substantives with only two cases: **fās, nefās,** Sing. N. Ac.; **īnstar,** Sing. N. Ac.; **interneciō,** Sing. Ac. Ab.; **naucum,** Sing. G. Ac.; **secus,** Sing. N. Ac.; **spinter,** Sing. N. Ac.; **suppetiae,** Plur. N. Ac., and a few others. Some verbals in **-us** have in Plural only Nom. and Acc., as **impetūs, monitūs.** Greek neuters in **-os** have only Nom. and Acc. Singular.

C. Substantives with three cases: **faex,** Sing. N., D., Plur. Ab.; **vīrus,** *slime;* Sing. N., G., Ab.

D. Defective substantives with more than three cases are numerous, but in the classical period the most important are: **calx,** *lime,* **cōs, [daps], dica, [diciō], flāmen,** *blast,* **forum, [frūx], [indāgo], later, lūx, [ops], ōs,** *mouth,* **pāx, rēmex, vīs, [vix],** and most substantives of the Fifth Declension. The Nominatives in brackets do not occur, but only oblique cases.

E. **Nēmō,** *nobody,* substitutes for Gen. and Abl. **nūllīus hominis,** and **nūllō homine.** In the Dat. and Acc. it is normal; **nēminī, nēminem.**

71. III. Peculiarities.

ās, assis (m.), *a copper.*
auceps, aucupis, *fowler.*
bōs (for **bovs**), **bovis** (c.), *ox, cow.*
G. Pl. **boum.**
D. Ab. **būbus, bōbus.**
caput, capitis (n.), *head.*
anceps, ancipitis, *two-headed.*
praeceps, -cipitis, *headlong.*
carō, carnis (f.), *flesh.*
Pl. G. **carnium.**
Cerēs, Cereris, *Ceres.*
fār, farris (n.) *spelt.*
fel, fellis (n.), *gall.*
femur, femoris (n.), *thigh.*
feminis.
iter, itineris (n.), *way, route.*
iecur, iecoris (n.), *liver.*
iecinoris, iecineris, iocineris.
Iūppiter, Iovis.
mel, mellis (n.), *honey.*
nix, nivis (f.), *snow.*
os, ossis (n.), *bone* (48 R.).
ōs, ōris (n.), *mouth.*
pollis, pollinis (m.), *flour.*
sanguis, sanguinis (m.), *blood.*
senex, senis, *old man.*
supellēx, supellēctilis (f.), *furniture.*
Venus, Veneris, *Venus.*

ADJECTIVES.

72. The adjective adds a quality to the substantive. Adjectives have the same declension as substantives, and according to the stem-characteristic are of the First and Second, or Third Declension.

Adjectives of the First and Second Declension.

73. Stems in **-o** for masculine and neuter, **-a** for feminine; nominative in **-us, -a, -um**; **(er), -a, -um.** The same variations in termination occur as in the substantives; except that adjectives in **-ius** form Singular Genitive and Vocative regularly. See 33, R. 1 and 2.

Bonus, bona, bonum, *good.*

	M.	F.	N.		M.	F.	N.
SG.—N.	**bonus,**	**bona,**	**bonum.**	PL.—	**bonī,**	**bonae,**	**bona.**
G.	**bonī,**	**bonae,**	**bonī.**		**bonōrum,**	**bonārum,**	**bonōrum.**
D.	**bonō,**	**bonae,**	**bonō.**		**bonīs,**	**bonīs,**	**bonīs.**
Ac.	**bonum,**	**bonam,**	**bonum.**		**bonōs,**	**bonās,**	**bona.**
V.	**bone,**	**bona,**	**bonum.**		**bonī,**	**bonae,**	**bona.**
Ab.	**bonō,**	**bonā,**	**bonō.**		**bonīs,**	**bonīs,**	**bonīs.**

Miser, misera, miserum, *wretched.*

SG.—N.	**miser,**	**misera,**	**miserum.**	PL.—	**miserī,**	**miserae,**	**misera.**
G.	**miserī,**	**miserae,**	**miserī.**		**miserōrum,**	**miserārum,**	**miserōrum.**
D.	**miserō,**	**miserae,**	**miserō.**		**miserīs,**	**miserīs,**	**miserīs.**
Ac.	**miserum,**	**miseram,**	**miserum.**		**miserōs,**	**miserās,**	**misera.**
V.	**miser,**	**misera,**	**miserum.**		**miserī,**	**miserae,**	**misera.**
Ab.	**miserō,**	**miserā,**	**miserō.**		**miserīs,**	**miserīs,**	**miserīs.**

Piger, pigra, pigrum, *slow.*

Sg.—N.	**piger,**	**pigra,**	**pigrum.**	Pl.—**pigrī,**	**pigrae,**	**pigra.**
G.	**pigrī,**	**pigrae,**	**pigrī.**	**pigrōrum,**	**pigrārum,**	**pigrōrum.**
D.	**pigrō,**	**pigrae,**	**pigrō.**	**pigrīs,**	**pigrīs,**	**pigrīs.**
Ac.	**pigrum,**	**pigram,**	**pigrum.**	**pigrōs,**	**pigrās,**	**pigra.**
V.	**piger,**	**pigra,**	**pigrum.**	**pigrī,**	**pigrae,**	**pigra.**
Ab.	**pigrō,**	**pigrā,**	**pigrō.**	**pigrīs,**	**pigrīs,**	**pigrīs.**

Remark.—For irregularities in the declension of **ambō,** *both,* **duo,** *two,* see 95 ; for **meus,** *my,* see 100, r. i.

74. Stems in **-ro** follow the same principle in the formation of the Nominative masculine as the substantives, except that **-us** is retained in **ferus,** *wild,* **properus,** *quick,* **praeproperus, praeposterus,** *absurd,* **īnferus,** *lower* (**īnfer** is early), **superus,** *upper* (**super** is early), and a few others in late Latin ; also when **-ro** is preceded by a long vowel ; as, **austērus,** *harsh,* **mātūrus,** *early,* **prōcērus,** *tall,* **pūrus,** *pure,* **sevērus,** *serious,* **sincērus,** *sincere,* **sērus,** *late,* **vērus,** *true.*

Remarks.—1. **Dextera, dexterum,** *etc., right,* are found side by side with **dextra, dextrum,** *etc.,* throughout the language (see 8, 2). Caesar uses only the shorter form.

2. A few adjectives of this class lack the Nom. Sing. wholly or in part ; so there is no **cēterus** or **posterus** in the classical period.

75. Notes on the Cases.—1. The Gen. Sing. in **-ī** from adjectives in **-ius** occurs occasionally in inscriptions and in late authors. The Gen. Sing. fem. in early Latin had sometimes **āī,** and in inscriptions occasionally **-aes** and **-es.**

2. The Dat. Sing. fem. in early Latin occasionally ended in **-āī,** and in the oldest inscriptions in **-ā.**

3. In early inscriptions the **-d** of the Abl. is occasionally retained.

4. Very rarely in early inscriptions does the Nom. Pl. masc. end in **-ēīs,** and in one case the Nom. Pl. fem of a perfect participle ends in **-āī.**

5. In poetry, but at all periods, we find **-um** alongside of **-ōrum** and **-ārum** in the Gen. Plural.

6. In the Dat. and Abl. Pl. **-iīs** from adjectives in **-ius** is often contracted to **īs**; usually in names of months and in adjectives formed from proper names. In early inscriptions **-ābus** is found occasionally for **-īs** in the Dat. and Abl. Pl. feminine.

76. The so-called pronominal adjectives **alter,** *one of the two ;* **alteruter** (a combination of **alter** and **uter**), *either of the two ;* **alius,** *other ;* **neuter,** *neither ;* **nūllus,** *none ;* **sōlus,** *sole ;* **tōtus,** *whole ;* **ūllus,** *any ;* **ūnus,** *one ;* **uter,** *which of the two,* and their compounds, show the following variations in declension :

1. They usually make the Gen. Sing. in **-īus** for all genders.

REMARKS.—1. The Gen. **alīus** is very rare, and as a possessive its place is usually taken by **aliēnus.**

2. The **ī** of the ending **-īus** (except in **alīus**) could be shortened in poetry. This was usually the case with **alter**, and regularly in the compounds of **uter**; as, **utrĭusque.**

NOTE.—The regular forms are early and rare; in classical prose only **nūllī** (CIC. *Rosc. Com.* 16, 48) and occasionally **aliae.**

2. They usually make the Dat. Sing. in **-ī.**

NOTE.—Regular forms are sometimes found, but in classical prose only **alterae, nūllō, tōtō**, and perhaps **tōtae. Alī** is found in early Latin for **aliī.**

3. In the compound **alteruter** we find usually both parts declined; sometimes the second only.

4. **Alius** makes Nom. and Acc. Sing. neuter irregularly: **aliud.**

NOTE.—**Alis** and **alid**, for **alius** and **aliud**, are early and rare; the latter, however occurs several times in LUCR. and once in CATULLUS.

Adjectives of the Third Declension.

77. The declension of the adjectives of the Third Declension follows the rules given for the substantives.

Most adjectives of the Third Declension are vowel stems in **-i**, with two (rarely three) endings in the Nominative.

The remaining adjectives of the Third Declension are consonant stems and have one ending only in the Nominative.

ADJECTIVES OF TWO ENDINGS.

78. 1. These have (except stems in **-ri**) one ending in the Nominative for masculine and feminine, one for neuter.

Most stems in **-i** form the masculine and feminine alike, with Nominative in **s**; but the Nominative neuter weakens the characteristic **i** into **e.** (Compare **mare,** *sea.*)

2. Several stems in **-i**, preceded by **r** (**cr, tr, br**), form the Nominative masculine, not by affixing **s**, but by dropping the **i** and inserting short **e** before the **r**, as, stem **ācri,** *sharp,* Nom., **ācer** (m.), **ācris** (f.), **ācre** (n.).

These adjectives are **ācer, alacer, campester, celeber, celer, equester, palūster, pedester, puter, salūber, silvester, terrester, volucer,** and the last four months; and are sometimes called adjectives of *three endings.*

The **e** belongs to the stem in **celer, celeris, celere,** *swift,* and therefore appears in all cases.

	M. and F.	N.	M.	F.	N.
SG.—N.	**facilis**, *easy*.	**facile**,	**ācer**, *sharp*,	**ācris**,	**ācre**,
G.	**facilis**,	**facilis**,	**ācris**,	**ācris**,	**ācris**,
D.	**facilī**,	**facilī**,	**ācrī**,	**ācrī**,	**ācrī**,
Ac.	**facilem**,	**facile**,	**ācrem**,	**ācrem**,	**ācre**,
V.	**facilis**,	**facile**,	**ācer**,	**ācris**,	**ācre**,
Ab.	**facilī**.	**facilī**.	**ācrī**.	**ācrī**.	**ācrī**.
PL.—N.	**facilēs**,	**facilia**,	**ācrēs**,	**ācrēs**,	**ācria**,
G.	**facilium**,	**facilium**,	**ācrium**,	**ācrium**,	**ācrium**,
D.	**facilibus**,	**facilibus**,	**ācribus**,	**ācribus**,	**ācribus**,
Ac.	**facilēs (īs)**,	**facilia**,	**ācrēs (īs)**,	**ācrēs (īs)**,	**ācria**,
V.	**facilēs**,	**facilia**,	**ācrēs**,	**ācrēs**,	**ācria**,
Ab.	**facilibus**.	**facilibus**.	**ācribus**.	**ācribus**.	**ācribus**.

REMARK.—Stems in **-āli** and **-āri** differ from the substantival declension in not suffering apocope in the Nom. Sing. neuter, except occasionally **capital**. See 56.

79. REMARKS.—1. Many adjectives of two endings (except stems in **-ri**) have also **-e** in the Ablative. This is found chiefly in the poets, very rarely, if ever, in classical prose, occasionally in early and pre-Augustan prose, and more often in inscriptions. When, however, these adjectives become proper names, **-e** is the rule. See 57, R. 2, N.

2. The Gen. Pl. in **-um** is found occasionally in inscriptions, frequently in the poets. In classical prose are found only **Titiēnsum** and **familiārum**.

NOTES.—1. The Nom. Pl. has in early Latin not unfrequently **-īs**.

2. In the Acc. Pl., masc. and fem., of adjectives, the ending **-īs** (**ēis**) is found alongside of **-ēs** in every period of the language, though in decreasing proportion, and after the Augustan period principally in **omnīs**.

ADJECTIVES OF ONE ENDING.

80. Adjective stems of one ending (consonant stems) close with **l**, **r**, **s**, a **p** mute, a **k** mute, or a **t** mute. Examples are:

vigil, *alert*, **vigilis**. **memor**, *mindful*, **memoris**. **pauper**, *poor*, **pauperis**. **cicur**, *tame*, **cicuris**. **pūbēs**, *adult*, **pūberis**. **vetus**, *old*, **veteris**.

particeps, *sharing*, **participis**. **caelebs**, *unmarried*, **caelibis**. **inops**, *poor*, **inopis**.

audāx, *bold*, **audācis**. **fēlīx**, *lucky*, **fēlīcis**. **duplex**, *double*, **duplicis**. **ferōx**, *fierce*, **ferōcis**. **trux**, *savage*, **trucis**.

dīves, *rich*, **dīvitis**. **dēses**, *slothful*, **dēsidis**. **compos**, *possessed of*, **compotis**. **prūdēns**, *wise*, **prūdentis**. **concors**, *harmonious*, **concordis**.

Present active participles are also consonant stems and follow the same declension.

81. The stem varieties are:

1. Liquid stems in (*a*) **-l**: **vigil** (G. **vigil-is**), *alert*, **pervigil**; (*b*) **-r**: **pār** (G. **par-is**), *equal*, **impār** (these two lengthen the vowel in the Nom.), **compar**, and three others; **pauper** (G. **pauper-is**), *poor*, **ūber**; **memor** (G. **memor-is**), *mindful*, **immemor**; **concolor** (G. **-ōr-is**), and three other compounds of **color**; **dēgener** (G. **-er-is**), from **genus** (G. **gener-is**).

2. Sibilant stems in (*a*) **-s**: **exos** (G. **exoss-is**), *boneless* (Lucr.); (*b*) **-r**: **gnārus** (G. **gnārur-is**; Plaut.), **Ligus**, **vetus**; **pūbēs** (G. **pūber-is**), **impūbēs**.

3. Mute stems in (*a*) a K-mute: **audāx** (G. **audāc-is**), *bold*, and four others; **fēlīx** (G. **fēlīc-is**), **pernīx**, **atrōx** (G. **atrōc-is**), **ferōx**, **vēlōx**; **exlēx** (G. **-lēg-is**); **trux** (G. **truc-is**), **redux**; the multiplicatives in **-plex** (G. **-plic-is**), as **simplex**, *etc.* (*b*) A P-mute: **inops** (G. **inop-is**); **caelebs** (G. **caelib-is**); compounds of **-ceps** (G. **-cip-is**, from **capere**), as **particeps**, and of **-ceps** (G. **-cipit-is**, from **caput**), as **anceps**, **praeceps** (Plaut. sometimes uses, in the Nom., **ancipes**, **praecipes**, *etc.*). (*c*) A T-mute: **hebes** (G. **hebet-is**) and three others; **locuplēs** (G. **-plēt-is**) and three others; **dīves** (G. **dīvit-is**), for which in poetry **dīs** (G. **dīt-is**), **sōspes**; **compos** (G. **compot-is**), **impos**; **superstes** (G. **-sti-tis**), **āles**; **exhērēs** (G. **ēd-is**); **dēses** (G. **dēsid-is**), **reses**; compounds from substantives: **cōnsors** (G. **-sort-is**), **exsors**; **concors**, **discors**, **misericors**, **sōcors**, **vēcors**; **expers** (G. **-ert-is**), **iners**, **sollers**; **āmēns** (G. **āment-is**), **dēmēns**; **intercus** (G. **cut-is**); **pernox** (G. **-noct-is**); **bipēs** (G. **-ped-is**), **quadrupēs**, **ālipēs**; adjectives and participles in **-āns**, **-ēns** (G. **-ant-is**, **-ent-is**); and proper names in **-ās** (G. **āt-is**), **-īs** (G. **-īt-is**), **-ns** (G. **-nt-is**), **-rs** (G. **-rt-is**), **Arpīnās**, **Samnīs**, **Veiēns**, **Camers**.

82. The consonant stems have the same forms in all the genders, except that in the Accusative Singular, and in the Nominative, Accusative, and Vocative Plural, the neuter is distinguished from the masculine and feminine.

In the oblique cases they follow in part the declension of vowel stems; thus,

1. In the Ablative Singular they have **ī** and **e**—when used as adjectives commonly **ī**; when used as substantives commonly **e**.

The participles, as such, have **e**; but used as substantives or adjectives, either **e** or **ī**, with tendency to **ī**.

2. In the neuter Plural they have **ia**; except **vetus**, *old*, which has **vetera**. Many have no neuter.

3. In the Genitive Plural they have: **ium**, when the stem-characteristic is preceded by a long vowel or a consonant; **um**, when the characteristic is preceded by a short vowel. The participles have **ium**.

	M. and F.	N.	M. and F.	N.	M. and F.	N.
Sg.—N.	**fēlīx,** *lucky,*	**fēlīx,**	**prūdēns,** *wise,*	**prūdēns,**	**vetus,** *old,*	**vetus,**
G.	**fēlīcis,**	**fēlīcis,**	**prūdentis,**	**prūdentis,**	**veteris,**	**veteris,**
D.	**fēlīcī,**	**fēlīcī,**	**prūdentī,**	**prūdentī,**	**veterī,**	**veterī,**
Ac.	**fēlīcem,**	**fēlīx,**	**prūdentem,**	**prūdēns,**	**veterem,**	**vetus,**
V.	**fēlīx,**	**fēlīx,**	**prūdēns,**	**prūdēns,**	**vetus,**	**vetus,**
Ab.	**fēlīcī (e)**	**fēlīcī (e)**	**prūdentī (e)**	**prūdentī (e)**	**vetere (ī)**	**vetere (ī)**
Pl.—N.	**fēlīcēs,**	**fēlīcia,**	**prūdentēs,**	**prūdentia,**	**veterēs,**	**vetera,**
G.	**fēlīcium,**	**fēlīcium,**	**prūdentium,**	**prūdentium,**	**veterum,**	**veterum,**
D.	**fēlīcibus,**	**fēlīcibus,**	**prūdentibus,**	**prūdentibus,**	**veteribus,**	**veteribus,**
Ac.	**fēlīcēs,**	**fēlīcia,**	**prūdentēs,**	**prūdentia,**	**veterēs,**	**vetera,**
V.	**fēlīcēs,**	**fēlīcia,**	**prūdentēs,**	**prūdentia,**	**veterēs,**	**vetera,**
Ab.	**fēlīcibus,**	**fēlīcibus.**	**prūdentibus,**	**prūdentibus.**	**veteribus,**	**veteribus.**

	M. and F.	N.		M. and F.	N.
Sg.—N.	**amāns,** *loving,*	**amāns,**	Pl.—N.	**amantēs,**	**amantia,**
G.	**amantis,**	**amantis,**	G.	**amantium,**	**amantium,**
D.	**amantī,**	**amantī,**	D.	**amantibus,**	**amantibus,**
Ac.	**amantem,**	**amāns,**	Ac.	**amantēs (īs),**	**amantia,**
V.	**amāns,**	**amāns,**	V.	**amantēs,**	**amantia,**
Ab.	**amante (ī).**	**amante (ī).**	Ab.	**amantibus.**	**amantibus.**

83. Remark.—In early and late Latin, and at all periods in the poets, **-e** is often found for **-ī** in the Abl. Singular. In classical prose we find regularly **compote, dēside, impūbere, participe, paupere, pūbere, superstite, vetere,** and frequently **dīvite** (but always **dītī**), **quadrupede, sapiente.** With participles, **-ī** is usual when they are used as adjectives, but classical prose shows **-e** also in **antecēdēns, candēns, cōnsentiēns, dēspiciēns, effluēns, hiāns, imminēns, īnfluēns, prōfluēns, cōnsequēns** (but **sequēns** not before Livy), **titubāns, vertēns.**

Notes.—1. In the Nom. and Acc. Pl. **-īs** for **ēs** belongs to early Latin and the poets, but a few cases of the Acc. are still found in Cicero. In the case of participles **-īs** is very common, and is the rule in Vergil and Horace. In the neuter, **-a** for **-ia** is found only in **ūbera, vetera**; **dītia** is always used for the unsyncopated form **dīvitia.**

2. Compound adjectives, whose primitives had **-um** in Gen. Pl., have usually **-um** instead of **-ium**; **quadrupēs, quadrupedum,** and other compounds of **pēs**; **inops, inopum**; **supplex, supplicum.** Also, **cicur, cicurum**; **vetus, veterum**; **dīves, dīvitum**; **locuplēs, locuplētum** (rare, usually **-ium**). In the poets and in later writers, **-um** is not unfrequently found where classical prose uses **-ium.**

Irregular Adjectives.

84. A. Abundantia.

1. Some adjectives which end in **-us, -a, -um,** in the classical times, show occasionally in early Latin, in the poets, and in later Latin, forms in **-is, -e,** *e. g.*, **imbēcillus** and **imbēcillis**; **īnfrēnus** and **īnfrēnis**; **biiugus** and **biiugis**; **violentus** and **violēns**; **indecōrus** and **indecoris**; so also **perpetuus** and **perpes.** In a number of other adjectives the variant forms are very rare or disputed.

2. Many adjectives which end in **-is, -e,** in the classical times, show parallel forms in **-us, -a, -um,** in early Latin, and more rarely in late Latin. Adjectives in **-us, -a, -um,** in early Latin, seem to have had a tendency to go over into forms in **-is, -e.** Thus, **hilarus** is the regular form in early Latin ; in CICERO it is used side by side with **hilaris,** and later **hilaris** is universal. Other examples in the classical period are **inermis** and **inermus** ; **imberbis** and **imberbus** ; **ālāris** and **ālārius** ; **auxiliāris** and **auxiliārius** ; **intercalāris** and **intercalārius** ; **tālāris** and **tālārius.**

85. B. DEFECTIVE.

1. Several adjectives lack a Nom. Singular, wholly or in part : as, **cētera** (f.), **cēterum, perperum** (n.), **nūperum** (n.), **prīmōris** (G.), **bimaris** (G.), **bimātris** (G.), **tricorporis** (G.), and a few others.

2. Some adjectives are defective in other cases : thus, **exspēs** and **perdius, -a** are found only in the Nom.; **exlēx** only in the Nom. and Acc. (**exlēgem**) ; **pernox** only in Nom., Abl. (**pernocte**), and Nom. Pl. (**pernoctēs,** rare) ; **centimanus** has only the Acc. Sing. (HOR., OV.) ; also **ūnimanus** (LIV.), and a few others.

C. INDECLINABLES.

Nēquam ; **potis,** and **pote** (early) ; **frūgī** ; **macte** (**mactus, -um,** very rare) ; **necesse, necessum,** and **necessus** (early and poetical) ; **volup** and **volupe** (early) ; and the judicial **damnās.**

COMPARISON OF ADJECTIVES.

86. The Degrees of Comparison are : Positive, Comparative, and Superlative.

The Comparative is formed by adding to the consonant stems the endings **-ior** for the masculine and feminine, and **-ius** for the neuter.

The Superlative is formed by adding to the consonant stems the endings **-is-simus, -a, -um** (earlier **-is-sumus**).

Vowel stems, before forming the Comparative and Superlative, drop their characteristic vowel.

POSITIVE.		COMPARATIVE. M. and F.	N.	SUPERLATIVE.
altus, a, um,	*high,*	**altior,** *higher,*	**altius,**	**altissimus, a, um,** *highest.*
fortis, e,	*brave,*	**fortior,**	**fortius,**	**fortissimus.**
ūtilis, e,	*useful,*	**ūtilior,**	**ūtilius,**	**ūtilissimus.**
audāx,	*bold,*	**audācior,**	**audācius,**	**audācissimus.**
prūdēns,	*wise,*	**prūdentior,**	**prūdentius,**	**prūdentissimus.**

NOTE.—In early Latin we find very rarely **-iōs** for **ior** ; also **-ior** used for the neuter as well.

Peculiarities.

87. 1. Adjectives in **-er** add the Superlative ending (**-rumus**) **-rimus** (for **-simus** by assimilation ; see 9, 1) directly to the Nominative masculine. The Comparative follows the rule.

Positive.		Comparative.		Superlative.
miser, a, um,	*wretched,*	**miserior,**	**miserius,**	**miserrimus.**
celer, is, e,	*swift,*	**celerior,**	**celerius,**	**celerrimus.**
ācer, ācris, ācre,	*sharp,*	**ācrior,**	**ācrius,**	**ācerrimus.**

Remarks.—1. **Dexter,** *right,* and **sinister,** *left,* have always **dexterior** and **sinisterior** in the Comparative. **Dēterior,** *worse,* **dēterrimus,** lacks a Positive.

2. **Vetus,** *old,* has Comp. **veterior** (archaic) or **vetustior**; Sup., **veterrimus. Mātūrus,** *ripe,* has occasionally Sup. **mātūrrimus** in addition to the normal **mātūrissimus.**

Note.—In early Latin and in inscriptions this rule is occasionally violated. Thus **celerissimus** in Ennius ; **integrissimus, miserissimus,** in inscriptions.

2. Some Comparatives in **-er-ior,** whose Positive is lacking or rare, form the Superlative either in **-rēmus** by metathesis ; or in **-imus** or **-umus** ; or in both. These are : **citerior,** *on this side,* **citimus** (rare) ; **exterior,** *outer,* **extrēmus, extimus** (latter not in Cic.) ; **dexterior** (87, 1, r. 1 ; once in Cic.), **dextimus** (rare ; not in Cic.) ; **īnferior,** *lower,* **īnfimus, īmus** ; **interior,** *inner,* **intimus** ; **posterior,** *hinder,* **postrēmus, postumus** ; **superior,** *upper,* **suprēmus, summus.**

3. Six adjectives in **-ilis** add **-limus** to the stem, after dropping **-i,** to form the Superlative ; perhaps by assimilation : **facilis,** *easy ;* **difficilis,** *hard ;* **similis,** *like ;* **dissimilis,** *unlike ;* **gracilis,** *slender,* and **humilis,** *low.*

facilis, Comp. **facilior,** Sup. **facillimus.**

4. Adjectives in **-dicus, -ficus, -volus,** borrow the Comparative and Superlative from the participial forms in **-dīcēns, -ficēns,** and **-volēns.**

benevolus,	*benevolent,*	Comp. **benevolentior,**	Sup. **benevolentissimus.**
maledicus,	*scurrilous.*	**maledīcentior,**	**maledīcentissimus.**
māgnificus,	*distinguished.*	**māgnificentior,**	**māgnificentissimus.**

Note.—**Benevolēns, malevolēns, maledīcēns,** still occur in early Latin.

5. In like manner **egēnus** and **prōvidus** form their Comparative and Superlative.

egēnus,	*needy,*	**egentior,**	**egentissimus.**
prōvidus,	*far-sighted,*	**prōvidentior,**	**prōvidentissimus.**

6. Adjectives in **-us** (**os**), preceded by a vowel (except those in **-quos**), form the Comparative and Superlative by means of **magis** and **māximē**, *more* and *most.*

idōneus, *fit,* Comp. **magis idōneus,** Sup. **māximē idōneus.**

But

antīquos, *old,* Comp. **antīquior,** Sup. **antīquissimus.**

REMARK.—But **pius,** *pious,* which lacks the Comparative, forms the Superlative regularly, **piissimus** (in inscriptions also **pientissimus**); likewise in late Latin, **impius.**

NOTES.—1. A few words, chiefly in early Latin, show the normal comparison. In CIC. only, **assiduissimē** (adv.) and **alsius.**

2. Comparison by means of **plūs** and **plūrimum** is late.

7. Some Comparatives and Superlatives are in use, whilst the corresponding Positive is either lacking or rare.

So **dēterior** (87, 1, R. 1); **ōcior,** *swift,* **ōcissimus; potior,** *better,* **potissimus; exterior,** *outer* (87, 2), from **exterus,** *on the outside,* and prep. **extra,** *without;* **superior,** *upper* (87, 2), from **superus,** *on the top,* and prep. **suprā,** *above;* **īnferior,** *lower* (87, 2), from **īnferus,** *below,* and prep. **īnfrā,** *below;* **posterior,** *hinder* (87, 2), from **posterus,** *coming after,* and prep. **post,** *after;* **citerior,** *on this side* (87, 2), from **citer,** and prep. **citrā,** *on this side.*

8. The Positive stem of existing Comparatives is sometimes met with only in a preposition or an adverb; as, **ante,** *before;* **anterior,** *that is before;* **prope,** *near;* **propior, proximus**; **ūlterior,** *further,* **ūltimus,** from **ūltrā,** *beyond;* **interior,** *inner,* **intimus,** from **intrā,** *within;* **prior,** *former,* **prīmus,** *first,* from **prō,** *before;* **sequior** (late), *worse,* from **secus.**

9. Many adjectives lack one or both of the degrees of comparison; especially those denoting *material, relationship, time, etc.*

Novus, *new,* **falsus,** *untrue,* **meritus,** *deserved,* have no Comparative.

Longinquos, *afar,* **propinquos,** *near,* **salūtāris,** *healthful,* **iuvenis,** *young* (Comparative **iūnior**), and **senex,** *old* (Comparative **senior**), have no Superlative.

"*Youngest*" and "*oldest*" are expressed by **minimus, māximus** (**nātū**).

NOTE.—The Plautine and late **medioximus,** *middlemost,* lacks Positive and Comparative.

10. **Dīves,** *rich,* shows in CIC. only **dīvitior** and **dīvitissimus**; otherwise the Comparative and Superlative are found principally in poetry and later prose, the more usual forms being the syncopated **dītior, dītissimus.**

88. Participles used as adjectives are subject also to the same laws of comparison: as, **amāns,** *loving,* **amantior, amantissimus**; **apertus,** *open,* **apertior, apertissimus.**

89. The Superlative follows the declension of adjectives of Three Endings of the First and Second Declensions. The Comparative is declined according to the Third Declension, thus:

	M. and F.	N.		M. and F.	N.
SG.—N.	**altior,**	**altius.**	PL.—	**altiōrēs,**	**altiōra.**
G.	**altiōris,**	**altiōris.**		**altiōrum,**	**altiōrum.**
D.	**altiōrī,**	**altiōrī.**		**altiōribus,**	**altiōribus.**
Ac.	**altiōrem,**	**altius.**		**altiōrēs,**	**altiōra.**
V.	**altior,**	**altius.**		**altiōrēs,**	**altiōra.**
Ab.	**altiōre** and **-ī,**	**altiōre** and **-ī.**		**altiōribus,**	**altiōribus.**

REMARKS.—1. In classical prose the Abl. Sing. ends in **-e.** In the poets and in early and late prose often in **-ī.**

2. Extremely rare is the ending **-īs** for **-ēs** in the Nom. Plural. In the Acc. Pl. this ending **-īs** (**-ēīs**) is more common but still not frequent, and confined mainly to **plūrīs, minōrīs, māiōrīs, meliōrīs.** The neuter in **-ia** is found rarely in **complūria,** and perhaps once in **plūria.**

3. The Gen. Pl. in **-ium** is found in **plūrium** and **complūrium** only.

90. Irregular Comparison.

bonus,	*good,*		**melior,**	**melius,**	**optimus.**
malus,	*bad,*		**pēior,**	**pēius,**	**pessimus.**
māgnus,	*great,*		**māior,**	**māius,**	**māximus.**
parvus,	*small,*		**minor,**	**minus,**	**minimus.**
multus,	*much,*	S.	——	**plūs** (no Dat. nor Abl.),	**plūrimus.**
		Pl.	**plūrēs,**	**plūra.**	
			complūrēs,	**complūra** and **-ia.**	
nēquam,	*worthless,*		**nēquior,**	**nēquius,**	**nēquissimus.**
frūgī (indecl.),	*frugal,*		**frūgālior,**		**frūgālissimus.**

ADVERBS.

91. Most adverbs are either oblique cases or mutilated forms of oblique cases of nominal or pronominal stems.

The cases from which they are derived are principally the Accusative and the Ablative.

1. (*a*) From the Accusative are Substantival Adverbs in **-tim.** This was a favorite formation, and is used very often in all periods. In the classical times the adverbs of this form are:

Acervātim, articulātim, centuriātim, certātim, generātim, gradātim, gregātim, membrātim, paulātim, prīvātim, sēparātim, singulātim, statim, summātim, virītim, tribūtim, strictim, pedetemptim, raptim, fūrtim, partim, praesertim, cōnfēstim, and a few others; disguised forms of **-tim** are: **caesim, incīsim, sēnsim, cursim, passim, vicissim,** for **caed-tim** (9, 1-3), *etc.:* also **interim.**

(*b*) A few very common adverbs are, perhaps, from Accusative Singular feminine of adjectives and pronominal stems. Chiefly **clam**, *secretly*, **cōram**, *in one's presence*, **palam**, *openly*, **perperam**, *wrongly*, **tam**, *so*, **quam**, *as*, **aliquam**, *some*, **iam**, *already;* and forms in **-fāriam**, as **bifāriam**, **multifāriam**, *etc.*

(*c*) The Accusative Singular neuter of many adjectival and pronominal stems is used as an adverb. *This is true of all Comparatives.*

Multum, *much;* **paulum**, *a little;* **nimium**, *too much;* **cēterum**, *for the rest;* **prīmum**, *first;* **postrēmum**, *finally;* **potissimum**, *chiefly;* **facile**, *easily;* **dulce**, *sweetly;* **trīste**, *sadly;* **impūne**, *scot-free;* **aliquantum**, *somewhat*, and others.

To the Comparatives belong **magis**, *more;* **nimis**, *too;* **satis**, *enough.*

(*d*) The Accusative Plural feminine is found in **aliās**, *at other times*, perhaps in **forās**, *out-of-doors.* The Accusative Plural neuter is found in **alia**, **cētera**, **omnia**, and occasionally in **reliqua** and a few others.

2. (*a*) From the Ablative are some substantival adverbs; the principal ones in classical Latin being **domō**, *at home;* **impendiō**, *greatly;* **initiō**, *at the outset;* **modo**, *only;* **oppidō**, *very;* **prīncipiō**, *in the beginning;* **prīvātō**, *privately;* **vulgō**, *commonly;* **forte**, *by chance;* **māgnopere**, *greatly*, and other compounds of **-opere**; **grātiīs**, *for nothing*, and **ingrātiīs**, and a few others.

(*b*) Ablatives are also adverbs in **ē** from adjectives in **-us** and **-er**:

altus, *lofty*, **altē**; **pulcher**, *beautiful*, **pulchrē**; **miser**, *wretched*, **miserē**.

Also **ferē** and **fermē** (Sup.), *almost.*

(*c*) The Ablative of some adjectives and pronouns serves as an adverb:

tūtō, *safely;* **falsō**, *falsely;* **perpetuō**, *ceaselessly;* **continuō**, *forthwith;* **imprōvīsō**, *unexpectedly;* **prīmō**, *at first;* **hōc**, *here;* **istō**, *there, etc.*

(*d*) In a few cases the adverbial form is the Abl. Sing. feminine:

aliā, *otherwise;* **aliquā**, *somehow;* **dexterā** and **dextrā**, *to the right;* **sinistrā** and **laevā**, *to the left hand;* **quā**, *on which side;* **rēctā**, *straightway*, and some others.

(*e*) A large number of these adjectives show adverbs in two endings, sometimes with a difference in meaning:

cōnsultē and **cōnsultō**, *purposely;* **certē**, *at least*, and **certō**, *certainly* (**certē sciō**, *I certainly know:* **certō sciō**, *I know for certain*); **rārē**, *thinly*, and **rārō**, *seldom;* **vērē**, *in truth*, and **vērō**, *true but;* **rēctē**, *correctly*, and **rēctā**, *straightway;* **dexterā** or **dextrā**, *to the right;* and **dexterē**, *skilfully.*

(*f*) Ablatives are also **quī**, *how* (archaic), **nēquīquam**, *to no purpose;* **aliōquī**, *otherwise;* perhaps also **diū**, *by day*, and its compounds.

3. Locative in origin are the following, in addition to those mentioned under 37, 5: **diē** (in combination with numeral adjectives in early Latin, as **diē septimī**) and its compounds **cottīdiē**, *daily*, **hodiē**, *to-day*, **prīdiē**, *the day before*, **postrīdiē**, *the day after;* **quotannīs**, *yearly;* **forīs**, *outside*. Also many forms from the pronominal stems, as **hīc**, **illīc**, **istīc** (**istī** belongs to early Latin and VERG.); **sīc**, *so*, **ut** (**utī**, **uteī**), *as;* **ibi**, *there*, and its compounds **alibi**, **ibīdem**; **ubi** (**cubi**), *where*, and its compounds.

4. A number of adverbs cannot be referred to a definite case, as: adverbs of *separation:* **hinc**, *hence*, **illinc** (**illim**), **istinc** (**istim**), *thence; temporal* adverbs: **tunc**, *then*, **cum**, *when*, **quondam**, *once*, **quandō**, *when?* and its compounds; also, **ante**, *before;* **post** (**poste**), *after;* **paene**, *almost;* **prope**, **propter**, *near;* **saepe**, *often;* **circiter**, *around;* **praeter**, *past;* **ergō**, *therefore;* **crās**, *to-morrow;* **haud** (**hau**, **haut**), *not;* **item**, *likewise;* **susque dēque**, *up and down;* **vix**, *scarcely*.

92. 1. Adjectives and participles of the Third Declension form their adverbs by adding **-ter** (**-iter**) to the stem; stems in **-nt** dropping the **t**, and stems in a **k**-mute inserting the connecting vowel **i** before the ending; also a few adjectives of the Second Declension:

fortis, *brave*, **fortiter**; **ferōx**, *wild*, **ferōciter**; **prūdēns**, *foreseeing*, **prūdenter**.

Exceptions: **audāx**, *bold*, **audāc-ter** (seldom **audāciter**); **difficilis**, *hard to do*, **difficulter**, **difficiliter** (but generally, **nōn facile**, **vix**, **aegrē**), and others.

2. A large number of adjectives of the Second Declension in **-us**, **-a**, **-um**, and **-er**, **-era**, **-erum**, form in early and late Latin their adverbs by dropping the stem vowel and adding **-iter** (those in **-tus** added **-er** only). Many of these occur in classical writers alongside of the normal form in **-ē**: **hūmāniter** and **hūmānē**, *humanely;* **largiter** and **largē**, *lavishly;* **turbulenter** and **turbulentē**, *riotously*.

3. Some adverbs of *origin* are formed from substantival or adjectival stems by the ending **-tus**. In classical Latin mainly **antīquitus**, *from early time;* **dīvīnitus**, *from the gods;* **funditus**, *from the foundation;* **penitus**, *from the depths;* **rādīcitus**, *from the roots;* also **intus**, *from within*.

4. The termination **-vorsus**, **-vorsum**, is used to show *direction whither;* but in classical Latin it is found principally in the adverbs: **intrōrsus** (**intrōvorsus**), *inwards;* **prōrsus** (**-um**), *onwards;* **rūrsus** (**-um**, **rūsum**), *back;* **sūrsum** (**sūsum**), *up;* **vorsum**, *towards*.

5. A very large number of adverbs are formed by adding various other terminations; as, ***-de:*** **inde**, *thence*, **unde**, *whence;* ***-dem:*** **prīdem**, *long ago*, **itidem**, *likewise*, *etc.;* ***-dō:*** **quandō**, *when*, *etc.;* ***-dam:*** **quondam**, *once;* ***-dum:*** **dūdum**, *a while ago;* **vixdum**, *hardly yet*, *etc.;* ***-per:*** **nūper**, *lately*, **parumper**, *a little*, **semper**, *always*, *etc.;* ***-quam:*** **umquam**, *ever*, **numquam**, *never*, *etc.;* ***-secus:*** **extrīnsecus**, *outside*, *etc.;* ***-tenus:*** **quātenus**, *how far?* *etc.*

6. Syntactical and miscellaneous: **admodum,** *very* (*to a degree*), **dēnuō,** *anew,* **imprīmis**; **super,** *above,* and its compounds, **dēsuper, īnsuper**; **extemplō,** *at once;* **ūsque,** *to,* and its compounds; **invicem,** *in turn;* **adeō,** *so;* **anteā,** *before;* **intereā,** *meanwhile;* **posteā,** *after;* **praetereā,** *besides;* **proptereā,** *on that account,* and a few others.

COMPARISON OF ADVERBS.

93. The Comparative of the adverb is the Accusative neuter of the Comparative of the adjective. The Superlative ends in **-is-simē, -er-rimē,** *etc.,* according to the Superlative of the adjective.

Positive.		Comparative.	Superlative.
altē,	*loftily,*	**altius,**	**altissimē.**
pulchrē,	*beautifully,*	**pulchrius,**	**pulcherrimē.**
miserē,	*poorly,*	**miserius,**	**miserrimē.**
fortiter,	*bravely,*	**fortius,**	**fortissimē.**
audācter,	*boldly,*	**audācius,**	**audācissimē.**
tūtō,	*safely,*	**tūtius,**	**tūtissimē.**
facile,	*easily,*	**facilius,**	**facillimē.**
bene,	*well,*	**melius,**	**optimē.**
male,	*ill,*	**pēius,**	**pessimē.**
[parvus],	*small,*	**minus,** *less,*	**minimē,** *least.*
[māgnus],	*great,*	**magis,** *more,*	**māximē,** *most.*
multum,	*much,*	**plūs,** *more,*	**plūrimum.**
cito,	*quickly,*	**citius,**	**citissimē.**
diū,	*long,*	**diūtius,**	**diūtissimē.**
saepe,	*often,*	**saepius,**	**saepissimē.**
nūper,	*recently,*	——,	**nūperrimē.**
satis,	*enough,*	**satius,** *better,*	

NUMERALS.

NUMERAL ADJECTIVES.

94. The Cardinal numerals answer the question **quot,** *how many?* and are the numbers used in counting. The Ordinal numerals are derived from these and answer the question **quotus,** *which one in the series?* They are as follows:

		1. Cardinal Numbers.	2. Ordinal Numbers.
1	I	**ūnus, ūna, ūnum**	**prīmus, -a, -um (prior)**
2	II	**duo, duae, duo**	**secundus (alter)**
3	III	**trēs, tria**	**tertius**
4	IV	**quattuor**	**quārtus**
5	V	**quīnque**	**quīntus**
6	VI	**sex**	**sextus**
7	VII	**septem**	**septimus**

		1. Cardinal Numbers.	2. Ordinal Numbers.
8	VIII	octō	octāvus
9	IX	novem	nōnus
10	X	decem	decimus
11	XI	ūndecim	ūndecimus
12	XII	duodecim	duodecimus
13	XIII	tredecim	tertius decimus
14	XIV	quattuordecim	quārtus decimus
15	XV	quīndecim	quīntus decimus
16	XVI	sēdecim	sextus decimus
17	XVII	septendecim	septimus decimus
18	XVIII	duodēvīgintī	duodēvīcēsimus
19	XIX	ūndēvīgintī	ūndēvīcēsimus
20	XX	vīgintī	vīcēsimus
21	XXI	vīgintī ūnus	vīcēsimus prīmus
22	XXII	vīgintī duo	vīcēsimus secundus
23	XXIII	vīgintī trēs	vīcēsimus tertius
24	XXIV	vīgintī quattuor	vīcēsimus quārtus
25	XXV	vīgintī quīnque	vīcēsimus quīntus
26	XXVI	vīgintī sex	vīcēsimus sextus
27	XXVII	vīgintī septem	vīcēsimus septimus
28	XXVIII	duodētrīgintā	duodētrīcēsimus
29	XXIX	ūndētrīgintā	ūndētrīcēsimus
30	XXX	trīgintā	trīcēsimus
40	XL	quadr*ā*gintā	quadrāgēsimus
50	L	quīnqu*ā*gintā	quīnquāgēsimus
60	LX	sex*ā*gintā	sexāgēsimus
70	LXX	sept*uā*gintā	septuāgēsimus
80	LXXX	oct*ō*gintā	octōgēsimus
90	XC	nōn*ā*gintā	nōnāgēsimus
100	C	centum	centēsimus
101	CI	centum et ūnus	centēsimus prīmus
115	CXV	centum et quīndecim	centēsimus (et) quīntus decimus
120	CXX	centum et vīgintī	centēsimus vīcēsimus
121	CXXI	centum vīgintī ūnus	centēsimus vīcēsimus prīmus
200	CC	ducentī, -ae, -a	ducentēsimus
300	CCC	trecentī	trecentēsimus
400	CCCC	quadr*in*gentī	quadringentēsimus
500	D (IↃ)	*quīn*gentī	quīngentēsimus
600	DC	*sēs*centī	sēscentēsimus
700	DCC	sept*in*gentī	septingentēsimus
800	DCCC	oct*in*gentī	octingentēsimus
900	DCCCC	*nōn*gentī	nōngentēsimus
1000	M (CIↃ)	mīlle	mīllēsimus

		1. Cardinal Numbers.	2. Ordinal Numbers.
1001	MI	mīlle et ūnus	mīllēsimus prīmus
1101	MCI	mīlle centum ūnus	mīllēsimus centēsimus prīmus
1120	MCXX	mīlle centum vīgintī	mīllēsimus centēsimus vīcē-
		[ūnus	simus [simus prīmus
1121	MCXXI	mīlle centum vīgintī	mīllēsimus centēsimus vīcē-
1200	MCC	mīlle ducentī	mīllēsimus ducentēsimus
2000	MM	duo mīlia (mīllia)	bis mīllēsimus
		bīna mīlia	
2222		duo mīlia ducentī vī- gintī duo	bis mīllēsimus ducentēsimus vīcēsimus secundus
5000	IↃↃ	quīnque mīlia	quīnquiēs mīllēsimus
		quīna mīlia	
10,000	CCIↃↃ	decem mīlia	deciēs mīllēsimus
		dēna mīlia	
21,000		ūnum et vīgintī mīlia	semel et vīciēs mīllēsimus
100,000		centum mīlia	centiēs mīllēsimus
		centēna mīlia [mīlia	
1,000,000		deciēs centēna (centum)	deciēs centiēs mīllēsimus

95. The Cardinal numerals are indeclinable, except: **ūnus**, *one*, **duo**, *two*, **trēs**, *three*, the hundreds beginning with **ducentī**, *two hundred*, and the plural **mīlia**, *thousands*, which forms **mīlium** and **mīlibus**.

				M and F.	N.
N.	**duo**, *two*,	**duae**,	**duo**,	**trēs**, *three*,	**tria**.
G.	**duōrum**,	**duārum**,	**duōrum**,	**trium**,	**trium**.
D.	**duōbus**,	**duābus**,	**duōbus**,	**tribus**,	**tribus**.
A.	**duōs**, **duo**,	**duās**,	**duo**,	**trēs**, **trīs**,	**tria**.
Ab.	**duōbus**,	**duābus**,	**duōbus**,	**tribus**,	**tribus**.

Like **duŏ** is declined **ambō**, **-ae**, **-ō**, *both*.

Remarks.—1. For the declension of **ūnus** see 76. It occurs also in plural forms in connection with **plūrālia tantum**, as **ūnīs lītterīs** (Cic. *Att.*, v. 9, 2), or with another numeral in the sense *only*; in the latter sense also with substantives.

2. The Gen. of the hundreds, **ducentī**, *etc.*, ends in **-um** and not **-ōrum**. This must be distinguished from the use of the neuter singular in **-um** as a *collective*, as **argentī sēscentum** (Luc.), *a six hundred of silver*.

3. The Pl. **mīlia**, **mīlium**, **mīlibus**, are treated almost always as substantives, the adjectival form being the Singular.

Notes.—1. The form **oinos** for **ūnus** is found in early Latin. A Voc. **ūne** is occasional (Cat., 37, 17).

2. For **duae** late Latin shows occasionally **duo**, and in inscriptions **dua**, for neuter

duo, is sometimes found. The Gen. **duum** (old **duom**) for **duōrum** is not unfrequent. In the Dat. and Abl., **duo** is found in inscriptions, and for **ambōbus** occasionally **ambīs.** In the Acc. Pl. masc., **duo** and **ambō** for **duōs** and **ambōs** are quite common in early Latin, and also in classical times, but the better forms are **duōs, ambōs.**

3. **Quattor** is found for **quattuor** occasionally in inscriptions, and in early poetry **quattuor** was sometimes scanned as a dissyllable.

4. In inscriptions the forms **mēilia** and **mīllia** are also found.

5. In regard to spelling of the Ordinals we find in early Latin **quīnctus** as well as **quīntus; septumus** and **decumus** regularly, and often the endings **-ēnsimus** and **-ēnsumus** in Ordinals from **vīcēsimus** on.

96. 1. Compound Numerals.

1. From 10 to 20, as in the tables, or separately : **decem et trēs.**

2. The numbers 18, 19, 28, 29, etc., are commonly expressed by subtraction ; occasionally, as in English, but never in CICERO, and very rarely in other classical authors. **duodēcentum** is not found, and **ūndēcentum** but once (PLIN. MAI.).

3. From 20 to 100, the compound numerals stand in the same order as the English : *twenty-one,* **vīgintī ūnus** ; or, *one and twenty,* **ūnus et (atque) vīgintī** ; as, *twenty-one years old :* **annōs ūnum et vīgintī (vīgintī ūnum), ūnum et vīgintī annōs nātus.** But compounds like **septuāgintā et trēs** are not uncommon, though avoided by good writers.

4. From 100 on, **et** may be inserted after the first numeral, if there be but two numbers ; as, **centum quattuor,** or **centum et quattuor.** If the smaller number precedes, the **et** should be inserted; likewise in all cases where a word is inserted within the compound numeral, as **ducentī annī et vīgintī.** If there be three numerals, the **et** is regularly omitted ; exceptions are very rare.

5. In compound ordinals **alter** is preferred to **secundus.**

6. **Centēna mīlia** is often omitted after the numeral adverb **deciēs** = 1,000,000 ; especially in stating sums of money.

7. Fractions are expressed by **pars** (omitted or expressed) in combination with **dīmidia** ($\frac{1}{2}$), **tertia** ($\frac{1}{3}$), **quārta** ($\frac{1}{4}$), *etc.* A Plural numerator is expressed by a Cardinal ; as, **duae quīntae** ($\frac{2}{5}$). The fraction is often broken up ; as, **pars dīmidia et tertia** ($\frac{5}{6} = \frac{1}{2} + \frac{1}{3}$). The even denominators could be divided ; as, **dīmidia tertia** ($\frac{1}{2} \times \frac{1}{3} = \frac{1}{6}$). Instead of **dīmidia** without **pars, dīmidium** is used.

2. Numeral Signs.

D is short for IƆ, M for CIƆ. Adding Ɔ on the right of IƆ multiplies by 10 ; IƆƆ = 5000 ; IƆƆƆ = 50,000. Putting C before as often as Ɔ stands after multiplies the right-hand number by 2 ; CIƆ = 1000 ; CCIƆƆ = 10,000 ; CCCIƆƆƆ = 100,000. A line above multiplies by 1000 ; $\overline{\text{V}}$ = 5000. A line above and at each side multiplies by 100,000 : $|\overline{\text{XIIII}}|$ = 1,400,000. These signs may be combined : thus, $|\overline{\text{XIII}}|$ $\overline{\text{XXXVII}}$ D or $|\overline{\text{XIII}}|$ XXXVII MD = 1,337,500. PLIN., *N. H.* IV., 12, 24. Other signs are ↆ, ⊥ (inscr.) for 50, ∽, ∞, ↀ (inscr.) for 1000, and ↈ for 100,000 (inscr.), and **q** for 500,000 (inscr.).

97. 3. Distributive Numerals.

1	**singulī, -ae, -a,** *one each.*	30	**trīcēnī**
2	**bīnī, -ae, -a,** *two each.*	40	**quadrāgēnī**
3	**ternī (trīnī)**	50	**quīnquāgēnī**
4	**quaternī**	60	**sexāgēnī**
5	**quīnī**	70	**septuāgēnī**
6	**sēnī**	80	**octōgēnī**
7	**septēnī**	90	**nōnāgēnī**
8	**octōnī**	100	**centēnī**
9	**novēnī**	102	**centēnī bīnī**
10	**dēnī**	125	**centēnī vīcēnī quīnī**
11	**ūndēnī**	200	**ducēnī**
12	**duodēnī**	300	**trecēnī**
13	**ternī dēnī**	400	**quadringēnī**
14	**quaternī dēnī**	500	**quīngēnī**
15	**quīnī dēnī**	600	**sexcēnī (sēscēnī)**
16	**sēnī dēnī**	700	**septingēnī**
17	**septēnī dēnī**	800	**octingēnī**
18	**octōnī dēnī, duodēvīcēnī**	900	**nōngēnī**
19	**novēnī dēnī, ūndēvīcēnī**	1000	**singula mīlia**
20	**vīcēnī**	2000	**bīna mīlia**
21	**vīcēnī singulī**	3000	**trīna mīlia**
22	**vīcēnī bīnī, bīnī et vīcēnī**	10,000	**dēna mīlia**
28	**duodētrīcēnī**	100,000	**centēna mīlia**
29	**ūndētrīcenī**		

These answer the question **quotēnī**, *how many each?*

REMARKS.—1. The Gen. Pl. masc. and neuter ends usually in **-um**, except that **singulus** has always **singulōrum**, and CICERO uses **bīnōrum.**

2. The Distributives are used with an exactness which is foreign to our idiom, whenever repetition is involved, as in the multiplication table. But when **singulī** is expressed, the Cardinal may be used.

3. The Distributives are used with **plūrālia tantum**: **bīnae litterae,** *two epistles.* But with these **ūnī** is used for *one*, **trīnī** for *three*: **ūnae lītterae, trīnae lītterae.**

4. The same rules as to the insertion or omission of **et** apply to the Distributives as to the Ordinals (96, 1. 3, 4).

NOTES.—1. The poets and later prose writers occasionally use the Distributives for Cardinals, with words other than **plūrālia tantum** (R. 3); also some forms of the Singular. Especially noteworthy is the combination **trīnum nūndinum,** which is technical, and therefore found also in model prose.

2. Parallel forms not found in classical times are **quadrīnī** (early, late), and the late **du(o)centēnī, trecentēnī, quadringentēnī, quīngentēnī, ses(x)centēnī, millēnī,** *etc.*

4. Multiplicative Numerals.

Only the following forms occur:

1	**simplex,**	*single,*	5	**quīncuplex**
2	**duplex,**	*double,*	7	**septemplex**
3	**triplex,**	*triple,*	10	**decemplex**
4	**quadruplex,**	*quadruple.*	100	**centuplex**

These answer the question, *how many fold?*

5. Proportional Numerals.

Only the following forms occur:

1	**simplus, -a, -um,**	*single,*	4	**quadruplus**
2	**duplus,**	*double.*	7	**septuplus**
3	**triplus**		8	**octuplus**

These answer the question, *how many times as great?*

98. NUMERAL ADVERBS.

1	**semel,** *once,*	22	**bis et vīciēs, vīciēs et bis, vīciēs bis** *
2	**bis,** *twice.*	30	**trīciēs**
3	**ter**	40	**quadrāgiēs**
4	**quater**	50	**quīnquāgiēs**
5	**quīnquiēs (-ēns)**	60	**sexāgiēs**
6	**sexiēs (-ēns)**	70	**septuāgiēs**
7	**septiēs (-ēns)**	80	**octōgiēs**
8	**octiēs (-ēns)**	90	**nōnāgiēs**
9	**noviēs (-ēns)**	100	**centiēs**
10	**deciēs (-ēns)**	200	**ducentiēs**
11	**ūndeciēs (-ēns)**	400	**quadringentiēs**
12	**duodeciēs,** *etc.*	500	**quīngentiēs**
13	**ter deciēs, tredeciēs**	600	**sexcentiēs (sēscentiēs)**
14	**quater deciēs, quattuordeciēs**	700	**septingentiēs**
15	**quīnquiēs deciēs, quīndeciēs**	800	**octingentiēs**
16	**sexiēs deciēs, sēdeciēs**	900	**nōngentiēs**
17	**septiēs deciēs**	1,000	**mīlliēs**
18	**duodēvīciēs, octiēs deciēs**	2,000	**bis mīlliēs**
19	**ūndēvīciēs, noviēs deciēs**	100,000	**centiēs mīlliēs**
20	**vīciēs**	1,000,000	**mīlliēs mīlliēs, deciēs centiēs mīlliēs**
21	**semel et vīciēs, vīciēs et semel, vīciēs semel** *		

These answer the question **quotiēns (ēs)**: *how often?*

* Not **semel vīciēs, bis vīciēs,** *etc.*, because that would be, once twenty times = 20 times; twice twenty times = 40 times; this, however, does not hold for numerals between 10 and 20.

REMARKS.—1. These adverbs, from **quīnquiēs** on, have an older form in **-ēns**; **quīnquiēns**. In **totiēns**, *so often*, and **quotiēns**, *how often*, this remained the more usual form in classical times.

2. The combination of an adverb with a distributive adjective was much liked by the Romans: as **bis bīna** for **quaterna**, *etc.* But the normal forms are not unfrequent.

NOTE.—For the adverbs from **ūndeciēs** on, examples are very rare, and some are cited only from the grammarians. So, when two forms are given, one is often due to the grammarians; thus **quīnquiēs deciēs, sexiēs deciēs**, are cited only from PRISCIAN. The order, too, of compound adverbs varies.

PRONOUNS.

99. Pronouns point out without describing.

NOTE.—The pronoun is not a word used instead of a noun. The noun says too much, for all nouns (proper as well as common) are originally descriptive; the pronoun simply points out. The noun says too little, because it cannot express person, as **ego**, *I*, **tū**, *thou*; it cannot express local appurtenance, as **hīc**, *this (here)*, **ille**, *that (there)*.

A. PERSONAL PRONOUNS.

100. I. **Personal Pronouns of the First Person.**

	SUBSTANTIVE.		POSSESSIVE.
SG.—N.	**ego,**	*I,*	
G.	**meī,**	*of me,*	**meus, -a, -um,** *mine* or *my.*
D.	**mihĭ,**	*to, for me,*	
Ac.	**mē,**	*me,*	
Ab.	**mē,**	*from, with, by me.*	
PL.—N.	**nōs,**	*we,*	
G.	**nostrī,**	*of us,*	
	nostrum,		**noster, nostra, nostrum,** *our* or *ours.*
D.	**nōbīs,**	*to, for us,*	
Ac.	**nōs,**	*us,*	
Ab.	**nōbīs**	*from, with, by us.*	

REMARKS.—1. The Voc. Sing. masc. of **meus** is **mī**, except when **meus** is used with a substantive which does not change its form in the Voc.; thus, **meus ocellus** (PLAUT.; possibly, however, appositional), but **mī anime.**

2. **Nostrum** in the Gen. Pl. is the form for the Partitive Genitive.

NOTES.—1. Early Latin shows the following: Sg., N. **egō**; G. **mīs**; D. **mī, mihei** (inscr.); **mihē** (inscr.); Ac. **mēd, mēmē**; Ab. **mēd** (**mēmē** is doubtful); Pl., N. Ac. **ēnōs** (in *Carmen Arvale* only); G. **nostrōrum, nostrārum** (for **nostrum**); D. Ab. **nōbeīs** (inscr.).

2. In late Latin **mī** also serves for the Voc. Sing. fem. and Voc. Pl. masc. **Meum, nostrum**, in the Gen. Pl. of the Possessives, are not unfrequent in early Latin.

3. The forms of **meus**, of **tuī** and **tuos**, of **suī** and **suos**, very frequently suffer Synizesis (727) in early Latin.

4. On the combination of these pronouns with **-met** and **-pte** see 102, N. 2, 3.

101. II. Personal Pronouns of the Second Person.

	Substantive.		Possessive.
Sg.—N. V.	**tū,**	*thou,*	
G.	**tuī,**	*of thee,*	
D.	**tibī,**	*to, for thee,*	**tuus** (-os), **-a, -um** (-om), *thy* or *thine.*
Ac.	**tē,**	*thee,*	
Ab.	**tē,**	*from, with, by thee.*	
Pl.—N.	**vōs,**	*ye* or *you,*	
G.	**vestrī,**	*of you,*	
	vestrum,		**vester** (archaic **voster**), **vestra, vestrum,**
D.	**vōbīs,**	*to, for you,*	*your* or *yours.*
Ac.	**vōs,**	*you,*	
Ab.	**vōbīs,**	*from, with, by you.*	

Notes.—1. Early forms are: G. **tis**; D. **tibei** (inscr.), **tibē** (inscr.); Ac. Ab. **tēd, tētē**; Pl. G. **vostrī, vostrōrum, -ārum.**

2. **Vestrum** is for the Partitive Genitive.

3. **Tuom** and **vostrom** in the Gen. Pl. of the Possessives are rare and confined to early Latin.

4. On Synizesis see 100, N. 3. On combination with **-met** or **-pte** see 102, N. 2, 3.

III. Personal Pronouns of the Third Person.

102. The original personal pronoun of the third person, together with its possessive, is used only as a reflexive in Latin, and therefore lacks a Nominative. Its place is taken in the oblique cases by the Determinative **is** (103).

DETERMINATIVE.

	Substantive.		Possessive.
Sg.—N.	[**is, ea, id**],	*he, she, it,*	supplied by the Genitive.
G.	**ēius,**	*of him,*	**ēius,** *his, hers, its.*
	etc.		
Pl.—N.	[**eī, iī, ī; eae, ea**],	*they,*	
G.	**eōrum, eārum, eōrum,**	*of them,*	**eōrum, eārum, eōrum,** *their* or *theirs.*
	etc.		

REFLEXIVE.

	Substantive.		Possessive.
Sg.—N.	——		
G.	**suī,**	*of him, her, it(self),*	**suus** (-os), **-a, -um** (-om), *his,*
D.	**sibī,**	*to, for, him(self), her(self),*	*her(s), its (own).*
Ac.	**sē, sēsē,**	*him(self), her(self),*	
Ab.	**sē, sēsē,**	*from, with, by him(self).*	
Pl.—N.	——		
G.	**suī,**	*of them(selves),*	**suus** (-os), **-a, -um** (-om), *their*
D.	**sibī,**	*to, for them(selves),*	*(own), theirs.*
Ac.	**sē, sēsē,**	*them(selves),*	
Ab.	**sē, sēsē,**	*from, with, by them(selves).*	

NOTES.—1. Inscriptions show **sibeī**. The use of **sēsē** in classical prose is regulated mainly by artistic reasons. **Suom** in Gen. Pl. from **suus** is rare and early.

2. The enclitic **-met** may be added to all the forms of **ego** (except **nostrum**), to all the forms of **tū** (except **tū** and **vestrum**), to **sibi, sē**, and some forms of **suus**; **egomet**, *I myself*. Instead of **tūmet, tūte** is found; from which early poets formed occasionally **tūtemet, tūtimet. Met** is also occasionally appended to forms of **meus** (early) and **tuus** (late).

3. The enclitic **-pte** is joined very rarely to forms of the Personal Pronoun (**mēpte**, PL., *Men.* 1059); more often to the Abl. Sing. of the Possessives; it is especially common with **suō**; **suōpte ingeniō**, *by his own genius.*

4. From **noster** and **vester** and also from **cūius**, *whose?* are formed the Gentile adjectives of one ending: **nostrās**, of *our country;* **vestrās**, of *your country;* **cūiās**, of *whose country?* G. **nostrātis, vestrātis, cūiātis.**

103. B. DETERMINATIVE PRONOUNS.

1. is, *he, that.*

	Singular.			Plural.		
N.	**is,**	**ea,**	**id,**	**iī, eī, ī,**	**eae,**	**ea,**
G.	**ēius,**	**ēius,**	**ēius,**	**eōrum,**	**eārum,**	**eōrum,**
D.	**eī,**	**eī,**	**eī,**		**iīs, eīs, īs,**	
Ac.	**eum,**	**eam,**	**id,**	**eōs,**	**eās,**	**ea,**
Ab.	**eō,**	**eā,**	**eō.**		**iīs, eīs, īs.**	

NOTE.—The following variations in the forms are found: N. **it** for **id** (post-cl.); G. **eiius** (inscr.), **eiūs** (early poetry); D. **eieī** (inscr.), **ēī, eī** (early poetry), **eae** (f.); Ac. **em, im** (early), for **eum**; Pl. N. **eīs, eeīs, ieīs, ieī** (early and rare), for **eī**; the usual classical form is **iī**; G. **eum** (inscr.) for **eōrum**; D. **eieīs, eeīs, ieīs** (inscr.), **ībus** (early poetry and rare); the usual classical form is **iīs.** The early forms **sum, sam, sōs, sās**, for **eum, eam, eōs, eās**, are cited by FESTUS. Acc. and Abl. Sing. and Gen. Pl. often suffer Synizesis in early poetry.

2. īdem (is + dem), *the same.*

	Singular.			Plural.		
N.	**īdem,**	**eadem,**	**idem,**	**īdem, eīdem, iīdem,**	**eaedem,**	**eadem,**
G.	**ēiusdem,**	**ēiusdem,**	**ēiusdem,**	**eōrundem,**	**eārundem,**	**eōrundem,**
D.	**eīdem,**	**eīdem,**	**eīdem,**	**īsdem, eīsdem, iīsdem,**		
Ac.	**eundem,**	**eandem,**	**idem,**	**eōsdem,**	**eāsdem,**	**eadem,**
Abl.	**eōdem,**	**eādem,**	**eōdem.**	**īsdem, eīsdem, iīsdem.**		

NOTE.—Variations in form: N. **ēīdem, isdem** (inscr., early) for **īdem**; D. **īdem** (inscr.) for **eīdem**; Pl. N. **īdem** (more usual in poetry), **ēīsdem, īsdem** (inscr.); D. Ab. **iīsdem** (rare), **eīsdem** (uncommon in classical prose). Synizesis is common.

3. ipse (perhaps is + pse), *he, self.*

	Singular.			Plural.		
N.	**ipse,**	**ipsa,**	**ipsum,**	**ipsī,**	**ipsae,**	**ipsa,**
G.	**ipsīus,**	**ipsīus,**	**ipsīus,**	**ipsōrum,**	**ipsārum,**	**ipsōrum,**
D.	**ipsī,**	**ipsī,**	**ipsī,**	**ipsīs,**	**ipsīs,**	**ipsīs,**
Ac.	**ipsum,**	**ipsam,**	**ipsum,**	**ipsōs,**	**ipsās,**	**ipsa,**
Ab.	**ipsō,**	**ipsā**	**ipsō.**	**ipsīs,**	**ipsīs,**	**ipsīs.**

NOTES.—1. In the earlier time the first part of **ipse** was also declined, thus: N. **eapse**; Ac. **eumpse, eampse**; Ab. **eōpse, eāpse**. Other forms are doubtful.

2. For **ipse** the form **ipsus** was very commonly employed in early Latin, but fades out with TERENCE, and later is only sporadic.

3. Inflectional variations are: D. **ipsō, ipsae** (late); Pl. N. **ipseī** (inscr.). The few other forms are uncertain. **Ipsīus** is dissyllabic twice in TERENCE.

4. PLAUTUS shows **ipsissimus** (comp. Gr. αὐτότατος), and in late Latin **ipsimus** and **ipsima** are found. A post-Ciceronian colloquialism was **isse, issa.**

5. **Ipse** combines with **-met**: **ipsemet** and **ipsīmet** (N. Pl.), both rare.

104. C. DEMONSTRATIVE PRONOUNS.

I. Demonstrative Pronoun for the First Person.

hīc, *this.*

SG.—N.	**hīc,**	**haec,**	**hōc,**	PL.—**hī,**	**hae,**	**haec,**	*these,*
G.	**hūius,**	**hūius,**	**hūius,**	**hōrum,**	**hārum,**	**hōrum,**	
D.	**huīc,**	**huīc,**	**huīc,**	**hīs,**	**hīs,**	**hīs,**	
Ac.	**hunc,**	**hanc,**	**hōc,**	**hōs,**	**hās,**	**haec,**	
Abl.	**hōc,**	**hāc,**	**hōc.**	**hīs,**	**hīs,**	**hīs.**	

NOTES.—1. The full forms of **hīc** in **-ce** are still found in limited numbers in early Latin; G. **hōiusce** (in the phrase **hūiusce modī**, the form is common in the classical period and later); D. **hōīce** (inscr.); Pl. N. **hēīsce, hīsce** (not uncommon); G. **hōrunce** (rare); D., Ab. **hīsce** (in PLAUT. and TER. usually before vowels); Ac. **hōsce, hāsce** (not uncommon; occasionally in CIC.).

2. Other variations in form are: G. **hŭius** and **hūīus** (in early poetry for metrical reasons); D. **hae** (rare and early); Ac. **honc**; Pl. N. **hēī, hēīs** for **hī, haec** for **hae** (in PLAUT. and TER. regularly before vowels or **h,** occasionally before consonants; occasionally also in classical times and later); G. **hōrunc, hārunc** (early). Pl. N. **hīc** for **hī** and D. Ab. **hībus** for **hīs** are doubtful.

3. **Hīc** combines with **-ne.** Usually **-ne** was appended to **hīce**, *etc.*, and the **e** weakened to **i.** Sometimes **-ne** is added directly to the regular forms. The examples are frequent in early Latin, but occur also in CIC. and later writers: **hīcine, haecine, hōcine, huīcine, huncine, hancine, hōcine, hācine, haecine** (N. Pl. fem.), **haecine** (N. Pl. neut.), **hīscine, hōscine, hāscine**; also **hīcne, haecne, hōcne, hūiusne, huncne, hancne, hōcne, hācne, haecne, hōsne, hāsne.**

II. Demonstrative Pronoun for the Second Person.

iste, *that.*

SG.—N.	**iste,**	**ista,**	**istud,**	PL.—**istī,**	**istae,**	**ista,**
G.	**istīus,**	**istīus,**	**istīus,**	**istōrum,**	**istārum,**	**istōrum,**
D.	**istī,**	**istī,**	**istī,**	**istīs,**	**istīs,**	**istīs,**
Ac.	**istum,**	**istam,**	**istud,**	**istōs,**	**istās,**	**ista,**
Abl.	**istō,**	**istā,**	**istō.**	**istīs,**	**istīs,**	**istīs.**

NOTES.—1. The Dat. Sing. shows **istō** in late and **istae** in early Latin.

2. **Iste** combines with **-ce.** In a very few cases (three times in early, once in late Latin) this **-ce** is retained unchanged, but usually it is shortened to **-c.** The following forms occur, all except **istuc** (more common than **istud** in classical Latin) and **istaec**

(neuter, occasionally in CIC., *Ep.* and later), being wholly confined to early and late Latin. N. **istic, istaec, istuc** (**istoc**, once); D. **istīc**; Ac. **istunc, istanc**; Ab. **istōc, istāc.** Pl. N. **istaec** (f.), **istaec** (n.).

3. In a few cases in PLAUT. and TER. **-ne** is appended to **istice,** *etc.*, the preceding **e** being weakened to **i**: **istucine, istōcine, istācine, istōscin'.**

III. Demonstrative Pronoun for the Third Person.

SG.—N.	**ille,**	**illa,**	**illud,**	PL.—**illī,**	**illae,**	**illa,**
G.	**illīus,**	**illīus,**	**illīus,**	**illōrum,**	**illārum,**	**illōrum,**
D.	**illī,**	**illī,**	**illī,**	**illīs,**	**illīs,**	**illīs,**
Ac.	**illum,**	**illam,**	**illud,**	**illōs,**	**illās,**	**illa,**
Ab.	**illō,**	**illā,**	**illō.**	**illīs,**	**illīs,**	**illīs.**

NOTES.—1. The older forms from stem **ollo-** occur on early inscriptions, in laws, and in the poets (except PLAUT. and TER.), even to a very late period, as follows: N. **ollus, -e** (early); D. **ollī**; Pl. N. **ollī, olla**; G. **ollom, ollārum** (early); D. **ollēis, ollīs**; Ac. **ollōs** (early).

2. Inscriptions show **illut** occasionally for **illud.** Other rare forms are: G. **illī** (doubtful); D. **illae**; Pl. N. **illēī. Illīus** is often dissyllabic in early Latin.

3. **Ille** often combines with **-ce,** which is, however, usually shortened to **-c**: **illīusce, illāce, illōce, illōsce, illāsce, illīsce,** all in early Latin; shortened forms: N. **illic, illaec, illuc**; D. **illīc**; Ac. **illunc, illanc**; Ab. **illōc, illāc**; Pl. N. **illaec** (f.), **illaec** (n.), all with rare exceptions confined to PLAUTUS and TERENCE.

4. A few cases of combination with **-ne**: **illicine, illancine** occur in PLAUTUS and TERENCE.

105. D. RELATIVE PRONOUNS.

quī (Substantive and Adjective), *who.*

SG.—N.	**quī,**	**quae,**	**quod,**	PL.—**quī,**	**quae,**	**quae,**
G.	**cūius,**	**cūius,**	**cūius,**	**quōrum,**	**quārum,**	**quōrum,**
D.	**cuī,**	**cuī,**	**cuī,**	**quibus,**	**quibus,**	**quibus,**
Ac.	**quem,**	**quam,**	**quod,**	**quōs,**	**quās,**	**quae,**
Ab.	**quō,**	**quā,**	**quō.**	**quibus,**	**quibus,**	**quibus.**

General Relatives are:

Substantive.	**quisquis,** *whoever,*	**quidquid,**	**quicquid,**	*whatever.*
Adjective.	(**quīquī,** **quaequae,**	**quodquod**),		*whosoever.*
	quīcunque, quaecunque,	**quodcunque,**		*whichever.*

NOTES.—1. Archaic and legal are **quis** and **quid** as relatives.

2. The prevalent form of Gen. on inscriptions of the Republican period and in early Latin is **quōius**; **quius, cuiius,** and other variations are also found. Other archaic forms are: D., **quoi.** D. Pl., **quēīs.** D. Pl. **quīs** is common in the poets at all periods; and also in prose writers; but not cited from CAESAR, and only from the letters of CICERO.

3. The Abl. Sing. **quī** for all genders is the prevalent form in early times, and in combination with **cum** is preferred to **quō, quā** by CICERO.

4. **Quisquis** is occasionally used as an adjective, but not in classical Latin. Occasionally, also, but rarely in CICERO, it is used for **quisque, quidque.** The Nom. Sing. of the adjective **quīquī,** *etc.*, probably does not occur. In the other cases the forms are

the same as those of **quisquis** and can be distinguished only by the usage. In combination with **modī** we find **cuīcuī** in Gen. sometimes in CICERO. In the Plural the only form found is **quibusquibus.** (LIV. XLI., 8, 10.)

5. In **quīcumque** the **-cumque** is often separated by tmesis. The only variations in form are **queīquomque, quēscumque** in early Latin, and occasionally **quīscumque** for **quibuscumque** (several times in CICERO).

106. E. INTERROGATIVE PRONOUNS.

Substantive.	**quis ?** *who ?*		**quid ?**	*what ?*
Adjective.	**quī ?**	**quae ?**	**quod ?**	*which ?*
Subst. and Adj.	**uter ?**	**utra ?**	**utrum ?**	*who, which of two ?*

SG. N.	**quis ?**	**quid ?**	*who ? what ?*	POSSESSIVE.
G.	**cūius ?**	**cūius ?**	*whose?*	**cūius, cūia, cūium,** *whose !*
D.	**cuī ?**	**cuī ?**	*to, for whom ?*	
Ac.	**quem ?**	**quid ?**	*whom ? what ?*	
Ab.	**quō ?**	**quō ?**	*from, with, by whom* or *what ?*	

The plural of the substantive interrogative pronoun and both numbers of the adjective interrogative pronoun coincide with the forms of the relative **quī, quae, quod,** *who, which.*

Strengthened Interrogatives.

Substantive.	**quisnam ?** *who, pray ?*		**quidnam ?** *what, pray ?*
	ecquis ? *is there any one who ?*		**ecquid ?**
Adjective.	**quīnam ?**	**quaenam ?**	**quodnam ?** *which, pray ?*
	ecquī ?	**ecqua ? (ecquae) ?**	**ecquod ?**

REMARK.—In the poets **quī** is sometimes found as a substantive for **quis** in independent sentences. In dependent sentences the use always fluctuates. A difference in meaning can hardly be made other than that **quī** is generally used in much the same sense as **quālis.** On the other hand, **quis** is often used as an adjective for **quī** ; usually, however, the substantive which follows is best looked upon as in apposition. In the classical period **quī** is the normal form for the adjective in dependent questions.

NOTES.—1. Inscriptions show here and there **quit** and **quot** for **quid** and **quod. Quid** is sometimes used for **quod,** but usually in the phrase **quid nōmen tibi est** and only in early Latin. Sometimes **quae** seems to be used as a substantive, but another explanation is always possible.

2. In the oblique cases the same variations occur as in the oblique cases of the relative. The Abl. **quī** means *how ?*

3. For the declension of **uter** see 76.

4. The possessive **cūius (quōius), -a, -um** was used both as relative and as interroga-

tive. It is frequent in PLAUT. and TER., but rare in other authors. Besides the Nom. the only forms found are Ac. **quōium, quōiam**; Ab. **quōiā**; Pl. N. **quōiae**, and, perhaps, G. Pl. **quōium.**

5. **Quisnam** is sometimes used as an adjective for **quīnam** and **quīnam** occasionally for **quisnam** as a substantive. The **-nam** may be separated by tmesis. **Ecquis** and **ecquī** are not common, and are subject to the same fluctuations as **quis** and **quī. Ecquis** combines with **-nam** to form **ecquisnam** and a few other occasional forms, as: **ecquaenam, ecquidnam, ecquodnam, ecquōnam, ecquōsnam.**

107. F. INDEFINITE PRONOUNS.

1. *Substantive.*	**aliquis,**	**aliqua** (rare),	**aliquid,**	*somebody, some one or other.*
	quis,	**qua,**	**quid,**	
Adjective.	**aliquī,**	**aliqua,**	**aliquod,**	*some, any.*
	quī,	**quae, qua,**	**quod,**	

REMARK.—The common rule is that **quis** and **quī** occur properly only after **sī, nisi, nē, num,** or after a relative; otherwise **aliquis, aliquī.**

NOTES.—1. **Aliquis** and **quis** are not unfrequently used as adjectives instead of **aliquī, quī,** but rarely in early Latin. Occasionally (not in early Latin) **aliquī** is used as a substantive. **Quī** is also so used, but only after **sī, sīn, sīve, nē.**

The use of **quid** and **aliquid** for **quod** and **aliquod,** and of **aliquod** for **aliquid,** is very rare and late.

2. Besides the variations in form mentioned under the relative and interrogative, the indefinitive **quis** shows **quēs** as an early form for **quī** (N. Pl.), and in Pl. Nom. Acc. neut. **quae** and **qua** in equally good usage. **Aliquis** shows in Abl. Sing. **aliquī** (rare and early), in the Pl. Nom. Acc. neut. always **aliqua,** and not unfrequently in postclassical Latin **aliquīs** for **aliquibus.**

2. **quīdam, quaedam, quiddam** (and **quoddam**), *a certain, certain one.*

REMARK.—**Quīdam, quaedam** occur both as substantives and adjectives, but **quiddam** is always substantive, **quoddam** always adjective. The Plural is rare in early Latin (never in PLAUTUS).

3. **quispiam, quaepiam, quidpiam** (and **quodpiam**), *some one, some.*
quisquam, ———, **quicquam,** *any one* (*at all*). No plural.

NOTES.—1. **quispiam, quaepiam** are rare as adjectives. In the neuter, **quippiam** and **quoppiam** occur rarely. The comic poets do not use the Plural, and it is rare elsewhere.

2. **Quisquam** is seldom used as an adjective, except with designations of persons: **scrīptor quisquam,** *any writer* (*at all*), **Gallus quisquam,** *any Gaul* (*at all*). The corresponding adjective is **ūllus.** The use of **quisquam** as a feminine is only in early Latin. **Quidquam** is a poor spelling for **quicquam.** In Abl. Sing. **quīquam** occurs occasionally. In Sing. Gen. Dat. Acc. frequently, and in Plural always, forms of **ūllus** were used.

4. **quīvīs, quaevīs, quidvīs** (and **quodvīs**), **quīlibet, quaelibet, quidlibet** (and **quodlibet**), *any one you please, you like.*

NOTE.—**Quīvīs, quaevīs, quīlibet** (archaic **-lubet**), **quaelibet** may be used either as substantives or adjectives, but **quidvīs, quidlibet** are substantives only, **quodvīs, quodlibet** are adjectives only. Peculiar forms of **quīvīs** are G. **quoivīs** in **quoivīsmodī** (PLAUT.); D., **quōvīs** (late); Ab., **quīvīs** (PLAUT., TER.), and the compounds **cūiusvīscumque** (LUCR. III., 388) and **quōvīscumque** (MART. XIV., 2, 1). **Quīlibet** may be separated by tmesis into **quī** and **libet** (SALL., *Cat.* 5, 4).

5. **quisque, quaeque, quidque** and **quodque**, *each one.*
ūnusquisque, ūnaquaeque, ūnumquidque and **ūnumquodque**, *each one severally.*

NOTE.—**Quisque** occurs occasionally in early Latin as a feminine, and with its forms is not unfrequently found in early and late Latin for **quisquis**, or **quīcumque**. **Quidque** is substantive, **quodque** adjective. In the Abl. Sing. **quīque** occurs occasionally. The Plural is regular, but rare until post-classical times. In Nom. Pl. **quaeque** is either fem. or neuter.

108. The declension of the pronominal adjectives has been given in 76. They are:

ūllus, -a, -um, *any;* **nūllus, -a, -um,** *no one, not one.* The corresponding substantives are **nēmō** (76) and **nihil,** the latter of which forms only **nihilī** (Gen.) and **nihilō** (Abl.), and those only in certain combinations.

nōnnūllus, -a, -um, *some, many a,* declined like **nūllus.**
alius, -a, -ud, *another;* the Possessive of **alius** is **aliēnus.**
alter, -era, -erum, *the other, one (of two).*
neuter, neutra, neutrum, *neither of two.*
alteruter, alterutra, alterutrum, *the one or the other of the two.*
uterque, utraque, utrumque, *each of two, either.* **ambō, -ae, -ō,** *both.*
utervīs, utravīs, utrumvīs, uterlibet, utralibet, utrumlibet, *whichever you please of the two.*

CORRELATIVES.

109. I. CORRELATIVE PRONOMINAL ADJECTIVES.

INTERROGATIVES.		DEMONSTRATIVES.		RELATIVES.	
quis?	*who?*	**is,**	*that,*	**quī,**	*who.*
quālis?	*of what kind?*	**tālis,**	*such (of that kind),*	**quālis,**	*as (of which kind).*
quantus?	*how much?*	**tantus,**	*so much,*	**quantus,**	*as much.*
quot?	*how many?*	**tot,**	*so many,*	**quot,**	*as many.*

110. II. CORRELATIVE PRONOMINAL ADVERBS.

1. Pronominal adverbs of *place*.

ubĭ?	*where?*	**ibĭ,**	*there.*	**ubĭ,**	*where.*
quā?	*where, which way?*	**hīc, hāc,**	*here, this way.*	**quā,**	*where, which way.*
		istīc, istāc,	*there, that way.*		
		illīc, illāc,	*there, yonder way.*		
unde?	*whence?*	**inde,**	*thence.*	**unde,**	*whence.*
		hinc,	*hence.*		
		istinc,	*thence.*		
		illinc,	*thence, from yonder.*		
quō?	*whither?*	**eō,**	*thither.*	**quō,**	*whither.*
		hūc, (hōc,)	*hither.*		
		istūc, (istōc,)	*thither.*		
		illūc, (illōc,)	*thither, yonder.*		

2. Pronominal adverbs of *time*.

quandō?	*when?*	**tum,**	*then.*	**quandō,** *when.*
		tunc,	*at that time.*	**quom, cum.**
		nunc,	*now.*	
quotiēns?	*how often?*	**totiēns,**	*so often.*	**quotiēns,** *as often as.*

3. Pronominal adverbs of *manner*.

quōmodo? quī?	*how?*	**ita, sīc,**	*so, thus.*	**ut, utī,**	*as.*
quam?	*how much?*	**tam,**	*so much.*	**quam,**	*as.*

111. III. COMPOUNDS OF THE RELATIVE FORMS.

1. The relative pronouns become *indefinite* by prefixing **ali-**:

aliquantus, *somewhat great;* **aliquot**, *several, some;* **alicubĭ**, *somewhere;* **alicunde**, *from somewhere;* **aliquandō**, *at some time.*

2. The simple relatives become *universal* by doubling themselves, or by suffixing **-cunque (-cumque)**, sometimes **-que**:

quantuscunque, *however great;* **quāliscunque**, *of whatever kind;* **quotquot**, *however many;* **ubĭcunque**, *wheresoever;* **quandōcunque, quandŏque**, *whenever;* **quotiēscunque**, *however often;* **utut**, *in whatever way;* **utcunque**, *howsoever;* **quamquam**, *however, although.*

3. Many of the relatives are further compounded with **-vīs** or **-libet**:

quantuslibet, quantusvīs, *as great as you please;* **ubivīs**, *where you will;* **quamvīs**, *as you please, though.*

THE VERB.

112. The inflection given to the verbal stem is called Conjugation, and expresses :

1. Person and Number ;

2. Voice—Active or Passive.

The Active Voice denotes that the action proceeds from the subject : **amō**, *I love.*

The Passive Voice denotes that the subject receives the action of the Verb : **amor,** *I am loved.*

3. Tense—Present, Imperfect, Future,
Perfect, Pluperfect, Future Perfect.

The Present, **amō,** *I love ;* Future, **amābō,** *I shall love ;* Pure Perfect, **amāvī,** *I have loved ;* Future Perfect, **amāverō,** *I shall have loved,* are called *Principal Tenses.*

The Imperfect, **amābam,** *I was loving ;* Historical Perfect, **amāvī,** *I loved ;* Pluperfect, **amāveram,** *I had loved,* are called *Historical Tenses.*

REMARK.—The Pure and Historical Perfects are identical in form.

4. Mood—Indicative, Subjunctive, Imperative.

The Indicative Mood is the mood of the *fact :* **amō,** *I love.*

The Subjunctive Mood is the mood of the *idea :* **amem,** *may I love, I may love ;* **amet,** *may he love, he may love ;* **sī amet,** *if he should love.*

The Imperative Mood is the mood of *command :* **amā,** *love thou !*

For further distinctions see Syntax.

5. These forms belong to the Finite Verb. Outside of the Finite Verb, and akin to the noun, are the verbal forms called
Infinitive, Supine, Participle, Gerund.

The Infinitive active and the Supine are related to the noun, the former being originally a Dative or Locative and the Supine showing two cases, Accusative and Ablative.

No adequate uniform translation can be given, but for the general meaning see paradigms.

113. A large number of Verbs have the passive form but

are active in meaning : **hortor,** *I exhort.* These are called *deponent* (from **dēpōnere,** *to lay aside*).

114. The Inflection of the Finite Verb is effected by the addition of personal endings to the verb stems.

1. The personal endings are mostly pronominal forms, which serve to indicate not only person, but also number and voice. They are :

	Active.	Passive.
Sg.—1.	**-m** (or a vowel, coalescing with the characteristic ending); Pf. **ī**,	**-r.**
2.	**-s**; Pf. **-s-tī**; Impv. **-tō(d)** or wanting,	**-ris** or **-re**; Impv. **-re** or **-tor.**
3.	**-t**; Impv. **tō(d)**,	**-tur**; Impv. **-tor.**
Pl.—1.	**-mus,**	**-mur.**
2.	**-tis**; Pf. **-s-tis-**; Impv. **-te** or **-tōte,**	**-minī.**
3.	**-nt**; Pf. **ērunt** or **ēre**; Impv. **-ntō(d),**	**-ntur**; Impv. **-ntor.**

2. The personal endings are added directly to the stem in the Present Indicative and Imperative only, except in the third conjugation, in some forms of the Future Indicative. In the other tenses certain modifications occur in the stem, or tense signs are employed :

(*a*) In the Present Subjunctive final **ā** of the stem is changed to **ē (e)**; final **ē** to **eā (ea)**; final **ī** to **iā (ia)**; final **e** to **ā (a)**. In the Future Indicative final **e** is changed to **a** or **ē (e)**; final **ī** to **ia (iē, ie).**

(*b*) The tense signs are : for the Imperfect Indicative, **bā (ba)**; for the Imperfect Subjunctive, **rē (re)**; for the Future Indicative in **ā** and **ē** verbs **bĭ (b, bu)**; for the Perfect Indicative, **ī (i)**; for the Perfect Subjunctive, **-erī̆**; for the Pluperfect Indicative, **erā (era)**; for the Pluperfect Subjunctive, **issē (isse)**; for the Future Perfect Indicative, **erī̆ (er).**

3. The stem itself is variously modified ; either by change of vowel or by addition of suffixes, and appears in the following forms :

(*a*) The *Present* stem; being the stem of the Present, Imperfect, and Future tenses. These forms are called the *Present System.*

(*b*) The *Perfect* stem; being the stem of the Perfect, Pluperfect, and Future Perfect tenses. These forms are called the *Perfect System.*

(*c*) The *Supine** stem; being the stem of the Future Active and Perfect Passive Participles and of the Supine. These forms are called the *Supine System.*

Note.—For details as to the formation of these stems, see 132 ff.

*** This designation is retained because it is an established *terminus technicus*; as a matter of fact the Supine stem is not the stem of the Participles.**

115. 1. The Perfect, Pluperfect, and Future Perfect tenses in the Passive are formed by the combination of the Perfect Passive Participle with forms of the verb **sum,** *I am.*

2. The Future Passive Infinitive is formed by the combination of the Supine with the Present Passive Infinitive of **eō,** *I go.*

3. The infinite parts of the verb are formed by the addition of the following endings to the stems :

		Active.	Passive
Infinitive.	Pr.	**-re,**	**rī, ī.**
	Pf.	**-isse,**	**-tus** (**-ta, -tum**), **esse.**
	Fut.	**-tūrum** (**-a, -um**), **esse,**	**-tum īrī.**
Participles.	Pr.	**-ns** (G. **-ntis**),	
	Pf.	——	**-tus** (**-ta, -tum**).
	Fut.	**-tūrus** (**-a, -um**).	

Gerund.	Gerundive.	Supine.
-ndī (**-dō, -dum, -dō**).	**-ndus** (**-a, -um**).	**-tum** ; **-tū**

116. The Verb sum, *I am.*

(Pres. stem **es-**, Perf. stem **fu-**)

	Indicative.		Subjunctive.		
		Present.			
Sg.—1.	**sum,**	*I am,*	**sim,**	*I be,*	
2.	**es,**	*thou art,*	**sīs,**	*thou be,*	
3.	**est,**	*he, she, it is.*	**sit,**	*he, she, it be.*	
Pl.—1.	**sumus,**	*we are,*	**sīmus,**	*we be,*	
2.	**estis,**	*you are,*	**sītis,**	*you be,*	
3.	**sunt,**	*they are*	**sint,**	*they be.*	
		Imperfect.			
Sg.—1.	**eram,**	*I was,*	**essem,**	*I were*	(**forem**),
2.	**erās,**	*thou wast,*	**essēs,**	*thou wert*	(**forēs**),
3.	**erat,**	*he was.*	**esset,**	*he were*	(**foret**).
Pl.—1.	**erāmus,**	*we were,*	**essēmus,**	*we were,*	
2.	**erātis,**	*you were,*	**essētis,**	*you were,*	
3.	**erant,**	*they were,*	**essent,**	*they were*	(**forent**).
		Future.			
Sg.—1.	**erō,**	*I shall be,*			
2.	**eris,**	*thou wilt be,*			
3.	**erit,**	*he will be.*			
Pl.—1.	**erimus,**	*we shall be,*			
2.	**eritis,**	*you will be,*			
3.	**erunt,**	*they will be.*			

PERFECT.

SG.—1.	**fuī,**	*I have been, I was,*	**fuerim,**	*I have, may have, been,*
2.	**fuistī,**	*thou hast been, thou wast,*	**fuerīs,**	*thou have, mayest have, been,*
3.	**fuit,**	*he has been, he was.*	**fuerit,**	*he have, may have, been.*
PL.—1.	**fuimus,**	*we have been, we were,*	**fuerīmus,**	*we have, may have, been,*
2.	**fuistis,**	*you have been, you were,*	**fuerītis,**	*you have, may have, been,*
3.	**fuērunt, fuēre,**	*they have been, they were.*	**fuerint,**	*they have, may have, been.*

PLUPERFECT.

SG.—1.	**fueram,**	*I had been,*	**fuissem,**	*I had, might have, been,*
2.	**fuerās,**	*thou hadst been,*	**fuissēs,**	*thou hadst, mightst have, been,*
3.	**fuerat,**	*he had been.*	**fuisset,**	*he had, might have, been.*
PL.—1.	**fuerāmus,**	*we had been,*	**fuissēmus,**	*we had, might have, been,*
2.	**fuerātis,**	*you had been,*	**fuissētis,**	*you had, might have, been,*
3.	**fuerant,**	*they had been.*	**fuissent,**	*they had, might have, been.*

FUTURE PERFECT.

SG.—1.	**fuerō,**	*I shall have been,*
2.	**fuerīs,**	*thou wilt have been,*
3.	**fuerit,**	*he will have been.*
PL.—1.	**fuerīmus,**	*we shall have been,*
2.	**fuerītis,**	*you will have been,*
3.	**fuerint,**	*they will have been.*

IMPERATIVE.

	PRESENT.	FUTURE.
SG.—1.	——,	——,
2.	**es,** *be thou,*	**estō,** *thou shalt be,*
3.	——,	**estō,** *he shall be.*
PL.—1.	——,	
2.	**este,** *be ye,*	**estōte,** *you shall be,*
3.	——,	**suntō,** *they shall be.*

INFINITIVE.

PRES. **esse,** *to be,*
PERF. **fuisse,** *to have been,*
FUT. **futūrum (-am, -um) esse (fore),** *to be about to be.*

PARTICIPLE.

FUT. **futūrus, -a, -um,** *about to be.*

NOTES.—1. Early forms are:

(*a*) In the Pres. Ind. **ēs** for **es**; regularly in PLAUTUS and TERENCE, but the quantity of the vowel is disputed.

(*b*) In the Pres. Subjv. **siem, siēs, siet, sient**; regular in inscriptions until the first century B. C. and common in early poets chiefly for metrical reasons; side by side with this occur **fuam, fuās, fuat, fuant** (also LUCR. IV., 637, VERG. X., 108, LIV. XXV., 12, 6), which are taken up again by very late poets. **Sīt** is also common.

(*c*) In the Impf. Subjv. the forms **forem, forēs, foret, forent** were probably in very early times equivalent to **futūrus essem,** *etc.;* and occasionally this force seems to be still present in the later period, especially in SALLUST; usually, however, they are equivalent to **essem, essēs, esset, essent**; in the Inf. **fore** always remained the equivalent of **futūrum esse.**

(*d*) In all the Perfect forms the original length was **fū-**, which is still found occasionally in early Latin.

(*e*) Early and principally legal are the rare forms **escit, escet, esit,** for **erit**; **-essint** for **erunt.**

2. The Pres. Part. is found only in the compounds; **ab-sēns,** *absent,* and **prae-sēns,** *present.*

117. COMPOUNDS OF **sum,** *I am.*

ab-sum, *I am away, absent.* Pf. (**abfuī**) **āfuī.**
ad-sum, *I am present.* Pf. **affuī.**
dē-sum, *I am wanting.*
in-sum, *I am in.*
inter-sum, *I am between.*
ob-sum, *I am against, I hurt.* Pf. **obfuī** or **offuī.**
pos-sum, *I am able.*
prae-sum, *I am over, I superintend*
prō-sum, *I am for, I profit.*
sub-sum, *I am under.* No Pf.
super-sum, *I am, or remain, over.*

These are all inflected like **sum**; but **prōsum** and **possum** require special treatment by reason of their composition.

Prōsum, *I profit.*

118. In the forms of **prōsum, prōd-** is used before vowels.

	INDICATIVE.	SUBJUNCTIVE.
PRESENT.	**prō-sum, prōd-es, prōd-est,** **prō-sumus, prōd-estis, prō-sunt,**	**prō-sim,**
IMPERFECT.	**prōd-eram,**	**prōd-essem,**
FUTURE.	**prōd-erō,**	
PERFECT.	**prō-fuī,**	**prō-fuerim,**
PLUPERFECT.	**prō-fueram,**	**prō-fuissem.**
FUT. PERF.	**prō-fuerō,**	

INFINITIVE. PRES. **prōd-esse**; FUT. **prō-futūrum esse** (**-fore**); PERF. **prō-fuisse.**

Possum, *I am able, I can.*

119. **Possum** is compounded of **pot** (**potis, pote**) and **sum**; **t** becomes **s** before **s**; in the perfect forms, **f** (**pot-fui**) is lost.

	INDICATIVE.	SUBJUNCTIVE.
	Present.	
Sg.—1.	**pos-sum**, *I am able, can,*	**pos-sim**, *I be able.*
2.	**pot-es,**	**pos-sīs,**
3.	**pot-est.**	**pos-sit.**
Pl.—1.	**pos-sumus,**	**pos-sīmus,**
2.	**pot-estis,**	**pos-sītis,**
3.	**pos-sunt.**	**pos-sint.**
	Imperfect.	
Sg.—1.	**pot-eram**, *I was able, could,*	**pos-sem**, *I were, might be, able.*
2.	**pot-erās,**	**pos-sēs,**
3.	**pot-erat.**	**pos-set.**
Pl.—1.	**pot-erāmus,**	**pos-sēmus,**
2.	**pot-erātis,**	**pos-sētis,**
3.	**pot-erant.**	**pos-sent.**
	Future	
Sg.—1.	**pot-erō**, *I shall be able.*	
2.	**pot-eris,**	
3.	**pot-erit.**	
Pl.—1.	**pot-erimus,**	
2.	**pot-eritis,**	
3.	**pot-erunt.**	
	Perfect.	
Sg.—1.	**pot-uī**, *I have been able,*	**pot-uerim**, *I have, may have, been able.*
2.	**pot-uistī,**	**pot-uerĭs,**
3.	**pot-uit.**	**pot-uerit.**
Pl.—1.	**pot-uimus,**	**pot-uerĭmus,**
2.	**pot-uistis,**	**pot-uerĭtis,**
3.	**pot-uērunt.**	**pot-uerint.**
	Pluperfect.	
Sg.—1.	**pot-ueram**, *I had been able.*	**pot-uissem**, *I had, might have, been able.*
2.	**pot-uerās,**	**pot-uissēs,**
3.	**pot-uerat.**	**pot-uisset.**
Pl.—1.	**pot-uerāmus,**	**pot-uissēmus,**
2.	**pot-uerātis,**	**pot-uissētis,**
3.	**pot-uerant.**	**pot-uissent.**

FUTURE PERFECT.

SG.—1. **pot-uerō,** *I shall have been* [*able,*	PL.—1. **pot-uerĭmus,**
2. **pot-uerĭs,**	2. **pot-uerĭtis,**
3. **pot-uerit.**	3. **pot-uerint.**

INFINITIVE. PRES., **posse,** *to be able.* PERF., **potuisse,** *to have been able.*

NOTES.—1. In the early Latin the fusion of the two parts of the compound has not fully taken place ; we accordingly find not unfrequently : **potis sum, potis es, potis est, potis sunt ; potis siem, potis sīs, potis sit, potis sint ; potis erat ; pote fuisset ;** and sometimes (even in classical and Augustan poets) **potis** and **pote** alone, the copula being omitted. Partial fusion is seen in Inf. **pot-esse, potisse ;** Subjv. **poti-sit** (inscr.). **poti-sset.**

2. Occasional passive forms (followed by a passive infinitive) are found in early Latin (not in PLAUT. or TER.) and LUCRETIUS : **potestur, possētur, possitur, poterātur. Poterint** for **poterunt** is doubtful.

REGULAR VERBS.

SYSTEMS OF CONJUGATION.

120. 1. There are two Systems of Conjugation, the Thematic and the Non-thematic (132). The Non-thematic is confined to a small class. The Thematic System comprises four Conjugations, distinguished by the vowel characteristics of the present stem, **ā, ē, ĕ, ī,** which may be found by dropping **-re** from the Present Infinitive Active. The consonant preceding the short vowel stem-characteristic is called the consonant stem-characteristic.

2. From the *Present* stem, as seen in the Present Indicative and Present Infinitive active ; from the *Perfect* stem, as seen in the Perfect Indicative active ; and from the *Supine* stem, can be derived all the forms of the verb. These tenses are accordingly called the *Principal Parts ;* and in the regular verbs appear in the four conjugations as follows :

	PRES. IND.	PRES. INF.	PERF. IND.	SUPINE.	
I.	**am-ō,**	**amā-re,**	**amā-vī,**	**amā-tum,**	*to love.*
II.	**dēle-ō,**	**dēlē-re,**	**dēlē-vī,**	**dēlē-tum,**	*to blot out.*
	mone-ō,	**monē-re,**	**mon-uī,**	**mon-i-tum,**	*to remind.*
III.	**em-ō,**	**eme-re,**	**ēm-ī,**	**ēm(p)-tum,**	*to buy.*
	statu-ō,	**statue-re,**	**statu-ī,**	**statū-tum,**	*to settle.*
	scrīb-ō,	**scrībe-re,**	**scrīp-sī,**	**scrīp-tum,**	*to write.*
	capi-ō,	**cape-re,**	**cēp-ī,**	**cap-tum,**	*to take.*
IV.	**audi-ō,**	**audī-re,**	**audī-vī,**	**audī-tum,**	*to hear.*

Rules for forming the Tenses.

121. 1. The *Present System.* From the Present stem as obtained by dropping **-re** of the Pres. Inf. Active, form

a. Pres. Subjv. by changing final **ā** to **e, ē** to **ea, e** to **a** (or **-ia**), **ī** to **ia,** and adding **-m** for active, **-r** for passive ; *Pres. Impv. Passive* by adding **-re;** *Fut. Impv.* by adding **-to** for Active and **-tor** for the Passive ; *Pres. Part.* by adding **-ns** and lengthening preceding vowel ; *Gerund* by adding **-ndī** after shortening **ā** and **ē**, changing **ī** to **ie**, and in a few verbs **e** to **ie.** *Pres. Impv. Active* is the same as the stem ; *Pres. Indic. Passive* may be formed from Pres. Indic. Act. by adding **-r** (after shortening **ō**).

b. Impf. Indic. by adding **-bam** for active and **-bar** for passive to the stem in the first and second conjugations ; to the lengthened stem in the third and fourth (**e** to **ē** or **iē, ī** to **iē**) ; *Impf. Subjv.* by adding the endings **-rem** and **-rer,** or by adding **-m** and **-r** respectively to the Pres. Inf. Active.

c. Future, by adding **-bō** and **-bor** to the stem in the first and second conjugations ; **-m** and **-r** in the third and in the fourth (**e** being changed to **a** (**ia**) ; **ī,** to **ia**).

2. The *Perfect System.* From the Perfect stem as obtained by dropping final **ī** of the Perfect, form

a. Perf. Subjv. Active by adding **-erim**; *Perf. Inf. Active* by adding **-isse.**

b. Plupf. Indic. Active by adding **-eram;** *Plup. Subjv. Active* by adding **-issem.**

c. Fut. Perf. Active by adding **-erō.**

3. The *Supine System.* From the Supine stem as obtained by dropping final **-m** of the Supine, form

a. Perf. Part. Passive by adding **-s.**

b. Fut. Part. Active by adding **-rus** (preceding **u** being lengthened to **ū**).

c. The Compound Tenses in the Passive and the Periphrastic forms by combining these Participles with forms of **esse,** *to be.*

REMARK.—*Euphonic changes in the consonant stem-characteristic.* Characteristic **b** before **s** and **t** becomes **p**; **g** and **qu** before **t** become **c**; **c, g, qu,** with **s,** become **x**; **t** and **d** before **s** are assimilated, and then sometimes dropped. See further, 9.

scrīb-ō, scrīp-sī, scrīp-tum ; legō, lēc-tum ; coqu-ō, coc-tum ; dīc-ō, dīxī (dīc-sī) ; iung-ō, iūnx-ī (iūng-sī) ; coqu-ō, coxī (coqu-sī) ; ed-ō, ē-sum (ed-sum) ; cēd-ō, cēs-sī (cēd-sī) ; mitt-ō, mī-sī (mit-sī), mis-sum (mit-sum).

122 First Conjugation.

Conjugation of amāre, *to love.*

Prin. Parts : **am-ō, amā-re, amā-vī, amā-tum.**

ACTIVE.

	INDICATIVE.	SUBJUNCTIVE.
	Present.	
	Am loving, do love, love.	*Be loving, may love.*
Sg.—1.	am-**ō**,	ame-**m**,
2.	amā-**s**,	amē-**s**,
3.	ama-**t**,	ame-**t**.
Pl.—1.	amā-**mus**,	amē-**mus**,
2.	amā-**tis**,	amē-**tis**,
3.	ama-**nt**,	ame-**nt**.
	Imperfect.	
	Was loving, loved.	*Were loving, might love.*
Sg.—1.	amā-**ba-m**,	amā-**re-m**,
2.	amā-**bā-s**,	amā-**rē-s**,
3.	amā-**ba-t**,	amā-**re-t**.
Pl.—1.	amā-**bā-mus**,	amā-**rē-mus**,
2.	amā-**bā-tis**,	amā-**rē-tis**,
3.	amā-**ba-nt**,	amā-**re-nt**.
	Future.	
	Shall be loving, shall love.	
Sg.—1.	amā-**b-ō**,	
2.	amā-**bi-s**,	
3.	amā-**bi-t**,	
Pl.—1.	amā-**bi-mus**,	
2.	amā-**bi-tis**,	
3.	amā-**bu-nt**.	
	Perfect.	
	Have loved, did love.	*Have, may have, loved.*
Sg.—1.	amā-**v-ī**,	amā-**v-eri-m**,
2.	amā-**v-istī**,	amā-**v-erī-s**,
3.	amā-**v-it**,	amā-**v-eri-t**.
Pl.—1.	amā-**v-imus**,	amā-**v-erī-mus**,
2.	amā-**v-istis**,	amā-**v-erī-tis**,
3.	amā-**v-ērunt (-ēre)**,	amā-**v-eri-nt**.

First Conjugation.

ACTIVE.

INDICATIVE.	SUBJUNCTIVE.
PLUPERFECT.	
Had loved.	*Had, might have, loved.*
SG.—1. amā-v-era-m,	amā-v-isse-m,
2. amā-v-erā-s,	amā-v-issē-s,
3. amā-v-era-t,	amā-v-isse-t.
PL.—1. amā-v-erā-mus,	amā-v-issē-mus,
2. amā-v-erā-tis,	amā-v-issē-tis,
3. amā-v-era-nt,	amā-v-isse-nt.

FUTURE PERFECT.

Shall have loved.

SG.—1. amā-v-er-ō,
2. amā-v-erĭ-s,
3. amā-v-eri-t.

PL.—1. amā-v-erĭ-mus,
2. amā-v-erĭ-tis,
3. amā-v-eri-nt.

IMPERATIVE.

	PRESENT.		FUTURE.	
SG.—1.	——,		——,	
2.	amā,	*love thou,*	amā-tō,	*thou shalt love.*
3.	——.		amā-tō,	*he shall love.*
PL.—1.	——,		——,	
2.	amā-te,	*love ye,*	amā-tōte,	*ye shall love.*
3.	——,		ama-ntō,	*they shall love.*

INFINITIVE.

PRES. amā-re, *to love.*
PERF. amā-v-isse, *to have loved.*
FUT. amā-tūr-um, -am, -um esse, *to be about to love.*

GERUND.	SUPINE.
N. [amā-re], *loving.*	
G. ama-nd-ī, *of loving.*	
D. ama-nd-ō, *to loving.*	
Ac. [amā-re], (ad) ama-nd-um, *loving, to love.*	Ac. amā-tum, *to love.*
Ab. ama-nd-ō, *by loving.*	Ab. amā-tū, *to love, in the loving*

PARTICIPLES.

PRESENT. N. amā-n-s (G. ama-nt-is), *loving.*
FUTURE. amā-tūr-us, -a, -um, *being about to love.*

First Conjugation.

PASSIVE.

Present.

	INDICATIVE.	SUBJUNCTIVE.
	Am loved.	*Be, may be, loved.*
SG.—1.	amo-r,	ame-r,
2.	amā-ris (-re),	amē-ris (-re),
3.	amā-tur,	amē-tur.
PL.—1.	amā-mur,	amē-mur,
2.	amā-minī,	amē-minī,
3.	ama-ntur,	ame-ntur.

Imperfect.

	INDICATIVE.	SUBJUNCTIVE.
	Was loved.	*Were, might be, loved.*
SG.—1.	amā-ba-r,	amā-re-r,
2.	amā-bā-ris (-re),	amā-rē-ris (-re),
3.	amā-bā-tur,	amā-rē-tur.
PL.—1.	amā-bā-mur,	amā-rē-mur,
2.	amā-bā-minī,	amā-rē-minī,
3.	amā-ba-ntur,	amā-re-ntur.

Future.

	INDICATIVE.
	Shall be loved.
SG.—1.	amā-bo-r,
2.	amā-be-ris (-re),
3.	amā-bi-tur.
PL.—1.	amā-bi-mur,
2.	amā-bi-minī,
3.	amā-bu-ntur.

Perfect.

	INDICATIVE.		SUBJUNCTIVE.	
	Have been loved, was loved.		*Have, may have, been loved.*	
SG.—1.	amā-t-us, -a, -um	sum,	amā-t-us, -a, -um	sim,
2.		es,		sīs,
3.		est,		sit,
PL.—1.	amā-t-ī, -ae, -a	sumus,	amā-t-ī, -ae, -a	sīmus,
2.		estis,		sītis,
3.		sunt.		sint.

First Conjugation.

PASSIVE.

	INDICATIVE.		SUBJUNCTIVE.	
	PLUPERFECT.			
	Had been loved.		*Had, might have, been loved.*	
SG.—1.	amā-t-us, -a, -um	eram,	amā-t-us, -a, -um	essem,
2.		erās,		essēs,
3.		erat,		esset,
PL.—1.	amā-t-ī, -ae, -a	erāmus,	amā-t-ī, -ae, -a	essēmus,
2.		erātis,		essētis,
3.		erant.		essent.

FUTURE PERFECT.

Shall have been loved.

SG.—1.	amā-t-us, -a, -um	erō,
2.		eris,
3.		erit.
PL.—1.	amā-t-ī, -ae, -a	erimus,
2.		eritis,
3.		erunt.

IMPERATIVE.

	PRESENT.		FUTURE.	
SG.—1.	——,		——,	
2.	amā-re,	*be thou loved.*	amā-tor,	*thou shalt be loved.*
3.	——,		amā-tor,	*he shall be loved.*
PL.—1.	——,		——,	
2.	amā-minī,	*be ye loved.*	——,	
3.	——.		ama-ntor,	*they shall be loved.*

INFINITIVE.

PRES.	amā-rī,	*to be loved.*
PERF.	amā-t-um, -am, -um esse,	*to have been loved.*
FUT.	amā-tum īrī,	*to be about to be loved.*
FUT. PF.	amā-t-um, -am, -um fore.	

	PARTICIPLE.	GERUNDIVE.
PERF.	amā-t-us, -a, -um, *loved.*	ama-nd-us, -a, -um, (*one*) *to be loved.*

123. Second Conjugation.

Conjugation of **dēlēre**, *to destroy (blot out).*

Prin. Parts: **dēle-ō, dēlē-re, dēlē-vī, dēlē-tum.**

	ACTIVE.		PASSIVE.	
	INDIC.	SUBJV.	INDIC.	SUBJV.
		Present.		
Sg.	dēle-ō,	dēlea-m,	dēle-o-r,	dēlea-r,
	dēlē-s,	dēleā-s,	dēlē-ris (-re),	dēleā-ris (-re),
	dēle-t,	dēlea-t,	dēlē-tur,	dēleā-tur,
Pl.	dēlē-mus,	dēleā-mus,	dēlē-mur,	dēle-ā-mur,
	dēlē-tis,	dēleā-tis,	dēlē-minī,	dēle-ā-minī,
	dēle-nt.	dēlea-nt.	dēle-ntur.	dēle-a-ntur.
		Imperfect.		
Sg.	dēlē-ba-m,	dēlē-re-m,	dēlē-ba-r,	dēlē-re-r,
	dēlē-bā-s,	dēlē-rē-s,	dēlē-bā-ris (-re),	dēlē-rē-ris (-re),
	dēlē-ba-t,	dēlē-re-t,	dēlē-bā-tur,	dēlē-rē-tur,
Pl.	dēlē-bā-mus,	dēlē-rē-mus,	dēlē-bā-mur,	dēlē-rē-mur,
	dēlē-bā-tis,	dēlē-rē-tis,	dēlē-bā-minī,	dēlē-rē-minī,
	dēlē-ba-nt.	dēlē-re-nt.	dēlē-ba-ntur,	dēlē-re-ntur.
		Future.		
Sg.	dēlē-b-ō,		dēlē-bo-r,	
	dēlē-bi-s,		dēlē-be-ris (ro),	
	dēlē-bi-t,		dēlē-bi-tur,	
Pl.	dēlē-bi-mus,		dēlē-bi-mur,	
	dēlē-bi-tis,		dēlē-bi-minī,	
	dēlē-bu-nt.		dēlē-bu-ntur.	
		Perfect.		
Sg.	dēlē-v-ī,	dēlē-v-eri-m,	dēlē-t-us sum,	dēlē-t-us sim,
	dēlē-v-istī,	dēlē-v-erī-s,	es,	sīs,
	dēlē-v-it,	dēlē-v-eri-t,	est,	sit.
Pl.	dēlē-v-imus,	dēlē-v-erī-mus,	dēlē-t-ī sumus,	dēlē-t-ī sīmus,
	dēlē-v-istis,	dēlē-v-erī-tis,	estis,	sītis,
	dēlē-v-ērunt (-ēre),	dēlē-v-eri-nt.	sunt,	sint.

Second Conjugation.

	ACTIVE. INDIC.	ACTIVE. SUBJV.	PASSIVE. INDIC.	PASSIVE. SUBJV.
	PLUPERFECT.			
Sg.—	dēlē-v-era-m,	dēlē-v-isse-m,	dēlē-t-us eram,	dēlē-t-us essem,
	dēlē-v-erā-s,	dēlē-v-issē-s,	erās,	essēs,
	dēlē-v-era-t,	dēlē-v-isse-t.	erat,	esset.
Pl.—	dēlē-v-erā-mus,	dēlē-v-issē-mus,	dēlē-t-ī erāmus,	dēlē-t-ī essēmus,
	dēlē-v-erā-tis,	dēlē-v-issē-tis,	erātis,	essētis,
	dēlē-v-era-nt,	dēlē-v-isse-nt.	erant,	essent.
	FUTURE PERFECT.			
Sg.—	dēlē-v-er-ō,		dēlē-t-us erō,	
	dēlē-v-erĭ-s,		eris,	
	dēlē-v-eri-t,		erit.	
Pl.—	dēlē-v-erĭ-mus,		dēlē-t-ī erimus,	
	dēlē-v-erĭ-tis,		eritis,	
	dēlē-v-eri-nt,		erunt.	

IMPERATIVE.

	PRESENT.	FUTURE.	PRESENT.	FUTURE.
Sg.	——,	——,	——,	——,
	dēlē,	dēlē-tō,	dēlē-re,	dēlē-tor,
	——,	dēlē-tō,	——,	dēlē-tor.
Pl.	——,	——,	——,	——,
	dēlē-te,	dēlē-tōte,	dēlē-minī,	——,
	——,	dēle-ntō.	——,	dēle-ntor.

INFINITIVE.

	Active		Passive
Pres.	dēlē-re.	Pres.	dēlē-rī.
Perf.	dēlē-v-isse.	Perf.	dēlē-t-um, -am, -um esse.
Fut.	dēlē-tūr-um, -am, -um esse.	Fut.	dēlē-tum īrī.
		Fut. Pf.	dēlē-t-um, -am, -um fore.

GERUND.		SUPINE.		PARTICIPLES.
N.	[dēlē-re].			Pres. N. dēlē-n-s ; G. dēle-nt-is.
G.	dēle-nd-ī.			Fut. dēlē-tūr-us, -a, -um.
D.	dēle-nd-ō.			Perf. dēlē-t-us, -a, -um.
Ac.	[dēlē-re]	Ac.	dēlē-tum.	
	(ad) dēle-nd-um.			GERUNDIVE.
Ab.	dēle-nd-ō.	Ab.	dēlē-tū.	dēle-nd-us, -a, -um.

124. Like **dēlēre,** *to destroy,* are conjugated only, **nēre,** *to spin,* **flēre,** *to weep,* and the compounds of **-plēre,** *fill,* and **-olēre** *grow* (the latter with Supine in **-ıtum**); also **ciēre,** *to stir up.* See 137(*b*).

All other verbs of the Second Conjugation retain the characteristic **e** in the Present System, but drop it in the Perfect System, changing **vī** to **uī**, and weaken it to **i** in the Supine System.

Second Conjugation.

Conjugation of **monēre,** *to remind.*

Prin. Parts : **mone-ō, monē-re, mon-uī, moni-tum.**

	ACTIVE.		PASSIVE.	
	INDIC.	SUBJV.	INDIC.	SUBJV.
			PRESENT.	
Sg.	mone-**ō**,	monea-**m**,	mone-**o-r**,	monea-**r**,
	monē-**s**,	moneā-**s**,	monē-**ris** (**-re**),	moneā-**ris** (**-re**),
	mone-**t**,	monea-**t**,	monē-**tur**,	moneā-**tur**,
Pl.	monē-**mus**,	moneā-**mus**,	monē-**mur**,	mone-**ā-mur**,
	monē-**tis**,	moneā-**tis**,	monē-**minī**,	mone-**ā-minī**,
	mone-**nt**.	monea-**nt**.	mone-**ntur**.	mone-**a-ntur**.
			IMPERFECT.	
Sg.	monē-**ba-m**,	monē-**re-m**,	monē-**ba-r**,	monē-**re-r**,
	monē-**bā-s**,	monē-**rē-s**,	monē-**bā-ris** (**-re**),	monē-**rē-ris** (**-re**),
	monē-**ba-t**,	monē-**re-t**,	monē-**bā-tur**,	monē-**rē-tur**,
Pl.	monē-**bā-mus**,	monē-**rē-mus**,	monē-**bā-mur**,	monē-**rē-mur**,
	monē-**bā-tis**,	monē-**rē-tis**,	monē-**bā-minī**,	monē-**rē-minī**,
	monē-**ba-nt**.	monē-**re-nt**.	monē-**ba-ntur**.	monē-**re-ntur**.
			FUTURE.	
Sg.	monē-**b-ō**,		monē-**bo-r**,	
	monē-**bi-s**,		monē-**be-ris** (**-re**),	
	monē-**bi-t**,		monē-**bi-tur**,	
Pl.	monē-**bi-mus**,		monē-**bi-mur**,	
	monē-**bi-tis**,		monē-**bi-minī**,	
	monē-**bu-nt**.		monē-**bu-ntur**.	
			PERFECT.	
Sg.	mon-**u-ī**,	mon-**u-eri-m**,	moni-**t-us sum**,	moni-**t-us sim**,
	mon-**u-istī**,	mon-**u-erī-s**,	**es**,	**sīs**,
	mon-**u-it**,	mon-**u-eri-t**,	**est**,	**sit**,
Pl.	mon-**u-imus**,	mon-**u-erī-mus**,	moni-**t-ī sumus**,	moni-**t-ī sīmus**,
	mon-**u-istis**,	mon-**u-erī-tis**,	**estis**,	**sītis**,
	mon-**u-ērunt** (**-ēre**).	mon-**u-eri-nt**.	**sunt**.	**sint**.

Second Conjugation.

	ACTIVE. INDIC.	ACTIVE. SUBJV.	PASSIVE. INDIC.	PASSIVE. SUBJV.
	Pluperfect.			
Sg.	mon-u-era-m,	mon-u-isse-m,	moni-t-us eram,	moni-t-us essem,
	mon-u-erā-s,	mon-u-issē-s,	erās,	essēs,
	mon-u-era-t,	mon-u-isse-t.	erat,	esset,
Pl.	mon-u-erā-mus,	mon-u-issē-mus,	moni-t-ī erāmus,	moni-t-ī essēmus,
	mon-u-erā-tis,	mon-u-issē-tis,	erātis,	essētis,
	mon-u-era-nt.	mon-u-isse-nt.	erant.	essent.
	Future Perfect.			
Sg.	mon-u-er-ō,		moni-t-us erō,	
	mon-u-erĭ-s,		eris,	
	mon-u-eri-t,		erit,	
Pl.	mon-u-erĭ-mus,		moni-t-ī erimus,	
	mon-u-erĭ-tis,		eritis,	
	mon-u-eri-nt.		erunt.	

IMPERATIVE.

	Present.	Future.	Present.	Future.
Sg.	——	——	——	——
	monē,	monē-tō,	monē-re,	monē-tor,
	——	monē-tō,	——	monē-tor,
Pl.	——	——	——	——
	monē-te,	monē-tōte,	monē-minī,	——
	——	mone-ntō.	——	mone-ntor.

INFINITIVE.

	Active		Passive
Pres.	monē-re.	Pres.	monē-rī.
Perf.	mon-u-isse.	Perf.	moni-t-um, -am, -um esse.
Fut.	moni-tūr-um, -am, um esse.	Fut.	moni-t-um īrī.
		Fut. Pf.	moni-t-um, -am, -um fore.

GERUND.		SUPINE.	PARTICIPLES.
N.	[monē-re].		Pres. N. monē-n-s; G. mone-nt-is
G.	mone-nd-ī.		Fut. moni-tūr-us, -a, -um.
D.	mone-nd-ō.		Perf. moni-t-us, -a, -um.
Ac.	[monē-re] (ad) mone-nd-um.	Ac. moni-tum.	**GERUNDIVE.**
Ab.	mone-nd-ō.	Ab. moni-tū.	mone-nd-us, -a, -um.

125 Third Conjugation.

Conjugation of emere, *to buy.*

Prin. Parts : **em-o, eme-re, ēm-ī, ēm(p)-tum.**

	ACTIVE.		PASSIVE.	
	INDIC.	SUBJV.	INDIC.	SUBJV.
	Present.			
Sg.—	em-o,	ema-m,	em-o-r,	ema-r,
	emi-s,	emā-s,	eme-ris (-re),	emā-ris (-re),
	emi-t,	ema-t,	emi-tur,	emā-tur,
Pl.—	emi-mus,	emā-mus,	emi-mur,	emā-mur,
	emi-tis,	emā-tis,	emi-minī,	emā-minī,
	emu-nt.	ema-nt.	emu-ntur.	ema-ntur.
	Imperfect.			
Sg.—	emē-ba-m,	eme-re-m,	emē-ba-r,	eme-re-r,
	emē-bā-s,	eme-rē-s,	emē-bā-ris (-re,)	eme-rē-ris (-re),
	emē-ba-t,	eme-re-t,	emē-bā-tur,	eme-rē-tur,
Pl.—	emē-bā-mus,	eme-rē-mus,	emē-bā-mur,	eme-rē-mur,
	emē-bā-tis,	eme-rē-tis,	emē-bā-minī,	eme-rē-minī,
	emē-ba-nt.	eme-re-nt.	emē-ba-ntur.	eme-re-ntur.
	Future.			
Sg.—	ema-m,		ema-r,	
	emē-s,		emē-ris (-re),	
	eme-t,		emē-tur,	
Pl.—	emē-mus,		emē-mur,	
	emē-tis,		emē-minī,	
	eme-nt.		eme-ntur.	
	Perfect.			
Sg.—	ēm-ī,	ēm-eri-m,	ēmp-t-us sum,	ēmp-t-us sim,
	ēm-istī,	ēm-erĭ-s,	es,	sīs,
	ēm-it,	ēm-eri-t,	est,	sit,
Pl.—	ēm-imus,	ēm-erĭ-mus,	ēmp-t-ī sumus,	ēmp-t-ī sīmus,
	ēm-istis,	ēm-erĭ-tis,	estis,	sītis,
	ēm-ērunt (-ēre).	ēm-eri-nt.	sunt.	sint.

Third Conjugation.

	ACTIVE. INDIC.	ACTIVE. SUBJV.	PASSIVE. INDIC.	PASSIVE. SUBJV.
	Pluperfect.			
Sg.—	ēm-era-m,	ēm-isse-m,	ēmp-t-us eram,	ēmp-t-us essem,
	ēm-erā-s,	ēm-issē-s,	erās,	essēs,
	ēm-era-t,	ēm-isse-t,	erat,	esset,
Pl.—	ēm-erā-mus,	ēm-issē-mus,	ēmp-t-ī erāmus,	ēmp-t-ī essēmus,
	ēm-erā-tis,	ēm-issē-tis,	erātis,	essētis,
	ēm-era-nt.	ēm-isse-nt.	erant.	essent.
	Future Perfect.			
Sg.—	ēm-er-ō,		ēmp-t-us erō,	
	ēm-eris,		eris,	
	ēm-eri-t,		erit,	
Pl.—	ēm-eri-mus,		ēmp-t-ī erimus,	
	ēm-eri-tis,		eritis,	
	ēm-eri-nt.		erunt.	

IMPERATIVE.

	Present.	Future.	Present.	Future.
Sg.	——	——	——	——
	eme,	emi-tō,	eme-re,	emi-tor,
	——	emi-tō,	——	emi-tor,
Pl.	——	——	——	——
	emi-te.	emi-tōte,	emi-minī.	——
	——	emu-ntō.	——	emu-ntor.

INFINITIVE.

Active		Passive	
Pres.	eme-re.	Pres.	em-ī.
Perf.	ēm-isse.	Perf.	ēmp-t-um, -am, -um esse.
Fut.	ēmp-tūr-um, -am, -um esse.	Fut.	ēmp-tum īrī.
		Fut. Pf.	ēmp-t-um, -am, -um fore.

GERUND.	SUPINE.	PARTICIPLES.
N. [eme-re].		Pres. N. emē-n-s; G. eme-nt-is
G. em-e-nd-ī.		Fut. ēmp-tūr-us, -a, -um.
D. em-e-nd-ō.		Perf. ēmp-t-us, -a, -um.
Ac. [em-e-re]	Ac. ēmp-tum.	
(ad) em-e-ndum.		GERUNDIVE.
Ab. em-e-nd-ō.	Ab. ēmp-tū.	em-e-nd-us, -a, -um.

126. Many verbs of the third conjugation with stem in **ie** (Pres. Indic. in **iō**) weaken this **ie** to **e** before **-re,** and to **i** before **m, s,** and **t** in all tenses of the Present System except the Future. Otherwise they follow the inflection of **eme-re.**

These verbs are **capiō, cupiō, faciō, fodiō, fugiō, iaciō, pariō, quatiō, rapiō, sapiō,** and their compounds; also compounds of **-liciō, -spiciō,** and the deponents **gradior** and its compounds, **morior** and its compounds, **patior** and its compounds.

SYNOPSIS OF PRESENT SYSTEM OF **cape-re,** *to take.*

PRIN. PARTS: **capi-ō, cape-re, cēp-ī, cap-tum.**

	ACTIVE.		PASSIVE.	
	INDIC.	SUBJV.	INDIC.	SUBJV.
		PRESENT.		
SG.—	capi-**ō**,	capia-**m**,	capi-o-**r**,	capia-**r**,
	capi-**s**,	capiā-**s**,	cape-**ris** (-**re**),	capiā-**ris** (-**re**),
	capi-**t**,	capia-**t**,	capi-**tur**,	capiā-**tur**,
PL.—	capi-**mus**,	capiā-**mus**,	capi-**mur**,	capiā-**mur**,
	capi-**tis**,	capiā-**tis**,	capi-**minī**,	capiā-**minī**,
	capiu-**nt**.	capia-**nt**.	capiu-**ntur**.	capia-**ntur**.
		IMPERFECT.		
SG.—	capiē-**ba-m**, *etc.*	cap-**e-re-m**, *etc.*	capi-**ē-ba-r**, *etc.*	cape-**re-r**, *etc.*
		FUTURE.		
SG.—	capia-**m**,		capia-r,	
	capiē-**s**,		capiē-**ris** (-**re**),	
	etc.		*etc.*	
		IMPERATIVE.		
	PRES.	FUT.	PRES.	FUT.
SG.—	cape,	cap-**i-tō**,	cape-**re**,	capi-**tor**,
		cap-**i-tō**,		capi-**tor**,
	capi-**te**.	capi-**tōte**,	capi-**minī**.	
		capiu-**ntō**.		capiu-**ntor**.

INFINITIVE.

PRES. cape-**re**. cap-**ī**.

PARTICIPLE.	GERUND.	GERUNDIVE.
PRES. capiē-**n-s**.	G. capie-**nd-ī**.	capie-**nd-us, -a, -um**.

127. **Fourth Conjugation.**

CONJUGATION OF **audīre**, *to hear*.

PRIN. PARTS: **audi-ō, audī-re, audī-vī, audī-tum.**

	ACTIVE INDIC.	ACTIVE SUBJV.	PASSIVE INDIC.	PASSIVE SUBJV.
		PRESENT.		
Sg.—	audi-ō,	audia-m,	audi-o-r,	audia-r,
	audī-s,	audiā-s,	audī-ris (re),	audiā-ris (-re),
	audi-t,	audia-t,	audī-tur,	audiā-tur,
Pl.—	audī-mus,	audiā-mus,	audī-mur,	audiā-mur,
	audī-tis,	audiā-tis,	audī-minī,	audiā-minī,
	audiu-nt.	audia-nt.	audi-u-ntur.	audia-ntur.
		IMPERFECT.		
Sg.—	audiē-ba-m,	audī-re-m,	audiē-ba-r,	audī-re-r,
	audiē-bā-s,	audī-rē-s,	audiē-bā-ris (re),	audī-rē-ris (-re),
	audiē-ba-t,	audī-re-t,	audiē-bā-tur,	audī-rē-tur,
Pl.—	audiē-bā-mus,	audī-rē-mus,	audiē-bā-mur,	audī-rē-mur,
	audiē-bā-tis,	audī-rē-tis,	audiē-bā-minī,	audī-rē-minī,
	audiē-ba-nt.	audī-re-nt.	audiē-ba-ntur.	audī-re-ntur.
		FUTURE.		
Sg.—	audia-m,		audia-r,	
	audiē-s,		audiē-ris (-re),	
	audie-t,		audiē-tur,	
Pl.—	audiē-mus,		audiē-mur,	
	audiē-tis,		audiē-minī,	
	audie-nt.		audie-ntur.	
		PERFECT.		
Sg.—	audī-v-ī,	audī-v-eri-m,	audī-t-us sum,	audī-t-us sim,
	audī-v-istī,	audī-v-erĭ-s,	es,	sīs,
	audī-v-it,	audī-v-eri-t,	est,	sit,
Pl.—	audī-v-imus,	audī-v-erĭ-mus,	audī-t-ī sumus,	audī-t-ī sīmus,
	audī-v-istis,	audī-v-erĭ-tis,	estis,	sītis,
	audī-v-ērunt (-ēre).	audī-v-eri-nt.	sunt.	sint.

Fourth Conjugation.

	ACTIVE.		PASSIVE.	
	INDIC.	SUBJV.	INDIC.	SUBJV.
	Pluperfect.			
Sg.—	audī-v-era-m,	audī-v-isse-m,	audī-t-us eram,	audī-tu-s essem,
	audī-v-erā-s,	audī-v-issē-s,	erās,	essēs,
	audī-v-era-t,	audī-v-isse-t,	erat,	esset,
Pl.—	audī-v-erā-mus,	audī-v-issē-mus,	audī-t-ī erāmus,	audī-t-ī essēmus
	audī-v-erā-tis,	audī-v-issē-tis,	erātis,	essētis,
	audī-v-era-nt.	audī-v-isse-nt.	erant.	essent.
	Future Perfect.			
Sg.—	audī-v-er-ō,		audī-t-us erō,	
	audī-v-erĭ-s,		eris,	
	audī-v-eri-t,		erit,	
Pl.—	audī-v-erĭ-mus,		audī-t-ī erimus,	
	audī-v-erĭ-tis,		eritis,	
	audī-v-eri-nt.		erunt.	

IMPERATIVE.

	Present.	Future.	Present.	Future.
Sg.—	——	——	——	——
	audī,	audī-tō,	audī-re,	audī-tor,
	——	audī-tō,	——	audī-tor,
Pl.—	——	——	——	——
	audī-te.	audī-tōte,	audī-minī.	——
	——	audiu-ntō.	——	audiu-ntor.

INFINITIVE.

Active		Passive	
Pres.	audī-re.	Pres.	audī-rī.
Perf.	audī-v-isse.	Perf.	audī-t-um, -am, um esse.
Fut.	audī-tūr-um, -am, -um esse.	Fut.	audī-tum īrī.
		Fut. Pf.	audī-t-um, -am, -um fore.

GERUND.	SUPINE.	PARTICIPLES.
N. [audī-re].		Pres. N. audiē-n-s, G. audie-nt-is.
G. audie-nd-ī.		Fut. audī-tūr-us, -a, -um.
D. audie-nd-ō.		Perf. audī-t-us, -a, -um.
Ac. [audī-re] (ad) audie-nd-um.	Ac. audī-tum.	GERUNDIVE.
Ab. audie-nd-ō.	Ab. audī-tū.	audie-nd-us, -a, -um.

DEPONENT VERBS.

128. Deponent verbs have the passive form, but are active in meaning. They have also the Present and Future Active Participles, and the Future Active Infinitive. Thus a deponent verb alone can have a Present, Future, and Perfect Participle, all with active meaning. The Gerundive, however, is passive in meaning as well as in form.

The conjugation differs in no particular from that of the regular conjugation.

I. First Conjugation.

Conjugation of **hortārī**, *to exhort*.

Prin. Parts: **hort-or, hortā-rī, hortā-tus sum.**

INDICATIVE.	SUBJUNCTIVE.
	Present.
Exhort.	*Be exhorting, may exhort.*
Sg.—hort-**o-r**,	horte-**r**,
hortā-**ris** (-**re**),	hortē-**ris** (-**re**),
hortā-**tur**,	hortē-**tur**,
Pl.—hortā-**mur**,	hortē-**mur**,
hortā-**minī**,	hortē-**minī**,
horta-**ntur**.	horte-**ntur**.
	Imperfect.
Was exhorting.	*Were exhorting, might exhort.*
Sg.—hortā-**ba-r**,	hortā-**re-r**,
hortā-**bā-ris** (-**re**),	hortā-**rē-ris** (-**re**),
hortā-**bā-tur**,	hortā-**rē-tur**,
Pl.—hortā-**bā-mur**,	hortā-**rē-mur**,
hortā-**bā-minī**,	hortā-**rē-minī**,
hortā-**ba-ntur**.	hortā-**re-ntur**.
	Future.
Shall exhort.	
Sg.—hortā-**bo-r**,	
hortā-**be-ris** (-**re**),	
hortā-**bi-tur**,	
Pl.—hortā-**bi-mur**,	
hortā-**bi-minī**,	
hortā-**bu-ntur**.	

PERFECT.

Have exhorted, exhorted.		*Have, may have, exhorted.*	
SG.—hortā-t-us, -a, -um	sum,	hortā-t-us, -a, -um	sim,
	es,		sīs,
	est,		sit,
PL.—hortā-t-ī, -ae, -a	sumus,	hortā-t-ī, ae, -a	sīmus,
	estis,		sītis,
	sunt.		sint.

PLUPERFECT.

Had exhorted.		*Had, might have, exhorted.*	
SG.—hortā-t-us, -a, -um	eram,	hortā-t-us, -a, -um	essem,
	erās,		essēs,
	erat,		esset,
PL.—hortā-t-ī, -ae, -a	erāmus,	hortā-t-ī, -ae, -a	essēmus,
	erātis,		essētis,
	erant.		essent.

FUTURE PERFECT.

Shall have exhorted.	
SG.—hortā-t-us, -a, -um	erō,
	eris,
	erit,
PL.—hortā-t-ī, -ae, -a	erimus,
	eritis,
	erunt.

IMPERATIVE.

	PRESENT.	FUTURE.
SG.	——	——
	hortā-re, *exhort thou.*	hortā-tor, *thou shalt exhort.*
	——	hortā-tor, *he shall exhort.*
PL.	——	——
	hortā-minī, *exhort ye.*	——
	——	horta-ntor, *they shall exhort.*

INFINITIVE.

PRES. hortā-rī, *to exhort.*

FUT. hortā-tūr-um, am, -um esse, *to be about to exhort.*

PERF. hortā-t-um, -am, -um esse, *to have exhorted.*

F. P. hortā-t-um, -am, -um fore.

SUPINE.

AC. hortā-tum, *to exhort, for exhorting.*

Ab. hortā-tū, *to exhort, in the exhorting.*

PARTICIPLES.

PRES. hortā-n-s, *exhorting.*

FUT. hortā-tūr-us, -a, um, *about to exhort.*

PERF. hortā-t-us, -a, -um, *having exhorted.*

GERUNDIVE.

horta-nd-us, -a, -um, [*one*] *to be exhorted.*

GERUND.

G. horta-nd-ī, *of exhorting.*

2. Second, Third, Fourth Conjugations.

SYNOPSIS OF **verērī**, *to fear;* **loquī**, *to speak;* **mentīrī**, *to lie.*

PRIN. PARTS: **vere-or, verē-rī, veri-tus sum; loqu-or, loqu-ī, locū-tus sum; menti-or, mentī-rī, mentī-tus sum.**

INDICATIVE.

	II.	III.	IV.
PRES.	vere-**o-r**,	loqu-**o-r**,	menti-**o-r**,
	verē-**ris** (-**re**), *etc.*,	loque-**ris** (-**re**), *etc.*,	mentī-**ris** (-**re**), *etc.*,
IMPERF.	verē-**ba-r**,	loquē-**ba-r**,	mentiē-**ba-r**,
FUT.	verē-**bo-r**,	loqua-**r**,	mentia-**r**,
PERF.	veri-**t-us sum**,	locū-**t-us sum**,	mentī-**t-us sum**,
PLUPF.	veri-**t-us eram**,	locū-**t-us eram**,	mentī-**t-us eram**,
FUT. PF.	veri-**t-us erō**.	locū-**t-us erō**.	mentī-**t-us erō**.

SUBJUNCTIVE.

PRES.	verea-**r**,	loqua-**r**,	mentia-**r**,
	vereā-**ris** (-**re**), *etc.*,	loquā-**ris** (-**re**), *etc.*,	mentiā-**ris** (-**re**), *etc.*,
IMPERF.	verē-**re-r**,	loque-**re-r**,	mentī-**re-r**,
PERF.	veri-**t-us sim**,	locū-**t-us sim**,	mentī-**t-us sim**,
PLUPF.	veri-**t-us essem**.	locū-**t-us essem**.	mentī-**t-us essem**.

IMPERATIVE.

PRES.	verē-**re**,	loque-**re**,	mentī-**re**,
FUT.	verē-**tor**.	loqui-**tor**.	mentī-**tor**.

INFINITIVE.

PRES.	verē-**rī**,	loqu-**ī**,	mentī-**rī**,
FUT.	veri-**tūr-um esse**,	locū-**tūr-um esse**,	mentī-**tūr-um esse**,
PERF.	veri-**t-um esse**,	locū-**t-um esse**,	mentī-**t-um esse**,
FUT. PF.	veri-**t-um fore**.	locū-**t-um fore**.	mentī-**t-um fore**.

PARTICIPLES.

PRES.	verē-**n-s**,	loquē-**n-s**,	mentiē-**n-s**,
FUT.	veri-**tūr-us**,	locū-**tūr-us**,	mentī-**tūr-us**,
PERF	veri-**t-us**.	locū-**t-us**.	mentī-**t-us**.
GERUND.	vere-**nd-ī**, *etc.*,	loque-**nd-ī**,	mentie-**nd-ī**,
GERUNDIVE.	vere-**nd-us**,	loque-**nd-us**,	mentie-**nd-us**,
SUPINE.	veri-**tum**,	locū-**tum**,	mentī-**tum**,
	veri-**tū**.	locū-**tū**.	mentī-**tū**.

Periphrastic Conjugation.

129. The Periphrastic Conjugation arises from the combination of the Future Participle active and the Gerundive with forms of the verb **sum**.

ACTIVE.

	INDICATIVE.	SUBJUNCTIVE.
PRES.	**amātūrus (-a, -um) sum,** *Am about to love.*	**amātūrus (-a, -um) sim,** *Be about to love.*
IMPF.	**amātūrus eram,** *Was about to love.*	**amātūrus essem,** *Were about to love.*
FUT.	**amātūrus erō,** *Shall be about to love.*	
PERF.	**amātūrus fuī,** *Have been, was, about to love.*	**amātūrus fuerim,** *Have, may have, been about to love.*
PLUPF.	**amātūrus fueram,** *Had been about to love.*	**amātūrus fuissem,** *Had, might have, been about to love.*
FUT. PERF.	**amātūrus fuerō,** *Shall have been about to love.*	

INFINITIVE. PRES. **amātūr-um (-am, -um) esse,** *To be about to love.*

PERF. **amātūr-um fuisse,** *To have been about to love.*

PASSIVE.

PRES.	**amandus (-a, -um) sum,** *Have to be loved.*	**amandus (-a, -um) sim,** *Have to be loved.*
IMPF.	**amandus eram,** *Had to be loved.*	**amandus essem, forem,** *Had to be loved.*
FUT.	**amandus erō,** *Shall have to be loved.*	
PERF.	**amandus fuī,** *Have had to be loved.*	**amandus fuerim,** *Have had to be loved.*
PLUPF.	**amandus fueram,** *Had had to be loved.*	**amandus fuissem,** *Should have had to be loved.*

INFINITIVE. PRES. **amandum (-am, -um) esse,** *To have to be loved.*

PERF. **amandum fuisse,** *To have had to be loved.*

Notes on the Four Conjugations.

130. *The Present System.*

1. Present Indicative.—(*a*) In the third person Singular active, early Latin, and occasionally later poets, often retain the original length of vowel in the endings **-āt, -ēt,** and **-īt** of the first, second, and fourth conjugations. Final **-īt** in the third conjugation is rare, and due, perhaps, to analogy or to metrical necessity. In the first person Plural the ending **-mūs** is found a few times in poetry. In third person Plural an earlier ending, **-onti,** is found only in a *Carmen Saliare*, and is disputed. The ending **-ont** is frequent in early Latin for **-unt.**

(*b*) In the second Singular, passive, in all tenses of the Present stem, the ending **-re** is much more common in early Latin than **-ris,** and is regular in Cic. except in the Pr. Indic., where he prefers **-ris** on account of confusion with Pr. Inf., admitting **-re** only in deponents, and then but rarely. In general, in the Pr. Indic. **-re** is rare in the first and second conjugations, more rare in the third, and never found in the fourth, in prose authors. Post-Ciceronian prose writers, *e. g.*, Livy, Tacitus, prefer **-ris,** even in the other tenses of the Present stem. The poets use **-ris** or **-re** to suit the metre.

2. Imperfect Indicative.—In the fourth conjugation, instead of **-iē-,** we find in early times **-ī-.** This is common in early Latin (especially **scībam**), in the poets to suit the metre, and occasionally in later prose. In the verb **eō,** and its compounds (but **ambīre** varies), this form was regular always.

3. Future Indicative.—Plautus shows sporadic cases of **-īt,** as **erīt, vēnībīt (vēneō).** In the fourth conjugation **-ībō** for **-iam** is very common in early Latin (especially **scībō**), and forms in **-ībō** of the third conjugation are occasional.

4. Present Subjunctive.—Final **-āt** of the third person Singular active is occasional in early Latin and also in later poets. In early Latin the active endings **-im, -īs, -it, -int** are found in **dare** (and some compounds), which forms very often **duim, duīs, duit, duint.** On similar forms from **esse,** see 116; from **edere,** see 172.

5. Imperative.—(*a*) Four verbs, **dīcere, dūcere, facere, ferre** (171), form the Pr. Impv. active **dīc, dūc, fac, fer.** But in early Latin **dīce, dūce, face** are not uncommon. The compounds follow the usage of the simple verbs, except non-prepositional compounds of **faciō. Scīre,** *to know*, lacks the Pr. Impv. **scī.**

(*b*) The original ending of the Fut. Impv. active **-tōd** is found in early inscriptions, but very rarely.

(*c*) The Pr. Impv. passive (second and third Singular) ends occasionally in early Latin in **-minō.**

6. Present Infinitive Passive.—The early ending **-rier (-ier)** is very common in early Latin and occasionally in poetry at all periods. Plautus shows about 140 such formations. In literary prose it does not appear till very late.

7. The Present Participle occurs sporadically in early Latin with the ending **-ās, -ēs,** the **n** having been omitted owing to its weak sound; see 12, r. 1.

8. The older ending of the Gerund and Gerundive in the third and fourth conjugations was **-undus;** and **-endus** was found only after **u.** In classical times **-undus** is frequent, especially in verbs of third and fourth conjugations. Later, **-endus** is the regular form.

131. *The Perfect System.*

1. Syncopated Forms.—The Perfects in **-āvī, -ēvī, -īvī,** often drop the **v** before **s** or **r,** and contract the vowels throughout, except those in **-īvī,** which admit the contraction only before **s.**

The syncopated forms are found in all periods, and in the poets **are** used to suit the metre.

PERFECT.

SING. 1.	—	—	—
2.	**amāvistī, amāstī.**	**dēlēvistī, dēlēstī.**	**audīvistī, audīstī.**
3.	—	—	—
PLUR. 1.	—	—	—
2.	**amāvistis, amāstis.**	**dēlēvistis, dēlēstis.**	**audīvistis, audīstis.**
3.	**amāvērunt, amārunt.**	**dēlēvērunt, dēlērunt.**	**audīvērunt, audiērunt.**
SUBJV.	**amāverim, amārim,** *etc.*	**dēlēverim, dēlērim,** *etc.*	**audīverim, audierim,** *etc.*

PLUPERFECT.

INDIC.	**amāveram, amāram,** *etc.*	**dēlēveram, dēlēram,** *etc.*	**audīveram, audieram,** *etc.*
SUBJV.	**amāvissem, amāssem,** *etc.*	**dēlēvissem, dēlēssem,** *etc.*	**audīvissem, audīssem,** *etc.*

FUTURE PERFECT.

amāverō, amārō, *etc.*	**dēlēverō, dēlērō,** *etc.*	**audīverō, audierō,** *etc.*

INFINITIVE PERFECT.

amāvisse, amāsse.	**dēlēvisse, dēlēsse.**	**audīvisse, audīsse.**

2. In the first and third persons Sing. and in the first person Pl. of the Perfect, syncope occurs regularly only in Perfects in **īvī**, and no contraction ensues. It is most common in the Perfects of **īre** (169) and **petere.** In other verbs this syncopation is post-Ciceronian, except in a few forms. So CICERO uses **dormiit, ērudiit, expediit, molliit, cupiit** (also PLAUTUS); CAESAR, **commūniit, resciit, quaesiit. Dēsinere** forms **desiī** and **dēsiit,** once each in early Latin (CICERO uses **dēstitī** and **dēstitit** instead), and then in post-Augustan Latin; **dēsiimus** is cited once from CICERO. The unsyncopated forms are always common except those of **īre** (169), which are very rare in classical prose, but occur more often in the poets for metrical reasons.

NOTE.—The forms **nōmus** (ENN. = **nōvimus**), **ēnārrāmus** (TER., *Ad.*, 365), **flēmus, mūtāmus,** and **nārrāmus** (PROP.), **suēmus** (LUCR.), in the Perfect, are sporadic and sometimes doubtful.

3. **nōvī**, *I know*, and **mōvī**, *I have moved*, are also contracted, in their compounds especially.

SING.—2. **nōstī.** PLUR.—2. **nōstis.** 3. **nōrunt.** SUBJV. **nōrim,** *etc.*
PLUPF. **nōram,** *etc.* SUBJV. **nōssem,** *etc.* INF. **nōsse.**
But the Fut. Perf. **nōrō** is found only in compounds.
Similar contractions are seen in **mōvī**, but not so often; **iūvī** shows also a few cases of syncope in poetry.

4. (*a*) In the early Latin poets frequently and occasionally in later, syncope takes place in Perfects in **-sī.** These drop the **s** and contract. A few cases are found in CICERO, especially in the letters. Examples are **dīxtī** (found also in CIC. and probably an earlier formation, and not by syncope for **dīxistī**); **dūxtī,** principally in compounds; **intellextī** (once in CIC.); **scrīpstī**; **mīstī** (**mīsistī**) and several others; also **scrīpstis.**

(*b*) Akin to these are a number of forms in **-sō** for Fut. Perfect; **-sim** for Pf. Subjv. and more rarely **-sem** for Plupf. Subjv. These forms are most usual in the third conjugation, but are also not unfrequent in the other three; thus,

1. *Future Perfect:* **faxō** (facere); **capsō** (capere) and compounds; **iūssō** (**iubēre**; VERG.); **amāssō** (**amāre**); **servāssō** (**servāre**) and compounds, together with some others.

2. *Perfect Subjunctive:* **faxim** and compounds; **dūxim**; **ausim** (**audēre**, also used by CIC.); **iūssim**; **ēmpsim** (emere); **locāssim** (**locāre**); **negāssim** (**negāre**). In the second and third persons Sing., where the Fut. Pf. Indic. and the Pf. Subjv. are identical, the forms are much more common. The plural forms are much less frequent.

3. *Pluperfect Subjunctive:* **faxem**; **prō-mīssem**; **intel-lexēs**; **re-cēsset** and a few other forms; **ērēpsēmus** (HOR., *S*, i. 5, 79). These forms are rare.

4. *Infinitive:* **dīxe**; **dē-spexe**; **ad-dūxe**, *etc.*; **intel-lexe**; **dē-trāxe**, *etc.*; **ad-vexe**; **ad-mīsse**, and a few others. Also the Future forms **āveruncāssere**, **reconciliāssere**, **impetrāssere**, **oppūgnāssere**.

The exact origin of these forms is still a matter of dispute, but the common view is that they are aoristic formations.

5. From the earliest times the third Plural of the Pf. Indic. active shows two endings, **-ēront** (later **-ērunt**) and **-ēre**. The form in **-ērunt** was always preferred, and in classical prose is the normal form. The form in **-ēre** seems to have been the popular form, and is much liked by LIVY and later writers. TACITUS seems to have preferred **-ērunt** for the Pure Perfect, and **-ēre** for the Historical Perfect. The poets scan, according to the exigencies of the metre, at all periods also **ĕrunt**.

6. In regard to the other endings, we have to notice in early Latin **-īs** occasionally in the Pf. Subjv. and Fut. Pf. Indic. active; Perfects in **-iī** are always written with **-iēī-** on inscriptions; in other Perfects the third person Singular in **-ēit** (older **-ēt**), or **-īt**; as **dedet**; occasionally the first person ends in **-ēī** and the second in **-istēī**. Peculiar forms are **dedrot** (**dedro**), (for **dederunt**), **fēcēd** (for **fēcit**), and a few others.

THE STEM.

132. With the exception of the verbs **sum**, *I am*, **edō**, *I eat*, **eō**, *I go*, **ferō**, *I bear*, **volō**, *I wish* (perhaps **dō**, *I give*), and their compounds, most of whose forms come directly from the root, all verbs in Latin form their stems from the root by the addition of a vowel or of a combination of a vowel with a consonant. This vowel is called the *thematic* vowel; see 190.

In the first, second, and fourth conjugations, and in some verbs of the third conjugation, the stem thus formed is found throughout the whole conjugation; in other verbs the present stem shows different forms from the other stems.

1. THE PRESENT STEM.

133. I. *The Stem* or *Thematic class:* To this class belong those verbs whose stems are formed by the addition of a thematic vowel (usually **i**, sometimes **u**) to the root, as in the third conjugation, or to a stem formed by the addition of **ā**, **ĕ**, or **i** to the root, as in the first, second, and fourth conjugations. The stem thus formed is seen (with lengthened vowel sometimes) in all forms of the verb. To this class belong verbs of the first, second, and fourth conjugations, and in the third (*a*) verbs formed from a strong root, *i. e.*, verbs with **ī, ū, ā, ē, ō, ae, au**; and with **e** in the stem; as **dīcō** (= **deicō**), **dūcō** (= **doucō**), **rādō, cēdō, rōdō, caedō, plaudō**; **vehō, vergō, pendō**, *etc.*; (*b*) verbs formed from a weak root, *i. e.*, those with vowel **ĭ, ŭ, ŏ**, and probably those with **ă**: as **dī-vidō, furō, olō (olere), ago.**

II. *The Reduplicated class:* The Present stem is formed by reduplication, with **i** in the reduplicated syllable:

gen-, gī-gnō (for GI-GEN-O), **gī-gne-re**, *to beget;* **sta-, si-stō, si-ste-re**, *to set, stand.* Compare **stāre**, *to stand.* Other forms, as **sīdō** (for SI-S(E)DO), **serō** (for SI-SO), and perhaps **bibō**, have the Reduplication concealed.

III. *The* **T** *class:* The root, which usually ends in a guttural, is strengthened by **to, te**: **flectō** (FLEC-), **flecte-re**, *to bend.*

IV. *The Nasal class:* In this class the root is strengthened by **no, ne,** the nasal being inserted

A. In vowel-stems: **sinō** (SI-), **sine-re**, *to let;* **linō** (LI-), **line-re**, *to besmear.*

B. After the characteristic liquid: **cernō** (CER-), **cerne-re**, *to sift, separate;* **temnō** (TEM-), **temne-re**, *to scorn.*

NOTES.—1. After **l** assimilation takes place: **pellō** (for **pel-nō**), **pelle-re**, *to drive.*
2. In a few verbs the strengthened forms (**-no** after a vowel, **-ino** after a liquid) are confined mainly to the third person Plural active of the Present, and are found not later than the close of the sixth century of the city: **danunt** (= **dant**), **explēnunt** (= **explent**), **nequīnont** (= **nequeunt**), and a few others.

C. Before the characteristic mute: **vincō** (VIC-), **vince-re**, *to conquer;* **frangō** (FRAG-), **frange-re**, *to break;* **fundō** (FUD-), **funde-re**, *to pour.*

Before a **p**-mute **n** becomes **m**: **rumpō** (RUP-), **rumpe-re**, *to rend;* **cumbō** (CUB-), **cumbe-re**, *to lie down.*

D. Here belong also those verbs in which the root is strengthened by **-nuō, nue**; as **sternuō** (STER-), **sternue-re**, *to sneeze.*

NOTE.—In verbs like **tinguō**, *I soak*, the consonantal **u** disappears before a consonant in the Pf. and Supine: **tinxī, tinc-tum.**

V. *The Inchoative class:* The Present stem has the suffix **-sco, -sce.**

irā-scor, *I am in a rage;* **crē-scō**, *I grow;* **ob-dormī-scō**, *I fall asleep;* **apī-scor**, *I reach;* **pro-ficī-scor**, *I set out;* **nancī-scor** (NAC-), *I get;* **nō-scō** (= **gnō-scō**), *I become acquainted;* **pō-scō** (= **porc-scō**), *I demand;* **mis-ceō** (= **mic-sc-eō**), *I mix;* **discō** (= **di-dc-scō**), *I learn.* A number of Inchoatives are derivative formations from substantives; as, **lapidēscō** (from **lapis**), *I become stone.*

VI. *The* **I** *class:* Instead of the simple thematic vowel **i** the root is increased by the form **ie.** In some forms of the Present stem, *i. e.*, the Pr. Inf., Impf. Subjv., second Sing., Pr. Impv., this appears in the form **e**; in some other forms it appears as **i**: **capi-ō** (CAP-), **cape-re**, *to take.*

NOTE.—Verbs of the fourth conjugation also belong to the **i** class; but for convenience the **i** class is here restricted as above.

VII. *The Mixed class:* Some verbs that originally belong to the **i**-class have gone over in the Present stem to the forms of the stem class: as **veniō** (VEN-), **venī-re,** *to come;* **videō** (VID-), **vidē-re,** *to see;* **sonō** (SON-), **sonā-re,** *to sound.*

II. THE PERFECT STEM.

134. I. *Perfect in* **-vī** (or **-uī**): These are formed by the addition

(*a*) Of **-vī** to the stem as it appears in the Present Inf. in combination with the thematic vowel. To this class belong the Perfects of the first and fourth conjugations, and the few verbs of the second conjugation mentioned in 124; **amā-re, amā-vī; audī-re, audī-vī; delē-re, delē-vī.**

(*b*) Of **-uī** to the Present stem after its characteristic vowel is dropped. Here belong the majority of the verbs of the second conjugation; **monē-re, mon-uī.**

II. *Perfect in* **-sī**: These are formed by the addition of **-sī** to the root; which is, as a rule, long either by nature or position. This class comprises a large number of verbs in the third conjugation in which the stem-characteristic consonant is a mute; three in which it is **-m** (**preme-re,** *to press;* **sūme-re,** *to take;* **con-tem(n)e-re,** *to scorn*); and a few in which it is **-s,** as **ūr-ō,** *I burn,* **ūs-sī; haereō,** *I stick,* **haesī** (= **haes-sī**).

Examples are **rēpō,** *I creep,* **rēp-sī; scrībō,** *I write,* **scrīp-sī; dīcō,** *I say,* **dīxī** (= **dīc-sī**); **carpō,** *I pluck,* **carp-sī; rādō,** *I scrape,* **rāsī** (= **rād-sī**).

NOTE.—But verbs in **-ndō,** take **ī** in the Perfect: **dēfend-ō,** *I strike (ward) off,* **dēfend-ī;** perhaps because they formed originally a *reduplicated perfect;* as, **mandō,** *I chew,* **man(di)dī;** so **(fe)fendī,** *I have struck.*

III. *Reduplicated Perfects:* These are formed by prefixing to the unstrengthened root its first consonant (or consonantal combination) together with the following vowel, **a** and **ae** being weakened to **e,** or, if the root began with a vowel, by prefixing **e,** and adding the termination **-ī.** In Latin but few of these forms remain, and they have been variously modified: **discō,** *I learn,* **di-dicī; spondeō,** *I pledge,* **spo(s)pondī; tangō,** *I touch,* **te-ti-gī; tundō,** *I strike,* **tu-tud-ī; ago,** *I act,* **ēgī** (= **e-ag-ī**); **emo,** *I buy,* **ēmī** (= **e-em-ī**).

In composition the reduplication is in many cases dropped; so always in compounds of **cade-re,** *to fall;* **caede-re,** *to fell;* **cane-re,** *to sing;* **falle-re,** *to deceive;* **pange-re,** *to fix;* **parce-re,** *to spare;* **pare-re.** *to bear;* **pende-re,** *to hang;* **punge-re,** *to prick;* **tange-re,** *to touch;* **tende-re,** *to stretch* (occasionally retained in late Latin); **tondē-re,** *to shear* (but occasionally retained in late Latin); **tunde-re,** *to strike.* **Disc-ere,** *to learn,* always retains it, and so **pōsce-re,** *to demand,* and **ad-mordēre,** *to bite.* Of compounds of **curre-re,** *to run,* **succurrere** always drops the reduplication, **praecurrere** always retains it; the others vary. Of compounds of **dare**, **abscondere** usually drops it, but all trisyllabic compounds that change the **a**, and all quadrisyllabic compounds, retain it. Compounds of **sistere**, *to set*, and **stāre**, *to stand*, retain it.

IV. *Perfect in* **ī**. Verbs of the third conjugation, with a *short* stem-syllable, take **ī** in the Perfect, after lengthening the stem-syllable and changing **ă** into **ē**. In many cases these Perfects are the remains of reduplicated forms: **legō**, *I read*, **lēg-ī**; **vide-ō**, *I see*, **vīd-ī**; **fodi-ō**, *I stab*, **fōd-ī**; **fugi-ō**, *I flee*, **fūg-ī**; **frang-ō**, *I break*, **frēg-ī**.

V. Denominative verbs in **-uō**, like **acuō**, *I sharpen*; **metuō**, *I fear*; also **sternuō**, *I sneeze*, form the Perfect in **-u-ī** after the analogy of primary verbs, and the formation in **-uī** gradually extended in Latin.

III. THE SUPINE STEM.

135. I. *Supine in* **-tum**, *Perfect Passive Participle in* **-tus**: The stems are formed by the addition of **-tu** or **-to**

(*a*) To the stem as it appears in the Present Infinitive active. Here belong most verbs of the first and fourth conjugations, and those verbs of the second conjugation that are mentioned in 124: **amā-tum, dēlē-tum, audī-tum.** Those verbs of the second conjugation which form Perfect in **-uī**, form the Supine stem by weakening the thematic vowel **e** to **i**, and adding **-tu, -to,** except **cēnsē-re**, *to deem*, **docē-re**, *to teach*, **miscē-re**, *to mix*, **tenē-re**, *to hold*, **torrē-re**, *to scorch*, which omit the thematic vowel, and form **cēnsum, doctum, mixtum,** (**tentum**), **tōstum.**

(*b*) To the unstrengthened stem. Here belong most verbs of the third conjugation and the five verbs of the second just given, with sporadic forms in the other conjugations: **cap-tum** (**capiō**, *I take*), **rēp-tum** (**rēpō**, *I creep*), **dic-tum** (**dīcō**, *I say*), **fac-tum** (**faciō**, *I do*).

In combinations of **-t-** with a dental, assimilation took place, giving usually **ss** after a short vowel and **s** after a long vowel: **scissum** (**scindō**, *I cleave*), **caesum** (**caedō**, *I fell*). On the analogy of this and under the influence often of Perfect in **-sī**, we find **-s-** also in some other stems:

1. In stems with a guttural characteristic; as, **fīx-um** (**fīgō**, *I fix*); often with a preceding liquid: **mersum** (**mergō**, *I dip*; Pf. **mersī**); **tersum** (**tergeō**, *I wipe*; Pf. **tersī**); **parsum** (**parcō**, *I spare*; Pf. **parsī**, old); **spar-sum** (**spargō**, *I sprinkle*; Pf. **sparsī**); **mul-sum** (**mulgeō**, *I milk*; Pf. **mul-sī**); but **far-tum** (**farciō**, *I stuff*; Pf. **farsī**); **tortum** (**torqueō**, *I twist*; Pf. **torsī**); **indul-tum** (rare and post-classical, from **indulgeō**, *I indulge*; Pf. **indulsī**).

2. In one with a labial characteristic: **lāp-sum** (**lābor**, *I slip*).

3. In some stems with characteristic **s**; as, **cēnsum** (**cēnseō**, *I deem*; see I. *a*.); **haesum** (**haereō**, *I stick*); **pīnsum** (**pīnsō**, *I pound*).

4. In some stems with a nasal characteristic: **pressum** (**premō**, *I press*; Pf. **pressī**); **mānsum** (**maneō**, *I remain*; Pf. **mānsī**).

5. In stems where **ll, rr** has arisen by assimilation: **pulsum** (**pellō**, *I drive*); **falsum** (**fallō**, *I falsify*); **vulsum** (**vellō**, *I pluck*); **cursum** (**currō**, *I run*); **versum** (**verrō**, *I sweep*).

II. Future Active Participle in **-tūrus**.—The same changes occur in the stem as are found in the case of the Supine.

1. In some stems ending in -u a thematic vowel **i** is inserted; as **arguitūrus** (**arguere**, *to prove*); **luitūrus** (**luere**, *to loose*); **abnuitūrus** (**abnuere**, *to deny*); **ruitūrus** (**ruere**, *to rush*); **ēruitūrus** (**ēruere**, *to root out*); **fruitūrus** (**fruī**, *to enjoy*).

2. Some Future Participles are found without corresponding Perfect: **calitūrus** (**calēre**, *to be warm*); **caritūrus** (**carēre**, *to lack*); **dolitūrus** (**dolēre**, *to grieve*); **iacitūrus** (**iacēre**, *to lie*); **pāritūrus** (**pārēre**, *to obey*); **valitūrus** (**valēre**, *to be well*).

3. Irregular are: **āgnōtūrus**, **āgnitūrus** (**āgnōscere**, *to know well*); **dīscitūrus** (**dīscere**, *to learn*); **hausūrus**, **haustūrus** (**haurīre**, *to drain*); **nīsūrus** (**nītī**, *to lean*); **moritūrus** (**morī**, *to die*); **nōscitūrus** (**nōscere**, *to know*); **oritūrus** (**orīrī**, *to arise*); **paritūrus** (**parere**, *to bear*).

Change of Conjugation.

136. A change of Conjugation occurs in verbs which show a long thematic vowel in the Present stem, but not in the Perfect stem, or the reverse.

1. Verbs with Perfect and Supine formed regularly, according to the third conjugation, have the Present stem formed according to one of the other three:

auge-ō,	**augē-re,**	**aux-ī,**	**auc-tum,**	*to increase.*
senti-ō,	**sentī-re,**	**sēn-sī,**	**sēn-sum,**	*to feel.*
saepi-ō,	**saepī-re,**	**saep-sī,**	**saep-tum,**	*to hedge about.*
veni-ō,	**venī-re,**	**vēn-ī,**	**ven-tum,**	*to come.*
vide-ō,	**vidē-re,**	**vīd-ī,**	**vī-sum,**	*to see.*
vinci-ō,	**vincī-re,**	**vinx-ī,**	**vinc-tum,**	*to bind.*

2. Verbs with Perfect and Supine formed according to the first, second, or fourth conjugations, have the Present stem formed according to the third, in consequence of strengthening:

ster-n-ō,	**ster-ne-re,**	**strā-vī,**	**strā-tum,**	*to strew.*
crē-sc-ō,	**crē-sce-re,**	**crē-vī,**	**crē-tum,**	*to grow.*
li-n-ō,	**line-re,**	**lē-vī (lī-vī),**	**li-tum,**	*to smear.*

3. Verbs with the Present formed regularly according to the third conjugation, have the Perfect and Supine formed according to (*a*) the second, or (*b*) the fourth conjugation:

(*a*) **accumbere**, *to recline*, **fremere**, *to rage*, **gemere**, *to groan*, **gīgnere**, *to beget*, **molere**, *to grind*, **strepere**, *to resound*, **vomere**, *to vomit*, form Perfect in **-uī**, Supine in **-itum**.

alere, *to nourish*, **colere**, *to cultivate*, **cōnsulere**, *to consult*, **frendere**, *to show the teeth*, **occulere**, *to conceal*, **rapere**, *to snatch*, and its compounds form Perfect in **-uī**, Supine in **-tum** (**-sum**). For **ali-tus**, see 142, 3.

compēscere, *to check,* **con-cinere,** *to sing together,* and other compounds of **canere,** *to sing,* **excellere,** *to excel,* **stertere,** *to snore,* **tremere,** *to tremble,* form Perfect in **-uī,** but no Supine.

(*b*) **arcessere,** *to summon,* **incessere,** *to enter,* **cupere,** *to desire,* **petere,** *to seek,* **quaerere,** *to search,* and its compounds, **rudere,** *to roar,* **sapere,** *to savor,* form Perfect in **-īvī,** Supine in **-ītum.**

4. Stems vary among the first, second, and fourth conjugations.

(*a*) Verbs with the Present formed according to the first, and Perfect and Supine according to the second conjugation :

crepāre, *to crackle,* **cubāre,** *to lie,* **domāre,** *to conquer,* **micāre,** *to flash,* **plicāre,** *to fold,* **sonāre,** *to sound,* **tonāre,** *to thunder,* **vetāre,** *to forbid,* with Perfect in **-uī,** Supine in **-itum :**

fricare, *to rub,* **necāre,** *to kill,* **secāre,** *to cut,* with Perfect in **-uī,** Supine in **-tum** (but participles in **ātus** are occasional, principally in later Latin).

(*b*) Verbs with Present formed according to fourth, and Perfect and Supine according to the second : **amicīre,** *to wrap,* **aperīre,** *to open,* **operīre,** *to cover,* **salīre,** *to leap,* and compounds.

(*c*) Of the second and fourth conjugations is **cie-ō (ci-o), ciē-re (cī-re), cīvī, cītum (ci-tum),** *to stir up,* and its compounds ; while **pōtō, pōtāre,** *to drink,* forms Sup. **pō-tum** or **pō-tātum,** and Fut. Part. **pō-tūrus** or **pōtā-tūrus.**

5. **dare,** *to give,* and **stāre,** *to stand,* pass over to the third conjugation in the Perfect, in consequence of reduplication.

LIST OF VERBS ACCORDING TO THE PERFECT FORM.

PERFECT: -vī; SUPINE: -tum.

137. *Stem class:*

(*a*) Verbs of *first* and *fourth* conjugations, except those mentioned in 136, 4. Irregular in Supine is

sepeli-ō,	**sepelī-re,**	**sepelī-vī,**	**sepul-tum,**	*to bury.*

(*b*) In the *second* conjugation :

dēle-ō,	**dēlē-re,**	**dēlē-vī,**	**dēlē-tum,**	*to destroy.*
fle-ō,	**flē-re,**	**flē-vī,**	**flē-tum,**	*to weep.*
ne-ō,	**nē-re,**	**nē-vī,**	**nē-tum,**	*to spin.*
-ole-ō (ab-, in-),	**-olē-re,**	**-olē-vī,**	—	*to grow.*

These compounds form Supine in **itum ; abolitum, inolitus.**

-pleō,	**-plē-re,**	**plē-vī,**	**plē-tum,**	*to fill.*

So the compounds with **com-, in-, ex-, re-, sup-.**

vie-ō,	**viē-re,**	—	**viē-tus,**	*to plait.*

Irregular is

cie-ō (ci-ō),	**ciē-re (cīre),**	**cī-vī,**	**cī-tum (ci-tum),**	*to stir up.*

In the compounds we find the Participles **concitus** or **concītus, percitus, excītus** or **excitus,** but **accītus.**

(*c*) In the *third* conjugation :

arcess-ō, **arcesse-re,** **arcessī-vī,** **arcessī-tum,** *to send for.*
So, too, **lacess-ō,** *I tease*, **capess-ō,** *I lay hold of*. In early Latin we often find **accersō,** the relation of which to **arcessō** is variously explained. The forms **arcessiri,** and later **arcessīrētur,** from the fourth conjugation, also occur.

in-cess-ō, **in-cesse-re,** **in-cessī-vī** (**cessī**), *to attack.*
So **facess-ō,** *I cause, make off.*

pet-ō, **pete-re,** **petī-vī,** **petī-tum,** *to seek (fly at).*
quaer-ō, **quaere-re,** **quaesī-vī,** **quaesī-tum,** *to seek.*
con-quīr-ō, **con-quīre-re,** **conquīsī-vī,** **con-quīsī-tum,** *to hunt up.*
So other compounds of **-quīrō** (**quaerō**).
rud-ō, **rude-re,** **rudī-vī,** **rudī-tum,** *to roar.*
ter-ō, **tere-re,** **trī-vī,** **trī-tum,** *to rub.*
TIB., I. 4, 48, has **at-teruisse,** and APULEIUS has similar forms.

138. *Reduplicated class:*

ser-ō, **sere-re,** **sē-vī,** **sa-tum,** *to sow.*
So **cōnserō,** but with Sup. **cōn-situm.**

139. *Nasal class:*

A. **li-n-ō,** **li-ne-re,** **lē-vī,** **li-tum,** *to besmear.*
So compounds of **linō.** Pf. **lī-vī** is rare.

si-n-ō, **si-ne-re,** **sī-vī,** **si-tum,** *to let.*
So **dē-sinō,** *I leave off*, and in early Latin, **pōnō** (= **po-sinō**), *I put.*

B. **cer-n-ō,** **cer-ne-re,** **crē-vī,** (**crē-tum**), *to separate.*
So **dēcernō,** *I decide.*

sper-n-ō, **sper-ne-re,** **sprē-vī,** **sprē-tum,** *to despise.*
ster-n-ō, **ster-ne-re,** **strā-vī,** **strā-tum,** *to strew.*

140. *Inchoative class:*

keterā-sc-ō, **inveterā-sce-re,** **inveterā-vī,** **inveterā-tum,** *to grow old.*
pā-sc-ō, **pā-sce-re,** **pā-vī,** **pās-tum,** *to graze* (trans.).
vesperā-sc-ō, **vesperā-sce-re,** **vesperā-vī,** —— *to become evening.*
So **advesperāscō.**

crē-sc-ō, **crē-sce-re,** **crē-vī,** **crē-tum,** *to grow.*
So the compounds.

con-cupī-sc-ō, **-cupī-sce-re,** **-cupī-vī,** **-cupī-tum,** *to long for.*
ob-dormī-sc-ō, **-dormī-sce-re,** **-dormī-vī,** **-dormī-tum,** *to fall asleep.*
So **condormīscō, ēdormīscō.**

ex-olē-sc-ō, **-olē-sce-re,** **-olē-vī,** **-olē-tum,** *to get one's growth.*
So **ob-solēscō,** *I grow old.* But **ab-olēscō,** *I disappear*, has **abolitum; co-alēscō,** *I grow together*, **co-alitum; ad-olēscō,** *I grow up*, **ad-ultum** in the Sup.; and **inolēscō** lacks the Supine.

quiē-sc-ō, **quiē-sce-re,** **quiē-vī,** **quiē-tum,** *to rest.*
scī-sc-ō, **scī-sce-re,** **scī-vī,** **scī-tum,** *to decree.*
So **ad-scīscō,** *I take on.*

su-ēsc-ō, **suē-sce-re,** **suē-vī,** **suē-tum,** *to accustom one's self.*
So compounds **as-, con-, dē-, man-.**

(g)nō-sc-ō, **nō-sce-re,** **nō-vī,** **(nō-tum),** *to know.*
So **ignōscō,** *I pardon;* but **cō-gnōsco,** *I recognise,* and other compounds of **nōsco,** have Sup. in **-itum.**

re-sip-īsc-ō, **-sipī-sce-re,** **-sipī-vī,** —— *to come to one's senses.*

141. *I-class:*

cupi-ō, **cupe-re,** **cupī-vī,** **cupī-tum,** *to desire.*
sapi-ō, **sape-re,** **sapī-vī (-uī),** —— *to have a flavor.*

PERFECT: -uī; SUPINE: (i)tum.

142. *Stem class:*

1. The majority of the verbs of the *second* conjugation; see 134, I, *b*, and 135, *a*. But

sorbe-ō, **sorbē-re,** **sorb-uī,** —— *to sup up.*
Pf. **sorp-sī** occurs in VAL. MAX. and LUCAN.

2. Of the *first* conjugation:

crep-ō, **crepā-re,** **crep-uī,** **crepi-tum,** *to rattle.*
So the compounds, but in early and late Latin the regular forms of **dis-crepāre** and **in-crepāre** are occasional.

cub-ō, **cubā-re,** **cub-uī,** **cubi-tum,** *to lie.*
Occasional regular forms in post-Ciceronian Latin.

dom-ō, **domā-re,** **dom-uī,** **domi-tum,** *to tame.*

fric-ō, **fricā-re,** **fric-uī,** **fric-tum (-ā-tum),** *to rub.*
Occasionally in early and more often in post-classical Latin, the regular forms are found in the compounds; so always **-fricā-tūrus.**

mic-ō, **micā-re,** **mic-uī,** —— *to quiver, flash.*
But **dī-micāre,** *to fight (out),* is regular, except occasionally in OVID.

nec-ō, **necā-re,** **necā-vi (nec-uī** rare), **necā-tum,** *to kill.*
The compound **ēnecā-re,** *to kill off,* has **ēnecāvī** in early Latin, otherwise **ēnecuī** (rare); and **ēnectus** (but PLIN. MAI., **ēnecātus**).

plic-ō, **plicā-re,** **(plicā-vī),** **plici-tum,** *to fold.*
The simple forms of **plicāre** are rare. The compounds **ap-, com-, ex-, im-,** vary between **-āvī** and **-uī** in the Pf., and **-ātum** and **-itum** in the Sup.; but CICERO uses always **applicāvī, applicātum; complicāvī, complicātum;** and usually **explicāvī,** always **explicātum;** always **implicātum; circumplicāre** is always regular; forms of **replicāre** are rare.

sec-ō, **secā-re,** **sec-uī,** **sec-tum,** *to cut.*
Regular forms are early, late, and rare.

son-ō, **sonā-re,** **son-uī,** **soni-tum,** *to sound.*
But regularly **sonātūrus.** Regular forms are late. In early Latin the forms **sonere, sonit, sonunt, resonit, resonunt,** show that the simple verb was **sonere.**

ton-ō, **tonā-re,** **ton-uī,** —— *to thunder.*
But **at-tonitus** and **intonātus** (HOR., *Epod.* 2, 51).

vet-ō,	**vetā-re,**	**vet-uī,**	**veti-tum,**	*to forbid.*

But PERSIUS (5, 90) uses **vetā-vī.**

3. Of the *third* conjugation :

frem-ō,	**freme-re,**	**frem-uī,**	—	*to roar, rage.*
gem-ō,	**geme-re,**	**gem-uī,**	—	*to groan.*
vom-ō,	**vome-re,**	**vom-uī,**	**vomi-tum,**	*to vomit.*
al-ō,	**ale-re,**	**al-uī,**	**al-tum,**	*to nourish.*

Participle **ali-tus** occurs from LIVY on.

col-ō,	**cole-re,**	**col-uī,**	**cul-tum,**	*to cultivate.*
con-cin-ō,	**-cine-re,**	**-cin-uī,**	—	*to sing together.*

So **occinere, praecinere.**

cōn-sul-ō,	**cōn-sule-re,**	**cōn-sul-uī,**	**cōn-sul-tum,**	*to consult.*
deps-ō,	**depse-re,**	**deps-uī,**	**deps-tus,**	*to knead.*
mol-ō,	**mole-re,**	**mol-uī,**	**moli-tum,**	*to grind.*
occul-ō,	**occule-re,**	**occul-uī,**	**occul-tum,**	*to conceal.*
pīns-ō,	**pīnse-re,**	**pīns-uī,**	**pīnsi-tum,**	*to pound.*

Sup. also **pīnsum, pīstum.** Collateral forms of **pīsō, pīsere,** are early and rare, so also is **pīnsībant.**

ser-ō,	**sere-re,**	—	(**ser-tum**),	*to string (out).*

Common in compounds: as, **dēserō, dēserere, dēseruī, dēsertum,** *to desert.* The same forms are found occasionally in compounds of **serere,** *to sow* (138), but not in classical Latin.

stert-ō,	**sterte-re,**	**stert-uī,**	—	*to snore.*
strep-ō,	**strepe-re,**	**strep-uī,**	(**strepi-tum**),	*to make a din.*
tex-ō,	**texe-re,**	**tex-uī,**	**tex-tum,**	*to weave.*

Irregular are

met-ō,	**mete-re,**	**mess-uī,**	**mes-sum,**	*to mow.*
vol-ō,	**vel-le,**	**vol-uī,**	—	*to wish.*

So **nōlō, mālō**; see 174.

4. In the *fourth* conjugation :

amici-ō,	**amicī-re,**	**amic-uī** (**amixī**),	**amic-tum,**	*to clothe.*
aperi-ō,	**aperī-re,**	**aper-uī,**	**aper-tum,**	*to open.*
operi-ō,	**operī-re,**	**oper-uī,**	**oper-tum,**	*to cover up.*
sali-ō,	**salī-re,**	**sal-uī,**	**sal-tum,**	*to leap.*

The regular Perfects **salīvī, saliī,** are found in compounds, but usually in post-classical writers, and often syncopated.

143. *Reduplicated class :*

gī-gn-ō (GEN-),	**gī-gne-re,**	**gen-uī,**	**geni-tum,**	*to beget.*

Early Latin has the Present forms **genit, genunt, genat, genitur, genuntur, genendī, genī.**

144. *Nasal class:*

frend-ō,	**frende-re,**	—	**frē-sum, frēs-sum,**	*to gnash.*

Also in the form **frende-ō, frendē-re.**

ac-cumb-ō,	**-cumbe-re,**	**cub-uī,**	**cubi-tum,**	*to lie down.*

So also the compounds **con-, dis-, in-**; but **re-cumbō** lacks the Supine.

ex-cell-ō,	**-celle-re,**	**(cell-uī),**	**(cel-sus),**	*to surpass.*

But **per-cellere,** *to beat down,* has Pf. **per-culī,** Sup. **per-culsum. Excelluērunt** is found in GELL. XIV. 3, 7, and in AUGUSTINE; otherwise forms of Pf. and Sup. do not occur.

145. *The Inchoative class:*

dispēsc-ō,	**dispēsce-re,**	**dispēsc-uī,**	—	*to let loose.*

So **compēscere,** *to check.*

A large number of verbs are formed from verbs of the second conjugation, or from substantives or adjectives, and take Pf. in **-uī**; as,

co-alēsc-ō,	**alēsce-re,**	**al-uī,**	**ali-tum,**	*to grow together.*

See 140.

ē-vānēsc-ō,	**vānēsce-re,**	**vān-uī,**	—	*to disappear.*
con-valēsc-ō,	**valēsce-re,**	**val-uī,**	**vali-tum,**	*to get well.*
in-gemīsc-ō,	**gemīsce-re,**	**gem-uī,**	—	*to sigh.*
nōtēsc-ō,	**nōtēsce-re,**	**nōt-uī,**	—	*to become known.*
incalēsc-ō,	**incalēsce-re,**	**incal-uī,**	—	*to get warm.*

146. *The I-class:*

rapi-ō,	**rape-re,**	**rap-uī,**	**rap-tum,**	*to snatch.*
cor-ripiō,	**ripe-re,**	**rip-uī,**	**rep-tum,**	*to seize.*

So other compounds. In early Latin, **surripere** syncopates some of its forms, as **surpuit, surpere; surpuerat** occurs in HOR.; aoristic forms, as **rapsit, surrepsit,** belong also to the early period. 131, 4, *b.* 2.

PERFECT: -sī; SUPINE: -tum, -sum.

147. *Stem class:*

1. In the *second* conjugation:

iube-ō,	**iubē-re,**	**iūs-sī,**	**iūs-sum,**	*to order.*

On **sorbeō** see 142, 1.

ārde-ō,	**ārdē-re,**	**ār-sī,**	**ār-sum,**	*to be on fire.*
rīde-ō,	**rīdē-re,**	**rī-sī,**	**rī-sum,**	*to laugh (at).*
haere-ō,	**haerē-re,**	**hae-sī,**	**(hae-sum),**	*to stick (to).*
mane-ō,	**manē-re,**	**mān-sī,**	**mān-sum,**	*to remain.*
suāde-ō,	**suādē-re,**	**suā-sī,**	**suā-sum,**	*to counsel.*

With dental dropped before ending of Pf. and Supine.

auge-ō,	**augē-re,**	**auxī,**	**auc-tum,**	*to cause to wax.*
frīge-ō,	**frīgē-re,**	**(frīxī),**	—	*to be chilled.*
lūce-ō,	**lūcē-re,**	**lūxī,**	—	*to give light.*

lūge-ō,	**lūgē-re,**	**lūxī,**	—	*to be in mourning.*
alge-ō,	**algē-re,**	**al-sī,**	—	*to freeze.*
fulge-ō,	**fulgē-re,**	**ful-sī,**	—	*to glow.*

In early Latin, forms of the third conjugation occur: **fulgit, fulgere, effulgere** (VERG., *A*, VIII. 677).

indulge-ō,	**indulgē-re,**	**indul-sī,**	**(indul-tum),**	*to give way.*
mulce-ō,	**mulcē-re,**	**mul-sī,**	**mul-sum,**	*to stroke.*

Rarely **mulc-tus** in compounds.

mulge-ō,	**mulgē-re,**	**mul-sī,**	**mul-sum(ctum),**	*to milk.*
terge-ō,	**tergē-re,**	**ter-sī,**	**ter-sum,**	*to wipe.*

Forms of the third conjugation: **tergit, tergitur, terguntur,** are occasionally found; and so too in some late compounds. VARRO has **tertus.**

torque-ō,	**torquē-re,**	**tor-sī,**	**tor-tum,**	*to twist.*
turge-ō,	**turgē-re,**	**tur-sī,**	—	*to swell.*
urge-ō,	**urgē-re,**	**ur-sī,**	—	*to press.*
cō-nīve-ō (gnigv),	**-nīvē-re,**	**-nīxī (īvī),**	—	*to close the eyes.*

2. In the *third* conjugation:

carp-ō,	**carpe-re,**	**carp-sī,**	**carp-tum,**	*to pluck.*
dē-cerp-ō,	**dē-cerpe-re,**	**dē-cerp-sī,**	**dē-cerp-tum,**	*to pluck off.*
clep-ō,	**clepe-re,**	**clep-sī (clēp-ī),**	**clep-tum,**	*to filch.*

Rare and ante-classic.

nūb-ō,	**nūbe-re,**	**nūp-sī,**	**nūp-tum,**	*to put on a veil (as a bride).*
rēp-ō,	**rēpe-re,**	**rēp-sī,**	**rēp-tum,**	*to creep.*
scalp-ō,	**scalpe-re,**	**scalp-sī,**	**scalp-tum,**	*to scrape.*
scrīb-ō,	**scrībe-re,**	**scrīp-sī,**	**scrīp-tum,**	*to write.*
sculp-ō,	**sculpe-re,**	**sculp-sī,**	**sculp-tum,**	*to chisel.*
serp-ō,	**serpe-re,**	**serp-sī,**	**serp-tum,**	*to creep.*
prem-ō (-primō),	**preme-re,**	**pres-sī,**	**pres-sum,**	*to press.*

Some compounds of **emo,** *I take, buy,* have Pf. in **-sī,** Sup. in **-tum,** before which a euphonic **p** developes:

cōm-ō,	**cōme-re,**	**cōm-p-sī,**	**cōm-p-tum,**	*to adorn.*
dēm-ō,	**dēme-re,**	**dēm-p-sī,**	**dēm-p-tum,**	*to take away.*
prōm-ō,	**prōme-re,**	**prōm-p-sī,**	**prōm-p-tum,**	*to take out.*
sūm-ō,	**sūme-re,**	**sūm-p-sī,**	**sūm-p-tum,**	*to take.*

On **contemn-ō** see 149, *c*.

dīc-ō,	**dīce-re,**	**dīxī (dīc-sī),**	**dic-tum,**	*to say.*

Impv. **dīc,** see 130, 5. Occasionally in old Latin **dīcēbō** for Future.

dūc-ō,	**dūce-re,**	**dūxī,**	**duc-tum,**	*to lead.*

Imperative **dūc,** see 130, 5.

fīg-ō,	**fīge-re,**	**fīxī,**	**fīxum,**	*to fasten.*

Part. **fīctus** for **fīxus** is occasional in early Latin.

-flīg-ō (con-, af-, in-),	**-flīge-re,**	**-flīxī,**	**-flīc-tum,**	*to strike.*

Simple verb is found occasionally in early Latin.

frīg-ō,	**frīge-re,**	**frīxī,**	**frīc-tum,**	*to parch.*

sūg-ō,	**sūge-re,**	**sūxī,**	**sūc-tum,**	*to suck.*

Fut. **exsūgēbō** is found in PLAUT., *Ep.* 188.

merg-ō,	**merge-re,**	**mer-sī,**	**mer-sum,**	*to plunge.*
sparg-ō,	**sparge-re,**	**spar-sī,**	**spar-sum,**	*to strew.*
cōn-sperg-ō,	**cōn-sperge-re,**	**cōn-sper-sī,**	**cōn-sper-sum,**	*to besprinkle.*
coqu-ō,	**coque-re,**	**coxī,**	**coc-tum,**	*to cook.*
[**-lig-ō** (**leg-**),	**-lige-re,**	**-lēxī,**	**-lēc-tum.**]	
dī-lig-ō,	**dī-lige-re,**	**dī-lēxī,**	**dīlēc-tum,**	*to love.*
intelligō, *or* **intellegō,**	**intellege-re,**	**intel-lēxī,**	**intel-lēc-tum,**	*to understand.*
negligō, *or* **neg-leg-ō,**	**neg-lege-re,**	**neg-lēxī,**	**neg-lēc-tum,**	*to neglect.*

Other compounds have **lēgī**. SALL., *J.* 40, 1, has **neglēgisset**.

reg-ō,	**rege-re,**	**rēxī,**	**rēc-tum,**	*to keep right.*
dī-rig-ō,	**dī-rige-re,**	**dī-rēxī,**	**dī-rēc-tum,**	*to guide.*
per-g-ō,	**per-ge-re,**	**per-rēxī,**	**per-rēc-tum,**	*to go on.*
su-rg-ō,	**su-rge-re,**	**sur-rēxī,**	**sur-rēc-tum,**	*to rise up.*

But **expergō** formed **expergitus** in earry and late Latin.

teg-ō,	**tege-re,**	**tēxī,**	**tēc-tum,**	*to cover.*
claud-ō,	**claude-re,**	**clau-sī,**	**clau-sum,**	*to shut.*
con-, ex-clūd-ō,	**ex-clūde-re,**	**ex-clū-sī,**	**ex-clū-sum,**	*to shut up, out.*

Early Latin shows also **clūdō, clūdere.**

laed-ō,	**laede-re,**	**lae-sī,**	**lae-sum,**	*to harm.*
col-līd-ō,	**col-līde-re,**	**col-lī-sī,**	**col-lī-sum,**	*to strike together.*
lūd-ō,	**lūde-re,**	**lū-sī,**	**lū-sum,**	*to play.*
plaud-ō (**ap-plaud-ō**),	**plaude-re,**	**plau-sī,**	**plau-sum,**	*to clap.*
ex-plōd-ō,	**ex-plōde-re,**	**ex-plō-sī,**	**ex-plō-sum,**	*to hoot off.*
rād-ō,	**rāde-re,**	**rā-sī,**	**rā-sum,**	*to scratch.*
rōd-ō,	**rōde-re,**	**rō-sī,**	**rō-sum,**	*to gnaw.*
trūd-ō,	**trūde-re,**	**trū-sī,**	**trū-sum,**	*to push.*
vād-ō (**in-, ē-**),	**-vāde-re,**	**-vā-sī,**	**-vā-sum,**	*to go.*
cēd-ō,	**cēde-re,**	**cēs-sī,**	**cēs-sum,**	*to give way.*
quati-ō,	**quate-re,**	(**quas-sī**),	**quas-sum,**	*to shake.*
con-cutiō (**per-, ex-**),	**con-cute-re,**	**con-cus-sī,**	**con-cus-sum,**	*to shatter.*
mitt-ō,	**mitte-re,**	**mī-sī,**	**mis-sum,**	*to send.*
dī-vid-ō,	**dī-vide-re,**	**dī-vī-sī,**	**dī-vī-sum,**	*to part.*
ūr-ō,	**ūre-re,**	**ūs-sī,**	**ūs-tum,**	*to burn.*
com-būr-ō,	**com-būre-re,**	**com-būs-sī,**	**com-būs-tum,**	*to burn up.*
ger-ō,	**gere-re,**	**ges-sī,**	**ges-tum,**	*to carry.*
flu-ō (**flugv-**),	**flue-re,**	**fluxī,**	(**flux-us**),	*to flow.*
stru-ō (**strugv-**),	**strue-re,**	**strūxī,**	**strūc-tum,**	*to build.*
trah-o (**tragh-**),	**trahe-re,**	**trāxī,**	**trāc-tum,**	*to drag.*
veh-ō (**vegh**),	**vehe-re,**	**vexī,**	**vec-tum,**	*to carry.*
vīv-ō (**vigv-**),	**vīve-re.**	**vīxī,**	**vīc-tum,**	*to live.*

148. *The T-class:*

flect-ō,	**flecte-re,**	**flexī,**	**flexum,**	*to bend.*
nect-ō,	**necte-re,**	**nexī (nexuī),**	**nexum,**	*to knot.*

The Pf. forms: **in-nexuī** (VERG., *A.* v., 425).

pect-ō,	**pecte-re,**	**pexī,**	**pexum,**	*to comb.*
plect-ō,	**plecte-re,**	**(plexī),**	**plexum,**	*to plait.*

149. *The Nasal class:*

(*a*) Supine without N:

fing-ō,	**finge-re,**	**finxī,**	**fic-tum,**	*to form.*
ming-ō,	**minge-re,**	**minxī,**	**mic-tum,**	*to urinate.*
ping-ō,	**pinge-re,**	**pinxī,**	**pic-tum,**	*to paint.*
string-ō,	**stringe-re,**	**strinxī,**	**stric-tum,**	*to draw tight.*

(*b*) Supine with N:

ang-ō,	**ange-re,**	**anxī,**	——	*to throttle, vex.*
cing-ō,	**cinge-re,**	**cinxī,**	**cinc-tum,**	*to gird.*
ē-mung-ō,	**ē-munge-re,**	**ē-munxī,**	**ē-munc-tum,**	*to wipe the nose.*
iung-ō,	**iunge-re,**	**iūnxī,**	**iūnc-tum,**	*to yoke, join.*
ling-ō,	**linge-re,**	**linxī,**	**linc-tum,**	*to lick.*
ning-ō,	**ninge-re,**	**ninxī,**	——	*to snow.*
pang-ō,	**pange-re,**	**panxī,**	**panc-tum,**	*to drive in.*

Perfect also **pēgī**, and Supine **pāctum**. Compare 155 and **pacīscor**, 165.

plang-ō,	**plange-re,**	**planxī,**	**planc-tum,**	*to smite.*
-stingu-ō,	**-stingue-re,**	**-stinxī,**	**-stinc-tum,**	*to put out.*

So the compounds **ex-, dis-, re-**; the simple verb is ante-classic.

ting-ō (**tingu-ō**),	**ting**(**u**)**e-re,**	**tinxī,**	**tinc-tum,**	*to wet, dye.*
ung-ō (**ungu-ō**),	**ung**(**u**)**e-re,**	**ūnxī,**	**ūnc-tum,**	*to anoint.*

(*c*) **tem-n-ō** (rare) and its compounds form the Pf. with a euphonic **p:**

con-tem-n-ō,	**-temne-re,**	**-tem-p-sī,**	**-tem-p-tum,**	*to despise.*

150. *The I-class:*

I. In the *third* conjugation:

[**-lici-ō** (LAC),	**lice-re,**	**-lexī,**	**-lec-tum**],	*to lure.*
pel-lici-ō,	**pel-lice-re,**	**pel-lexī,**	**pel-lec-tum,**	*to allure.*

So **allicere, illicere,** which, however, have early Pf. in **-uī**, as does **pellicere** also. But **ē-licere** has **-uī** regularly in classical times, and **ē-lexī** only later.

[**-spici-ō** (SPEC),	**-spice-re,**	**-spexī,**	**-spec-tum**],	*to peer.*
per-spici-ō,	**per-spice-re,**	**per-spexī,**	**per-spec-tum,**	*to see through.*

So the compounds with **ad-, con-, dē-, in-.**

2. In the *fourth* conjugation :

saepi-ō,	**saepī-re,**	**saep-sī,**	**saep-tum,**	*to hedge in.*
sanci-ō,	**sancī-re,**	**sānxī,**	**sānc-tum,**	*to hallow.*

The Sup. **sancī-tum** is rare.

vinci-ō,	**vincī-re,**	**vinxī,**	**vinc-tum,**	*to bind.*
farci-ō (**-ferci-ō**),	**farcī-re,**	**far-sī,**	**far-tum,**	*to stuff.*
fulci-ō,	**fulcī-re,**	**ful-sī,**	**ful-tum,**	*to prop.*
sarci-ō,	**sarcī-re,**	**sar-sī,**	**sar-tum,**	*to patch.*
senti-ō,	**sentī-re,**	**sēn-sī,**	**sēn-sum,**	*to feel.*
hauri-ō,	**haurī-re,**	**hau-sī,**	**haus-tum,**	*to drain.*

VERG., *A.* iv., 383, has **hausūrus.** Early Latin shows **haurībant** (LUCR.) and **haurierint** ; **haurītūrus** is very late.

rauci-ō,	**raucī-re,**	**rau-sī,**	**rau-sum,**	*to be hoarse.*

This verb is very rare.

PERFECT : -ī WITH REDUPLICATION ; SUPINE : -sum, -tum.

151. In the *first* conjugation :

1. **d-ō,** **da-re,** **ded-ī,** **da-tum,** *to give, put, do.*

Everywhere **ă**, except in **dās**, *thou givest*, and **dā**, *give thou.*

1. Like **dō**, are conjugated the compounds with dissyllabic words, such as : **circum-d-ō**, *I surround ;* **satis-dō**, *I give bail ;* **pessum-dō**, *I ruin ;* **vēnum-dō**, *I sell ;* thus :

circum-d-ō, **circum-da-re,** **circum-de-dī,** **circum-da-tum,** *to surround.*

2. The compounds of **da-re** with monosyllabic words pass over wholly into the Third Conjugation.

ab-d-ō,	**ab-de-re,**	**ab-did-ī,**	**ab-di-tum,**	*to put away.*
ad-d-ō,	**ad-de-re,**	**ad-did-ī,**	**ad-di-tum,**	*to put to.*
con-d-ō,	**con-de-re,**	**con-did-ī,**	**con-di-tum,**	*to put up (found).*
abs-con-dō,	**abs-con-de-re,**	**abs-con-d-ī,**	**abs-con-di-tum,**	*to put far away.*

Pf. **abscondidī** is found in PL., *Mer.* 360, then not until late Latin.

crē-d-ō,	**crē-de-re,**	**crē-did-ī,**	**crē-di-tum,**	*to put faith.*
dē-d-ō,	**dē-de-re,**	**dē-did-ī,**	**dē-di-tum,**	*to give up.*
ē-d-ō,	**ē-de-re,**	**ē-did-ī,**	**ē-di-tum,**	*to put out.*
in-d-ō,	**in-de-re,**	**in-did-ī,**	**in-di-tum,**	*to put in.*
per-d-ō,	**per-de-re,**	**per-did-ī,**	**per-di-tum,**	*to fordo (ruin).*
prō-d-ō,	**prō-de-re,**	**prō-did-ī,**	**prō-di-tum,**	*to betray.*
red-d-ō,	**red-de-re,**	**red-did-ī,**	**red-di-tum,**	*to give back.*
trā-d-ō,	**trā-de-re,**	**trā-did-ī,**	**trā-di-tum,**	*to give over.*
vēn-d-ō,	**vēn-de-re,**	**vēn-did-ī,**	**vēn-di-tum,**	*to put up to sale.*

NOTE.—In early Latin **dare** formed the Pr. Subjv., also **duim.** So in some of its compounds, as **perduim.** See 130, 4.

2. **st-ō,** **stā-re,** **stet-ī,** (**stā-tū-rus**), *to stand.*

So the compounds :

ad-st-ō,	**ad-stā-re,**	**ad-stit-ī,**	—	*to stand by.*
cōn-st-ō,	**cōn-stā-re,**	**cōn-stit-ī,**	—	*to stand fast.*

in-st-ō,	**in-stā-re,**	**in-stit-ī,**	—	*to stand upon.*
ob-st-ō,	**ob-stā-re,**	**ob-stit-ī,**	—	*to stand out against.*
per-st-ō,	**per-stā-re,**	**per-stit-ī,**	—	*to stand firm.*
prae-st-ō,	**prae-stā-re,**	**prae-stit-ī,**	—	*to stand ahead.*
re-st-ō,	**re-stā-re,**	**re-stit-ī,**	—	*to stand over.*
dī-st-ō,	**dī-stā-re,**	—	—	*to stand apart.*
ex-st-ō,	**ex-stā-re,**	—	—	*to stand out.*

All compounds of **stāre** with dissyllabic prepositions have, however, **-stetī** in the Perfect, as: **ante-stō,** *I am superior;* **inter-stō,** *I am between;* **super-stō,** *I stand upon;* thus:

circum-st-ō,	**circum-stā-re,**	**circum-stet-ī,**	—	*to stand round.*

NOTE.—Compare **sistō** and its compounds; 154, I.

152. In the *second* conjugation:

morde-ō,	**mordē-re,**	**mo-mord-ī,**	**mor-sum,**	*to bite.*
pende-ō,	**pendē-re,**	**pe-pend-ī,**	—	*to hang* (intr.).
sponde-ō,	**spondē-re,**	**spo-pond-ī,**	**spōn-sum,**	*to pledge oneself.*

Compounds omit the reduplication, but PLAUT. shows also **dē-spo-pondisse** and **dē-spo-ponderās.**

tonde-ō,	**tondē-re,**	**to-tond-ī,**	**tōn-sum,**	*to shear.*

153. In the *third* conjugation:

(*a*) *Stem class.*

Reduplication lost in the compounds:

cad-ō,	**cade-re,**	**ce-cid-ī,**	**cā-sum,**	*to fall.*
oc-cid-ō,	**oc-cide-re,**	**oc-cid-ī,**	**oc-cā-sum,**	*to perish.*

re-cidere sometimes forms **reccidī,** as well as **recidī,** in the Perfect.

caed-ō,	**caede-re,**	**ce-cīd-ī,**	**cae-sum,**	*to fell.*
oc-cīd-ō,	**oc-cīde-re,**	**oc-cīd-ī,**	**oc-cī-sum,**	*to kill.*
can-ō,	**cane-re,**	**ce-cin-ī,**	**(can-tum),**	*to sing.*

Compounds form the Pf. in **-uī.** For **(cantum), cantātum** was used.

parc-ō,	**parce-re,**	**pe-perc-ī (par-sī), (par-sūrus),**		*to spare.*
com-parcō (-percō),	**com-parce-re,**	**com-pars-ī,**	**com-par-sum,**	*to save.*

parsī is common in early Latin, and is the only form used by PLAUTUS. Early Latin shows rarely **parcuī.** TER. uses **compersit.**

154. (*b*) *Reduplicated class:*

I. **sistō** (= **si-st-ō**), as a simple verb, has the transitive meaning, *I (cause to) stand,* but in its compounds, the intransitive meaning, *I stand.* Compare **stō,** *I stand,* and its compounds (151):

sist-ō,	**siste-re,**	**(stit-ī),**	**sta-tum,**	*to (cause to) stand.*

So the compounds:

cōn-sist-ō,	**cōn-siste-re,**	**cōn-stit-ī,**	**cōn-sti-tum,**	*to come to a stand.*
dē-sist-ō (ab-),	**dē-siste-re,**	**dē-stit-ī,**	**dē-sti-tum,**	*to stand off.*

ex-sist-ō,	**ex-siste-re,**	**ex-stit-ī,**	**ex-sti-tum,**	*to stand up.*
ob-sist-ō,	**ob-siste-re,**	**ob-stit-ī,**	**ob-sti-tum,**	*to take a stand against.*
re-sist-ō,	**re-siste-re,**	**re-stit-ī,**	**re-sti-tum,**	*to withstand.*
ad-sist-ō,	**ad-siste-re,**	**ad-stit-ī,**	——	*to stand near.*
īn-sist-ō,	**īn-siste-re,**	**īn-stit-ī,**	——	*to stand upon.*
circum-sist-ō,	**circum-siste-re,**	**circum-stet-ī,**		*to take a stand round.*

2. **bi-bō,** **bi-be-re,** **bi-bī,** **(bi-bi-tus),** *to drink.*

No Supine. The Pf. Part. is late.

155. (*c*) *Nasal class:*

fall-ō, **falle-re,** **fe-fell-ī,** **fal-sum,** *to cheat.*

The compound **refellō** has the Perfect **refellī,** and lacks Supine.

pell-ō, **pelle-re,** **pe-pul-ī,** **pul-sum,** *to push, drive back.*

repellō loses the reduplicating vowel in Pf. **reppulī.**

toll-ō, **tolle-re,** —— —— *to lift up.*

Pf. and Sup. are formed **sus-tulī** (from reduplicated Pf. **tetulī,** 171, N. 1) and **sub-lātum** (for **t'lā-tum**); a recent view makes **su-stulī** from **(s)tollō.**

(pang-ō), **(pange-re),** **pe-pig-ī,** **pāc-tum,** *to drive a bargain.*

The Pr. forms are supplied by **pacīscor,** 165. The Pf. **pēgī,** rare in the simple form, is regular in the compounds **com-, im-, op-.** See 149, *b*.

tang-ō (TAG), **tange-re,** **te-tig-ī,** **tāc-tum,** *to touch.*
at-ting-ō, **at-tinge-re,** **at-tig-ī,** **at-tāc-tum,** *to border upon.*

So with other compounds.

pend-ō, **pende-re,** **pe-pend-ī,** **pēn-sum,** *to hang* (trans.).

tend-ō, **tende-re,** **te-tend-ī,** **tēn-sum** and **-tum,** *to stretch.*
ex-tend-ō, **ex-tende-re** **ex-tend-ī,** **ex-tēn-sum** and **-tum,** *to stretch out.*
os-tend-ō, **os-tende-re,** **os-tend-ī,** **os-tēn-sum** (**-tus**), *to stretch at, show.*

The compounds prefer the Sup. in **-tum;** so always **attentus, contentus,** usually **distentus** and **intentus.**

pung-ō, **punge-re,** **pu-pug-ī,** **punc-tum,** *to prick.*
inter-pungō, **inter-punge-re,** **inter-punxī,** **inter-punc-tum,** *to place points between.*

tund-ō, **tunde-re,** **tu-tud-ī,** **tūn-sum, tū-sum,** *to thump.*

Simple form has usually **tūnsus** in the Participle; in the compounds more often **tūsus.** The reduplicating vowel is lost in **rettudī.**

curr-ō, **curre-re,** **cu-curr-ī,** **cur-sum,** *to run.*

The compounds vary in their use of the reduplication; **praecurrere** always has the reduplication, **succurrere** always omits it; other compounds vary. See 134, III.

156. (*d*) *Inchoative class:*

discō (= **di-d(e)c-scō**), **dīsce-re,** **di-dic-ī,** —— *to learn.*

A late form is Fut. Part. **dīscitūrus.** Compounds retain reduplication. See 134, III.

pōsc-ō (= **porc-scō**), **pōsce-re,** **po-pōsc-ī,** —— *to claim.*

Compounds retain the reduplication. See 134, III.

157. (*e*) *The I-class:*

pari-ō, **pare-re,** **pe-per-ī,** **par-tum** (**paritūrus**), *to bring forth.*

The compounds drop the reduplication and form the Inf. in **-īre.** But **reperīre,** *to find*, forms its Pf., **repperī,** with omission of the vowel of reduplication.

PERFECT: -ī; SUPINE: -tum, -sum.

158. In the *first* conjugation:

iuv-ō,	**iuvā-re,**	**iūv-ī,**	**iū-tum (iuvātūrus),**	*to help.*
ad-iuv-ō,	**-iuvā-re,**	**-iūv-ī,**	**-iū-tum (-iū-tūrus),**	*to stand by as aid.*
(lav-ō),	**(lav-ere),**	**lāv-ī,**	**lau-tum (lō-tum),**	*to wash.*
lav-ō,	**lavā-re,**	**(lavā-vī),**	**lavā-tum,**	*to wash.*

The Present forms of **lavere** belong principally to early Latin, with occasional forms in Augustan poets and late writers; **lautum** and **lōtum** are both used in classical times; but **lautum** belongs rather to early, **lōtum** to post-classical Latin. The form **lavātum** is early and poetical.

159. In the *second* conjugation:

cave-ō,	**cavē-re,**	**cāv-ī,**	**cau-tum,**	*to take heed.*
fave-ō,	**favē-re,**	**fāv-ī,**	**fau-tum,**	*to be well-disposed.*
ferve-ō (o),	**fervē-re (ere),**	**ferv-ī (ferb-uī),**	——	*to seethe.*

The Pr. forms of the third conjugation belong to early Latin and the poets. The Pf. in **-uī** is post-Ciceronian.

fove-ō,	**fovē-re,**	**fōv-ī,**	**fō-tum,**	*to keep warm.*
move-ō,	**movē-re,**	**mōv-ī,**	**mō-tum,**	*to move.*
pave-ō,	**pavē-re,**	**pāv-ī,**	——	*to quake (with fear).*
prande-ō,	**prandē-re,**	**prand-ī,**	**prān-sum,**	*to breakfast.*
sede-ō,	**sedē-re,**	**sēd-ī,**	**ses-sum,**	*to sit.*
strīde-ō (-dō),	**strīdē-re(-e-re),**	**strīd-ī,**	——	*to whistle, screech.*
vove-ō,	**vovē-re,**	**vōv-ī,**	**vō-tum,**	*to vow.*

The Present forms of the third conjugation belong almost entirely to Augustan poets and later writers.

vide-ō,	**vidē-re,**	**vīd-ī,**	**vī-sum,**	*to see.*

160. In the *third* conjugation:

With long vowel in the Perfect.

1. *The Stem class:*

ag-o,	**age-re,**	**ēg-ī,**	**āc-tum,**	*to do, drive.*
cō-g-ō,	**cō-ge-re,**	**co-ēg-ī,**	**co-āc-tum,**	*to compel.*
dē-g-ō,	**dē-ge-re,**	——	——	*to pass (time).*
red-ig-ō,	**red-ige-re,**	**red-ēg-ī,**	**red-āc-tum,**	*to bring back.*
em-o,	**eme-re,**	**ēm-ī,**	**ēmp-tum,**	*to take, to buy.*
inter-im-ō,	**-ime-re,**	**-ēm-ī,**	**-ēmp-tum,**	*to make away with.*

co-em-ō, *I buy up*, is conjugated like **em-o.** But the compounds with **ad-, ex-, inter-, red-,** take **-im-ō.** So, too, **dir-im-ō**, *I sever.*

ed-ō,	**ede-re,**	**ēd-ī,**	**ē-sum,**	*to eat.*

Note.—In **agere, edere, emere,** the reduplication has coalesced with the root; as, **ēgī = eagī.**

cūd-ō,	**cūde-re,**	**(cūd-ī),**	**(cū-sum),**	*to hammer.*

The Pf. and Sup. occur in compounds only.

leg-o,	**lege-re,**	**lēg-ī,**	**lēc-tum,**	*to pick up, read.*
col-lig-ō,	**col-lige-re,**	**col-lēg-ī,**	**col-lēc-tum,**	*to gather.*

So the other compounds, except **dī-lig-ō, intel-leg-ō, neg-leg-ō,** see 147, 2.

īc-ō (defective),	**īce-re,**	**īc-ī,**	**īc-tum,**	*to strike.*

Present stem rare: **īc-it, īc-itur, īc-imur.**

sīd-ō,	**sīde-re,**	**sīd-ī,**		*to sit down.*

The Pf. was originally reduplicated as the Present; see 133, II. In composition the Pf. is **-sēdī, -sessum,** *from* **sede-ō,** thus:

cōn-sīd-ō,	**cōn-sīde-re,**	**cōn-sēd-ī,**	**cōn-ses-sum,**	*to settle down.*
scab-ō,	**scabe-re,**	**scāb-ī,**	—	*to scratch.*
solv-ō,	**solve-re,**	**solv-ī,**	**solū-tum,**	*to loose, pay.*
vert-ō,	**verte-re,**	**vert-ī,**	**ver-sum,**	*to turn.*
re-vert-or,	**re-vert-ī,**	**revert-ī** (active),	**re-ver-sum,**	*to turn back.*
verr-ō,	**verre-re,**	**verr-ī** (rare),	**ver-sum,**	*to sweep.*
vīs-ō,	**vīse-re,**	**vīs-ī,**	—	*to visit.*
volv-ō,	**volve-re,**	**volv-ī,**	**volū-tum,**	*to roll.*

On **percellō, perculī,** see 144. On **tollō, sustulī,** see 155.

2. *The Nasal class:*

psall-ō,	**psalle-re,**	**psall-ī,**	—	*to play on the cithern.*
sall-ō,	**salle-re,**	(**sall-ī**),	**sal-sum,**	*to salt.*

Very rare except in the past participle **salsus.**

vell-ō,	**velle-re,**	**vell-ī** (**vul-sī**),	**vul-sum,**	*to pluck.*

The Pf. **vulsī** is post-Augustan.

lamb-ō,	**lambe-re,**	**lamb-ī,**	—	*to lick.*
rump-ō,	**rumpe-re,**	**rūp-ī,**	**rup-tum,**	*to break.*
ac-cend-ō,	**ac-cende-re,**	**ac-cend-ī,**	**ac-cēn-sum,**	*to kindle.*
dē-fend-ō,	**dē-fende-re,**	**dē-fend-ī,**	**dē-fēn-sum,**	*to strike away, defend.*
fund-ō (FUD),	**funde-re,**	**fūd-ī,**	**fū-sum,**	*to pour.*
mand-ō,	**mande-re,**	**mand-ī,**	**mān-sum,**	*to chew.*
pand-ō,	**pande-re,**	**pand-ī,**	**pas-sum,**	*to spread out.*

pān-sum in Supine is late.

prehend-ō,	**prehende-re,**	**prehend-ī,**	**prehēn-sum,**	*to seize.*

Often shortened to **prēndō, prēndere, prēndī, prēnsum.**

scand-ō,	**scande-re,**	**scand-ī,**	**scān-sum,**	*to climb.*
ā(d)-, dē-scend-ō,	**dē-scende-re,**	**dē-scend-ī,**	**dē-scēn-sum,**	*to climb up, down.*
frang-ō,	**frange-re,**	**frēg-ī,**	**frāc-tum,**	*to break.*
per-fring-ō,	**per-fringe-re,**	**per-frēg-ī,**	**per-frāc-tum,**	*to shiver.*
linqu-ō,	**linque-re,**	**līqu-ī,**		*to leave.*
re-linqu-ō,	**re-linque-re,**	**re-līqu-ī,**	**re-lic-tum,**	*to leave behind.*
(**pang-ō**),	(**pange-re**),	(**pēg-ī**),	(**pāc-tum**),	*to drive in.*
com-ping-ō,	**com-pinge-re,**	**com-pēg-ī,**	**com-pāc-tum,**	*to drive tight.*

See 149, *b*, 155.

vinc-ō (VIC),	**vince-re,**	**vīc-ī,**	**vic-tum,**	*to conquer.*

3. *The I-class.*

(*a*) With long vowel in the Perfect.

capi-ō (cap-),	**cape-re,**	**cēp-ī,**	**cap-tum,**	*to take.*
ac-cipi-ō,	**ac-cipe-re,**	**ac-cēp-ī,**	**ac-cep-tum,**	*to receive.*
faci-ō,	**face-re,**	**fēc-ī,**	**fac-tum,**	*to make.*
cale-faci-ō (calf.),	**cale-face-re,**	**cale-fēc-ī,**	**cale-fac-tum,**	*to make warm.*
per-fici-ō,	**per-fice-re,**	**per-fēc-ī,**	**per-fec-tum,**	*to achieve.*

The Pf. was originally reduplicated; on Impv. **fac,** see 130, 5.

fodi-ō,	**fode-re,**	**fōd-ī,**	**fos-sum,**	*to dig.*
fugi-ō,	**fuge-re,**	**fūg-ī,**	**(fug-i-tūrus),**	*to flee.*
iaci-ō,	**iace-re,**	**iēc-ī,**	**iac-tum,**	*to cast.*
con-ici-ō,	**con-ice-re,**	**con-iēc-ī,**	**con-iec-tum,**	*to gather.*

(*b*) With short vowel in the Pf. due to the loss of the reduplication:

find-ō,	**finde-re,**	**fid-ī,**	**fis-sum,**	*to cleave.*
scind-ō,	**scinde-re,**	**scid-ī,**	**scis-sum,**	*to split.*

The reduplicated form **sci-cidī** is found in early Latin.

161. In the *fourth* conjugation:

amici-ō forms rarely in late Latin **amicī**; see 142, 4.

com-peri-ō,	**com-perī-re,**	**com-per-ī,**	**com-per-tum,**	*to find out.*
re-peri-ō,	**re-perī-re,**	**rep-per-ī,**	**re-per-tum,**	*to find.*

See the simple verb **parere,** 157.

veni-ō,	**venī-re,**	**vēn-ī,**	**ven-tum,**	*to come.*

In early Latin sporadic tenses from a form **venere** occur, as **advenat, ēvenat.**

162. A number of verbs of the *third* conjugation have a characteristic **-u-**; these form the perfect in **-ī.**

ab-lu-ō,	**ab-lue-re,**	**ab-lu-ī,**	**ab-lū-tum,**	*to wash off.*
ab-nu-ō,	**ab-nue-re,**	**ab-nu-ī,**	**(ab-nu-itūr-us),**	*to dissent.*
acu-ō,	**acue-re,**	**acu-ī,**	**acū-tum,**	*to sharpen.*
ad-nu-ō(an-nu-ō),	**ad-nue-re,**	**ad-nu-ī,**		*to nod assent.*
argu-ō,	**argue-re,**	**argu-ī,**	**argū-tum,**	*to accuse.*
batu-ō,	**batue-re,**	**batu-ī,**	—	*to beat.*
con-gru-ō,	**con-grue-re,**	**con-gru-ī,**	—	*to agree.*
dē-libu-ō,	**dē-libue-re,**	**dē-libu-ī,**	**dē-libū-tum,**	*to anoint.*
ex-u-ō,	**ex-ue-re,**	**ex-u-ī,**	**ex-ū-tum,**	*to put off, doff.*
im-bu-ō,	**im-bue-re,**	**im-bu-ī,**	**im-bū-tum,**	*to dip, dye.*
in-du-ō,	**in-due-re,**	**in-du-ī,**	**in-dū-tum,**	*to put on, don.*
lu-ō,	**lue-re,**	**lu-ī,**	**lu-itūr-us,**	*to atone for.*
metu-ō,	**metue-re,**	**metu-ī,**	—	*to fear.*
minu-ō,	**minue-re,**	**minu-ī,**	**minū-tum,**	*to lessen.*
plu-ō,	**plue-re,**	**plu-it, plūv-it,**	—	*to rain.*
ru-ō,	**rue-re,**	**ru-ī,**	**ru-tum (ruitūrus),**	*to rush down.*
spu-ō,	**spue-re,**	**spu-ī,**	**spū-tum,**	*to spew.*
statu-ō,	**statue-re,**	**statu-ī,**	**statū-tum,**	*to settle.*
sternu-ō,	**sternue-re,**	**sternu-ī,**	—	*to sneeze.*
su-ō,	**sue-re,**	**su-ī,**	**sū-tum,**	*to sew.*
tribu-ō,	**tribue-re,**	**tribu-ī,**	**tribū-tum,**	*to allot.*

DEPONENTS.

163. The majority of the deponent verbs belong to the *first* conjugation. In many instances they have parallel active forms in early or in late Latin. The principal verbs are as follows:

In the *first* conjugation:

adūl-or, adūlā-rī, adūlā-tus sum, *to fawn upon.*
Occasionally active in ante-classical Latin (LUCR. v., 1070) and more often in later Latin.

alterc-or, altercā-rī, altercā-tus sum, *to wrangle.*
In early Latin **altercāstī** (TER., *And.* 653), **altercās.** Active forms more common in late Latin.

arbitr-or, arbitrā-rī, arbitrā-tus sum, *to think.*
PLAUT. uses this verb also as an active, but later this usage is rare.

aucup-or, aucupā-rī, aucupā-tus sum, *to try to catch.*
Active forms are common in early Latin.

augur-or, augurā-rī, augurā-tus sum, *to take the auguries.*
Active forms are early, legal, and late. Use as a passive is occasional in the classical period.

auspic-or, auspicā-rī, auspicā-tus sum, *to take the auspices.*
Active forms are early and late. CIC. and LIVY use the verb as a passive in a few instances.

comit-or, comitā-rī, comitā-tus sum, *to accompany.*
Poets (OV., PROP., *etc.*) use the active forms frequently. The Perfect Part. **comitātus** is common as a passive, also in classical Latin.

comment-or, commentā-rī, commentā-tus sum, *to discuss.*
CIC. uses **commentātus** as a passive in *Br.* 88, 301, *Fam.* XVI., 26, 1.

cōnflīct-or, cōnflīctā-rī, cōnflīctā-tus sum, *to struggle.*
Occasionally found for **cōnflīctāre.** See TER., *And.*, 93.

cōnspic-or, cōnspicā-rī, cōnspicā-tus sum, *to descry.*
So **dēspicor, sūspicor.** But a few forms are occasionally (usually in early Latin) used as passives, especially **dēspicātus** (PLAUT., TER.), compared **dēspicātissimus** by CIC. (*Sest.* 16, 36, *Verr.* III., 41, 98). PLAUT., *Cas.* 394, **sūspicēs.**

contempl-or, contemplā-rī, contemplā-tus sum, *to survey.*
The active forms are used frequently in early Latin (regularly by PLAUT.).

cōpul-or, cōpulā-rī, cōpulā-tus sum, *to join.*
So PLAUT., *Aul.* 116. Otherwise everywhere **cōpulāre.**

crīmin-or, crīminā-rī, crīminā-tus sum, *to charge.*
PLAUT. uses **crīmināret,** ENNIUS **crīmināt.**

cunct-or, cunctā-rī, cunctā-tus sum, *to delay.*
Active forms are occasional in early and late Latin.

dīgn-or, dīgnā-rī, dīgnā-tus sum, *to deem worthy.*
This verb is predominantly post-classical and poetical. The active forms are early and rare; perhaps once in CICERO.

fabric-or, **fabricā-rī,** **fabricā-tus sum,** *to forge.*
The active forms belong to poetry and to post-Augustan prose.

faener-or, **faenerā-rī,** **faenerā-tus sum,** *to lend on interest.*
Active forms occasional in early Latin and more frequent in late Latin.

fluctu-or, **fluctuā-rī,** **fluctuā-tus sum,** *to undulate.*
Active forms are rare in PLAUT. and in CIC., but not uncommon later. The deponent forms are post-Ciceronian.

(for), **fā-rī,** **fā-tus sum,** *to speak.*
See 175, 3.

frūstr-or, **frūstrā-rī,** **frūstrā-tus sum,** *to deceive.*
Active forms rare, but at all periods.

illacrim-or, **illacrimā-rī,** **illacrimā-tus sum,** *to weep over.*
In CIC. and HOR.; otherwise active.

interpret-or, **interpretā-rī,** **interpretā-tus sum,** *to interpret.*
CIC. uses **interpretātus** occasionally as a passive; likewise LIVY and others.

luct-or, **luctā-rī,** **luctā-tus sum,** *to wrestle.*
PLAUT., TER., ENNIUS, VARRO show sporadic forms of the active.

lūdific-or, **lūdificā-rī,** **lūdificā-tus sum,** *to make sport.*
Active frequent in PLAUT., and occasionally later.

medic-or, **medicā-rī,** **medicā-tus sum,** *to heal.*
The active is once in PLAUT., and frequent in poets and post-Augustan prose.

medit-or, **meditā-rī,** **meditā-tus sum,** *to think over*
The form **meditātus** is very commonly found as a passive.

mūner-or, **mūnerā-rī,** **mūnerā-tus sum,** *to bestow.*
Active forms in early Latin and occasionally in CIC. and later.

nūtrīc-or, **nūtrīcā-rī,** **nūtrīcā-tus sum,** *to suckle.*
Active forms in early Latin.

odōr-or, **odōrā-rī,** **odōrā-tus sum,** *to smell.*
Active forms occasional at all periods.

opīn-or, **opīnā-rī,** **opīnā-tus sum,** *to think.*
opīnō is frequent in early Latin, and **opīnātus** as passive is common in CICERO.

palp-or, **palpā-rī,** **palpā-tus sum,** *to stroke.*
Is occasional (principally in early Latin) for **palpāre.**

popul-or, **populā-rī,** **populā-tus sum,** *to ravage.*
Active forms in simple verb and compounds are early, poetical, and post-classic

scīscit-or, **scīscitā-rī,** **scīscitā-tus sum,** *to inquire.*
PLAUT., *Merc.* 389, **scīscitāre** (active).

scrūt-or, **scrūtā-rī,** **scrūtā-tus sum,** *to search.*
PLAUT., *Aul.* 657, **perscrūtāvī.** The use as a passive occurs first in SENECA

sect-or, **sectā-rī,** **sectā-tus sum,** *to pursue.*
Active forms and passive usages are early.

stabul-or, **stabulā-rī,** **stabulā-tus sum,** *to stable.*
Active forms begin with VERGIL.

tūt-or, **tūtā-rī,** **tūtā-tus sum,** *to protect.*
Active forms and passive usages are early and rare.

tumultu-or, tumultuā-rī, tumultuā-tus sum, *to raise a riot.*
But PLAUTUS uses active forms; and passive uses are occasional later.

vag-or, vagā-rī, vagā-tus sum, *to wander.*
Active forms belong to early Latin.

vener-or, venerā-rī, venerā-tus sum, *to reverence.*
But PLAUT. uses **venerō, venerem**; VERG., HOR., and later writers show passive uses.

164. In the *second* conjugation:

fate-or, fatē-rī, fas-sus sum, *to confess.*
cōn-fite-or, cōn-fitē-rī, cōn-fes-sus sum, *to confess.*
Both **fateor** and **cōnfiteor** are used occasionally as passives by CIC. and later.

lice-or, licē-rī, lici-tus sum, *to bid* (*at a sale*).

mere-or, merē-rī, meri-tus sum, *to deserve.*
Especially in the phrases **merērī bene dē aliquō,** *to deserve well of any one.* Otherwise the active is usual.

misere-or, miserē-rī, miseri-tus sum, *to pity.*
In early Latin the active forms are found occasionally, *e. g.*, LUCR. III., 881.

pollice-or, pollicē-rī, pollici-tus sum, *to promise.*
Occasionally used as a passive in post-classical Latin.

re-or, rē-rī, ra-tus sum, *to think.*
Pr. Part. Active is wanting.

tue-or, tuē-rī, tui-tus (tūtus) sum, *to protect.*
In early Latin and occasionally later, a parallel form, **tuor, tuī, tuitus sum,** occurs. For **tuitus** usually **tūtātus.**

vere-or, verē-rī, veri-tus sum, *to fear.*

165. In the *third* conjugation:

apīsc-or, apīsc-ī, ap-tus sum, *to get.*
Simple verb is frequent in early and late Latin. Of the compounds, **adipīscor, adipīscī, adeptus sum,** is usually deponent in classical times, but occurs occasionally as a passive in SALL. and later writers. The compounds **ind-, red-,** are rare.

am-plect-or, am-plect-ī, am-plex-us sum, *to twine round, embrace.*
So the compounds **complector, circumplector.** In early Latin active forms are occasionally found; *e. g.*, **amplectitōte, circumplecte** (PLAUT.).

com-min-īsc-or, com-min-īsc-ī, com-men-tus sum, *to think up, devise.*
OVID and later writers use **commentus** as a passive.

experg-īsc-or, (-reg-) ex-perg-īsc-ī, ex-per-rēc-tus sum, *to (right one's self up) awake.*

fung-or, fung-ī, fūnc-tus sum, *to discharge.*
This verb is used passively very rarely: TER., *Ad.* 508. LUCR. III., 968. CIC., *Sest.* 4, 10.

fru-or (frugv-), fru-ī, frūc-tus (fru-i-tus) sum, *to enjoy.*
The form **fruitus** is rare and late.

gradi-or,	**grad-ī,**	**gres-sus sum,**	*to step,*
ag-gredi-or,	**ag-gred-ī,**	**ag-gres-sus sum,**	*to attack.*

Occasionally active forms of the fourth conjugation are found in early Latin.

lāb-or,	**lāb-ī,**	**lāp-sus sum,**	*to glide.*
loqu-or,	**loqu-ī,**	**locū-tus sum,**	*to speak.*
mori-or,	**mor-ī,**	**mortu-us sum,**	*to die.*

Early Latin shows parallel forms of the fourth conjugation, as **morīrī, ēmorīrī.** Fut. Part. **moritūrus**; see 135, II., 3.

nanc-īsc-or,	**nanc-īsc-ī,**	**nac-tus** (**nanc-tus**) **sum,**	*to get.*
nāsc-or (**gnā-**),	**nāsc-ī,**	**nā-tus sum,**	*to be born.*

Fut. Part. **nāscitūrus.**

nīt-or (**gnict-** from **genū**),	**nīt-ī,**	**nī-sus** (**nīx-us**) **sum, nī-sūrus,**	*to stay one's self on.*
ob-līv-īsc-or,	**ob-līv-īsc-ī,**	**ob-lī-tus sum,**	*to forget.*
pac-īsc-or,	**pac-īsc-ī,**	**pac-tus sum** (**pepigī**),	*to drive (a bargain).*

Occasionally active forms are found in early Latin; in Cic. **pactus** is frequently used as a passive. See **pangō.**

pati-or,	**pat-ī,**	**pas-sus sum,**	*to suffer.*
per-peti-or,	**per-pet-ī,**	**per-pes-sus sum,**	*to endure to the end.*
pro-fic-īsc-or,	**pro-fic-īsc-ī,**	**pro-fec-tus sum,**	*to (get forward) set out.*

But Plaut., *M. G.* 1329, **proficīscō.**

quer-or,	**quer-ī,**	**ques-tus sum,**	*to complain.*
sequ-or,	**sequ-ī,**	**secū-tus sum,**	*to follow.*
ulc-īsc-or,	**ulc-īsc-ī,**	**ul-tus sum,**	*to avenge.*

Active forms are rare; so once in Ennius. But Sall., Livy, and later writers use the verb as a passive sometimes.

ūt-or,	**ūt-ī,**	**ū-sus sum,**	*to use.*

Plaut. shows the compound **abūsā** as a passive (*Asin.* 196).

veh-or,	**veh-ī,**	**vec-tus sum,**	*to (wagon) ride.*
vesc-or,	**vesc-ī,**	——	*to feed.*

166. In the *fourth* conjugation:

assenti-or,	**assentī-rī,**	**assēn-sus sum,**	*to assent.*

Active forms are not uncommon in early Latin. Cic. uses the Pf. active forms frequently; likewise later writers.

com-peri-or,	**comperī-rī,**	——	*to find out.*

Occasionally found (but rarely in classical Latin; as, Sall., *J.*, 45, 1; 108, 3) for **comperiō, comperīre.** But **experior, experīrī, expertus sum,** *to try*, is regularly deponent; though Cic. and others use often the Pf. active forms.

largi-or,	**largī-rī,**	**largī-tus sum,**	*to bestow.*
menti-or,	**mentī-rī,**	**mentī-tus sum,**	*to lie.*

The poets and later prose writers use this as a passive also.

mēti-or,	**mētī-rī,**	**mēn-sus sum,**	*to measure.*

Passive usage is common, especially in the compounds: **dēmēnsus, dīmēnsus, ēmēnsus, permēnsus, remēnsus.**

ōrdi-or, ōrdī-rī, ōr-sus sum, *to begin.*
ōrsus, and more commonly **exōrsus,** are also found as passives.

ori-or, orī-rī, or-tus sum, *to arise.*
The Pr. Indic. is usually formed according to the third conjugation; the Impf. Subjv. always **orerer**; but the Fut. Part. is **oritūrus.** The compounds follow the same usage except **adorīrī,** *to rise up at, attack,* which follows the fourth conjugation.

parti-or, partī-rī, partī-tus sum, *to share.*
Active forms and passive uses are found in early Latin, and sporadically in Cic. and later.

poti-or, potī-rī, potī-tus sum, *to get possession of.*
The Pr. Indic., Impf. Subjv., and occasionally other forms, are also found in early Latin and the poets, inflected according to the third conjugation; so regularly after Plaut. **potitur,** frequently **poterētur, poterēmur.**

pūni-or, pūnī-rī, pūnī-tus sum, *to punish.*
Occasionally in Cic. and late writers for **pūnīre.**

sorti-or, sortī-rī, sortī-tus sum, *to cast lots.*
Active occasionally in early Latin, and passive uses later of the Pf. Participle.

SEMI-DEPONENTS.

167. 1. A few verbs form the Perfect forms only as deponents:

aude-ō, audē-re, au-sus sum, *to dare.*
On the aorist forms **ausim,** *etc.*, see 131, 4, *b.*

fīd-ō, fīd-ere, fī-sus sum, *to trust.*

gaude-ō, gaudē-re, gāv-īsus sum, *to rejoice.*

sole-ō, solē-re, sol-itus sum, *to be wont.*
The Pf. active is found in early Latin; but rarely.

2. The reverse usage is found in:

re-vert-or, re-vert-ī, re-vert-ī, *to turn back.*
So also **dēvertī,** but without Pf. Part. **Reversus** is also used actively, but **reversus sum** for **revertī** is post-classic.
See also **assentior,** *etc.*, 166.

Notes.—1. Some active verbs have a Perfect Participle passive with active meaning, as: **cēnātus,** *one who has dined,* from **cēnāre,** *to dine;* **prānsus,** *having breakfasted,* from **prandeō,** *I breakfast;* **pōtus,** *drunken,* from **pōtō,** *I drink;* **iūrātus,** *having taken the oath, sworn,* from **iūrō,** *I swear;* **coniūrātus,** *a conspirator,* from **coniūrō,** *I conspire.* Many such are used purely as Adjectives: **cōnsīderātus,** *circumspect,* from **cōnsīderō**; **cautus,** *wary,* from **caveō,** *I beware.*

2. The Perfect Participle of many deponent Verbs has both active and passive meaning: **adeptus (adipīscor),** *having acquired,* or *being acquired;* **comitātus (comitor,** *I accompany*); **effātus (effor,** *I speak out*); **expertus (experior,** *I try*); **exsecrātus (exsecror,** *I curse*); **imitātus (imitor,** *I copy*); **meritus (mereor,** *I deserve*); **opīnātus, necopīnātus (opīnor,** *I think*); **pactus (pacīscor,** *I contract*); **partītus (partior,** *I distribute*); **sortītus (sortior,** *I cast lots*); **tueor,** *I protect;* **tūtus,** *safe.*
For others, see the list of deponents.

IRREGULAR VERBS.

168. Irregular in the formation of the tense-stems :

1. Nine verbs of the third conjugation, which have, in spite of the short stem-syllable, the Pf. in **-sī**, viz. :

clepō, *I filch ;* **rego**, *I keep right ;* **tego**, *I cover in ;* **coquō**, *I bake ;* and the compounds of **lego**, *I pick up ;* **laciō**, *I lure ;* **speciō**, *I spy* (**-ligō**, **-liciō**, **-spiciō**) ; **dīvidō**, *I part ;* **quatiō**, *I shake.* See 147, 2.

From **lego**, however, only **dīligō**, *I love ;* **intellegō**, *I understand ;* and **neglegō**, *neglect*, are irregular. The other compounds are regular. See 147, 2.

2. Five verbs of the third conjugation, which, in spite of long stem-syllable, have the Pf. in **-ī**, viz. :

lambō *I lick ;* **cūdō**, *I hammer ;* **sīdō**, *I sit* (160, 1) ; **strīdeō**, *I whistle* (159) ; **vertō**, *I turn* (160, 1).

3. Assimilation between **bs** and **ms** occurs in the **Pf.** and Sup. of

iube-ō,	*I order.*	See 147, 1.
prem-ō (**-prim-ō**),	*I press.*	See 147, 2.

4. Special irregularities occur in :

bib-ō,	*I drink.*	154, 2.
mane-ō,	*I remain.*	147, 1.
mēti-or,	*I measure.*	166.
met-ō,	*I mow.*	142, 3.
mori-or,	*I die.*	165.
rauci-ō,	*I am hoarse.*	150, 2.
re-or,	*I think.*	164.

5. Formed from different tense-stems, are the tenses of

fer-ō,	*I bear.*	171.
toll-ō,	*I lift.*	155.

169. Irregular in the conjugation of the Present-stem :

1. **ori-or, orī-rī, or-tus sum,** *to arise.*
See 166.

2. **ī-re,** *to go.*

The stem is **i**, which, before **a**, **o**, **u**, becomes **e**.

PRIN. PARTS : **eō, īre, īvī** (**iī**), **itum.**

	INDICATIVE. *I go.*		SUBJUNCTIVE. *I be going.*	
PRES.	SG.—1. **e-ō,**	PL.—**ī-mus,**	SG.—**ea-m,**	PL.—**eā-mus,**
	2. **ī-s,**	**ī-tis,**	**eā-s,**	**eā-tis,**
	3. **i-t,**	**eu-nt.**	**ea-t,**	**ea-nt.**

Impf.	**ī-ba-m**, *I went.*	**ī-re-m**, *I were going.*
Fut.	**ī-b-ō**, *I shall go.*	
Perf.	**ī-v-ī** (i-ī), *I have gone.*	**ī-v-eri-m** (i-eri-m).
Plupf.	**ī-v-era-m** (i-era-m), *I had gone.*	**ī-v-isse-m** (i-isse-m, ī-sse-m).
Fut. Pf.	**ī-v-er-ō** (i-er-ō), *I shall have gone.*	

IMPERATIVE.

Sg.—2.	**ī**,	*go thou.*	**ī-tō**,	*thou shalt go.*
3.	——		**ī-tō**,	*he shall go.*
Pl.—2.	**ī-te**,	*go ye.*	**ī-tōte**,	*ye shall go.*
3.	——		**eu-ntō**,	*they shall go.*

INFINITIVE.

Pres. **ī-re.**
Fut. **i-tūr-um esse.**
Perf. **ī-v-isse (ī-sse).**

PARTICIPLES.

Pres. **iē-ns** (G. **eu-nt-is**).
Fut. **i-tūr-us.**

GERUND.

eu-nd-ī, *etc.*

SUPINE.

i-tum, *to go.*

Remarks.—1. Like the simple verb are inflected most of the compounds, except in the Perfect system, where syncope regularly takes place (see 131, 2). **Vēn-eō**, *I am for sale*, and **per-eō**, *I perish*, serve as passives to **vēn-dō**, *I sell*, and **per-dō**, *I destroy*, whose regular passives occur only in the forms **vēnditus, vēndendus**, and **perditus** (but see Hor., *Sat.*, ii. 6, 59). **Amb-iō**, *I solicit*, follows the fourth conjugation throughout, but in post-Ciceronian writers (Livy, Tac., Plin. Min.) shows occasional forms like those of **eō**. Some compounds show occasionally Fut. in **-eam** after the time of Seneca.

2. The passive of the simple verb is found only in the impersonal forms **ītur, ībātur, itum est, īrī** (in combination with the Supine). But compounds with transitive force are conjugated regularly; so, **praeter-eō** forms **praeter-eor, -īris, ītur, -īmur, -īminī, -euntur, ībar**, *etc.*, **-itus sum, eram, erō, -euntor, -ītor, -īrī, -eundus.**

3. quīre, *to be able*; nequīre, *to be unable.*

170. (*a*) **que-ō**, *I am able*, is found in the following forms, of which those in parenthesis are unclassical, occurring in early and late Latin and the poets; Cæsar uses no form of **queō.**

Pr. Indic. **queō, (quīs), (quit), quīmus, (quītis), queunt.** Pr. Subjv. **queam, queās, queat, queāmus, queātis, queant.** Impf. **(quībam), (quīrem).** Fut. **(quībō).** Pf. **quīvī**, *etc.;* **quīverim**, *etc.* Plupf. **quīveram**, *etc.;* **quīvissem**, *etc.* Fut. Pf. **quīverō**, *etc.* Pr. Inf. **quīre.** Pf. **quīvisse.** Part. **quiēns.**

(*b*) **neque-ō**, *I am unable*, has the same forms, all of which seem to be classic excepting the Future Indicative, which is not cited.

4. **fer-re**, *to bear.*

171. The endings beginning with **t**, **s**, and **r** are added directly to the root (132). Some parts are supplied by **tul-** (**tol-**, **tla-**).

PRIN. PARTS: **ferō, ferre, tulī, lātum.**

ACTIVE.

	INDICATIVE.		SUBJUNCTIVE.	
PRES.	*I bear.*		*I be bearing.*	
SG.—1.	**fer-ō,**	PL.—**fer-i-mus,**	SG.—**fera-m,**	PL.—**ferā-mus,**
2.	**fer-s,**	**fer-tis,**	**ferā-s,**	**ferā-tis,**
3.	**fer-t,**	**fer-u-nt.**	**fera-t,**	**fera-nt.**
IMPF.	**ferē-ba-m,** *I was bearing.*		**fer-re-m,** *I were bearing.*	
FUT.	**fera-m,** *I shall bear.*			
PERF.	**tul-ī,** *I have borne.*		**tul-eri-m.**	
PLUPF.	**tul-era-m.**		**tul-isse-m.**	
FUT. PF.	**tul-er-ō.**			

IMPERATIVE.

SG.—2.	**fer,**	*bear thou.*	**fer-tō,**	*thou shalt bear.*
3.	——		**fer-tō,**	*he shall bear.*
PL.—2.	**fer-te,**	*bear ye.*	**fer-tōte,**	*ye shall bear.*
3.	——		**feru-ntō,**	*they shall bear.*

INFINITIVE.	PARTICIPLES.
PRES. **fer-re.**	PRES. **ferē-ns,** *bearing.*
FUT. **lā-tūr-um esse.**	FUT. **lā-tūr-us.**
PERF. **tul-isse.**	

GERUND.	SUPINE.
fere-nd-ī, *etc.*	**lā-tum** (**t**(o)**lā-tum**).

PASSIVE.

		INDICATIVE.		SUBJUNCTIVE.	
		I am borne.		*I be borne.*	
PRES.	SG.—1.	**fer-o-r,**	PL.—**feri-mur,**	SG.—**fera-r,**	PL.—**ferā-mur,**
	2.	**fer-ris,**	**feri-minī,**	**ferā-ris,**	**ferā-minī,**
	3.	**fer-tur,**	**feru-ntur.**	**ferā-tur,**	**fera-ntur.**
IMPF.		**ferē-ba-r.**		**fer-re-r.**	
FUT.		**fera-r.**			
PERF.		**lā-tus sum.**		**lā-tus sim.**	
PLUPF.		**lā-tus eram.**		**lā-tus essem.**	
FUT. PF.		**lā-tus erō.**			

IMPERATIVE.

Sg.—2.	fer-re,	*be thou borne.*	fer-tor,	*thou shalt be borne.*
3.	——		fer-tor,	*he shall be borne.*
Pl.—2.	feri-minī,	*be ye borne.*	——	
3.	——		feru-ntor,	*they shall be borne.*

INFINITIVE.			PARTICIPLE.
Pres.	fer-rī,	*to be borne.*	Perf. lā-t-us, -a, -um, *borne.*
Fut.	lā-tum īrī.		GERUNDIVE.
Perf.	lā-tum esse,	*to have been borne.*	fere-nd-us.

COMPOUNDS.

af-fer-ō,	af-fer-re,	at-tul-ī,	al-lā-tum,	*to bear to.*
au-fer-ō,	au-fer-re,	abs-tul-ī,	ab-lā-tum,	*to bear away.*
cōn-fer-ō,	cōn-fer-re,	con-tul-ī,	col-lā-tum,	*to collect.*
dif-fer-ō,	dif-fer-re,	dis-tul-ī,	dī-lā-tum,	*to put off.*
ef-fer-ō,	ef-fer-re,	ex-tul-ī,	ē-lā-tum,	*to carry out.*
of-fer-ō,	of-fer-re,	ob-tul-ī,	ob-lā-tum,	*to offer.*

Notes.—1. The Pf. **tulī** was originally reduplicated **te-tulī.** See 134, iii., 155. Traces of this are seen in **rettulī.**

2. **Suf-ferō,** *I undergo,* has the Pf. **sus-tin-uī** (**sus-tul-ī, sub-lā-tum,** being appropriated to **toll-ō**). (155.)

5. ed-ere, *to eat.*

172. In certain forms the endings beginning with **s, t,** and **r** are added directly to the root (132); **d** before **s** (**r**) is dropped or assimilated (as **ss**), and before **t** becomes **s.**

Prin. Parts: **edō, edere (ēsse), ēdī, ēsum.**

ACTIVE.

INDICATIVE.			SUBJUNCTIVE.	
	Present.			
	I eat.		*I be eating.*	
Sg.—1.	ed-ō,	Pl.—edi-mus,	Sg.—eda-m,	Pl.—edā-mus,
2.	edi-s, ē-s,	edi-tis, ēs-tis,	edā-s,	edā-tis,
3.	edi-t, ē-st,	edu-nt.	eda-t,	eda-nt.
Impf.	edē-ba-m,	*I ate.*	ede-re-m, ēs-se-m, *I were eating*	
Fut.	eda-m.			
Perf.	ēd-ī.		ēd-eri-m.	
Plupf.	ēd-era-m.		ēd-isse-m.	
Fut. Pf.	ēd-er-ō.			

IMPERATIVE.

Sg.—2.	**ede, ēs,**	*eat thou.*	**edi-to, ēs-tō,**	*thou shalt eat.*
3.	——		**edi-to, ēs-tō,**	*he shall eat.*
Pl.—2.	**edi-te, ēs-te,**	*eat ye.*	**edi-tōte, ēs-tōte,**	*ye shall eat.*
3.	——		**edu-ntō,**	*they shall eat*

INFINITIVE.

Pres. **ede-re, ēs-se,** *to eat.*
Fut. **ēs-ūr-um esse.**
Perf. **ēd-isse.**

PARTICIPLE.

Pres. (**edē-ns**).
Fut. **ēs-ūr-us.**

GERUND.

ede-nd-ī, *etc.*

SUPINE.

ēs-um, ēs-ū.

PASSIVE.

In the passive voice the only peculiarities are as follows: Pr. Indic. Sing. Third, **editur** and **ēstur.** Impf. Subjv. Sing. Third, **ederētur** and **ēssētur.** The Pf. Part. is **ēsus** and the Gerundive **edendus.**

Note.—In the Pr. Subjv. Active, early Latin shows **edim, edīs, edit, edīmus, edītis, edint.** Also **ēssum** and **ēssū** in the Sup., **ēssūrus** in the Fut. Part. **Comedere** also shows **comestus** for **comēsus.**

6. fi-erī, *to become.*

173. Fī-ō is conjugated in the Present, Imperfect, and Future, according to the fourth conjugation, but in the Subjunctive Imperfect and in the Infinitive the stem is increased by **e**; thus, **fi-e-rem,** *I were becoming;* **fi-e-rī,** *to become.* In these forms the **i** is short, but elsewhere it is long even before another vowel.

The Infinitive ends in **-rī**, and the whole Verb in the Present-stem is treated as the Passive to **faciō,** *I make.* The rest of the Passive is formed regularly from **faciō.**

Prin. Parts: **fīō, fierī, factus sum.**

	ACTIVE.			PASSIVE.
Pres.	**faciō,**	*I make.*	INDIC.	**fīō,** *I am made, I become.*
				fīs, fit (fīmus, fītis), fīunt.
Impf.	**faciēbam,**	*I made.*		**fīēbam,** *I was made, I became.*
Fut.	**faciam,**	*I shall make.*		**fīam,** *I shall be made* (*become*).
Perf.	**fēcī.**			**factus sum.**
Plupf.	**fēceram.**			**factus eram.**
Fut. Pf.	**fēcerō.**			**factus erō.**
			SUBJV.	**fīam, fīās, fīat,** *etc.*
	etc.			**fierem, fierēs,** *etc.*
				INFINITIVE.
			Pres.	**fierī.**
	IMPERATIVE.		Perf.	**factum esse,** *to have become.*
	(**fī**),	(**fī-tō**).	Fut.	**futūrum esse** *or* **fore.**
	(**fī-te**).		Fut. Pf.	**factum fore.**

NOTES.—1. Occasionally in early Latin the form **fiere** is found for the Infinitive, which indicates that the verb was originally active. The forms **fierī** and **fierem** are very common in early Latin, along with the normal forms. Of the forms in parenthesis **fīmus** and **fītis** do not certainly occur, and the Imperative forms are early. Passive forms of **fīō** are very rare; never in PLAUTUS or TERENCE.

2. The compounds of **faciō** with Prepositions change the **a** of the stem into **i**, and form the Passive in classical Latin regularly from the same stem: **perficiō,** *I achieve*, Pass. **perficior**; **interficiō,** Pass. **interficior,** *I am destroyed*. But **interfierī, cōnfierent, cōnfierī,** and several other forms are found in early Latin, and occasionally in classical times. When compounded with words other than prepositions, **faciō** retains its **a,** and uses **fīō** as its Passive:

patefaciō, *I lay open*, Pass. **patefīō**; **calefaciō,** *I warm*, Pass. **calefīō.**

For the accent, see 15, 2, R. 2.

174. 7. vel-le, *to be willing.*

nōlle, *to be unwilling*; mālle, *to be willing rather.*

PRIN. PARTS: **volō, velle, voluī; nōlō, nōlle, nōluī; mālō, mālle, māluī.**

INDICATIVE.

PRES.	**volō,**	**nōlō,**	**mālō,**
	vīs,	**nōn vīs,**	**māvīs,**
	vult,	**nōn vult,**	**māvult,**
	volumus,	**nōlumus,**	**mālumus,**
	vultis,	**nōn vultis,**	**māvultis,**
	volunt.	**nōlunt.**	**mālunt.**
IMPF.	**volēbam,**	**nōlēbam,**	**mālēbam.**
FUT.	**volam,**	**nōlam,**	**mālam,**
	volēs, *etc.*	**nōlēs,** *etc.*	**mālēs,** *etc.*
PERF.	**voluī,**	**nōluī,**	**māluī,** *etc.*
PLUPF.	**volueram,**	**nōlueram,**	**mālueram,** *etc.*
FUT. PF.	**voluerō,**	**nōluerō,**	**māluerō,** *etc.*

SUBJUNCTIVE.

PRES.	**velim,**	**nōlim,**	**mālim,**
	velīs,	**nōlīs,**	**mālīs,**
	velit,	**nōlit,**	**mālit,**
	velīmus,	**nōlīmus,**	**mālīmus,**
	velītis,	**nōlītis,**	**mālītis,**
	velint.	**nōlint.**	**mālint.**
IMPF.	**vellem,**	**nōllem,**	**māllem.**
PERF.	**voluerim,**	**nōluerim,**	**māluerim,** *etc.*
PLUPF.	**voluissem,**	**nōluissem,**	**māluissem,** *etc.*

IMPV.		Sg.—**nōlī, nōlītō.**	
		Pl.—**nōlīte, nōlītōte, nōluntō.**	
INF.	Pr. **velle,**	**nōlle,**	**mālle.**
	Pf. **voluisse,**	**nōluisse,**	**māluisse.**
PART.	**volēns,**	**nōlēns.**	

Notes.—1. To the time of Cicero, and occasionally later, **volt, voltis,** are employed for **vult, vultis.** In familiar language **sī vīs, sī vultis,** were contracted to **sīs, sultis ; vīs** was further combined with **-ne** into **vīn.**

2. **Nōlō** is a contraction of **nevolō** (= **nōn volō**), and in early Latin we find, along with the forms given above, also **nevīs, nevolt ;** also occasionally we find **nōn velīs, nōn velit, nōn velint, nōn vellem,** for **nōlīs,** *etc.;* but the feeling is slightly different.

3. **Mālō = ma volō,** from **mag(mage, magis)-volō.** Frequently in Plaut., but rarely in Ter., we find **mavolō, mavolunt, mavolet, mavelim, -īs, -it, mavellem,** instead of **mālō, mālim, mālīs,** *etc.*

175. DEFECTIVE VERBS.

1. āiō, *I say aye.*

INDIC.	Pres. Sg.—1. **āiō,**	2. **ais,**	3. **ait,**	Pl.—3. **āiunt.**
	Impf. **āiēbam,** *etc.*			
	Perf.		3. **ait.**	
SUBJV.	Pres. Sg.—	2. **āiās,**	3. **āiat,**	3. **āiant.**
PART.	**āiēns** (as adj.), *affirmative.*		IMPV. **aī.**	

Note.—In early Latin **ain** (= **aisne ?**) was scanned often as a monosyllable ; and in the Impf., **aībam, aībās, aībat, aībant** were frequently employed along with the normal forms. The Impv. is rare, and found only in early Latin. Pr. Subjv. **āiam** is emended into Pl., *Ep.*, 281.

2. inquam, *I say, quoth I.*

INDIC.	Pres.	Sg.—1. **inquam,**	2. **inquis,**	3. **inquit.**
		Pl.—1. **inquimus,**	2. **inquitis,**	3. **inquiunt.**
	Impf.	Sg.—		3. **inquiēbat.**
	Fut.	Sg.—	2. **inquiēs,**	3. **inquiet.**
	Perf.	Sg.—1. **inquiī,**	2. **inquistī,**	3. **inquit.**

IMPV. **inque, inquitō.**

3. fā-rī, *to speak.*

INDIC. Pres. **fātur.** Fut. **fābor, fābitur.** Perf. **fātus sum,** *etc.* IMPV. **fāre.**
PART. Pres. **fāns, fantis, fantī, fantem.** GER. **fandī, fandō.** SUP. **fātū.**

Note.—In addition to these, compounds show also Pres. : **-fāris, -fāmur, -fāminī, -fantur ;** Impf. : **-fābar, -fābantur ;** Fut. : **-fābere, -fābimur ;** Part. : **-fante** and others. These forms, as well as the uncompounded forms, though occasionally found in prose, are peculiar to the poets until post-Augustan times. The Pf. Part. is sometimes used passively ; so especially **fātum,** *fate ;* **effātus,** *designated.*

4. havē-re (avē-re), salvē-re.

IMPV.	**havē,**	**salvē, salvēbis,**	*hail thou!*
	havētō,	**salvētō.**	
	havēte,	**salvēte,**	*hail ye!*
INF.	**havēre,**	**salvēre.**	

Corresponding to these are the forms of **valēre,** viz.: **valē, valēte, valēre,** *farewell.*

5. coepī, meminī, ōdī, nōvī.

In use only in the Perfect-stem are **coepī,** *I have begun,* which serves as a Perfect to **incipiō,** and **meminī,** *I remember,* **ōdī,** *I hate,* **nōvī** (from **nōscō,** see 131, 3, 140), *I know, am aware,* **cōnsuēvī** (from **consuēscō**), *I am wont,* which have the force of Presents.

a.	INDIC.	**coepī,**	*I have begun.*	SUBJV.	**coeperim.**	
		coeperam.			**coepissem.**	
		coeperō.		INF.	**coepisse,**	*to have begun.*

NOTE.—Early Latin shows **coepiō, coepiās, coepiat, coepiam, coepere, coeperet.** Future Participle **coeptūrus** is Post-Augustan. **Incēpī** is ante-classical.

Passive forms **coeptus sum,** *etc.*, occur with the same meaning in combination with a Passive Infinitive. See 423, N. 3.

b.	INDIC.	**meminī,**	*I remember.*	SUBJV.	**meminerim.**	
		memineram.			**meminissem.**	
		meminerō.		INF.	**meminisse,**	*to remember.*
	IMPV.	SG.—**mementō.**		PL.—**mementōte.**		
c.	INDIC.	**ōdī,**	*I hate.*	SUBJV.	**ōderim.**	
		ōderam.			**ōdissem.**	
		ōderō.		INF.	**ōdisse,**	*to hate.*
	FUT. PART.	**ōsūrus.**				

NOTE.—Occasionally in early Latin, the poets, and later prose, deponent forms of the Perfect are found, **ōsus sum,** *etc.* For the Passive the phrase **odiō esse** is used.

d.	INDIC.	**nōvī.**		SUBJV.	**nōverim (nōrim).**	
		nōveram (nōram).			**nōvissem (nōssem).**	
		nōverō (nōrō).		INF.	**nōvisse (nōsse)**	*to know.*

6. cedo, quaesō.

Other defective forms are:

SG.—**cedo,** *give!* (old Impv.) PL.—**cette.**

INDIC. PRES. **quaesō,** *please* (i. e., *I seek, beg*), **quaesumus.**

NOTE.—Other forms of **quaesō** are found occasionally in early Latin, and sporadically in CIC., SALL., and later: the Pf. forms have been attached to **quaerere,** 137. *c.*

FORMATION OF WORDS.

176. By the formation of words is meant the way in which stems are made of roots, new stems of old, and in which words are compounded.

177. All roots of the Latin language are probably monosyllabic.* They can be ascertained only by scientific analysis.

The difference between Root and Stem has been set forth in 25, NN. Sometimes the Stem is the same as the Root; so especially in the Root Verbs (132). But it is usually different.

178. Words are either *simple* or *compound.*

A *simple* word is one that is formed from a single root: **sōl,** *sun;* **stā-re,** *stand, stay.*

A *compound* word is one that is made up of two or more roots: **sōl-stiti-um,** *sun-staying, solstice.*

A.—Simple Words.

179. Simple words are partly *primitive,* partly *derivative* or *secondary.*

1. Primitive words come from the root, and as this usually appears in the simplest form of the verb-stem, primitive words are called *verbals.* Examples are the root-verbal forms (134, II., 132, 135, I.), some substantives of the third declension, as **dux** (**duc-s**), *leader,* root **duc** (see 183, 1), many substantives of the first, second, and fourth declensions, as: **scrīb-a** (**scrībō,** *I write*), *scribe.*

2. Derivative words are formed from a noun-stem; hence called *denominatives:* **vetus-tās,** *age,* from **vetes-** (N. **vetus**), *old.*

NOTE.—Denominative verbs include many verbs which cannot definitely be referred to any substantive; such as many frequentatives and intensives. In its narrower signification the term refers to the special class of verbs made from substantives in use.

180. Substantives are generally formed by means of a *suffix.* A suffix is an addition to a stem, and serves to define its meaning or show its relations. So from the verbal stem **scrīb-** (**scrībō,** *I write*) comes **scrīp-tor,** *writ-er;* **scrīp-tiō(n),** *writ-ing.*

---

* The theory of monosyllabic roots is adopted here as being somewhat more convenient than the theory of polysyllabic roots, now held by some important scholars. Of course it will be understood that the actual existence of mere roots can be assumed only for a very early period in the development of language, long before the independent existence of Latin.

Suffixes are either *primary* or *secondary*. A primary suffix is one added to a root (or verb stem) to form primitive words. A secondary suffix is one used in the formation of derivative words. Thus, **-tor** in **scrīp-tor** is a primary suffix ; **-tās** in **vetus-tās** is secondary.

NOTES.—1. By the fading out of the difference between primary and secondary suffixes, primary suffixes come to be used sometimes to form secondary derivatives.

2. Consonant stems before consonant suffixes undergo the usual changes (9). So **scrīb-tor** becomes **scrīp-tor ; rēg-s** becomes **rēx.** Stems are sometimes extended by a vowel, usually **i,** less often **u,** to facilitate pronunciation : **val-i-dus,** *strong ;* **doc-u-mentum,** *proof ;* sometimes they change the stem vowel : **teg,** *cover ;* **tog-a,** *toga ;* **tug-urium,** *hut.*

3. Vowel stems lengthen the final vowel : **acu-,** *sharpen ;* **acū-men,** *sharp part, point.*

The final vowel often disappears before the suffix : **opta-,** *choose ;* **opt-iō,** *choice.*

181. FORMATION OF SUBSTANTIVES.

The suffixes, as applied to various roots, have often special functions, and form words of definite meaning. The most important are as follows :

1. *Agency* is indicated by

-tor, -trīc (N. **tor** (*m.*), **trīx** (*f.*)) : **amā-tor,** *lover ;* **vic-trīx,** *conqueress ;* occasionally ***-ter*** (N. **ter,** G. **-trī**) : **ar-bi-ter** (= **ad** + **ba,** *step*), *umpire;* ***-ōn*** (N. **ō,** G. **ōnis**) : **com-bib-ō** (*fellow-drinker*), *boon companion ;* occasionally ***-o, -a*** (N. **-us, -a**) : **serv-os,** *slave ;* **scrīb-a,** *scribe ;* ***-ōno, -ōna*** (N. **ōnu-s, -ōna**) : **col-ōnu-s,** *settler ;* ***-(i)t*** (N. **es,** G. **itis**) : **mīl-es,** *soldier,* and a few others.

2. *Action, Activity,* and *Event* are indicated by

a. ***-tu*** (N. **tu-s, su-s,** G. **-ūs**) : **ad-ven-tus,** *arrival ;* ***-trī-na*** (N. **trīna**) : **doc-trīna,** *instruction;* ***-īn-a*** (N. **-īna**) : **rap-īna,** *rapine;* ***-men*** (N. **men,** G. **min-is**) : **āg-men,** *train ;* ***-mento*** (N. **mentum**) : **tor-mentu-m,** *torture ;* ***-ē-la*** (***ella***) **:** **loqu-ēla,** *speech ;* **quer-ēla,** *complaint ;* ***-cinio*** (N. **-u-m**) : **latrō-ciniu-m,** *highway robbery ;* ***-mōnio, -mōnia*** (N. **mōnia, mōniu-m**) : **queri-mōnia,** *complaint ;* **tēsti-mōniu-m,** *testimony.*

b. Abstracts. Masculine : ***-ōs-*** (N. **-or,** G. **-ōr-is**) : **ang-or,** *anguish.* Feminine : ***-on*** (N. **dō, gō,** G. **in-is**) : **imā-gō,** *image ;* **cup-ī-dō,** *desire ;* ***-ia :*** **audāc-ia,** *boldness ;* ***-iōn*** (N. **iō**) : **leg-iō,** *legion;* ***-tia :*** **avāri-tia,** *avarice ;* collateral are some with Nom. in ***-tiēs,*** as **dūri-tiēs,** *hardness;* ***-tiōn*** (N. **tiō, siō**) : **amb-i-tiō,** *ambition ;* **cōn-fū-siō,** *confusion ;* ***-tāt*** (N. **tās**) : **aequāli-tās,** *equality;* ***-tūra :*** **pic-tūra,** *painting;* ***-tūt-*** (N. **tūs, sus**) : **iuven-tūs,** *youth ;* ***-tu*** (***-su***) (N. **tu-s, su-s**), **sēn-sus,** *perception ;* ***-tūdon*** (N. **tūd-ō,** G. **-inis**): **aegri-tūdō,** *sickness of heart.* Neuter: ***-tio*** (N. **tiu-m**) : **servi-tiu-m,** *bondage.*

3. An *Artisan* or *Tradesman* is indicated by

-ārio (N. **āriu-s**) : **argent-āriu-s,** *money changer.*

4. The *Trade* is indicated by

-āria : **argent-āria,** *silver mine, bank.*

5. The *Locality* of the work (or trade) is indicated by

-ārio (N. **āriu-m**) : **sēmin-āriu-m,** *seed-plot ;* ***-ōnio*** (N. **ōniu-m**) : **full-ōnium,** *fuller's shop;* ***-īna :*** **offic-īna,** *workshop;* ***-cro, -culo*** (N. **-cru-m, -culu-m**) : **lavā-cru-m,** *bath ;* ***-trīno, -trīna*** (N. **trīna, trīnu-m**) : **sū-trīna,** *shoemaker's shop ;* **pis-trīnu-m,** *mill.*

6. *Instrument* and *Means* are indicated by

-bro, -bra (N. **bra, bru-m**) : **lī-bra,** *balance ;* **crī-brum,** *sieve;* ***-cro, -culo*** (N. **cru-m, culu-m**) : **ba-culu-m,** *walking stick;* ***-lo, -la*** (N. **-la, -lu-m**) : **pī-la,** *pillar ;* **tē-lu-m,** *weapon;* ***-ulo, -ula*** (N. **ulu-s, ula, ulu-m**) : **cap-ulu-s,** *handle ;* **rēg-ula,** *rule ;* **cing-ulu-m,** *girdle ;* ***-mento*** (N. **mentu-m**) : **al-i-mentu-m,** *nourishment ;* ***-tro, -tra*** (N. **tra, tru-m**) : **fenes-tra,** *window ;* **arā-tru-m,** *plough.*

7. *Relationship* is indicated by

-ter (N. **ter,** G. **tr-is**) : **pa-ter,** *father;* **mā-ter,** *mother.*

8. *Condition* or *Relation* by

-īna : **dīscipl-īna,** *discipline;* **medic-īna,** *medicine.*

9. *Function* is indicated by

-tūra (***sūra***) : **cul-tūra,** *cultivation.*

10. *Office* is indicated by

-ātu (N. **ātus,** G. **ātūs**) : **cōnsul-ātus,** *consulship;* ***-tūra (-sūra) :*** **dictā-tūra,** *dictatorship.*

11. *Dense Growths* are indicated by

-ēto (N. **ētu-m**) : **murt-ētu-m,** *myrtle grove;* ***-to*** (N. **tu-m**) : **virgul-tu-m,** *brushwood.*

12. *Diminutives* are indicated by

-lo, -la (N. **lu-s,** *etc.*), before which a liquid is assimilated (9, 3) : (**ager**), **agel-lu-s,** *little field ;* (**tabul-a**), **tabel-la,** *tablet ;* (**corōn-a**), **corōl-la,** *chaplet ;* **Catul-lu-s** (= **Catōn-lu-s**) ; **homul-lu-s** (= **homōn-lu-s**), *manikin ;* ***-olo, -ulo :*** **olo** after **e, i, v,** otherwise **-ulo** (N. **olu-s, ola, ulu-s, ula**) : (**alve-us**), **alve-olu-s,** *little hollow ;* (**fīli-a**), **fīli-ola,** *little daughter ;* (**valv-a**), **valv-olae,** *pod* (*little flaps*); (**circu-s**), **circ-ulu-s,** *little ring.* ***-culo, -cula*** (N. **culu-s,** *etc.*), after **e, i, u,** and consonant stems : (**spēs**), **spē-cula,** *slight hope ;* (**amni-s**), **amni-culu-s,** *streamlet ;* (**versu-s**), **versi-culu-s,** *versicle ;* (**homō̆, homin-**), **homun-culu-s,** *manikin ;* (**flōs**), **flōs-culu-s,** *floweret ;* (**cor, cord-**), **cor-culu-m,** *dear heart.*

NOTE.—Diminutives have, as a rule, the gender of their primitives. Exceptions are sometimes due to difference in signification.

182. FORMATION OF ADJECTIVES.

The significance of the most important adjective suffixes, which are often identical with the substantive suffixes, are as follows:

1. *Action* is indicated by

-bundo, -bunda **:** **cunctā-bundu-s,** *lingering. Repeated action* by ***-ulo, -ula*** **:** **crēd-ulu-s,** *quick to believe;* **quer-ulu-s,** *complaining. Passive action* is indicated by ***-bili*** **:** **amā-bili-s,** *lovable;* **vēnd-i-bili-s,** *to be sold.*

2. *Capacity* and *Inclination* are indicated by

-cundo, -cunda: **fā-cundu-s,** *of ready speech;* **verē-cundu-s,** *modest. Passive Capacity* by ***-ili*** **:** **ag-ili-s,** *readily moved, quick,* **doc-ili-s,** *teachable.* The *Capacity* and *Resulting Condition* by ***-tili*** **:** **duc-tili-s,** *ductile;* **fic-tili-s,** *capable of being moulded, of clay.*

3. *Tendency* is indicated by

-āci (N. **āx**) : **aud-āx,** *bold;* **rap-āx,** *greedy.*

4. *Likeness* and *Composition* or *Material* are indicated by

-āceo, -ācea **:** **arundin-āceu-s,** *reedy;* **crēt-āceu-s,** *chalky;* ***-icio*** **:** **later-iciu-s,** *made of brick;* ***-no, -na*** **:** **acer-nu-s,** *of maple;* ***-neo, -nea*** **:** **ae-neu-s,** *brazen.*

5. *Belonging to* is indicated by

-io, -ia **:** **imperātōr-iu-s,** *belonging to a general;* ***-icio, -icia*** **:** **aedīl-iciu-s,** *belonging to an ædile;* ***-āno, -āna*** **:** **hūm-ānu-s,** *human;* **urb-ānu-s,** *urbane, city.*

6. *Appurtenance* and *Medium* are indicated by

-tico, -tica **:** **aquā-ticu-s,** *aquatic;* ***-tili-*** **:** **aquā-tili-s,** *aquatic;* **plūmā-tili-s,** (*embroidered*) *like feathers.*

7. *Origin* is indicated by

-io, -ia **:** **Cornēl-ia (lēx), Corinth-iu-s**; ***-āno, -āna, -īno, -īna*** **:** **Rōm-ānu-s, Lat-īnu-s.**

8. *Time* is indicated by

-tino, -tina **:** **crās-tinu-s,** *of to-morrow;* ***-terno, -terna*** **:** **hes-ternu-s,** *of yesterday;* ***-urno, -urna*** **:** **noct-urnu-s,** *by night;* ***-tīno, -tīna*** **:** **mātū-tīnu-s,** *of early morning.*

9. *Locality, where, whence,* is indicated by

-ia **:** **Gall-ia,** *Gaul;* ***-tīno*** **:** **intes-tīnu-s,** *inner, intestine;* ***-ēnsi*** **:** **circ-ēnsi-s,** *from the circus;* **Sicili-ēnsi-s,** *Sicilian;* ***-āti*** (N. **-ās**) : **cūi-ās,** *of what country?*

10. *Fulness* is indicated by

-ōso, -ōsa : **anim-ōsu-s,** *full of spirit;* **verb-ōsu-s,** *wordy;* ***-lento, lenta :*** **sanguin-o-lentu-s,** *bloody;* **op-u-lentu-s,** *with abundant means.*

11. *Descent* and *Relationship* are indicated in Latin mainly by Greek adjectives, made by the addition of Greek suffixes to proper names. These suffixes are

M. ***-idēs*** (G. **idae**), F. ***-is*** (G. **idis**), from Nominatives in **us, or, ōs,** and **s** preceded by a consonant; M. ***-īdēs*** (G. **īdae**), F. ***-ēis*** (G. **ēidis**), from Nominatives in **-eus**; M. ***-adēs*** (G. **adae**), F. ***-ēis*** (G. **ēidis**), from Nominatives in **ās** (G. **ae**) and **-ēs** (G. **-ae**); M. ***-iadēs*** (G. **iadae**), F. ***-ias*** (G. **iadis**), from Nominatives in **ius, ēs, ōn, o**; F. ***-īnē,*** from Nominatives in **-us** and **-eus**; F. ***-iōnē,*** from Nominatives in **ius**: (**Tantalus**) **Tantal-idēs,** *son of Tantalus;* **Tantal-is,** *daughter of Tantalus;* (**Pelops**) **Pelopidēs**; (**Thēs-eus**) **Thēs-īdēs, Thēsēis**; (**Aenēās**) **Aene-adēs** (**Aeneadae** also); (**Lāertēs**) **Lāert-iadēs**; (**Neptūnus**) **Neptūn-īnē**; (**Acrisius**) **Acrisiōnē,** *etc.*

12. *Diminutive* adjectives are formed by the same suffixes as diminutive substantives (181, 12): **albus,** *white,* **albu-lus,** *whitish;* **miser,** *wretched,* **mis-ellus,** *poor* (*little*); **ācer,** *sharp,* **ācri-culu-s,** *somewhat sharp.*

183. SUBSTANTIVES WITHOUT SUFFIXES.

(Root Substantives.)

A few substantives are formed from roots without a suffix:

1. With weak root: **duc-s** (**dux**), *leader,* from root **duc,** *lead;* **nec-s** (**nex**), *killing,* from root **nec,** *kill.*

2. With strong root: **lūc-s** (**lūx**), *light,* from root **lūc,** *light;* **rēg-s** (**rēx**), *king,* from root **rēg,** *rule.*

3. With reduplication: **car-cer,** *jail;* **mar-mor,** *marble;* **mur-mur,** *murmur.*

THE SUFFIXES IN DETAIL.

184 Vowels.

-o, -a (N. **u-s, a, u-m**). Primary and secondary adjectives, and primary substantives. The primary adjectives resemble somewhat active participles in meaning; **fer-u-s,** *wild;* **vag-u-s,** *wandering.* Secondary are especially adjectives in **-ōrus,** as **dec-ōru-s,** *graceful,* from **decor,** *grace,* and many others. Masculine substantives in **-u-s** are often nouns of *agency,* sometimes *nōmina āctiōnis* and concretes therefrom: **coqu-o-s,** *cook;* **rog-u-s,** *pyre.* Those in **-a** (**ā**) are regularly *nōmina agentis,* especially in composition; **scrīb-a,** *scribe;* **agri-cola,** *husbandman* (*land-tiller*). Feminines are in **-o** (which are principally names of *trees:* **pir-us,** *pear tree*) and in **-a**: **lup-a,** *she-wolf,* as well as **lup-u-s.** Neuters are those in **-u-m,** especially names of *fruits:* **pir-u-m,** *pear.*

-i (N. **i-s, e**). Substantives: M. **orb-i-s**, *circle;* **pisc-i-s**, *fish, etc.;* F. **av-i-s**, *bird;* **nāv-i-s**, *ship;* N. **mar-e**, *sea;* **conclāv-e**, *room.* Adjectives: **dulc-i-s**, *sweet;* **turp-i-s**, *ugly.*

NOTE.—In adjectives especially, **i** is often weakened from **-o**, as **inermis** and **inermus**, *etc.* Sometimes in substantives the Nom. shows **ēs** instead of **is**, as **caedēs** and **caedis**, *etc.*

-io, -ia (N. **iu-s, ia, iu-m**).—1. This is the principal secondary suffix, and is found in many combinations; but it is also found as primary in substantives: M. **gen-iu-s**, *genius;* **glad-iu-s**, *sword;* F. **pluv-ia**, *rain;* **tīb-ia**, *fife;* N. **fol-iu-m**, *leaf;* **od-iu-m**, *hate;* and in adjectives **ex-im-iu-s**, *pre-eminent* (*taken out*); **sauc-iu-s**, *wounded*, **pluv-iu-s**, *rainy.*

2. The suffix occurs as secondary in the forms **-ēio** (**-aeo**), **-io, eo, io**, in a large number of Gentile names: **Flāv-ēiu-s, Flāv-iu-s**; **Lūc-ēiu-s, Lūc-īu-s, Lūc-iu-s**; similar to these are those in **ed-iu-s, īd-iu-s, id-iu-s, -ēl-iu-s, īl-iu-s**, as **Lūc-id-iu-s, Corn-ēl-iu-s, Lūc-īl-iu-s.** Also in some adjectives of *material* in **eu-s**, as **aur-eu-s**, *golden;* **ferr-eu-s**, *iron.* It occurs, moreover, in many compound adjective and substantive endings, to be discussed later, and in many abstract substantives in **-antia, -entia**, as **abund-ant-ia**, *abundance;* **sci-ent-ia**, *knowledge, etc.*

NOTE.—Instead of **-ia**, we find **-ea** in a few words: **cav-ea**, *cage;* **cochl-ea**, *snail.*

-u (N. **u-s, u**). M. **arc-u-s**, *bow;* **curr-u-s**, *chariot;* F. **ac-u-s**, *needle;* **man-u-s**, *hand;* N. **gel-ū**, *frost;* **gen-u**, *knee.* Secondary is **socr-u-s**, *mother-in-law.* This suffix is found occasionally in adjectives compounded with **manus**, as **centi-manus**, *hundred-handed;* also in the form **-ui** in a few adjectives, as **ten-ui-s**, *thin.*

NOTE.—The suffix **-o** often alternates with **-u.**

-uo, -ua (N. **uo-s, ua, uo-m**). Primary and secondary substantives and adjectives. Primary: M. **eq-uo-s**, *horse;* F. **al-vo-s**, *belly;* N. **ar-vo-m**, *field;* **par-vo-s**, *small.* Secondary: M. **patr-uo-s**, *uncle;* **cer-vo-s**, *stag;* F. **iān-ua**, *gate;* **cern-uo-s**, *stooping;* **aestī-vo-s**, *of the summer.*

NOTE.—**īvo-s** is found in **voc-īvo-s** (**vacuos**), **rediv-īvo-s**, *etc.* **-vo** is weakened to **-vi** in **pel-vi-s**, *basin.*

185. Suffixes with Gutturals.

1. ***-co, -ca*** (N. **cu-s, ca, cu-m**). This forms both adjectives and substantives, but is usually secondary. As primary it is found in: **io-cu-s**, *jest;* **lo-cu-s**, *place;* as secondary in: **medi-cu-s**, *physician;* **ped-i-ca**, *fetter.* Adjectives are primary: **cas-cu-s**, *very old;* or secondary: **cīvi-cu-s**, *civic.*

2. ***-āco, -āca*** (N. **ācu-s, āca, ācu-m**). Primary in **clo-āca**, *sewer;* secondary in **ver-bēn-āca**, *vervain*, and in adjectives, as **mer-ācu-s**, *pure.*

3. ***-īco, -īca*** (N. **īcu-s, īca, īcu-m**). In substantives, such as: M. **umbil-īcu-s**, *navel;* F. **lect-īca**, *litter;* **urt-īca**, *nettle.* In adjectives, as: **am-īcu-s**, *friendly, etc.*

4. ***-ūco, -ūca*** (N. **ūcu-s, ūca, ūcu-m**). Primary in the adjectives: **cad-ūcu-s**, *tottering;* **mand-ūcu-s**, *voracious;* secondary in **alb-ūcu-s**, *asphodel;* and in substantives 'n **-ūca**, as **ēr-ūca**, *caterpillar;* **verr-ūca**, *wart.*

NOTE.—Similar is the secondary suffix **-inquo** in **long-inquo-s**, *distant;* **propinquo-s**, *near.*

5. ***-āc*** (N. **āx**) forms substantives and adjectives; the latter expressing *inclination.* Primary: **aud-āx**, *bold;* **fug-āx**, *fleeing.* Secondary: F. **forn-āx**, *furnace;* **līm-āx**, *snail;* **vēr-āx**, *truthful.*

6. ***-ēc*** (N. **ēx**) is found in **verv-ēx**, *wether.*

7. ***-ic*** (N. **ex**) forms a number of substantives that are mainly *masculine,* except names of *plants* and *trees.* Primary: M. **ap-ex**, *point;* **cort-ex**, *bark;* F. **il-ex**, *holm-oak.* Secondary: F. **imbr-ex**, *gutter-tile.*

8. ***-īc*** (N. **īx**) forms substantives and adjectives. Primary: F. **rād-īx**, *root;* **fēl-īx**, *happy.* Secondary; **corn-īx**, *crow,* and feminines in **-trīx.**

9. ***-ōc*** (N. **ōx**) is found in the substantive **cel-ōx**, *yacht,* and in a number of adjectives: **atr-ōx**, *ferocious.*

10. ***-āceo, -ācea*** (N. **āceu-s, ācea, āceu-m**), forms adjectives of *material* or *likeness:* **crēt-āceu-s**, *chalk-like.*

NOTE.—Notice also the suffix **-āc-io**, especially in proper names: **Vēr-ācia.**

11. ***-ic-eo, -ic-io*** (N. **iceu-s**, *etc.*, **iciu-s**, *etc.*), form adjectives indicating *material,* the latter suffix also some indicating *relation:* **palm-iceu-s**, *of palms;* **tribūn-iciu-s**, *proceeding from a tribune.*

12. ***-īc-io*** (N. **īciu-s**, *etc.*) is found in **nov-īciu-s**, *new,* and in words of participial meaning coming from forms in **-to**, as **advent-īciu-s**, *stranger.*

13. ***-ūc-eo, -ūc-io,*** occurs in **pann-ūceu-s** or **pann-ūciu-s.**

14. ***-ci-no*** and ***ci-n'-io*** occur (perhaps) in **vāti-cinu-s**, *prophetic,* and in some secondary neuter substantives, which denote *action* or *event,* as **latrō-ciniu-m**, *robbery.*

15. ***-cro, -cri, -clo, -culo*** (N. **cer, cris, clu-m, culu-m**) are found in some adjectives with participial force, and in a few neuter substantives indicating *instrument* or *locality;* as **ala-cer**, *quick;* **medio-cris**, *mediocre;* **perī-clum** (**-culu-m**), *danger;* **ba-culu-m**, *stick* (also m.); **sepul-crum**, *grave.* Also the primary **rīdi-culu-s**, *laughable,* and the secondary **anni-culu-s**, *aged.*

186. Suffixes with a Dental.

1. ***-d*** (N. **(d)s**). Substantives only : **frau-s**, *cheatery;* **mercē-s**, *pay;* **cūstō-s**, *guard.*

2. ***-do, -di*** (N. **du-s**, *etc.*, **di-s**). A secondary suffix used especially for the formation of adjectives : **frīg-i-du-s**, *cold;* **vir-i-dis**, *blooming.*

3. ***-to*** (***-so***) (N. **tu-s, ta, tu-m**). This forms substantives and adjectives, and is both primary and secondary. Primary : M. **cub-i-tu-s**, *elbow;* **dig-i-tus**, *finger;* also substantives in **-ta** after Greek analogy : **poē-ta**, *poet;* F. **has-ta**, *spear;* **am-i-ta**, *aunt;* N. **lu-tu-m**, *mud;* **tēc-tum**, *roof;* **ap-tu-s**, *fit;* **beā-tu-s**, *blessed.* Secondary : M. **nau-ta**, *sailor;* F. **iuven-ta**, *youth;* N. dense growths in **ē-tu-m** : **frutic-ē-tu-m**, *copse;* **iūs-tu-s**, *just;* and passive adjectives like **barb-ā-tus**, *bearded.*

4. ***-ti*** (***-si***) [N. **tis (sis)**] forms primary and secondary substantives and adjectives. Primary : M. **fūs-ti-s**, *club;* **cas-si-s**, *hunting-net;* F. **cu-ti-s**, *skin;* **si-ti-s**, *thirst;* **for-ti-s**, *brave;* **mī-ti-s**, *mild.* Secondary : (1) in adjectives and substantives indicating *home, origin,* usually preceded by **ā**, **ī**, more rarely **ē** : **Camer-s (Camer-ti-s)**, *from Camerinum;* **Arpīnā-s (Arpīnā-ti-s)**, *of Arpinum;* **nostr-ās**, *from our country;* (2) in the form **-ēnsi** (for **ent-ti**) in adjectives of *origin* and *locality :* **Sicili-ēn-si-s**, *from Sicily;* **castr-ēnsi-s**, *belonging to a camp.*

5. ***-t*** (N. **(t)s**) forms primary and secondary substantives and adjectives. Primary : M. **com-e-s**, *companion;* **dēn-s**, *tooth;* F. **qui-ē-s**, *rest;* **ar-s**, *art;* **locupl-ē-s**, *wealthy;* with preceding **e** : **dīv-e-s**, *rich.* Note also the Participles in **-ns**. Secondary : M. **āl-e-s**, *bird;* **eque-s**, *horseman.*

6. ***-ento-*** (N. **-entu-s**, *etc.*) forms substantives and adjectives ; the latter are participial in nature. M. **v-entu-s**, *wind;* F. **pol-enta**, *cluster;* N. **ungu-entu-m**, *salve;* **cru-entu-s**, *bloody.* Secondary adjectives : **gracil-entu-s**, *slender;* and by false analogy **corpul-entu-s**, *corpulent,* and the like.

7. ***-tāt, -tūt*** (M. **tā-s, tū-s**), forms secondary feminine abstracts and collectives : **cīv-i-tā-s**, *citizenship;* **līber-tā-s**, *freedom;* **iuven-tū-s**, *youth;* **vir-tū-s**, *manliness.*

8. ***-tio, -tia, -tiē*** (N. **tiu-m, tia, tiē-s**), likewise form abstracts and collectives, some neuter, most masculine : **servi-tiu-m**, *slavery;* **molli-tia** and **molli-tiē-s**, *gentleness, etc.*

NOTES.—1. In **in-i-tiu-m**, *beginning*, and **spa-tiu-m**, *room*, the suffix is primary.

2. Many roots form various derivatives of similar meaning, thus : **dūr-i-tia, dūr-i-tiē-s, dūr-i-tā-s**, *hardness, etc.*

9. ***-ti-co*** (N. **ti-cu-s**, *etc.*) forms secondary adjectives signifying *pertaining to :* **domes-ticu-s**, *domestic;* **aquā-ticu-s**, *aquatic.*

NOTE.—In such substantives as **canti-cu-m, trīti-c-um,** the ending **-co** has been added to a participial form in **-to (canto, trīto).**

10. ***-ter*** forms primary substantives of *kinship;* as, **pa-ter,** *etc.* Different in formation is **soror,** which, like **ux-or,** has no feminine ending.

11. ***-tor*** (***-sor***), F. ***-trīc*** (N. **tor, trīx**), form substantives of *agency,* those in **trīx** being all secondary : **aud-ī-tor,** *hearer ;* **vēnā-trīx,** *huntress ;* **-tor** is secondary in **gladiā-tor,** *etc.*

12. ***-tūro-, -tūr-a*** (N. **tūru-s,** *etc.*), forms participles in **tūru-s,** as **amā-tūru-s,** and feminine substantives denoting *activity* or *office :* **cul-tūr-a,** *cultivation ;* **cēn-sūr-a,** *censorship.*

13. ***-tōr-io*** (***-sōr-io***) (N. **tōriu-s,** *etc.*), form neuter substantives of *place* and *instrument,* and adjectives denoting that *which pertains to the actor :* **audī-tōr-iu-m,** *lecture hall ;* **āleā-tōr-iu-s,** *pertaining to a dice-player.*

14. ***-tro, -tra*** (N. **tra, tru-m**), forms substantives, mostly neuter, of *means :* **arā-tru-m,** *plough ;* **fenes-tra** (f.), *window.* From words like **mōn-s-tru-m,** *monster,* come by false analogy those in **-ster,** as **pīn-aster,** *wild pine.*

15. ***-tero, -tera*** (N. **ter, tra, tru-m**) forms comparatives : **al-ter,** *other ;* **dex-ter,** *right ;* **nos-ter,** *our ;* perhaps also adjectives of *relation, appurtenance,* or *locality* in **-s-ter** (G. **stris**), such as : **palūs-ter** (= **palūd-ter**), *swampy ;* **eques-ter,** *equestrian ;* **campes-ter,** *champaign ;* **terres-ter,** *of the earth, terrestrial.*

16. ***-trīno, -trīna*** (N. **trīna, trīnu-m**), forms substantives of *activity* (f.), or of *locality* (f., n.) : **doc-trīna,** *instruction ;* **pīs-trīna,** *bakery ;* **pīs-trīnu-m,** (*pounding*) *mill.*

17. ***-tili-*** (***-sili***) (N. **tili-s, tile**) forms primary adjectives of *capacity* and *adaptation,* and with preceding **ā** secondary adjectives of *relation* or *belonging :* **duc-tili-s,** *ductile ;* **mis-sili-s,** *missile ;* **aquā-tili-s,** *belonging to the water.*

18. ***-ter-no*** (N. **ternu-s,** *etc.*) forms adjectives indicating *time :* **hes-ternu-s,** *of yesterday.*

19. ***-tur-no*** (N. **turnu-s,** *etc.*) forms substantives and adjectives indicating *continuance,* from which come proper names : **Sā-turnu-s, Vol-turnu-s, tac-i-turnu-s,** *silent.*

20. ***-tino, -tīno*** (N. **tinu-s, tīnu-s,** *etc.*), forms adjectives of *time,* the latter also of *place :* **crās-tinu-s,** *of to-morrow ;* **intes-tīnu-s,** *inner, intestine ;* **mātū-tīnu-s,** *of early morning.*

21. ***-tu*** (***-su***) (N. **tu-s, su-s**) forms substantives of *action* and its *result :* **adven-tu-s,** *arrival ;* **cur-su-s,** *course ;* **or-tu-s,** *rising.*

22. ***-ā-tu*** (N. **ā-tu-s**) forms secondary substantives of *office :* **cōnsul-ā-tu-s,** *consulship ;* **sen-ā-tu-s,** *senate.*

187. Suffixes with a Labial.

1. ***-bo, -ba*** (N. **bu-s**, *etc.*), forms substantives and adjectives: M. **mor-bu-s**, *disease;* F. **bar-ba**, *beard;* N. **ver-bu-m**, *word;* **pro-bu-s**, *upright.*

2. ***-bro, -bra*** (N. **bra, bru-m**), forms substantives indicating *means* or *instrument.* Primary: F. **dolā-bra**, *celt;* **lī-bra**, *balance;* **ter-e-bra**, *borer;* N. **crī-bru-m**, *sieve.* Secondary: **candēlā-bru-m**, *candlestick.*

NOTE.—Very rare are masculines; as, **fa-ber**, *wright;* **Mulci-ber**, *Vulcan.*

3. ***-bulo, -bula*** (N. **bula, bulu-m**), form substantives: F. **fā-bula**, *tale;* **fī-bula** (**fig-**), *brooch;* N. **pā-bulu-m**, *fodder;* **sta-bulu-m**, *stall.*

4. ***-bili*** (N. **bili-s**) forms adjectives, mostly of *passive meaning* in classical prose: **amā-bili-s**, *lovable;* **nō-bili-s**, *noble;* **flē-bili-s**, *weeping.*

188. Suffixes with an original S.

1. ***-is*** (N. **is**, G. **er-is**) forms a few substantives: **vōm-is** (also **vōm-er**), *ploughshare;* **cin-is**, *ashes;* **pulv-is**, *dust;* **cucum-is**, *cucumber.*

2. ***-us*** (N. **us**, G. **er-is, or-is**) forms primary and secondary neuter substantives. Primary: **foed-us**, *bond;* **gen-us**, *race;* **temp-us**, *time.* Secondary: **pect-us**, *breast;* **fūn-us**, *funeral.*

NOTE.—Some such words have become monosyllabic, as **aes, iūs, rūs.**

3. ***-ōs*** (***-ōr***) (N. **ōs, or**, G. **ōr-is**) forms many primary and a few secondary masculine abstracts. Primary: **fl-ōs**, *flower;* **am-or**, *love.* Secondary: **aegr-or**, *sickness.*

NOTE.—Noteworthy are M. **lep-us**, *hare;* F. **arb-ōs**, *tree* (45 N.); **Ven-us** (G. **Veneris**), and the adjective **vet-us** (G. **veteris**), *old.*

4. ***-es*** (N. **es, ēs**, G. **is, ĕī**) forms a few substantives of the third and fifth declension: **vāt-ēs**, *bard;* **fam-ēs**, *hunger;* **plēb-ēs**, *people.*

5. ***-ōr-o*** (N. **ōru-s**, *etc.*) forms secondary adjectives, as: **can-ōru-s**, *sounding;* **hon-ōru-s**, *honourable;* and a few substantives, as: **aur-ōra**, *morning;* **Flōra**, *etc.*

189. Suffixes with a Liquid.

1. ***-lo, -la*** (N. **lu-s**, *etc.*), forms many feminine and neuter, and a few masculine substantives: M. **mā-lu-s**, *mast;* F. **pī-la**, *pillar;* N. **cae-lu-m** (= **caed-lu-m**), *chisel;* **fī-lu-m**, *thread.*

2. ***-i-lo, -i-la*** (N. **ilu-s**, *etc.*), forms primary and secondary sub-

stantives and adjectives. M. **sīb-i-lu-s**, *hissing;* N. **cae-lu-m** (= **cav-i-lu-m**, *hollow*), *heaven;* **nūb-i-lu-s**, *cloudy.*

3. ***(-o-lo), -u-lo, -u-la*** (N. **ulu-s**, *etc.*), form primary and secondary substantives, most of which indicate *instrument*, and primary adjectives indicating *repeated action* or *tendency:* M. **ang-u-lu-s**, *corner;* **oc-u-lu-s**, *eye;* F. **rēg-u-la**, *rule;* **tēg-u-la**, *tile;* N. **iac-u-lu-m**, *javelin;* **spec-u-lu-m**, *mirror;* **bib-u-lu-s**, *bibulous;* **crēd-u-lu-s**, *quick to believe;* **quer-u-lu-s**, *complaining;* **caer-u-lu-s**, *blue* (secondary), and **caer-u-leu-s.** Also **fam-u-lu-s**, *servant*, and the extension **fam-ili-a**, *family.*

4. ***-li*** (N. **li-s, le**) occurs in the substantive: M. **cau-li-s**, *stalk;* and in adjectives: **subtī-li-s**, *fine;* **incī-li-s**, *cut in.* Secondary in **fidē-li-s**, *faithful.*

5. ***-i-li*** (N. **ili-s, ile**) forms a few substantives and many adjectives indicating *passive capacity:* F. **strig-i-li-s**, *scraper;* N. **teg-i-le**, *roof.* Also **vig-il**, *watchman;* **ag-i-li-s**, *readily moved;* **doc-ili-s**, *teachable.* Secondary in **hum-i-li-s**, *low*, and in the terminations **-tili-s, -sili-s.**

6. ***-olo, -ola*** (after **e, i, v**), ***-ulo, -ula*** (N. **olu-s, ulu-s**, *etc.*), form diminutives: **alve-olu-s**, *little belly;* **fīli-olu-s**, *little son;* **rīv-ulu-s**, *brooklet;* **rēg-ulu-s**, *chief;* **vōc-ula**, *voice;* **grān-ulu-m**, *grain;* **alb-ulu-s**, *whitish;* **parv-olu-s**, *small.*

7. ***-ello, -ella*** (N. **ellu-s**, *etc.*), forms diminutives after **l** and by assimilation after **n, r**: **pop-ellu-s**, *tribelet;* **tab-el-la**, *tablet;* **pu-el-la**, *girl;* **bel-lu-s (bonus)**, *good;* **misel-lus (miser)**, *wretched.* Doubly diminutive are **catel-lu-s**, *puppy;* **cistel-la**, *basket;* **capitel-lu-m**, *head.*

8. ***-illo, -illa*** (N. **illu-s**, *etc.*), forms diminutives, and is formed like **ello**, but usually after a preceding **i**: **pulv-illu-s**, *small cushion;* **pīstr-illa**, *small mill;* **sig-illu-m**, *small image;* **bov-illu-s**, *bovine.* Also **cōdic-illī**, *billets;* **paux-illu-s**, *slight;* **pus-illu-s**, *tiny.*

9. ***-olla*** is found in **cor-ōl-la**, *wreath;* **ōl-la**, *jar* **(aula).**

10. ***-ullo, -ulla,*** occurs in **ūl-lu-s**, *any.* **Sul-la (= Sūr-u-la), Catul-lu-s (Catōn-lus), homullus (= homōn-lu-s).**

11. ***(-co-lo), -cu-lo*** (N. **culu-s**, *etc.*), forms diminutives, especially after consonantal and **e, i, u** stems: M. **flōs-culu-s**, *floweret;* **homun-culu-s**, *manikin* (irregular); **avu-n-culu-s**, *uncle* (*mother's brother*, irregular); F. **spē-cula**, *little hope;* **auri-cula**, *ear;* **arbus-cula**, *little tree* (irregular); **domu-n-cula**, *little house* (irregular); N. **cor-culu-m**, (*dear*) *heart;* **mūnus-culu-m**, *little gift.* Adjectives are **dulci-culu-s**, *sweetish*, and especially diminutives from comparative stems, **melius-culu-s.**

12. ***-cello (-cillo)*** (N. **cellu-s**, *etc.*) stands to **culo** as **ello** to **ulo**: M. **pēni-cillu-s, -m**, *painter's brush;* **ōs-cillu-m**, *little mouth;* **molli-cellu-s**, *softish.*

13. ***-uleo*** (N. **ūleu-s**) forms substantives that were originally adjectival : **acūleu-s**, *sting.*

14. ***-āli, -āri*** (N. **āli-s, āri-s**, *etc.*), form secondary adjectives, some of which are substantivised in the neuter, and a few substantives : **vēn-ālis**, *venal;* **mort-āli-s**, *mortal;* **singul-āri-s**, *unique;* **vulg-āri-s**, *common;* **can-āli-s**, *canal;* **animal**, *living being;* **calc-ar**, *spur.*

15. ***-ēla*** (***-ella***) forms primary and secondary substantives, most of which indicate *action :* **loqu-ēla** (**loqu-ella**), *talking ;* **cand-ēla**, *candle ;* **cūstōd-ēla**, *watching.*

16. ***-ēli*** (N. **ēli-s**, *etc.*) forms secondary substantives and adjectives: **cardu-ēli-s**, *linnet;* **crūd-ēli-s**, *cruel.*

REMARK.—A further development of **-ēli** is **-ēlio**, **-ēlia** : **Aur-ēli-us**, **contum-ēli-a**, *contumely.*

17. ***-īli*** (N. **īli-s, īle**) forms secondary substantives and adjectives : M. **aed-īli-s**, *ædile;* N. **cub-īle**, *couch;* **sed-īle**, *seat;* **cīv-īli-s**, *civic;* **erī-li-s**, *master's.*

18. ***-mo, -ma*** (N. **mu-s**, *etc.*), forms primary substantives and primary and secondary adjectives. The feminine substantives express usually the *result of an action:* M. **an-i-mu-s**, *spirit;* **cal-mu-s, cal-a-mu-s**, *stalk ;* F. **fā-ma**, *fame ;* **flam-ma**, *flame;* N. **ar-ma**, *arms ;* **pō-mum**, *fruit.* Adjectives, primary: **al-mu-s**, *fostering;* **fīr-mu-s**, *strong.* Secondary: **op-ī-mu-s**, *fat ;* **patr-ī-mu-s, mātr-ī-mu-s**, *with father, mother, living.*

19. ***-men*** (N. **men**, G. **min-is**) forms primary, neuter substantives, mostly indicating *activity* or *results of activity*: **āg-men**, *train;* **flū-men**, *river ;* but M. **flā-men**, *priest.*

20. ***-men-to*** (N. **mentu-m**) forms substantives (mostly primary) indicating *instrument :* **al-i-mentu-m**, *nourishment ;* **tor-mentu-m**, *torture.*

NOTES.—1. **-men** and **-mentum** are often formed from the same radical. In that case **mentu-m** is the more common : **teg-u-men, teg-u-mentu-m**, *covering.*

2. Rare and archaic are feminines in **-menta** : **armenta** = **armentu-m**.

3. **-menti** occurs in **sēmenti-s** (f.), *seed* = **sēmen** (n.).

21. ***-met*** (N. **mes**, G. **mit-is**) forms a few masculine substantives : **trā-mes**, *path ;* **fō-mes**, *fuel ;* **lī-mes**, *cross-path.*

22. ***-mino, -mina, -mno, -mna*** (N. **minu-s**, *etc.*), form substantives : M. **ter-minu-s**, *boundary ;* F. **al-u-mna**, *foster-daughter ;* **fē-mina**, *woman ;* N. **da-mnu-m**, *loss.*

23. ***-mōn*** (N. **mō**, G. **mōn-is**) forms primary and secondary masculine substantives : **pul-mō**, *lung ;* **ser-mō**, *discourse ;* **tē-mō**, *pole (of a chariot).*

24. ***-mōn-io, -mōn-ia*** (N. **mōnia, mōniu-m**), forms primary and

secondary substantives. Primary: F. **al-i-mōnia**, *nourishment*; **quer-i-mōnia**, *complaint*; N. **al-i-mōniu-m**, *nourishment*. Secondary: F. **ācri-mōnia**, *tartness*; N. **mātr-i-mōniu-m**, *marriage*.

25. ***-mōr*** forms primary masculine substantives: **cre-mor**, *broth*; **rū-mor**, *rumour*.

26. ***-mic*** (N. **mex**, G. **mic-is**) forms a few substantives: **cī-mex**, *bug*; **pū-mex**, *pumice*.

27. *a*. ***-no, -na*** (N. **nu-s**, *etc.*), forms primary and secondary adjectives; the primary are participial in meaning; the secondary indicate *material* or *relation*, and occasionally *locality*; when added to local comparatives and adverbs, *distributive numerals* are also formed with this suffix. Primary: **dīg-nu-s**, *worthy*; **plē-nu-s**, *full*. Secondary: **diur-nu-s**, *daily*; **frāter-nu-s**, *brotherly*; **acer-nu-s**, *maple*; **ex-ter-nu-s**, *outer*; **bī-nī**, *two each*.

NOTE.—Adjectives denoting *material* have also **-neo** (= **n'-eo**), as **ae-neu-s**, *brazen*; **īlīg-neu-s, quer-neu-s**.

b. ***-no, -na*** (N. **nu-s**, *etc.*), forms primary and a few secondary substantives. Primary: M. **fur-nu-s**, *oven*; **pūg-nu-s**, *fist*; F. **cē-na**, *meal*; **lā-na**, *wool*. N. **dō-nu-m**, *gift*; **rēg-nu-m**, *kingdom*. Secondary: M. **tribū-nu-s**, *tribune*; F. **fortū-na**, *fortune*; **albur-nu-m**, *sap-wood*.

NOTE.—This suffix is extended in **pecū-nia**, *money*.

28. ***-bundo-, -cundo*** (N. **bundu-s**, *etc.*, **cundu-s**, *etc.*), form adjectives of *activity*: **cunct-ā-bundu-s**, *delaying*; **fā-cundu-s**, *eloquent*.

29. ***-ni*** (N. **ni-s**) forms primary substantives and adjectives: **am-ni-s**, *stream*; **pē-ni-s**, *tail*; **pā-ni-s**, *bread*; **im-mā-ni-s**, *wild*; **sēg-ni-s**, *lazy*.

30. ***-ino, -ina*** (N. **inu-s**, *etc.*), forms primary and secondary substantives and adjectives. Primary: M. **dom-inu-s**, *lord*; F. **pāg-ina**, *page*; **lic-inu-s**, *curled upwards*. Secondary: M. **ped-ic-inu-s**, *foot*; F. **fisc-ina**, *basket*; N. **sūc-inu-m**, *amber*; **faec-inu-s**, *making dregs*.

NOTE.—The suffix is extended in the proper name **Lic-iniu-s**.

31. ***-āno, -āna*** (N. **ānu-s**, *etc.*), forms secondary adjectives, some of which are substantivised. They indicate *origin* or *appurtenance*; **decum-ānu-s**, *belonging to the tenth*; **hūm-ānu-s**, *human*; **alt-ānu-s**, *sea-wind*. Primary in **Volc-ānu-s, Di-āna**.

32. ***-ān-eo*** (N. **āneu-s**, *etc.*) forms primary and secondary adjectives. Primary: **cōnsent-āneu-s**, *harmonious*. Secondary: **subit-āneu-s**, *sudden*. This suffix becomes **ānio** (= **ān'io**) in proper names: **Afr-āniu-s, Fund-āniu-s**.

33. ***-ēno, -ēna*** (N. **ēnu-s**, *etc.*), forms secondary substantives and

adjectives: M. **Vībidi-ēnu-s**; F. **cat-ēna**, *chain;* **hab-ēna**, *rein;* **N. ven-ēnu-m**, *poison;* **eg-ēnu-s**, *needy;* **ali-ēnu-s**, *strange.*

NOTE.—This is extended to **ēn-on** in **toll-ēnō**, *(well) sweep.*

34. ***-īno, -īna*** (N. **īnu-s**, *etc.*), forms primary and secondary substantives and adjectives. Primary: M. **cat-īnu-s, -m**, *dish;* F. **rap-īna**, *rapine;* **ru-īna**, *ruin;* **nec-op-īnu-s**, *unexpected.* Secondary: M. **pulv-īnu-s**, *cushion;* **sal-īnu-m**, *salt-cellar*, and many feminines, especially those denoting *shops* and *factories;* **rēg-īna**, *queen;* **cul-īna**, *kitchen;* **offic-īna**, *workshop;* **āgn-īnu-s**, *belonging to a lamb;* **dīv-īnu-s**, *divine.*

NOTE.—An extension of this suffix is found in **rīc-īniu-m**, *veil.*

35. ***-en*** (N. **-en**, G. **-in-is**) forms a few substantives: M. **pect-en**, *comb;* N. **glūt-en**, *glue.*

36. ***-ōn*** (N. **ŏ**, G. **in-is**) forms a few substantives: M. **card-ō**, *hinge;* **marg-ō**, *rim;* **ōrd-ō**, *row;* F. **a-sperg-ō**, *sprinkling;* **virg-ō**, *maid;* **car-ŏ**, *flesh.*

NOTES.—1. Noteworthy is **hom-ŏ, hom-in-is**, *man.*
2. This suffix occurs very commonly in compounds forming feminine abstracts:
-ēdōn (N. **ēdō**), **dulc-ēdō**, *sweetness;* ***-īdōn*** (N. **īdō**), **cup-īdō**, *desire;* **form-īdō**, *fear;* ***-ūdōn*** (N. **ūdō**), **tēst-ūdō**, *tortoise;* ***-tūdōn*** (N. **tūdō**), **aegri-tūdō**, *sickness;* ***-āgōn*** (N. **āgō**), **im-āgō**, *image;* ***-ūgōn*** (N. **ūgō**), **aer-ūgō**, *rust;* ***-īgōn*** (N. **īgō**), **cāl-īgō**, *thick darkness;* **or-īgō**, *origin, etc.*

37. ***-ōn*** (N. **ō**, G. **ōnis**) forms primary and secondary substantives. The primary are nouns of *agency:* **combib-ō**, *fellow-drinker;* **prae-c-ō**, *herald;* **tī-rō**, *recruit.* The secondary indicate often the possession of some bodily or mental peculiarities; **āle-ō**, *dice-player;* **centuri-ō**, *centurion.*

38. ***-iōn*** (N. **iō**) forms a few masculine and many feminine primary and secondary substantives. Primary: M. **pūg-iō**, *dagger;* F. **opīn-iō**, *opinion;* **reg-iō**, *region.* Secondary: M. **pell-iō**, *furrier;* **vespertīl-iō**, *bat;* F. **com-mūn-iō**, *communion.*

NOTE.—Especially frequent are feminine abstracts in **t-iō** (**s-iō**): **amb-i-tiō**, *ambition;* **op-pūgnā-tiō**, *siege.* Noteworthy are the secondary diminutives, **homunc-iō**, **senec-iō.**

39. ***-ōno, -ōna*** (N. **ōnu-s, ōna**), forms few primary and many secondary substantives; the masculines indicate *agents*, especially *person employed:* M. **col-ōnu-s**, *settler;* F. **mātr-ōna**, *matron;* **Bell-ōna.**

40. ***-ōnio, -ōnia*** (N. **ōniu-s**, *etc.*), forms substantives and adjectives: M. **Fav-ōniu-s**, *zephyr;* **Pomp-ōniu-s**, *etc.;* **caup-ōniu-s**, *belonging to a host.* Neuters indicate the *trade* or *shop:* **full-ōniu-m**, *fuller's-shop.*

41. ***-ro, -ra*** (N. **(e)r, -ra, ru-m**), forms primary substantives and adjectives: M. **ag-e-r**, *field;* **cap-e-r**, *goat;* **mū-ru-s**, *wall;* F. **lau-ru-s**, *laurel;*

ser-ra, *saw;* N. **flag-ru-m**, *whip;* **lab-ru-m**, *lip;* **clā-ru-s**, *bright;* **pū-rus**, *clean.*

Often a short vowel precedes: M. **num-e-ru-s**, *number;* F. **cam-era**, *vault;* N. **iūg-eru-m**, *measure of land.* So **hil-aru-s**, *joyous;* **līb-er**, *free;* **cam-uru-s**, *vaulted;* **sat-ur**, *full.*

NOTES.—1. Extensions are **Mer-curiu-s**, **tug-uriu-m**, *hut.*

2. In a number of primary substantives and adjectives simple **r** is preceded by a short vowel: M. **late-r**, *tile;* **āns-er**, *goose;* F. **mul-i-er**, *woman;* N. **ac-er**, *maple;* **vēr** (= **ves-er**), *spring;* **cic-ur**, *tame.*

42. ***-ri*** (N. **-(e)-r**, **-ris**, G. **ris**) forms substantives and adjectives: M. **imb-e-r**, *rain-storm;* **āc-e-r**, *sharp;* **fūneb-ri-s**, *funeral;* perhaps **celeb-er**, *thronged.*

43. ***-āro*** forms adjectives, as: **av-āru-s**, *greedy;* **am-āru-s**, *bitter.*

44. ***-āri, -āli*** (N. **āri-s**, **āli-s**, *etc.*), forms secondary substantives and adjectives; **-āri** when the stem has **l**, **-āli** when it has an **r**: **pugill-ārē-s**, *tablets;* **prīmipīl-āri-s**, *one who has been primipilus;* some neuters in **ar** (from **-āre**): **calc-ar**, *spur;* **ex-em-p-l-ar**, *pattern;* **pulvīn-ar**, *(sacred) couch;* **auxili-āri-s**, *auxiliary;* **mīlit-āri-s**, *military;* **cōnsul-āri-s**, *consular.*

45. ***-ārio, -āria*** (N. **āriu-s**, *etc.*), forms substantives and adjectives. There are sometimes collateral forms in **-āri-s**. The substantives, when masculine, indicate *artisans;* when feminine, *business* or *profession;* when neuter, the *place* where the work is carried on. M. **argent-āriu-s**, *money-changer;* **ferr-āriu-s**, *iron-worker;* F. **argent-āria**, *silver mine, bank or banking;* N. **api-āriu-m**, *beehive;* **pōm-āriu-m**, *apple orchard.*

46. ***-ēro*** (N. **ēru-s**, *etc.*) forms **sev-ērus**, *earnest,* and the substantive **gal-ēru-s**, **-m**, *bonnet.*

47. ***-ūri*** forms the substantive **sec-ūri-s**, *axe,* and by extension **pēn-ūria**, *want.*

48. The letter ***r*** appears often in combination with other suffixes, as: **-er-co** in **lup-ercu-s**, *Pan;* **nov-erca**, *step-mother;* **-er-to** in **lac-ertu-s**, *arm;* **lac-ertu-s**, *a lizard;* **-er-bo** in **ac-erbu-s**, *sour;* **sup-erbu-s**, *proud;* **-er-vo** in **ac-ervo-s**, *heap;* **cat-erva**, *crowd;* **-er-na** in **cav-erna**, *hollow;* **lu-cerna**, *lamp;* **-ter-na** in **lan-ter-na**, *lantern;* **-ur-no** in **alb-urnu-s**, *white fish;* **lab-urnu-m**, *laburnum.*

190. FORMATION OF VERBS.

1. Primitives are confined to the Third Conjugation, to some forms of the Irregular verbs, and to some Inchoatives. The various stem-formations are shown in 133.

2. Derivatives comprise the verbs of the First, Second, and Fourth

Conjugations, and some verbs of the Third Conjugation. They are all (except the Inchoatives and the Meditatives) formed with the suffix **io, ie** (**yo, ye**), which is added either to simple verbal stems, or to noun (16) stems already existing or presupposed. The **i** in **io, ie,** contracts with the preceding vowels **ā, ĕ, i, u,** leaving the ordinary forms of the regular conjugations. Certain categories of these verbs have obtained special names according to their various meanings:

The *Causatives*, formed by a change in the stem-vowel.

The *Desideratives*, formed by the addition of **-io** to *nōmina agentis* in **-tor**; afterwards a desiderative force was associated with the combination **-tor-io** (**-tar-io**), and it was applied indiscriminately.

The *Frequentatives* come originally probably from participial stems in **-to**; Latin developed also the suffix **-ito**; further, this being added again to **-to** gave rise to **-tito** (**-sito**).

The *Inchoatives*, formed by a special suffix, **-sco** (**sko**), are treated in conjugation as primitives belonging to the Third Conjugation.

The *Meditatives* have not been explained.

NOTE.—Theoretically the *Verbālia* are all *Dēnōminātīva*, but owing to the wide working of Analogy, it has been impossible in many cases, as in **amā-re, monē-re,** to discover an original noun; while in other cases, as the verbal is formed from a part of a denominative verb, it is convenient to retain the division.

191. A. *Verbālia* (derived from verb-stems, 190, N.):

1. ***Frequentatives*** or ***Intensives,*** denoting *repeated* or *intense Action.* These verbs end in **-tāre** (**-sāre**), **-itāre, -titāre** (**-sitāre**), and follow the supine stem (perfect passive form).

(*a*) **cantāre,** *sing;* compare **canō** (**cantum**): **cursāre,** *run to and fro;* compare **currō** (**cursum**): **dictāre,** *dictate;* compare **dīcō** (**dictum**): **dormītāre,** *be sleepy;* compare **dormiō** (**dormītum**): **habitāre,** *keep, dwell;* compare **habeō** (**habitum**): **pollicitārī,** *promise freely;* compare **polliceor** (**pollicitus**): **pulsāre,** *beat;* compare **pellō** (**pulsum**).

(*b*) **agitāre** (**ago**), **nōscitāre** (**nōscō**), **scīscitāre** (**scīscō**), **vīsitāre** (**vīsō**), **vocitāre** (**vocō**), **volitāre** (**volō**).

(*c*) **cantitāre** (**cantāre**), **dictitāre** (**dictāre**), **cursitāre** (**cursāre**).

NOTES.—1. The simple verb presupposed by the frequentative or intensive is often out of use, as in the case of: **gus-tāre,** *taste;* **hor-tārī,** *exhort.* The frequentative or intensive in **-tāre** is often out of use: **āctitāre,** *repeatedly* or *zealously agitate* (no **āctāre**), from **ago, āctum**: **lēctitāre,** *read carefully* (no **lēctāre**), from **legō, lēctum.**

2. The verbs of the Fourth Conjugation form no frequentatives except **dormiō,** *sleep,* **dormītō**; **mūniō,** *fortify,* **mūnītō** (rare); **saliō,** *leap,* **saltō**; **apertō,** *lay bare,* and **opertō,** *cover,* and compounds of **ventō** (**veniō,** *come*).

2. ***Inchoatives*** indicate *entrance upon an action.* For their formation see 133, V.

3. ***Desideratives*** denote *Desire* or *Tendency.* They are formed

by means of the suffix **-turiō** (**-suriō**) : **ēsurīre** (for **ed-t**), *to be sharp-set for eating, hungry ;* **ēm-p-turīre**, *to be all agog for buying.*

4. ***Causatives*** signify the *Effecting* of the *Condition* indicated by their original verb. They are found mainly in the Second Conjugation, and show usually a change in the stem-vowel.

Change : **cadere**, *fall*, and **caedere**, *fell ;* **liquēre**, *melt* (trans.), and **līquere**, *melt* (intr.) ; from root **men-** (as in **me-men-tō**) comes **monēre**, *remind ;* **necāre**, *kill*, and **nocēre**, *be death to ;* **placēre**, *please*, and **plācāre**, *cause to be pleased, appease ;* **sedēre**, *sit*, and **sēdāre**, *settle.*

No change ; **fugere**, *flee*, and **fugāre**, *put to flight ;* **iacere**, *throw*, and **iacēre**, (*lie*) *thrown ;* **pendere** (*hang*) *weigh*, and **pendēre**, *hang* (intr.).

5. ***Meditatives :*** (verbs that look forward to an action). These end in **-essere** : **arcessere**, *to summon ;* **capessere**, *to catch at ;* **facessere**, *to do eagerly ;* **incessere**, *to enter ;* **lacessere**, *to irritate* (136, 3, *b*).

192. B. *Denominatives* (derived from noun-stems) :

1. These are most commonly found in the First Conjugation, even though the stem-vowel of the noun is **i** or **u**.

(*a*) **acervā-re**, *heap up* (from **acervo-s**); **aestuā-re**, *seethe* (**aestu-s**) ; **corōnā-re**, *wreathe* (**corōna**) ; **levā-re**, *lighten* (**lev-i-s**) ; **maculā-re**, *besmirch* (**macula**) ; **nōminā-re**, *name* (**nōmen, nōmin-is**) ; **onerā-re**, *load* (**onus, oner-is**).

The Deponents signify *Condition, Employment :* **ancillā-rī**, *be maid* (**ancilla**) ; **aquā-rī**, *be a drawer of water* (**aqua**) ; **fūrā-rī**, *thieve* (**fūr**) ; **laetā-rī**, *be glad* (**laetu-s**).

(*b*) **albē-re**, *be white* (**albu-s**) ; **flōrē-re**, *be in bloom* (**flōs, flōris**) ; **frondē-re**, *be in leaf* (**frōns. frondi-s**) ; **lūcē-re**, *be light* (**lūx, lūc-is**).

(*c*) **argue-re** (*be bright, sharp*), *prove ;* **laede-re**, *hurt ;* **metue-re**, *be in fear* (**metu-s**).

(*d*) **cūstōdī-re**, *guard* (**cūstōs, cūstōd-is**) ; **fīnī-re**, *end* (**fīni-s**) ; **lēnī-re** *soften* (**lēni-s**) ; **vestī-re**, *clothe* (**vesti-s**).

3. Noteworthy are the *Diminutives* formed by the suffix **-illāre :** **st-illāre**, *drop* (**st-illa**) ; **scint-illare**, *sparkle* (**scint-illa**) ; **ōsc-illāre**, *to swing* (**ōsc-illum**). Similar in function but of different formation are **pullulāre**, *sprout* (**pul-lus**) ; **fodic-āre**, *punch* (**fodere**, *dig*) ; **albicāre**, *whiten* (**albu-s**).

NOTES.—1. The Denominatives of the First, Third, and Fourth Conjugations are regularly *transitive*, those of the Second Conjugation are regularly *intransitive*.

2. These verbs are often found only in combination with prepositions : **ab-undāre**, *run over, abound* (from **unda**, *wave*) ; **ac-cūsāre**, *accuse* (from **causa**, *case*) ; **ex-aggerāre**, *pile up* (from **agger**) ; **ex-stirpāre**, *root out* (**stirp-s**) ; **il-lūmināre**, *illumine* (from **lūmen, lūmin-is**).

B.—Compound Words.

I. FORMATION OF COMPOUND WORDS.

193. 1. By composition words are so put together that a new word is made with a signification of its own. The second word is regularly the fundamental word, the first the modifier.

NOTE.—Properly speaking, composition occurs only in the case of substantives, *i. e.*, where two or more simple stems come together. In verbs, there is either juxtaposition, where the parts still retain their original force, or the combination of a verb with a preposition. Broadly speaking, however, composition applies to all combinations of words.

2. Composition is either *proper* or *improper*.

194. *Substantive.*

In *Composition Improper* there are either traces of construction or the first part is still inflected: **ē-nōrmis** = **ex nōrmā**, *out of all rule*; **lēgis-lātor**, *lawgiver*; **Senātūs-cōnsultum**, *decree of the Senate.*

Many of these compounds have gradually become inflectional: **dēlīrus** (**dē-līra**), *crazy from fear*; **ēgregius** (**ē-grege**), *distinguished* (*from the crowd*); **prōcōnsul** (for **prō cōnsule**); **trium-vir** (from **trium virum**), *etc.*

NOTE.—From composition we must distinguish juxtaposition. So a preposition is brought into juxtaposition with a substantive, or a substantive with a substantive: **ad-modum**, *to a degree, very*; **ob-viam**, *in the way, meeting*; **ūsusfrūctus**, *usufruct*; **Iūppiter**, *Father Jove.* Noteworthy are the *Copulative* compounds; such are compound numerals like **ūn-decim, duo-decim,** *etc.*, and occasional others: **su-ove-taur-īlia,** *offerings of swine, sheep, and bulls.*

195. *Composition Proper.*

1. The first part of the compound may be a particle, as **ne-fār-iu-s,** *nefarious*; **vē-sānu-s,** *mad, out of one's sound senses*: or a substantive.

If it is a substantive—

(*a*) The stems in **-a, -o, -u** regularly weaken these vowels into **-i** before the consonants of the second part, which **i** may vanish: **causi-dicus,** *pleader, lawyer* (**causa**); **sīgni-fer,** *standard-bearer* (**sīgnu-m**); **corni-ger,** *horn-wearer* (**cornū**); **man-ceps** (**manu-** and **cap-**), *one who takes in hand, contractor.* The **i**-stems retain **i** or drop it: **īgni-vomu-s,** *fire-vomiting* (**īgni-s**); **nau-fragu-s,** *shipwrecked* (**nāvi-s**).

(*b*) Vowel-stems drop their vowel before the vowel of the second part: **māgn-animu-s,** *great-souled*; **ūn-animu-s,** *of one mind.*

(*c*) Consonant-stems either drop their consonants or add **i**: **homi-cīd-a,** *manslayer* (**homin-**); **lapi-cīd-a,** *stone-cutter* (**lapid-**); **mātr-i-cīd-a,** *mother-murderer, matricide.*

NOTE.—The first part is rarely, if ever, a verb. APULEIUS uses the form **pōsci-nummius.**

2. The second part of the composition is a noun : **tri-enn-iu-m,** *space of three years* (**annus**); **miseri-cor-s,** *tender-hearted* (**cor**).

When the second part ends in a vowel, it adapts itself, if an adjective, to changes of gender, as **flāvi-comus,** *yellow-haired* (**coma,** *hair*), but more often this final vowel becomes **i** and the adjective follows the third declension : **tri-rēmi-s,** *trireme* (**rēmu-s,** *oar*); **ab-nōrmi-s,** *abnormal* (**nōrma,** *norm*).

When the second part ends in a consonant, the last term usually undergoes no change : **bi-dēn-s,** *two-pronged ;* **simplex (sim-plec-s),** *simple.*

NOTE.—From **genus** (G. **generis**), is formed **dē-gener.**

II. SIGNIFICATION OF COMPOUNDS.

196. Compound substantives and adjectives are divided according to their signification into two main classes : Determinative and Possessive.

In Determinative compounds one of the terms is subordinate to the other. They fall into two classes : Attributive or Appositional, and Dependent.

197. 1. *Attributive compounds.* The first part is the attribute of the second.

The first word is, (1) a substantive : **āli-pēs,** *wing-foot(ed) ;* (2) an adjective : **māgn-animus,** *great-hearted ;* **lāti-fundium,** *large estate ;* (3) a numeral : **bi-enni-um** (*i. e.*, **spatium**), *space of two years.*

2. *Dependent compounds.* In these the second word is simply limited by the other, its signification not being altered.

(*a*) The first word is : (1) an adjective : **merī-diēs** (from **medī-diē** = **mediō diē**), *mid-day ;* (2) an adverb : **bene-ficus** (*well-doing*), *beneficent ;* **male-ficus,** *evil-doing ;* (3) a numeral : **ter-geminus,** *triple ;* (4) a particle : **dis-sonus,** *harsh-sounding ;* **per-māgnus,** *very large ;* **in-dīgnus,** *unworthy ;* (5) a verb-stem : **horr-i-ficus,** *horrible* (*horror-stirring*).

(*b*) The first word gives a case relation, such as (1) the Accusative : **armi-ger** = **arma gerēns,** *armour-bearer ;* **agri-cola** = **agrum colēns** (*land-tiller*), *husbandman ;* (2) the Genitive : **sōl-stitium** = **sōlis statiō** (*sun-staying*), *solstice ;* (3) the Locative : **aliēni-gena** (*born elsewhere*), *alien ;* (4) the Instrumental : **tībī-cen** = **tībiā canēns,** *flute-player.*

198. *Possessive Compounds* are adjectival only, and are so called because they imply the existence of a Subject possessing the quality indicated.

The first term is, (1) a substantive : **angui-manus,** (*having a*) *snake-hand* (*elephant*) : (2) an adjective : **flāvi-comus,** (*having*) *yellow hair ;* (3) a numeral : **bi-frōns,** (*having*) *two front*(*s*) *;* (4) a particle : **dis-cors,** *discordant ;* **in-ers,** *inactive.*

NOTE.—Notice that these divisions run into each other: thus **māgn-animus** is possessive, attributive, and dependent.

199. *Verb.*

In *Composition Improper* the verb is joined to a verb, substantive, or adverb. In *Composition Proper* the verb is combined with a preposition.

200. 1. *Composition Improper.*

(*a*) *Verb with verb:* This only takes place when the second part of the compound is **faciō** or **fīō** (173, N. 2). The first part of the compound is regularly an intransitive of the second conjugation: **cale-faciō, cale-fīō,** *warm, am warmed.*

(*b*) *Verb with substantive:* **anim-advertō = animum advertō,** *take notice;* **manū-mittō,** *set free;* **ūsū-capiō,** *acquire by use.*

(*c*) *Verb with adverb:* **bene-dīcō,** *bless;* **male-dīcō,** *curse;* **mālō, nōlō** (for **mage** (**magis**) **volō, ne- volō**), **satis-faciō,** *satisfy.*

2. *Composition Proper.*

The verb combines with separable or inseparable prepositions. Compare 413, R. 3.

(*a*) *With inseparable prepositions:* **amb-eō,** *go about;* **am-plector,** *enfold;* **an-hēlō,** *draw deep breath, pant;* **dis-currō,** *run apart;* **dir-imō,** 160, 1, and 715, R. 1; **por-tendō,** *hold forth, portend;* **red-dō,** *give back;* **re-solvō,** *resolve;* **sē-iungō,** *separate.*

(*b*) *With separable prepositions:* **ab-eō,** *go away;* **ad-eō,** *come up;* **ante-currō,** *run in advance;* **com-pōnō,** *put together;* **dē-currō,** *run down, finish a course;* **ex-cēdō,** *overstep;* **in-clūdō,** *shut in;* **ob-dūcō,** *draw over;* **per-agrō,** *wander through;* **post-habeō,** *keep in the background;* **prae-dīcō,** *foretell;* **praeter-eō,** *pass by;* **prōd-eō,** *go forth;* **prae-videō,** *foresee;* **sub-iciō,** *put under;* **subter-fugiō,** *flee from under;* **super-sum,** *remain over;* **trāns-gredior,** *pass beyond.*

SYNTAX.

201. SYNTAX treats of the formation and combination of sentences.

A sentence is the expression of a thought (**sententia**) in words.

Sentences are divided into *simple* and *compound.*

A simple sentence is one in which the necessary parts occur but once; for the compound sentence see 472.

The necessary parts of the sentence are *the subject* and *the predicate.*

The predicate is that which is said of the subject.

The subject is that of which the predicate is said.

Lūna fulget, *The moon shines.*

Lūna is the *subject;* **fulget,** the *predicate.*

REMARKS.—1. The Interjection (16, R. 2) and the Vocative case (23, 5) stand outside the structure of the sentence, and therefore do not enter as elements into Syntax, except that the Vocative is subject to the laws of Concord. See R. 3.

2. The Vocative differs from the Nominative in form in the second declension only, and even there the Nominative is sometimes used instead, especially in poetry and solemn prose.

Almae fīlius Māiae, H., *O.*, I. 2, 43; *son of mild Maia!* **Audī tū, populus Albānus,** L., I. 24, 7; *hear thou, people of Alba!*

Ō is prefixed to give emphasis to the address:

Ō fōrmōse puer, nimium nē crēde colōrī, V., *Ec.* 2, 17; *O shapely boy! trust not complexion all too much.*

The Vocative is commonly interjected in prose, except in highly emotional passages.

3. On the use of the Vocative of an adjective or participle in apposition, attribution, or predication, see 289, 325, R. 1.

SYNTAX OF THE SIMPLE SENTENCE.

202. The most simple form of the sentence is the finite verb: **su-m,** *I am;* **docē-s,** *thou teachest;* **scrībi-t,** *he writes*

REMARK.—Here the form contains in itself all the necessary elements (compare 114), the persons being indicated by the endings. From the expansion and modification of the finite verb arise all the complicated forms of the compound sentence.

203. SUBJECT.—The subject of the finite verb is always in the Nominative Case, or so considered.

REMARKS.—1. The subj. of the Inf. is in the Accusative (343, 2).

2. The use of the Nom. in Latin is the same as in English.

204. The subject may be a substantive or a pronoun, or some other word, phrase, or clause used as a substantive:

Deus mundum gubernat, GOD *steers the universe.* **Ego rēgēs ēiēcī,** [C.] *ad Her.*, IV. 53, 66; I *drove out kings.* **Sapiēns rēs adversās nōn timet,** THE SAGE *does not fear adversity.* **Victī in servitūtem rediguntur,** THE VANQUISHED *are reduced to slavery.* **Contendisse decōrum est,** OV., *M.*, IX. 6; TO HAVE STRUGGLED *is honourable.* **Māgnum beneficium [est] nātūrae quod necesse est morī,** SEN., *E.M.*, 101, 14; *it is a great boon of nature,* THAT WE MUST NEEDS DIE. **Vidēs habet duās syllabās,** (the word) "VIDES" *has two syllables.*

NOTES.—1. Masculine and feminine adjectives, and to a less degree participles, are used as substantives, but with the following limitations:

(*a*) Many adjectives in **-ārius** and **-icus** (the latter mostly Greek), designating *office* or *occupation*, and words expressing *friendship*, *kinship*, or other *relationship*, are used often as substantives both in the Sing. and the Pl. of the masculine and feminine: **aquārius,** *waterman;* **librārius,** *bookman (-seller, writer, etc.);* **grammaticus,** *grammarian;* **amīcus,** *friend;* **cōgnātus,** *kinsman;* **socius,** *partner.* Many of these have become almost wholly fixed as substantives, as **amīcus,** *friend.* See 16, N. 1.

(*b*) Adjectives are very often used as substantives in the masc. Pl. when they designate a *class:* **pauperēs,** *the poor;* **dīvitēs,** *the rich.* In the oblique cases of the Sing., this use is also not uncommon; but in the Nom. the substantive is generally expressed: **vir bonus,** *a good man;* **mulier peregrīna,** *a foreign woman.* So regularly, if used with a proper name: **Platō, doctissimus homŏ,** *the learned Plato.* Exceptions are rare and scattering in prose: **ego et suāvissimus Cicerō valēmus,** C., *Fam.*, XIV. 5, 1.

(*c*) On the use of participles as substantives see 437, N.

(*d*) When persons are not meant, a substantive is understood: **cānī (capillī),** *gray hairs;* **calida (aqua),** *warm water;* **dextra (manus),** *right hand.*

2. Neuter adjectives and participles are freely employed as substantives in both numbers; in the Pl. usually in Nom. and Acc., in the Sing. in all cases, but especially in connection with prepositions: **medium,** *the midst;* **extrēmum,** *the end;* **reliquom,** *the residue;* **futūrum,** *the future;* **bonum,** *good;* **bona,** *blessings, possessions;* **malum,** *evil;* **mala,** *misfortunes.* The Plural is frequently employed when the English idiom prefers the Singular: **vēra,** *the truth;* **omnia,** *everything.*

3. Adjectives of the Second Declension are sometimes used as neuter substantives in the Gen., after words of quantity or pronouns: **aliquid bonī,** *something good;* **nihil malī,** *nothing bad.* Adjectives of the Third Declension are thus employed only in combination with those of the Second, and even then very rarely (369, R. 1).

Usually the adjective of the Third Declension draws the adjective of the Second into its own construction: **Quid habet ista rēs aut laetābile aut glōriōsum?** C., *Tusc.*, I. 21, 49; *what is there to be glad of or to brag about in that?*

4. Instead of the neuter adjective, the word **rēs,** *thing*, is frequently used, especially in forms which are identical for different genders, and consequently ambiguous; so **bonārum rērum,** *of blessings*, rather than **bonōrum** (masc. and neut.).

5. In Latin the Pl. of abstract substantives occurs more frequently than in English; **adventūs imperātōrum,** *the arrival(s) of the generals* (because there were several generals, or because they arrived at different times). Pluralising abstract substantives often makes them concrete: **fortitūdinēs,** *gallant actions*; **formīdinēs,** *bugbears*; **īrae,** *quarrels*.

6. Other Pl. expressions to be noted are: **nivēs,** *snow(-flakes)*; **grandinēs,** *hail (-stones)*; **pluviae,** *(streams of) rain*; **līgna,** *(logs of) wood*; **carnēs,** *pieces of meat*; **aera,** *articles of bronze*; also symmetrical parts of the human body: **cervīcēs,** *neck*; **pectora,** *breast*.

The Pl. is freely used in poetry and in later prose: **Ōtia sī tollās, periēre Cupīdinis arcūs,** Ov., *Rem.Am.*, 139; *if you do away with holidays, Cupid's bow* (and arrows) *are ruined.*

7. The rhetorical Roman often uses the First Person Pl. for the First Person Singular. The usage originates in modesty, but mock modesty is the worst form of pomposity. It is never very common, and is not found before CICERO: **Librum ad tē dē senectūte mīsimus,** C., *Cat. M.*, 1, 3; *we* (I) *have sent you a treatise on old age.*

In poetry there is often an element of shyness; **Sitque memor nostrī necne, referte mihī,** Ov., *Tr.*, IV. 3, 10; *bring me back (word) whether she thinks of us* (me among others) *or no.*

8. (*a*) The Sing., in a collective sense, is also used for the Pl., but more rarely: **faba,** *beans*; **porcus,** *pig (meat)*; **gallīna,** *fowl* (as articles of food); **vestis,** *clothing.*

(*b*) The use of the Sing. in designations of nationalities and divisions of troops is introduced by LIVY: **Rōmānus,** *the Roman forces*; **Poenus,** *the Carthaginians*; **hostis,** *the enemy*; **mīles,** *the soldiery*; **pedes,** *the infantry*; **eques,** *the cavalry.*

205. PREDICATE and COPULA.—When the predicate is not in the form of a verb, but in the form of an adjective or substantive, or equivalent, the so-called copula is generally employed, in order to couple the adjective or substantive with the subject.

The chief copula is the verb **sum,** *I am.*

Fortūna caeca est, C., *Lael.*, 15, 54; *fortune is blind.* **Ūsus magister est optimus,** C., *Rab. Post.*, 4, 9; *practice is the best teacher.*

NOTE.—Strictly speaking, the copula is itself a predicate, as is shown by the trans lation when it stands alone or with an adverb: **est Deus,** *there is a God, God exists*; **rēctē semper erunt rēs,** *things will always be (go on) well*; **sīc vīta hominum est,** C., *Rosc. Am.*, 30, 84; *such is human life*; "*So runs the world away.*"

206. Other copulative verbs are: **vidērī,** *to seem;* **nāscī,** *to be born;* **fierī,** *to become;* **ēvādere,** *to turn out;* **creārī,** *to be created;* **dēligī,** *to be chosen;* **putārī,** *to be thought;* **habērī,** *to be held;* **dīcī,** *to be said;* **appellārī,** *to be called;* **nōminārī,** *to be named.* Hence the rule:

Verbs of *seeming, becoming,* with the passive of verbs of

making, choosing, showing, thinking, and *calling,* take **two** Nominatives, one of the subject, one of the predicate :

Nēmō nāscitur dīves, Sen., *E.M.*, 20, 13; *no one is born rich.* **Aristīdēs iūstus adpellātur,** *Aristides is called just.* [**Servius**] **rēx est dēclārātus,** L., I. 46, 1; *Servius was declared king.* [**Thūcȳdidēs**] **numquam est numerātus ōrātor,** C., *O.*, 9, 31 ; *Thucydides has never been accounted an orator.*

Remarks.—1. With **esse,** *serve as;* **vidērī,** *seem;* **habērī,** *be held;* **dūcī,** *be deemed,* and rarely with other verbs, instead of the Predicate Nom., a phrase may be employed, as : **prō** with Abl., (**in**) **locō, in numerō,** with Gen., *etc.*

Audācia prō mūrō habētur, S., *C.*, 58, 17 ; *boldness is counted as a bulwark.* **In fīliī locō,** C., *Red. in Sen.*, 14, 35 ; *as a son.*

2. The previous condition is given by **ex** or **dē** and the Abl. (396, n. 2).

Ex ōrātōre arātor factus, C., *Ph.*, III. 9, 22; *a pleader turned plowman.*

3. All copulative verbs retain the Nom. with the Inf. after auxiliary verbs (423).

Beātus esse sine virtūte nēmō potest, C., *N.D.*, I. 18, 48 ; *no one can be happy without virtue.*

4. On the Double Acc. after Active Verbs, see 340.

Notes.—1. The verbs mentioned, with some others, are found in good prose. Others are either poetical or unclassical, thus : **perhibērī,** *to be held,* is early ; **appārēre,** *to appear,* is poetic and post-classical for **vidērī**; **reddī** is *not* used for **fierī**; **sistī,** *to be set down,* is Plautine ; **manēre,** *to remain,* is late (**permanēre** once in Cicero).

2. Noteworthy is the use of **audīre,** like the Greek ἀκούειν, *to be called,* which is confined to Horace ; **rēxque paterque audīstī,** *Ep.*, I. 7, 38 ; *S.*, II. 6, 20, just as "hear" in this sense is said to be confined to Milton.

207. Subject Omitted.—The personal pronoun is not expressed in classical prose, unless it is emphatic, as, for example, in contrasts :

Amāmus parentēs, *We love* (*our*) *parents.* **Ego rēgēs ēiēcī, vōs tyrannōs intrōdūcitis,** [C.] *ad Her.*, IV. 53, 66 ; I *drove out kings,* ye *are bringing in tyrants.*

Note.—The insertion of the pronoun without emphasis is very common in the comic poets, and seems to have been a colloquialism. Also common in Catullus, Sallust (as an archaism), and Petronius.

208. Impersonal Verbs.—Impersonal Verbs are verbs in which the agent is regularly implied in the action, the subject in the predicate, so that the person is not expressed. Chief of these are :

1. Verbs pertaining to the state of the weather : **tonat,** *it thunders, the thunder thunders,* or rather, *the Thunderer thunders;* **fulget, fulgu-**

rat (less common), **fulminat** (poet.), *it lightens;* **pluit** (poet.), *it rains;* **ningit**, *it snows, etc.*

Nocte pluit tōtā, V., (POET. LAT. MIN., IV. 155, B.); *all night it (he, Jupiter) rains.*

NOTE.—The divine agent is sometimes expressed; so, naturally, in religious or popular language: **Iove tonante, fulgurante**, C., *Div.*, II. 18, 43; **Iove fulgente**, C., *N. D.*, II. 25, 65.

2. The passive of intransitive verbs is often used impersonally; so regularly of verbs which in the active are construed with the Dat. (217): **vīvitur**, *people live;* **curritur**, *there is a running;* **pūgnātur**, *there is a battle;* **mihi invidētur**, *I am envied.* The subject is contained in the verb itself: **sīc vīvitur = sīc vīta vīvitur**, *such is life;* **pūgnātur = pūgna pūgnātur**, *a battle is (being) fought.* In the same way explain **taedet**, *it wearies;* **miseret**, *it moves to pity;* **piget**, *it disgusts;* **pudet**, *it puts to shame.*

NOTES.—1. With all other so-called Impersonal Verbs an Inf. (422, 535) or an equivalent (523) is conceived as a subject: **Nōn lubet mihī dēplōrāre vītam**, C., *Cat. M.*, 23, 84. **Sed accidit perincommodē quod eum nūsquam vīdistī**, C., *Att.*, I. 17, 2.

2. Other uses coincide with the English. So the Third Person Pl. of verbs of Saying, Thinking, and Calling. Also the ideal Second Person Singular (258). To be noticed is the occasional use of **inquit**, *quoth he*, of an imaginary person, but not by CAESAR, SALLUST, or TACITUS: **Nōn concēdō, inquit, Epicūrō**, C., *Ac.*, II. 32, 101; *I do not yield the point, quoth he (one), to Epicurus.*

209. COPULA OMITTED.—**Est** or **sunt** is often omitted in saws and proverbs, in short statements and questions, in rapid changes, in conditional clauses, and in tenses compounded with participles:

Summum iūs summa iniūria, C., *Off.*, I. 10, 33; *the height of right (is) the height of wrong.* **Nēmo malus fēlīx**, JUV., IV. 8; *no bad man (is) happy.* **Quid dulcius quam habēre quīcum omnia audeās loquī?** C., *Lael.*, 7, 22; *what sweeter than to have some one with whom you can venture to talk about everything?* **Sed haec vetera; illud vērō recēns**, C., *Ph.*, II. 11, 25. **Aliquamdiū certātum**, S., *Iug.*, 74, 3. **Cūr hostis Spartacus, sī tū cīvis?** C., *Parad.*, 4, 30.

So also **esse**, with participles and the like:

Caesar statuit exspectandam clāssem, CAES., *B. G.*, III. 14, 1; *Caesar resolved that the fleet must be waited for.*

NOTES.—1. The omission of **esse** is not common with the Nom. and Infinitive.

2. Popular speech omits freely; so, **mīrum nī, mīrum quīn, factum**, in Latin comedy; likewise **potis** and **pote** for forms of **posse**. To a like origin are due **mīrum quantum, nimium quantum**, *etc.*, found at all periods.

3. The ellipsis of other forms of the copula is unusual. Thus CICERO occasionally omits **sit** in the Indirect Question, and TACITUS other forms of the Subjv. besides. **Fuisse** is omitted by LIVY, and not unfrequently by TACITUS.

4. The Ellipsis of **esse** was sometimes due to the desire of avoiding the heaping up

of Infinitives. Thus sentences like **nōn dubitō tē esse sapientem dīcere** (*to declare you to be wise*) were regularly cut down to **nōn dubitō tē sapientem dīcere** (*to declare you wise*).

5. The ellipsis of other verbs, such as **facere, īre, venīre, dīcere,** *etc.*, is characteristic of popular speech; it is therefore not uncommon in CICERO's letters (*ad Att.*), in PLINY's letters, and in works involving dialogue, such as CICERO's philosophical writings. The historians avoid it, and it never occurs in CAESAR and VELLEIUS.

CONCORD.

210. THE THREE CONCORDS.—There are three great concords in Latin:

1. The agreement of the predicate with the subject (211).
2. The agreement of attributive or appositive with the substantive (285, 321).
3. The agreement of the relative with antecedent (614).

211. Agreement of the Predicate with the Subject.

The verbal predicate agrees with its subject { in number and person.

The adjective predicate agrees with its subject { in number, gender, and case.

The substantive predicate agrees with its subject in case.

Substantīva mōbilia (21, 2) are treated as adjectives, and follow the number and gender of the subject.

Ego rēgēs ēiēcī, vōs tyrannōs intrōdūcitis, [C.] *ad Her.*, IV. 53, 66 (207). **Vērae amīcitiae sempiternae sunt,** C., *Lael.*, 9, 32; *true friendships are abiding.* **Dōs est decem talenta,** TER., *And.*, 950; *the dowry is ten talents.* **Ūsus magister est optimus,** C., *Rab. Post.*, 4, 9 (205). **Arx est monosyllabum,** "*Arx*" *is a monosyllable.* Compare **Īgnis cōnfector est et cōnsūmptor omnium,** C., *N.D.*, II. 15, 41; *fire is the doer-up* (*destroyer*) *and eater-up* (*consumer*) *of everything,* with **cōnfectrīx rērum omnium vetustās,** C., *Frag.*

REMARKS.—1. The violation of the rules of agreement is due chiefly to one of two causes; *either* the natural relation is preferred to the artificial (**cōnstrūctiō ad sēnsum, per synesin,** *according to the sense*), *or* the nearer is preferred to the more remote. Hence the following

EXCEPTIONS.—(*a*) Substantives of multitude often take the predicate in the Plural: **pars,** *part*; **vīs** (*power*), *quantity*; **multitūdō,** *crowd*; organized bodies more rarely. Also, but not often, such words as **quisque, uterque, nēmō,** *etc.*

Pars māior recēperant sēsē, L., XXXIV. 47, 6; *the greater part had retired.* **Omnis multitūdō abeunt,** L., XXIV. 3, 15; *all the crowd depart.*

Māgna vīs ēminus missa tēlōrum multa nostrīs vulnera īnferēbant, Caes., *B.C.*, II. 6, 5. **Uterque eōrum ex castrīs exercitum ēdūcunt**, Caes., *B.C.*, III. 30, 3.

Note.—This usage is very common in comedy, but extremely rare in model prose. Livy shows a greater variety and a larger number of substantives than any other author, and poets and late prose writers are free. Yet Horace uses regularly the Sing. with a collective, while Vergil varies, often employing first a Sing. and then a Pl. verb with the same substantive (as *A.*, II. 64). Tacitus often uses **quisque** with a Plural.

(*b*) The adjective predicate often follows the natural gender of the subject; so especially with **mīlia.** This usage belongs pre-eminently to the historians.

Capita coniūrātiōnis virgīs caesī (sunt), L., x. 1, 3; *the heads of the conspiracy were flogged.* **Samnītium caesī tria mīlia**, *Cf.* L., x. 34, 3; *of the Samnites* (*there*) *were slain three thousand.*

The passive verb often agrees in gender with the predicate: **Nōn omnis error stultitia dīcenda est**, C., *Div.*, II. 43, 90; *not every false step is to be called folly.*

(*c*) The copula often agrees with the number of the predicate ("the wages of sin *is* death"):

Amantium īrae (204, N. 5) **amōris integrātiō est**, Ter., *And.*, 555; *lovers' quarrels are love's renewal.*

2. A superlative adjective defined by a Partitive Gen. follows the gender of the subj. when it precedes:

Indus, quī est omnium flūminum māximus, C., *N.D.*, II. 52, 130; *the Indus, which is the greatest of all rivers.*

Otherwise it follows the Genitive; but this usage is post-classic:

Vēlōcissimum omnium animālium est delphīnus, Plin., *N.H.*, IX. 8, 20; *the dolphin is the swiftest of all animals.*

3. The Voc. is sometimes used by the poets in the predicate, either by anticipation or by assimilation. (See 325, R. 1.)

4. The neuter adjective is often used as the substantive predicate of a masculine or feminine subject:

Trīste lupus stabulīs, V., *Ec.*, 3, 80; *the wolf is a baleful thing to the folds.* **Varium et mūtābile semper fēmina**, V., *A.*, IV. 569; *"a thing of moods and fancies" is woman ever.*

This construction is poetical; in Cicero it is used with a few words only; such as **extrēmum, commūne**:

Omnium rērum (204, N. 4) **mors** [est] **extrēmum**, *Cf.* C., *Fam.*, VI. 21, 1; *death is the end of all things.*

5. The demonstrative pronoun is commonly attracted into the gender of the predicate:

Negat Epicūrus; hōc enim vostrum lūmen est, C., *Fin.*, II. 22, 70; *Epicurus says No; for he is your great light.* **Ea nōn media sed nūlla via est**, L., XXXII., 21, 33; *that is not a middle course, but no course at all.*

F

But in negative sentences, and when the pronoun is the predicate, there is no change. So in definitions :

Quid aut quāle [**est**] **Deus ?** *Cf.* C., *N.D.*, I. 22, 60 ; *what or what manner of thing is God ?* **Nec sopor illud erat,** V., *A.*, III. 173. **Quod ita erit gestum, id lēx erit,** C., *Ph.*, I. 10, 26.

Exceptions are but apparent. C., *O.*, II. 38, 157.

6. The adjective predicate sometimes agrees with a substantive in apposition to the subject. So especially when the appositive is **oppidum, cīvitās,** and the like :

Coriolī oppidum captum [**est**], L., II. 33, 9 ; *Corioli-town was taken.* **Corinthum, tōtīus Graeciae lūmen, exstinctum esse voluērunt,** C., *Imp.*, 5, 11 ; *they would have Corinth, the eye of all Greece, put out.*

NOTES.—1. Peculiar is the occasional use of the Fut. participle in **-ūrum** for feminines in early Latin : **Alterō (gladiō) tē occīsūrum ait (Casina), alterō vīlicum.** PL., *Cas.*, 693. So *Truc.*, 400.

2. **Age** is often used in early Latin as if it were an adverb, with the Plural ; occasionally also **cavĕ : Age modo fabricāminī.** PL., *Cas.*, 488.

Akin is the use of a Voc. Sing. with a Pl. verb, which is occasionally found in classical prose also : **Tum Scaevola ; quid est, Cotta ? inquit, quid tacētis ?** C., *O.*, I. 35, 160.

The use of **aliquis,** *some one of you*, in this way is early : **Aperīte aliquis āctūtum ōstium,** TER., *Ad.*, 634.

3. Other less usual constructions **ad sēnsum** are : the use of a neuter demonstrative where a substantive of a different gender is expected, and the construction of **rēs** as if it were neuter (both found also in CICERO) ; the neuter Singular summing up a preceding Plural :

In Graeciā mūsicī floruērunt, dīscēbantque id (*that* [*accomplishment*]) **omnēs,** C., *Tusc.*, I. 2, 4. **Servitia repudiābat, cūius** (*of which* [*class*]) **initiō ad eum māgnae cōpiae concurrēbant,** S., *C.*, 56, 5. See also C., *Div.*, II. 57, 117.

Forms of the Verbal Predicate.

VOICES OF THE VERB.

212. There are two Voices in Latin—Active and Passive.

REMARK.—The Latin Passive corresponds to the Greek Middle, and, like the Greek Middle, may be explained in many of its uses as a Reflexive.

213. ACTIVE.—The Active Voice denotes that the *action proceeds from the subject.* Verbs used in the Active Voice fall into two classes, as follows :

Verbs are called *Transitive* when their action *goes over* to an object (**trānseō,** *I go over*) ; *Intransitive* when their action *does not go beyond* the subject : **occīdere,** *to fell = to kill* (Transitive) ; **occidere,** *to fall* (Intransitive).

REMARK.—Properly speaking, a Transitive Verb in Latin is one that forms a personal passive, but the traditional division given above has its convenience, though it does not rest upon a difference of nature, and a verb may be trans. or intrans. according to its use. So

(*a*) Transitive verbs are often used intransitively, in which case they serve simply to characterize the agent. This is true especially of verbs of *movement;* as **dēclīnāre, inclīnāre, movēre, mūtāre, vertere,** and the like, and is found at all periods.

(*b*) On the other hand, many intrans. verbs are often used transitively. This occurs also at all periods, but the Acc. is usually the *inner* object (332).

(*c*) On the use of the Inf. active, where English uses the passive, see 532, N. 2.

214. PASSIVE.—The Passive Voice denotes that the *subject receives the action* of the verb.

The instrument is put in the Ablative.

Virgīs caedētur, C., *Verr.*, III. 28, 69 ; *he shall be beaten with rods.* **[Īgnis] lūmine prōditur suō,** Ov., *Her.*, 15, 8 ; *the fire is betrayed by its own light.*

The agent is put in the Ablative with **ab (ā).**

Ab amīcīs prōdimur, C., *Cluent.*, 52, 143 ; *we are betrayed by friends.* **Virgīs caesī tribūnī ab lēgātō sunt,** L., XXIX. 18, 13 ; *the tribunes were beaten with rods by the lieutenant.*

REMARKS.—1. Intrans. verbs of passive signification are construed as passives : **famĕ perīre,** C., *Inv.*, II. 57, 172, *to perish of hunger.* So **vēnīre,** *to be sold;* **vāpulāre** (chiefly vulgar), *to be beaten,* **ab aliquō,** *by some one.*

Ab reō fūstibus [vāpulāvit], *Cf.* QUINT., IX. 2, 12; *he was whacked with cudgels by the defendant.* **Salvēbis ā meō Cicerōne,** C., *Att.*, VI. 2, 10 ; *greeting to you from Cicero.*

2. When the instrument is considered as an agent, or the agent as an instrument, the constructions are reversed :

Vincī ā Voluptāte, C., *Off.*, I. 20, 68 ; *to be overcome by Dame Pleasure.* **Patriciīs iuvenibus saepserant latera,** L., III. 37, 6 ; *they had flanked him with a guard of patrician youths.*

The latter construction is very rare in CICERO, and seems to belong pre-eminently to the historians.

Animals, as independent agents, are treated like persons.

Ā cane nōn māgnō saepe tenētur aper, Ov., *Rem.Am.*, 422 ; *a boar is often held fast by a little dog.*

Animals, as instruments, are treated like things.

Compare **equō vehī,** *to ride a horse* (*to be borne by a horse*), with **in equō,** *on horseback.*

215. The person in whose interest an action is done is put in the Dative. Hence the frequent inference that the person interested is the agent. See 354.

1. With the Perfect passive it is the *natural* inference, and common in prose.

Mihĭ rēs tōta prōvīsa est, C., *Verr.*, IV. 42, 91; *I have had the whole thing provided for.* **Carmina nūlla mihī sunt scrīpta**, Ov., *Tr.*, V. 12, 35; *poems—I have none written* (I have written no poems).

2. With the Gerundive it is the *necessary* inference, and the Dative is the reigning combination.

Nihil [est] hominī tam timendum quam invidia, C., *Cluent.*, 3, 7; *there is nothing that one has to fear to the same extent as envy.*

216. The Direct Object of the Active Verb (the Accusative Case) becomes the Subject of the Passive.

Alexander Dārēum vīcit, *Alexander conquered Darius.*

Dārēus ab Alexandrō victus est, *Darius was conquered by Alexander.*

217. The Indirect Object of the Active Verb (Dative Case) cannot be properly used as the Subject of the Passive. The Dative remains unchanged, and the verb becomes a Passive in the Third Person Singular (Impersonal Verb). This Passive form may have a neuter subject corresponding to the Inner object (333, 1).

Active: **Miserī invident bonīs**, *The wretched envy the well-to-do.*

Passive: **mihĭ invidētur**, *I am envied*,
tibĭ invidētur, *thou art envied*,
eī invidētur, *he is envied*,
nōbīs invidētur, *we are envied*,
vōbīs invidētur, *you are envied*,
iīs invidētur, *they are envied*,
} **ab aliquō**, *by some one.*

Nihil facile persuādētur invītīs, QUINT., IV. 3, 10; *people are not easily persuaded of anything against their will.* **Ānulīs nostrīs plūs quam animīs crēditur**, SEN., *Ben.*, III. 15, 3; *our seals are more trusted than our souls*

REMARKS.—1. In like manner a Gen. or Abl. in dependence upon an active verb cannot be made the subj. of the passive.

2. On the exceptional usage of personal Gerundives from intrans. verbs see 427, N. 5.

NOTES.—1. The poets and later prose writers sometimes violate the rule, under Greek influence or in imitation of early usage: **Cūr invideor?** (for **cūr invidētur mihĭ?**), H., *A.P.*, 56; **vix equidem crēdar**, Ov., *Tr.*, III. 10, 35; **persuāsus vidētur**

esse, [C.] *ad Her.*, I. 6, 9. (**Persuādeō hospitem,** Petr., 62, 2, is perhaps an intentional solecism.)

2. Similar liberties are taken by poets and late prose writers with the passive of other intrans. verbs, such as **concēdere, permittere, praecipere, prōnūntiāre**: **Fātīs numquam concēssa** (= **cuī concēssum est**) **movērī Camarīna,** V., *A.*, III. 700.

218. Reflexive.—Reflexive relations, when emphatic, are expressed as in English:

Omne animal sē ipsum dīligit, C., *Fin.*, V. 9, 24, *Every living creature loves itself.*

But when the reflexive relation is more general, the passive (middle) is employed: **lavor,** *I bathe, I bathe myself.*

Pūrgārī [**nequīvērunt**], *Cf.* L., XXIV. 18, 4; *they could not clear themselves.* **Cum in mentem vēnit, pōnor ad scrībendum,** C., *Fam.*, IX. 15, 4; *when the notion strikes me I set myself to writing.*

Note.—Some of these verbs approach the deponents, in that the reflexive meaning of the passive extends also to some active forms; thus, from **vehor,** *I ride*, we get the form **vehēns,** *riding* (rare): **Adulēscentiam per mediās laudēs quasi quadrīgīs vehentem,** C., *Br.*, 97, 331.

219. As the active is often used to express what the subject suffers or causes to be done, so the passive in its reflexive (middle) sense is often used to express an action which the subject suffers or causes to be done to itself: **trahor,** *I let myself be dragged;* **tondeor,** *I have myself shaved.*

Duōs Mȳsōs [**īnsuistī**] **in cūleum,** *Cf.* C., *Q.F.*, I. 2, 2, 5; *you sewed two Mysians into a sack* (*had them sewn*). **Sine gemitū adūruntur,** C., *Tusc.*, V. 27, 77; *they let themselves be burned without a moan.* **Dīruit, aedificat,** H., *Ep.*, I. 1, 100; *he is pulling down, he is building.* **Ipse docet quid agam; fās est et ab hoste docērī,** Ov., *M.*, IV. 428; *he himself teaches* (*me*) *what to do; it is* (*but*) *right to let oneself be taught even by an enemy* (*to take a lesson from a foe*).

220. Deponent.—The Deponent is a passive form which has lost, in most instances, its passive (or reflexive) signification. It is commonly translated as a transitive or intransitive active: **hortor,** *I am exhorting* (trans.); **morior,** *I am dying* (intrans.).

Notes.—1. A number of intrans. verbs show also a Perfect Part. passive used actively; not, however, in classical prose combined with **esse** to take the place of the regular Perfect. On the use of such participles as substantives, see 167, N. 1.

Quid causae excōgitārī potest, cur tē lautum voluerit, cēnātum nōluerit occīdere? C., *Dei.*, 7, 20.

2. Many verbs show both active and deponent forms side by side. **In this case the active forms belong more often to early authors. See 163–167.**

221. RECIPROCAL.—Reciprocal relations (*"one another"*) are expressed by **inter,** *among,* and the personal pronouns, **nōs,** *us;* **vōs,** *you;* **sē,** *themselves.* **Inter sē amant,** *They love one another.*

REMARKS.—1. Combinations of **alter alterum, alius alium, uterque alterum,** and the like, also often give the reciprocal relation: sometimes there is a redundancy of expression.

Placet Stōicīs hominēs hominum causā esse generātōs, ut ipsī inter sē aliī aliīs prōdesse possent, C., *Off.*, I. 7, 22; *it is a tenet of the Stoics that men are brought into the world for the sake of men, to be a blessing to one another.*

2. Later writers use **invicem** or **mūtuō, inter sē, vicissim**; and early Latin shows occasionally **uterque utrumque.**

Quae omnia hūc spectant, ut invicem ārdentius dīligāmus, PLIN., *Ep.*, VII. 20, 7; *all these things look to our loving one another more fervently.* **Uterque utrīquest cordī,** TER., *Ph.*, 800; *either is dear to other.*

TENSES.

222. The Tenses express the relations of time, embracing:

1. The stage of the action (duration in time).
2. The period of the action (position in time).

The first tells whether the action is *going on,* or *finished.* The second tells whether the action is *past, present,* or *future.*

Both these sets of relations are expressed by the tenses of the Indicative or Declarative mood—less clearly by the Subjunctive.

223. There are six tenses in Latin:

1. The *Present,* denoting *continuance* in the *present.*
2. The *Future,* denoting *continuance* in the *future.*
3. The *Imperfect,* denoting *continuance* in the *past.*
4. The *Perfect,* denoting *completion* in the *present.*
5. The *Future Perfect,* denoting *completion* in the *future.*
6. The *Pluperfect,* denoting *completion* in the *past.*

224. An action may further be regarded simply as *attained,* without reference to its *continuance* or *completion.* *Continuance* and *completion* require a point of reference for definition; *attainment* does not. This gives rise to the aoristic or *indefinite* stage of the action, which has no especial tense-form. It is expressed by the Present tense for the present; by the Future and Future Perfect tenses for the future; and by the Perfect tense for the past.

Of especial importance are the *Indefinite* or *Historical* Present and the *Indefinite* or *Historical* Perfect (Aorist), which differ materially in syntax from the *Definite* or *Pure* Present and Perfect.

225. The Tenses are divided into *Principal* and *Historical*. The *Principal Tenses* have to do with the Present and Future. The *Historical Tenses* have to do with the Past.

The Present, Pure Perfect, Future, and Future Perfect are *Principal Tenses.*

The Historical Present, Imperfect, Pluperfect, and Historical Perfect are *Historical Tenses.*

The Historical Tenses are well embodied in the following distich:

> **Tālia tentābat, sīc et tentāverat ante,**
> **Vixque dedit victās ūtilitāte manūs.** Ov., *Tr.*, I. 3, 87.

226. Table of Temporal Relations.

INDICATIVE MOOD.

ACTIVE.

	Continuance.	*Completion.*	*Attainment.*
PRES.	**scrībō,** *I am writing.*	**scrīpsī,** *I have written.*	**scrībō,** *I write.*
FUT.	**scrībam,** *I shall be writing.*	**scrīpserō,** *I shall have written.*	**scrībam (scrīpserō),** *I shall write.*
PAST.	**scrībēbam,** *I was writing.*	**scrīpseram,** *I had written.*	**scrīpsī,** *I wrote.*

PASSIVE.

	Continuance.	*Completion.*	*Attainment.*
PRES.	**scrībitur (epistula),** *The letter is written (writing).*	**scrīpta est,** *has been written, is written.*	**scrībitur,** *is written.*
FUT.	**scrībētur,** *The letter will be written (writing).*	**scrīpta erit,** *will have been, will be written.*	**scrībētur,** *will be written.*
PAST.	**scrībēbātur,** *The letter was written (writing).*	**scrīpta erat.** *had been written, was written.*	**scrīpta est,** *was written.*

REMARK.—The English passive is ambiguous. The same form is currently used for continuance, attainment, and completion. The context alone can decide. A convenient test is the substitution of the active.

A letter was written : { Continuance, *Some one was writing* a letter.
Completion, *Some one had written* a letter.
Attainment, *Some one wrote* a letter. }

Present Tense.

227. The Present Tense is used as in English of *that which is going on now* (Specific Present), and of statements *that apply to all time* (Universal Present).

Specific Present:

Auribus teneō lupum, TER., *Ph.*, 506; *I am holding a wolf by the ears.*

Universal Present:

Probitās laudātur et alget, JUV., I. 74; *honesty is bepraised and freezes.* **Dulce et decōrum est prō patriā morī,** H., *O.*, III. 2, 13; *sweet and seemly 'tis to die for fatherland.*

So regularly of the quoted views of authors, the inscriptions of books, etc.:

Dē iuvenum amōre scrībit Alcaeus, C., *Tusc.*, IV. 33, 71; *Alcaeus writes concerning the love of youths.*

NOTES.—1. The Specific Pr. is often to be translated by the English Progressive Present. The Universal Pr. is Aoristic, true at any point of time.

2. As continuance involves the notion of incompleteness the Pr. (see 233) is used of *attempted* and *intended* action (Present of Endeavor). But on account of the double use of the Pr. this signification is less prominent and less important than in the Impf. Do not mistake the Endeavor which lies in the *verb* for the Endeavor which lies in the *tense.*

Perīculum vītant, C., *Rosc.Am.*, I. 1; *they are trying to avoid danger.* In the example sometimes cited: **Quīntus frāter Tūsculānum vēnditat,** C., *Att.*, I. 14, 7; *Brother Quintus is "trying to sell" his Tusculan villa;* **vēnditāre** itself means *to offer for sale.* Translate: *intends to offer for sale,* if the notion lies in the Tense.

3. The Pr. when used with a negative often denotes *Resistance to Pressure* (233); this is, however, colloquial: **Tacē: nōn taceō,** PL., *Cas.*, 826; *keep quiet!* I WON'T.

4. The ambiguity of our English passive often suggests other translations. Use and Wont make Law; hence the frequent inference that what is done is what ought to be done; what is not done is not to be done: **(Deus) nec bene prōmeritīs capitur, nec tangitur īrā,** LUCR., II. 651; *God is not to be inveigled by good service, nor touched by anger.*

228. The Present Tense is used more rarely than in English *in anticipation of the future,* chiefly in compound sentences:

Sī vincimus, omnia tūta erunt, S., *C.*, 58, 9; *if we conquer* (= *shall conquer*) *everything will be safe.* **Antequam ad sententiam redeō dē mē pauca dīcam,** C., *Cat.*, IV. 10, 20; *before I return to the subject, I will* *say a few things of myself.* **Exspectābō dum venit**, TER., *Eun.*, 206; *I will wait all the time that he is coming*, or, *until he comes.*

NOTES.—1. This construction is archaic and familiar. It is very common in the Comic Poets, very rare in CICERO and CAESAR, but more common later. Some usages have become phraseological, as **sī vīvō**, *if I live, as I live.*

2. On the Pr. Indic. for the Deliberative Subjv., see 254, N. 2.

229. The Present Tense is used far more frequently than in English, *as a lively representation of the past* (Historical Present):

Cohortīs incēdere iubet, S., *C.*, 60, 1; *he orders the cohorts to advance.* **Mātūrat proficīscī**, CAES., *B. G.*, I. 7, 1; *he hastens to depart.*

REMARK.—**Dum**, *while* (*yet*), commonly takes a Pr., which is usually referred to this head. **Dum**, *so long as*, follows the ordinary law, 571, ff.

Dum haec in colloquiō geruntur, Caesarī nūntiātum est, CAES., *B. G.*, I. 46, 1; *while these things were transacting in the conference, word was brought to Caesar.*

230. The Present is used in Latin of actions *that are continued into the present*, especially with **iam**, *now*; **iam diū**, *now for a long time*; **iam prīdem**, *now long since.* In English we often translate by a Progressive Perfect.

(Mithridātēs) annum iam tertium et vīcēsimum rēgnat, C., *Imp.*, 3, 7; *Mithridates has been reigning now going on twenty-three years.* **Līberāre vōs ā Philippō iam diū magis vultis quam audētis**, L., XXXII. 21, 36; *you have this long time had the wish rather than* (= *though not*) *the courage to deliver yourselves from Philip.*

"How does your honor for this many a day?" SHAK., *Ham.*, III. 1, 91.

NOTES.—1. The Pr. sometimes gives the resulting condition:

Quī mortem nōn timet, māgnum is sibĭ praesidium ad beātam vītam comparat, C., *Tusc.*, II. 1, 2; *he who fears not death gets for himself great warrant for a happy life.* **(Dīcunt) vincere** (= **victōrem esse**) **bellō Rōmānum**, L., II. 7, 2.

2. More free is this usage in the poets, sometimes under Greek influence:

Auctōre Phoebō gīgnor (γίγνομαι = γόνος εἰμί); **haud generis pudet.** SEN., *Ag.*, 295.

VERGIL is especially prone to use a Pr. after a Past, denoting by the Past the *cause*, by the Pr. the *effect*: **Postquam altum tenuēre ratēs nec iam amplius ūllae adpārent terrae**, *A.*, III. 192.

Imperfect Tense.

231. The Imperfect Tense denotes *continuance in the past*: **pūgnābam**, *I was fighting.*

The Imperfect is employed to represent *manners, customs, situations*; to describe and to particularise. A good example is TER., *And.*, 74 ff.

The Imperfect and the Historical Perfect serve to illustrate one another. The Imperfect dwells on the *process;* the Historical Perfect states the *result.* The Imperfect counts out the *items;* the Historical Perfect gives the *sum.* A good example is NEP., II. 1, 3.

232. The two tenses are often so combined that the general statement is given by the Historical Perfect, the particulars of the action by the Imperfect:

(Verrēs) in forum vēnit; ārdēbant oculī; tōtō ex ōre crūdēlitās ēminēbat, C., *Verr.*, v. 62, 161; *Verres came into the forum, his eyes were blazing, cruelty was standing out from his whole countenance.*

233. The Imperfect is used of *attempted* and *interrupted, intended* and *expected* actions (*Imperfect of Endeavor*). It is the Tense of *Disappointment* and (with the negative) of *Resistance to Pressure.* (Mere negation is regularly Perfect.)

Cūriam relinquēbat, TAC., *Ann.*, II. 34, 1; *he was for leaving the senate-house.* [**Lēx**] **abrogābātur,** *Cf.* L., XXXIV. 1, 7; *the law was to be abrogated.* **Simul ostendēbātur** (*an attempt was made to show*) **quōmodo cōnstitūtiōnem reperīrī oportēret,** [C.] *ad Her.*, II. 1, 2. **Dīcēbat** (positive) **melius quam scrīpsit** (negative) **Hortēnsius,** C., *Or.*, 38, 132; *Hortensius spoke better than he wrote.* **Aditum nōn dabat,** NEP., IV. 3, 3; *he* WOULD *not grant access* (**dedit,** DID *not*). See also MART., XI. 105.

NOTES.—1. The Impf. as the Tense of Evolution is a Tense of Vision. But in English, Impf. and Hist. Pf. coincide; hence the various translations to put the reader in the place of the spectator.

2. The continuance is in the mind of the narrator; it has nothing to do with the absolute duration of the action. The mind may dwell on a rapid action or hurry over a slow one. With definite numbers, however large, the Hist. Pf. must be used, unless there is a notion of continuance into another stage (overlapping).

(Gorgiās) centum et novem vīxit annōs, QUINT., III. 1, 9; *Gorgias lived one hundred and nine years.* **Biennium ibi perpetuom misera illum tulī,** TER., *Hec.*, 87; *I bore him there—poor me!—for two long years together.*

3. As the Tense of Disappointment, the Impf. is occasionally used, as in Greek, to express a startling appreciation of the real state of things (*Imperfect of Awakening*). Greek influence is not unlikely.

Tū aderās, TER., *Ph.*, 858; (so it turns out that) *you were here* (all the time). **Peream male sī nōn optimum erat,** H., *S.*, II. 1, 6; *perdition catch me if that was not the best course* (*after all*).

Hence the modal use of **dēbēbam** and **poteram** (254, R. 2).

234. The Imperfect is used as the English Pluperfect, which often takes a progressive translation; especially with **iam, iam diū, iam dūdum.**

Iam dūdum tibi adversābar, Pl., *Men.*, 420; *I had long been opposing you.* **(Archiās) domicilium Rōmae multōs iam annōs [habēbat]**, *Cf.* C., *Arch.*, 4, 7; *Archias had been domiciled at Rome now these many years.*

Remark.—As the Hist. Pr. is used in lively *narrative*, so the Hist. Inf. is used in lively *description*, parallel with the Imperfect (647).

Perfect Tense.

The Perfect Tense has two distinct uses:

1. Pure Perfect. 2. Historical Perfect (Aorist).

1. PURE PERFECT.

235. The Pure Perfect Tense expresses completion in the Present, and hence is sometimes called the Present Perfect.

1. The Pure Perfect differs from the Historical Perfect, in that the Pure Perfect gives from the point of view of the Present an instantaneous view of the development of an action from its origin in the Past to its completion in the Present, that is, it looks at both ends of an action, and the time between is regarded as a Present. The Historical Perfect obliterates the intervening time and contracts beginning and end into one point in the Past.

2. An intermediate usage is that in which the Perfect denotes an action in the Past (Historical), whose effect is still in force (Pure).

236. Accordingly, the Perfect is used:

1. Of an action that is now *over and gone.*

Vīximus, C., *Fam.*, XIV. 4, 5; *we have lived* (*life for us has been*). **Fīlium ūnicum habeō, īmmo habuī**, Ter., *Heaut.*, 94; *I have an only son—nay, have had an only son.* **Tempora quid faciunt: hanc volo, tē voluī**, Mart., VI. 40, 4; *what difference times make!* (Time IS) *I want* HER, (Time HAS BEEN) *I wanted* YOU.

2. Far more frequently of the present result of a more remote action (*resulting condition*):

Equum et mūlum Brundisiī tibĭ relīquī, C., *Fam.*, XVI. 9, 3; *I have left a horse and mule for you at Brundusium*—(they are still there). **Perdidī spem quā mē oblectābam**, Pl., *Rud.*, 222; *I've lost the hope with which I entertained myself.* **Āctumst, perīstī**, Ter., *Eun.*, 54; *it is all over; you're undone.*

Remark.—The Pure Pf. is often translated by the English Present: **nōvī**, *I have become acquainted with, I know*; **meminī**, *I have recalled, I remember*; **ōdī**, *I have conceived a hatred of, I hate*; **cōnsuēvī**, *I have made it a rule, I am accustomed, etc.*

Ōdērunt hilarem trīstēs trīstemque iocōsī, H., *Ep.*, I. 18, 89; *the long-faced hate the lively man, the jokers hate the long-faced man.*

But the Aorist force is sometimes found:

Tacē, inquit, ante hōc nōvī quam tū nātus es, PHAED., V. 9, 4; *silence, quoth he, I knew this ere that you were born.*

NOTE.—The Pf. is used of that which has been and shall be (Sententious or Gnomic Perfect, 242, N. 1), but usually in poetry, from CATULLUS on, and frequently with an indefinite adjective or adverb of number or a negative. It is seldom an Aorist (Greek).

Ēvertēre domōs tōtās optantibus ipsīs dī facilēs, JUV., X. 7; *whole houses at the masters' own request the (too) compliant gods o'erturn.* **Nēmo repente fuit turpissimus**, JUV., II. 83; *none of a sudden (hath ever) reach(ed) the depth of baseness.*

237. As the Present stands for the Future, so the Perfect stands for the Future Perfect.

(Brūtus) sī cōnservātus erit, vīcimus, C., *Fam.*, XII. 6, 2; *Brutus!—if* HE *is saved, we are victorious, we (shall) have gained the victory.*

238. Habeō or **teneō**, *I hold, I have,* with the Accusative of the Perfect Participle Passive, is not a mere circumlocution for the Perfect, but lays peculiar stress on the *maintenance of the result.*

Habeō statūtum, *Cf.* C., *Verr.*, III. 41, 95; *I have resolved, and hold to my resolution.* **Perspectum habeō**, *Cf.* C., *Fam.*, III. 10, 7; *I have perceived, and I have full insight.* **Excūsātum habeās mē rogo, cēno domī**, MART., II. 79, 2; *I pray you have me excused, I dine at home.*

2. HISTORICAL PERFECT.

239. The Historical or Indefinite Perfect (Aorist) states a *past action, without reference to its duration, simply as a thing attained.*

Milō domum vēnit, calceōs et vestīmenta mūtāvit, paulīsper commorātus est, C., *Mil.*, 10, 28; *Milo came home, changed shoes and garments, tarried a little while.* **(Gorgiās) centum et novem vīxit annōs**, QUINT., III. 1, 9 (233, N. 2). **Vēnī, vīdī, vīcī**, SUET., *Iul.*, 37; *I came, saw, overcame.*

NOTE.—The Pf., as the "short hand" for the Plupf., is mainly post-Ciceronian, but begins with CAESAR. It is never common: **superiōribus diēbus nōna Caesaris legiō castra eō locō posuit**, CAES., *B.C.*, III. 66, 2.

240. The Historical Perfect is the great narrative tense of the Latin language, and is best studied in long connected passages, and by careful comparison with the Imperfect. See C., *Off.*, III. 27, 100; *Tusc.*, I. 2, 4.

Pluperfect Tense.

241. The Pluperfect denotes *Completion in the Past*, and is used of an action that was completed before another was begun. It is, so to speak, the Perfect of the Imperfect. Hence it is used:

1. Of an action *just concluded* in the past.

Modo Caesarem rēgnantem vīderāmus, C., *Ph.*, II. 42, 108; *we had just seen Caesar on the throne.*

2. Of an action that was *over and gone.*

Fuerat inimīcus, C., *Red. in Sen.*, 10, 26; *he had been my enemy.*

3. Of a *resulting condition* in the past.

Massiliēnsēs portās Caesarī clauserant, Caes., *B.C.*, I. 34, 4; *the Marseillese had shut their gates against Caesar.* (*Their gates were shut.*)

Remark.—When the Pf. of Resulting Condition is translated by an English Pr. (236, 2, r.), the Plupf. is translated by an English Imperfect: **nōveram**, *I had become acquainted with, I knew;* **memineram**, *I remembered;* **ōderam**, *I hated;* **cōnsuēveram**, *I was accustomed, etc.*

Notes.—1. Not unfrequently in early Latin, rarely in classical prose, but more often in the poets, the Plupf. seems to be used as an Aorist; so very often **dīxerat: Nīl equidem tibĭ abstulī.** Ev. **At illud quod tibĭ abstulerās cedo**, Pl., *Aul.*, 635. **Nōn sum ego quī fueram**, Prop., I. 12, 11. See Ov., *Tr.*, III. 11, 25.

2. The Periphrastic Plupf. with **habeō** corresponds to the Perfect (238). It is rare, and shows two forms, one with the Imperfect and one with the Plupf., the latter being post-classical.

Equitātum, quem ex omnī prōvinciā coāctum habēbat, praemittit, Caes., *B.G.*, I. 15, 1. **Multōrum aurēs illa lingua attonitās habuerat**, Val. M., III. 3.

Future Tense.

242. The Future Tense denotes *Continuance in the Future:* **scrībam**, *I shall be writing.*

The Future Tense is also used to express indefinite action in the Future: **scrībam**, *I shall write.*

Remarks.—1. In subordinate clauses the Latin language is more exact than the English in the expression of future relations.

Dōnec eris fēlīx, multōs numerābis amīcōs, Ov., *Tr.*, I. 9, 5; *so long as you shall be* (*are*) *happy, you will count many friends.*

2. Observe especially the verbs **volō**, *I will*, and **possum**, *I can.*

Ōdero sī poterō; sī nōn, invītus amābō, Ov., *Am.*, III. 11, 35; *I will hate if I shall be able* (*can*); *if not, I shall love against my will.* **Quī**

adipīscī vēram glōriam volet, iūstitiae fungātur officiīs, C., *Off.*, II. 13, 43; *whoso shall wish to obtain true glory, let him discharge the calls of justice.*

3. The Fut. is often used in conclusions, especially in CICERO:

Sunt illa sapientis; aberit igitur ā sapiente aegritūdō, C., *Tusc.*, III. 8, 18.

NOTES.—1. The Fut. is used sometimes as a gnomic (236, N.) tense:

Haut facul fēmina inveniētur bona, AFR., 7; *unneth (= hardly) a woman shall be found that's good.* **Et tremet sapiēns et dolēbit, et expallēscet**, SEN., *E.M.*, 71, 29.

2. Observe the (principally comic) use of the Future to indicate likelihood:

Verbum hercle hōc vērum erit, TER., *Eun.*, 732; *this will be God's own truth.*

243. The Future is used in an imperative sense, as in English, chiefly in familiar language.

Tū nihil dīcēs, H., *A.P.*, 385; *you will (are to) say nothing (do you say nothing).* **Cum volet accēdēs, cum tē vītābit abībis**, OV., *A.A.*, II. 529; *when she wants you, approach; and when she avoids you, begone, sir.* **Nōn mē appellābis, sī sapis**, PL., *Most.*, 515; see C., *Fam.*, V. 12, 10. Compare **ūtētur** and **ūtātur**, CORN., II. 3, 5.

Similar is the Future in Asseverations (comic).

Ita mē amābit Iūppiter, PL., *Trin.*, 447; *so help me God!*

Future Perfect Tense.

244. The Future Perfect is the Perfect, both Pure and Historical, transferred to the future, and embraces both *completion* and *attainment*: **fēcerō**, TER., *Ph.*, 882; *I shall have done it*, or *I shall do it* (once for all); **vīderō**, TER., *Ad.*, 538; *I will see to it;* **prōfēcerit**, C., *Fin.*, III. 4, 14; *it will prove profitable.*

REMARKS.—1. Hence, when the Pf. is used as a Pr., the Fut. Pf. is used as a Future: **nōverō**, *I shall know;* **cōnsuēverō**, *I shall be accustomed;* **Ōdero, sī poterō**, OV., *Am.*, III. 11, 35 (242, R. 2).

2. In subordinate sentences, the Latin language is more exact than the English in the use of the Fut. Perfect; hence, when one action precedes another in the future, the action that precedes is expressed by the Fut. Perfect.

Quī prior strinxerit ferrum, ēius victōria erit, L., XXIV. 38, 5; *who first draws the sword, his shall be the victory.*

3. The Fut. Pf. is frequently used in **volō**, *I will;* **nōlō**, *I will not;* **possum**, *I can;* **licet**, *it is left free;* **libet**, *it is agreeable;* **placet**, *it is the pleasure;* whereas the English idiom familiarly employs the Present.

Sī potuerō, faciam vōbīs satis, C., *Br.*, 5, 21; *if I can, I shall satisfy you.*

4. The Fut. Pf. in both clauses denotes simultaneous accomplishment or attainment ; one action involves the other.

Quī Antōnium oppresserit, is bellum cōnfēcerit, C., *Fam.*, x. 19, 2 ; *he who shall have crushed* (*crushes*) *Antony, will have finished* (*will finish*) *the war.* [**Ea**] **vitia quī fūgerit, is omnia ferē vitia vītāverit,** C., *Or.*, 69, 231 ; *he who shall have escaped these faults, will have avoided almost all faults.*

Sometimes, however, the first seems to denote *antecedence*, the second *finality*. An Impv. is often used in the first clause.

Immūtā (**verbōrum collocātiōnem**), **perierit tōta rēs,** C., *Or.*, 70, 232 ; *change the arrangement of the words, the whole thing falls dead.*

NOTES.—1. The independent use of the Fut. Pf. is characteristic of Comedy, but occurs occasionally later in familiar style. Sometimes it gives an air of positiveness :

Bene merentī bene prōfuerit, male merentī pār erit, PL., *Capt.*, 315 ; *good desert shall have good issue ; ill desert shall have its due.* **Ego crās hīc erō : crās habuerō, uxor, ego tamen convīvium,** PL., *Cas.*, 786. **Nūsquam facilius hanc miserrimam vītam vel sustentābō vel abiēcerō,** C., *Att.*, III. 19, 1. See also C., *Ac.*, II. 44, 135 ; L., I. 58, 10.

2. The Periphrastic Fut. Pf. with **habeō** is rare. It corresponds to the Pf. and Pluperfect.

Quod sī fēceris, mē māximō beneficiō dēvinctum habēbis, C., *Att.*, XVI. 16 B. 9.

245. As the Future is used as an Imperative, so the Future Perfect approaches the Imperative.

Dē tē tū vīderis ; ego dē mē ipse profitēbor, C., *Ph.*, II. 46, 118 ; *do you see to yourself ; I myself will define my position.*

NOTE.—This is confined in CICERO almost entirely to **vīderis,** which is suspiciously like the familiar Greek future ὄψει, and is used in the same way.

Periphrastic Tenses.

246. The Periphrastic Tenses are formed by combining the various tenses of **esse,** *to be,* with participles and verbal adjectives. See 129.

I. PERIPHRASTIC CONJUGATION—ACTIVE VOICE.

247. The Periphrastic Tenses of the Active are chiefly combinations of **esse** and its forms with the so-called Future Participle Active. The Future Participle is a verbal adjective denoting *capability* and *tendency*. Compare **amātor** and **amātūrus.** The translation is very various :

1. **Scrīptūrus sum,** *I am about to write, I am to write, I purpose to write, I am likely to write.*

2. **Scrīptūrus eram,** *I was about to write, etc.*

3. **Scrīptūrus fuī,** *I have been* or *was about to write* (often = ***I should have written***).

4. **Scrīptūrus fueram,** *I had been about to write, etc.*

5. **Scrīptūrus erō,** *I shall be about to write, etc.*

6. **Scrīptūrus fuerō,** *I shall have made up my mind to write, etc.* (of course very rare).

1. **Fīet illud quod futūrum est,** C., *Div.*, II. 8, 21; *what is to be, will be.*

2. **[Rēx] nōn interfutūrus nāvālī certāminī erat,** L., XXXVI. 43, 9; *the king did not intend to be present at the naval combat.*

3. **Fascīs ipsī ad mē dēlātūrī fuērunt,** C., *Ph.*, XIV. 6, 15; *they themselves were ready to tender the fasces to me.* **Dēditōs ūltimīs cruciātibus adfectūrī fuērunt,** L., XXI. 44, 4; *they would have put the surrendered to extreme tortures.*

4. **Māior Rōmānōrum grātia fuit quam quanta futūra Carthāginiēnsium fuerat,** L., XXII. 22, 19; *the Romans' credit for this was greater than the Carthaginians' would have been.*

5. **Eōrum apud quōs aget aut erit āctūrus, mentēs sēnsūsque dēgustet,** C., *Or.*, I. 52, 223; *he must taste-and-test the state of mind of those before whom he will plead or will have to plead.*

6. **(Sapiēns) nōn vīvet, sī fuerit sine homine vīctūrus,** SEN., *E.M.*, 9, 17; *The wise man will not continue to live, if he finds that he is to live without human society.* (The only example cited, and that doubtful.)

REMARKS.—1. The forms with **sum, eram,** and the corresponding Subjv. forms with **sim, essem,** are much more common than those with **fuī,** *etc.*, probably for euphonic reasons.

2. The Subjv. and Inf. **scrīptūrus sim, essem, fuerim, fuissem, scrīptūrum esse, fuisse,** are of great importance in subordinate clauses. (656.)

NOTES.—1. The use of **forem** for **essem** appears first in SALLUST, but is not uncommon in LIVY, and occurs sporadically later. **Fore** for **esse** is post-classical.

Dīcit sē vēnisse quaesītum pācem an bellum agitātūrus foret, S., *Iug.*, 109, 2.

2. The periphrastic use of the Pr. Part. with forms of **esse** is rare, and in most cases doubtful, as the question always arises whether the Part. is not rather a virtual substantive or adjective. So with the not uncommon **ut sīs sciēns** of the Comic Poets. The effect of this periphrasis is to emphasise the continuance.

Nēmō umquam tam suī dēspiciēns (*despiser of self, self-depreciator*) **fuit quīn spērāret melius sē posse dīcere,** C., *Or.*, II. 89, 364.

II. PERIPHRASTIC TENSES OF THE PASSIVE.

A.—Of Future Relations.

248. The periphrases **futūrum esse** (more often **fore**) **ut,** (*that*) *it is to be that*, and **futūrum fuisse ut,** (*that*) *it was to be that*, with the Subjunctive, are very commonly used to take the place of the Future Infinitive active; necessarily so when the verb forms no Future Participle. In the passive they are more common than the Supine with **īrī**.

Spērō fore ut contingat id nōbīs, C., *Tusc.*, I. 34, 82 ; *I hope that we shall have that good fortune.* **In fātīs scrīptum Vēientēs** [**habēbant**] **fore ut brevī ā Gallīs Rōma caperētur**, C., *Div.*, I. 44, 100 ; *the Veientes had it written down in their prophetic books that Rome would shortly be taken by the Gauls.*

REMARK.—**Posse**, *to be able*, and **velle**, *to will*, on account of their future sense, do not require a periphrasis. In the absence of periphrastic forms, the forms of **posse** are often used instead. (656, R.)

NOTES.—1. These periphrases do not occur in early Latin.

2. **Fore ut** is used chiefly with Pr. and Impf. Subjv. ; Pf. and Plupf. are very rare. (C., *Att.*, XVI. 16 E. 16.)

3. The form **futūrum fuisse ut** is used with passive and Supineless verbs, to express the dependent apodosis of an unreal conditional sentence.

Nisi eō ipsō tempore nūntiī dē Caesaris victōriā essent allātī, exīstimābant plērīque futūrum fuisse utī (**oppidum**) **āmitterētur**, CAES., *B. C.*, III. 101, 3. (656, 2.)

4. The Subjv. forms **futūrum sit, esset, fuerit ut**, are used in the grammars to supply the periphrastic Subjv. of passive and Supineless verbs (see 515, R. 2). Warrant in real usage is scarce.

An utique futūrum sit ut Carthāginem superent Rōmānī? QUINT. III. 8, 17 (not merely periphrastic).

249. In eō est, *it is on the point*, } **ut**, *that* (*of*), with the subjunctive.
erat, fuit, } *was* (Impersonal),

In eō [**erat**] **ut** (**Pausaniās**) **comprehenderētur**, NEP., IV. 5, 1 ; *it was on the point that Pausanias should be* (*P. was on the point of being*) *arrested.*

NOTE.—This phrase occurs in NEPOS and LIVY, seldom in earlier writers.

B.—Of Past Relations.

250. The Perfect Participle passive is used in combination with **sum**, *I am*, and **fuī**, *I have been*, *I was*, to express the Pure Perfect and Historical Perfect of the Passive Voice. **Eram**, *I was*, and **fueram**, *I had been*, stand for the Pluperfect ; and **erō**, *I shall be*, and **fuerō**, *I shall have been*, for the Future Perfect.

REMARKS.—1. **Fuī** is the *favorite* form when the participle is frequently used as an adjective : **convīvium exōrnātum fuit**, *the banquet was furnished forth* ; **fuī** is the *necessary* form when the Pf. denotes that the action is over and gone ; **amātus fuī**, *I have been loved* (but I am loved no longer). The same principle applies to **fueram** and **fuerō**, though not so regularly.

Simulācrum ē marmore in sepulcrō positum fuit; hōc quīdam homō nōbilis dēportāvit, C., *Dom.*, 43, 111; *a marble effigy* WAS *deposited in the tomb; a certain man of rank has carried it off.* **Arma quae fīxa in parietibus fuerant, ea sunt humī inventa**, C., *Div.*, I. 34, 74; *the arms which had been fastened to the walls were found on the ground.* **Quod tibĭ fuerit persuāsum, huīc erit persuāsum**, C., *Rosc. Com.*, I, 3; *what is (shall have proved) acceptable to you will be acceptable to him.*

2. To be distinguished is that use of the Pf. where each element has its full force, the Participle being treated as an adjective. In this case the tense is not past.

Gallia est omnis dīvīsa in partēs trēs, CAES., *B.G.*, I, 1.

NOTES.—1. The **fuī**, *etc.*, forms are rarely found in CICERO, never in CAESAR, but are characteristic of LIVY and SALLUST.

2. **Forem** for **essem** is common in the Comic Poets, occurs twice in CICERO's letters (*Att.*, VII. 21, 2; X. 14, 3), never in CAESAR, but in LIVY and NEPOS is very common, and practically synonymous with **essem.**

C.—Periphrastic Conjugation—Passive Voice.

251. 1. The combination of the Tenses of **esse**, *to be*, with the Gerundive (verbal in **-ndus**), is called the Periphrastic Conjugation of the Passive, and follows the laws of the simple conjugation (129). The idea expressed is usually one of *necessity.*

Praepōnenda [est] dīvitiīs glōria, C., *Top.*, 22, 84; *glory is to be preferred to riches.*

2. According to the rule (217) the Gerundive of intransitive verbs can be used only in the Impersonal form:

Parcendum est victīs, *The vanquished must be spared.*

NOTES.—1. The Gerundive is a verbal adjective, which produces the effect of a Progressive Participle. Whenever a participle is used as a predicate it becomes characteristic, and good for all time. As **amāns** not only = **quī amat,** but also = **quī amet,** so **amandus** = **quī amētur.** Compare 438, R.

2. **Forem** for **essem** is post-classical and comparatively uncommon.

TENSES IN LETTERS.

252. The Roman letter-writer not unfrequently puts himself in the position of the receiver, more especially at the beginning and at the end of the letter, often in the phrase **Nihil erat (habēbam) quod scrīberem**, *I have nothing to write.* This permutation of tenses is never kept up long, and applies only to temporary situations, never to general statements.

Table of Permutations.

scrībō,	*I am writing,*	becomes	**scrībēbam.**
	I write,	"	**scrīpsī.**
scrīpsī,	*I have written,*	"	**scrīpseram.**
	I wrote,	"	**scrīpseram.**
	or remains unchanged.		
scrībam,	*I shall write,*	"	**scrīptūrus eram.**

The adverbial designations of time remain unchanged—or

herī,	*yesterday,*	becomes	**prīdiē.**
hodiē,	*to-day,*	"	**quō diē hās litterās dedī, dabam.**
crās,	*to-morrow,*	"	**posterō diē, postrīdiē.**
nunc,	*now,*	"	**tum.**

Formiās mē continuō recipere cōgitābam, C., *Att.*, VII. 15, 3; *I am thinking of retiring forthwith to Formiae.* **Cum mihĭ dīxisset Caecilius puerum sē Rōmam mittere, haec scrīpsī raptim,** C., *Att.*, II. 9, 1; *as Caecilius has told me that he is sending a servant to Rome, I write in a hurry.* **(Lītterās) eram datūrus postrīdiē eī quī mihĭ prīmus obviam vēnisset,** C., *Att.*, II. 12, 4; *I will give the letter to-morrow to the first man that comes my way.*

NOTE.—CICERO is much more consistent in this tense-shifting than PLINY; and exceptions are not numerous proportionally: **Ego etsī nihil habeō quod ad tē scrībam, scrībō tamen quia tēcum loquī videor,** C., *Att.*, XII. 53.

MOODS.

253. Mood signifies manner. The mood of a verb signifies the manner in which the predicate is said of the subject.

There are three moods in Latin:

1. The Indicative.
2. The Subjunctive.
3. The Imperative.

NOTE.—The Infinitive form of the verb is generally, but improperly, called a mood.

The Indicative Mood.

254. The Indicative Mood represents the predicate *as a reality*. It is sometimes called the Declarative Mood, as the mood of direct assertion.

The use of the Latin Indicative differs little from the English.

REMARKS.—1. The Latin language expresses *possibility* and *power*, *obligation* and *necessity*, and abstract relations generally, as *facts*; whereas, our translation often *implies the failure to realise*. Such expressions are: **dēbeō**, *I ought, it is my duty;* **oportet,** *it behooves;* **necesse est,** *it is absolutely necessary;* **possum,** *I can, I have it in my power;* **convenit,** *it is fitting;* **pār, aequom est,** *it is fair;* **īnfīnītum,** *endless;* **difficile,** *hard to do;* **longum,** *tedious;* and many others; also the Indic. form of the passive Periphrastic Conjugation. Observe the difference between the use of the Inf. in Eng. and in Latin after past tenses of **dēbeō, possum, oportet,** *etc.*

Possum persequī permulta oblectāmenta rērum rūsticārum, C., *Cat.M.*, 16, 55; *I might rehearse very many delights of country life.* **Longum est persequī ūtilitātēs asinōrum,** C., *N.D.*, II. 64, 159; *it would be tedious to rehearse the useful qualities of asses* (I will not do it). **Ad mortem tē dūcī oportēbat,** C., *Cat.*, I. 1, 2; *it behooved you to be (you ought to have been) led to execution* (you were not). **Volumnia dēbuit in tē officiōsior esse, et id ipsum, quod fēcit, potuit dīligentius facere,** C., *Fam.*, XIV. 16; *it was Volumnia's duty to be (V. ought to have been) more attentive to you; and the little she did do, she had it in her power to do (she might have done) more carefully.* **Quae condiciō nōn accipienda fuit potius quam relinquenda patria?** C., *Att.*, VIII. 3, 3; *what terms ought not to have been accepted in preference to leaving thy country?* **[Eum] vīvum illinc exīre non oportuerat,** C., *Mur.*, 25, 51; *he ought never to have gone out thence alive.*

The Pf. and Plupf. always refer to a special case.

2. The Impf. as the Tense of Disappointment is sometimes used in these verbs to denote opposition to a present state of things: **dēbēbam,** *I ought* (but do not); **poterās,** *you could* (but do not). These may be considered as conditionals in disguise. (See R. 3.)

Poteram morbōs appellāre, sed nōn convenīret ad omnia, C., *Fin.*, III. 10, 35; *I might translate* (that Greek word) "*diseases,*" *but that would not suit all the cases* (**poteram sī convenīret**). **At poterās, inquis, melius mala ferre silendō,** Ov., *Tr.*, V. 1, 49; "*But,*" *you say,* "*you could* (you do not) *bear your misfortunes better by keeping silent*" (**poterās sī silērēs**).

3. The Indic. is sometimes used in the leading clause of conditional sentences (the Apodosis), thereby implying the certainty of the result, had it not been for the interruption. The Indic. clause generally precedes, which is sufficient to show the rhetorical character of the construction.

With the Impf. the action is often really begun:

Lābēbar longius, nisi mē retinuissem, C., *Leg.*, I. 19, 52; *I was letting myself go on (should have let myself go on) too far, had I not checked myself.* **Omnīnō supervacua erat doctrīna, sī nātūra sufficeret,** QUINT., II. 8, 8; *training were wholly superfluous, did nature suffice.* **Praeclārē vīcerāmus, nisi Lepidus recēpisset Antōnium,** C., *Fam.*, XII. 10, 3: *we had (should have) gained a brilliant victory, had not Lepidus received Antony.*

In all these sentences the English idiom requires the Subjv., which is disguised by coinciding with the Indic. in form, except in "were."

4. In general relative expressions, such as the double formations, **quisquis**, *no matter who*, **quotquot**, *no matter how many*, and all forms in **-cumque**, *-ever*, the Indic. is employed in classical Latin where we may use in English a Subjv. or its equivalent : **quisquis est**, *no matter who he is, be, may be ;* **quālecumque est**, *whatever sort of thing it is, be, may be.*

Quidquid id est, timeō Danaōs et dōna ferentēs, V., *A.*, II. 49 ; *whatever it (may) be, I fear the Danai even when they bring presents.*

CICERO has occasional exceptions (Ideal Second Person or by attraction) to this rule, and later writers, partly under Greek influence, frequently violate it. Exceptions in early Latin are not common.

NOTES.—1. CICERO introduces (**nōn**) **putāram**, "*I should (not) have thought so,*" and **mālueram**, *I could have preferred.* LUCAN and TACITUS alone imitate the latter; the former was never followed.

Mālueram, quod erat susceptum ab illīs, silentiō trānsīrī, C., *Att.*, II. 19, 3. **Feriam tua vīscera, Māgne ; māllueram socerī**, LUCAN, VIII. 521.

2. In early Latin, occasionally in the more familiar writings of CICERO, and here and there later we find the Pr. Indic. (in early Latin occasionally the Fut.) used in place of the Subjv. in the Deliberative Question.

Compressān palmā an porrēctā feriō ? PL., *Cas.*, 405. **Advolōne an maneō?** C., *Att.*, XIII. 40, 2. **Quoi dōnō lepidum novom libellum**, CAT., I, 1.

Subjunctive Mood.

255. The Subjunctive Mood represents the predicate *as an idea*, as something merely conceived in the mind (abstracts from reality).

REMARK.—The Latin Subjv. is often translated into English by the auxiliary verbs *may, can, must, might, could, would, should.* When these verbs have their full signification of *possibility* and *power, obligation* and *necessity*, they are represented in Latin by the corresponding verbs, thus : *may, can, might, could* by the forms of **posse**, to be *able*, **licet**, *it is left free ; will* and *would* by **velle**, *to will, to be willing ; must*, by **dēbeō** or **oportet** (of moral obligation), by **necesse est** (of absolute obligation).

Nostrās iniūriās nec potest nec possit alius ulcīscī quam vōs, L., XXIX. 18, 18 ; *our wrongs no other than you has the power or can well have the power to avenge.**

NOTE.—In the Latin Subjv. are combined two moods, the Subjv. proper, and the Optative, sometimes distinguished as the moods of the *will* and the *wish.* This fusion has rendered it difficult to define the fundamental conceptions of certain constructions.

---

* In this unique passage **nec potest** denies with the head, **nec possit** refuses to believe with the heart.

256. 1. The realisation of the idea may be *in suspense*, or it may be *beyond control*. The first, or purely Ideal Subjunctive, is represented by the Present and Perfect Tenses; the second, or Unreal, is represented by the Imperfect and Pluperfect.

NOTES.—1. The Subjv., as the name implies (**subiungō**, *I subjoin*), is largely used in dependent sentences, and will be treated at length in that connection.

2. The following modifications of the above principles must be carefully observed:

(*a*) The Romans, in lively discourse, often represent the unreal as ideal, that which is beyond control as still in suspense. (596, R. 1.)

(*b*) In transfers to the past, the Impf. represents the Pr., and the Plupf. the Pf. Subjunctive. (510.)

2. The idea may be a *view*, or a *wish*. In the first case the Subjunctive is said to be Potential, in the second case Optative. The Potential Subjunctive is nearer the Indicative, from which it differs in tone; the Optative Subjunctive is nearer the Imperative, for which it is often used.

Potential Subjunctive.

257. 1. The Potential Subjunctive represents the opinion of the speaker as an opinion. The tone varies from vague surmise to moral certainty, from "may" and "might" to "must." The negative is the negative of the Indicative, **nōn.**

2. The Potential of the Present or Future is the Present or Perfect Subjunctive. The verification is in suspense, and so future; the action may be present or future: with Perfect sometimes past.

Velim, *I should wish;* **nōlim,** *I should be unwilling;* **mālim,** *I should prefer;* **dīcās,** *you would say;* **crēdās,** *you would believe, you must believe;* **dīcat, dīxerit aliquis,** *some one may undertake to say, go so far as to say.*

Caedī discipulōs minimē velim, QUINT., I. 3, 13; *I should by no means like pupils to be flogged.* **Tū Platōnem nec nimis valdē nec nimis saepe laudāverīs,** C., *Leg.*, III. 1, 1; *you can't praise Plato too much nor too often.*

NOTES.—1. The Pf. Subjv. as a Potential seems to have been very rare in early Latin. CICERO extended the usage slightly and employed more persons; thus First Person Pl. and Second Sing. occur first in CICERO. From CICERO's time the usage spreads, perhaps under the influence of the Greek Aorist. It was always rare with Deponents and Passives. Another view regards this **dīxerit** as a Fut. Pf. Indicative.

2. The Potential Subjv. is sometimes explained by the ellipsis of an Ideal or of an

Unreal Conditional Protasis. But the free Potential Subjv. differs from an elliptical conditional sentence in the absence of definite ellipsis, and hence of definite translation. Compare the two sentences above with :

Eum quī palam est adversārius facile cavendō (sī caveās) vītāre possīs, C., *Verr.*, I. 15, 39 ; *an open adversary you can readily avoid by caution (if you are cautious).* **Nīl ego contulerim iūcundō sānus (= dum sānus erō) amīcō,** H., *S.*, I. 5, 44 ; *there is naught I should compare to an agreeable friend, while I am in my sound senses.*

3. The Potential Subjv., as a modified form of the Indic., is often found where the Indic. would be the regular construction. So after **quanquam** (607, R. 1).

258. The Potential of the Past is the Imperfect Subjunctive, chiefly in the Ideal Second Person, an imaginary "you."

Crēderēs victōs, L., II. 43, 9 ; *you would, might, have thought them beaten.* **Haud facile discernerēs utrum Hannibal imperātōrī an exercituī cārior esset,** L., XXI. 4, 3 ; *not readily could you have decided whether Hannibal was dearer to general or to army.* **Mīrārētur quī tum cerneret,** L., XXXIV. 9, 4 ; *any one who saw it then must have been astonished.*

Vellem, *I should have wished;* **nōllem,** *I should have been unwilling;* **māllem,** *I should have preferred* (it is too late).

NOTES.—1. With **vellem, nōllem, māllem,** the inference points to non-fulfilment of the wish in the Present (261, R.) ; with other words there is no such inference.

2. The Unreal of the Present and the Ideal of the Past coincide. What is unreal of a real person is simply ideal of an imaginary person The Impf. is used as the tense of Description.

The Aoristic Pf. Subjv. and the Plupf. Subjv. are rarely used as the Ideal of the Past: **Hī ambō saltūs ad Libuōs Gallōs dēdūxerint** (var. **dēdūxissent**), L., XXI. 38, 7. **Eā quā minimum crēdidisset (cōnsul) resistēbant hostēs,** L., XXXII. 17, 4.

259. The Mood of the Question is the Mood of the expected or anticipated answer (462). Hence the Potential Subjunctive is used in questions which serve to convey a negative opinion on the part of the speaker.

Quis dubitet (= nēmŏ dubitet) quīn in virtūte dīvitiae sint ? C., *Parad.*, VI. 2, 48 ; *who can doubt that true wealth consists in virtue ?* (No one.) **Quis tulerit Gracchōs dē sēditiōne querentēs ?** JUV., II. 24 ; *who could bear the Gracchi complaining of rebellion ?* (No one.) **Apud exercitum fuerĭs ?** C., *Mur.*, 9, 21; *can you have been with the army ?* **Hōc tantum bellum quis umquam arbitrārētur ab ūnō imperātōre cōnficī posse ?** C., *Imp.*, 11, 31 ; *who would, could, should have thought that this great war could be brought to a close by one general ?*

Optative Subjunctive.

260. The Subjunctive is used as an *Optative* or *wishing* mood.

The regular negative is **nē**. **Nōn** is used chiefly to negative a single word; but very rarely in the classical period. A second wish may be added by **neque** or **nec** (regularly if a positive wish precedes), but this is also rare in the classical period, and is denied for CAESAR.

The Pr. and Pf. Subjv. are used *when the decision is in suspense*, no matter how extravagant the wish; the Impf. and Plupf. are used *when the decision is adverse*. The Pf. is rare and old.

Stet haec urbs, C., *Mil.*, 34, 93; *may this city continue to stand!* **Quod dī ōmen āvertant**, C., *Ph.*, III. 14, 35; *which omen may the gods avert.* **Ita dī faxint** (= **fēcerint**), PL., *Poen.*, 911; *the gods grant it!* **Nē istūc Iūppiter optimus māximus sīrit** (= **sīverit**)! L., XXXIV. 24, 2; *may Jupiter, supremely great and good, suffer it not!*

261. The Optative Subjunctive frequently takes **ut** (archaic and rare), **utinam, utinam nē, utinam nōn**; also **ō sī**, *oh if* (poetical and very rare); **quī** (chiefly in early Latin and in curses).

Valeās beneque ut tibi sit, PL., *Poen.*, 912; *farewell! God bless you!* **Utinam modo cōnāta efficere possim**, C., *Att.*, IV. 16; *may I but have it in my power to accomplish my endeavours.* **Utinam revīvīscat frāter!** GELL., X. 6, 2; *would that my brother would come to life again!* **Utinam īnserere iocōs mōris esset**, QUINT., II. 10, 9; *would that it were usual to introduce jokes!* **Illud utinam nē vērē scrīberem**, C., *Fam.*, V. 17, 3; *would that what I am writing were not true!* **Utinam susceptus nōn essem**, C., *Att.*, III. 11, 8; *would I had not been born!* (CICERO's only example of **nōn**.) **Ō mihi praeteritōs referat sī Iūppiter annōs**, V., *A.*, VIII. 560; *O if Jove were to bring me back the years that are gone by!*

REMARK.—For the wish with adverse decision, **vellem** and **māllem** (theoretically also **nōllem**) may be used with the Impf. and sometimes (especially **vellem**) with the Plupf. Subjunctive.

Vellem adesse posset Panaetius! C., *Tusc.*, I. 33, 81; *would that Panaetius could be present!* **Vellem mē ad cēnam invītāssēs**, C., *Fam.*, XII. 4, 1; *would that you had invited* ME *to your dinner-party.*

So **velim, nōlim**, *etc.*, for the simple wish (546, R. 2).

Tuam mihĭ darī velim ēloquentiam, C., *N. D.*, II. 59, 147; *I could wish your eloquence given to me.*

NOTES.—1. **Utinam** was perhaps originally an interrogative, *How, pray?* If so, it belongs partly to the potential; hence the frequent occurrence of **nōn**. **Ō sī** (occasionally **sī**, V., *A.*, VI. 187) introduces an elliptical conditional sentence, which is not intended to have an Apodosis. When the Apodosis comes, it may come in a different form; as in the example: V., *A.*, VIII. 560, 568.

2. The Impf. Subjv. is occasionally used in early Latin to give an unreal wish in the Past. This is almost never found in the later period.

Utinam tē dī prius perderent, quam periistī ē patriā tuā, PL., *Capt.*, 537. **Tunc mihi vīta foret**, TIB., I. 10, 11.

262. The Optative Subjunctive is used in *asseverations:*

Ita vīvam ut māximōs sūmptūs faciō, C., *Att.*, v. 15, 2 ; *as I live, I am spending very largely* (literally, *so may I live as I am making very great outlay*). **Moriar, sī magis gaudērem sī id mihĭ accidisset,** C., *Att.*, VIII. 6, 3 ; *may I die if I could be more glad if that had happened to me.*

NOTE.—The Fut. Indic. in this sense is rare : **Sīc mē dī amābunt ut mē tuārum miseritumst fortūnārum,** TER., *Heaut.*, 463.

263. The Subjunctive is used as an *Imperative:*

1. In the First Person Plural Present, which has no Imperative form :

Amēmus patriam, C., *Sest.*, 68, 143; *let us love our country.* **Nē difficilia optēmus,** C., *Verr.*, IV. 7, 15 ; *let us not desire what is hard to do.*

NOTE.—In the First Person Singular, the command fades into the wish.

2. In the Second Person.

(*a*) In the Present chiefly in the Singular, and chiefly of an imaginary "you" :

Istō bonō ūtāre, dum adsit, cum absit, nē requīrās, C., *Cat.M.*, 10, 33 ; *you must enjoy that blessing so long as 'tis here, when it is gone you must not pine for it.*

NOTE.—The Comic Poets use the Pr. negatively very often of a definite person, sometimes combining it with an Impv.: **īgnōsce, īrāta nē siēs,** PL., *Am.*, 924 ; but in the classical period such usage is rare, and usually open to other explanations ; a definite person may be used as a type, or the sentence may be elliptical.

(*b*) In the Perfect negatively :

Nē trānsierīs Hibērum, L., XXI. 44, 6; *do not cross the Ebro.* **Nē vōs mortem timuerītis,** C., *Tusc.*, I. 41, 98; *have no fear of death!*

3. In the Third Person Present (regularly) :

Suum quisque nōscat ingenium, C., *Off.*, I. 31, 114 ; *let each one know his own mind.* **Dōnīs impiī nē plācāre audeant deōs,** C., *Leg.*, II. 16, 41 ; *let the wicked not dare to try to appease the gods with gifts.*

NOTE.—The Pf. in this usage is very rare. S., *Iug.*, 85, 47 ; TAC., *Ann.*, IV. 32, 1.

264. The Subjunctive is used as a *Concessive:*

Sit fūr, C., *Verr.*, v. 1, 4 ; (*granted that*) *he be a thief.* **Fuerit (malus cīvis),** C., *Verr.*, I. 14, 37; (*suppose*) *that he was a bad citizen.*

For other examples with **ut** and **nē**, see 608.

NOTE.—The past tenses are very rarely used concessively ; see C., *Tusc.*, III. 19, 75 (Impf.) ; *Sest.*, 19, 43 (Plupf.).

265. The Subjunctive is used in Questions which expect an Imperative answer (**cōniūnctīvus dēlīberātīvus**).

Genuine questions are commonly put in the First Person, or the representative of the First Person :

Utrum superbiam prius commemorem an crūdēlitātem, C., *Verr.*, I. 47, 122 ; *shall I mention the insolence first or the cruelty ?* **Māgna fuit contentiō utrum moenibus sē dēfenderent an obviam īrent hostibus**, NEP., I. 4, 4 ; *there was a great dispute whether they should defend themselves behind the walls or go to meet the enemy.* (**Utrum nōs dēfendāmus an obviam eāmus ?**) [Example of Third Person, 428, N. I.]

Rhetorical questions (questions which anticipate the answer), under this head, are hardly to be distinguished from Potential.

Quō mē nunc vertam ? Undique cūstōdior, C., *Att.*, X. 12, 1 ; *whither shall I now turn ? Sentinels on every side.* **Quid agerem ?** C., *Sest.*, 19, 42 ; *what was I to do ?*

REMARK.—The answer to the Deliberative Question is the Impv. or the Imperative Subjv. of the Present (263, 2) or Past (272, 3).

Imperative Mood.

266. The Imperative is the mood of the will. It wills that the predicate be made a reality. The tone of the Imperative varies from stern command to piteous entreaty. It may appear as a demand, an order, an exhortation, a permission, a concession, a prayer.

Abī in malam rem, PL., *Capt.*, 877 ; *go (to the mischief), and be hanged.* **Compēsce mentem**, H., *O.*, I. 16, 22 ; *curb your temper.* **Dā mihĭ hōc, mel meum !** PL., *Trin.*, 244 ; *give me this, honey dear !*

267. The Imperative has two forms, known as the First and the Second Imperative (also, but less accurately, as the Present and Future Imperative). The First Imperative has only the Second Person ; the Second Imperative has both Second and Third Persons. The First Person is represented by the Subjunctive (263, 1).

REMARK.—Some verbs have only the second form. This may be due to the signification : so **scītō**, *know thou ;* **mementō**, *remember thou ;* and **habētō**, in the sense of *know, remember.*

On violation of Concord with the Imperative, see **211**, N. 2.

NOTE.—The use of the Pronouns **tū**, **vōs**, *etc.*, with the Impv., is colloquial, hence common in Comedy; or solemn: see V., *A.*, VI. 95, 365, 675, 834, *etc.*

268. 1. The First Imperative looks forward to immediate fulfilment (Absolute Imperative):

Special: **Patent portae; proficīscere**, C., *Cat.*, I. 5, 10, *Open stand the gates; depart.*

General: **Iūstitiam cole et pietātem**, C., *Rep.*, VI. 16, 16, *Cultivate justice and piety.*

2. The Second Imperative looks forward to contingent fulfilment (Relative Imperative), and is chiefly used in laws, legal documents, maxims, recipes, and the like; likewise in familiar language.

RĒGIŌ IMPERIŌ DUO SUNTŌ; IĪQUE CŌNSULĒS APPELLĀMINŌ (130, 5, *c*); NĒMINĪ PĀRENTŌ; OLLĪS (104, III. N. 1) SALŪS POPULĪ SUPRĒMA LĒX ESTŌ, C., *Leg.*, III. 3, 8; *there shall be two (officers) with royal power; they shall be called consuls; they are to obey no one; to them the welfare of the people must be the paramount law.* **Rem vōbīs prōpōnam: vōs eam penditōte**, C., *Verr.*, IV. 1, 1; *I will propound the matter to you; do you thereupon perpend it.* **Percontātōrem fugitō, nam garrulus īdem est**, H., *Ep.*, I. 18, 69; *avoid your questioner, for he is a tell-tale too.*

269. STRENGTHENING WORDS.—The Imperative is often strengthened and emphasised by the addition of Adverbs, fossilised Imperatives, Phrases, *etc.*: **age, agite, agedum, agitedum**, *come;* enclitic **dum**, *then;* **modo**, *only:* **iamdūdum**, *at once;* **proinde**, *well, then;* **quīn**, *why not?* **sānē**, *certainly;* **amābō, obsecrō, quaesō**, *please;* **sīs** (= **sī vīs**), **sultis** (= **sī voltis**), **sōdēs** (= **sī audēs**), *if you please.* Most of these belong to familiar language, and are therefore found in great numbers in Comedy and in CICERO's letters. In the classical prose, and even later, they are not common. **Dum** in classical times is confined to **agedum**; **quīn** is cited twice in CICERO (*Mil.*, 29, 79; *Rosc. Com.*, 9, 25), and rarely later. **Iamdūdum** begins with VERGIL, and belongs to poetry and late prose. **Sānē** is not cited for the classical period. **Sultis** is confined to early Latin; and **sōdēs** occurs but once in CICERO (*Att.*, VII. 3, 11).

Mittite, agedum, lēgātōs, L., XXXVIII. 47, 11. **Quīn tū ī modō**, PL., *Cas.*, 755.

NOTE.—On the violation of Concord with **age**, see 211, N. 2.

270. NEGATIVE OF THE IMPERATIVE.—1. The regular negative of the Imperative is **nē** (**nēve, neu**), which is found with the Second Imperative; with the First Imperative, it is poetical or colloquial.

Hominem mortuum in urbe nē sepelītō nēve ūritō, C., *Leg.*, II. 23, 58; *thou shalt not bury nor burn a dead man in the city.* **Impius nē audētō plācāre dōnīs īram deōrum**, C., *Leg.*, II. 9, 22; *the impious man must not* *dare attempt to appease by gifts the anger of the gods.* **Tū nē cēde malīs, sed contrā audentior ītō**, V., *A.*, VI. 95 ; *yield not thou to misfortunes, but go more boldly (than ever) to meet them.*

REMARKS.—1. **Nōn** may be used to negative a single word:

Ā lēgibus nōn recēdāmus, C., *Cluent.*, 57, 155 ; *let us not recede from (let us stick to) the laws.* **Opus poliat līma, nōn exterat**, *Cf.* QUINT., X. 4, 4 ; *let the file rub the work up, not rub it out.*

2. Instead of **nē** with the First Imperative was employed either **nōlī** with the Infinitive (271, 2) ; or **nē** with the Pf. Subjv., but the latter is very rare in elevated prose (263, 2, *b*). On **nē** with Pr. Subjv. see 263, 2, *a*.

NOTE.—The use of **nōn** with the actual Impv. is found only in OVID ; but the addition of a second Impv. by **neque, nec**, instead of **nēve, neu**, begins in classical times (C., *Att.*, XII. 22, 3), and becomes common later. The use of **neque** (**nec**), **nihil, nēmō̆, nūllus** with the Subjv. in an Impv. sense has recently been claimed for the Potential Subjv. (*must*, 257, 1) on account of the negative.

271. PERIPHRASES.—1. **Cūrā (cūrātō) ut**, *take care that ;* **fac (facitō) ut**, *cause that ;* **fac (facitō)**, *do*, with the Subjunctive, are common circumlocutions for the Positive Imperative.

Cūra ut quam prīmum (303, R. 1) **veniās**, C., *Fam.*, IV. 10, 1 ; *manage to come as soon as possible.* **Fac cōgitēs**, C., *Fam.*, XI. 3, 4, *Do reflect !*

NOTES.—1. **Facitō** is almost wholly confined to early Latin, especially PLAUTUS ; so also **cūrātō**.

2. Early Latin also shows **vidē̆** and **vidētō** with Subjv. TERENCE introduces **volō, velim**, with Subjv., which is found also in later times ; as, C., *Fam.*, IX. 12, 2.

2. **Cavē̆** and **cavē̆ (cavētō) nē**, *beware lest*, with the Subjunctive, and **nōlī**, *be unwilling*, with the Infinitive, are circumlocutions for the Negative Imperative (Prohibitive). **Fac nē** is also familiarly used.

Cavē̆ fēstīnēs, C., *Fam.*, XVI. 12, 6 ; *do not be in a hurry.* **Tantum cum fingēs nē sīs manifēsta cavētō**, OV., *A.A.*, III. 801 ; *only when you pretend, beware that you be not detected.* **Nōlī, amābō, verberāre lapidem, nē perdās manum**, PL., *Curc.*, 197 ; *don't beat a stone, I pray you, lest you spoil your hand.* **Fac nē quid aliud cūrēs hōc tempore**, C., *Fam.*, XVI. 11, 1 ; *see that you pay no attention to anything else, at this time.*

NOTES.—1. Rare and confined to early Latin is the use of **cavē̆** with any but the second person. *Cf.* PL., *Aul.*, 660 ; TER., *And.*, 403.

2. Other phrases are those with **vidē nē** and **cūrātō nē**, with Subjv. ; **comperce, compēsce** with Inf. (all ante-classical) ; **parce, mitte, omitte** with Inf. (poetical and post-classical) ; **nōlim** with Subjv. (CIC.) ; **fuge** with Inf. (HOR.) ; **absiste with Inf.** (VERG.).

272. Representatives of the Imperative.—1. Instead of the Positive Imperative, may be employed :

(*a*) The Second Person of the Present Subjunctive (263, 2).
(*b*) The Second Person of the Future Indicative (243).
(*c*) The Third Person of the Present Subjunctive (263, 3).

2. Instead of the Negative Imperative (Prohibitive), may be employed :

(*a*) The Second Person of the Present Subjunctive, with **nē** (263, 2, N.).
(*b*) The Second Person of the Perfect Subjunctive, with **nē** (263, 2).
(*c*) The Second Person of the Future, with **nōn** (243).
(*d*) The Third Person of the Present or Perfect Subjunctive, with **nē** (263, 3).

Remark.—The Pr. Subjv. is employed when stress is laid on *the continuance of the action ;* the Pf., when stress is laid on the *completion.* Hence the use of the Pf. Subjv. in total prohibitions and passionate protests.

3. The Imperative of the Past is expressed by the Imperfect and Pluperfect Subjunctive (unfulfilled duties). Compare 265, R.

Dōtem darētis ; quaereret alium virum, Ter., *Ph.*, 297 ; *you should have given her a portion ; she should have sought another match.* **Crās īrēs potius, hodiē hīc cēnārēs. Valē,** Pl., *Pers.*, 710 ; *you ought rather to have put off going till to-morrow, you ought to (have) dine(d) with us to-day. Good-bye.* (Anything decided is regarded as past.) **Potius docēret (causam) nōn esse aequam,** C., *Off.*, iii. 22, 88 ; *he should rather have shown that the plea was not fair.* **Nē popōscissēs (librōs),** C., *Att.*, ii. 1, 3 ; *you ought not to have asked for the books.*

Observe the difference between the Unfulfilled Duty and the Unreal of the Past (597).

Morerētur ; fēcisset certē sī sine māximō dēdecore potuisset, C., *Rab. Post.*, 10, 29 ; *he ought to have died ; he would certainly have done so, could he have (done so) without the greatest disgrace.*

Note.—The Plupf. tense in this usage is not ante-classical.

273. Passionate questions are equivalent to a command :

Nōn tacēs ? Pl., *Am.*, 700 ; *won't you hold your tongue ?* **Quīn tacēs ?** *Why don't you hold your tongue ?* **Quīn datis, sī quid datis ?** Pl., *Cas.*, 765 ; *why don't you give, if you are going to do it ?* (Compare **Fac, sī quid facis,** Mart., i. 46, 1.) **Cūr nōn ut plēnus vītae convīva recēdis ?** Lucr., iii. 938 ; *why do you not withdraw as a guest sated with life ?*

274. **Puta, ut puta,** *for example,* begins with [C.] *ad Her.*, II. 11, 16 (reading doubtful); then H., *S.*, II. 5, 32, **Quīnte, puta, aut Pūblī.** Later it becomes more common, especially with the Jurists. See C., *Ph.*, II. 6, 15.

275. Summary of Imperative Constructions.

Positive.

2d P. **Audī,** *hear thou;* **audītō** (legal or contingent); **audiēs** (familiar); **audiās** (ideal Second Person chiefly).

3d P. **Audītō** (legal), *let him hear;* **audiat.**

Negative.

2d P. **Nē audī,** *hear not* (poetic); **nē audītō** (legal); **nōn audiēs** (familiar); **nē audiās** (chiefly ideal); **nōlī audīre** (common); **nē audīveris** (rare).

3d P. **Nē audītō** (legal), *let him not hear;* **nē audiat; nē audīverit.**

Tenses of the Moods and Verbal Substantives.

276. The Indicative alone expresses with uniform directness the period of time.

277. 1. The Present and Imperfect Subjunctive have to do with *continued* action, the Perfect and Pluperfect with *completed* action. The Perfect Subjunctive is also used to express the *attainment*.

2. In simple sentences Present and Perfect Subjunctive postpone the ascertainment of the Predicate to the Future. The action itself may be Present or Future for the Present Subjunctive; Present, Past, or Future for the Perfect Subjunctive.

Crēdat. *He may believe* (now *or* hereafter).

Crēdiderit. *Let him have had the belief* (heretofore), *he may have come to the belief* (now), *he may come to the belief* (hereafter).

3. In simple sentences the Imperfect and Pluperfect Subjunctive are Past Tenses, and regularly serve to indicate unreality. (See 597.)

Note.—A Subjv. of the Past, being a future of the past, gives a prospective (or future) action the time of which is over (or past), so that the analysis of the past tenses of the Subjv. shows the same elements as the Periphrastic Conjugation with **eram** and **fuī.** Hence the frequent parallel use. See 254, R. 2, and 597, R. 3.

4. In dependent sentences the Subjunctive is future if the leading verb has a future signification (515, R. 3); otherwise

the Subjunctive represents the Indicative. The tense is regulated by the law of sequence. (See 509.)

278. The Imperative is necessarily Future.

279. The Infinitive has two uses:

1. Its use as a Substantive.
2. Its use as a representative of the Indicative.

280. THE INFINITIVE AS A SUBSTANTIVE.—As a Substantive the Infinitive has two tenses, Present and Perfect. (See 419.)

1. The Present Infinitive is the common form of the Infinitive, used as a Substantive. It has to do with *continued* action.

(*a*) The Present Infinitive is used as a subject or predicate. (See 423, 424.)

Quibusdam tōtum hōc displicet philosophārī, C., *Fin.*, I. 1, 1; *to some this whole business of metaphysics is a nuisance.*

(*b*) The Present Infinitive is used as the object of Verbs of Creation (*Auxiliary Verbs,* Verbs that *help* the Infinitive into being; see 423.)

Catō servīre quam pūgnāre māvult, C., *Att.*, VII. 15, 2; *Cato prefers to be a slave rather than to fight* (*being a slave to fighting*).

2. The Perfect Infinitive is comparatively little used as a Substantive. It has to do with *completed* action, and is also used to express *attainment.*

(*a*) As a subject, it is used chiefly in fixed expressions or in marked opposition to the Present.

Plūs prōderit dēmōnstrāsse rēctam prōtinus viam quam revocāre ab errōre iam lāpsōs, QUINT., II. 6, 2; *it will be more profitable to have pointed out the right path immediately than to recall from wandering those that have already gone astray.* **[Nōn] tam turpe fuit vincī quam contendisse decōrum est,** Ov., *M.*, IX. 5; *'twas not so much dishonour to be beaten as 'tis an honour to have struggled.*

REMARKS.—1. By a kind of attraction **decuit,** *became,* takes occasionally a Pf. Inf. (*emotional*).

Tunc flēsse decuit, L., XXX. 44, 7; *that was the time when it would have been becoming to weep* (*to have wept*). **Et ērubuisse decēbat,** Ov., *M.*, IV. 330; *the very flush of shame was becoming.*

2. So **oportuit**, *behooved*, is frequently followed by the Pf. Part. passive, with or without **esse.** This seems to have belonged to familiar style ; it is accordingly very common in early Latin.

[**Hōc**] **iam prīdem factum esse oportuit,** C., *Cat.*, I. 2, 5 ; *this ought to have been done long ago.*

(*b*) As an object, the Perfect Infinitive is seldom found in the active, except after **velle,** *to wish,* which seems to have been a legal usage.

Nēminem notā strēnuī aut īgnāvī mīlitis notāsse voluī, L., XXIV. 16, 11 ; *I wished to have marked* (*to mark finally, to brand*) *no soldier with the mark of bravery or of cowardice.* **Annālēs, quibus crēdidisse mālīs,** L., XLII. 11, 1. NEIQUIS EŌRUM BACĂNAL HABUISE VELET, S. C. DE BAC.

Otherwise it is found mainly in the poets (after the fashion of the Greek Aorist Inf.), and usually with the Pf. and Plupf. tenses, **voluī,** *etc.*, **potuī, dēbueram** (**dēbuī**).

Frātrēs tendentēs opācō Pēlion imposuisse Olympō, H., *O.*, III. 4, 52 ; *The brothers striving to pile Pelion on shady Olympus.*

NOTES.—1. This usage with **velle** seems to have approached often the Fut. Pf. in force. A Pf. Inf. after the Pr. of **posse** occurs very rarely : **Nōn potes probāsse nūgās,** PL., *Aul.*, 828 ; see V., *A.*, VI. 78, and several cases in OVID and MARTIAL.

2. The Pf. Inf. act. (subj. or obj.) is often found in the poets, especially in elegiac poetry, as the first word in the second half of a pentameter, where it can hardly be distinguished from a Present. This usage may be due partly to analogy with verbs of wishing, partly to the exigencies of the metre, partly to the influence of the Greek Aorist. It must be distinguished from the normal use of the Perfect: **Quam iuvat immītēs ventōs audīre cubantem Et dominam tenerō dētinuisse sinū!** TIB., I. 1, 45.

3. Noteworthy is the occasional use of **dēbeō** with the Pf. Inf. act. in the sense "must have": **statim vīcisse dēbeō,** C., *Rosc. Am.*, 23, 73 ; **dēbēs adnotāsse,** PLIN., *Ep.*, VII. 20, 6.

(*c*) In the Passive, the Perfect Infinitive is used after verbs of Will and Desire, to denote impatience of anything except entire fulfilment. See 537.

[**Patriam**] **exstinctam cupit,** C., *Fin.*, IV. 24, 66 ; *he desires his country blotted out.*

Here the Infinitive **esse** is seldom expressed.

Corinthum patrēs vestrī tōtīus Graeciae lūmen exstinctum esse voluērunt, C., *Imp.*, 5, 11 (211, R. 6).

NOTE.—This usage is common in Comedy and in CICERO, rare, if at all, in CAESAR and SALLUST ; and later also it is rare, surviving chiefly in phrases. The principal verb is **volō,** less often **cupiō,** very rarely **expetō** and **nōlō.**

281. THE INFINITIVE AS THE REPRESENTATIVE OF THE INDICATIVE.—As the representative of the Indicative, the

Infinitive has all its Tenses: Present, Past, Future, and Future Periphrastics.

1. The Present Infinitive represents *contemporaneous action*—hence the Present Indicative after a Principal Tense, and the Imperfect after a Historical Tense:

Dīcō eum venīre, *I say that he is coming;* **dīcēbam eum venīre,** *I said that he was coming.*

2. The Perfect Infinitive represents *Prior Action*—hence the Perfect and Imperfect Indicative after a Principal Tense, and the Pluperfect, Imperfect, and Historical Perfect Indicative after a Historical Tense:

Dīcō eum vēnisse, *I say that he came, has come, used to come.*
Dīxī eum vēnisse, *I said that he had come, used to come, did come.*

NOTE.—**Meminī,** *I remember*, when used of *personal experience*, commonly takes the Present: **Tum mē rēgem appellārī ā vōbīs meminī, nunc tyrannum vocārī videō,** L., XXXIV. 31, 13; *I remember being styled by you a king then, I see that I am called a tyrant now.*

So also rarely **memoriā teneō, recordor,** *I remember, I recall*, and **fugit mē,** *I do not remember.* When the experience is not personal, the ordinary construction is followed: **Memineram Marium ad īnfimōrum hominum misericordiam cōnfūgisse,** C., *Sest.*, 22, 50; *I remembered that Marius had thrown himself on the mercy of a set of low creatures.*

The peculiar construction with the Pr. arises from the liveliness of the recollection. When the action is to be regarded as a bygone, the Pf. may be used even of personal experience: **Mē meminī īrātum dominae turbāsse capillōs,** Ov., *A.A.*, II. 169; *I remember in my anger having tousled my sweetheart's hair.*

282. The Present Participle active denotes *continuance;* the Perfect passive, *completion* or *attainment.*

NOTE.—The Latin is more exact than the English in the use of the tenses. So the Pf. Part. is frequently employed when we use the Present; especially in classical prose, with verbs that indicate a condition, mental or physical, where the action of the participle is conceived as continuing *up to*, and sometimes *into*, that of the leading verb, as **ratus,** *thinking;* **veritus,** *fearing;* **gāvīsus,** *rejoicing, etc.* This usage spreads later: **complexus,** *embracing;* **hortātus,** *exhorting.*

283. The Future Participle (active) is a verbal adjective, denoting capability and tendency, chiefly employed in the older language with **sum,** *I am,* as a periphrastic tense. In later Latin it is used freely, just as the Present and Perfect Participles, to express subordinate relations.

NOTES.—1. The so-called Fut. Part. passive is more properly called the Gerundive, and has already been discussed (251).

2. The Supine, being without tense relations, does not belong here.

SIMPLE SENTENCE EXPANDED.

284. The sentence may be expanded by the *multiplication* or by the *qualification*, A, of the subject, B, of the predicate.

A.

1. Multiplication of the Subject.

Concord.

285. Number.—The common predicate of two or more subjects is put in the Plural number :

Lūcius Tarquinius et Tullia minor iunguntur nūptiīs, L., I. 46, 9 ; *Lucius Tarquinius and Tullia the younger are united in marriage.* **Pater et māter mortuī [sunt],** Ter., *Eun.*, 518 ; *father and mother are dead.*

Exceptions.—1. The common predicate may agree with a Sing. subject when that subject is the nearest or the most important: "My flesh and my heart *faileth*," Psa., LXXIII. 26.

Aetās et fōrma et super omnia Rōmānum nōmen tē ferōciōrem facit, L., XXXI. 18, 3 ; *your youth and beauty, and, above all, the name of Roman, makes you too mettlesome.* **Latagum saxō occupat ōs faciemque adversam** V., *A.*, X. 698 (323, N. 2).

The agreement depends largely also upon the position of the verb. If it precedes or follows the first subj., the Sing. is more apt to stand.

2. Two abstracts in combination, when conceived as a unit, take a Sing. verb : "When distress and anguish *cometh* upon you," Prov., I. 27.

Religiō et fidēs antepōnātur amīcitiae, C., *Off.*, III. 10, 46 ; *let the religious obligation of a promise be preferred to friendship.*

So any close union : "Your gold and silver *is* cankered," Jas., V. 3.

Senātus populusque Rōmānus intellegit, C., *Fam.*, V. 8, 2; *the senate and people of Rome perceives* (= *Rome perceives*). **Tua fāma et gnātae vīta in dubium veniet,** Ter., *Ad.*, 340 ; *your good name will be jeoparded and your daughter's life.*

3. When the same predicate is found with two or more subjects, who are conceived as acting independently, classical usage requires that the predicate be in the Singular. Livy introduces the Pl., which grows, and becomes the rule in Tacitus : **Palātium Rōmulus, Remus Aventīnum ad inaugurandum templa capiunt,** L., I. 6, 4.

Notes.—1. **Neque—neque,** *neither—nor*, allows the Pl. chiefly when the Persons are different : **Haec neque ego neque tū fēcimus,** Ter., *Ad.*, 103 ; *neither you nor I did this.*

The same is true, but not so common, of **et—et** (*as well as*), **aut—aut**, *either—or*.

2. A Sing. subj. combined with another word by **cum**, *with*, is treated properly as a Singular. It is treated as a Pl. once each by CATO, TERENCE (*Heaut.*, 473), CICERO (by anacoluthon), CAESAR (*B.C.*, III. 88), more often by SALLUST and his imitators, LIVY, and later writers. VELLEIUS, VALERIUS M., and TACITUS follow the classical usage.

Sulla cum Scīpiōne . . . . lēgēs inter sē contulērunt, C., *Ph.*, XII. 11, 27. **Ipse dux cum aliquot prīncipibus capiuntur,** L., XXI. 60, 7; *the general himself with some of the leading men are captured.*

3. In the Abl. Abs. the Part. stands usually in the Pl. with persons, usually in the Sing. with things. **C. Gracchō et M. Fulviō Flaccō interfectīs,** S., *Iug.*, 16, 2. **Cāritāte benevolentiāque sublātā,** C., *Lael.*, 27, 102.

286. GENDER.—When the Genders of combined subjects are the same, the adjective predicate agrees in gender; when the genders are different, the adjective predicate takes either the strongest gender or the nearest.

1. In things with life, the masculine gender is the strongest; in things without life, the neuter.

(*a*) The strongest:

Pater et māter mortuī [**sunt**], TER., *Eun.*, 518 (285). **Mūrus et porta dē caelō tācta erant,** L., XXXII. 29, 1; *wall and gate had been struck by lightning.* **Hōc anima atque animus vinctī sunt foedere semper,** LUCR., III. 416.

(*b*) The nearest:

Convicta est Messālīna et Silius, *Cf.* TAC., *Ann.*, XII. 65; *Messalina was convicted and* (*so was*) *Silius.* **Hippolochus Lārissaeōrumque dēditum est praesidium,** L., XXXVI. 9, 14; *Hippolochus and the Larissaean garrison* (*were*) *surrendered.*

2. When things with life and things without life are combined, the gender varies.

(*a*) Both as persons:

Rēx rēgiaque clāssis profectī (**sunt**), L., XXI. 50, 11; *the king and the king's fleet set out.*

(*b*) Both as things:

Nātūrā inimīca [**sunt**] **lībera cīvitās et rēx,** *Cf.* L., XLIV. 24, 2; *a free state and a king are natural enemies.*

3. When the subjects are feminine abstracts the predicate may be a neuter Plural (211, R. 4).

Stultitiam et intemperantiam dīcimus esse fugienda, C., *Fin.*, III. 11, 39; *folly and want of self-control* (*we say*) *are* (*things*) *to be avoided.*

NOTE.—This usage does not appear in early Latin, nor in CAESAR or SALLUST.

287. Persons.—When the persons of combined subjects are different, the First Person is preferred to the Second, the Second to the Third :

Sī tū et Tullia, lūx nostra, valētis, ego et suāvissimus Cicerō valēmus, C., *Fam.*, xiv. 5, 1; *if Tullia, light of my life, and you are well, dearest Cicero and I are well.*

Remark.—(*a*) In contrasts, and when each person is considered separately, the predicate agrees with the person of the nearest subject. **Et ego et Cicerō meus flāgitābit,** C., *Att.*, iv. 18, 5 ; *my Cicero will demand it and (so will) I.* **Beātē vīvere aliī in aliō, vōs in voluptāte pōnitis,** C., *Fin.*, ii. 27, 86 ; *some make a blessed life to rest on one thing, some on another, you on pleasure.*

So regularly with disjunctives, see 285, n. 1.

(*b*) The order is commonly the order of the persons, not of modern politeness : **Ego et uxor mea,** *Wife and I.*

2. Qualification of the Subject.

288. The subject may be qualified by giving it an attribute. An attribute is that which serves to give a specific character.

The chief forms of the attribute are :

I. The adjective and its equivalents : **amīcus certus,** *a sure friend.*

Remark.—The equivalents of the adjective are : 1. The pronouns **hīc,** *this,* **ille,** *that, etc.* 2. Substantives denoting *rank, age, trade* : **servus homō,** *a slave person ;* **homō senex,** *an old fellow ;* **homō gladiātor,** *a gladiator-fellow ;* **mulier ancilla,** *a servant-wench.* 3. The Genitive (360, 1). 4. The Ablative (400). 5. Preposition and case : **excēssus ē vītā,** *departure from life.* 6. Adverbs, chiefly with substantival participles : **rēctē facta,** *good actions.* 7. Relative clauses (505).

II. The substantive in apposition : **Cicerō ōrātor,** *Cicero the orator.*

I. ADJECTIVE ATTRIBUTE.

Concord.

289. The Adjective Attribute agrees with its substantive in gender, number, and case :

Gender.	Number.
Vir sapiēns, *a wise man,*	**virī sapientēs,** *wise men.*
Mulier pulchra, *a beautiful woman,*	**mulierēs pulchrae,** *beautiful women.*
Rēgium dōnum, *royal gift,*	**rēgia dōna,** *royal gifts.*

CASE.

Virī sapientis, *of a wise man.*
Mulierī pulchrae, *for a beautiful woman.*
Virum sapientem, *wise man.*
bone fīlī! *good son!*
rēgiō dōnō, *by royal gift.*
mulierēs pulchrās, *beautiful women.*

290. The common attribute of two or more substantives agrees with the nearest; rarely with the most important.

Volusēnus, vir et cōnsiliī māgnī et virtūtis, CAES., *B. G.*, III. 5, 2; *Volusenus, a man of great wisdom and valour.* **Cūncta maria terraeque patēbant**, S., *C.*, 10, 1; *all seas and lands lay open.* **Multa alia castella vīcīque aut dēlēta hostīliter aut integra in potestātem vēnēre**, L., IX. 38, 1.

REMARKS.—1. For emphasis, or to avoid ambiguity, the adj. is repeated with every substantive. Sometimes also for rhetorical reasons simply.

(Semprōniae) multae facētiae, multusque lepōs inerat, S., *C.*, 25, 5; *Sempronia had a treasure of witticisms, a treasure of charming talk.*

2. When a substantive is construed with several *similar* adjectives in the Sing., it may be in agreement with one in the Sing. or may stand in the Pl., according to its position:

Quārta et Mārtia legiōnēs, C., *Fam.*, XI. 19, 1, but **Legiō Mārtia quārtaque**, C., *Ph.*, V. 17, 46, *The fourth and Martian legions.*

NOTES.—1. A common surname is put in the Plural: **M. (et) Q. Cicerōnēs**, *Marcus and Quintus Cicero*; **C., Cn., M. Carbōnēs**, *Gaius, Gnaeus* (and) *Marcus Carbo*; otherwise, **M. Cicerō et Q. Cicerō**, *Marcus and Quintus Cicero.*

2. Poets are free in regard to the position of the adjective: **Semper honōs nōmenque tuum laudēsque manēbunt**, V., *A.*, I. 609.

291. *Position of the Attribute.*—1. When the attribute is emphatic, it is commonly put before the substantive, otherwise in classical Latin ordinarily after it. But see 676.

1. **Fugitīvus servus**, *a runaway slave* (one complex).
2. **Servus fugitīvus**, *a slave* (that is) *a runaway* (two notions).

Many expressions, however, have become fixed formulæ, such as **cīvis Rōmānus**, *Roman citizen*; **populus Rōmānus**, *people of Rome.*

Compare *body politic*, *heir apparent* in English.

REMARKS.—1. Variation in the position of the adj. often causes variation in the meaning of the word. Thus **rēs bonae**, *good things*; **bonae rēs**, *articles of value*, or *good circumstances*; **rēs urbānae**, *city matters*; **urbānae rēs**, *witticisms*; **mēnsa secunda**, *a second table*; **secunda mēnsa**, *dessert.*

2. Superlatives which denote order and sequence in time and space are often used partitively, and then *generally* precede their substantive: **summa aqua**, *the surface of the water;* **summus mōns**, *the top of the mountain;* **vēre prīmō, prīmō vēre**, *in the beginning of spring.* Similarly **in mediā urbe**, *in the midst of the city;* **reliqua, cētera Graecia**, *the rest of Greece*, and the like.

2. When the attribute belongs to two or more words, it is placed sometimes after them all, sometimes after the first, sometimes before them all.

Dīvitiae, nōmen, opēs vacuae cōnsiliō dēdecoris plēnae sunt, C., *Rep.*, I. 34, 51; *riches, name, resources (when) void of wisdom are full of dishonour.*

For examples of the other positions see 290.

Numerals.

292. **Duo** means simply *two*, **ambō**, *both* (two considered together), **uterque**, *either* (two considered apart, as, "They crucified two other with him, on either side one," JOHN, XIX. 18):

Supplicātiō ambōrum nōmine et triumphus utrīque dēcrētus est, L., XXVIII. 9, 9; *a thanksgiving in the name of both and a triumph to either (each of the two) was decreed.* **Quī utrumque probat, ambōbus dēbuit ūtī**, C., *Fin.*, II. 7, 20; *he who approves of either ought to have availed himself of both.*

REMARK.—**Uterque** is seldom Pl., except of sets; so with **plūrālia tantum.**

Utrīque (*i.e.*, **plēbis fautōrēs et senātus**) **victōriam crūdēliter exercēbant**, S., *C.*, 38, 4; *either party* (democrats and senate) *made a cruel use of victory.* **Duae fuērunt Ariovistī uxōrēs: utraeque in eā fugā periērunt**, CAES., *B.G.*, I. 53, 4; *Ariovistus's wives were two in number; both perished in that flight.* **Proximō diē Caesar ē castrīs utrīsque cōpiās suās ēdūxit**, CAES., *B.G.*, I. 50, 1.

On **uterque** with the Pl., see 211, R. 1; with Gen., see 371, R.

293. **Mīlle**, *a thousand*, is in the Sing. an indeclinable adj. and is less frequently used with the Genitive: **mīlle mīlitēs**, rather than **mīlle mīlitum**, *a thousand soldiers;* in the Pl. it is a declinable substantive, and must have the Genitive: **duo mīlia mīlitum**, *two thousand(s of) soldiers = two regiments of soldiers.* If a smaller number comes between, the substantive usually follows the smaller number:

3500 *cavalry*, { **tria mīlia quīngentī equitēs,**
tria mīlia equitum et quīngentī, but
equitēs tria mīlia quīngentī, or
equitum tria mīlia quīngentī. }

But **duo mīlia quīngentī hostium in aciē periēre,** L., XXII. 7, 3.

NOTE.—The use of **mīlle** as a substantive with the Part. Gen. is found mostly in ante-classical and post-classical Latin. CICERO and CAESAR use it but rarely, and in phrases such as **mīlle nummum, mīlle passuum.** LIVY is fonder of it.

294. ORDINALS.—The Ordinals are used more often in Latin than in English; thus always in dates: **annō ducentēsimō quārtō,** *in the year 204.* Sometimes they are used for the cardinals with a carelessness that gives rise to ambiguity:

Quattuor annī sunt, ex quō tē nōn vīdī,
It is four years, that I have not seen you (*since I saw you*).
Quārtus annus est, ex quō tē nōn vīdī.
It is the fourth year (*four years, going on four years*).

NOTE.—To avoid this ambiguity forms of **incipere,** *to begin*, and **exigere,** *to finish*, seem to have been used. *Cf.*, PL., *Capt.*, 980; *Cist.*, 161.

On **quisque** with the ordinal, see 318, 2.

295. DISTRIBUTIVES.—The distributives are used with an exactness which is foreign to our idiom wherever repetition is involved, as in the multiplication table.

Bis bīna quot [sunt]? C., *N.D.*, II. 18, 49; *how many are twice two?* **Scrīptum eculeum cum quīnque pedibus, pullōs gallīnāceōs trīs cum ternīs pedibus nātōs esse,** L., XXXII. 1, 11; *a letter was written to say that a colt had been foaled with five feet* (and) *three chickens hatched with three feet* (*apiece*).

With **singulī** the distributive is preferred, but the cardinal may be used.

Antōnius (**pollicitus est**) **dēnāriōs quīngēnōs singulīs mīlitibus datūrum,** C., *Fam.*, X. 32, 4; *Antonius promised to give five hundred denarii to each soldier.* **Singulīs cēnsōribus dēnāriī trecentī** (so all MSS.) **imperātī sunt,** C., *Verr.*, II. 55, 137; *the censors were required to pay three hundred denarii apiece.*

NOTE.—Poets and later prose writers often use the distributive when the cardinal would be the rule; thus **bīnī** is not unfrequently used of a pair even in CICERO: **bīnōs** (**scyphōs**) **habēbam,** *Verr.*, IV. 14, 32. When there is an idea of grouping, the distributive is often broken up into a multiplicative and a distributive; as,

Carmen ab ter novēnīs virginibus canī iūssērunt, L., XXXI. 12, 9; *they ordered a chant to be sung by thrice nine virgins.*

On the other hand, prose sometimes shows a cardinal when exact usage **would** require a distributive. So regularly **mīlia.**

Mīlia talentum per duodecim annōs (**dabitis**), L., XXXVII. 45, 15.

On the distributives with **plūrālia tantum,** see 97, R. 3.

Comparatives and Superlatives.

296. COMPARATIVE.—The comparative degree generally takes a term of comparison either with **quam,** *than,* or in the Ablative :

Īgnōrātiō futūrōrum malōrum ūtilior est quam scientia, C., *Div.*, II. 9, 23; *ignorance of future evils is better than knowledge* (*of them*). **Nihil est virtūte amābilius,** C., *Lael.*, 8, 28 ; *nothing is more lovable than virtue.*

REMARKS.—I. (*a*) The Abl. is used only when the word with **quam** would stand in the Nom. or Acc. (644).

Caesar minor est { **quam Pompēius,** / **Pompēiō,** } *Caesar is younger than Pompey.*

Caesarem plūs amāmus { **quam Pompēium,** / **Pompēiō,** } *we love Caesar more than Pompey.*

In the second example the use of the Abl. may give rise to ambiguity, as the sentence may also mean "*we love Caesar more than Pompey loves him.*" This ambiguity is always present when adverbs are used, and hence good prose avoids using a comparative adv. with an Ablative. See H., *S.*, I. I, 97.

(*b*) With cases other than Nom. or Acc., **quam** is regularly used to avoid ambiguity.

Ānulīs nostrīs plūs quam animīs crēditur, SEN., *Ben.*, III. 15, 3 (217).

2. The Abl. is very common in negative sentences, and is used exclusively in negative relative sentences.

Polybium sequāmur, quō nēmō fuit dīligentior, C., *Rep.*, II. 14, 27 ; *let us follow Polybius, than whom no one was more careful.*

3. Measure of difference is put in the Ablative (403).

4. **Quam** is often omitted after **plūs, amplius,** *more,* and **minus,** *less* and the like, without affecting the construction :

Hominī miserō plūs quīngentōs colaphōs īnfrēgit mihī, TER., *Ad.*, 199 ; *he has dealt me, luckless creature, more than five hundred crushing boxes on the ear.* **Spatium est nōn amplius pedum sēscentōrum,** CAES., *B.C.*, I. 38, 5 ; *the space is not more than* (*of*) *six hundred feet.*

But the normal construction is not excluded :

Palūs nōn lātior pedibus quīnquāgintā, CAES., *B.G.*, VII. 19, 1 ; *a swamp not broader than fifty feet* (or **pedēs quīnquāgintā**). **Nostrī mīlitēs amplius hōrīs quattuor pūgnāvērunt,** CAES., *B.G.*, IV. 37, 3.

5. In statements of age we may have a variety of expressions; thus, *more than thirty years old* may be:

1. **Nātus plūs (quam) trīgintā annōs.** 3. **Māior (quam) trīgintā annōs nātus.**
2. **Nātus plūs trīgintā annīs** (rare). 4. **Māior trīgintā annīs (nātus).**
5. **Māior trīgintā annōrum.**

6. On the combination of the comparative with **opīniōne,** *opinion,* **spē,** *hope,* and the like, see 398, N. 1.

NOTES.—1. Verbs and other words involving comparison sometimes have the Abl. where another construction would be more natural. Thus, **mālle,** *to prefer* (poet. and post-classical), **aequē, adaequē,** *equally* (early and late), **alius,** *other* (mainly poetic and rare): **Nūllōs hīs māllem lūdōs spectāsse,** H., *S.*, II. 8, 79. **Quī mē in terrā aequē fortūnātus erit?** PL., *Curc.*, 141. **Nē putēs alium sapiente bonōque beātum,** *Ep.*, I. 16, 20.

2. Instead of the Abl., the Gen. is found occasionally in late Latin.

3. Instead of **quam** or the Abl., prepositional uses with the positive are often found; as **prae,** *in comparison with,* **praeter, ante,** *beyond;* also **suprā quam.** Poetical is the circumlocution with **quālis,** as HOR., *Epod.*, 5, 59. **Īnferior** is sometimes constructed with the Dat., according to the sense; *inferior to* instead of *lower than.*

4. **Atque** for **quam** is mainly poetical; see 644, N. 2.

297. *Standard of Comparison omitted.*—When the standard of comparison is omitted, it is supplied: 1. By the context; 2. By the usual or proper standard; 3. By the opposite.

1. By the context:

Solent rēgēs Persārum plūrēs uxōrēs habēre, *Cf.* C., *Verr.*, III. 33, 76; *the kings of Persia usually have more wives* [than one].

2. By the proper standard:

Senectūs est nātūrā loquācior, C., *Cat.M.*, 16, 55, *Old age is naturally rather* (or *too*) *talkative.*

3. By the opposite:

Quiēsse erit melius, L., III. 48, 3; *it will be better to be-perfectly-quiet* (than to make a disturbance).

298. *Disproportion.*—Disproportion is expressed by the comparative with **quam prō,** *than for,* and the Ablative, or with **quam ut,** *that,* or **quam quī,** *who,* and the Subjunctive:

Minor caedēs quam prō tantā victōriā fuit, L., X, 14, 21; *the loss was (too) small for so great a victory.* **Quis nōn intellegit Canachī sīgna rigidiōra esse quam ut imitentur vēritātem?** C., *Br.*, 18, 70; *who does not perceive that Canachus' figures are too stiff to imitate the truth of nature?* **Māior sum quam cui possit Fortūna nocēre,** Ov., *M.*, VI. 195; *I am too great for Fortune possibly to hurt me.*

REMARK.—Disproportion may also be expressed by the positive in combination with prepositional phrases, *etc.*: **prō multitūdine angustī fīnēs**, CAES., *B.G.*, I. 2, 5; *boundaries too small for their multitude.*

NOTES.—1. The constructions **quam prō** and **quam quī** are both post-Ciceronian.

2. The **ut** is frequently omitted after **quam,** as: **Dolābella celerius Asiā [excēssit], quam eō praesidium addūcī potuisset,** C., *Fam.*, XII. 15, 1. This is especially common after **potius quam.**

299. *Two Qualities compared.*—When two qualities of the same substantive are compared, we find either **magis** and **quam** with the positive, or a double comparative:

Celer tuus disertus magis est quam sapiēns, C., *Att.*, X. 1, 4; *your* (friend) *Celer is eloquent rather than wise—more eloquent than wise.* **Acūtiōrem sē quam ōrnātiōrem [vult],** C., *Opt. Gen.*, 2, 6; *he wishes to be acute rather than ornate.*

NOTES.—1. There is no distinction to be made between the two expressions. In the latter turn, which is found first, but rarely, in CICERO, the second comparative is merely attracted into the same form as the first. The same rule applies to the adverb: **fortius quam fēlīcius,** *with more bravery than good luck.*

2. Post-Augustan Latin shows occasionally the comparative followed by **quam,** and the positive: **Nimia pietās vestra ācrius quam cōnsīderātē excitāvit,** TAC., *H.*, I. 83.

300. *Restriction to the Comparative.*—When but two objects are compared, the comparative exhausts the degrees of comparison, whereas, in English, the superlative is employed, unless the idea of duality is emphatic.

Nātū māior, *the eldest* (of two), *the elder;* **nātū minor,** *the youngest, the younger.* **Prior,** *the first;* **posterior,** *the last.*

Posteriōrēs cōgitātiōnēs, ut āiunt, sapientiōrēs solent esse, C., *Ph.*, XII. 2, 5; *afterthoughts, as the saying is, are usually the wisest.*

REMARK.—The same rule applies to the interrogative **uter,** *which of two?* (*whether?*): **Ex duōbus uter dīgnior? ex plūribus, quis dīgnissimus?** QUINT., VII. 4, 21; *of two, which is the worthier? of more* (than two), *which is the worthiest?*

NOTE.—**Quis** is rarely used instead of **uter,** as C., *Fam.*, VI. 3, 1; V., *A.*, XII. 725.

301. *Comparative Strengthened.* The comparative is often strengthened during the classical period by the insertion of **etiam,** *even*; later also by **adhūc,** *still.* **Multō** is properly the Ablative of difference, and is the normal form until the time of VERGIL, when its place is taken largely by **longē,** except in HORACE, who retains **multō.** Ante-classical and post-classical Latin occasionally doubles the comparative: **magis dulcius,** PL., *Stich.*, 699. **Nihil inveniēs magis hōc certō certius,** PL.,

Capt., 643. Even in CICERO a word involving Preference is sometimes strengthened by **potius**:

[**Themistoclī fuit**] **optābilius oblīvīscī posse potius quam meminisse**, C., *Or.*, II. 74, 300; *Themistocles thought it (more) preferable to be able to forget (rather) than to be able to remember.*

302. *Superlative.*—The Latin superlative is often to be rendered by the English positive, especially of persons:

Quīntus Fabius Māximus, *Quintus Fabius the Great.* **Māximō impetū, māiōre fortūnā**, L., XXVIII. 36, 2; *with great vigour, with greater luck.* **Tam fēlīx essēs quam fōrmōsissima vellem**, Ov., *Am.*, I. 8, 27; *would thou wert fortunate as* (thou art) *fair.*

303. *Superlative Strengthened.*—The superlative is strengthened by **multō**, *much* (especially in early Latin); **longē**, *by far* (the normal usage in the classical period); **vel**, *even;* **ūnus, ūnus omnium**, *one above all others;* **quam** (with adverbs and adjectives), **quantus** (with **māximus**), **ut** (with adverbs)—**potest, potuit**, *as—as possible.*

Ex Britannīs omnibus longē sunt hūmānissimī quī Cantium incolunt, CAES., *B.G.*, V. 14, 1; *of all the Britons by far the most cultivated are those that inhabit Kent.* **Prōtagorās sophistēs illīs temporibus vel māximus**, C., *N.D.*, I. 23, 63; *Protagoras, the very greatest sophist* (= professor of wisdom) *in those times.* **Urbem ūnam mihĭ amīcissimam dēclīnāvī**, C., *Planc.*, 41, 97; *I turned aside from a city above all others friendly to me.* (**Caesar**) **quam aequissimō locō potest castra commūnit**, CAES., *B.G.*, V. 49, 7; *Caesar fortifies a camp in as favourable a position as possible.*

REMARKS.—1. The omission of **potest** leaves **quam** with the superlative, which becomes a regular combination: *as (great) as possible.*

2. For **tam, tantum**, with positive followed by **quam, quantum quī**, and the **superlative**, see 642, R. 5.

PRONOUNS.

I. Personal Pronouns.

304. 1. The personal Pronoun is usually omitted when **it** is the subject of a verb; see 207.

2. The Genitive forms, **meī, tūī, suī, nostrī, vestrī**, are used mainly as *Objective* Genitives; see 364, N. 2.

(**Mārcellīnus**) **sē ācerrimum tuī dēfēnsōrem fore ostendit**, C., *Fam.*, I. 1, 2; *Marcellinus showed that he would be your keenest defender.*

NOTES.—1. **Nostrum** and **vestrum** for **nostrī, vestrī**, are very rare: [**Iūppiter, cūstōs**] **hūius urbis āc vestrum**, *Cf.* C., *Cat.*, III. 12, 29.

2. The Possessive pronouns sometimes are found in place of this Genitive: **Neque neclegentiā tuā neque odiō id fēcit tuō**, TER., *Ph.*, 1016; *he did this neither from*

neglect of thee nor from hatred of thee. **Vester cōnspectus reficit et recreat mentem meam,** C., *Planc.*, I, 2; *the sight of you refreshes and renews my spirits.*

"If I be a master, where is my fear?" MAL., I. 6.

3. The Genitive forms, **nostrum** and **vestrum**, are used *partitively*; see 364, R.

Tē ad mē venīre uterque nostrum cupit, C., *Att.*, XIII. 33, 2; *each of us two desires that you should come to me.*

NOTES.—1. So regularly also in certain phraseological uses which may be partitive at basis. **Frequentia vestrum, cōnsēnsus vestrum,** regularly in combination with **omnium** (364, R.), and occasionally when the Possessive is more natural; **is enim splendor est vestrum,** C., *Att.*, VII. 13A, 3.

2. For a Part. Gen. of the third person (reflexive) a circumlocution must be used, such as **ex sē** or the Possessive **suōrum.**

2. Demonstrative Pronouns.

305. Hīc, *this* (the Demonstrative of the First Person), refers to *that which is nearer the speaker,* and may mean:

1. The speaker himself: **hīc homō = ego,** PL., *Trin.*, 1115.

2. The persons with whom the speaker identifies himself, *e. g.*, the judges in a suit at law: **sī ego hōs nōvī,** *if I know these men* (= the jury).

3. The most important subject immediately in hand: **hīc sapiēns dē quō loquor,** C., *Ac.*, II. 33, 105; *this* (imaginary) *wise man of whom I am speaking.*

4. That in which the speaker is peculiarly interested: **hōc studium,** *this pursuit of mine, of ours.*

5. That which has just been mentioned: **haec hāctenus,** *these things thus far = so much for that.*

6. Very frequently, that which is about to be mentioned: **hīs condiciōnibus,** *on the following terms.*

7. The current period of time: **hīc diēs,** *to-day;* **haec nox,** *the night just past* or *just coming;* **hīc mēnsis,** *the current month.*

306. Iste, *that* (of thine, of yours), refers to *that which belongs more peculiarly to the Second Person* (Demonstrative of the Second Person):

Perfer istam mīlitiam, C., *Fam.*, VII. 11, 2; *endure that military service of yours.* **Adventū tuō ista subsellia vacuēfacta sunt,** C., *Cat.*, I. 7, 16; *at your approach the benches in your neighbourhood were vacated.*

NOTE.—The supposed contemptuous character of **iste** arises from the refusal to take any direct notice of the person under discussion, "the person *at* whom one speaks or points," and precisely the same thing is true of **hīc** and **ille,** but less common.

307. Ille, *that* (the Demonstrative of the Third Person), denotes *that which is more remote from the speaker,* and is often used in contrast to **hīc,** *this.*

Sōl mē ille admonuit, C., *Or.*, III., 55, 209 ; *that* (*yon*) *sun reminded me.* **Q. Catulus nōn antīquō illō mōre sed hōc nostrō ērudītus,** C., *Br.*, 35, 132; *Q. Catulus, a cultivated man, not after the old-fashioned standard of a by-gone time* (**illō**) *but by the standard of to-day* (**hōc**).

Ille may mean :

1. That which has been previously mentioned (often **ille quidem**): **illud quod initiō vōbīs prōposuī,** C., *Font.*, 7, 17; *that which I propounded to you at first.*

2. That which is well known, notorious (often put after the substantive) : **tēstula illa,** *that* (notorious) *potsherd = institution of ostracism ;* **illud Solōnis,** *that* (famous saying) *of Solon's.*

3. That which is to be recalled : **illud imprīmīs mīrābile,** *that* (which I am going to remind you of) *is especially wonderful.*

4. That which is expected :

Illa diēs veniet mea quā lūgubria pōnam, Ov., *Tr.*, IV. 2, 73 ; *the day will come when I shall lay aside* (*cease*) *my mournful strains.*

REMARKS.—1. **Hīc** and **ille** are used together in contrasts : as, *the latter—the former, the former—the latter.*

(*a*) When both are matters of indifference the natural signification is observed : **hīc,** *the latter ;* **ille,** *the former.*

Īgnāvia corpus hebetat, labor fīrmat ; illa mātūram senectūtem, hīc longam adolēscentiam reddit, CELS., I. 1; *laziness weakens the body, toil strengthens it ; the one* (the former) *hastens old age, the other* (the latter) *prolongs youth.*

(*b*) When the former is the more important, **hīc** is *the former*, **ille,** *the latter :*

Melior tūtiorque est certa pāx quam spērāta victōria ; haec in nostrā, illa in deōrum manū est, L., XXX. 30, 19 ; *better and safer is certain peace than hoped-for victory ; the former is in our hand(s), the latter in the hand(s) of the gods.*

2. **Hīc et ille ; ille et ille ; ille aut ille,** *this man and* (or) *that man = one or two.*

Nōn dīcam hōc sīgnum ablātum esse et illud ; hōc dīcō, nūllum tē sīgnum relīquisse, C., *Verr.*, I. 20, 53 ; *I will not say that this statue was taken off and that ;* (what) *I say* (is) *this, that you left no statue at all.*

3. The derived adverbs retain the personal relations of **hīc, iste, ille :** **hīc,** *here* (where I am) ; **hinc,** *hence* (from where I am) ; **hūc,** *hither* (where I am) ; **istīc,** *there* (where you are) ; **illīc,** *there* (where he is), *etc.*

4. The Demonstratives **hīc, iste, ille,** and the Determinative **is,** are often strengthened by **quidem,** *indeed.* The second member is then introduced by **sed, sed tamen** (more rarely **tamen, vērum, autem, vērō**), **vērumtamen,** and sometimes is added asyndetically. The sentence often requires that either the demonstrative or the particle be left untranslated.

Optāre hōc quidem est, nōn docēre, C., *Tusc.*, II. 13, 30; THAT *is a* (pious) *wish, not a* (logical) *proof.* **Nihil perfertur ad nōs praeter rūmōrēs satis istōs quidem cōnstantēs sed adhūc sine auctōre,** C., *Fam.* XII. 9, 1; *nothing is brought to us except reports, consistent enough, it is true, but thus far not authoritative.*

Ille is most often used thus; **is, iste, hīc,** more rarely.

NOTES.—1. **Hīc** and **ille** are sometimes employed to add a qualification to a substantive by means of a contrast: **Ōrātor nōn ille vulgāris sed hīc excellēns,** C., *Or.*, 14, 45; *an orator, not of the (yon) common type, but of the ideal excellence (we seek).*

2. Not unfrequently in poetry, very rarely in prose, in a long sentence a substantive is repeated by means of **ille**: V., *A.*, I. 3, **ille et terrīs iactātus**; H., *O.*, IV. 9, 51.

3. Sometimes two forms of **hīc, ille,** or **is** are found in the same clause referring to different substantives: **Ēvolve dīligenter ēius** [*i. e.*, **Platōnis**] **eum librum, quī est dē animō,** C., *Tusc.*, I. 11, 24.

4. **Ille** may refer to an oblique form of **is**: **Nōn est amīcī tālem esse in eum, quālis ille in sē est,** C., *Lael.*, 16, 59.

5. **Ille** is found chiefly in poetry with the personal pronouns **ego, tū,** and occasionally with **hīc,** and when so used takes its fullest force. **Hunc illum fātīs externā ab sēde profectum portendī generum,** V., *A.*, VII. 255.

3. Determinative and Reflexive Pronouns.

308. Is, *that,* is the determinative pronoun, and serves as the lacking pronoun of the Third Person. It furnishes the regular antecedent of the relative:

Mihĭ vēnit obviam tuus puer; is mihĭ litterās abs tē reddidit, C., *Att.*, II. 1, 1; *I was met by your servant; he delivered to me a letter from you.* **Is minimō eget mortālis quī minimum cupit,** SYRUS, 286 (Fr.); *that mortal is in want of least, who wanteth least.*

REMARKS.—1. **Is,** as the antecedent of the relative, is often omitted, chiefly in the Nom., more rarely in an oblique case (619).

Bis dat quī dat celeriter, SYRUS, 235 (Fr.); *he gives twice who gives in a trice.*

Often it has the force of **tālis** (631, 1) in this connection:

Ego is sum quī nihil umquam meā potius quam meōrum cīvium causā fēcerim, C., *Fam.*, V. 21, 2; *I am a man never to have done anything for my own sake, rather than for the sake of my fellow-citizens.*

2. **Is,** with a copulative or adversative particle, is used as *he* or *that* in English, for the purpose of emphasis. Such expressions are: **et is, atque is, isque,** *and he too, and that too;* **neque is, et is nōn,** *and he not, and that not;* **sed is,** *but he,* further strengthened by **quidem,** *indeed.* To refer to the whole action **id** is employed.

Exempla quaerimus et ea nōn antīqua, C., *Verr.*, III. 90, 210; *we are looking for examples, and those, too, not of ancient date.* **Epicūrus ūnā in domō et eā quidem angustā quam māgnōs tenuit amīcōrum gregēs,** C., *Fin.*, I. 20, 65; *what shoals of friends Epicurus had in one house, and* *that a pinched-up one!* **Negōtium māgnum est nāvigāre atque id mēnse Quīnctīlī,** C., *Att.* v. 12, 1; *it is a big job to take a voyage and that in the month of July.*

3. **Is** does not represent a substantive before a Gen., as in the English *that of.* In Latin the substantive is omitted, or repeated, or a word of like meaning substituted.

Nōn iūdiciō discipulōrum dīcere dēbet magister sed discipulī magistrī, QUINT., II. 2, 13; *the master is not to speak according to the judgment of the pupils; but the pupils according to that of the master.* **Nūlla est celeritās quae possit cum animī celeritāte contendere,** C., *Tusc.*, I. 19, 43; *there is no speed that can possibly vie with that of the mind.* **M. Coelius tribūnal suum iūxtā C. Trebōnī sellam collocāvit,** CAES., *B.C.*, III. 20, 1; *Marcus Coelius placed his chair of office next to that of Gaius Trebonius.*

Of course **hīc, ille,** and **iste** can be used with the Gen. in their proper sense.

309. REFLEXIVE. Instead of forms of **is**, the Reflexive Pronoun **suī, sibĭ, sē,** together with the Possessive of the Reflexive **suos (-us), sua, suom (-um)** is used. (See 521.)

1. *Regularly* when reference is made to the *grammatical* subject of the sentence:

Ipse sē quisque dīligit quod sibĭ quisque cārus est, C., *Lael.*, 21, 80; *every one loves himself, because every one is dear to himself.* **(Fadius) ā mē dīligitur propter summam suam hūmānitātem,** C., *Fam.*, XV. 14, 1; *Fadius is a favourite of mine by reason of his exceeding kindliness.*

The subject may be indefinite or (occasionally) impersonal.

Contentum suīs rēbus esse māximae sunt dīvitiae, C., *Par.*, VI. 3, 51; *to be content with one's own things (with what one hath) is the greatest riches.* **Perventum ad suōs erat,** L., XXXIII. 8, 6.

"Pure religion and undefiled is this . . . to keep himself unspotted from the world." JAMES, I. 27.

2. *Frequently* when reference is made to the *actual* subject (521, R. 2):

Suos rēx rēgīnae placet, PL., *St.*, 133; *every queen favours her own king (every Gill loves her own Jack).* **Ōsculātur tigrim suus cūstōs,** SEN., *E.M.*, 85, 41; *her own keeper kisses the tigress (the tigress is kissed by her own keeper).* **Cuī prōposita sit cōnservātiō suī necesse est huīc partēs quoque suī cārās esse,** C., *Fin.*, V. 13, 37; *he who has in view the preservation of himself (self-preservation) must necessarily hold dear the parts of (that) self also.*

This is especially common with **suos,** which when thus employed has usually its emphatic sense: *own, peculiar, proper.*

3. **Suī, sibĭ, sē** are the regular complements of the infinitive and its equivalents when a reflexive idea is involved; they are also used with prepositions **ergā, inter, propter, per,** for especial emphasis.

(Rōmānī) suī colligendī hostibus facultātem (nōn) relinquunt, CAES., *B.G.*, III. 6, 1; *the Romans do not leave the enemy a chance to rally.* **Ipsum Furnium per sē vīdī libentissimē,** C., *Fam.*, X. 3, 1.

4. **Suos (-us)** is also used in prepositional phrases that are joined closely with the substantives; so after **cum, inter,** and more rarely after **in, intrā,** and **ad.**

Māgōnem cum clāsse suā in Hispāniam mittunt, L., XXIII. 32, 11; *they sent Mago with his fleet to Spain.* **Helvētiōs in fīnēs suōs revertī iūssit,** CAES., *B.G.*, I. 28, 3; *he ordered the Helvetians to return to their own country.*

So the phrases **suō tempore,** *at the right time;* **suō locō,** *at the right place.*

Cōmoediae quem ūsum in puerīs putem suō locō dīcam, QUINT., I. 8, 7; *what I consider to be the good of comedy in the case of boys I will mention in the proper place.*

NOTES.—1. The writer may retain forms of **is,** if he desires to emphasise his own point of view. So too in prepositional combinations.

(Caesar) Cicerōnem prō ēius meritō laudat, CAES., *B.G.*, V. 52, 4; *Caesar praises Cicero according to his desert.* **[Pompēius] cum dēcrētum dē mē Capuae fēcit, ipse cūnctae Ītaliae ēius fidem implōrantī sīgnum dedit,** C., *Mil.*, 15, 39.

2. In early comedy and then again in late Latin, **suos** is sometimes strengthened by **sibĭ: Suō sibĭ gladiō hunc iugulō,** TER., *Ad.*, 958; very rarely in classical Latin (C., *Ph.*, II. 37, 96). Similarly **meā mihĭ,** PL., *Truc.*, 698.

3. On **suum quisque,** see 318, 3.

4. In dependent clauses the reflexive is used with reference either to the principal or to the subordinate subject. See for fuller treatment 521.

310. Īdem, *the same,* serves to unite two or more attributes or predicates on a person or thing; it is often to be translated by *at the same time; likewise, also; yet, notwithstanding.*

(Cimōn) incidit in eandem invidiam quam pater suus, NEP., V. 3, 1; *Cimon fell into the same odium as his father.* **Quidquid honestum [est] idem [est] ūtile,** C., *Off.*, II. 3, 10; *whatever is honourable is also* (at the same time) *useful.* **Nīl prōdest quod nōn laedere possit idem,** OV., *Tr.*, II. 266; *nothing helps that may not likewise hurt.* **(Epicūrus), cum optimam et praestantissimam nātūram deī dīcat esse, negat īdem esse in deō grātiam,** C., *N.D.*, I. 43, 121; *although Epicurus says that the nature of God is* *transcendently good and great, yet* (at the same time) *he says that there is no sense of favour in God.* **Difficilis facilis, iūcundus acerbus, es īdem,** MART., XII. 47, 1; *crabbed* (*and*) *kindly, sweet* (*and*) *sour, are you at once.*

REMARKS.—1. When a second attribute is to be added to a substantive it is often connected by **īdemque, et īdem, atque īdem: Vir doctissimus Platō atque īdem gravissimus philosophōrum omnium,** C., *Leg.*, II. 6, 14; *Plato, a most learned man, and at the same time weightiest of all the philosophers.*

2. *The same as* is expressed by **īdem** with **quī,** with **atque** or **āc,** with **ut,** with **cum,** and poetically with the Dative. See 359, N. 6, 642, 643.

Tibĭ mēcum in eōdem est pīstrīnō vīvendum, C., *Or.*, II. 33, 144; *you have to live in the same treadmill with me.*

3. **Īdem** cannot be used with **is,** of which it is only a stronger form **(is + dem).**

311. 1. **Ipse,** *self,* is the distinctive pronoun, and separates a subject or an object from all others:

Ipse fēcī, *I myself did it and none other, I alone did it, I did it of my own accord, I am the very man that did it.* **Nunc ipsum,** *at this very instant, at this precise moment.*

Valvae subitō sē ipsae aperuērunt, C., *Div.*, I. 34, 74; *the folding-doors suddenly opened of their own accord.* **(Catō) mortuus est annīs octōgintā sex ipsīs ante [Cicerōnem] cōnsulem,** C., *Br.*, 15, 61; *Cato died just eighty-six years before Cicero's consulship.* **Huīc reī quod satis esse vīsum est mīlitum relīquit (Caesar); ipse cum legiōnibus in fīnēs Trēverōrum proficīscitur,** CAES., *B.G.*, V. 2, 4.

REMARKS.—1. Owing to this distinctive character, **ipse** is often used of *persons* in opposition to *things; riders* in opposition to *horses; inhabitants* in opposition to the *towns* which they inhabit; the *master* of the house in opposition to his *household, etc.*

Eō quō mē ipsa mīsit, PL., *Cas.*, 790; *I am going where mistress sent me.* **Ipse dīxit,** C., *N.D.*, I. 5, 10; *the master said* (αὐτὸς ἔφα).

2. **Et ipse,** *likewise, as well,* is used when a new subject takes an old predicate:

[Locrī urbs] dēscīverat et ipsa ad Poenōs, L., XXIX. 6, 1; *Locri-city had likewise* (as well as the other cities) *revolted to the Carthaginians.* **[Camillus] ex Volscīs in Aequōs trānsiit et ipsōs bellum mōlientēs,** L., VI. 2, 14; *Camillus went across from the Volscians to the Aequians, who were likewise* (as well as the Volscians) *getting up war.*

CICERO prefers in this meaning **ipse** alone, but **et ipse** occurs occasionally (not in CAESAR or SALLUST), and becomes the prevailing form in LIVY and later.

2. **Ipse** is used to lay stress on the reflexive relation; in

the Nominative when the subject is emphatic, in the Oblique Cases when the object is emphatic.

Sē ipse laudat, *he* (and not another) *praises himself.* **Sē ipsum laudat,** *he praises himself* (and not another).

Piger ipse sibĭ obstat, PROV. (SEN., *E.M.*, 94, 28); *the lazy man stands in his own way, is his own obstacle.* **Nōn egeō medicīnā; mē ipse cōnsōlor,** C., *Lael.*, 3, 10; *I do not need medicine; I comfort myself* (I am my only comforter). **Eōdem modō sapiēns erit affectus ergā amīcum quō in sē ipsum,** C., *Fin.*, I. 20, 68; *the wise man will feel towards his friend as he feels towards himself.*

Exceptions are common:

Quīque aliīs cāvit, nōn cavet ipse sibī, Ov., *A.A.*, I. 84; *and he who cared for others, cares not for himself.*

NOTE.—LIVY seems to use sometimes **ipse** in connection with a reflexive as if it were indeclinable or absolute: **cum diēs vēnit, causā ipse prō sē dictā, damnātur,** L., IV. 44, 10; *when the appointed day came he pleaded his own cause and was condemned.*

4. Possessive Pronouns.

312. The Possessive Pronouns are more rarely used in Latin than in English, and chiefly for the purpose of contrast or clearness.

Manūs lavā et cēnā, C., *Or.*, II. 60, 246; *wash* (*your*) *hands and dine.* **Praedia mea tū possidēs, ego aliēnā misericordiā vīvō,** C., *Rosc. Am.*, 50, 145; *you are in possession of my estates,* (*while*) *I live on the charity of others.*

REMARKS.—1. Observe the intense use of the Possessive in the sense of *property, peculiarity, fitness:* **suum esse,** *to belong to one's self, to be one's own man.*

Tempore tuō pūgnāstī, L., XXXVIII. 45, 10; *you have fought at your own time* (= when you wished). **Hōc honōre mē adfēcistis annō meō,** C., *Leg. Agr.*, II. 2, 4; *you visited me with this honour in my own year* (= the first year in which I could be made consul). **Pūgna suum fīnem, cum iacet hostis, habet,** Ov., *Tr.*, III. 5, 34; *a fight has reached its fit end when the foe is down.*

2. On the use of the Possessive Pronouns for the Gen., see 364.

5. Indefinite Pronouns.

313. Quīdam means *one, a, a certain one,* definite or indefinite to the speaker, but not definitely designated to the hearer. In the Plural, it is equivalent to *some, sundry,* without emphasis.

Intereā mulier quaedam commigrāvit hūc, Ter., *And.*, 69; *meanwhile a certain woman took up her quarters here.* **Intellegendum est quibusdam quaestiōnibus aliōs, quibusdam aliōs esse aptiōrēs locōs**, C., *Top.*, 21, 79; *it is to be observed that some grounds are more suitable for some questions, for some, others.* **Tam nescīre quaedam mīlitēs quam scīre oportet**, Tac., *H.*, I. 83.

Remarks.—1. With an adjective **quīdam** often serves to heighten the attribute by adding a vagueness to it. (Gr. **τις**).

Est quōdam incrēdibilī rōbore animī, C., *Mil.*, 37, 101; *really he is endowed with a strange strength of mind (one that is past belief).*

2. **Quīdam** is often used with or without **quasi**, *as if*, to modify an expression:

Nōn sunt istī audiendī quī virtūtem dūram et quasi ferream esse quandam volunt, C., *Lael.*, 13, 48; *those friends of yours are not to be listened to who will have it (maintain) that virtue is hard, and, as it were, made of iron.* **Est quaedam virtūtum vitiōrumque vīcīnia**, Quint., II. 12, 4 (*cf.* III. 7, 25); *there is a certain neighborly relation between virtues and vices.*

3. **Quīdam** may be strengthened by the addition of **certus** or **ūnus**:

Vīta agenda est certō genere quōdam, nōn quōlibet, C., *Fin.*, III. 7, 24. **Est ēloquentia ūna quaedam dē summīs virtūtibus**, C., *Or.*, III. 14, 55.

314. Aliquis (aliquī) means, *some one, some one or other*, wholly indefinite to the speaker as well as to the hearer:

[Dēclāmābam] cum aliquō cottīdiē, C., *Br.*, 90, 310; *I used to declaim with somebody or other daily.*

In the predicate it is often emphatic (by Lītotēs, 700): **sum aliquis, aliquid**, *I am somebody = a person of importance, something = of some weight;* opposed to: **nūllus sum, nihil sum**, *I am a nobody, nothing.*

This force is often heightened by a following contrast:

Est hōc aliquid, tametsī nōn est satis, C., *Div. in Caec.*, 15, 47; *this is something, although it is not enough.* **Fac, ut mē velīs esse aliquem, quoniam, quī fuī et quī esse potuī, iam esse nōn possum**, C., *Att.*, III. 15, 8; *do make out that I am somebody, since I can no longer be the man I was and the man I might have been.*

Remarks.—1. **Aliquis** and **aliquī** are distinguished as substantive and adjective; accordingly, when **aliquis** is used with a substantive the relation is appositional. This always occurs with Proper names; and even with other substantives the Romans seem to have preferred **aliquis** to **aliquī**. (See 107, n. 1.)

2. With numerals, **aliquis** is used like English *some.* Occasionally also it has the force of *many a.* So in Caes., *B.C.*, I. 2, 2, **dīxerat aliquis lēniōrem sententiam**, where **aliquis** refers to three persons, named later.

315. Quis (quī), fainter than **aliquis**, is used chiefly after **sī**, *if;* **nisi**, *unless;* **nē**, *lest;* **num**, *whether,* and in relative sentences. See 107, R.

Nē quid nimis! TER., *And.*, 61; *nothing in excess!* **Fit plērumque ut iī quī bonī quid volunt adferre, adfingant aliquid, quō faciant id, quod nūntiant, laetius**, C., *Ph.*, I. 3, 8; *it often happens that those who wish to bring* (*some*) *good tidings, invent something more, to make the news more cheering.*

NOTES.—1. **Aliquis** is used after **sī**, *etc.*, when there is stress: **sī quis**, *if any;* **sī aliquis**, *if some;* **sī quid**, *if anything;* **sī quidquam**, *if anything at all.*

Sī aliquid dandum est voluptātī, senectūs modicīs convīviīs dēlectārī potest, C., *Cato. M.*, 14, 44; *if something is to be given to pleasure* (as something or other must), *old age can take delight in mild festivities.*

Aliquis is regular if the sentence contains two negatives: **[Verrēs] nihil umquam fēcit sine aliquō quaestū**, C., *Verr.*, V. 5, 11. (446.)

2. **Quis** and **quī** are distinguished as **aliquis** and **aliquī**, but the distinction is often neglected, even in classical Latin. See 107, N. 1.

316. Quispiam is rarer than **aliquis**, but not to be distinguished from it, except that **quispiam** never intimates importance. **Dīxerit quispiam**, C., *Cat.M.*, 3, 8; *some one may say.*

317. I. **Quisquam** and **ūllus** (adjective) mean *any one* (at all), and are used chiefly in negative sentences, in sentences that imply total negation, and in sweeping conditions:

[Iūstitia] numquam nocet cuīquam, C., *Fin.*, I. 16, 50; *justice never hurts anybody.* **Quis umquam Graecōrum rhētorum ā Thūcȳdide quidquam dūxit?** C., *Or.*, 9, 317; *what Greek rhetorician ever drew anything from Thucydides?* [None]. **Sī quisquam, ille sapiēns fuit**, C., *Lael.*, 2, 9; *if any one at all* (was) *wise, he was.* **Quamdiū quisquam erit quī tē dēfendere audeat, vīvēs**, C., *Cat.*, I. 2, 6; *so long as there shall be any one to dare defend you, live on.* **Hostem esse in Syriā negant ūllum**, C., *Fam.*, III. 8, 10; *they say that there is not any enemy in Syria.* **Omnīnō nēmō ūllīus reī fuit ēmptor cuī dēfuerit hīc vēnditor**, C., *Ph.*, II. 38, 97; *generally there was never a buyer of anything who lacked a seller in him* (*no one ever wanted to buy anything that he was not ready to sell*).

So after comparatives:

Sōlis candor inlūstrior est quam ūllīus īgnis, C., *N.D.*, II. 15, 40; *the brilliancy of the sun is more radiant than that of any fire.*

NOTES.—1. **Quisquam** is occasionally (principally in LIVY) strengthened by **ūnus**, especially after a negative: **Cum multī magis fremerent, quam quisquam ūnus recūsāre audēret**, L., III. 45, 4.

2. After **sine**, *without*, **omnī** is often used instead of **ūllō** (**ūllā**) in early Latin: **Sine omnī cūrā dormiās**, PL., *Trin.*, 621.

3. On the use of **quisquam** as an adj., see 107, 3, N. 2.

2. The negative of **quisquam** is **nēmō**, *nobody;* **nihil**, *nothing* (108). The negative of **ūllus** is **nūllus**, *no, none,* which is also used regularly as a substantive in the Genitive and Ablative instead of **nēminis** and **nēmine**.

Nēmō is also sometimes used apparently as an adjective, though the conception is usually appositional.

Nēmō vir māgnus, C., *N.D.*, II. 66, 167; *no great man, no one (who is) a great man.*

NOTES.—1. On **neque quisquam** and **et nēmō**, see 480.

2. **Nūllus** is used in familiar language instead of **nōn** (so sometimes in English): **Philippus nūllus ūsquam**, L., XXXII. 35, 2; *no Philip anywhere.* **Quis** is also used familiarly: **Prōspectum petit, Anthea sī quem videat**, V., *A.*, I. 181; *an Antheus, i.e., Antheus or somebody who would answer for him.*

3. **Nēmō** and **nūllus** are occasionally strengthened by **ūnus**.

318. 1. **Quisque** means *each one,* as opposed to **omnis**, *every,* and is usually post-positive.

Mēns cūiusque, is est quisque, C., *Rep.*, VI. 24, 26; *each man's mind is each man's self.* **Laudātī omnēs sunt dōnātīque prō meritō quisque**, L., XXXVIII. 23; *all were praised and rewarded, each one according to his desert.* **Quam quisque nōrit artem in hāc sē exerceat**, [C.], *Tusc.*, I. 18, 41. (616.)

2. With superlatives and ordinals **quisque** is loosely translated *every:*

Optimum quidque rārissimum est, C., *Fin.*, II. 25, 81; *every good thing is rare;* more accurately, *the better a thing, the rarer it is.* (645, R. 2.) **Quīntō quōque annō Sicilia tōta cēnsētur**, C., *Verr.*, II. 56, 139; *every fifth year all Sicily is assessed.*

3. **Quisque** combines readily with the reflexives, **suī, sibĭ, sē, suus**, in their emphatic sense (309, 2). Here, except for special reasons, the reflexive precedes. **Suum cuīque** has become a standing phrase.

Sua quemque fraus et suus terror vexat, C., *Rosc.Am.*, 24, 67; *it is his own sin and his own alarm that harasses a man.*

NOTES.—1. After CICERO's time, owing to the phraseological character of the combination, **suī** *etc.* **quisque**, we find it used without agreement.

Exercitus āmissō duce āc passim multīs sibĭ quisque imperium petentibus brevī dīlābitur, S., *Iug.*, 18, 3. **Īnstīgandō suōs quisque populōs effēcēre ut omne Volscum nōmen dēficeret**, L., II. 38, 6.

2. Classical but not common is the attraction of **quisque** into the case of the reflexive. **Haec prōclīvitās ad suum quodque genus ā similitūdine corporis aegrōtātiō dīcātur**, C., *Tusc.*, IV. 12, 28.

3. **Quisque** combined with **prīmus** has two meanings: (*a*) *as early as possible*, (*b*) *one after the other in order* (**deinceps**).

Prīmō quōque tempore, C., *Ph.*, III. 15, 39; *at the earliest time possible.* **Prīmum quidque** (*each thing in order*) **cōnsīderā quāle sit**, C., *N.D.*, I. 27, 77.

4. The various uses of **quisque** are well summed up in NÄGELSBACH's formulæ:

a. **Nōn omnia omnibus tribuenda sunt, sed suum cuīque;**
b. **Omnēs idem faciunt, sed optimus quisque optimē;**
c. **Nōn omnibus annīs hōc fit, sed tertiō quōque annō;**
d. **Nōn omnēs idem faciunt, sed quod quisque vult.**

319. **Alter** and **alius** are both translated *other, another,* but **alter** refers to one of two, **alius** to diversity. They are used in various phraseological ways, which can be best shown by examples:

Sōlus aut cum alterō, *alone or with* (only) *one other;* **alter Nerō**, *a second Nero.*

Alter alterum quaerit, *one* (definite person) *seeks the other* (definite person); **alius alium quaerit**, *one seeks one, another another;* **alterī—alterī**, *one party—another party* (already defined); **aliī—aliī**, *some—others.* **Alter** often means *neighbor, brother, fellow-man;* **alius**, *third person.*

Alter:

(Āgēsilāüs) fuit claudus alterō pede, NEP., XVII. 8, 1; *Agesilaüs was lame of one foot.* **Alterā manū fert lapidem, pānem ostentat alterā**, PL., *Aul.*, 195; *in one hand a stone he carries, in the other holds out bread.* **Mors nec ad vīvōs pertinet nec ad mortuōs: alterī nūllī** (317, 2, N. 2) **sunt, alterōs nōn attinget**, C., *Tusc.*, I. 38, 91; *death concerns neither the living nor the dead: the latter are not, the former it will not reach.*

Alius:

Fallācia alia aliam trūdit, TER., *And.*, 779; *one lie treads on the heels of another* (indefinite series). **Aliī voluptātis causā omnia sapientēs facere dīxērunt; aliī cum voluptāte dīgnitātem cōniungendam putāvērunt**, C., *Cael.*, 15, 41; *some have said that wise men do everything for the sake of pleasure, others have thought that pleasure is to be combined with dignity.* **Dīvitiās aliī praepōnunt, aliī honōres**, C., *Lael.*, 6, 20; *some prefer riches, others honors.* **Aliī vestrum ānserēs sunt, aliī canēs**, C., *Rosc.Am.*, 20, 57; *some of you are geese, others dogs.* **Aliud aliī nātūra iter ostendit**, S., *C.*, 2, 9; *nature shows one path to one man, another path to another man.*

Alter and **alius:**

Ab aliō expectēs alterī quod fēcerīs, SYRUS, 2 (Fr.); *you may look for from another what you've done unto your brother* (from No. 3, what No. 1 has done to No. 2).

NOTES.—1. **Alius** is found occasionally, especially in late Latin, for **alter**: **alius Nerō**, SUET., *Tit.* 7; but in CAES., *B.G.*, I. 1, 1, **alius** follows **ūnus**. **Aliī** for **reliquī** or **cēterī** is occasional, in the earlier times, but more common in LIVY and later.

2. The Greek usage of **alius** in the meaning *besides*, is post-Ciceronian and rare. **Eō missa plaustra iūmentaque alia**, L., IV. 41, 8.

APPOSITION.

320. By apposition one substantive is placed by the side of another, which contains it:

Cicerō ōrātor, *Cicero the orator*. **Rhēnus flūmen**, *the river Rhine*.

CONCORD.

321. The word in apposition agrees with the principal word (or words) in case, and as far as it can in gender and number:

Nom. **Hērodotus pater historiae**, *Herodotus the father of history;* Gen. **Hērodotī patris historiae**; Dat. **Hērodotō patrī historiae.**

Cnidus et Colophōn, nōbilissimae urbēs, captae sunt, *Cf.* C., *Imp.*, 12, 33; *Cnidus and Colophon, most noble cities, were taken.* **Omnium doctrīnārum inventrīcēs Athēnae**, *Cf.* C., *Or.*, I. 4, 13; *Athens, the inventor of all branches of learning.*

REMARKS.—1. Exceptions in *number* are due to special uses, as, for example, when **dēliciae** or **amōrēs**, *etc.*, are used of a Singular:

Pompēius, nostrī amōrēs, ipse sē afflīxit, C., *Att.*, II. 19, 2; *Pompey, our special passion, has wrecked himself.*

2. The Possessive Pronoun takes the Gen. in apposition:

Tuum, hominis simplicis, pectus vīdimus, C., *Ph.*, II. 43, 111; *we have seen your bosom bared, you open-hearted creature!* **Urbs meā ūnīus operā fuit salva**, *Cf.* C., *Pis.*, 3, 6; *the city was saved by my exertions alone.*

3. On the agreement of the predicate with the word in apposition, see 211, R. 6.

NOTES.—1. In poetry, instead of the Voc. in apposition, the Nom. is often found. **Semper celebrābere dōnīs, Corniger Hesperidum, fluvius rēgnātor aquārum**, V., *A.*, VIII. 77. In prose not before PLINY.

2. Very rarely persons are looked upon as things, and the Appositives used in the neuter: **Dum patrēs et plēbem, invalida et inermia, lūdificētur**, TAC., *Ann.*, I. 46.

322. *Partitive Apposition.*—Partitive Apposition is that form of Apposition in which a part is taken out of the whole. It is sometimes called Restrictive Apposition.

Māxuma pars ferē mōrem hunc hominēs habent, PL., *Capt.*, 232; *mankind—pretty much the greatest part of them—have this way.* **Cētera multitūdō sorte decumus quisque ad supplicium lēctī (sunt)**, L., II. 59, 11; (of) *the rest of the crowd every tenth man was chosen by lot for punishment.*

323. *Distributive Apposition.*—Distributive Apposition is that form of Apposition in which the whole is subdivided into its parts, chiefly with **alter—alter,** *the one—the other;* **quisque, uterque,** *each one;* **aliī—aliī, pars—pars,** *some—others.* (It is often called Partitive Apposition.)

Duae fīliae altera occīsa altera capta est, Caes., *B.G.*, I. 53, 4; *(of) two daughters, the one was killed, the other captured.*

Remark.—The Part. Gen. is more commonly employed than either of these forms of apposition.

Notes.—1. Partitive Apposition is not found in Cicero or Caesar, and Distributive Apposition rarely. They are more frequent in Sallust, and not uncommon in Livy.

2. The Greek figure of *the whole and the part* (σχῆμα καθ' ὅλον καὶ μέρος) is rare and poetical in Latin. **Latagum saxō occupat ōs faciemque adversam,** V., *A.*, X. 698; *smites Latagus with a bowlder, full (in) mouth and face* (*Cf.* Eng. "*hand and foot*").

324. *Apposition to a Sentence.*—Sometimes an Accusative stands in apposition to a whole preceding sentence; either explaining the contents of the sentence or giving the end or the aim of the action involved in the sentence. The latter usage, however, is not found in Cicero or Caesar.

Admoneor ut aliquid etiam dē sepultūrā dīcendum exīstimem, rem nōn difficilem, C., *Tusc.*, I. 43, 102; *I am reminded to take into consideration that something is to be said about burial also—an easy matter.* **Dēserunt tribūnal, ut quis praetōriānōrum mīlitum occurreret manūs intentantēs, causam discordiae et initium armōrum,** Tac., *Ann.*, I. 27.

If the main verb is passive the Appositive may be in the Nominative: Tac., *Ann.*, III. 27.

Notes.—1. Neuter adjectives and participles are occasionally used in the same way, and some regard such neuters as Nominatives.

2. This Acc. is to be regarded as the object effected (330) by the general action of the sentence.

Predicative Attribution and Predicative Apposition.

325. Any case may be attended by the same case in Predicative Attribution or Apposition, which differ from the ordinary Attribution or Apposition in translation only.

Nominative: **Fīlius aegrōtus rediit.**

Ordinary Attribution: *The sick son returned.*

Predicative Attribution: *The son returned sick = he was sick when he returned.*

Herculēs iuvenis leōnem interfēcit.

Ordinary Apposition: *The young man Hercules slew a lion.*

Predicative Apposition : *Hercules, when a young man, slew a lion = he was a young man when he slew a lion.*

GENITIVE : **Potestās ēius adhibendae uxōris,** *the permission to take her to wife.*

DATIVE : **Amīcō vīvō nōn subvēnistī,** *you did not help your friend (while he was) alive.*

ACCUSATIVE : **Herculēs cervam vīvam cēpit.**

Ordinary Attribution : *Hercules caught a living doe.*

Predicative Attribution : *Hercules caught a doe alive.*

ABLATIVE : **Aere ūtuntur importātō,** *they use imported copper = the copper which they use is imported.*

REMARKS.—1. The Voc., not being a case proper, is not used predicatively. Exceptions are apparent or poetical.

Quō, moritūre, ruis? V., *A.*, x. 810 ; "*whither dost thou rush to die*" (*thou doomed to die*)? **Sīc veniās, hodierne,** TIB., I. 7, 53.

Notice here the old phrase : **Macte virtūte estō,** H., *S.*, I. 2, 31 ; *increase in virtue = heaven speed thee in thy high career.*

Macte is regarded by some as an old Voc., from the same stem as **māgnus**; by others as an adverb. A third view is that **macte** with **estō** is an adverb, and only when used absolutely a Vocative.

2. **Victōrēs rediērunt** may mean, *the conquerors returned,* or, *they returned conquerors;* and a similar predicative use is to be noticed in **īdem,** *the same:* **Iīdem abeunt quī vēnerant,** C., *Fin.*, IV. 3, 7 ; *they go away just as they had come* (literally, *the same persons as they had come*).

3. Predicative Attribution and Apposition are often to be turned into an abstract substantive :

Dēfendī rem pūblicam adulēscēns, nōn dēseram senex, C., *Ph.*, II. 46, 118; *I defended the state in my youth, I will not desert her in my old age.*

So with prepositions :

Ante Cicerōnem cōnsulem, *before the consulship of Cicero;* **ante urbem conditam,** *before the building of the city.*

4. Do not confound the "as" of apposition with the "as" of comparison—**ut, quasi, tamquam, sīcut, velut** (602, N. 1, 642): **Hanc (virtūtem) vōbīs tamquam hērēditātem māiōres vestrī relīquērunt,** C., *Ph.*, IV. 5, 13 ; *your ancestors left you this virtue as (if it were) a legacy.*

5. When especial stress is laid on the adjective or substantive predicate, in combination with the verbal predicate, the English language is prone to resolve the sentence into its elements :

Fragilem trucī commīsit pelagō ratem prīmus, H., *O.*, I. 3, 10; *his frail bark to the wild waves he trusted first = to trust his frail bark to the wild waves he was first.* **Ūna salūs victīs nūllam spērāre salūtem,** V., *A.*, II. 353 ; *sole safety for the vanquished 'tis, to hope for none—the only safety that the vanquished have is to hope for none.*

6. The English idiom often uses the adverb and adverbial expressions instead of the Latin adjective : so in adjectives of *inclination* and *disinclination*, *knowledge* and *ignorance*, of *order* and *position*, of *time* and *season*, and of temporary condition generally : **libēns**, *with pleasure;* **volēns**, *willing(ly) ;* **nōlēns**, *unwilling(ly) ;* **invītus**, *against one's will ;* **prūdēns**, *aware ;* **imprūdēns**, *unawares ;* **sciēns**, *knowing(ly) ;* **prīmus, prior,** *first ;* **ūltimus**, *last ;* **medius**, *in, about the middle ;* **hodiernus**, *to-day ;* **mātūtīnus**, *in the morning ;* **frequēns**, *frequent(ly) ;* **sublīmis**, *aloft ;* **tōtus**, *wholly ;* **sōlus, ūnus**, *alone*, and many others.

Ego eum ā mē invītissimus dīmīsī, C., *Fam.*, XIII. 63, 1 ; *I dismissed him most unwillingly.* **Plūs hodiē bonī fēcī imprūdēns quam sciēns ante hunc diem umquam**, TER., *Hec.*, 880 ; *I have done more good to-day unawares than I have ever done knowingly before.* **Adcurrit, mediam mulierem complectitur**, TER., *And.*, 133 ; *he runs up, puts his arms about the woman's waist.* **Quī prior strinxerit ferrum ēius victōria erit**, L., XXIV. 38, 5 (244, R. 2). **Vespertīnus pete tēctum**, H., *Ep.*, I. 6, 20 ; *seek thy dwelling at eventide.* **Rārus venit in cēnācula mīles**, JUV., X. 18 ; *the soldiery rarely comes into the garret.* **Sē tōtōs trādidērunt voluptātibus**, C., *Lael.*, 23, 86 ; *they have given themselves wholly to pleasure.* **Sōlī hōc contingit sapientī**, C., *Par.*, V. 1, 34 ; *this good luck happens to the wise man alone = it is only the wise man who has this good luck.*

7. Carefully to be distinguished are the uses of **prīmus**, and the adverbs **prīmum**, *first, for the first time*, and **prīmō**, *at first.* **Prīmum** means first in a series ; **prīmō**, first in a contrast. But these distinctions are not always observed.

Prīmum docent esse deōs, deinde quālēs sint, tum mundum ab iīs administrārī, postrēmō cōnsulere eōs rēbus hūmānīs, C., *N.D.*, II. 1, 3 ; *first, they teach us that there are gods, next of what nature they are, then that the world is ruled by them, finally, that they take thought for human affairs.* **Prīmō Stōicōrum mōre agāmus, deinde nostrō īnstitūtō vagābimur**, C., *Tusc.*, III. 6, 13 ; *let us treat the subject at first after the manner of the Stoics, afterwards we will ramble after our own fashion.*

B.

1. Multiplication of the Predicate.

326. The Multiplication of the Predicate requires no further rules than those that have been given in the general doctrine of Concord.

2. Qualification of the Predicate.

327. The Qualification of the Predicate may be regarded as an External or an Internal change :

I. External change : combination with an object.

1. Direct Object, Accusative. 2. Indirect Object, Dative.

II. Internal change : combination with an attribute which may be in the form of

1. The Genitive case.
2. The Ablative.
3. Preposition with a case.
4. An Adverb.

NOTE.—The Infinitive forms (Infinitive, Gerund, Gerundive, and Supine) appear now as objects, now as attributes, and require a separate treatment.

I. External Change.

Accusative.

The great function of the Accusative is to form temporary compounds with the verb, as the great function of the Genitive is to form temporary compounds with the noun. Beyond this statement everything is more or less extra-grammatical, and sharp subdivisions are often unsatisfactory. Still it may be said that

328. The Accusative is the case of the Direct Object.

The Direct Object is the object which defines directly the action of the verb.

REMARK.—The Dative defines indirectly because it involves an Accusative ; and the Genitive with the verb depends upon the nominal idea contained in the verb.

1. (*a*) The Object may be contained in the verb (Inner Object, Object Effected) :

Deus mundum creāvit, *God made a creation—the universe.*

(*b*) Akin to this is the Accusative of Extent :

Ā rēctā cōnscientiā trāversum unguem nōn oportet discēdere, C., *Att.*, XIII. 20, 4 ; *one ought not to swerve a nailbreadth from a right conscience.* **Decem annōs (Trōia) oppūgnāta est,** L., V. 4, 11 ; *ten years was Troy besieged.* **Māximam partem lacte vīvunt,** CAES., *B.G.*, IV. 1, 8 ; *for the most part they live on milk.*

2. The object may be distinct from the verb (Outer Object, Object Affected) :

Deus mundum gubernat, *God steers the universe.*

General View of the Accusative.

329. I. Inner Object: Object Effected:
Cognate Accusative.
Accusative of Extent.
1. In Space.
2. In Time.
3. In Degree.
Terminal Accusative (Point Reached).

II. Outer Object: Object Affected:
1. Whole.
2. Part (so-called Greek Accusative).

III. Inner and Outer Objects combined:
1. Asking and Teaching.
2. Making and Taking.

IV. Accusative as the most general form of the object (object created or called up by the mind):
1. In Exclamations.
2. Accusative and Infinitive.

DIRECT OBJECT (Inner and Outer).

Note.—The Accusative is the object reached by the verb. This object is either in apposition to the result of the action of the verb, and then it is called the Inner Object or Object Effected; or it is in attribution to the result of the action, and then it is said to be the Outer Object or Object Affected. The Inner Object is sometimes called the Voluntary Accusative, because it is already contained in the verb; the Outer Object is sometimes called the Necessary Accusative, because it is needed to define the character of the action; both verb and substantive contribute to the result; compare **hominem caedere** (**occīdere**), *to slay a man* (Object Affected), with **homicīdium facere** (*Cf.* Quint., v. 9, 9), *to commit manslaughter* (Object Effected).

330. Active Transitive Verbs take the Accusative case:

Rōmulus Urbem Rōmam condidit, *Cf.* C., *Div.*, I. 17, 30; *Romulus founded the City of Rome.* (Object Effected.)

[**Mēns**] **regit corpus,** C., *Rep.*, VI. 24, 26; *mind governs body.* (Object Affected.)

Remark.—Many verbs of Emotion which are intrans. in English are trans. in Latin, as: **dolēre,** *to grieve* (*for*); **dēspērāre,** *to despair* (*of*); **horrēre,** *to shudder* (*at*); **mīrārī,** *to wonder* (*at*); **rīdēre,** *to laugh* (*at*).

Honōrēs dēspērant, C., *Cat.*, II. 9, 19; *they despair of honours* (*give them up in despair*). **Necāta est Vitia quod fīliī necem flēvisset** (541), Tac., *Ann.*, VI. 10, 1; *Vitia was executed for having wept* (*for*) *her son's execution.* **Cōnscia mēns rēctī Fāmae mendācia rīsit,** Ov., *F.*, IV. 311; *conscious of right, her soul* (but) *laughed* (*at*) *the falsehoods of Rumour.*

NOTES.—1. From the definition of transitive given above (213, R.) it will be seen that this traditional rule reverses the poles; it is retained merely for practical purposes.

2. This Acc. with verbs of Emotion is very rare in early Latin, and is not widely extended even in the classical period. With most verbs an Abl. of Cause or a prepositional phrase is much more common, as: **Cūr dē suā virtūte dēspērārent?** CAES., *B.G.*, I. 40, 4.

3. The Acc. with verbal substantives is confined to PLAUTUS: **quid tibī nōs tāctiōst, mendīce homō?** *Aul.*, 423.

4. The Acc. with verbal adjectives in **-undus** is rare and mainly post-classical: **Haec prope cōntiōnābundus circumībat hominēs,** L., III. 47, 2.

331. Verbs compounded with the prepositions **ad, ante, circum, con, in, inter, ob, per, praeter, sub, subter, super,** and **trāns,** which become transitive, take the Accusative.

All with **circum, per, praeter, trāns,** and **subter.**

Many with **ad, in,** and **super.**

Some with **ante, con, inter, ob,** and **sub.** See 347.

Pȳthagorās Persārum magōs adiit, C., *Fin.*, V. 29, 87; *Pythagoras applied to (consulted) the Persian magi.* **Stella Veneris antegreditur sōlem,** C., *N.D.*, II. 20, 53; *the star Venus goes in advance of the sun.* **Omnēs Domitium circumsistunt,** CAES., *B.C.*, I. 20, 5; *all surround Domitius.* **Eam, sī opus esse vidēbitur, ipse conveniam,** C., *Fam.*, V. 11, 2; *I will go to see her, myself, if it shall seem expedient.* **Convīvia cum patre nōn inībat,** C., *Rosc.Am.*, 18, 52; *he would not go to banquets with his father.* **Fretum, quod Naupactum et Patrās interfluit,** L., XXVII. 29, 9; *the frith that flows between Naupactus and Patrae.* **Alexander tertiō et trīcēsimō annō mortem obiit,** C., *Ph.*, V. 17, 48; *Alexander died in his thirty-third year.* **Caesar omnem agrum Pīcēnum percurrit,** CAES., *B.C.*, I. 15, 1; *Caesar traversed rapidly all the Picenian district.* **[Populus] solet dīgnōs praeterīre,** C., *Planc.*, 3, 8; *the people is wont to pass by the worthy.* **Epamīnōndās poenam subiit,** *Cf.* NEP., XV. 8, 2; *Epaminondas submitted to the punishment.* **Crīminum vim subterfugere nūllō modō poterat,** C., *Verr.*, I. 3, 8; *he could in no way evade the force of the charges.* **Rōmānī ruīnās mūrī supervādēbant,** L., XXXII. 24, 5; *the Romans marched over the ruins of the wall.* **Crassus Euphrātem nūllā bellī causā trānsiit,** *Cf.* C., *Fin.*, III. 22, 75; *Crassus crossed the Euphrates without any cause for war.*

REMARKS.—1. If the simple verb is trans., it can take two Accusatives: **Equitum māgnam partem flūmen trāiēcit,** CAES., *B.C.*, I. 55, 1; *he threw a great part of the cavalry across the river.*

2. With many of these verbs the preposition may be repeated; but never **circum**: **Cōpiās trāiēcit Rhodanum,** or **trāns Rhodanum,** *he threw his troops across the Rhone.*

3. Sometimes a difference of signification is caused by the addition of the preposition:

Adīre ad aliquem, *to go to a man;* **adīre aliquem,** *to apply to (to consult) a man.*

INNER OBJECT.

332. Any verb can take an Accusative of the Inner Object, when that object serves to define more narrowly or to explain more fully the contents of the verb.

The most common form of this object is a neuter pronoun or adjective.

The most striking form is the so-called Cognate Accusative.

333. 1. Neuter Pronouns and Adjectives are often used to define or modify the substantive notion that lies in the verb.

Xenophōn eadem ferē peccat, C., *N.D.*, I. 12, 31; *Xenophon makes very much the same mistakes.* **Vellem equidem idem possem glōriārī quod Cȳrus,** C., *Cat.M.*, 10, 32; *for my part I could wish that it were in my power to make the same boast as Cyrus.*

With trans. verbs an Acc. of the person can be employed besides:

Discipulōs id ūnum moneō ut praeceptōrēs suōs nōn minus quam ipsa studia ament, Quint., II. 9, 1; *I give pupils this one piece of advice, that they love their teachers no less than their studies themselves.*

Remarks.—1. The usage is best felt by comparing the familiar English *it* after intrans. verbs, "to walk it, to foot it," *etc.*, where "it" represents the substantive that lies in "walk, foot," *etc.*

2. In many cases the feeling of the case is lost to the consciousness, so especially with the interrogative **quid,** which has almost the force of **cūr. Quid rīdēs?** *what (laughter) are you laughing = what means your laughter?*

Id nōs ad tē, sī quid vellēs, vēnimus, Pl., *M.G.*, 1158; *that's why we have come to you, to see if you wanted anything.*

Notes.—1. With verbs of Emotion this Acc. gives the ground of the emotion:

Utrumque laetor *(I have a double gladness, I am doubly glad)*, **et sine dolōre tē fuisse et animō valuisse,** C., *Fam.*, VII. 1, 1. **Laetae exclāmant: vēnit! id quod** *(in this that, for this that)* **mē repente aspexerant,** Ter., *Hec.*, 368.

From this arises the causal force of **quod,** *in that = because.*

2. Occasionally, but at all periods, the relative is used thus, to facilitate connection with a demonstrative clause:

Quae hominēs arant *(what men do in the way of plowing, etc.)*, **nāvigant, aedificant, omnia virtūtī pārent,** S., *C.*, 2, 7. **Id ipsum quod maneam in vītā** *(in the very fact of my remaining in life)* **peccāre mē [exīstimō],** C., *Fam.*, IV. 13, 2.

2. *Cognate Accusative.*—When the dependent word is of the same origin or of kindred meaning with the verb, it is called the Cognate Accusative, and usually has an attribute.

Faciam ut meī memineris dum vītam vīvās, Pl., *Pers.*, 494 ; *I'll make you think of me the longest day you live.* **Mīrum atque īnscītum somniāvī somnium,** Pl., *Rud.*, 597; *a marvellous and uncanny dream I've dreamed.* **Iūrāvī vērissimum iūs iūrandum,** C., *Fam.*, v. 2, 7; *I swore the truest of oaths.*

Remark.—After the analogy of the Cognate Acc. are many phraseological usages, such as **rem certāre,** *to fight a case ;* **foedus ferīre,** *to make a treaty* (compare, *to strike a bargain*)*;* **iūs respondēre,** *to render an opinion ;* **causam vincere,** *to win a case, etc.* Also the phrases with **īre : exsequiās īre,** *to attend a funeral ;* **īnfitiās īre,** *to deny, etc.*

Notes.—1. The omission of the attribute is found most often in legal phraseology, proverbs, and the like :

Māiōrum nēmō servitūtem servīvit, C., *Top.*, 6, 29 ; *of our ancestors no one ever slaved* (*what you would call*) *a slavery.* **Sī servos fūrtum faxit noxiamve noxit,** xii. *Tab.*

2. When the Cognate Acc. is replaced by a word of similar meaning, but of a different root, the effect is much the same as when an adjective is employed with the normal Accusative. This usage, however, is rare, and mainly poetical.

Tertiam iam aetātem hominum (Nestor) vīvēbat, C., *Cat. M.*, 10, 31 (reading doubtful). **Omne mīlitābitur bellum,** H., *Epod.*, 1, 23.

3. Interesting extensions are found in the poets, and rarely in prose.

Quī Curiōs simulant et Bacchānālia vīvunt, Juv., ii. 3. **Nunc Satyrum, nunc agrestem Cyclōpa movētur,** H., *Ep.*, ii. 2, 125.

4. Instead of the Inner Acc. the Abl. is occasionally found : **lapidibus pluere,** *to rain stones ;* **sanguine sūdāre,** *to sweat blood.*

Herculis simulācrum multō sūdōre mānāvit, C., *Div.*, i. 34, 74; *the statue of Hercules ran freely with sweat.*

5. Verbs of Smell and Taste have the Inner Object, which is an extension of the Cognate variety.

Piscis sapit ipsum mare, *Cf.* Sen., *N. Q.*, iii. 18, 2; *the fish tastes of the very sea.* **Nōn omnēs possunt olēre unguenta exōtica,** Pl., *Most.*, 42 ; *it is not every one can smell of foreign perfumes.*

6. A poetical and post-classical construction is that which makes a substantival neuter adjective the object of a verb. This occurs chiefly with verbs of sound : **nec mortāle sonāns,** V., *A.*, vi. 50; **māgna sonātūrum,** H., *S.*, i. 4, 44. Yet bolder is **nec vōx hominem sonat,** V., *A.*, i. 328. A verb of sight is found in **tam cernis acūtum,** H., *S.*, i. 3, 26. *Cf.* **dulce rīdentem,** H., *O.*, i. 22, 23.

Accusative of Extent.

The Accusative of Extent has to do with Degree, Space, or Time.

334. The Accusative of Extent in Degree is confined to neuter adjectives and pronouns used substantively, **multum, plūs, tantum, quantum,** *etc.*

Sī mē amās tantum quantum profectō amās, C., *Att.*, ii. 20, 5 ; *if you love me as much as in fact you do love me.*

REMARKS.—1. The number of adjectives and pronouns so used is large, and in many cases the form is felt more as an adverb than as a substantive.

2. Here belong the adverbial Accusatives **tuam,** *etc.*, **partem, vicem,** which occur occasionally at all periods.

335. The Accusative of Extent in Space is used properly only with words that involve a notion of space. When space is not involved in the governing word the idea of extent is given by the use of **per,** *through.*

Trabēs, dīstantēs inter sē bīnōs pedēs, in solō collocantur, CAES., *B.G.*, VII. 23, 1 ; *beams two feet apart are planted in the ground.* **Ā rēctā cōnscientiā trāversum unguem nōn oportet discēdere,** C. *Att.*, XIII. 20, 4 (328, *b*). **Equitēs per ōram maritimam dispositī sunt,** *Cf.* CAES., *B.C.*, III. 24, 4 ; *cavalry were posted along the sea shore.* **Phoebidās iter per Thēbās [fēcit],** NEP., XVI. 1, 2 ; *Phoebidas marched through Thebes.* **Mīlitēs aggerem lātum pedēs trecentōs trīgintā altum pedēs octōgintā exstrūxērunt,** CAES., *B.G.*, VII. 24, 1; *the soldiers raised an embankment three hundred and thirty feet wide* (and) *eighty feet high.*

REMARKS.—1. The adjectives in most common use with this Accusative are **longus,** *long,* **lātus,** *wide,* **altus,** *deep, high. Thickness,* which was indicated in early times by **crassus,** is expressed by phrases with **crassitūdō.** Similarly occur phrases with **māgnitūdō, longitūdō, lātitūdō, altitūdō. Profundus,** *deep,* never occurs with the Accusative.

2. With **abesse** and **dīstāre,** an Abl. of Measure may also be used :

Mīlibus passuum quattuor et vīgintī abesse, CAES., *B.G.*, I. 41, 5 ; *to be twenty-four miles from....*

NOTE.—When the point of reference is taken for granted, **ab (ā)** with the Abl. is occasionally used ; but only by CAESAR and LIVY. Here it has been suggested that **ab** is used adverbially, and the Abl. is one of Measure.

(Hostēs) ab mīlibus passuum minus duōbus castra posuērunt, CAES., *B.G.*, II. 7, 3 ; *the enemy pitched their camp less than two miles off.*

336. The Accusative of Extent in Time accompanies the verb, either with or without **per,** in answer to the question, *How long?*

Duodēquadrāgintā annōs tyrannus Syrācūsānōrum fuit Dionȳsius, C., *Tusc.*, V. 20, 57 ; *thirty-eight years was Dionysius tyrant of Syracuse.* **(Gorgiās) centum et novem vīxit annōs,** QUINT., III. 1, 9 (233, N. 2). **Lūdī per decem diēs factī sunt,** C., *Cat.*, III. 8, 20 ; *games were performed for ten days.* **Est mēcum per diem tōtum,** PLIN., *Ep.*, I. 16, 7 ; *he is with me the livelong day.* **Sedet aeternumque sedēbit īnfēlīx Thēseus,** V., *A.*, VI. 617 ; *there sits and shall forever sit unhappy Theseus.*

REMARKS.—1. In giving definite numbers with **iam, iam diū, iam dūdum,** *etc.*, the Latin often employs the ordinal where the English prefers the cardinal. Compare the Ablative of Measure (403).

Mithridātēs annum iam tertium et vīcēsimum rēgnat, C., *Imp.*, 3, 7 (230).

2. **Per** with the Acc. is frequently used like the Abl. of Time Within Which. **Per illa tempora = illīs temporibus,** *in those times.*

So especially with the negative :

Nūlla rēs per triennium nisi ad nūtum istīus iūdicāta est, C., *Verr.*, I. 5, 13 ; *no matter was decided during* (*in*) *the three years except at his beck.*

3. With an Aoristic tense the dating point is given by **abhinc,** which usually precedes the temporal designation.

Abhinc annōs factumst sēdecim, PL., *Cas.*, 39 ; *'twas done sixteen years ago.* **Dēmosthenēs abhinc annōs prope trecentōs fuit,** C., *Div.*, II. 57, 118; *Demosthenes lived nearly three hundred years ago.*

The use of an Acc. with an Aoristic tense without a dating word, like **abhinc,** is very rare and doubtful. CAES., *B. G.*, II. 35, 4, has been emended.

4. **Nātus,** *old* (*born*), seems to be an exception to R. 3, but it is only an apparent one, as the dating point is involved in the verb with which it is construed. For various constructions with **nātus,** see 296, R. 5.

Puer decem annōs nātus est, *the boy is ten years old.* **Quadrāgintā annōs nātus rēgnāre** [**coepit**], C., *Div.*, I. 23, 46 ; (he was) *forty years old* (when) *he began to reign.*

NOTES.—1. The use of the indefinite substantival adjective is rare. PLAUTUS uses **sempiternum,** VERGIL introduces **aeternum** (see example above), while **perpetuum** does not appear until APULEIUS.

2. Here belong the phraseological uses **id temporis, id aetātis,** which belonged to the popular speech, and never became firmly rooted in literature. Thus CICERO rarely uses them, except in his earliest works and his letters. **Id genus** is used after the same general analogy, but is not temporal. This occurs in CICERO but once, *Att.*, XIII. 12, 3. CAESAR never uses any of these forms.

3. Poetical and rare is the extension which makes the Accusative of Extent the subject of a passive verb.

Nunc tertia vīvitur aetās, OV., *M.*, XII. 188 = **nunc tertiam vīvitur aetātem. Tōta mihī dormītur hiems,** MART., XIII. 59, 1 = **tōtam dormiō hiemem.**

Normally the verb becomes impersonal or is regularly used with a proper subject, and the Accusative of Extent is unchanged : [**Bellum**] **quō duodecimum annum Ītalia ūrēbātur,** L., XXVII. 39, 9.

Accusative of the Local Object.

Terminal Accusative.

337. The activity of a verb may be defined by the Point Reached. Hence the rule : **Names of Towns and small Islands, when used as limits of Motion Whither, are put in the Accusative.**

So also **rūs**, *into the country*, **domum, domōs**, *home*.

Missī lēgātī Athēnās sunt, L., III. 31, 8; *envoys were sent to Athens.* **Lātōna cōnfūgit Dēlum**, *Cf.* C., *Verr.*, I. 18, 48; *Latona took refuge in Delos.* **Ego rūs ībō atque ibi manēbō**, TER., *Eun.*, 216; *I shall go to the country and stay there.* **Innumerābilēs (philosophī) numquam domum revertērunt**, C., *Tusc.*, V. 37, 107; *innumerable philosophers never returned home.*

REMARKS.—1. Countries and large islands being looked upon as areas, and not as points, require prepositions, such as: **in**, *into*; **ad**, *to*; **versus**, *-ward*; **in Graeciam proficīscī**, *to set out for Greece.*

2. When **urbem**, *city*, or **oppidum**, *town*, precedes the name of the city or town, the idea of area is emphasised, and the preposition **in** or **ad** is prefixed; if **urbem** or **oppidum** follows, **in** or **ad** may be omitted: **In (ad) oppidum Cirtam**, *to, in (at) the town* (of) *Cirta.*

When **urbem** or **oppidum** is qualified by an adjective, it regularly follows the name of the town, and has the preposition:

Iugurtha Thalam pervēnit in oppidum māgnum et opulentum, S., *Iug.*, 75, 1; *Jugurtha arrived at Thala, a great and wealthy town.*

3. **Domum**, with a possessive pronoun, or Gen., may mean *house* as well as *home*, and accordingly may or may not have **in** before it: **domum meam**, or, **in domum meam**, *to my house*; **domum Pompēiī**, or, **in domum Pompēiī**, *to Pompey's house*; also **domum ad Pompēium.** Otherwise: **in māgnificam domum venīre**, *to come into a grand house.*

4. **Ad** means *to the neighbourhood of*, often *before*, of military operations. **Ad Mutinam**, *to the neighbourhood (siege of) Mutina* (Modena).

5. The simple Acc. will suffice even for *extent*:

Omnia illa mūnicipia, quae sunt ā Vibōne Brundisium, C., *Planc.*, 41, 97; *all the free towns from Vibo to Brundisium.*

6. Motion *to a place* embraces all the local designations:

Phalara in sinum Māliacum prōcēsserat, L., XXXV. 43, 8; *he had advanced to Phalara on the Maliac Gulf.* **Tarentum in Ītaliam īnferiōrem proficīscī**, *to set out for Tarentum in Lower Italy.*

NOTES.—1. The omission of the preposition before countries and large islands is poetical and post-classical. CAESAR shows such omission with **Aegyptus** only, CICERO not at all.

2. Poets and later prose writers extend the Acc. also to names of peoples and streams. Beginnings of this are seen in CICERO: **cum Bosphorum cōnfūgisset**, *Mur.*, 16, 34.

3. The insertion of the preposition with names of towns and small islands is rare in good prose, but is always legitimate when the preposition is to be emphasised.

4. The use of **ūsque** with this Acc. to emphasise the continuity of the motion is found first in TERENCE, occasionally in CICERO. From LIVY on it spreads and is used also with other local designations.

5. Verbal substantives are also occasionally followed by this Accusative: **Reditus Rōmam**, C., *Ph.*, II. 42, 108; *return to Rome.*

OUTER OBJECT.

Accusative of Respect.

338. The Accusative of the object affected sometimes specifies that *in respect to which* the statement of a passive or intransitive verb, or an adjective, applies. There are two varieties:

1. *Definite:* The Accusative of the part affected.

Percussa novā mentem formīdine, V., *G.*, IV. 357; *her mind stricken with a new dread.* **Iam vulgātum āctīs quoque saucius pectus**, QUINT., IX. 3, 17; *by this time "breast-wounded" is actually become a common newspaper phrase.*

2. *Indefinite:* **cētera, alia, reliqua, omnia, plēraque, cūncta**; *in other respects, in all respects, in most respects.*

Cētera adsentior Crassō, C., *Or.*, I. 9, 35; *in all other points I agree with Crassus.* **Omnia Mercuriō similis**, V., *A.*, IV. 558; *in all respects like unto Mercury.*

NOTES.—1. This is commonly called the Greek Accusative, because it is so much more common in Greek, and because its extension in Latin is due to Greek influence. The first variety is very rare in early Latin; introduced into prose by SALLUST, it is extended in LIVY, but in both is applied usually to wounds. It is much more common in the poets. Of the second variety **cētera** is found here and there at all periods; the others are very rare. Good prose uses the Ablative for the first variety, and for the second, **ad cētera, in cēterīs, per cētera**, *etc.*

2. Different is the Accusative with **induor**, *I don*; **exuor**, *I doff*; **cingor**, *I gird on myself*, and other verbs of *clothing* and *unclothing*, as well as *passives*, where the Subject is also the Agent; in which verbs the reflexive or middle signification is retained. These uses are poetical or post-classical.

Inūtile ferrum cingitur, V., *A.*, II. 510; *he girds on (himself) a useless blade.* **Lōrīcam induitur fīdōque accingitur ēnse**, V., *A.*, VII. 640; *he dons a corselet and begirds himself with his trusty glaive.* **(Arminius) impetū equī pervāsit oblitus faciem suō cruōre nē nōscerētur**, TAC., *Ann.* II. 17, 7; *Hermann pushed his way through, thanks to the onset of his charger, having smeared his face with his own gore, to keep from being recognised.*

DOUBLE ACCUSATIVE (Inner and Outer).

When two Accusatives depend on the same verb, one is the Inner and the other the Outer object. Theoretically any combination of Inner and Outer objects is allowable; practically the language has restricted its usage to varieties *a* and *b*.

339. (*a*) Active verbs signifying to Inquire, to Require, to Teach, and **cēlāre**, *to conceal*, take two Accusatives, one of the Person, and the other of the Thing.

Pūsiōnem quendam Sōcratēs interrogat quaedam geōmetrica, C., *Tusc.*, I. 24, 57; *Socrates asks an urchin sundry questions in geometry.* **Caesar Aeduōs frūmentum flāgitābat**, CAES., *B.G.*, I. 16, 1; *Caesar kept demanding the corn of the Aedui.* **Quid nunc tē, asine, litterās doceam?** (265), C., *Pis.*, 30, 73; *why should I now give you a lesson in literature,* *you donkey?* **Nōn tē cēlāvī sermōnem Ampiī,** C., *Fam.*, II. 16, 3, *I did not keep you in the dark about my talk with Ampius.*

REMARKS.—1. The expressions vary a good deal. Observe:

This then is not the only way,
For it is also right to say,
Docēre and **cēlāre dē,**
Interrogāre dē quā rē.

Pōscō, *I claim,* and **flāgitō,**
And always **petō, pōstulō,**
Take **aliquid ab aliquō,**
While **quaerō** takes **ex, ab, dē, quō.**

Adherbal Rōmam lēgātōs mīserat, quī senātum docērent dē caede frātris, S., *Iug.*, 13, 3; *Adherbal had sent envoys to Rome to inform the senate of the murder of his brother.* **Bassus noster mē dē hōc librō cēlāvit,** C., *Fam.*, VII. 20, 3; *our friend Bassus has kept me in the dark about this book.* **Aquam ā pūmice nunc pōstulās,** PL., *Pers.*, 41; *you are now asking water of a pumice-stone* (blood of a turnip).

2. With **doceō** the Abl. of the Instrument is also used: **docēre fidibus, equō,** *to teach the lyre, to teach riding;* with **ērudīre,** the Abl., **in** with the Abl. or (rarely) **dē. Doctus** and **ērudītus** generally take the Abl.: **Doctus Graecīs lītterīs,** *a good Grecian.*

3. With **cēlārī** the Acc. of the Thing becomes the subject, and the Acc. of the Person is retained; or the Acc. of the Person is made the subject, and instead of the Acc. of the Thing, **dē** with the Abl. is used.

NOTES.—1. There is a great deal of difference in the relative frequency of these verbs. So **doceō** and its compounds, **rogō, pōscō, repōscō, cēlō,** are common; **interrogō, ōrō, expōscō, pōstulō, flāgitō, cōnsulō,** are rare, **exigō** (in passive), **percontor,** are ante-classical and post-classical. So, too, the classical Latin *in general* avoids two Accusatives, unless one is a neuter pronoun.

2. The construction with **ab,** with verbs of Requiring, is much more common than the double Acc., and in some cases is necessary; so, too, the construction with **dē** after verbs of Inquiring.

3. Other verbs of teaching than **doceō** and its compounds, and **ērudīre,** always have **dē** until late Latin, as **īnstruere,** *etc.* So **docēre,** when it means *to inform.*

4. The Passive form, with the Nom. of the Person and the Acc. of the Thing, is sparingly used. **Dīscere** is the prose word for **docērī,** except that the past participle **doctus** is classical but rare.

Mōtūs docērī gaudet Iōnicōs mātūra virgō, H., *O.*, III. 6, 21; *the rare ripe maid delights to learn Ionic dances.* **Vir omnēs bellī artēs ēdoctus,** L., XXV. 40, 5; *one who had learned (been taught) thoroughly all the arts of war.*

340. (*b*) Verbs of Naming, Making, Taking, Choosing, Showing, may have two Accusatives of the same Person or Thing:

[**Īram**] **bene Ennius initium dīxit īnsāniae,** C., *Tusc.*, IV. 23, 52; *well did Ennius call anger the beginning of madness.* **Ancum Mārcium rēgem populus creāvit,** L., I. 32, 1; *the people made Ancus Marcius king.* **Catō Valerium Flaccum habuit collēgam,** *Cf.* NEP., XXIV. 1, 2; *Cato had Valerius Flaccus* (as) *colleague.* **Eum simillimum deō iūdicō,** C., *Marc.*, 3, 8; *I judge him (to be) very like unto a god.* **Athēniēnsibus Pȳthia praecēpit ut**

Miltiadem sibĭ imperātōrem sūmerent, Nep., i. 1, 3 ; *the Pythia instructed the Athenians to take Miltiades* (as) *their commander.* **Praestā tē eum quī mihĭ es cōgnitus,** C., *Fam.*, i. 6, 2 ; *show yourself the man that I know you to be.* **Quem intellegimus dīvitem?** C., *Par.*, vi. 1, 42 ; *whom do we understand by the rich man?*

Remarks.—1. The Double Acc. is turned into the Double Nom. with the Passive (206). **Reddō,** *I render*, is not used in the Passive, but, instead thereof, **fīō,** *I become.*

Habeō, with two Accusatives, commonly means to *have ;* in the sense of *hold, regard,* other turns are used ; usually **prō.**

Utrum prō ancillā mē habēs an prō filiā? Pl., *Pers.*, 341 ; *do you look upon me as a maid-servant or as a daughter?*

Similarly **habēre servōrum locō, (in) numerō deōrum,** *to regard as slaves, as gods.*

2. With verbs of Taking and Choosing the *end* is indicated by the Dat. or **ad** with Accusative.

(Rōmulus) trecentōs armātōs ad cūstōdiam corporis habuit, L., i. 15, 8 ; *Romulus had three hundred armed men as a body-guard.*

341. (*c*) Double Accusatives, where one is the cognate, are very uncommon :

Tē bonās precēs precor, Cato, *R.R.*, i. 3, 4. **Tam tē bāsia multa bāsiāre vēsānō satis et super Catullōst,** Cat., vii. 9.

Notes.—1. Curious extensions occasionally occur :

Idem iūs iūrandum adigit Afrānium, Caes., *B.C.*, i. 76.

2. In early Latin frequently, and in later times occasionally, the Inner object is given by a neuter pronoun, in the simplest form. **Quid mē vīs?** *what do you want of me? what do you want me for?* So with **prohibēre** ; also with **iubēre** (once in Cicero and Caesar), **admonēre,** *etc.*

Neque mē Iūppiter neque dī omnēs id prohibēbunt, Pl., *Am.*, 1051. **Lītterae quae tē aliquid iubērent,** C., *Fam.*, xiii. 26, 3.

342. (*d*) In early Latin we find cases of two Accusatives with a single verb, where the verb forms a single phrase with one of the Accusatives, and the second Accusative is the object of the phrase : **animum advertere,** *to perceive ;* **lūdōs facere,** *to make game of ;* **manum inicere,** *to lay hands on, etc.* In classical Latin these phrases have been usually, where possible, formed into a single word : **animadvertere, lūdificārī.**

Animum advertit Gracchus in cōntiōne Pīsōnem stantem, C., *Tusc.*, iii. 20, 48 ; *Gracchus perceived Piso standing in the assembly.*

Note.—On the Double Accusative with compound verbs, see 331, r. 1.

ACCUSATIVE AS A GENERAL OBJECTIVE CASE.

343. The Accusative as the Objective Case generally is used as an object of Thought, Perception, Emotion ; an object created by the mind, evoked or deprecated by the will. Hence the use of the Accusative :

(*a*) In Exclamations. (*b*) With the Infinitive.

1. The Accusative is used in Exclamations as the general object of Thought, Perception, or Emotion :

Mē miserum, C., *Fam.*, XIV. 1, 1 ; *poor me!* **Mē caecum quī haec ante nōn vīderim**, C., *Att.*, X. 10, 1 ; *blind me! not to have seen all this before.*

So in Exclamatory Questions :

Quō mihi fortūnam, sī nōn concēditur ūtī? H., *Ep.*, I. 5, 12 ; *what* (is the object of) *fortune to me if I'm not allowed to enjoy it?*

Interjections are used :

Heu mē miserum! *Alas! poor me!* **Ō miserās hominum mentēs, Ō pectora caeca**, LUCR., II. 14 ; *oh, the wretched minds of men, oh, the blind hearts!*

So, in apposition to a sentence, see 324.

NOTES.—1. **Ō** with the Voc. is an address ; with the Nom. a characteristic ; with the Acc. an object of emotion.

2. **Em**, *Lo!* and **Ecce**, *Lo here!* have the Acc. in the earlier language :

Em tibĭ hominem! PL., *Asin.*, 880 ; *here's your man!* **Ecce mē!** PL., *Ep.*, 680 ; *here am I!*

So **eccum, ellum, eccam, eccillam,** in comic poetry.

Ecce takes only the Nom. in classical Latin. Distinguish between **em** and **ēn,** the latter of which, in the sense *lo!* does not appear until CICERO's time, and takes the Nominative.

Prō takes the Vocative : **Prō dī immortālēs!** *Ye immortal gods!* The Accusative occurs in : **Prō deum atque hominum fidem!** C., *Tusc.*, V. 16, 48 ; *for heaven's sake!* and similar phrases.

Ei (hei)! and **Vae!** take the Dative.

Ei mihĭ! *Ah me!* **Vae victīs!** *Woe to the conquered!*

2. The Accusative and the Infinitive are combined so as to present the notion of Subject and Predicate as an object of thought or perception (527). Hence the Accusative with the Infinitive is used :

(*a*) In Exclamations. (See 534.)
(*b*) As an Object. (See 527.)
(*c*) As a Subject. (See 535.)

DATIVE.

344. The Dative is the case of the Indirect Object, and always involves a Direct Object, which may be contained in the verb or expressed by the complex of verb and object.

Nēmō errat ūnī sibī, SEN., *E.M.*, 94, 54 ; *no one errs* (makes mistakes) *to* (*for*) *himself alone.* **Nōn omnibus dormiō**, C., *Fam.*, VII. 24, 1 ; *it is not for everybody that I am asleep.* **Tibī exercitum patria prō sē dedit**, C., *Ph.*, XIII. 6, 14 ; *your country gave you an army for its own defence.* **Mulier sibī fēlīcior quam virīs**, C., *Ph.*, V. 4, 11.

NOTE.—In English the form of the Indirect Object is the same as that of the Direct : "He showed *me* (Dat.) a pure river ; " "he showed *me* (Acc.) to the priest." Originally a case of Personal Interest, it is used freely of Personified Things, sparingly of Local Relations, and this despite the fact that Locative and Dative are blended in the First and Third Declensions. If a Locative, the Dative is a sentient Locative.

Dative with Transitive Verbs.

345. The Indirect Object is put in the Dative with Transitive verbs, which already have a Direct Object in the Accusative. Translation, *to, for, from.* This Accusative becomes the Nominative of the Passive. The Dative depends on the complex.

Active Form :

TO : **Facile omnēs, quom valēmus, rēcta cōnsilia aegrōtīs damus**, TER., *And.*, 309 ; *readily all of us, when well, give good counsel to the sick.*

FOR : **Frangam tōnsōrī crūra manūsque simul**, MART., XI. 58, 10 ; *I'd break the barber's legs for him and hands at once.*

FROM : **Somnum mihī [adēmit]**, C., *Att.*, II. 16, 1 ; *it took my sleep away from me.*

Passive Form :

Mercēs mihi glōria dētur, OV., *F.*, III. 389 ; *let glory be given* TO *me as a reward.* **Immeritīs franguntur crūra caballīs**, JUV., X, 60 ; *the innocent hacks get their legs broken* FOR *them.* **Arma [adimuntur] mīlitibus**, L., XXII. 44, 6 ; *the soldiers have their arms taken* FROM *them.* **Domus pulchra dominīs aedificātur nōn mūribus**, *Cf.* C., *N.D.*, III. 10, 26 ; *a handsome house is built for its owners, not for the mice.*

REMARKS.—1. These constructions are found with more or less frequency at all periods. But the Dat. with verbs of Taking Away, Prohibiting, and the like, is mostly confined to poetry and later prose. The translation *from* is merely approximate, instead of *for*. When the idea of Personal Interest is not involved, the Abl. is necessary.

Is frāter, quī ēripuit frātrem carcere, nōn potuit ēripere fātō, SEN., *Dial.*, XI. 14, 4.

A good example of a play on construction is PL., *Aul.*, 635 :

ST. **Nihil equidem tibī abstulī.** EU. **At illud quod tibī abstulerās cedo.**

2. The translation *For* is nearer the Dat. than *To*. It is the regular

form when the Acc. is that of the object *effected ;* when it is that of the object *affected* the translation is more often *to ;* but *for* (*in defence of*) is **prō**: **prō patriā morī,** *to die for one's country.* *To* (*with a view to*) is **ad** or **in,** and when the idea of motion is involved, the preposition must be used, even with **dare,** which gives its name to the Dative :

Lītterās alicuī dare, *to give one a letter* (to carry or to have).

Lītterās ad aliquem dare, *to indite a letter to one.*

Rogās ut mea tibĭ scrīpta mittam, C., *Fam.*, I. 9, 23 ; *you ask me to send you my writings* (you wish to have them). **Librōs iam prīdem ad tē mīsissem sī esse ēdendōs putāssem,** C., *Fam.*, I. 9, 23 ; *I should have sent the books to you long since if I had thought they ought to be published.*

Dative with Intransitive Verbs.

346. The Indirect Object is put in the Dative with many Intransitive Verbs of Advantage or Disadvantage, Yielding and Resisting, Pleasure and Displeasure, Bidding and Forbidding.

Fuit mīrificus in Crassō pudor, quī tamen nōn obesset ēius ōrātiōnī, C., *Or.*, I. 26, 122 ; *Crassus had a marvellous modesty, not, however, such as to be a bar to the effectiveness of his oratory.* **Ipsa sibĭ imbēcillitās indulget,** C., *Tusc.*, IV. 18, 42 ; *weakness gives free course to itself.* **Probus invidet nēminī,** C., *Tim.*, 3, 9 ; *your upright man cherishes envy to no one.* **Catilīna lītterās mittit sē fortūnae cēdere,** S., *C.*, 34, 2; *Catiline writes that he gives way to fortune.* **Diēs stultīs quoque medērī solet,** C., *Fam.*, VII., 28, 3 ; *time is wont to prove a medicine even to fools.* **Moderārī et animō et ōrātiōnī, est nōn mediocris ingenii,** C., *Q.F.*, I. II. 13, 38 ; *to put bounds both to temper and to language is the work of no mean ability.* **Sīc agam, ut ipsī auctōrī hūius dīsciplīnae placet,** C., *Fin.*, I. 9, 29 ; *I will act as it seems good to the head of this school* (*of thought*) *himself.* [**Mundus**] **deō pāret et huīc oboediunt maria terraeque,** C., *Leg.*, III. 1, 3 ; *the universe is obedient to God, and seas and lands hearken unto him.* **Virtūtī suōrum satis crēdit,** *Cf.* S., *Iug.*, 106, 3 ; *he puts full confidence in the valour of his men.* **Illī poena, nōbīs lībertās** [**appropinquat**], C., *Ph.*, IV. 4, 10; *to him punishment, to us freedom, is drawing nigh.*

Remarks.—1. Of course the passives of these verbs are used impersonally (208) :

Quī invident egent, illīs quibus invidētur, ī rem habent, Pl., *Truc.*, 745; *those who envy are the needy, those who are envied have the stuff.*

2. The verbs found with this Dat. in classical Latin are : **prōdesse, obesse, nocēre, condūcit, expedit ; assentīrī, blandīrī, cupere, favēre, grātificārī, grātulārī, ignōscere, indulgēre, mōrigerārī, studēre, suffrāgārī ; adversārī, īnsidiārī, invidēre, īrāscī, maledīcere, minārī, minitārī, obtrectāre,**

efficere, refrāgārī, suscēnsēre ; cēdere, concēdere ; resistere ; auxiliārī, cōnsulere, medērī, opitulārī, parcere, prōspicere ; moderārī, temperāre (sibī) ; placēre, displicēre ; auscultāre, imperāre, oboedīre, obsequī, obtemperāre, pārēre, persuādēre, servīre, suādēre ; crēdere, fīdere, cōnfīdere, diffīdere, dēspērāre ; accidit, contingit, ēvenit ; libet, licet ; appropinquāre, repūgnāre. Also **nūbere,** *to marry* (of a woman) ; **supplicāre,** *to implore.*

NOTES.—1. Some other verbs are used occasionally in the same way, as **incommodāre,** which CICERO uses once. Also, **dolēre,** with Dat. of suffering person, is found sometimes in CICERO, though it belongs rather to the Comic Poets.

2. Some of these words have also other constructions. These occur usually in ante-classical and post-classical Latin ; if in classical Latin a different meaning is usually found in the new construction. Thus **indulgēre aliquid,** *to grant a thing,* **invidēre alicuī aliquid, obtrēctāre,** with Acc., **suādēre, persuādēre,** with Acc. of the Person, are post-classical and late ; **moderārī,** with Acc., is found in LUCRETIUS and in Silver Latin ; **temperāre,** meaning *mix,* takes Acc. at all periods. **Fīdere, cōnfīdere, diffīdere** are found also with Ablative.

Sometimes the personal interest is emphasised when the Dat. is employed, as over against the Accusative. So regularly with verbs of Fearing, as : **metuere aliquem,** *to dread some one,* but **metuere alicuī,** *to fear for some one* ; **cavēre alicuī,** *to take precautions for some one,* but **cavēre aliquem** (also **dē, ab aliquō**), *to take precautions against some one* ; **cavēre aliquā rē** (early), *to beware of a thing.* **Cōnsulere aliquem,** *to consult a person* ; **cōnsulere alicuī,** *to consult for a person.* On **convenīre,** see 347, R. 2.

Noteworthy are the constructions of **invidēre** and **vacāre** :

Invidēre alicuī (in) aliquā rē (CIC. uses prep.) } *to begrudge a man a thing.*
alicuī aliquid (VERG., HOR., LIVY, *etc.*) }
alicūius reī (once in HORACE, *S.*, II. 6, 84), *to begrudge a thing.*
(alicūius) alicuī reī (common), *to envy something belonging to a man.*

Vacāre reī, *to be at leisure for, to attend to* } *a matter.*
rē, ā rē, *to be at leisure from* }

Sometimes there is hardly any difference in meaning :

Comitor aliquem, *I accompany a man* ; **comitor alicuī,** *I act as companion to a man* ; **praestōlor alicuī** (better) or **aliquem,** *I wait for.*

3. Some words with similar meanings take the Accusative ; the most notable are : **aequāre,** *to be equal* ; **decēre** (*to distinguish*), *to be becoming* ; **dēficere,** *to be wanting* ; **dēlectāre,** *to please* ; **iuvāre,** *to be a help* ; **iubēre,** *to order* ; **laedere,** *to injure* ; and **vetāre,** *to forbid.*

Eam pictūram imitātī sunt multī, aequāvit nēmō, PLIN., *N.H.*, XXXV. 11, 126 ; *that style of painting many have imitated, none equalled.* **Fōrma virōs neglēcta decet,** OV., *A.A.*, I. 509 ; *a careless beauty is becoming to men.* **Mē diēs dēficiat,** *Cf.* C., *Verr.*, II. 21, 52 ; *the day would fail me.* **Fortīs fortūna adiuvat,** TER., *Ph.*, 203 ; *fortune favours the brave.*

TACITUS is the first to use **iubēre** with Dative ; *Ann.*, IV. 72, *etc.*

4. The Dat. use is often obscured by the absence of etymological translation. So **nūbere alicuī,** *to marry a man* (to veil for him) ; **medērī alicuī,** *to heal* (to take one's measures for) *a man* ; **supplicāre,** *to beg* (to bow the knee to) ; **persuādēre,** *to persuade* (to make it sweet).

5. After the analogy of verbs the phrases **audientem esse,** *to hear,* i.e., *to obey,* **supplicem esse,** *to entreat,* **auctōrem esse,** *to advise,* **fidem habēre,** *to have faith in,* are also found with the Dative :

Sī potest tibī dictō audiēns esse quisquam, C., *Verr.*, I. 44, 114.

6. The poets are very free in their use of the Dat. with verbs of the same general

meaning as those given. So **sē mīscēre**, *to mingle with*; **coīre, concurrere**, *to meet*; verbs of *contending*, as **contendere, bellāre, pūgnāre, certāre**; verbs of *disagreement*, as **differre, discrepāre, dīstāre, dissentīre.** Here belongs **haerēre** with the Dat., as V., *A.*, IV. 73, which may, however, be a Locative construction.

Dative and Verbs Compounded with Prepositions.

347. Many verbs compounded with the prepositions **ad, ante, con, in, inter, ob, (post), prae, sub,** and **super,** take the Dative, especially in moral relations.

Transitive Verbs have an Accusative case besides.

Plēbēs cūncta comitiīs adfuit, C., *Planc.*, 8, 21; *the entire commonalty was present at the election.* **Omnis sēnsus hominum multō antecellit sēnsibus bēstiārum,** C., *N.D.*, II. 57, 145; *every sense of man is far superior to the senses of beasts.* **(Ennius) equī fortis et victōris senectūtī comparat suam,** C., *Cat.M.*, 5, 14; *Ennius compares his (old age) to the old age of a gallant and winning steed.* **Imminent duo rēgēs tōtī Asiae,** C., *Imp.*, 5, 12; *two kings are menaces to all Asia.* **Interes cōnsiliīs,** C., *Att.*, XIV. 22, 2; *you are in their councils, are privy to their plans.* **Piger ipse sibĭ obstat,** PROV. (311, 2). **Omnibus Druidibus praeest ūnus,** CAES., *B.G.*, VI. 13, 8; *at the head of all the Druids is one man.* **Anatum ōva gallīnīs saepe suppōnimus,** C., *N.D.*, II. 48, 124; *we often put ducks' eggs under hens* (for them to hatch). **Neque dēesse neque superesse reī pūblicae volō,** C. (POLLIO), *Fam.*, X. 33, 5; *no life that is not true to the state, no life that outlives the state's—that is my motto.*

REMARKS.—1. The Dat. is found, as a rule, only when these verbs are used in a transferred sense. In a local sense the preposition should be employed, although even classical Latin is not wholly consistent in this matter. In poetry and later prose the Dat. is extended even to the local signification. In early Latin the repetition of the preposition is the rule.

So **incumbere in gladium,** C., *Inv.*, II. 51, 154, *to fall upon one's sword.*

2. The principal intrans. verbs with the Dat. in classical Latin are: **Accēdere** (*to join*, or, *to be added*; otherwise usually preposition **ad**); **accumbere** (once in CIC.); **adesse** (also with **ad, in,** and, in PLAUT., **apud**); **adhaerēscere** (**ad** of local uses); **arrīdēre** (once in CIC.); **annuere** (occasionally with Acc.); **assentīrī**; **assidēre**; **antecēdere** (also with Acc.); **anteīre** (also with Acc.); **antecellere** (with Acc. from LIVY on); **congruere** (also with **cum**); **cōnsentīre** (also with **cum**); **cōnstāre**; **convenīre** (*to suit*; with **cum**, *to agree with*, especially in the phrase **convenit mihĭ cum aliquō**, *I agree with*); **illūdere** (also with Acc. and occasionally **in** and Acc.); **impendēre** (with Acc. is archaic; occasionally **in**); **incēdere** (SALL., LIVY, *etc.*); **incidere** (twice in CIC.; regularly **in**); **incubāre** (but **incumbere** regularly with **in** or **ad**); **inesse** (once in CIC.); **inhaerēre** (occa-

sionally ad or **in** with Abl.); **inhiāre** (PLAUT. has Acc. only); **innāscī** (**innātus**); **inservīre**; **insinuāre** (once in CIC.; usually **in**); **insistere** (locally, **in** with Abl.; occasionally Acc.); **instāre**; **invādere** (once in CIC.; occasionally Acc.; regularly **in**); **intercēdere**; **intercurrere**; **interesse** (also with **in** and Abl.); **intervenīre**; **obesse**; **obrēpere** (usually **in**, **ad**); **obsistere**; **obstāre**; **obstrepere**; **obtingere**; **obvenīre**; **obversārī**; **occurrere**; **occursāre**; **praestāre**; **praesidēre**; **subesse**; **subvenīre**; **succēdere**; **succumbere**; **succrēscere** (once in CIC.); **succurrere**; **superesse.**

3. The same variety of construction is found with transitive verbs, in composition.

4. After the analogy of **praestāre, excellere,** *to excel,* is also found with the Dative.

5. Some trans. verbs, compounded with **dē** and **ex** (rarely with **ab**), take the Dat., but it properly comes under 345.

Caesar Dēiotarō tetrarchian ēripuit, eīdemque dētrāxit Armeniam, *Cf.* C., *Div.*, II. 37, 79; *Caesar wrested from Dejotarus his tetrarchy, and stripped from him Armenia.*

Dative with Verbs of Giving and Putting.

348. A few verbs, chiefly of Giving and Putting, take a Dative with an Accusative, or an Accusative with an Ablative, according to the conception.

Praedam mīlitibus dōnat, CAES., *B.G.*, VII. 11, 9; *he presents the booty to the soldiers.* But **Rubrium corōnā dōnāstī,** C., *Verr.* III. 80, 185; *thou didst present Rubrius with a crown.*

Nātūra corpus animō circumdedit, SEN., *E.M.*, 92, 13; *Nature has put a body around the mind.* But **Deus animum circumdedit corpore,** *Cf.* C., *Tim.*, 6, 20; *God has surrounded the mind with a body.*

REMARKS.—1. These are: **aspergere,** *to besprinkle* and *to sprinkle on;* **circumdare, circumfundere,** *to surround;* **dōnāre,** *to present;* **impertīre,** *to endow* and *to give;* **induere,** *to clothe* and *to put on;* **exuere,** *to strip of* and *to strip off;* **interclūdere,** *to shut off;* **miscēre,** *to mix* and *to mix in.*

2. In general, classical Latin here prefers the Dat. of the person, but no fixed rule is followed.

Dative of Possessor.

349. Esse, *to be,* with the Dative, denotes an inner connection between its subject and the Dative, and is commonly translated by the verb *to have:*

[Contrōversia] mihī fuit cum avunculō tuō, C., *Fin.*, III. 2, 6; *I had a debate with your uncle.* **An nescīs longās rēgibus esse manūs?** Ov., *Her.*,

XVI. 166 ; *or perhaps you do not know that kings have long arms?* Compare **nōn habet, ut putāmus, fortūna longās manūs**, SEN., *E.M.*, 82, 5.

REMARKS.—1. The predicate of **esse**, with the Dat., is translated in the ordinary manner : **Caesar amīcus est mihĭ**, *Caesar is a friend to me* (**amīcus meus**, MY *friend, friend of* MINE).

2. The Dat. is never simply equivalent to the Genitive. The Dat. is the Person interested in the Possession, hence the Possession is emphatic; the Gen. characterises the Possession by the Possessor, hence the Possessor is emphatic. The Gen. is the permanent Possessor, or owner; the Dat. is the temporary Possessor. The one may include the other:

Latīnī concēdunt Rōmam caput Latiō esse, *Cf.* L., VIII. 4, 5; *the Latins concede that Latium has its capital in* ROME. (**Latiī**: *that* LATIUM'S *capital is Rome.*)

3. Possession of qualities is expressed by **esse** with **in** and the Abl., by **inesse** with Dat. or with **in**, or by some other turn :

Fuit mīrificus in Crassō pudor, C., *Or.*, I. 26, 122 (346). **Cimōn habēbat satis ēloquentiae**, NEP., V. 2, 1 ; *Cimon had eloquence enough.*

SALLUST introduces the Dat. also for these relations.

4. **Abesse** and **dēesse**, *to be wanting, to fail*, take also the Dat. of Possessor.

5. The Dat. of the person is regular with the phrases **nōmen** (**cōgnōmen**) **est, inditum est**, *etc.* Here the name is in the Nom. in apposition to **nōmen**, in the best usage. Rarely in CICERO, once in SALLUST, never in CAESAR, more often in early and post-Ciceronian Latin, the name is found in the Dat.; either by attraction with the Dat. of the person or on the analogy of the Double Dative. The Appositional Genitive (361) is first cited from VELLEIUS. The undeclined Nom. after an active verb appears first in OVID; then in SUETONIUS.

Fōns aquae dulcis, cuī nōmen Arethūsa est, C., *Verr.*, IV. 53, 118 ; *a fountain of sweet water named Arethusa.* **Apollodōrus, cuī Pyragrō cōgnōmen est**, C., *Verr.*, III. 31, 74 ; *Apollodorus, surnamed Pyragrus* (*fire-tongs*). **Nōmen Arctūrō est mihĭ**, PL., *Rud.*, 5 ; *my name is Arcturus.* **Tibi nōmen īnsānō posuēre**, H., *S.*, II. 3, 47 ; *they called you "cracked."* [**Samnītēs**] **Maleventum, cuī nunc urbī Beneventum nōmen est, perfūgērunt**, L., IX. 27, 14 ; *the Samnites fled to Maleventum* (Ilcome), *a city which now bears the name Beneventum* (Welcome). **Aetās, cuī fēcimus 'aurea' nōmen**, OV., *M.*, XV. 96 ; *the age to which we have given the name 'Golden.'*

Dative of Personal Interest.

In its widest sense this category includes the Dative with Transitive and Intransitive Verbs, already treated, and the Ethical Dative, Dative of Reference, and Dative of Agent, to follow. In its narrower sense it applies only to persons or their equivalents who are essential to, but not necessarily participant in or affected by, the result, and differs from the Dative with Transitive and Intransitive Verbs, in that the connection with the verb is much more remote.

350. 1. The person from whose point of view the action is observed, or towards whom it is directed, may be put in the Dative. A convenient but not exact translation is often the English Possessive (*Datīvus Energicus*).

Eī libenter mē ad pedēs abiēcī, *Cf.* C., *Att.*, VIII. 9, 1 ; *I gladly cast myself at his feet.* **In cōnspectum vēnerat hostibus,** Hirt., VIII. 27 ; *he had come into the sight of the enemy.* **Tuō virō oculī dolent,** *Cf.* Ter., *Ph.*, 1053 ; *your husband's* EYES *ache;* nearer, *your husband has a pain in his eyes* (**tuī virī oculī,** *your* HUSBAND'S *eyes*).

Note.—This Dative is not common in Cicero and is not cited for early Latin. But it becomes common from Livy on. With Relative and Demonstrative pronouns it is often used by Ciceronian and Augustan poets. In the case of many of the examples we have parallel constructions with the Gen. of Possessor, which is the normal usage.

2. The Dative is used of the person in whose honour, or interest, or advantage, or for whose pleasure, an action takes place, or the reverse (*Datīvus Commodī et Incommodī*):

Cōnsurrēxisse omnēs [Lȳsandrō] dīcuntur, C., *Cat.M.*, 18, 63; *all are said to have risen up together in honour of Lysander.* **[Deō] nostra altāria fūmant,** V., *Ec.*, I. 43; *our altars smoke in honour of the god.* **Sī quid peccat mihi peccat,** Ter., *Ad.*, 115 ; *if he commits a fault, it is at my cost.*

Ethical Dative.

351. The Ethical Dative indicates special interest in the action. It may be called the Dative of Feeling, and its use is confined to the personal pronouns (*Datīvus Ēthicus.*)

Tū mihĭ Antōniī exemplō istīus audāciam dēfendis? C., *Verr.*, III. 91, 213 ; *do you defend me (to my face) by Antony's example that fellow's audacity?* **Ecce tibĭ Sēbōsus!** C., *Att.*, II. 15 ; *here's your Sebosus!*

"She's a civil modest wife, one (I tell you) that will not miss *you* morning nor evening prayer."—Shakespeare.

Notes.—1. This is essentially a colloquialism, common in comedy, especially with **ecce** and **em,** frequent in Cicero's letters, occasionally found elsewhere. In poetry, notably Augustan, it is almost wholly absent; but there are several cases in Horace. Cicero does not use **em.** Livy does not use **ecce.**

2. Especially to be noted is **sibĭ velle,** *to want, to mean:* **Quid tibĭ vīs, īnsāne,** C., *Or.*, II. 67, 269 ; *what do you want, madman?* **Quid volt sibĭ haec ōrātiō?** Ter., *Heaut.*, 615 ; *what does all this holding forth mean?*

Dative of Reference.

352. This indicates the person in whose eyes the statement of the predicate holds good (*Datīvus Iūdicantis*).

Ut mihĭ dēfōrmis, sīc tibĭ māgnificus, Tac., *H.*, XII. 37 ; *to me a monster, to yourself a prodigy of splendour.* **Quīntia fōrmōsa est multīs,** Cat., 86, 1; *Quintia is a beauty in the eyes of many.*

NOTE.—This Dative is characteristic of the Augustan poets, but it is also common enough in CICERO and the prose authors.

353. Noteworthy is the use of this Dative in combination with participles, which shows two varieties, one giving the *local* point of view, the other the *mental*, both post-Ciceronian and rare. CAESAR gives the first local usage, LIVY the first mental.

[**Hōc**] **est oppidum prīmum Thessaliae venientibus ab Ēpīrō,** CAES., *B.C.*, III. 80 ; *this is the first town of Thessaly to those coming* (*as you come*) *from Epirus.* **Vērē aestimantī,** L., XXXVII. 58, 8 ; *to one whose judgment was true.*

NOTES.—1. This construction is probably drawn from the Greek, although VITRUVIUS shows several examples.

2. Certainly Greek is the Dat. of the person with **volentī, cupientī, invītō** (**est**), *etc.*, which is found first in SALLUST, once in LIVY, and sporadically in TACITUS, and later.

Dative of the Agent.

354. The Dative is used with Passive Verbs, in prose chiefly with the Perfect Passive, to show the interest which the agent takes in the result. That the person interested is the agent is only an inference. (See 215.)

Mihī rēs tōta prōvīsa est, C., *Verr.*, IV. 42, 91 ; *I have had the whole matter provided for.* **Cui nōn sunt audītae Dēmosthenis vigiliae?** C., *Tusc.*, IV. 19, 44 ; *to whom are not Demosthenes' long watchings a familiar hearsay?*

NOTES.—1. Instances of this Dat. with the Tenses of Continuance are poetical, or admit of a different explanation :

Barbarus hīc ego sum quī nōn intellegor ūllī, OV., *Tr.*, V. 10, 37 ; *I am a barbarian here because I can't make myself intelligible to any one.*

Whenever an adj. or an equivalent is used, the Dat. Pl. may be an Ablative :

Sīc dissimillimīs bēstiolīs commūniter cibus quaeritur, C., *N.D.*, II. 48, 123 ; *so, though these little creatures are so very unlike, their food is sought in common.* **Carmina quae scrībuntur aquae pōtōribus,** H., *Ep.*, I. 19, 3 ; *poems which are written when people are water-drinkers.* **Cēna ministrātur puerīs tribus,** H., *S.*, I. 6, 116 ; *Dinner is served,* (*the waiters being*) *the waiters are* (but) *three.*

2. This Dat. is rare in early Latin, rare, if ever, in CAESAR, not uncommon in CICERO. But it is much liked by the poets and by some prose writers, notably by TACITUS.

355. The agent of the Gerund and Gerundive is put in the Dative, at all periods.

Dīligentia praecipuē colenda est nōbīs, C., *Or.*, II. 35, 148 ; *carefulness is to be cultivated by us first and foremost.* **Dēspēranda tibī salvā concordia socrū,** JUV., VI. 231 ; *you must despair of harmony while Mother-in-law's alive.*

REMARK.—To avoid ambiguity, especially when the verb itself takes the Dat., the Abl. with **ab** (**ā**) is employed for the sake of clearness:

Cīvibus ā vōbīs cōnsulendum, C., *Imp.*, 2, 6; *the interest of the citizens must be consulted by you.* **Supplicātiō ab eō dēcernenda nōn fuit,** C., *Ph.*, XIV. 4, 11.

Where there is no ambiguity there is no need of **ab**:

Linguae moderandum est mihī, PL., *Curc.*, 486; *I must put bounds to my tongue.*

NOTE.—Poets are free in their use of this Dative; so with verbals in **bilis**; as, **multīs ille bonīs flēbilis occidit,** H., *O.*, I. 24, 9; **nūllī exōrābilis,** SIL. ITAL., V. 131.

Dative of the Object For Which.

356. Certain verbs take the Dative of the Object For Which (to what end), and often at the same time a Dative of the Personal Object For Whom, or To Whom.

Nēminī meus adventus labōrī aut sūmptuī fuit, C., *Verr.*, I. 6, 16; *to no one was my arrival a burden or an expense.* **Virtūs sōla neque datur dōnō neque accipitur,** S., *Iug.*, 85, 38; *virtue alone is neither given nor taken as a present.* **Habēre quaestuī rem pūblicam turpe est,** C., *Off.*, II., 22, 77; *it is base to have the state for one's exchequer.*

REMARKS.—1. Noteworthy is the legal phrase **cuī bonō?** *to whom is it for an advantage? = who is advantaged?*

2. In the classical times the principal verbs in this construction are **esse, dare, dūcere, habēre, vertere,** and a few others which occur less frequently. Later Latin extends the usage to many other verbs, and especially to Gerundive constructions. **Dare** is used principally in the phrase **dōnō dare.**

3. The Double Dative is found principally with **esse,** but occasionally with other verbs. Here there seems to have been a tendency, mainly post-Ciceronian, to use the predicative Nom. instead of the Dative. Interesting sometimes is the shift in usage; thus, CICERO says **est turpitūdō,** NEPOS, **fuit turpitūdinī.**

NOTES.—1. In the same category, but with the idea of finality more clearly indicated, are the agricultural usages, **alimentō serere, conditū̄ legere**; the medical, **remediō adhibēre**; the military terms, **praesidiō, auxiliō, mittere, esse,** *etc.*

2. With LIVY we notice the great extension of this Dat. with verbs of *seeking, choosing, etc.*, where classical Latin would prefer some other construction. So **locum īnsidiīs** (**īnsidiārum** is classical) **circumspectāre Poenus coepit,** L., XXI. 53, 11. TACITUS goes furthest in such usages. CAESAR, however, shows a few instances (*B. G.*, I. 30, 3).

3. The Final Dative with intrans. verbs is military and rare. So **receptuī canere,** *to sound a retreat*, is found first in CAES., *B. G.*, VII. 47. SALLUST shows a few examples. The Dat., with similar substantives, is an extension, and is very rare. CICERO, *Ph.*, XIII. 7, 15, says **receptuī signum.**

4. The origin of this usage may have been mercantile (Key). In English we treat Profit and Loss as persons : **Quem fors diērum cumque dabit lucrō appōne,** H., *O.*, I. 9, 14 ; "*Every day that Fate shall give, set down to Profit.*"

On the Dative of the Gerund and Gerundive in a similar sense, see 429.

Dative with Derivative Substantives.

357. A few derivative substantives take the Dative of their primitives :

Iūstitia est obtemperātiō lēgibus, C., *Leg.*, I. 15, 42 ; *justice is obedience to the laws.*

NOTE.—We find a few examples in PLAUTUS, several in CICERO, and only sporadically elsewhere. Usually the verbal force is very prominent in the substantives ; as, **Insidiās cōnsulī mātūrāre,** S., *C.*, 32, 2.

Local Dative.

358. The Dative is used in poetry to denote the *place whither.*

Karthāginī iam nōn ego nūntiōs mittam superbōs, H., *O.*, IV. 4, 69 ; *to Carthage no more shall I send haughty tidings.* **Iam satis terrīs nivis atque dīrae grandinis mīsit pater,** H., *O.*, I. 2, 1 ; *full, full enough of snow and dire hail the Sire hath sent the Land.*

NOTES.—1. This construction begins with ACCIUS, and is not uncommon in the Augustan poets. No examples are cited from PLAUTUS or TERENCE, hence the inference is fair that it was not a colloquialism. As a poetical construction it seems to have sprung from personification.

2. Occasionally the substantive is also thus construed ; as in the **facilis dēscēnsus Avernō** of VERGIL (*A.*, VI. 126).

The extreme is reached when the Dative follows **īre** and the like :

It caelō clāmorque virum clangorque tubārum, V., *A.*, XI. 192 ; *mounts to High Heaven warriors' shout and trumpets' blare.*

3. **Tendere manūs** has a few times, even in CICERO and CAESAR, the Dat. of the person, which is sometimes referred to this head. But the usual construction is **ad.**

Mātrēs familiae Rōmānīs dē mūrō manūs tendēbant, CAES., *B. G.*, VII. 48.

Dative with Adjectives.

359. Adjectives of Likeness, Fitness, Friendliness, Nearness, and the like, with their opposites, take the Dative :

Canis similis lupō est, C., *N. D.*, I. 35, 97 ; *the dog is like unto the wolf.* **Castrīs idōneus locus,** CAES., *B. G.*, VI. 10, 2 ; *a place suitable for a camp.* **Ūtile est reī pūblicae nōbilēs hominēs esse dīgnōs māiōribus suīs,** C., *Sest.*, 9, 21 ; *it is to the advantage of the state that men of rank should be worthy of their ancestors.* **Vir mihĭ amīcissimus, Q. Fabricius,** C., *Sest.*, 35, 75 ; *my very great friend, Q. Fabricius.* **Proxumus sum egomet mihĭ,** TER., *And.*, 636 ; *myself am nearest to me.* **Omnī aetātī mors est com-**

mūnis, *Cf.* C., *Cat.M.*, 19, 68 ; *death is common to every time of life.* **(Tēstis) id dīcit quod illī causae māximē est aliēnum,** C., *Caec.*, 9, 24 ; *the witness says what is especially damaging to that case (side).*

Remarks.—1. Many adjectives which belong to this class are used also as substantives, and as such are construed with the Genitive: **amīcus,** *friend ;* **affīnis,** *connection ;* **aequālis,** *contemporary ;* **aliēnus** (rare), *foreign, strange ;* **cōgnātus,** *kinsman ;* **commūnis,** *common ;* **contrārius,** *opposite ;* **pār,** *match ;* **proprius, pecūliāris,** *own, peculiar ;* **similis,** *like* ("we ne'er shall look upon *his like* again"), especially of gods and men, and regularly with personal pronouns, and in early Latin ; **sacer,** *set apart, sacred ;* **superstes** (rare), *survivor.* Comparatives have regularly the Dative ; Superlatives vary.

[Ille], cūius paucōs parēs haec cīvitās tulit, C., *Pis.*, 4, 8 ; *(he was) a man few of whose peers the state hath borne.* **Utinam tē nōn sōlum vītae, sed etiam dīgnitātis meae superstitem relīquissem,** C., *Q.F.*, I. 3, 1 ; *would that I had left thee survivor not only of my life but also of my position.*

2. The *object toward which* is expressed by the Acc. with **in, ergā, adversus :**

Manlius (fuit) sevērus in fīlium, C., *Off.*, III. 31, 112 ; *Manlius was severe toward his son.* **Mē esse scit sēsē ergā benivolum,** Pl., *Capt.*, 350 ; *he knows that I am kindly disposed toward him.* **Vir adversus merita Caesaris ingrātissimus,** *Cf.* Vell., II. 69, 1 ; *a man most ungrateful towards Caesar's services (to him).*

3. The *object for which* may be expressed by the Acc. with **ad,** *to :*

Homō ad nūllam rem ūtilis, C., *Off.*, III. 6, 29 ; *a good-for-nothing fellow.*

This is the more common construction with adjectives of Fitness.

Notes.—1. **Propior,** *nearer*, **proximus,** *next*, are also construed (like **prope,** *near*) occasionally with the Acc. (principally by Caesar, Sallust, Livy), the adverbial forms also with the Abl. with **ab,** *off :*

Crassus proximus mare Ōceanum hiemārat, Caes., *B.G.*, III. 7, 2 ; *Crassus had wintered next the ocean.* **Id propius fidem est,** L., II. 41, 11 ; *that is nearer belief*, i.e., *more likely.*

2. **Aliēnus,** *foreign, strange,* is also construed with the Abl., with or without **ab (ā)** ; so commonly **absonus.**

Homō sum, hūmānī nīl ā mē aliēnum putō, Ter., *Heaut.*, 77 ; *I am a man, and nothing that pertains to man do I consider foreign to me.*

3. **Iūnctus, coniūnctus,** *joined*, are also construed frequently with **cum** and the Abl.; sometimes with the Abl. only : **improbitās scelere iūncta,** C., *Or.*, II. 58, 237.

4. **Similis** is said to be used with the Gen. when the likeness is general and comprehensive ; with the Dat. when it is conditional or partial ; hence, in classical prose, always **vērī simile,** Livy being the first to say **vērō simile.**

5. **Adversus,** *opponent*, seems to be construed with the Gen. once in Sallust (*C.*, 52, 7) and once in Quintilian (XII. 1, 2). **Invidus,** *envious*, is cited with the Gen. once in Cicero (*Flac.*, 1, 2), then not till late Latin ; with the Dat. it is poetical ; otherwise the possessive pronoun is used, as **tuī invidī** (C., *Fam.*, I. 4, 2). **Prōnus,** *inclined*, with the Dat., occurs in Sallust (*Iug.*, 114, 2), then not till Tacitus ; the usual construction is **ad.** **Intentus,** *intent upon*, has Abl. in Sallust (*C.*, 2, 9, *etc.*) ;

otherwise Dat., or **ad (in)** with Acc. Notice the use of **āversus** with Dat. in Tac., *Ann.*, I. 66, 2; some other examples are doubtful.

6. In poetry, **idem,** *the same*, is often construed after Greek analogy, with the Dative.

Invītum quī servat idem facit occīdentī, H., *A.P*, 467; *he who saves a man('s life) against his will does the same thing as one who kills him (as if he had killed him).*

7. Adverbs of similar meaning sometimes take the Dative: **Congruenter nātūrae convenienterque vīvere,** C., *Fin.*, III. 7, 26.

II. Internal Change.

Genitive.

360. I. The Genitive Case is the Case of the Complement, and is akin to the Adjective, with which it is often parallel. It is the substantive form of the Specific Characteristic.

The chief English representatives of the Genitive are:

(*a*) The Possessive case: **Domus rēgis,** *the king's palace.*

(*b*) The Objective case with *of*: **Domus rēgis,** *the palace of the king.*

(*c*) Substantives used as adjectives or in composition: **Arbor abietis,** *fir-tree.*

Remarks.—1. Other prepositions than *of* are not unfrequently used, especially with the Objective Genitive. (363, R. 1.)

Patriae quis exsul sē quoque fūgit? H., *O.*, II. 16, 19; *what exile* FROM *his country ever fled himself as well?* **Boiōrum triumphī spem collēgae relīquit,** L., XXXIII. 37, 10; *he left the hope of a triumph* OVER *the Boii to his colleague.*

Via mortis may be considered *the way (mode) of death* or *the death-path,* instead of **via ad mortem** (L., XLIV. 4, 14).

2. An abstract substantive with the Gen. is often to be translated as an attribute:

Vernī temporis suāvitās, C., *Cat.M.*, 19, 70; *the sweet spring-time.* **Fontium gelidae perennitātēs,** C., *N.D.*, II. 39, 98; *cool springs that never fail.* Compare S., *C.*, 8, 3.

And, on the other hand, the predicative attribute is often to be translated as an abstract substantive with *of*:

Ante Rōmam conditam, *before the founding of Rome.* (325, R. 3.)

Notice also **hīc metus,** *this fear* = *fear of this,* and kindred expressions: **Quam similitūdinem** = **cūius reī similitūdinem,** C., *N.D.*, II. 10, 27.

2. The Genitive is employed:

I. and II. Chiefly as the complement of Substantives and Adjectives.

III. Occasionally as the complement of Verbs.

Note.—As the Accusative forms a complex with the verb, so the Genitive forms a complex with the Substantive or equivalent. No logical distribution can be wholly satisfactory, and the following arrangement has regard to convenience.

I. GENITIVE WITH SUBSTANTIVES.

Adnominal Genitive.

Appositive Genitive, or Genitive of Specification.

361. The Genitive is sometimes used to specify the contents of generic words instead of Apposition in the same case; there are two varieties:

1. *Appositional Genitive.*—Genitive after such words as, **vōx**, *expression;* **nōmen**, *name, noun;* **verbum**, *word, verb;* **rēs**, *thing, etc.*

Nōmen amīcitiae, C., *Fin.*, II. 24, 78; *the name friendship.*

2. *Epexegetical Genitive.*—Genitive after such words as **genus**, *class;* **vitium**, *vice;* **culpa**, *fault, etc.*

[**Virtūtēs**] **continentiae, gravitātis, iūstitiae, fideī**, C., *Mur.*, 10, 23; *the virtues of self-control, earnestness, justice, honour.*

NOTES.—1. The former variety is very rare in CICERO, the latter much more common. A special variety is the use of the Gen. after such words as **urbs, oppidum, flūmen**, *etc.* This is not found in PLAUTUS and TERENCE, occurs perhaps but once in CICERO, and seems to be confined to a few cases in poetry and later prose. Often personification is at work; thus, in **fōns Timāvī** (V., *A.*, I. 244), **Timāvus** is a river god, and **fōns** is not equal to **Timāvus.**

2. Examples like **arbor abietis** (L., XXIV. 3, 4), *fir-tree;* **arbor fīcī** (*Cf.* C., *Flac.*, 17, 41), *fig-tree, etc.*, occur only here and there.

3. Colloquial, and probably belonging here, are: **scelus virī** (PL., *M.G.*, 1434), *a scoundrel of a man;* **flāgitium hominis** (PL., *Asin.*, 473), *a scamp of a fellow*, and the like. **Quaedam pēstēs hominum**, C., *Fam.*, V. 8, 2; *certain pestilent fellows.*

Possessive Genitive, or Genitive of Property.

362. The Possessive Genitive is the substantive form of an adjective attribute with which it is often parallel; it is used only of the Third Person.

Domus rēgis = **domus rēgia**, *the palace of the king, the king's palace = the royal palace.*

REMARKS.—1. The Possession in the First and Second Person (and in the Reflexive) is indicated by the Possessive Pronouns (until after LIVY): **amīcus meus**, *a friend of mine;* **gladius tuus**, *a sword of thine.* But when **omnium** is added, **vestrum** and **nostrum** are used; **ārīs et focīs omnium nostrum inimīcus**, C., *Ph.*, XI. 4, 10. Sometimes the adjective form is preferred also in the Third Person: **canis aliēnus**, *a strange dog, another man's dog;* **fīlius erīlis**, *master's son.*

2. The attention of the student is called to the variety of forms which possession may take. **Statua Myrōnis**, *Myron's statue*, may mean: 1. A statue which Myron owns; 2. Which Myron has made; 3. Which represents Myron.

3. Sometimes the governing word is omitted, where it can be easily

supplied, so especially **aedēs** or **templum**, after **ad**, and less often **after** other prepositions: **Pecūnia utinam ad Opis manēret**, C., *Ph.*, I. 7, 17; *would that the money were still at Ops's* (temple).

NOTES.—1. The *Family* Genitive, as **Hasdrubal Gisgōnis** (L., XXVIII., 12, 13), *Gisgo's Hasdrubal, Hasdrubal, Gisgo's son* (as it were, *Hasdrubal O' Gisgo*), **Hectoris Andromachē** (V., *A.*, III. 319), *Hector's* (*wife*) *Andromache*, is found twice only in CICERO, otherwise it is poetical and post-Ciceronian. **Servos**, however, is regularly omitted; **Flaccus Claudī**, *Flaccus, Claudius' slave.*

2. The *Chorographic* (*geographic*) Genitive is rare and post-Ciceronian: **Rēx Chalcidem Euboeae vēnit**, L., XXVII. 30, 7; *the king came to Chalcis of* (in) *Euboea.*

The *Chorographic* Genitive is not found with persons. Here an adjective or a prepositional phrase is necessary: **Thalēs Mīlēsius**, or **ex Mīlētō**, *Thales of Miletus.*

Active and Passive Genitive.

363. When the substantive on which the Genitive depends contains the idea of an action (**nōmen āctiōnis**), the possession may be *active* or *passive*. Hence the division into

1. The Active or Subjective Genitive: **amor Deī**, *the love of God, the love which God feels* (God loves); **patriae beneficia**, *the benefits of* (*conferred by*) *one's country* (376, R. 2).

2. Passive or Objective Genitive: **amor Deī**, *love of God, love toward God* (God is loved).

REMARKS.—1. The English form in *of* is used either *actively* or *passively*: *the love of women.* Hence, to avoid ambiguity, other prepositions than *of* are often substituted for the Passive Genitive, such as *for, toward*, and the like. So, also, sometimes in Latin, especially in LIVY, and later Historians generally:

Voluntās Servīliī ergā Caesarem, *Cf.* C., *Q.F.*, III. 1. 6, 26; *the good-will of Servilius toward Caesar.* **Odium in bonōs inveterātum**, C., *Vat.*, 3, 6; *deep-seated hate toward the conservatives.*

2. Both Genitives may be connected with the same substantive:

Veterēs Helvētiōrum iniūriae populī Rōmānī, *Cf.* CAES., *B.G.*, I. 30, 2; *the ancient injuries of the Roman people by the Helvetians.*

NOTE.—The use of the Genitive with substantives whose corresponding verbs take other cases than the Accusative, gradually increases in Latin, beginning with the earliest times, but it is not very common in the classical language.

364. The Subjective Genitive, like the Possessive, is used only of the Third Person. In the First and Second Persons the possessive pronoun is used, thus showing the close relationship of Agent and Possessor.

Amor meus, *my love* (*the love which I feel*). **Dēsīderium tuum**, *your longing* (*the longing which you feel*).

Additional attributives are put in the Genitive (321, R. 2):

Iūrāvī hanc urbem meā ūnīus operā salvam esse, C., *Pis.*, 3, 6 ; *I swore that this city owed its salvation to my exertions alone.*

REMARK.—**Nostrum** and **vestrum** are used as Partitive Genitives:

Māgna pars nostrum, *a great part of us ;* **uterque vestrum,** *either (both) of you.*

Nostrī melior pars means *the better part of our being, our better part.*

With **omnium,** the forms **nostrum** and **vestrum** must be used (362, R. 1).

NOTES.—1. Occasionally, however, in Latin, as in English, the Gen. is used instead of the possessive pronoun; so CICERO says **splendor vestrum** (*Att.*, VII. 13 *a*, 3), and **cōnsēnsus vestrum** (*Ph.*, V. 1, 2), and one or two others ; but other examples are very rare until after TACITUS, when the Singular forms, after the example of OVID (*M.*, I. 30), become not uncommon. See 304, 3, N. 1. "For the life of me" = "for my life."

2. On the other hand the Genitives of the personal pronouns are used regularly as the Objective Genitive :

Amor meī, *love to me.* **Dēsīderium tuī,** *longing for thee.* **Memoria nostrī,** *memory of us* (our memory).

Occasionally the possessive pronoun is used even here ; see 304, 2, N. 2, and compare "The deep damnation of *his* taking off."

Genitive of Quality.

365. The Genitive of Quality must always have an adjective or its equivalent.

Vir māgnae auctōritātis, CAES., *B.G.*, V. 35, 6; *a man of great influence.* **Homō nihilī** (= **nūllīus pretiī**), PL., *B.*, 1188 ; *a fellow of no account.* **Trīduī via,** CAES., *B.G.*, I. 38, 1; *a three days' journey.* **Nōn multī cibī hospitem accipiēs, multī iocī,** C., *Fam.*, IX. 26, 4; *you will receive a guest who is a small eater but a great joker.*

REMARKS.—1. The Genitive of Quality, like the adjective, is not used with a proper name. Exceptions are very rare in classical Latin (CAES., *B.G.*, V. 35, 6, **Quīntus Lūcānius, ēiusdem ōrdinis**). But later they are more common.

2. The Genitive of Quality is less common than the Ablative, being used chiefly of the essentials. The Genitive always of Number, Measure, Time, Space; the Ablative always of externals, so of parts of the body. Often the use seems indifferent. (400.)

NOTE.—The omission of the adjective is not found before APULEIUS, in whom, as in English, *a man of influence* may be for *a man of great influence.*

Genitive as a Predicate.

366. The Genitives of Possession and Quality may be used as Predicates.

Hic versus Plautī nōn est, hic est, C., *Fam.*, IX. 16, 4; *this verse is not* *by Plautus, this is.* **Omnia quae mulieris fuērunt, virī fīunt dōtis nōmine,** C., *Top.*, IV. 23; *everything that was the woman's becomes the husband's under the title of dowry.* **Virtūs tantārum vīrium est ut sē ipsa tueātur,** C., *Tusc.*, V. 1, 2; *virtue is of such strength as to be her own protector.*

REMARKS.—1. The Possession appears in a variety of forms, and takes a variety of translations:

Hūius erō vīvus, mortuus hūius erō, PROP., II. 15, 35; *hers I shall be, living; dead, hers I shall be.* **Nōlae senātus Rōmānōrum, plēbs Hannibalis erat,** L., XXIII. 39, 7; *at Nola the senate was* (on the side) *of the Romans, the common folk* (on) *Hannibal's.* **Damnātiō est iūdicum, poena lēgis,** C., *Sull.*, 22, 63; *condemning is the judges'* (business), *punishment the law's.* **Est animī ingenuī cuī multum dēbeās eīdem plūrimum velle dēbēre,** C., *Fam.*, II. 6, 2; *it shows the feeling of a gentleman to be willing to owe very much to him to whom you already owe much.* **Pauperis est numerāre pecus,** OV., *M.*, XIII. 823; *'tis only the poor man that counts his flock* (*'tis the mark of a poor man to count the flock*).

Observe the special variety, *Genitīvus Auctōris:* **Is [Herculēs] dīcēbātur esse Myrōnis,** C., *Verr.*, IV. 3, 5; *that* (statue of) *Hercules was said to be Myron's* (work), *by Myron.*

So also with **facere,** *to make* (*cause to be*), which is common in LIVY especially:

Rōmānae diciōnis facere, L., XXI. 60, 3; *to bring under the Roman sway.* **Summum imperium in orbe terrārum Macedonum fēcerant,** L., XLV. 7, 3; *the paramount authority of the world they had brought* (*into the hands*) *of the Macedonians.*

2. For the personal representative of a quality, the quality itself may be used sometimes with but little difference, as: **stultitiae est,** *it is the part of folly;* **stultī est,** *it is the part of a fool.* So, too, **stultum est,** *it is foolish.* But when the adj. is of the Third Declension, the neuter should not be used, except in combination with an adj. of the Second.

Temporī cēdere semper sapientis est habitum, C., *Fam.*, IV. 9, 2; *to yield to the pressure of the times has always been held wise.* **Pigrum et iners vidētur sūdōre adquīrere quod possīs sanguine parāre,** TAC., *G.*, 14, 17; *it is thought slow and spiritless to acquire by sweat what you can get by blood.*

Some combinations become phraseological, as: **cōnsuētūdinis, mōris est** (the latter post-classical), *it is the custom.*

3. The same methods of translation apply to the Possessive Pronoun in the Predicate ("Vengeance is *mine*"): **meum est,** *it is my property, business, way.*

Nōn est mentīrī meum, TER., *Heaut.*, 549; *lying is not my way* (*I do not lie*). **Hīs tantīs in rēbus est tuum vidēre, quid agātur,** C., *Mur.*, 38, 83; *in this important crisis it is your business to see what is to be done.*

Partitive Genitive.

367. The Partitive Genitive stands for the Whole to which a Part belongs. It is therefore but an extension of the Possessive Genitive. It may be used with any word that involves partition, and has the following varieties (368–372) :

368. The Partitive Genitive is used with substantives of Quantity, Number, Weight.

Māximus vīnī numerus fuit, permāgnum pondus argentī, C., *Ph.*, II. 27, 66 ; *there was a large amount of wine, an enormous mass of silver.* **In iūgerō Leontīnī agrī medimnum trīticī seritur,** C. *Verr.*, III. 47, 112 ; *on a juger of the Leontine territory a medimnus of wheat is sown.* **Campānōrum ālam, quīngentōs ferē equitēs excēdere aciē iubet,** L., x. 29, 2 ; *he orders a squadron of Campanians, about* 500 *horsemen, to leave the line.*

REMARK.—This is sometimes called the *Genitīvus Generis,* Whether the conception be partitive or not, depends on circumstances. **Medimnus trīticī,** *a medimnus of wheat,* may be *a medimnus of* WHEAT (*Genitīvus Generis*) or a MEDIMNUS *of wheat* (*Partitive*).

NOTE.—The reversed construction is occasionally found. **Sex diēs ad eam rem cōnficiendam spatiī pōstulant,** CAES., *B. C.*, I. 3, 6, instead of **spatium sex diērum.**

369. The Partitive Genitive is used with the Neuter Singular of the following and kindred words, but only in the Nominative or Accusative.

tantum, *so much,*	**quantum,** *as* (*how much*),	**aliquantum,** *somewhat,*
multum, *much,*	**plūs,** *more,*	**plūrimum,** *most,*
paulum, *little,*	**minus,** *less,*	**minimum,** *least,*
satis, *enough,*	**parum,** *too little,*	**nihil,** *nothing,*
hōc, *this,*	**id, illud, istud,** *that,*	**idem,** *the same,*

quod and **quid,** *which* and *what ?* with their compounds.

Quod in rēbus honestīs operae cūraeque pōnētur, id iūre laudābitur, C., *Off.*, I. 6, 19 ; *what* (*of*) *effort and pains shall be bestowed on reputable deeds, will receive a just recompense of praise.* **Is locus ab omnī turbā id temporis** (336, N. 2) **vacuus** [**erat**], C., *Fin.*, v. 1, 1 ; *that place was at that* (*point of*) *time free from anything like a crowd.* **Satis ēloquentiae, sapientiae parum,** S., *C.*, 5, 4 ; *enough* (*of*) *eloquence, of wisdom too little.*

REMARKS.—1. Neuter adjectives of the Second Declension can be treated as substantives in the Gen.; not so adjectives of the Third, except in combination with adjectives of the Second, but here usually the Second Declension adjective is attracted : **aliquid bonum,** or **bonī,** *something good ;* **aliquid memorābile,** *something memorable ;* **aliquid bonī**

et memorābilis, *something good and memorable* (better **aliquid bonum et memorābile**).

Quid habet ista rēs aut laetābile aut glōriōsum? C., *Tusc.*, I. 21, 49 (204, N. 3).

2. A familiar phrase is: **Nihil reliquī facere.** 1. *To leave nothing* (*not a thing*). 2. (Occasionally), *to leave nothing undone.*

NOTES.—1. The conception is often not so much partitive as characteristic. So **Quodcumque hōc rēgnī,** V., *A.*, I. 78; *this realm, what* (little) *there is of it* (*what little realm I have*). Perhaps, too, such combinations as **flāgitium hominis** may be classed under this head. See 361, N. 3.

2. The partitive construction, with a preposition, is not found in CICERO or CAESAR, but begins with SALLUST:

Ad id locī, S., *C.*, 45, 3; **ad id locōrum,** S., *Iug.*, 63, 6.

370. The Partitive Genitive is used with numerals both general and special.

Special:

Centum mīlitum, *a hundred* (of the) *soldiers, a hundred* (of) *soldiers.*

(**Centum mīlitēs,** *a, the hundred soldiers.*)

Quīntus rēgum, *the fifth* (*of the*) *king*(*s*).

(**Quīntus rēx,** *the fifth king.*)

General:

Multī mīlitum, *many of the soldiers, many soldiers.*

(**Multī mīlitēs,** *many soldiers.*)

REMARKS.—1. The English language commonly omits the partition, unless it is especially emphatic:

Multī cīvium adsunt, *many* CITIZENS *are present.* **Multī cīvēs adsunt,** MANY *are the citizens present.*

2. When all are embraced, there is no partition in Latin:

(Nōs) trecentī coniūrāvimus, L., II. 12, 15; *three hundred of us have bound ourselves by an oath.* **Volnera quae circum plūrima mūrōs accēpit patriōs,** V., *A.*, II. 277; *wounds which he received in great numbers before his country's walls.*

Quī omnēs, *all of whom.* **Quot estis?** *how many are* (*there of*) *you?* So always **quot, tot, totidem.**

Here the English language familiarly employs the partition. Exceptions are very rare.

3. On **mīlle** and **mīlia,** see 293. On prepositions with numerals, see 372, R. 2.

371. The Partitive Genitive is used with Pronouns.

Iī mīlitum, *those* (of the) *soldiers.* **Iī mīlitēs,** *those soldiers.*

Illī Graecōrum, *those* (of the) *Greeks.*

Fīdēnātium quī supersunt, ad urbem Fīdēnās tendunt, L., IV. 33, 10; *the surviving Fidenates take their way to the city of Fidenae.*

REMARKS.—1. **Uterque**, *either* (*both*), is commonly used as an adjective with substantives : **uterque cōnsul**, *either consul = both consuls ;* as a substantive with pronouns, unless a substantive is also used: **uterque hōrum**, *both of these ;* but **uterque ille dux**. So, too, with relatives in the neuter, and with Plural forms of **uterque**, concord is the rule. Compare **uterque nostrum**, C., *Sull.*, 4, 13, with **utrīque nōs**, C., *Fam.*, XI. 20, 3. See 292.

2. On the use of prepositions instead of the Genitive, see 372, R. 2.

NOTE.—The use of the relative with the Genitive is characteristic of LIVY.

372. The Partitive Genitive is used with Comparatives and Superlatives :

Prior hōrum in proeliō cecidit, NEP., XXI. 1, 2 ; *the former of these fell in an engagement.* **Indus est omnium flūminum māximus**, C., *N.D.*, II. 52, 130 (211, R. 2).

REMARKS.—1. When there are only two, the comparative exhausts the degrees of comparison (300).

2. Instead of the Partitive Genitive with Numerals, Pronouns, Comparatives, and Superlatives, the Abl. may be employed with **ex**, *out of*, **dē**, *from* (especially with proper names and singulars), **in**, *among* (rare), or the Acc. with **inter**, *among*, **apud** : **Gallus prōvocat ūnum ex Rōmānīs**, *the Gaul challenges one of the Romans ;* **ūnus dē multīs**, *one of the many* (the masses) ; **Croesus inter rēgēs opulentissimus**, *Croesus, wealthiest of kings.* With **ūnus**, **ex** or **dē** is the more common construction, except that when **ūnus** is *first* in a series, the Gen. is common.

3. On the concord of the Superlative see 211, R. 2.

NOTES.—1. The Partitive Genitive with positives is occasional in poetry ; in prose it begins with LIVY and becomes more common later.

Sequimur tē, sāncte deōrum, V., *A.*, IV. 576 ; *we follow thee, holy deity.* **Canum dēgenerēs (caudam) sub alvom flectunt**, PLIN., *N.H.*, XI., 50, 265 ; *currish dogs curl the tail up under the belly.*

2. Substantival neuters, with no idea of quantity, were rarely followed by the Gen. in early Latin. CICERO shows a few cases of Plurals of superlatives, and one case of a Plural of a comparative in this construction : **in interiōra aedium Sullae** (*Att.* IV., 3, 3). CAESAR shows one case of a positive : **in occultīs āc reconditīs templī** (*B. C.*, III. 105, 5). SALLUST shows the first case of the Singular : **in praeruptī montis extrēmō** (*Iug.*, 37, 4). Then the usage extends and becomes common, especially in TACITUS. In the poets it begins with LUCRETIUS.

Ardua dum metuunt āmittunt vēra viāī (29, N. 2), LUCR., I. 660 ; *the while they fear the steeper road, they miss the true.*

So **amāra cūrārum**, H., *O.*, IV. 12, 19 ; *bitter elements of cares, bitter cares ;* **strāta viārum**, V., *A.*, I. 422 = **strātae viae**, *the paved streets.*

3. The Partitive Genitive is also used with Adverbs of Quantity, Place, Extent : **armōrum adfatim**, L., XXVII. 17, 7 ; *abundance of arms ;* **ubi terrārum, gentium?** *where in the world?* (Very late Latin, **tum temporis**, *at that time.*) The usage with **hūc, eō**, as **hūc, eō arrogantiae prōcēssit**, *he got to this, that pitch of presumption,* is a colloquialism, which begins with SALLUST, but is not found in CICERO or CAESAR.

Notice especially the phrase: **quod** (or **quoad**) **ēius** (**facere**) **possum,** *as far as I can do so:* C., *Fam.*, III. 2, 2; *Att.*, XI. 12, 4; *Inv.*, II., 6, 20.

4. The Partitive Genitive with proper names is rare, and mostly confined to LIVY: **Cōnsulum Sulpicius in dextrō Poetelius in laevō cornū cōnsistunt,** L., IX. 27, 8.

5. The Partitive Genitive as a Predicate is Greekish: **Fiēs nōbilium tū quoque fontium,** H., *O.*, III., 13, 13; *thou too shalt count among the famous fountains.*

Genitive with Prepositional Substantives.

373. Causā, grātiā, ergō, and **īnstar** are construed with the Genitive.

[**Sophistae**] **quaestūs causā philosophābantur,** C., *Ac.*, II. 23, 72; *the professors of wisdom dealt in philosophy for the sake of gain.* **Tū mē amōris magis quam honōris servāvistī grātiā,** ENN., *F.*, 287 (M.); *thou didst save me more for love's* (sake) *than* (thou didst) *for honour's sake.* **Virtūtis ergō,** C., *Opt. Gen.*, 7, 19; *on account of valor.* **Īnstar montis equus,** V., *A.*, II. 15; *a horse the bigness of a mountain.* **Platō mihī ūnus īnstar est omnium,** C., *Br.*, 51, 191; *Plato by himself is in my eyes worth them all.*

REMARKS.—1. **Causā** and **grātiā,** *for the sake,* commonly follow the Gen. in classical Latin and also in the Jurists. In LIVY and later they often precede. **Ergō,** *on account,* belongs especially to early Latin, except in formulæ and laws, and follows its Genitive. It is rare in the poets. **Īnstar** is probably a fossilised Infinitive (**īnstāre**), meaning "*the equivalent,*" whether of size or value.

2. Except for special reasons **causā** takes the possessive pronoun in agreement, rather than the personal pronoun in the Genitive; more rarely **grātiā**:

Vestrā reīque pūblicae causā, C., *Verr.*, v. 68, 173; *for your sake and that of the commonwealth.* But in antithesis, **multa quae nostrī causā numquam facerēmus, facimus causā amīcōrum!** C., *Lael.*, 16, 57 (disputed).

II. GENITIVE WITH ADJECTIVES.

374. Adjectives of Fulness, of Participation, and of Power, of Knowledge and Ignorance, of Desire and Disgust, take the Genitive.

Plēnus rīmārum, TER., *Eun.*, 105; *full of chinks* ("a leaky vessel"). **Particeps cōnsiliī,** C., *Sull.*, 4, 12; *a sharer in the plan.* **Mentis compos,** C., *Ph.*, II. 38, 97; *in possession of* (one's) *mind.* **Multārum rērum perītus,** C., *Font.*, 11, 25; *versed in many things.* **Cupidus pecūniae,** *Cf.* C., *Verr.*, I. 3, 8; *grasping after money.* **Fāstīdiōsus Latīnārum** (**lītterārum**), C., *Br.*, 70, 247; *too dainty for Latin.* **Omnium rērum īnscius,** C., *Br.*, 85, 292; *a universal ignoramus.* **Cūr nōn ut plēnus vītae convīva recēdis?** LUCR., III. 938 (273). **Sitque memor nostrī necne, referte mihī,** Ov., *Tr.*, IV.

3, 10 (204, N. 7). **Cōnscia mēns rēctī Fāmae mendācia rīsit,** Ov., *F.*, IV. 311 (330, R.). **Agricolam laudat iūris lēgumque perītus,** H., *S.*, I. 1, 9; *the husbandman('s lot) is praised by the counsel learned in the law.* **Omnēs immemorem beneficiī ōdērunt,** C., *Off.*, II. 18, 63; *all hate a man who has no memory for kindness.* **(Bēstiae) sunt ratiōnis et ōrātiōnis expertēs,** C., *Off.*, I. 16, 50; *beasts are devoid of reason and speech (lack discourse of reason).* **Omnia plēna cōnsiliōrum, inānia verbōrum vidēmus,** C., *Or.*, I. 9, 37; *we see a world that is full of wise measures, void of eloquence.* **Gallia frūgum fertilis fuit,** L., V. 34, 2; *Gaul was productive of grain.*

NOTES.—1. Of adjectives of *Fulness*, with the Gen., only **plēnus, replētus, inops,** and **inānis** are classical and common; single instances are found of **līberālis, profūsus,** in SALLUST (*C.*, 7, 6; 5, 4), and **ieiūnus** occurs once in CICERO. PLAUTUS also uses **onustus** and **prōdigus.** Poets and later prose writers are free. **Plēnus** occurs very rarely with the Abl. in CICERO and CAESAR, more often in LIVY. **Refertus** is used by CICERO usually with the Abl. of the Thing and with the Gen. of the Person.

2. *Participation:* Classical are **particeps, expers, cōnsors,** with some adjectives expressing guilt, as **manifēstus** (archaic), **affīnis, reus.** Of these **particeps** takes also the Dat. in post-classical Latin, and **expers** has also the Abl. (not classical) from PLAUTUS on. (See S., *C.*, 33, 1.) **Affīnis** has the Dat. in LIVY, in local sense also in CICERO; **reus** takes Abl. or **dē.**

3. *Power:* **Compos** alone is classical, and is occasionally found with Abl. in SALLUST, VERGIL, LIVY. **Potēns** is found in PLAUTUS, the poets, and post-classical prose; **impos** in PLAUTUS, and then not until SENECA.

4. *Knowledge and Ignorance:* Classical are some eighteen. Of these **perītus** has also Abl., and rarely **ad**; **īnsuētus** takes also Dat. as well as **dē**; **prūdēns** has also **ad**; **rudis** has Abl. with **in** more often than the Gen. in CICERO, but also **ad.** Ante-classical Latin shows a few more adjectives.

5. *Desire and Disgust:* Classical are **avidus, cupidus, fāstīdiōsus, studiōsus.** Of these **avidus** has also **in** with Acc. and with Abl.; **studiōsus** has Dat. in PLAUTUS (*M. G.*, 801); single examples are cited with **ad** and **in.** **Fāstīdiōsus** occurs but once in CICERO (see above); see H., *O.*, III. 1, 37.

6. In later Latin and in the poets almost all adjectives that denote an affection of the mind take a Gen. of the Thing to which the affection refers, where model prose requires the Abl. or a preposition: **cōnsiliī ambiguus,** TAC., *H.*, IV. 21; *doubtful of purpose.* **Ingrātus salūtis,** V., *A.*, X. 665.

The analogy of these adjectives is followed by others, so that the Gen. becomes a complement to the adjective, just as it is to the corresponding substantive.

Integer vītae, H., *O.*, I. 22, 1; *spotless of life;* like **integritās vītae.** (Compare **fāmā et fortūnīs integer,** S., *H.*, II. 41, 5 D; *in fame and fortunes intact.*)

7. The seat of the feeling is also put in the Gen., chiefly with **animī** and **ingeniī** (which were probably Locatives originally). **Aeger animī,** L., I. 58, 9; *sick at heart, heartsick.* **Audāx ingeniī,** STAT., *S.*, III. 2, 64; *daring of disposition.* The Pl. is **animīs.**

8. The Gen. with adjectives involving *Separation* instead of the Abl. (390, 3) begins with the Augustan poets; though SALLUST shows **nūdus** and **vacuus** (*Iug.*, 79, 6; 90, 1); **līber labōrum,** H., *A.P.*, 212.

9. Classical Latin uses **certus** with Gen. only in the phrase **certiōrem facere,** *to inform,* which has also **dē** (always in CAESAR).

10. **Dīgnus,** *worthy,* and **indīgnus,** *unworthy,* with Gen. are poetical and rare.

11. On **aliēnus,** *strange,* see 359, N. 2. On **aequālis, commūnis, cōnscius, contrārius, pār, proprius, similis, superstes,** and the like, see 359, R. 1.

Genitive with Verbals.

375. Some Present Participles take the Genitive when they lose their verbal nature; and so occasionally do verbals in **-āx** in poetry and later prose.

(Epamīnōndās) erat adeō vēritātis dīligēns ut nē iocō quidem mentīrētur, NEP., XV. 3, 1; *Epaminondas was so careful (such a lover) of the truth as not to tell lies even in jest.* **Omnium cōnsēnsū capāx imperiī nisi imperāsset,** TAC., *H.*, I. 49; *by general consent capable of empire, had he not become emperor.*

NOTES.—1. The participle is transient; the adjective permanent. The simple test is the substitution of the relative and the verb: **amāns** (participle), *loving* (*who is loving*); **amāns** (adjective), *fond*, (substantive), *lover*; **patiēns** (participle), *bearing* (*who is bearing*); **patiēns** (adjective), *enduring*, (substantive), *a sufferer*.

2. Ante-classical Latin shows only **amāns, cupiēns, concupiēns, fugitāns, gerēns, persequēns, sciēns, temperāns.** CICERO carries the usage very far, and it is characteristic of his style. CAESAR, on the other hand, has very few cases (*B. C.*, I. 69, 3).

CICERO also shows the first case of a Gen. after a compared participle. **Sumus nātūrā appetentissimī honestātis,** C., *Tusc.*, II. 24, 58. These participles can also revert to the verbal constructions.

3. Of verbals with the Gen., PLAUTUS shows one example: **mendāx** (*Asin.*, 855); CICERO perhaps one: **rapāx** (*Lael.*, 14, 50). The usage in later Latin and the poets is confined at most to about one dozen verbals.

III. GENITIVE WITH VERBS.

Genitive with Verbs of Memory.

376. Verbs of Reminding, Remembering, and Forgetting, take the Genitive.

Tē veteris amīcitiae commonefēcit, [C.] *ad Her.*, IV. 24, 33; *he reminded you of your old friendship.* **Est proprium stultitiae aliōrum vitia cernere, oblīvīscī suōrum,** C., *Tusc.*, III. 30, 73; *the fact is, it shows a fool to have keen eyes for the faults of others, to forget one's own.* **Ipse iubet mortis tē meminisse deus,** MART., II. 59; *a god himself bids you remember death.*

REMARKS.—1. Verbs of Reminding take more often the Abl. with **dē** (so regularly in CICERO), and the Acc. neut. of a pronoun or Numeral adjective. TACITUS alone uses **monēre** with the Gen. (*Ann.*, I. 67, 1).

Ōrō ut Terentiam moneātis dē tēstāmentō, C., *Att.*, XI. 16, 5; *I beg you to put Terentia in mind of the will.* **Discipulōs id ūnum moneō,** QUINT., II. 9, 1 (333, 1).

2. Verbs of Remembering and Forgetting also take the Acc., especially of Things;

Haec ōlim meminisse iuvābit, V., *A.*, I. 203 ; *to remember these things one day will give us pleasure.* **Quī sunt bonī cīvēs, nisi quī patriae beneficia meminērunt?** C., *Planc.*, 33, 80 ; *who are good citizens except those who remember the benefits conferred by their country?* **Oblīvīscī nihil solēs nisi iniūriās**, C., *Lig.*, 12, 35 ; *you are wont to forget nothing except injuries.*

Recordor (literally = *I bring to heart, to mind*) is construed with the Acc. of the Thing, except in three passages from CICERO ; **dē** is found with Persons.

Et vōcem Anchīsae māgnī voltumque recordor, V., *A.*, VIII. 156 ; *and I recall* (call to mind) *the voice and countenance of Anchises the Great.*

Meminī, *I bear in mind, I* (am old enough to) *remember*, takes the Accusative :

[**Antipatrum**] **tū probē meministī**, C., *Or.*, III. 50, 194 ; *you remember Antipater very well.*

3. **Venit mihĭ in mentem**, *it comes into* (up to) *my mind*, may be construed impersonally with the Gen., or personally with a subject ; the latter by CICERO only when the subject is a neuter pronoun.

Venit mihĭ Platōnis in mentem, C., *Fin.*, V. 1, 2 ; *Plato rises before my mind's eye.*

Genitive with Verbs of Emotion.

377. Misereor, *I pity*, takes the Genitive, and **miseret**, *it moves to pity*, **paenitet**, *it repents*, **piget**, *it irks*, **pudet**, *it makes ashamed*, **taedet** and **pertaesum est**, *it tires*, take the Accusative of the Person Who Feels, and the Genitive of the Exciting Cause.

Miserēminī sociōrum, C., *Verr.*, I. 28, 72 ; *pity your allies!* **Suae quemque fortūnae paenitet**, C., *Fam.*, VI. 1, 1; *each man is discontented with his lot.* **Mē nōn sōlum piget stultitiae meae, sed etiam pudet**, C., *Dom.*, 11, 29 ; *I am not only fretted at my folly, but actually ashamed of it.*

REMARKS.—1. **Pudet** is also used with the Gen. of the Person whose Presence excites the shame :

Pudet deōrum hominumque, L., III. 19, 7 ; *it is a shame in the sight of gods and men.*

2. These Impersonals can also have a subject, chiefly a Demonstrative or Relative pronoun : **Nōn tē haec pudent?** TER., *Ad.*, 754 ; *do not these things put you to the blush?*

3. Other constructions follow from general rules. So the Inf. (422) and **quod** (542).

Nōn mē vīxisse paenitet, C., *Cat.M.*, 23, 84 (540). **Quīntum paenitet quod animum tuum offendit**, *Cf.* C., *Att.*, XI. 13, 2; *Quintus is sorry that he has wounded your feelings.*

NOTES.—1. With the same construction are found **misereō** (early Latin), **miserēscō** (poetical), **dispudet** (early Latin), **distaedet** (early Latin), **vereor** (mostly in early Latin), and a few others.

2. **Miserārī** and **commiserārī**, *to pity*, *commiserate*, take Acc. until very late Latin.

Genitive with Judicial Verbs.

The Genitive with Judicial Verbs belongs to the same category as the Genitive with Verbs of Rating, both being extensions of the Genitive of Quality.

378. Verbs of Accusing, Convicting, Condemning, and Acquitting take the Genitive of the Charge.

(Miltiadēs) accūsātus est prōditiōnis, NEP., I. 7, 5; *Miltiades was accused of treason.* [**Fannius**] **C. Verrem īnsimulat avāritiae**, C., *Verr.*, I. 49, 128; *Fannius charges Gaius Verres with avarice.* **Videō nōn tē absolūtum esse improbitātis sed illōs damnātōs esse caedis**, C., *Verr.*, I. 28, 72; *I see not that you are acquitted of dishonour, but that they are convicted of murder.*

REMARKS.—1. Judicial Verbs include a number of expressions and usages. So **capī, tenērī, dēprehendī, sē adstringere, sē adligāre, sē obligāre** (ante-classical), and others, mean *to be found guilty*; **increpāre, increpitāre, urgēre, dēferre, arguere**, *etc.*, mean *charge.*

So also kindred expressions: **reum facere**, (*to make a party*) *to indict, to bring an action against*; **nōmen dēferre dē**, *to bring an action against*; **sacrilegiī compertum esse**, *to be found* (*guilty*) *of sacrilege.*

2. For the Gen. of the Charge may be substituted **nōmine** or **crīmine** with the Gen., or the Abl. with **dē**: **nōmine (crīmine) coniūrātiōnis damnāre**, *to find guilty of conspiracy*; **accūsāre dē vī**, *of violence* (Gen. **vis** rare); **dē venēficiō**, *of poisoning*; **dē rēbus repetundīs**, *of extortion.* **Pōstulāre** always has **dē** in CICERO. We find sometimes **in** with Abl.; **convictus in crīmine**, *on the charge*; or, **inter**: **inter sīcāriōs damnātus est**, *convicted of homicide* (C., *Cluent.*, 7, 21; *Cf. Ph.*, II. 4, 8).

3. Verbs of Condemning and Acquitting take the Abl. as well as the Gen. of the Charge and the Punishment, and always the Abl. of the definite Fine; the indefinite Fine, **quantī, duplī, quadruplī**, *etc.*, is in the Genitive.

Accūsāre capitis, or **capite**, *to bring a capital charge.* **Damnāre capitis**, or **capite**, *to condemn to death.* **Damnārī decem mīlibus**, *to be fined ten thousand.*

Multāre, *to mulct*, is always construed with the Ablative: **Multāre pecūniā**, *to mulct in* (*of*) *money.*

Manlius virtūtem fīliī morte multāvit, QUINT., V. 11, 7; *Manlius punished the valour of his son with death.*

4. Destination and Enforced Labor are expressed by **ad** or **in**, but all examples are post-classical: **damnārī ad bēstiās**, *to be condemned* (to be

thrown) *to wild beasts*; **ad (in) metalla**, *to the mines*; **ad (in) opus pūblicum**, *to hard labour*. **Vōtī damnārī**, *to be bound to fulfil a vow*, is Livian (except NEP., XX. 5, 3, where it has a different sense).

5. Verbs of Accusing may have also the Acc. of the Thing and the Gen. of the Person: **inertiam accūsās adulēscentium**, C., *Or.*, I. 58, 246.

Genitive with Verbs of Rating and Buying.

379. Verbs of Rating and Buying are construed with the Genitive of the general value or cost, and the Ablative of the particular value or cost. (404.)

Verbs of Rating are: **aestimāre, exīstimāre** (rare), *to value*; **putāre**, *to reckon*; **dūcere** (rare in CICERO), *to take*; **habēre**, *to hold*; **pendere** (mostly in Comedy), *to weigh*; **facere**, *to make, put*; **esse**, *to be* (worth); **fierī**, *to be considered*.

Verbs of Buying are: **emere**, *to buy*; **vēndere**, *to sell*; **vēnīre**, *to be for sale*; **stāre** and **cōnstāre**, *to cost, to come to*; **prōstāre, licēre**, *to be exposed, left* (*for sale*); **condūcere**, *to hire*; **locāre**, *to let*.

380. I. Verbs of Rating take:

Māgnī, *much*,	**plūris**, *more*,	**plūrimī, māximī**, *most*,
Parvī, *little*,	**minōris**, *less*,	**minimī**, *least*,
Tantī, tantīdem, *so much*,	**quantī** (and compounds), *how much*,	**nihilī**, *naught*.

Equivalents of **nihilī**, *nothing*, are **floccī**, *a lock of wool*, **naucī**, *a trifle*, **assis**, *a copper*, **pilī** (both in CATULLUS, mainly), and the like, and so also **hūius**, *that* (a snap of the finger), all usually with the negative.

Dum nē ob malefacta, peream; parvī exīstumō, PL., *Capt.*, 682, ; *so long as it be not for misdeeds, let me die; little do I care*. [**Voluptātem**] **virtūs minimī facit**, C., *Fin.*, II. 13, 42; *virtue makes very little account of the pleasure of the senses*. [**Iūdicēs**] **rem pūblicam floccī nōn faciunt**, *Cf.* C., *Att.*, IV. 15, 4; *the judges do not care a fig for the State*. **Nōn habeō naucī Marsum augurem**, C., *Div.*, I. 58, 132; *I do not value a Marsian augur a bawbee*.

REMARK.—**Tantī** is often used in the sense of **operae pretium est** = *it is worth while*.

Est mihĭ tantī hūius invidiae tempestātem subīre, C., *Cat.*, II. 7, 15; *it is worth while* (*the cost*), *in my eyes, to bear this storm of odium*.

NOTES.—1. **Aestimō** is found with the Abl. as well as with the Genitive. So **aestimāre māgnō** and **māgnī**, *to value highly*. CICERO prefers the Ablative.

2. Observe the phrases: **bonī (aequī bonīque) faciō** (a colloquialism), **bonī cōnsulō** (an old formula), *I put up with, take in good part*. **Nōn pēnsī habēre (dūcere)**, *to consider not worth the while*, is post-Augustan and rare.

2. Verbs of Buying take **tantī, quantī, plūris,** and **minōris.** The rest are put in the Ablative.

Vēndō meum (frūmentum) nōn plūris quam cēterī, fortasse etiam minōris, C., *Off.*, III. 12, 51; *I sell my corn not dearer than everybody else, perhaps even cheaper.* **Magis illa iuvant quae plūris emuntur,** JUV., XI. 16; *things give more pleasure which are bought for more.* **Ēmit (Canius hortōs) tantī quantī Pȳthius voluit,** C., *Off.*, III. 14, 59; *Canius bought the gardens at the price Pythius wanted.*

Quantī cēnās? *What do you give for your dinner?*

Quantī habitās? *What is the rent of your lodgings?*

But:

Parvō famēs cōnstat, māgnō fāstīdium, SEN., *E.M.*, 17, 4; *hunger costs little, daintiness much.*

An instructive shift:

Ēmit? periī hercle: quantī?—Vīgintī minīs, TER., *Eun.*, 984; *he bought her? I'm undone. For how much?—Twenty minae.*

REMARK.—**Bene emere,** *to buy cheap;* **bene vēndere,** *to sell dear;* **male emere,** *to buy dear;* **male vēndere,** *to sell cheap.* So, too, other adverbs: **melius, optimē, pēius, pessimē.**

Genitive with Interest and Rēfert.

381. Interest and **Rēfert** take a Genitive of the Person, seldom of the Thing, concerned.

Interest omnium rēctē facere, C., *Fin.*, II. 22, 72; *it is to the interest of all to do right.* **Rēfert compositiōnis quae quibus antepōnās,** QUINT., IX. 4, 44; *it is of importance for the arrangement of words, which you put before which.*

Instead of the Genitive of the personal pronouns, the Ablative Singular feminine of the possessives is employed.

Meā interest, meā rēfert, *I am concerned.*

NOTES.—1. **Rēfert** is commonly used absolutely, occasionally with **meā,** *etc.*, seldom with the Gen., in the classical language.

2. Instead of Apposition use the Relative:

Vehementer intererat vestrā, quī patrēs estis, līberōs vestrōs hīc potissimum dīscere, PLIN., *Ep.*, IV. 13, 4; *it were vastly to the interest of you parents, that your children, if possible, were taught at home.*

3. The Nom. as a subject is rare, except in PLINY's *Natural History:*

Ūsque adeō māgnī rēfert studium atque voluptās, LUCR., IV. 984.

Occasionally the Nom. of a neuter pronoun is found:

Quid (Acc.) **tuā id** (Nom.) **rēfert?** TER., *Ph.*, 723; *what business is that of yours?*

4. **Rēfert** is the more ancient, and is employed by the poets (**interest** is excluded from Dactylic poetry by its form) to the end of the classical period. **Interest** is peculiar to prose, employed exclusively by CAESAR, and preferred by CICERO when a complement is added.

5. No satisfactory explanation has been given of this construction. One view is that **meā rēfert** was originally [**ex**] **meā rē fert** (like **ex meā rē est**), *it is to my advantage*, and that the **ex** was lost. **Interest** having much the same force, but being later in development, took the constructions of **rēfert** by false analogy. The Gen. would be but parallel to the possessive.

382. 1. The Degree of Concern is expressed by an Adverb, Adverbial Accusative, or a Genitive of Value.

Id meā minumē rēfert, TER., *Ad.*, 881; *that makes no difference at all to me.* **Theodōrī nihil interest**, C., *Tusc.*, I. 43, 102; *It is no concern of Theodorus.* **Māgnī interest meā ūnā nōs esse**, C., *Att.*, XIII. 4; *it is of great importance to me that we be together.*

2. The Object of Concern is commonly put in the Infinitive, Accusative and Infinitive, **ut** or **nē** with the Subjunctive, or an Interrogative Sentence.

Quid Milōnis intererat interficī Clōdium? C., *Mil.*, 13, 34; *what interest had Milo in Clodius' being killed?* [**Caesar dīcere solēbat**] **nōn tam suā quam reī pūblicae interesse utī salvus esset**, SUET., *Iul.*, 86; *Caesar used to say that it was not of so much importance to him(self) as to the State that his life should be spared.* **Vestrā interest nē imperātōrem pessimī faciant**, TAC., *H.*, I. 30; *it is to your interest that the dregs of creation do not make the emperor.* **Quid rēfert tālēs versūs quā vōce legantur?** JUV., XI. 182; *what matters it what voice such verses are recited with?*

3. The Thing Involved is put in the Accusative with **ad**:

Māgnī ad honōrem nostrum interest quam prīmum mē ad urbem venīre, C., *Fam.*, XVI. 1, 1; *it makes a great difference touching our honour that I should come to the city as soon as possible.*

Occasional Uses.

383. 1. The Genitive is found occasionally with certain Verbs of Fulness: in classical Latin principally **implēre, complēre, egēre, indigēre.**

Pīsō multōs cōdicēs implēvit eārum rērum, C., *Verr.* I. 46, 119; *Piso filled many books full of those things.* **Virtūs plūrimae commentātiōnis et exercitātiōnis indiget**, *Cf.* C., *Fin.*, III. 15, 50; *virtue stands in need of much (very much) study and practice.*

NOTES.—1. Classical Latin shows in all cases the Abl. much more frequently than the Gen., except in the case of **indigēre**, where CICERO prefers the Genitive. LIVY likewise prefers the Gen. with **implēre.**

2. Ante-classical and poetic are **explēre** (VERG.), **abundāre** (LUC.), **scatēre** (LUCR.), **saturāre** (PLAUT.), **obsaturāre** (TER.), **carēre** (TER.). **Carēre** and **egēre** have the Acc. occasionally in early Latin.

3. Other Grecisms are **labōrum dēcipitur**, H., *O.*, II. 13, 38 (reading doubtful).

Rēgnāvit populōrum, H., *O.*, III. 30, 12. Also **mīrārī** with Gen. in VERGIL (*A.*, XI. 126). Noteworthy is the occasional use of **crēdere** with Gen. in PLAUTUS; so once **fallī.**

2. A Genitive of Separation, after the analogy of the Greek, is found in a few cases in the poets.

Ut mē omnium iam labōrum levās, PL., *Rud.* 247; *how you relieve me at last of all my toils and troubles.* **Dēsine mollium tandem querēllārum,** H., *O.*, II. 9, 17; *cease at last from womanish complainings.*

3. The Genitive in Exclamations occurs in a very few instances in the poets. CAT., IX. 5; PROP., IV. (V.) 7, 21; compare PL., *Most.*, 912; LUCAN, II. 45.

On the Genitive after comparatives, see 296, N. 2.

ABLATIVE.

384. The Ablative is the Adverbial, as the Genitive is the Adjective case. It contains three elements:

A. Where? B. Whence? C. Wherewith?

In a literal sense, the Ablative is commonly used with prepositions; in a figurative sense, it is commonly used without prepositions.

A. The Ablative of the Place Where appears in a figurative sense as the Ablative of the Time When.

B. The Ablative of the Place Whence appears as:

1. The Ablative of Origin. 2. The Ablative of Measure.

C. The Ablative of the Thing Wherewith appears in a figurative sense, as:

1. The Ablative of Manner. 2. The Ablative of Quality. 3. The Ablative of Means.

REMARK.—It is impossible to draw the line of demarcation with absolute exactness. So the Ablative of Cause may be derived from any of the three fundamental significations of the case, which is evidently a composite one.

To these we add:

D. The Ablative of Cause. E. The Ablative Absolute.

I. The Literal Meanings of the Ablative.

A. ABLATIVE OF THE PLACE WHERE.

Ablātīvus Locālis.

385. The Ablative answers the question *Where?* and takes as a rule the preposition **in.**

In portū nāvigō, TER., *And.*, 480; *I am sailing* IN *harbour.* **Póns in Hibērō prope effectus (erat),** CAES., *B.C.*, I. 62, 3; *the bridge* OVER *the*

Ebro was nearly finished. **Histriō in scaenā [est]**, PL., *Poen.*, 20; *the actor is* ON *the stage.* **Haeret in equō senex,** *Cf.* C., *Dei.*, 10, 28; *the old man sticks* TO *his horse.*

REMARKS.—1. Verbs of Placing and kindred significations take the Abl. with **in**, to designate the result of the motion: classical are **pōnere,** *to place,* and compounds; **locāre, collocāre,** *to put;* **statuere, cōnstituere,** *to set;* **cōnsīdere,** *to settle;* **dēfīgere,** *to plant;* **dēmergere,** *to plunge;* **imprimere,** *to press upon;* **īnsculpere,** *to engrave* (figurative); **īnscrībere,** *to write upon;* **incīdere,** *to carve upon;* **inclūdere,** *to shut into.*

Platō ratiōnem in capite posuit, īram in pectore locāvit, C., *Tusc.*, I. 10, 20; *Plato has put reason in the head, has placed anger in the breast.* **(Lucrētia) cultrum in corde dēfīgit,** L., I. 58, 11; *Lucretia plants a knife in (thrusts a knife down into) her heart.* **Philosophī in iīs librīs ipsīs quōs scrībunt dē contemnendā glōriā sua nōmina īnscrībunt,** C., *Tusc.*, I. 15, 34; *philosophers write their own names on* (the titles of) *the very books which they write about contempt of glory.* **(Foedus) in columnā aēneā incīsum,** C., *Balb.*, 23, 53; *a treaty cut upon a brazen column.*

The same observation applies to **sub**:

Pōne sub currū nimium propinquī sōlis in terrā domibus negātā, H., *O.*, I. 22, 21; *put* (me) *under the chariot of the all-too neighboring sun, in a land denied to dwellings.*

2. Verbs of Hanging and Fastening take **ex, ab,** or **dē.**

Cui spēs omnis pendet ex fortūnā, huic nihil potest esse certī, C., *Par.*, II. 17; *to him who has all his hopes suspended on fortune, nothing can be certain.*

3. *Here and there in* is often rendered by **per**: C., *Fam.*, I. 7, 6, **per prōvinciās,** *here and there in the provinces;* V., *A.*, III. 236.

NOTES.—1. In classical prose the use of the Abl. without **in** is confined to a few words, mostly phraseological. So **terrā,** *on land;* **marī,** *by sea;* usually in the phrase **terrā marīque** (rarely in the reversed order), *on land and sea.* **In terrā** is more common otherwise than **terrā. Locō** and **locīs,** especially when used with adjectives, usually omit **in.** The same is true of **parte** and **partibus**; so regularly **dextrā (parte), sinistrā, laevā,** *etc., on the right, on the left.* LIVY uses **regiō** like **locus.** The tendency, however, is observable as early as CICERO's time to omit the **in** when an adjective is employed, even in words other than those given above; this tendency becomes more marked in LIVY and is very strong in later Latin. The poets are free. Regard must always be had to 389.

2. The Acc. with **in** after verbs of Placing is very rare in classical prose. In early Latin it is more common; so with **pōnere, impōnere, collocāre.** The examples with Acc. in classical Latin are principally with compounds of **pōnere,** as **impōnere** (usually), **repōnere, expōnere. Collocāre** with **in** and Acc. in CAES., *B.G.*, I. 18, 7, is not in a local sense. Sometimes the Dat. is found with **impōnere.**

3. With a verb of Rest the motion antecedent to the rest is often emphasised by construing the verb with **in** and the Acc. instead of with **in** and the Abl. This occurs most often with **esse** and **habēre,** and seems to have been colloquial, as it is very rare in classical prose.

Numerō mihī in mentem fuit dīs advenientem grātiās agere, PL., *Am.*, 180.

Adesse in senātum iūssit, C., *Ph.*, v. 7, 19 (*Cf.* **hūc ades,** *come hither*). **Parcere victīs in animum habēbat,** L., xxxiii. 10, 4.

386. Names of Towns in the Singular of the Third Declension, and in the Plural of all Declensions, take the Ablative of Place Where without **in.**

Ut Rōmae cōnsulēs sīc Carthāgine quotannīs bīnī rēgēs creābantur, Nep., xxiii. 7, 4 ; *as at Rome* (two) *consuls, so in Carthage two kings, were created yearly.* **Tālis (Rōmae Fabricius), quālis Aristīdēs Athēnīs, fuit,** C., *Off.*, iii. 22, 87; *Fabricius was just such a man at Rome as Aristides was at Athens.*

Remarks.—1. Appositions are put in the Abl. commonly with **in;** when the appositive has an attribute, the proper name regularly precedes : **Neāpolī, in celeberrimō oppidō,** C., *Rab.Post.*, 10, 26; *at Naples, a populous town.*

2. *In the neighborhood of, at,* is **ad** with Acc., especially of military operations: **pūgna ad Cannās** (better **Cannēnsis**), *the battle at Cannae;* **pōns ad Genāvam,** Caes., *B.G.*, i. 7; *the bridge at Geneva.*

Note.—The Abl. in names of Towns of the Second Declension is found once in Caesar (*B.C.*, iii. 35, but the reading is questioned) ; more often in Vitruvius and later Latin, but in Greek words only. Apparent exceptions in Caesar and Cicero are to be referred to the Abl. of Separation. The poets, however, are free.

387. In citations from Books and in Enumerations, the Ablative of the Place Where is used without **in.**

Librō tertiō, *third book;* **versū decimō,** *tenth verse;* **aliō locō,** *elsewhere.*

But **in** is necessary when a passage in a book and not the whole book is meant : **Agricultūra laudātur in eō librō quī est dē tuendā rē familiārī,** C., *Cat. M.*, 17, 59; *agriculture is praised in the work on domestic economy.*

388. In designations of Place, with **tōtus, cūnctus,** *whole;* **omnis,** *all;* **medius,** *middle,* the Ablative of the Place Where is generally used without **in.**

Menippus, meō iūdiciō, tōtā Asiā disertissimus, C., *Br.*, 91, 315 ; *Menippus, in my judgment, the most eloquent man in all Asia* (Minor). **Battiadēs semper tōtō cantābitur orbe,** Ov., *Am.*, i. 15, 13; *Battiades* (Callimachus) *will always be sung throughout the world.*

Remark.—**In** is not excluded when the idea is *throughout,* in which case **per** also may be used. **Negō in Siciliā tōtā** (*throughout the whole of Sicily*) **ūllum argenteum vās fuisse,** *etc.*, C., *Verr.*, iv. 1, 1.

389. In all such designations of Place as may be regarded in the light of Cause, Manner, or Instrument, the Ablative is used without a preposition.

Ut terrā Thermopylārum angustiae Graeciam, ita marī fretum Eurīpī claudit, L., XXXI. 23, 12 ; *as the pass of Thermopylae bars Greece by land, so the frith of Euripus by sea.* **Ariovistus exercitum castrīs continuit,** CAES., *B.G.*, I. 48, 4 ; *Ariovistus kept his army within the camp.* **Ēgressus est nōn viīs sed trāmitibus,** C., *Ph.*, XIII. 9, 19 ; *he went out not by high roads but by cross-cuts.* **Nēmō īre quemquam pūblicā prohibet viā,** PL., *Curc.*, 35 ; *no man forbiddeth (any one to) travel by the public road.* **Mātris cinerēs Rōmam Tiberī subvectī sunt,** *Cf.* SUET., *Cal.*, 15 ; *his mother's ashes were brought up to Rome by the Tiber.*

So **recipere aliquem tēctō, oppidō, portū,** *to receive a man into one's house, town, harbour;* where, however, the Acc. with **in** is not excluded: **gentēs ūniversae in cīvitātem sunt receptae,** C., *Balb.*, 13, 31.

B. ABLATIVE OF THE PLACE WHENCE.

Ablātīvus Sēparātīvus.

390. 1. The Ablative answers the question Whence? and takes as a rule the prepositions **ex,** *out of,* **dē,** *from,* **ab,** *off.*

(Eum) exturbāstī ex aedibus? PL., *Trin.*, 137 ; *did you hustle him out of the house?* **Arāneās dēiciam dē pariete,** PL., *St.*, 355 ; *I will get the cobwebs down from the wall.* **Alcibiadem Athēniēnsēs ē cīvitāte expulērunt,** *Cf.* NEP., VII. 6, 2 ; *the Athenians banished Alcibiades from the state.* **Dēcēdit ex Galliā Rōmam Naevius,** C., *Quinct.*, 4. 16 ; *Naevius withdrew from Gaul to Rome.* **Unde dēiēcistī sive ex quō locō, sive ā quō locō** (*whether* OUT OF *or* FROM *which place*), **eō restituās,** C., *Caec.*, 30, 88.

2. The prepositions are often omitted with Verbs of Abstaining, Removing, Relieving, and Excluding ; so regularly with **domō,** *from home,* **rūre,** *from the country.*

With Persons a preposition (chiefly **ab**) must be used.

(Verrēs) omnia domō ēius abstulit, C., *Verr.*, II. 34, 83 ; *Verres took everything away from his house.* **Ego, cum Tullius rūre redierit, mittam eum ad tē,** C., *Fam.*, V. 20, 9 ; *when Tullius returns from the country, I will send him to you.*

Compare **Aliēnō manum abstineant,** CATO, *Agr.*, 5, 1 ; *let them keep their hand(s) from other people's property,* with [**Alexander**] **vix ā sē manūs abstinuit,** C., *Tusc.*, IV. 37, 79 ; *Alexander hardly kept (could hardly keep) his hands from himself (from laying hands on himself).*

Compare **Lapidibus optimōs virōs forō pellis,** C., *Har. Res.*, 18, 39 ; *you drive men of the best classes from the forum with stones,* with **Istum aemulum ab eā pellitō,** TER., *Eun.*, 215 ; *drive that rival from her.*

Compare **Omnium rērum nātūrā cōgnitā līberāmur mortis metū,** C., *Fin.*, I. 19, 63; *by the knowledge of universal nature we get rid of the* *fear of death*, with **Tē ab eō līberō**, C., *Q.F.*, III. i. 3, 9; *I rid you of him.*

Compare **Amīcitia nūllō locō exclūditur**, C., *Lael.*, 6, 22; *friendship is shut out from no place*, with **Ab illā exclūdor, hōc conclūdor**, *Cf.* TER., *And.*, 386; *I am shut out from* HER (and) *shut up here* (*to live with* HER).

NOTES.—1. In classical Latin the preposition is usually employed in local relations, and omitted in metaphorical relations; though there are some exceptions.

2. It is to be noted that in the vast majority of cases the separation is indicated by a verb; hence this Abl. is found commonly with verbs compounded with prepositions. Thus, classical Latin shows but few simple verbs with the Abl., as follows: **movēre**, chiefly in general or technical combinations: **movēre locō, senātū, tribū** (CAESAR, however, has no case); **pellere**, in technical language with **cīvitāte, domō, forō, patriā, possessiōnibus, suīs sēdibus**; **cēdere** is found with **patriā, vītā, memoriā, possessiōne, Ītaliā**; **cadere**, technical with **causā**; **solvere** with **lēge** (**lēgibus**), **religiōne**, *etc.*, **somnō**; **levāre** and **līberāre** are found chiefly in metaphorical combinations, and especially in CICERO; **arcēre** has peculiarly **ab** with metaphorical, Abl. with local forces. In the case of most of these verbs, the preposition with the Abl. is also found.

3. Of compound verbs with the Abl., CICERO shows only **sē abdicāre** (principally technical), **abesse** (rarely), **abhorrēre** (once); **abīre** (in technical uses = **sē abdicāre**), **abrumpere** (once), **absolvere, abstinēre** (intrans. without, trans. more often with, preposition), **dēicere** (with **aedīlitāte**, *etc.*), **dēmovēre** (once), **dēpellere, dēsistere, dēturbāre**; **ēdūcere** (rare); **efferre** (rare); **ēgredī**; **ēicere**; **ēlābī** (rare); **ēmittere** (CAES.); **ēripere** (rare; usually Dat.); **ēvertere**; **excēdere**; **exclūdere**; **exīre** (rare); **expellere**; **exsolvere**; **exsistere** (rare); **exturbāre**; **interclūdere**; **interdīcere** (**alicuī aliquā rē**; also **alicuī aliquid**); **praecipitāre** (CAES.); **prohibēre**; **supersedēre**.

Early Latin shows a few more verbs with this construction. The poets are free with the Abl., and also later prose writers, beginning with LIVY.

4. **Humō**, *from the ground*, begins with VERGIL. The preposition **ā** is found occasionally with **domō**; necessarily with a word (adjective or adverb) involving measurement, as; **longinquē, longē, procul.**

5. Compounds with **dī** (**dis**) also take the Dative (in poetry):

Paulum sepultae dīstat inertiae cēlāta virtūs, H., *O.*, IV. 9, 29; *little doth hidden worth differ from buried sloth.*

6. The Place Whence gives the Point of View from which. In English a different translation is often given, though not always necessarily: **ā tergō**, *in the rear;* **ex parte dextrā**, *on the right side;* **ab oriente**, *on the east;* **ā tantō spatiō**, *at such a distance;* **ex fugā**, *on the flight;* **ā rē frūmentāriā labōrāre**, *to be embarrassed in the matter of provisions.*

3. The prepositions are also omitted with kindred Adjectives.

Animus excelsus omnī est līber cūrā, C., *Fin.*, I. 15, 49; *a lofty mind is free from all care.* (**Catō**) **omnibus hūmānīs vitiīs immūnis, semper fortūnam in suā potestāte habuit**, VELL., II. 35, 2; *Cato, exempt from all human failings, always had fortune in his own power.* **Iugurtha** (**Adherbalem**) **extorrem patriā effēcit**, S., *Iug.*, 14, 11; *Iugurtha rendered Adherbal an exile from his country.* **Utrumque** (**fraus et vīs**) **homine aliēnissimum**, C., *Off.*, I. 13, 41.

NOTES.—1. The preposition is more usual in most cases. **Pūrus** and **immūnis**, with simple Abl., are poetical and post-Augustan. **Expers**, with Abl. instead of with Gen., belongs to early Latin and SALLUST. **Recēns**, *fresh from*, with Abl., belongs to TACITUS.

2. **Procul**, *far from*, regularly takes the preposition **ab**, except in the poets and later prose.

3. The Abl. of the Supine is early and late, as CATO, *Agr.*, 5; **Vīlicus prīmus cubitū surgat, postrēmus cubitum eat.** See 436, N. 4.

391. Names of Towns and Small Islands are put in the Ablative of the Place Whence.

Dēmarātus fūgit Tarquiniōs Corinthō, C., *Tusc.*, V. 37, 109; *Demaratus fled to Tarquinii from Corinth.* **Dolābella Dēlō proficīscitur**, C., *Verr.*, I. 18, 46; *Dolabella sets out from Delos.*

REMARKS.—1. The prepositions **ab** (**ā**) and **ex** (**ē**) are sometimes used for the sake of greater exactness, but rarely in model prose. So regularly **ab** with the Place from which distance is measured:

[**Aesculāpiī templum**] **quīnque mīlibus passuum ab urbe** [**Epidaurō**] **distat**, *Cf.* L., XLV. 28, 3 (403, N. 1).

When the substantives **urbe**, *city*, and **oppidō**, *town*, are employed, the use of the preposition is the rule, as also when not the town, but the neighbourhood is intended; also always with **longē**. When the Appositive has an attribute the proper name regularly precedes.

Aulide, ex oppidō Boeōtiae, *from Aulis, a town of Boeotia.* **Ex Apollōniā Pontī urbe**, *from Apollonia, a city of Pontus.* **Ex oppidō Gergoviā**, CAES., *B.G.*, VII. 4, 2; *from the town of Gergovia.*

Early Latin is free in the use of prepositions; and also from LIVY on the usage seems to increase.

2. The Place Whence embraces all the local designations:

Agrigentō ex Aesculāpiī fānō whereas we should say, *from the temple of Aesculapius at Agrigentum.* **Unde domō?** V., *A.*, VIII. 114; *from what home?*

3. Letters are dated *from* rather than *at* a place.

NOTE.—Names of countries are but rarely used in the Ablative. CICERO, SALLUST, and LIVY show no instance, CAESAR only one (*B.C.*, III. 58, 4). Occasional examples are found in early Latin and in old inscriptions; then in later historians, beginning with VELLEIUS. The use of prepositions with towns seems in general to have been a colloquialism, *Cf.* SUET., *Aug.*, 86. The poets are free in their usage.

C. ABLATIVE OF THE THING WHEREWITH.

Ablātīvus Sociātīvus.

392. The Ablative of Attendance takes the preposition **cum**, *with.*

Cum febrī domum rediit, C., *Or.*, III. 2, 6; *he returned home with a* *fever.* **Catilīna stetit in comitiō cum tēlō,** *Cf.* C., *Cat.*, I. 6, 15; *Catiline stood in the place of election with a weapon* (*on him*). **Cum baculō pērāque [senex],** MART., IV. 53, 3; *an old man with stick and wallet.* **Nec tēcum possum vīvere nec sine tē,** MART., XII. 47, 2; *I can't live either with you or without you.*

REMARKS.—1. In military phrases, the troops with which a march is made are put in the Ablative, with or without **cum**; generally without **cum** when an adjective is used (Ablative of Manner), with **cum** when no adjective is used (Ablative of Attendance). With definite numbers, however, **cum** is regularly employed.

Albānī ingentī exercitū in agrum Rōmānum impetum fēcēre, L., I. 23, 3; *the Albans attacked the Roman territory with a huge army.* **Caesar cum equitibus DCCCC in castra pervēnit,** CAES., *B.C.*, I. 41, 1; *Caesar arrived in camp with nine hundred cavalry.*

2. Not to be confounded with the above is the Instrumental Ablative:

Nāvibus profectus est, C., *Fam.*, XV. 3, 2; *he set out by ship.*

So also with verbs which denote other military actions:

Hasdrubal mediam aciem Hispānīs firmat, L., XXIII. 29, 4; *Hannibal strengthens the centre with Spanish troops.* **Āctum nihil est nisi Poenō mīlite portās frangimus,** JUV., X. 155; *naught is accomplished unless we break the gates with the Punic soldiery* (as if with a battering-ram).

II. The Figurative Meanings of the Ablative.

A. The Place Where is transferred to the Time When.

Ablative of Time. Ablātīvus Temporis.

393. Time When or Within Which is put in the Ablative.

Quā nocte nātus Alexander est, eādem Diānae Ephesiae templum dēflagrāvit, *Cf.* C., *N.D.*, II. 27, 69; *on the same night on which Alexander was born, the temple of Diana of Ephesus burned to the ground.* **Sāturnī stella trīgintā ferē annīs cursum suum cōnficit,** C., *N.D.*, II. 20, 52; *the planet Saturn completes its period in about thirty years.*

Many adverbial forms of time are really Locative Ablatives:

So **hodiē**, *to-day;* **herī(e)**, *yesterday;* **māne**, *in the morning.*

REMARKS.—1. Time Within Which may be expressed by **per** and the Accusative:

Per eōs ipsōs diēs quibus Philippus in Achāiā fuit, Philoclēs saltum Cithaerōnis trānscendit, L., XXXI. 26, 1; *during those very days, while Philip was in Achaia, Philocles crossed the range of Cithaeron.*

2. Time Within Which may embrace both extremities so usually with **tōtus**, *all, whole:*

Nocte pluit tōtā, redeunt at māne serēna, V. (Poet. Lat. Min., iv. 155 B); *all night* (Jupiter) *rains; clear skies come back in the morning. Cf.* Caes., *B.G.*, i. 26, 5.

So with definite numbers; but rarely, until the post-Augustan period:

Scrīptum est trīgintā annīs vīxisse Panaetium, posteāquam illōs librōs ēdidisset, C., *Off.*, iii. 2, 8; *it is written that Panaetius lived for thirty years after he had published those books* (not to be confounded with the Abl. of Difference, 403). **Apud Pȳthagoram discipulīs quīnque annīs tacendum erat,** Sen., *E.M.*, 52, 10; *in the school of Pythagoras the disciples had to keep silence five years.*

3. When the Notion is Negative, the English Time For Which is the Latin Within Which.

[**Rōscius**] **Rōmam multīs annīs nōn vēnit,** C., *Rosc.Am.*, 27, 74; *Roscius has not come to Rome in* (*for*) *many years.* Not always, however; compare **Sex mēnsīs iam hīc nēmō habitat,** Pl., *Most.*, 954; *no one has been living here these six months.*

4. Especially to be noted is the Abl. of Time with **hīc,** *this;* **ille,** *that:*

Cui vīgintī hīs annīs supplicātiō dēcrēta est? C., *Ph.*, xiv. 4, 11; *to whom during these last twenty years has a supplication been decreed?* [**Karthāginem**] **hōc bienniō ēvertēs,** C., *Rep.*, vi. 11, 11; *Carthage you will overturn in the next two years.*

Transferred to **Ōrātiō Oblīqua, hīc** becomes **ille** (660, 3):

Diodōrus [**respondit**] **illud argentum sē paucīs illīs diēbus mīsisse Lilybaeum,** C., *Verr.*, iv. 18, 39; *Diodorus answered that he had sent that silver plate to Lilybaeum within a few days* (*a few days before*).

5. The Abl. of Time is regularly accompanied by an attribute in classical Latin, except in the case of a number of common designations, as **aestāte, diē, hieme, nocte, vespere (vesperī).** Exceptions are rare, such as **comitiīs, lūce, pāce, mīlitiā,** and some names of games.

394. The Ablative with the preposition **in** is used of points within a period of time, or of the character of the time.

Bis in diē, *twice a day;* **in pueritiā,** *in boyhood;* **in adulēscentiā,** *in youth.*

Nūllō modō mihī placuit bis in diē saturum fierī, C., *Tusc.*, v. 35, 100; *it did not suit me in any way to eat my fill twice a day.* **Fēcī ego istaec itidem in adulēscentiā,** Pl., *B.*, 410; *I did those things too in my youth.*

Remark.—The use or omission of **in** sometimes changes the meaning. So **bellō Persicō,** *at the time of the Persian war;* but **in bellō,** *in war times;* **in pāce,** *in peace times.* Phraseological is **in tempore,** more frequent than **tempore,** *at the right time.* But **in illō tempore** means *in those circumstances, at that crisis. At present, for the present,* is always **in praesentiā** or **in praesentī (rare).**

NOTES.—1. Classical Latin confines the use of **in** to designations **of Time of Life** (though here, when an adjective is employed, **in** is usually omitted) and to the periods of time. Later **in** is used much more extensively. With numerals **in** is the rule. CATO and the poets have sometimes **bis diē**, as **diēs** = **ūnus diēs.**

2. **Dē**, *from*, is also used in designations of time: principally in the phrase **dē diē, dē nocte. Ut iugulent hominem surgunt dē nocte latrōnēs,** H., *Ep.*, I. 2, 32; *to kill a man, highwaymen rise by night*, i. e., *while it is yet night.*

Inter, *between:* **Quae prandia inter continuom perdidī triennium,** PL., *St.*, 213; *what luncheons I have lost during three years together.*

Intrā, *within:* **Subēgit sōlus intrā vīgintī diēs,** PL., *Curc.*, 448; *he quelled them all alone in less than twenty days.*

On **per,** *through,* see 336, R. 2.

Cum, *with,* is found occasionally in phrases, as **cum prīmā lūce,** *with daybreak.*

B. The Place Whence is transferred:

1. To Origin. 2. To Respect or Specification.

I. Ablative of Origin.

395. Participles which signify Birth take the Ablative of Origin; sometimes with the prepositions **ex** and **dē.**

Amplissimā familiā nātī adulēscentēs, CAES., *B.G.*, VII. 37, 1; *young men born of a great house.* **Numae Pompiliī rēgis nepōs, fīliā ortus, Ancus Mārcius erat,** L., I. 32, 1; *King Numa Pompilius's grandson, a daughter's issue, was Ancus Marcius.* **Maecēnās atavīs ēdite rēgibus,** H., *O.*, I. 1, 1; *Maecenas, offshoot of great-grandsire kings.* **Dīs genite et genitūre deōs,** V., *A.*, IX. 639; *begotten of gods, and destined to beget gods!* **Sate sanguine dīvum!** V., *A.*, VI. 125; *seed of blood divine!* **Ex mē atque ex hōc nātus es,** TER., *Heaut.*, 1030; *you are his son and mine.* **Ōdērunt nātōs dē paelice,** JUV., VI. 627; *they hate the offspring of the concubine.*

Ab, and occasionally **ex,** are employed of remote progenitors:

Plērīque Belgae sunt ortī ab Germānīs, *Cf.* CAES., *B.G.*, II. 4, 1; *Belgians are mostly of German descent.* **Oriundī ex Etrūscīs,** *Cf.* L., II. 9, 1; *of Etruscan origin.*

NOTES.—1. The principal participles thus used are **nātus, prōgnātus, oriundus; ortus, genitus,** and **satus** begin in prose with LIVY; **ēditus** and **crētus** are poetic; **prōcreātus** is late. CICERO uses **oriundus** but once; it denotes remote origin.

2. With names of Places the preposition is the rule (362, N. 2); but there are a few exceptions in early Latin and in CICERO, and a couple of examples in CAESAR. Later the simple Abl. disappears. The Abl. was the rule with names of Tribes.

Periphanēs Rhodō mercātor, PL., *Asin.*, 499. **Magius Cremōnā,** CAES., *B.C.*, I. 24, 4. **Q. Verrēs Rōmiliā,** C., *Verr.*, I. 8, 23; *Q. Verres of the Romilian tribe.*

3. With finite verbs denoting Origin, the preposition is regular, except occasionally with **nāscī.**

4. The Ablative of Agent properly belongs here. But for convenience of contrast it is treated under 401.

396. The Ablative of Material takes **ex** in classical Latin.

Ex animō cōnstāmus et corpore, *Cf.* C., *Fin.*, IV. 8, 19 ; *we consist of mind and body.*

Statua ex aurō, ex aere, facta, *a statue made of gold, of bronze.* Often an adjective is used : **aureus,** *golden ;* **līgneus,** *wooden.*

NOTES.—1. After CICERO **cōnstāre** is used more often with the Abl.; **cōnsistere** (with the Abl.) is poetical. **Continērī,** *to be contained in,* i.e., almost "*to consist of,*" takes the Abl. only, but with a different conception.

Medicīna tōta cōnstat experīmentīs, QUINT., II. 17, 9 ; *all medicine is made up of experiments (is empirical).*

2. With **fierī** the previous state is indicated by **dē** as well as by **ex.**

Dē templō carcerem fierī! C., *Ph.*, V. 7, 18 ; *from a temple to become a jail.* **Fīēs dē rhētore cōnsul,** JUV., VII. 197 ; *from* (having been) *rhetorician you will become consul.* **Ex ōrātōre arātor factus,** C., *Ph.*, III. 9, 22 (206, R. 2).

3. Otherwise the simple Ablative of Material is poetic or late :

Māvors caelātus ferrō, V., *A.*, VIII. 700 ; *Mars carven of iron.*

Meliōre lutō finxit, JUV., XIV. 35 ; *he fashioned it of better clay.*

2. Ablative of Respect.

397. The Ablative of Respect or Specification gives the Point From Which a thing is measured or treated, and is put in answer to the questions From What Point of View ? According to What ? By What ? In Respect of What ?

Dīscrīptus populus cēnsū, ōrdinibus, aetātibus, C., *Leg.*, III. 19, 44 ; *a people drawn off according to income, rank,* (and) *age.* **Ennius ingeniō māximus, arte rudis,** OV., *Tr.*, II. 424 ; *Ennius in genius great, in art unskilled.* **Animō īgnāvus, procāx ōre,** TAC., *H.*, II. 23, 18 ; *coward of soul, saucy of tongue.*

Noteworthy are the phrases : **crīne ruber,** *red-haired ;* **captus oculīs** (literally, *caught in the eyes*), *blind ;* **captus mente,** *insane ;* **meā sententiā,** *according to my opinion ;* **iūre,** *by right ;* **lēge,** *by law,* etc. ; and the Supines in **-ū** (436).

NOTES.—1. Prepositions are also used, which serve to show the conception :

(Caesaris) adventus ex colōre vestītūs cōgnitus, *Cf.* CAES., *B. G.*, VII. 88, 1 ; *the arrival of Caesar was known by the color of his clothing.* **Dē gestū intellegō quid respondeās,** C., *Vat.*, 15, 35 ; *I understand by your gesture what answer you are giving.* **Ab animō aeger fuī,** PL., *Ep.*, 129 ; *at heart I was sick.* **Ōtiōsum ab animō,** TER., *Ph.*, 340 ; *easy in mind.*

Similarly **ex lēge,** *according to law ;* **ex pactō,** *according to agreement ;* **ex (dē) mōre,** *according to custom ;* **ex animī sententiā,** *according to (my) heart's desire ;* **ex ūsū,** *useful.*

2. A special category is formed by words indicating *eminence* or *superiority ;* so **excellere, antecellere, praestāre, superāre, vincere ;** and the adjectives : **īnsīgnis, illūstris, dīgnus ; excellēns, praecellēns. Praecellere** is found in early and late Latin, while **dīgnārī** is poetic and post-Augustan.

Māximē populus Rōmānus animī māgnitūdine excellit, C., *Off.*, I. 18, 61 ; *the Roman people excel most in loftiness of mind.*

On **dīgnus** with Gen., see 374, N. 10.

A curious usage is that of **decōrus** and **decēre**, with Abl., in Pl., *M. G.*, 619; *Asin.*, 577

3. The origin of these constructions is still undetermined. They may be deduced also from the Instrumental side of the Abl., or from the Locative side.

398. The Ablative of Respect is used with the Comparative instead of **quam**, *than*, with the Nominative or Accusative; but in the classical language mainly after a negative, or its equivalent. (*Ablātīvus Comparātiōnis.*)

Tunica propior palliōst, Pl., *Trin.*, 1154; *the shirt is nearer than the cloak.* **Nihil est virtūte amābilius,** C., *Lael.*, 8, 28; *nothing is more attractive than virtue.* **Quid est in homine ratiōne dīvīnius?** C., *Leg.*, I. 7, 22; *what is there in man more godlike than reason?*

So also after adverbs, but not so freely in prose:

Lacrimā nihil citius ārēscit, C., *Inv.*, I. 56, 109; *nothing dries more quickly than a tear.* **Nēmō est quī tibĭ sapientius suādēre possit tē ipsō,** C., *Fam.*, II. 7, 1; *there is no one who can give you wiser advice than you yourself.* **Pulcrum ōrnātum turpēs mōrēs pēius caenō conlinunt,** Pl., *Most.*, 291; *foul behavior doth bedraggle fine apparel worse than mud.*

Remark.—When the word giving the point of view is a relative, the Abl. must be used. See 296, R. 2.

Phīdiae simulācrīs quibus nihil in illō genere perfectius vidēmus, cōgitāre tamen possumus pulchriōra, C., *Or.*, 2, 8; *the statues of Pheidias, than which we see nothing more perfect in their kind, still leave room for us to imagine those that are more beautiful.*

Notes.—1. The comparative is also employed with the Abl. of certain abstract substantives and adjectives used as substantives; so **opīniōne, spē, exspectātiōne; aequō, iūstō, solitō,** and the like, all post-Ciceronian except **aequō, opīniōne.**

(Cōnsul) sērius spē (= quam spēs fuerat) Rōmam vēnit, L., XXVI. 26, 4; *the consul came to Rome later than was hoped.* **Solitō citātior amnis,** L., XXIII. 19, 11; *the river running faster than usual.*

2. **Aequē** and **adaequē** are found once each in Plautus with the Abl.; and then **not** till the time of the elder Pliny.

3. For other details, see 296 and 644.

C. ABLATIVE OF THE THING WHEREWITH.

Ablātīvus Sociātīvus. Ablative of Attendance.

1. Ablative of Manner.

399. The Ablative of Manner answers the question How? and is used with the Preposition **cum** when it has no Adjective; with or without **cum** when it has an Adjective or its equivalent. (*Ablātīvus Modī.*)

[**Stellae**] **circulōs suōs orbēsque cōnficiunt celeritāte mīrābilī,** C., *Rep.*, VI. 15, 15; *the stars complete their orbits with wonderful swiftness.* **Vōs**

ōrō ut attentē bonāque cum veniā verba mea audiātis, C., *Rosc. Am.*, 4, 9; *I beg you to hear my words attentively and with kind indulgence.* **Beātē vīvere, honestē, id est cum virtūte, vīvere**, C., *Fin.*, III. 8, 29; *to live happily is to live honestly, that is, virtuously.*

NOTES.—1. The simple Abl. without an attribute is confined to a few substantives, which have acquired adverbial force; early Latin shows **astū, curriculō, dolō, ergō, grātiīs** and **ingrātiīs, ioculō, meritō, numerō, optātō, ōrdine, sortītō, voluntāte, vulgō.** TERENCE adds: **vī, iūre, iniūriā.** Classical Latin shows some of these, also **ratiōne, ratiōne et viā, mōribus, cōnsuētūdine, silentiō, cāsū, lēge, fraude, vitiō, sacrāmentō** (beginning with LIVY), and a few others. Sometimes the idea of Specification is prominent, as in **lēge, iūre** (397); sometimes it is hard to distinguish between the Manner and the Instrument: **vī**, *violently* and *by violence;* **vī et armīs**, *by force of arms;* **pedibus**, *afoot;* **nāvibus**, *by ship.* Notice, also, the use of **per**, *through*, with the Accusative: **per vim**, *by violence;* **per litterās**, *by letter.*

2. The post-Ciceronian Latin extends the use of the Abl. without an attribute.

3. The phrases **sub condiciōne, sub lēge**, *etc.*, begin with LIVY.

2. Ablative of Quality.

(*Descriptive Ablative.*)

400. The Ablative of Quality has no Preposition, and always takes an Adjective or an equivalent.

[**Hannibalis**] **nōmen erat māgnā apud omnēs glōriā**, C., *Or.*, II. 18, 75; *the name of Hannibal was glorious in the esteem of all the world.* (**Āgēsilāus**) **statūrā fuit humilī**, NEP., XVII. 8, 1; *Agesilāus was* (a man) *of low stature.* **Ista turpiculō puella nāsō**, CAT., 41, 3; *that girl of yours with the ugly nose.* **Clāvī ferreī digitī pollicis crassitūdine**, *Cf.* CAES., *B.G.*, III. 13, 4; *iron nails of the thickness of your thumb.*

REMARKS.—1. External and transient qualities are put by preference in the Ablative; Measure, Number, Time, and Space are put in the Genitive only; parts of the body in the Ablative only. Otherwise there is often no difference.

2. Of unnatural productions **cum** may be used: **āgnus cum suillō capite**, L., XXXI. 12, 7; *a lamb with a swine's head.*

3. Ablative of Means.

401. The Means or Instrument is put in the Ablative without a Preposition.

The Agent or Doer is put in the Ablative with the Preposition **ab** (**ā**). The Person Through Whom is put in the Accusative with **per**.

Xerxēs certior factus est, *Xerxes was informed*,
1. **nūntiō**, *by a message.*
2. **ā nūntiō**, *by a messenger.*
3. **per nūntium**, *by means of a messenger.*

Quī sunt hominēs, ā quibus ille sē lapidibus adpetītum, etiam percussum esse dīxit? C., *Dom.*, 5, 13; *who are the men by whom he said he had been thrown at with stones, and even hit?* **Vulgō occīdēbantur? Per quōs et ā quibus?** C., *Rosc.Am.*, 29, 80; *were they cut down openly? Through whose instrumentality and by whose agency?* **Nec bene prōmeritīs capitur neque tangitur īrā,** Lucr., II. 651 (227, N. 4). **Ipse docet quid agam: fās est et ab hoste docērī,** Ov., *M.*, IV. 428 (219). **Discite sānārī per quem didicistis amāre,** Ov., *Rem. Am.*, 43; *learn to be healed by means of* (him by) *whom you learned to love.*

Remarks.—1. When the Instrument is personified and regarded as an Agent, or the Agent is regarded as an Instrument, the constructions are reversed; when an adjective is used, the construction may be doubtful; see 354, N. 1, and 214, R. 2.

So **iacent suīs tēstibus,** C., *Mil.*, 18, 47; *they are cast by their own witnesses;* or, *they are cast, their own men being witnesses.*

2. A quality, when personified, has the construction of the person. So **dēserī ā mente, ā spē.**

Vōbīs animus ab īgnāviā atque sōcordiā conruptus [est], S., *Iug.*, 31, 2; *you have had your soul(s) debauched by sloth and indifference.*

Notes.—1. The number of verbs construed with this Abl. is very large and comprises several categories; so verbs of Clothing and Providing, Adorning and Endowing, Training (**ērudīre** also takes **in**; others take Acc., see 339), Living and Nourishing, *etc.*

2. Of special importance are **assuēscō, assuēfaciō, assuētus; (Catilīna) scelerum exercitātiōne assuēfactus,** C., *Cat.*, II. 5, 9. The Dat. is found first in Livy in prose. **Ad** with the Acc. is also classical.

3. **Afficere,** *to treat,* with the Ablative, is a favorite turn; see the Lexicons.

4. Verbs of *sacrificing,* such as **sacrificāre, sacrum facere, dīvīnam rem facere, facere** and **fierī** (mostly poetical), **immolāre, litāre** (poetical), have the Abl. of Means. But **immolāre** usually has Acc. and Dat., and so the others occasionally, except **facere.**

Quīnquāgintā caprīs sacrificāvērunt, L., XLV. 16, 6; *they sacrificed fifty she-goats.*

5. Here belong also verbs like **pluere, sūdāre** (not classic), **stīllāre** (not classic), **fluere, mānāre,** and the like: **sanguine pluisse,** L., XXIV. 10, 7. The Acc. is also common.

6. **Nītor,** *I stay myself,* is construed with the Abl.; occasionally with **in. Fīdō, cōnfīdō,** *I trust, rely on,* have the Abl.; but with persons the Dat., sometimes also with things. On the other hand, **diffīdō,** *I distrust,* always has the Dat. in classical Latin, but Tacitus shows Abl., and so do other later writers. **Stāre,** *to abide by,* usually has the Abl., but occasionally **in; manēre** has usually **in**; the Abl. is poetical. **Acquiēscere,** *to acquiesce in,* with Abl. is rare. **Frētus,** *supported,* takes the Abl. regularly; Livy alone uses the Dative. **Contentus,** *satisfied with (by),* is used only of one's own possessions (**rēbus, fortūnā,** *etc.*), and has the Ablative.

Salūs omnium nōn vēritāte sōlum sed etiam fāmā nītitur, *Cf.* C., *Q.F.*, I. ii. 1, 2; *the welfare of all rests not on truth alone, but also on repute.* **Eius iūdiciō stāre nōlim,** C., *Tusc.*, II. 26, 63; *I should not like to abide by his judgment.*

7. A remnant of the old usage is found with **fīō, faciō,** and **esse:**

Quid fēcistī scīpiōne? Pl., *Cas.*, 975; *what have you done with the wand?* **Quid**

mē fiet? Pl., *Most.*, 1166; *what will become of me?* **Quid tē futūrumst**? Ter., *Ph.*, 137; *what is to become of you?* **Quid hōc homine faciās**? C., *Verr.*, II. 16, 39; *how will you dispose of this man?* **Quid huīc hominī faciās**? C., *Caecin.*, 11, 30; *what will you do to this man?* **Quid dē nōbīs futūrum** [est]? C., *Fam.*, IX. 17, 1; *what is to happen in our case?*

The use of the Dative is rare, and still more rare the use of **dē**.

The construction is colloquial, and never found in Caesar and Tacitus; it is always in an interrogative sentence, except in Cato and Ovid.

4. Ablative of Standard. Ablātīvus Mēnsūrae.

402. The Standard of Measure is put in the Ablative with verbs of Measurement and Judgment.

Benevolentiam nōn ārdōre amōris sed stabilitāte iūdicēmus, C., *Off.*, I. 15, 47; *good will we are to judge not by ardour but by steadfastness.* **Māgnōs hominēs virtūte mētīmur, nōn fortūnā**, Nep., XVIII. 1, 1; *we measure great men by worth, not by fortune.* **Sonīs hominēs ut aera tinnītū dīgnōscimus**, Quint., XI. 3, 31; *we distinguish men by sound, as coppers by ring.*

Remarks.—1. It is often hard to distinguish the Measure from the Respect (see 397).

2. **Ex** with the Abl. is frequently found with these verbs; so regularly with **aestimāre, exīstimāre, spectāre**, in the sense of *judge, value.*

Dīcendum erit nōn esse ex fortūnā fidem ponderandam, C., *Part. Or.*, 34, 117; *the plea will have to be made that faith is not to be weighed by fortune.* **Sīc est vulgus: ex vēritāte pauca, ex opīniōne multa aestimat**, C., *Rosc. Com.*, 10, 29; *this is the way of the rabble: they value few things by (the standard of) truth, many by (the standard of) opinion.*

403. Measure of Difference is put in the Ablative.

Sōl multīs partibus māior (est) quam terra ūniversa, C., *N.D.*, II. 36, 92; *the sun is many parts larger than the whole earth.* **(Via) alterō tantō longiōrem habēbat ānfrāctum**, Nep., XVIII. 8, 5; *the road had a bend (that made it) longer by as much again, as long again.* **Quīnquiēns tantō amplius Verrēs, quam licitum est, cīvitātibus imperāvit**, *Cf.* C., *Verr.*, III. 97, 225; *Verres levied on the various cities five times more than was allowed by law.* **Turrēs dēnīs pedibus quam mūrus altiōrēs sunt**, Curt., V. 1, 26; *the towers are* (by) *ten feet higher than the wall.* **Tantō est accūsāre quam dēfendere, quantō facere quam sānāre vulnera, facilius**, Quint., V. 13, 3; *it is as much easier to accuse than to defend, as it is easier to inflict wounds than to heal them.* **Perfer et obdūrā: multō graviōra tulistī**, Ov., *Tr.*, V. 11, 7; *endure to the end and be firm: you have borne much more grievous burdens.*

Notes.—1. This rule applies to verbs involving difference (such as **abesse, dīstāre, mālle, praestāre, excellere**, *etc.*), as well as to comparatives, with which must be reckoned **īnfrā, suprā, ūltrā.**

[Aesculāpiī templum] quīnque mīlibus passuum ab urbe [Epidaurō] distat, *Cf.* L., XLV. 28, 3; *the temple of Aesculapius is five miles from the city of Epidaurus.*

2. The Acc. is sometimes employed (see 335); especially with neuter adjectives **multum, tantum,** *etc.*, but this is not common except with verbs.

3. The Plautine Abl. **nimiō,** with the comparative, is not classical (compare [C.], *Att.*, X. 8 A, 1), but reappears in LIVY. **Aliter** with this Abl. is very rare and is not classical. So also the Abl. with the positive, of which a few examples are cited from early Latin, as TER., *Heaut.*, 205.

4. (*a*) Especially to be noted is the use of the Abl. of Measure with **ante,** *before,* and **post,** *after:*

Paucīs ante diēbus, Paucīs diēbus ante, *a few days before.*

Paucīs post diēbus, Paucīs diēbus post, *a few days after, afterward.*

Duōbus annīs postquam Rōma condita est, *two years after Rome was founded.*

Paulō post Trōiam captam, *a little while after the taking of Troy.*

The Acc. can also be employed: **post paucōs annōs,** *after a few years;* **ante paucōs annōs,** *a few years before;* and the ordinal as well as the cardinal numbers (but only when **quam** follows): *two hundred years after(ward)* may be:

Ducentīs annīs post	*or*	**Ducentēsimō annō post,**
Post ducentōs annōs	*or*	**Post ducentēsimum annum.**

(*b*) **Ante** and **post** do not precede the Abl. in classical Latin except with **aliquantō** (rare) and **paulō. Ante** and **post,** with the Acc. followed by **quam,** instead of **antequam** and **postquam** with the Abl., belong preëminently to post-classical Latin; classical examples are rare. CICERO never has **ante.**

(*c*) **Ante hōs sex mēnsēs,** *six months ago* (compare 393, R. 4) more frequently **abhinc sex mēnsēs** (336, R. 3); **abhinc sex mēnsibus,** means *six months before.*

(*d*) With a relative sentence the Abl. of the relative may be used alone, instead of **ante (post) quam:**

Mors Rōsciī quadriduō quō is occīsus est, Chrȳsogonō nūntiātur, C., *Rosc. Am.*, 37, 105; *the death of Roscius was announced to Chrysogonus four days after he was killed* (*in the course of the four days within which he was killed*). See 393.

(*e*) *Hence* is **ad: ad sex mēnsēs,** *six months hence.*

(*f*) Do not confuse the Acc. with **ante** and **post** with the Acc. of Duration of Time.

5. Ablative of Price.

404. Definite Price is put in the Ablative.

Eriphȳla aurō virī vītam vēndidit, C., *Inv.*, I. 50, 94; *Eriphyle sold her husband's life for gold.* **Vīgintī talentīs ūnam ōrātiōnem Īsocratēs vēndidit,** PLIN., *N.H.*, VII. 31, 110; *Isocrates sold one speech for twenty talents.* **Ēmit morte immortālitātem,** QUINT., IX. 3, 71; *he purchased deathlessness with death.* **Argentum accēpī, dōte imperium vēndidī,** PL., *Asin.*, 87; *the cash I took,* (and) *for a dowry sold my sway.*

NOTES.—1. **Mūtāre,** *to exchange,* is sometimes Give, sometimes Get; sometimes Sell, sometimes Buy. The latter use is confined to poetry and later prose.

Nēmō nisi victor pāce bellum mūtāvit, S., *C.*, 58, 15; *no one unless victorious* (*ever*) *exchanged war for peace.* **Misera pāx vel bellō bene mūtātur,** *Cf.* TAC., *Ann.*, III. 44, 10; *a wretched peace is well exchanged even for war.*

But **cūr valle permūtem Sabīnā dīvitiās operōsiōrēs?** H., *O.*, III. 1, 47; *why should I exchange my Sabine vale for riches sure to breed* (me) *greater trouble?*

2. So **vēnālis, vīlis,** *cheap;* **cārus,** *dear.* **Nōn, edepol, minīs trecentīs cārast,** PL., *Pers.*, 668; *she is not dear, 'fore George, at three hundred minae.*

3. For Genitive of Price, see 379.

6. Ablative with Verbs of Plenty and Want.

405. Verbs of Depriving and Filling, of Plenty and Want, take the Ablative.

[Dēmocritus] dīcitur oculīs sē prīvāsse, C., *Fin.*, v. 29, 87; *Democritus is said to have deprived himself of his eyes.* **Deus bonīs omnibus explēvit mundum,** *Cf.* C., *Univ.*, 3, 9; *God has filled the universe with all blessings.* **Capua fortissimōrum virōrum multitūdine redundat,** C., *Pis.*, 11, 25; *Capua is full to overflowing with a multitude of gallant gentlemen.* **Nōn caret effectū quod voluēre duo,** Ov., *Am.*, ii. 3, 16; *what two have resolved on never lacks execution.* **Quō māior est in [animīs] praestantia, eō māiōre indigent dīligentiā,** C., *Tusc.*, iv. 27, 58.

Notes.—1. Verbs of Depriving are commonly referred to the Ablative of Separation, rather than to the Instrumental Ablative, and are put here for convenience of contrast. But it must be remembered that in the classic tongues the construction of opposites is identical.

2. **Egeō** and (more frequently) **indigeō** also take the Genitive:

Nōn tam artis indigent quam labōris, C., *Or.*, i. 34, 156; *they are not so much in need of skill as of industry.* So **implērī,** V., *A.*, i. 214.

3. Adjectives of Plenty and Want take the Gen., but some of them follow the analogy of the verb (374, n. 1). So **onustus, orbus,** have Abl. more often than Gen.; **indigus, egēnus,** and **inops** have the Gen. more commonly. **Plēnus** has usually the Gen.; the Abl. in increasing proportion from Lucretius on. **Frequēns** and **validus** do not take the Gen. until the post-Augustan period. See 374.

Asellus onustus aurō, C., *Att.*, i. 16, 12; *a donkey laden with gold.* **Pollicitīs dīves quīlibet esse potest,** Ov., *A.A.*, i. 444; *anybody can be rich in promises.* **Amor et melle et felle est fēcundissimus,** Pl., *Cist.*, 67; *love is (very) fruitful both in honey and in gall* (of acrimony).

406. Opus and **ūsus** take the Dative of the Person who Wants and the Ablative of the Thing Wanted; but the Thing Wanted may be the subject, and **opus** (not **ūsus**) the predicate.

Novō cōnsiliō mihi nunc opus est, Pl., *Ps.*, 601; *a new device is what I'm needing now.* **Vīgintī iam ūsust fīliō argentī minīs,** Pl., *Asin.*, 89; *my son has urgent need of twenty silver minae.* **Nihil opus est simulātiōne et fallāciīs,** C., *Or.*, ii. 46, 191; *there is no need of making believe, and of cheating tricks.* **Nōn opus est verbīs sed fūstibus,** C., *Pis.*, 30, 73; *there is need not of words, but of cudgels.* **Emās nōn quod opus est, sed quod necesse est; quod nōn opus est asse cārum est,** Cato (Sen., *E.M.*, 94, 27); *buy not what you want, but what is absolutely needful; what you do not want* (have no use for) *is dear at a penny.*

So with the Perfect Participle Passive.

Quod parātō opus est parā, Ter., *And.*, 523; *what must be got ready, get ready.* **Vīcīnō conventōst opus,** Pl., *Cas.*, 502; *the neighbour must* *be called on.* **Citius quod nōn factōst ūsus fit quam quod factōst opus,** Pl., *Am.*, 505.

Notes.—1. **Opus est** means properly: *there is work to be done with*; **ūsus est,** *there is making use of* (like **ūtor**); hence the Ablative. Some think that **opus** takes Abl. by analogy with **ūsus.**

2. **Opus est** is common throughout; **ūsus est** is very rarely found after the early period. It belongs especially to comedy.

3. The Gen. with **opus** occurs twice in Livy; also in Propertius, Quintilian, and Apuleius.

4. The neut. Acc. is usually adverbial (333, 1):

Quid (Acc.) **digitōs opus est graphiō lassāre tenendō?** Ov., *Am.*, I. 11, 23; *what is the use of tiring the fingers by holding the stylus?*

5. Besides the Pf. Part. pass., we find the Infin. and sometimes **ut**; in this case the Person is usually in the Dat. with **opus (ūsus),** but may be in the Acc. with the Inf., or may be omitted.

Opus est tē animō valēre ut corpore possīs, C., *Fam.*, XVI. 14, 2; *you must be well in mind in order to be well in body.* **An quoiquamst ūsus hominī sē ut cruciet?** Ter., *Heaut.*, 81; *of what good is it to any man to torture himself?*

The Supine is found occasionally; in Cicero only **scītū** (*Inv.*, I. 20, 28; disputed).

6. In Plautus and Lucretius are occasional examples of **ūsus** as a predicate, with the Thing Wanted as the subject.

7. Ablative with Sundry Verbs.

407. The Deponent Verbs **ūtor, abūtor, fruor, fungor, potior,** and **vescor,** take the Ablative.

Victōriā ūtī nescīs, L., XXII. 51, 4; *how to make use of victory you know not.* **Quō ūsque tandem abūtēre patientiā nostrā,** C., *Cat.*, I. 1, 1; *how long, tell me, will you abuse our patience?* **Lūx quā fruimur ā Deō nōbīs datur,** *Cf.* C., *Rosc. Am.*, 45, 131; *the light which we enjoy is given to us by God.* **Funguntur officiō; dēfendunt suōs,** C., *Cael.*, 9, 21; *they acquit themselves of a duty; they defend their own people.* **Fungar vice cōtis,** H., *A.P.*, 304; *I shall acquit myself of, discharge, the office of a whetstone.* **Tūtius esse arbitrābantur sine ūllō vulnere victōriā potīrī,** Caes., *B.G.*, III. 24, 2; *they thought it safer to make themselves masters of the victory without any wound.* **Numidae lacte vescēbantur,** S., *Iug.*, 89, 7; *the Numidians made their food of milk (fed on milk).*

Notes.—1. These Ablatives are commonly regarded as Ablatives of the Instrument: but **fruor,** *I get fruit*, and **vescor,** *I feed myself from*, and perhaps **fungor,** may take the Abl. as a Whence-case.

2. These verbs seem to have been originally construed with the Acc.; but this case is not found in classical Latin except in the Gerundive construction (427, n. 5).

(*a*) **Ūtor** with Acc. is very common in Plautus, less so in Terence, but only with neuter pronouns. Cato uses also the neuter of substantives. **Abūtor** is combined only with Acc. in early Latin.

(*b*) **Fruor** with Acc. is not in Plautus, but occasionally in Terence and Cato. **Frūnīscor** (rare) is transitive in Plautus and Quadrigarius (ap. Gell.).

(*c*) **Fungor** with Acc. is the rule in early Latin (Ter., *Ad.*, 603, is disputed), then in Nepos, Tacitus, Suetonius, and later.

(*d*) **Potior** has Gen. at all periods (rare in Cicero; once in Caesar); the Acc.

occasionally in early and late Latin, in the *b. Afr.*, the *b. Hisp.*, and in SALLUST. Noteworthy is the use of an act. **potīre** with Gen. in PL., *Am.*, 178, and a pass. **potītus** with Gen. in several places in PLAUTUS.

(*e*) **Vescor** takes the Acc. rarely in early Latin, in the poets, and in later Latin. **Vīvere, hēlluārī,** take Abl. like **vescī.**

3. **Ūtor** is a favorite word, and has a most varied translation :

Ūtī aliquō amīcō, *to avail one's self of* (*to enjoy*) *a man's friendship* (*to have a friend in him*) *;* **ūtī cōnsiliō,** *to follow advice ;* **ūtī bonō patre,** *to have the advantage of having a good father ;* **ūtī lēgibus,** *to obey the laws.* See the Lexicons.

D. ABLATIVE OF CAUSE.

408. The Ablative of Cause is used without a preposition, chiefly with Verbs of Emotion. *Ablātīvus Causae.*

In culpā sunt quī officia dēserunt mollitiā animī, C., *Fin.*, I. 10, 33 ; *they are to blame who shirk their duties from effeminacy of temper.* **Ōdērunt peccāre bonī virtūtis amōre,** H., *Ep.*, I. 16, 52 ; *the good hate to sin from love of virtue.* **Dēlictō dolēre, corrēctiōne gaudēre (oportet),** C., *Lael.*, 24, 90 ; *one ought to be sorry for sin, to be glad of chastisement.* **Nōn dīcī potest quam flagrem dēsīderiō urbis,** C., *Att.*, V. 11, 1 ; *I burn* (*am afire*) *beyond expression with longing for Rome.*

NOTES.—1. A number of combinations become phraseological, as the verbals : **arbitrātū, hortātū, impulsū, iūssū, missū, rogātū,** *etc.;* also **cōnsiliō, auctōritāte,** with a Gen. or possessive pronoun : **iūssū cīvium,** *at the bidding of the citizens ;* **meō rogātū,** *at my request.*

2. The moving cause is often expressed by a participle with the Abl., which usually precedes : **adductus,** *led ;* **ārdēns,** *fired ;* **commōtus,** *stirred up ;* **incitātus,** *egged on ;* **incēnsus,** *inflamed ;* **impulsus,** *driven on ;* **mōtus,** *moved,* and many others ; **amōre,** *by love ;* **īrā,** *by anger ;* **odiō,** *by hate ;* **metū,** *by fear ;* **spē,** *by hope, etc.* **Metū perterritus,** *sore frightened ;* **verēcundiā dēterritus,** *abashed, etc.*

3. Instead of the simple Abl. the prepositions **dē** and **ex** (sometimes **in**), with the Abl., **ob** and **propter** with the Acc., are often used ; perhaps occasionally **ab.**

4. The preventing cause is expressed by **prae,** *for* (417, 9) : **Prae gaudiō ubi sim nesciō,** TER., *Heaut.*, 308 ; *I know not where I am for joy.*

5. On **causā** and **grātiā** with the Gen., see 373.

6. The use of the Abl. for the *external* cause, as **rēgāle genus nōn tam rēgnī quam rēgis vitiīs repudiātum est** (C., *Leg.*, III. 7, 15), *the kingly form of government was rejected not so much by reason of the faults of the kingly form, as by reason of the faults of the king,* is not common in the early and in the classical period, except in certain formulæ ; but it becomes very common later.

7. The Ablative of Cause may have its origin in the Instrumental Ablative, in the Ablative of Source, or in the Comitative Ablative.

E. ABLATIVE ABSOLUTE.

409. The so-called Ablative Absolute is an Ablative combined with a participle, and serves to modify the verbal predicate of a sentence. Instead of the participle, a predicative substantive or adjective can be employed.

NOTE.—This Ablative, which may be called the Ablative of Circumstance, springs from the Temporal Use of the Ablative—the Temporal from the Local. Another view regards it as an Ablative of Manner, with a predicate instead of an attribute.

410. The Ablative Absolute may be translated by the English so-called Nominative (originally Dative) Absolute, which is a close equivalent; but for purposes of style, it is often well to analyse the thought, to change Passive into Active, to make use of an abstract substantive.

Xerxe rēgnante (= **cum Xerxēs rēgnāret**), *Xerxes reigning. When Xerxes was reigning. In the reign of Xerxes.*

Xerxe victō (= **cum Xerxēs victus esset**), *Xerxes being, having been, defeated. When Xerxes had been defeated. After the defeat of Xerxes.*

Xerxe rēge (= **cum Xerxēs rēx esset**), *Xerxes [being] king. When Xerxes was king.*

Patre vīvō, WHILE *father is, was alive* (*in father's lifetime*).

Urbe expūgnātā imperātor rediit:

PASSIVE FORM: *The city* [being] *taken* (*after the city was taken*), *the general returned.*

ACTIVE FORM: *Having taken the city* (*after he had taken the city*), *the general returned.*

ABSTRACT FORM: *After the taking of the city. After taking the city.*

Māximās virtūtēs iacēre omnēs necesse est voluptāte dominante, C., *Fin.*, II. 35, 117; *all the great(est) virtues must necessarily lie prostrate,* IF (or WHEN) *the pleasure* (of the senses) *is mistress.* **Rōmānī veterēs rēgnārī omnēs volēbant lībertātis dulcēdine nōndum expertā,** L., I. 17, 3; *the old Romans all wished to have a king over them* (BECAUSE they had) *not yet tried the sweetness of liberty.*

REMARKS.—1. As the Latin language has no Pf. Part. active, except when the Deponent is thus used, the passive construction is far more common than in English:

Iuvenēs veste positā corpora oleō perūnxērunt, C., *Tusc.*, I. 47, 113; *the youths,* (*having*) *laid aside their clothing, anointed their bodies with oil;* or, *laid aside their clothing, and anointed their bodies with oil.*

2. The Abl. Abs., though often to be rendered by a coördinate sentence, for convenience' sake, always presents a subordinate conception:

(**Lȳsander**) **suādet Lacedaemoniīs ut rēgiā potestāte dissolūtā ex omnibus dūx dēligātur ad bellum gerendum,** NEP., VI. 3, 5; *Lysander advises the Lacedaemonians that the royal power be done away with,* AND *a leader be chosen from all, to conduct the war.* Here the one is necessary to the other.

3. As a rule, the Abl. Abs. can stand only when it is not identical

with the subject, object, or dependent case of the verbal predicate. *Manlius slew the Gaul and stripped him of his necklace* is to be rendered : **Mānlius caesum Gallum torque spoliāvit.**

This rule is frequently violated at all periods of the language, for the purpose either of emphasis or of stylistic effect. The shifted construction is clearer, more vigorous, more conversational.

Neque illum mē vīvō corrumpī sinam, PL., *B.*, 419 ; *nor will I suffer him to be debauched while I am alive.*

The violation is most frequent when the dependent case is in the Genitive :

Iugurtha frātre meō interfectō rēgnum ēius sceleris suī praedam fēcit, S., *Iug.*, 14, 11 ; *Jugurtha killed my brother, and* (= after killing my brother) *made his throne the booty of his crime.*

NOTES.—1. The Pf. Part. of Deponents and Semi-deponents as an active in the Abl. Abs. is not found in early Latin, and is not common in classical Latin, where it is always without an object and is confined to verbs of Growth (principally **ortus, coortus, nātus**), Death, and Motion. It becomes common later, being used with an object from SALLUST on.

2. The Pf. Part. of Deponents as a passive in the Abl. Abs. is confined in classical Latin to **ēmeritus, pactus, partītus.** SALLUST and LIVY, as well as later writers, extend the usage. TACITUS, however, shows but two cases : **adeptus** (*Ann.*, I. 7, 8) and **ausus** (*Ann.*, III. 67, 4).

3. The Fut. Part. act. in the Abl. Abs. is post-Ciceronian, beginning with POLLIO and LIVY.

4. The impersonal use of the Abl. Abs. is found not unfrequently in early Latin and CICERO, rarely in CAESAR and SALLUST. Most of the forms so used have become adverbial in character, as **optātō, sortītō, intēstātō, cōnsultō, auspicātō, dīrēctō, meritō,** *etc.* The use of a following clause dependent upon the Abl. is begun in CICERO : **adiūnctō ut** (*Off.*, II. 12, 42). SALLUST uses **audītō** and **compertō** with the Infinitive. But LIVY extends this construction very greatly, and introduces the use of neuter adjectives in the same way : **incertō prae tenebrīs quid aut peterent aut vītārent,** L., XXVIII. 36, 12. It is frequent in TACITUS.

5. The use of adjectives and substantives in the Abl. is not common in early Latin, but is a favorite usage of the classical period and later : **mē auctōre,** C., *Or.*, III. 14, 54.

6. A predicate substantive, with the participle, is rare, but occurs in good prose : **Praetōre dēsīgnātō mortuō fīliō,** C., *Tusc.*, III. 28, 70.

LOCATIVE.

411. In the Singular of the First and Second Declensions, names of Towns and Small Islands are put in the Locative of the Place Where.

Pompēius hiemāre Dyrrhachiī, Apollōniae omnibusque oppidīs cōnstituerat, CAES., *B.C.*, III. 5, 1 ; *Pompey had determined to winter at Dyrrhachium, Apollonia, and all the towns.* **Tīmotheus Lesbī** (**vīxit**), NEP., XII. 3, 4 ; *Timotheus lived at Lesbos.* **Rhodī ego nōn fuī, sed fuī in Bīthȳniā,** C., *Planc.*, 34, 83 ; *I was not at Rhodes, but I was in Bithynia.*

REMARKS.—1. A few substantives of the Third Declension also form sporadic Locatives; so **Carthāginī**, in PLAUTUS, CICERO, and later; **Tīburī** in CICERO, LIVY, and later, and a few others. See 386.

2. Other Locative forms are, **domī**, *at home* (61, R. 2), **humī**, *on the ground* (first in CICERO), **bellī**, and **mīlitiae**, in the combinations **domī mīlitiaeque, bellī domīque**, *in peace and in war, at home and in the field;* **rūrī**, *in the country* (but **rūre meō**, *on my farm*).

Parvī sunt forīs arma nisi est cōnsilium domī, C., *Off.*, I. 22, 76; *of little value are arms abroad unless there is wisdom at home.* **Iacēre humī**, C., *Cat.*, I. 10, 26; *to lie on the ground.* **Humī prōsternere**, L., XLV. 20, 9; *to throw flat on the ground.*

Bellī is found alone occasionally in TERENCE and CICERO; ENNIUS, VERGIL, and OVID have **terrae**; VERGIL also **campī**.

3. Appositions are put in the Ablative, commonly with **in**, and regularly follow when qualified by an attribute:

Mīlitēs Albae cōnstitērunt in urbe opportūnā, C., *Ph.*, IV. 2, 6; *the soldiers halted at Alba, a conveniently situated town.* **Archiās Antiochīae nātus est celebrī quondam urbe**, C., *Arch.*, 3, 4; *Archias was born at Antioch, once a populous city.*

When **urbe**, *city*, **oppidō**, *town*, or **īnsulā**, *island*, precedes, the preposition is always employed:

In urbe Rōmā, *in the city* (of) *Rome.* **In oppidō Citiō**, *in the town of Citium.* **In īnsulā Samō**, *in the island* (of) *Samos.*

4. **Domī** takes the possessive pronoun in the Genitive:

Domī suae senex est mortuus, C., *N.D.*, III. 32, 81; *the old man died at his own house.* **Metuis ut meae domī cūrētur dīligenter**, TER., *Hec.*, 257; *you fear that she will not be carefully nursed at my house.* Also **aliēnae domuī** (61, R. 2), C., *Tusc.*, I. 22, 51; *in a strange house;* **domī illīus**, C., *Div. in Caec.*, 18, 58; *in his house.*

But **in domō Periclī** (65), NEP., VII. 2, 1; *in the house*(hold) *of Pericles.* **In domō castā**, *in a pure house.* **In domō**, *in the house* (not, *at home*).

NOTES.—1. Early Latin shows a number of Locative forms that have disappeared for the most part in the classical period. So **temperī (temporī)** replaced by **tempore** in CICERO (LIVY and TACITUS only **in tempore**); **mānī**, replaced by **māne**; **vesperī** and **herī**; and rare forms like **diē, crāstinī, proximī.** See 37, 5.

2. On Locative forms of the pronouns, see 91, 3. On **animī**, see 374, N. 7.

PREPOSITIONS.

412. The Prepositions are originally local adverbs, which serve to define more narrowly the local ideas involved in the cases. The analogy of the local adverbs is followed by other adverbs, which are not so much prepositions as prepositional adverbs. Of the Prepositions proper, that is, Prepositions used in composition (see Note), as well as in the regimen of cases, **cum (con)** does not clearly indicate a local relation.

The only cases that involve local ideas are the Accusative and Ablative. The Accusative, as the case of the Direct Object, represents the relation *whither?* the Ablative represents the relations *whence?* and *where?*

REMARKS.—1. In verbs of Motion, the Result of the Motion is often considered as Rest in a place (where). See 385, N. 2.

2. In verbs of Rest, the Rest is sometimes conceived as the Result of Motion (whither). See 385, N. 3.

NOTE.—Prepositions derive their name from the fact that they are prefixed in composition. Many of the Latin Prepositions are not used in composition, and these may be called improper Prepositions. The prefixes **amb-** (**am- an-**), **dis** (**dī**), **por-** (**porr-**, **pol-**), **red-** (**re-**), **sēd-** (**sē-**) and **vē-** are sometimes called inseparable prepositions.

413. *Position of the Preposition.*—The Preposition generally precedes the case.

REMARKS.—1. **Cum** always follows a personal pronoun, and may or may not follow a relative pronoun: **mēcum,** *with me;* **quōcum** or **cum quō,** *with whom.* **Dē** is not uncommonly placed after **quō** and **quā**, rarely after **quibus.** Position after the relative is found here and there also in the case of other Prepositions, but principally in early Latin or the poets, as follows: **ab, ad** (also in CICERO), **ex, in, per, post** (after **hunc,** C., *Tusc.*, II. 6, 15), and **prō.**

Dissyllabic Prepositions are postponed more often, but CICERO restricts this to pronouns, with the following Prepositions: **ante, circā, contrā, inter, penes, propter, sine, ūltrā.** CAESAR postpones **intrā** also.

Tenus, *as far as,* and **versus,** *-ward,* always follow.

2. When the substantive has an attribute the Preposition may come between; **hanc igitur ob causam** (C., *Br.*, 24, 94), *for this reason, therefore.*

3. The Preposition may be separated from its case by an attributive adjective or its equivalent, or other modifier of the case: **post vērō Sullae victōriam,** *but after Sulla's victory;* **ad beātē vīvendum,** *for living happily.* But model prose usually avoids separating the Preposition by more than a word or two. The poets have no scruples.

NOTES.—1. A peculiarity of poetry, LIVY, and later prose is the post-position of both Preposition and attribute: **metū in māgnō,** L., IX. 37, 11; *in great fear.*

2. Especially to be noted is the position of **per,** *through* (by), in adjurations: **Lȳdia dīc per omnēs tē deōs ōrō,** H., *O.*, I. 8, 1; *Lydia, tell, by all the gods, I pray thee.* **Per ego tē deōs ōrō,** TER., *And.*, 834; *I pray thee, by the gods.*

3. Between the Preposition and its case are often inserted the enclitics **que, ne, ve;** and after **ante, post,** and **praeter** the conjunctions **autem, enim, quidem, tamen, vērō,** occur, but not frequently. The first word in the combinations **et—et, aut—aut,**

simul—simul, vel—vel, sometimes follows the Preposition; **cum et diurnō et nocturnō metū,** C., *Tusc.*, v. 23, 66.

414. *Repetition and Omission of the Preposition.*—With different words which stand in the same connection, the Preposition is repeated, when the Preposition is emphatic, or the individual words are to be distinguished; so regularly after **aut—aut, et—et, nec—nec, vel—vel, nōn modo—sed etiam, sed, nisi, quam,** and in comparative clauses with **ut.** Otherwise it is omitted; so always with **que.**

Et ex urbe et ex agrīs, C., *Cat.*, II. 10, 21; *both from* (the) *city and from* (the) *country.* **Dē honōre aut dē dīgnitāte contendimus,** C., *Tusc.*, III. 21, 50; *we are striving about office, or about position.*

REMARKS.—1. When a relative follows in the same construction as its antecedent, the Preposition is usually omitted.

(Cimōn) incidit in eandem invidiam (in) quam pater suus, NEP., v. 3, 1; *Cimon fell into the same disrepute into which his father had fallen.*

2. So in questions: **Ante tempus morī miserum. Quod tandem tempus?** C., *Tusc.*, I. 39, 93; *a hard case 'tis, to die before the time.* (*Before*) *what time, pray?*

3. After **quasi, tamquam, sīcut,** the Preposition is more often inserted.

Rūs ex urbe tamquam ē vinclīs ēvolāvērunt, *Cf.* C., *Or.*, II. 6, 22; *they sped from the city to the country as if from a jail.*

4. Two Prepositions are rarely used with the same word. Either the word is repeated, a form of **is** used, or one Prep. turned into an adverb:

Prō Scīpiōne et adversus Scīpiōnem, *for and against Scipio.* **Ante pūgnam et post eam,** *before and after the battle.* **Et in corpore et extrā [sunt] quaedam bona,** C., *Fin.*, II. 21, 68. But **intrā extrāque mūnītiōnēs,** CAES., *B.C.*, III. 72, 2.

415. As adverbs without a case are used:

Ad, *about,* with numerals in CAESAR, LIVY, and later; **adversus,** *to meet,* especially in PLAUTUS and TERENCE; **ante** and **post** of Time (403, N. 4); **contrā,** *opposite, on the other hand;* **circā,** *round about,* and **circum** (rare); **prae,** *forward,* in PLAUTUS and TERENCE; **prope,** *near,* and **propter** (rare); **iūxtā,** *near by* (rare); **intrā,** *inside* (post-classical); **extrā,** *outside;* **īnfrā,** *below;* **suprā,** *above;* **subter,** *beneath,* and **super,** *above,* both rare; **citrā,** *on this side;* **ūltrā,** *beyond;* **cōram,** *in the presence of;* **clam,** *secretly.*

I.—Prepositions Construed with the Accusative.

416. The Prepositions construed with the Accusative are: **Ad, adversus, ante, apud, circā, circum, circiter, cis, citrā,**

clam, contrā, ergā, extrā, īnfrā, inter, intrā, iūxtā, ob, penes, per, post (pōne), praeter, prope, propter, secundum, suprā, trāns, ūltrā, ūsque, versus.

1. **Ad**. Of Motion Whither, *to, up to.* Of Direction, *towards* (**ad orientem**). Of Respect, *for, with regard to* (**ad hās rēs perspicāx**); found first in TERENCE. Of Manner, *after, according to* (**ad hunc modum**); colloquial (in CICERO's speeches only **quem ad modum**). Of Place, *at* (= **apud**), colloquial (**ad montem**, C., *Fam.*, XV. 2, 2) and legal (**ad forum, ad tē**), rare in CICERO's speeches. Of Time, *at*, refers only to future, and gives either a point (**ad vesperum**, *at evening*), an interval (**ad paucōs diēs**, *a few days hence*), or an approaching time, *towards.* With Numerals, *about.* Of Purpose, *for* (**castra hostī ad praedam relinquunt**, L., III. 63, 4). Also in phrases. Post-Ciceronian Latin extended the sphere of **ad**, and colloquially it was often a substitute for the Dative.

2. **Adversus** (**-um**), [*i.e., turned to*]. *Towards, over against, against.* Rare in early Latin and in CAESAR and SALLUST. In the sense, *over against*, it is found first in LIVY. In the transferred sense, *towards*, it expresses usually hostile disposition, but begins to indicate friendly disposition in CICERO. **Exadversus** (**-um**) is found occasionally, beginning with CICERO, and is always local.

3. **Ante** [*i.e., over against, facing*]. Of Place Where, *before.* Of Place Whither, *before;* rarely (not in CICERO). Of Time, *before;* the most frequent use. Of Degree, *before;* not in CICERO or CAESAR.

4. **Apud** is used chiefly of Persons. *At the house of* (characteristic locality). *In the presence of* (**iūdicem**). *In the writings of* (**Platōnem**). *In the view of.* Of Place, *at, in* (= **in**); common in comedy (**apud vīllam**); rare elsewhere, especially with proper names, where **ad** was preferred, except by SALLUST. In phrases like **apud sē esse**, *to be in one's senses.*

5. **Circā** (**circum**). *Around.* **Circum** is exclusively local (except once in VITRUVIUS, where it is temporal). **Circā** in the local sense is found first in CICERO. In the meaning *about*, of Time or Number, it is found first in HORACE. So, too, in the transferred sense of the sphere of mental action: **circā virentīs est animus campōs**, H., *O.*, II. 5, 5.

6. **Circiter.** Of Place, *about;* once in PLAUTUS. Usually of Time, *about*, especially with numerals; but the prepositional usage is on the whole small.

7. **Cis, citrā.** *This side, short of.* Of Place; **cis** found first in VARRO, **citrā** in CICERO. **Cis** is occasionally temporal in PLAUTUS, SALLUST, OVID. **Citrā**, of Time, *within, this side of;* found first in OVID. *Without* (*stopping short of*); found first in LIVY, then in OVID, and

the post-Augustan prose writers. In C., *Or.*, 18, 50, **citrā** may be rendered *further back; i.e.*, nearer the beginning.

8. **Clam.** *Secretly.* With Acc. in early Latin, in the *b. Hisp.*, and in the Jurists. With Abl. in CAESAR (*B.C.*, II. 32, 8), and in the *b. Afr.*, 11, 4 (both passages disputed). **Clanculum** with Acc., only in TERENCE.

9. **Contrā.** *Opposite to, over against, opposed to, against.* It appears as a Preposition first in the classical period, and is used both in local and transferred senses. In the latter case the force is predominantly hostile.

10. **Ergā.** *Opposite, towards.* Of Place ; very rarely, in early and late Latin. Usually in the transferred sense of friendly relations. The hostile sense is occasional in comedy, NEPOS, and later writers. **Ergā** is used always of Persons or personified Things until the time of TACITUS.

11. **Extrā.** *Without, outside of, beside.* It is used of local and transferred relations ; rarely in the sense of **sine** (TAC., *H.*, I. 49) ; occasionally in sense of **praeter**, *except.*

12. **Īnfrā.** *Beneath, lower down.* Of Space ; more frequently in classical Latin, of Rank or Grade ; Temporal but once (C., *Br.*, 10, 40). It occurs but rarely in later Latin, and is cited only once from early Latin (TER., *Eun.*, 489).

13. **Inter.** *Between.* Of Place Where, rarely of Place Whither. Colloquial were phrases like **inter viam (viās)**, *on the road*, **inter nōs**, *between ourselves.* **Inter paucōs**, *preëminently*, is post-classical. Of Time, *during;* at all periods, but in CICERO principally in the *Letters.*

14. **Intrā.** *Within.* Of Local and Temporal (not in CICERO) relations. The usage in transferred relations is post-classical, and mainly poetical.

15. **Iūxtā** [*i.e.*, *adjoining*]. *Hard by, near, next to.* It appears as a Preposition first in VARRO, then in CAESAR, but not in CICERO. It is used locally until LIVY, who employs it also in transferred senses of Time, Order, *etc.*

16. **Ob** [*i.e.*, *over against, opposite to*]. *Right before.* Of Place occasionally at all periods (not in CAESAR, LIVY, CURTIUS, TACITUS). Of Cause, *for;* found in early Latin (not with personal pronouns in PLAUTUS), in classical and post-classical Latin in increasing proportion. CAESAR uses it only in formulæ with **rem (rēs)** and **causam.** CICERO and CAESAR do not use **ob id** or **ob ea**, which, found in early Latin, reappear in SALLUST. **Ob** has almost completely supplanted **propter** in TACITUS. With the substantive and participle (**ob dēfēnsum Capitōlium**) **ob** is found first in LIVY.

17. **Penes.** *With = in the hands of;* of Persons. Applied to

Things, it is found in poetry first in HORACE ; in prose first in TACITUS. It is found wholly with **esse** until later Latin.

18. **Per.** Of Space, *through ;* of Time, *during ;* of Cause, *owing to ;* of Instrument, *by* (both persons and things) ; of Manner, *by, in.* It is used phraseologically in oaths, *by ;* also with persons (sometimes things), as **per me licet,** *as far as I am concerned you may.* **Per = ab** of Agent is found only in late Latin.

19. **Pōne.** *Behind,* only in Local relations; it is most frequent in PLAUTUS, occurs but once in CICERO, never in CAESAR or HORACE, and is rare in general.

20. **Post.** Of Place, *behind;* rare, but in good usage. Of Time, *after.* Of Rank, *subordinate to ;* in SALLUST, poets, and late prose.

21. **Praeter.** Of Place, *in front of, on before, past.* In a transferred sense, *except ; contrary to* (**opīniōnem** and the like). Of Rank, *beyond* (**praeter omnēs** is cited only from PLAUTUS and HORACE ; usually **praeter cēterōs**).

22. **Prope.** Of Place, *near ;* found first in the classical period. It sometimes has the constructions of adjectives of Nearness. Of Time, *near ;* very rare and post-classical, as LIVY, SUETONIUS. **Propius** is found first in CAESAR as a preposition.

23. **Propter.** Of Place, *near.* Of Cause, *on account of ;* very common in early and classical Latin, but avoided by many authors, notably TACITUS. With substantive and participle it appears first in VARRO ; then is common in LIVY, and later.

24. **Secundum** [*i.e., following*]. Of Place, *along* (**lītus**), *close behind ;* very rare (C., *Fam.*, IV. 12, 1). Of Time, *immediately after ;* in early Latin and CICERO, common in LIVY, but never in CAESAR, SALLUST, TACITUS. Of Series, *next to ;* in PLAUTUS and CICERO. Of Reference, *according to ;* at all periods. **Secus** is ante-classical and rare.

25. **Suprā.** Of Place, *above, beyond ;* so CICERO almost exclusively. Of Time, *beyond ;* very rare. Of Grade, *above.* Of Authority, *in charge of ;* VITRUVIUS and later.

26. **Trāns.** *On the other side, beyond, across ;* only in Local relations.

27. **Ūltrā.** Of Space and Measure, *on that side, beyond.* Of Time ; only in late Latin. The early form **ūls** is very rare and in formulæ, as, **Cis Tiberim et ūls Tiberim.** In late Latin **ūltrā** supplants **praeter** almost wholly.

28. **Ūsque,** *up to,* is found once in TERENCE, several times in CICERO, and occasionally later, with the Acc. of the name of a town. With other names of localities it appears first in LIVY.

29. **Versus,** *-ward.* As a preposition it first appears in the classical period and is found usually with names of Towns, and small Islands ; with other words it is regularly combined with the prepositions **ad** (not in CICERO) or **in.**

II. Prepositions Construed with the Ablative.

417. Prepositions construed with the Ablative are **ā (ab, abs), absque, cōram, cum, dē, ē (ex), prae, prō, sine, tenus;** rarely **fīne, palam, procul, simul.**

1. **Ā** (**ab, abs**). Of Place Whence, *from*, especially of the point of departure; so in phrases, **ā tergō, ā capite,** *etc.* Of Cause, *from* (**īrā**); beginning with Livy. Of Agent, *by*. Of Remote Origin, *from*. Of Time, *from*. Of Reference, *according to, after*. Of Specification, *in* (**doleō ab oculīs**); often with compound verbs.

Note.—The form before vowels and **h** is always **ab**; before consonants usually **ā**, though **ab** is not uncommon before consonants other than the labials **b, f, p, v,** and is frequent before **l, n, r, s,** and **i (j)**; **abs** is found only before **tē** and in the combination **absque.** Cicero uses **abs tē** in his early writings, but prefers **ā tē** in his later ones.

2. **Absque** [*i.e., off*]. *Without.* Peculiar to early Latin, where it is used in conditional sentences only. Occasionally in later Latin, as, **absque sententiā** (Quint., VII. 2, 44), for **praeter sententiam.**

3. **Cōram.** *Face to face with, in the presence of;* it is used with Persons only, and is found first in Cicero, and then in later writers, but in general it is rare until the time of Tacitus, who uses it very often in the *Annals* and always postpones.

4. **Cum.** *With;* of Accompaniment in the widest sense. With Abl. of Manner regularly when there is no attributive; often when there is one. Sometimes it is used of mutual action: **ōrāre cum,** *plead with* (Plautus), *etc.*

5. **Dē.** Of Place, *down from*, and then *from;* especially with compounds of **dē** and **ex.** Of Source, *from;* with verbs of Receiving (actual and mental). Of Origin; but mainly in poetry and later prose. Of Object, *concerning*. Of Time; in phrases **dē nocte, dē diē (diem dē diē,** *day after day*). Of the Whole *from* which a part is taken. Of Reference, *according to* (**dē sententiā**). Of Material; poetical and late.

6. **Ē** (**ex**). Of Place, *out of, from*. Often in phraseological usages, as **ex parte,** *partly;* **ex asse,** and the like. With verbs of Receiving, *from*. Of Time, *from;* **ex tempore** is phraseological. Of Origin, *from*. Of Reference, *according to*. Of Manner; in many phrases, as **ex aequō, ex ōrdine. Ē** is used before consonants only, **ex** before both vowels and consonants.

7. **Fīne** (or **fīnī**). *Up to;* found in Plautus and Cato, then not until very late Latin. With the Gen. it occurs in *b. Afr.* and in Sallust, *Fr.;* then not until Ovid and very late Latin.

8. **Palam,** in the sense of **cōram,** *in the presence of,* is found first in Horace and Livy, and is rare.

9. **Prae.** Of Place, *in front of;* with verbs of Motion only, in classical Latin. In early Latin in the phrase **prae manū**, *at hand.* Of the Preventive Cause, *for;* with negatives only, in and after the classical period; in early Latin, also in positive sentences. Of Comparison, *in comparison with;* occasionally at all periods.

10. **Prō.** Of Place, *before;* not in early Latin, but found first in the classical period, where it is confined to certain combinations, as **prō rōstrīs, castrīs, aede, vāllō,** *etc.*, and means *before and on.* *In behalf of;* not cited for early Latin. *Instead of;* very common at all periods. *In proportion to;* at all periods. **Quam prō**; found first in Livy.

11. **Procul,** *far from,* is poetical, and begins in prose with Livy. In classical Latin prose always with **ab.**

12. **Simul,** in the sense of **cum,** belongs to poetry and Tacitus (*Ann.*, III. 64).

13. **Sine,** *without,* is opposed to **cum.**

14. **Tenus,** *to the extent of.* Of Space (actual and transferred), *as far as.* It is found occasionally with the Gen., but almost wholly with Pl., and perhaps but once in Cicero (*Arat.*, 83); otherwise it belongs to poetry, making its first appearance in prose in Cicero (*Dei.*, 13, 36) and Livy. It occurs with the Acc. in late Latin. **Tenus** is always postponed.

III. Prepositions Construed with the Accusative and Ablative.

418. Prepositions construed with the Accusative and Ablative are **in, sub, subter, super.**

1. **In** (the forms **endo, indu,** are early and rare). (*a*) With Accusative: Of Place, *into, into the midst of.* Of Disposition and Direction, *towards.* Of Time, *into* (**multam noctem**), *for* (**diem, multōs annōs, posterum**). Of Purpose or Destination, *for;* mostly post-classical. Of Manner, *in, after.* Phraseologically with neuter adjectives: **in dēterius,** *for the worse;* but mainly post-classical. With Distributives, *to, among.*

(*b*) With Ablative: Of Place, *in, on.* Of Time, *within.* Of Reference, *in the case of, in regard to, in the matter of.* Of Condition, *in* (**armīs**). In many phrases, especially with neuter adjectives, **in incertō, dubiō, integrō, ambiguō,** *etc.*

2. **Sub.** (*a*) With Accusative: Of Place Whither, *under.* Of Time Approaching, *about* (**noctem, vesperum**); just Past, *immediately after.* Of Condition, *under* (**sub potestātem redigī**).

(*b*) With Ablative: Of Place Where, *under;* also in phrases, **sub armīs,** *etc.* Of Time When, *about;* rare, and first in Caesar. Of Position, *under* (**rēge, iūdice,** *etc.*). Of Condition, *under* (**eā condiciōne**); first in Livy.

3. **Subter.** (*a*) With Accusative ; rare, and locally equal to **sub.**

(*b*) With the Ablative ; more rare and almost wholly poetical (CATULLUS and VERGIL). *Cf.* C., *Tusc.*, v. 1, 4, which may be Acc. **Subtus** occurs only in VITR., IV. 2, 5, and then with the Accusative.

4. **Super.** (*a*) With Accusative but once before the classical time : Of Place, *over*, *above*. Of Time, *during ;* found first in PLINY, *Epp.* Metaphorically of Degree, *beyond* (**super modum**) ; post-classical.

(*b*) With the Ablative : Of Space, *above*. Of Time, *during* (not until the Augustan poets). Metaphorically = **praeter** ; very rare : = **dē**, *concerning ;* colloquial ; hence in PLAUTUS, CATO, CICERO's *Letters* (*ad Att.*), SALLUST, HORACE, LIVY; but uncommon.

INFINITIVE.

The Infinitive as a Substantive.

419. The Infinitive is the substantive form of the verb.

NOTE.—The Infinitive differs from a verbal substantive in that it retains the adverbial attribute, the designations of voice and time, and the regimen of the verb :

Amāre, *to love ;* **valdē amāre,** *to love hugely ;* **amārī,** *to be loved ;* **amāvisse,** *to have loved ;* **amāre aliquem,** *to love a man ;* **nocēre alicuī,** *to hurt a man.*

But the great claim of the Infinitive to be considered a verb lies in the involution of predicate and subject. Like the finite verb, the Infinitive involves predicate and subject ; but the subj. is indefinite and the predication is dependent.

420. The Infinitive, when it stands alone, involves an indefinite Accusative Subject, and the Predicate of that Subject is, of course, in the Accusative Case.

Rēgem esse, *to be king.* **Bonum esse,** *to be good.* Compare **quid stultius quam aliquem eō sibĭ placēre quod ipse nōn fēcit,** SEN., *E.M.*, 74, 17 ; *what is more foolish than for a man to* (*that a man should*) *pride himself on what he has not done himself.*

So in the paradigm of the verb :

Amātūrum esse, *to be about to love.*

NOTE.—On the Nom. with the Inf. by Attraction, see 528.

In consequence of this double nature, the Infinitive may be used as a substantive or as a verb.

421. The Infinitive, as a substantive, is used regularly in two cases only—Nominative and Accusative. In the other cases its place is supplied by the Gerund and the Ablative Supine.

NOTES.—1. Traces of the original Dat. (or Loc.) nature of the Infinitive are still apparent in many constructions, which are, however, mostly poetical :

(*a*) With verbs of Motion in early Latin and the later poets, when **ut, ad** with Gerundive or Sup. is to be expected.

Abiīt aedem vīsere Minervae, Pl., *B.*, 900; *she went away to visit the temple of Minerva.* **Semper in Ōceanum mittit mē quaerere gemmās,** Prop., II. (III.) 16 (8), 17; *she is always sending me to the Ocean to look for* (*in quest of*) *pearls.*

(*b*) With verbs of Giving, Rendering, and the like, in early Latin and the poets, where the Acc. of the Gerundive is to be expected. Classical is the use of **bibere** only, in this way. (The old form **biber** points to the effacement of the final sense of this Inf.)

Iovī bibere ministrāre, *Cf.* C., *Tusc.*, I. 26. **Quem virum aut hērōa lyrā vel ācrī tībiā sūmēs celebrāre, Cliō?** H., *O.*, I. 12, 1. Different, of course, are cases like **dī tibi posse tuōs tribuant dēfendere semper,** Ov., *Tr.*, III. 5, 21, where **posse dēfendere** is felt as **potestātem dēfendendī.**

(*c*) With many adjectives where the Sup. in **ū,** or some construction of Purpose, is to be expected.

In early Latin the adjectives are **parātus, cōnsuētus, dēfessus.** But this usage is widely extended by the Augustan poets Vergil and Horace, and later.

It is confined principally, however, to adjectives of *capability, ability, necessity, etc.*, and adjectives like **facilis** (with act. as well as pass. Inf., first in Prop.), **difficilis,** and the like: **Rōma capī facilis,** Lucan, II. 656. Note the strange usage **dissentīre manifēstus,** Tac., *Ann.*, II. 57, 4, and occasionally elsewhere.

2. The Inf. may take an adj. attribute, but in classical prose this is limited to **ipsum, hōc ipsum,** and **tōtum hōc:**

Vīvere ipsum turpe est nōbīs, *living itself is a disgrace to us.* **Quibusdam tōtum hōc displicet philosophārī** (280, 1, *a*).

The Infinitive as a Subject.

422. The Infinitive, as a Subject, is treated as a neuter substantive.

Incipere multō est quam inpetrāre facilius, Pl., *Poen.*, 974; *beginning is much easier* (*work*) *than winning.* **Miserum est dēturbārī fortūnīs omnibus,** C., *Quinct.*, 31, 95; *it is wretched to find one's self turned rudely out of all one's fortunes.* **Nōn tam turpe fuit vincī quam contendisse dēcōrum est,** Ov., *M.*, IX. 6 (280, 2, *a*).

Notes.—1. The use of the Inf. as a subj. grew out of its use as an obj., but the original Dat. (Loc.) sense was lost to the consciousness just as the prepositional sense of our own *to* is lost when our Inf. becomes a subj.; as in, *to err is human, to forgive divine.* No Roman felt **turpe fuit vincī,** as, *there was disgrace in being beaten;* **bonum est legere** was to him another **bona est lēctiō** (see Priscian, 408, 27).

2. The substantives used as predicates are not common in early Latin. **Lubīdō est** is confined to Plautus. **Stultitia est, cōnsilium est,** and **tempus est** are universal. Cicero introduces the not uncommon **mōs est,** and many others with **est,** as: **cōnsuētūdō (-inis), vitium, iūs, fās, nefās, facinus, fātum, caput, rēs** (Caesar), **opus, mūnus, officium, onus, sapientia,** and a few others. Still more are found later. Many of these also take **ut**; so **officium** always in comedy (except Ter., *And.*, 331).

3. Neuter adjectives are used as predicates in great variety. Ciceronian are **certius (quam), cōnsentāneum, falsum, incrēdibile, integrum, glōriōsum, māius (quam), mīrum, novom, optimum, rēctum, singulāre, trītum, vērīsimile, vērum.** Most of them, however, but once. Some of these also take **ut,** but not often in good prose.

4. In early Latin many impersonal verbs are used as predicates. Classical Latin retains most of them, but drops **condecet, dispudet, subolet,** and adds some, such as **paenitet, dēdecet, displicet, prōdest, obest, attinet.** Others come in later. Some, such as **oportet,** also take **ut** or the simple Subjv. Noteworthy is **est,** *it is possible*, found first in VARRO and LUCR., then not till VERG. and HOR., and never common.

5. Certain abstract phrases, whose meanings are akin to the words already mentioned, take the Inf. as a subject. So especially predicate Genitives, as **cōnsuētūdinis** and **mōris**; or combinations like **quid negōtiī, nihil negōtiī est**; predicate Datives such as **cordī est, cūrae est,** both unclassical; or phrases, as **operae pretium, in animō esse, in mentem venīre,** of which the last two were introduced by CICERO.

The Infinitive as an Object.

423. 1. The Infinitive is used as the Object of Verbs of Creation, commonly known as Auxiliary Verbs.

These Verbs *help* the Infinitive into existence.

2. Such verbs denote Will, Power, Duty, Habit, Inclination, Resolve, Continuance, End, and the like, with their opposites.

Ēmorī cupiō, TER., *Heaut.*, 971; *I want to die.* [**Catō**] **esse quam vidērī bonus mālēbat,** S., *C.*, 54, 5; *Cato preferred being* (*good*) *to seeming good.* **Sed precor ut possim tūtius esse miser,** Ov., *Tr.*, v. 2, 78; *but I pray that I may be more safely wretched.* **Vincere scīs, Hannibal; victōriā ūtī nescīs,** L., XXII. 51; *how to win victory, you know, Hannibal; how to make use of victory, you know not.* **Quī morī didicit, servīre dēdidicit,** SEN., *E.M.*, 26, 10; *he who has learned to die has unlearned to be a slave.* **Maledictīs dēterrēre nē scrībat parat,** TER., *Ph.*, 3; *he is preparing* (trying) *to frighten* (him) *from writing, by abuse.* **Quī mentīrī solet, pēierāre cōnsuēvit,** C., *Rosc. Com.*, 16, 46; *he who is wont to lie is accustomed to swear falsely.* **Vulnera quae fēcit dēbuit ipse patī,** Ov., *Am.*, II. 3, 4; *the wounds he gave he should himself have suffered.* **Vereor laudāre praesentem,** C., *N.D.*, I. 21, 58; *I feel a delicacy about praising a man to his face.* **Rēligiōnum animum nōdīs exsolvere pergō,** LUCR., I. 932; *I go on to loose the spirit from the bonds of superstitious creeds.* **Tuā quod nīl rēfert, percontārī dēsinās,** TER., *Hec.*, 810; *cease to inquire what is not to your advantage.*

So **habeō,** *I have* (it in my power).

Tantum habeō pollicērī mē tibī cumulātē satisfactūrum, C., *Fam.*, I. 5A, 3; *so much I can promise, that I will give you abundant satisfaction.*

NOTES.—1. The original force of the Inf. is, in most of these constructions, hard to determine, and was certainly not felt by the Romans themselves. In many cases the Inf. seems to have been used because the governing word or phrase was felt to be more or less equivalent to a Verb of Creation.

2. The principal verbs, construed thus with the Inf., are as follows:

Will: **velle, mālle, nōlle, cupere, optāre** (rare, except in passive), **petere, pōstulāre, avēre, audēre, dēsīderāre** (first in CIC.), **praegestīre, gestīre, ārdēre,**

metuere (ante-class.), **verērī, timēre, formīdāre** (ante-class.), **reformīdāre, horrēre, horrēscere, hortārī** and compounds, **monēre** and compounds, **suādēre** (first in Cic.), **persuādēre, iubēre, imperāre, praecipere, cōgere, permittere** (once in Cic., then later), **concēdere** (first in Cic.), **cūrāre** (not in Caes., Sall., Livy), **vetāre, recūsāre** (first in Cic.), **mittere, omittere, intermittere, cunctārī, cēssāre, morārī, dubitāre, gravārī, prohibēre, impedīre, dēterrēre.**

Power: **posse, quīre, nequīre, sustinēre** (first in Cic.), **valēre** (first in Cic.), **pollēre** (first in Cic.), **habēre** (rare, except in Cic.), **scīre, nescīre.**

Duty: **dēbēre, necesse habeō.**

Habit: **assuēscere, assuēfacere** (first in Cic.), **cōnsuēscere, solēre.**

Inclination: **cōnārī** (only with Inf.), **studēre, contendere, intendere** (Caes.), **labōrāre** (always with neg. in Cic.), **mōlīrī** (rare), **aggredī, ingredī, adorīrī, nītī** (first in Caes.), **ēnītī** (ante-class. and post-class.), **quaerere** (first in Cic.), **temptāre** (first in Hirtius).

Resolve: **cōgitāre, meditārī, meminī** (mostly poet.), **parāre, statuere** (first in Cic.), **cōnstituere** (first in Ter.), **dēcernere** (not class. in pass.), **iūdicāre** (first in Cic.), **dēstināre** (first in Caes.), **certum est, dēlīberātum est, prōpositum est** (first in Cic.).

Continuance: **stāre** (first in Cic.), **īnstāre, perstāre** (once in Cic., then late), **persevērāre** (first in Cic.), **properāre** (only word used in early Latin), **fēstīnāre** (first in Cic.), **mātūrāre** (first in Cic.).

Beginning and End: **coepī, incipere** (first in Cic.), **exōrdīrī, pergere, dēsinere.**

Poets are free in using the Inf. after other verbs.

3. Notice that **coepī**, *I have begun*, and **dēsinō**, *I cease*, are used in Pf. pass. with passive Infinitives, in early Latin, Cicero, Caesar, always; later the construction varies, and Tacitus does not observe the rule.

Bellō Athēniēnsēs undique premī sunt coeptī, Nep., xiii. 3, 1; *the Athenians began to feel the pressure of war on (from) all sides.* **Veterēs ōrātiōnēs legī sunt dēsitae,** C., *Br.*, 32, 123; *the old speeches have ceased to be read.*

When the passives are really reflexives or neuter, the active forms may be used.

4. Verbs of Will and Desire take **ut** as well as the Infinitive. So regularly **optō**, *I choose*, in classical prose.

5. Verbs which denote Hope, Promise, and Threat are treated as verbs of Saying and Thinking (530), but also occasionally as in English:

Spērant sē māximum frūctum esse captūrōs, C., *Lael.*, 21, 79; *they hope that they will derive great advantage.* **Subruptūrum pallam prōmīsit tibī,** Pl., *Asin.*, 930; *he promised to steal the mantle from you.*

6. **Doceō**, *I teach*, **iubeō**, *I bid*, **vetō**, *I forbid*, **sinō**, *I let*, take the Inf. as a Second Accusative (339):

(Dionȳsius) nē collum tōnsōrī committeret tondēre fīliās suās docuit, C., *Tusc.*, v. 20, 58; *Dionysius, to keep from trusting his neck to a barber, taught his daughters to shave* (taught them shaving). **Ipse iubet mortis tē meminisse deus,** Mart., ii. 59 (376). **Vītae summa brevis spem nōs vetat inchoāre longam,** H., *O.*, i. 4, 15; *life's brief sum forbids us open (a) long (account with) hope.* **Neu sinās Mēdōs equitāre inultōs,** H., *O.*, i. 2, 51; *nor let the Median ride and ride unpunished.*

The Infinitive as a Predicate.

424. The Infinitive, as a verbal substantive, may be used as a Predicate after the copula **esse**, *to be*, and the like.

Doctō hominī et ērudītō vīvere est cōgitāre, C., *Tusc.*, v. 38, 111; *to a learned and cultivated man to live is to think.*

GERUND AND GERUNDIVE.

425. The other cases of the Infinitive are supplied by the Gerund. With Prepositions, the Gerund, and not the Infinitive, is employed.

N. **Legere difficile est,** *reading (to read) is hard to do.*
G. **Ars legendī,** *the art of reading.*
Puer studiōsus est legendī, *the boy is zealous of reading.*
D. **Puer operam dat legendō,** *the boy devotes himself to reading.*
Ac. **Puer cupit legere,** *the boy is desirous to read.*
Puer prōpēnsus est ad legendum, *the boy has a bent toward reading.*
Ab. **Puer dīscit legendō,** *the boy learns by reading.*

Note.—Of course the Inf. may be quoted as an abstract notion, a form of the verb: **Multum interest inter "dare" et "accipere,"** Sen., *Ben.*, 5, 10; *there is a vast difference between "Give" and "Receive."*

426. As a verbal form, the Gerund, like the Infinitive, takes the same case as the verb.

Hominēs ad deōs nūllā rē propius accēdunt, quam salūtem hominibus dandō, C., *Lig.*, 12, 38; *men draw nearer to the gods by nothing so much as by bringing deliverance to their fellow-men.*

Notes.—1. The Gerund is the substantive of the Gerundive (251, n. 1). The most plausible theory connects the forms in **-ndu-** with those in **-nt-** (Pr. Part. active) as being verbal nouns originally without any distinction of voice. The signification of necessity comes mainly from the use as a predicate, *i.e.*, through the characteristic idea. Thus, *he who is being loved*, implies *he who is of a character to be loved* (**quī amētur**), and then *he who should be loved.*

The Gerundive is passive: the Gerund, like other verbal nouns (363), is theoretically active or passive, according to the point of view. Practically, however, the passive signification of the Gerund is rare.

Iugurtha ad imperandum (= **ut eī imperārētur,** perhaps an old military formula) **Tisidium vocābātur,** *Cf.* S., *Iug.*, 62, 8.

2. Gerundive and Pf. Part. passive are often translated alike; but in the one case the action is progressive or prospective, in the other it is completed.

Caesare interficiendō Brūtus et Cassius patriae lībertātēm restituere cōnātī sunt; *by the murder of Caesar (by murdering Caesar), Brutus and Cassius endeavoured to restore their country's freedom to her.* **Caesare interfectō, Brūtus et Cassius patriae lībertātem nōn restituērunt;** *by murdering Caesar, Brutus and Cassius did not restore their country's freedom to her.*

427. *Gerundive for Gerund.*—Instead of the Gerund, with an Accusative Object, the object is generally put in the case of the Gerund, with the Gerundive as an Attribute.

G. **Plācandī Deī,** *of appeasing God.*
D. **Plācandō Deō,** *for appeasing God.*
Ab. **Plācandō Deō,** *by appeasing God.*

In model prose this construction is invariably employed with Prepositions.

Ad plācandōs Deōs, *for appeasing the gods* (C., *Cat.*, III. 8, 20).

In plācandīs Diīs, *in appeasing the gods.*

NOTES.—1. It is impossible to make a distinction between the Gerund and the Gerundive form. They are often used side by side, where there can be no difference (L., XXI. 5, 5; XXV. 40, 6; XXVIII. 37, 1; XXXI. 26, 6). The preference for the Gerundive is of a piece with the use of the Pf. Part. pass. in preference to an Abstract Substantive (360, R. 2).

2. The impersonal Gerundive is found with an Acc. obj. once in PLAUTUS (**agitandumst vigiliās,** *Trin.*, 869), and occasionally elsewhere in early Latin (principally VARRO); very rarely in CICERO and for special reasons (*Cat. M.*, 2, 6); here and there later (not in CAESAR, HORACE, OVID, and, perhaps, LIVY).

Aeternās quoniam poenās in morte timendumst, LUCR., I. 111; *since we must fear eternal punishments in death.*

3. Neuter adjectives and pronouns are not attracted: **aliquid faciendī ratiō,** C., *Inv.*, I. 25, 36; *method of doing something.* **Cupiditās plūra habendī,** *greed for having more.* But when the neuter adjective has become a substantive (204, N. 2), the Gerundive form may be used: **cupiditās vērī videndī,** C., *Fin.*, II. 14, 46; *the desire of seeing the truth.*

4. The Gerundive with personal construction can be formed only from Transitive Verbs, like other passives (217). Hence the impersonal form must be used for all verbs that do not take the Acc., but with such verbs prepositions are rarely found.

Ad nōn pārendum senātuī, L., XLII. 9; *for not obeying the senate.*

5. But the Gerundives from **ūtor, fruor, fungor, potior, vescor** (407) have the personal construction, but usually only in the oblique cases (C., *Fin.*, I. 1, 3, is an exception), as a remnant of their original usage. The poets and later prose writers use still more forms in the same way, as **laetandus, dolendus, medendus, paenitendus,** *etc.* CICERO also shows single instances of **glōriandus, disserendus, respondendus.**

6. The use of the Nom. of the Gerundive follows the ordinary rules of the Nominative.

Genitive of the Gerund and Gerundive.

428. The Genitive of the Gerund and Gerundive is used chiefly after substantives and adjectives which require a complement:

Sapientia ars vīvendī putanda est, C., *Fin.*, I. 13, 42; *philosophy is to be considered the art of living.* **Et propter vītam vīvendī perdere causās,** JUV., VIII. 84; *and on account of life, to lose the reasons for living.* **Raucaque garrulitās studiumque immāne loquendī,** OV., *M.*, V. 678; *and hoarse chattiness, and a monstrous love of talking.* **Trīste est nōmen ipsum carendī,** C., *Tusc.*, I. 36, 87; *dismal is the mere word* "**carēre**" (*go without*). **Nōn est plācandī spēs mihi nūlla Deī,** OV., *Tr.*, V. 8, 22; *I am not without hope of appeasing God.* **Īgnōrant cupidī maledīcendī plūs invidiam quam convīcium posse,** QUINT., VI. 2, 16; *those who are eager to abuse know not that envy has more power than billingsgate.* **(Titus) equitandī perītissimus fuit,** SUET., *Tit.*, 3; *Titus was exceedingly skilful in riding.* **Neuter suī prōtegendī corporis memor (erat),** L., II. 6, 9; *neither* *thought of shielding his own body.* **Quī hīc mōs obsidendī viās et virōs aliēnōs appellandī?** L., xxxiv. 2, 9; *what sort of way is this of blocking up the streets and calling upon other women's husbands?* **Summa ēlūdendī occāsiōst mihi nunc senēs,** Ter., *Ph.*, 885; *I have a tip-top chance to fool the old chaps now.*

Remarks.—1. As **meī, tuī, suī, nostrī, vestrī,** are, in their origin, neuter singulars, from **meum,** *my being,* **tuum,** *thy being,* **suum,** *one's being, etc.*, the Gerundive is put in the same form: **cōnservandī suī,** *of preserving themselves;* **vestrī adhortandī,** *of exhorting you;* and no regard is had to number or gender.

Cōpia plācandī sit modo parva tuī, Ov., *Her.*, 20, 74; *let* (me) *only have a slight chance of trying to appease you* (feminine).

2. The Gen. of the Gerund and Gerundive is used very commonly with **causā,** less often with **grātiā,** and rarely with (antiquated) **ergō,** *on account of,* to express Design: **Dissimulandī causā in senātum vēnit,** S., *C.*, 31, 52; *he came into the senate for the purpose of dissimulation.*

The Gen. alone in this final sense is found once in Terence, several times in Sallust, occasionally later, especially in Tacitus.

(Lepidus arma) cēpit lībertātis subvortundae, S., *Phil.Fr.*, 10; *Lepidus took up arms as a matter of (for the purpose of) subverting freedom.*

More commonly **ad,** rarely **ob.** See 432.

Esse with this Gen. may be translated by *serve to;* this is occasional in Cicero; see 366, 429, 1.

Omnia discrīmina tālia concordiae minuendae [**sunt**], L., xxxiv. 54, 5; *all such distinctions are matters of (belong to) the diminishing of concord (serve to diminish concord).* Compare Caes., *B.G.*, v. 8, 6: [**nāvēs**] **quās suī quisque commodī fēcerat,** *ships which each one had (had) made* (as a matter) *of personal convenience.*

Notes.—1. In early Latin, in Cicero (early works, *Philippics* and philosophical writings), then in later authors, we find occasionally a Gen. Sing. of the Gerund, followed by a substantive in the Plural. Here it is better to conceive the second Gen. as objectively dependent upon the Gerund form.

Agitur utrum Antōniō facultās dētur agrōrum suīs latrōnibus condōnandī, C., *Ph.*, v. 3, 6; *the question is whether Antony shall receive the power of giving away (of) lands to his pet highwaymen.*

2. **Fās est, nefās est, iūs est, fātum est, cōpia est, ratiō est, cōnsilium est, cōnsilium capere, cōnsilium inīre,** and a few others, have often the Inf. where the Gerund might be expected. Sometimes there is a difference in meaning; thus **tempus,** with Gerund, *the proper time (season)*, with Inf., *high time.*

The poets and later prose writers extend this usage of the Infinitive.

3. Another peculiarity of the poets is the construction of the adj. or subst. like the cognate verb with the Inf., instead of with the Gen. of the Gerund. **(At) sēcūra quiēs et nescia fallere** (= **quae nesciat fallere**) **vīta,** V., *G.*, ii. 467; *quiet without a care, and a life that knoweth not how to disappoint (ignorant of disappointment).*

Later prose is more careful in this matter.

4. The Gen. of Gerund, depending upon a verb, is rare and Tacitean (*Ann.*, ii. 43). Tacitus also uses the appositional Gerund with a substantival neuter (*Ann.*, xiii. 26).

5. Some substantives, like **auctor, dux,** may have a Dat. instead of a Gen.; LIV., I. 23 : **mē Albānī gerendō bellō ducem creāvēre.**

Dative of the Gerund and Gerundive.

429. The Dative of the Gerund and Gerundive is used chiefly after words that denote Fitness and Function.

1. The usage is rare in classical Latin, and begins with a few verbs and phrases : **esse** (= **parem esse**), *to be equal to ;* **praeesse** and **praeficere,** *to be (put) in charge of;* **studēre** and **operam addere, labōrem impertīre,** *to give one's attention to;* then it is used with a few substantives and adjectives to give the object *for which,* and with names of Boards.

Solvendō cīvitātēs nōn erant, *Cf.* C., *Fam.*, III. 8, 2 ; *the communities were not equal to (ready for) payment (were not solvent).* **[Sapiēns] vīrēs suās nōvit, scit sē esse onerī ferendō,** SEN., *E.M.*, 71, 26 ; *the wise man is acquainted with his own strength ; he knows that he is* (equal) *to bearing the burden.*

So **comitia decemvirīs creandīs** (C., *Leg.Agr.*, 2, 8) ; **triumvir colōniīs dēdūcendīs** (S., *Iug.*, 42) ; **reliqua tempora dēmetendīs frūctibus accommodāta sunt,** C., *Cat. M.*, 19, 70.

2. Classical Latin requires **ad** with the Acc., but from LIVY on the use of this Dat. spreads, and it is found regularly after words which imply Capacity and Adaptation. It is found also technically with verbs of Decreeing and Appointing, to give the Purpose.

Aqua nitrōsa ūtilis est bibendō, *Cf.* PLIN., *N.H.*, XXXI. 32, 59; *alkaline water is good for drinking (to drink).* **Līgnum āridum māteria est idōnea ēliciendīs īgnibus,** *Cf.* SEN., *N.Q.*, II. 22, 1 ; *dry wood is a fit substance for striking fire (drawing out sparks).* **Referundae ego habeō linguam nātam grātiae,** PL., *Pers.*, 428 ; *I have a tongue that's born for showing thankfulness.*

NOTES.—1. In early Latin the use of this Dat. is very restricted, it being found principally after **studēre** ; **operam dare,** or **sūmere** (both revived by LIVY) ; **fīnem** (or **modum**) **facere** ; and a few adjectival forms. Of the latter, CICERO uses only **accommodātus,** CAESAR only **pār.**

2. Rare and unclassical is the Acc. in dependence upon a Dat. of the Gerund. **Epidicum operam quaerendō dabō,** PL., *Ep.*, 605.

Accusative of the Gerundive.

430. The Gerundive is used in the Accusative of the Object to be Effected, after such verbs as Giving and Taking, Sending and Leaving, Letting, Contracting, and Undertaking. (Factitive Predicate.)

Dīvitī hominī id aurum servandum dedit, PL., *B.*, 338 ; *he gave that* *gold to a rich man to keep.* **Conōn mūrōs reficiendōs cūrat,** NEP., IX. 4, 5; *Conon has the walls rebuilt.* **Patriam dīripiendam relīquimus,** C., *Fam.*, XVI. 12, 1; *we have left our country to be plundered.* **[Carvilius] aedem faciendam locāvit,** L., X. 46, 14; *Carvilius let the* (contract of) *building the temple.*

Of course, the passive form has the Nominative:

Fīlius Philippī Dēmētrius ad patrem redūcendus lēgātīs datus est, L., XXXVI. 35, 13; *the son of Philip, Demetrius, was given to the envoys to be taken back to his father.*

NOTES.—1. Early Latin shows with this construction **dare, condūcere, locāre, rogāre, petere, habēre, prŏpīnāre.** Classical Latin gives up **rogāre, petere, propīnāre,** but adds others, as **trādere, obicere, concēdere, committere, cūrāre, relinquere, prōpōnere.** LIVY introduces **suscipere.** The use of **ad** in place of the simple Acc. is not common.

[Caesar] oppidum ad dīripiendum mīlitibus concēssit, CAES., *B.C.*, III. 80, 6. But **ad** is necessary in **nēminī sē ad docendum dabat,** C., *Br.*, 89, 306; *he would yield to no one for teaching,* i.e., *would accept no one as a pupil.*

2. **Habeō dīcendum** and the like for **habeō dīcere,** or, **habeō quod dīcam,** belongs to later Latin (TAC., *Dial.*, 37; *Ann.* IV. 40, *etc.*).

Ablative of the Gerund and Gerundive.

431. The Ablative of the Gerund or Gerundive is used as the Ablative of Means and Cause, seldom as the Ablative of Manner or Circumstance.

Ūnus homō nōbīs cunctandō restituit rem, ENNIUS (C., *Cat.M.*, 4, 10); *one man by lingering raised our cause again.* **Hominis mēns dīscendō alitur et cōgitandō,** C., *Off.*, I. 30, 105; *the human mind is nourished by learning and thinking.* **Plausum meō nōmine recitandō dedērunt,** *Cf.* C., *Att.*, IV. 1, 6; *they clapped when my name was read.* **Exercendō cottīdiē mīlite hostem opperiēbātur,** L., XXXIII. 3, 5; *drilling the soldiers daily he waited for the enemy.*

NOTES.—1. The Abl. with adjectives is post-Ciceronian: **dīgna stirps suscipiendō** (instead of **quae susciperet**) **patris imperiō,** TAC., *Ann.*, XIII. 14. So too with verbs: **continuandō abstitit magistrātū,** L., IX. 34, 2.

2. The Abl. after a comparative is cited only from C., *Off.*, I. 15, 47.

3. In post-Augustan Latin, and occasionally earlier, we find the Abl. of the Gerund paralleled by the Pr. participle: **Bocchus, seu reputandō** (= **reputāns**) . . . **seu admonitus,** *etc.*, S., *Iug.*, 103, 2.

Prepositions with the Gerund and Gerundive.

432. The Accusative of the Gerund and Gerundive follows the preposition **ad,** seldom **ante, circā, in, inter, ob,** and **propter.** See 427.

Nūlla rēs tantum ad dīcendum prōficit quantum scrīptiō, C., *Br.* 24, 92;

nothing is as profitable for speaking as writing. **Atticus philosophōrum praeceptīs ad vītam agendam nōn ad ostentātiōnem ūtēbātur,** *Cf.* NEP., XXV. 17, 3; *Atticus made use of the precepts of philosophers for the conduct of life, not for display.* **Inter spoliandum corpus hostis exspīrāvit,** *Cf.* L., II. 20, 9; *while in the act of stripping the body of the enemy he gave up the ghost.*

REMARK.—**Ad** is very common; noteworthy is its use with verbs of Hindering (**palūs Rōmānōs ad īnsequendum tardābat,** CAES., *B. G.*, VII. 26, 2); with substantives to give the End (*for*); with adjectives of Capacity and Adaptation (**aptus, facilis,** *etc.*). See **429, 2.**

NOTES.—1. **Ante** is very rare (L., *Praef.*, 6; V., *G.*, III. 206). **Circā** and **ergā** are post-Augustan and very rare. **In** gives the End For Which, and is classical but not common. **Inter** is temporal, *during*, *while*, and is found rarely in early, more often in later, but not in classical prose. **Ob** is used first by CICERO (not by CAESAR), and is rare. **Propter** occurs first in VALERIUS MAXIMUS; **super** first in TACITUS.

2. On the Infinitive after a Preposition, see 425.

433. The Ablative of the Gerund and Gerundive takes the prepositions **ab, dē, ex,** often **in,** but seldom **prō.** Post-classic and rare are **cum** and **super.**

Prohibenda māximē est īra in pūniendō, C., *Off.*, I. 25, 89; *especially to be forbidden is anger in punishing.* [**Brūtus**] **in līberandā patriā** (= **dum līberat**) **est interfectus,** C., *Cat.M.*, 20, 75; *Brutus was slain in the effort to free his country.* **Philosophī in iīs librīs ipsīs quōs scrībunt dē contemnendā glōriā sua nōmina īnscrībunt,** C., *Tusc.*, I. 15, 34 (385, R. 1). **Ex dīscendō capiunt voluptātem,** *Cf.* C., *Fin.*, V. 18, 48; *they receive pleasure from learning.*

NOTES.—1. **In** with Abl. is sometimes almost equivalent to a Pr. participle: **In circumeundō exercitū animadvertit,** *b.Afr.*, 82.

2. **Sine** is used once in VARRO, *L.L.*, 6, 75, and in DONATUS (TER., *And.*, 391).

3. Even when the word and not the action is meant, the Gerund is the rule: **Discrepat ā timendō cōnfīdere,** C., *Tusc.*, III. 7, 14; the Inf. in VARRO, *L.L.*, 6, 50.

SUPINE.

434. The Supine is a verbal substantive, which appears only in the Accusative and Ablative cases.

The Accusative Supine.

435. The Accusative Supine (Supine in **-um**) is used chiefly after verbs of Motion, to express Design.

Galliae lēgātī ad Caesarem grātulātum convēnērunt, CAES., *B.G.*, I. 30, 1; *the commissioners of Gaul came to congratulate Caesar.* **Spectātum**

veniunt; veniunt spectentur ut ipsae, Ov., *A.A.*, I. 99; *they come to see the show; they come to be themselves a show.* **(Gallī gallīnāceī) cum sōle eunt cubitum,** Plin., *N.H.*, x. 24, 46; *cocks go to roost at sunset.* **Stultitia est vēnātum dūcere invītās canēs,** Pl., *St.*, 139; *'tis foolishness to take unwilling dogs a-hunting.*

Notes.—1. **Īre** and **venīre** are the most common verbs with the Supine, and they form many phraseological usages, as: **īre coctum, cubitum, dormītum, pāstum, supplicātum, sessum, salūtātum,** *etc.* Similarly **dare** is found in phrases with **nūptum, vēnum, pessum.**

2. The Supine is very common in early Latin, less so in Cicero, comparatively rare in Caesar, frequent again in Sallust and Livy. Later Latin, and especially the poets, show but few examples, as the final Inf. takes its place.

3. The Acc. Supine may take an object, but the construction is not very common:

(Hannibal) patriam dēfēnsum (more usual, **ad dēfendendam patriam**) **revocātus (est),** Nep., xxiii. 6, 1; *Hannibal was recalled to defend his country.*

4. The Fut. Inf. passive is actually made up of the passive Inf. of **īre,** *to go,* **īrī** (*that a movement is made,* from **ītur**; 208, 2), and the Supine:

Rūmor venit datum īrī gladiātōrēs, Ter., *Hec.*, 39; *the rumour comes that gladiators (gladiatorial shows) are going to be given.*

The consciousness of this is lost, as is shown by the Nom. (528).

Reus damnātum īrī vidēbātur, Quint., ix. 2, 88; *the accused seemed to be about to be condemned.*

The Ablative Supine.

436. The Ablative Supine (Supine in -ū) is used chiefly with Adjectives, as the Ablative of the Point of View From Which (397). It never takes an object.

Mīrābile dictū, *wonderful (in the telling) to tell,* **vīsū,** *to behold.*

Id dictū quam rē facilius est, L., xxxi. 38, 4; *that is easier in the saying than in the fact (easier said than done).*

Notes.—1. Cicero and Livy are the most extensive users of this Supine; Caesar has but two forms: **factū** and **nātū**; Sallust but three; Cicero uses twenty-four. In early Latin and in the poets the usage is uncommon; in later Latin it grows. Altogether there are over one hundred Supines, but only about twenty-five Supines occur in Abl. alone; the most common are **dictū,** *to tell,* **factū,** *to do,* **audītū,** *to hear,* **vīsū,** *to see,* **memorātū, relātū, trāctātū**; then, less often, **cōgnitū,** *to know,* **inventū, intellēctū, scītū, adspectū.**

2. The adjectives generally denote Ease or Difficulty, Pleasure or Displeasure, Right or Wrong (**fās** and **nefās**). These adjectives are commonly used with Dative, and a plausible theory views the Supine in **ū** as an original Dative (**uī**).

3. **Ad,** with the Gerundive, is often used instead: **Cibus facillimus ad concoquendum,** C., *Fin.*, ii. 20, 64; *food* (that is) *very easy to digest.*

The Infinitive, **facilis concoquī,** is poetical. Common is **facile concoquitur.**

Other equivalents are active Infin., a verbal substantive, a Pf. Part. pass. (with **opus**), or a relative clause (with **dīgnus**).

4. The use of the Abl. Supine with verbs is very rare.

(Vīlicus) prīmus cubitū surgat, postrēmus cubitum eat, Cato, *Agr.*, 5, 5; *the steward must be the first to get out of bed, the last to go to bed.* **Obsōnātū redeō,** Pl., *Men.*, 277; *I come back from marketing* (imitated by Statius).

PARTICIPLE.

437. The Participle may be used as a substantive, but even then generally retains something of its predicative nature.

Nihil est māgnum somnianti, C., *Div.*, II. 68, 141 ; *nothing is great to a dreamer* (*to a man, when he is dreaming*). **Rēgia, crēde mihī, rēs est succurrere lāpsīs**, Ov., *Pont.*, II. 9, 11; *it is a kingly thing, believe me,* (*to run to catch those who have slipped,*) *to succour the fallen.*

REMARK.—The Attribute of the Participle, employed as a substantive, is generally in the adverbial form : **rēctē facta**, *right actions ;* **facētē dictum**, *a witty remark.*

NOTES.—1. This use as a substantive is rare in classical prose, but more common in the poets and in post-classical prose. In the Pr. Part., principally **sapiēns, adulēscēns, amāns** ; in the Pf. more often, but usually in the Plural ; **doctī**, *the learned*, **victī**, *the conquered.* The first examples of Fut. Part. used as substantives are **nūntiātūrī** (CURT., VII. 4, 32), **peccātūrōs** (TAC., *Agr.*, 19).

2. The use of an attributive or predicative Pf. Part. with a substantive is a growth in Latin. Early Latin shows very few cases, and those mostly with **opus** and **ūsus.** CATO has **post dīmissum bellum,** and this innovation is extended by VARRO, with **propter.** CICERO is cautious, employing the prepositions **ante, dē, in, post, praeter,** but SALLUST goes much farther, as the strange sentence **inter haec parāta atque dēcrēta** (664, R. 2) indicates. LIVY and TACITUS are, however, characterised by these prepositional uses more than any other authors. The use of a Part. in the Nom. in this way is found first in LIVY.

438. The Participle, as an adjective, often modifies its verbal nature, so as to be characteristic, or descriptive.

(Epamīnōndās) erat temporibus sapienter ūtēns, NEP., XV. 3, 1; *Epaminondas was a man who made* (*to make*) *wise use of opportunities* (= **is quī ūterētur**). **Senectūs est operōsa et semper agēns aliquid et mōliēns,** *Cf.* C., *Cat.M.*, 8, 26; *old age is busy, and always doing something and working.*

REMARK.—Especial attention is called to the parallelism of the participle or adjective with the relative and Subjunctive:

Rēs parva dictū, sed quae studiīs in māgnum certāmen excēsserit, L. XXXIV. 1; *a small thing to mention, but one which, by the excitement of the parties, terminated in a great contest.* **Mūnera nōn ad dēliciās muliebrēs quaesīta nec quibus nova nūpta cōmātur,** TAC., *Germ.*, 18.

NOTE.—The Fut. Part. active is rarely used adjectively in classical Latin except the forms **futūrus, ventūrus.** The predicate use after verbs of Motion to express Purpose is found first in CICERO (*Verr.*, I. 21, 56), though very rarely, but becomes increasingly common from LIVY's time. LIVY is the first to use the Fut. Part. as an adjective clause, a usage which also becomes common later.

(Maroboduus) mīsit lēgātōs ad Tiberium ōrātūrōs auxilia, TAC., *Ann.*, II. 46; *Marbod sent commissioners to Tiberius, to beg for reinforcements.* **Servīlius adest**

dē tē sententiam lātūrus (perhaps due to **est**), C., *Verr.*, I. 21, 56. **Rem ausus plūs fāmae habitūram** (*that was likely to have*) **quam fideī,** L., II. 10, 11. (**Dictātor**) **ad hostem dūcit, nūllō locō, nisi quantum necessitās cōgeret, fortūnae sē commissūrus** (*with the intention of submitting*), L., XXII. 12, 2.

ADVERB.

439. 1. The Predicate may be qualified by an Adverb.

2. Adverbs qualify verbs, adjectives, and other adverbs, and sometimes substantives, when they express or imply verbal or adjective relations.

Male vīvit, *he lives ill;* **bene est,** *it is well;* **ferē omnēs,** *almost all;* **nimis saepe,** *too often;* **admodum adulēscēns,** *a mere youth;* **lātē rēx** (V., *A.*, I. 21), *wide-ruling;* **bis cōnsul,** *twice consul;* **duo simul bella,** *two simultaneous wars.*

NOTES.—1. The form of the Adverb does not admit of any further inflection, and therefore the Adverb requires no rules of Syntax except as to its position.

2. With other adverbs and with adjectives, adverbs of *degree* only are allowable, to which must be reckoned **bene, ēgregiē,** and (later) **īnsīgniter.** Poetical are such expressions as **turpiter āter, splendidē mendāx** (H., *A.P.*, 3; *O.*, III. 11, 35). **Male** as a negative is found with **sānus** only in CICERO (*Att.*, IX. 15, 5); other combinations are poetical, or post-classical.

3. The translation for *very* varies at different periods; **multum** is common in PLAUTUS and in HORACE'S *Satires* and *Epistles*, rare elsewhere; **valdē** is introduced by CICERO, but did not survive him, to any extent. **Sānē** is also frequent in CICERO, especially in the *Letters ad Atticum.* CORNIFICIUS affected **vehementer,** and so do colloquial authors, as VITRUVIUS; **fortiter** comes in later; **bene** is occasional in PLAUTUS and TERENCE, more common in CICERO; **oppidō** is characteristic of early Latin, and LIVY and the Archaists; **admodum** is Ciceronian, but **adfatim** comes later and is rare. **Abundē** is rare before the time of SALLUST. **Nimium** (**nimiō**) belongs to early Latin, as do **impēnsē** and **impendiō. Satis** is common in the classical period, and also **nimis,** but mainly with negatives.

4. The Adverb as an attribute of substantives is rare. CICERO shows **tum, saepe, quasi, tamquam.** LIVY uses more.

440. *Position of the Adverb.*—Adverbs are commonly put next to their verb, and before it when it ends the sentence, and immediately before their adjective or adverb.

Iniūstē facit, *he acts unjustly.* **Admodum pulcher,** *handsome to a degree, very handsome.* **Valdē dīligenter,** *very carefully.*

REMARK.—Exceptions occur chiefly in rhetorical passages, in which great stress is laid on the adverb, or in poetry:

[**Īram**] **bene Ennius initium dīxit īnsāniae,** C., *Tusc.*, IV. 23, 52; *well did Ennius call anger the beginning of madness.* **Vīxit dum vīxit bene** TER., *Hec.*, 461; *he lived while he lived* (and lived) *well.*

One class of Adverbs demands special notice—the Negatives.

Negative Adverbs.

441. There are two original negatives in Latin, **nē** and **haud** (**haut, hau**). From **nē** is derived **nōn** [**nē-oinom** (**ūnum**), *no-whit, not*]. **Nē** is used chiefly in compounds, or with the Imperative and Optative Subjunctive. The old use appears in **nē—quidem**. **Nōn** is used with the Indicative and Potential Subjunctive; **haud** negatives the single word, and is used mainly with adjectives and adverbs.

442. **Nōn** (the absolute *not*) is the regular Negative of the Indicative and of the Potential Subjunctive.

Quem amat, amat; quem nōn amat, nōn amat, PETR., 37; *whom she likes, she likes; whom she does not like, she does not like.*

Nōn ausim, *I should not venture.*

REMARKS.—1. **Nōn**, as the emphatic, specific negative, may negative anything. (See 270, R. 1.)

2. **Nōn** is the rule in antitheses: **Nōn est vīvere sed valēre vīta,** MART., VI. 70, 15; *not living, but being well, is life.*

NOTES.—1. **Nōn** in combination with adjectives and adverbs, and rarely with substantives and verbs, takes the place of negative **in-** or **ne-**. **Nōn arbitrābātur quod efficeret aliquid posse esse nōn corpus** (ἀσώματον), C., *Ac.*, I. 11, 39; *Cat. M.*, 14, 47.

2. Other negative expressions are **neutiquam,** *by no means;* **nihil,** *nothing* ("Adam, with such counsel *nothing* swayed"). On **nūllus,** see 317, 2, N. 2.

3. **Nec** = **nōn** is found in early Latin, here and there in VERG., LIVY, and TACITUS. In classical Latin it is retained in a few compounds, as: **necopīnāns, negōtium,** and in legal phraseology.

443. **Haud** is the negative of the single word, and in model prose is not common, being used chiefly with adjectives and adverbs: **haud quisquam,** *not any;* **haud māgnus,** *not great;* **haud male,** *not badly.*

NOTES.—1. **Hau** is found only before consonants, and belongs to early Latin and VERGIL. **Haut** (early) and **haud** are found indiscriminately before vowels.

2. **Haud** is very rarely or never found in Conditional, Concessive, Interrogative, Relative, and Infinitive sentences.

3. CAESAR uses **haud** but once, and then in the phrase **haud sciō an** (457, 2). CICERO says also **haud dubitō, haud īgnōrō, haud errāverō,** and a few others; and combines it also with adjectives and adverbs, but not when they are compounded with negative particles, *i.e.*, he does not say **haud difficilis,** and the like.

4. **Haud** with verbs is very common in early Latin, and then again in LIVY and TACITUS. In antitheses it is not uncommon in comedy, but usually in the second member: **inceptiōst āmentium haud amantium,** TER., *And.* 218; *the undertaking is one of lunatics, not lovers.*

5. A strengthened expression is **haud quāquam.**

444. 1. **Nē** is the Negative of the Imperative and of the Optative Subjunctive.

Tū nē cēde malīs, V., *A.*, VI. 95; *yield not thou to misfortunes.* **Nē trānsierīs Hibērum,** L., XXI. 44, 6; *do not cross the Ebro.* **Nē vīvam, sī sciō,** C., *Att.*, IV. 16, 8; *may I cease to live* (strike me dead), *if I know.*

NOTES.—1. On the negative with the Imperative, see 270, N.

2. **Nē** as a general negative particle, = **nōn,** is found very rarely in early Latin, mostly with forms of **velle** (**nē parcunt,** PL., *Most.*, 124, is disputed). Classical Latin retains this only in **nē—quidem,** in compound **nēquāquam,** and in a shortened form in **nefās, negō, neque,** *etc.*

2. **Nē** is continued by **nēve** or **neu.** See 260.

Nē illam vēndās neu mē perdās hominem amantem, PL., *Ps.*, 322; *don't sell her, and don't ruin me, a fellow in love.*

445. *Subdivision of the Negative.*—A general negative may be subdivided by **neque—neque,** as well as by **aut—aut,** or strengthened by **nē—quidem,** *not even.*

Nihil umquam neque īnsolēns neque glōriōsum ex ōre [Tīmoleontis] prōcēssit, NEP., XX. 4, 2; *nothing insolent or boastful ever came out of the mouth of Timoleon.* **Cōnsciōrum nēmŏ aut latuit aut fūgit,** L., XXIV. 5, 14; *of the accomplices no one either hid or fled.* **Numquam [Scīpiōnem] nē minimā quidem rē offendī,** C., *Lael.*, 27, 103; *I never wounded Scipio's feelings, no, not even in the slightest matter.*

("I will give *no* thousand crowns *neither*."—SHAKESPEARE.)

NOTE.—In the same way **negō,** *I say no,* is continued by **neque—neque** (**nec—nec**): **Negant nec virtūtēs nec vitia crēscere,** C., *Fin.*, III. 15, 48; *they deny that either virtues or vices increase* (*that there are any degrees in*).

446. *Negative Combinations.*—In English, we say either *no one ever*, or, *never any one; nothing ever*, or, *never anything;* in Latin, the former turn is invariably used: **nēmŏ umquam,** *no one ever.*

Verrēs nihil umquam fēcit sine aliquō quaestū, C., *Verr.*, V. 5, 11; *Verres never did anything without some profit or other.*

NOTES.—1. *No one yet* is **nōndum quisquam**; *no more, no longer,* is **iam nōn.**

2. The resolution of a negative **nōn ūllus** for **nūllus, nōn umquam** for **numquam, nōn sciō** for **nesciō,** is poetical, except for purposes of emphasis, or when the first part of the resolved negative is combined with a coördinating conjunction (480): **Nōn ūlla tibĭ facta est iniūria,** *Cf.* C., *Div. in Caec.*, 18, 60.

3. **Nēmŏ** often equals **nē quis**: **Nēmŏ dē nōbīs ūnus excellat,** C., *Tusc.*, V. 36, 105.

447. Negō (*I say no, I deny*) is commonly used instead of **dīcō nōn,** *I say—not.*

Assem sēsē datūrum negat, C., *Quinct.*, 5, 19; *he says that he will not give a copper.* **Vel aī vel negā,** Accius, 125 (R.); *say yes or say no!*

Remark.—The positive (**āiō,** *I say*) is sometimes to be supplied for a subsequent clause, as C., *Fin.*, I. 18, 61. The same thing happens with the other negatives, as **volō** from **nōlō, iubeō** from **vetō, sciō** from **nesciō, queō** from **nequeō, quisquam** from **nēmō, ut** from **nē.**

POSITION OF THE NEGATIVE.

448. The Negative naturally belongs to the Predicate, and usually stands immediately before it, but may be placed before any emphatic word or combination of words.

Potes nōn revertī, Sen., *E.M.*, 49, 10; *possibly you may not return.* (**Nōn potes revertī,** *you cannot possibly return.*) **Saepe virī fallunt; tenerae nōn saepe puellae,** Ov., *A.A.*, III. 31; *often do men deceive; soft-hearted maidens not often.* **Nōn omnis aetās, Lȳde, lūdō convenit,** Pl., *B.*, 129; *not every age,* (good) *Lydus* (Playfair), *sorts with play.* **Nōn ego ventōsae plēbis suffrāgia vēnor,** H., *Ep.*, I. 19, 37; *I do not hunt the voices of the windy commons, no, not I.*

Notes.—1. As the Copula **esse,** *to be,* is, strictly speaking, a predicate, the Negative generally precedes it, contrary to the English idiom, except in contrasts. The difference in position can often be brought out only by stress of voice: **fēlīx nōn erat,** *he wasn't happy;* **nōn fēlīx erat,** *he was* NOT *happy, he was* FAR FROM *happy.*

2. **Nē—quidem** straddles the emphatic word or emphatic group (445); but very rarely does the group consist of more than two words.

3. A negative with an Inf. is often transferred to the governing verb: **nōn putant lūgendum (esse) virīs,** C., *Tusc.*, III. 28, 70; on **negō,** see 447.

449. Two negatives in the same sentence destroy one another, and make an affirmative, but see 445:

Nōn negō, *I do not deny* (*I admit*).

Remarks.—1. **Nōn possum nōn,** *I cannot but* (*I must*):

Quī mortem in malīs pōnit nōn potest eam nōn timēre, C., *Fin.*, III. 8, 29; *he who classes death among misfortunes cannot but* (*must*) *fear it.*

2. The double Negative is often stronger than the opposite Positive; this is a common form of the figure **Lītotēs,** *understatement* (700).

Nōn indoctus, *highly educated;* **nōn sum nescius,** *I am well aware.*

Nōn indecōrō pulvere sordidī, H., *O.*, II. 1, 22; *swart* (*soiled*) *with* (*no dis*)*honourable dust.* **Nōn ignāra malī miserīs succurrere discō,** V., *A.*, I. 630; *not unacquainted* (= *but too well acquainted*) *with misfortune, I learn to succour the wretched.*

3. It follows from R. 2 that **nec nōn** is not simply equivalent to **et**, *and;* **nec** belongs to the sentence, **nōn** to the particular word:

Nec hōc [**Zēnō**] **nōn vīdit,** C., *Fin.*, IV. 22, 60; *nor did Zeno fail to see this.* **At neque nōn** (**dī**) **dīligunt nōs,** C., *Div.*, II. 49, 102; *but neither* (is it true that) *the gods do not love us, etc.*

In the classical Latin this form of connection is used to connect clauses but not single words, and the words are regularly separated. VARRO, the poets, and later prose use **necnōn** like **et**, and connect with it also single ideas.

4. Of especial importance is the position of the Negative in the following combinations;

Indefinite Affirmative.		*General Affirmative.*	
nōnnihil,	*somewhat;*	**nihil nōn,**	*everything;*
nōnnēmŏ,	*some one, some;*	**nēmŏ nōn,**	*everybody;*
nōnnūllī,	*some people;*	**nūllī nōn,**	*all;*
nōnnumquam,	*sometimes;*	**numquam nōn,**	*always;*
nōnnūsquam,	*somewhere;*	**nūsquam nōn,**	*everywhere.*

In ipsā cūriā nōnnēmŏ hostis est, C., *Mur.*, 39, 84; *in the senate-house itself there are enemies* (**nēmŏ nōn hostis est,** *everybody is an enemy*). **Nōn est plācandī spēs mihi nūlla Deī,** Ov., *Tr.*, v. 8, 22 (428); *I have some hope of appeasing God* (**nūlla spēs nōn est,** *I have every hope*). **Nēmŏ nōn didicisse māvult quam dīscere,** QUINT., III. 1, 6; *everybody prefers having learned to learning.*

INCOMPLETE SENTENCE.

Interrogative Sentences.

450. An interrogative sentence is necessarily incomplete. The answer is the complement.

451. A question may relate:

(*a*) To the existence or the non-existence of the Predicate: Predicate Question.

Vīvitne pater? *Is my father alive?*

(*b*) To some undetermined essential part of the sentence, such as Subject, Object, Adjective, Adverbial modifier: Nominal Question.

Quis est? *Who is it?* **Quid ais?** *What do you say?* **Quī hīc mōs?** *What sort of way is this?* **Cūr nōn discēdis?** *Why do you not depart?*

For a list of Interrogative Pronouns see 104.

REMARKS.—1. The second class requires no rules except as to mood (462).

2. The form of the question is often used to imply a negative opin-

ion on the part of the speaker: **Quid interest inter periūrum et mendācem?** C., *Rosc. Com.*, 16, 46; *what is the difference between a perjured man and a liar?* All questions of this kind are called *Rhetorical.*

452. 1. Interrogative sentences are divided into *simple* and *compound* (disjunctive). *Am I?* (simple); *Am I, or am I not?* (disjunctive).

NOTE.—Strictly speaking, only the simple interrogative sentence belongs to this section; but for the sake of completeness, the whole subject will be treated here.

2. Interrogative sentences are further divided into *direct* and *indirect*, or *independent* and *dependent*. *Am I?* (direct); *He asks whether I am* (indirect).

DIRECT SIMPLE QUESTIONS.

453. Direct simple questions sometimes have no interrogative sign. Such questions are chiefly passionate in their character, and serve to express Astonishment, Blame, Disgust.

Īnfēlīx est Fabricius quod rūs suum fodit? SEN., *Dial.*, I. 3, 6; *Fabricius is unhappy because he digs his own field?* (Impossible!) **Heus, inquit, linguam vīs meam praeclūdere?** PHAEDR., I. 23, 5; *Ho! ho! quoth he, you wish to shut my mouth, you do?* (You shall not.) **Tuom parasītum nōn nōvistī?** PL., *Men.*, 505; *you don't know your own parasite?* (Strange!) **Hunc tū vītae splendōrem maculīs adspergis istīs?** C., *Planc.*, 12, 30; *you bespatter this splendid life with such blots as those?*

NOTES.—1. Questions of this kind are characteristic of the Comic Poets. In CICERO they are found especially in expressions of doubt, with **posse,** and with an emphatic personal pronoun.

2. Such a question may have the force of a command. So in the phrase **etiam tū tacēs?** *won't you keep quiet?* common in comedy (PL., *Trin.*, 514).

3. Noteworthy is the occasional usage of the question in place of a condition. **Amat? sapit,** PL., *Am.*, 995; *is he in love? he is sensible.* **Trīstis es? indīgnor quod sum tibi causa dolōris,** OV., *Tr.*, IV. 3, 33 (542). See 593, 4.

4. When several questions follow in immediate succession, only the first generally takes the Interrogative Pronoun, or **-ne.** Repeated questioning is passionate.

5. On **ut** in the exclamatory question, see 558.

454. *Interrogative Particles.*—**-Ne** (enclitic) is always appended to the emphatic word, and generally serves to denote a question, without indicating the expectation of the speaker.

Omnisne pecūnia dissolūta est? C., *Verr.*, III. 77, 180; *is* ALL *the money paid out?* (**Estne omnis pecūnia dissolūta?** IS *all the money paid out?*)

REMARKS.—1. As the emphatic word usually begins the sentence, so **-ne** is usually appended to the first word in the sentence. But exceptions are not uncommon.

2. **-Ne** is originally a negative. Questioning a negative leans to the affirmative; and **-ne** is not always strictly impartial.

NOTES.—1. **-Ne** sometimes cuts off a preceding **-s** (in which case it may shorten a preceding long vowel), and often drops its own **e.** **Viden?** *Seest?* **Tūn?** *You?* **Satin?** *For certain?* Also **scīn, ain, vīn, itan,** *etc.* This occurs especially in early Latin.

2. This **-ne** is not to be confounded with the asseverative **-ne,** which is found occasionally in PLAUTUS and TERENCE, CATULLUS, HORACE (**ō sērī studiōrum, quīne putētis,** *etc.*, H., *S.*, I. 10, 21, a much discussed passage), and later appended to personal, demonstrative, and relative pronouns.

3. In poetry **-ne** is sometimes appended to interrogative words, to heighten the effect: **utrumne** (H., *S.*, II. 3, 251), **quōne** (H., *S.*, II. 3, 295).

4. **-Ne** is often added to personal pronouns in indignant questions: **tūne ināne quicquam putēs esse?** C., *Ac.*, II. 40, 125.

5. In early Latin **-ne** seems to be used sometimes with a force similar to that later exercised by **nōnne;** but in most of the examples the expectation of an affirmative answer seems to be due rather to the context than to **ne;** see, however, R. 2.

455. Nōnne expects the answer *Yes.*

Nōnne meministī? C., *Fin.*, II. 3, 10; *do you not remember?* **Nōnne is generōsissimus quī optimus?** QUINT., V. 11, 4; *is he not the truest gentleman who is the best man?*

So the other negatives with **-ne: nēmōne, nihilne,** and the like.

NOTE.—**Nōnne** is denied for PLAUTUS, but wrongly, though it occurs but rarely, and regularly before a vowel. It is also rare in TERENCE. In classical Latin it is frequent, but is never found in CATULLUS, TIBULLUS, and SENECA RHETOR.

456. Num expects the answer *No.*

Numquis est hīc alius praeter mē atque tē? Nēmō est, PL., *Tr.*, 69; *is anybody here besides you and me? No.* **Num tibi cum faucēs ūrit sitis, aurea quaeris pōcula?** H., *S.*, I. 2, 114; *when thirst burns your throat for you, do you ask for golden cups?* [No.]

NOTE.—**Numne** is found very rarely, perhaps only in C., *N.D.*, I. 31, 88, and *Lael.*, 11, 36. **Numnam** belongs to early Latin. In many cases in early Latin, **num** seems to introduce a simple question for information, without expecting a negative answer.

457. 1. **An** (*or*) belongs to the second part of a disjunctive question.

Sometimes, however, the first part of the disjunctive question is suppressed, or, rather, involved. The second alternative with **an** serves to urge the acceptance of the positive or negative proposition involved in the preceding statement. This abrupt form of question (*or, then*) is of frequent use in Remonstrance, Expostulation, Surprise, and Irony.

Nōn manum abstinēs? An tibi iam māvīs cerebrum dispergam hīc? TER., *Ad.* 781; *are you not going to keep your hands off? Or would* *you rather have me scatter your brains over the place now?* (**Vir cūstōdit absēns**, *my husband keeps guard, though absent. Is it not so?*) **An nescīs longās rēgibus esse manūs?** Ov., *Her.*, 16, 166; *or perhaps you do not know* (*you do not know, then*) *that kings have long hands* (arms).

NOTES.—1. This usage is found in early Latin, but is a characteristic of CICERO especially.

2. **An** is strengthened by **ne.** This is found frequently in early Latin, more rarely later. CICERO uses **anne** only in disjunctive questions, and HORACE, TIBULLUS, PROPERTIUS not at all.

3. In early Latin very frequently, less often in the poets; occasionally in prose, beginning with LIVY, **an** is used as a simple interrogative; so **nesciō an** = **nesciō num.** There seems to be good reason for believing that **an** was originally a simple interrogative particle, but became identified later with disjunctive questions.

2. Especially to be noted, in connection with **an**, are the phrases, **nesciō an** (first in CICERO, and not common), **haud sciō an** (this is the usual phrase: **haud sciam an** is rare), *I do not know but;* **dubitō an**, *I doubt, I doubt but = I am inclined to think;* **incertum an** (once in CICERO), and rarely **dubitārim** and **dubium an**, which give a modest affirmation; very rarely a negation. Negative particles, added to these expressions, give a mild negation.

Haud sciō an ita sit, C., *Tusc.*, II. 17, 41; *I do not know but it is so.* **Haud sciō an nūlla (senectūs) beātior esse possit**, C., *Cat.M.*, 16. 56; *I do not know but it is impossible for any old age to be happier.* **Dubitō an [Thrasybūlum] prīmum omnium pōnam**, NEP., VIII. 1, 1; *I doubt but I should* (*= I am inclined to think I should*) *put Thrasybulus first of all.*

NOTE.—In early Latin these phrases are still dubitative. The affirmative force comes in first in CICERO, and seems to have been equivalent to **fōrsitan**, *perhaps*, with the Potential Subjunctive: **Fōrsitan et Priamī fuerint quae fāta requīrās**, V., *A.*, II. 506; *perhaps you may ask what was the fate of Priam, too.*

DIRECT DISJUNCTIVE QUESTIONS.

458. Direct Disjunctive Questions have the following forms:

First Clause.	*Second and Subsequent Clauses.*
utrum, *whether*,	**an (anne)**, *or*
-ne,	**an**,
———	**an (anne).**

Utrum nescīs quam altē ascenderīs, an prō nihilō id putās? C., *Fam.*, X. 26, 3; *are you not aware how high you have mounted, or do you count that as nothing?* **Vōsne Lūcium Domitium an vōs Domitius dēseruit?** CAES., *B.C.*, II. 32, 8; *have you deserted Lucius Domitius, or has Domitius deserted you?* **Ēloquar an sileam?** V., *A.*, III. 39; *shall I speak, or hold my peace?* **Utrum hōc tū parum commeministī, an ego nōn satis intellēxī, an mūtāstī sententiam?** C., *Att.*, IX. 2; *do you not remember this, or did I misunderstand you, or have you changed your view?*

NOTES.—1. **Utrumne—an** is found once in CICERO (*Inv.*, I. 31, 51), not in CAESAR or LIVY, occasionally elsewhere (H., *Epod.*, 1, 7); **utrum—ne—an** is more common. **Ne—an**, which is common in prose, is not found in CAT., TIB., PROP., HOR., LUCAN.

2. **Ne** in the second member, with omitted particle in first member, occurs only in H., *Ep.*, I. 11, 3 (disputed), in the direct question, except in the combination **necne** (459).

3. **Ne—ne** is very rare; V., *A.*, II. 738; XI. 126.

4. **Aut** (*or*), in questions, is not to be confounded with **an.** **Aut** gives another part of a simple question, or another form of it (*or, in other words*). **An** excludes, **aut** extends.

(Voluptās) meliōremne efficit aut laudābiliōrem virum? C., *Parad.*, I. 3, 15; *does pleasure make a better or more praiseworthy man?* (Answer: *neither.*) **Tū virum mē aut hominem dēputās adeō esse?** TER., *Hec.*, 524; *do you hold me to be your husband or even a man?*

459. In direct questions, *or not* is **annōn,** rarely **necne**; in indirect, **necne,** rarely **annōn.**

Isne est quem quaerō, annōn? TER., *Ph.*, 852; *is that the man I am looking for, or not?* **Sitque memor nostrī necne, referte mihī,** OV., *Tr.*, IV. 3, 10 (204, N. 7).

NOTES.—1. **Necne** is found in direct questions in CICERO, *Tusc.*, III. 18, 41 (**sunt haec tua verba necne?**), *Flacc.*, 25, 59; and also LUCR., III. 713. **Annōn** in indirect questions occurs in CICERO, *Inv.*, I. 50, 95; II. 20, 60; *Cael.*, 21, 52; *Balb.*, 8, 22, *etc.*

2. **Utrum** is sometimes used with the suppression of the second clause for *whether or no?* but not in early Latin. So C., *Flacc.*, 19, 45, *etc.*

INDIRECT QUESTIONS.

460. Indirect questions have the same particles as the direct, with the following modifications.

1. Simple Questions.

(*a*) **Num** loses its negative force, and becomes simply *whether.* It decays in later Latin.

Speculārī (iūssērunt) num sollicitātī animī sociōrum essent, L., XLII. 19, 8; *they ordered them to spy out whether the allies had been tampered with.*

(*b*) **Sī,** *if,* is used for *whether,* chiefly after verbs and sentences implying trial. Compare **Ō sī** (261).

Temptāta rēs est sī prīmō impetū capī Ardea posset, L., I. 57, 2; *an attempt was made* (in case, in hopes that, to see) *if Ardea could be taken by a dash* (coup-de-main). **Ībō, vīsam sī domī est** (467, N.), TER., *Heaut.*, 170; *I will go* (to) *see if he is at home.*

NOTES.—1. **An** is sometimes used for **num** and **ne,** but never in model prose.

Cōnsuluit deinde (Alexander) an tōtīus orbis imperium fātīs sibi dēstinārētur, CURT., IV. 7, 26; *Alexander then asked the oracle whether the empire of the whole world was destined for him by the fates.*

2. **Nōnne** is cited only from CICERO and only after **quaerere** (*Ph.*, XII. 7, 15).

2. Disjunctive Questions.

In addition to the forms for Direct Questions (458), a form with **-ne** in the second clause only is found in the Indirect Question, but is never common; see 458, N. 2.

Tarquinius Prīscī Tarquiniī rēgis fīlius nepōsne fuerit parum liquet, L., I. 46, 4; *whether Tarquin was the son or grandson of king Tarquin the Elder does not appear.*

NOTES.—1. The form **-ne** is not found in CAESAR or SALLUST.

2. The form **ne—ne** is poetical, except once in CAESAR (*B. G.*, VII. 141, 8).

3. **Utrum—ne—an** is rare but classical. **Utrumne—an** begins with HORACE, is not found in LIVY, VELL., VAL. M., and both PLINYS. In TACITUS only in the *Dialogus*.

SUMMARY OF DIRECT AND INDIRECT DISJUNCTIVE QUESTIONS.

461. Direct.

Is the last syllable short or long? *Cf.* C., *Or.*, 64, 217.

Postrēma syllaba **utrum brevis est an longa?**
brevisne est an longa?

Indirect.

In a verse it makes no difference whether the last syllable be short or long:

In versū nihil rēfert
- **utrum postrēma syllaba brevis sit an longa.**
- **postrēma syllaba brevisne sit an longa.**
- **postrēma syllaba brevis an longa sit** (CICERO).
- **postrēma syllaba brevis sit longane.**

MOODS IN INTERROGATIVE SENTENCES.

1. In Direct Questions.

462. The Mood of the question is the Mood of the expected or anticipated answer.

463. Indicative questions expect an Indicative answer, when the question is *genuine*.

A. **Quis homō est?** B. **Ego sum,** TER., *And.*, 965; *who is that? It is I.*

A. **Vīvitne (pater)?** B. **Vīvom līquimus,** PL., *Capt.*, 282; *is his father living? We left him alive.*

464. Indicative questions anticipate an Indicative answer in the negative when the question is *rhetorical*.

Quis nōn paupertātem extimēscit? C., *Tusc.*, V. 31, 89; *who does not dread poverty?*

REMARK.—**Nōnne** and **num** in the direct question are often rhetorical (see PL., *Am.*, 539; C., *Div.*, I. 14, 24). With **nōnne** a negative answer is anticipated to a negative, hence the affirmative character. Compare further, 451, R. 2.

465. Subjunctive questions which expect Imperative answers are put chiefly in the First Person, when the question is *deliberative.*

A. **Abeam?** B. **Abī,** PL., *Merc.*, 749; *shall I go away? Go.*

A. **Quid nunc faciam?** B. **Tē suspenditō,** PL., *Ps.*, 1229; *what shall I do now? Hang yourself.*

REMARK.—So in the representative of the First Person in dependent discourse (265).

466. Subjunctive questions anticipate a potential answer in the negative, when the question is *rhetorical.*

Quis hōc crēdat? *who would believe this?* [No one would believe this.] **Quid faceret aliud?** *what else was he to do?* [Nothing.]

Quis tulerit Gracchōs dē sēditiōne querentēs? JUV., II. 24 (259).

REMARK.—On the Exclamatory Question see 534, 558.

2. In Indirect Questions.

467. The Dependent Interrogative is always in the Subjunctive.

The Subjunctive may represent the Indicative.

[**Cōnsīderābimus**] **quid fēcerit** (Indic. **fēcit**), **quid faciat** (Indic. **facit**), **quid factūrus sit** (Indic. **faciet** *or* **factūrus est**), *Cf.* C., *Inv.*, I. 25, 36; *we will consider what he has done, what he is doing, what he is going to do (will do).* (**Epamīnōndās**) **quaesīvit salvusne esset clipeus,** C., *Fin.*, II. 30, 97; *Epaminondas asked whether his shield was safe.* (**Salvusne est?**)

The Subjunctive may be original. See 265.

Ipse docet quid agam; fās est et ab hoste docērī, OV., *M.*, IV. 428 (219); (**Quid agam,** *what I am to do;* not *what I am doing*). **Quaerō ā tē cūr C. Cornēlium nōn dēfenderem,** C., *Vat.*, 2, 5; *I inquire of you why I was not to defend C. Cornelius.* (**Cūr nōn dēfenderem?** *why was I not to defend?*)

REMARKS.—1. **Nesciō quis, nesciō quid, nesciō quī, nesciō quod,** *I know not who, what, which,* may be used exactly as indefinite pronouns, and then have no effect on the construction. This usage is found at all periods.

Nesciō quid māius nāscitur Īliade, PROP., II. (III.) 32 (34), 66; *something, I know not what, is coming to the birth, greater than the Iliad.*

2. The Relative has the same form as the Interrogative **quis ?** except in the Nom. Sing.; hence the importance of distinguishing between them in dependent sentences. The interrogative depends on the leading verb, the relative belongs to the antecedent. (611, R. 2.)

Interrogative : **dīc quid rogem,** *tell me what it is I am asking.*

Relative : **dīc quod rogō,** TER., *And.*, 764 ; *tell me that which I am asking* (the answer to my question).

The relative is not unfrequently used where we should expect the interrogative, especially when the facts of the case are to be emphasised :

Dīcam quod sentiō, C., *Or.*, I. 44, 195 ; *I will tell you my real opinion.*

Incorporated relatives are not to be confounded with interrogatives:

Patefaciō vōbīs quās istī penitus abstrūsās īnsidiās (= **īnsidiās quās**) **sē posuissse arbitrantur,** C., *Agr.*, II. 18, 49; *I am exposing to your view the schemes which those people fancy they have laid in profound secrecy.*

NOTE.—In the early Latin of Comedy the leading verb is very frequently disconnected from the interrogative, which consequently appears as an independent sentence with the Indicative. This is most common after **dīc, respondē, loquere,** and kindred Imperatives; **vidĕ** (PLAUTUS also **circumspice, respice**); **tē rogō, interrogō, quaerō,** and similar phrases ; **audīre, vidēre,** *etc.*, **scīn ;** relative words, **ut, quōmodō,** *etc.*, where the modal and not interrogative force is prominent. Classical prose has given up all these usages. A few cases in CICERO are contested or differently explained. In poetry and later prose the examples are found only here and there.

Dīc, quid est ? PL., *Men.*, 397; *tell me, what is it?* (**Dīc quid sit,** *tell me what it is.*) **Quīn tū ūnō verbō dīc: quid est quod mē velīs ?** TER., *And.*, 45 ; *won't you tell me in one word: What is it you want of me?* **Dīc mihi quid fēcī nisi nōn sapienter amāvī,** OV., *Her.*, II. 27 ; *tell me what have I done, save that I have loved unwisely.*

So also, **nesciō quōmodō,** *I know not how = strangely ;* and **mīrum quantum,** *it* (is) *marvellous how much = wonderfully*, are used as adverbs :

Mīrum quantum prōfuit ad concordiam, L., II. 1, 11 ; *it served wonderfully to promote harmony.* **Nesciō quō pactō vel magis hominēs iuvat glōria lāta quam māgna,** PLIN., *Ep.*, IV. 12, 7 ; *somehow or other, people are even more charmed to have a widespread reputation than a grand one.*

Early Latin shows also **perquam, admodum quam, nimis quam, incrēdibile quantum ;** CICERO **mīrum** (**mīrē**) **quam, nimium quantum, sānē quam, valdē quam;** CAESAR none of these ; SALLUST **immāne quantum;** LIVY adds **oppidō quantum ;** PLINY MAI. **immēnsum, īnfīnītum quantum ;** FLORUS **plūrimum quantum.** The position excludes a conscious ellipsis of the Subjunctive.

PECULIARITIES OF INTERROGATIVE SENTENCES.

468. The subject of the dependent clause is often treated as the object of the leading clause by Anticipation (**Prolēpsis**).

Nōstī Mārcellum quam tardus sit, CAELIUS (C., *Fam.*, VIII. 10, 3); *you know Marcellus, what a slow creature he is.*

NOTE.—This usage is very common in Comedy, and belongs to conversational style in general.

469. Contrary to our idiom, the interrogative is often used in participial clauses. In English, the participle and verb change places, and a Causal sentence becomes Final or Consecutive.

Quam ūtilitātem petentēs scīre cupimus illa quae occulta nōbīs sunt? C., *Fin.*, III. 11, 37; *what advantage do we seek when we desire to know those things which are hidden from us?* [**Solōn Pīsistratō tyrannō**] **quaerentī quā tandem rē frētus sibĭ tam audāciter resisteret, respondisse dīcitur senectūte,** C., *Cat.M.*, 20, 72; *Solon, to Pisistratus the usurper, asking him* (= when Pisistratus the usurper asked him) *on what thing relying* (= on what he relied that) *he resisted him so boldly, is said to have answered* "*old age.*"

NOTE.—The Abl. Abs. with the interrogative is rare. C., *Verr.*, III. 80, 185.

470. Final sentences (sentences of Design) are used in questions more freely than in English.

Sessum it praetor. Quid ut iūdicētur? C., *N.D.*, III. 30, 74; *the judge is going to take his seat. What is to be adjudged?* (*To adjudge what?*)

REMARK.—The Latin language goes further than the English in combining interrogative words in the same clause; thus two interrogatives are not uncommon:

Cōnsīderā quis quem fraudāsse dīcātur, C., *Rosc.Com.*, 7, 21.

Yes and No.

471. (*a*) *Yes* is represented:

1. By **sānē**, (literally) *soundly*, **sānē quidem**, *yes indeed*, **etiam**, *even* (so), **vērō** (rarely **vērum**), *of a truth*, **ita**, *so*, **omnīnō**, *by all means*, **certē**, *surely*, **certō**, *for certain*, **admodum**, *to a degree, etc.*

Aut etiam aut nōn respondēre [**potest**], C., *Ac.*, II. 32, 104; *he can answer either yes or no.*

2. By **cēnseō**, *I think so;* **scīlicet**, *to be sure.*

Quid sī etiam occentem hymenaeum? Cēnseō, PL., *Cas.*, 806; *what if I should also sing a marriage-song? I think you had better.*

3. By repeating the emphatic word either with or without the confirmatory particles, **vērō** (principally with pronouns), **sānē**, **prōrsus**, *etc.*

Estisne? Sumus, *are you? We are.* **Dāsne? Dō sānē,** C., *Leg.*, I. 7, 21; *do you grant? I do indeed.*

(*b*) *No* is represented:

1. By **nōn**, **nōn vērō**, **nōn ita**, **minimē**, *by no means*, **nihil**, *nothing*, **minimē vērō**, **nihil sānē**, **nihil minus**.

2. By repeating the emphatic word with the negative:

Nōn īrāta es? Nōn sum īrāta, PL., *Cas.*, 1007; *you are not angry? I am not.*

(*c*) YEA or NAY.—**Immō** conveys a correction, and either removes a doubt or heightens a previous statement: *yes indeed, nay rather.*

Ecquid placeant (aedēs) mē rogās? Immō perplacent, PL., *Most.*, 907; *do I like the house, you ask me? Yes indeed, very much.* **Causa igitur nōn bona est? Immō optima,** C., *Att.*, IX. 7, 4; *the cause, then, is a bad one? Nay, it is an excellent one.*

REMARK.—*Yes, for,* and *no, for,* are often expressed simply by **nam** and **enim**: **Tum Antōnius: Herī enim, inquit, hōc mihĭ prōposueram,** C., *Or.*, II. 10, 40; *then quoth Antony: Yes, for I had proposed this to myself yesterday.*

SYNTAX OF THE COMPOUND SENTENCE.

472. 1. A compound sentence is one in which the necessary parts of the sentence occur more than once; one which consists of two or more clauses.

2. Coördination **(Parataxis)** is that arrangement of the sentence according to which the different clauses are merely placed side by side.

3. Subordination **(Hypotaxis)** is that arrangement of the sentence according to which one clause depends on the other.

He became poor and we became rich; the second clause is a coördinate sentence.

He became poor that we might be rich; the second clause is a subordinate sentence.

4. The sentence which is modified is called the Principal Clause, that which modifies is called the Subordinate Clause. "*He became poor*" is the Principal Clause, "*that we might be rich*" is the Subordinate Clause.

REMARK.—Logical dependence and grammatical dependence are not to be confounded. In the conditional sentence, **vīvam sī vīvet,** *let me live if she lives,* my living depends on her living; yet "**vīvam**" is the principal, "**sī vīvet**" the subordinate clause. It is the dependence of the introductory particle that determines the grammatical relation.

COÖRDINATION.

473. Coördinate sentences are divided into various classes, according to the particles by which the separate clauses are bound together.

REMARK.—Coördinate sentences often dispense with conjunctions (*Asyndeton*). Then the connection must determine the character.

Copulative Sentences.

474. The following particles are called Copulative Conjunctions: **et, -que, atque (āc), etiam, quoque.**

NOTE.—The Copulative Conjunctions are often omitted, in climax, in enumerations in contrasts, in standing formulæ, particularly in dating by the consuls of a year, if the **praenōmina** are added; and finally, in summing up previous enumerations by such words as **aliī, cēterī, cūnctī, multī, omnēs, reliquī.**

475. Et is simply *and*, the most common and general particle of connection, and combines likes and unlikes.

Pānem et aquam nātūra dēsīderat, SEN., *E.M.*, 25, 4; *bread and water* (is what) *nature calls for.* **Probitās laudātur et alget,** JUV., I. 74; *honesty is bepraised and—freezes.*

NOTES.—1. We find sometimes two clauses connected by **et** where we should expect **et tamen.** This usage is characteristic of TACITUS, but is found all through the language. **Fierī potest, ut rēctē quis sentiat et id, quod sentit, polītē ēloquī nōn possit,** C., *Tusc.*, I. 3, 6.

2. **Et** sometimes introduces a conclusion to a condition expressed in the Imperative, but only once in early Latin, never in classical prose. **Dīc quibus in terrīs; et eris mihi māgnus Apollō,** V., *Ec.*, III. 104.

3. **Et,** instead of a temporal conjunction, begins with CAESAR (*Cf. B.G.*, I. 37, 1) and SALLUST (*Iug.*, 97, 4); it is never common.

4. On **neque ūllus** for **et nūllus** and the like, see 480. On **et** after words indicating Likeness, see 643. On **et** for **etiam,** see 478, N. 2.

476. -Que (enclitic) unites things that belong closely to one another. The second member serves to *complete* or *extend* the first.

Senātus populusque Rōmānus, C., *Planc.*, 37, 90; *the Senate and people of Rome.* **Ibi mortuus sepultusque Alexander,** L., XXXVI. 20, 5; *there Alexander died and was buried.* [**Sōl**] **oriēns et occidēns diem noctemque cōnficit,** C., *N.D.*, II. 40, 102; *the sun by its rising and setting makes day and night.*

NOTES.—1. **Que** was very common in early Latin, especially in legal phraseology, where it was always retained.

2. **Que—que—que** is ante-classical and poetic.

3. **Que** is always added to the first word in the clause it introduces, in PLAUTUS as well as in classical prose; but the Augustan poets are free in their position, for metrical reasons. As regards prepositions, **que** is never appended to **ob** and **sub,** rarely to **ā** and **ad,** but frequently to other monosyllabic prepositions; it is always appended to dissyllabic prepositions in **-ā,** and often to other dissyllabic prepositions.

4. On **que** for **quoque** see 479, N. 2.

5. Combinations:

(*a*) **et—et;**

(*b*) **que—et;** rare in early Latin, never in CICERO, CAESAR; begins with SALLUST.

Sallust and **Tacitus** always add the **que** to the pronoun, **Livy** and later prose writers to the substantive.

(*c*) **et—que**; rare, and beginning with Ennius.

(*d*) **que—que** begins with Plautus, Ennius. Cicero has it but once (**noctēsque diēsque**, *Fin.*, I. 16, 51); it enters prose with Sallust, and poets are fond of it.

Et dominō satis et nimium fūrīque lupōque, Tib., IV. 1, 187; *enough for owner, and too much for thief and wolf.*

477. Atque (compounded of **ad** and **-que**) adds a more important to a less important member. But the second member often owes its importance to the necessity of having the complement (**-que**).

Āc (a shorter form, which does not stand before a vowel or **h**) is fainter than **atque**, and almost equivalent to **et**.

Intrā moenia atque in sinū urbis sunt hostēs, S., *C.*, 52, 35; *within the walls, ay, and in the heart of the city, are the enemies.* A. **Servos? Ego?** B. **Atque meus**, Pl., *Cas.*, 735; *a slave? I? And mine to boot.*

Notes.—1. The confirmative force of **atque**, as in the second example, is found especially in Plautus, occasionally later.

2. **Atque** adds a climax, and then is often strengthened by **ēcastor, profectō, vērō**, *etc.*, Pl., *B.*, 86; C., *Tusc.*, I. 20, 46.

3. In comedy, **atque** has sometimes demonstrative force: **atque eccum**, Pl., *St.*, 577.

4. Occasionally in Cicero, then in the Augustan poets, Livy and later prose writers, notably Tacitus, **atque** or **āc** is often used to connect the parts of a clause in which **et** or **que** (sometimes both) has been already employed:

Et potentēs sequitur invidia et humilēs abiectōsque contemptus et turpēs āc nocentēs odium, Quint., IV. 1, 14; *the powerful are followed by envy; the low and grovelling, by contempt; the base and hurtful, by hatred.*

5. **Atque—atque** is found occasionally in Cato, Catullus, Cicero, and Vergil. **Que—atque** begins in poetry with Vergil, in prose with Livy, and is very rare.

6. **Atque**, introducing a principal clause after a temporal conjunction, belongs exclusively to Plautus: **Dum circumspectō mē, atque ego lembum cōnspicor**, *B.*, 279. Also *Ep.*, 217.

7. **Atque** is used before consonants, as well as **āc**, to connect single notions: when sentences or clauses are to be connected, **āc** only is allowable; either **atque** or **āc** with expressions of Likeness.—Stamm.

8. On **atque**, after words indicating Likeness, see 643. **Atque** follows a comparative only after a negative in early and classical Latin. Horace is first to use it after a positive.

9. Phraseological is **alius atque alius**, *one or another*, found first in Livy, and rare.

478. Etiam, *even* (*now*), *yet, still*, exaggerates (heightens), and generally precedes the word to which it belongs.

Nōbīs rēs familiāris etiam ad necessāria deest, *Cf.* S., *C.*, 20, 11; *we lack means even for the necessaries of life.* **Ad Appī Claudī senectūtem accēdēbat etiam ut caecus esset**, C., *Cat.M.*, 6, 16 (553, 4).

Notes.—1. **Etiam** as a temporal adverb refers to the Past or Present, and means *still*; it is sometimes strengthened by **tum** (**tunc**) or **num** (**nunc**). But beginning with

LIVY, **adhūc,** which properly refers only to the Present, is extended to the Past and used like **etiam** (**tum**).

Nōn satis mē pernōstī etiam quālis sim, TER., *And.*, 503; *you still do not know well enough* (= little know) *what manner of person I am.* **Cum iste** (*i.e.*, **Polemarchus**) **etiam cubāret, in cubiculum intrōductus est,** C., *Verr.*, III. 23, 56; *while the defendant* (*Polemarchus*) *was still in bed, he was introduced into the bedroom.*

2. Instead of **etiam, et** is occasional in PLAUTUS, in a change of person. CICERO uses it also after an adversative conjunction, as **vērum et**; also after **nam** and **simul**; more often when a pronoun follows, as **et ille, et ipse.** CAESAR never uses it so, SALLUST rarely, but it becomes common from LIVY on.

3. Phraseological is **etiam atque etiam,** *time and again.* On **etiam** for *yes*, see 471, I.

479. Quoque, *so also,* complements (compare **que**) and always follows the words to which it belongs.

Cum patrī (Tīmotheī) populus statuam posuisset, fīliō quoque dedit, *Cf.* NEP., XIII. 2, 3; *the people, having erected a statue in honour of the father of Timotheus, gave one to the son also* (*likewise*).

REMARK.—The difference between **etiam** and **quoque** is not to be insisted on too rigidly:

Grande et cōnspicuum nostrō quoque tempore mōnstrum, JUV., IV. 115; *a huge and conspicuous prodigy, even in our day.*

NOTES.—1. In ante-classical and post-classical Latin the double forms **etiam — quoque, etiam quoque,** are sometimes found, and in classical Latin also **quoque etiam** occasionally: **nunc vērō meā quoque etiam causā rogō,** C., *Or.*, I. 35, 164.

2. **Que** in the sense of **quoque** is rare (compare **mēque,** CAT., CII. 3; *me too*), and is found chiefly in the post-Augustan **hodiēque,** *to-day also.*

480. *Copulation by means of the Negative.*—Instead of **et** and the negative, **neque (nec)** and the positive is the rule in Latin.

Opīniōnibus vulgī rapimur in errōrem nec vēra cernimus, C., *Leg.*, II. 17, 43; *by the prejudices of the rabble we are hurried into error, and do not distinguish the truth.* (**Caesar**) **properāns noctem diēī cōniūnxerat neque iter intermīserat,** CAES., *B.C.*, III. 13, 2; *Caesar in his haste had joined night with day and had not broken his march.*

REMARKS.—I. **Et—nōn,** *and—not,* is used when the negation is confined to a single word, or is otherwise emphatic; but **neque** is found occasionally here, even in CICERO (*Off.*, III. 10, 41).

Et mīlitāvī nōn sine glōriā, H., *O.*, III. 26, 2; *and I have been a soldier not without glory.*

On **nec nōn,** the opposite of **et nōn,** see 449, R. 3.

2. In combination with the negative we have the following

Paradigms:	*And no one,*	**neque quisquam,**	*nor any one.*
	And no,	**neque ūllus,**	*nor any.*
	And nothing,	**neque quidquam,**	*nor anything.*
	And never,	**neque umquam,**	*nor ever.*

Neque amet quemquam nec amētur ab ūllō, Juv., XII. 130; *may he love no one, and be loved by none.*

3. **Nec** is often nearly equivalent to **nec tamen**, *and yet not:*

Extrā invidiam nec extrā glōriam erat, Tac., *Agr.*, 8, 3; *he was beyond the reach of envy, and yet not beyond the reach of glory. Cf.* Ter., *Eun.*, 249; C., *Tusc.*, II., 25, 60.

Notes.—1. **Neque = nē quidem**, is ante-classical and post-classical: **nec nunc, cum mē vocat ūltrō, accēdam?** H., *S.*, II. 3, 262 (the only case in Horace).

2. Caesar, Lucretius, Vergil, and Propertius use **neque** regularly before vowels.

3. Combinations:

(*a*) **neque—neque; nec—nec; neque—nec; nec—neque.** Sometimes the first **neque** has the force of *and neither;* but this is limited in prose to Caesar, Sallust, and Livy; in poetry to Catullus and Propertius.

(*b*) **neque—et; neque—que; neque—āc.** Of these **neque—et** is rare in early Latin, but more common in Cicero and later; **neque—que** is rare, and found first in Cicero; **neque—atque (āc)** is very rare, and begins in Tacitus.

(*c*) **et—neque** is found first in Cicero, who is fond of it, but it fades out after him.

4. **Neque** is usually used for **nōn**, when followed by the strengthening words **enim, tamen, vērō,** *etc.*

481. 1. *Insertion and Omission of Copulatives.*—When **multus**, *much, many,* is followed by another attribute, the two are often combined by copulative particles: *many renowned deeds,* **multa et praeclāra facinora**; *many good qualities,* **multae bonaeque artēs.**

2. Several subjects or objects, standing in the same relations, either take **et** throughout or omit it throughout. The omission of it is common in emphatic enumeration.

Phrygēs et Pīsidae et Cilicēs, C., *Div.*, I. 41, 92; or, **Phrygēs, Pīsidae, Cilicēs**, *Phrygians, Pisidians,* and *Cilicians.*

Note.—**Et** before the third member of a series is rare, but occurs here and there at all periods; in Cicero it usually draws especial attention to the last member. **Atque (āc)** is used thus a little more frequently (**mōrēs īnstitūta atque vīta**, C., *Fam.*, XV. 4, 14), and **que** is not uncommon: **aegritūdinēs, īrae libīdinēsque**, C., *Tusc.*, I. 33, 80.

3. **Et** is further omitted in *climaxes,* in *antitheses,* in *phrases,* and in *formulæ.*

Virī nōn [est] dēbilitārī dolōre, frangī, succumbere, C., *Fin.*, II. 29, 95; *it is unmanly to allow one's self to be disabled* (unnerved) *by grief, to be broken-spirited, to succumb.* **Difficilis facilis, iūcundus acerbus, es īdem**, Mart., XII. 47, 1 (310).

Patrēs Cōnscrīptī, *Fathers* (and) *Conscript* (Senators).

Iūppiter Optimus Māximus, *Father Jove, supremely good* (and) *great.*

Other Particles Employed.

482. Other particles are sometimes employed instead of the copulative in the same general sense.

1. Temporal: **tum—tum,** *then—then;* **aliās—aliās,** *at one time—at another;* **iam—iam, nunc—nunc, modo—modo,** *now—now;* **simul—simul,** *at the same time.*

Tum Graecē—tum Latīnē, *partly in Greek, partly in Latin.* **Horātius Cocles nunc singulōs prōvocābat, nunc increpābat omnēs,** *Cf.* L., II. 10, 8; *Horatius Cocles now challenged them singly, now taunted them all.* **Modo hūc, modo illūc,** C., *Att.*, XIII. 25, 3; *now hither, now thither* (*hither and thither*). **Simul spernēbant, simul metuēbant,** *they despised and feared at the same time* (*they at once despised and feared*).

NOTES.—1. Of these **tum—tum** is not ante-classical, **nunc—nunc** is found first in LUCR., and is introduced into prose by LIVY: **simul—simul** is found first in CAESAR, but not in CICERO; **iam—iam** begins with VERGIL and LIVY. **Aliquandō—aliquandō, quandōque—quandōque,** are post-Augustan; **interdum—interdum** is rare, but occurs in CICERO.

2. The combinations vary in many ways. Ciceronian are **tum—aliās; aliās—plērumque; interdum—aliās; modo—tum; modo—vicissim;** most of them found but once. Some fifteen other combinations are post-Ciceronian.

3. On **cum—tum,** see 588.

2. Local: In CICERO only **aliō—aliō; hinc—illinc.** Others are: **hīc—illīc** (first in VERGIL); **hinc—hinc** (VERGIL, LIVY); **hinc—inde** (TACITUS); **illinc—hinc** (LIVY); **inde—hinc** (TACITUS); **alibi—alibi** (LIVY); **aliunde—aliunde** (PLINY).

3. Modal: **aliter—aliter; quā—quā,** rare, and lacking in many authors (*e.g.*, CAESAR, SALLUST). In CICERO only four times, and confined to the *Letters;* **pariter—pariter** is poetical and post-classical; **aequē—aequē** is found once in HORACE and once in TACITUS.

4. Comparative: **ut—ita,** *as—so:*

Dolābellam ut Tarsēnsēs ita Lāodicēnī ūltrō arcessiērunt, C., *Fam.*, XII. 13, 4; *as the people of Tarsus so the people of Laodicea* (= both the people of Tarsus and those of Laodicea) *sent for Dolabella of their own accord.*

Often, however, the actions compared are adversative; and **ut** may be loosely translated *although, while.*

Haec omnia ut invītīs ita nōn adversantibus patriciīs trānsācta, L., III. 55, 15; *all this was done, the patricians, though unwilling, yet not opposing* (= against the wishes, but without any opposition on the part of the patricians).

NOTE.—There are also many other similar combinations, as: **quemadmodum—sīc; ut—sīc; tamquam—sīc,** *etc.* The adversative use of **ut—ita** is rare in the classical period, but extends later.

5. Adversative: **nōn modo, nōn sōlum, nōn tantum,** *not only;* **sed, sed etiam, sed—quoque, vērum etiam,** *but even, but also:*

Urbēs maritimae nōn sōlum multīs perīculīs oppositae [sunt] sed etiam caecīs, C., *Rep.*, II. 3, 5: *cities on the seaboard are liable not only to many dangers, but even (also) to hidden* (ones). **[Nōn] docērī tantum sed etiam dēlectārī volunt,** QUINT., IV. 1, 57; *they wish not merely to be taught, but to be tickled to boot.*

In the negative form, **nōn modo nōn,** *not only not;* **sed nē—quidem,** *but not even;* **sed vix,** *but hardly.*

Ego nōn modo tibĭ nōn īrāscor, sed nē reprehendō quidem factum tuum, C., *Sull.*, 18, 50; *I not only am not angry with you, but I do not even find fault with your action.*

REMARKS.—1. Instead of **nōn modo (sōlum) nōn—sed nē—quidem,** the latter **nōn** is generally omitted, when the two negative clauses *have a verb in common,* the negative of the first clause being supplied by the second; otherwise both negatives are expressed.

Pīsōne cōnsule senātuī nōn sōlum iuvāre rem pūblicam sed nē lūgēre quidem licēbat, *Cf.* C., *Pis.* 10, 23; *when Piso was consul, it was not only not left free for the senate* (= the senate was not only not free) *to help the commonwealth, but not even to mourn* (for her).

2. **Nēdum,** *not* (to speak of) *yet, much less,* is also used, either with or without a verb in the Subjunctive; it is found first and only once in TERENCE, never in CAESAR and SALLUST, in CICERO only after negative sentences; from LIVY on it is used after affirmative clauses as well.

Satrapa numquam sufferre ēius sūmptūs queat, nēdum tū possīs, TER., *Heaut.*, 454; *a nabob could never stand that girl's expenditures, much less could you.*

NOTES.—1. **Nōn tantum** is never found in early Latin, CAESAR and SALLUST, rarely in CICERO. **Sed—quoque** is found first in CICERO; so, too, **sed** simply, but rarely. LIVY is especially free in his use of **sed. Vērum,** in the second member, is not ante-classical nor Tacitean. **Nōn** alone in the first member is rare, but Ciceronian, it is usually followed by **sed** only; occasionally by **sed etiam. Sed** is sometimes omitted from LIVY on. *Cf.* L., XXVIII. 39, 11; TAC., *Ann.*, III. 19, 2, *etc.*

2. **Sed et,** for **sed etiam,** belongs to post-Augustan Latin.

Adversative Sentences.

483. The Adversative particles are: **autem, sed, vērum, vērō, at, atquī, tamen, cēterum.** Of these only **sed** and **tamen** are really adversative.

NOTE.—The Adversative particles are often omitted: as when an affirmative is followed by a negative, or the reverse, or in other contrasts.

484. Autem (post-positive) is the weakest form of *but,* and indicates a *difference* from the foregoing, a *contrast* rather than a *contradiction*. It serves as a particle of *transition* and *explanation* (= *moreover, furthermore, now*), and of *resumption* (= *to come back*), and is often used in syllogisms.

Modo accēdēns, tum autem recēdēns, C., *N.D.*, II. 40, 102; *now approaching, then again receding.* **Rūmōribus mēcum pūgnās, ego autem ā tē ratiōnēs requīrō**, C., *N.D.*, III. 5, 13; *you fight me with rumours, whereas I ask of you reasons.* **Quod est bonum, omne laudābile est; quod autem laudābile est, omne est honestum; bonum igitur quod est, honestum est**, C., *Fin.*, III. 8, 27; *everything that is good is praiseworthy; but everything that is praiseworthy is virtuous; therefore, what is good is virtuous.*

REMARK.—**Autem** commonly follows the first word in the sentence or clause; but when an unemphatic **est** or **sunt** occupies the second place, it is put in the third. So **igitur** and **enim.**

NOTES.—1. Noteworthy is the use of **autem** in lively questions. CICERO employs it in this way, also to correct his own previous questions (*Epanorthōsis*).

Egon dēbacchātus sum autem an tū in mē? TER., *Ad.*, 185. **Num quis tēstis Postumium appellāvit? Tēstis autem? nōn accūsātor?** C., *Rab.Post.*, 5, 10.

2. **Autem** is a favorite word with CICERO, especially in his philosophical and moral works, but not with the Historians, least of all with TACITUS, who uses it only nine times in all.

485. Sed (set) is used partly in a stronger sense, to denote *contradiction*, partly in a weaker sense, *to introduce a new thought*, or *to revive an old one.*

Nōn est vīvere sed valēre vīta, MART., VI. 70, 15 (442, R. 2). **Domitius nūllā quidem arte sed Latīnē tamen dīcēbat**, C., *Br.*, 77, 267; *Domitius spoke with no art it is true, but for all that, in good Latin.*

NOTES.—1. The use of **sed** to carry on a narrative is characteristic of the historians, though found also in CICERO. **Sed in eā coniūrātiōne fuit Q. Cūrius**, S., *C.*, 23, 1.

2. **Sed** is repeated by anaphora (682), occasionally in CICERO (*Verr.*, III. 72, 169), more often later.

3. **Sed** may be strengthened by **tamen**; by **vērō, enimvērō, enim**; by **autem,** but only in connection with **quid,** and then only in comedy and in VERGIL. Sometimes it is equal to **sed tamen,** as in V., *A.*, IV. 660.

486. Vērum, *it is true, true,* always takes the first place in a sentence, and is practically equivalent to **sed** in its stronger sense.

Sī certum est facere, faciam; vērum nē post cōnferās culpam in mē, TER., *Eun.*, 388; *if you are determined to do it, I will arrange it; but you must not afterward lay the blame on me.*

NOTE.—**Vērum** gradually gives place to **sed** in CICERO. It is used occasionally to return to the subject (**vērum haec quidem hāctenus,** C., *Tusc.*, III. 34, 84), and in yielding a point (**vērum estō,** C., *Fin.*, II. 23, 75), where **sed** is the usual word.

487. Vērō, *of a truth,* is generally put in the second place, asserts with conviction, and is used to heighten the statement.

[**Platōnem**] **Diōn adeō admīrātus est ut sē tōtum eī trāderet. Neque vērō minus Platō dēlectātus est Diōne,** NEP., X. 2, 3; *Dion admired Plato to such a degree that he gave himself wholly up to him; and indeed Plato was no less delighted with Dion.*

NOTES.—1. **Vērō** is properly an affirmative adverb, and such is its only use in PLAUTUS. In TERENCE it has also acquired adversative force, which it preserves throughout the language in greater or less degree; so in the historians it is hardly more than **autem.**

2. The combination **vērum vērō** is ante-classical; on combinations with **enim,** see 498, N. 6.

3. **Vērō** is also, but not so commonly, used in transitions; especially in the formulæ **age vērō, iam vērō.**

488. At (another form of **ad** = *in addition to*) introduces *startling transitions, lively objections, remonstrances, questions, wishes,* often by way of quotation.

"Philoctēta, St! brevis dolor." At iam decimum annum in spēluncā iacet, C., *Fin.*, II. 29, 94; *"Philoctetes, still! the pain is short." But he has been lying in his cave going on ten years.* **"At multīs malīs affectus?" Quis negat?** C., *Fin.*, V. 30, 92; *"but he has suffered much?" Who denies it?* **At vidēte hominis intolerābilem audāciam!** C., *Dom.*, 44, 115; *well, but see the fellow's insufferable audacity!* **At vōbīs male sit!** CAT., III. 13; *and ill luck to you!*

NOTES.—1. **Ast** is the archaic form of **at,** and is found occasionally in CICERO, *de Leg.* and *ad Att.*, but more often in the poets and the later archaists.

2. **At** is used in anaphora, and also, especially in the poets, in continuing the narrative. Noteworthy is its use after conditional sentences (in CICERO only after negatives, never in SALLUST), where it is frequently strengthened by **certē, tamen, saltem: sī minus suppliciō adficī, at cūstōdīrī oportēbat,** C., *Verr.*, V. 27, 69.

489. Atquī (*but at any rate, but for all that*) is still stronger than **at,** and is used chiefly in argument.

Vix crēdibile. Atquī sīc habet, H., *S.*, I. 9, 52; *scarce credible. But for all that, 'tis so.*

NOTES.—1. **Atquīn** is occasional in early Latin, and even in CICERO.

2. **At** seems sometimes to be used for **atquī.** C., *Tusc.*, III. 9, 19.

490. Tamen (literally, *even thus*), *nevertheless,* is often combined with **at, vērum, sed.**

It is commonly prepositive, unless a particular word is to be made emphatic.

Nātūram expellēs furcā, tamen ūsque recurret, H., *Ep.*, I. 10, 24 ; *you may drive out Dame Nature with a pitchfork, for all that she will ever be returning.* **Domitius nūllā quidem arte sed Latīnē tamen dīcēbat,** C., *Br.*, II. 77, 267 (485).

REMARK.—**Nihilōminus** (*nothing the less*), *nevertheless*, is used like **tamen,** by which it is occasionally strengthened.

491. **Cēterum,** *for the rest*, is used by the Historians as an adversative particle.

Duo imperātōrēs, ipsī parēs cēterum opibus disparibus, S., *Iug.*, 52, 1 ; *two commanders, equal in personal qualities, but of unequal resources.*

NOTE.—**Cēterum** is found once in TERENCE (*Eun.*, 452), once in CICERO (*Q.F.*, II. 12, 1), otherwise not before SALLUST.

Disjunctive Sentences.

492. The Disjunctive particles are **aut, vel, -ve, sīve (seu).**

NOTE.—The Disjunctive particles are but rarely omitted, and then mainly in contrasted opposites like **pauper dīves, plūs minus,** and the like.

493. 1. **Aut,** *or*, denotes absolute exclusion or substitution.

Vinceris aut vincis, PROP., II. 8, 8 ; *you are conquered or conquering.*

2. **Aut** is often corrective = *or at least, at most, rather* (**aut saltem, aut potius**).

Cūnctī aut māgna pars fidem mūtāvissent, S., *Iug.*, 56, 5 ; *all, or at least a great part, would have changed their allegiance.* **Duo aut summum trēs iuvenēs,** L., XXXIII. 5, 8 ; *two, or at most three, youths.*

3. **Aut—aut,** *either—or.*

Quaedam terrae partēs aut frīgore rigent aut ūruntur calōre, *Cf.* C., *Tusc.*, I. 28, 68 ; *some parts of the earth are either frozen with cold or burnt with heat.* **Aut dīc aut accipe calcem,** JUV., III. 295 ; *either speak or take a kick.*

NOTES.—1. The use of **aut** to carry on a preceding negative is found first in CICERO, but becomes more common later : **nēmō tribūnōs aut plēbem timēbat,** L., III. 16, 4.

2. **Aut** is sometimes equivalent to *partly—partly* in TACITUS :

Hausta aut obruta Campāniae ōra, *H.*, I. 2.

3. On **aut** in interrogative sentences, see 458, N. 4.

494. 1. **Vel** (literally, *you may choose*) gives a choice, often with **etiam,** *even*, **potius,** *rather.*

Ego vel Cluviēnus, JUV., I. 80 ; *I, or, if you choose, Cluvienus.* **Per mē vel stertās licet, nōn modo quiēscās**, C., *Ac.*, II. 29, 93 ; *for all I care, you may* (*even*) *snore, if you choose, not merely take your rest* (*sleep*). **Satis vel etiam nimium multa**, C., *Fam.*, IV. 14, 3 ; *enough, or even too much.* **Epicūrus homŏ minimē malus vel potius vir optimus**, C., *Tusc.*, II. 19, 44 ; *Epicurus* (was) *a person by no means bad, or, rather, a man of excellent character.*

2. **Vel—vel**, *either—or* (whether—or).

[**Miltiadēs dīxit**] **ponte rescissō rēgem vel hostium ferrō vel inopiā paucīs diēbus interitūrum**, NEP., I. 3, 4 ; *Miltiades said that if the bridge were cut the king would perish in a few days, whether by the sword of the enemy, or for want of provisions.*

NOTES.—1. **Vel**, *for example*, is rare in PLAUTUS and TERENCE, but common in CICERO, especially in the *Letters*.

2. **Vel** in the sense of **aut** is rare in the classical period (C., *Rep.*, II. 28, 50), but is more common later, beginning with OVID. See TAC., *Ann.*, I. 59.

3. **Vel—vel** is found in PLAUTUS occasionally in the sense *as well as*, but in classical Latin is rigidly distinguished from **et—et.**

4. **Aut** is not uncommonly subdivided by **vel—vel: aut canere vel vōce vel fidibus**, C., *Div.*, II. 59, 122.

495. **-Ve** (enclitic) is a weaker form of **vel**, and in CICERO is used principally with numerals, in the sense *at most*, or with words from the same stem or of similar formation.

Bis terve, C., *Fam.*, II. 1, 1 ; *twice or at most thrice* (**bis terque**, *twice and indeed as much as thrice, if not more*).

Cūr timeam dubitemve locum dēfendere? JUV., I. 103 ; *why should I fear or hesitate to maintain my position?* **Aliquid faciendī nōn faciendīve ratiō**, C., *Inv.*, II. 9, 31 ; *the method of doing something or not doing it.*

NOTES.—1. In early Latin **ve** is more often copulative than adversative.

2. **Ve—ve** is poetical only.

496. 1. **Sīve (seu)**, *if you choose*, gives a choice between two designations of the same object.

Urbem mātrī seu novercae relinquit, L., I. 3, 3 ; *he leaves the city to his mother or* (*if it seems more likely*) *to his step-mother.*

2. **Sīve—sīve (seu—seu)**, *whether—or* (indifference).

Sīve medicum adhibueris sīve nōn adhibueris nōn convalēscēs, C., *Fat.*, 12, 29 ; *whether you employ a physician, or do not employ* (one), *you will not get well.* **Seu vīsa est catulīs cerva fidēlibus seu rūpit teretēs Marsus aper plagās**, H., *O.*, I. 1, 27 ; *whether a doe hath appeared to the faithful hounds, or a Marsian boar hath burst the tightly-twisted toils.*

NOTES.—1. Single **sīve** (= *or*) is not found in PLAUTUS or TERENCE (*Cf. And.*, 190), but it occurs in LUCRETIUS, LUCILIUS, and is common in CICERO. CAESAR and SAL-

LUST, however, do not use it, and it is rare in the Poets. In the sense of **sīve—sīve** it is found occasionally in poetry; but in prose only three times in TACITUS.

2. **Sīve—sīve** is not found in TERENCE, but from CICERO on becomes common.

3. No distinction seems possible between **sīve** and **seu.**

497. **An** is used in the sense of *or* not uncommonly in CICERO, especially in the *Letters;* occasionally in LIVY, and frequently in TACITUS. Elsewhere it is rare. See 457.

Tiberius cāsū an manibus [Haterii] impedītus prōciderat, TAC., *Ann.*, I. 13, 7; *Tiberius had fallen forward, either by chance or tripped by Haterius' hands.*

Causal and Illative Sentences.

498. A. The Causal particles are **nam, enim, namque,** and **etenim,** *for.*

Nam is put at the beginning of a sentence; **enim** is post-positive (484, R.): **namque** and **etenim** are commonly put in the first place.

Sēnsūs mīrificē conlocātī sunt; nam oculī tamquam speculātōrēs altissimum locum obtinent, C., *N.D.*, II. 56, 140; *the senses are admirably situated; for the eyes, like watchmen, occupy the highest post.* **Piscēs ōva relinquunt, facile enim illa aquā sustinentur,** C., *N.D.*, II. 51, 129; *fish leave their eggs, for they are easily kept alive by the water.* **[Themistoclēs] mūrōs Athēniēnsium restituit suō perīculō; namque Lacedaemoniī prohibēre cōnātī sunt,** NEP., II. 6, 2; *Themistocles restored the walls of Athens with risk to himself; for the Lacedaemonians endeavoured to prevent it.*

NOTES.—1. The Augustan poets postpone both **nam** and **namque** according to the requirements of the metre, and in prose, beginning with LIVY, **namque** is found sometimes in the second place, but more often in LIVY than later.

In early Latin **enim** is often first in the sentence; **etenim** is postponed in prose only in the elder PLINY and APULEIUS; in the poets, not uncommonly, so in AFRANIUS, TIBULLUS, PROPERTIUS, and HORACE.

2. These particles are originally asseverative, and are often used not only to furnish a reason, but also to give an explanation or illustration (*as for instance*). **Quid enim agās?** *what, for instance, can you do?* This is especially true of **enim,** but is also common enough with **nam** (N. 3), and a broad difference between **nam** and **enim** (which is of common origin with **nam**) cannot be proved. **Etenim** is often used to carry on the argument, and gives an additional ground.

3. The asseverative force of **nam** is retained in conversational style occasionally, even in CICERO (*Verr.*, I. 51, 133). **Enim** is almost wholly asseverative in PLAUTUS and TERENCE. **Namque** is very rare in PLAUTUS and TERENCE, and is found before vowels only. In classical Latin it is also rare, and found usually before vowels. With LIVY it comes into general use before vowels and consonants equally. **Etenim** is found but once in PLAUTUS (*Am.*, 26, an interpolation) and four times in TERENCE; in post-classical Latin also it is not common, but it is very frequent in classical Latin, especially in CICERO.

4. Noteworthy is the use of **nam,** in passing over a matter: **nam quid ego dē āctiōne ipsā plūra dīcam?** (C., *O.*, I. 5, 18), which is especially common in CICERO.

5. **Nam** shows an affinity for interrogative particles. Here it sometimes precedes **in**

the early language (TER., *Ph.*, 932), but becomes firmly attached in the classical period in the forms **quisnam, ubinam,** *etc.*, which, however, sometimes suffer tmesis and transposition in poetry (V., *G.*, 4, 445).

6. In **atenim** (first in CICERO), **nempe enim** (ante-classical and post-classical), **sed enim** (rare), **vērumenim, enimvērō, vērum enimvērō,** as in **etenim,** the **enim** gives a ground or an illustration of the leading particle, but translation by an ellipsis would be too heavy, and **enim** is best left untranslated :

A. **Audī quid dīcam.** B. **At enim taedet iam audīre eadem mīliēns,** TER., *Ph.*, 487 ; A. *Hear what I say.* B. *But (I won't, for) I am tired of hearing the same things a thousand times already.*

7. **Enim** is used pleonastically after **quia** in early Latin, and then again in PETRONIUS and GELLIUS ; also after **ut** and **nē** in early Latin.

8. **Quīppe** is originally interrogative. From this the causal force developes, which is not uncommon in CICERO. In SALLUST, and especially in LIVY and later writers, **quīppe** is equal to **enim.**

499. B. Illative particles are **itaque, igitur, ergō ; eō, hinc, inde, ideō, idcircō, quōcircā, propterea, quāpropter, proin, proinde.**

500. Itaque (literally, *and so*), *therefore,* is put at the beginning of the sentence by the best writers, and is used of *facts* that follow from the preceding statement.

Nēmŏ ausus est Phōciōnem līber sepelīre ; itaque ā servīs sepultus est, *Cf.* NEP., XIX. 4, 4; *no free man dared to bury Phocion, and so he was buried by slaves.*

REMARK.—**Itaque** in early and classical Latin has first place in a sentence. It is first postponed by LUCRETIUS, then by CORNIFICIUS and HORACE, and more often later.

501. Igitur, *therefore,* is used of *opinions* which have their natural ground in the preceding statement ; in CICERO it is usually post-positive, in SALLUST never.

Mihĭ nōn satisfacit. Sed quot hominēs tot sententiae ; fallī igitur possumus, C., *Fin.*, I. 5, 15 ; ME *it does not satisfy. But many men many minds. I may therefore be mistaken.*

NOTE.—In historical writers **igitur** is sometimes used like **itaque.** Occasionally also (not in classical Latin), it seems to have the force of **enim** (PL., *Most.*, 1102, MSS.).

502. Ergō denotes *necessary consequence,* and is used especially in arguments, with somewhat more emphasis than **igitur.**

Negat haec fīliam mē suam esse ; nōn ergō haec māter mea est, PL., *Ep.*, 590 ; *she says that I am not her daughter, therefore she is not my mother.*

NOTES.—1. In the Poets **ergō** sometimes introduces a strong conclusion in advance of the premise (H., *O.*, I. 24, 5). In the classical period, however, its predominant use is to introduce the logical conclusion.

2. **Ergō** usually comes first, but its position is apt to vary in accordance with the stress laid upon it.

3. **Itaque ergō** is found in TERENCE and LIVY; **ergō igitur** in PLAUTUS.

503. Other Coördinating Conjunctions: **hinc,** *hence,* is found not unfrequently: **hinc illae lacrumae,** TER., *And.*, 126. **Inde,** *thence, therefore,* is rare, and first in CICERO, but more common in later Latin. **Eō,** *therefore,* is found in early Latin, rarely in CICERO (*Fam.*, VI. 20, 1), not in CAESAR or SALLUST; again in LIVY and later; so **ideō,** *on that account,* but **atque ideō** is found once in CAESAR. **Idcircō,** *on that account,* is rare, but from the earliest times. **Quōcircā,** *on which account,* is found first in the classical period; **quāpropter** is found here and there in early Latin, but more commonly in the classical time, rarely later; **propterea,** *on that account,* is rare, and belongs to early Latin. **Proin, proinde,** *accordingly,* are employed in *exhortations, appeals,* and the like.

Quod praeceptum (nōsce tē ipsum), quia māius erat quam ut ab homine vidērētur, idcircō assīgnātum est deō, C., *Fin.*, V. 16, 44; *this precept (know thyself), because it was too great to seem to be of man, was, on that account, attributed to a god.* **Proinde aut exeant aut quiēscant,** C., *Cat.*, II. 5, 11; *let them then either depart or be quiet.*

SUBORDINATION.

504. Subordinate sentences are only extended forms of the simple sentence, and are divided into *Adjective* and *Substantive* sentences, according as they represent *adjective* and *substantive* relations.

This arrangement is a matter of convenience merely, and no attempt is made to represent the development of the subordinate sentence from the coördinate.

505. Adjective sentences express an attribute of the subject in an expanded form.

Uxor quae bona est, PL., *Merc.*, 812 (624) = **uxor bona.**

506. Substantive sentences are introduced by particles, which correspond in their origin and use to the Oblique Cases, Accusative and Ablative.

These two cases furnish the mass of adverbial relations, and hence we make a subdivision for this class, and the distribution of the subordinate sentence appears as follows:

507. A. Substantive sentences.

I. Object sentences.

II. Adverbial sentences:
1. Of Cause. (Causal.)
2. Of Design and Tendency. (Final and Consecutive.)
3. Of Time. (Temporal.)
4. Of Condition and Concession. (Conditional and Concessive.)

B. Adjective sentences. (Relative.)

Moods in Subordinate Sentences.

508. 1. Final and Consecutive Clauses always take the Subjunctive. Others vary according to their conception. Especially important are the changes produced by **Ōrātiō Oblīqua.**

2. **Ōrātiō Oblīqua,** or *Indirect Discourse,* is opposed to **Ōrātiō Rēcta,** or *Direct Discourse,* and gives the main drift of a speech and not the exact words. **Ōrātiō Oblīqua,** proper, depends on some Verb of Saying or Thinking expressed or implied, the Principal Declarative Clauses being put in the Infinitive, the Dependent in the Subjunctive.

Sōcratēs dīcere solēbat:

Ō. R. Omnēs in eō quod sciunt satis sunt ēloquentēs.
Socrates used to say: "All men ARE *eloquent enough in what they* UNDERSTAND."

Ō. O. Omnēs in eō quod scīrent satis esse ēloquentēs, C., *Or.*, I. 14, 63.
Socrates used to say that all men WERE *eloquent enough in what they* UNDERSTOOD.

3. The oblique relation may be confined to a dependent clause and not extend to the whole sentence. This may be called *Partial Obliquity.*

Ō. R. Nova nūpta dīcit: Fleō quod īre necesse est.
The bride says: I weep because I must needs go.

Ō. O. Nova nūpta dīcit sē flēre quod īre necesse sit.
The bride says that she weeps because she must needs go.

Ō. R. Nova nūpta flet quod īre necesse est, *Cf.* CAT., LXI. 81.
The bride weeps because she must go.

Ō. O. Nova nūpta flet quod īre necesse sit.
The bride is weeping because "she must go" (quoth she).

4. Akin to **Ō. O.** is the so-called Attraction of Mood, by which clauses originally Indicative are put in the Subjunctive because they depend on Infinitives or Subjunctives. (663.)

Nōn dubitō quīn nova nūpta fleat quod īre necesse sit. *I do not doubt that the bride is weeping because she must go.*

REMARK.—The full discussion of Ō. O. must, of course, be reserved for a later period. See 648.

SEQUENCE OF TENSES.

509. 1. In those dependent sentences which require the Subjunctive, the choice of the tenses of the dependent clause is determined largely by the time of the leading or principal clause, so that Principal Tenses are ordinarily followed by Principal Tenses; Historical, by Historical.

NOTE.—As the subordinate sentence arose out of the coördinate, hypotaxis out of parataxis, the tenses of the Subjv. had originally an independent value, and the association was simply the natural association of time. But in some classes of sentences a certain mechanical levelling has taken place, as in the Final sentence; and in others, as in the Interrogative sentence, the range of the Subjv. is restricted by the necessity of clearness, just as the range of the Inf. is restricted by the necessity of clearness (530); so that a conventional Sequence of Tenses has to be recognised. To substitute for every dependent tense a corresponding independent tense, and so do away with the whole doctrine of Sequence, is impossible. At the same time it must be observed that the mechanical rule is often violated by a return to the primitive condition of parataxis, and that

2. This rule is subject to the following modifications:

1. Tense means time, not merely tense-form, so that

(*a*) The Historical Present may be conceived according to its sense (Past) or according to its tense (Present). (229.)

(*b*) In the Pure Perfect may be felt the past inception or origin (Past), or the present completion (Present). (235, 1.)

2. The effect of a past action may be continued into the present or the future of the writer (513).

3. The leading clause may itself consist of a principal and dependent clause, and so give rise to a conflict of tenses with varying Sequence (511, R. 2).

4. An original Subjunctive (467) of the past (265) resists levelling, especially in the Indirect Question.

510.

All forms that relate to the Present and Future (so especially Principal Tenses)	are followed by	the Present Subjunctive (for continued action); the Perfect Subjunctive (for completed action).
All forms that relate to the Past (so especially Historical Tenses)	are followed by	the Imperfect Subjunctive (for continued action); the Pluperfect Subjunctive (for completed action).

REMARK.—The action which is completed with regard to the leading verb may be in itself a continued action. So in English: *I do not know what he has been doing, I did not know what he had been doing.* The Latin is unable to make this distinction, and accordingly the Imperfect Indicative (*I was doing*) is represented in this dependent form by the Perfect and Pluperfect, when the action is completed as to the leading verb.

511.

PR. (PURE OR HIST.),	**cōgnōscō,**	*I am finding out,*	**quid faciās,** *what you are doing;* **quid fēcerīs,** *what you have done, what you have been doing* (*what you did*), *what you were doing* (*before*).
FUT.,	**cōgnōscam,**	*I shall* (try to) *find out,*	
PURE PF.,	**cōgnōvī,**	*I have found out* (*I know*),	
FUT. PF.,	**cōgnōverō,**	*I shall have found out* (*shall know*),	
HIST. PR.,	**cōgnōscō,**	*I am* (*was*) *finding out,*	**quid facerēs,** *what you were doing;* **quid fēcissēs,** *what you had done, what you had been doing, what you were doing* (*before*).
IMPF.,	**cōgnōscēbam,**	*I was finding out,*	
HIST. PF.,	**cōgnōvī,**	*I found out,*	
PLUPF.,	**cōgnōveram,**	*I had found out* (*I knew*),	

When the Subjunctive is original, we have:

cōgnōscō, *etc., I am finding out,*	**quid faciās,**	*what you are to do.*
	quid facerēs,	*what you were to do.*
cōgnōvī, *etc., I knew,*	**quid facerēs,**	*what you were to do.*

Principal Tenses.

Nihil rēfert postrēma syllaba brevis an longa sit, *Cf.* C., *Or.*, 64, 217 (461). **Ubiī (Caesarem) ōrant** (historical) **ut sibī parcat,** CAES., *B.G.*, VI. 9,

7 (546, 1). **Nēmō adeō ferus est ut nōn mītēscere possit**, H., *Ep.*, I. 1, 39 (552). **Nec mea quī digitīs lūmina condat erit**, Ov., *Her.*, 10, 120 (631, 2). **Rūsticus exspectat dum dēfluat amnis**, H., *Ep.*, I. 2, 42 (572). **Post mortem in morte nihil est quod metuam malī**, PL., *Capt.*, 741 (631, 2). **Ārdeat ipsa licet, tormentīs gaudet amantis**, JUV., VI. 209 (607).

Utrum nescīs quam altē ascenderīs an prō nihilō id putās? C., *Fam.*, X. 26, 3 (458). **Laudat Āfricānum Panaetius quod fuerit abstinēns**, C., *Off.*, II. 22, 76 (542). **Nōn is es ut tē pudor umquam ā turpitūdine revocārit**, C., *Cat.*, I. 9, 22 (552). **Quem mea Calliopē laeserit ūnus egō (sum)**, Ov., *Tr.*, II. 568 (631, 1). **Sim licet extrēmum, sīcut sum, missus in orbem**, Ov., *Tr.*, IV. 9, 9 (607). **Multī fuērunt quī tranquillitātem expetentēs ā negōtiīs pūblicīs sē remōverint**, C., *Off.*, I. 20, 69 (631, 2).

Historical Tenses.

Epamīnōndās quaesīvit salvusne esset clipeus, C., *Fin.*, II. 30, 97 (467). **Noctū ambulābat in pūblicō Themistoclēs quod somnum capere nōn posset**, C., *Tusc.*, IV. 19, 44 (541). **[Athēniēnsēs] creant decem praetōrēs quī exercituī praeessent**, NEP., I. 4, 4 (545). **Accidit ut ūnā nocte omnēs Hermae dēicerentur**, NEP., VII. 3, 2 (513, R. 2). **Ad Appī Claudī senectūtem accēdēbat etiam ut caecus esset**, C., *Cat.M.*, 6, 16 (553, 4). **Hannibal omnia priusquam excēderet pūgnā (erat) expertus**, L., XXX. 35, 4 (577). **(Āgēsilāus) cum ex Aegyptō reverterētur dēcēssit**, NEP., XVII. 8, 6 (585).

Tanta opibus Etrūria erat ut iam nōn terrās sōlum sed mare etiam fāmā nōminis suī implēsset, L., I. 2, 5 (521, R. 1). **Cum prīmī ōrdinēs hostium concidissent, tamen ācerrimē reliquī resistēbant**, CAES., *B.G.*, VII. 62, 4 (587). **Dēlēta (est) Ausonum gēns perinde āc sī internecīvō bellō certāsset**, L., IX. 25, 9 (602).

Original Subjunctive Retained.

Ipse docet quid agam (original, **agam**); **fās est et ab hoste docērī**, Ov., *M.*, IV. 428 (219). **Quaerō ā tē cūr ego C. Cornēlium nōn dēfenderem** (original, **dēfenderem**), C., *Vat.*, 2, 5 (467). **Mīsērunt Delphōs cōnsultum quid facerent** (original, **faciāmus**), NEP., II. 2, 6 (518).

REMARKS.—1. The treatment of the Hist. Pr. according to its sense (past) is the rule in classical Latin, especially when the dependent clause precedes. But there are many exceptions.

Agunt grātiās quod sibī pepercissent; quod arma cum hominibus cōnsanguineīs contulerint queruntur, CAES., *B. C.*, I. 74, 2; *they return thanks to them for having spared them, and complain that they had crossed swords with kinsmen.*

2. Noteworthy is the shift from the primary to the secondary sequence; this is mostly confined to clauses of double dependence, *i.e.*, where one subordinate clause is itself principal to a second subordinate clause.

Here the first has usually the primary, the second the secondary sequence.

Rogat ut cūret quod dīxisset, C., *Quinct.*, 5, 18 ; *he asks him to attend to what he had said* (he would).

So of authors :

[Chrȳsippus] disputat aethera esse eum quem hominēs Iovem appellārent, C., *N.D.*, I. 15, 40 ; *Chrysippus maintains that to be ether which men call Jove.*

3. The Pure Pf. is usually treated as a Hist. Pf. in the matter of sequence :

Quae subsidia habērēs et habēre possēs, exposuī, Q. CICERO, 4, 13 ; *what supports you have or can have I have set forth.*

4. The reverse usage, when an Hist. Pf. is followed by a primary Subjv., is not common. Many of those cited from CICERO are from the *Letters*, where the shift of tense might be influenced by the letter-tense principle (252).

Sed quō cōnsiliō redierim, initiō audīstis, post estis expertī, C., *Ph.*, X. 4, 8. **Quis mīles fuit, quī Brundisiī illam nōn vīderit**, C., *Ph.*, II. 25, 61. (The context shows that **fuit** cannot be Pure Pf.)

512. *Sequence of Tenses in Sentences of Design.*—Sentences of Design have, as a rule, only the Present and Imperfect Subjunctive. The Roman keeps the purpose and the process, rather than the attainment, in view.

PR.,	**edunt,**	*they are eating,*	**ut vīvant,** *that they may live* (to live).
PURE PF.,	**ēdērunt,**	*they have eaten,*	
FUT.,	**edent,**	*they will eat,*	
FUT. PF.,	**ēderint,**	*they will have eaten,*	
IMPF.,	**edēbant,**	*they were eating,*	**ut vīverent,** *that they might live* (to live).
PLUPF.,	**ēderant,**	*they had eaten,*	
HIST. PF.,	**ēdērunt,**	*they ate,*	

Spectātum veniunt, veniunt spectentur ut ipsae, Ov., *A.A.*, I. 99 (435). **Sed precor ut possim tūtius esse miser**, Ov., *Tr.*, V. 2, 78 (424). **Gallīnae pennīs fovent pullōs nē frīgore laedantur**, *Cf.* C., *N.D.*, II. 52, 129 (545). **Lēgem brevem esse oportet quō facilius ab imperītīs teneātur**, SEN., *E.M.*, 94, 38 (545). **Mē praemīsit domum haec ut nūntiem uxōrī suae**, PL., *Am.*, 195 ; *he has sent me home ahead of him, to take the news to his wife.* **Oculōs ecfodiam tibī nē mē observāre possīs**, PL., *Aul.*, 53 ; *I will gouge out your eyes for you, to make it impossible for you to watch me.*

[Laelius] veniēbat ad cēnam ut satiāret dēsīderia nātūrae, C., *Fin.* II. 8, 25 ; *Laelius used to go to table, to satisfy the cravings of nature.* **(Phaëthōn) optāvit ut in currum patris tollerētur**, C., *Off.*, III. 25, 94 (546, 1).

REMARK.—Parenthetical final sentences like **ut ita dīcam, nē errētis,** are really dependent on the thought or utterance of the speaker, and have the present sequence everywhere.

Nē longior sim, valē, C., *Fam.*, XV. 19; *not to be tedious, farewell!* **Nē tamen īgnōrēs, virtūte Nerōnis Armenius cecidit,** H., *Ep.*, I. 12, 25; *but that you may not fail to know it, it was by the valour of Nero that the Armenian fell.*

NOTES.—1. The Pf. and Plupf. Subjv. are sometimes found in sentences of Design, chiefly in earlier and later Latin (no example is cited from CAESAR or SALLUST), when stress is laid on completion, or when an element of Hope or Fear comes in: **Ut sīc dīxerim** (first found in QUINT.), *if I may be allowed to use the expression.*

Affīrmāre audeō mē omnī ope adnīsūrum esse nē frūstrā vōs hanc spem dē mē concēperītis, L., XLIV. 22; *I dare assure you that I will strain every nerve to keep you from having conceived this hope of me in vain.* (After a past tense, **nē concēpissētis.**) **Nunc agendum est nē frūstrā oppressum esse Antōnium gāvīsī sīmus,** C., *ad Br.*, I. 4, 3. **Hīc obsistam, nē imprūdentī hūc ea sē subrēpsit** (131, 4, *b.* 2) **mihī,** PL., *M.G.*, 333. **Effēcit nē cūius alterīus sacrilegium rēs pūblica quam Nerōnis sēnsisset,** TAC., *Agr.*, 6.

When the tense is compound, the participle is usually to be considered as a mere adjective.

Patrōnus extitī utī nē [Sex. Rōscius] omnīnō dēsertus esset, C., *Rosc.Am.*, 2, 5; where **dēsertus = sōlus.**

2. Occasional apparent exceptions are to be explained in various ways. Thus, in C., *Sest.*, 14, 32: **etiamne ēdīcere audeās nē maerērent,** we have a repetition as an indignant question of the preceding statement: **ēdīcunt** (Hist. Pr.) **duo cōnsulēs ut ad suum vestītum senātōres redīrent.**

513. *Exceptional Sequence of Tenses:—Sentences of Result (Consecutive Sentences).* In Sentences of Result, the Present Subjunctive is used after Past Tenses to denote the continuance into the Present, the Perfect Subjunctive to imply final result. This Perfect Subjunctive may represent either the Pure Perfect or Aorist, the latter especially with the negative: the action happened once for all or not at all.

Present Tense:

[Siciliam Verrēs] per triennium ita vexāvit ut ea restituī in antīquum statum nūllō modō possit, C., *Verr.*, I. 4, 12; *Verres so harried Sicily for three years as to make it utterly impossible for it to be restored to its original condition.* **In [Lūcullō] tanta prūdentia fuit ut hodiē stet Asia,** C., *Ac.*, II. 1, 3; *Lucullus's forethought was so great that Asia stands firm to-day.*

Perfect Tense (Pure):

(Mūrēna) Asiam sīc obiit ut in eā neque avāritiae neque lūxuriae vēstīgium relīquerit, C., *Mur.*, 9, 20; *Murena so administered Asia as not to have* (*that he has not*) *left in it a trace either of greed or debauchery* (there is no trace there).

Perfect Tense (Aorist):

Equitēs hostium ācriter cum equitātū nostrō cōnflīxērunt, tamen ut nostrī eōs in silvās collēsque compulerint, CAES., *B.G.*, V. 15, 1; *the cavalry of the enemy engaged the cavalry on our side briskly, and yet* (the upshot was that) *our men forced them into the woods and hills.* **Neque vērō tam remissō āc languidō animō quisquam omnium fuit quī eā nocte conquiēverit,** CAES., *B.C.*, I. 21, 5; *and indeed there was no one at all of so slack and indifferent a temper as to take (a wink of) sleep that night.*

REMARKS.—1. After a Pure Pf., if the dependent clause is affirmative, CICERO prefers the Impf. (he has but five cases of Pf.); if negative the Pf. (in the proportion 2 to 1).

2. After **accidit, contigit,** and other verbs of Happening, the Impf. is always used, the result being already emphasised in the Indic. form.

Accidit ut ūnā nocte omnēs Hermae dēicerentur, NEP., VII., 3, 2; *it happened that in one night all the Hermae were thrown down.*

NOTES.—1. The use of the Aoristic Pf. Subjv. after an Aoristic Pf. Indic. seems to have been an attempt of the Romans to replace the consecutive Aor. Inf. in Greek with ὥστε. Examples are not found in early Latin, are rare in CICERO, very rare in CAESAR, perhaps not at all in SALLUST; more frequent in LIVY, common in TACITUS, very common in NEPOS and SUETONIUS, *etc.*

2. In two coördinated clauses depending on the same verb we find the tenses occasionally varying. The Pf. in the first subordinate, with Impf. in the second, is doubtful in any case, rare in CICERO, and is cited but once each from CAESAR (*B.G.*, VII. 17) and VELLEIUS (I. 9, 1). The reverse construction, Impf. followed by Pf., is more common, but found first (though rarely) in LIVY, and belongs mainly to late Latin.

Zēnō nūllō modō is erat quī nervōs virtūtis inciderit, sed contrā quī omnia in virtūte pōneret, C., *Ac.*, I. 10, 35. Here the shift is due to the negative. **Tantus pavor omnēs occupāvit ut nōn modo alius quisquam arma caperet—sed etiam ipse rēx perfūgerit,** L., XXIV. 40, 12. Here the tenses depend on the ideas of continuance and completion, of the many and the single (**nōn capiēbant—rēx perfūgit**).

3. In relative sentences of coincident action with causal coloring, either the coincidence is retained, or a principal clause in the Past is followed by the Impf. Subjunctive.

Tū hūmānissimē fēcistī quī mē certiōrem fēcerīs, C., *Att.*, XIII. 43, 1. **Cum hōc Pompēius vehementer ēgit cum dīceret,** *etc.*, C., *Att.*, II. 22, 2. **Videor mihi grātum fēcisse Siculīs, quod eōrum iniūriās sim persecūtus,** C., *Verr.*, II. 6, 15 (518, R.).

Representation of the Subjunctive in the Future and Future Perfect Tenses.

514. The Subjunctive has no Future or Future Perfect, which are represented either by the other Subjunctives, or in the Active by the Subjunctive of the Periphrastic Conjugation.

RULE I.—(*a*) After a Future or Future Perfect Tense, the Future relation (contemporary with the leading Future) is represented by the Present Subjunctive; the Future Perfect (prior to the leading Future) by the Perfect Subjunctive, according to the rule.

Cōgnōscam, *I shall* (try to) *find out*, } **quid faciās,** *what you are doing* (will be doing).
Cōgnōverō, *I shall have found out* (shall know), } **quid fēcerīs,** *what you have done* (will have done).

(*b*) But whenever the dependent Future is subsequent to the leading Future, the Periphrastic Tense must be employed.

Cōgnōscam, *I shall* (try to) *find out*,
Cōgnōverō, *I shall have found out* (shall know), } **quid factūrus sīs,** *what you are going to do* (what you will do).

[**Cōnsīderābimus**], [*we shall consider*].

A. **Quid fēcerit aut quid ipsī acciderit aut quid dīxerit,** *what he has done, or what has happened to him, or what he has said.*

B. **Aut quid faciat, quid ipsī accidat, quid dīcat,** *or, what he is doing, what is happening to him, what he is saying.*

C. **Aut quid factūrus sit, quid ipsī cāsūrum sit, quā sit ūsūrus ōrātiōne,** C., *Inv.*, I. 25, 36; *or what he is going to do* (will do), *what is going to* (will) *happen to him, what plea he is going to employ* (will employ).

Tū quid sīs āctūrus pergrātum erit sī ad mē scrīpserīs, C., *Fam.*, IX. 2, 5; *it will be a great favour if you will write to me what you are going to do.*

REMARK.—In some of these forms ambiguity is unavoidable. So A may represent a real Perfect, B a real Present.

515. RULE II.—After the other tenses, the Future relation is expressed by the Active Periphrastic Subjunctive, Present or Imperfect.

Cōgnōscō, *I am finding out*,
Cōgnōvī, *I have found out* (know), } **quid factūrus sīs** (*what you are going to do*), *what you will do.*

Cōgnōscēbam, *I was trying to find out*,
Cōgnōveram, *I had found out*, } **quid factūrus essēs** (*what you were going to do*), *what you would do.*

Tam ea rēs est facilis ut innumerābilīs nātūra mundōs effectūra sit, efficiat, effēcerit, *Cf.* C., *N.D.*, I. 21, 53; *the thing is so easy that nature will make, is making, has made, innumerable worlds.*

Incertum est quam longa cūiusque nostrum vīta futūra sit, C., *Verr.*, I. 58, 153; *it is uncertain how long the life of each one of us is going to be* (will be).

Anteā dubitābam ventūraene essent legiōnēs; nunc mihī nōn est dubium quīn ventūrae nōn sint, C., *Fam.*, II. 17, 5; *before, I was doubtful whether the legions would come* (or no); *now I have no doubt that they will not come.*

REMARKS.—1. The Pf. and Plupf. Subjv. of the Periphrastic are used only to represent the Apodosis of an Unreal Conditional Sentence.

Cōgnōscō, *I am finding out,*	**Cōgnōvī,** *I have found out* (know),	**quid factūrus fuerīs,** *what you would have done,*	(*what you have been going to do*).
Cōgnōscēbam, *I was trying to find out,*	**Cōgnōveram,** *I had found out,*	[**quid factūrus fuissēs,** *what you would have done,* rare.]	(*what you had been going to do*).

2. There is no Periphrastic for the Fut. Pf. active, no Periphrastic for passive and Supineless Verbs. The Grammars make up a Periphrastic for all these from **futūrum sit, esset ut,** as:

Nōn dubitō quīn futūrum sit, *I do not doubt*
- **ut redierit,** *that he will have returned.*
- **ut maereat,** *that he will grieve.*
- **ut necētur,** *that he will be killed.*

But there is no warrant in actual usage.

For the dependent Fut. Pf. act. TERENCE says (*Hec.*, 618): **Tuā rēfert nīl utrum illaec fēcerint quandō haec aberit.**

For the dependent Fut. Pf. pass. CICERO says (*Fam.*, VI. 12, 3): **Nec dubitō quīn cōnfecta rēs futūra sit,** *nor do I doubt but the matter will have been settled.*

In the absence of the Periphrastic forms, use the proper tenses of **posse.** (248, R.)

3. When the preceding verb has a future character (Fear, Hope, Power, Will, and the like), the simple Subjv. is sufficient.

Gallī, nisi perfrēgerint mūnītiōnēs, dē omnī salūte dēspērant; Rōmānī, sī rem obtinuerint, fīnem labōrum omnium exspectant, CAES., *B.G.*, VII. 85, 3; *the Gauls despair of all safety unless they break through (shall have broken through) the fortifications; the Romans look forward to an end of all their toils, if they hold their own (shall have held).* **Vēnērunt querentēs nec spem ūllam esse resistendī, nisi praesidium Rōmānus mīsisset,** L., XXXIV. 11, 2; *they came with the complaint that there was no hope of resistance unless the Roman sent a force to protect them.* **Intentī quandō hostis inprūdentiā rueret,** TAC., *H.*, II. 34.

Of course the Deliberative Subjunctive is future: Examples, 265.

Et certāmen habent lētī, quae vīva sequātur cōniugium, PROP., IV. 12, 19 (M.).

516. *Sequence of Tenses in* **Ōrātiō Oblīqua**: In **Ōrātiō Oblīqua** and kindred constructions, the attraction of tenses applies also to the representatives of the Future and Future Perfect Subjunctive.

In [clāvā] erat scrīptum nisi domum reverterētur sē capitis eum damnātūrōs, NEP., IV. 3, 4; *it was written on the staff that if he did not return home, they would condemn him to death.* (**Ōrātiō Rēcta: nisi domum revertēris, tē capitis damnābimus,** *unless you* (shall) *return home, we will condemn you to death*). **Pȳthia praecēpit ut Miltiadem sibĭ imperātōrem sūmerent; id sī fēcissent (Ō. R., fēcerĭtis) incepta prōspera futūra (Ō. R., erunt),** NEP., I. 1, 3; *the Pythia instructed them to take Miltiades for their general; that if they did that, their undertakings would be successful.* **Lacedaemoniī, Philippō minitante per lītterās sē omnia quae cōnārentur (Ō. R., cōnābiminī) prohibitūrum, quaesīvērunt num sē esset etiam morī prohibitūrus (Ō. R., prohibēbis),** C., *Tusc.*, V. 14, 42; *the Lacedaemonians, when Philip threatened them by letter that he would prevent everything they undertook (should undertake), asked whether he was going to (would) prevent them from dying too.*

517. *Sequence of Tenses after the other Moods.*—The Imperative and the Present and Perfect Subjunctive have the Sequences of the Principal Tenses; the Imperfect and Pluperfect have the Sequences of the Historical Tenses.

[Nē] compōne comās quia sīs ventūrus ad illam, OV., *Rem. Am.*, 679; *do not arrange (your) locks because* (forsooth) *you are going to see her.* **Excellentibus ingeniīs citius dēfuerit ars quā cīvem regant quam quā hostem superent,** L., II. 43, 10; *great geniuses would be more likely to lack the skill to control the citizen than the skill to overcome the enemy.* **Quid mē prohibēret Epicūrēum esse, sī probārem quae ille dīceret?** C., *Fin.*, I. 8, 27; *what would prevent me from being an Epicurean if I approved what he said* (says)? **Tum ego tē prīmus hortārer diū pēnsitārēs quem potissimum ēligerēs,** PLIN., *Ep.*, IV. 15, 8; *in that case I should be the first to exhort you to weigh long whom you should choose above all others.* **Quae vīta fuisset Priamō sī ab adulēscentiā scīsset quōs ēventūs senectūtis esset habitūrus?** C., *Div.*, II. 9, 22; *what sort of life would Priam have led if he had known, from early manhood, what were to be the closing scenes of his old age?*

REMARKS.—1. Of course, when the Pf. Subjv. represents an Historical Tense, it takes the historical Sequence:

Māgna culpa Pelopis quī nōn docuerit fīlium quātenus esset quidque cūrandum, C., *Tusc.*, I. 44, 107; *greatly to blame is Pelops for not having taught his son how far each thing was to be cared for.* **Quī scīs an eā causā mē ōdisse adsimulāverit, ut cum mātre plūs ūnā esset?** TER., *Hec.*, 235; *how do you know but she has pretended to hate me in order to be more with her (own) mother?*

So also in the Conditional proposition, when the action is past. For varying conception, see C., *Off.*, III. 24, 92.

2. The Impf. Subjv., being used in opposition to the Present, might be treated as a Principal Tense, but the construction is less usual :

Verērer nē immodicam ōrātiōnem putārēs nisi esset generis ēius ut saepe incipere saepe dēsinere videātur, PLIN., *Ep.*, IX. 4, 1; *I should be afraid of your thinking the speech of immoderate length, if it were not of such kind as to produce the effect of often beginning, often ending.* **Ō ego nē possim tālēs sentīre dolōrēs quam māllem in gelidīs montibus esse lapis!** TIB., II. 4, 7.

518. *Sequence of Tenses after an Infinitive or Participle.* —When a subordinate clause depends on an Infinitive or Participle, Gerund or Supine, the tense of that clause follows the tense of the Finite verb, if the Finite verb is Past; if the Finite verb is Present, it follows the tense that the dependent verb would have had, if it had been independent.

Dīcit sē interrogāre (original **interrogō**), *He says that he is asking,*	**quid agās,** **quid ēgerīs,** **quid āctūrus sīs,**	*what you are doing.* *what you have done.* *what you are going to do* (will do).
Dīcit sē interrogāsse (original **interrogāvī**), *He says that he asked,* **Dīxit sē interrogāre** (original **interrogō**), *He said that he was asking,*	**quid agerēs,** **quid ēgissēs,** **quid āctūrus essēs,**	*what you were doing.* *what you had done.* *what you were going to do* (would do).

Mihī interrogantī, *when I ask him,* (literally : *to me asking*),	**quid agat,** **quid ēgerit,** **quid āctūrus sit,**	*what he is doing,* *what he has done,* *what he is going to do* (will do),	**nōn respondet,** *he gives no answer.*
Mihī interrogantī, *when I asked him,* (literally : *to me asking*),	**quid ageret,** **quid ēgisset,** **quid āctūrus esset,**	*what he was doing,* *what he had done,* *what he was going to do,*	**nōn respondit,** *he gave no answer.*

Apud Hypanim fluvium Aristotelēs ait bēstiolās quāsdam nāscī quae ūnam diem vīvant, C., *Tusc.*, I. 39, 94 (650). **Satis mihī multa verba fēcisse videor quārē esset hōc bellum necessārium,** C., *Imp.*, 10, 27; *I think I have said enough* (to show) *why this war* IS *necessary.* **Apellēs pictōrēs eōs**

peccāre dīcēbat quī nōn sentīrent quid esset satis, C., *Or.*, 22, 73; *Apelles used to say that those painters blundered who did not perceive what was* (is) *enough.* **Athēniēnsēs Cyrsilum quendam suādentem ut in urbe manērent lapidibus obruērunt,** C., *Off.*, III. 11, 48 (546). **Cupīdō incēssit animōs iuvenum scīscitandī ad quem eōrum rēgnum Rōmānum esset ventūrum,** L., I. 56, 10; *the minds of the young men were seized by the desire of inquiring to which of them the kingdom of Rome would come.* **Mīsērunt Delphōs cōnsultum quid facerent,** Nep., II. 2, 6; *they sent to Delphi to ask the oracle what they should do.* See 265.

Remark.—Nevertheless examples are not unfrequent where the sequence of the governing verb is retained: **Videor mihī grātum fēcisse Siculīs quod eōrum iniūriās meō perīculō sim persecūtus,** C., *Verr.*, II. 6, 15; *I seem to have pleased the Sicilians, in that I have followed up their injuries at my own risk* (on account of the coincidence, 513, n. 3).

519. *Original Subjunctives in Dependence.*—1. The Potential of Present or Future after a Past tense goes into the Past; the same is true of Deliberative Questions (465). On the other hand, the Potential of the Past must be retained even after a Present tense (467).

Videō causās esse permultās quae [Titum Rōscium] impellerent, C., *Rosc. Am.*, 33, 92; *I see that there are very many causes which might have impelled Titus Roscius.* **Quaerō ā tē cūr Gāium Cornēlium nōn dēfenderem,** C., *Vat.*, 2, 5 (467).

2. On the behaviour of Conditional Subjunctives in dependence see 597, r. 4.

Remark.—The Sequence of Tenses is not unfrequently deranged by the attraction of parenthetic clauses or, especially in long sentences, by the shifting of the conception. Examples are C., *Balb.*, I. 2; *Ph.*, III. 15, 39; *Ac.*, II. 18, 56, and many others.

USE OF THE REFLEXIVE IN SUBORDINATE SENTENCES.

520. In subordinate clauses, the Reflexive is used with reference either to the subject of the principal, or to the subject of the subordinate, clause; and sometimes first to the one and then to the other.

521. The Reflexive is used of the principal subject when reference is made to the thought or will of that subject; hence, in Infinitive Sentences, in Indirect Questions, in Sentences of Design, and in Sentences which partake of the Oblique Relation.

Sentit animus sē vī suā, nōn aliēnā movērī, C., *Tusc.*, I. 23, 55; *the mind feels that it moves by its own force,* (and) *not by that of another.* **Quaesīvērunt num sē esset etiam morī prohibitūrus,** C., *Tusc.*, V. 14, 42 (516). **Pompēius ā mē petīvit ut sēcum et apud sē essem cottīdiē,** *Cf.* C., *Att.*, V. 6, 1; *Pompey asked me to be with him, and at his house, daily.* **Paetus omnēs librōs quōs frāter suus relīquisset mihī dōnāvit,** C., *Att.*, II. 1, 12; *Paetus presented to me all the books* (as he said) *that his brother had left* (**quōs frāter ēius relīquerat,** would be the statement of the narrator).

REMARKS.—1. Sentences of Tendency and Result have forms of **is**, when the subj. is not the same as that of the leading verb; otherwise the Reflexive:

Tarquinius sīc Servium dīligēbat ut is ēius vulgō habērētur fīlius, C., *Rep.* II. 21, 38; *Tarquin loved Servius so that he was commonly considered his son.* But **Tanta opibus Etrūria erat ut iam nōn terrās sōlum sed mare etiam fāmā nōminis suī implēsset,** L., I. 2, 5; *so great in means* (= *so powerful*) *was Etruria that she had already filled not only the land, but even the sea, with the reputation of her name.*

2. The Reflexive may refer to the real agent, and not to the grammatical subj. of the principal clause. (309, 2.)

Ā Caesare invītor sibī ut sim lēgātus, C., *Att.*, II. 18, 3; *I am invited by Caesar* (= Caesar invites me) *to be lieutenant to him.*

Especially to be noted is the freer use of **suus** (309, 4). The other forms are employed chiefly in reflexive formulæ (309, 3), as **sē recipere,** *to withdraw, etc.*

(**Rōmānī**) **suī colligendī hostibus facultātem** (**nōn**) **relinquunt,** CAES., *B.G.*, III. 6, 1 (309, 3).

3. The Reflexive is used in general sentences, as *one, one's self, etc.* (309, 1): **Dēfōrme est dē sē ipsum praedicāre,** C., *Off.*, I. 38, 137; *it is unseemly to be bragging about one's self.*

With the Inf. this follows naturally from 420.

4. In Indic. relative sentences, which are mere circumlocutions (505), **is** is the rule:

Sōcratēs inhonestam sibī crēdidit ōrātiōnem quam eī Lȳsiās reō composuerat, QUINT., II. 15, 30; *Socrates believed the speech which Lysias had composed for him when he was arraigned, dishonoring to him.*

Sometimes, however, the Reflexive is put contrary to the rule:

Metellus in iīs urbibus quae ad sē dēfēcerant praesidia impōnit, S., *Iug.*, 61, 1; *Metellus put garrisons in those towns which had gone over to him;* regularly, **ad eum.**

Ille habet quod sibī dēbēbātur, PETR., 43, 1; *he has his due;* regularly, **eī.**

5. Sometimes the Demonstrative is used instead of the Reflexive, because the narrator presents his point of view:

Solōn, quō tūtior vīta ēius esset, furere sē simulāvit, C., *Off.*, I. 30, 108; *Solon feigned madness that his life might be the safer.* (The notion of Result intrudes.) **Pompēius īgnēs fierī prohibuit, quō occultior esset ēius adventus,** CAES., *B.C.*, III. 30, 5; *Pompey forbade fires to be kindled in order that his approach might be the better concealed.*

NOTES.—1. Occasionally, principally in early Latin, the Reflexive seems to be used with the force merely of a third personal pronoun:

Vītis sī macra erit, sarmenta sua concīditō minūtē, CATO, *Agr.*, 37, 3.

But sentences like **eum fēcisse āiunt quod sibi faciundum fuit** (PL., *Poen.*, 956), where the relative clause is but a circumlocution for **officium suom**, belong properly under R. 4. Similarly, C., *Inv.*, I. 33, 55. In the sentence, **Cicerō tibĭ mandat, ut Aristodēmō idem dē sē respondeās quod dē frātre suō respondistī** (C., *Att.*, II. 7, 5), **dē frātre ēius** would jar on account of the **sē** to which it refers.

2. Examples of Reflexives pointing both ways:

[Rōmānī] lēgātōs mīsērunt quī ā [Prūsiā] peterent nē inimīcissimum suum (= Rōmānōrum) apud sē (= Prūsiam) habēret, NEP., XXIII. 12, 2; *the Romans sent ambassadors to ask Prusias not to keep their bitterest enemy at his court.* **Agrippa Atticum flēns ōrābat atque obsecrābat ut sē sibĭ suīsque reservāret,** *Cf.* NEP., XXV. 22, 2; *Agrippa begged and conjured Atticus with tears to save himself* [Atticus] *for him* [Agrippa] *and for his own family* [Atticus].

Hopeless ambiguity:

Hērēs meus dare illī damnās estō omnia sua, QUINT., VII. 9, 12; *my heir is to give him all that is his.*

3. For the sake of clearness, the subj. of the leading sentence is not unfrequently referred to in the form of the Demonstrative instead of the Reflexive:

(Helvētiī) Allobrogibus sēsē vel persuāsūrōs exīstimābant vel vī coāctūrōs ut per suōs fīnēs eōs īre paterentur, CAES., *B.G.*, I. 6, 3; *the Helvetians thought that they would persuade or force the Allobroges to let them* [the Helvetians] *go through their territory.*

4. **Ipse** is always used in its proper distinctive sense; so, when it represents the speaker in **Ō. O.** (660.)

Ēius and Suī.

522. **Alexander moriēns ānulum suum dederat Perdiccae,** NEP., XVIII. 2, 1; *Alexander,* [when] *dying, had given his ring to Perdiccas.*

Perdiccās accēperat ēius ānulum, *Perdiccas had received his ring.*

Quārē Alexander dēclārāverat sē rēgnum eī commendāsse, *thereby, Alexander had declared that he had committed the kingdom to him.*

Ex quō Perdiccās coniēcerat eum rēgnum sibĭ commendāsse, *from this Perdiccas had gathered that he had committed the kingdom to him.*

Ex quō omnēs coniēcerant eum rēgnum eī commendāsse, *from this, all had gathered that he had committed the kingdom to him.*

Perdiccās pōstulāvit ut sē rēgem habērent cum Alexander ānulum sibĭ dedisset, *Perdiccas demanded that they should have him for king, as Alexander had given the ring to him.*

Amīcī pōstulāvērunt ut omnēs eum rēgem habērent cum Alexander ānu-

lum eī dedisset, (his) *friends demanded that all should have him for king, as Alexander had given the ring to him.* (Lattmann and Müller.)

Ita sē gesserat Perdiccās ut eī rēgnum ab Alexandrō commendārētur, *Perdiccas had so behaved himself that the kingdom was intrusted to him by Alexander.*

OBJECT SENTENCES.

523. Verbs of Doing, Perceiving, Conceiving, of Thinking and Saying, often take their object in the form of a sentence.

Notes.—1. These sentences are regarded, grammatically, as neuter substantives. The Accusative of neuter substantives is employed as a Nominative. Hence, a passive or intransitive verb may take an object sentence as a subject.

2. To object sentences belong also Dependent Interrogative clauses, which have been treated elsewhere for convenience of reference. See 452, I, N., 460, 467.

I. Object Sentences introduced by QUOD.

524. Clauses which serve merely as periphrases (circumlocutions) or expansions of elements in the leading sentence are introduced by **quod,** *that.*

Notes.—1. This usage seems to be in origin explanatory; that is, a demonstrative in the leading clause is explained by the **quod** clause. But as the relative can always include the antecedent demonstrative, the prevailing usage is without an antecedent. In any case, however, the connection is essentially relative.

2. The original relation of **quod** and its antecedent is adverbial. They are Accusatives of Extent, *that = in that,* and are to be classed under the Inner Object (332). But after transitive verbs **quod** and its antecedent are felt as Outer Objects, though whenever the notion of Cause intrudes (*in that = because*), the original relation comes back, as in causal sentences proper.

3. The antecedent demonstrative (whether omitted or inserted) would therefore be either the direct object of the verb or it would be in adverbial or prepositional relation. We have then two uses of the explanatory clause; (*a*) with *verbs,* with or without an antecedent demonstrative; (*b*) as explanatory of an *antecedent* (expressed or implied) in adverbial relation to the verb or dependent upon a preposition.

525. I. **Quod** (*the fact that, the circumstance that, in that*) is used to introduce explanatory clauses, after verbs of Adding and Dropping, and after verbs of Doing and Happening with an adverb.

Adde hūc quod perferrī lītterae nūllā condiciōne potuērunt, Pollio (C., *Fam.*, X. 31, 4); *add to this the fact that letters could under no circumstances be got through.* **Adde quod ingenuās didicisse fidēliter artēs ēmollit mōrēs nec sinit esse ferōs,** Ov., *Pont.*, II. 9, 47; *add* (*the fact*) *that to have acquired faithfully the accomplishments* (*education*) *of a gentleman, softens the character, and does not let it be savage.* **Praetereō quod**

eam sibī domum dēlēgit, C., *Cluent.*, 66, 188; *I pass over the fact that he chose that house for himself.* **Bene facis quod mē adiuvās**, C., *Fin.*, III. 4, 16; *you do well* (in) *that you help me.* **Accidit perincommodē quod eum nūsquam vīdistī**, C., *Att.*, I. 17, 2; *it happened very unfortunately that you saw him nowhere.* **Bene mihī ēvenit quod mittor ad mortem**, C., *Tusc.*, I. 41, 97; *it is fortunate for me that I am sent to death* (*execution*).

NOTES.—1. Of verbs of Adding **adicere** is introduced by LIVY, **addere** is cited once each from ACCIUS (209, R.) and TERENCE (*Ph.*, 168), then more often from LUCRETIUS, HORACE, and OVID, but not from CICERO and VERGIL. **Accēdere** is the passive of **addere** and occurs at all periods. Of verbs of Dropping, only **praetereō, mittō,** and **omittō** (C., *Att.*, VIII. 3, 3) are cited (all classical).

2. **Esse** is found mostly in the combinations **quid (hōc) est quod,** *why is it that, this is why*, which are confined to early Latin: **Scīn quid est quod ego ad tē veniō?** PL., *Men.*, 677; **hōc est quod ad vōs veniō,** PL., *St.*, 127. **Est quod, nihil est quod,** *etc.*, occur here and there later, but the effect of the negative on the mood is noteworthy. Compare positive **sed est quod suscēnset tibī** (TER., *And.*, 448); *there is something that makes him angry with you*, with negative **nihil est iam quod mihi suscēnseās** (PL., *Merc.*, 317); *there is nothing to make you angry with me.*

3. To this group belongs the exclamatory interrogation **Quid? quod,** or **quid quod ——?** *what of this, that?*

Quid quod simulāc mihī collibitum est praestō est imāgō? C., *N.D.*, I. 38, 108; *what is to be said of the fact that the image presents itself as soon as I see fit?* (*Nay, does not the image present itself?*)

4. The use of **quod** after verbs of Doing and Happening is found first in CICERO: PLAUTUS uses **quia** in this construction.

5. With several of the above-mentioned verbs **ut** can be employed, as well as **quod** (**ut,** of the tendency—**quod,** of the fact):

Ad Appī Claudī senectūtem accēdēbat ut etiam caecus esset, C., *Cat.M.*, 6, 16 (553, 4), or, **quod caecus erat. Accēdit quod patrem plūs etiam quam ipse scit amō,** C., *Att.*, XIII. 21, 7; *besides, I love the father even more than he himself knows.*

But when the action is prospective or conditional, **ut** must be used:

Additur ad hanc dēfīnītiōnem ā Zēnōne rēctē ut illa opīniō praesentis malī sit recēns, C., *Tusc.*, III. 31, 75.

6. **Quod** with verbs of Motion as an adverbial Acc. is confined to early Latin and to **veniō** (PL., *Men.*, 677) and **mittō** (PL., *Ps.*, 639).

7. The extension of **quod** to **verba sentiendī et dīcendī** is very unusual. One example in early Latin (PL., *Asin.*, 52) is much disputed; suspicious examples are C., *Fam.*, III. 8, 6; CAES., *B.C.*, I. 23, 3, but a certain example is in *b.Hisp.* (10, 2), **renūntiārunt quod habērent.** The only case in Augustan poets is V., *A.*, IX. 289; it is doubtful in LIVY; perhaps twice in TACITUS (*Ann.*, III. 54; XIV. 6). In later Latin, from PETRONIUS on, it becomes frequent.

2. **Quod** (*in that, as to the fact that*) is used to introduce explanatory clauses after demonstratives (expressed or implied), independent of the leading verb. See 627, R. 2.

Mihī quidem videntur hominēs hāc rē māximē bēstiīs praestāre, quod loquī possunt, C., *Inv.*, I. 4: *to me men seem to excel beasts most in this, that they have the power of speech.* **Praeterquam quod fierī nōn potuit, nē fingī quidem potest,** C., *Div.*, II. 12, 28; *besides the fact that this could not be done, it could not even be made up.* **Nīl habet īnfēlīx paupertās**

dūrius in sē quam quod (= **id quod**) **rīdiculōs hominēs facit**, Juv., III. 152; *unhappy poverty hath in itself nothing harder (to bear) than that it makes people ridiculous.* **Māgnum beneficium** [**est**] **nātūrae quod necesse est morī**, Sen., *E.M.*, 101, 14 (204). **Quod spīrō et placeō, sī placeō, tuum est**, H., *O.*, IV. 3, 24; *that I do breathe and please, if that I please, is thine.*

Notes.—1. In early usage the antecedent is not common, but it is employed very often by Cicero, for the purposes of argument.

2. Prepositional usages with the Abl. are **ex eō, dē eō, in eō, prō eō, cum eō quod.** Of these **cum eō quod,** *with the proviso that,* is very rare, occurring but once in Cicero (*Att.*, VI. 1, 7). The prepositional usages with the Acc. are **ad id quod** (only in Livy); **super id quod** (only in Tacitus); **praeter quod** (Florus and late writers); **prae quod** (Plautus only). Similar is **exceptō quod** (Hor., Quint.). As **praeter** and **super** are comparative in force, we find **praeter quam quod** (early Latin, Cic., and later), **super quam quod** (only in Livy). Similar to **praeter quod** is **nisi quod** (Plaut., Cicero [not *Orations*], Sall., Livy, and later). **Tantum quod** = **nisi quod,** once in Cicero (*Verr.*, I. 45, 116) and is rare; **tantum quod,** temporal, "just," is colloquial, and found first in Cicero's *Letters*, then not till the post-Augustan period.

3. **Quod,** "*as to the fact that,*" is combined also with the Subjv. in early Latin: **quod ille gallīnam sē sectārī dīcat,** *etc.* (Pl., *M.G.*, 162). This is explained as being the Potential Subjv., inasmuch as all the examples cited involve supposed statements or actions of a second or third (often indefinite) person, which the speaker merely wishes to anticipate. The usage is occasional, also, later: C., *Pis.*, 27, 66; *Verr.*, V. 68, 175, and sporadically in Fronto and Gaius. Sometimes the idea of Partial Obliquity enters, as in C., *Br.*, 18, 73, **quod aequālis fuerit Līvius, minor fuit aliquantō**; *Inv.*, II. 29, 89, (reading doubtful).

In general the usage of **quod,** "*as to the fact that,*" is familiar. Cicero uses it often in his *Letters*. But Caesar is fond of it too. Tacitus has it but once (*Dial.*, 25).

3. The reigning mood is the Indicative. The Subjunctive is only used as in **Ōrātiō Oblīqua.**

Cum Castam accūsārem nihil magis pressī quam quod accūsātor ēius praevāricātiōnis crīmine corruisset, Plin., *Ep.*, III. 9, 34; *when I accused Casta there was no point that I laid more stress on than (what I stated) "that her accuser had gone to pieces under a charge of collusion."*

Remark.—Verbs of Emotion, such as Rejoicing, Sorrowing, *etc.*, take **quod** with the Indic. or Subjunctive. See Causal Sentences, 539.

II. Object Sentences, with Accusative and Infinitive.

526. *Preliminary Observation.*—On the simple Infinitive as an object, see 423.

The Inf., as a verbal predicate, has its subject in the Accusative. (420.)

527. Active verbs of Saying, Showing, Believing, and Perceiving (**verba sentiendī et dēclārandī**), and similar expressions, take the Accusative and Infinitive:

Thalēs Mīlēsius aquam dīxit esse initium rērum, C., *N.D.*, I. 10, 25;

Thales of Miletus said that water was the first principle of things. [**Solōn**] **furere sē simulāvit,** C., *Off.*, I. 30, 108; *Solon pretended to be mad.* **Medicī causā morbī inventā cūrātiōnēm esse inventam putant,** C., *Tusc.*, III. 10, 23; *physicians think that,* (when) *the cause of disease* (is) *discovered, the method of treatment is discovered.* **Volucrēs vidēmus fingere et cōnstruere nīdōs,** C., *Or.*, II. 6, 23; *we see that birds fashion and build nests.* **Audiet cīvēs acuisse ferrum,** H., *O.*, I. 2, 21; [the youth] *shall hear that citizens gave edge to steel.* **Tīmāgenēs auctor est omnium in lītterīs studiōrum antīquissimam mūsicēn extitisse,** QUINT., I. 10, 10; *Timagenes is the authority* (for the statement) *that of all intellectual pursuits music was the most ancient.*

The sentence very often passes over into the Acc. and Inf. (Ō. O.) without any formal notice.

REMARKS.—1. **Verba sentiendī** comprise two classes, those of (*a*) Actual and those of (*b*) Intellectual Perception. Some verbs, such as **sentīre, vidēre, cernere, audīre,** belong to both classes. Otherwise the most common are:

(*a*) **Cōnspicārī, cōnspicere, aspicere, sūspicere, prōspicere,** also rarely **tuērī** and **somniāre** (early).

(*b*) **Intellegere, cōgnōscere, comperīre, scīre, nescīre,** and less commonly, but Ciceronian, **dīscere, īgnōrāre, accipere, animadvertere, perspicere,** *etc.*

2. **Verba dēclārandī** can likewise be divided into two classes: (*a*) those of Actual and (*b*) those of Intellectual Representation; but the classes often fade into each other, or, rather, a verb of Intellectual Representation can be readily used as one of Actual Representation. In general, verbs of Intellectual Representation are those of Thinking, Remembering, Belief and Opinion, Expectation, Trust and Hope. Verbs of Actual Representation are those of Saying, Showing, Approving, Boasting, Pretending, Promising, Swearing, Threatening, Accusing (the last have more often **quod**). Verbs of Concluding belong always to both classes. The principal of these verbs are: **putāre, dūcere, arbitrārī, cēnsēre, sūspicārī, crēdere, exīstimāre, meminisse, cōnfīdere, spērāre, dēspērāre.** Then **dīcere, ēdīcere, affirmāre, cōnfirmāre, āiō** (rare), **loquī** (rare), **negāre, fatērī, nārrāre, trādere, scrībere, nūntiāre, ostendere, probāre, glōriārī, dēmōnstrāre, persuādēre, sīgnificāre, pollicērī, prōmittere, minārī, simulāre, dissimulāre,** *etc.*; **conclūdere, colligere, efficere.** Also **pōnere,** *to suppose* (rare), **facere,** *to represent.* Similar expressions are **spēs est, opīniō est, fāma est, auctor sum, tēstis sum, certiōrem aliquem facere,** *etc.*

3. When the subj. of the Inf. is a personal or reflexive pronoun, that subj. may be omitted—chiefly with Fut. Inf.—and then **esse** also is dropped. This occurs rarely in CICERO, more frequently in early Latin, CAESAR, and later.

Refrāctūrōs carcerem minābantur, L., VI. 17, 6; *they threatened to break open the jail.*

4. The simple Inf. is often used in English, where the Latin takes Acc. and Infinitive. This is especially true of verbs of Hoping and Promising. **Spērō mē hōc adeptūrum esse,** *I hope to (that I shall) obtain this.* **Prōmittēbat sē ventūrum esse,** *he promised to (that he would) come.*

5. When the Acc. with the Inf. is followed by a dependent Acc., ambiguity may arise:

Āiō tē, Aeacidā, Rōmānōs vincere posse (C., *Div.*, II. 56, 116), in which **tē** may be subject or object.

Real ambiguity is to be avoided by giving the sentence a passive turn:

Āiō ā tē, Aeacidā, Rōmānōs vincī posse, *I affirm that the Romans can be conquered by thee, son of Aeacus.*

Āiō tē, Aeacidā, ā Rōmānīs vincī posse, *I affirm that thou, son of Aeacus, canst be conquered by the Romans.*

When the context shows which is the real subj., formal ambiguity is of no importance. But see QUINT., VII. 9, 10.

NOTES.—1. Verbs of Perception and Representation take the Part. to express the actual condition of the object of Perception or Representation (536). As there is no Pr. Part. pass., the Inf. must be used, and thus the difference between Intellectual and Actual Perception is effaced, sometimes even in the active, and, in fact, the use of the Part. is confined to authors who are consciously influenced by a rivalry with the Greek.

Audiō cīvēs acuentēs ferrum, *Cf.* H., *O.*, I. 2, 21; *I hear citizens sharpen(ing) the steel.* **Audiō ā cīvibus acuī ferrum,** *I hear that the steel is sharpened by citizens;* or, *the steel as it is sharpened by citizens.* **Octāvium (dolōre) cōnficī vīdī,** C., *Fin.*, II. 28, 93; *I have seen Octavius* (when he was) *wearing out with anguish.* **Vīdī histriōnēs flentēs ēgredī,** QUINT., VI. 2, 35; *I have seen actors leave the stage weeping.*

(Platō) ā Deō aedificārī mundum facit, C., *N.D.*, I. 8, 19; *Plato makes out that the universe is built by God.* **Polyphēmum Homērus cum ariete conloquentem facit,** C., *Tusc.*, V. 39, 115 (536). **Fac, quaesō, quī ego sum esse tē,** C., *Fam.*, VII. 23, 1; *suppose, I pray, yourself to be me.*

2. The (Greek) attraction of the predicate of the Inf. into the Nom. after the Verb of Saying or Thinking, is poetical; the first example is PL., *Asin.*, 634.

Phasēlus ille, quem vidētis, hospitēs, ait fuisse nāvium celerrimus, CAT., IV. 1; *that pinnace yonder, which you see, my stranger guests, declares she used to be (claims to have been) the fastest craft afloat.*

There is one example in CICERO (*Agr.*, II. 21, 57).

3. The use of the Acc. and Inf. with **verba dēclārandī** is an outgrowth of the use after verbs of Creation (423), just as in English "I declare him to be," is an extension of "I make him to be," in which Acc. and Inf. have each its proper force. This is the origin of the so-called **Ōrātiō Oblīqua,** or Indirect Discourse, which represents not the exact language used, but the general drift, and in which the tenses of the Inf. seem to represent approximately the tenses of the Indicative. It was to complete the scheme of the Tenses that the Fut. Inf. was developed, and this is the sole use of that tense. The use of the Acc. and Inf. after **verba sentiendī,** like the use in English "I see him go," is more primitive, but the original case of the Inf. is no longer felt.

Nominative with Infinitive.

528. Passive verbs of Saying, Showing, Believing, and Perceiving :

1. In the Simple tenses prefer the personal construction, in which the Accusative Subject of the Infinitive appears as the Nominative Subject of the leading verb.

2. In the Compound tenses prefer the impersonal construction, which is the rule with Gerund and Gerundive.

Thus, instead of

Trādunt Homērum caecum fuisse, *they say that Homer was blind,*

we should have,

Trāditur Homērus caecus fuisse, *Homer is said to have been blind,*

or,

[**Trāditum**] **est Homērum caecum fuisse,** C., *Tusc.*, v. 39, 114 ; *there is a tradition that Homer was blind.*

[**Aristaeus**] **inventor oleī esse dīcitur,** C., *Verr.*, IV. 57, 128 ; *Aristaeus is said to be the inventor of oil.* **Terentī fābellae propter ēlegantiam sermōnis putābantur ā Laeliō scrībī,** C., *Att.*, VII. 3, 10 ; *Terence's plays, on account of the elegance of the language, were thought to be written by Laelius.* [**Sī Vēiōs migrābimus**] **āmīsisse patriam vidēbimur,** L., v. 53, 5 ; *if we remove to Veji, we shall seem to have lost our country.* **Reus damnātum īrī vidēbātur,** QUINT., IX. 2, 88 (435, N. 4). **Crēditur Pȳthagorae audītōrem fuisse Numam,** L., XL. 29, 8 ; *it is believed that Numa was a hearer of Pythagoras.*

But :

[**Venerem**] **Adōnidī nūpsisse prōditum est,** C., *N.D.*, III. 23, 59 ; *it is recorded that Venus married Adonis.* (**Philōnem**) **exīstimandum est disertum fuisse,** C., *Or.*, I. 14, 62 ; *we must suppose that Philo was eloquent.*

REMARKS.—1. The impersonal construction is the rule if a Dat. is combined with the verb : **mihī nūntiābātur Parthōs trānsīsse Euphrātem,** C., *Fam.*, XV. 1, 2 ; *it was announced to me that the Parthians had crossed the Euphrates.*

2. Various peculiarities are noteworthy in the matter of these verbs. Thus, **dīcitur** usually means *it is maintained*, **dictum est,** *it is said.* **Crēditur,** *etc.* (impersonal), is the regular form in classical prose ; the personal construction is poetical and late. **Vidērī** is used, as a rule, personally ; the impersonal construction **vidētur** is rare. The active forms **trādunt, crēdunt,** *etc.*, are everywhere common.

NOTES.—1. In early Latin the personal construction is found with **arguī, cluēre** (a virtual passive), **dīcī, exīstimārī, invenīrī, iubērī, nūntiārī, perhibērī, reperīrī.** All these, except **cluēre,** are retained in the classical period. CICERO and CAESAR add twenty-five new verbs, and from this time on the construction increases.

2. Virtual passives, on the analogy of **cluēre,** are rare ; **appārēre, cōnstāre, venīre in sūspīciōnem,** are Ciceronian ; so also **opus est** in [C.], *Fam.*, XI. 11, 2, and perhaps TER., *And.*, 337.

3. A second clause following a Nom. with the Inf. takes its subj. in the Accusative C., *Or.*, II. 74, 299.

4. In verbs of Saying, except **dīcō** (compare TAC., *Ann.*, IV. 34, 3), the personal construction is confined to the third person. The poets are free in treating verbs under this head.

Tenses of the Infinitive with Verba Sentiendī et Dēclārandī.

529. The Infinitive denotes only the stage of the action, and determines only the relation to the time of the leading verb (281).

530. After verbs of Saying, Showing, Believing, and Perceiving, and the like,

The Present Infinitive expresses contemporaneous action ;
The Perfect Infinitive expresses prior action ;
The Future Infinitive expresses future action.

REMARK.—The action which is completed with regard to the leading verb may be in itself a continued action. So in English: *I have been studying, I had been studying.* Hence, the Impf. Indic. (*I was studying*) is represented in this dependent form by the Pf. Inf., because it is prior to the leading verb.

☞ In this table the Present is taken as the type of the Principal, the Imperfect as the type of the Historical, Tenses.

531. *Contemporaneous Action.*

	ACTIVE.	PASSIVE.
P. T.	**Dīcit: tē errāre,** *He says, that you are going wrong,*	**tē dēcipī,** *that you are (being) deceived* (**217, R.**).
H. T.	**Dīcēbat: tē errāre,** *He was saying, that you were going wrong,*	**tē dēcipī,** *that you were (being) deceived.*

Prior Action.

	ACTIVE.	PASSIVE.
P. T.	**Dīcit: tē errāsse,** *He says, that you have gone wrong, that you went wrong, that you have been going wrong,*	**tē dēceptum esse,** *that you have been (are) deceived, that you were deceived* (AOR.), *(that people have been deceiving you).*

H. T. Dīcēbat: tē errāsse, *He was saying, that you had gone wrong, that you went wrong, that you had been going wrong,*

tē dēceptum esse, *that you had been deceived, that you were deceived* (Aor.). (*that people had been deceiving you*)

Subsequent Action.

P. T. Dīcit: tē errātūrum esse, *He says, that you (are about to go wrong), will (be) go(ing) wrong,*

tē dēceptum īrī, *that you (are going to) will be deceived.*

H. T. Dīcēbat: tē errātūrum esse, *He was saying, that you were about to (would) go wrong,*

tē dēceptum īrī, *that you were going to (would) be deceived.*

Periphrastic Future.

The following form (the *Periphrastic Future*) is necessary when the verb has no Sup. or Fut. participle. It is often formed from other verbs to intimate an interval, which cannot be expressed by other forms, and is more common in the passive than the Fut. Inf. pass. of the paradigms.

P. T. Dīcit: fore (futūrum esse) ut errēs (metuās), fore (futūrum esse) ut errāverīs (rare),

fore ut dēcipiāris (metuāris), fore ut dēceptus sīs (rare), usually **dēceptum fore** (not **futūrum esse**).

H. T. Dīcēbat: fore (futūrum esse) ut errārēs (metuerēs), errāssēs (rare),

fore ut dēciperēris (metuerēris), dēceptum fore (rarely: **fore ut dēceptus essēs**).

Notes.—1. For examples of the Periphrastic, see 248.

Carthāginiēnsēs dēbellātum mox fore rēbantur, L., xxiii. 13, 6; *the Carthaginians thought that the war would soon be (have been) brought to an end.* From **dēbellātum erit,** *it will be (have been) brought to an end.* So in the deponent **adeptum fore.**

2. Ponderous periphrastics are of rare occurrence. So **fētiālēs dēcrēvērunt utrum eōrum fēcisset rēctē factūrum** (L., xxxi. 8); not **fore ut fēcisset,** although the Ō. R. requires **utrum fēcerīs, rēctē fēcerīs.** (244, r. 4.) See Weissenborn's note.

3. **Posse, velle,** *etc.*, do not require the Periphrastic, and seldom take it. (248, r.)

4. **Spērāre,** *to hope*, **prōmittere (pollicērī),** *to promise*, which regularly take the Fut. Inf., have occasionally the Pr. when an immediate realisation of the hope is anticipated. With **spēs est** the Pr. Inf. is more common.

Lēgātī veniunt quī polliceantur obsidēs dare, Caes., *B. G.*, iv. 21, 5; *ambassadors come to promise the giving of (to give) hostages.*

So, too, when the Fut. Inf. is not available, sometimes also when it is, **posse** and the Pr. is a fair substitute. **Tōtīus Galliae sēsē potīrī posse** (= **potītūrōs esse**) **spērant,** Caes., *B. G.*, i. 3, 8; *they hope they can (will) get possession of the whole of Gaul.* See 423, n. 5.

Of course **spērāre** may be used simply as a verb of Thinking.

Accusative and Infinitive with Verbs of Will and Desire.

532. Verbs of Will and Desire take a Dependent Accusative and Infinitive.

The relation is that of an Object to be Effected.

Sī vīs mē flēre, dolendum est prīmum ipsī tibi, H., *A.P.*, 102; *if you wish me to weep, you must first feel the pang yourself.* **Utrum [Milōnis] corporis an Pȳthagorae tibĭ mālīs vīrēs ingeniī darī?** C., *Cat. M.*, 10, 33; *which (whether) would you rather have given to you, Milo's strength of body or Pythagoras' strength of mind?* **Ipse iubet mortis tē meminisse deus,** MART., II. 59 (376). **Vītae summa brevis spem nōs vetat inchoāre longam,** H., *O.*, I. 4, 15 (423, N. 6). **Nēmō īre quemquam pūblicā prohibet viā,** PL., *Curc.*, 35 (389). **Germānī vīnum ad sē omnīnō importārī nōn sinunt,** CAES., *B.G.*, IV. 2, 6; *the Germans do not permit wine to be imported into their country at all.*

REMARKS.—1. A list of these verbs is given in 423, N. 2.

2. When the subj. of the Inf. is the same as the subj. of the leading verb, the subj. of the Inf. is usually not expressed:

Nī pārēre velīs, pereundum erit ante lucernās, JUV., X. 339; *unless you resolve to obey, you will have to perish before candle-light.* **Et iam māllet equōs numquam tetigisse paternōs,** OV., *M.*, II. 182; *and now he could have wished rather never to have touched his father's horses.*

But the subj. may be expressed, and commonly is expressed, when the action of the Inf. is not within the power of the subject; so especially with an Inf. passive:

(Tīmoleōn) māluit sē dīligī quam metuī, NEP., XX. 3, 4; *Timoleon preferred that he should be loved rather than that he should be feared.* **Ego rūs abitūram mē certō dēcrēvī,** TER., *Hec.*, 586. **Prīncipem sē esse māvult quam vidērī,** C., *Off.*, I. 19, 65.

NOTES.—1. On the construction of this class of verbs with **ut (nē, quōminus)**, see 546. **Imperō,** *I command*, in model prose takes only the Inf. passive or deponent; in SALLUST, HIRTIUS, CURTIUS, TACITUS, and the Poets sometimes the active.

(Hannibal) imperāvit quam plūrimās venēnātās serpentēs vīvās colligī, NEP., 23, 10; *Hannibal ordered as many poisonous serpents as possible to be caught alive.*

Permittō seldom takes the Inf. (*e.g.*, C., *Verr.*, V. 9, 22); the Acc. with Inf. begins in TACITUS; **concēdō** takes Inf. pass. only, in classical prose. **Iubeō,** *I bid*; **sinō,** *I let*; **vetō,** *I forbid*; **prohibeō,** *I prohibit*, always have the Inf. of passive verbs. With **sinō** and **vetō** the model construction is Inf. only. **Sinō** takes **ut** occasionally in early and late Latin, **vetō** does not have **nē** till in the post-Ciceronian period. **Iubēre** takes **ut** when it is applied to decrees of the Senate, and from LIVY on when used of the orders of generals; **prohibēre** takes **nē** and **quōminus.** These verbs may themselves be turned into the passive: **iubeor, sinor, vetor, prohibeor.**

2. After **iubeō,** *I bid*, and **vetō,** *I forbid*, the Inf. act. can be used without a subj. (even an imaginary or indefinite one):

Iubet reddere, *he bids return (orders the returning).*

Vetat adhibēre medicīnam, C., *Att.*, XVI. 15, 5; *he forbids the administration of medicine.* **Īnfandum, rēgīna, iubēs renovāre dolōrem,** V., *A.*, II. 3; *unspeakable, O queen, the anguish which you bid* (me, us) *revive.*

3. After **volō, nōlō, mālō** in early Latin, **ut** and the Subjv. is proportionally more common than in the classical time. But with the Potential forms, **velim, mālim, vellem, māllem,** CICERO uses only the Subjv. (without **ut**). When **volō** means *maintain*, it takes the Inf. only; see 546, R. 1.

4. It is noteworthy that in classical Prose **cupere** never takes **ut,** while **optāre** never takes the Infinitive.

5. On the use of the Pf. Inf. instead of the Pr. after these verbs, see 537, N. 1.

6. The Poets go much further in using verbs and phrases as expressions of Will and Desire. See 423, N. 4.

Accusative and Infinitive with Verbs of Emotion.

533. Verbs of Emotion take a dependent Accusative and Infinitive, inasmuch as these verbs may be considered as verbs of Saying and Thinking. (542.)

Salvom tē advēnisse gaudeō, TER., *Ph.*, 286; *I rejoice that you should have arrived safe* (*to think that you have arrived safe, at your arriving safe*). **Quod salvos advēnistī,** *that you have arrived safe.* **Quod salvos advēnerīs,** *that* (as you say) *you have arrived safe.*

Īnferiōres nōn dolēre [dēbent] sē ā suīs dīgnitāte superārī, C., *Lael.*, 20, 71; *inferiors ought not to consider it a grievance that they are surpassed in rank by their own* (*friends*).

REMARKS.—1. This construction, outside of a few verbs, is not common, though found in a wide range of authors. **Gaudēre, laetārī, dolēre, querī** (beginning in CIC.), **mīrārī,** are common; in addition CICERO uses, rarely, however, more than once each, **maerēre, lūgēre, cōnficī, discruciārī, angī, sollicitārī, indīgnārī, fremere, dēmīrārī, admīrārī, subesse timōrem.** Early Latin shows **rīdēre** (NAEV.), **gestīre, mihĭ dolet** (TER.), **maestus sum** (PLAUT.), **cruciārī** (PLAUT.), **lāmentārī** (PLAUT., HOR.), **sūspīrāre** (LUCR.), **incendor īrā** (TER.), **ferōx est** (PLAUT.), **invidēre** (PLAUT., HOR.), **formīdāre, verērī,** in addition to the common **gaudēre,** *etc.*, already cited.

2. On the Participle after a verb of Emotion, 536, N. 2.

Accusative and Infinitive in Exclamations.

534. The Accusative with the Infinitive is used in Exclamations and Exclamatory Questions as the object of an unexpressed thought or feeling.

Hem, mea lūx, tē nunc, mea Terentia, sīc vexārī, C., *Fam.*, XIV. 2, 2; *h'm, light of my life, for you to be so harassed now, Terentia dear.* **Hominemne Rōmānum tam Graecē loquī?** PLIN., *Ep.*, IV. 3, 5; *a Roman speak such good Greek?* (*To think that a Roman should speak such* *good Greek.*) **Mēne inceptō dēsistere— ?** V., *A.*, I. 37; *I—desist from my undertaking?* **Hinc abīre mātrem ?** Ter., *Hec.*, 612; *mother go away from here?*

Remarks.—1. Different is **quod**, which gives the ground.

Ei mihi quod nūllīs amor est sānābilis herbīs, Ov., *M.*, I. 523; *woe's me that (in that, because) love is not to be cured by any herbs.*

2. On **ut**, with the Subjv. in a similar sense, see 558. Both forms offer an objection.

Accusative and Infinitive as a Subject.

535. The Accusative with the Infinitive may be treated as the Subject of a sentence. The Predicate is a substantive or neuter adjective, an impersonal verb or abstract phrase.

In the English "for—to," the "*for*" belongs not to the case but to the Infinitive, but the object relation has been effaced here as it has been in Latin. See 422, N. 1.

Est inūsitātum rēgem reum capitis esse, C., *Dei.*, I. 1; *it is an extraordinary thing that a king should (for a king to) be tried for his life.* **Facinus est vincīre cīvem Rōmānum**, C., *Verr.*, V. 66, 170; *it is an outrage to put a Roman citizen in chains.* **Necesse est facere sūmptum quī quaerit** (= **eum quī quaerit**) **lucrum**, Pl., *As.*, 218; *need is that he make outlay who an income seeks.* **Lēgem brevem esse oportet, quō facilius ab imperītīs teneātur**, Sen., *E.M.*, 94, 38; *it is proper that a law should be brief (a law ought to be brief), that it may the more easily be grasped by the uneducated.* **Quid Milōnis intererat interficī Clōdium**, C., *Mil.*, 13, 34 (382, 2). **Opus est tē animō valēre**, C., *Fam.*, XVI. 14, 2 (406, N. 5).

Remarks.—1. A list of expressions taking the Inf. as a subj. is given in 422, NN.

2. **Oportet**, *it is proper*, and **necesse est**, *must needs*, are often used with the Subjunctive. So also many other phrases with **ut.** (See 557.)

Necesse also takes the Dat. of the Person:

Ut culpent aliī, tibi mē laudāre necesse est, Ov., *Her.*, 12, 131; *let others blame, but you must give me praise.*

3. When the indirect obj. of the leading verb is the same as the subj. of the Inf. the predicate of the subj. is put in the same case as the indirect object: in standard prose chiefly with **licet**, *it is left (free)*; in poetry and later prose with **necesse**, with **satius est**, *it is better*, **contingit**, *it happens*, **vacat**, *there is room.*

Licuit esse ōtiōsō Themistoclī, C., *Tusc.*, I. 15, 33; *Themistocles was free to live a life of leisure.*

The Acc. is occasionally found; always if the Dat. is not expressed.

Mediōs esse iam nōn licēbit (nōs), C., *Att.*, X. 8, 4; *it will no longer be allowable to be neutral.*

Object Sentences Represented by the Participle.

536. The Participle is used after verbs of Perception and Representation, to express the actual condition of the object of perception or representation.

Catōnem vīdī in bibliothēcā sedentem multīs circumfūsum Stōicōrum librīs, C., *Fin.*, III. 2, 7; *I saw Cato sitting in the library with an ocean of Stoic books about him.* **Prōdiga nōn sentit pereuntem fēmina cēnsum,** Juv., VI. 362; *the lavish woman does not perceive* (how) *the income* (is) *dwindling.* **Saepe illam audīvī fūrtīvā vōce loquentem,** Cat., LXVII. 41; *I have often heard her talking in a stealthy* (*in an under-*) *tone.* **Gaudē quod spectant oculī tē mīlle loquentem,** H., *Ep.*, I. 6, 19 (542). **Polyphēmum Homērus cum ariete conloquentem facit,** C., *Tusc.*, V. 39, 115; *Homer represents Polyphemus* (as) *talking with the ram.*

Notes.—1. This construction is found but once in early Latin (Piso), then in Cicero, Sallust, Nepos, Vitruvius, Livy, Horace. The naturalisation of it is due to Cicero and other students of Greek models. The poverty of Latin in participles was a serious drawback to the convenient distinction from the Infinitive; and it may be said that the participle was never perfectly at home.

2. On the Inf., see 527, n. 1. The Greek construction of Part. agreeing with the leading Nom. after verbs of Perception and Emotion, is rare and poetical:

Gaudent scrībentēs, H., *Ep.*, II. 2, 107; *they have joy while writing.* **Sēnsit mediōs dēlāpsus in hostēs,** V., *A.*, II. 377; *he perceived* (it) *having fallen* (*that he had fallen*) *'midst the enemy.* **Gaudent perfūsī sanguine frātrum,** V., *G.*, II. 510; *they rejoice, bedrenched with brothers' blood.*

537. The Perfect Participle Passive is used after verbs of Causation and Desire, to denote impatience of anything except entire fulfilment:

Sī quī voluptātibus dūcuntur missōs faciant honōrēs, C., *Sest.*, 66, 138; *if any are led captive by sensual pleasures, let them dismiss honours* (*at once and forever*). **Huīc mandēs sī quid rēctē cūrātum velīs,** Ter., *Ad.*, 372; *you must intrust to him whatever you want properly attended to.*

Notes.—1. After verbs of Will and Desire, the Inf. **esse** is occasionally found with this Part., and hence it may be considered a Pf. Infinitive (280, 2, *c*). Compare, however, Pf. Part. pass. with **opus est, ūsus est** (406).

2. The verbs of Causation thus employed are **cūrāre, dare, facere, reddere.** The usage is most common in early Latin. In the classical period only **missum facere.**

CAUSAL SENTENCES.

538. Causal sentences are introduced:

1. By **quia,** *because,* **quod,** (*in that*) *because.*
2. By **quoniam** (**quom iam**), *now that,* **quandŏ, quandŏquidem,** *since.*

} (Cause Proper.)

3. By **cum (quom)**, *as.* (Inference.)

4. By the Relative Pronoun, partly alone, partly with **ut, utpote, quīppe,** *etc.* (See 626, 634.)

NOTES.—1. **Quod** is the Acc. Sing. neuter, and **quia** is probably the Acc. Pl. neuter from the relative stem. They have accordingly often a correlative demonstrative; so with **quod**: **eō, eā rē, ideō, idcircō, eā grātiā** (in SALLUST only), **hōc, hāc mente** (H., *S.*, II. 2, 90), **proptereā,** and a few combinations with **ob** and **propter**; with **quia** are found **eō, eā rē, ideō, idcircō, proptereā,** and **ergō** (in PLAUTUS only).

2. **Quod** and **quia** differ in classical prose, chiefly in that **quod** is used, and not **quia,** when the causal sentence is at the same time an object sentence.

3. **Quoniam** is originally temporal, and as such is still found in PLAUTUS. The causal use of it becomes much more extensive in classical prose, and, like **quandō̆** (**quandō̆quidem**), it is used of *evident* reasons.

4. **Quandō̆** is used principally as a temporal particle. In a causal sense it is very rare in CICERO (in the *Orations* never, unless compounded with **quidem**), and is not found in CAESAR. The compound with **quidem** is more common.

5. **Quātenus,** *in so far as*, is poetical and in late prose. HORACE shows first example, *O.*, III. 24, 30. VALERIUS M., QUINTILIAN, TACITUS, PLINY MINOR, and SUETONIUS show occasional examples.

Causal Sentences with QUOD, QUIA, QUONIAM, and QUANDŌ̆.

539. Causal sentences with **quod, quia, quoniam,** and **quandō̆** are put in the Indicative, except in oblique relation (Partial or Total).

REMARK.—The other person of the oblique clause may be imaginary, and the writer or speaker may quote from himself indirectly:

Laetātus sum, quod mihi licēret rēcta dēfendere, C., *Fam.*, I. 9, 18; *I was glad* (to say to myself) *that I was free to champion the right.*

540. Causal sentences with **quod, quia, quoniam,** and **quandō̆** take the Indicative in Direct Discourse.

Torquātus fīlium suum quod is contrā imperium in hostem pūgnāverat necārī iūssit, S., *C.*, 52, 30; *Torquatus bade his son be put to death because he had fought against the enemy contrary to order*(s) [**quod pūgnāsset** = because, as Torquatus said or thought]. **Amantēs dē fōrmā iūdicāre nōn possunt, quia sēnsum oculōrum praecipit animus,** QUINT., VI. 2, 6; *lovers cannot judge of beauty, because the heart forestalls the eye.* **Quia nātūra mūtārī nōn potest idcircō vērae amīcitiae sempiternae sunt,** C., *Lael.*, 9, 32; *because nature cannot change, therefore true friendships are everlasting.* **Neque mē vīxisse paenitet quoniam ita vīxī ut nōn frūstrā mē nātum exīstumem,** C., *Cat.M.*, 23, 84; *and I am not sorry for having lived, since I have so lived that I think I was born not in vain.* **Sōlus erō quoniam nōn licet esse tuum,** PROP., II. 9, 46; *I shall be alone since I may not be thine.* **Voluptās sēmovenda est quandō̆ ad māiōra quaedam nātī sumus,** *Cf.* C., *Fin.*, V. 8, 21; *pleasure is to be put aside* *because we are born for greater things.* **Erant quibus appetentior fāmae [Helvidius] vidērētur quandŏ etiam sapientibus cupīdō glōriae novissima exuitur,** TAC., *H.*, IV. 6, 1; *there were some to whom Helvidius seemed too eager for fame, since, even from the wise, ambition is the last* (infirmity) *that is put off.* **Sequitur ut līberātōrēs (sint), quandŏquidem tertium nihil potest esse,** C., *Ph.*, II. 13, 31.

541. Causal sentences with **quod, quia, quoniam,** and **quandō** take the Subjunctive in Oblique Discourse (Partial or Total).

Noctū ambulābat in pūblicō Themistoclēs quod somnum capere nōn posset, C., *Tusc.*, IV. 19, 44; *Themistocles used to walk about in public at night because* (as he said) *he could not get to sleep.* **Aristīdēs nōnne ob eam causam expulsus est patriā quod praeter modum iūstus esset?** C., *Tusc.*, V. 36, 105; (*there is*) *Aristides; was he not banished his country for the* (*alleged*) *reason "that he was unreasonably just"?* **[Nē] compōne comās quia sīs ventūrus ad illam,** Ov., *Rem.Am.*, 679 (517). **Quoniam** (so most MSS.) **ipse prō sē dīcere nōn posset, verba fēcit frāter ēius Stēsagorās,** NEP., I. 7, 5; *"as* [Miltiades] *could not speak for himself," his brother, Stesagoras, made a speech.* (Indirect quotation from the speech of Stesagoras.)

A good example is PL., *M.G.*, 1412–15.

NOTES.—1. **Quia** is the usual particle in the causal sense in PLAUTUS, **quod** being very rare; but **quod** is more common in TERENCE, and is the regular particle in classical prose (CAESAR has but one case of **quia**), though the use of **quia** revives in post-classical Latin. CICERO makes a point on the difference in meaning in *Rosc.Am.*, 50, 145: **concēdō et quod** (*by reason of the fact that*) **animus aequus est, et quia** (*because*) **necesse est.**

2. A rejected reason is introduced by **nōn quod** with the Subjv. (as being the suggestion of another person). The Indic., which is properly used of excluded facts, is also used of flat denials, like the negative and Indic. in the independent sentence, but the Subjv. is the rule. **Nōn quia** is the rule in early Latin, but classical prose shows very few examples. From LIVY on it becomes common. Other equivalents are **nōn quō, nōn eō quod, nōn eō quō**; further, **nōn quīn** for **nōn quō nōn.** All of these are found with Subjv. only. The corresponding affirmative is given by **sed quod** or **sed quia** indiscriminately, regularly with the Indicative.

Subjunctive:

Pugilēs in iactandīs caestibus ingemīscunt, nōn quod doleant, sed quia profundendā vōce omne corpus intenditur venitque plāga vehementior, C., *Tusc.*, II. 23, 56; *boxers in plying the caestus heave groans, not that* (as you might suppose) *they are in pain, but because in giving full vent to the voice all the body is put to the stretch and the blow comes with a greater rush.* **Māiōrēs nostrī in dominum dē servō quaerī nōluērunt; nōn quīn posset vērum invenīrī, sed quia vidēbātur indīgnum esse,** C., *Mil.*, 22, 59; *our ancestors would not allow a slave to be questioned by torture against his master, not because* (not as though they thought) *the truth could not be got at, but because such a course seemed degrading.* **Ā [Lacedaemoniōrum exulibus] praetor vim arcuerat, nōn quia salvōs vellet sed quia perīre causā indictā nōlēbat,** L., XXXVIII. 33, 11; *the praetor had warded off violence from the*

Lacedaemonian exiles, not (as you might have supposed) *because he wished them to escape, but because he did not wish them to perish with their case not pleaded* (unheard).

The same principle applies to **magis quod (quō), quia—quam quō** (first in Cicero), **quod** (first in Sallust), **quia** (first in Livy), with the moods in inverse order.

Lībertātis orīginem inde, magis quia annuum imperium cōnsulāre factum est quam quod dēminūtum quidquam sit ex rēgiā potestāte, numerēs, L., II. 1, 7; *you may begin to count the origin of liberty from that point, rather because the consular government was limited to a year, than because aught was taken away from the royal power.*

Indicative:

Sum nōn dīcam miser, sed certē exercitus, nōn quia multīs dēbeō sed quia saepe concurrunt aliquōrum bene de mē meritōrum inter ipsōs contentiōnēs, C., *Planc.*, 32, 78; *I am, I will not say, wretched, but certainly worried, not because I am in debt to many, but because the rival claims of some who have deserved well of me often conflict.* Compare also H., *S.*, II. 2, 89.

3. Verbs of Saying and Thinking are occasionally put in the Subjv. with **quod** by a kind of attraction. Compare 585, N. 3.

Impetrāre nōn potuī, quod rēligiōne sē impedīrī dīcerent, C., *Fam.*, IV. 12, 3; *I could not obtain permission, because they said they were embarrassed (prevented) by a religious scruple* (= **quod impedīrentur,** *because* (as they said) *they were prevented*).

This attraction is said to occur not unfrequently in Cicero, several times in Caesar and Sallust, but is not cited from any other author. Compare, however, **crēderent,** L., XXI. 1, 3.

4. On the use of **tamquam,** *etc.*, to indicate an assumed reason, see 602, N. 4.

5. **Quandōque** is archaic and rare. It is found first in the Twelve Tables, a few times in Cicero and Livy, three times in Horace, and occasionally later.

6. Causal sentences may be represented by a participle (669), or by the relative (626).

QUOD with Verbs of Emotion.

542. Quod is used to give the ground of Emotions and Expressions of Emotion, such as verbs of Joy, Sorrow, Surprise, Satisfaction and Anger, Praise and Blame, Thanks and Complaint.

The rule for the Mood has been given already: 539.

Indicative:

Gaudē quod spectant oculī tē mīlle loquentem, H., *Ep.*, I. 6, 19; *rejoice that a thousand eyes are gazing at you* (while you are) *speaking.* **Dolet mihī quod tū nunc stomachāris,** C., *ad Br.*, I. 17, 6; *it pains me that you are angry now.* **Quīntum paenitet quod animum tuum offendit,** *Cf.* C., *Att.*, XI. 13, 2 (377, R. 3). **Iuvat mē quod vigent studia,** Plin., *Ep.*, I. 13, 1; *I am charmed that studies are flourishing.* **Trīstis es? indīgnor quod sum tibi causa dolōris,** Ov., *Tr.*, IV. 3, 33; *are you sad? I am provoked* (with myself) *that I am a cause of pain to you.* **Tibī grātiās agō, quod mē omnī molestiā līberāstī,** C., *Fam.*, XIII. 62; *I thank you, that you freed me from all annoyance.*

Subjunctive:

Gaudet mīles quod vīcerit hostem, Ov., *Tr.*, II. 49; *the soldier rejoices* *at having conquered the enemy.* **Neque mihĭ umquam veniet in mentem poenitēre quod ā mē ipse nōn dēscīverim,** C., *Att.*, II. 4, 2 ; *it will never occur to me to be sorry for not having been untrue to myself.* **Laudat Āfricānum Panaetius quod fuerit abstinēns,** C., *Off.*, II. 22, 76 ; *Panaetius praises Africanus for having been abstinent.* **Nēmŏ est ōrātōrem quod Latīnē loquerētur admīrātus,** C., *Or.*, III. 14, 52; *no one* (ever) *admired an orator for speaking* (good) *Latin.* **Sōcratēs accūsātus est quod corrumperet iuventūtem,** QUINT., IV. 4, 5 ; *Socrates was accused of corrupting youth.* **Meminī glōriārī solitum esse Quīntum Hortēnsium quod numquam bellō cīvīlī interfuisset,** C., *Fam.*, II. 16, 3; *I remember that Quintus Hortensius used to boast of never having engaged in civil war.* **Agunt grātiās quod sibĭ pepercissent,** CAES., *B.C.*, I. 74, 2 (511, R. 1).

REMARK.—This class of verbs may be construed with the Acc. and Inf.: **salvom tē advēnisse gaudeō** (533) ; also with **quia,** principally in early Latin, and in CICERO's *Letters,* then occasionally in LIVY, TACITUS, SUETONIUS, and later. But in Expressions of Praise and Blame, Thanks and Complaint, **quod** is more common. On **cum,** see 564, N. 2.

Amō tē et nōn neglēxisse habeō grātiam, TER., *Ph.*, 54 ; *I love you* (= much obliged), *and I am thankful to you for not having neglected* (it). **Grātulor ingenium nōn latuisse tuum,** Ov., *Tr.*, I. 9, 54; *I congratulate* (you) *that your genius has not lain hidden.* **[Īsocratēs] queritur plūs honōris corporum quam animōrum virtūtibus darī,** QUINT., III. 8, 9 ; *Isocrates complains that more honour is paid to the virtues of the body than to those of the mind.*

NOTES.—1. Perplexing Emotion (Wonder) may be followed by a Conditional, or by a Dependent Interrogative, as in English, but this construction is not found in VERGIL, CAESAR, SALLUST, and is never common.

Mīror sī [Tarquinius] quemquam amīcum habēre potuit, C., *Lael.*, 15, 54 ; *I wonder if Tarquin could ever have had a friend.*

Besides **mīror** (and **mīrum**), there is one case of **gaudeō sī** in CICERO (*Verr.*, IV. 17, 37), and a few cases after expressions of Fear in TACITUS. There are also sporadic cases of **indīgnārī (indīgnitās) sī.**

2. Noteworthy is the phrase **mīrum (-a) nī (nisi),** *'tis a wonder that—not,* which belongs to the colloquialisms of early Latin (PL., *Capt.*, 820), but reappears once in LIVY.

SENTENCES OF DESIGN AND TENDENCY.

543. 1. Sentences of Design are commonly called Final Sentences. Sentences of Tendency are commonly called Consecutive Sentences. Both contemplate the end—the one, as an aim ; the other, as a consequence.

2. They are alike in having the Subjunctive and the particle **ut** (*how, that*), a relative conjunction.

3. They differ in the Tenses employed. The Final Sentence, as a rule, takes only the Present and Imperfect Subjunctive. Consecutive Sentences may take also Perfect and Pluperfect.

4. They differ in the kind of Subjunctive employed. The Final Sentence takes the Optative. The Consecutive Sentence takes the Potential. Hence the difference in the Negative.

Final:	**nē** (**ut nē**),	*Consecutive:*	**ut nōn**, *that not.*
	nē quis,		**ut nēmŏ**, *that no one.*
	nē ūllus,		**ut nūllus**, *that no.*
	nē umquam, (**nē quandŏ**,)		**ut numquam**, *that never,*
	nē ūsquam, (**nēcubi**,)		**ut nūsquam**, *that nowhere.*
	nē aut—aut, (**ut nēve—nēve**,)		**ut neque—neque**, *that neither—nor.*

Remarks.—1. Verbs of Effecting have the Final Sequence.

2. Verbs of Hindering have the sequence of the Final Sentence, but often the signification of the Consecutive.

3. Verbs of Fearing belong to the Final Sentence only so far as they have the Optative Subjunctive; the subordinate clause is only semi-dependent upon the principal, and we have a partial survival of original parataxis.

Notes.—1. Inasmuch as the Subjv. cannot express a fact, the Latin Consecutive clause does not properly express actual result, but only a tendency, which may, we *infer*, lead to a result. To obviate this difficulty, the Latin has recourse to the circumlocutions with **accidit, ēvenit,** *etc.*

2. It is to be remarked that the difference between Final and Consecutive often consists only in the point of view. What is final from the point of view of the doer is consecutive from the point of view of the spectator; hence the variation in sequence after verbs of Effecting. A frustrated purpose gives a negative result; hence the variation in negative after verbs of Hindering.

3. Here and there in Cicero, more often in Livy and later writers, instead of **nēve** (**neu**), a second clause is added by **neque**, the force of the final particle being felt throughout the sentence.

Monitor tuus suādēbit tibĭ ut hinc discēdās neque mihĭ verbum ūllum respondeās, C., *Div. in Caec.*, 16, 52; *your adviser will counsel you to depart hence and answer me never a word.*

FINAL SENTENCES.

544. Final Sentences are divided into two classes:

I. Final Sentences in which the Design is expressed by the particle; Pure Final Sentences (Sentences of Design).

Oportet ēsse, ut vīvās, nōn vīvere ut edās, [C.], *ad Her.*, iv. 28, 39; *you must eat in order to live, not live in order to eat.*

This form may be translated by, (*in order*) *to;* sometimes by *that may, that might, that,* with the Subjunctive and the like.

II. Final Sentences in which the Design lies in the leading verb (**verba studiī et voluntātis,** verbs of Will and Desire); Complementary Final Sentences.

Volō utī mihĭ respondeās, C., *Vat.*, 7, 17; *I wish you to answer me.*

This form is often rendered by *to,* never by *in order to,* sometimes by *that* and the Subjunctive, or some equivalent.

Of the same nature, but partly Final and partly Consecutive in their sequence, are:

Verbs of Hindering.

Peculiar in their sequence are:

III. Verbs of Fearing.

REMARKS.—1. The use of the Subjv. with Temporal Particles often adds a final sense, inasmuch as the Subjv. regularly looks forward to the future. So **dum, dōnec, quoad** (572), **antequam, priusquam** (577).

2. The general sense of a Final Sentence may also be expressed:

(1) By the Relative **quī** with the Subjunctive. (630.)

(2) By the Genitive of Gerund or Gerundive, with (seldom without) **causā** or **grātiā.** (428, R. 2.)

(3) By **ad** with Gerund and Gerundive. (432.)

(4) By the Dative of the Gerund and Gerundive. (429, 2.)

(5) By the Accusative of the Gerund and Gerundive after verbs of Giving, *etc.* (430.)

(6) By the Accusative Supine after verbs of Motion. (435.)

(7) By the Future Participle Active (post-Ciceronian). (438, N.)

(8) By the Infinitive (poetic and rare). (421, N. 1, *a.*)

I. Pure Final Sentences.

545. Pure Final Sentences are introduced by:

1. **Ut** (**utī**) (*how*) *that,* and other relative pronouns and adverbs. (630.)

Ut and **nē** are often preceded by a demonstrative expression, such as: **idcircō,** *therefore;* **eō,** *to that end;* **propterea,** *on that account;* **eō cōnsiliō,** *with that design;* **eā causā, rē,** *for that reason.*

2. **Quō** = **ut eō,** *that thereby;* with comparatives, *that the . . . —:*

3. **Nē**, *that not, lest,* continued by **nēve, neu.** (444.)

Oportet ēsse, ut vīvās, nōn vīvere ut edās, [C.], *ad Her.*, IV. 28, 39 (544, I.). **Inventa sunt specula, ut homō ipse sē nōsset,** SEN., *N.Q.*, I. 17, 4; *mirrors were invented, to make man acquainted with himself.* **Ut amēris, amābilis estō,** Ov., *A.A.*, II. 107; *that you may be loved (to make yourself loved, in order to be loved), be lovable.* **Lēgem brevem esse oportet, quō facilius ab imperītīs teneātur,** SEN., *E.M.*, 94, 38 (535). **[Senex] serit arborēs, quae alterī saeclō prōsint,** CAECILIUS (C., *Tusc.*, I. 14, 31); *the old man sets out trees, to do good to the next generation.* **Semper habē Pyladēn aliquem quī cūret Orestem,** Ov., *Rem. Am.*, 589; *always have some Pylades, to tend Orestes.* **[Athēniēnsēs] creant decem praetōrēs quī exercituī praeessent,** NEP., I. 4, 4; *the Athenians make ten generals to command their army.* **[Māgnēsiam Themistoclī Artaxerxēs] urbem dōnārat, quae eī pānem praebēret,** NEP., II. 10, 3; *Artaxerxes had given Themistocles the city of Magnesia, to furnish him with bread.* **Gallīnae pennīs fovent pullōs, nē frīgore laedantur,** *Cf.* C., *N.D.*, II. 52, 129; *hens keep (their) chickens warm with (their) wings, that they may not be (to keep them from being) hurt by the cold.* **Dionȳsius, nē collum tōnsōrī committeret, tondēre fīliās suās docuit,** C., *Tusc.*, V. 20, 58 (423, N. 6).

REMARKS.—1. **Ut nē** is found for **nē** with apparently no difference in signification, occasionally at all periods, but not in CAESAR, SALLUST, LIVY. **Quō** without comparative is rare and cited only from PLAUTUS, TERENCE, SALLUST, OVID, and late Latin; **quōnē** (= **ut nē**) is not found till the time of DICTYS; apparent examples in classical Latin are to be otherwise explained. **Quōminus** and **quīn** occur in special uses.

2. **Ut nōn** is used when a particular word is negatived:

Cōnfer tē ad Māllium, ut nōn ēiectus ad aliēnōs sed invītātus ad tuōs īsse videāris, C., *Cat.*, I. 9, 23; *betake yourself to Mallius, that you may seem to have gone not as an outcast to strangers but as an invited guest to your own* (friends).

3. **Ut** and **nē** are used parenthetically at all periods, depending on a suppressed word of Saying or the like.

Utque magis stupeās lūdōs Paridemque relīquit, JUV., VI. 87; *and to stun you more* (I tell you that) *she left Paris and the games.*

The verb of Saying may be inserted: **atque ut omnēs intellegant dīcō,** C., *Imp.*, 8, 20; *and that all may understand, I say.*

II. Complementary Final Sentences.

A. *Verbs of Will and Desire.*

546. Complementary Final Sentences follow verbs of Willing and Wishing, of Warning and Beseeching, of Urging and Demanding, of Resolving and Endeavouring (**verba studiī et voluntātis**).

1. Positive : **ut.**

Volō utī mihĭ respondeās, C., *Vat.*, 7, 17 (544, II.). **(Phaëthōn) optāvit ut in currum patris tollerētur**, C., *Off.*, III. 25, 94; *Phaethon desired to be lifted up into his father's chariot.* **Admoneō ut cottīdiē meditēre resistendum esse īrācundiae**, C., *Q.F.*, I. I. 13, 38; *I admonish you to reflect daily that resistance must be made to hot-headedness.* **Ubiī (Caesarem) ōrant, ut sibĭ parcat**, CAES., *B.G.*, VI. 9, 7 ; *the Ubii beg Cæsar to spare them.* **Sed precor ut possim tūtius esse miser**, Ov., *Tr.*, v. 2, 78 (423, 2). **Exigis ut Priamus nātōrum fūnere lūdat**, Ov., *Tr.*, v. 12, 7; *you exact that Priam sport at* (his) *sons' funeral.* **Athēniēnsēs cum statuerent ut nāvēs cōnscenderent, Cyrsilum quendam suādentem ut in urbe manērent lapidibus obruērunt**, C., *Off.*, III. 11, 48; *the Athenians, resolving to go on board their ships, overwhelmed with stones* (= stoned) *one Cyrsilus, who tried to persuade them to remain in the city.*

So also any verb or phrase used as a verb of Willing or Demanding.

Pȳthia respondit ut moenibus līgneīs sē mūnīrent, NEP., II. 2, 6 ; *the Pythia answered that they must defend themselves with walls of wood.*

2. Negative : **nē, ut nē**; continued by **nēve (neu)**, *and not.*

Caesar suīs imperāvit nē quod omnīnō tēlum in hostēs rēicerent, CAES., *B.G.*, I. 46, 2; *Caesar gave orders to his* (men) *not to throw back any missile at all at the enemy.* **Themistoclēs [collēgīs suīs] praedīxit ut nē prius Lacedaemoniōrum lēgātōs dīmitterent quam ipse esset remissus**, NEP., II. 7, 3 ; *Themistocles told his colleagues beforehand not to dismiss the Lacedaemonian envoys before he were sent back.* **Pompēius suīs praedīxerat ut Caesaris impetum exciperent nēve sē locō movērent**, CAES., *B.C.*, III. 92, 1 ; *Pompey had told his men beforehand to receive Caesar's charge and not to move from their position.*

REMARKS.—1. When verbs of Willing and Wishing are used as verbs of Saying and Thinking, Knowing and Showing, the Inf. must be used. The English translation is *that*, and the Indic. : **volō**, *I will have it* (maintain), **moneō**, *I remark*, **persuādeō**, *I convince*, **dēcernō**, *I decide*, **cōgō**, *I conclude*.

[Moneō] artem sine adsiduitāte dīcendī nōn multum iuvāre, *Cf.* [C.], *ad Her.*, I. 1, 1 ; *I remark that art without constant practice in speaking is of little avail.* **Vix cuīquam persuādēbātur Graeciā omnī cēssūrōs (Rōmānōs)**, L., XXXIII. 32, 3 ; *scarce any one could be persuaded that the Romans would retire from all Greece.* **Nōn sunt istī audiendī quī virtūtem dūram et quasi ferream esse quandam volunt**, C., *Lael.*, 13, 48 (318, R. 2). **Est**

mōs hominum ut nōlint eundem plūribus rēbus excellere, C., *Brut.*, 21, 84; *it is the way of the world not to allow that the same man excels in more things* (than one).

2. When the idea of Wishing is emphatic, the simple Subjv., without **ut,** is employed, and the restriction of sequence to Pr. and Impf. is removed:

Velim exīstimēs nēminem cuīquam cāriōrem umquam fuisse quam tē mihī, C., *Fam.*, I. 9, 24; *I wish you to think that no one was ever dearer to any one than you to me.* **Mālō tē sapiēns hostis metuat quam stultī cīvēs laudent,** L., XXII. 39, 20; *I had rather a wise enemy should fear you than foolish citizens should praise you.* **Excūsātum habeās mē rogo, cēno domī,** MART., II. 79, 2 (238). **Hūc ades, īnsānī feriant sine lītora fluctūs,** V., *Ec.*, 9, 43; *come hither* (and) *let the mad waves lash the shores.* **Tam fēlīx essēs quam fōrmōsissima vellem,** Ov., *Am.*, I. 8, 27 (302). **Vellem mē ad cēnam invītāssēs,** C., *Fam.*, XII. 4, 1 (261, R.). **Occidit occideritque sinās cum nōmine Trōia,** V., *A.*, XII. 828; *'tis fallen, and let Troy be fallen, name and all.*

So **iubeō** in poetry and later prose. Compare also **potius quam,** 577, N. 6.

3. **Ut nē** is not used after verbs of negative signification, as **impediō,** *I hinder,* **recūsō,** *I refuse* (548). Otherwise there seems to be no difference in meaning between it and **nē,** except that sometimes the **nē** seems to apply more to a single word in the sentence.

4. On **nēdum,** see 482, 5, R. 2.

NOTES.—1. Such verbs and phrases are: *Willing* and *Wishing:* **volō, nōlō, mālō, optō, studeō.** *Warning* and *Beseeching:* **hortor, adhortor, moneō, admoneō, auctor sum, cōnsilium dō, ōrō, rogō, petō, precor, pōscō, pōstulō, flāgitō, obsecrō.** *Urging* and *Demanding:* **suādeō, persuādeō, cēnseō, imperō, mandō, praecipiō, ēdīcō, dīcō, scrībō.** *Resolving* and *Endeavouring:* **statuō, cōnstituō, dēcernō, nītor, contendō, labōrō, pūgnō, id agō, operam dō, cūrō, videō, prōvideō, prōspiciō, legem ferō, lēx est,** *etc.*

2. Substantives of kindred meaning, in combination with the copula or other verbs, take similar constructions. Such are **voluntās, cupiditās, spēs, ārdor, auctōritās, cōnsilium** (especially in the combination **eō, hōc cōnsiliō**), **sīgnum, praeceptum, exemplum, prōpositum, officium, negōtium, mūnus, verba,** and **lītterae** (with **dare, mittere,** *etc.*), **sententia, animus** (especially **eō animō**), **condiciō** (especially **eā condiciōne**), **foedus, iūs, lēx** (**eā lēge**), **cūra, opera, causa, ratiō.**

3. Instead of **ut** with the Subjv., the Inf. is frequently used with this class of verbs. So, generally, with **iubeō,** *I order,* 532. With verbs of Asking, however, the Inf. is not common until VERGIL. **Ōrāre** has Inf. once in PLAUTUS, then in VERGIL and later poets; in prose first in TACITUS. **Rogāre** has **ut** regularly, Inf. only once (CAT., XXXV. 10). **Quaesō, implōrō, obsecrō, obtēstor,** never have Inf., **flāgitāre** only once (H., *S.*, II. 4, 61) until SUETONIUS; **pōstulāre** very often, especially in early Latin in the sense *expect;* **pōscere** not till the Augustan poets. Authors vary. The use of the Inf. is wider in poetry and silver prose.

B. *Verbs of Hindering.*

547. The dependencies of verbs of Hindering may be regarded as partly Final, partly Consecutive. **Nē** and **quōminus** are originally final, but the final sense is often effaced, especially in **quōminus. Quīn** is a consecutive particle. The sequence of verbs of Hindering is that of the Final Sentence.

The negative often disappears in the English translation.

548. Verbs and phrases signifying to Prevent, to Forbid, to Refuse, and to Beware, may take **nē** with the Subjunctive, if they are not negatived.

Impedior nē plūra dīcam, C., *Sull.*, 33, 92 ; *I am hindered from saying more* (*I am hindered that I should say no more*). "Who did hinder you that ye should not obey the truth ?" GAL., V. 7.

Servitūs mea mihi interdīxit nē quid mīrer meum malum, PL., *Pers.*, 621 ; *my slavery has forbidden me to marvel aught at ill of mine.* **Histiaeus nē rēs cōnficerētur obstitit**, NEP., I. 3, 5 ; *Histiaeus opposed the thing's being done.* (**Rēgulus**) **sententiam nē dīceret recūsāvit**, C., *Off.*, III. 27, 100 ; *Regulus refused to pronounce an opinion.* **Maledictīs dēterrēre nē scrībat parat**, TER., *Ph.*, 3 (423, 2). **Tantum cum fingēs nē sīs manifēsta cavētō**, OV., *A.A.*, III. 801 (271, 2). **Tantum nē noceās dum vīs prōdesse vidētō**, OV., *Tr.*, I. 1, 101 ; *only see* (*to it*) *that you do not do harm while you wish to do good.*

NOTES.—1. The most important of these words are : *Preventing :* **impedīre, impedīmentō esse, prohibēre, tenēre, retinēre, dēterrēre, interclūdere, interpellāre, dēprecārī, obsistere, obstāre, intercēdere, interpōnere.** *Forbidding :* **interdīcere.** *Refusing :* **recūsāre, repūgnāre, resistere, sē tenēre, sē reprimere, sibĭ temperāre, morārī.** *Beware :* **cavēre, vidēre,** and a few others, especially the phrase **per aliquem stāre** (more often with **quōminus**).

2. Many verbs of Preventing and Refusing also take **quōminus** (549), and some also the Infinitive (423, 2, N. 2).

3. **Cavēre,** *to beware*, and **praecavēre** belong to verbs of Hindering only so far as action is contemplated. **Cavēre,** followed by **ut,** means *to be sure to ;* by **nē** or **ut nē,** *to see to it that not ;* by **nē,** *to take precautions against.* When **nē** is omitted, **cavē, cavētō,** with the Subjv., form circumlocutions for the negative Imperative (271, 2). So with **vidē ut, nē. Cavēre** also has the Inf. occasionally as a verb of negative Will (423, 2, N. 2), beginning with PLAUTUS. In prose it is cited only from CATO (once), CICERO (*Att.*, III. 17, 3), SALLUST (*Iug.*, 64, 2), and PLINY MAI.

4. **Vidē nē** (**nē nōn**), *see to it lest*, is often used as a polite formula for **dubitō an** (457, 2), *I am inclined to think.* **Crēdere omnia vidē nē nōn sit necesse,** C., *Div.*, II. 13, 31.

549. Verbs of Preventing and Refusing may take **quōminus** (= **ut eō minus**), *that thereby the less*, with the Subjunctive.

Aetās nōn impedit quōminus agrī colendī studia teneāmus, C., *Cat.M.*, 17, 60 ; *age does not hinder our retaining interest in agriculture.* **Nōn dēterret sapientem mors quōminus reī pūblicae cōnsulat**, C., *Tusc.*, I. 38, 91 ; *death does not deter the sage from consulting the interest of the State.* **Quid obstat quōminus (Deus) sit beātus ?** C., *N.D.*, I. 34, 95 ; *what* *is in the way of God's being happy?* **Caesar cōgnōvit per Afrānium stāre quōminus proeliō dīmicārētur,** CAES., *B.C.*, I. 41, 3; *Caesar found that it was Afranius's fault that there was no decisive fight* (**stat,** *there is a stand-still*).

NOTES.—1. With **impedīre** and **prohibēre** CAESAR never uses **quōminus**; CICERO rarely. But with other words implying Hindrance CICERO uses **quōminus** not unfrequently. With **prohibēre** the regular construction is the Inf., but this is rare with **impedīre, quōminus** being the rule. With **recūsāre,** the Inf. is rare (CAES., *B.G.*, III. 22, 3) but classical, becoming more frequent from LIVY on. The passive of **dēterrēre** is also construed with the Inf. occasionally.

2. PLAUTUS does not use **quōminus,** TERENCE first, but seldom. It is especially common from the time of CICERO. In TERENCE the elements are sometimes separated (**quō—minus**), thus emphasising the relative character. But it is not so used in the classical Latin, and in the Silver Age the force of its origin ceases to be felt, so that it is construed like **quīn.** The fact that it is not found in PLAUTUS nor in VITRUVIUS has led to the suggestion that it is a book-word.

3. The difference in usage between **quōminus** and **quīn** seems to be that while **quīn** is always used with negatives, **quōminus** occurs sometimes with positives, so that according to the connection it is either Final or Consecutive.

4. **Quō sētius** for **quōminus** is archaic, but occurs twice in CORNIFICIUS and twice in CICERO (*Inv.*, II. 45, 132; 57, 170).

III. Verbs of Fearing.

550. 1. Verbs of Fearing, and expressions that involve Fear, take the Present and Perfect, Imperfect and Pluperfect Subjunctive.

The Present Subjunctive represents the Present and Future Indicative. The Perfect Subjunctive regularly represents the Perfect Indicative.

Present and Perfect Subjunctive become Imperfect and Pluperfect after a Past Tense.

These constructions are survivals of the original parataxis, when **nē** and **ut** were particles of wish. Thus, **timeō: nē veniat,** *I am afraid; may he not come* (i.e., *I am afraid that he will*), becomes, when the two clauses are combined, **timeō nē veniat,** *I am afraid lest* (*that*) *he may* (*will*) *come.* Similarly with **ut,** which in this usage was originally *how.* Hence,

2. With verbs of Fearing, **nē,** *lest,* shows that the negative is wished and the positive feared; **ut** (**nē nōn**) shows that the positive is wished and the negative feared: **nē nōn** is used regularly after the negative, or an interrogative with negative force.

Vereor nē hostis veniat, *I fear lest the enemy come, that he is coming, that he will come.* (*I wish he may not come.*)

Vereor nē hostis vēnerit, *I fear lest the enemy have come, that* (*it will turn out that*) *he has come.*

Vereor ut amīcus veniat, *I fear (how my friend can come) lest my friend come not, that he is not coming, will not come. (I wish he may come.)*

Vereor ut amīcus vēnerit, *I fear lest my friend have not come, that he has not come.*

Nōn vereor nē amīcus nōn veniat, *I do not fear that my friend is not coming, will not come.*

Nōn vereor nē amīcus nōn vēnerit, *I do not fear that my friend has not come.*

Id pavēs, nē dūcās tū illam, tū autem ut dūcās, TER., *And.*, 349; *that's what you dread,* YOU *lest you marry her* (**nē dūcam!**); YOU, *on the other hand, lest you don't* (**utinam dūcam!**).

Vereor nē dum minuere velim labōrem augeam, C., *Leg.*, I. 4, 12; *I fear lest, while I wish to lessen the toil, I increase it (that I am increasing it).* **Verēmur nē parum hīc liber mellis et absinthiī multum habēre videātur,** QUINT., III. 1, 5; *I am afraid that this book will seem to have too little honey and* (too) *much wormwood.* **Timeō nē tibī nihil praeter lacrimās queam reddere,** C., *Planc.*, 42, 101; *I am afraid that I can give you nothing in return save tears.* **Aurum īnspicere volt nē subruptum siet,** PL., *Aul.*, 39; *he wishes to inspect the gold (for fear) lest it be filched.*

Timeō ut sustineās (**labōrēs**), C., *Fam.*, XIV. 2, 3; *I fear that you will not hold out under your toils.* **Vereor nē dum dēfendam meōs, nōn parcam tuīs,** C., *Att.*, I. 17, 3; *I fear lest in defending my own I may not spare thine.* **Nōn vereor nē tua virtūs opīniōnī hominum nōn respondeat,** *Cf.* C., *Fam.*, II. 5, 2; *I do not fear that your virtue will not answer to* (come up to) *public expectation.* **Metuō nē id cōnsiliī cēperīmus quod nōn facile explicāre possīmus,** C., *Fam.*, XIV. 12; *I fear that we have formed a plan that we cannot readily explain.* **Ūnum illud extimēscēbam nē quid turpius facerem, vel dīcam, iam effēcissem,** C., *Att.*, IX. 7, 1; *the only thing I feared was, lest I should act disgracefully, or, I should* (rather) *say,* (lest) *I had already acted disgracefully.*

NOTES.—1. **Ut** seems to be used only after **metuō, paveō, timeō,** and **vereor.** Most common is **vereor**; **metuō** is common in early Latin, but is cited but rarely later (HORACE, CICERO); **paveō** has to be supplied once with **ut** in TER., *And.*, 349. **Timeō ut** is found first in CICERO, and is very rare.

2. **Nē nōn** is very rare in early Latin, but becomes more frequent from CICERO on. **Ut nē** is never found for **nē.**

3. Two strange cases are cited where, instead of **nē, ut** seems to be used, *viz.*, HOR., *S.*, I. 3, 120, **nam ut ferulā caedās meritum māiōra subīre verbera, nōn vereor,** and L., XXVIII. 22, 12, **nihil minus, quam ut ēgredī obsessī moenibus audērent, timērī poterat.** In the first case the **ut** clause precedes, and the **nōn vereor** is used by anacoluthon; in the second the **ut** clause is a circumlocution for an omitted **illud,** parallel to **nihil.** This is also helped by the antecedence of the **ut** clause.

4. When a verb of Fear is a verb of Uncertainty an indirect question may follow: **vereor quō modō acceptūrī sītis,** [C.], *ad Her.*, IV. 37, 49.

5. (*a*) With the Inf. verbs of Fear are verbs of (negative) Will: **vereor = prae timōre nōlō.**

Vōs Allobrogum tēstimōniīs nōn crēdere timētis? C., *Font.*, 12, 26; *are ye afraid to disbelieve the testimony of the Allobroges?* **Vereor laudāre praesentem,** C., *N.D.*, I. 21, 58 (423, 2). **Nīl metuunt iūrāre,** CAT., LXIV. 146; *they have no fear to take an oath.*

These constructions are found at all periods and with a wide range of words. CICERO, however, is restrained in his usage, and the most examples are found in the poets and later prose writers.

(*b*) With the Acc. and Inf. verbs of Fear are verbs of Thinking or of Perception: **vereor = cum timōre putō** or **videō.**

Verēbar nōn omnēs causam vincere posse suam [Ov., *Her.*, 16, 75]. **Tēlumque īnstāre tremēscit,** V., *A.*, XII. 916.

This construction is rare, but occurs at all periods; more often, however, it involves the substantives **timor** and **metus,** especially in LIVY, who shows seven cases altogether.

CONSECUTIVE SENTENCES.

Sentences of Tendency and Result.

551. 1. Consecutive Sentences are those sentences which show the Consequence or Tendency of Actions. In Latin, Result is a mere inference from Tendency, though often an irresistible inference. In other words, the Latin language uses *so as* throughout, and not *so that,* although *so that* is often a convenient translation. The result is only implied, not stated.

2. Consecutive Sentences are divided into two classes:

I. Consecutive Sentences in which the Tendency is expressed by the Particle: Pure Consecutive Sentences.

II. Consecutive Sentences in which the Tendency lies in the leading Verb: (*a*) after verbs of Effecting; (*b*) after negatived verbs of Preventing, Doubt, and Uncertainty; (*c*) after words and phrases requiring expansion.

I. Pure Consecutive Sentences.

552. Pure Consecutive Sentences are introduced by

1. **Ut (utī),** *that, so that,* and other relative pronouns and adverbs (631).

2. **Ut—nōn,** *that, so that, as—not,* continued by **neque, nec** (543, 4).

3. **Quīn = ut nōn,** after a negative sentence (554).

Correlative demonstratives occur very often: **ita (sīc), tam,**

tantopere, tantō, tantum, adeō, eō, huc; tālis, tantus, tot, is, ēius modī, and others of similar meaning.

In virtūte multī sunt adscēnsūs, ut is māximē glōriā excellat, quī virtūte plūrimum praestet, C., *Planc.*, 25, 60 ; *in virtue there are many degrees, so that he excels most in glory who is most advanced in virtue.* **Neque mē vīxisse paenitet quoniam ita vīxī ut nōn frūstrā mē nātum exīstumem,** C., *Cat.M.*, 23, 84 (540). **Tanta vīs probitātis est, ut eam in hoste etiam dīligāmus,** C., *Lael.*, 9, 29 ; *so great is the virtue of uprightness, that we love it even in an enemy.* **Nōn is es ut tē pudor umquam ā turpitūdine revocārit,** C., *Cat.*, I. 9, 22 ; *you are not the man for shame ever to have recalled you* (= *ever to have been recalled by shame*) *from baseness.* **Nēmŏ adeō ferus est ut nōn mītēscere possit,** H., *Ep.*, I. 1, 39 ; *no one is so savage that he cannot* (*be made to*) *soften.* **Nīl tam difficile est quīn quaerendō invēstīgārī possiet,** Ter., *Heaut.*, 675 ; *naught is so hard but it can* (= *that it cannot*) *be tracked out by search.* **Numquam tam male est Siculīs quīn aliquid facētē et commodē dīcant,** C., *Verr.*, IV. 43, 95 ; *the Sicilians are never so badly off as not to* (have) *something or other clever and pat* (to) *say.*

Remarks.—1. Notice especially the impersonal **tantum abest, āfuit** (rarely **aberat**)—**ut**—**ut.** The phrase originates with an abstract Abl. dependent on a personal **absum,** which abstract Abl. is afterward expanded into a consecutive clause with **ut.**

[**Āgēsilāus**] **tantum āfuit ab īnsolentiā glōriae ut commiserātus sit fortūnam Graeciae,** Nep., XVII. 5, 2 ; *Agesilaus was so far from the insolence of glory that he pitied the* (*mis*)*fortune of Greece.* **Tantum abest ab eō ut malum mors sit ut verear nē hominī sit nihil bonum aliud,** C., *Tusc.*, I. 31, 76 ; *so far is it from death* (= so far is death from) *being an evil that I fear man has no other blessing.* **Tantum āfuit, ut illōrum praesidiō nostram fīrmārēmus clāssem, ut etiam ā Rhodiīs urbe prohibērentur nostrī mīlitēs,** Lentulus [C., *Fam.*, XII. 15, 2] ; *so far were we from strengthening our fleet by reinforcements from them that our soldiers were actually kept away from the city by the Rhodians.* **Tantum abest ut nostra mīrēmur ut ūsque eō difficilēs sīmus ut nōbīs nōn satisfaciat ipse Dēmosthenēs,** C., *Or.*, 29, 104 ; *so far are we from admiring our own* (compositions) *that we are so hard to please that Demosthenes himself fails to satisfy us.*

The personal construction is extremely rare.

The second **ut** may be omitted, and a declarative sentence follow asyndetically : **Tantum aberat ut bīnōs (librōs) scrīberent : vix singulōs cōnfēcērunt,** C., *Att.*, XIII. 21, 5 ; *so far were they from writing two copies of each book, they with difficulty finished up one.*

2. **Dīgnus,** *worthy,* **indīgnus,** *unworthy,* **aptus, idōneus,** *fit,* take a consecutive sentence with **quī.** Occasionally in early, more often in later

Latin, **dīgnus** and **indīgnus** take **ut.** In poetry all these words are found sometimes with the Infinitive.

Quī modestē pāret, vidētur quī aliquandō imperet dīgnus esse, C., *Leg.*, III. 2, 5 ; *he who obeys duly seems to be worthy to command some day.*

3. While **ita** (**sīc**) is usually antecedent to a consecutive **ut,** it may also be antecedent to a final **ut** or **nē** when the *design* or *wish* intrudes. **Ita mē gessī nē tibī pudōrī essem,** L., XL. 15, 6 ; *I behaved myself so as not to be a disgrace to you.*

So not unfrequently when a restriction or condition is intended :

Ita probanda est mānsuētūdō ut adhibeātur reī pūblicae causā sevēritās, C., *Off.*, I. 25, 88 ; *mildness is to be approved, so that* (*provided that*) *strictness be used for the sake of the commonwealth.* **Ita fruī volunt voluptātibus ut nūllī propter eās cōnsequantur dolōrēs,** C., *Fin.*, I. 14, 48 ; *they wish to enjoy pleasures without having any pain to ensue on account of them.* **[Pȳthagorās et Platō] mortem ita laudant ut fugere vītam vetent,** C., *Scaur.*, 4, 5; *Pythagoras and Plato so praise death, that they* (while they praise death) *forbid fleeing from life.* **Ita tū istaec tua mīscētō nē mē admīsceās,** TER., *Heaut.*, 783 ; *mix up your mixings so you mix me not withal.* **Tantum ā vāllō [Pompēī] prīma aciēs aberat, utī nē tēlō adicī posset,** CAES., *B.C.*, III. 55.

Ut alone may also be used thus : **Rēx esse nōlim ut esse crūdēlis velim,** SYR., 577 ; *king I would not be, if I must school myself to cruelty.*

4. **Ut nōn** is often = *without*, and the English verbal in *-ing :*

(Octāviānus) numquam fīliōs suōs populō commendāvit ut nōn adiceret : sī merēbuntur, SUET., *Aug.*, 56; *Octavianus* (*Augustus*) *never recommended his sons to the people in such a way as not to add* (= *without adding*) *: if they are worthy.* **Quī nē malum habeat abstinet sē ab iniūriā certē mālet exīstimārī bonus vir ut nōn sit quam esse ut nōn putētur,** C., *Fin.*, II. 22, 71 ; *he who, to avoid misfortune, abstains from injury, will certainly prefer being thought a good man without being such, to being* (a good man) *without being believed* (to be such).

II. Complementary Consecutive Sentences.

A. *Verbs of Effecting.*

553. Verbs of Effecting belong partly to the Consecutive, partly to the Final Sentence. The negative is **nōn** or **nē** ; the sequence, final.

Such verbs are :

1. Verbs of Causation : **facere, efficere, perficere,** *I make, effect, achieve ;* **assequī, cōnsequī,** *I attain, accomplish,* and many others.

The following are cited as more or less common in CICERO : **prōficere,**

impetrāre, valēre, committere, tenēre, adipīscī, praestāre, ferre (in phrases **cōnsuētūdō, nātūra, fortūna fert**), **adferre, adiuvāre, expūgnāre, extorquēre, exprimere,** and a few others.

Efficiam ut intellegātis, C., *Cluent.*, 3, 7; *I will cause you to understand.* **Sed perfice, ut Crassus haec quae coartāvit nōbīs explicet,** C., *Or.*, I. 35, 163; *but bring it about that Crassus (make Crassus) unfold to us what he has condensed.* **Nōn committam ut causam aliquam tibī recūsandī dem,** C., *Or.*, II. 57, 233; *I shall not make the blunder of giving you an excuse for refusing.*

Negatives:

Rērum obscūritās nōn verbōrum facit ut nōn intellegātur ōrātiō, C., *Fin.*, II. 5, 15; *it is the obscurity of the subject, not of the words, that causes the language not to be understood.* **Potestis efficere ut male moriar, ut nōn moriar nōn potestis,** Plin., *Ep.*, III. 16, 11; *you may make me die a hard death, keep me from dying you cannot.* **Efficiam posthāc nē quemquam vōce lacessās,** V., *Ec.*, 3, 51; *I will bring it about that you challenge no one hereafter in song.*

Facere ut is often little more than a periphrasis; especially in the forms **fac ut** and **faxō, faxit** (both peculiar to Comedy).

Fortūna vestra facit ut īrae meae temperem, L., XXXVI. 35, 3; *your fortune causes that I (makes me) restrain my anger (put metes to my anger).* **Invītus** (325, R. 6) **faciō ut recorder ruīnās reī pūblicae,** C., *Vat.*, 9, 21; (it is) *against my will that I (am doing so as to) recall the ruined condition of the commonwealth.*

2. Verbs of Compelling and Permitting:

Cōgere, adigere, impellere, dūcere, with its compounds, **movēre, commovēre,** to which must be added **exōrāre,** *to force by pleading.* **Permittere, sinere, concēdere, dare, (nōn) patī,** and less often **largīrī, tribuere, ferre.**

Tenēmus memoriā Catulum esse coāctum ut vītā sē ipse prīvāret, C., *Or.*, III. 3, 9; *we remember that Catulus was forced to take his own life.* **Illud nātūra nōn patitur, ut aliōrum spoliīs nostrās cōpiās augeāmus,** C., *Off.*, III. 5, 22; *nature does not allow us to increase our wealth by the spoils of others.* **Collēgam perpulerat nē contrā rem pūblicam sentīret,** S., *C.*, 26, 4; *he had prevailed upon his colleague, not to take sides against the commonwealth.*

Note.—**Cōgere** has usually the Inf. (423, 2, N. 2), so occasionally **sinere, patī.** On **permittere,** see 532, N. 1. **Cōgere** in the sense *conclude* is a verb of Saying (546, R. 1). **Facere** and **efficere,** in the sense *cause*, are very rarely used with the Infinitive. Compare C., *Br.*, 38, 142, (**āctiō**) **tālēs ōrātōrēs vidērī facit, quālēs ipsī sē vidērī volunt.** This becomes more common in very late Latin.

3. Passive verbs of Causation, and their equivalents,

namely, many Impersonal Verbs of Happening and Following, of Accident and Consequent.

Such verbs are **cōnficī, efficī, fit, accidit, contingit, obtingit, ēvenit,** *it happens,* **ūsū venit,** *it occurs,* **sequitur,** *it follows,* and many others. So also **est,** *it is the case.*

Ex quō efficitur, nōn ut voluptās nē (the design of the arguer) **sit voluptās, sed ut voluptās nōn** (the result of the argument) **sit summum bonum,** C., *Fin.*, II. 8, 24; *from which it results, not that pleasure is not pleasure, but that pleasure is not the supreme good.* **Potest fierī ut fallar,** C., *Fam.*, XIII. 73, 2 ; *(it) may be (that) I am mistaken.* **Potest fierī ut is unde tē audīsse dīcis īrātus dīxerit,** C., *Or.*, II. 70, 285; *(it) may be (that) he from whom you say you heard (it) said it in anger.* **Persaepe ēvenit ut ūtilitās cum honestāte certet,** C., *Part.Or.*, 25, 89; *it very often (so) happens that profit is at variance with honor.*

NOTE.—Noteworthy is the early Latin use of **(fierī) potis ut nē,** as in **fierī potis est ut nē quā exeat,** TER., *Ad.*, 626.

4. Very many impersonal verbs and combinations of neuter adjectives with **est,** after the analogy of the impersonals just mentioned.

Such are: **additur, accēdit,** *it is added;* **restat, reliquom est,** *it remains;* **appāret,** *it is plain.* Enumerations, as, **proximum, tertium, extrēmum est; inūsitātum, rārum est,** *it rarely happens that;* **novom, singulāre, mīrum, inaudītum, vērum, falsum, (nōn) vērīsimile, cōnsequēns,** *etc.* Also rarely, **interest, necesse est, necessārium est,** and the like.

Ad Appī Claudī senectūtem accēdēbat etiam ut caecus esset, C., *Cat.M.*, 6, 16; *to the old age of Appius Claudius was further added his being blind.* **Eī ne integrum quidem erat ut ad iūstitiam remigrāret,** C., *Tusc.*, V. 21, 62 ; *for him it was not even an open question to go back to justice.* **Rārum (= rārō accidit) ut sit idōneus suae reī quisque dēfēnsor,** QUINT., IV. 1, 46; *it is rare for a man to be a good defender of his own case.*

REMARKS.—1. **Necesse est,** *it is necessary,* generally, and **oportet,** *it behooves,* always omit **ut**:

[Leuctrica pūgna] immortālis sit necesse est, NEP., XV. 10, 2 ; *the battle of Leuctra must needs be immortal.* **Sed nōn effugiēs; mēcum moriāris oportet,** PROP., II. 8, 25 ; *but you shall not escape; you must die with me.*

2. The neuter adjectives with **ut** are very rare until the post-classical period and are far more commonly construed with the Infinitive.

3. Very common is the periphrasis **fore (futūrum) ut,** which gives the common form of the Fut. Infinitive. See 248.

B. *Verbs of Hindering.*

554. **Quīn** is used like **quōminus**, with Verbs of Preventing, Refusing, *etc.*, but only when they are negatived or questioned.

Notes.—1. **Quīn** is compounded of **quī**—an interrogative-relative Ablative or Locative—and **nĕ** (**nōn**). Its first use is interrogative: "why not" in an indignant question; almost equivalent to an indignant Imperative, with which, through the fading out of its composition, it is occasionally connected, especially in early and later Latin, rarely in Cicero (269).

2. An indignant question (*How not? Why not?*) objects to opposition, and is therefore naturally construed with the negative of a verb of Hindering. Hence **quīn,** as an interrogative (*How not?*), takes the sequence of the Interrogative Sentence. But this shows itself only after words of doubt; after verbs of Preventing the sequence coincides with that of the Final Sentence, and after other negative sentences the sequence coincides with that of the Consecutive Sentence.

3. By its combination with verbs of Preventing, **quīn** came to be felt as a consecutive particle = **ut nōn,** and was then used in other consecutive connections for **ut nōn.**

555. **Quīn** is used when Verbs and Phrases of Preventing, Omitting, Refraining, Refusing, and Delaying, Doubt, and Uncertainty, are negatived or questioned.

1. Verbs of Preventing and the like (sequence of the Final Sentence).

Vix nunc obsistitur illīs quīn lanient mundum, Ov., *M.*, I. 58; *they are now hardly to be kept* (*that they should not rend*) *from rending the universe.* **Antiochus nōn sē tenuit quīn contrā suum doctōrem librum ēderet,** C., *Ac.*, II. 4, 12; *Antiochus did not refrain from publishing a book against his teacher.* **Vix reprimor quīn tē manēre iubeam,** Pl., *M.G.*, 1368; *I am scarcely kept back* (*keep myself back*) *from bidding you remain.* **Neque mē Iūppiter [prohibēbit] quīn sīc faciam utī cōnstituī,** Pl., *Am.*, 1051; *nor will Jupiter prevent me from doing just as I determined to do.*

Remark.—The list of verbs is given in 548, n. 1.

2. Verbs of Doubt and Uncertainty (sequence of the Interrogative Sentence).

Nōn dubium est quīn uxōrem nōlit fīlius, Ter., *And.*, 172; *there is no doubt that* (my) *son does not want a wife.* **Quis dubitet (= nēmŏ dubitet) quīn in virtūte dīvitiae sint?** C., *Parad.*, VI. 2, 48 (259). **Nōn dubitārī dēbet quīn fuerint ante Homērum poētae,** C., *Br.*, 18, 71; *it is not to be doubted that there were poets before Homer.* **Nunc mihĭ nōn est dubium quīn ventūrae nōn sint (legiōnēs),** C., *Fam.*, II. 17, 5 (515).

Occasionally verbs of Saying and Thinking are found with the same construction, because they are near equivalents.

Negārī nōn potest quīn rēctius sit etiam ad pācātōs barbarōs exercitum mittī, *Cf.* L., XL. 36, 2; *it cannot be denied* (doubted) *that it is better for an army to be sent to the barbarians even though they be quiet.* **Nōn abest sūspīciō (Lītotēs** [700] for **dubitārī nōn potest) quīn (Orgetorīx) ipse sibĭ mortem cōnscīverit,** CAES., *B. G.*, I. 4, 4; *there is no lack of ground to suspect* (= *there is no doubt that*) *Orgetorix killed himself.*

REMARKS.—1. The principal gain of the interrogative sequence is that the Periphrastic Fut. may be employed (of which, however, the first example is cited from CICERO), but according to 515, R. 3, **nōn dubitō quīn** may have the simple Subjv. instead of the Periphrastic:

Nōn dubitāre quīn dē omnibus obsidibus supplicium sūmat (Ariovistus), CAES., *B. G.*, I. 31, 15; "*he did not doubt that Ariovistus would put all the hostages to death.*" Compare CAT., CVIII. 3.

So when there is an original Subjv. notion:

Nōn dubitō quīn ad tē statim veniam, C., *Att.*, VIII. 11 B, 3; *I do not doubt that I ought to come to you forthwith.* (**Veniam?** *Shall I come?*)

2. Of course **dubitō** and **nōn dubitō** may have the ordinary interrogative constructions (467). On **dubitō an,** see 457, 2.

3. **Nōn dubitō,** with the Inf., usually means *I do not hesitate to:*

Nōn dubitem dīcere omnēs sapientēs semper esse beātōs, C., *Fin.*, V. 32, 95; *I should not hesitate to say that all wise men are always happy.* **Et dubitāmus adhūc virtūtem extendere factīs?** V., *A.*, VI. 806; *and do we still hesitate to spread our* (fame for) *valour by our deeds?* Compare **vereor, timeō,** *I fear, hesitate to* (550, 2, N. 5).

So occasionally **nōn dubitō quīn.** See R. 1.

(Rōmānī) arbitrābantur nōn dubitātūrum fortem virum quīn cēderet aequō animō lēgibus, C., *Mil.*, 23, 63; *the Romans thought that a brave man would not hesitate to yield with equanimity to the laws.*

NOTE.—**Nōn dubitō** with the Inf. for **nōn dubitō quīn** occurs chiefly in NEPOS, LIVY, and later writers.

Sunt multī quī quae turpia esse dubitāre nōn possunt ūtilitātis speciē ductī probent, QUINT., III. 8, 3; *there are many who, led on by the appearance of profit, approve what they cannot doubt to be base.*

556. Quīn, equivalent to **ut nōn,** may be used after any negative sentence (sequence of the Consecutive Sentence). Here it may often be translated "*without.*"

Nīl tam difficile est quīn quaerendō invēstīgārī possiet, TER., *Heaut.*, 675 (552). **Nūllum adhūc intermīsī diem quīn aliquid ad tē litterārum darem,** C., *Att.*, VII. 15, 1; *I have thus far not allowed a day to pass but I dropped you* (*without dropping you*) *something of a letter* (*a line or two*).

Note the combination **(facere) nōn possum quīn**, *I cannot but*, and similar combinations ; **nōn possum nōn** with Inf. is also classical.

Facere nōn possum quīn cottīdiē ad tē mittam (lītterās), C., *Att.*, XII. 27, 2; *I cannot do without* (*I cannot help*) *sending a letter to you daily.* **Nōn possum quīn exclāmem**, PL., *Trin.*, 705; *I cannot but* (*I must*) *cry out.* (**Nūllō modō facere possum ut nōn sim populāris**, C., *Agr.*, II. 3, 7 (reading doubtful); *I cannot help being a man of the people.*)

Nihil abest quīn sim miserrimus, C., *Att.*, XI. 15, 3; *there is nothing wanting that I should be* (= *to make me*) *perfectly miserable.* **Fierī nūllō modō poterat quīn Cleomenī parcerētur**, C., *Verr.*, V. 40, 104; *it could in nowise happen but that Cleomenes should be spared* (= *Cleomenes had to be spared*). **Paulum āfuit quīn (Fabius) Vārum interficeret**, CAES., *B.C.*, II. 35, 2; *there was little lacking but Fabius* (had) *killed Varus* (= *Fabius came near killing Varus*).

Explanatory Ut.

557. A Consecutive Sentence with **ut** is often used to give the contents or character of a preceding substantive, adjective, or pronoun.

Est mōs hominum ut nōlint eundem plūribus rēbus excellere, C., *Br.*, 21, 84 (546, R. 1). **An quoiquamst ūsus hominī sē ut cruciet?** TER., *Heaut.*, 81 (406, N. 5). **Est miserōrum ut malevolentēs sint atque invideant bonīs**, PL., *Capt.*, 583; *the wretched have a way of being ill-natured and envying the well-to-do.* **Nec meum ad tē ut mittam grātiīs**, PL., *Asin.*, 190; *nor is it my style to let her go to you as a gracious gift.* **Id est proprium cīvitātis ut sit lībera**, C., *Off.*, II. 22, 78; *it is the peculiar privilege of a state, to be free.* **Illud ipsum habet cōnsul ut eī reliquī magistrātūs pāreant**, C., *Leg.*, III. 7, 16; *the consul has this very prerogative, that the other magistrates be obedient unto him.* **Tōtum in eō est, ut tibī imperēs**, C., *Tusc.*, II. 22, 53; *all depends upon this* (one thing), *your self-command.*

REMARK.—These are principally **mōs, cōnsuētūdō**, *habit, wont*; **opus, ūsus**, *need*; many substantives of *opinion* and *perception*, as **opīniō, sententia, cōgitātiō, mēns, sapientia, scientia, cōgnitiō**; **nātūra, genus, status**, and others, usually with a demonstrative attached; adjectives indicating possession: **meum, tuom, suom** (all mainly ante-class.), **proprium, commūne, praecipuum** (LIVY), and predicate Genitives with **esse**: **id, hōc, illud**, *etc.* These should be distinguished from final usages.

NOTES.—1. Tendency and Character lend themselves readily to circumlocution, and **ut** with Subjv. becomes a manner of equivalent to the Inf., which, however, is by far the more common construction.

2. To the same principle is to be referred the use of **ut** after **māior (magis) quam, nōn aliter quam** (*without*), first in LIVY; after **nisi** (591, *b*, R. 3). See 298.

Praeceptum māius erat quam ut ab homine vidērētur, C., *Fin.*, V. 16, 44 (503).

Exclamatory Questions.

558. **Ut** with the Subjunctive is used in Exclamatory Questions, usually with the insertion of **-ne.**

Egone ut tē interpellem? C., *Tusc.*, II. 18, 42; *I interrupt you?* **Tū ut umquam tē corrigās?** C., *Cat.*, I. 9, 22; *you—ever reform yourself?* **Dī māgnī, ut quī cīvem Rōmānum occīdisset, impūnitātem acciperet,** SEN., *Ben.*, V. 16, 3; *Great Gods! that one who had slain a Roman citizen, should escape unpunished!*

NOTE.—The expression is closely parallel with the Acc. and Infinitive. The one objects to the idea; the other, to any state of things that could produce the result. In neither case is there any definite or conscious ellipsis. Compare TER., *Hec.*, 589, with 613.

TEMPORAL SENTENCES.

559. The action of the Temporal or Dependent clause may stand to the action of the Principal clause in one of three relations:

I. It may be *antecedent.*

CONJUNCTIONS: **Postquam** (**Posteā quam,** not ante-class.), *after that, after;* **ut,** *as;* **ubi,** *when* (literally, *where*); **simulāc,** *as soon as;* **ut prīmum, cum prīmum,** *the first moment that.*

II. It may be *contemporaneous.*

CONJUNCTIONS: **Dum, dōnec,** *while, until;* **quoad,** *up to* (the time) *that;* **quamdiū,** *as long as;* **cum,** *when.*

III. It may be *subsequent.*

CONJUNCTIONS: **Antequam, priusquam,** *before that, before.*

A special chapter is required by

IV. **Cum (quom),** *when.*

MOODS IN TEMPORAL SENTENCES.

560. 1. The mood of Temporal clauses is regularly the Indicative.

2. The Subjunctive is used only:

(1) In **Ōrātiō Oblīqua** (508), Total or Partial. So also in the Ideal Second Person.

(2) When the idea of Design or Condition is introduced.

I. ANTECEDENT ACTION.

561. In historical narrative, Temporal Clauses with **postquam (posteāquam), ubi, ut, simulāc, ut prīmum,** and **cum prīmum** commonly take the Historical Perfect or the Historical Present Indicative.

The English translation is not unfrequently the Pluperfect.

Postquam Caesar pervēnit, obsidēs popōscit, CAES., *B.G.*, I. 27, 3 ; *after Caesar arrived, he demanded hostages.* **Quae ubi nūntiantur Rōmam, senātus extemplō dictātōrem dīcī iūssit,** L., IV. 56, 8 ; *when these tidings were carried to Rome, the senate forthwith ordered a dictator to be appointed.* **Pompēius ut equitātum suum pulsum vīdit, aciē excēssit,** CAES., *B.C.*, III. 94, 5 ; *as Pompey saw his cavalry beaten, he left the line of battle.* **(Pelopidās) nōn dubitāvit, simul āc cōnspexit hostem, cōnflīgere** (555, 2, R. 3), NEP., XVI. 5, 3 ; *as soon as he* (had) *caught sight of the enemy, Pelopidas did not hesitate to engage* (*him*).

Subjunctive in **Ōrātiō Oblīqua.**

Ariovistum, ut semel Gallōrum cōpiās vīcerit (Ō. R. vīcit), superbē imperāre, CAES., *B.G.*, I. 31, 12 ; "*that Ariovistus, as soon as he had once beaten the forces of the Gauls, exercised his rule arrogantly.*"

562. The Imperfect is used to express an action continued into the time of the principal clause (overlapping).

The translation often indicates the spectator (233, N. 1).

Tū postquam quī tibī erant amīcī nōn poterant vincere, ut amīcī tibī essent quī vincēbant effēcistī, C., *Quinct.*, 22, 70 ; *after* (*you saw*) *that those who were friendly to you could not be victorious you managed that those should be friendly to you who were going to be victorious.* **Ubi nēmō obvius ībat, ad castra hostium tendunt,** L., IX. 45, 14 ; *when* (they saw that) *no one was coming to meet them, they proceeded to the camp of the enemy.*

Subjunctive in **Ōrātiō Oblīqua.**

Scrīpsistī (eum) posteāquam nōn audēret (Ō. R. nōn audēbat) reprehendere, laudāre coepisse, C., *Att.*, I. 13, 4 ; *you wrote that, after he could not get up the courage to blame, he began to praise.*

563. 1. The Pluperfect is used to express an action completed before the time of the principal clause ; often of the Resulting Condition.

Albīnus postquam dēcrēverat nōn ēgredī prōvinciā, mīlitēs statīvīs castrīs habēbat, S., *Iug.*, 44, 4 ; *after Albinus had fully determined not to depart* *from the province, he kept his soldiers in cantonments.* **Posteāquam multitūdinem collēgerat emblēmatum, īnstituit officīnam,** C., *Verr.*, IV. 24, 54 ; *after he had got together a great number of figures, he set up shop.*

2. The Pluperfect is used with **postquam** when a definite interval is mentioned. Rarely also the Historical Perfect (Aorist).

Post and **quam** are often separated. With an Ablative of Measure, **post** may be omitted (403, N. 4, *d*).

(Aristīdēs) dēcēssit ferē post annum quārtum quam Themistoclēs Athēnīs erat expulsus, NEP., III. 3, 3 ; *Aristides died about four years after Themistocles had been* (was) *banished from Athens.* **Post diem tertium gesta rēs est quam dīxerat,** C., *Mil.*, 16, 44; *the matter was accomplished three days after he had said it would be.* **[Hamilcar] nōnō annō postquam in Hispāniam vēnerat occīsus est,** NEP., XXII. 4, 2 ; *Hamilcar was killed nine years after he came to Spain.* **(Aristīdēs) sextō ferē annō quam erat expulsus in patriam restitūtus est,** NEP., III. 1, 5 ; *Aristides was restored to his country about six years after he was exiled.* **Trīduō ferē postquam Hannibal ā rīpā Rhodanī mōvit, ad castra hostium vēnerat,** L., XXI. 32, 1 ; (*within*) *about three days after Hannibal moved from the banks of the Rhone he had come to the camp of the enemy.*

Subjunctive in Ōrātiō Oblīqua.

Scrīptum ā Posīdōniō est trīgintā annīs vīxisse Panaetium posteāquam librōs [dē officiīs] ēdidisset, C., *Off.*, III. 2, 8; *it is recorded by Posidonius that Panaetius lived thirty years after he put forth his books on Duties.*

The attraction is sometimes neglected.

NOTES.—1. The most common of these conjunctions is **postquam,** but the others also occur at all periods. **Simul (atque)** is rare in early Latin. In the following notes the usage in Iterative action is excluded.

2. The Impf. with **postquam** is cited but once from early Latin (PL., *Most.*, 640), it becomes more common in CICERO, but is distinctive of LIVY, who shows nearly one hundred examples. The Impf. with **ubi** is cited once in early Latin (TER., *Eun.*, 405), where, however, it is Iterative, not at all from CICERO, once from CAESAR, after which it is found more frequently, but never becomes common. The Impf. with **ut** is found first in CICERO, never in CAESAR, SALLUST, VERGIL, but not uncommonly in LIVY ; only once in TACITUS (*H.*, III. 31), where it is Iterative. The Impf. with **simul (atque)** is not cited from CICERO and CAESAR, but appears once in SALLUST, where it is Iterative ; it is very rare.

3. The Plupf. with **postquam** is not cited from PLAUTUS or HORACE, and but once from TERENCE (*And.* 177) ; CICERO uses it but rarely, CAESAR but once (*B. C.*, III. 58, 5) ; LIVY uses it often, and TACITUS is fond of it. The Plupf. with **ubi** is found once in PLAUTUS, twice each in CICERO and CAESAR, and then more frequently. The Plupf. with **ut (prīmum)** is found first in CICERO, perhaps but once in CAESAR (*B. C.*, III. 63, 6), more often later. The Plupf. with **simul (atque)** is cited once from CICERO, not at all from CAESAR, and rarely later.

4. Some dozen cases are cited, principally from CICERO, of the Subjv. with **post-**

quam not in Ō.O. Most of these are disputed. If the Subjv. is to remain in these passages it is to be explained as due either to Partial Obliquity or to the intrusion of the **cum** Subjv. into other temporal constructions. The Subjv. appears in late Latin.

5. The Subjv. with **ubi** occurs occasionally in early Latin, but only once in CICERO, not unfrequently in LIVY and TACITUS. This is usually explained as either the Iterative or Potential Subjunctive. The Subjv. with **ut** is post-classical, and the Subjv. with **simul** does not occur.

564. Postquam and the like, with the Present and Perfect Indicative, assume a causative signification (compare **quoniam,** *now that* = *since*).

[Cūria] minor mihĭ vidētur posteāquam est māior, C., *Fin.*, v. 1, 2; *the senate-house seems to me smaller now that it is* (really) *greater.* **Tremō horreōque postquam aspexī hanc,** TER., *Eun.*, 84; *I quiver and shiver since I have seen her.*

NOTES.—1. The use of temporal conjunctions, especially **postquam** in the Present Sphere, is much more common in early Latin than later. **Ubi** and **ut** occur at all periods, but rarely; **ubi** has almost the same force as **sī**; **ut** means **ex quō,** *since.* **Simul** is rare, and found first in LUCRETIUS.

2. **Cum,** also, has sometimes the causal signification.

Grātulor tibĭ cum tantum valēs, C., *Fam.*, IX. 14, 3; *I wish you joy now that you have so much influence.*

565. Ubi and **simul** are occasionally found with the Future and Future Perfect; not so **postquam** and **ut.**

Ubī mē aspiciet ad carnuficem rapiet continuō, PL., *B.*, 689; *as soon as he shall catch (catches) sight of me he will hurry me at once to the hangman.* **Id tibi quidem hercle fīet, Dēmaenetum simulāc cōnspexerō,** PL., *Asin.*, 477; *that indeed shall certainly be your fate, as soon as I shall have espied Demaenetus.*

NOTE.—When thus used **ubi** and **simul** approach almost the meaning of **cum** (580). So also **quandō**; see 580, N. 3. These uses should be distinguished from those of Iterative Action.

Iterative Action.

566. RULE I.—When two actions are repeated contemporaneously, both are put in tenses of continuance.

Humilēs labōrant ubi potentēs dissident, PHAED., I. 30, 1; *the lowly suffer when the powerful disagree.* **Populus mē sībilat; at mihi plaudō ipse domī simul āc nummōs contemplor in arcā,** H., *S.*, I. 1, 66; *the people hiss me; but I clap myself at home as soon as I gloat o'er my cash in the strong box.* **Ubi frūmentō opus erat, cohortēs praesidium agitābant,** S., *Iug.*, 55, 4; *when there was need of corn, the cohorts would serve as an escort.*

The Subjunctive with the Ideal Second Person.

Bonus sēgnior fit ubi neglegās, S., *Iug.*, 31, 28 ; *a good man becomes more spiritless when you neglect him.*

567. Rule II.—When one action is repeated before another, the antecedent action is put in the Perfect, Pluperfect, or Future Perfect ; the subsequent action in the Present, Imperfect, or Future, according to the relation.

☞ As this use runs through all sentences involving antecedent action, all the classes are represented in the following examples.

Observe the greater exactness of the Latin expression. Compare 244, R. 2.

Quotiēns cecidit,	**surgit,**	*As often as he falls, he rises.*
Quotiēns ceciderat,	**surgēbat,**	*As often as he fell, he rose.*
Quotiēns ceciderit,	**surget,**	*As often as he falls, he will rise.*

Simul īnflāvit tībīcen ā perītō carmen āgnōscitur, C., *Ac.*, II. 27, 86; *as soon as the fluter blows, the song is recognised by the connoisseur.* **[Alcibiadēs] simul āc sē remīserat, lūxuriōsus reperiēbātur,** Nep., VII. 1, 4; *as soon as Alcibiades relaxed, he was found a debauchee.* **Dociliōra sunt ingenia priusquam obdūruērunt,** Quint., I. 12, 9 ; *minds are more teachable before they* (have) *become hardened.* **[Ager] cum multōs annōs quiēvit, ūberiōrēs efferre frūgēs solet,** C., *Br.*, 4, 16 ; *when a field has rested* (rests) *many years, it usually produces a more abundant crop.* **Cum pālam ēius ānulī ad palmam converterat (Gȳgēs) ā nūllō vidēbātur,** C., *Off.*, III. 9, 38; *when*(ever) *Gyges turned the bezel of the ring toward the palm* (*of his hand*), *he was to be seen by no one.* **Sī pēs condoluit, sī dēns, ferre nōn possumus,** C., *Tusc.*, II, 22, 52; *if a foot, if a tooth ache*(*s*), *we cannot endure it.* **Stomachābātur senex, sī quid asperius dīxeram,** C., *N.D.*, I. 33, 93; *the old man used to be fretted, if I said anything* (*that was*) *rather harsh.* **Quōs labōrantēs cōnspexerat, hīs subsidia submittēbat,** Caes., *B.G.*, IV. 26, 4; *to those whom he saw* (*had espied*) *hard pressed he would send reinforcements.* **Haerēbant in memoriā quaecumque audierat et vīderat (Themistoclēs),** C., *Ac.*, II. 1, 2 ; *whatever Themistocles had heard and seen* (= heard and saw) *remained fixed in his memory.* **Quī timēre dēsierint, ōdisse incipient,** Tac., *Agr.*, 32; *those who cease to fear will begin to hate.*

The Subjunctive with the Ideal Second Person.

Ubi cōnsulueris, mātūrē factō opus est, S., *C.*, 1, 6 ; *when you have deliberated, you want speedy action.*

The Subjunctive in **Ōrātiō Oblīqua.**

[Catō] mīrārī sē āiēbat quod nōn rīdēret haruspex haruspicem cum vīdis-

set, C., *Div.*, II. 24, 51 ; *Cato said that he wondered that an haruspex did not laugh when he saw* (another) *haruspex.* (**Nōn rīdet cum vīdit.**)

The Subjunctive by Attraction.

[**Arāneolae**] **rēte texunt ut sī quid inhaeserit cōnficiant**, C., *N.D.*, II. 48, 123 ; *spiders weave webs to despatch anything that gets caught* (**sī quid inhaesit, cōnficiunt**). **Quārē fīēbat, ut omnium oculōs, quotiēscunque in pūblicum prōdīsset, ad sē converteret**, NEP., VII. 3, 5 ; *whereby it happened that he attracted the eyes of all every time he went out in public* (**quotiēscunque prōdierat, convertēbat**).

NOTE.—The Subjunctive in Iterative Tenses may be accounted for on the principle that a repeated action which is retrospective from the point of view of the narrator, and so naturally takes the Indicative, becomes prospective from the point of view of the agent, and so takes the Subjunctive. But, however the construction is justified, the fact remains that the Subjunctive in Iterative Sentences is a growth in Latin. With the principal tenses it is confined mostly to the Ideal Second Person. Indefinite **quis** is very near to this. So CICERO, *Rab. Post.*, 13, 36 : **ubi semel quis pēierāverit–oportet.** With Impf. and Plupf. the first examples (excluding **cum**) are in CATULLUS (LXXXIV. 1), and CAESAR (*e.g. B. C.*, II. 15, 3). Then it spreads, probably under Greek influence, and is very common in the historians, especially LIVY and TACITUS. **Ubi** and **ut** are the particles employed ; also very often **sī** and relatives, in general **quīcumque, quotiēns**, *etc.* With **cum**, Iterative Subjunctives are found to a limited extent also in CICERO and CAESAR ; but all cases of principal tenses in third person have been emended, and those with historical tenses are not common, and sometimes doubtful.

Cum ferrum sē īnflexisset, neque ēvellere neque pūgnāre poterant (= **vidēbant sē nōn posse**), CAES., *B. G.*, I. 25, 3 ; *when the iron had bent, they found that they could neither pluck it out nor fight.* **Incurrere ea gēns in Macedoniam solita erat** (as if **cōnstituerat**) **ubi rēgem occupātum externō bellō sēnsisset**, L., XXVI. 25, 7 ; *that tribe was wont to make a raid on Macedonia whenever they perceived the king engrossed in foreign war.* **Quī ūnum ēius ōrdinis offendisset omnēs adversōs habēbat** (as if **certō sciēbat sē habitūrum**), L., XXXIII. 46, 1 ; *whoso had offended one of that order was sure to have all against him.* **Modum adhibendō ubi rēs pōsceret, priōrēs erant**, L., III. 19, 3 ; *by the use of moderation, when the case demanded it, they were his superiors.*

II. CONTEMPORANEOUS ACTION.

568. Conjunctions used of Contemporaneous Action are : **Dum, dōnec**, *while, so long as, until* ; **quoad**, *up to* (the time) *that* ; **quamdiū**, *as long as* ; **cum**, *when.*

An action may be contemporaneous in Extent—*so long as, while.*

An action may be contemporaneous in Limit—*until.*

REMARK.—**Dum**, (*while*) *yet*, denotes duration, which may be coëxtensive, *so long as*, or not. It is often causal. **Dōnec** (old form **dōnicum**, used only in the sense *until*), is parallel with **dum** in the sense *so long as, until.* CICERO uses it only as *until.*

1. Contemporaneous in Extent.

(*So long as, while.*)

569. *Complete Coextension.*—**Dum, dōnec, quoad, quamdiū,** *so long as, while,* take the Indicative of all the tenses.

Vīta dum superest, bene est, MAECENAS (SEN., *E.M.*, 101, 11); *while (so long as) life remains, 'tis well.* **Sibi vērō hanc laudem relinquont, "Vīxit, dum vīxit, bene,"** TER., *Hec.*, 461; *they leave indeed this praise for themselves, "He lived well while he lived" (all the time).* **Tiberius Gracchus tam diū laudābitur dum memoria rērum Rōmānārum manēbit,** C., *Off.*, II. 12, 43; *Tiberius Gracchus shall be praised so long as the memory of Roman history remains (shall remain).* **Fuit haec gēns fortis dum Lycūrgī lēgēs vigēbant,** C., *Tusc.*, I. 42, 101; *this nation was brave so long as the laws of Lycurgus were in force.* **Dōnec grātus eram tibī, Persārum viguī rēge beātior,** H., *O.*, III. 9, 1; *while I was pleasing in your sight, I throve more blessed than Persia's king.* **Quoad potuit, restitit,** CAES., *B.G.*, IV. 12, 5; *as long as he could, he withstood.*

Subjunctive in **Ōrātiō Oblīqua.**

(Rēgulus dīxit) quam diū iūre iūrandō hostium tenērētur nōn esse sē senātōrem, C., *Off.*, III. 27, 100; [Regulus said] *that as long as he was bound by his oath to the enemy he was not a senator.* (**Quamdiū teneor nōn sum senātor.**)

Subjunctive by Attraction.

Faciam ut meī meminerīs dum vītam vīvās, PL., *Pers.*, 494 (333, 2).

NOTES.—1. **Dum.**—In the Past Sphere we have the Pf. (Aor.), Hist. Pr., and Imperfect. Of these the Hist. Pr. is found first in SALLUST (*C.*, 36, 1), and the Impf., while occurring at all periods, is rare. The Pf. is not in CAESAR. **Dum** in the Present Sphere is rare; the Pure Pr. has been observed in PL., *B.*, 737: **mane dum scrībit,** which looks much like parataxis, and occasionally in CICERO and later; the Pure Pf. is cited only from TERENCE (*And.*, 556, 597), and is only apparent. Several examples of the Future Sphere are cited, PL., *B.*, 225, **nōn metuō mihi dum hōc valēbit pectus;** TER., *Heaut.*, 107; C., *Rosc.Am.*, 32, 991; V., *A.*, I. 607, *etc.*

Dōnec is not found in the sense "so long as," until LUCR., V. 178; then H., *O.*, I. 9, 16; III, 9, 1. Also OV., *Tr.*, I. 9, 5. LIVY uses it occasionally, but TACITUS affects it, and employs Hist. Pf., Impf., and Fut. tenses.

Quoad (correlative with **adeō**) belongs especially to the classical poets, but is also found in prose. Compare C., *Ph.*, III. 11, 28, *etc.* It is usually found in the Past Sphere; in the Present the adverbial force, "so far as," seems to preponderate; PL., *Asin.*, 296: **quoad vīrēs valent.** The Future tenses are more common.

Quamdiū (correlative with **tamdiū**) is found with this usage first in CICERO.

2. When the actions are coëxtensive, the tenses are generally the same in both members, but not always.

570. *Partial Coextension.*—**Dum,** *while, while yet, dur-*

ing, commonly takes the Present Indicative after all Tenses: so especially in narrative.

Cape hunc equum, dum tibĭ vīrium aliquid superest, L., XXII. 49, 7; *take this horse, while you have yet some strength left.* **Dum haec Rōmae aguntur, cōnsulēs ambō in Liguribus gerēbant bellum,** L., XXXIX. 1, 1; *while these things were going on at Rome, both consuls were carrying on war in Liguria.* **Praetermissa ēius reī occāsiō est, dum in castellīs recipiendīs tempus teritur,** L., XXXIII. 18, 20; *the opportunity was allowed to slip by, while time was wasted in recovering miserable forts.*

☞ **Dum** in this sense often resists the change into Subjv. in **Ō. O.**, especially in post-classical Latin. (655, R. 3.)

NOTES.—1. **Quamdiū** and **quoad** are, by their composition, incapable of being used in this sense, and as **dōnec** was avoided, **dum** is the only temporal conjunction of limit that is loose enough in its formation to serve for partial coextension. The Pr. after it, formally an Hist. Pr., always connotes continuance, and the construction becomes practically a periphrasis for a missing Pr. participle.

2. The Pure Pr. of the Present Sphere is found occasionally, principally in early Latin. In this sense the relation is often causal, and the construction is parallel with the Pr. participle, the lack of which in the passive it supplies.

Ardua dum metuunt (= metuentēs) āmittunt vēra viāī, LUCR., I. 660 (372, N. 2).

The causal relation is also often present with the other tenses.

3. Other tenses are extremely rare, as the Future; PL., *Men.*, 214, **dum coquētur, interim pōtābimus**; the Impf., NEP., XXIII. 2, 4, **quae dīvīna rēs dum cōnficiēbātur, quaesīvit ā mē.**

4. LIVY, XXXII. 24, 5, shows one case of the Plupf. as a shorthand to express the maintenance of the result, **dum āverterat = dum āversōs tēnēbat.**

2. Contemporaneous in Limit.

(*Until.*)

571. Dum, dōnec, quoad, *up to* (the time) *that, until*, have the Present, Historical Present, Historical Perfect, and Future Perfect Indicative.

Tītyre, dum redeō, brevis est via, pāsce capellās, V., *Ec.*, 9, 23; *Tityrus, while I am returning* (= till I return)—*the way is short—feed my kids.* **Epamīnōndās ferrum in corpore ūsque eō retinuit, quoad renūntiātum est vīcisse Boeōtiōs,** *Cf.* NEP., XV. 9, 3; *Epaminondas retained the iron in his body, until word was brought back that the Boeotians had conquered.* **Dōnec rediīt Mārcellus, silentium fuit,** L., XXIII. 31, 9; *until Marcellus returned, there was silence.* **Haud dēsinam dōnec perfēcerō hōc,** TER., *Ph.*, 420; *I will not cease until I have* (shall have) *accomplished it.* **Expectābō dum venit,** TER., *Eun.*, 206; *I will wait until he comes.*

Subjunctive in **Ōrātiō Oblīqua.**

Scīpiōnī Sīlānōque dōnec revocātī ab senātū forent prōrogātum imperium

est, L., XXVII. 7, 17; *Scipio and Silanus had their command extended until "they should have been recalled by the senate."*

NOTES.—1. With the Past Sphere the idea of limit precludes the employment of a tense of continuance, which would naturally involve the notion of Overlapping Action. The Impf. is, therefore, not found until the time of TACITUS (once with **dōnec,** *H.*, I. 9). With the Present Sphere the tense must be iterative or historical. Otherwise the Pr. is used by anticipation for the Future.

2. The Fut. Indic. is found occasionally in early Latin, usually, however, the Present. In the classical times, and afterwards, the Subjv. takes its place. Thus CICERO uses the Subjv. regularly, after **verba exspectandī,** except in possibly four passages of the earlier *Orations* and *Letters*.

3. **Dōnec** is not uncommon in early Latin, but is very rare in CICERO, and never occurs in CAESAR. On the other hand, TACITUS shows one hundred and thirty-eight cases of it.

4. **Dōnicum** belongs to early Latin, but is not found in TERENCE; one case with the Subjv. is found in NEPOS. **Dōnique** is found in LUCRETIUS four times with the Indic., always before vowels; in VITRUVIUS once with Indic., three times with Subjv.; otherwise it is not cited.

5. **Quoad,** *until,* occurs once in PLAUTUS, and with the Subjunctive. Otherwise it is found with both moods occasionally throughout the language.

6. LIVY introduces **dōnec inversum** like **cum inversum** (581). See XXI. 46, 6: XXXV. 50, 4, *etc.*

572. Dum, dōnec, and **quoad,** *until,* take the Subjunctive when Suspense and Design are involved.

Vergīnius dum collēgam cōnsuleret morātus (est), L., IV. 21, 10; *Verginius delayed until he could* (long enough to) *consult his colleague.* **At tantī tibi sit nōn indulgēre theātrīs, dum bene dē vacuō pectore cēdat amor,** Ov., *Rem.Am.*, 751; *but let it be worth the cost to you* (= deem it worth the cost) *not to indulge in play-going, until love be fairly gone from* (your) *untenanted bosom.*

Often with **verba exspectandī,** especially **exspectō,** *I wait.*

Rūsticus exspectat dum dēfluat amnis, H., *Ep.*, I. 2, 42; *the clown waits for the river to run off* (dry).

REMARKS.—1. The Subjv. is sometimes used in narrative with **dum,** *while,* and **dōnec,** *while, until,* to express subordination. The principle is that of Partial Obliquity. There is often a Causal or Iterative sense (like **cum,** 584, R.).

Dum intentus in eum sē rēx tōtus āverteret, alter ēlātam secūrim in caput dēiēcit, L., I. 40, 7; *while the king, intent upon him, was turning quite away, the other raised his axe and planted it in his skull.* (**Āverteret** from the point of view of **alter** = **dum videt āvertentem.**)

2. **Verba exspectandī** have also other constructions, as **ut, sī, quīn,** but not the Infinitive.

573. Dum, modŏ, and **dummodŏ,** *if only, provided only,*

only, are used with the Present and Imperfect Subjunctive in Conditional Wishes.

The negative is **nē** (**dum nē** = **nē interim**).

Ōderint dum metuant, Accius (C., *Off.*, I. 28, 97); *let them hate so long as they fear* (provided that, if they will only fear). **Quō lubeat nūbant, dum dōs nē fīat comes**, Pl., *Aul.*, 491; *let them marry where* (= *whom*) *they please, if but the dowry do not go with them.* **Dummodō mōrāta rēctē veniat, dōtāta est satis**, Pl., *Aul.*, 239; *provided only she come with a good character, she is endowed* (= her dowry is) *enough.* **In eō multa admīranda sunt: ēligere modo cūrae sit**, Quint., x. 1, 131; *many things in him are to be admired; only you must be careful to choose.* **Cōpia plācandī sit modo parva tuī**, Ov., *Her.*, 20, 74 (428, R. 1).

Notes.—1. It has been noticed that Tacitus uses **dummodŏ** only in the *Germania* and *Dialogus*, otherwise **dum.**

2. **Dummodŏ nē** and **modŏ nē** are found first in Cicero. In post-Augustan Latin **nōn** is sometimes used for **nē**; Juv., vii. 222, **dummodo nōn pereat.**

III. SUBSEQUENT ACTION.

Antequam and Priusquam with the Indicative.

574. Antequam and **priusquam**, *before*, take the Present, Perfect, and Future Perfect Indicative, when the limit is stated as a fact. The Present is used in anticipation of the Future.

Remarks.—1. The elements **ante, anteā, prius,** and **quam** are often separated.

2. As **prius** (**ante**) **-quam** is negative in its signification (= **necdum**), the Indic. is sometimes found where we should expect the Subjunctive.

Note.—**Antequam** is much rarer than **priusquam**, especially in early Latin, where it is cited only from Cato, Caelius, Terence (*Hec.*, 146, with Subjv. in Ō. O.), and Varro. Cicero prefers it before a Pr. Indic., **priusquam** elsewhere.

575. The Present Indicative is used after positive sentences.

Antequam ad sententiam redeō, dē mē pauca dīcam, C., *Cat.*, iv. 10, 20; *before I return to the subject, I will say a few things of myself.* **Omnia experīrī certum est prius quam pereō**, Ter., *And.*, 311; *I am determined to try everything before I perish.* (**Prius quam peream** = *sooner than perish, to keep from perishing.*)

Notes.—1. The Pure Pf. Indic. is used of Iterative Action, and is rare. (567.) **Dociliōra sunt ingenia priusquam obdūruērunt**, Quint., i. 12, 9 (567). Instead of this, the Pr. Subjv. is more common in general statements. (567, N.)

2. Tacitus shows no example of the Pr. Indicative.

576. The Perfect (Aorist) and Future Perfect Indicative are used both after positive and after negative clauses, chiefly the latter.

Hēracliō, aliquantō ante quam est mortuus, omnia trādiderat, C., *Verr.*, II. 18, 46; *some time before he died he had handed over everything to Heraclius.* **Lēgātī nōn ante profectī quam impositōs in nāvēs mīlitēs vīdērunt**, L., XXXIV. 12, 8; *the envoys did not set out until they saw the soldiers on board.* **Neque dēfatīgābor ante quam illōrum viās ratiōnēsque et prō omnibus et contrā omnia disputandī percēperō**, C., *Or.*, III. 36, 145; *I will not let myself grow weary before* (until) *I learn* (shall have learned) *their methods of disputing for and against everything.*

Subjunctive in **Ōrātiō Oblīqua.**

Themistoclēs [collēgīs suīs] praedīxit, ut nē prius Lacedaemoniōrum lēgātōs dīmitterent quam ipse esset remissus, NEP., II. 7, 3 (546, 2). (**Nōn prius dīmittētis quam ego erō remissus.**)

REMARK.—After negative clauses containing a historical tense the Pf. is the rule and the connection is always close: **nōn priusquam** = **dum**. Violations of this rule are very rare; see 577, 2.

NOTES.—1. The Fut. is found occasionally in PLAUTUS, but has disappeared by the time of TERENCE. The Fut. Pf. is never common, but is found at all periods. TACITUS avoids it, and so do other authors.

2. The Impf. is confined to LIVY, who shows four examples, and to one case in late Latin. The Plupf. is found once in CICERO (*Dom.*, 30, 78), where it may be Iterative, and once in early Latin.

Antequam and Priusquam with the Subjunctive.

577. Antequam and **priusquam** are used with the Subjunctive when an ideal limit is given; when the action is expected, contingent, designed, or subordinate.

1. An ideal limit involves necessary antecedence, but not necessary consequence. After positive sentences, the Subjunctive is the rule, especially in generic sentences and in narrative. (Compare **cum**, 585.) After Historical Tenses the Subjunctive is almost invariable when the action does not, or is not to, take place. The translation is often *before*, and the verbal in *-ing* (Greek πρίν with the Infinitive).

Ante vidēmus fulgōrem quam sonum audiāmus, SEN., *N.Q.*, II. 12, 6; *we see the flash of lightning before hearing the sound* (we may never hear it). But compare LUCR., VI. 170. **In omnibus negōtiīs prius quam aggrediāre adhibenda est praeparātiō dīligēns**, C., *Off.*, I. 21, 73; *in all affairs, before addressing yourself* (*to them*), *you must make use of careful preparation* (Ideal Second Person). **[Collem] celeriter priusquam ab**

adversāriīs sentiātur commūnit, Caes., *B.C.*, I. 54, 4; *he speedily fortified the hill before he was* (too soon to be) *perceived by the enemy* (**prius quam = prius quam ut**). **Hannibal omnia priusquam excēderet pūgnā (erat) expertus,** L., XXX. 35, 4; *Hannibal had tried everything before withdrawing from the fight* (= *to avoid withdrawing from the fight*). **Saepe māgna indolēs virtūtis priusquam reī pūblicae prōdesse potuisset exstincta est,** C., *Ph.*, V. 17, 47; *often hath great native worth been extinguished before it could be of service to the State.* **Ducentīs annīs ante quam urbem Rōmam caperent in Ītaliam Gallī trānscendērunt,** L., V. 33, 5; (*it was*) *two hundred years before their taking Rome* (*that*) *the Gauls crossed into Italy* (here the Subjv. gives the natural point of reference).

2. After an historical tense in the negative, the Subjunctive is exceptional. (576, R.)

Inde nōn prius ēgressus est quam (= ibi manēbat dum) rēx eum in fidem reciperet, Nep., II. 8, 4; *he did not come out until the king should take him under his protection* (he stayed to make the king take him under his protection). See Caes., *B.G.*, VI. 37, 2; L., XLV. 11, 3.

Notes.—1. The Pr. Subjv. is common, but is usually generic; the few cases of Final Subjv. are confined to early Latin. Very rarely the Hist. Pr. is found after a Hist. Present. See Caes., *B.C.*, I. 22.

2. The Pf. occurs occasionally; it is usually in a final sense.

Nōn prius dīmittunt quam ab hīs sit concēssum, Caes., *B.G.*, III. 18.

3. In Livy we find the Impf. Subjv. used not unfrequently, where the idea of suspense or design is very slight, much after the manner of **cum nōndum** (as C., *Ph.*, V. 1, 4).

4. The Plupf. Subjv. is cited five times from Cicero and four times from Livy. In these passages the completion rather than the continuance is in suspense.

5. **Postrīdiēquam** is found in Plautus, Cicero (*Letters*), and Suetonius with the Indicative. In Cicero, *Ac.*, II. 3, 9, with the Subjunctive. **Prīdiēquam** is found in Plautus and Cicero with the Indicative; in Livy, Val. Max., and Suetonius with the Subjunctive. Both are very rare.

6. When the will is involved, **potius quam** is used in the same way as **prius quam.**

Dēpūgnā potius quam serviās, C., *Att.* VII. 7, 7; *fight it out rather than be a slave.*

IV. CONSTRUCTIONS OF CUM (QUOM).

578. **Cum** is a (locative) relative conjunction.

Note.—Originally locative (*where*), **quom** became temporal (*when*) like **ubi.** When time is not defined by a fixed date, it readily becomes *circumstance*, and this circumstance is interpreted as cause, condition, and the like. Compare the circumstantial relative itself. The first construction was with the Indicative as with any other merely relative clause, and this is the sole construction in earliest Latin. But, beginning with Terence, we can observe the drift ever increasing in Latin towards the expression of character by tendency (Subjv.) rather than by fact (Indic.), so that the relative of character takes more and more the Subjunctive, and **cum** follows the lead of **ut** and of the inflected relative pronoun.

579. There are two great uses of **cum**:

I. Temporal **cum** (*when, then*), with the Indicative.

II. Circumstantial **cum** (*as, whereas*), with the Subjunctive.

In the second usage the relation is still purely a matter of inference; but according to this inferential connection we distinguish:

(*a*) Historical **cum**, *as*, giving the attendant circumstances, mainly temporal, under which an action took place.

(*b*) Causal **cum**, *as, whereas, since*, indicating that the main action proceeded from the subordinate one.

(*c*) Concessive **cum**, *whereas, although*, indicating that the main action was accomplished in spite of that of the subordinate clause.

I. **Cum vēr appetit, mīlitēs ex hībernīs movent,** *when spring approaches, soldiers move out of winter-quarters.*

II. (*a*) **Cum vēr appeteret, Hannibal ex hībernīs mōvit,** *as spring was approaching* (*spring approaching*), *Hannibal moved out of winter-quarters.*

(*b*) **Cum vēr appetat, ex hībernīs movendum est,** *as* (*since*) *spring is approaching, we must move out of winter-quarters.*

(*c*) **Cum vēr appeteret, tamen hostēs ex hībernīs nōn mōvērunt,** *whereas* (*although*) *spring was approaching, nevertheless the enemy did not move out of winter-quarters.*

1. Temporal Cum.

580. Cum, *when*, is used with all the tenses of the Indicative to designate merely temporal relations.

In the Principal clause, a temporal adverb or temporal expression is frequently employed, such as **tum, tunc,** *then*; **nunc,** *now*; **diēs,** *day*; **tempus,** *time*; **iam,** *already*; **vix,** *scarcely*, and the like.

Animus, nec cum adest nec cum discēdit, appāret, C., *Cat.M.*, 22, 80; *the soul is not visible, either when it is present, or when it departs.* **Stomachor cum aliōrum nōn mē dīgna in mē cōnferuntur,** C., *Planc.*, 14, 35; *I get fretted when other people's jokes that are not worthy of me are foisted on me.* **[Sex librōs dē rē pūblicā] tum scrīpsimus cum gubernācula reī pūblicae tenēbāmus,** C., *Div.*, II. 1, 3; *I wrote the six books about the State at the time when I held the helm of the State.* **Recordāre tempus illud cum pater Cūriō maerēns iacēbat in lectō,** C., *Ph.*, II. 18, 45; *remember the time when Curio the father lay abed from grief.* **Longum illud tempus cum nōn erō magis mē movet quam hōc exiguum,** C., *Att.*, XII. 18, 1; *that long time* (to come), *when I shall not exist, has more effect on me than this scant* (*present time*). **Iam dīlūcēscēbat cum signum cōnsul**

dedit, L., XXXVI. 24, 6; *by this time day was beginning to dawn, when the consul gave the signal.* (See 581.)

Ideal Second Person with the Subjunctive:

Pater, hominum inmortālis est īnfāmia. Etiam tum vīvit quom esse crēdās mortuam, PL., *Pers.*, 355; *Father, immortal is the ill-fame of the world. It lives on even when you think that it is dead.*

But the presence of a temporal adverb does not mean necessarily that the **cum** clause is merely temporal.

REMARKS.—1. **Fuit cum** commonly follows the analogy of other characteristic relatives (631), and takes the Subjunctive:

Fuit tempus cum (= **fuit cum**) **rūra colerent hominēs,** VARRO, *R.R.*, III. I, 1; *there was a time when all mankind tilled fields = were countrymen.*

The Indic. is rare.

2. **Meminī cum,** *I remember the time when,* takes the Indic., but **audīre cum** takes the Subjv. parallel with the participle:

Meminī cum mihĭ dēsipere vidēbāre, C., *Fam.*, VII. 28, 1; *I remember the time when you seemed to me to show the worst possible taste.* **Audīvī Mētrodōrum cum dē iīs ipsīs rēbus disputāret,** C., *Or.*, II. 90, 365; *I have heard Metrodorus discuss*(ing) *these very matters.*

3. Peculiar is the use of **cum** with Lapses of Time. Lapses of Time are treated as Designations of Time in Accusative or Ablative:

Multī annī sunt cum (= **multōs annōs**) **in aere meō est,** C., *Fam.*, XV. 14, 1; (*it is*) *many years* (*that*) *he has been* (230) *in my debt.* **Permultī annī iam erant cum inter patriciōs magistrātūs tribūnōsque nūlla certāmina fuerant,** L., IX. 33, 3; *very many years had elapsed since there had been any struggles between the patrician magistrates and the tribunes.* **Nōndum centum et decem annī sunt cum** (= **ex quō** = **abhinc annōs**) **dē pecūniīs repetundīs lāta lēx est,** C., *Off.*, II. 21, 75; *it is not yet one hundred and ten years since the law concerning extortion was proposed.*

NOTES.—1. In PLAUTUS **cum** with the Indic. may be explicative, causal, concessive, adversative. *Explicative:* **salvos quom** (*that*) **advenīs, gaudeō,** *Most.*, 1128. *Causal:* **salvos quom** (*since*) **peregrē advenīs, cēna dētur,** *B.*, 536. *Concessive:* **[servī] quom** (*although*) **culpā carent, tamen malum metuont,** *Most.*, 859. *Adversative:* **īnsānīre mē āiunt, ūltrō quom** (*whereas*) **ipsī īnsāniunt,** *Men.*, 831.

The same holds true for TERENCE, except that the Subjv. is now making its appearance in cases where it can be neither potential, ideal, nor attracted, as *Hec.*, 341: **nōn vīsam uxōrem Pamphilī, quom in proxumō hīc sit aegra?**

Of course, this prevalence of the Indic. does not exclude the attraction into the Subjv., nor does it exclude the regular potential use.

2. The explicative use dies out, except where it is akin to the conditional; but it always retains the Indicative. With Causal and Concessive-Adversative uses, the Subjv. is used more and more in place of the Indicative.

3. In early Latin we find **quoniam** and **quandō,** used sometimes with the force of **quom.** In the case of **quoniam** several examples are cited from PLAUTUS, in most of which, however, the causal conception lies very close at hand; the temporal force seems to have disappeared by the time of TERENCE, and only reappears in GELLIUS. The

temporal usage of **quandō** is still the prevailing one in PLAUTUS, over seventy instances having been collected. Of these the majority are in the Present and Future Spheres, in which the shift to the causal conception is very easy; many of them are also iterative. In TERENCE the temporal usage of **quandō** has disappeared unless possibly in one passage (*Ad.*, 206), but sporadic cases are found later, even in CICERO.

Quoniam hinc est prōfectūrus peregrē thēnsaurum dēmōnstrāvit mihi, PL., *Trin.*, 149. **Tum, quandŏ lēgātōs Tyrum mīsimus,** C., *Leg.Agr.*, II. 16, 41.

581. Cum *Inversum.* When the two actions are independent, **cum** is sometimes used with the one which seems to be logically the principal clause, just as in English.

Iam nōn longius bīduī viā aberant, cum duās vēnisse legiōnēs cōgnōscunt, CAES., *B.G.*, VI. 7, 2; *they were now distant not more than two days' march, when they learned that two legions were come.*

Similar is the addition of an illustrative fact, often causal or adversative, by **cum intereā (interim), quidem, tamen,** *etc.*, with the Indicative.

582. *Explicative* **cum.**—When the actions of the two clauses are coincident, **cum** is almost equivalent to its kindred relative **quod,** *in that.*

Āiācem, hunc quom vidēs, ipsum vidēs, PL., *Capt.*, 615; *when you see him, you see Ajax himself.* **Cum tacent, clāmant,** C., *Cat.*, I. 8, 21; *when* (= in that) *they are silent, they cry aloud.* **Dīxī omnia cum hominem nōmināvī,** PLIN., *Ep.*, IV. 22, 4; *I have said everything, in naming the man.*

583. *Conditional* **cum.—Cum** with the Future, Future Perfect, or Universal Present, is often almost equivalent to **sī,** *if,* with which it is sometimes interchanged.

Cum pōscēs, pōsce Latīnē, JUV., XI. 148; *when* (if) *you* (shall) *ask* (for anything), *ask in Latin.* **Cum veniet contrā, digitō compēsce labellum,** JUV., I. 160; *when* (if) *he meets you, padlock your lip with your finger.*

584. *Iterative* **cum.—Cum** in the sense of **quotiēns,** *as often as,* takes the Tenses of Iterative Action.

Solet cum sē pūrgat in mē cōnferre omnem culpam, C., *Att.*, IX. 2 A, 1; *he is accustomed, when he clears himself, to put off all the blame on me.* **[Ager] cum multōs annōs requiēvit ūberiōrēs efferre frūgēs solet,** C., *Br.*, 4, 16 (567). **Cum pālam ēius ānulī ad palmam converterat (Gȳgēs) ā nūllō vidēbātur,** C., *Off.*, III. 9, 38 (567).

REMARK.—The Subjv. is also found (567, N.):

Cum in iūs dūcī dēbitōrem vīdissent, undique convolābant, L., II. 27, 8; *whenever they saw a debtor taken to court, they made it a rule to hurry together from all quarters.*

2. Circumstantial Cum.

585. *Historical* **cum.—Cum,** *when* (*as*), is used in narrative with the Imperfect Subjunctive of contemporaneous action, with the Pluperfect Subjunctive of antecedent action, to characterise the temporal circumstances under which an action took place.

[**Āgēsilāus**] **cum ex Aegyptō reverterētur dēcēssit,** NEP., XVII. 8, 6; *Agesilaus died as he was returning from Egypt.* **Zēnōnem cum Athēnīs essem audiēbam frequenter,** C., *N.D.*, I. 21, 59; *when I was* (*being*) *at Athens, I heard Zeno* (*lecture*) *frequently.* **Athēniēnsēs cum statuerent ut nāvēs cōnscenderent, Cyrsilum quendam suādentem ut in urbe manērent, lapidibus obruērunt,** C., *Off.*, III. 11, 48 (546).

Cum Caesar Ancōnam occupāvisset, urbem relīquimus, C., *Fam.*, XVI. 12, 2; *when* (as) *Caesar had occupied Ancona* (Caesar having occupied Ancona), *I left the city.* **Attalus moritur alterō et septuāgēsimō annō, cum quattuor et quadrāgintā annōs rēgnāsset,** L., XXXIII. 21, 1; *Attalus died in his seventy-second year, having reigned forty-four years.*

REMARK.—The subordinate clause generally precedes. The circumstantiality often appears as causality, but sometimes the exact shade cannot be distinguished. Owing to this implicit character, **cum** with the Subjv. is a close equivalent to the participle, and often serves to supply its absence. Compare 611 with 631, 2.

NOTES.—1. How closely allied the ideas of time and circumstance are, in these constructions, is seen from such examples as this:

Cum varicēs secābantur C. Mariō, dolēbat, C., *Tusc.*, II. 15, 35 (time). **Marius cum secārētur, ut suprā dīxī, vetuit,** *etc.*, C., *Tusc.*, II. 22, 53 (circumstances). **Cum ad tribum Polliam ventum est,** (date) **et praecō cunctārētur** (circumstances) **citāre ipsum cēnsōrem; Citā, inquit Nerō, M. Līvium,** L., XXIX. 37, 8.

2. The use of temporal particles with the Pr. is necessarily limited to iterative or causal (adversative) relations. Hence there is no room for the circumstantial **cum** with the Subjv. except so far as it is causal-adversative. Fut. and Fut. Pf. are found chiefly in general or iterative relations.

3. By attraction similar to that with **quod** (541, N. 3) and other relatives, **cum dīceret,** with an Inf., is found where **dīceret** would be more naturally omitted or inserted as (**ut dīcēbat**); so **cum adsentīre sē dīceret** for **cum adsentīret,** L., I. 54, 1. Similarly with **cum** causal: "saying, as he did," C., *Mil.*, 5, 12.

586. *Causal* **cum.—Cum,** *when, whereas, since, seeing that,* with any tense of the Subjunctive, is used to denote the reason, and occasionally the motive, of an action (580, N. 1).

Quae cum ita sint, effectum est nihil esse malum quod turpe nōn sit, C., *Fin.*, III. 8, 29; *since these things are so, it is made out* (proved) *that nothing is bad that is not dishonourable.* **Cum** [**Athēnās**] **tamquam ad**

mercātūram bonārum artium sīs profectus, inānem redīre turpissimum est, C., *Off.*, III. 2, 6; *as (since) you set out for Athens as if to market for accomplishments, it would be utterly disgraceful to return empty (handed).* **Dolō erat pūgnandum, cum pār nōn esset armīs,** NEP., XXIII. 10, 4; *he had to fight by stratagem, as he (seeing that he) was not a match in arms.*

REMARKS.—1. The characteristic nature of the Subjv. with **cum** comes out more clearly in the causal connection, owing to the parallel with **utpote, quīppe,** and the relative (626, N.).

2. The primary tenses are more common, in this connection, but the historical tenses are abundant enough. With the latter the causal relation need never be emphasised.

587. *Concessive* and *Adversative* **cum.**—Causal **cum,** *whereas,* becomes Concessive **cum,** *whereas, although,* with the Subjunctive, when the cause is not sufficient; the relation is often adversative, and there is no limitation as to tense.

The temporal notion is still at work; whether the times are for or against an action is a matter outside of language (580, N. 1).

Nihil mē adiūvit cum posset, C., *Att.*, IX. 13, 3; *he gave me no assistance, although (at a time when) he had it in his power.* **Cum prīmī ōrdinēs hostium concidissent, tamen ācerrimē reliquī resistēbant,** CAES., *B.G.*, VII. 62, 4; *although the first ranks of the enemy had fallen (been cut to pieces), nevertheless the rest resisted most vigorously.* **Perīre artem putāmus nisi appāret, cum dēsinat ars esse, sī appāret,** QUINT., IV. 2, 127; *we think that (our) art is lost unless it shows, whereas it ceases to be art if it shows.*

REMARKS.—1. To emphasise the adversative idea, **tamen** is often added in the principal clause.

2. Adversative **cum nōn,** *whereas not,* is often conveniently translated *without;* **cum nōn īnferior fuisset,** C., *Off.*, I. 32, 116; *without being inferior.*

588. Cum—tum. 1. When **cum,** *when,* **tum,** *then,* have the same verb, the verb is put in the Indicative. **Cum—tum** then has the force of *both—and especially,* and a strengthening adverb, such as **māximē, praecipuē,** is often added to the latter.

(Pausaniās) cōnsilia cum patriae tum sibī inimīca capiēbat, NEP., IV. 3, 3; *Pausanias conceived plans that were hurtful both to his country and especially to himself.*

2. When they have different verbs, the verb with **cum** is usually in the Indicative, but *may* be in the Subjunctive, especially when the actions of the two verbs are not contemporary; this Subjunctive often has a concessive force.

[**Sīsennae historia**] **cum facile omnēs vincat superiōrēs, tum indicat tamen quantum absit ā summō**, C., *Br.*, 64, 228; *although the history of Sisenna easily surpasses all former histories, yet it shows how far it is from the highest* (*mark*).

CONDITIONAL SENTENCES.

589. In Conditional Sentences the clause which contains the condition (supposed cause) is called the **Prŏtasis**, that which contains the consequence is called the **Apŏdosis.**

Logically, **Protasis** is *Premiss;* and **Apodosis**, *Conclusion.*

Grammatically, the **Apodosis** is the *Principal,* the **Protasis** the *Dependent,* clause.

590. *Sign of the Conditional.*—The common conditional particle is **sī**, *if.*

NOTES.—1. **Sī** is a locative case, literally, *so, in those circumstances* (comp. **sī-c**, *so*, and the English: "I would by combat make her good, *so* were I a man."—SHAKESPEARE). Hence, conditional clauses with **sī** may be regarded as adverbs in the Abl. case, and are often actually represented by the Abl. Absolute.

Sīc is found as the correlative of **sī** in the colloquial language, as: **sīc scrībēs aliquid, sī vacābis** (C., *Att.*, XII. 38, 2); **sīc ignōvisse putātō mē tibi, sī cēnās hodiē mēcum** (H., *Ep.*, I. 7, 69). Instead of **sīc**, its equivalent **tum** occurs at all periods, being in the Augustan time restricted to formal uses. **Igitur** is also found as late as CICERO, who likewise uses **ita.** Other particles are post-classical.

2. The connection with the Causal Sentence is shown by **sĭ quidem**, which in later Latin is almost = **quoniam**; see 595, R. 5.

3. The temporal particles **cum** and **quandŏ**, *when*, and the locative **ubi**, are also used to indicate conditional relations in which the idea of Time or Space is involved.

591. *Negative of* **sī.**—The negative of **sī** is **sī nōn** or **nisi.**

(*a*) With **sī nōn**, *if not,* the **nōn** negatives the single word; hence an opposing positive is expected, either in a preceding condition, or in the conclusion. Therefore, **sī nōn** is the rule:

1. When the positive of the same verb precedes.

Sī fēcerĭs, māgnam habēbō grātiam; sī nōn fēcerĭs, ignōscam, C., *Fam.*, V. 19; *if you do it, I will be very grateful to you; if you do not, I will forgive* (*you*).

2. When the Condition is concessive; in this case the principal clause often contains an adversative particle.

Sī mihī bonā rē pūblicā fruī nōn licuerit, at carēbō malā, C., *Mil.*, 34, 93; *if I shall not be allowed to enjoy good government, I shall at least be rid of bad.*

(*b*) With **nisi**, *unless*, the negative **ni-** refers to the principal clause, which is thus denied, if the conditional clause is accepted; hence:

1. **Nisi** adds an exception or restriction to the leading statement. Compare the general use of **nisi**, *except* (R. 2).

Nisi molestumst, paucīs percontārier (130, 6) **volō ego ex tē**, PL., *Rud.*, 120; *if it is not disagreeable, I wish to ask you a few questions.*

So the formulæ **nisi fallor** (**nī fallor** is found first in OVID), **nisi mē omnia fallunt** (C., *Att.*, VIII. 7, 1), and the like.

2. **Nisi** is in favorite use after negatives.

Parvī (= **nihilī**) **sunt forīs arma nisi est cōnsilium domī**, C., *Off.*, I. 22, 76 (411, R. 2). **[Nōn] possem vīvere nisi in litterīs vīverem**, C., *Fam.*, IX. 26, 1; *I could not live unless I lived in study.* **Memoria minuitur nisi eam exerceās**, C., *Cat.M.*, 7, 21; *memory wanes unless (except) you exercise it.* (**Sī nōn exerceās**, *in case you fail to exercise it.*)

So more often than **sī nōn**, in asseverations. **Peream nisi sollicitus sum**, C., *Fam.*, XV. 19, 4; *may I die if I am not troubled.*

REMARKS.—1. Sometimes the difference is unessential:

Nisi Cūriō fuisset, hodiē tē mūscae comēdissent, *Cf.* QUINT., XI. 3, 129; *if it had not been for Curio, the flies would have eaten you up this day.* **Sī nōn fuisset** would be equally correct.

2. **Nisi** is often used after negative sentences or equivalents in the signification of *but, except, besides, only:*

Īnspice quid portem; nihil hīc nisi trīste vidēbis, Ov., *Tr.*, III. 1, 9; *examine what I am bringing; you will see nothing here except* (what is) *sad.* **Falsus honor iuvat et mendāx īnfāmia terret, quem nisi mendōsum et medicandum?** H., *Ep.*, I. 16, 39; "*false honour charms and lying slander scares,*" *whom but the faulty and the fit for physic?*

So **nisi sī**, *except in case*, with a following verb; occasional in early Latin, more common later, but not in CAES. (*B.G.*, I. 31, 14, is disputed), SALL., VERG., HOR. **Nisi ut**, *except on condition that*, is post-classical.

Necesse est Casilīnēnsēs sē dēdere Hannibalī; nisi sī mālunt famĕ perīre, C., *Inv.*, II. 57, 171; *the people of Casilinum must needs surrender to Hannibal; unless* (except in case) *they prefer to perish by hunger.*

3. **Nisi quod** introduces an actual limitation—*with the exception, that* (525, 2, N. 2); so **praeterquam quod**; **nisi ut** (*e.g.* C., *Imp.*, 23, 67).

Nihil acciderat [Polycratī] quod nōllet nisi quod ānulum quō dēlectābātur in marī abiēcerat, C., *Fin.*, v. 30, 92; *nothing had happened to Polycrates that he could not have wished, except that he had thrown into the sea a ring in which he took delight* (= *a favorite ring*). **Nihil peccat nisi quod nihil peccat,** Plin., *Ep.*, ix. 26, 1; *he makes no blunder except —that he makes no blunder* ("faultily faultless").

4. **Nisi forte** (found very often in Cicero, very rarely earlier), *unless, perhaps,* **nisi vērō** (peculiar to Cicero), *unless, indeed,* with the Indic., either limit a previous statement, or make an ironical concession:

Nēmŏ ferē saltat sōbrius nisi forte īnsānit, C., *Mur.*, 6, 13; *there is scarce any one that dances* (when) *sober, unless perhaps he is cracked.* **Plēnum forum est eōrum hominum, . . . nisi vērō paucōs fuisse arbitrāminī,** C., *Sull.*, 9, 28; *the forum is full of those men; unless, indeed, you think they were* (but) *few.*

Notes.—1. **Nisi** is sometimes strengthened by **tamen,** *but, yet.*

Nisi etiam hīc opperiar tamen paulisper, Pl., *Aul.*, 805; *Cf.* C., *Att.*, v. 14, 3. Even without **tamen** it is adversative in colloquial Latin, especially after **nesciō.**

2. **Nī** is found mostly in early Latin and the poets, and in legal formulæ and colloquial phrases. It is rare in Cicero, and never used in Caesar.

Peream nī piscem putāvī esse, Varro, *R.R.*, iii. 3, 9; *may I die if I did not think it was a fish.*

3. **Nisi forte** is found occasionally with the Subjv. from Apuleius on.

592. *Two Conditions excluding each the other.*—When two conditions exclude each the other, **sī** is used for the first; **sīn,** *if not* (*but if*), for the second.

Sīn is further strengthened by **autem, vērō** (rare), *but;* **minus,** *less* (*not*)*;* **secus** (rare), *otherwise;* **aliter,** *else.*

Mercātūra, sī tenuis est, sordida putanda est; sīn māgna et cōpiōsa, nōn est admodum vituperanda, C., *Off.*, i. 42, 151; *mercantile business, if it is petty, is to be considered dirty* (work)*; if* (*it is*) *not* (*petty, but*) *great and abundant* (= *conducted on a large scale*), *it is not to be found fault with much.*

Remark.—If the verb or predicate is to be supplied from the context, **sī minus,** *if less* (*not*), **sīn minus, sīn aliter,** *if otherwise,* are commonly used, rarely **sī nōn**:

Ēdūc tēcum omnēs tuōs; sī minus, quam plūrimōs, C., *Cat.*, i. 5, 10; *take out with you all your* (*followers*)*; if not, as many as possible.* **Ōdero sī poterō; sī nōn, invītus amābō,** Ov., *Am.*, iii. 11, 35 (242, r. 2).

Note.—Much less common are simple **sī,** or **sī** strengthened by **nōn, nihil, nūllus, minus,** or by **autem, vērō**; or **sed sī, at sī** (Col.), **sī contrā** (Hor., Plin.). **Sīn** may also be followed by **nōn,** but commonly only when one or more words intervene.

Pōma crūda sī sunt, vix ēvelluntur; sī mātūra, dēcidunt, C., *Cat.M.*, 19, 71; *if fruit is green it can hardly be plucked, if ripe it falls* (*of itself*).

593. *Other Forms of the Protasis.*—1. The Protasis may be expressed by a Relative.

Quī vidēret, urbem captam dīceret, C., *Verr.*, IV. 23, 52; *whoso had seen it, had said that the city was taken.* **Mīrārētur quī tum cerneret,** L., XXXIV. 9, 4 (258).

2. The Protasis may be contained in a Participle.

Sī latet ars, prōdest; affert dēprēnsa pudōrem, Ov., *A.A.*, II. 313; *art, if concealed, does good; detected, it brings shame.* **Māximās virtūtēs iacēre omnēs necesse est voluptāte dominante,** C., *Fin.*, II. 35, 117; *all the greatest virtues must necessarily lie prostrate, if the pleasure (of the senses) is mistress.* **Nihil [potest] ēvenīre nisi causā antecēdente,** C., *Fat.*, 15, 34; *nothing can happen, unless a cause precede.*

3. The Protasis may be involved in a modifier.

Fēcērunt id servī Milōnis quod suōs quisque servōs in tālī rē facere voluisset, C., *Mil.*, 10, 29; *the servants of Milo did what each man would have wished his servants to do in such case* (**sī quid tāle accidisset**). **At bene nōn poterat sine pūrō pectore vīvī,** LUCR., V. 18; *but there could be no good living without a clean heart* (**nisi pūrum pectus esset**). **Neque enim māteriam ipsam (cēnsēbant) cohaerēre potuisse sī nūllā vī continērētur, neque vim sine aliquā māteriā,** C., *Ac.*, I. 6, 24.

4. The Protasis may be expressed by an Interrogative, or, what is more common, by an Imperative or equivalent.

Trīstis es? indīgnor quod sum tibi causa dolōris, Ov., *Tr.*, IV. 3, 33 (542). **Cēdit amor rēbus: rēs age, tūtus eris,** Ov., *Rem.Am.*, 144; *love yields to business; be busy (if you plunge into business), you will be safe.* **Immūtā (verbōrum collocātiōnem), perierit tōta rēs,** C., *Or.*, 70, 232 (244, R. 4).

Classification of Conditional Sentences.

594. Conditional sentences may be divided into three classes, according to the character of the Protasis:

I. Logical Conditional Sentences: **sī,** with the Indicative.

II. Ideal Conditional Sentences: **sī,** chiefly with Present and Perfect Subjunctive.

III. Unreal Conditional Sentences: **sī,** with Imperfect and Pluperfect Subjunctive.

NOTES.—1. In some grammars of Greek and Latin, conditional sentences, and sentences involving conditional relations, have been divided into *particular* and *general*. Whether a condition be particular or general depends simply on the character of the Apodosis. Any form of the Conditional Sentence may be general, if it implies a rule of action. The forms for Iterative action have been given (566, 567).

2. Conditional Sentences with the Subjunctive (Ideal and Unreal) are best understood by comparing the forms of the Ideal and Unreal wish which have the same mood and the same tenses. The Unreal wish of the Past is the Plupf., that of the Present is the Impf. Subjunctive. The Ideal wish is the Pr. and Pf. Subjunctive. The same temporal relations appear in the conditional.

I. LOGICAL CONDITIONAL SENTENCES.

595. The Logical Conditional Sentence simply states the elements in question, according to the formula : if this is so, then that is so ; if this is not so, then that is not so.

It may be compared with the Indicative Question.

The Protasis is in the Indicative : the Apodosis is generally in the Indicative ; but in future relations any equivalent of the Future (Subjunctive, Imperative) may be used.

Protasis.	Apodosis.
Sī id crēdis, *If you believe that,*	**errās,** *you are going wrong.*
Sī id crēdēbās, *If you believed that,*	**errābās,** *you were going wrong.*
Sī id crēdidistī, *If you* (have) *believed that,*	**errāstī,** *you went* (have gone) *wrong.*
Sī id crēdēs, *If you* (shall) *believe that,*	**errābis,** *you will* (be) *go*(ing) *wrong* (234, R.).
Sī id crēderĭs, *If you* (shall have) *believe*(d) *that,*	**errāverĭs,** *you will have gone* (will go) *wrong.*
Sī quid crēdidistī, *If you have believed anything* (= when you believe anything),	**errās,** *you go wrong.* Comp. 569.
Sī quid crēdiderās, *If you had believed anything* (= when you believed anything),	**errābās,** *you went wrong.*

Sī spīritum dūcit, vīvit, C., *Inv.*, I. 46, 86; *if he is drawing* (his) *breath* (breathing) *he is living.* **Parvī sunt forīs arma nisi est cōnsilium domī,** C., *Off.*, I. 22, 76 (411, R. 2). **Sī occīdī, rēctē fēcī ; sed nōn occīdī,** QUINT., IV. 5, 13; *if I killed him, I did right ; but I did not kill him.* **[Nātūram] sī sequēmur ducem, numquam aberrābimus,** C., *Off.*, I. 28, 100; *if we* (shall) *follow nature* (as our) *guide, we shall never go astray.* **[Improbōs] sī meus cōnsulātus sustulerit, multa saecula prŏpāgārit reī pūblicae,** C., *Cat.*, II. 5, 11; *if my consulship shall have done away with the destructives, it will have added many ages to the life of the State.* **Sī pēs condoluit, sī dēns, ferre nōn possumus,** C., *Tusc.*, II. 22, 52 (567). **Stomachābātur senex, sī quid asperius dīxeram,** C., *N.D.*, I. 33, 93 (567). **Vīvam, sī vīvet ; sī cadet illa, cadam,** PROP., II. (III.) 28 (25), 42 (8); *let me live, if she lives ; if she falls, let me fall.* **Nunc sī forte potes, sed nōn potes, optima cōniūnx, fīnītīs gaudē tot mihi morte malīs,** OV., *Tr.*, III. 3, 55;

now, if haply you can, but you cannot, noble wife, rejoice that so many evils have been finished for me by death. **Flectere sī nequeō superōs, Acheronta movēbō**, V., *A.*, VII. 312; *if I can't bend the gods above, I'll rouse* (*all*) *hell below.* **Sī tot exempla virtūtis nōn movent, nihil umquam movēbit; sī tanta clādēs vīlem vītam nōn fēcit, nūlla faciet**, L., XXII. 60, 14; *if so many examples of valour stir you not, nothing will ever do it; if so great a disaster has not made life cheap, none* (ever) *will.* **Dēsinēs timēre, sī spērāre dēsierīs**, SEN., *E.M.*, I. 5, 7; *you will cease to fear, if you* (*shall have*) *cease*(*d*) *to hope.* **Peream male, sī nōn optimum erat**, H., *S.*, II. 1, 6; *may I die the death if it was not best.* **Sī volēbās participārī, auferrēs** (= **auferre dēbēbās**) **dīmidium domum**, PL., *Truc.*, 748; *if you wished to share in it, you should have taken the half home.* **Respīrārō sī tē vīderō**, C., *Att.*, II. 24, 5; *I shall breathe again, if I shall have seen you.*

REMARKS.—1. After a verb of Saying or Thinking (**Ōrātiō Oblīqua**), the Protasis must be put in the Subjv., according to the rule.

(**Sī id crēdis, errās.**)	**Dīcō, tē, sī id crēdās, errāre.**
	Dīxī, tē, sī id crēderēs, errāre.
(**Sī id crēdēs, errābis.**)	**Dīcō, tē, sī id crēdās, errātūrum esse.**
	Dīxī, tē, sī id crēderēs, errātūrum esse.
(**Sī id crēdidistī, errāstī.**)	**Dīcō, tē, sī id crēdiderīs, errāsse.**
	Dīxī, tē, sī id crēdidissēs, errāsse.

For examples, see **Ōrātiō Oblīqua, 657.**

2. The Subjv. is used by Attraction:

[**Arāneolae**] **rēte texunt ut sī quid inhaeserit cōnficiant**, C., *N.D.*, II. 48, 123 (567). (**Sī quid inhaesit cōnficiunt.**)

3. The Ideal Second Person takes the Subjv. in connection with the Universal Present:

(**Senectūs**) **plēna est voluptātis sī illā sciās ūtī**, SEN., *E.M.*, 12, 4; *old age is full of pleasure if you know* (*if one knows*) *how to enjoy it.* **Memoria minuitur nisi eam exerceās**, C., *Cat.M.*, 7, 21 (591, *b.* 2).

4. **Sīve—sīve** (**seu—seu**) almost invariably takes the Logical form. (496, 2.) The Subjv. is occasionally used by Attraction or with the Ideal Second Person.

Seu vīcit, ferōciter īnstat victīs; seu victus est, īnstaurat cum victōribus certāmen, L., XXVII. 14, 1; *if he vanquishes* (567), *he presses the vanquished furiously; if he is vanquished, he renews the struggle with the vanquishers.*

5. **Sīquidem**, as giving the basis for a conclusion, often approaches the causal sense (590, N. 2). In this case the Apodosis precedes.

Molesta vēritās, sīquidem ex eā nāscitur odium, C., *Lael.*, 24, 89; *truth is burdensome, if indeed* (*since*) *hatred arises from it.*

6. **Sī modŏ**, *if only*, serves to limit the preceding statement.

Ā deō tantum ratiōnem habēmus, sī modo habēmus, C., *N.D.*, III. 28, 71; *all that we have from God is* (bare) *reason, if only we have it.*

Sī vērō when thus used is ironical (C., *Ph.*, VIII. 8, 24). **Sī tamen** seems to be post-classical.

NOTES.—1. Phraseological are **sī quaeris (quaerimus)** in a sense approaching that of **profectō** (C., *Off.*, III. 20, 80; *Tusc.*, III. 29, 73): **Sī dīs placet,** *if the gods will,* often ironical (*Cf.* TER., *Eun.*, 919; C., *Fin.*, II. 10, 31). **Sī forte,** *peradventure* (C., *Or.*, III. 12, 47; *Mil.*, 38, 104).

2. It will be observed that the tense involved depends in each member upon the sense. But for this very reason certain combinations would be uncommon. Thus Pr.—Impf. and Fut.—Pr. are rare; Pr.—Fut. is more common in ante-classical and post-classical Latin than Fut.—Fut., the Pres. being used by anticipation. CICERO prefers Fut.—Fut. CICERO also uses frequently Fut. Pf.—Fut. Pf., which is also found elsewhere, but rarely. Pf.—Fut. is found first in CICERO, and is never common; also Impf.—Impf. Plupf.—Impf. is mostly found in ante-classical and post-classical Latin. The Pf., by anticipation for Fut. Pf., is not unfrequent in early Latin. So C., *Fam.*, XII. 6, 2: **(Brūtus) sī cōnservātus erit, vīcimus** (237); *Cf.* SEN., *Ben.*, III. 62, 145. PL., *Poen.*, 671, shows us our only example of Pr.—Fut. Pf.: **Rēx sum, sī ego illum ad mē adlexerō.**

II. IDEAL CONDITIONAL SENTENCES.

596. The Ideal Conditional Sentence represents the matter as still in suspense. The supposition is more or less fanciful, and no real test is to be applied. There is often a wish for or against. The point of view is usually the Present.

1. The Protasis is put in the Present Subjunctive for continued action, and in the Perfect Subjunctive for completion or attainment.

The Apodosis is in the Present or Perfect Subjunctive. The Imperative and Future Indicative or equivalents are often found. The Universal Present is frequently used, especially in combination with the Ideal Second Person (595, R. 3; 663, 2).

On the difference between Subjunctive and Future, see 257.

PROTASIS.	APODOSIS.
Sī id crēdās,	**errēs,**
If you should (were to) *believe that,*	*you would be going wrong.*
Sī id crēdās,	**errāverīs,**
If you should (were to) *believe that,*	*you would go wrong.*
Sī id crēdiderīs,	**errēs,**
1. *If you should* (prove to) *have believed that* (Perfect; Action Past or Future),	*you would be going wrong.*
2. *If you should* (come to) *believe that* (Aor.; Action Future),	*you would be going wrong.*
Sī id crēdiderīs,	**errāverīs** (rare),
If you (should have) *believe*(d) *that,*	*you would* (have) *go*(ne) *wrong.*

Sī vīcīnus tuus equum meliōrem habeat quam tuus est, tuumne equum mālīs an illīus? C., *Inv.*, I. 31, 52; *if your neighbour (were to) have a better horse than yours is, would you prefer your horse or his?* **Sī gladium quis apud tē sānā mente dēposuerit, repetat īnsāniēns, reddere peccātum sit, officium nōn reddere,** C., *Off.*, III. 25, 95; *if a man in sound mind were to deposit (to have deposited) a sword with you,* (and) *reclaim it (when) mad, it would be wrong to return it, right not to return it.* **Hanc viam sī asperam esse negem, mentiar,** C., *Sest.*, 46, 100; *if I should say that this way is not rough, I should lie.* **Sī nunc mē suspendam meam operam lūserim, et meīs inimīcīs voluptātem creāverim,** PL., *Cas.*, 424; *should I hang myself now, I should* (thereby) *(have) fool(ed) my work away, and give(n) to my enemies a charming treat.* **Cicerōnī nēmo ducentōs nunc dederit nummōs nisi fulserit ānulus ingēns,** JUV., VII. 139; *no one would give Cicero nowadays two hundred two-pences unless a huge ring glittered (on his hand).* **Sī quis furiōsō praecepta det, erit ipsō quem monēbit, īnsānior,** SEN., *E.M.*, 94, 17; *if one should give advice to a madman, he will be more out of his mind than the very man whom he advises.* **Sī valeant hominēs, ars tua, Phoebe, iacet,** OV., *Tr.*, IV. 3, 78; *should men keep well, your art, Phoebus, is naught.* **Ōtia sī tollās, periēre Cupīdinis arcūs,** OV., *Rem.Am.*, 139 (204, N. 6). **(Senectūs) est plēna voluptātis, sī illā sciās ūtī,** SEN., *E.M.*, 12, 4 (595, R. 3). **Memoria minuitur nisi eam exerceās,** C., *Cat.M.*, 7, 21 (591, *b.* 2). **Nūlla est excūsātiō peccātī, sī amīcī causā peccāverīs,** C., *Lael.*, 11, 37; *it is no excuse for a sin to have sinned for the sake of a friend.*

2. The Point of View may be the Past. In that case the Protasis is found in the Imperfect, very rarely the Pluperfect Subjunctive, and the Apodosis has corresponding forms. This usage, however, is rare, inasmuch as it coincides in form with the Unreal Condition, from which it is distinguishable only by a careful study of the context. When found with indefinite persons, the construction is the Potential of the Past.

The idea of Partial Obliquity frequently enters, in which case **sī** may often be translated, *in case that.*

Quod ūsū nōn veniēbat dē eō sī quis lēgem cōnstitueret nōn tam prohibēre vidērētur quam admonēre, C., *Tull.*, 4, 9; *if one should make a law about that which was not customary, he would seem not so much to prevent as to warn.* (Present: **sī quis cōnstituat, videātur.**) **Sī Alfēnus tum iūdicium accipere vellet, dēnique omnia quae pōstulārēs facere voluisset, quid agerēs?** C., *Quinct.*, 26, 83; *in case Alfenus was willing then to undertake the trial, and should have been willing afterwards to do all that you required, what were you to do?* (See the whole passage—Present:

sī nunc velit, . . . voluerit, agās.) **Sī tribūnī mē triumphāre prohibērent, Fūrium et Aemilium tēstēs citātūrus fuī,** L., XXXVIII. 47; *should the tribunes prevent me from triumphing, I was going to summon Furius and Aemilius as witnesses.* **Quid faceret? sī vīvere vellet, Sēiānus rogandus erat,** SEN., *Cons.Marc.*, 22, 6; *what was he to do? if he wished to live Sejanus was* (*the man*) *to be asked.* See TAC., *Ann.*, III. 13. **Erat Quīnctius, sī cēderēs, plācābilis,** L., XXXVI. 32, 5; *Quinctius was, if you yielded to him,* (sure to be) *placable.* (**Est sī cēdās.**) **Sī lūxuriae temperāret, avāritiam nōn timērēs,** TAC., *H.*, II. 62; *if he were to control his love of pleasure, you should not have feared avarice.* (**Sī temperet, nōn timeās.**) **Cūr igitur et Camillus dolēret, sī haec . . . ēventūra putāret? et ego doleam sī. . .putem?** C., *Tusc.*, I. 37, 90. (Present: **doleat sī putet.**)

REMARKS.—1. The Ideal is not controlled by impossibility or improbability, and the lively fancy of the Roman often employs the Ideal where we should expect the Unreal. (Comp. 256, N. 2.) This is more common in early Latin.

Tū sī hīc sīs, aliter sentiās, TER., *And.*, 310; *if you were I* (put yourself in my place), *you would think differently.* **Haec sī tēcum patria loquātur, nōnne impetrāre dēbeat?** C., *Cat.*, I. 8, 19; *if your country should* (were to) *speak thus with you, ought she not to get* (what she wants)? So C., *Fin.*, IV. 22, 61.

2. Sometimes the conception shifts in the course of a long sentence:

Sī revīvīscant et tēcum loquantur—quid tālibus virīs respondērēs? C., *Fin.*, IV. 22, 61: *if they should come to life again, and speak with you —what answer would you make to such men?*

3. When **nōn possum** is followed by **nisi (sī nōn)**, the Protasis has the Ideal of the Past, after the past tense, and *may* have the ideal of the Present after a primary tense.

Neque mūnītiōnēs Caesaris prohibēre poterat, nisi proeliō dēcertāre vellet, CAES., *B.C.*, III. 44. See MADVIG on C., *Fin.*, III. 21, 70.

4. In comparing Ideal and Unreal Conditionals, exclude future verbs such as **posse, velle,** *etc.* The future sense of such Unreal Conditionals comes from the auxiliary.

5. In **Ōrātiō Oblīqua** the difference between Ideal and Logical Future is necessarily effaced, so far as the mood is concerned. (656.)

III. UNREAL CONDITIONAL SENTENCES.

597. The Unreal Conditional sentence is used of that which is Unfulfilled or Impossible, and is expressed by the Imperfect Subjunctive for continued action—generally, in opposition to the Present; and by the Pluperfect Subjunctive—uniformly in opposition to the Past.

The notion of Impossibility comes from the irreversible character of the Past Tense. Compare the Periphrastic Conjug. Perfect and Imperfect. Any action that is decided is considered Past (compare C., *Off.*, II. 21, 75). (See 277, 3, N.)

PROTASIS.	APODOSIS.
Sī id crēderēs, *If you believed* (were believing) *that*, [you do not,]	**errārēs,** *you would be going wrong.*
Sī id crēdidissēs, *If you had believed that*, [you did not,]	**errāvissēs,** *you would have gone wrong.*

Sapientia nōn expeterētur, sī nihil efficeret, C., *Fin.*, I. 13, 42 ; *wisdom would not be sought after, if it did no practical good.* **Caederem tē, nisi īrāscerer,** SEN., *Ira*, I. 15, 3; *I should flog you, if I were not getting angry.* **Sī ibi tē esse scīssem, ad tē ipse vēnissem,** C., *Fin.*, I. 8 ; *if I had known you were there, I should have come to you myself.* **Hectora quis nōsset, fēlīx sī Trōia fuisset ?** Ov., *Tr.*, IV. 3, 75 ; *who would know* (of) *Hector, if Troy had been happy ?* **Nisi ante Rōmā profectus essēs, nunc eam certē relinquerēs,** C., *Fam.*, VII. 11, 1; *if you had not departed from Rome before, you would certainly leave it now.* **Ego nisi peperissem, Rōma nōn oppūgnārētur ; nisi fīlium habērem, lībera in līberā patriā mortua essem,** L., II. 40, 8 ; *had I not become a mother, Rome would not be besieged ; had I not a son, I should have died a free woman in a free land.*

REMARKS.—1. The Impf. Subjv. is sometimes used in opposition to continuance from a point in the Past into the Present. This is necessarily the case when the Protasis is in the Impf., and the Apodosis in the Plupf., except when the Impf. denotes opposition to a general statement, which holds good both for Past and for Present :

Nōn tam facile opēs Carthāginis tantae concidissent, nisi Sicilia clāssibus nostrīs patēret, *Cf.* C., *Verr.*, II. 1, 3; *the great resources of Carthage* (*Carthage with her great resources*) *would not have fallen so readily, if Sicily had not been* (as it still continues to be) *open to our fleets.* **Sī pudōrem habērēs, ūltimam mihĭ pēnsiōnem remīsissēs,** SEN., *E.M.*, 29, 10 ; *if you had* (= *you had not, as you have not*) *any delicacy, you would have let me off from the last payment.* **Memoriam ipsam cum vōce perdidissēmus, sī tam in nostrā potestāte esset oblīvīscī quam tacēre,** TAC., *Agr.*, 2, 4 ; *we should have lost memory itself, together with utterance, if it were as much in our power to forget as to keep silent.*

The Impf. in both members, referring to the Past, always admits of another explanation than that of the Unreal ; thus we have a case of Representation (654, N.) in

Prōtogenēs sī Iālȳsum illum suum caenō oblitum vidēret, māgnum, crēdō, acciperet dolōrem, C., *Att.*, II. 21, 4; *if Protogenes could see that famous Ialysus of his besmeared with mud, he would feel a mighty pang.* See PL., *Aul.*, 742.

2. In Unreal Conditions, after a negative Protasis, the Apodosis is sometimes expressed by the Impf. Indic., when the action is represented as interrupted (233); by the Plupf. and Hist. Pf., when the conclusion is confidently anticipated (254, R. 3).

Lābēbar longius, nisi mē retinuissem, C., *Leg.*, I. 19, 52 (254, R. 3).

This usage after a positive is cited first in the post-Augustan writers. Cases like C., *Verr.*, V. 42, 129; L., XXII. 28, 13, do not belong here.

Omnīnō supervacua erat doctrīna, sī nātūra sufficeret, QUINT., II. 8, 8 (254, R. 3). **Perāctum erat bellum, sī Pompēium Brundisiī opprimere potuisset,** FLOR., II. 13, 19; *the war was (had been) finished, if he had been able to crush Pompey at Brundusium.*

The Impf. Indic. is sometimes found in the Protasis:

Ipsam tibĭ epistolam mīsissem, nisi (*v.l.*, **sed**) **tam subitō frātris puer profi-cīscēbātur,** C., *Att.*, VIII. 1, 2; *I should have sent you the letter itself, if my brother's servant was not starting so suddenly.*

3. (*a*) The Indicative is the regular construction in the Apodosis with verbs which signify Possibility or Power, Obligation or Necessity—so with the active and passive Periphrastic—**vix, paene,** *scarcely, hardly*, and the like. In many cases it is difficult to distinguish this usage from that of the Ideal (596, 2).

Cōnsul esse quī potuī, nisi eum vītae cursum tenuissem? C., *Rep.*, I. 6, 10; *how could I have been consul, if I had not kept that course of life?* **Antōnī gladiōs potuit contemnere, sī sīc omnia dīxisset,** JUV., X. 123; *he might have despised Antony's swords, if he had thus said all (that he did say).* **Ēmendātūrus, sī licuisset, eram,** OV., *Tr.*, I. 7, 40; *I should have removed the faults, if I had been free* (to do it). **Pōns iter paene hostibus dedit (paene dedit = dabat = datūrus erat), nī ūnus vir fuisset,** L., II. 10, 2; *the bridge well nigh gave a passage to the enemy, had it not been for one man.*

(*b*) With the Indic. the Possibility and the rest are stated absolutely; when the Subjv. is used the Possibility and the rest are conditioned as in any other Unreal sentence.

Compare **quid facere potuissem, nisi tum cōnsul fuissem,** with **cōnsul esse quī potuī, nisi eum vītae cursum tenuissem,** C., *Rep.*, I. 6, 10. **Quī sī fuisset meliōre fortūnā, fortasse austērior et gravior esse potuisset,** C., *Pis.*, 29, 71.

4. In **Ōrātiō Oblīqua** the Protasis is unchanged; the Apodosis is formed by the Periphrastic Pr. and Pf. Inf. (149), for the Active, **futūrum (fore) ut, futūrum fuisse ut** for passive and Supineless verbs.

A. **Dīcō (dīxī), tē, sī id crēderēs, errātūrum esse.**
B. **Dīcō (dīxī), tē, sī id crēdidissēs, errātūrum fuisse.**
A. **Dīcō (dīxī), sī id crēderēs, fore ut dēciperēris.**
B. **Dīcō (dīxī), sī id crēdidissēs, futūrum fuisse ut dēciperēris.**

A is very rare; *A*, theoretical. For the long form, *B*, the simple

Perfect Infinitive is found. Examples, see 659, N. In B, **fuisse** is omitted occasionally in later Latin ; TAC., *Ann.*, I. 33, *etc.*

5. (*a*) When the Apodosis of an Unreal Conditional is made to depend on a sentence which requires the Subjv., the Plupf. is turned into the Periphrastic Pf. Subjv.; the Impf. form is unchanged.

Nōn dubitō, *I do not doubt,*	**quīn, sī id crēderēs, errārēs,** *that, if you believed that, you would be going wrong.*
Nōn dubitābam, *I did not doubt,*	**quīn, sī id crēdidissēs, errātūrus fuerīs,** *that, if you had believed that, you would have gone wrong.*

Honestum tāle est ut, vel sī īgnōrārent id hominēs, esset laudābile, *Cf.* C., *Fin.*, II. 15, 49; *virtue is a thing to deserve praise, even if men did not know it.* **Ea rēs tantum tumultum āc fugam praebuit ut nisi castra Pūnica extrā urbem fuissent, effūsūra sē omnis pavida multitūdō fuerit,** L., XXVI. 10, 7 ; *that matter caused so much tumult and flight* (= so wild a panic), *that had not the Punic camp been outside the city the whole frightened multitude would have poured forth.* **Nec dubium erat quīn, sī tam paucī simul obīre omnia possent, terga datūrī hostēs fuerint,** L., IV. 38, 5 ; *there was no doubt that, if it had been possible for so small a number to manage everything at the same time, the enemy would have turned their backs.* **Dīc quidnam factūrus fuerīs, sī eō tempore cēnsor fuissēs ?** L., IX. 33, 7 ; *tell* (me) *what you would have done, if you had been censor at that time ?* See C., *Pis.*, 7, 14.

(*b*) The Periphrastic Plupf. Subjv. occurs rarely, and then only in the Dependent Interrogative. The only examples cited are from LIVY.

Subībat cōgitātiō animum, quōnam modō tolerābilis futūra Etrūria fuisset sī quid in Samniō adversī ēvēnisset, L., X. 45, 3.

(*c*) **Potuī** (254, R. 1) commonly becomes **potuerim**, and **fuī** with the Periphrastic passive in **-dus** becomes **fuerim,** after all tenses.

Haud dubium fuit quīn, nisi ea mora intervēnisset, castra eō diē Pūnica capī potuerint, L., XXIV. 42, 3; *there was no doubt that, had not that delay interfered, the Punic camp could have been taken on that day.* **Quae (rēs) suā sponte nefāria est ut etiamsī lēx nōn esset, māgnopere vītanda fuerit,** C., *Verr.*, I. 42, 108.

(*d*) The passive Conditional is unchanged :

Id ille sī repudiāsset, dubitātis quīn eī vīs esset allāta ? C., *Sest.*, 29, 62 ; *if he had rejected that, do you doubt that force would have been brought* (to bear) *on him ?*

The active form is rarely unchanged (L., II. 33, 9). In the absence of the Periphrastic tense the Inf. with **potuerim** is often a sufficient substitute; see L., XXXII. 28, 6.

NOTE.—In PLAUTUS and TERENCE, **absque** with the Abl. and **esset** (**foret**) is found a few times instead of **nisi** (**sī nōn**) with Nom., and **esset** (**fuisset**) in the sense *if it were not* (*had not been*) *for.*

Nam absque tē esset, hodiē numquam ad sōlem occāsum vīverem, PL., *Men.*, 1022. *Cf.* LIV., II. 10, 2 (R. 3, above).

INCOMPLETE CONDITIONAL SENTENCES.

598. *Omission of the Conditional Sign.*—Occasionally the members of a Conditional sentence are put side by side without a Conditional sign.

An ille mihī̆ (351) **līber, cuī mulier imperat? pōscit, dandum est; vocat, veniendum est; ēicit, abeundum; minātur, extimēscendum,** C., *Parad.*, 5, 2; *or is he free (tell) me, to whom a woman gives orders? she asks, he must give; she calls, he must come; she turns out (of door), he must go; she threatens, he must be frightened.* **Ūnum cōgnōrĭ̄s, omnīs nōrĭ̄s,** Ter., *Ph.*, 265; *you know one, you know all.* **Dedissēs huīc animō pār corpus, fēcisset quod optābat,** Plin., *Ep.*, I. 12, 8; *had you given him a body that was a match for his spirit, he would have accomplished what he desired.*

599. *Omission of the Verb of the Protasis.*—When the verb of the Protasis is omitted, either the precise form or the general idea of the verb is to be supplied from the Apodosis.

Sī quisquam (= **sī quisquam fuit**), **Catō sapiēns fuit,** *Cf.* C., *Lael.*, 2, 9; *if any one was wise, Cato was.* **Ēdūc tēcum omnēs tuōs; sī minus, quam plūrimōs,** C., *Cat.*, I. 5, 10 (592, R.).

600. *Total Omission of the Protasis.*—1. The Protasis is often contained in a participle or involved in the context; for examples see 593, 2 and 3.

2. The Potential Subjunctive is sometimes mechanically explained by the omission of an indefinite Protasis (257, N. 2).

Nimiō plūs quam velim [Volscōrum] ingenia sunt mōbilia, L., II. 37, 4; *the dispositions of the Volscians are (too) much more unstable than I should like.* **Tuam mihī̆ darī vellem ēloquentiam,** C., *N.D.*, II. 59, 147; *I could wish to have your eloquence given me.* **Tam fēlīx essēs quam fōrmōsissima vellem,** Ov., *Am.*, I. 8, 27 (302). **(Utinam essēs!)**

601. *Omission and Involution of the Apodosis.*—The Apodosis is omitted in *Wishes* (261), and implied after verbs and phrases denoting *Trial* (460, 2). It is often involved in **Ōrātiō Oblīqua,** and sometimes consists in the general notion of *Result, Ascertainment,* or the like.

Sī vērum excutiās, faciēs nōn uxor amātur, Juv., VI. 143; *if you were to get out the truth* (you would find that) *it is the face, not the wife, that* *is loved.* **(Iugurtha) timēbat īram (= nē īrāscerētur) senātūs, nī pāruisset lēgātīs,** S., *Iug.*, 25, 7; *Iugurtha was afraid of the anger of the senate* (that the senate would get angry) *in case he did not* (should not have) *obey*(ed) *the legates.*

CONDITIONAL SENTENCES OF COMPARISON.

602. The Apodosis is omitted in comparisons with **ut sī, velut sī, āc sī, quam sī** (rare), **tamquam sī, quasi,** or simply **velut** and **tamquam,** *as if.*

The verb is to be supplied from the Protasis, as is common in correlative sentences. The Mood is the Subjunctive.

The tenses follow the rule of sequence, rather than the ordinary use of the conditional. In English, the translation implies the unreality of the comparison.

Nōlī timēre quasi [= quam timeās sī] assem elephantō dēs, QUINT., VI. 3, 59; *don't be afraid, as if you were giving a penny to an elephant.* **Parvī prīmō ortū sīc iacent tamquam [= iaceant sī] omnīnō sine animō sint,** C., *Fin.*, V. 15, 42; *babies, when first born, lie (there), as if they had no mind at all.* **Hīc est obstandum, mīlitēs, velut sī ante Rōmāna moenia pūgnēmus,** L., XXI. 41, 15; *here (is where) we must oppose them, soldiers, as if we were fighting before the walls of Rome* (**velut obstēmus, sī pūgnēmus,** *as we would oppose them, if we were to fight*). **Mē iuvat, velut ipse in parte labōris āc perīculī fuerim, ad fīnem bellī Pūnicī pervēnisse,** L., XXXI. 1; *I am delighted to have reached the end of the Punic war, as if I had shared in the toil and danger (of it).* **Tantus patrēs metus cēpit velut sī iam ad portās hostis esset,** L., XXI. 16, 2; *a great fear took hold of the senators, as if the enemy were already at their gates.* **Dēlēta (est) Ausonum gēns perinde āc sī internecīvō bellō certāsset,** L., IX. 25, 9; *the Ausonian race was blotted out, just as if it had engaged in an internecine war (war to the knife).*

REMARKS.—1. Occasionally the sequence is violated out of regard to the Conditional:

Massiliēnsēs in eō honōre audīmus apud [Rōmānōs] esse āc sī medium umbilīcum Graeciae incolerent, L., XXXVII. 54, 21; *we hear that the people of Marseilles are in as high honour with the Romans as if they inhabited the mid-navel* (= the heart) *of Greece.* **Ēius negōtium sīc velim suscipiās, ut sī esset rēs mea,** C., *Fam.*, II. 14, 1; *I wish you would undertake his business just as if it were my affair.*

2. The principal clause often contains correlatives, as: **ita, sīc, perinde, proinde, similiter, nōn (haud) secus,** *etc.*

NOTES.—1. **Tamquam** and **quasi** are also used in direct comparison with the Indicative. Here the verbs with both clauses are apt to be the same, in which case the verb with **quasi** or **tamquam** is usually omitted in model prose.

Quasi pōma ex arboribus, crūda sī sunt, vix ēvelluntur, sīc vītam adulēscentibus vīs aufert, C., *Cat.M.*, 19, 71.

2. **Quasi** is used to soften or apologise for a single word (= **ut ita dīcam**).

Mors est quaedam quasi migrātiō commūtātiōque vītae, *Cf.* C., *Tusc.*, I. 12, 27; *death is as it were a shifting of life's quarters.*

3. As in the ordinary Conditional sentence, so in the Comparative sentence, the Protasis may be expressed by a participle:

Gallī laetī ut explōrātā victōriā ad castra Rōmānōrum pergunt, *Cf.* CAES., *B.G.*, III. 18, 8; *the Gauls in their joy, as if* (their) *victory had been fully ascertained, proceeded to the camp of the Romans.* **Antiochus sēcūrus dē bellō Rōmānō erat tamquam nōn trānsitūrīs in Asiam Rōmānīs,** L., XXXVI. 41, 1; *Antiochus was as unconcerned about the war with Rome as if the Romans did not intend to cross over into Asia Minor.*

4. In CELSUS, QUINTILIAN, JUVENAL, PLINY MIN., and especially in TACITUS and SUETONIUS, we find **tamquam** used almost like **quod** (541), to indicate an assumed reason, in imitation of the similar Greek use of ὡς with the participle, and occasionally where we might have expected the Acc. and Infinitive.

Prīdem invīsus tamquam plūs quam cīvīlia agitāret, TAC., *Ann.*, I. 12, 6; *long misliked as* (in Tiberius' judgment) *plotting high treason.* **Sūspectus tamquam ipse suās incenderit aedēs,** JUV., III. 222; *suspected of having* (*as if he had*) *set his own house on fire.* **Vulgī opīniō est tamquam (comētēs) mūtātiōnem rēgnī portendat,** TAC. *Ann.*, XIV. 22, 1; *it is the popular belief that a comet portends a change in the kingdom.*

Other particles, **quasi, sīcut,** and **ut,** occur much more rarely and are cited mainly from TACITUS (**quasi** only in the *Annals*). Compare SUET., *Tit.*, 5.

5. **Ut sī** is rare in early Latin, not being found at all in PLAUTUS. It is found but once in LIVY, but frequently in CICERO and later Latin. **Velut sī** is found first in CAESAR. **Velut** for **velut sī** is found first in LIVY. **Āc sī** is equivalent to **quasi** only in late Latin.

CONCESSIVE SENTENCES.

603. Concessive Sentences are introduced by:

1. The Conditional particles, **etsī, etiamsī, tametsī (tamenetsī).**
2. The generic relative, **quamquam.**
3. The compounds, **quamvīs, quantumvīs.**
4. The verb **licet.**
5. The Final particles, **ut (nē).**
6. **Cum (quom).**

These all answer generally to the notion *although.*

NOTE.—**Etsī** (**et** + **sī**), *even if;* **etiamsī,** *even now if;* **tametsī,** *yet even if;* **quamquam** (**quam** + **quam**), *to what extent soever;* **quamvīs,** *to what extent you choose;* **quantumvīs,** *to what amount you choose;* **licet,** *it is left free* (perhaps intrans. of **linquō,** *I leave*).

604. Etsī, etiamsī, and **tametsī,** take the Indicative or Subjunctive, according to the general principles which regulate the use of **sī**, *if* The Indicative is more common, especially with **etsī**.

Dē futūrīs rēbus etsī semper difficile est dīcere, tamen interdum coniectūrā possīs accēdere, C., *Fam.*, VI. 4, 1; *although it is always difficult to tell about the future, nevertheless you can sometimes come near it by guessing.* **[Hamilcar] etsī flagrābat bellandī cupiditāte, tamen pācī serviundum putāvit**, NEP., XXII. 1, 3; *although Hamilcar was on fire with the desire of war, nevertheless he thought that he ought to subserve (to work for) peace.* **Inops ille etiamsī referre grātiam nōn potest, habēre certē potest**, C., *Off.*, II. 20, 69; *the needy man (spoken of), if he cannot return a favour, can at least feel it.* **Mē vēra prō grātīs loquī, etsī meum ingenium nōn monēret, necessitās cōgit**, L., III. 68, 9; *even if my disposition did not bid me, necessity compels me to speak what is true instead of what is palatable.*

REMARKS.—1. **Sī** itself is often concessive (591, 2), and the addition of **et, etiam,** and **tamen** serves merely to fix the idea.

2. **Etiamsī** is used oftener with the Subjv. than with the Indic., and seems to be found only in conditional sentences. On the other hand, **etsī** is also used like **quamquam** (605, R. 2), in the sense "*and yet;*" **virtūtem sī ūnam āmīserīs—etsī āmittī nōn potest virtūs**, C., *Tusc.*, II. 14, 32; so too, but rarely, **tametsī**. **Etsī** is a favorite word with CICERO, but does not occur in QUINTILIAN nor in SALLUST, the latter of whom prefers **tametsī**. **Tametsī** is not found in the Augustan poets nor in TACITUS, and belongs especially to familiar speech.

3. **Tamen** is often correlative even with **tametsī**.

605. Quamquam, *to what extent soever*, falls under the head of generic relatives (254, R. 4), and, in the best authors, is construed with the Indicative.

Medicī quamquam intellegunt saepe, tamen numquam aegrīs dīcunt, illō morbō eōs esse moritūrōs, C., *Div.*, II. 25, 54; *although physicians often know, nevertheless they never tell their patients that they will die of that* (particular) *disease.*

REMARKS.—1. The Potential Subjv. (257, N. 3) is sometimes found with **quamquam**: **Quamquam exercitum quī in Volscīs erat māllet, nihil recūsāvit**, L., VI. 9, 6; *although he might well have preferred the army which was in the Volscian country, nevertheless he made no objection.*

So especially with the Ideal Second Person.

2. **Quamquam** is often used like **etsī**, but more frequently, at the beginning of sentences, in the same way as the English, *and yet, although, however*, in order to limit the whole preceding sentence.

3. The Indic., with **etsī** and **quamquam**, is, of course, liable to attraction into the Subjv. in **Ōrātiō Oblīqua** (508).

NOTE.—The Subjv. with **quamquam** (not due to attraction) is first cited from CICERO (perhaps *Tusc.*, v. 30, 85), NEPOS (XXV. 13, 6), after which, following the development in all generic sentences in Latin, it becomes more and more common; thus, in post-Augustan Latin, JUVENAL uses it exclusively, and PLINY MIN. and TACITUS regularly.

606. Quamvīs follows the analogy of **volō**, *I will*, with which it is compounded, and takes the Subjunctive (usually the principal tenses).

Quantumvīs and **quamlibet** (as conjunctions) belong to poetry and silver prose.

Quamvīs sint sub aquā, sub aquā maledīcere temptant, Ov., *M.*, VI. 376; *although they be under the water, under the water they try to revile.* **Quamvīs ille niger, quamvīs tū candidus essēs**, V., *Ec.*, II. 16; *although he was black, although you were fair.* **[Vitia mentis], quamvīs exigua sint, in māius excēdunt**, SEN., *E.M.*, 85, 12; *mental ailments* (= *passions*), *no matter how slight they be, go on increasing.* **Quamvīs sīs molestus numquam tē esse cōnfitēbor malum**, C., *Tusc.*, II. 25, 61; *although you be troublesome, I shall never confess that you are evil.*

NOTES.—1. The Indic. with **quamvīs** is cited in prose first from C., *Rab.Post.*, 2, 4; NEP., I. 2, 3 (except in fragments of VARRO and VATINIUS); in poetry it appears first in LUCRETIUS. Then it grows, so that in the post-Augustan period it is used just like **quamquam** with the Indic., though the Subjv. is also common:

Quamvīs ingeniō nōn valet, arte valet, Ov., *Am.*, I. 15, 14; *although he does not tell by genius, he does tell by art.*

2. The verb of **quamvīs** is sometimes inflected: **Quam volet Epicūrus iocētur, tamen numquam mē movēbit**, C., *N.D.*, II. 17, 46.

607. Licet retains its verbal nature, and, according to the Sequence of Tenses, takes only the Present and Perfect Subjunctive:

Licet irrīdeat sī quī vult, C., *Parad.*, I. 1, 8; *let any one laugh who will.* **Ārdeat ipsa licet, tormentīs gaudet amantis**, JUV., VI. 209; *though she herself is aglow, she rejoices in the tortures of her lover.* **Sim licet extrēmum, sīcut sum, missus in orbem**, Ov., *Tr.*, IV. 9, 9; *although I be sent, as I have been, to the end of the world.*

NOTES.—1. Exceptions are extremely rare: JUV., XIII. 56.

2. **Quamvīs** is sometimes combined with **licet**, as: **quamvīs licet īnsectēmur istōs—metuō nē sōlī philosophī sint**, C., *Tusc.*, IV. 24, 53.

3. Occasionally **licet** is inflected; *e.g.*, H., *Epod.*, 15, 19; *S.*, II. 1, 59. From the time of APULEIUS **licet** is construed with the Indicative.

608. Ut and **nē** are also used concessively for the sake of argument; this is common in CICERO, who often attaches to it **sānē**; the basis of this is the Imperative Subjunctive.

Ut dēsint vīrēs, tamen est land nda voluntās, Ov., *Pont.*, III. 4, 79;

granted that strength be lacking, nevertheless you must praise (my) good will. **Nē sit summum malum dolor, malum certē est,** C., *Tusc.*, II. 5, 14; *granted that pain be not the chief evil, an evil it certainly is.*

REMARKS.—1. **Ut nōn** can be used on the principle of the Specific Negative: **Hīc diēs ūltimus est; ut nōn sit, prope ab ūltimō est,** SEN., *E.M.*, 15, 12; *this is your last day; granted that it be not, it is near the last.*

2. Examples with past tenses are rare: C., *Mil.*, 17, 46; L., XXXVIII 46, 3, *etc.*

3. On **ita—ut,** see 262; on **ut—ita,** see 482, 4.

609. *Concessive Sentence represented by a Participle or Predicative Attribute.*—The Concessive sentence may be represented by a Participle or Predicative Attribute.

[**Rīsus**] **interdum ita repente ērumpit, ut eum cupientēs tenēre nequeāmus,** *Cf.* C., *Or.*, II. 58, 235; *laughter between whiles* (occasionally) *breaks out so suddenly that we cannot keep it down, although we desire to do so.* **Multōrum tē oculī et aurēs nōn sentientem cūstōdient,** C., *Cat.*, I. 2, 6; (*of*) *many* (*the*) *eyes and ears will keep guard over you, though you perceive it not* (WITHOUT *your perceiving it*). **Quis Aristīdem nōn mortuum dīligit?** C., *Fin.*, V. 22, 62; *who does not love Aristides,* (*though*) *dead?*

NOTES.—1. **Quamquam, quamvīs,** and **etsī** are often combined with the participle. This, however, is rare in classical Latin, but becomes more common later.

(Caesar), quamquam obsidiōne Massiliae retardante, brevī tamen omnia subēgit, SUET., *Iul.*, 34.

2. With adjectives and adverbs this is much more common, so especially with **quamvīs,** which is used with a positive as a circumlocution for the superlative. With the superlative **quamvīs** is rare.

Etsī nōn inīquum, certē trīste senātūs cōnsultum, L., XXV. 6, 2. **Cum omnia per populum geruntur, quamvīs iūstum atque moderātum tamen ipsa aequābilitās est inīqua,** C., *Rep.*, I. 27, 43.

RELATIVE SENTENCES.

610. The Latin language uses the relative construction far more than the English: so in the beginning of sentences, and in combination with Conjunctions and other Relatives.

REMARKS.—1. The awkwardness, or impossibility, of a literal translation may generally be relieved by the substitution of a demonstrative with an appropriate conjunction, or the employment of an abstract noun:

Quae cum ita sint, *now since these things are so* (Ciceronian formula).

Futūra modo exspectant; quae quia certa esse nōn possunt, cōnficiuntur et angōre et metū, C., *Fin.*, I. 18, 60; *they only look forward to the future; and because that cannot be certain, they wear themselves out* *with distress and fear.* [**Epicūrus**] **nōn satis polītus iīs artibus quās quī tenent, ērudītī appellantur**, C., *Fin.*, I. 7, 26; *Epicurus is not sufficiently polished by those accomplishments, from the possession of which people are called cultivated.*

2. Notice especially **quod** in combination with **sī** and its compounds **ubi, quia, quoniam, ut** (poetic and post-class.), **utinam, nē, utinam nē, quī** (rare), in which **quod** means *and as for that,* and is sometimes translated by *and, but, therefore, whereas,* sometimes not at all.

Quod nī fuissem incōgitāns ita eum exspectārem ut pār fuit, Ter., *Ph.*, 155; *whereas, had I not been heedless, I should be awaiting him in proper mood.*

Notes.—1. The use of the Relative to connect two independent clauses instead of a demonstrative, is very rare in Plautus, more common in Terence, but fully developed only in the classical period.

2. The Relative is the fertile source of many of the introductory particles of the compound sentence (**quom, quia, quoniam,** compounds of **quam, ut, ubi,** *etc.*), and is therefore treated last on account of the multiplicity of its uses.

611. Relative sentences are introduced by the Relative pronouns in all their forms: adjective, substantive, and adverbial. (See Tables 109 foll.)

Remarks.—1. The Relative adverbs of Place, and their correlatives, may be used instead of a preposition with a Relative. **Unde,** *whence,* is frequently used of persons, but the others rarely; occasional examples are cited for **ubi** and **quō**, the others less frequently: **ibi = in eō,** *etc.;* **ubi = in quō,** *etc.;* **inde = ex eō,** *etc.;* **unde = ex quō,** *etc.;* **eō = in eum,** *etc.;* **quō = in quem,** *etc.*

Potest fierī ut is, unde tē audīsse dīcis, īrātus dīxerit, C., *Or.*, II. 70, 285; *it may be that he, from whom you say you heard* (it), *said it in anger.* **Quō (= quibus) lubeat nūbant, dum dōs nē fīat comes**, Pl., *Aul.*, 491 (573).

2. The Relative is not to be confounded with the Dependent Interrogative sentence (469, R. 2).

Quae probat populus ego nesciō, Sen., *E.M.*, 29, 10; *the things that the people approves, I do not know* (**quid probet,** *what it is the people approves*). **Et quid ego tē velim, et tū quod quaeris, sciēs**, Ter., *And.*, 536; *you shall know both what* (*it is*) *I want of you, and what* (the thing which) *you are asking* (*= the answer to your question*).

612. *Position of Relatives.*—The Relative and Relative forms are put at the beginning of sentences and clauses. The preposition, however, generally, though not invariably, precedes its Relative (413).

613. *Antecedent.*—The word to which the Relative refers is called the Antecedent, because it precedes in thought even when it does not in expression.

REMARK.—The close connection between Relative and Antecedent is shown by the frequent use of one preposition in common (414, R. 1).

CONCORD.

614. The Relative agrees with its Antecedent in Gender, Number, and Person.

Is minimō eget mortālis, quī minimum cupit, SYRUS, 286 (Fr.) (308). **Uxor contenta est quae bona est ūnō virō,** PL., *Merc.*, 812; *a wife who is good is contented with one husband.* **Malum est cōnsilium quod mūtārī nōn potest,** SYRUS, 362 (Fr.); *bad is the plan that cannot (let itself) be changed.* **Hōc illīs nārrō quī mē nōn intellegunt,** PHAEDR., 3, 128; *I tell this tale for those who understand me not.* **Ego quī tē cōnfīrmō, ipse mē nōn possum,** C., *Fam.*, XIV. 4, 5; *I who reassure you, cannot reassure myself.*

REMARKS.—1. The Relative agrees with the Person of the true Antecedent, even when a predicate intervenes; exceptions are very rare:

Tū es is, quī (mē) summīs laudibus ad caelum extulistī, C., *Fam.*, XV. 4, 11; *you are he that has(t) praised me to the skies.*

The Latin rule is the English exception: Acts, xxi. 38; Luke, xvi. 15.

2. When the Relative refers to a sentence, **id quod,** *that which,* is commonly used (parenthetically). So also **quae rēs,** or simple **quod,** and, if reference is made to a single substantive, **is quī** or some similar form.

Sī ā vōbīs id quod nōn spērō dēserar, tamen animō nōn dēficiam, C., *Rosc.Am.*, 4, 10; *if I should be deserted by you (which I do not expect), nevertheless I should not become faint-hearted.* **Nec audiendus [Theophrastī] audītor, Stratō, is quī physicus appellātur,** C., *N.D.*, I. 13, 35.

3. The gender and number of the Relative may be determined:

(*a*) By the sense, and not by the form; that is, a collective noun may be followed by a Plural Relative, a neuter numeral by a masculine Relative, a possessive pronoun by a Relative in the person indicated by the possessive, *etc.*

Caesa sunt ad sex mīlia quī Pydnam perfūgerant, L., XLIV. 42, 7; *there were slain up to six thousand who had fled to Pydna.* **Equitātum omnem praemittit, quī videant,** CAES., *B.G.*, I. 15; *he sent all the cavalry ahead, who should see (that they might see, to see).*

(*b*) By the predicate or the apposition, and not by the antecedent; so especially when the Relative is combined with the copula or with a copulative verb.

Thēbae, quod Boeōtiae caput est, L., XLII. 44, 3; *Thebes, which is the capital of Boeotia.* **Flūmen Scaldis, quod īnfluit in Mosam,** CAES., *B.G.*,

VI. 33, 3; *the river Scheldt, which empties into the Maas.* **Iūsta glōria, quī est frūctus virtūtis**, C., *Pis.*, 24, 57; *real glory, which is the fruit of virtue.*

Exceptions are not unfrequent, especially when the predicative substantive in the Relative clause is a foreign word or a proper name.

Stellae quās Graecī comētās vocant, C., *N.D.*, II. 5, 14; *the stars which the Greeks call comets.* **Est genus quoddam hominum quod Helōtae vocātur**, NEP., IV. 3, 6; *there is a certain class of men called Helots.*

4. The pronominal apposition may be taken up into the Relative and disappear:

Tēstārum suffrāgiīs quod illī ostracismum vocant, NEP., V. 3, 1; *by potsherd votes*—(a thing) *which they call "ostracism."*

5. When the Relative refers to the combined antecedents of different gender, the strongest gender is preferred, according to 282:

Grandēs nātū mātrēs et parvī līberī, quōrum utrumque aetās misericordiam vestram requīrit, C., *Verr.*, V. 49, 129; *aged matrons and infant children, whose age on either hand demands your compassion.* **Ōtium atque dīvitiae, quae prīma mortālēs putant**, S., *C.*, 36, 4; *leisure and money, which mortals reckon as the prime things.*

Or, the nearest gender may be preferred:

Eae frūgēs atque frūctūs quōs terra gignit, C., *N.D.*, II. 14, 37; *those fruits of field and tree which earth bears.*

6. Combined Persons follow the rule, 287.

NOTE.—A noteworthy peculiarity is found in early Latin, where a generic Relative sentence with **quī** is made the subject of an abstract substantive with **est**, and represented by a demonstrative in agreement with that substantive.

Istaec virtūs est, quandō ūsust, quī malum fert fortiter, PL., *Asin.*, 323; *that's manhood who* (if one) *bears evil bravely, when there's need.*

The parallel Greek construction suggests Greek influence.

615. *Repetition of the Antecedent.*—The Antecedent of the Relative is not seldom repeated in the Relative clause, with the Relative as its attributive.

(Caesar) intellēxit diem īnstāre, quō diē frūmentum mīlitibus mētīrī oportēret, CAES., *B.G.*, I. 16, 5; *Caesar saw that the day was at hand, on which day it behooved to measure corn* (corn was to be measured out) *to the soldiers.*

NOTE.—This usage belongs to the formal style of government and law. CAESAR is very fond of it, especially with the word **diēs**. It is occasional in PLAUTUS and TERENCE, and not uncommon in CICERO; but after CICERO it fades out, being found but rarely in LIVY, and only here and there later.

616. *Incorporation of the Antecedent.*—1. The Antecedent substantive is often incorporated into the Relative clause; sometimes there is a demonstrative antecedent, sometimes not.

In quem prīmum ēgressī sunt locum Trōia vocātur, L., I. 1, 3; *the first place they landed at was called Troy.* **Quam quisque nōrit artem, in hāc sē exerceat,** [C.], *Tusc.*, I. 18, 41; *what trade each man is master of, (in) that let him practise (himself), that let him ply.*

NOTES.—1. Incorporation, while much less frequent than Repetition, is still not unfrequently met with in LIVY; after LIVY it decays. No examples are cited from SALLUST with a demonstrative antecedent, and but one from CAESAR. No example is cited from CAESAR without a demonstrative antecedent.

2. Instead of a principal clause, followed by a consecutive clause, the structure is sometimes reversed. What would have been the dependent clause becomes the principal clause, and an incorporated explanatory Relative takes the place of the demonstrative. This is confined to certain substantives, and is found a number of times in CICERO, but rarely elsewhere (SALL., HOR., LIVY, OVID, SEN., TAC., PLINY MIN.).

Quā enim prūdentiā es, nihil tē fugiet (= **eā prūdentiā es, ut nihil tē fugiat**), C., *Fam.*, XI. 13, 1. **Velīs tantummodo; quae tua virtūs** (**est**), **expūgnābis,** H., *S.*, I. 9, 54.

2. An appositional substantive, from which a Relative clause depends, is regularly incorporated into the Relative clause.

[**Amānus**] **Syriam ā Ciliciā dīvidit, quī mōns erat hostium plēnus,** C., *Att.*, V. 20, 3; *Syria is divided from Cilicia by Amanus, a mountain which was full of enemies.*

NOTE.—This usage is found first in CICERO. The normal English position is found first in LIVY, but it becomes more common in later Latin.

Prīscus, vir cūius prōvidentiam in rē pūblicā ante experta cīvitās erat, L., IV. 46, 10.

3. Adjectives, especially superlatives, are sometimes transferred from the substantive in the principal clause and made to agree with the Relative in the Relative clause.

[**Themistoclēs**] **dē servīs suīs quem habuit fidēlissimum ad rēgem mīsit,** NEP., II. 4, 3; *Themistocles sent the most faithful slave he had to the king.* **Nēminī crēdō, quī largē blandust dīves pauperī,** PL., *Aul.*, 196; *I trust no rich man who is lavishly kind to a poor man.*

617. *Attraction of the Relative.*—The Accusative of the Relative is occasionally attracted into the Ablative of the antecedent, rarely into any other case.

Hōc cōnfirmāmus illō auguriō quō dīximus, C., *Att.*, X. 8, 7; *we confirm this by the augury which we mentioned.*

NOTES.—1. This attraction takes place chiefly when the verb of the Relative clause must be supplied from the principal sentence; that is, with auxiliary verbs like **velle, solēre, iubēre**; and after verbs of Saying and the like.

It is rare in early Latin. but common from CICERO on.

Quibus poterat sauciīs ductīs sēcum ad urbem pergit, L., IV. 39, 9; *having taken with him all the wounded he could, he proceeded to the city.*

2. *Inverted Attraction.*—So-called Inverted Attraction is found only in poetry, and then usually in the Acc., which may be considered as an object of thought or feeling.

This Acc. stands usually for a Nom., sometimes, but only in Comedy, for the Gen. Dat. or Abl. A strange usage is the Nom. where the Acc. would be expected. This may be **nōminātīvus pendēns,** a form of *anacoluthon* (697), and is found only in early Latin.

Urbem quam statuō, vestra est, V., *A.*, I. 573; (*as for*) *the city which I am rearing*, (it) *is yours.* **Istum quem quaeris, ego sum,** PL., *Curc.*, 419; (*as for*) *that man whom you are looking for, I am he.* **Ille quī mandāvit eum exturbāstī ex aedibus?** PL., *Trin.*, 137. ("*He* that hath ears to hear, let *him* hear.")

618. *Correlative Use of the Relative.*—The usual Correlative of **quī** is **is,** more rarely **hīc, ille.**

Is minimō eget mortālis, quī minimum cupit, SYRUS, 286 (Fr.) (308). **Hīc sapiēns, de quō loquor,** C., *Ac.*, II. 33, 105 (305, 3). **Illa diēs veniet, mea quā lūgubria pōnam,** OV., *Tr.*, IV. 2, 73 (307, 4).

619. *Absorption of the Correlative.*—The Correlative, **is,** is often absorbed, especially when it would stand in the same case as the Relative. This is a kind of Incorporation.

Postume, nōn bene olet, quī bene semper olet, MART., II. 12, 4; *Postumus,* (*he*) *smells not sweet, who always smells sweet.* **Quem arma nōn frēgerant vitia vīcērunt,** CURT., VI. 2, 1; (*him*) *whom arms had not crushed did vices overcome.* **Quem dī dīligunt adulēscēns moritur,** PL., *B.*, 816; (*he*) *whom the gods love dies young.* **Xerxēs praemium prōposuit quī** [= **eī quī**] **invēnisset novam voluptātem,** C., *Tusc.*, V. 7, 20; *Xerxes offered a reward to him who should invent a new pleasure.* **Miseranda vīta quī** [= **eōrum quī**] **sē metuī quam amārī mālunt,** NEP., X. 9, 5; *pitiable is the life of those who would prefer being feared to being loved.* **Discite sānārī per quem** [= **per eum, per quem**] **didicistis amāre,** OV., *Rem. Am.*, 43 (401).

Difficult and rare are cases like:

Nunc redeō ad quae (for **ad ea quae**) **mihĭ mandās,** C., *Att.*, V. 11, 6.

620. *Position of the Correlative clause.*—The Relative clause naturally follows its Correlative, but it often precedes; incorporation also is common.

Male sē rēs habet cum quod virtūte efficī dēbet id temptātur pecūniā, C., *Off.*, II. 6, 22; *it is a bad state of affairs when what ought to be accomplished by worth, is attempted by money.* **Quod vidēs accidere puerīs hōc nōbīs quoque māiusculīs puerīs ēvenit,** SEN., *E.M.*, 24, 13; *what you see befall children* (*this*) *happens to us also, children of a larger growth.* **Quam quisque nōrit artem, in hāc sē exerceat,** [C.], *Tusc.*, I. 18, 41 (616, 1).

The Correlative absorbed:

Quod nōn dedit fortūna, nōn ēripit, Sen., *E.M.*, 59, 18; *what fortune has not given* (does not give), *she does not take away*. **Per quās nōs petitis saepe fugātis opēs**, Ov., *A.A.*, III. 132; *the means you take to win us often scare us off.*

621. *Indefinite Antecedent.*—The Indefinite Antecedent is generally omitted.

Ēlige cui dīcās: tū mihi sōla placēs, Ov., *A.A.*, I. 42; *choose some one to whom you may say: You alone please me.*

Remark.—Such sentences are sometimes hardly to be distinguished from the Interrogative: **[Conōn] nōn quaesīvit ubi ipse tūtō vīveret**, Nep., IX. 2, 1; *Conon did not seek a place to live in safety himself*, might be either Relative or Deliberative (265).

TENSES IN RELATIVE SENTENCES.

622. *Future and Future Perfect.*—The Future and Future Perfect are used with greater exactness than in current English (242, 244).

Sit līber, dominus quī volet esse meus, Mart., II. 32, 8; *he must be free who wishes* (shall wish) *to be my master*. **Quī prior strinxerit ferrum, ēius victōria erit**, Liv. (244, R. 2).

623. *Iterative Action.*—Relative sentences follow the laws laid down for Iterative action (566, 567).

I. Contemporaneous action:

Ōre trahit quodcumque potest, atque addit acervō, H., *S.*, I. 1, 34; *drags with its mouth whatever it can, and adds to the treasure* (*heap*). **Quācumque incēdēbat āgmen, lēgātī occurrēbant**, L., XXXIV. 16, 6; *in whatever direction the column advanced, ambassadors came to meet them.*

II. Prior action:

[Terra] numquam sine ūsūrā reddit, quod accēpit, C., *Cat.M.*, 15, 51; *the earth never returns without interest what it has received* (*receives*). **Quod nōn dedit fortūna, nōn ēripit**, Sen., *E.M.*, 59, 18 (620). **Nōn cēnat quotiēns nēmo vocāvit eum**, Mart., V. 47, 2; *he does not dine as often as* (*when*) *no one has invited* (*invites*) *him*. **Haerēbant in memoriā quaecumque audierat et vīderat [Themistoclēs]**, C., *Ac.*, II. 1, 2 (567). **Sequentur tē quōcumque pervēneris vitia**, Sen., *E.M.*, 28, 1; *vices will follow you whithersoever you go*. **Quī timēre dēsierint, ōdisse incipient**, Tac., *Agr.*, 32 (567).

Remark.—On the Subjv. in Iterative Sentences, see 567, N.

MOODS IN RELATIVE SENTENCES.

624. The Relative clause, as such—that is, as the representative of an adjective—takes the Indicative mood.

Uxor quae bona est, Pl., *Merc.*, 812; *a wife who is good* (*a good wife*).

Remark.—The Relative in this use often serves as a circumlocution for a substantive, with this difference: that the substantive expresses a permanent relation; the Relative clause, a transient relation: **iī quī docent** = *those who teach* = *the teachers* (inasmuch as they are exercising the functions). On the Relative with Subjv. after an adj. clause, see 438, r.

625. *Indefinite and Generic Relatives.*—1. **Quīcumque, quisquis**, and the like, being essentially Iterative Relatives, take the Indicative according to the principles of Iterative action (254, r. 4). So also simple Relatives when similarly used.

Quācumque incēdēbat āgmen, lēgātī occurrēbant, Liv., xxxiv. 16, 6 (623).

Remark.—According to 567, n., the Subjv. is used:

(1) In **Ōrātiō Oblīqua** (Total or Partial):

Mārtī Gallī quae bellō cēperint (Pf. Subjv.) **dēvovent** (= **sē datūrōs vovent**), *Cf.* Caes., *B.G.*, vi. 17, 3; *the Gauls devote* (*promise to give*) *to Mars whatever they* (*shall*) *take in war* (**Ō. R., Quae cēperimus, dabimus**).

(2) By Attraction of Mood (Complementary Clauses):

Quis eum dīligat quem metuat? C., *Lael.*, 15, 53 (629).

(3) In the Ideal Second Person:

Bonus sēgnior fit ubi neglegās, S., *Iug.*, 31, 28 (566).

(4) By the spread of the Subjv. in post-classical Latin:

Quī ūnum ēius ōrdinis offendisset omnēs adversōs habēbat, L., xxxiii. 46, 1 (567).

2. **Quī** = **sī quis**, *if any*, has the Indicative when the Condition is Logical.

[Terra] numquam sine ūsūrā reddit, quod accēpit, C., *Cat.M.*, 15, 51 (623). (**Sī quid accēpit.**) **Quī morī didicit, servīre dēdidicit**, Sen., *E.M.*, 26, 10 (423).

Remark.—When the Condition is Ideal, the Subjv. is necessary (596). In post-classical Latin the Subjv. is the rule with all conditionals.

626. *Explanatory Relative.*—**Quī**, with the Indicative (= **is enim**, *for he*), often approaches **quod**, *in that*.

Habeō senectūtī māgnam grātiam, quae mihi sermōnis aviditātem

auxit, C., *Cat.M.*, 14, 46; *I am very thankful to old age, which* (for it, in that it) *has increased me* (= in me) *the appetite for talk.*

REMARK.—**Quī** with the Subjv. gives a ground, = **cum is** (586); **quī** with the Indic., *a fact;* and in many passages the causal sense seems to be inevitable:

Īnsānit hīc quidem, quī ipse male dīcit sibī, PL., *Men.*, 309; *cracked is this man, who calls* (= for calling) *down curses on himself.* **Errāverim fortasse quī mē aliquid putāvī**, PLIN., *Ep.*, I. 23, 2; *I may have erred in thinking myself to be something.*

NOTES.—1. This causal sense is heightened by **ut, utpote**, *as;* **quīppe**, *namely.* **Ut quī** is rare in early Latin, CAESAR, and CICERO, and is not found at all in TERENCE and SALLUST. LIVY, however, is fond of it. The mood is everywhere the Subjunctive. **Utpote** is found only here and there in Latin, and not at all in TERENCE, CAESAR, LIVY; but once in PLAUTUS. The mood is the Subjv. until late Latin. **Quīppe quī** is the most common of the three, but does not occur in CAESAR. In early Latin the mood is the Indic. (except PL., *Pers.*, 699); also in SALLUST. CICERO uses the Subjv.; LIVY uses both moods; later the Subjv. is the rule until the time of APULEIUS.

2. Simple Explanatory **quī** has the Indic. most commonly in early Latin, and in general developes on the same line that **cum** follows.

627. The Subjunctive is employed in Relative clauses when it would be used in a simple sentence.

POTENTIAL: **Habeō quae velim**, C., *Fin.*, I. 8, 28; *I have what I should like.*

OPTATIVE: **Quod faustum sit, rēgem creāte**, L., I. 17, 10; *blessing be on your choice, make ye a king.*

REMARKS.—1. Especially to be noted is the Subjv. in restrictive phrases. Here the Relative often takes **quidem**, sometimes **modo**.

The early Latin shows only **quod sciam** (as if **dum aliquid sciam**), *so far as I may be permitted to know anything about it* (= **quantum sciō**, *as far as I know, for all I know*), which is used throughout the language, and **quod quidem veniat in mentem** (PL., *Ep.*, 638). CICERO, however, shows a great variety. **Quantum sciam** is found first in QUINTILIAN.

Omnium ōrātōrum quōs quidem cōgnōverim acūtissimum iūdicō Sertōrium, C., *Br.*, 48, 180; *of all orators, so far as I know them, I consider Sertorius the most acute.* **Nūllum ōrnātum quī modo nōn obscūret subtrahendum putō**, QUINT., V. 14, 33; *I think no ornament is to be withdrawn, provided that it do not cause obscurity.*

2. Restrictions involving **esse, posse, attinet**, are regularly in the Indicative. CICERO and CAESAR, however, show a very few cases of the Subjv., especially with **possīs**.

Prōdidistī et tē et illam, quod quidem in tē fuit, TER., *Ad.*, 692; *you have betrayed both her and yourself, so far as in you lay.* **Ego quod ad mē attinet, iūdicēs, vīcī**, C., *Verr.*, II. I. 8, 21; *I, judges, so far as pertains to me, have conquered.*

628. The Subjunctive is used in Relative clauses which form a part of the utterance or the view of another than the narrator, or of the narrator himself when indirectly quoted (539, R.). So especially in **Ōrātiō Oblīqua** and Final Sentences.

Rēctē Graecī praecipiunt, nōn temptanda quae efficī nōn possint, QUINT., IV. 5, 17; *right are the Greeks in teaching that those things are not to be attempted which cannot be accomplished.* **Apud Hypanim fluvium Aristotelēs ait, bēstiolās quāsdam nāscī quae ūnum diem vīvant,** C., *Tusc.*, I. 39, 94 (650). **Virtūs facit ut eōs dīligāmus in quibus ipsa inesse videātur,** C., *Off.*, I. 17, 56; *virtue makes us love those in whom she seems to reside.* **Pōstulātur ab hominibus ut ab iīs sē abstineant māximē vitiīs, in quibus alterum reprehenderint,** C., *Verr.*, III. 2, 4; *it is demanded of men that they refrain from those faults most of all as to which they have blamed another.* **Senātus cēnsuit utī quīcumque Galliam prōvinciam obtinēret, Haeduōs dēfenderet,** CAES., *B.G.*, I. 35; *the senate decreed that whoever obtained Gaul as his province should defend the Haedui.* **Paetus omnēs librōs quōs frāter suus relīquisset mihi dōnāvit,** C., *Att.*, II. 1, 12; (this is Paetus' statement; otherwise: **quōs frāter ēius** (521) **relīquit**; compare C., *Att.*, I. 20, 7). **Xerxēs praemium prōposuit quī** [= **eī quī**] **invēnisset novam voluptātem,** C., *Tusc.*, V. 7, 20 (619).

REMARK.—Even in **Ōrātiō Oblīqua** the Indic. is retained:

(*a*) In explanations of the narrator:

Nūntiātur Afrāniō māgnōs commeātūs quī iter habēbant ad Caesarem ad flūmen cōnstitisse, CAES., *B.C.*, I. 51, 1; *it is* (was) *announced to Afranius that large supplies of provisions* (which were on their way to Caesar) *had halted at the river.*

In the historians this sometimes occurs where the Relative clause is an integral part of the sentence, especially in the Impf. and Pluperfect; partly for clearness, partly for liveliness. For shifting Indic. and Subjv., see L., XXVI. 1.

(*b*) In mere circumlocutions:

Quis neget haec omnia quae vidēmus deōrum potestāte administrārī? *Cf.* C., *Cat.*, III. 9, 21; *who would deny that this whole visible world is managed by the power of the gods?* **Prōvidendum est nē quae dīcuntur ab eō quī dīcit dissentiant,** QUINT., III. 8, 48; *we must see to it that the speech be not out of keeping with the speaker.*

629. Relative sentences which depend on Infinitives and Subjunctives, and form an integral part of the thought, are put in the Subjunctive (Attraction of Mood).

Pigrī est ingeniī contentum esse iīs quae sint ab aliīs inventa, QUINT., X.

2, 4; *it is the mark of a slow genius to be content with what has been found out by others.* **Quis aut eum dīligat quem metuat aut eum ā quō sē metuī putet?** C., *Lael.*, 15, 53; *who could love a man whom he fears, or by whom he deems himself feared?* **Nam quod emās possīs iūre vocāre tuum,** MART., II. 20, 2; *for what you buy you may rightly call your own.* **Ab aliō exspectēs alterī quod fēceris,** SYRUS, 2 (Fr.) (319). **In virtūte sunt multī ascēnsūs, ut is glōriā māximē excellat, quī virtūte plūrimum praestet,** C., *Planc.*, 25, 60 (552). **Sī sōlōs eōs dīcerēs miserōs quibus moriendum esset, nēminem eōrum quī vīverent exciperēs; moriendum est enim omnibus,** C., *Tusc.*, I. 5, 9; *if you called only those wretched who had* (*have*) *to die, you would except none who lived* (*live*)*; for all have to die.*

REMARK.—The Indic. is used :

(*a*) In mere circumlocutions ; so, often in Consecutive Sentences :

Necesse est facere sūmptum quī quaerit lucrum, PL., *As.*, 218 (535). **Efficitur ab ōrātōre, ut iī quī audiunt ita adficiantur ut ōrātor velit,** *Cf.* C., *Br.*, 49, 185; *it is brought about by the orator that those who hear him* (= his auditors) *are affected as he wishes* (*them to be*).

(*b*) Of individual facts :

Et quod vidēs perīsse perditum dūcās, CAT., VIII. 2; *and what you see* (definite thing, definite person) *is lost for aye, for aye deem lost.* (**Quod videās,** anybody, anything.)

630. *Relative Sentences of Design.*—Optative Relative sentences are put in the Subjunctive of Design, when **quī = ut is.**

Sunt multī quī ēripiunt aliīs quod aliīs largiantur, C., *Off.*, I. 14, 43; *many are they who snatch from some to lavish on others.* [**Senex**] **serit arborēs, quae alterī saeclō prōsint,** CAECILIUS (C., *Tusc.*, I. 14, 31) (545). **Semper habē Pyladēn aliquem quī cūret Orestem,** OV., *Rem.Am.*, 589 (545). [**Māgnēsiam Themistoclī Artaxerxēs**] **urbem dōnārat, quae eī pānem praebēret,** NEP., II. 10, 3 (545).

NOTES.—1. The basis of this construction is the characteristic Subjv., and the conception seems Potential rather than Optative ; but in many cases the characteristic force is no longer felt.

2. After **mittere** there are a few cases where the Impf. Indic. is used with much the same force as the Impf. Subjv., but the purpose is merely inferential from the continuance in the tense.

Inmittēbantur illī canēs, quī invēstīgābant omnia, C., *Verr.*, IV. 21, 47.

3. By attraction similar to that with **quod** (541, N. 3) and **quom** (585, N. 3), the Relative is sometimes found with an Inf. and **dīceret,** where the Subjv. of the verb in the Inf., or the Indic. with a parenthetical **ut dīxit,** is to be expected.

Litterās quās mē sibī mīsisse dīceret (= **mīsisset,** or **mīserat, ut dīxit**) **recitāvit,** C., *Ph.*, II. 4, 7.

631. *Relative Sentences of Tendency.*—Potential Relative sentences are put in the Subjunctive of Tendency, when **quī = ut is.**

The notion is generally that of Character and Adaptation, and we distinguish three varieties :

1. With a definite antecedent, when the character is emphasised ; regularly after **idōneus**, *suitable ;* **aptus**, *fit ;* **dīgnus**, *worthy ;* **indīgnus**, *unworthy ;* after **is**, **tālis**, **ēiusmodī**, **tam**, **tantus**, and the like ; after **ūnus** and **sōlus**.

Est innocentia adfectiō tālis animī, quae noceat nēminī, C., *Tusc.*, III. 8, 16 ; *harmlessness* (*innocence*) *is that state of mind that does harm to no one* (*is innocuous to any one*). **Ille ego sim cūius laniet furiōsa capillōs**, Ov., *A.A.*, II. 451 ; *may I be the man whose hair she tears in her seasons of frenzy.* **Sōlus es, C. Caesar, cūius in victōriā ceciderit nēmŏ**, C., *Dei.*, 12, 34; *thou art the only one, Caesar, in whose victory no one has fallen.* **Quem mea Calliopē laeserit ūnus egŏ**, Ov., *Tr.*, II. 568; *I am the only one that my Calliope* (= *my Muse*) *has hurt.* (**Acadēmicī**) **mentem sōlam cēnsēbant idōneam cuī crēderētur**, C., *Ac.*, I. 8, 30; *the Academics held that the mind alone was fit to be believed* (trustworthy).

REMARKS.—1. **Ut** is not unfrequently found instead of **quī** after the correlatives.

2. **Idōneus, dīgnus,** *etc.*, take also **ut**, and the Infinitive (552, R. 2).

2. With an indefinite antecedent ; so especially after negatives of all kinds, and their equivalents, and in combinations of **multī**, **quīdam**, **aliī**, **nōnnūllī**, *etc.*, with **est**, **sunt**, **exsistit**, *etc.*

Est quī, sunt quī, *there is, there are some who ;* **nēmŏ est quī,** *there is none to ;* **nihil est quod,** *there is nothing ;* **habeō quod,** *I have to ;* **reperiuntur quī,** *persons are found who* (*to*) . . . . ; **quis est quī ?** *who is there who* (*to*) . . . . ? **est cūr,** *there is reason for, etc.* So, also, **fuit cum,** *there was a time when* (580, R. 1).

Sunt quī discēssum animī ā corpore putent esse mortem, C., *Tusc.*, I. 9, 18 ; *there are some who* (to) *think that death is the departure of the soul from the body.* **Fuit quī suādēret appellātiōnem mēnsis Augustī in Septembrem trānsferendam**, SUET., *Aug.*, 100 ; *there was a man who urged* (= *to urge*) *that the name of the month* (*of*) *August should be transferred to September.* **Multī fuērunt quī tranquillitātem expetentēs ā negōtiīs pūblicīs sē remōverint**, C., *Off.*, I. 20, 69; *there have been many who, in the search for quiet, have withdrawn themselves from public engagements.* **Omnīnō nēmŏ ūllīus reī fuit ēmptor cuī dēfuerit hīc vēnditor**, C., *Ph.*, II. 38, 97 (317, 1). **Post mortem in morte nihil est quod metuam malī**, PL., *Capt.*, 741; *after death there is no ill in death for me to dread.* **Nec mea quī digitīs lūmina condat erit**, Ov., *Her.*, 10, 120 ; *and there will be no one to close mine eyes with his fingers.* **Miserrimus est**

quī quom ēsse cupit quod edit (172, N.) **nōn habet,** PL., *Capt.*, 463; *he is a poor wretch who, when he wants to eat, has not anything to eat* (**nōn habet quid edat** would mean *does not know what to eat*). **Quotus est quisque quī somniīs pāreat,** C., *Div.*, II. 60, 125; (*how many men in the world*), *the fewest men in the world obey dreams.*

REMARKS.—I. The Indic. may be used in the statements of definite facts, and not of general characteristics:

Multī sunt quī ēripiant,	**Multī sunt quī ēripiunt,**
There are many to snatch away.	*Many are they who snatch away.*

Of course this happens only after affirmative sentences. The poets use the Indic. more freely than prose writers:

Sunt-quī (= **quīdam**) **quod sentiunt nōn audent** (so MSS.) **dīcere,** C., *Off.*, I. 24, 84; *some dare not say what they think.* **Sunt-quibus ingrātē timida indulgentia servit,** OV., *A.A.*, II. 435; *to some trembling indulgence plays the slave all thanklessly.* **Sunt quī** (indefinite) **nōn habeant, est-quī** (definite) **nōn cūrat habēre,** H., *Ep.*, II. 2, 182.

2. When a definite predicate is negatived, the Indic. may stand on account of the definite statement, the Subjv. on account of the negative:

A. **Nihil bonum est quod nōn eum quī id possidet meliōrem facit;** or,
B. **Nihil bonum est quod nōn eum quī id possideat meliōrem faciat.**
A. *Nothing that does not make its owner better is good.*
B. *There is nothing good that does not make its owner better.*

3. After comparatives with **quam** as an object clause.

Māiōra in dēfectiōne dēlīquerant, quam quibus īgnōscī posset, L., XXVI. 12, 6; (*in that revolt*) *they had been guilty of greater crimes than could be forgiven* (*had sinned past forgiveness*). **Nōn longius hostēs aberant, quam quō tēlum adicī posset,** CAES., *B.G.*, II. 21, 3; *the enemy were not more than a javelin's throw distant.*

REMARKS.—I. Classical Latin prefers **ut** after comparatives.

2. Instead of **quam ut, quam** is not unfrequently found alone, especially after **potius,** but also after **amplius, celerius,** *etc.;* in which case the construction resembles that of **antequam.**

4. Parallel with a descriptive adjective with which it is connected by **et** or **sed.**

Exierant (duo) **adulēscentēs et Drūsī māximē familiārēs, et in quibus māgnam spem māiōrēs collocārent,** C., *Or.*, I. 7, 25; *two young men had come out* (who were) *intimates of Drusus and in whom their elders were putting great hopes.*

632. Quīn *in Sentences of Character.*—After negative clauses, usually with a demonstrative **tam, ita,** *etc.*, **quīn** is often used (556) where we might expect **quī nōn,** and sometimes where we should expect **quae nōn,** or **quod nōn.**

Sunt certa vitia quae nēmō est quīn effugere cupiat, C., *Or.*, III. 11, 41; *there are certain faults which there is no one but* (= everybody) *desires to escape.* **Nīl tam difficile est quīn quaerendō invēstīgārī possiet** (= **possit**), TER., *Heaut.*, 675 (552).

REMARK.—That **quīn** was felt not as **quī nōn,** but rather as **ut nōn,** is shown by the fact that the demonstrative may be expressed:

Nōn cum quōquam arma contulī quīn is mihī succubuerit, NEP., XVIII. 11, 5; *I have never measured swords with any one that he has not* (*but he has*) *succumbed to me.*

633. *Relative in a Causal Sense.*—When **quī** = **cum is,** *as he,* the Subjunctive is employed. (See 586, R. 1.)

The particles **ut, utpote, quīppe,** *as,* are often used in conjunction with the Relative; for their range, see 626, N. 1.

(Canīnius) fuit mīrificā vigilantiā quī suō tōtō cōnsulātū somnum nōn vīderit, C., *Fam.*, VII. 30, 1; *Caninius has shown marvellous watchfulness, not to have seen* (= *taken a wink of*) *sleep in his whole consulship.* **Ō fortūnāte adulēscēns, quī tuae virtūtis Homērum praecōnem invēnerīs!** C., *Arch.*, 10, 24; *lucky youth! to have found a crier* (= *trumpeter*) *of your valor* (in) *Homer!* **Māior glōria in Scīpiōne, Quīnctiī recentior ut quī eō annō triumphāsset,** L., XXXV. 10, 5; *Scipio's glory was greater, Quinctius' was fresher, as* (*was to be expected in*) *a man who* (*inasmuch as he*) *had triumphed in that year.*

REMARK.—On the use of the Indic. after **quīppe,** *etc.*, see 626, N. 1. On the sequence of tenses, see 513, N. 3.

634. *Relative in a Concessive or Adversative Sense.*—**Quī** is sometimes used as equivalent to **cum is** in a Concessive or Adversative Sense.

Ego quī leviter Graecās lītterās attigissem, tamen cum vēnissem Athēnās complūrēs ibi diēs sum commorātus, C., *Or.*, I. 18, 82; *although I had dabbled but slightly in Greek, nevertheless, having come to Athens, I stayed there several days.*

NOTE.—The Indic. is the rule for this construction in early Latin (580, N. 1).

635. *Relative and Infinitive.*—The Accusative and Infinitive may be used in **Ōrātiō Oblīqua** after a Relative, when the Relative is to be resolved into a Coördinating Conjunction and the Demonstrative.

(Philosophī cēnsent) ūnum quemque nostrum mundī esse partem, ex quō illud nātūrā cōnsequī ut commūnem ūtilitātem nostrae antepōnāmus, C.,

Fin., III. 19, 64; *philosophers hold that every one of us is a part of the universe, and that the natural consequence of this is for us to prefer the common welfare to our own.*

NOTES.—1. This usage is not cited earlier than CICERO, and seems to be found principally there, with sporadic examples from other authors.

2. Occasional examples are also found of the Inf. after **etsī** (LIVY), **quamquam** (TAC.), in the sense *and yet*; **cum interim** (LIVY), **quia** (SEN.), **nisi** (TAC.), **sī nōn** (LIVY); and after **quem admodum, ut** (CIC., LIVY, TAC.), in comparative sentences.

636. *Combination of Relative Sentences.*—Relative Sentences are combined by means of Copulative Conjunctions *only when they are actually coördinate.*

When the second Relative would stand in the same case as the first, it is commonly omitted (*a*).

When it would stand in a different case (*b*), the Demonstrative is often substituted (*c*); or, if the case be the Nominative (*d*) or Accusative (*e*), the Relative may be omitted altogether.

(*a*) **Dumnorīx quī prīncipātum obtinēbat āc plēbī acceptus erat** (CAES., *B.G.*, I. 3, 5),
Dumnorix, who held the chieftaincy, and (*who*) *was acceptable to the commons;*
(*b*) **Dumnorīx quī prīncipātum obtinēbat cuīque plēbs favēbat,**
Dumnorix, who held the chieftaincy, and whom the commons favoured;
(*c*) **Dumnorīx quī prīncipātum obtinēbat eīque plēbs favēbat,**
Dumnorix, who held the chieftaincy, and whom the commons favoured;
(*d*) **Dumnorīx quem plēbs dīligēbat et prīncipātum obtinēbat,**
Dumnorix, whom the commons loved, and (*who*) *held the chieftaincy;*
(*e*) **Dumnorīx quī prīncipātum obtinēbat et plēbs dīligēbat,**
Dumnorix, who held the chieftaincy, and (*whom*) *the commons loved.*

Examples: (*a*) CAES., *B.G.*, IV. 34, 4; (*b*) C., *Lael.*, 23, 87; *Tusc.*, I. 30, 72; (*c*) C., *Br.*, 74, 258; *Tusc.*, V. 13, 38; (*e*) C., *Off.*, II. 6, 21; L., X. 29, 3; (*d*) S., *Iug.*, 101, 5; TER., *Ad.*, 85.

NOTES.—1. The insertion of a demonstrative is almost confined to early Latin, LUCRETIUS, and CICERO. CAESAR and SALLUST have no examples, and LIVY very few. On the other hand, the use of a relative by *zeugma* (690) in connection with two or more verbs governing different cases is found at all periods.

2. (*a*) The Relative is not combined with adversative or illative conjunctions (*but who, who therefore*) except at the beginning of a sentence, when it represents a *following* demonstrative or anticipates it (620).

Quī fortis est, īdem fīdēns est; quī autem fīdēns est, is nōn extimēscit, C., *Tusc.*, III. 7, 14; *he who is brave is confident, but he who is confident is not afraid.*

(*b*) **Sed quī, quī tamen,** can be used in antithesis to adjectives.

Sōphrōn mīmōrum quidem scrīptor sed quem Platō probāvit, QUINT., I. 10, 17; *Sophron, a writer of mimes, 'tis true, but* (one) *that Plato approved.*

(*c*) **Quī tamen** may be added to explain a foregoing statement.

Causam tibĭ exposuimus Ephesī, quam tū tamen cōram facilius cōgnōscēs, C., *Fam.*, XIII. 55, 1.

3. Two or more Relative clauses may be connected with the same antecedent when the one serves to complete the idea of the principal clause, the other to modify it;

Illa vīs quae invēstīgat occulta, quae inventiō dīcitur, C., *Tusc.*, I. 25, 61; *the faculty that tracks out hidden things, which is called* (the faculty of) *research.*

4. The Relative is often repeated by *anaphora* (682) for stylistic reasons. Compare C., *Tusc.*, I. 25, 62; *Planc.*, 33, 81; L., XXIII. 14, 3.

637. *Relative Sentence represented by a Participle.*—The Relative sentence is sometimes represented by a Participle, but generally the Participle expresses a closer connection than the mere explanatory Relative.

Omnēs aliud agentēs, aliud simulantēs perfidī (sunt), C., *Off.*, III. 14, 60; *all who are driving at one thing and pretending another are treacherous.* [**Pīsistratus**] **Homērī librōs cōnfūsōs anteā sīc disposuisse dīcitur ut nunc habēmus,** C., *Or.*, III. 34, 137; *Pisistratus is said to have arranged the books of Homer, which were* (whereas they were) *in confusion before, as we have them now.*

COMPARATIVE SENTENCES.

638. A peculiar phase of the Relative sentence is the Comparative, which is introduced in English by *as* or *than,* in Latin by a great variety of relative forms:

(*a*) By correlatives; (*b*) by **atque** or **āc**; (*c*) by **quam.**

639. *Moods in Comparative Sentences.*—The mood of the Dependent clause is the Indicative, unless the Subjunctive is required by the laws of oblique relation, or by the conditional idea (602).

REMARK.—On **potius quam** with the Subjv., see below, 644, R. 3.

640. The dependent clause often borrows its verb from the leading clause. Compare 602.

Īgnōrātiō futūrōrum malōrum ūtilior est quam scientia, C., *Div.*, II. 9, 23 (296). **Servī mōribus īsdem erant quibus dominus,** *Cf.* C., *Verr.*, III. 25, 62; *the servants had the same character as the master.*

641. When the dependent clause (or standard of comparison) borrows its verb from the leading clause, the dependent clause is treated as a part of the leading clause; and if the first or leading clause stands in the Accusative with the Infinitive, the second or dependent clause must have the Accusative likewise.

Ita sentiō Latīnam linguam locuplētiōrem esse quam Graecam, C., *Fin.*, I. 3, 10; *it is my opinion that the Latin language is richer than the*

Greek. **Ego Gāium Caesarem nōn eadem dē rē pūblicā sentīre quae mē sciō**, C., *Pis.*, 32, 79; *I know that Gaius Caesar has not the same political views that I* (have).

I. Correlative Comparative Sentences.

642. Correlative Sentences of Comparison are introduced by Adjective and Adverbial Correlatives:

1. Adjective correlatives:

tot, totidem	**quot,**	(so) *as many*	*as.*
tantus	**quantus,**	(so) *as great*	
tālis	**quālis,**	*such*	
īdem	**quī,**	*the same*	

2. Adverbial correlatives:

tam	**quam,**	(so) *as much*	*as.*
tantopere	**quantopere,**	(so) *as much*	
totiēns (ēs)	**quotiēns (ēs),**	*as often*	
tamdiū	**quamdiū,**	*as long*	
ita, sīc / **item, itidem**	**ut, utī, sīcut, tamquam** (rare), **quasi** (rare), **quemadmodum, quōmodo,**		*so* (as) = ***as.***

Quot hominēs, tot sententiae, (*as*) *many men,* (*so*) *many minds,* TER., *Ph.*, 454. **Frūmentum tantī fuit quantī iste aestimāvit,** C., *Verr.*, III. 84, 194; *corn was worth as much as he valued it.* **Plērīque habēre amīcum tālem volunt, quālēs ipsī esse nōn possunt,** C., *Lael.*, 22, 82; *most people wish to have a friend of a character such as they themselves cannot possess.* **Cimōn incidit in eandem invidiam quam pater suus,** NEP., V. 3, 1 (310). **Nihil est tam populāre quam bonitās,** C., *Lig.*, 12, 37; *nothing is so winning as kindness.* **Sīc dē ambitiōne quōmodo dē amīcā queruntur,** SEN., *E.M.*, 22, 10; *they complain of ambition as they do of a sweetheart.* **Tamdiū requiēscō quamdiū ad tē scrībō,** C., *Att.*, IX. 4, 1; *I rest as long as I am writing to you.* **Optō ut ita cuīque ēveniat, ut dē rē pūblicā quisque mereātur,** C., *Ph.*, II. 46, 119; *I wish each one's fortune to be such as he deserves of the state.*

3. The Correlative is sometimes omitted.

Homō, nōn quam istī sunt, glōriōsus, L., XXXV. 49, 7; *a man, not* (*so*) *vainglorious as they are.* **Discēs quamdiū volēs,** C., *Off.*, I. 1, 2; *you shall learn* (*as long*) *as you wish.*

REMARKS.—1. Instead of **īdem quī, īdem ut** is sometimes found.

Disputātiōnem expōnimus eīsdem ferē verbīs ut āctum disputātumque

est, C., *Tusc.* II. 3, 9; *we are setting forth the discussion in very much the same words in which it was actually carried on.*

On **īdem** with **atque, āc, et,** see 643; on **īdem** with Dat., see 359, N. 6; on **īdem** with **cum**, see 310, R. 2.

2. (*a*) *The more—the more,* may be translated by **quō (quisque)—eō,** and the like, with the comparatives; but usually by **ut (quisque), quam—ita, tam,** *etc.*, with the superlative, especially when the subj. is indefinite.

Tantō brevius omne quantō fēlīcius tempus, PLINY, *Ep.*, VIII. 14, 10; *time is the shorter, the happier it is.* **Quam citissimē cōnficiēs, tam māximē expediet,** CATO, *Agr.*, 64, 2; *the quicker the better.* **Ut quisque sibĭ plūrimum cōnfīdit, ita māximē excellit,** C., *Lael.*, 9, 30; *the more a man trusts himself, the more he excels.*

(*b*) When the predicate is the same, one member often coalesces with the other: **Optimum quidque rārissimum est,** C., *Fin.*, II. 25, 81 (318, 2), = **ut quidque optimum est, ita rārissimum.**

3. **Ut—ita** is often used adversatively (482, 4). On **ita—ut,** in asseverations, see 262.

4. **Ut** and **pro eō ut** are frequently used in a limiting or causal sense, *so far as, inasmuch as;* **prō eō ut temporum difficultās tulit** (C., *Verr.*, III. 54, 126), *so far as the hard times permitted;* **ut tum rēs erant,** *as things were then;* **ut temporibus illīs** (C., *Verr.*, III. 54, 125), *for those times;* **ut erat furiōsus** (C., *Rosc.Am.*, 12, 33), *stark mad as he was;* **ut Siculī** (C., *Tusc.*, I. 8, 15), *as (is, was, to be expected of) Sicilians.*

Vir ut inter Aetōlōs fācundus, L., XXXII. 33, 9; *a man of eloquence for an Aetolian.* **Ut sunt hūmāna, nihil est perpetuom datum,** PL., *Cist.*, 194; *as the world wags, nothing is given for good and all.*

5. On **quam, quantus,** and the Superlative, see 303.

Notice in this connection **quam quī, ut quī,** and the like, with the Superlative (usually **māximē**):

Tam sum amīcus reī pūblicae quam quī māximē (= est), C., *Fam.*, V. 2, 6; *I am as devoted a friend to the state as he who is most* (= as any man). **Proelium, ut quod māximē umquam, commissum est,** L., VII. 33, 5. **Domus celebrātur ita, ut cum māximē,** C., *Q.F.*, II. 4, 6.

6. The Correlative forms do not always correspond exactly.

Subeunda dīmicātiō totiēns, quot coniūrātī superessent, L., II. 13, 2.

II. Comparative Sentences with ATQUE (ĀC).

643. Adjectives and Adverbs of Likeness and Unlikeness may take **atque** or **āc**.

Virtūs eadem in homine āc deō est, C., *Leg.*, I. 8, 25; *virtue is the same in man as in god.* **Date operam nē similī ūtāmur fortūnā atque ūsī sumus,** TER., *Ph.*, 30; *do your endeavour that we have not* (ill)-*luck like that we had before.* **Dissimulātiō est cum alia dīcuntur āc sentiās,** C.,

Or., II. 67, 269; *dissimulation is when other things are said than what you mean* (something is said other than what you mean). **Similiter** (602, R. 2) **facis āc sī mē rogēs cūr tē duōbus contuear oculīs, et nōn alterō cōnīveam**, C., *N.D.*, III. 3, 8; *you are acting (like) as if you were to ask me why I am looking at you with two eyes, and not blinking with one.* **Nōn dīxī secus āc sentiēbam**, C., *Or.*, II. 6, 24; *I did not speak otherwise than I thought.*

NOTES.—1. The expression is commonly explained by an ellipsis: **Aliter dīxī atque [aliter] sentiēbam,** *I spoke one way and yet I was thinking another way.*

So we find: **Timeō nē aliud crēdam atque aliud nūntiēs,** TER., *Hec.*, 844; *I fear that I believe one thing, and you are telling another.*

2. Instead of **atque, et** is sometimes used; this is not common, but the greater proportion of cases occurs in the classical period: **Solet enim aliud sentīre et loqu**., C., *Fam.*, VIII. 1, 3; *for he has a way of thinking one thing and saying another.*

3. These words are principally: **aequos, pār, pariter, īdem, iūxtā** (from the classical period on), **perinde, proinde, prō eō; alius, aliter, secus** (usually with a negative), **contrā, contrārius, similis, dissimilis, simul**; and rarely **item, tālis, totidem, proximē,** and a few others. PLAUTUS uses thus some words which involve a similar meaning, as **(dē)mūtāre** (*M.G.*, 1130). Compare also *M.G.*, 763; *B.*, 725.

4. **Alius** and **secus** have **quam** occasionally at all periods. On the other hand, **nōn alius** and other negative combinations seldom have **atque,** commonly **quam** or **nisi.** After negative forms of **alius** CICERO has regularly **nisi,** occasionally **praeter.**

Philosophia quid est aliud (= nihil est aliud) nisi dōnum deōrum? C., *Tusc.*, I. 26, 64; *philosophy—what else is it but the gift of the gods?*

III. Comparative Sentences with QUAM.

644. Comparative Sentences with **quam** follow the comparative degree or comparative expressions.

The Verb of the dependent clause is commonly to be supplied from the leading clause, according to 640.

In Comparative Sentences **quam** takes the same case after it as before it.

Melior tūtiorque est certa pāx quam spērāta victōria, L., XXX. 30, 19 (307, R. 1). **Potius amīcum quam dictum perdidī,** QUINT., VI. 3, 20; *I preferred to lose my friend rather than my joke.* **Velim exīstimēs nēminem cuīquam cāriōrem umquam fuisse quam tē mihī,** C., *Fam.*, I. 9, 24 (546, R. 1).

REMARKS.—1. When the second member is a subj., and the first member an oblique case, the second member *must* be put in the Nom., with the proper form of the verb **esse,** unless the oblique case be an Accusative:

Vīcīnus tuus equum meliōrem habet quam tuus est, *Cf.* C., *Inv.*, I. 31, 52 (596). **Ego hominem callidiōrem vīdī nēminem quam Phormiōnem,** TER., *Ph.*, 591; *I have seen no shrewder man than Phormio* (= **quam Phormiō est**). **Tibī, multō māiōrī quam Āfricānus fuit, mē nōn multō minōrem quam Laelium adiūnctum esse patere,** *Cf.* C., *Fam.*, V. 7, 3.

2. On **quam prō**, and **quam quī**, see 298. On the double comparative, see 299.

3. (*a*) When two clauses are compared by **potius**, *rather*, **prius**, *before*, **citius**, *quicker*, *sooner*, the second clause is put in the Pr. or Impf. Subjv. (512), with or (in CICERO) without **ut.**

Dēpūgnā potius quam serviās, C., *Att.*, VII. 7, 7 (577, N. 6). **(Dīxērunt) sē miliēns moritūrōs potius quam ut tantum dēdecoris admittī patiantur**, L., IV. 2, 8; *they said that they would rather die a thousand times than* (to) *suffer such a disgrace to slip in.* **Moritūrōs sē affirmābant citius quam in aliēnōs mōrēs verterentur**, L., XXIV. 3, 12 ; *they declared that they had rather die, than let themselves be changed to foreign ways.*

(*b*) If the leading clause is in the Inf., the dependent clause may be in the Inf. likewise, and this is the regular construction in classical Latin when the Inf. follows a verb of Will and Desire ; CICERO uses the Inf. regularly, CAESAR generally, though examples of the simple Subjv. are not uncommon in both ; LIVY is very fond of the Subjv., especially with **ut**, which is cited first from him.

Sē ab omnibus dēsertōs potius quam abs tē dēfēnsōs esse mālunt, C., *Div. in Caec.*, 6, 21; *they prefer to be deserted by all rather than defended by you.*

NOTES.—1. Instead of **tam—quam**, *so—as*, the Roman prefers the combinations **nōn minus quam—nōn magis quam** (by Lītotēs).

(*a*) **Nōn minus quam** means *no less than = quite as much :*

Patria hominibus nōn minus quam līberī cāra esse dēbet, (*Cf.* C.,) *Fam.*, IV. 5, 2 ; *country ought to be no less dear to men than children* (= quite as dear as).

The meaning *as little as* is cited only from TER., *Hec.*, 647 : **nōn tibi illud factum minus placet quam mihi**, where *not less than* = quite as much as = *as little as.*

(*b*) **Nōn magis quam** means *quite as little*, or *quite as much :*

Animus nōn magis est sānus quam corpus, *Cf.* C., *Tusc.*, III. 5, 10 ; *the mind is no more sound than the body = as little sound as the body.* (Or it might mean : *The mind is no more sound than the body = the body is quite as sound as the mind.*)

So with other comparatives.

Fabius nōn in armīs praestantior fuit quam in togā, *Cf.* C., *Cat.M.*, 4, 11; *Fabius was not more distinguished in war than in peace* (*no less distinguished in peace than in war, quite as distinguished in peace as in war*).

2. After a negative comparative, **atque** is occasionally found for **quam** in PLAUTUS, TERENCE, CATULLUS, VERGIL ; much more often in HORACE (nine times in the *Satires*, twice in the *Epodes*), who uses it also after a positive.

Nōn Apollinis magis vērum atque hōc respōnsumst, TER., *And.*, 698. **Illī nōn minus āc tibī pectore ūritur intimō flamma**, CAT., LXI. 176. *Cf.* H., *S.*, II. 7, 96.

THE ABRIDGED SENTENCE.

645. The compound sentence may be reduced to a simple sentence, by substituting an Infinitive or a Participle for the dependent clause.

THE INFINITIVE AND INFINITIVE FORMS.

646. The practical uses of the Infinitive and its kindred forms, as equivalents of dependent clauses, have already been considered:

Infinitive after Verbs of Creation: 423.
Gerund and Gerundive: 425–433.
Supine: 434–436.
Infinitive in Object Sentences: 526–531.
Infinitive in Complementary Final Sentences: 532.
Infinitive in Relative Sentences: 635.

NOTE.—Under the head of the Abridged Sentence will be treated the Historical Infinitive and **Ōrātiō Oblīqua**: the Historical Infinitive, because it is a compendious Imperfect: **Ōrātiō Oblīqua**, because it foreshortens, if it does not actually abridge, and effaces the finer distinctions of **Ōrātiō Rēcta.**

HISTORICAL INFINITIVE.

647. The Infinitive of the Present is sometimes used by the historians to give a rapid sequence of events, with the subject in the Nominative; generally, several Infinitives in succession.

(Verrēs) minitārī Diodōrō, vōciferārī palam, lacrimās interdum vix tenēre, C., *Verr.*, IV. 18, 39; *Verres threatened* (was for threatening) *Diodorus, bawled out before everybody, sometimes could hardly restrain his tears.*

NOTES.—1. The ancient assumption of an ellipsis of **coepit,** *began* (QUINT., IX. 3, 58), serves to show the conception, although it does not explain the construction, which has not yet received a convincing explanation. A curious parallel is *de* with Infinitive in French. The Final Infinitive (*to be*) *for*, may help the conception, as it sometimes does the translation. It takes the place of the Imperfect, is used chiefly in rapid passages, and gives the outline of the thought, and not the details; it has regularly the sequence of a Past tense.

2. The Historical Infinitive is sometimes found after **cum, ubi,** *etc.* See S., *Iug.*, 98, 2; L., III. 37, 6; TAC., *Ann.*, II. 4, 4; *H.*, III. 31; *Ann.*, III. 26, 2. No examples are cited from CICERO and CAESAR; this usage is characteristic of TACITUS.

ŌRĀTIŌ OBLĪQUA.

648. The thoughts of the narrator, or the exact words of a person, as reported by the narrator, are called **Ōrātiō Rēcta,** or Direct Discourse.

Indirect Discourse, or **Ōrātiō Oblīqua,** reports not the exact words spoken, but the general impression produced.

REMARKS.—1. Under the general head of **Ōrātiō Oblīqua** are embraced also those clauses which imply Indirect Quotation (Partial Obliquity). See 508.

2. **Inquam,** *quoth I,* is used in citing the **Ōrātiō Rēcta**; **āiō,** *I say,* generally in **Ōrātiō Oblīqua. Inquam** never precedes the **Ōrātiō Oblīqua,** but is always parenthetic; **āiō** may or may not be parenthetic. **Ōrātiō Rēcta** may also be cited by a parenthetic **"ut ait," "ut āiunt,"** rarely **ait,** *(as) he says, (as) they say.* The subject of **inquit** often precedes the quotation, but when it is mentioned in the parenthesis it is almost always put after the verb.

Tum Cotta: rūmōribus mēcum, inquit, pūgnās, C., *N.D.*, III. 5, 13 (484).
Aliquot somnia vēra, inquit Ennius, C., *Div.*, II. 62, 127; *"some dreams are true," quoth Ennius.*

3. The lacking forms of **inquam** are supplied by forms of **dīcere.**

649. **Ōrātiō Oblīqua** differs from **Ōrātiō Rēcta,** partly in the use of the Moods and Tenses, partly in the use of the pronouns.

NOTES.—1. It must be remembered that as a rule the Roman thought immediately in **Ō. O.**, and did not think first in **Ō. R.** and then transfer to **Ō. O.**; also that **Ō. O.** is necessarily less accurate in its conception than **Ō. R.**, and hence it is not always possible to construct the **Ō. R.** from the **Ō. O.** with perfect certainty. What is ideal to the speaker may become unreal to the narrator, from his knowledge of the result, and hence, when accuracy is aimed at, the narrator takes the point of view of the speaker, and in the last resort passes over to **Ō. Rēcta.**

2. **Ō. Oblīqua** often comes in without any formal notice, and the governing verb has often to be supplied from the context, sometimes from a preceding negative.

(Rēgulus) sententiam nē dīceret recūsāvit; *(saying that)* **quam diū iūre iūrandō hostium tenērētur, nōn esse sē senātōrem,** C., *Off.*, III. 27, 100.
(Īdem Rēgulus) reddī captīvōs negāvit esse ūtile; *(saying that)* **illōs enim adulēscentēs esse, sē iam cōnfectum senectūte,** *Ib.*

3. Sometimes, after a long stretch of **Ō. Oblīqua,** the writer suddenly shifts to the **Ō. Rēcta.** Examples: C., *Tusc.*, II. 25, 61; L., II. 7, 9, *etc.*

Moods in Ōrātiō Oblīqua.

650. In **Ōrātiō Oblīqua** the *principal clauses* (except Interrogatives and Imperatives) are put in the *Infinitive,* the *subordinate* clauses in the *Subjunctive.*

Ōrātiō Rēcta:	**Apud Hypanim fluvium, inquit Aristotelēs,**
Ōrātiō Oblīqua:	**Apud Hypanim fluvium Aristotelēs ait**
Ō. R.:	**bēstiolae quaedam nāscuntur,**
Ō. O.:	**bēstiolās quāsdam nāscī,**
Ō. R.:	**quae ūnum diem vīvunt,**
Ō. O.:	**quae ūnum diem vīvant,** C., *Tusc.*, I. 39, 94.

Ō. R.—*On the river Bog, says Aristotle,* } *little creatures are born, that live (but) one day.*
Ō. O.—*Aristotle says that on the river Bog,* }

Sōcratēs dīcere solēbat:
Ō. R. Omnēs in eō quod sciunt satis sunt ēloquentēs,
Ō. O. Omnēs in eō quod scīrent satis esse ēloquentēs, C., *Or.*, I. 14, 63.

Ō. R. *Socrates used to say: "All men* ARE *eloquent enough in what they* UNDERSTAND."

Ō. O. *Socrates used to say that all men* WERE *eloquent enough in what they* UNDERSTOOD.

REMARK.—When the Principal Clause, or Apodosis, is in the Indic., the Inf. is used according to the rule for Verbs of Saying and Thinking. When the Principal Clause, or Apodosis, is in the Subjv., as in the Ideal and Unreal Conditions, special rules are necessary (656).

Otherwise, Subjv. in **Ō. R.** continues to be Subjv. in **Ō. O.**

NOTE.—In CAESAR, *B. C.*, III. 73, 6, where a principal clause is apparently put in the Subjv., instead of **dētrīmentum in bonum verteret,** read (**fore ut**) . . . **verteret,** with Vossius, Dübner, Perrin, Hoffmann. NEP., II. 7, 6, is disputed.

651. Interrogative sentences are put in the Subjunctive, according to 467; inasmuch as the verb of Saying involves the verb of Asking.

Ariovistus respondit sē prius in Galliam vēnisse quam populum Rōmānum: quid sibī vellet cūr in suās possessiōnēs venīret, CAES., *B. G.*, I. 44, 7; *Ariovistus replied that he had come to Gaul before the Roman people; what did he* (Caesar) *mean by coming into his possessions?* (**Quid tibī vīs?**)

REMARKS.—I. Indicative Rhetorical Questions (464), being substantially statements, are transferred from the Indic. of **Ō. R.** to the Acc. and Inf. of **Ō. O.** when they are in the First and Third Persons. The Second Person goes into the Subjunctive.

Ō. R. Num possum? *Can I?* [No.] **Ō. O. Num posse?** CAES., *B. G.*, I. 14; *Could he?*

Quid est turpius? *What is baser?* [Nothing.] **Quid esse turpius?** CAES., *B. G.*, V. 28, 6; *What was baser?*

Quō sē repulsōs ab Rōmānīs itūrōs? L., XXXIV. 11, 6; *whither should they go, if repelled by the Romans?* (**Quō ībimus?**) **Cui nōn appārēre ab eō quī prior arma intulisset iniūriam ortam (esse)?** L., XXXII. 10, 6; *to whom is it not evident that the wrong began with him, who had been the first to wage war?* (**Cui nōn appāret?**)

Examples are not found in early Latin, are rare in classical period, but are especially common in LIVY.

Sī bonum dūcerent, quid prō noxiō damnāssent? L., XXVII. 34, 13; *if they thought him a good man, why had they condemned him as guilty?* (**Sī bonum dūcitis, quid prō noxiō damnāstis?**)

The Question in the Second Person often veils an Imperative. Here from LIVY on the Subjv. is the rule.

Nec cēssābant Sabīnī īnstāre rogitantēs quid tererent tempus, L., III. 61, 13. (**Ō. R., Quid teritis?**)

Exceptions are rare; Subjv. with Third Person, CAES., *B.C.*, I. 32, 8; Inf. with Second Person, L., VI. 39, 10.

2. In Subjv. Rhetorical Questions the Subjv. is either retained or transferred to the Infinitive. *The Deliberative Subjv. is always retained.*

Quis sibī persuādēret sine certā rē Ambiorigem ad ēiusmodī cōnsilium dēscendisse? CAES., *B.G.*, V. 29, 5; *who could persuade himself that Ambiorix had proceeded to an extreme measure like that, without* (having made) *a sure thing* (of it)? (**Quis sibī persuādeat?**)

The Inf. form would be the Future: **quem sibī persuāsūrum?** (659), and is not to be distinguished from the Fut. Indicative.

652. Imperative sentences are put in the Subjunctive, sometimes with, usually without, **ut**; the Negative is, of course, **nē** (never **ut nē**).

Redditur respōnsum: nōndum tempus pūgnae esse; castrīs sē tenērent, L., II. 45, 8; *there was returned for answer, that it was not yet time to fight, that they must keep within the camp.* (**Ō. R., castrīs vōs tenēte.**) (**Vercingetorīx) cohortātus est: nē perturbārentur incommodō,** CAES., *B.G.*, VII. 29, 1; *Vercingetorix comforted them (by saying) that they must not allow themselves to be disconcerted by the disaster.* (**Ō. R., nōlīte perturbārī.**)

REMARKS.—1. **Ut** can be used according to 546, after verbs of Will and Desire and their equivalents.

Pȳthia respondit ut moenibus līgneīs sē mūnīrent, NEP., II. 2, 6; *the Pythia answered that they must defend themselves with walls of wood.*

2. Verbs of Will and Desire, being also **verba dīcendī,** frequently have an **ut** clause followed by an Acc. with the Inf., the second clause adding a statement to the request.

Ubiī ōrābant ut sibī auxilium ferret; ad auxilium spemque reliquī temporis satis futūrum, CAES., *B.G.*, IV. 16, 5.

Tenses in Ōrātiō Oblīqua.

653. The Tenses of the Infinitive follow the laws already laid down (530):

The Present Infinitive expresses contemporaneous action;
The Perfect Infinitive expresses prior action;
The Future Infinitive expresses future action.

REMARK.—The Impf. Indic., as expressing prior continuance, becomes the Pf. Inf. in **Ō. O.**, and hence loses its note of continuance.

654. The Tenses of the Subjunctive follow the laws of

sequence (510). The choice is regulated by the point of view of the Reporter, or the point of view of the Speaker.

NOTE.—By assuming the point of view of the speaker, greater liveliness as well as greater accuracy is imparted to the discourse. This form is technically called **Repraesentātiō.** In Conditional Sentences **Repraesentātiō** often serves to prevent ambiguity. The point of view not unfrequently shifts from reporter to speaker, sometimes in the same sentence; this has the effect of giving additional emphasis to the primary verb, and is therefore common in commands and in favourable alternatives.

Point of View of the Reporter:

Lēgātiōnī Ariovistus respondit: sibī mīrum vidērī quid in suā Galliā quam bellō vīcisset, Caesarī negōtiī esset, CAES., *B.G.*, I. 34, 4; *to the embassy Ariovistus replied, that it seemed strange to him* (he wondered) *what business Caesar had in his Gaul, which he had conquered in war.*

Point of View of the Speaker:

[Lēgātīs Helvētiōrum] Caesar respondit: cōnsuēsse deōs immortālēs, quō gravius hominēs ex commūtātiōne rērum doleant, quōs prō scelere eōrum ulcīscī velint, hīs secundiōrēs interdum rēs concēdere, CAES., *B.G.*, I. 14, 5; *to the envoys of the Helvetians Caesar replied, that the gods were* (are) *wont, that men might* (may) *suffer the more severely from change in their fortunes, to grant occasional increase of prosperity to those whom they wished* (wish) *to punish for their crime.* (A long passage is L., XXVIII. 32.)

Point of View shifted:

Ad haec Mārcius respondit: Sī quid ab senātū petere vellent, ab armīs discēdant, S., *C.*, 34, 1; *thereto Marcius replied: If they wished to ask anything of the senate, they must lay down their arms.*

Proinde aut cēderent (undesired alternative) **animō atque virtūte gentī per eōs diēs totiēns ab sē victae, aut itineris fīnem spērent** (desired alternative) **campum interiacentem Tiberī āc moenibus Rōmānīs,** L., XXI. 30, 11; *therefore they should either yield in spirit and courage to a nation which during those days they had so often conquered, or they must hope as the end of their march the plain that lies between the Tiber and the walls of Rome.*

655. Object, Causal, Temporal, and Relative Clauses follow the general laws for Subordinate Clauses in **Ōrātiō Oblīqua.**

For examples of Object Clauses, see 525; for Causal, see 541; for Temporal, see 561-564, 569-577; for Relative, see 628.

REMARKS.—1. Coördinate Relative Clauses are put in the Acc. and Infinitive (635).

2. Relative Clauses are put in the Indicative: (*a*) In mere circumlocutions. (*b*) In explanations of the narrator (628, R.).

3. **Dum**, with the Indic., is often retained as a mere circumlocution: **Dīc, hospes, Spartae nōs tē hīc vīdisse iacentīs, dum sānctīs patriae lēgibus obsequimur**, C., *Tusc.*, I. 42, 101; *tell Sparta, stranger, that thou hast seen us lying here obeying (in obedience to) our country's hallowed laws.*

So also sometimes **cum**; see C., *Lael.*, 3, 12.

656. Conditional Sentences in Ōrātiō Oblīqua, Total and Partial.

1. The Protasis follows the rule.

2. The Indicative Apodosis follows the rule, but Present, Imperfect, and Perfect Subjunctive are turned into the Future Infinitive or its periphrases.

The Pluperfect Subjunctive is transferred to the Perfect Infinitive of the Active Periphrastic Conjugation.

Passive and Supineless Verbs take the circumlocution with **futūrum fuisse ut** . . . . 248, N. 3.

REMARK.—**Posse** needs no Fut. (248, R.), and **potuisse** no Periphrastic Pf. Inf., so that these forms are often used to lighten the construction.

3. *Identical Forms.*—In the transfer of Conditions to **Ō. O.**, the difference between many forms disappears. For instance,

I.	1.	**Sī id crēdis, errābis.**	**Dīcō tē, sī id crēdās, errātūrum esse.**
	2.	**Sī id crēdēs, errābis.**	
	3.	**Sī id crēdās, errēs.**	
II.	1.	**Sī id crēdis, errābis.**	**Dīxī tē, sī id crēderēs, errātūrum esse.**
	2.	**Sī id crēdēs, errābis.**	
	3.	**Sī id crēdās, errēs.**	
	4.	**Sī id crēderēs, errārēs.**	
III.	1.	**Sī id crēdiderīs, errābis.**	**Dīxī tē, sī id crēdidissēs, errātūrum esse.**
	2.	**Sī id crēdiderīs, errēs.**	
	3.	**Sī id crēdiderīs, errāverīs.**	
	4.	**Sī id crēdidissēs, errārēs,**	

NOTES.—1. In No. I. the difference is not vital, though exactness is lost.

2. (*a*) In No. II. the ambiguity lies practically between 2 and 3; inasmuch as **Repraesentātiō** is usually employed for the Logical Condition, and the Periphrastic Pf. Inf. is employed in the Unreal, wherever it is possible. The difference between an Unfulfilled Present and an Unfulfilled Past would naturally vanish to the narrator, to whom both are Past.

Ariovistus respondit: sī quid ipsī ā Caesare opus esset, sēsē ad illum ventūrum fuisse: sī quid ille sē velit, illum ad sē venīre oportēre, CAES., *B.G.*, I.

34, 2; *Ariovistus answered, that if he had wanted anything of Caesar he would have come to him; if he* (Caesar) *wanted anything of him, he ought to come to him* (Ariovistus). **Ō. R.: sī quid mihĭ ā Caesare opus esset, ego ad illum vēnissem; sī quid ille mē vult, illum ad mē venīre oportet.**

Fatentur sē virtūtis causā, nisi ea voluptātem faceret, nē manum quidem versūrōs fuisse, C., *Fin.*, v. 31, 93; *they confess that for virtue's own sake, if it did not cause pleasure, they would not even turn a hand.* **Ō. R.: nisi ea voluptātem faceret nē manum quidem verterēmus.**

(*b*) Occasionally in the Logical Condition the Fut. Indic. is changed to the Fut. Periphrastic Subjv., thus: **sī adsēnsūrus esset, etiam opīnātūrum** is an **Ō. O.** quotation for **sī... adsentiētur, opīnābitur** in C., *Ac.*, II. 21, 67.

3. No. III., like No. II., is used chiefly of the future. But in 3 the periphrases with **fore (futūrum esse)** are commonly employed for the active and the Pf. participle, with **fore** for the passive. In 4 the same fading out of the difference between Unfulfilled Present and Past occurs as in II.

657. Logical Conditions in Ōrātiō Oblīqua.

1. **Ad haec Ariovistus respondit: sī ipse populō Rōmānō nōn praescrīberet quemadmodum suō iūre ūterētur, nōn oportēre sēsē ā populō Rōmānō in suō iūre impedīrī,** Caes., *B.G.*, I. 36, 2; *to this Ariovistus made answer: If he did not prescribe to the Roman people how to exercise their right, he ought not to be hindered by the Roman people in the exercise of his right.* (**Ō. R.: sī ego nōn praescrībō, nōn oportet mē impedīrī.**)

2. **Sī bonum dūcerent, quid prō noxiō damnāssent? Sī noxium comperissent, quid alterum (cōnsulātum) crēderent?** L., XXVII. 34, 13; *if they thought him a good man, why had they condemned him as guilty; if, on the other hand, they had found him guilty, why did they intrust him with a second consulship?* (**Ō. R.: sī—dūcitis, quid damnāstis? sī—comperistis, quid crēditis?**)

3. **Titurius clāmitābat, suam sententiam in utramque partem esse tūtam; sī nihil esset** (**Ō. R.: sī nihil erit**) **dūrius, nūllō perīculō ad proximam legiōnem perventūrōs** (**Ō. R.: perveniētis**); **sī Gallia omnis cum Germānīs cōnsentīret** (**Ō. R.: sī cōnsentit**) **ūnam esse** (**Ō. R.: est**) **in celeritāte positam salūtem,** Caes., *B.G.*, v. 29, 6; *Titurius kept crying out that his resolution was safe in either case: if there were (should be) no especial pressure, they would get to the next legion without danger; if all Gaul was in league with the Germans, their only safety lay in speed.*

4. **Eum omnium labōrum fīnem fore exīstimābant sī hostem Hibērō interclūdere potuissent,** Caes., *B.C.*, I. 68, 3; *they thought that would be the end of all (their) toils, if they could cut off the enemy from the Ebro.* (**Ō. R.: is labōrum fīnis erit** (or **fuerit**) **sī hostem interclūdere potuerĭmus.**)

5. **[Hī] Iugurthae nōn mediocrem animum pollicitandō accendēbant sī Micipsa rēx occidisset, fore utī sōlus imperī Numidiae potīrētur,** S., *Iug.*, 8, 1; *these persons kindled no little courage in Jugurtha*('s heart) *by promising over and over that if King Micipsa fell, he alone should possess the rule over Numidia.* (**Ō. R.: sī Micipsa occiderit, tū sōlus imperī potiēris.**)

6. [**Fidēs data est**] **sī Iugurtham vīvom aut necātum sibĭ trādidisset fore ut illī senātus inpūnitātem et sua omnia concēderet**, S., *Iug.*, 61, 5; *his word was pledged that if he delivered to him Jugurtha, alive or dead, the senate would grant him impunity, and all that was his.* (**Ō. R.: sī mihĭ trādiderĭs, tibĭ senātus tua omnia concēdet.**)

7. **Nōn multō ante urbem captam exaudīta vōx est . . . futūrum esse, nisi prōvīsum esset, ut Rōma caperētur**, C., *Div.*, I. 45, 101; *not long before the taking of the city, a voice was heard* (saying), *that unless precautions were adopted, Rome would be taken.* (**Ō. R.: nisi prōvīsum erit, Rōma capiētur.**)

8. **Ariovistus respondit sī quid ille sē velit illum ad sē venīre oportēre**, CAES., *B.G.*, I. 34, 2 (656, 3, N. 2).

9. **Ariovistus respondit nisi dēcēdat** [**Caesar**] **sēsē illum prō hoste habitūrum; quod sī eum interfēcerit, multīs sēsē nōbilibus prīncipibusque populī Rōmānī grātum esse factūrum**, CAES., *B.G.*, I. 44, 12; *Ariovistus replied, that unless Caesar withdrew, he should regard him as an enemy, and in case he killed him, he would do a favour to many men of the highest position among the Roman people.* (**Ō. R.: nisi dēcēdēs tē prō hoste habēbō . . . sī tē interfēcerō grātum fēcerō**; 244, R. 4.)

REMARK.—**Posse** is used as has been stated (656, 2, R.).

Negārunt dirimī bellum posse nisi Messēniīs Achaeī Pylum redderent, L., XXVII. 30, 13; *they said that the war could not be stopped unless the Achaeans restored Pylos to the Messenians.* (**Ō. R.: bellum dirimī nōn potest (poterit) nisi Pylum reddent.**)

Docent, sī turris concidisset, nōn posse mīlitēs continērī quīn spē praedae in urbem irrumperent, CAES., *B.C.*, II. 12, 4; *they show that if the tower fell, the soldiers could not be kept from bursting into the city in the hope of booty.* (**Ō. R.: sī conciderit, nōn possunt (poterunt) continērī.**)

658. Ideal Conditions in Ōrātiō Oblīqua.

1. **Ait sē sī ūrātur "Quam hōc suāve" dictūrum**, C., *Fin.*, II. 27, 88; *he declares that if he were to be burnt he would say, "How sweet this is."* (**Ō. R.: sī ūrar, dīcam**, same form as Logical.)

2. **Voluptātem sī ipsa prō sē loquātur concēssūram arbitror Dīgnitātī**, C., *Fin.*, III. 1, 1; *I think that if Pleasure were to speak for herself, she would yield* (*the palm*) *to Virtue.* The context shows that the condi tion is Ideal, not Logical. **Sī loquātur, concēdat.** Compare 596, R. 1.

659. Unreal Conditions in Ōrātiō Oblīqua.

1. **Titurius clāmitābat Eburōnēs, sī** [**Caesar**] **adesset, ad castra ventūrōs** [**nōn**] **esse**, CAES., *B.G.*, V. 29, 2; *Titurius kept crying out that if Caesar were there, the Eburones would not be coming to the camp.* (**Ō. R.; sī Caesar adesset, Eburōnēs nōn venīrent.**) On the rareness of

this form, see 599, R. 4; and even this passage has been emended into **ventūrōs sēsē** (for esse).

2. **[Appārēbat] sī diūtius vīxisset, Hamilcare duce Poenōs arma Ītaliae inlātūrōs fuisse**, L., XXI. 2, 2; *it was evident that if he had lived longer, the Punics would have carried their arms into Italy under Hamilcar's conduct.*

3. **Nisi eō ipsō tempore nūntiī dē Caesaris victōriā essent allātī exīstimābant plērīque futūrum fuisse ut (oppidum) āmitterētur**, CAES., *B.C.*, III. 101, 3; *had not news of Caesar's victory been brought at that very time, most persons thought the city would have been lost.* (**Ō. R.: nisi nūntiī allātī essent, oppidum āmissum esset.**)

NOTE.—As the Plupf. Indic. is sometimes used (rhetorically) for the Subjv. (254, R. 3), so the ordinary Pf. Inf. is sometimes employed instead of the Periphrastic:

Nemō mihī persuādēbit multōs praestantēs virōs tanta esse cōnātōs (= **cōnātūrōs fuisse**) **nisi animō cernerent** (597, R. 1) **posteritātem ad sē pertinēre**, C., *Cat.M.*, 23, 82; *no one will persuade me that* (so) *many eminent men had made such mighty endeavours, had they not seen with their minds'* (eye) *that posterity belonged to them.* **Agricola solēbat nārrāre sē prīmā in iuventā studium philosophiae ācrius hausisse** (**Ō. R.: hauserat**), **nī prūdentia mātris coercuisset**, *Cf.* TAC., *Agr.*, 4, 5; *Agricola used to relate that in his earliest youth he would have drunk in more eagerly the study of philosophy, had not his mother's prudence restrained him.*

So with **potuisse**:

(Pompēium) plērīque exīstimant sī ācrius īnsequī voluisset bellum eō diē potuisse fīnīre, CAES., *B.C.*, III. 51, 3; *most people think that if Pompey had* (*but*) *determined to follow up more energetically, he could have finished the war on that day.* (**Ō. R.: sī voluisset, potuit**, 597, R. 3.) **Namque illā multitūdine sī sāna mēns esset** (597, R. 1) **Graeciae, supplicium Persās dare potuisse**, NEP., XVII. 5, 2; *for with that number, if Greece had had* (*had been in her*) *sound mind, the Persians might have paid the penalty* (due). (**Ō. R.: sī sāna mēns esset Graeciae, supplicium Persae dare potuērunt.**)

Pronouns in Ōrātiō Oblīqua.

660. 1. The Reflexive is used according to the principles laid down in 520 ff.

2. The person addressed is usually **ille**; less often **is.**

Ariovistus respondit nisi dēcēdat [Caesar] sēsē illum prō hoste habitūrum: quod sī eum interfēcerit, multīs sēsē nōbilibus prīncipibusque populī Rōmānī grātum esse factūrum, CAES., *B.G.*, I. 44, 12 (657, 9).

Of course, this does not exclude the ordinary demonstrative use.

3. **Hīc** and **iste** are commonly changed into **ille** or **is, nunc** is changed into **tum** and **tunc,** except when already contrasted with **tunc,** when it is retained (S., *Iug.*, 109, 3; 111, 1).

Diodōrus [respondit] illud argentum sē paucīs illīs diēbus mīsisse Lilybaeum, C., *Verr.*, IV. 18, 39 (393, R. 4).

4. **Nōs** is used when the narrator's party is referred to; compare Caes., *B.G.*, I. 44, below.

5. **Ipse** seems to be used sometimes in **Ō. O.** with reference to the principal subject, as contrasted with the person addressed. Usually, however, **ipse** would have occurred in the **Ō. R.** as well.

Ariovistus respondit: Sī ipse populō Rōmānō nōn praescrīberet, quemadmodum suō iūre ūterētur, nōn oportēre sēsē ā populō Rōmānō in suō iūre impedīrī, Caes., *B.G.*, I. 36, 2 (657).

661. *Specimens of the conversion* of **Ōrātiō Oblīqua** *into* **Ōrātiō Rēcta.**

Ōrātiō Oblīqua.

I. *Ariovistus respondit:*

Trānsī*sse* Rhēnum *sēsē* nōn *suā* sponte sed rogātu*m* et arcessītu*m* ā Gallīs; nōn sine māgnā spē māgnīsque praemiīs domum propinquōsque relīqu*isse;* sēdēs hab*ēre* in Galliā ab ipsīs concēssās, obsidēs ipsōrum voluntāte datōs; stīpendium cap*ere* iūre bellī, quod victōrēs victīs impōnere cōnsuēr*int.* Nōn *sēsē* Gallīs sed Gall*ōs* *sibī* bellum intul*isse;* omnēs Galliae cīvitātēs ad *sē* oppūgnandum vēn*isse* et contrā *sē* castra habuisse; *eās* omnēs cōpi*ās* ā *sē* ūnō proeliō puls*ās* āc superāt*ās* *esse.* Sī iterum experīrī *velint*, *sē* iterum parātu*m* *esse* dēcertāre; sī pāce ūtī *velint*, inīquum *esse* dē stīpendiō recūsāre, quod suā voluntāte ad id tempus pepend*erint.* Amīcitiam populī Rōmānī *sibī* ōrnāmentō et praesidiō, non dētrīmentō esse oport*ēre* idque *sē* eā spē pet*īsse.* Sī per populum Rōmānum stīpendium remitt*ātur* et dēditīciī subtrah*antur*, nōn minus libenter *sēsē* recūsā*tūrum* populī Rōmānī amīcitiam quam appet*ierit.* Quod multitūdinem Germānōrum in Galliam trādūc*at*, id *sē* *suī* mūniendī, nōn Galliae impūgnandae causā fac*ere;* ēius reī tēstimōniō *esse* quod nisi rogātus nōn vēn*erit* et quod bellum nōn intul*erit* sed dēfend*erit.*

Caes., *B.G.*, I. 44.

Ōrātiō Rēcta.

Trāns*iī* Rhēnum nōn *meā* sponte sed rogātu*s* et arcessītu*s* ā Gallīs; nōn sine māgnā spē māgnīsque praemiīs domum propinquōsque relīqu*ī;* sēdēs hab*eō* in Galliā ab ipsīs concēssās, obsidēs ipsōrum voluntāte datōs; stīpendium cap*iō* iūre bellī, quod victōrēs victīs impōnere cōnsuē*runt.* Nōn *ego* Gallīs sed Gall*ī* *mihī* bellum intulē*runt;* omnēs Galliae cīvitātēs ad *mē* oppūgnandum vēn*ērunt* et contrā *mē* castra habu*ērunt;* *eae* omnēs cōpi*ae* ā *mē* ūnō proeliō puls*ae* āc superāt*ae* *sunt.* Sī iterum experīrī *volunt*, iterum parātu*s* *sum* dēcertāre, sī pāce ūtī *volunt*, inīquum *est* dē stīpendiō recūsāre, quod suā voluntāte ad hōc tempus pepend*ērunt.* Amīcitiam populī Rōmānī *mihī* ōrnāmentō et praesidiō, nōn dētrīmentō esse oport*et* idque eā spē pet*iī.* Sī per populum Rōmānum stīpendium remitt*ētur* et dēditīciī subtrah*entur*, nōn minus libenter recūsā*bō* populī Rōmānī amīcitiam quam appet*iī.* Quod multitūdinem Germānōrum in Galliam trādūc*am*,* id meī mūniendī, nōn Galliae impūgnandae causā fac*iō;* ēius reī tēstimōniō *est* quod nisi rogātus nōn vēn*ī* et quod bellum nōn intul*ī* sed dēfend*ī.*

* Allusion to the preceding speech, otherwise **trādūcō.**

Ōrātiō Oblīqua.

2. *Hīs Caesar ita respondit:*
Eō sibĭ minus dubitātiōnis *darī* quod eās rēs quās lēgātī Helvētiī commemor*āssent* memoriā ten*ēret* atque *eō* gravius fer*re* quō minus meritō populī Rōmānī accid*issent;* quī sī alicūius iniūriae sibĭ cōnscius fuisset nōn fu*isse* difficile cavēre; sed eō dēceptu*m* quod neque commissum ā sē intelleg*eret* quārē timēret neque sine causā timendum put*āret*. Quod sī veteris contumēliae oblīvīscī *vellet*, num etiam recentium iniūriārum, quod *eō* invītō iter per prōvinciam per vim tempt*āssent*, quod Aeduōs, quod Ambarrōs, quod Allobrogas vex*āssent* memoriam dēpōnere po*sse*? Quod *suā* victōriā tam īnsolenter glōriā*rentur*, quodque tam diū *sē* impūne tulisse iniūriās admīr*ārentur* eōdem pertin*ēre*. Cōnsu*ēsse* enim *deōs* immortālēs quō gravius hominēs ex commūtātiōne rērum doleant, quōs prō scelere eōrum ulcīscī *velint*, hīs secundiōrēs interdum rēs et diūturniōrem impūnitātem concēdere. Cum *ea* ita sint, tamen sī obsidēs ab *iīs sibĭ dentur*, utī ea quae pollic*eantur* factūrōs intelleg*at*, et sī Aeduīs dē iniūriīs quās ipsīs sociīsque eōrum intul*erint*, item sī Allobrogibus satisfaci*ant*, *sēsē* cum *iīs* pācem *esse factūrum*.

Caes., *B.G.*, I. 14.

Ōrātiō Rēcta.

Hōc mihĭ minus dubitātiōnis *datur* quod eās rēs quās *vōs*, lēgātī Helvētiī, commemor*āstis*, memoriā ten*eō* atque *hōc* gravius fer*ō* quō minus meritō populī Rōmānī accid*ērunt;* quī sī alicūius iniūriae sibĭ cōnscius fuisset, nōn fu*it* difficile cavēre; sed eō dēceptu*s* quod neque commissum ā sē intelleg*ēbat* quārē timēret neque sine causā timendum put*ābat*. Quod sī veteris contumēliae oblīvīscī *volō*, num etiam recentium iniūriārum, quod *mē* invītō iter per prōvinciam per vim tempt*āstis*, quod Aeduōs, quod Ambarrōs, quod Allobrogas vex*āstis*, memoriam dēpōnere pos*sum*? Quod *vestrā* victōriā tam īnsolenter glōriā*minī*, quodque tam diū *vōs* impūne tulisse iniūriās admīr*āminī* eōdem pertin*et*. Cōnsuē*vērunt* enim *dī* immortālēs quō gravius hominēs ex commūtātiōne rērum doleant, quōs prō scelere eōrum ulcīscī *volunt*, hīs secundiōrēs interdum rēs et diūturniōrem impūnitātem concēdere. Cum *haec* ita sint, tamen sī obsidēs ā *vōbīs mihĭ dabuntur*, utī ea, quae pollic*ēminī*, factūrōs intelleg*am* et sī Aeduīs dē iniūriīs quās ipsīs sociīsque eōrum intul*istis*, item sī Allobrogibus satisfaci*ētis*, *ego vōbīs*cum pācem *faciam*.

3. *Sulla rēgī patefēcit:*
Quod pollic*ēātur*, senātu*m* et populu*m* Rōmānu*m*, quoniam amplius armīs valu*issent*, nōn in grātiam hab*itūrōs;* faciundum aliquid, quod illōrum magis quam *suā* rētulisse vid*ērētur;* id ideō in prōmptū *esse*, quoniam Iugurthae cōpiam hab*ēret*, quem sī Rōmānīs trādid*isset*, *fore ut illī* plūrimum dēbē*rētur;* amīcitia*m*, foedus, Numidiae *partem*, quam nunc pet*eret*, tunc ūltrō adven*tūram*.

S., *Iug.*, 111.

Quod pollic*ēris*, senātu*s* et populu*s* Rōmānu*s* quoniam amplius armīs valu*ērunt*, nōn in grātiam hab*ēbunt*; faciundum aliquid, quod illōrum magis quam *tuā* rētulisse vid*eātur;* id ideō in prōmptū *est*, quoniam Iugurthae cōpiam hab*ēs*, quem sī Rōmānīs trādid*eris tibĭ* plūrimum dēbē*bitur;* amīcitia, foedus, Numidiae *pars*, quam nunc pet*is*, tunc ūltrō adven*iet*.

Ōrātiō Oblīqua.

4. *Athēniēnsēs dēplōrāvērunt vāstātiōnem populātiōnemque miserābilem agrōrum.* Neque *sē* id que*rī* quod hostīlia ab hoste passī *forent; esse* enim quaedam bellī iūra quae ut facere ita patī *sit* fās. Sata exūrī, dīruī tēcta, praedās hominum pecorumque agī misera magis quam indīgna patientī *esse;* vērum enim vērō id *sē* que*rī*, quod is, quī Rōmānōs aliēnigenās et barbarōs voc*et*, adeō omnia simul dīvīna hūmānaque iūra pollu*erit* ut priōre populātiōne cum īnfernīs diīs, secundā cum superīs bellum nefārium gesserit. Omnia sepulcra monumentaque dīruta *esse* in fīnibus *suīs*, omnium nūdāt*ōs* mānēs, nūllīus ossa terrā teg*ī*. Quālem terram Atticam fēc*erit*, exōrnātam quondam opulentamque, tālem *eum* sī lic*eat* Aetōliam Graeciamque omnem fac*tūrum*. Urbis quoque *suae* simil*em* dēfōrmit*ātem futūram fuisse*, nisi Rōmānī subvēnissent.

L., XXXI. 30.

Ōrātiō Rēcta.

Nōn id que*rimur* quod hostīlia ab hoste passī *sumus*. *Sunt* enim quaedam bellī iūra quae ut facere ita patī *est* fās. Sata exūrī, dīruī tēcta, praedās hominum pecorumque agī misera magis quam indīgna patientī *sunt;* vērum enim vērō id que*rimur* quod is, quī Rōmānōs aliēnigenās et barbarōs voc*at*, adeō omnia simul dīvīna hūmānaque iūra pollu*it* ut priōre populātiōne cum īnfernīs diīs, secundā cum superīs bellum nefārium gesserit. Omnia sepulcra monumentaque dīruta *sunt* in fīnibus *nostrīs*, omnium nūdāt*ī* mānēs, nūllīus ossa terrā teg*untur*. Quālem terram Atticam fēc*it*, exōrnātam quondam opulentamque, tālem *is*, sī lic*ēbit* (or: lic*eat*) Aetōliam Graeciamque omnem fac*iet* (or: fac*iat*). Urbis quoque *nostrae* simil*is* dēfōrmit*ās fuisset*, nisi Rōmānī subvēnissent.

INVOLVED ŌRĀTIŌ OBLĪQUA. ATTRACTION OF MOOD.

662. **Ōrātiō Oblīqua** proper depends on some verb of Thinking or Saying, expressed or understood. In a more general sense the term **Ō. Oblīqua** is used of all complementary clauses that belong to ideal relations. The principle is the same in both sets of sentences, for in the one, as in the other, the Infinitive takes its dependencies in the Subjunctive, on account of the close relation between the Ideal mood and the Substantive Idea of the verb. Hence the favourite combination of the Infinitive and the Ideal Second person:

Difficile est amīcitiam manēre sī ā virtūte dēfēcerīs, C., *Lael.*, 11, 37; *it is hard for friendship to abide if you (one) have fallen away from virtue.* **Proprium hūmānī ingeniī est ōdisse quem laeserīs**, Tac., *Agr.*, 42, 4; *it is (peculiar to) human nature to hate whom you have injured.* (But **ōdistī quem laesistī.**)

The so-called attraction of mood, by which clauses originally Indicative become Subjunctive in dependence on Subjunctives, is another phase of the same general principle.

663. 1. All clauses which depend on Infinitives and Subjunctives, and form an integral part of the thought, are put in the Subjunctive (Subjunctive by Attraction).

Recordātiōne nostrae amīcitiae sīc fruor ut beātē vīxisse videar quia cum Scīpiōne vīxerim, C., *Lael.*, 4, 15: *I enjoy the remembrance of our friendship so much that I seem to have lived happily because I lived with Scipio.* **Vereor nē dum minuere velim labōrem augeam,** C., *Leg.*, I, 4, 12; *I fear lest while I am wishing to lessen the toil I may increase it* (**dum minuere volō, augeō**). **Istō bonō ūtāre dum adsit, cum absit, nē requīrās,** C., *Cat.M.*, 10, 33 (263, 2, *a*). **Quārē fīēbat ut omnium oculōs quotiēscumque in pūblicum prōdīsset ad sē converteret,** Nep., VII. 3, 5 (567; **quotiēscumque prōdierat convertēbat**). **Nescīre quid antequam nātus sīs acciderit, id est semper esse puerum,** C., *Or.*, 34, 120; *not to know what happened before you were born,* (that) *is to be always a boy.* **Fraus fidem in parvīs sibī praestruit ut cum operae pretium sit, cum mercēde māgnā fallat,** L., XXVIII. 42, 7; *fraud lays itself a foundation of credit in small things in order that when it is worth while it may make a great profit by cheating.* **[Arāneolae] rēte texunt ut sī quid inhaeserit cōnficiant,** C., *N.D.*, II. 48, 123 (567; **sī quid inhaesit cōnficiunt**). **Abeuntī sī quid popōscerit concēdere mōris,** Tac., *G.*, 21, 4; *to the departing (guest) it is customary to grant anything that he asks* (**sī quid popōscit concēdunt**).

Notes.—1. **Dum** not unfrequently resists the Attraction both in prose and poetry: **Tantum nē noceās dum vīs prōdesse vidētō,** Ov., *Tr.*, I. 1, 101 (548).
2. On the retention of the Indic. in Relative clauses, see 628, R.

2. Partial Obliquity.—(*a*) From this it is easy to see how the Subjunctive came to be used in a Generic or Iterative sense after Tenses of Continuance. Present, Imperfect, and Future Indicative may all involve the Notion of Habit, Will, Inclination, Endeavour, and the complementary clauses would follow the sense rather than the form. For examples, see 567, N.

(*b*) So also is explained the use of the Subjunctive in Causal Sentences, and especially in Conditional Sentences, where the Apodosis is embodied in the leading verb.

(Iugurtha) timēbat īram senātūs (= nē īrāscerētur senātus) nī pāruisset lēgātīs, S., *Iug.*, 25, 7 (601). **[Ubiis] auxilium suum (= sē auxiliātūrum) pollicitus est, sī ab Suēbīs premerentur,** Caes., *B.G.*, IV. 19, 1. **Praetor aedem (= sē aedificātūrum) Diovī vōvit sī eō diē hostīs fūdisset,** L., XXXI. 21, 12.

The idea of **Ō. O.** is shown in the tense:

Sī per Metellum licitum esset mātrēs veniēbant (= ventūrae erant), C., *Verr.*, V. 49, 129. **[Dictātor] ad hostem dūcit nūllō locō nisi necessitās cōgeret fortūnae sē commissūrus,** L., XXII. 12, 2 (438, N.).

PARTICIPIAL SENTENCES.

664. Participles are used in Latin even more extensively than in English, to express a great variety of subordinate relations, such as Time and Circumstance, Cause and Occasion, Condition and Concession. The classification cannot always be exact, as one kind blends with another.

REMARKS.—1. It is sometimes convenient to translate a Participial Sentence by a coördinate clause, but the Participle itself is never coördinate, and such clauses are never equivalents. (410, R. 2.)

Mānlius Gallum caesum torque spoliāvit, L., VI. 42, 5; *Manlius slew the Gaul and stripped him of his neckchain* (after slaying the Gaul stripped him of his neckchain, having slain, *etc.*). **(Miltiadēs) capitis absolūtus, pecūniā multātus est,** NEP., I. 7, 6; *Miltiades (though) acquitted of a capital charge, was mulcted in (a sum of) money (was acquitted, but mulcted).*

2. A common translation of the Participle is an abstract substantive; see 325, R. 3; 437, N. 2.

Nec terra mūtāta mūtāvit mōrēs, L., XXXVII. 54, 18; *nor hath the change of land changed the character.* **Teucer Ulixēn reum facit Āiācis occīsī,** QUINT., IV. 2, 13; *Teucer indicts Ulysses for the murder of Ajax.* **Inter haec parāta atque dēcrēta,** S., *C.*, 43, 3.

3. On the Participle after verbs of Perception and Representation, see 536.

665. Participles may represent Time When.

Alexander moriēns ānulum suum dederat Perdiccae, NEP., XVIII. 2, 1; *Alexander* (when he was) *dying, had given his ring to Perdiccas.* **Dionȳsius tyrannus Syrācūsīs expulsus Corinthī puerōs docēbat,** C., *Tusc.*, III. 12, 27; *Dionysius the tyrant,* (after he had been) *exiled from Syracuse* (after his exile from Syracuse), *taught (a) boys' (school) at Corinth.*

Ablative Absolute.

(Solōn et Pīsistratus) Serviō Tulliō rēgnante viguērunt, C., *Br.*, 10, 39; *Solon and Pisistratus flourished when Servius Tullius was king (in the reign of Servius Tullius).* **Sōle ortō Volscī sē circumvāllātōs vīdērunt,** *Cf.* L., IV. 9, 13; *when the sun was risen* (after sunrise), *the Volscians saw that they were surrounded by lines of intrenchment.*

NOTES.—1. On the Abl. Abs. of the simple Participle, see 410, N. 4.

2. SUETONIUS uses the Abl. Abs. as well as the simple Participle with **ante (prius) quam: (Tiberius) excēssum Augustī nōn prius palam fēcit quam Agrippā iuvene interēmptō,** *Tib.*, 22; see also *Iul.*, 58.

666. Participles may represent Cause Why.

Arēopagītae damnāvērunt puerum coturnīcum oculōs ēruentem, *Cf.* QUINT., V. 9, 13; *the court of Mars' Hill condemned a boy for plucking out* (because he plucked out) *the eyes of quails.* **Athēniēnsēs Alcibiadem corruptum ā rēge Persārum capere nōluisse Cȳmēn arguēbant,** *Cf.* NEP., VII. 7, 2; *the Athenians charged Alcibiades with having been unwilling to take Cyme* (because he had been) *bribed by the King of Persia.*

Ablative Absolute.

(**Rōmānī veterēs**) **rēgnārī omnēs volēbant lībertātis dulcēdine nōndum expertā,** L., I. 17, 3; *the old Romans all wished to have a king over them* (because they had) *not yet tried the sweetness of liberty.*

NOTE.—An apparent cause is given by **ut,** *as,* **velut,** *as, for instance,* **tamquam,** (so) *as,* **quasi,** *as if,* see 602, N. 3.

In this usage CICERO and CAESAR are very careful, employing only **quasi, ut.** LIVY introduces **tamquam, utpote, velut,** and the tendency grows until it reaches its culmination in TACITUS.

667. Participles may represent Condition and Concession.

Sī latet ars prōdest, affert dēprēnsa pudōrem, OV., *A.A.*, II. 313 (593, 2). [**Rīsus**] **interdum ita repente ērumpit ut eum cupientēs tenēre nequeāmus,** *Cf.* C., *Or.*, II. 58, 235 (609). (**Miltiadēs**) **capitis absolūtus, pecūniā multātus est,** NEP., I. 7, 6 (664, R. 1).

Ablative Absolute.

Māximās virtūtēs iacēre omnēs necesse est voluptāte dominante, C., *Fin.*, II. 35, 117 (593, 2).

NOTE.—On the combination of **quamquam, quamvīs,** and **etsī** with the Participle, see 609, N. 1; **nisi** also is not uncommon; **tamen** is sometimes added in the principal clause.

668. Participles may represent Relative Clauses (637).

Omnēs aliud agentēs, aliud simulantēs, perfidī (**sunt**), C., *Off.*, III. 14, 60 (637). [**Pīsistratus**] **Homērī librōs cōnfūsōs anteā sīc disposuisse dīcitur ut nunc habēmus,** C., *Or.*, III. 34, 137 (637).

REMARK.—*So-called,* **quī dīcitur, vocātur, quem vocant;** *above-mentioned,* **quem anteā, suprā dīximus.**

669. *Future Participle* (*Active*).—The Future Participle is a verbal adjective, denoting Capability and Tendency, chiefly employed in the older language with **sum,** *I am,* as a periphrastic tense. In later Latin it is used freely, just as the Present and Perfect Participles, to express subordinate relations.

Peculiar is the free use of it in Sentences of Design, and especially noticeable the compactness gained by the employment of it in Conditional Relations.

670. In later Latin, the Future Participle (active) is used to represent subordinate relations (438, N.):

1. Time When.

(Tiberius) trāiectūrus (= **cum trāiectūrus esset**) **Rhēnum commeātum nōn trānsmīsit,** SUET., *Tib.*, 18; *when Tiberius was about to cross the Rhine, he did not send over the provisions.*

2. Cause Why.

Dērīdiculō fuit senex foedissimae adūlātiōnis tantum īnfāmiā ūsūrus, TAC., *Ann.*, III. 57, 3; *a butt of ridicule was the old man, as infamy was the only gain he would make by his foul fawning.* **Antiochus sēcūrus dē bellō Rōmānō erat tamquam nōn trānsitūrīs in Asiam Rōmānīs,** L., XXXVI. 41, 1 (602, N. 3).

3. Purpose (usually after a verb of Motion).

(Maroboduus) mīsit lēgātōs ad Tiberium ōrātūrōs auxilia, TAC., *Ann.* II. 46 (438, N.). **Cōnsul Lārīsam est profectus, ibi dē summā bellī cōnsultātūrus,** L., XXXVI. 14, 5.

NOTE.—The Pr. Participle is sometimes used in a similar sense, but the Purpose is only an inference:

Lēgātī vēnērunt nūntiantēs Asiae quoque cīvitātēs sollicitārī, L., XXXI. 2, 1; *envoys came with the announcement that the states of Asia also were tampered with.*

4. Condition and Concession.

(1) Protasis.

Dēditūrīs sē Hannibalī fuisse accersendum Rōmānōrum praesidium? L., XXIII. 44, 2; *if they had been ready to surrender to Hannibal, would they have had to send for a Roman garrison?* (= **sī dēditūrī fuissent, Ō. R.: sī dēditūrī fuērunt.**)

(2) Apodosis.

Quatiunt arma, ruptūrī imperium nī dūcantur, TAC., *H.*, III. 19, 3; *they clash their arms, ready to break orders, if they be not led forward.* **Librum mīsī exigentī tibĭ, missūrus etsī nōn exēgissēs,** PLIN., *Ep.*, III. 13, 1; *I have sent you the book, as you exacted it, although I should have sent it even if you had not exacted it.*

ARRANGEMENT OF WORDS.

671. The Latin language allows greater freedom in the arrangement of words than the English. This freedom is, of course, due to its greater wealth of inflections.

Two elements enter into the composition of a Latin Sentence, governing to some extent its arrangement: Grammar and Rhetoric.

672. 1. Grammatical arrangement has for its object clearness. It shows the ideas in the order of development in the mind of the speaker. By Grammatical arrangement the sentence grows under the view.

2. Rhetorical arrangement has for its objects Emphasis and Rhythm. It presents a sentence already developed in such a way that the attention is directed to certain parts of it especially.

(*a*) *Emphasis* is produced:

1. By reversing the ordinary position.
2. By approximation of similars or opposites.
3. By separation.

In all sentences Beginning and End are emphatic points. In long sentences the Means as well as the Extremes are the points of emphasis.

(*b*) *Rhythm.*—Much depends on the rhythmical order of words, for which the treatises of the ancients are to be consulted. Especially avoided are poetic rhythms. So, for example, the Dactyl and Spondee, or close of an Hexameter at the end of a period.

673. Two further principles seem to underlie the arrangement of Latin sentences: (*a*) that of the ascending construction; (*b*) that of the descending construction. In the ascending construction, which is more common, the principal word is placed last, and the subordinate ones, in the order of their importance, precede. In the descending construction the reverse is the process. The descending construction is regular in definitions.

674. Rule I.—The most simple arrangement of a sentence is as follows:

1. The Subject and its Modifiers.
2. The Predicate and its Modifiers.

1. **Dionȳsius tyrannus, Syrācūsīs expulsus,** 2. **Corinthī puerōs docēbat,** C., *Tusc.*, III. 12, 27 (665).

Rhetorical positions:

Potentēs sequitur invidia. Quint., IV. 1, 14 (477, N. 4). **Nōbīs nōn satis-**

facit ipse Dēmosthenēs, *Cf.* C., *Or.*, 29, 104 (552, R. 1). **Dīscrīptus (erat) populus cēnsū, ōrdinibus, aetātibus,** C., *Leg.*, III. 19, 44 (397). **Intrā moenia sunt hostēs,** S., *C.*, 52, 35 (477).

REMARK.—The modifiers of the predicate stand in the order of their importance. The following arrangement is common :

1. Place, Time, Cause, or Means. 2. Indirect Object. 3. Direct Object. 4. Adverb. 5. Verb.

NOTE.—The postponement of the subject is rare and always for definite reasons in the classical period ; later it becomes a mannerism, especially in the elder PLINY ; to a less degree in NEPOS and LIVY.

675. RULE II.—Interrogative Sentences begin with the interrogative, subordinate clauses with the leading particle or relative.

Quis eum dīligat quem metuat ? C., *Lael.*, 15, 53 (629). **Postquam Caesar pervēnit obsidēs popōscit,** CAES., *B.G.*, I. 27, 3 (561). **Sī spīritum dūcit vīvit,** C., *Inv.*, I. 46, 86 (595). **Quī timēre dēsierint ōdisse incipient,** TAC., *Agr.*, 32 (567).

Rhetorical position :

[Nātūram] sī sequēmur ducem, numquam aberrābimus, C., *Off.*, I. 28, 100 (595). **Dē futūrīs rēbus etsī semper difficile est dīcere, tamen interdum coniectūrā possīs accēdere,** C., *Fam.*, VI. 4, 1 (604). **[Catō] mīrārī sē āiēbat quod nōn rīdēret haruspex, haruspicem cum vīdisset,** C., *Div.*, II. 24, 51 (567).

676. RULE III.—An Adjective usually precedes, but often follows, the word to which it belongs ; a dependent Genitive usually follows the governing word ; so too does a word in Apposition.

Saepe māgna indolēs virtūtis priusquam reī pūblicae prōdesse potuisset exstincta est, C., *Ph.*, V. 17, 47 (577). **Sēnsum oculōrum praecipit animus,** QUINT., VI. 2, 6 (540).

Rhetorical position :

[Īsocratēs] queritur plūs honōris corporum quam animōrum virtūtibus darī, QUINT., III. 8, 9 (542, R.). **[Ager], cum multōs annōs quiēvit, ūberiōrēs efferre frūgēs solet,** C., *Br.*, 4, 16 (567). **Verēmur nē parum hīc liber mellis et absinthiī multum habēre videātur,** QUINT., III. 1, 5 (550).

REMARKS.—1. The demonstrative pronouns regularly precede; the possessives regularly follow.

Verēmur nē hīc liber absinthiī multum habēre videātur, QUINT., III. 1, 5 (550). **Torquātus fīlium suum necārī iūssit,** S., *C.*, 52, 30 (540).

Rhetorical position:

Recordāre tempus illud, cum pater Cūriō maerēns iacēbat in lectō, C., *Ph.*, II. 18, 45 (580). **Ōsculātur tigrim suus cūstōs,** SEN., *E.M.*, 85, 41 (309, 2).

2. Ordinals regularly follow, Cardinals regularly precede the substantive.

3. Many expressions have become fixed formulae: so titles, proper names, and the like; see 288.

Facinus est vincīre cīvem Rōmānum, C., *Verr.*, v. 66, 170 (535).

4. The titles **rēx, imperātor,** *etc.*, frequently precede the proper name with which they are in apposition.

5. New modifiers of either element may be inserted, prefixed, or added:

Catōnem vīdī in bibliothēcā sedentem multīs circumfūsum Stōicōrum librīs, C., *Fin.*, III. 2, 7 (536). **Saepe māgna indolēs virtūtis priusquam reī pūblicae prōdesse potuisset exstincta est,** C., *Ph.*, v. 17, 47 (577). **At vidēte hominis intolerābilem audāciam,** C., *Dom.*, 44, 115 (488). **(Aristīdēs) interfuit pūgnae nāvālī apud Salamīna,** NEP., III. 2, 1.

NOTES.—1. The tendency in Latin was to reverse the Indo-Germanic rule by which an attributive adjective and a dependent Genitive preceded the governing word. But in early Latin the adjective still holds its place more often before its substantive, while the Genitive has already succumbed for the most part to the tendency. In the classical period the adjective is more often used after its substantive. But neither position can be strictly called rhetorical. The same is true of the possessive pronoun.

2. The original force of a following adjective or Genitive was restrictive or appositional, while, when it preceded, it formed a close compound with its substantive; thus, **bonus homō,** *a good man* (one idea); **homō bonus,** *a man* (one idea) *who is good* (another idea). In classical Latin this distinction is no longer inevitable, though it is often essential.

677. RULE IV.—Adverbs are commonly put next to their verb (before it when it ends a sentence), and immediately before their adjective or adverb.

Zēnōnem cum Athēnīs essem audiēbam frequenter . . . ., C., *N.D.*, I. 21, 59 (585). **Caedī discipulōs minimē velim,** QUINT., I. 3, 13 (257). **Vix cuiquam persuādēbātur Graeciā omnī cēssūrōs (Rōmānōs),** L., XXXIII. 32, 3 (546, R. 1). **[Rīsus] interdum ita repente ērumpit ut eum cupientēs tenēre nequeāmus,** C., *Or.*, II. 58, 235 (609).

Rhetorical positions:

[Īram] bene Ennius initium dīxit īnsāniae, C., *Tusc.*, IV. 23, 52 (440). **Saepe māgna indolēs virtūtis priusquam reī pūblicae prōdesse potuisset exstincta est,** C., *Ph.*, v. 17, 47 (577).

REMARKS.—1. **Ferē, paene, prope,** usually follow:

Nēmō ferē saltat sōbrius nisi forte īnsānit, C., *Mur.*, 6, 13 (591, R. 4).

2. Negatives always precede, see 448.

NOTE.—The separation of adverbs from their adjectives is rare, except in the case of **tam** and **quam,** which PLAUTUS, TERENCE, CICERO, and later authors often separate, *e.g.*, by a preposition : **tam ab tenuī exitiō.** Hyperbaton with other adverbs is rare.

678. RULE V.—Prepositions regularly precede their case (413).

Ā rēctā cōnscientiā trāversum unguem nōn oportet discēdere, C., *Att.*, XIII. 20, 4 (328, 1).

REMARKS.—1. On **versus, tenus,** and the postposition of **cum** in combination with the personal pronouns and the relative, see 413, R. 1.

2. Monosyllabic prepositions are not unfrequently put between the adjective and substantive : **māgnā cum cūrā.** See 413, R. 2.

Less frequently they are placed between the Gen. and substantive; except when the relative is employed.

3. Dissyllabic prepositions are sometimes put after their case (Anastrophé), especially after a relative or demonstrative: most frequently **contrā, inter, propter.** So also adverbs. See 413, R. 1.

4. The preposition may be separated from its case by a Gen. or an adverb (413, R. 3) : **ad Appī Claudī senectūtem accēdēbat etiam ut caecus esset,** C., *Cat.M.*, 6, 16 (553, 4).

5. Monosyllabic prepositions, such as **cum, ex, dē, post,** sometimes append the enclitics **-que, -ve, -ne,** as, **exque iīs,** *and from them.* Usually, however, the enclitics join the dependent substantive: **in patriamque rediit,** *and returned to his country.* See 413, N. 3.

On the position of **per,** see 413, N. 2.

679. RULE VI.—Particles vary.

Enim commonly takes the second, seldom the third place; **nam** and **namque** are regularly prepositive. See 498, N. 1.

Ergō in the syllogism precedes, elsewhere follows; **igitur** is commonly second or third; **itaque** regularly first. See 502, N. 2; 500, R.

Tamen is first, but may follow an emphatic word. See 490.

Etiam usually precedes, **quoque** always follows. See 478, 479.

Quidem and **dēmum** (*at length*) follow the word to which they belong.

680. RULE VII.—A word that belongs to more than one word regularly stands before them all, or after them all, sometimes after the first (291).

Ariovistus respondit multīs sēsē nōbilibus prīncipibusque populī Rōmānī grātum esse factūrum, CAES., *B.G.*, I. 44, 12 (657, 9). [**Īsocratēs**] **queritur plūs honōris corporum quam animōrum virtūtibus darī,** QUINT., III. 8, 9 (542, R.). **Longum est mūlōrum persequī ūtilitātēs et asinōrum,** C., *N.D.*, II. 64, 159 (254, R. 1).

681. Rule VIII.—Words of kindred or opposite meaning are often put side by side for the sake of complement or contrast.

Manus manum lavat, *one hand washes the other.* **[Catō] mīrārī sē āiēbat quod nōn rīdēret haruspex, haruspicem cum vīdisset,** C., *Div.*, II. 24, 51 (567). **Ēmit morte immortālitātem,** Quint., IX. 3, 71 (404).

682. Rule IX.—*Contrasted Pairs.*—When pairs are contrasted, the second is put in the same order as the first, but often in inverse order. The employment of the same order is called *Anaphora* (repetition). The inverse order is called *Chiasmus*, or crosswise position, and gives alternate stress. The principle is of wide application, not merely in the simple sentence but also in the period.

Same order (Anaphora).

Fortūna (1) **vestra** (2) **facit ut īrae** (1) **meae** (2) **temperem,** L., XXXVI. 35, 3 (553, 1). **Mālō tē sapiēns** (1) **hostis** (2) **metuat quam stultī** (1) **cīvēs** (2) **laudent,** L., XXII. 39, 20 (546, R. 2).

Inverse order (Chiasmus).

Ante vidēmus (1) **fulgōrem** (2) **quam sonum** (2) **audiāmus** (1), Sen., *N. Q.*, II. 12, 6 (577). **Parvī sunt forīs** (1) **arma** (2) **nisi est cōnsilium** (2) **domī** (1), C., *Off.*, I. 22, 76 (411, R. 2).

Remark.—Chiasmus is from the Greek letter *X* (chi):

1. **Forīs**	*X*	2. **arma**
2. **cōnsilium**		1. **domī.**

683. *Poetical Peculiarities.*—In the poets we find many varieties of arrangement of substantive and adjective, designed to draw especial attention to the idea or to colour the verse. These occur chiefly in the Hexameter and Pentameter, but to a lesser degree also in other measures. Thus the substantive and adjective are put either at the end of each hemistich, or at the beginning of each hemistich, or one is at the end of the first and the other at the beginning of the second.

Cerberus et *nūllās* **hodiē petat improbus** *umbrās* | **et iaceat** *tacitā* **lapsa catēna** *serā*, Prop., IV. (V.) 11, 25. *Pūniceō* **stābis sūrās ēvincta** *cothurnō*, V., *Ec.*, 7, 32. **Mē similem** *vestrīs* *mōribus* **esse putās?** Prop., II. (III.) 29 (27), 32.

ARRANGEMENT OF CLAUSES.

684. A period is a compound sentence with one or more subordinate clauses, in which sentence the meaning is kept suspended to the close.

685. Latin periods may be divided into two classes:

1. Responsive or Apodotic, in which a Protasis has an Apodosis.

2. Intercalary or Enthetic, in which the various items are inserted in their proper place between Subject and Predicate.

Ut saepe hominēs aegrī morbō gravī, cum aestū febrīque iactantur, sī aquam gelidam bibērunt, prīmō relevārī videntur, deinde multō gravius vehementiusque afflīctantur: sīc hīc morbus, quī est in rē pūblicā, relevātus istīus poenā, vehementius, reliquīs vīvīs, ingravēscet, C., *Cat.*, I. 13, 31 (Apodotic).

Catuvolcus, rēx dīmidiae partis Eburōnum, quī ūnā cum Ambiorige cōnsilium inierat, aetāte iam cōnfectus, cum labōrem aut bellī aut fugae ferre nōn posset, omnibus precibus dētēstātus Ambiorigem, quī ēius cōnsiliī auctor fuisset, taxō, cūius māgna in Galliā Germāniāque cōpia est, sē exanimāvit, CAES., *B.G.*, VI. 31, 5 (Enthetic).

686. NÄGELSBACH's careful study of the subject has led to the following results. The simplest period is composed of one subordinate (*a*) and one principal (*A*) clause; the principal varieties are: (1) *a : A*, where the principal clause follows the subordinate; (2) *A* (*a*) *A*, where the subordinate clause is inserted within the principal clause; (3) *A* | *a*, where the principal clause precedes the subordinate clause; (4) *a* (*A*) *a*, where the principal clause is inserted within the subordinate clause. When two subordinate clauses (*a*, *b*), independent of each other, are used, the forms are: (5) *a : A* | *b*; (6) *a : A* (*b*) *a*; (7) *A* (*a*) *A* | *b*; (8) *A* (*a*) *A* (*b*) *A*; (9) *a* : (*b* : *A*). If the dependent clauses are of different degree (*α*, *a*, *A*), that is, one depending upon the other, some fifteen additional forms are allowable.

Some examples are:

a (*A*) *a* : **illōrum vidēs quam niteat ōrātiō**, C., *Fin.*, IV. 3, 5. *a* : (*b* : *A*): **cūr nōlint, etiamsī taceant, satis dīcunt**, C., *Div. in Caec.*, 6, 21. *α* : *a* : *A*: **quid agātur, cum aperuerō, facile erit statuere**, C., *Ph.*, V. 2, 6. *a* : *A* | *α*: **illud quid sit, scīre cupiō, quod iacis obscūrē**, C., *Att.*, II. 7, 4. *a* | *α* (*A*) *a*: **nōs utī exspectārēmus sē, relīquit quī rogāret**, VARRO, *R.R.*, I. 2, 32. *A* | *α* (*a*) *α* : **mandō tibī plānē, tōtum ut videās cūius modī sit**, C., *Att.*, I. 12, 2.

687. Periods are also divided into Historical and Oratorical. The former are, as a rule, simple. The most common form is *a : A*, *i.e.*, where a subordinate clause is followed by a leading clause: **Id ubi dīxisset hastam in hostium fīnēs ēmittēbat**, L., I. 42, 13. Another common period, developed and much liked by LIVY, and later by TACITUS, was *α : a : A*, consisting of (1) a participial clause; (2) a clause introduced by a conjunction; (3) the principal clause. *Cf.* TAC., *Ann.*,

II. 69, 3, **dētentus ubi . . . accēpit plēbem prōturbat.** Historians, having much occasion for description, are also prone to use the descending period, *i.e.*, the form in which the principal clause precedes. So especially NEPOS. LIVY likes also to use two independent subordinate clauses asyndetically.

The Oratorical periods are much more diverse and complicated, owing to the greater variety of effects at which they aim. We find, however, the ascending structure, where the emphasis is continually ascending until it culminates at the end, more common.

See an excellent example in C., *Imp.*, 5, 11:

Vōs eum rēgem inultum esse patiēminī quī **lēgātum populī Rōmānī cōnsulārem** VINCULĪS ĀC VERBERIBUS ATQUE OMNĪ SUPPLICIŌ EXCRUCIĀTUM NECĀVIT?

FIGURES OF SYNTAX AND RHETORIC.

688. Ellipsis is the omission of some integral part of the thought, such as the substantive of the adjective (204, N. 1), the copula of the predicate (209), the verb of the adverb.

Unde domō? V., *A.*, VIII. 114 (391, R. 2).

REMARK.—When the ellipsis is indefinite, do not attempt to supply it. The figure is still much abused by commentators in the explanation of grammatical phenomena.

689. Brachylogy (**breviloquentia**) is a failure to repeat an element which is often to be supplied in a more or less modified form.

Tam fēlīx essēs quam fōrmōsissima (=**es**) **vellem**, Ov., *Am.*, I. 8, 27 (302).

690. Zeugma or Syllēpsis is a junction of two words under the same regimen, or with the same modifier, although the common factor strictly applies but to one.

Manūs āc supplicēs vōcēs ad Tiberium tendēns, TAC., *Ann.*, II. 29, 2; *stretching out hands and* (uttering) *suppliant cries to Tiberius.*

691. Aposiōpēsis is a rhetorical breaking off before the close of the sentence, as in the famous Vergilian **Quōs ego**. . . . .

692. Pleonasm is the use of superfluous words.

693. Enallage is a shift from one form to another: **vōs ō Calliopē precor,** V., *A.*, IX. 525.

Hypallage is an interchange in the relations of words: **dare clāssibus austrōs,** V., *A.*, III. 61.

694. Oxymōron is the use of words apparently contradictory of each other: **cum tacent clāmant,** C., *Cat.*, I. 8, 21 (582).

695. Synecdoché is the use of the part for the whole, or the reverse: **tēctum** for **domum, puppis** for **nāvis, mucrō** for **gladius,** *etc.*

696. Hypérbaton, Trajection, is a violent displacement of words. **Lȳdia dīc per omnēs tē deōs ōrō,** H., *O.*, I. 8, 1 (413, N. 2).

697. Anacolūthon, or *want of sequence,* occurs when the scheme of a sentence is changed in its course.

698. Hendiadys (ἓν διὰ δυοῖν) consists in giving an analysis instead of a complex, in putting two substantives connected by a copulative conjunction, instead of one substantive and an adjective or attributive genitive.

Vulgus et multitūdō, *the common herd.* **Via et ratiō** (C., *Verr.*, I. 16, 47), *scientific method.* **Vī et armīs,** *by force of arms.*

So two verbs may be translated by an adverb and a verb: **fundī fugārīque,** *to be utterly routed.*

699. Cōnstrūctiō Praegnāns. So-called **cōnstrūctiō praegnāns** is nothing but an extended application of the accusative of the Inner Object (Object Effected). The result is involved, not distinctly stated.

Exitium inrītat, *Cf.* TAC., *Ann.*, XIII. 1, 1; *he provokes destruction* (**ad exitium inrītat**).

700. Lītotēs, or Understatement, is the use of an expression by which more is meant than meets the ear. This is especially common with the Negative.

Nōn indecōrō pulvere sordidī, H., *O.*, II. 1, 22 (449, R. 2).

PRINCIPAL RULES OF SYNTAX.

1. The Verb agrees with its subject in number and person (211).

2. The Adjective agrees with its subject in gender, number, and case (211).

3. The common Predicate of two or more subjects is put in the Plural (285); when the genders are different, it takes the strongest gender or the nearest (286); when the persons are different, it takes the first in preference to the second, the second in preference to the third (287).

4. The common Attribute of two or more substantives agrees with the nearest, rarely with the most important (290).

5. The Predicate substantive agrees with its subject in case (211).

6. The Appositive agrees with its subject in case; if possible, also in number and person (321).

7. The Relative agrees with its antecedent in gender, number, and person (614).

8. Disproportion is indicated by the comparative with **quam prō, quam ut, quam quī** (298).

9. In comparing two qualities, use either **magis quam** with the positive, or a double comparative (299).

10. Superlatives denoting order and sequence are often used partitively and then usually precede their substantive (291, R. 2).

11. The Genitive forms **meī, tuī, suī, nostrī, vestrī,** are used mainly as objective genitives; **nostrum** and **vestrum** as partitive (304, 2).

12. The Reflexive is used regularly when reference is made to the grammatical subject; frequently when reference is made to the actual subject (309).

13. The Reflexive is used of the principal subject, when reference is made to the thought or will of that subject; hence, in Infinitive clauses, or Indirect Questions, in Sentences of Design, and in Ōrātiō Oblīqua (521).

14. The Possessive Pronoun is used instead of the Possessive or Subjective Genitive in the First and Second Persons (362, 364).

15. The Appositive to a possessive pronoun is in the Genitive (321, R. 2).

16. With words of Inclination and Disinclination, Knowledge and Ignorance, Order and Position, Time and Season, the adjective is usually employed for the adverb (325, R. 6).

17. The Indicative, not the Subjunctive, is used in expressions of Possibility, Power, Obligation, and Necessity (254, R. 1).

18. The Potential of the Present or Future is the Present or Perfect Subjunctive (257); the Potential of the Past is the Imperfect Subjunctive (258).

19. The Optative Subjunctive may be used to express a Wish (260), an Asseveration (262), a Command (263), or a Concession (264).

20. The First Imperative looks forward to immediate, the Second to contingent, fulfilment (268).

21. The Negative of the Imperative is regularly **nōlī** with the Infinitive; sometimes **nē** with the Perfect Subjunctive (270, R. 2), or **cavĕ** with the Subjunctive (271) is also used.

22. The Infinitive, with or without a subject, may be treated as a neuter subject (422), object (423), or predicate (424).

23. The Infinitive is used as the object of verbs of Will, Power, Duty, Habit, Inclination, Resolve, Continuance, End, *etc.* (423).

24. The Accusative and Infinitive is used as the object of verbs of Will and Desire (532).

25. The Accusative and Infinitive is used as the object of verbs of Emotion (533).

26. The Accusative and Infinitive is used in Exclamation (534).

27. After verbs of Saying, Showing, Believing, and Perceiving, the Present Infinitive expresses action contemporary with that of the governing verb, the Perfect, action prior to it, the Future, action future to it (530).

28. The Genitive of the Gerund and Gerundive is used chiefly after substantives and adjectives that require a complement (428).

29. The Dative of the Gerund and Gerundive is used mainly in post-classical Latin after words of Fitness and Function; also after words of Capacity and Adaptation, and to express Design (429).

30. The Accusative of the Gerund and Gerundive is used after verbs of Giving and Taking, Sending and Leaving, *etc.*, to indicate Design (430).

31. The Ablative of the Gerund and Gerundive is used to denote Means and Cause, rarely Manner (431).

32. The Supine in **-um** is used chiefly after verbs of Motion to express Design (435).

33. The Supine in **-ū** is used chiefly with adjectives to indicate Respect (436).

34. The Present Participle denotes continuance, the Perfect, completion, at the time of the leading verb (282).

35. The Future Participle is used in post-Ciceronian Latin to express Design (438, N.).

36. The Participle is used after verbs of Perception and Representation to express the actual condition of the object (536).

37. The Perfect Participle passive is used after verbs of Causation and Desire, to denote impatience of anything except entire fulfilment (537).

38. The subject of a finite verb is in the Nominative (203).

39. Verbs of Seeming, Becoming, with the passive of verbs of Making, Choosing, Showing, Thinking, and Calling, take two Nominatives, one of the subject, one of the predicate (206).

40. With passive verbs of Saying, Showing, Believing, and Perceiving, the Accusative subject of the Infinitive becomes the Nominative subject of the leading verb (528).

41. The Appositional Genitive is used after **vōx, nōmen, verbum, rēs,** *etc.* (361, 1).

42. The Epexegetical Genitive (or Genitive of Explanation) is used after **genus, vitium, culpa,** *etc.* (361, 2).

43. The Possessive Genitive is used of the Third Person to denote possession (362).

44. The Subjective Genitive is used of the subject of the action indicated by the substantive (363, 1); the Objective Genitive of the object of that action (363, 2).

45. Essential or permanent qualities are put in the Genitive, always with an adjective (365); external and transient qualities in the Ablative, always with an adjective (400). See No. 82.

46. The Genitives of Quality and Possession may be used as predicates (366).

47. The Partitive Genitive stands for the whole to which a part belongs (367).

48. Adjectives of Fulness and Want, of Knowledge and Ignorance, of Desire and Disgust, of Participation and Power, may take the Genitive (374). Also some present participles used as adjectives, and in later Latin some verbals in **-āx** (375).

49. Verbs of Reminding, Remembering, and Forgetting take usually the Genitive (376); but sometimes the Accusative, especially of things (376, R.).

50. Impersonal verbs of Emotion take the Accusative of the Person Who Feels, and the Genitive of the Exciting Cause (371).

51. Verbs of Accusing, Convicting, Condemning, and Acquitting, take the Genitive of the Charge (378).

52. Verbs of Rating and Buying take the Genitive of the General, the Ablative of the Particular Value (379, 404). See No. 87.

53. **Interest** and **Rēfert** take the Genitive of the Person, **rarely of the** Thing concerned (381).

54. The Indirect Object is put in the Dative (345).

55. Verbs of Advantage and Disadvantage, Bidding and Forbidding, Pleasure and Displeasure, Yielding and Resisting, take the Dative (346).

56. Many intransitive verbs compounded with **ad, ante, con, in, inter, ob, post, prae, sub,** and **super** may take a Dative; transitive verbs also an Accusative besides (347).

57. Verbs of Giving and Putting take a Dative and Accusative, or an Accusative and Ablative (348).

58. The Dative is used with **esse** to denote possession (349).

59. The Dative is used of the Person Interested in the action (350).

60. The Ethical Dative is used of the personal pronouns only (351).

61. The Dative of Reference is used of the Person to whom a statement is referred (352).

62. The Dative of Agent is used with the Perfect passive, the Gerund, and the Gerundive (354).

63. The Dative may denote the Object For Which in combination with the Person To Whom (355).

64. Adjectives of Friendliness, Fulness, Likeness, Nearness, with their opposites, take the Dative (359).

65. Active transitive verbs take the Accusative case (330).

66. Many intransitive verbs, mostly those of Motion, compounded with **ad, ante, circum, con, in, inter, ob, per, praeter, sub, subter, super,** and **trans,** take the Accusative; transitive verbs thus compounded may have two Accusatives (331).

67. Intransitive verbs may take an Accusative of similar form or meaning (333, 2).

68. The Accusative may express Extent in Degree, Space, or Time (334–6).

69. Names of Towns and Small Islands are put in the Accusative of Place Whither; so also **domus** and **rūs** (337). See No. 74 and 92.

70. Verbs meaning to Inquire, Require, Teach, and Conceal, take two Accusatives, one of the Person, one of the Thing (339).

71. Verbs of Naming, Making, Taking, Choosing, and Showing, take two Accusatives of the same Person or Thing (340).

72. The subject of the Infinitive is regularly in the Accusative (420).

73. The Accusative may be used in Exclamations (343).

74. Place Where is denoted by the Ablative, usually with **in** (385);

Place Whence by the Ablative, usually with **ex, dē,** or **ab** (390). Names of Towns and Small Islands omit the prepositions (386, 391). See No. 69 and 92.

75. Attendance is denoted by the Ablative with **cum** (392).

76. Time When or Within Which is denoted by the Ablative (393).

77. Origin or Descent is denoted by the Ablative with or without **ex** and **dē** (395).

78. Material is denoted by the Ablative with **ex** (396).

79. The Point of View or Respect is denoted by the Ablative (397).

80. Comparatives without **quam** are followed by the Ablative (398).

81. Manner is denoted by the Ablative regularly with an adjective or **cum** (399).

82. External and transient qualities are denoted by the Ablative, always with an adjective (400); essential and permanent qualities by the Genitive, always with an adjective (365). See No. 45.

83. Cause, Means, and Instrument, are denoted by the Ablative (401, 408).

84. The Agent is denoted by the Ablative with **ā** (**ab**) (401).

85. The Standard of Measurement is denoted by the Ablative (402).

86. Measure of Difference is put in the Ablative (403).

87. Definite Price is put in the Ablative (404); General Price in the Genitive (379). See No. 52.

88. Verbs of Depriving and Filling, of Plenty and Want, take the Ablative (405).

89. The Ablative is used with **opus** and **ūsus** (406).

90. **Ūtor, fruor, fungor, potior,** and **vescor** take the Ablative (407).

91. The Ablative, combined with a participle, serves to modify the verbal predicate of a sentence: Ablative Absolute (409).

92. Names of Towns and Small Islands of the First and Second Declensions are put in the Locative of the Place Where (411). See No. 69 and 74.

93. Adverbs qualify verbs, adjectives, and other adverbs (439).

94. A question for information merely is introduced by **-ne** (454).

95. A question that expects the answer *yes* is introduced by **nōnne** (455).

96. A question that expects the answer *no* is introduced by **num** (456).

97. The Deliberative Question is in the Subjunctive (265).

98. The Indirect Question is in the Subjunctive (467).

99. *Sequence of Tenses.* Principal tenses are ordinarily followed by Principal tenses, Historical by Historical (509).

100. After a Future or Future Perfect, the Future relation is expressed by the Present, the Future Perfect by the Perfect Subjunctive (514). After other tenses the Future relation is expressed by the Active Periphrastic Present and Imperfect Subjunctive (515).

101. In Ōrātiō Oblīqua all subordinate tenses follow the general law of sequence (516).

102. **Quod,** *the fact that, in that,* is used with the Indicative to introduce explanatory clauses after Verbs of Adding and Dropping, Doing and Happening, and demonstratives (525).

103. **Quod, quia, quoniam,** and **quandō** take the Indicative in Direct Discourse, the Subjunctive in Indirect Discourse, to express Cause (540, 541).

104. **Quod** is used after verbs of Emotion with the Indicative in Direct, the Subjunctive in Indirect Discourse, to give the Ground (542).

105. Final Sentences have the Present and Imperfect Subjunctive with **ut** or **nē** (545).

106. Complementary Final Clauses are used after verbs of Will and Desire (546).

107. Positive verbs of Preventing, Refusing, Forbidding, and Bewaring, may take **nē** with the Subjunctive (548).

108. Verbs of Preventing and Refusing may take **quōminus** with the Subjunctive (549). See No. 112.

109. Verbs of Fear are followed by **nē** or **ut** (**nē nōn**) and all tenses of the Subjunctive (550).

110. Consecutive Sentences have the Subjunctive with **ut** and **ut nōn** (552).

111. Verbs of Effecting have the Subjunctive with **ut** and **nē,** or **ut nōn** (553).

112. Negatived or Questioned verbs of Preventing, Hindering, *etc.*, of Doubt and Uncertainty, may be followed by the Subjunctive with **quīn** (555). See No. 108.

113. A Consecutive Clause with **ut** is often used to give the contents or character of a preceding substantive, adjective, or pronoun (557).

114. **Ut, ut prīmum, cum, cum prīmum, ubi, ubi prīmum, simulāc, simul atque,** and **postquam** take the Perfect Indicative, in the sense of *as soon as;* but the Imperfect of Overlapping Action, and the Pluperfect when a definite interval is given (561, 562, 563).

115. When two actions are repeated contemporaneously, both are put in the Indicative in tenses of continuance (566).

116. When one action is repeated before another, the antecedent action is put in the Perfect, Pluperfect, or Future Perfect, the subsequent in the Present, Imperfect, or Future, according to the relation (567).

117. **Dum, dōnec, quoad, quamdiū,** *so long as, while,* take the Indicative of all tenses (569).

118. **Dum,** *while, while yet,* takes the Present Indicative after all tenses (570).

119. **Dum, dōnec, quoad,** *until,* take the Present, Historical Present, Historical Perfect, and Future Perfect Indicative (571).

120. **Dum, dōnec, quoad,** *until,* take the Subjunctive when Suspense or Design is involved (572).

121. **Dum, modŏ,** and **dummodŏ,** *if only, provided only,* take the Present and Imperfect Subjunctive in Conditional Wishes (573).

122. **Antequam** and **priusquam** take the Indicative Present, Perfect, and Future Perfect when the limit is stated as a fact; the Subjunctive when the action is expected, contingent, designed, or subordinate (574, 577).

123. Temporal **cum,** *when,* is used with all tenses of the Indicative to designate merely temporal relations (580).

124. Historical **cum,** *when,* is used with the Imperfect and Pluperfect Subjunctive to give the temporal circumstances under which an action took place (585).

125. Causal and Concessive **cum,** *when, whereas, although,* are used with all tenses of the Subjunctive (586, 587).

126. The Logical Condition has usually some form of the Indicative in both Protasis and Apodosis (595).

127. The Ideal Condition has usually the Present or Perfect Subjunctive, less often the Imperfect or Pluperfect, in both clauses (596).

128. The Unreal Condition has the Imperfect Subjunctive of opposition to present, the Pluperfect of opposition to past fact (597).

129. **Ut sī, āc sī, quasi, quam sī, tamquam, tamquam sī, velut,** and **velut sī,** introduce a comparison in the Subjunctive. The tense follows the rule of sequence (602).

130. Concessive clauses may be introduced by **etsī, etiamsī, tametsī,** with the Indicative or Subjunctive (604); by **quamquam,** with the Indicative (605); by **quamvīs,** with the Subjunctive (606).

131. Indefinite and generic relatives usually have the Indicative (625); so explanatory **quī,** when equivalent to **quod** (626).

132. The Subjunctive is used in Relative Clauses that form a part

of the utterance of another; so in Ōrātiō Oblīqua and Final Clauses (628).

133. Relative sentences that depend on Infinitives or Subjunctives, and form an integral part of the thought, are put in the Subjunctive by Attraction (629).

134. Relative sentences are put in the Subjunctive of Design when **quī** = **ut** (final) **is** (630).

135. Relative sentences are put in the Subjunctive of Tendency when **quī** = **ut** (consecutive) **is**; so after **dīgnus, indīgnus, idōneus, aptus,** *etc.;* after an indefinite antecedent; after comparatives with **quam** (631).

136. Comparative sentences after words of Likeness and Unlikeness may be introduced by **atque** or **āc** (643).

137. Comparative sentences after comparatives are introduced by **quam** (644).

138. In Ōrātiō Oblīqua, Principal Clauses are put in the Infinitive, except Interrogatives and Imperatives, which are put in the Subjunctive; Subordinate clauses are put in the Subjunctive (650, 651, 652).

PROSODY.

701. PROSODY treats of Quantity and Versification.

REMARKS.—1. Prosody originally meant Accent. Latin Accent is regulated by Quantity, and as classical Latin versification is also quantitative, Prosody is loosely used of both quantity and versification.

2. In the earliest Latin the Accent was not regulated by Quantity, but was on the initial syllable (15, N.). This often resulted in

(*a*) The disappearance of the vowel (8, 2) in the *antepenult* or *pro-antepenult*; this occurs especially in Greek words, but also in some common Latin words: **Poludeucēs, Poldeucēs, Pollūcēs, Pollūx**; **balineion, balineum, balneum**, *bath*; **māximus**, *greatest*, for **magisimos**; **optumus**, *best*, for **opitumus**, *etc.*

(*b*) The shortening of a *long penult* (8). This was still going on in the time of PLAUTUS, and occurs here and there in the poets: **anchora**, *anchor*, from **ankūra**; so **pēierō**, *I swear falsely*, for **periūrō**; **chorea**, *dance*, from **choreia**, *etc.*

(*c*) The weakening (8) of the *antepenult*, sometimes also of the *penult*, both in Greek words and Latin: **Massilia** from **Massalia**; **beni-** and **mali-** for **bene** and **male** in composition; **-hibeō** for **habeō** in composition; and a few others, as **-cīdō** for **caedō** in composition, *etc.*

QUANTITY.

702. RULE I.—A syllable is said to be long *by nature* when it contains a long vowel or diphthong: **ō, vae, lēgēs, saevae.**

REMARKS.—1. (*a*) A vowel before **-gm, -gn, -nf, -ns** is long *by nature*; (*b*) a vowel before **-nt, -nd** is short *by nature*.

EXCEPTIONS:

(*a*) **Egnātius, Theognis**, and some Greek words in **-egma**, as **phlegma**, *phlegm*; but **pēgma.**

(*b*) **Cōntiō** (for **coventiō**), *assembly*; **iēntāculum, iēntātiō**, *breakfast*; **nūntius**, *messenger*; **quīntus**, *fifth*; and Greek substantives in **-ūs, -ūntis, -ōn, -ōntis**; **Charōndās, Epamīnōndās**; also **nūndinae** (**noven-d-**), *market day*; **nōndum**, *not yet*; **prēndō**, *I seize*; **quīndecim**, *fifteen*; **vēndō**, *I sell*; **ūndecim**, *eleven*; **vīndēmia**, *vintage*.

2. Inchoative verbs have vowel before **-sc** long *by nature*; **dīscō**, *I learn*.

3. Noteworthy are the following: **quārtus**, *fourth*; **quīnque**, *five*, and its derivatives; **vīgintī**, *twenty*; **mīlle**, *thousand*, and its derivatives.

4. In verbs the quantity of the Present Stem is generally retained throughout before two consonants (except **-ns**).

Except **dīcō**, *I say;* Supine, **dictum**; **dūcō**, *I lead;* Supine, **ductum**; and their derivatives, like **dictiō**, *etc.*

5. Noteworthy are the following: **ago**, *I drive,* **ēgī, āctum**; **emo**, *I buy,* **ēmī, ēmptum**; **frangō**, *I break,* **frēgī, frāctum**; **fungor**, *I perform,* **fūnctus**; **iubeō**, *I order,* **iūssī, iūssum**; **iungō**, *I join,* **iūnxī, iūnctum**; **lego**, *I read,* **lēgī, lēctum**; **pangō**, *I fix,* **pāctum**; **rego**, *I govern,* **rēxī, rēctum**; **sanciō**, *I sanction,* **sānxī, sānctum, sāncītum**; **struo**, *I pile up,* **strūxī, strūctum**; **tangō**, *I touch,* **tāctum**; **tego**, *I cover,* **tēxī, tēctum**; **traho**, *I draw,* **trāxī, trāctum**; **ungō**, *I anoint,* **ūnxī, ūnctum**; **vincō**, *I conquer,* **vīxī, victum.**

6. In verbs, a vowel resulting from syncope is long before **ss, st** (131). Also, perhaps, **ī** before **s** and **t** in syncopated Pf. forms of **īre** and **petere.**

NOTE.—On the method of distinguishing long vowels on inscriptions, see 12, 1, N.

703. RULE II —A syllable is said to be long *by position* (12, 2) when a short vowel is followed by two or more consonants, or a double consonant: **_a_rs, c_o_llum, c_a_stra.**

REMARKS.—1. The consonants may be divided between two words: **per mare, in terrīs**; but when all the consonants are in the second word, the preceding short syllable commonly remains short, except in the Thesis (729) of a verse, when it is lengthened: **praemiă scrībae.**

2. Every vowel sound followed by **i** *consonant* (**j**) is long (except in the compounds of **iugum**, *yoke*). This is due sometimes to natural length of the vowel, sometimes to compensation: **Gāius** from **Gāvius, pēierō** for **periūrō**; but **biiugus**, *two-horse.*

NOTE.—In compounds of **iacere**, *to throw*, the **i** is often omitted, and the preceding vowel lengthened by compensation; so **cōnicere**; a short vowel with the **i** omitted is not found until OVID's time.

3. Final **s**, preceded by a short vowel, is dropped before a consonant in the older poetry; often too in LUCRETIUS.

Īn somnís vidít priu(s) quám sam (= eam) díscere cóepit.—ENNIUS.

NOTE.—In comic poetry, a short final syllable in **s** blends with **est**, and sometimes with **es**: **opust** (= **opus est**); **simili's** (= **similis es**).

704. RULE III.—A syllable ending in a short vowel before a mute, followed by **l** or **r**, is common (13): **tenĕ-brae**, *darkness.* In early Latin it is regularly short, so, too, when the mute and liquid begin a word.

REMARKS.—1. The syllable must *end* in a short vowel: **nāvĭ-fragus**, *ship-wrecking;* **mellĭ-fluus**, *flowing with honey;* but in **ab-rumpō** the **a** is long by position.

2. In Greek words **m** and **n** are included under this rule: **Tĕ-cmēssa, Cy̆-cnus.**

EXCEPTION.—Derivative substantives in **ābrum, ācrum, ātrum** from verbs; as **flābra,** *blasts.* **Zmarăgdos,** MART., V. 11, 1, cannot be paralleled.

705. RULE IV.—Every diphthong, and every vowel derived from a diphthong, or contracted from other vowels, is long (14): **saevos,** *cruel;* **conclūdō,** *I shut up* (from **claudō**); **inīquos,** *unfair* (from **aequos**); **cōgō,** *I drive together* (from **coigo = con + ago**).

EXCEPTION.—**Prae** in composition is shortened before a vowel until the time of STATIUS; **pr*ae*-ūstus,** *burnt at the point* (V., *A.*, VII. 524).

706. RULE V.—One simple vowel before another vowel-sound, or **h,** makes a short syllable: **dĕus,** *God;* **pŭer,** *boy;* **nĭhil,** *nothing.*

EXCEPTIONS:

1. **ā** in the old Gen. of the First Declension: **aurāī.**

2. **ē** in **-ēī** of the Fifth Declension, when a vowel precedes: **diēī,** but **fidĕī** (63, N. 1).

3. **a** and **e** before **i** in proper names in **-ius**: **Gāī, Pompēī.**

4. **i** in the Gen. form **-īus** (76, R. 2). **Alterĭus** is often shortened, perhaps even in prose: **ūnĭus, ūllĭus, nūllĭus, tōtĭus,** are found in poetry. In **alīus** the **i** is never shortened (**alīus** for **aliius**).

5. **i** in **fīō** is long, except before **er**: **fīō,** but **fĭeret** and **fĭerī.**

6. **ĕheu, Dīāna, ōhē, dīus** (= **dīvus**).

7. Many Greek words: **āēr, Menelāus, mūsēum, Mēdēa.**

8. In early Latin many words retain the original length of the vowel: **āis, rēī**; all forms of **fīō**; **clūō**; **fūī** and its forms; **plūit, lūit, adnūī,** *etc.* Most of the shortened forms also occur, and are more common.

Quantity of Final Syllables.

A. POLYSYLLABLES.

707. RULE VI.—In words of more than one syllable, final **a, e,** and **y** are *short;* **i, o,** and **u** are *long.*

1. **a** is short: **terră,** *earth;* **dōnă,** *gifts;* **capită,** *heads.*

EXCEPTIONS:

1. Abl. of the First Declension: **terrā.**

2. Voc. of words in **ās** (**Aenēā**), and Greek Nom. in **ā** (**Ēlectrā**).

3. Impv. of First Conjugation: **amā**

4. Most uninflected words : **trīgintā, iūxtā,** but **ită, quiă, ēiă. With pută,** *for instance,* compare **cavĕ** below.

2. **e** is short.

Exceptions :

1. Abl. of the Fifth Declension : **diē.**

2. Impv. of Second Conjugation : **monē** (but see Note).

3. Most adverbs of Second Declension : **rēctē**; but **benĕ, malĕ, īnfernĕ** (Lucr.), **māxumĕ** (Plaut.), **probĕ** (Plaut.), **supernĕ** (Lucr., Hor.), **temerĕ** (Plaut., Ter.).

4. Greek words in **ē** (η) : **Tempē, melē.**

5. **Que** is thought to be not unfrequently long in the Thesis of early Saturnians ; so in the hexameter of the classical period if a second **que** follows in the Arsis.

Note.—Observe that in Plautus and Terence any dissyllabic Iambic impv. may have the last **ē** shortened ; principally **cavē̆, habē̆, iubē̆, manē̆, monē̆, movē̆, tacē̆, tenē̆, valē̆, vidē̆.** See 716. Later poets also shorten sometimes when the penult is long ; **salve** (Mart.).

3. **y** is always short, except in contracted forms : **misȳ̆** (Dative **misȳ** = **misyi**).

4. **i** is long : **dominī, vīgintī, audī.**

Exceptions :

1. Greek Dat. **sĭ** : **Trōasĭ.**

2. Greek Nom., as **sināpĭ**; Voc., as **Parĭ**; Dat. Sing. (rarely), as **Mīnōidĭ.**

3, **quasĭ, nisĭ, cŭĭ** (when a dissyllable).

4. **i** is common in **mihī̆, tibī̆, sibī̆, ibī̆, ubī̆.**

Observe the compounds : **ibī̆dem, ibīque, ubīque, ubĭnam, ubĭvīs, ubĭcunque, nēcubĭ, utĭnam, utĭque, sīcutĭ**; (but **utī**).

5. **o** is long : **bonō, tūtō.**

Exceptions :

1. Common in **homō̆**; in the Augustan times in **leō̆** and many proper names ; as **Scīpiō̆**; in the post-Augustan times in many common substantives : **virgō̆. Nēmŏ** is found first in Ovid, **mentiŏ** in Horace.

2. Frequently short in Iambic words in early Latin, especially in verbs, many of which remained common in the Augustan times, as **volō̆, vetō̆, sciō̆, petō̆, putō̆,** *etc.;* so less often **nesciō̆, dēsinō̆, obsecrō̆, dīxerō̆, ōderō̆.** From Seneca on, the Gerund may be shortened : **amandō̆.**

3. **o** is usually short in **modŏ, citŏ, octŏ, egŏ, īlicŏ, immŏ, duŏ, ambŏ** (post-classical); and in many other words in later poetry.

6. **u** is always long : **cornū, frūctū, audītū.**

708. Rule VII.—All final syllables that end in a simple consonant other than **s** are short.

Exceptions :

1. **ālēc, liēn,** and many Greek substantives.

2. The adverbs and oblique cases of **illīc, illūc, istīc, istūc, can** hardly be considered exceptions, as **-c** is for **-ce,** and is merely enclitic.

3. Compounds of **pār : dispār, impār.**

4. **iīt, petiīt,** and their compounds.

5. Final **-at, -et, -it,** were originally long, and as such often occur in early Latin, and occasionally before a pause in the classical poets.

709. Rule VIII.—Of final syllables in **s**: **as, es, os, are** long ; **is, us, ys,** short.

1. **as** is long : **Aenēās, servās, amās.**

Exceptions :

1. Greek substantives in **ăs, ădis : Arcăs, Arcădis.**

2. Greek Acc. Pl., Third Declension : **hērōăs, Arcadăs.**

3. **anăs, anătis.**

2. **es** is long : **rēgēs, diēs, monēs.**

Exceptions :

1. Nom. and Voc. Sing., Third Declension, when the Gen. has **ĕtis, ĭtis, ĭdis : segĕs, mīlĕs, obsĕs ;** but **abiēs, ariēs, pariēs.**

2. Compounds of **ĕs,** *be* (long syllable in Plautus) : **adĕs, potĕs.**

3. **penĕs** (Preposition).

4. Greek words in **ĕs** (ες) : Nom. Pl., as **Arcadĕs ;** Voc., as **Dēmosthenĕs ;** Neuter, as **cacoēthĕs.**

5. Iambic verbal forms in Second Person Sing. in early Latin.

3. **os** is long : **deōs, nepōs.**

Exceptions :

1. **Compŏs, impŏs, exŏs ;** and as the Nom. ending in the Second Declension.

2. Greek words in **ŏs** (ος) : **melŏs.**

4. **is** is short : **canĭs, legĭs.**

Exceptions :

1. Dat. and Abl. Plural : **terrīs, bonīs.**

2. Acc. Pl. of the Third Declension : **omnīs = omnēs.**

3. In the Nom. of sundry Proper Names, increasing long in the Genitive : **Quirīs, Quirītis.**

4. Second Person Sing. Pr. Indic. active, Fourth Conjugation : **audīs.**

5. In the verbal forms from **vīs, sīs, fīs**, and **velīs**: **nō-līs, mā-līs, ad-sīs, cale-fīs.**

6. In the Second Person Sing. Fut. Pf. Indic. and Pf. Subjv., **is** is common: **vīderĭs.**

7. **Pulvīs, cinīs, sanguīs**, occasionally in early Latin.

5. **us** is short: **servŭs, currŭs.**

EXCEPTIONS:

1. Gen. Sing., Nom. and Acc. Pl., Fourth Declension: **currūs.**

2. Nom. Third Declension, when the Gen. has a long **u**: **virtūs, virtūtis; incūs, incūdis; tellūs, tellūris.**

3. In Greek words with **ū** (*ους*): **tripūs, Sapphūs**; but **Oedipŭs and polypŭs**

4. Occasionally the Dat. and Abl. Pl. of the Third Declension, the First Person Pl. active of verbs, seem to be long in early Latin.

6. **ys** is short: **chlamўs.**

B. MONOSYLLABLES.

710. RULE IX.—All monosyllables that end in a vowel are long: **ā, dā, mē, dē, hī, sī, ō, dō, tū.**

Except the enclitics: **-quĕ, -vĕ, -nĕ, -cĕ, -tĕ, -psĕ, ptĕ.**

711. RULE X.—Declined or conjugated monosyllables that end in a consonant follow the rules given: **dās, flēs, scīs, dăt, flĕt, ĭs, ĭd, quĭs, hīs, quīs, quōs.**

hic, *this one*, is sometimes short; **dīc** and **dūc** have the quantity of their verbs; **es**, *be*, is short in classical Latin, long in early Latin.

712. RULE XI.—Monosyllabic Nominatives of substantives and adjectives are long when they end in a consonant, even if the stem-syllable be short: **ōs, mōs, vēr, sōl, fūr, plūs; lār (lăris), pēs (pĕdis), bōs (bŏvis), pār (păris).**

EXCEPTIONS:
vir and **lac, os (ossis), mel;**
Also **cor, vas (vadis), fel.** Also **quot, tot.**

713. RULE XII.—Monosyllabic particles that end in a consonant are short: **ăn, cĭs, ĭn, nĕc, pĕr, tĕr.**

Excepting **ēn** and **nōn** and **quīn**;
And also **crās** and **cūr** and **sīn**;
Also the Adverbs in **c**: **hīc, hūc, hāc, sīc**; and **āc (atque).**

Quantity of Stem-Syllables.

714. RULE XIII.—The quantity of stem-syllables, when not determined by the general rules, is fixed by the usage of the poets (long or short *by authority*).

REMARKS.—1. The changes of quantity in the formation of tense-stems have been set forth in the conjugation of the verb (153, 2).

2. The occasional differences in the quantity of the stem-syllables which spring from the same radical can only be explained by reference to the history of each word, and cannot be given here. Some examples are:

păcīscor,	**pāx, pācis.**	**sĕdeō,**	**sēdēs.**
măcer,	**mācerō.**	**fĭdēs,**	**fīdō** (feido).
lĕgo,	**lēx, lēgis.**	**dux, dŭcis,**	**dūcō** (doucō).
rĕgo,	**rēx, rēgis.**	**vŏcō,**	**vōx.**
tĕgo,	**tēgula.**	**lūcerna,**	**lūceō** (louceō).
ācer,	**ăcerbus.**	**suspĭcor,**	**suspīciō.**
mōlēs,	**mŏlestus.**	**mŏveō,**	**mōbilis** (= **movbilis**).

Quantity in Compounds.

715. RULE XIV.—Compounds generally keep the quantity of their constituent parts: **(cēdō) ante-cēdō, dē-cēdō, prō-cēdō; (caedō), occīdō; (cădō), occĭdō.**

REMARKS.—1. Of the inseparable prefixes, **dī, sē,** and **vē** are long, **rĕ** short: **dīdūcō, sēdūcō, vēcors, rĕdūcō**; **di,** in **dĭsertus,** is shortened for **dis,** and in **dirimo, dĭr** stands for **dis.**

2. **Nĕ** is short, except in **nēdum, nēmŏ** (ne-hemŏ), **nēquam, nēquīquam, nēquāquam, nēquitia, nēve.**

3. **Rĕ** comes from **red,** which in the forms **redd, recc, repp, rell, rett,** occurs principally in poetry before many consonantal verb forms; but this doubling varies at different periods, and is found throughout only in **reddō. Rē** by compensation for the loss of the **d** is found, occasionally, principally in Perfect stems and in dactylic poetry, especially in **rēicere, rēligiō** (also **relligiō** and **religiō**), **rēdūcō** (once in PLAUT.).

4. **Prō** is shortened before vowels, and in many words before consonants, especially before **f**: **prŏavos, prŏhibeō, prŏinde, prŏfugiō, prŏfugus, prŏfundus, prŏfiteor, prŏfārī, prŏfānus, prŏficīscor, prŏcella, prŏcul, prŏnepōs.** The older language shortens less frequently than the later. In Greek words **pro** (*πρό*) is generally short: **prŏphēta**; but **prōlogus.**

5. The second part of the compound is sometimes shortened: **dēiĕrō,**

(from **iūrō**), **cognĭtus, agnĭtus** (from **nōtus**). Notice the quantity in the compounds of **-dicus: fātidĭcus, vēridĭcus** (**dīcō**), and **innŭba, prōnŭba** (**nūbō**).

6. Mechanical rules, more minute than those given above, might be multiplied indefinitely, but they are all open to so many exceptions as to be of little practical value. A correct pronunciation of Latin cannot be acquired except by constant practice, under the direction of a competent teacher, or by a diligent study of the Latin poets, and consequently of Latin versification.

Peculiarities of Quantity in Early Latin.

716. The *Iambic* (734) *Law*. Any combination of short and long, having an accent on the short, or immediately preceding or following an accented syllable, may be scanned as a Pyrrhic. This applies to

(*a*) Iambic words, especially imperatives, as: **rogŏ, vidĕ, manĕ**;

(*b*) Words beginning with an Iambus, when the second syllable is long by position, and the third syllable is accented, as: **senĕctūtem, volŭntātis**;

(*c*) Two monosyllables closely connected, or a monosyllable closely connected with a following long initial syllable, as: **quis hĭc est, ut ŏccēpī.** The monosyllable may have become so by elision.

(*d*) Trochaic words following a short accented syllable, as: **quid ĭstuc.**

(*e*) Cretic words, but more often in anapaestic measure, or at the beginning of a hemistich, as **vēnerănt.**

NOTES.—1. Before **quidem** a monosyllable is shortened: **tŭ quidem.**

2. A combination like **volŭptās mea** is looked upon as a single word.

3. Authorities are not agreed as to the shortening: in polysyllabic words, when the second syllable is long by nature and the third syllable accented; in trisyllables which have become Iambic by elision; in Cretics at Trochaic and Iambic close; in polysyllables like **simĭllumae.**

717. Personal pronouns and similar words of common occurrence forming Trochees (734) may shorten the initial syllable when followed by a long syllable or its equivalent, even in the oblique cases: **ílle mē, ómnium mē, ŭnde tíbí.**

NOTES.—1. The words involved are **ille, illic, iste, istic, ipse, ecquis, omnis, nempe, inde, unde, quĭppe, ĭmmo,** and a few others that are disputed, such as some dissyllabic imperatives like **mitte, redde,** and monosyllables followed by **-que, -ne, -ve,** and the like.

2. **Nempe, inde, unde, quippe, ille, iste,** may perhaps suffer *syncope* and be scanned as monosyllables.

3. **Nempe** never forms a whole foot. **Proin, dein, exin** are used only before consonants: **proinde** only before vowels; **deinde** usually before vowels, rarely before consonants.

4. Trochees also come under the operation of the *Iambic Law* when they follow a short accented syllable.

FIGURES OF PROSODY.

718. Poetry often preserves the older forms of language, and perpetuates peculiarities of pronunciation, both of which are too frequently set down to poetic license.

719. 1. *Elision.*—When one word ends with a vowel and another begins with a vowel, or **h**, the first vowel is *elided.* Elision is not a total omission, but rather a hurried half-pronunciation, similar to Grace notes in music.

Ō fēlīx ūn(a) ant(e) aliās Priamēïa virgō.—VERG.

2. *Ecthlipsis.*—In like manner **m** final (a faint nasal sound) is elided with its short vowel before a vowel or **h.**

Mōnstr(um), horrend(um), īnfōrm(e) ingēns cuī lūmen adēmptum.—VERG.

EXCEPTION.—After a vowel or **m** final, the word **est,** *is,* drops its **e** and joins the preceding syllable (*Aphæresis*).

Sī rixast ubi tū pulsās ego vāpulō tantum.—JUV.
Aeternās quoniam poenās in morte timendumst.—LUCR.

720. *Hiatus.*—Hiatus is the meeting of two vowels in separate syllables, which meeting produces an almost continuous opening (yawning) of the vocal tube. In the body of a word this hiatus, or yawning, is avoided sometimes by contraction, often by shortening the first vowel (13).

REMARKS.—1. The Hiatus is sometimes allowed : *a,* in the Thesis (729), chiefly when the first vowel is long ; *b,* in an Arsis (729), or resolved Thesis, when a long vowel is shortened (Semi-hiatus) ; *c,* before a pause, chiefly in the principal Caesura (750); *d,* in early Latin, in the principal Caesura, before a change of speakers, and occasionally elsewhere.

(*a*) **Stant et iūniperī** (*h*) **et castaneae** (*h*) **hīrsūtae.**—VERG.
(*b*) **Crēdimus ? an quĭ** (*h*) **amant ipsī sibi somnia fingunt ?**—VERG.
(*c*) **Prōmissam ēripuī generō.** (*h*) **Arma impia sūmpsī.**—VERG.
(*d*) A. **Abī.** B. **Quid abeam ?** A. **St ! abī** (*h*). B. **Abeam** (*h*) **?** A. **Abī.**—PLAUT.

2. Monosyllabic interjections are not elided.

3. On the elision of **e** in **-ne ?** see 456, R. 2.

721. *Diastolé.*—Many final syllables, which were originally long, are restored to their rights by the weight of the Thesis.

Uxōr, heus uxor, quamquam tū īrāta's mihī.—PLAUT.
Dummodō mōrāta rēctē veniat dōtātast satis.—PLAUT.
Perrūpit Acheronta Herculeus labor.—HOR.

Sometimes, however, Diastolé arises from the necessities of the verse (as in proper names), or is owing to a pause (Punctuation).

Nec quās Prīamidēs in aquōsīs vallibus Īdae.—OV.
Dēsine plūra puēr—et quod nunc īnstat agāmus.—VERG.
Pectoribūs inhiāns spīrantia cōnsulit exta.—VERG.

NOTE.—The extent to which diastolé is allowable is a matter of dispute, especially in early Latin.

On **quē**, see 707, 2, Ex. 5.

722. *Systolé.*—Long syllables which had begun to shorten in prose, are shortened (Systolé).

Obstupuī stetĕruntque comae vōx faucibus haesit.—VERG.
Ē terrā māgn(um) alterĭus spectāre labōrem.—LUCR.
Ūnĭus ad certam fōrmam prīmōrdia rērum.—LUCR.
Nūllĭus addictus iūrāre in verba magistrī.—HOR.

NOTE.—The short penult of the Pf. in **stetĕrunt, dedĕrunt,** was probably original (DEDRO in inscriptions). See 131, 4, *b*, 5 and 6.

723. *Hardening.*—The vowels **i** and **u** assert their half-consonant nature (Hardening): **ab*i*ĕtĕ (ăbĭĕtĕ), gen*v*ă (gĕnŭă), ten*v*ĭă (tĕnŭĭă).**

Flūv*i*ōrum rēx Ēridanus campōsque per omnēs.—VERG.
Nam quae tēn*v*ia sunt hīscendīst nūlla potestās.—LUCR.

724. *Dialysis.*—The consonants **i** and **v** assert their half-vowel nature: **dissŏl*ŭ*ō** (**dissolvō**), **Gā*ĭ*ūs** (**Gāius,** from **Gāvius**).

Adulterētur et columba mīluō.—HOR.
Stāmina nōn ūllī dissoluenda deō.—TIB.

725. *Syncopé.*—Short vowels are dropped between consonants, as often in prose: **calfaciō** for **calefaciō.**

Templōrum positor templōrum sāncte repostor.—OV.
Quiddam māgnum addēns ūnum mē surpite (= **surripite**) **mortī.**—HOR.

726. *Tmēsis.*—Compound words are separated into their parts.

Quō mē cunque (= **quōcumque mē**) **rapit tempestās dēferor hospes.**—HOR.

NOTE.—The earlier poets carry Tmesis much further, in unwise emulation of the Greek. Celebrated is: **Saxō cere comminuit brum.**—ENNIUS.

727. *Synizēsis.*—Vowels are connected by a slur, as often in the living language: **dĕinde, dĕinceps.**

Quid faciam roger anne rogem? quid dĕinde rogābō?—Ov.

So even when **h** intervenes, as **dehinc**:

Eurum ad sē Zephyrumque vocat, dehinc tālia fātur.—Verg.

Remark.—Synizēsis (*settling together*) is also called Synaerĕsis (*taking together*), as opposed to Diaeresis (5); but Synaeresis properly means *contraction*, as in **cōgō** (for **coagō**), and **nēmŏ** (for **nehemŏ**). Synaloepha is a general term embracing all methods of avoiding Hiatus.

Note.—1. Synizesis is very common in early Latin, especially in pronominal forms: **mī** (**mihi**), **mĕus**, and its forms, dissyllabic forms like **ĕō**, **ĕum**, *etc.*

728. *Synapheia.*—A line ends in a short vowel, which is elided before the initial vowel of a following line, or a word is divided between two lines, *i. e.*, the two lines are joined together.

Sors exitūra et nōs in aetern(um)
Exilium impositūra cumbae.—Hor., *O.*, II. 3, 27.
Gallicum Rhēn(um), horribile aequor, ūlti-
mōsque Britannōs.—Cat., II. 11.

VERSIFICATION.

729. *Rhythm.*—Rhythm means harmonious movement. In language, Rhythm is marked by the stress of voice (*Accent*). The accented part is called the Thesis;* the unaccented, the Arsis. The Rhythmical Accent is called the Ictus (*blow, beat*).

Remark.—Besides the dominant Ictus, there is a subordinate or secondary Ictus, just as there is a dominant and a secondary Accent in words.

730. *Metre.*—Rhythm, when represented in language, is embodied in Metre (*Measure*). A Metre is a system of syllables standing in a determined order.

* Thesis and Arsis are Greek terms, meaning the *putting down* and the *raising* of the foot in marching. The Roman Grammarians, misunderstanding the Greek, applied the terms to the *lowering* and *raising* of the voice, and thus reversed the significations. Modern scholars up to recent times followed the Roman habit, but at present the tendency is to use the terms in their original signification, as above.

731. *Unit of Measure.*—The Unit of Measure is the short syllable, (⏑), and is called **Mora, Tempus** (*Time*).

The value in music is ♪ = ⅛.

The long (–) is the double of the short.

The value in music is ♩ = ¼.

Remark.—An irrational syllable is one which is not an exact multiple of the standard unit. Feet containing such quantities are called irrational.

732. *Resolution and Contraction.*—In some verses, two short syllables may be used instead of a long (Resolution), or a long instead of two short (Contraction).

Resolution ⏑⏑ ♫ Contraction, ⏑⏑ ♫

733. *Feet.*—As elements of musical strains, Metres are called Bars. As elements of verses, they are called Feet.

As musical strains are composed of equal bars, so verses are composed of equal feet, marked as in music, thus | .

Remark.—Theoretically, the number of metres is unrestricted; practically, only those metres are important that serve to embody the principal rhythms.

734. *Names of the Feet.*—The feet in use are the following:

Feet of Three Times.

Trochee,	– ⏑	**lēgĭt.**	♩ ♪
Iambus,	⏑ –	**lĕgunt.**	♪ ♩
Tribrach,	⏑ ⏑ ⏑	**lĕgĭtĕ.**	♪ ♪ ♪

Feet of Four Times.

Dactyl,	– ⏑ ⏑	**lēgĭmŭs.**	♩ ♫
Anapaest,	⏑ ⏑ –	**lĕgĕrent.**	♫ ♩
Spondee,	– –	**lēgī.**	♩ ♩
Proceleusmaticus,	⏑ ⏑ ⏑ ⏑	**relegitur.**	♫ ♫

Feet of Five Times.

Cretic,	– ◡ –	lēgĕrint.	♩ ♪ ♩
First **Paeōn,**	– ◡ ◡ ◡	lēgĕrĭtĭs.	♩ ♪ ♫
Fourth **Paeōn,**	◡ ◡ ◡ –	lĕgĭmĭnī.	♫ ♪ ♩
Bacchīus,	◡ – –	lĕgēbant.	♪ ♩ ♩
Antibacchīus,	– – ◡	lēgistĭs.	♩ ♩ ♪

Feet of Six Times.

Iōnicus ā māiōre,	– – ◡ ◡	collēgĭmŭs.	♩ ♩ ♫
Iōnicus ā minōre,	◡ ◡ – –	rĕlĕgēbant.	♫ ♩ ♩
Choriambus,	– ◡ ◡ –	collĭgĕrant.	♩ ♫ ♩
Ditrochee,	– ◡ – ◡	collĭguntŭr.	♩ ♪ ♩ ♪
Diiambus,	◡ – ◡ –	lĕgāmĭnī.	♪ ♩ ♪ ♩

Remarks.—1. Other feet are put down in Latin Grammars, but they do not occur in Latin verse, if in any, such as:

Pyrrhic,	◡ ◡	lĕgĭt.	**Antispast,**	◡ – – ◡	lĕgēbārĭs.
First **Epitrite,**	◡ – – –	rĕlēgērunt.	**Dispondee,**	– – – –	sēlēgērunt.
Second **Epitrite,**	– ◡ – –	ēlĭgēbant.	Second **Paeōn,**	◡ – ◡ ◡	lĕgentĭbŭs.
Third **Epitrite,**	– – ◡ –	sēlēgĕrint.	Third **Paeōn,**	◡ ◡ – ◡	lĕgĭtōtĕ.
Fourth **Epitrite,**	– – – ◡	collēgistĭs.	**Molossus,**	– – –	lēgērunt.

2. For *Irrational Feet* see 743 and 744.

735. *Ascending and Descending Rhythms.*—Rhythms are divided into ascending and descending. If the Thesis follows, the Rhythm is called *ascending;* if it precedes, *descending.* So the Trochee has a descending, the Iambus an ascending, rhythm.

736. *Names of Rhythms.*—Rhythms are commonly called after their principal metrical representative. So the Trochaic Rhythm, the Anapaestic Rhythm, the Iambic Rhythm, the Dactylic Rhythm, the Ionic Rhythm.

737. *Classes of Rhythms.*—In Latin, the musical element of versification is subordinate, and the principles of Greek rhythm have but a limited application.

The Greek classes are based on the relation of Thesis to Arsis.

I. *Equal Class,* in which the Thesis is equal to the Arsis (γένος ἴσον). This may be called the Dactylico-Anapaestic class.

II. *Unequal Class,* in which the Thesis is double of the Arsis (γένος διπλάσιον). This may be called the Trochaico-Iambic class.

III. *Quinquepartite or Paeonian Class* (*Five-eighths class*), of which the Cretic and Bacchīus are the chief representatives (γένος ἡμιόλιον).

738. *Rhythmical Series.*—A Rhythmical Series is an uninterrupted succession of rhythmical feet, and takes its name from the number of feet that compose it.

Dipody	=	two feet.	Pentapody	=	five feet.
Tripody	=	three feet.	Hexapody	=	six feet.
Tetrapody	=	four feet.			

REMARKS.—1. The Dipody is the ordinary unit of measure (-meter) in Trochaic, Iambic, and Anapaestic verse. In these rhythms a monometer contains two feet, a dimeter four, a trimeter six, a tetrameter eight.

2. The single foot is the ordinary unit of measure (-meter) in Dactylic verse. Thus, a verse of one Dactyl is called a Monometer; of two, a Dimeter; of three, a Trimeter; of four, a Tetrameter; of five, a Pentameter; of six, a Hexameter.

3. There are limits to the extension of series. Four feet (in Greek, five) is the limit of the Dactylic and Anapaestic, six of the Trochaic and Iambic series. All beyond these are compounds.

739. *The Anacrustic Scheme.*—Ancient Metric discussed the colon, whether in Ascending or Descending Rhythm, according to the feet of which it was composed. Most modern critics, since the time of BENTLEY, regard the first Arsis in an ascending rhythm as taking the place of an upward beat in music (called by HERMANN Anacrŭsis; *i. e., upward stroke, signal-beat*), whereby all rhythms become descending.

In this way the Iambus is regarded as an Anacrustic Trochee, the Anapaest as an Anacrustic Dactyl, the Iōnicus a minōre as an Anacrustic Iōnicus ā māiōre. The sign of the Anacrŭsis is :

740. *Equality of the Feet.*—Every rhythmical series is composed of equal parts. To restore this equality, when it is violated by language, there are four methods:

1. Syllaba Anceps.
2. Catalēxis.
3. Protraction.
4. Correption.

741. *Syllaba Anceps.*—The final syllable of an independent series or verse may be short or long indifferently. It may be short when the metre demands a long; long when the metre demands a short. Such a syllable is called a Syllaba Anceps.

742. *Catalēxis and Pause.*—A complete series is called Acatalectic; an incomplete series is called Catalectic. A series or verse is said to be Catalectic *in syllabam, in dissyllabum, in trisyllabum,* according to the number of syllables in the catalectic foot.

–́ ⏑ ⏑ | –́ ⏑ ⏑ | –́ *Trimeter dactylicus catalēcticus in syllabam.*
–́ ⏑ ⏑ | –́ ⏑ ⏑ | –́ ⏑ *Trimeter dactylicus catalēcticus in dissyllabum.*

The time is made up by Pause.

The omission of one mora is marked ∧; of two $\bar{\wedge}$

743. *Protraction and Syncopé.*—Protraction (τονή) consists in drawing out a long syllable beyond its normal quantity. It occurs in the body of a verse, and serves to make up for the omission of one or more Arses, which omission is called Syncopé.

⌞ = 3 = ♩. (triseme long); ⌞⌟ = 4 = 𝅗𝅥 (tetraseme long).

744. *Correption.*—Correption is the shortening of a syllable to suit the measure.

1. So a long syllable sometimes takes the place of a short, and is marked >; similarly, two short syllables often seem to take the place of one, and may be marked ⏑⏑.

2. When a Dactyl is used as a substitute for a Trochee, the approximate value is often $1\frac{1}{2} + \frac{1}{2} + 1 = 3 =$ ♩. ♬ ♩; which may be indicated by –⏑ ⏑ (cyclic Dactyl).

The following line illustrates all the points mentioned:

a	b	c	b	c	b		d e
–>	–⏑ ⏑	⌞	–⏑ ⏑	⌞	–⏑ ⏑	– ⏑	– ∧
Nūllam	**Vāre sa-**	**crā** ‖	**vīte pri-**	**us** ‖	**sēveris**	**arbo**	**-rem.**—HOR.

(*a*) Irrational trochee (irrational long). (*b*) Cyclic dactyl. (*c*) Syncopé and Protraction (triseme long). (*d*) Syllaba anceps. (*e*) Catalēxis.

REMARK.—Under this head, notice the frequent use of the irrational long in Anacrusis.

745. *Verse.*—A Simple Rhythm is one that consists of a simple series; a Compound Rhythm is one that consists of two or more series.

A Verse is a simple or compound rhythmical series, which forms a distinct and separate unit. The end of a verse is marked

1. By closing with a full word. Two verses cannot divide a word between them, except very rarely by Synapheia (728).

2. By the *Syllaba Anceps,* which can stand unconditionally.

3. By the Hiatus, *i. e.*, the verse may end with a vowel, though the next verse begin with one. Occasionally such verses are joined by Synapheia (V., *A.*, I. 332–3, 448–9; II. 745–6).

746. *Methods of Combining Verses.*—The same verse may be repeated throughout without recurring groups (Stichic Composition); such as the Septenarius and Octonarius, the Trochaic Septenarius, the Heroic Hexameter, the Iambic Senarius (Trimeter). Or the same verse or different verses may be grouped in pairs (distichs), triplets (tristichs), fours (tetrastichs). Beyond these simple stanzas Latin versification seldom ventured.

Larger groups of series are called Systems.

Larger groups of verses are called Strophes, a name sometimes attached to the Horatian stanzas.

747. *Cantica and Dīverbia.*—In the Drama there is a broad division between that part of the play which was simply spoken, and is called *Dīverbium,* comprising the scenes in the Iambic Senarius, and that part which was either sung or recited to a musical accompaniment called *Canticum.* The Canticum is subdivided into: (1) Those scenes which were merely *recited* to the accompaniment of the flute, and were written in Trochaic and Iambic Septenarii and Iambic Octonarii; and (2) those parts which were written in varying measures (**mutātīs modīs cantica**) and sung. The latter division is also called "*Cantica* in the narrow sense," and may be divided into monologues, dialogues, etc. The greatest variety of measures is found in the monologues.

748. *Union of Language with Rhythm.*—When embodied

in language, rhythm has to deal with rhythmical groups already in existence. Every full word is a rhythmical group with its accent, is a metrical group with its long or short syllables, is a word-foot. Ictus sometimes conflicts with accent; the unity of the verse-foot breaks up the unity of the word-foot.

749. *Conflict of Ictus and Accent.*—In ordinary Latin verse, at least according to modern pronunciation, the Ictus overrides the Accent; this conflict seems, however, to have been avoided in the second half of the Dactylic Hexameter, and the Ictus made to coincide with the Accent.

Note.—The extent to which this conflict was felt by the Romans themselves is a matter of uncertainty, but it seems likely that the dominant accent of a word was not so sharp as in modern pronunciation, and consequently the conflict would not be serious.

750. *Conflict of Word-foot and Verse-foot.*—The conflict of word-foot and verse-foot gives rise to Caesura. Caesura means an incision produced by the end of a word in the middle of a verse-foot, and is marked †.

This incision serves as a pause, partly to rest the voice for a more vigorous effort, partly to prevent monotony by distributing the masses of the verse.

Remarks.—1. So in the Heroic Hexameter the great Caesura falls *before* the middle of the verse, to give the voice strength for the first Arsis of the second half.

″– ∪ ∪ | ∠ – | ∠ † – | ″– – | ∠ ∪ ∪ | ∠ –
Ūna salūs victīs † nūllam spērāre salūtem.—Verg.

It does not occur *at* the middle, as in that case the verse would become monotonous.

2. In many treatises any incision in a verse is called a Caesura.

751. *Varieties of Caesura.*—Caesurae have different names to show their position in the foot, as follows:

Sēmiternāria, after the third half foot, *i.e.*, in the second foot.
Sēmiquīnāria, after the fifth half foot, *i.e.*, in the third foot.
Sēmiseptēnāria, after the seventh half foot, *i.e.*, in the fourth foot.
Sēminovēnāria, after the ninth half foot, *i.e.*, in the fifth foot.

Remark.—These Caesurae are frequently called after their Greek names, thus: *trihemimeral, penthemimeral, hepthemimeral, etc.*

752. *Masculine and Feminine Caesurae.*—In trisyllabic metres, when the end of the word within the verse-foot falls on a Thesis, it is called a Masculine Caesura; when on an Arsis, a Feminine Caesura.

Ūna sa | lūs †[a] vi | ctīs †[b] nūl | lam †[c] spē | rāre †[d] sa | lūtem.

a, *b*, *c*, are Masculine Caesurae; *d*, a Feminine Caesura.

Especially noteworthy is the Feminine Caesura of the third foot in the Hexameter, called the Third Trochee (783, R. 2).

753. *Diaeresis.*—When verse-foot and word-foot coincide, Diaeresis arises, marked ‖

Īte domum saturae † venit ‖ Hesperus ‖ īte capellae.—VERG.

REMARKS.—1. Diaeresis, like Caesura, serves to distribute the masses of the verse and prevent monotony. What is Caesura in an ascending rhythm becomes Diaeresis as soon as the rhythm is treated anacrustically.

Suīs | et i | psa † Rō | ma vī | ribus ‖ ruit. Iambic Trimeter.
Su : īs et ‖ ipsa ‖ Rōma ‖ vīri | bus † ru | it. Troch. Trimeter Catal., with Anacrusis.

2. Diaeresis at the end of the fourth foot of a Hexameter is called Bucolic Caesura, and has a special effect (783, R. 3).

754. *Recitation.*—When the word-foot runs over into the next verse-foot, a more energetic recitation is required, in order to preserve the sense, and hence the multiplication of Caesurae lends vigour to the verse.

REMARK.—The ordinary mode of scanning, or singing out the elements of a verse, without reference to signification, cannot be too strongly condemned, as,

Unasa, lusvic, tisnul, lamspe, raresa, lutem!

Numerus Italicus.

755. The oldest remains of Italian poetry are found in some fragments of ritualistic and sacred songs, and seem to have had no regard to quantity. No definite theory can be formed of this so-called *Numerus Ītalicus* in which they were composed, but they seem to have been in series of four Theses, usually united in pairs or triplets, but sometimes separate. An example is the prayer to Mars, from CATO, *Agr.*, 141.

Márs páter té précor | quáesóque úti síēs | vólēns própítiús
Míhī dómṓ | fámiliaéque nóstraé. *etc.*

Saturnian Verse.

756. The Saturnian verse is an old Italian rhythm which occurs in the earlier monuments of Latin literature. It divides itself into two parts, with three Theses in each ; but the exact metrical composition has been a matter of much dispute, the remains not being sufficient to admit of any dogmatism. The two principal theories are :

1. *The Quantitative Theory.*—The Saturnian is a six-foot verse with Anacrusis, and a Caesura after the third Arsis, or more rarely after the third Thesis.

Dabúnt malúm Metéllī | Naéviō poḗtae.
Cornḗliūs Lūcíus | Scípiṓ Barbā́tus.
Quōīūs fṓrma vírtūtḗi | parísumá fúit.
Eōrúm sectám sequóntur | múltī mórtā́lēs.

Notes.—1. The Thesis is formed by a long or two shorts ; the Arsis by a short, a long, or two shorts (not immediately before the Caesura). The Arsis may be wholly suppressed, most often the second Arsis of the second hemistich. Short syllables under the Ictus may be scanned long. Hiatus occurs everywhere, but usually in Caesura.

2. This theory is held by many scholars, but with various modifications. Thus, some do not accept the lengthening of the short syllables, others would scan by protraction four feet in each half verse, *etc.*

Dabúnt malúm Metéllí | Naéviō poḗtae, *etc.*

2. *The Accentual Theory.*—The Saturnian verse falls into two halves, the first of which has three Theses, the second usually three, sometimes two, in which case there is usually Anacrusis in the second hemistich. Quantity is not considered.

Dábunt málum Metéllī | Naéviō poḗtae.
Quōius fṓrma virtū́tei | parísuma fúit.

Notes.—1. Two accented syllables are regularly divided by a single unaccented syllable, except that between the second and third there are always two. Hiatus allowed only at Caesura.

2. A modification of this theory would scan

Dábunt málum Métellí | Naéviō poḗtaé.

3. Very recently a modification of the Accentual Theory has been proposed, which has much in its favor :

(*a*) The accent must fall on the beginning of each line, though it may be a secondary accent ; the first hemistich has three, the second has but two Theses.

(*b*) The first hemistich has normally seven syllables, the second six ; but an extra short syllable may be admitted where it would be wholly or partially suppressed in current pronunciation.

(*c*) After the first two feet there is an alternation between words accented on the first and those accented on the second syllable.

(*d*) A final short vowel is elided, otherwise semi-hiatus is the rule ; but there may be full Hiatus at the Caesura.

Dábunt málum Metéllī | Naéviō poḗtae.
Prī́m(a) incédit Céreris | Prosérpina púer.

Iambic Rhythms.

757. The Iambic Rhythm is an ascending rhythm, in which the Thesis is double of the Arsis. It is represented

By the Iambus : ∪ ∠ ;
By the Tribrach : ∪ ∪́ ∪ ;
By the Spondee : — ∠ ;
By the Dactyl : — ∪́ ∪ ;
By the Anapaest : ∪ ∪ ∠ ; and
By the Proceleusmaticus : ∪∪ ∪́ ∪.

REMARK.—The Spondee, Dactyl, Anapaest, and Proceleusmaticus are all irrational, and are consequently marked on the schemes thus: >—, > ∪ ∪, ∪∪—, ∪∪ ∪ ∪; see 744.

758. *Iambic Octōnārius* (*Tetrameter Acatalectic*).

Iūss(ī) ádparārī prándium ‖ amī-
c(a) exspectat mé, sciō, PL., *Men.*, 599. > ∠ ∪ — > ∠ ∪ ∪̄ ‖ ∪ ∠ > — > ∠ ∪ —
Hīc fínis est iámbe salvō † víndi-
cis doctór malī, SERVIUS. > ∠ ∪ — ∪ ∠ ∪ — > ∠ ∪ — > ∠ ∪ —

Anacrustic Scheme :

$\overset{>}{\smile}$: ∠ $\overset{(>)}{\smile}$ | — $\overset{>}{\smile}$ | ∠ $\overset{(>)}{\smile}$ | — $\overset{>}{\smile}$ | ∠ $\overset{(>)}{\smile}$ | — $\overset{>}{\smile}$ | ∠ ∪ | — ∧

NOTE.—This verse is predominantly a comic verse, occurring most frequently in TERENCE, who shows five hundred lines, while PLAUTUS shows but three hundred. The substitutions are the same as in the Senarius (761, N. 1). There are two varieties :

(*a*) That which is divided into two equal halves by Diæresis at the end of the fourth foot. In this case the fourth foot as well as the eighth has all the privileges of the final foot of the Senarius (Hiatus, Syllaba Anceps), and conforms also to its rules, so that the line is practically a distich of two Quaternarii ; but Hiatus after the fourth foot is denied for TERENCE.

(*b*) That which is divided into two unequal halves by a Cæsura after the fifth Arsis. Here the rules of the final foot apply only to the eighth, and the fourth may be a Spondee. The principle which governs the choice of words after the *sēmiquīnāria* in the Senarius applies here after the dividing Cæsura. The Hiatus comes under the general rules. From the earliest period there is a tendency to keep the even feet pure. This variety is preferred by TERENCE to the former. Examples of the two forms are :

Ō Trōia, Ō patria, Ō Pergamum, ‖ Ō Priame, periistī senex, PLAUT.
Is porrō m(ē) autem verberāt ‖ incursat pūgnīs calcibus, PLAUT.
Facil(e) omnēs quom valēmus rēcta | cōnsilia aegrōtīs damus, TER.

759. *Iambic Septēnārius* (*Tetrameter Catalectic*).

Remítte palliúm mihī ‖ meúm quod
involástī, CAT. ∪ ∠ ∪ — ∪ ∠ ∪ — ‖ ∪ ∠ ∪ — ∪ ∠ — ∧

Anacrustic Scheme:

⏒ : ∠(⏒) | – ⏒ | ∠(⏒) | – † ⏒ | ∠(⏒) | – (⏒) | ⏑́ – | – ∧

NOTES.—1. This verse is confined principally to PLAUTUS and TERENCE; it is to be regarded as a compound of Dimeter + Dimeter Catalectic: hence regular Diæresis after the fourth foot, which is treated as a final foot. The same rules, in regard to the various word-feet allowable, apply here as in the case of the Senarius (761, N. 6). Substitutions are allowable in every foot except in the fourth, when followed by a Diæresis.

With Syllaba Anceps:

Sī abdūxerīs cēlābitūr ‖ itidem ut cēlāta adhūc est, PLAUT.

With Hiatus:

Sed sī tibi vīgintī minae ‖ argentī prōferuntur, PLAUT.

2. Exceptionally in PLAUTUS, more often in TERENCE, the line is cut by Cæsura after the fifth Arsis. In this case the fourth foot has no exceptional laws except that if the seventh foot is not pure the fourth should be, though this is not absolutely necessary.

760. *The Iambic Sēnārius (a Stichic measure).* This is an imitation of the Iambic Trimeter of the Greeks, but differs from it in that it is a line of six separate feet and not of three dipodies. In the early Latin there is no distinction between the odd and even feet, such as prevails in the Greek Trimeter, but the same substitutions were allowable in the one as in the other. This distinction is regained in HORACE and SENECA, who follow the Greek treatment closely, and with whom the line may be with some degree of justice called the Iambic Trimeter, but it is very doubtful whether the Roman felt the Iambic Trimeter as did the Greek. In both Senarius and Trimeter the *last foot is always pure.*

761. The Early Use (*Sēnārius*).

Any substitution is allowed in any foot except the last.

Quamvīs sermōnēs† póssunt longī téxier, PL., *Trin.*, 797. > ∠ | > – | > ∠ | > – | > ∠ | ⏑ –

Quī scīre possīs † aút ingenium nṓscere, TER., *And.*, 53. > ∠ | ⏑ – | > ∠ | > ⏑⏑ | > ∠ | ⏑ –

S(ī) uxṓris † propter amṓrem†nōlit dúcere, TER., *And.*, 155. > ∠ | > – | ⏑⏑∠ | > – | > ∠ | ⏑ –

Dī fórtūnābunt†vóstra cōnsili(a). Íta volō, PL., *Trin.*, 576. > ∠ | > – | > ∠ | ⏑ – | ⏑⏑́⏑ | ⏑ –

Eī r(eī) óperam dare tē†fúerat aliquant(ō) aéquius, PL., *Trin.*, 119. > ⏑́⏑ | > ⏑⏑ | > ⏑́⏑ | ⏑⏑⏑ | > ∠ | ⏑ –

NOTES.—1. In the Iambic measure two shorts at the end of a polysyllabic word cannot stand in either Thesis or Arsis; hence such feet as **genéra, ma | tería,** would not be allowable. But a Dactyl is sometimes found in the first foot (TER., *Eun.*, 348). The two shorts of a Thesis cannot be divided between two words, when the second word is a polysyllable with the accent on the second syllable; hence **fingít amōrem** is faulty. The two shorts of an Arsis should not be divided between two words if the first short ends a word; but there are sundry exceptions; especially the case where two words are closely connected, as, for instance, a preposition and its case; **propter amōrem.**

2. The most frequent Cæsura is the *sēmiquīnāria*. Next comes the *sēmiseptēnāria*, which is usually accompanied by the *sēmiternāria* or by Diæresis after second foot. Examples above.

3. Elision is more frequent in the Iambic Senarius than in the Dactylic Hexameter, and occurs especially before the first and fifth Theses; also not unfrequently in the fourth foot. The proportion of elision varies between TERENCE (four elisions in every three verses) and HORACE (one in five stichic verses, and one in seven in distichs).

4. Semi-hiatus (720), also called *Graecānicus* or *Lēgitimus*, is very common both in Thesis and Arsis; Hiatus is also admitted at a change of speaker; whether it is admissible before proper names, foreign words, and in the principal Cæsura, is still a matter of dispute.

5. If the line is divided by the *sēmiquīnāria* Cæsura, and the fifth foot is formed by a single word, the second half of the third foot, together with the fourth, may be formed by a single word only when that is a Cretic or a Fourth Pæon; as, **fīlius bonān fidē** (PL., *Most.*, 670). Thus **dēpinxtī verbīs probē** would not be allowable for **verbīs dēpinxtī probē** (PL., *Poen.*, 1114).

6. To close the line with two Iambic feet was not allowable, except as follows: (1) When the line ends with a word of four syllables or more. (2) When the line ends with a Cretic. (3) When the line ends with an Iambic word preceded by an anapaest or Fourth Pæon. (4) When a change of person precedes the sixth foot. (5) When elision occurs in the fifth or sixth foot.

762. The Later Use (*Trimeter*).

Suís et ipsa † Rṓma vīribús ruit	∪ ∠ ∪ – | ∪ ∠ ∪ – | ∪ ∠ ∪ –
Heu mḗ per urbem † nám pudet tantí malī	> ∠ ∪ – | > ∠ ∪ – | > ∠ ∪ –
Dērípere lūnam † vṓcibus possím meīs	> ∪́ ∪ ∪ – | > ∠ ∪ – | > ∠ ∪ –
Īnfā́mis Helenae † Cástor offēnsus vicem	> ∠ ∪ ∪ ∪ | > ∠ ∪ – | > ∠ ∪ –
Optát quiētem † Pélopis īnfīdí pater	> ∠ ∪ – | > ∪́ ∪ ∪ – | > ∠ ∪ –
Ālítibus atque † cánibus homicī-d(am) Héctorem	> ∪́ ∪ ∪ – | ∪ ∪́ ∪ ∪ ∪ ∪ | > ∠ ∪ –
Vectā́bor humerīs † túnc eg(o) inimīcís eques	> ∠ ∪ ∪ ∪ | > ∠ ∪ ∪ ∪ | > ∠ ∪ –
Pavidúmque lepor(em) et † ádvenam laqueṓ gruem, HOR.	∪∪ ∠ ∪ ∪ ∪ | ∪ ∠ ∪ – | ∪∪ ∠ ∪ –

Anacrustic Scheme: ∪ : – ∪ | – >/∪ | – ∪ | – >/∪ | – ∪ | – ∧

NOTES.—1. The Iambic Trimeter, when kept pure, has a rapid aggressive movement. Hence, it is thus used in lampoons and invectives. It admits the Spondee in the odd places (first, third, fifth foot); the Tribrach in any but the last, though in HORACE it is excluded from the fifth foot; the Dactyl in the first and third. The Anapaest is rare. The Proceleusmaticus occurs only in SENECA and TERENTIANUS. When carefully handled, the closing part of the verse is kept light, so as to preserve the character. The fifth foot is pure in CATULLUS, but is almost always a Spondee in SENECA and PETRONIUS.

2. Diæresis at the middle of the verse is avoided. Short particles, which adhere closely to the following word, do not constitute exceptions.

Labōriōsa nec cohors Ulixeī, HOR.

Adulterētur et columba mīluō, HOR.

In like manner explain—

Refertque tanta grex amīcus ūbera, HOR.

3. The Cæsura is usually the *sēmiquīnāria*, but the *sēmiseptēnāria* is found also, but either with the *sēmiquīnāria* or with Diæresis after the second foot.

4. The *Sēnārius pūrus*, composed wholly of Iambi, is found first in CATULLUS (IV. and XXIX.); also in HORACE (*Epod.*, XVI.), VERGIL (*Cat.*, 3, 4, 8), and the *Priāpēa*.

5. Of course, in the Anacrustic Scheme, the Cæsura of the ordinary scheme becomes Diæresis.

Le : vis cre | pante ‖ lympha ‖ dēsi | lit pe | de.

763. *Iambic Trimeter Catalectic.*

Meā renīdet ín domō lacúnar ◡ ⏑́ ◡ — ◡ ⏑́ ◡ — ◡ ⏑́ ◡

Rēgúmque puerīs néc satelles Órcī, HOR. > ⏑́ ◡◡◡ > ⏑́ ◡ — ◡ ⏑́ ⏓

Anacrustic Scheme: > ◡ : ⏑́ ◡ | — > | ⏑́ ◡ | — ◡ | ⏑́ | — ∧ (with Syncopé).

NOTES.—This occurs in HORACE (*O.*, I. 4; II. 18). No resolutions are found except in the second line quoted, where **puerīs** may be dissyllabic (27), and the Spondee alone is used for the Iambus, mainly in the third foot. The Cæsura is always *sēmiquīnāria*.

764. *Trimeter Iambicus Claudus* (Chōliambus); *Scazon* (= *Hobbler*) Hippōnactēus.

Misér Catulle dḗsinās inéptīre, CAT. ◡ ⏑́ ◡ — ◡ ⏑́ ◡ — ◡ ⏑́ ⏑́ ◡

Fulsḗre quondam cándidī tibí sōlēs, CAT. > ⏑́ ◡ — > ⏑́ ◡ — ◡ ⏑́ ⏑́ —

Dominís parantur ísta; serviúnt vṓbīs, MART. ◡◡ ⏑́ ◡ — ◡ ⏑́ ◡ — ◡ ⏑́ ⏑́ —

Anacrustic Scheme: > ◡ : ⏑́ ◡ | — > ◡ | ⏑́ ◡ | — ◡ | ⏑́ | ⏑́ > ◡. Trochaic Trimeter with Anacrusis, Syncopé, and Protraction.

NOTES.—1. In the Choliambus the rhythm is reversed at the close, by putting a Trochee or Spondee in the sixth foot. The lighter the first part of the verse, the greater the surprise. It is intended to express comic anger, resentment, disappointment.

2. This metre, introduced into Rome by MATTIUS, was used frequently by CATULLUS and MARTIAL. PERSIUS also has it in his Prologue.

3. The Dactyl is occasional in the first and third feet, the Tribrach occurs very rarely in the first, more often in the third and fourth, frequently in the second. The Spondee is found in the first and third feet; the Anapaest only in the first.

4. The Cæsura is usually *sēmiquīnāria*, sometimes *sēmiseptēnāria*, which is regularly supported by Diæresis after the second foot.

765. *Iambic Quaternārius* (*Dimeter*).

Inársit aestuṓsius ◡ ⏑́ ◡ — ◡ ⏑́ ◡ —

Imbrḗs nivēsque cómparat > ⏑́ ◡ — ◡ ⏑́ ◡ —

Vidḗre properantḗs domum ◡ ⏑́ ◡◡◡ > ⏑́ ◡ —

Ást égo vicissim rísero, HOR. > ◡́◡◡ — > ⏑́ ◡ —

Anacrustic Scheme:

⏒ : – ⏒ | – ⏒ | – ⏑ | – ∧

NOTE.—This verse is constructed according to the principles which govern the Senarius and Octonarius. It is rare in systems until the time of SENECA, and is usually employed as a Clausula in connection with Octonarii and Septenarii (PLAUTUS, TERENCE), Senarii (HORACE), or Dactylic Hexameter (HORACE).

766. *Iambic Ternārius* (*Dimeter Catalectic*).

Id réppperí i(am) exémplum > ⏑́ ⏑ – > ⏑́ – or > : ⏑́ ⏑ ⏑́ > ⏑́ – ∧

NOTE.—This verse is found mainly in PLAUTUS and TERENCE, and used as a Clausula to Bacchic Tetrameters (PLAUTUS), Iambic Septenarii (PLAUTUS); but twice in TERENCE (*And.*, 485; *Hec.*, 731). It is found in systems first in PETRONIUS.

767. The *Iambic Tripody Catalectic* and the *Dipody Acatalectic* are found here and there.

Inóps amátor, *Trin.*, 256. **Bonu(s) sít bonís,** *B.*, 660.

Trochaic Rhythms.

768. The Trochaic Rhythm is a descending rhythm, in which the Thesis is double of the Arsis. It is represented,

By the Trochee: ⏑́ ⏑;
By the Tribrach: ⏑́ ⏑ ⏑;
By the Spondee: ⏑́ –;
By the Anapaest: ⏑́ ⏑ –;
By the Dactyl: ⏑́ ⏑ ⏑.
By the Proceleusmaticus: ⏑́ ⏑ ⏑⏑.

REMARK.—The Spondee, Anapaest, Dactyl, and Proceleusmaticus are all irrational and are accordingly measured – >, ⏑⏑ >, –⏑ ⏑ or – ⏑⏑, ⏑⏑ ⏑⏑; see 744.

769. *Trochaic Octōnārius* (*Tetrameter Acatalectic*).

Scheme: ⏑́ ⏒ – ⏒ ⏑́ ⏒ – ⏒ ‖ ⏑́ ⏒ – ⏒ ⏑́ ⏒ – ⏒

Párce iam camoéna vātī ‖ párce iam sacró furōrī.—SERVIUS.
Dáte viam quā fúgere liceat, ‖ fácite, tōtae pláteae pateant, PL., *Aul.*, 407.

NOTE.—This verse belongs to the cantica of early Comedy. It is properly a compound of two Quaternarii. Hence Hiatus and Syllaba Anceps are admitted in the Diæresis. A fourth or sixth Thesis, formed by the last syllable of a word forming or ending in a Spondee or Anapaest, was avoided, as was also a monosyllabic close. The Substitutions were allowed in all feet except the eighth, where the Tribrach is rare.

770. *Trochaic Septēnārius* (*Tetrameter Catalectic*).

Scheme: ⏑́ ⏒ – ⏒ ⏑́ ⏒ – ⏒ ⏑́ ⏒ – ⏒ ⏑́ ⏑ – ∧

Crās amet qui númqu(am) amāvit ‖ quíqu(e) amāvit crās amet.—Pervig. Ven.

Tū m(ē) amōris mági' qu(am) honōris ‖ sérvāvistī grātiā.—Ennius.

Vāpulār(e) ego tē vehementer ‖ iúbeō: nē mē térritēs.—Plaut.

Notes.—1. This is usually divided by a Diæresis after the fourth Arsis into two halves, with the license of a closing verse before the Diæresis; this is often supported by Diæresis after the second foot. Not unfrequently the line is divided by Cæsura after the fourth Thesis, which may in this case be Anceps or have Hiatus, though not in Terence; but other critics refuse to admit such a division, and prefer Diæresis after the fifth foot. The substitutions are allowable in any foot except the seventh, which is regularly kept pure, though occasionally in early Latin a Tribrach or a Dactyl occurs even here. But the Dactyl is rare in the fourth foot.

2. The rule for the words allowable after the *sēmiquīnāria* Cæsura in the Senarius (761, n. 5) apply here after the Diæresis, with the necessary modifications; that is, the second hemistich cannot be formed by a word occupying the fifth and the Thesis of the sixth foot, followed by a word occupying the two succeeding half feet, unless the first word is a Cretic or a Fourth Pæon.

3. In regard to the close the same rules apply as in the case of the Iambic Senarius (761, n. 6); in regard to the fourth and sixth Theses the rules are the same as for the Octonarius (769, n.).

4. The strict Septenarius of the later poets keeps the odd feet pure, and rigidly observes the Diæresis.

771. *Trochaic Tetrameter Claudus.*

Húnc Cerēs, cibī ministra, frūgibus suīs pórcet, Varro. ∠ ⏑ – ⏑ ∠ ⏑ – ⏑ ∠ ⏑ – ⏑ ∠ ∠ ⏑

Note.—This verse is found only in the *Menippean Satires* of Varro, and is formed, like the Iambic Senarius Claudus, by reversing the last two quantities.

772. *Trochaic Quaternārius with Anacrūsis.*

Sī frāctus illābātur orbis, Hor. ⏒ : ∠ ⏑ | – – | ∠ ⏑ | – ⏑̄

Note.—This occurs only in the *Alcaic* Strophe of Horace.

773. *Trochaic Ternārius (Dimeter Catalectic).*

Réspice vērō Théspriō, Pl., *Ep.*, 3. ⏑́⏑ ⏑ – > ∠ ⏑ – ∧

Nōn ebur nequ(e) aúreum, Hor. ∠ ⏑ – ⏑ ∠ ⏑ – ∧

Note.—An uncommon measure, confined mainly to early poetry and to Horace; it is used as a Clausula between Tetrameters (Plautus) and Iambic Senarii Catalectic (Horace), or in series. The third foot was kept pure; also the others in the strict measure.

774. The *Trochaic Tripody Acatalectic (Ithyphallic).*

Qu(om) ūsus est ut púdeat, Plaut., ∠ ⏑ – > ⏑́ ⏑ ⏑

Note.—This is rare, and appears only in early Latin and as a Clausula, usually with Cretics. Substitutions were allowable in every foot.

775. *Trochaic Tripody Catalectic.*

Éheu, qu(am) égo malís ‖ pérdidí modís,
Pl., *Ps.*, 259. –́ > ⏑́⏑ ⏑ ⏑ –́ ‖ –́ ⏑ –́ ⏑ –́

Note.—This is found occasionally in early Latin; usually two at a time, otherwise as a Clausula. When the first word is a Cretic the line may end in two Iambi.

776. *Trochaic Dipody (Monometer).*

Nímis inépta's, Pl., *Rud.*, 681. ⏑́⏑ ⏑ ⏑ –́ >/⏑

Note.—This is found occasionally as a Clausula with Cretic Tetrameters.

Anapaestic Rhythms.

777. The Anapaestic Rhythm is an ascending rhythm, in which the Thesis is to the Arsis as 2 to 2. It is represented,

By the Anapaest: ⏑ ⏑ –́;
By the Spondee: – –́;
By the Dactyl: – ⏑́⏑;
By the Proceleusmaticus: ⏑ ⏑ ⏑́⏑.

Notes.—1. The Anapaestic measure is not uncommon in the Cantica of Plautus; but it is the metre most subject to license of all the early metres. Notice especially the operation of the Iambic Law (716, 717); the common occurrence of Synizesis, of Diastolé, and less often of Syncopé, *etc.*

2. Strict Anapaestic lines after the model of the Greek are found only in Varro, Seneca, and later authors.

778. *Anapaestic Octōnārius (Tetrameter Acatalectic),* and *Anapaestic Septēnārius (Tetrameter Catalectic).*

Hostíbŭs victīs, cīvíbŭs salvīs ‖ rē plá- – ⏑́⏑ – – – ⏑́⏑ – – ‖
cidā, pācibŭs pérfectīs, *Pers.*, 753. – ⏑́⏑ – – ⏑⏑ –́ – –
Septŭmās ess(e) aedīs ā portā † ‖ ub(i) – ⏑́⏑ – – – –́ – – ‖
ĭll(e) hábitat lēnō quoí iŭssit, *Ps.*, 597. ⏑ ⏑ ⏑́⏑ – – – –́ – –

Ait íllam miseram, crúciār(ī) et lacru- ⏑ ⏑ –́ – ⏑⏑ – ⏑́ ⏑ – – ‖
mántem s(ē) adflīctāre, Pl., *M.G.*, 1032. ⏑ ⏑ –́ – – – –́ – ⊼
Erit ét tib(i) ĕxoptāt(um) óbtinget ‖ bo- ⏑ ⏑ –́ ⏑ ⏑ – – –́ – – ‖
n(um) hab(e) ánimum nē formídā, Pl., *M.G.*, 1011. ⏑ ⏑ ⏑́⏑ – – – –́ – ⊼

Notes.—1. These have regularly the Diæresis after the fourth foot, dividing the line into Quaternarii. Before the Diæresis, the licenses of a closing foot (Hiatus and Syllaba Anceps) are occasionally found.

2. In the Septenarius the seventh Thesis may be resolved, but the resolution of the eighth in the Octonarius is avoided.

779. *Anapaestic Trimeter Catalectic.*

Perspíciō nihilī meám vōs grātíām fácere,
Pl., *Curc.*, 155. – ⏑́⏑ – ⏑⏑ – –́ – – – ⏑́⏑ – ∧

Note.—This verse is very rare, and is denied by some critics; it has the same treatment as the Septenarius.

780. *Anapaestic Quaternārius (Dimeter Acatalectic).*

Veniént annīs ‖ saecúla sērīs ∪ ∪ ∠ — — — ∪́∪ — —
Quibus Ōceanus ‖ vincúla rērum ∪ ∪ ∠ ∪ ∪ — — ∪́∪ — —
Laxét et ingēns ‖ pateát tellūs — ∪́∪ — — ∪ ∪ ∠ — —
Tēthýsque novōs ‖ dētégat orbēs — ∠ ∪ ∪ — — ∪́∪ — —
Nec sít terrīs ‖ ūltíma Thūlē.—SEN. TRAG. — ∠ — — — ∪́∪ — —

NOTE.—This verse avoids resolution of the fourth Thesis: Syllaba Anceps and Hiatus are rare.

781. *Anapaestic Dimeter Catalectic (Paroemiac).*

Volucér pede corpore púlcher ∪ ∪ ∠ ∪ ∪ — ∪ ∪ ∠ ∪
Linguá catus óre canṓrus — ∠ ∪ ∪ — ∪ ∪ ∠ ∪
Vērúm memoráre magís quam — ∠ ∪ ∪ — ∪ ∪ ∠ ∪
Fūnctúm laudāre decḗbit.—AUSON. — ∠ — — ∪ ∪ ∠ ∪

NOTES.—1. This verse is not common except as the close of a system of Anapaestic Acatalectic Dimeters. It allows in early Latin resolution of the third Thesis.

2. Latin Anapaests, as found in later writers, are mere metrical imitations of the Greek Anapaests, and do not correspond to their original in contents. The Greek Anapaest was an anacrustic dactylic measure or march (in ⁴⁄₄ time). Hence the use of Pause to bring out the four bars.

Paroemiacus: *Anacrustic Scheme.*

Volucer pede corpore pulcher ∪ ∪ : — ∪ ∪ | — ∪ ∪ | — — | — ∧

Dimeter Acatalectic: *Anacrustic Scheme.*

Quibus Ōceanus vincula rērum ∪ ∪ : — ∪ ∪ | — — | ∪ ∪ — ⁞ —

The Arses of the last feet are supplied by the Anacrusis of the following verse.

782. *Anapaestic Dipody (Monometer Acatalectic).*

Omné parātúmst, PL., *Min.*, 365 — ∪́∪ — ∠

NOTE.—This verse is found in anapaestic systems between Anapaestic Dimeters.

Dactylic Rhythms.

783. The Dactylic Rhythm is a descending rhythm, in which the Thesis is equal to the Arsis (2 = 2).

The Dactylic Rhythm is represented by the Dactyl: ∠ ∪ ∪.

Often, also, by the Spondee: ∠ —.

784. *Dactylic (Heroic) Hexameter.*—The Heroic Hexameter is composed of two Dactylic tripodies, the second of which ends in a Spondee. Spondees may be substituted for the Dactyl in the first four feet; in the fifth foot, only when a special effect is to be produced. Such verses are called Spondaic. The longest Hexameter contains five Dactyls and one Spondee (or Trochee)—in all, seventeen syllables; the shortest in use, five Spondees and one Dactyl—in all, thirteen syllables. This variety in the length of the verse, combined with the great number of cæsural pauses, gives the Hexameter peculiar advantages for continuous composition.

Scheme: ″́⏑⏑ | ́⏑⏑ | ́⏑⏑ | ″́⏑⏑ | ́⏑⏑ (–) | ́–

	Verse	
1.	**Ut fugiunt aquilās † timidissima ‖ turba columbae.** Ov.	Five Dactyls.
2.	**At tuba terribilī † sonitū † procul ‖ aere canōrō.** Verg.	
3.	**Quadrupedante putrem † sonitū | quatit ‖ ungula campum.** Verg.	
4.	**Cum mediō celerēs † revolant | ex aequore mergī.** Verg.	Four Dactyls.
5.	**Vāstius īnsurgēns † decimae | ruit ‖ impetus undae.** Ov.	
6.	**Et reboat raucum † regiō † cita ‖ barbara | bombum.** Lucr.	
7.	**Mūta metū terram † genibus † summissa petēbat.** Lucr.	Three Dactyls.
8.	**Inter cunctantēs † cecidit † moribunda ministrōs.** Verg.	
9.	**Nē turbāta volent † rapidīs † lūdibria ventīs.** Verg.	
10.	**Versaqu(e) in obnīxōs † urgentur ‖ cornua vāstō.** Verg.	Two Dactyls.
11.	**Prōcēssit longē † flammantia ‖ moenia mundī.** Lucr.	
12.	**Portam vī multā † conversō ‖ cardine torquet.** Verg.	One Dactyl.
13.	**Tēct(um) august(um) ingēns † centum sublīme columnīs.** Verg.	
14.	**Ollī respondit † Rēx Albāī Longāī.** Ennius.	No Dactyl.
15.	**Aut lēvēs ocreās † lentō † dūcunt argentō.** Verg.	Spondaic Verses.
16.	**Sunt apud īnfernōs † tot mīlia fōrmōsārum.** Prop.	
17.	**Āëriaeque Alpēs † et nūbifer ‖ Appennīnus.** Ov.	
18.	**Prōcubuit viridī- | qu(e) in lītore ‖ cōnspicitur—sūs.** Verg.	Monosyllabic ending.
19.	**Parturiunt montēs † nāscētur ‖ rīdiculus—mūs.** Hor.	
20.	10 +6 = 16 8 **Nāscere, praeque diem†veniēns age,‖Lūcifer,almum.** Verg.	Semiquin. and Bucolic.
21.	**Īnsīgnem pietāte † virum † tot adīre labōrēs.** Verg.	Third Trochee and Semisept.
22.	**Et nigrae violae † sunt ‖ et vaccīnia | nigra.** Verg.	Split in half.
23.	**Sparsīs ‖ hastīs ‖ longīs ‖ campus ‖ splendet et horret.** En.	Shivered.
24.	**Quamvīs sint sub aquā sub aquā maledīcere tentant.** Ov.	a - sound.
25.	**Mē m(ē) adsum qui fēc(ī) in mē convertite ferrum.** Verg.	e - sound.
26.	**Discissōs nūdōs laniābant dentibus artūs.** Verg.	s - sound.

Notes.—1. The two reigning ictuses are the first and fourth, and the pauses are so arranged as to give special prominence to them—the first by the pause at the end of the preceding verse, the fourth by pauses within the verse, both before and after the Thesis.

2. The principal Cæsura is the *sēmiquīnāria* or *penthemimeral*, *i. e.*, after the Thesis of the third foot, or Masculine Cæsura of the third foot; the next is the *sēmiseptēnāria* or *hepthemimeral*, after the Thesis of the fourth foot; but usually supplemented by the *sēmiternāria* in the Thesis of the second or by one after the second Trochee; then the Feminine Cæsura of the third foot, the so-called *Third Trochee*, which is less used among the Romans than among the Greeks. As Latin poetry is largely rhetorical, and the Cæsura is of more importance for recitation than for singing, the Roman poets are very exact in the observance of these pauses.

In verses with several Cæsuræ, the *sēmiseptēnāria* outranks the *sēmiquīnāria*, if it precedes a period, and the latter does not, or if it is perfect and the latter is imperfect (*i.e.*, formed by tmesis or by elision); it also as a masculine Cæsura outranks the Third Trochee as a feminine. In other cases there may be doubt as to the principal Cæsura.

3. The Diæresis which is most carefully avoided is the one after the third foot, especially if that foot ends in a Spondee, and the verse is thereby split in half.

Examples are found occasionally, and if the regular Cæsura precedes, the verse is not positively faulty.

Hīs lacrimīs vītam † damus ‖ — et miserēscimus ūltrō.—VERG.

It is abominable when no other Cæsura proper is combined with it.

Poenī ‖ pervortentēs ‖ omnia ‖ circumcursant.—ENNIUS.

On the other hand the Diæresis at the end of the fourth foot divides the verse into proportionate parts (sixteen and eight *morae*, or two to one), and gives a graceful trochaic movement to the hexameter. This is called the Bucolic Cæsura, and while common in Greek, is not so in Latin even in bucolic poetry. JUVENAL, however, is fond of it, showing one in every fifteen verses.

Īte domum saturae | venit Hesperus ‖ īte capellae.—VERG.

4. Verses without Cæsura are very rare; a few are found in ENNIUS (see No. 23) and LUCILIUS. HORACE uses one designedly in *A.P.*, 263.

5. Elision is found most often in VERGIL (one case in every two verses) and least often in LUCAN (leaving out ENNIUS and CLAUDIAN). CATULLUS, JUVENAL, HORACE, OVID stand about midway between these two extremes. It is very rare in the Thesis of the first foot, and is found oftenest in the following order: the Thesis of the second foot, the Arsis of the fourth, the Arsis of the first, the Thesis of the third.

6. Simple Hiatus is very rare in lines composed wholly of Latin words, except at the principal Cæsura; it is found after a final short syllable (excluding **-m**) but twice (V., *Ec.*, II. 53; *A.*, I. 405); after a long monosyllable (omitting Interjections **o** and **ā**) but once (V., *A.*, IV. 235). But before the principal Cæsura, or if the line contains a Greek word, examples are not very uncommon. VERGIL has altogether about forty cases; HORACE shows two cases (*S.*, I. 1, 108; *Epod.*, 13, 3); CATULLUS two in the Hexameter of the Elegiac Distich (66, 11; 107, 1); PROPERTIUS one (III. 7, 49).

7. Of Semi-hiatus VERGIL shows some ten examples at the close of the Dactyl, but all of Greek words except *A.*, III. 211; *Ec.*, 3, 79; there are occasional examples elsewhere, as in PROPERTIUS, HORACE, *etc.* There are also several examples of Semi-hiatus after a monosyllable in the first short of the Dactyl, as: CAT., XCVII. 1; V., *A.*, VI. 507; HOR., *S.*, I. 9, 38. Hiatus after *num* occurs in HOR., *S.*, II. 2, 28.

8. VERGIL is fond of Diastolé, showing fifty-seven cases, all except three (*A.*, III. 464, 702; XII. 648) of syllables ending in a consonant; HORACE, in *Satires* and *Epistles*, has eleven, once only of a vowel (*S.*, II. 3, 22); CATULLUS, three; PROPERTIUS, three; TIBULLUS, four; MARTIAL (in the Distich), two; VERGIL also lengthens **que** sixteen times, but only when **que** is repeated in the verse, and before two consonants or a double consonant (except *A.*, III. 91); OVID exercises no such care.

9. A short syllable formed by a final short vowel remains short before two consonants, of which the second is not a liquid (mainly **sc, sp, st**), especially in the fifth foot, less often in the first. LUCILIUS, LUCRETIUS, and ENNIUS have numerous examples of this; VERGIL but one case (*A.*, XI. 309), except before **z**; HORACE has eight cases in the *Satires*; PROPERTIUS six; TIBULLUS two cases, one before **smaragdos.**

10. A Hexameter should close (*a*) with a dissyllable preceded by a polysyllable of at least three syllables, or (*b*) with a trisyllable preceded by a word of at least two syllables. The preposition is proclitic to its case. Exceptions to this rule are common in early Latin, but decrease later. Thus ENNIUS shows fourteen per cent. of exceptional lines. In later times artistic reasons sometimes caused the employment even of a monosyllable at the end (see exs. 18, 19).

11. Spondaic lines are exceptional in ENNIUS and LUCRETIUS, more common in

CATULLUS, rare in VERGIL, OVID, HORACE, never in TIBULLUS. The stricter poets required that in this case the fourth foot should be a Dactyl, and then the two last feet were usually a single word. Entirely Spondaic lines are found in ENNIUS (three cases, as *Ann.*, I. 66, M.) and CAT. (116, 3).

12. ENNIUS shows three peculiar cases of the resolution of the Thesis in the Dactyl, *Ann.*, 267 ; *Sat.*, 53 and 59.

13. Hypermetrical verses running into the next by Synapheia are rare ; *e.g.*, LUCR., V. 846 ; CAT., 64, 298 ; 115, 5. VERGIL has twenty cases, usually involving **que** or **ve**, but twice **-m** (*A.*, VII. 160 ; *G.*, I., 295) ; three other cases are doubtful. HORACE has two cases (in the *Satires*), OVID three, VALERIUS FLACCUS one. HORACE has also four cases of two verses united by tmesis of a compound word.

14. Pure dactylic lines are rare ; the most usual forms of the first four feet of the stichic measure are these : DSSS, 15 per cent. ; DSDS, 11.8 per cent. ; DDSS, 11 per cent. ; SDSS, 10 per cent. The most uncommon are SSDD, 1.9 per cent. ; SDDD, 2 per cent. The proportion of Spondee to Dactyl in the first four feet varies from 65.8 per cent. of Spondee in CATULLUS to 45.2 per cent. in OVID. The following statements are from Drobisch : (*a*) Excepting ENNIUS, CICERO, and SILIUS ITALICUS, Latin poets have more Dactyls than Spondees in the first foot. (*b*) Excepting LUCRETIUS, more Spondees in the second. (*c*) Excepting VALERIUS FLACCUS, more Spondees in the third. (*d*) Without exception, more Spondees in the fourth.

15. Much of the beauty of the Hexameter depends on the selection and arrangement of the words, considered as metrical elements. The examples given above have been chosen with especial reference to the picturesque effect of the verse. Monosyllables at the end of the Hexameter denote surprise ; anapaestic words, rapid movement, and the like.

Again, the Hexameter may be lowered to a conversational tone by large masses of Spondees, and free handling of the Cæsura. Compare the Hexameters of HORACE in the *Odes* with those in the *Satires*.

785. *Elegiac Pentameter* (*Catalectic Trimeter repeated*).

The Elegiac Pentameter consists of two Catalectic Trimeters or Penthemimers, *the first of which admits Spondees, the second does not.* There is a fixed Diæresis in the middle of the verse, as marked above, which is commonly supplemented by the *sēmiternāria* Cæsura. The Pentameter derives its name from the old measurement: — ⏑ ⏑, — ⏑ ⏑, — —, ⏑ ⏑ —, ⏑ ⏑ — ; and the name is a convenient one, because the verse consists of 2½ + 2½ Dactyls. The Elegiac Distich is used in sentimental, amatory, epigrammatic poetry.

The musical measurement of the Pentameter is as follows :

— ⏑̄⏑ | — ⏑̄⏑ | ⌴ ‖ — ⏑ ⏑ | — ⏑ ⏑ | — —
^

This shows why neither Syllaba Anceps nor Hiatus is allowed at the Diæresis, and explains the preference for length by nature at that point.

Át dolor ín lacrimā́s ‖ vérterat ómne merúm, TIB.	⏒ ⏑ ⏑ ⏒ ⏑ ⏑ ⏒	
Mḗ legat ét lēctṓ ‖ cármine dóctus amét, OV.	⏒ ⏑ ⏑ ⏒ — ⏒	⏒ ⏑ ⏑ ⏒ ⏑ ⏑ ⏒
Át nunc bárbariḗs ‖ grándis habḗre nihíl, OV.	⏒ — ⏒ ⏑ ⏑ ⏒	
Cóncēssúm nūllā́ ‖ lḗge redíbit iter, PROP.	⏒ — ⏒ — ⏒	

The Elegiac Pentameter occurs only as a Clausula to the Heroic Hexameter, with which it forms the Elegiac Distich. Consequently the sense should not run into the following Hexameter (exceptions rare):

Saep(e) ego tentāvī cūrās dēpellere vīnō
At dolor in lacrimās ‖ verterat omne merum, TIB.
Ingenium quondam fuerat pretiōsius aurō
At nunc barbariēs ‖ grandis habēre nihil, OV.
Pār erat īnferior versus: rīsisse Cupīdō
Dīcitur atque ūnum ‖ surripuisse pedem, OV.
Saep(e) ego cum dominae dulcēs ā līmine dūrō
Āgnōscō vōcēs ‖ haec negat esse domī, TIB.

NOTES.—1. In the first two feet of the Pentameter, which alone can suffer variation, the forms are as follows: DS, 46 per cent.; DD, 24.5 per cent.; SS, 16 per cent.; SD, 13.5 per cent. CATULLUS, however, has SS, 34.5 per cent.

2. Elision is rare, especially in the second hemistich. When it occurs it is generally in the first Arsis or second Thesis, and usually affects a short vowel or **-m.** CATULLUS shows the greatest proportion of examples, OVID the smallest. Except in CATULLUS and LYGDAMUS there are fewer cases of Elision in the Pentameter than in the Hexameter.

3. Elision and Diastolé in the Diæresis are rare. CATULLUS especially, and PROPERTIUS occasionally, have Elision. PROPERTIUS and MARTIAL show each two cases of Diastolé (PROP., II. 8, 8; II. 24, 4; MART., IX. 101, 4; XIV. 77, 2).

4. A final short vowel before two consonants, one of which is a liquid or **s**, is lengthened twice in TIBULLUS, and remains short once in PROPERTIUS (TIB., I. 5, 28; I. 6, 34; PROP., IV. 4, 48).

5. Dialysis occurs in compounds of **solvō** and **volvō**; as, CAT., 66, 74; TIB., I. 7, 2, *etc.*

6. In the strict handling of the Pentameter by OVID, the rule was that it should close with a dissyllable. So in his *Amores*, OVID shows no example of any other ending; and in his *Tristia* the proportion is one in one hundred and forty lines. In earlier times, however, there was no especial avoidance of polysyllabic endings, though more are found in CATULLUS than in any other author. Peculiar is PROPERTIUS, who, while almost equalling CATULLUS in his disregard of the law of the dissyllabic ending in the first book, equals the *Tristia* of OVID in the observance of it in his fourth. With dissyllabic ending the prevailing forms of the second Hemistich are — ⏑ ⏑, — ⏑, ⏑ —, and — ⏑, ⏑ — ⏑, ⏑ —, but TIBULLUS and OVID, and in less degree CATULLUS, employ quite often — ⏑ ⏑ — ⏑, ⏑ — and —, ⏑ ⏑, — ⏑, ⏑ —.

786. *Dactylic Tetrameter Acat.* (*metrum Alcmānium*).

Núnc decet aút viridí nitidúm caput	∠ ⏑ ⏑ ∠ ⏑ ⏑ ∠ ⏑ ⏑ ∠ ⏑ ⏑
Pállida mórs aequṓ pulsát pede	∠ ⏑ ⏑ ∠ — ∠ — ∠ ⏑ ⏑
Vítae súmma brevís spem nṓs vetat	∠ — ∠ ⏑ ⏑ ∠ — ∠ ⏑ ⏑

This verse occurs mainly in combination with an *Ithyphallic* to form the *Greater Archilochian* verse; occasionally in stichic composition in SENECA; also in TER., *And.*, 625.

787. *Dactylic Tetrameter Cat. in Dissyllabum* (*Archilochium*).

Aút Ephesón bimarísve Corínthī	∠ ⏑ ⏑ ∠ ⏑ ⏑ ∠ ⏑ ⏑ ∠ ⏓
Ṓ fortēs pēiṓraque pássī	∠ — ∠ — ∠ ⏑ ⏑ ∠ ⏓
Mḗnsōrém cohibént Archȳ́ta, HOR.	∠ — ∠ ⏑ ⏑ ∠ — ∠ ⏓

NOTE.—This line, which only occurs in the *Alcmanian System*, may also be looked upon as an Acatalectic Tetrameter with a spondaic close.

788. *Dactylic Trimeter Catalectic in Syllabam (Lesser Archilochian).*

Púlvis et úmbra sumús, HOR. ∠ ∪ ∪ ∠ ∪ ∪ ∠

NOTE.—This line occurs mainly in the first three *Archilochian* Strophes.

789. *Dactylic Dimeter Catalectic in Dissyllabum* (***Adōnic***).

Térruit úrbem, HOR. ∠ ∪ ∪ ∠ ∪̲

NOTE.—Though generally measured thus, this verse is properly logaœdic, and will recur under that head (792). It occurs mainly in the *Sapphic* stanza, and at the close of series of Sapphic Hendecasyllabics in SENECA.

Logaœdic Rhythms.

790. The Logaœdic Rhythm is a peculiar form of the Trochaic rhythm, in which the Arsis has a stronger secondary ictus than the ordinary Trochee.

Instead of the Trochee, the cyclic Dactyl or the irrational Trochee may be employed. This cyclic Dactyl is represented in morae by $1\frac{1}{2}$, $\frac{1}{2}$, 1; in music, by  $= \frac{3}{16}, \frac{1}{16}, \frac{1}{8}$.

When Dactyls are employed, the Trochee preceding is called a Basis, or *Tread,* commonly marked ×. If the basis is double, the second is almost always irrational in Latin poetry. Instead of the Trochee, an Iambus is sometimes prefixed. Anacrusis and Syncopé are also found.

REMARKS.—1. Logaœdic comes from λόγος, *prose,* and ἀοιδή, *song,* perhaps because the rhythms seem to vary as in prose.

2. Dactyls are usually, but not necessarily, employed.

No Dactyl.

791. *Alcaic Enneasyllabic.*

Sí frāctus illābātur orbis, HOR. ⏑/> : ∠ ∪ ∠ > ∠ ∪ ∠ ∪

NOTE.—The Anacrusis should be long. HORACE shows no exceptions in the fourth book and very few in the first three. The regular Cæsura is the *sēmiquīnāria.*

One Dactyl.

792. *Adōnic.*

Térruit úrbem, HOR. ∠∪∪ | ∠ >/∪ |

NOTE.—Elision is not allowed in this verse. As far as its formation is concerned, it should consist either of a dissyllable + a trisyllable, or the reverse. Proclitics and enclitics go with their principals.

793. *Aristophanic* (*Choriambic*).

Lýdia díc per ómnēs, Hor. ⏖⏑ | –́⏑ | ⏕ | –́ ∧

Note.—This verse occurs mainly in the lesser *Sapphic* Strophe of Horace.

One Dactyl, with Basis.

794. *Pherecratēan.*

Nígrīs aéquora véntīs, Hor. ×–́> | ⏖⏑ | ⏕ | – ∧

Note.—This verse occurs in the fourth *Asclepiadēan* Strophe of Horace; also in Catullus (xvii.) and the *Priāpēa*. No Elision is allowed by Horace, and there is no regular Cæsura.

795. *Glycōnic.*

Ēmīrābitur ínsoléns, Hor. ×–́> | ⏖⏑ | –́⏑ | – ∧

Note.—This occurs in the second, third, and fourth *Asclēpiadēan* strophes of Horace; also in Catullus (xvii.) and the *Priāpēa*. There is generally the *sēmiternāria* Cæsura; occasionally instead of it a Second Trochee. Elision of long syllables is very rare in Horace; Elision of a short before the long of the Dactyl more often. Horace also shows occasional liberties, such as Diastolé (*O.*, iii. 24, 5), Dialysis (*O.*, i. 23, 4), and lines ending with monosyllables (*O.*, i. 3, 19; i. 19, 13; iv. 1, 33).

796. *Phalaecēan* (*Hendecasyllabic*).

Pásser mórtuus ést meaé puéllae. –́ ⏑ ×
Árida modo pūmic(e) éxpolítum –́ >
Tuaé Lésbia sínt satís supérque. Cat. ⏑ : ⏕
} ⏖⏑ | –́⏑ | –́⏑ | –́ ⏑̄

Notes.—1. This verse, introduced into Latin by Laevius, was used very often by Catullus, Martial, Pliny Minor, Petronius, and Statius, as well as in the *Priāpēa* and elsewhere.

2. In Greek the Basis was not unfrequently an Iambus. So, too, in Catullus, but the tendency in Latin was to make it a Spondee; thus, in the *Priāpēa*, Petronius, and Martial it is always so, while Statius has but one case of a Trochee, and Ausonius but one of an Iambus.

3. The principal Cæsura is the *sēmiquīnāria;* but Catullus uses also almost as frequently Diæresis after the second foot. Occasionally there is a Diæresis after the third foot, supplemented by a Second Trochee Cæsura.

4. Elision is very common in Catullus; in the *Priāpēa*, Martial, and later it is very rare, if we exclude Aphæresis from consideration. Hardening (723) is occasional, and Catullus shows a few cases of Semi-hiatus. A monosyllabic ending is very rare, with the exception of **es** and **est**.

5. Catullus, in 55, apparently shows a mixture of regular Phalaeceans and spurious Phalaeceans in which the Dactyl is supplanted by a Spondee. The poem is still under discussion.

One Dactyl, with Double Basis.

797. *Sapphic* (*Hendecasyllabic*).

Aúdiét cīvḗs † acuísse férrum, Hor. –×⏑ | –×> | – † ⏖ | – ⏑ | – ⏑

Notes.—1. In the Greek measure, often retained in Catullus, the Dactyl is measured ⏖⏑; in Horace, owing to a strong Cæsura after the long it is regularly – ⏖.

Further, CATULLUS, like the Greeks, employed occasionally a Trochee in the second foot ; HORACE made it a rule to employ only a Spondee there.

2. The regular Cæsura in Latin is the *sēmiquīnāria* ; but the *Third Trochee* (784, N. 2) is found not unfrequently in CATULLUS and HORACE, but not later. The usage of HORACE is peculiar in this respect : In the first and second books there are seven cases in two hundred and eighty-five verses ; in the third none at all ; in the fourth twenty-two in one hundred and five verses ; in the *Carmen Sæculare* nineteen in fifty-seven verses.

3. Elision is very common in CATULLUS, but occurs in HORACE only in about one verse in ten. Later usage tends to restrict Elision. Licenses are extremely rare in the classical period. So HORACE shows one example of Diastolé (*O.*, II. 6, 14). Monosyllabic endings are not common, but the word is usually attached closely with what precedes. The last syllable is regularly long.

4. SENECA shows some peculiarities : occasionally a Dactyl in the second foot, or a Spondee in the third ; occasionally also Dialysis.

One Dactyl with Double Basis and Anacrusis.

798. *Alcaic (Greater) Hendecasyllabic.*

Vidḗs ut áltā ‖ stḗt nive cándidúm > : –́ ⏑ | –́ > | –́⏑ ⏑ | –́ ⏑ | –́ ∧
Sōrácte néc iam ‖ sústineánt onús, HOR.

NOTES.—1. The second Basis is always a Spondee ; the few exceptions having been emended. The Anacrusis is regularly long ; HORACE shows no exception in the fourth book and very few in the first three. The last syllable may be long or short.

2. The regular Cæsura is a Diæresis after the second foot ; HORACE shows but two exceptions in six hundred and thirty-four verses (*O.*, I. 37, 14 ; IV. 14, 17). A few others show imperfect Cæsuræ, as *O.*, I. 16, 21 ; I. 37, 5 ; II. 17, 21.

3. In regard to Elision, the facts are the same as in the case of the Sapphic.

4. Licenses are not common : Diastolé occurs in H., *O.*, III. 5, 17 ; Hardening (723) occurs in H., *O.*, III. 4, 41 ; III. 6, 6. Tmesis is not unfrequent in forms of **quīcumque** (H., *O.*, I. 9, 14 ; I. 16, 2 ; I. 27, 14).

Two Dactyls.

799. *Alcaic (Lesser) or Decasyllabic.*

Vértere fūneribús triúmphōs, HOR. –́⏑ ⏑ | –́⏑ ⏑ | –́ ⏑ | –́ ⏑̄

NOTE.—The Cæsura is regularly the *sēmiternāria*, occasionally the Second Trochee. Elision occurs a little less often in this measure than in the Hendecasyllabic. The last syllable is usually long. Diastolé occurs in H., *O.*, II. 13, 16.

In all these, the Dactyl has a diminished value. More questionable is the logaœdic character of the Greater Archilochian :

800. *Archilochian (Greater) = Dactylic Tetrameter and Trochaic Tripody.*

–́ ⏑⏑ | –́ ⏑⏑ | –́ ⏑⏑ | –́ ⏑⏑ ‖ –́ ⏑ | –́ ⏑ | –́ ⏑̄
Sólvitur ācris hiéms grātā́ vice ‖ vḗris ét Favṓnī, HOR.

If measured logaœdically, the two shorts of the Dactyl must be reduced in value to one (⏖ = ⏑), and the logaœdic scheme is

– ⏖> | – ⏖> | – ⏖> | – ⏖> ‖ – ⏑ | – ⏑ | ⏗ | – ∧

Logaœdic tetrapody + Logaœdic tetrapody with Syncopé.

NOTE.—Diæresis is always found after the fourth foot, which is always Dactylic. The principal Cæsura is the *sēmiquīnāria*. In the third foot a Spondee is preferred, whereas the Greek model has more often the Dactyl.

801. *Choriambic Rhythms.*—When a logaœdic series is syncopated, apparent choriambi arise. What is | ⏘⏑ | ⏗ | seems to be – ⏑ ⏑ –. Genuine choriambi do not exist in Latin, except, perhaps, in the single line PL., *Men.*, 110.

802. *Asclēpiadēan* (*Lesser*).

This verse is formed by a Catalectic Pherecratean followed by a Catalectic Aristophanic.

Máecēnās atavís ‖ ēdite régibús, HOR.

×
–> | ⏘⏑ | ⏗ ‖ ⏘⏑ | ⏕⏑ | ⏕ ∧

NOTES.—1. There should be Diæresis, complete or incomplete (*i.e.*, weakened by Elision), between the two halves. Only two exceptions are cited (H., *O.*, II. 12, 25; IV. 8, 17). The Cæsura is regularly the *sēmiternāria* in HORACE, less often the Second Trochee.

2. Elision occurs about as often as in the Elegiac Pentameter. It occurs most often in the first Dactyl and in the stichic measure. The final syllable may be short or long; but a monosyllable is rare. Licenses are likewise rare, as Diastolé (H., *O.*, I. 3, 36).

803. *Asclēpiadēan* (*Greater*).

Nūllam Vāre sacrā ‖ víte priús ‖ sēveris árborem, HOR.

×
⏕> | ⏘⏑ | ⏗ ‖ ⏘⏑ | ⏗ ‖ ⏘⏑ | ⏕⏑ | ⏕ ∧

NOTE.—This verse differs from the preceding by having a Catalectic Adonic (792) inserted between the two halves. Diæresis always separates the parts in HORACE. The rules of Elision are the same as in the preceding verse.

804. *Sapphic* (*Greater*).

Tē deōs ōrō Sybarín ‖ cūr properās amándō, HOR.

× ×
⏕⏑ | ⏕> | ⏘⏑ | ⏗ ‖ ⏘⏑ | ⏕⏑ | ⏗ | – ∧

NOTE.—This verse differs from the lesser Sapphic by the insertion of a catalectic Adonic. It is found only in HORACE (*O.*, I. 8). Diæresis always occurs after the fourth foot, and there is also a *sēmiquīnāria* Caesura.

805. *Priăpēan* (*Glyconic* + *Pherecratēan*).

Hū́nc lūcū́m tibi dḗdicṓ ‖ cṓnsecrṓque Priā́pe, CAT.

× ×

–́ > | –́⏑⏑ | –́ ⏑ | –́ ‖ –́ > | –́⏑⏑ | –́ | –́ ∧

NOTE.—Diæresis always follows the Glyconic, but neither Hiatus nor **Syllaba Anceps is** allowable. The verse occurs in CAT. 17 and *Priap.* 85.

Cretic and Bacchic Rhythms.

806. These passionate rhythms are found not unfrequently in PLAUTUS and occasionally elsewhere. They both belong to the Quinquepartite or Five-Eighths class.

The distribution of the Crēticus is 3 + 2 morae.

The metrical value of the Crēticus is – ⏑ – (Amphimacer).

For it may be substituted the First Pæon, – ⏑ ⏑ ⏑, or the Fourth Pæon, ⏑ ⏑ ⏑ –.

NOTE.—Double resolution in the same foot is not allowable, and there is rarely more than one resolution in a verse. Instead of the middle short an irrational long is sometimes found.

807. *Tetrameter Acatalectic.* –́ ⏑ –́ | –́ ⏑ –́ | –́ ⏑ –́ | –́ ⏑ –́

Ḗx bonī́s péssum(ī) ét fraū́dulḗntíssumī́, PL., *Capt.*, 235.

NOTE.—Resolution is not allowed at the end nor in the second foot immediately before a Cæsura. The Arsis immediately preceding (*i.e.*, of the second and fourth foot) is regularly pure.

808. *Tetrameter Catalectic.* –́ ⏑ –́ | –́ ⏑ –́ | –́ ⏑ –́ | –́ –

Dá mi(hi) hṓc mél meū́m sí m(ē) amā́s s(ī)aúdēs, PL., *Trin.*, 244.

NOTE.—The existence of such lines is disputed, but the balance of authority seems to be in favor of recognising them.

809. *Dimeter Acatalectic.*

Nṓsce sált(em) hū́nc quis ést, PL., *Ps.*, 262. –́ ⏑ –́ | –́ ⏑ –́

NOTE.—This verse is found usually at the close of a Cretic system, or with Trochaic Septenarii. It follows the same rules as the Tetrameter, that is, the last long is not resolved and the second Arsis is kept pure.

810. *Acatalectic Cretic Trimeters* are rare and not always certain. Compare PL., *Trin.*, 267, 269, 271; *Ps.*, 1119; *Most.*, 338; *Catalectic Trimeters* and *Dimeters* are even more uncertain. Compare PL., *Trin.*, 275; *Truc.*, 121.

811. The Bacchīus has the following measure: ⏑ –́ –́, = 1 + 2 + 2 morae (♪♩♩), or if the descending form –́ –́ ⏑ be regarded as the normal one 2 + 2 + 1 morae (♩♩♪).

For the long two shorts are sometimes substituted. On the other hand, an irrational long may be used for the short, and occasionally two shorts are also thus used.

812. *Bacchic Tetrameter.*

Quibús néc locúst úllu' néc spés parátá ⏑ –́ –́ | ⏑ –́ –́ | ⏑ –́ –́ | ⏑ –́ ⏑́⏑
Misérícórdiór núlla mést féminárúm ⏑ ⏑́⏑ ⏑ –́ | ⏑ –́ –́ | ⏑ –́ –́ | ⏑ –́ ⏑́⏑

NOTE.—In this verse there is usually a Cæsura after either the second or third Iambus; rarely Diæresis after the second Bacchius. The Arsis is kept pure in the second and fourth feet if the following long closes a word. Not more than one dissyllabic Arsis is allowable. Usually there is only one resolved Thesis, very rarely two, never more than three.

813. *Dimeter Acatalectic.*

Ad áetát(em) agúndám, PL., *Trin.*, 232. ⏑ –́ –́ | ⏑ –́ –́

NOTE.—This is rare except at the close of a Bacchic series, to form the transition to another rhythm.

814. *Bacchic Hexameter* occurs in nine lines in a monologue in PL., *Am.*, 633–642. Hypermetric combination into systems is found in PL., *Men.*, 571 ff, and VARRO, *Sat.*, p. 195 (R.).

Ionic Rhythm.

815. The Ionic Rhythm is represented by Iōnicus ā māiōre – – ⏑ ⏑ ♩♩♫ For the Iōnicus ā māiōre may be substituted the Ditrochaeus – ⏑ – ⏑. This is called Anáclasis (*breaking-up*).

The verse is commonly anacrustic, so that it begins with the thesis ⏑ ⏑ : – –. Such verses are called Iōnicī ā minōre.

The second long has a strong secondary ictus.

In the early Latin, beginning with ENNIUS, the verse was used with much license. Resolution of the long syllables was common as well as the use of irrational long, and the contraction of two short syllables into a long. HORACE alone shows the pure Ionic.

The Iōnicus is an excited measure, and serves to express the frenzy of distress as well as the madness of triumph.

816. *Tetrameter Catalectic Ionic ā māiōre* (*Sōtadēan*).

This measure, introduced by ENNIUS, was used with great freedom by the earlier poets; but a stricter handling is found in later Latin poets, as PETRONIUS, MARTIAL, *etc.*

**Nám quam varia sínt genera
poḗmatōrum, Baébī,** ∠ – ⏑ ⏑⏑ | ∠⏑⏑⏑⏑ | ∠⏑ – > | ∠ ⋀
**Quámque longē díscinct(a) ali(a)
áb aliīs, sīc nṓsce.**—Accius. ∠ ⏑ – > | ∠ – ⏑ ⏑ | ∠⏑⏑⏑ – > | ∠ ⋀

Later Latin:

The most common scheme is the pure Ionic with Anaclasis, especially in the third foot. Irrational longs are not used, and there is rarely more than one resolution, as: ⏑⏑ – ⏑ ⏑ or – ⏑⏑⏑ ⏑.

Móllēs veterḗs Dēliacī́ manū recísí ∠ – ⏑ ⏑ ∠ – ⏑ ⏑ ∠ ⏑ ∠ ⏑ ∠ –
tér corripuī́ terribilém manū bipénnem. ∠ – ⏑ ⏑ ∠ – ⏑ ⏑ ∠ ⏑ ∠ ⏑ ∠ –
—Prop.

817. A combination of the *Ionic ā māiōre* into systems is found in Laevius, who has a system of ten followed by a system of nine. Some traces of similar arrangement have been observed in the *Satires* of Varro.

818. *Tetrameter Catalectic Ionic ā minōre* (*Galliambic*).

This verse was introduced by Varro in his *Menippēan Satires*, and appears also in Catullus, 63, and in some fragments of Maecenas.

In Catullus the two short syllables may be contracted (ten times in the first foot, six times in the third), and the long may be resolved, but not twice in the same Dimeter (except 63), and very rarely in the first foot of the second Dimeter (once in 91), but almost regularly in the penultimate long. Diæresis between the two Dimeters is regular. Anaclasis is found in the majority of the lines; regularly in the first Dimeter (except 18, 54, 75).

The frequent resolutions and conversions give this verse a peculiarly wild character.

Ordinary Scheme:

Without Anaclasis: ⏑ ⏑ ∠ – ⏑ ⏑ ∠ – ⏑ ⏑ ∠ – ⏑ ⏑ ∠
With Anaclasis: ⏑ ⏑ ∠ ⏑ – ⏑ ∠ – ⏑ ⏑ ∠ ⏑ – ⏑ ∠.

Anacrustic Scheme:

Without Anaclasis: ⏑ ⏑ : ∠ – ⏑ ⏑ | ∠ – † ⏑ ⏑ | ∠ – ⏑ ⏑ | ⏖ – ‖ ⋀
With Anaclasis: ⏑ ⏑ : ∠ ⏑ – ⏑ | ∠ – † ⏑ ⏑ | ∠ ⏑ – ⏑ | ⏖ – ‖ ⋀

**Et eā́r(um) omni(a) adī́rem furi-
búnda latibulá** ⏑ ⏑ ∠ – ⏑ ⏑ ∠ – ⏑ ⏑ ∠ ⏑ ⏑͡⏑ ⏑ ∠
**Quō nṓs decet citā́tīs celerā́re tri-
pudiīs** – ∠ ⏑ – ⏑ ∠ – ⏑ ⏑ ∠ ⏑ ⏑͡⏑ ⏑ ∠
**Itaqu(e) út domum Cybḗbēs teti-
gḗre lassulaé** ⏑ ⏑ ∠ ⏑ – ⏑ ∠ – ⏑ ⏑ ∠ ⏑ – ⏑ ∠

Super álta vectus Áttis celerí rate mariá ∪ ∪ ∠ ∪ — ∪ ∠ — ∪ ∪ ∠ ∪ ∪ ∪ ∪ ∠
Iam iám dolet quod ēgī iam iámque paenitét.—CAT. — ∠ ∪ — ∪ ∠ — — ∠ ∪ — ∪ ∠

819. *Dimeter Catalectic Ionic ā minōre* (*Anacreontic*).

This verse is found first in LAEVIUS, then in SENECA, PETRONIUS, and later. Anaclasis is regular in the first foot. The long syllable may be resolved, or the two shorts at the beginning may be contracted. The verse may end in a Syllaba Anceps.

Vener(em) ígitur álm(um) adōrāns ∪ ∪ ∪́ ∪ ∪ ∠ ∪ ∠ —
Seu fémin(a) ísve mās est — ∠ ∪ ∠ ∪ ∠ —
It(a) ut álba Nóctilúcast. ∪ ∪ ∠ ∪ ∠ ∪ ∠ —

NOTE.—Owing to the similarity of the verse to the Iambic Quaternarius Catalectic it is also called the *Hemiambic*.

Compound Verses.

820. *Iambelegus* (*Iambic Dimeter and Dactylic Trimeter Cat.*).

This verse occurs only in the *second Archilochian* Strophe of HORACE, and is often scanned as two verses:

Tū vína Tórquātō movē ‖ cōnsule préssa meō.—HOR.

$\overset{>}{\cup}$: ∠ ∪ | ∠ $\overset{>}{\cup}$ | ∠ ∪ | ∠ ∧ ‖

∠ ∪ ∪ | ∠ ∪ ∪ | ∠ $\overset{-}{\wedge}$ ‖

821. *Elegiambus* (*Dactylic Trimeter Cat. and Iambic Dimeter*).

This verse occurs only in the third *Archilochian* Strophe of HORACE, and is often scanned as two verses:

Dēsinet ímparibús ‖ certāre súbmōtús pudór.—HOR.

∠ ∪ ∪ | ∠ ∪ ∪ | ∠ $\overset{-}{\wedge}$ ‖

$\overset{>}{\cup}$: ∠ ∪ | ∠ $\overset{>}{\cup}$ | ∠ ∪ | ∠ ∧ ‖

822. *Versus Reiziānus* (*Iambic Dimeter and Anapaestic Tripody Catalectic*).

Redī, quō fugis nunc? ténĕ tenē. ‖ Quid stólidē clāmās?
Qui(a) ăd trís virōs i(am) ego dēferam ‖ Nōmén tuōm. Qu(am) óbrem?
PL., *Aul.*, 415.

⏖ ∠ ∪ — > ∪́ ∪ ∪ — ‖ — ∪́ ∪ — ∠ —
⏖ ∠ ∪ — ∪ ∪ ∠ ∪ — ‖ — ∠ — ∠ —

NOTE.—From the time of REIZ, after whom this verse has been named, it has been the subject of a great deal of discussion. In regard to the first part of the verse there is considerable unanimity, in regard to the second opinions differ. Some regard it as an Iambic Dimeter Catalectic Syncopated (⏑ ⏑́ ⏑ ⏗ ⏑́ ⏑); others as an Iambic Tripody Catalectic (⏑ ⏑́ ⏑ ⏑́ — ∧). SPENGEL regards it as a Hypercatalectic Anapaestic Monometer, and he has been followed with a variation in the nomenclature in the above scheme. LEO regards it as Logaœdic. The most recent view (KLOTZ) regards it as sometimes Logaœdic, and sometimes Anapaestic.

823. 1. PLAUTUS shows several verses compounded of a Cretic Dimeter and a Catalectic Trochaic Tripody. These verses are usually, but not always, separated by Diæresis. Examples: *Ps.*, 1285, 1287.

2. Some authorities consider verses like PL., *Most.*, 693, *Rud.*, 209, compounded of a Cretic Dimeter and a Clausula. Others regard them as Catalectic Cretic Tetrameters.

The Cantica of Early Latin.

824. The construction of the Cantica (in the narrow sense) of PLAUTUS and TERENCE is still a matter of dispute. Three opinions have been advanced. One looks at them as antistrophic, following the scheme A.B.B.; others hold that the scheme is A.B.A. The third view is that with some exceptions the Cantica are irregular compositions, without a fixed principle of responsion.

In TERENCE, Trochaic Octonarii are always followed by Trochaic Septenarii, and very frequently the Trochaic Septenarii are followed by Iambic Octonarii. In PLAUTUS there are long series of Cretic and Bacchic verses, and sometimes these alternate, without, however, any regular scheme, with other verses.

A Bacchic Trochaic Canticum is found in PL., *Merc.*, 335–363, as follows: I. 2 Bacc. Tetram.; II. 4 Anap. Dim.; III. 1 Troch. Octon.; IV. 13 Bacc. Tetram.; V. 1 Troch. Octon.; VI. 2 Bacc. Tetram.; VII. 1 Troch. Octon.; VIII. 2 Bacc. Tetram.; IX. 2 Troch. Octon.

A Trochaic Iambic Canticum is TER., *Ph.*, 153–163. A. 153–157: 2 Troch. Octon.; 1 Troch. Sept.; 1 Iamb. Octon. B. 158–163; 1 Troch. Octon.; 2 Troch. Sept.; 3 Iamb. Octon.; 1 Iamb. Quater. (Clausula).

The Cantica of Later Latin.

825. 1. The Cantica of SENECA are composed mostly in Anapaestic Dimeters, closed frequently, though not necessarily, by a Monometer. A Dactyl is common in the first and third feet. The Spondee is likewise very common, a favourite close being — ⏑́⏑ ⏑ — ⏑́. The Diæresis between the Dimeters is regular. Examples: *Herc. Fur.*, 125–203. In *Ag.*, 310–407, Dimeters and Monometers alternate.

2. Iambic Dimeters, occasionally alternating with Trimeters, but usually stichic, are found occasionally; as *Med.*, 771–786.

3. Peculiar to SENECA is the use of a large variety of Logaœdic measures in his Cantica. So we find not unfrequently the following in stichic repetition: Lesser Asclepiadēans, Glyconics, Sapphic Hendecasyllabics, Adonics, and other imitations of Horatian measures; but there are few traces of antistrophic arrangement.

Lyric Metres of Horace.

826. In the schemes that follow, the Roman numerals refer to periods, the Arabic to the number of feet or bars, the dots indicate the end of a line.

I. *Asclēpiadēan* Strophe No. 1. Lesser Asclepiadean Verse (802) repeated in tetrastichs.

×
–> | ⏖⏑ | └ ‖ ⏖⏑ | – ⏑ | – ∧ ‖ .3.3.
–> | ⏖⏑ | └ ‖ ⏖⏑ | – ⏑ | – ∧ ‖ 3.3.
–> | ⏖⏑ | └ ‖ ⏖⏑ | – ⏑ | – ∧ ‖ 3.3.
–> | ⏖⏑ | └ ‖ ⏖⏑ | – ⏑ | – ∧ ‖ 3.3.

O., I. 1; III. 30; IV. 8.

II. *Asclēpiadēan* Strophe No. 2. Glyconics (795) and Lesser Asclepiadean (802) alternating, and so forming tetrastichs.

×
–> | ⏖⏑ | – ⏑ | – ∧ ‖ .4.
–> | ⏖⏑ | └ ‖ ⏖⏑ | – ⏑ | – ∧ ‖ 3.3.
–> | ⏖⏑ | – ⏑ | – ∧ ‖ .4.
–> | ⏖⏑ | └ ‖ ⏖⏑ | – ⏑ | – ∧ ‖ 3.3.

O., I. 3, 13, 19, 36; III. 9, 15, 19, 24, 25, 28; IV. 1, 3.

III. *Asclēpiadēan* Strophe No. 3. Three Lesser Asclepiadean Verses (802) followed by a Glyconic (795).

×
–> | ⏖⏑ | └ ‖ ⏖⏑ | – ⏑ | – ∧ 3.3.
–> | ⏖⏑ | └ ‖ ⏖⏑ | – ⏑ | – ∧ 3.3.
–> | ⏖⏑ | └ ‖ ⏖⏑ | – ⏑ | – ∧ 3.3.
–> | ⏖⏑ | – ⏑ | – ∧ 4.

O., I. 6, 15, 24, 33; II. 12; III. 10, 16; IV. 5, 12.

IV. *Asclēpiadēan* Strophe No. 4. Two Lesser Asclepiadean Verses (802), a Pherecratean (794), and a Glyconic (795).

```
   ×
I. –> | ⏖⏑ | ∟ ‖ ⏖⏑ | – ⏑ | – ∧ ‖ I.   . 3 3
   –> | ⏖⏑ | ∟ ‖ ⏖⏑ | – ⏑ | – ∧ ‖      . 3 3
II. –> | ⏖⏑ | ∟ | – ∧ ‖          II.   . 4
   –> | ⏖⏑ | – ⏑ | – ∧ ‖               . 4 .
```

O., I. 5, 14, 21, 23; III. 7, 13; IV. 13.

V. *Asclēpiadēan* Strophe No. 5. Greater Asclepiadean (803), repeated in fours.

```
×
–> | ⏖⏑ | ∟ ‖ ⏖⏑ | ∟ ‖ ⏖⏑ | – ⏑ | – ∧ ‖    . 3 2 3
–> | ⏖⏑ | ∟ ‖ ⏖⏑ | ∟ ‖ ⏖⏑ | – ⏑ | – ∧ ‖    . 3 2 3
–> | ⏖⏑ | ∟ ‖ ⏖⏑ | ∟ ‖ ⏖⏑ | – ⏑ | – ∧ ‖    . 3 2 3
–> | ⏖⏑ | ∟ ‖ ⏖⏑ | ∟ ‖ ⏖⏑ | – ⏑ | – ∧ ‖    . 3 2 3
```

O., I. 11, 18; IV. 10.

VI. *Sapphic* Strophe. Three Lesser Sapphics (797), and an Adonic (792), which is merely a Clausula. In the Sapphic HORACE regularly breaks the Dactyl.

```
×     ×
– ⏑ | –> | –† ⏑⏑ | – ⏑ | – ⏑ ‖    . 5
×     ×
– ⏑ | –> | –† ⏑⏑ | – ⏑ | – ⏑ ‖    . 5
×     ×
– ⏑ | –> | –† ⏑⏑ | – ⏑ | – ⏑ ‖    . 5
⏖⏑ | – ⏑ ‖                         . 2 .
```

O., I. 2, 10, 12, 20, 22, 25, 30, 32, 38; II. 2, 4, 6, 8, 10, 16; III. 8, 11, 14, 18, 20, 22, 27; IV. 2, 6, 11; *Carmen Saeculāre*.

NOTE.—In Greek the third and fourth verses run together to form a single verse. In Latin this is rare; one case is found in CATULLUS, 11, 11, and three in HORACE, *O.*, I. 2, 19; 25, 11; II. 16, 7; but the occurrence of Hiatus between the two lines in HORACE (*O.*, I. 2, 47; 12, 7; 12, 31; 22, 15, *etc.*) may be considered as indicating that the verses were conceived as separate. Elision and Hiatus are also occasionally found in the lines. Elision, second and third: CAT., 11, 22; H., *O.*, II. 2, 18; 16, 34; IV. 2, 22; third and fourth: CAT., 11, 19; H., *O.*, IV. 2, 23; *C.S.*, 47. Hiatus, first and second: H., *O.*, I. 2, 41; 12, 25; II. 16, 5; III. 11, 29; 27, 33; second and third: H., *O.*, I. 2, 6; 12, 6; 25, 18; 30, 6; II. 2, 6; 4, 6; III. 11, 50; 27, 10.

VII. *Lesser Sapphic* Strophe. Aristophanic (793), and Greater Sapphic (804). Two pairs are combined into a tetrastich.

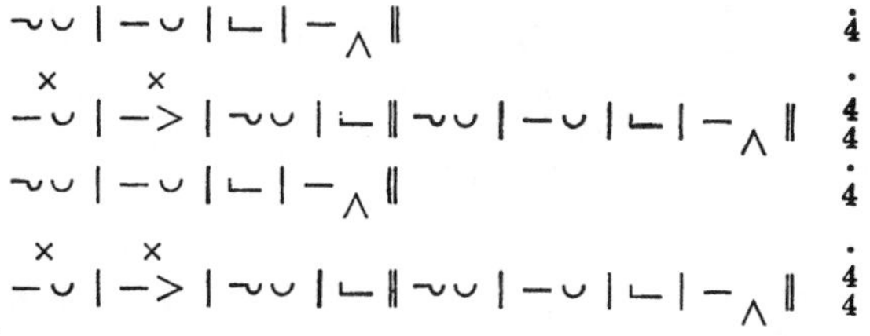

O., I. 8.

VIII. *Alcaic* Strophe. Two Alcaic verses of eleven syllables (798), a Trochaic Quaternarius with Anacrusis (772), and one Alcaic verse of ten (799).

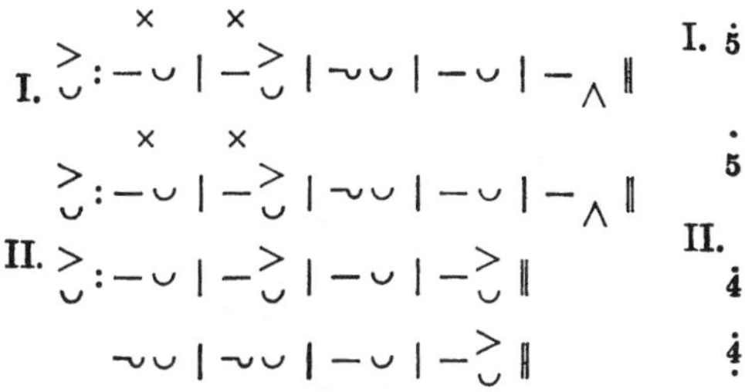

O., I. 9, 16, 17, 26, 27, 29, 31, 34, 35, 37; II. 1, 3, 5, 7, 9, 11, 13, 14, 15, 17, 19, 20; III. 1, 2, 3, 4, 5, 6, 17, 21, 23, 26, 29; IV. 4, 9, 15, 17.

NOTE.—Elision between the verses is much more rare than in the Sapphic strophe; it occurs but twice: *O.*, II. 3, 27; III. 29, 35. Hiatus, on the other hand, is very common.

IX. *Archilochian* Strophe No. 1. A Dactylic Hexameter (784), and a Lesser Archilochian (788), two pairs to a tetrastich.

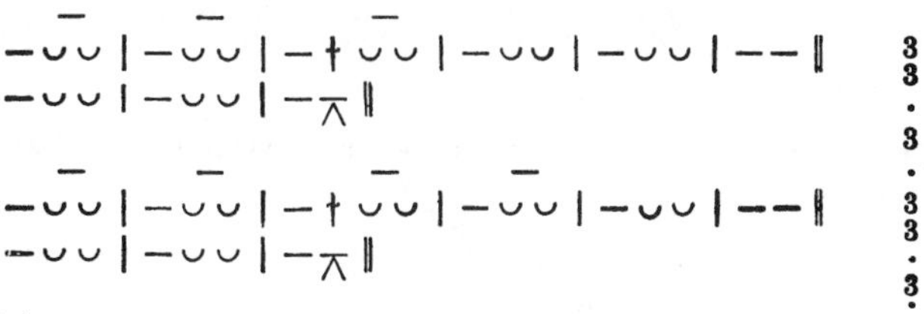

O., IV. 7.

X. *Archilochian* Strophe No. 2. A Dactylic Hexameter (784), and an Iambelegus (820).

Epod., 13.

XI. *Archilochian* Strophe No. 3. An Iambic Trimeter (762), followed by an Elegiambus (821).

⏓ : − ⏑ | − ⏓ | − ⏑ | − ⏓ | − ⏑ | − ∧ ‖
− ⏑ ⏑ | − ⏑ ⏑ | − ∧ ‖
⏓ : − ⏑ | − ⏓ | − ⏑ | − ∧ ‖

Epod., 11.

XII. *Archilochian* Strophe No. 4. A Greater Archilochian (800), and a Trimeter Iambic Catalectic (763). Two pairs combined to form a tetrastich.

∠ ⏑ ⏑ ∠ ⏒ ∠ ⏒ ∠ ⏑ ⏑ ‖ ∠ ⏑ − ⏑ − ⏒
⏒ ∠ ⏑ − ⏒ ∠ ⏑ − ⏑ ∠ ⏑

O., 1. 4.

This verse may be considered as Logaœdic, thus (800):

− ⏖ | − ⏖ | − ⏖ | − ⏑⏑ ‖ − ⏑ | − ⏑ | ⌊ | − ∧ ‖ 4/4
⏓ : − ⏑ | − ⏓ | − ⏑ | − ⏑ | ⌊ | − ∧ ‖ 6
− ⏖ | − ⏖ | − ⏖ | − ⏑⏑ ‖ − ⏑ | − ⏑ | ⌊ | − ∧ ‖ 4/4
⏓ : − ⏑ | − ⏓ | − ⏑ | − ⏑ | ⌊ | − ∧ ‖ 6

XIII. *Alcmanian* Strophe. A Dactylic Hexameter (784), followed by a Catalectic Dactylic Tetrameter (787).

∠ ⏒ ∠ ⏒ ∠ ⏒ ∠ ⏒ ∠ ⏑ ⏑ ∠ −
∠ ⏑ ⏑ ∠ ⏑ ⏑ ∠ ⏑ ⏑ ∠ ⏒

O., 1. 7, 28; *Epod.*, 12.

NOTE.—The Tetrameter may be considered acatalectic with a Spondee in the fourth place (787, N.).

XIV. *Iambic Trimeter* repeated (762).

⏓ : ∠ ⏑ | − ⏓ | − ⏑ | − ⏓ | − ⏑ | − ∧

Epod., 17.

XV. *Iambic* Strophe. Iambic Trimeter (762), and Dimeter (765).

⏓ : − ⏑ | − ⏓ | − ⏑ | − ⏓ | − ⏑ | − ∧
⏓ : − ⏑ | − ⏓ | − ⏑ | − ∧

Epod., 1–10.

XVI. *Pythiambic* Strophe No. 1. A Dactylic Hexameter (784), or Versus Pythius, and an Iambic Dimeter (765).

∠ ⏕ ∠ ⏕ ∠ ⏕ ∠ ⏒ ⏑ ∠ ⏑ ⏑ ∠ ⏒
⏒ ∠ ⏑ – ⏒ ∠ ⏑ –

Epod., 14, 15.

XVII. *Pythiambic* Strophe No. 2. A Dactylic Hexameter (784), and an Iambic Trimeter (760).

∠ ⏕ ∠ ⏕ ∠ ⏕ ∠ ⏕ ∠ ⏑ ⏑ ∠ ⏒
⏒ ∠ ⏑ – ⏒ ∠ ⏑ – ⏒ ∠ ⏑ –

Epod., 16.

XVIII. *Trochaic* Strophe. A Catalectic Trochaic Dimeter (772), and a Catalectic Iambic Trimeter (763). Two pairs make a tetrastich.

∠ ⏑ – ⏒ ∠ ⏑ –
⏒ ∠ ⏑ – ⏒ ∠ ⏑ – ⏑ ∠ ⏒

O., II. 18.

XIX. The *Ionic* System is found once in Horace; it consists of ten Iōnicī ā minōre feet, variously arranged by metrists. Some regard the system as composed of ten Tetrameters followed by a Dimeter. Others, with more probability, divide into two Dimeters followed by two Trimeters. The scheme may be made ā māiōre by Anacrusis.

Iōnicus ā minōre scheme:

Miserārum(e)st neque amōrī	⏑ ⏑ ∠ – ⏑ ⏑ ∠ – ‖
dare lūdum neque dulcī	⏑ ⏑ ∠ – ⏑ ⏑ ∠ – ‖
mala vīnō laver(e) aut exanimārī	⏑ ⏑ ∠ – ⏑ ⏑ ∠ – ⏑ ⏑ ∠ – ‖
metuentēs patruae verbera linguae	⏑ ⏑ ∠ – ⏑ ⏑ ∠ – ⏑ ⏑ ∠ – ‖

Iōnicus ā māiōre scheme:

⏑ ⏑ : – – ⏑ ⏑ | – – – ‖ ∧	I.	2
⏑ ⏑ : – – ⏑ ⏑ | – – – ‖ ∧		2
⏑ ⏑ : – – ⏑ ⏑ | – – ⏑ ⏑ | – – – ∧	II.	3
⏑ ⏑ : – – ⏑ ⏑ | – – ⏑ ⏑ | – – – ∧		3

O., III. 12.

827. Index of Horatian Odes and Metres.

Book.	Ode.	Metre.
I.	1	i.
	2	vi.
	3	ii.
	4	x.
	5	iv.
	6	iii.
	7	xiii.
	8	vii.
	9	viii.
	10	vi.
	11	v.
	12	vi.
	13	ii.
	14	iv.
	15	iii.
	16	viii.
	17	viii.
	18	v.
	19	ii.
	20	vi.
	21	iv.
	22	vi.
	23	iv.
	24	iii.
	25	vi.
	26	viii.
	27	viii.
	28	xiii.
	29	viii.
	30	vi.
	31	viii.
	32	vi.
	33	iii.
	34	viii.
	35	viii.
	36	ii.
	37	viii.
	38	vi.
II.	1	viii.
	2	vi.
	3	viii.
	4	vi.
	5	viii.
	6	vi.
	7	viii.
	8	vi.
	9	viii.
	10	vi.
	11	viii.
	12	iii.
	13	viii.
	14	viii.
	15	viii.
	16	vi.
	17	viii.
	18	xviii.
	19	viii.
	20	viii.
III.	1	viii.
	2	viii.
	3	viii.
	4	viii.
	5	viii.
	6	viii.
	7	iv.
	8	vi.
	9	ii.
	10	iii.
	11	vi.
	12	xix.
	13	iv.
	14	vi.
	15	ii.
	16	iii.
	17	viii.
III.	18	vi.
	19	ii.
	20	vi.
	21	viii.
	22	vi.
	23	viii.
	24	ii.
	25	ii.
	26	viii.
	27	vi.
	28	ii.
	29	viii.
	30	i.
IV.	1	ii.
	2	vi.
	3	ii.
	4	viii.
	5	iii.
	6	vi.
	7	ix.
	8	i.
	9	viii.
	10	v.
	11	vi.
	12	iii.
	13	iv.
	14	viii.
	15	viii.
Carmen Saeculāre		vi.
Epod.	1–10	xv.
	11	xi.
	12	xiii.
	13	x.
	14	xvi.
	15	xvi.
	16	xvii.
	17	xiv.

APPENDIX.

ROMAN CALENDAR.

The names of the Roman months were originally adjectives. The substantive **mēnsis**, *month*, may or may not be expressed: **(mēnsis) Iānuārius, Februārius**, and so on. Before Augustus, the months July and August were called, not **Iūlius** and **Augustus**, but **Quīntīlis** and **Sextīlis.**

The Romans counted backward from three points in the month, Calends (**Kalendae**), Nones (**Nōnae**), and Ides (**Īdūs**), to which the names of the months are added as adjectives: **Kalendae Iānuāriae, Nōnae Februāriae, Īdūs Mārtiae.** The Calends are the first day, the Nones the fifth, the Ides the thirteenth. In March, May, July, and October the Nones and Ides are two days later. Or thus:

> In March, July, October, May,
> The Ides are on the fifteenth day,
> The Nones the seventh; but all besides
> Have two days less for Nones and Ides.

In counting backward ("come next Calends, next Nones, next Ides") the Romans used for "the day before" **prīdiē** with the Acc.: **prīdiē Kalendās Iānuāriās**, Dec. 31; **prīdiē Nōnās Iān.** = Jan. 4; **prīdiē Īdūs Iān.** = Jan. 12.

The longer intervals are expressed by **ante diem tertium, quārtum,** *etc.*, before the Accusative, so that **ante diem tertium Kal. Iān.** means "two days before the Calends of January;" **ante diem quārtum,** or **a. d. iv.**, or **iv. Kal. Iān.**, "three days before," and so on. This remarkable combination is treated as one word, so that it can be used with the prepositions **ex** and **in**: **ex ante diem iii. Nōnās Iūniās ūsque ad prīdiē Kal. Septembrēs**, from June 3 to August 31; **differre aliquid in ante diem xv. Kal. Nov.**, *to postpone a matter to the* 18*th of October*.

Leap Year.—In leap year the intercalary day was counted between **a. d. vi. Kal. Mārt.** and **a. d. vii. Kal. Mārt.** It was called **a. d. bis sextum Kal. Mārt.**, so that **a. d. vii. Kal. Mārt.** corresponded to our February 23, just as in the ordinary year.

To turn Roman Dates into English.

For Nones and Ides.—I. Add one to the date of the Nones and Ides, and subtract the given number.

For Calends.—II. Add two to the days of the preceding month, and subtract the given number.

EXAMPLES: **a. d. viii. Īd. Iān.** (13 + 1 – 8) = Jan. 6; **a. d. iv. Nōn. Apr.** (5 + 1 – 4) = Apr. 2; **a. d. xiv. Kal. Oct.** (30 + 2 – 14) = Sept. 18.

Year.—To obtain the year B.C., subtract the given date from 754 (753 B.C. being the assumed date of the founding of Rome, **annō urbis conditae**). To obtain the year A.D., subtract 753.

Thus: *Cicero was born* 648, **a. u. c.** = 106 B.C.
Augustus died 767, **a. u. c.** = 14 A.D.

NOTE.—Before the reform of the Calendar by Julius Cæsar in B.C. 46, the year consisted of 355 days, divided into twelve months, of which March, May, Quintīlis (July), and October had 31 days, February 28, the remainder 29. To rectify the Calendar, every second year, at the discretion of the Pontifices, a month of varying length, called **mēnsis intercalāris**, was inserted after the 23d of February.

ROMAN SYSTEMS OF MEASUREMENT.

LONG MEASURE.

4	**digitī**	=	1 **palmus**.
4	**palmī**	=	1 **pēs** (11.65 in.).
6	**palmī**,	=	1 **cubitus**.
1½	**pedēs**		
2½	**pedēs**	=	1 **gradus**.
2	**gradūs**,	=	1 **passus**.
5	**pedēs**		
125	**passus**	=	1 **stadium**.
8	**stadia**	=	1 **mīlle passuum** (mile).

SQUARE MEASURE.

100	**pedēs, quadrātī**	=	1 **scrīpulum**.
36	**scrīpula**	=	1 **clima**.
4	**climata**	=	1 **āctus**.
2	**āctūs**	=	1 **iūgerum** (acre).

The **iūgerum** contains 28,800 sq. ft. Rom.;
Eng. acre = 43,560 sq. ft.

DRY MEASURE.

1½	**cyathī**	=	1 **acētābulum**.
2	**acētābula**	=	1 **quārtārius**.
2	**quārtāriī**	=	1 **hēmīna**.
2	**hēmīnae**	=	1 **sextārius**.
8	**sextāriī**	=	1 **sēmodius**.
2	**sēmodiī**	=	1 **modius** (peck).

LIQUID MEASURE.

1½	**cyathī**	=	1 **acētābulum**.
2	**acētābula**	=	1 **quārtārius**.
2	**quārtāriī**	=	1 **hēmīna**.
2	**hēmīnae**	=	1 **sextārius** (pint).
6	**sextāriī**	=	1 **congius**.
4	**congiī**	=	1 **ūrna**.
2	**ūrnae**	=	1 **amphora**.
20	**amphorae**	=	1 **culleus**.

ROMAN WEIGHTS.

3	**siliquae**	=	1 **obolus**.
2	**obolī**	=	1 **scrīpulum**.
2	**scrīpula**	=	1 **drachma**.
2	**drachmae**	=	1 **sicilicus**.
2	**sicilicī**	=	1 **sēmūncia**.
2	**sēmūnciae**	=	1 **ūncia**.
12	**ūnciae**	=	1 **lībra** (pound).

NOTES.—1. The multiples of the **ūncia** were **sēscūncia** (1½), **sextāns** (2), **quadrāns** (3), **triēns** (4), **quīncūnx** (5), **sēmis** (6), **septūnx** (7), **bēs** (8), **dodrāns** (9), **dextāns** (10), **deūnx** (11).

2. The **lībra** was also called **ās** (see below), which latter is taken as the unit in all measures, and the foregoing divisions applied to it. Hence, by substituting **ās** for **iūgerum**, we have **deūnx** as 11/12 of a **iūgerum**, **dextāns** as 10/12, *etc.*

ROMAN MONEY.

The unit was originally the **ās** (which was about a pound of copper), with its fractional divisions. This gradually depreciated, until, after the second Punic war, the unit had become a **sēstertius**, which was nominally 2½ **assēs**.

2½ **assēs**	= 1 **sēstertius** (about 4 cts.).	
2 **sēstertiī**	= 1 **quīnārius**.	
2 **quīnāriī**	= 1 **dēnārius**.	
25 **dēnāriī**	= 1 **aureus** (**nummus**).	
1000 **sēstertiī**	= 1 **sēstertium** ($42.94 to Augustus's time).	

NOTE.—**Sēstertium** (which may be a fossilised Gen. Pl. = **sēstertiōrum**) was modified by distributives (rarely by cardinals), thus: **bīna sēstertia**, 2000 sesterces. But in multiples of a million (**deciēns centēna mīlia sēstertium**, *i.e.*, **sēstertiōrum**), **centēna mīlia** was regularly omitted, and **sēstertium** declined as a neuter singular. HS stands as well for **sēstertius** as **sēstertium**; and the meaning is regulated by the form of the numeral; thus HS **vīgintī** (XX) = 20 **sēstertiī**; HS **vīcēna** ($\overline{\text{XX}}$) = 20 **sēstertia**, *i.e.*, 20,000 **sestertiī**.

ROMAN NAMES.

The Roman usually had three names; a **nōmen**, indicating the **gēns**, a **cōgnōmen**, indicating the **familia** in the **gēns**, and the **praenōmen**, indicating the individual in the **familia**.

The **nōmina** all end in **ius**. The **cōgnōmina** have various forms, in accordance with their derivation. For example: **Q. Mūcius Scaevola** (from **scaevos**, *left hand*).

The **praenōmina** are as follows, with their abbreviations:

Aulus,	A.	**Lūcius**,	L.	**Quīntus**,	Q.
Appius,	App.	**Mārcus**,	M.	**Servius**,	Ser.
Gāius,	C.	**Mānius**,	M'.	**Sextus**,	Sex.
Gnaeus,	Cn.	**Māmercus**,	Mam.	**Spurius**,	Sp.
Decimus,	D.	**Numerius**,	Num.	**Titus**,	T.
Kaesō,	K.	**Pūblius**.	P.	**Tiberius**,	Ti., Tib.

NOTES.—1. Adoption from one **gēns** into another was indicated by the termination **-iānus**. From the fourth century A.D. a second **cōgnōmen** was also called an **āgnōmen**.

2. Daughters had no peculiar **praenōmina**, but were called by the name of the **gēns** in which they were born. If there were two, they were distinguished as **māior** and **minor**; if more than two, by the numerals **tertia**, **quārta**, *etc.*

INDEX OF VERBS.

[The References are to the Sections.]

Ab-dō, ere, -didī, -ditum, 151, 1.
ab-igō (AGO), ere, -ēgī, -āctum, 160, 1.
ab-iciō (IACIŌ), ere, -iēcī, -iectum, 160, 3.
ab-luō, ere, -luī, -lūtum, 162.
ab-nuō, ere, -nuī (-nuitūrus), 162.
ab-oleō, ēre, ēvī, itum, 137, *b*.
ab-olēscō, -ere, -olēvī, -olitum, 140.
ab-ripiō (RAPIŌ), -ere, -ripuī, -reptum, 146.
abs-condō (DŌ), ere, -dī (-didī), ditum, 151, 1.
ab-sistō, -ere, -stitī, 154, 1.
ab-sum, -esse, ab-fuī, ā-fuī, 117.
ac-cendō, -ere, -cendī, -cēnsum, 160, 2.
ac-cidō (CADŌ), ere, -cidī, 165, *a*.
ac-cipiō (CAPIŌ), ere, -cēpī, -ceptum, 160, 3.
ac-colō (COLŌ), ere, -coluī, -cultum, 152, 3.
ac-cumbō, ere, -cubuī, -cubitum, 144.
ac-currō, ere, ac-currī, -cursum, 155, 134, III.
aceō, ēre, acuī, *to be sour.*
acēscō, ere, acuī, *to get sour.*
ac-quīrō (QUAERŌ), ere, -quīsīvī, -quīsītum, 137, *c*.
acuō, ere, acuī, acūtum, 162.
ad-dō, ere, -didī, -ditum, 151, 1.
ad-imō (EMO), ere, -ēmī, -ēmptum, 160, 1.
ad-ipīscor, ī, ad-eptus sum, 165.
ad-iuvō, āre, -iūvī, -iūtum, 158.
ad-olēscō, ere, -olēvī, -ultum, 140.
ad-orior, -orīrī, -ortus sum, 166.
ad-scīscō, ere, -scīvī, -scītum, 140.
ad-sistō, ere, -stitī, 154, 1.
ad-spiciō, ere, -spexī, -spectum, 150, 1.
ad-stō, -stāre, -stitī, 151, 2.
ad-sum, ad-esse, ad-fuī (af-fuī), 117.
ad-vesperāscō, ere, āvī, 140.
aegrēscō, ere, *to fall sick.*
af-ferō, -ferre, at-tulī, al-lātum, 171.
af-flīgō, ere, -flīxī, -flīctum, 147, 2.
ag-gredior, -gredī, -gressus, 165.
a-gnōscō, ere, a-gnōvī, a-gnitum (agnōtūrus), 140.
ago, ere, ēgī, āctum, 160, 1.
āiō, 175, 1.
albeō, ēre, *to be white.*
al-liciō, ere, -lexī, (-licuī) -lectum, 150, 1.
al-luō, ere, -luī, -lūtum, 162.
alō, ere, aluī, al(i)tum, 142, 3.
amb-igō (AGO), ere, 172, 1.
amb-iō (EŌ), īre, īvī (iī), ītum, 169, 2, R. 1.
amiciō, īre, (amicuī, amixī,) amictum 142, 4, 161.
amplector, ī, amplexus, 165.
angō, ere, anxī, 149, *b*.
an-nuō, ere, annuī (annūtum), 162.
ante-cellō, ere, 154.
ante-stō, -stāre, -stetī, 151, 2.
a-periō, -īre, aperuī, apertum, 142, 4.
apīscor, ī, aptus sum, 165.
ap-petō, ere, īvī, ītum, 147, *c*.
ap-plicō, āre, -plicuī, -plicitum, (-plicāvī, -plicātum), 152, 2.
ap-pōnō, ere, -posuī, -positum, 139, A.
arceō, ēre, arcuī {arctus, artus (adj.).
arcessō (accersō), ere, arcessīvī, -ītum, 137, *e*.
ārdeō, ēre, ārsī, ārsum, 147, 1.
ārēscō, ere, āruī, *to become dry.*
arguō, ere, arguī, (argūtum,) (arguitūrus,) 162.
ar-ripiō (RAPIŌ), ere, uī, -reptum, 146.
a-scendō (SCANDŌ), ere, ī, scēnsum, 160, 2.
ā-spiciō, ere, ā-spexī, ā-spectum, 150, 1.
as-sentior, īrī, assēnsus sum, 166.
as-sideō (SEDEŌ), ēre, -sēdī, -sessum, 159.
as-suēscō, ere, -suēvī, -suētum, 140.
at-tendō, ere, -tendī, -tentum, 155.

at-texō, ere, -texuī, -textum, 152, 3.
at-tineō (TENEŌ), ēre, uī, -tentum, 135, I. *a*.
at-tingō (TANGŌ), ere, attigī, attāctum, 155.
at-tollō, ere, *to raise up*.
audeō, ēre, ausus sum, 167.
audiō, īre, īvī, ītum. *See* 127.
au-ferō, -ferre, abstulī, ablātum, 171.
augeō, ēre, auxī, auctum, 147, I.
avē, 175, 4.

Balbūtiō, īre, *to stutter*.
batuō, ere, uī, 162.
bibō, ere, bibī, (bibitum), 154, 2.

Cadō, ere, cecidī, cāsum, 153.
caecūtiō, īre, *to be blind*.
caedō, ere, cecīdī, caesum, 153.
calefaciō, ere, -fēcī, -factum, 160, 3; 173, N. 2.
calēscō, ere, caluī, *to get warm*.
calleō, ēre, uī, *to be skilled*.
calveō, ēre, *to be bald*.
candeō, ēre, uī, *to shine*.
cāneō, ēre, *to be gray*.
canō, ere, cecinī, cantum, 153.
capessō, ere, īvī, ītum, 137, *c*.
capiō, ere, cēpī, captum, 126; 160, 3.
carpō, ere, carpsī, carptum, 147, 2.
caveō, ēre, cāvī, cautum, 159.
cedo, 175, 6.
cēdō, ere, cēssī, cēssum, 147, 2.
cēnātus, 167, N. 1.
cēnseō, ēre, uī, cēnsum, (cēnsītus), 135, I. *a*.
cernō, ere, crēvī, (crētum), 139.
cieō ciēre, / ciō cīre, cīvī, citum, 137, *b*.
cingō, ere, cinxī, cinctum, 149, *b*.
circum-dō, -dare, -dedī, -datum, 151, I.
circum-sistō, ere, stetī, 154, I.
circum-stō, stāre, stetī, 151, 2.
claudō, ere, clausī, clausum, 147, 2.
clepō, ere, clepsī, (clēpī,) cleptum, 147, 2.
co-alēscō, ere, -aluī, (-alitum), 140, 145.
co-arguō, ere, uī, 162.
co-emō, ere, -ēmī, -ēm(p)tum, 160, I.
coepī, coepisse, 175, 5, *a*.
cō-gnōscō, ere, -gnōvī, -gnitum, 140.
cō-gō (AGO), ere, co-ēgī, co-āctum, 160, I.
col-līdō (LAEDŌ), ere, -līsī, līsum, 147, 2.
col-ligō (LEGŌ), ere, -lēgī, -lectum, 160, I.
col-lūceō, ēre, -lūxī, 157, I.
colō, ere, coluī, cultum, 142, 3.
com-būrō, ere, -ūssī, -ūstum, 147, 2.
com-edō, ere, -ēdī, -ēsum (ēstum), 172.
comitātus, 167, N. 1.
comminīscor, ī, commentus sum, 165.
com-moveō, ēre, -mōvī, -mōtum, 159.
cō-mō (EMO), ere, cōmpsī, cōmptum, 147, 2.
com-parcō, ere, -parsī, -parsum, 153.
com-pellō, ere, com-pulī, -pulsum, 155.
com-periō (PARIŌ), īre, com-perī, com-per-tum, 161, 166.
compēscō, ere, uī, 145.
com-pingō, ere, -pēgī, -pāctum, 160, 2.
com-plector, ī, com-plexus, 165.
com-pleō, ēre, ēvī, ētum, 147.
com-primō (PREMŌ), ere, -pressī, -pressum, 147, 2.
com-pungō, ere, -punxī, -punctum, 155.
con-cidō (CADŌ), ere, -cidī, 153, *a*.
con-cīdō (CAEDŌ), ere, -cīdī, -cīsum, 153, *a*.
con-cinō (CANŌ), ere, -cinuī, 142, 3.
concitus (CIEŌ), 137, *b*.
con-clūdō (CLAUDŌ), ere, -clūsī, -clūsum, 147, 2.
con-cumbō, ere, -cubuī, -cubitum, 144.
con-cupīscō, ere, -cupīvī, cupītum, 140.
con-cutiō (QUATIŌ), ere, -cussī, -cussum, 147, 2.
con-dō, ere, -didī, -ditum, 151, I.
con-dormīscō, -ere, -īvī, ītum, 140.
cōn-ferciō (FARCIŌ), īre (fersī), fertum, 150, 2.
cōn-ferō, -ferre, -tulī, collātum, 171.
cōn-ficiō (FACIŌ), ere, -fēcī, -fectum, 160, 3.

cōn-fiteor (FATEOR), ērī, -fessus, 164.
con-flīgō, ere, -flīxī, -flīctum, 147, 2.
cōn-fringō (FRANGŌ), ere, -frēgī, -frāctum, 160, 2.
con-gruō, ere, congruī, 162.
con-iciō (IACIŌ), ere, -iēcī, -iectum, 160, 3.
coniūrātus, 167, N. 1.
co-nīveō, ēre, connixī, (connīvī), 147, 1.
con-quīrō (QUAERŌ), ere, -quīsīvī, -quīsītum, 137, c.
cōn-serō, ere, -seruī, -sertum, 152, 3.
cōn-serō, ere, -sēvī, -situm, 138.
cōn-sīderātus, 167, N. 1.
cōn-sīdō, ere, consēdī, -sessum, 160, 1.
cōn-sistō, ere, -stitī, -stitum, 154, 1.
cōn-spergō, ere, -spersī, -spersum, 147, 2.
cōn-spiciō, ere, -spexī, -spectum, 150, 1.
cōn-stituō (STATUŌ), ere, uī, -stitūtum, 162.
cōn-stō, -stāre, -stitī, (constātūrus), 151, 2.
cōn-suēscō, ere, -suēvī, suētum, 140; 175, 5.
cōnsulō, ere, cōnsuluī, -sultum, 142, 3.
con-temnō, ere, -tem(p)sī, -tem(p)tum, 149, c.
con-tendō, ere, -tendī, -tentum, 155.
con-texō, ere, -texuī, -textum, 152, 3.
con-tineō (TENEŌ), ēre, uī, -tentum, 135, 1. a.
con-tingō (TANGŌ), ere, contigī, contāctum, 155.
convalēscō, ere, -valuī, -valitum, 145.
coquō, ere, coxī, coctum, 147, 2, 168, 1.
cor-ripiō (RAPIŌ), ere, -ripuī, -reptum, 146.
cor-ruō, ere, corruī, 162.
crēbrēscō, ere, crēbruī, *to get frequent.*
crē-dō, ere, -didī, -ditum, 151, 1.
crepō, āre, crepuī, crepitum, 142, 2.
crēscō, ere, crēvī, crētum, 140.
cubō, āre, cubuī, cubitum, 142, 2.
cūdō, ere, cūdī, cūsum, 160, 1.
cupiō, ere, cupīvī, cupītum, 141.
currō, ere, cucurrī, cursum, 155.

Dē-cernō, ere, -crēvī, -crētum, 139.
dē-cerpō (CARPŌ), ere, sī, tum, 147, 2.
dē-dō, dēdere, dēdidī, dēditum, 151, 1.
dē-fendō, ere, -fendī, -fēnsum, 160, 2.
dēfetīscor, ī, *to be worn out.*
dē-gō (AGO), ere, 160, 1.
dēleō. *See Paradigm*, 123, 124.
dē-libuō, uēre, uī, ūtum, 162.
dē-ligō, ere, -lēgī, -lēctum, 160, 1.
dē-mō (EMO), ere, dēmpsī, dēmptum, 147, 2.
dēpellō, ere, dēpulī, dēpulsum, 155.
dē-primō (PREMŌ), ere, -pressī, pressum, 147, 2.
depsō, ere, depsuī, depstum, 142, 3.
dē-scendō (SCANDŌ), ere, -scendī, -scēnsum, 160, 2.
dē-serō, ere, -seruī, -sertum, 142, 3.
dē-siliō (SALIŌ), īre, (iī), uī, (dēsultum), 142, 4.
dē-sinō, ere, dēsīvī, dēsiī, dēsitum, 139.
dē-sipiō (SAPIŌ), -ere, 141.
dē-sistō, ere, -stitī, -stitum, 154, 1.
dē-spiciō, ere, -spexī, -spectum, 150, 1.
dē-suēscō, -ere, -ēvī, -ētum, 140.
dē-sum, -esse, -fuī, 117.
dē-tendō, ere, -tendī, -tentum, 155.
dē-tineō (TENEŌ), ēre, -uī, -tentum, 135, 1. a.
dē-vertor, -ī, 167.
dīcō, ere, dīxī, dictum, 147, 2.
dif-ferō, -ferre, distulī, dīlātum, 171.
dī-gnōscō (NŌSCŌ), ere, -gnōvī, 140.
dī-ligō, ere, -lēxī, -lēctum, 147, 2.
dī-micō, āre, āvī, ātum, 142, 2.
dī-rigō, ere, -rēxī, -rēctum, 147, 2.
dir-imō (EMO), ere, -ēmī, -ēmptum, 160, 1.
dīscō, ere, didicī, 156.
dis-crepō, āre, -crepuī (āvī), 142, 2.
dis-cumbō, ere, -cubuī, -cubitum, 144.
dis-pēscō, ere, -pēscuī, *to divide,* 145.
dis-sideō (SEDEŌ), ēre, -sēdī, 159.

dī-stinguō, ere, -stinxī, -stinctum, 149, *b*.
dī-stō, -stāre, 151, 2.
dītēscō, ere, *to grow rich*.
dīvidō, ere, dīvīsī, dīvīsum, 147, 2.
dō, dare, dedī, datum, 151, 1.
doceō, ēre, docuī, doctum, 135, 1, *a*.
domō, āre, uī, itum, 142, 2.
dūcō, ere, dūxī, ductum, 147, 2.
dulcēscō, ere, *to grow sweet*.
dūrēscō, ere, dūruī, *to grow hard*.

Edō, ere, ēdī, ēsum, 160, 1, 172.
ē-dō (DŌ), ēdere, ēdidī, ēditum, 151, 1.
ē-dormīscō, -ere, -īvī, -ītum, 140.
ef-ferō, -ferre, extulī, ēlātum, 171.
egeō, ēre, eguī, *to want*.
ē-liciō, ere, -licuī, -licitum, 150, 1.
ē-ligō (LEGŌ), ere, -lēgī, -lēctum, 160, 1.
ē-micō, āre, uī (ātūrus), 142, 2.
ēmineō, ēre, uī, *to stand out*.
emo, ere, ēmī, ēmptum, 160, 1.
ēmungō, ēre, ēmunxī, ēmunctum, 149, *b*.
ē-necō, āre, ēnecuī, (ēnecāvī), ēnectum, 142, 2.
eō, īre, īvī, itum, 169, 2.
ē-vādō, ere, ēvāsī, ēvāsum, 147, 2.
ē-vānēscō, ere, ēvānuī, 145.
ex-ārdēscō, ere, exārsī, exārsum, 147, 1.
ex-cellō, ere, uī (excelsus), 144.
excītus, 137.
ex-clūdō (CLAUDŌ), ere, -sī, -sum, 147, 2.
ex-currō, ere, ex(cu)currī, -cursum, 155.
ex-imō, ere, ēmī, -ēmptum, 160, 1.
ex-olēscō, ere, -olēvī, -olētum, 140.
ex-pellō, ere, -pulī, -pulsum, 155.
expergīscor, ī, experrēctus sum, 165.
ex-perior, īrī, -pertus sum, 166.
ex-pleō, ēre, ēvī, ētum, 124, 137, *b*.
ex-plicō, āre, uī (āvī), itum (ātum), 142.
ex-plōdō (PLAUDŌ), ere, -sī, -sum, 147, 2.
exsecrātus, 167, N. 2.
ex-stinguō, ere, -stinxī, -stinctum, 149, *b*.
ex-sistō, ere, -stitī, -stitum, 154, 1.
ex-stō, āre (exstātūrus), 151, 2.
ex-tendō, ere, dī, -sum (-tum), 155.
ex-tollō, ere, 155.
ex-uō, ere, -uī, -ūtum, 162.

Facessō, ere, īvī (-ī), ītum, 137, *c*.
faciō, ere, fēcī, factum, 160, 3.
fallō, ere, fefellī, falsum, 155.
farciō, īre, farsī, fartum, 150, 2.
fārī, 175, 3.
fateor, ērī, fassus sum, 164.
fatīscō, ere, *to fall apart*.
fatīscor, ī (fessus, *adj*.).
faveō, ere, fāvī, fautum, 159.
feriō, īre, *to strike*.
ferō, ferre, tulī, lātum, 171.
ferveō, ēre, fervī (ferbuī), 159.
fīdō, ere, fīsus sum, 167.
fīgō, ere, fīxī, fīxum, 147, 2.
findō, ere, fidī, fissum, 160, 3.
fingō, ere, finxī, fictum, 149, *a*.
fīō, fierī, factus sum, 173.
flectō, ere, flexī, flexum, 148.
fleō, ēre, ēvī, ētum, 137, *b*.
flīgō, ere, flīxī, flīctum, 147, 2.
flōreō, ēre, uī, *to bloom*.
fluō, ere, fluxī (fluxus, *adj*.), 147, 2.
fodiō, ere, fōdī, fossum, 160, 3.
forem, 116.
foveō, ēre, fōvī, fōtum, 159.
frangō, ere, frēgī, frāctum, 160, 2.
fremō, ere, uī, 142, 3.
frendō (eo), ere (uī), frēsum, frēssum, 144.
fricō, āre, uī, frictum (ātum), 142, 2.
frīgeō, ēre (frīxī), 147, 1.
frīgō, ere, frīxī, frīctum, 147, 2.
frondeō, ēre, uī, *to be leafy*.
fruor, ī, frūctus (fruitus) sum, 165.
fugiō, ere, fūgī, fugitum, 160, 3.
fulciō, īre, fulsī, fultum, 150, 2.
fulgeō, ēre, fulsī, 147, 1.
fundō, ere, fūdi, fūsum, 160, 2.
fungor, ī, fūnctus sum, 165.
(furō, *def*.), furere, *to rave*.

Ganniō, īre, *to yelp*.
gaudeō, ēre, gāvīsus sum, 167.
gemō, ere, uī, 142, 3.
gerō, ere, gessī, gestum, 147, 2.
gīgnō, ere, genuī, genitum, 143.
glīscō, ere, *to swell*.
gradior, ī, gressus sum, 165.

Haereō, ēre, haesī, (haesum), 147, 1.
hauriō, īre, hausī, haustum (hausūrus, haustūrus), 150, 2.
havē, 175, 4.
hīscō, ere, *to yawn.*
horreō, ēre, uī, *to stand on end*
hortor, ārī, ātus sum, 128.

Iaceō, ēre, iacuī, *to lie.*
iaciō, ere, iēci, iactum, 160, 3.
īcō, ere, īcī, īctum, 160, 1.
ī-gnōscō, ere, -gnōvī, -gnōtum, 140.
il-liciō, ere, -lexī, -lectum, 150, 1.
il-līdō (LAEDŌ), ere, -līsī, -līsum, 147, 2.
imbuō, ere, uī, ūtum, 162.
imitātus, 167, N. 2.
immineō, ēre, *to overhang.*
im-pingō (PANGŌ), ere, pēgī, pāctum, 160, 2.
in-calēscō, ere, -caluī, 145.
in-cendō, ere, -cendī, -cēnsum, 160, 2.
incessō, ere, īvī (ī), 137, *c.*
in-cidō (CADŌ), ere, -cidī, -cāsum, 152.
in-cīdō (CAEDŌ), ere, -cīdī, cīsum, 153.
in-cipiō (CAPIŌ), ere, -cēpī, -ceptum, 160, 3.
in-crepō, āre, uī, itum, 142, 2.
in-cumbō, ere, -cubuī, -cubitum, 144.
in-cutiō (QUATIŌ), ere, -cussī, -cussum, 147, 2.
ind-igeō (EGEŌ), ēre, uī, *to want.*
ind-ipīscor, ī, indeptus sum, 165.
in-dō, ere, -didī, -ditum, 151, 1.
indulgeō, ēre, indulsī (indultum), 147, 1.
in-duō, ere, -duī, -dūtum, 162.
ineptiō, īre, *to be silly.*
īn-flīgō, ere, -flīxī, -flīctum, 147, 2.
ingemīscō, ere, ingemuī, 145.
ingruō, ere, uī. *See* congruo, 162.
in-nōtēsco, ere, nōtuī, 145.
in-olēscō, ere, -olēvī, 140.
inquam, 175, 2.
īn-sideō (SEDEŌ), ēre, -sēdī, -sessum, 159.
īn-sistō, ere, -stitī, 154, 1.
īn-spiciō, ere, -spexī, -spectum, 150, 1.
inter-ficiō, ere, -fēcī, -fectum, 160, 3; 173, N. 2.
īn-stō, āre, -stitī (instātūrus), 151, 2.
īn-sum, -esse, -fuī, 117.
intel-legō, ere, -lēxī, -lēctum, 147, 2.
inter-imō (EMŌ), ere, -ēmī, -ēmptum, 160, 1.
inter-pungō, ere, -punxī, -punctum, 155.
inter-stō, āre, -stetī, 151, 2.
inter-sum, -esse, -fuī, 117.
inveterāscō, ere, -āvī, 140.
in-vādō, ere, invāsī, -vāsum, 147, 2.
īrāscor, ī, īrātus sum, *to get angry.*
iubeō, ēre, iūssī, iūssum, 147, 1.
iungō, ere, iūnxī, iūnctum, 149, *b.*
iūrātus, 167, N. 1.
iuvō, āre, iūvī, iūtum (iuvātūrus), 158.

Lābor, ī, lāpsus sum, 165.
lacessō, ere, lacessīvī, -ītum, 137, *c.*
laciō, 150.
laedō, ere, laesī, laesum, 147, 2.
lambō, ere, ī, 160, 2.
langueō, ēre, ī, *to be languid.*
largior, īrī, ītus sum, 166.
lateō, ēre, uī, *to lie hid.*
lavō, āre (ere), lāvī, lautum, lōtum, lavātum, 158.
lego, ere, lēgī, lēctum, 160, 1.
libet, libēre, libuit (libitum est), *it pleases.*
liceor, ērī, itus sum, 164.
licet, licēre, licuit (licitum est), *it is permitted.*
lingō, ere, linxī, linctum, 149, *b.*
linō, ere, lēvī (līvī), litum, 139.
linquō, ere, līquī, 160, 2.
liqueō, ēre, licuī, *to be clear.*
līveō, ēre, *to be livid.*
loquor, ī, locūtus sum, 128, 2; 165.
lūceō, ēre, lūxī, 147, 1.
lūdō, ere, lūsī, lūsum, 147, 2.
lūgeō, ēre, lūxī, 147, 1.
luō, ere, luī, { lūtum, *to wash,* luitum, *to atone for,* 162.

Maereō, ēre, *to grieve.*
mālō, mālle, māluī, 142, 3; 174.
mandō, ere, mandī, mānsum, 160, 2.
maneō, ēre, mānsī, mānsum, 147, 1.
mānsuēscō, -ere, -ēvī, -ētum, 140.

medeor, ērī, *to heal.*
meminī, 175, 5, *b.*
mentior, īrī, ītus, 128, 2; 166.
mereor, ērī, meritus sum, 164.
mergō, ere, mersī, mersum, 147, 2.
mētior, īrī, mēnsus sum, 166.
metō, ere, messuī (rare), messum, 142, 3.
metuō, ere, uī, 162.
micō, āre, uī, 142, 2.
mingō, ere, minxī, mictum, 149, *a.*
minuō, ere, minuī, minūtum, 162.
mīsceō, ēre, uī, mīxtum (mīstum).
misereor, ērī, miseritus (misertus) sum, 164.
mittō, ere, mīsī, missum, 147, 2.
molō, ere, moluī, molitum, 142, 3.
moneō, ēre, uī, itum, 131.
mordeō, ēre, momordī, morsum, 152.
morior, morī, mortuus sum (moritūrus), 165.
moveō, ēre, mōvī, mōtum, 159.
mulceō, ēre, mulsī, mulsum, 147, 1.
mulgeō, ēre, mulsī, mulsum (ctum), 157, 1.
mungō, ere, munxī, munctum, 160.

Nancīscor, ī, nactus (nanctus), 165.
nāscor, ī, nātus sum (nāscitūrus), 165.
necō, āre, āvī, ātum, 142, 2.
nectō, ere, nexī (nexuī), nexum, 148.
neg-legō, ere, -lēxī, -lēctum, 147, 2.
necopīnātus, 167, N. 2.
neō, nēre, nēvī, nētum, 137, *b.*
nequeō, īre, 170.
ningō, ere, ninxī, 149, *b.*
niteō, ēre, uī, *to shine.*
nītor, ī, nīxus (nīsus) sum, 165.
nōlo, nōlle, nōluī, 142, 3; 174.
noceō, ēre, uī (nocitūrus), *to be hurtful.*
nōscō, ere, nōvī, nōtum, 140; 175, 5, *d.*
nōtēscō, ere, nōtuī, 145.
nūbō, ere, nūpsī, nūptum, 147, 2.

Ob-dō, ere, -didī, -ditum, 151, 1.
ob-dormīscō, ere, -dormīvī, -dormītum, 140.
oblīvīscor, ī, oblītus sum, 165.
ob-sideō (SEDEŌ), ēre, -sēdī, -sessum, 159.
ob-sistō, ere, -stitī, -stitum, 154, 1.
obs-olēscō, ere, -olēvī, -olētum, 140.
ob-stō, stāre, stitī (obstātūrus), 151, 2.
obtineō (TENEŌ), ēre, -tinuī, -tentum, 135, 1, *a.*
oc-cidō (CADŌ), ere, -cidī, -cāsum, 153.
oc-cīdō (CAEDŌ), ere, -cīdī, -cīsum, 153.
oc-cinō (CANŌ), ere, -cinuī, 142, 3; 153.
oc-cipiō (CAPIŌ), ere, -cēpī, -ceptum, 160, 3.
occulō, ere, occuluī, occultum, 142, 3.
ōdī, *def.*, 175, 5, *a.*
of-fendō, ere, -fendī, -fēnsum, 160, 2.
of-ferō, -ferre, obtulī, oblātum, 171.
oleō, ēre, uī, *to smell.*
operiō, īre, operuī, opertum, 142, 4.
opīnātus, 167, N. 2.
opperior, īrī, oppertus (*or* ītus), 166.
ōrdior, īrī, ōrsus sum, 166.
orior, īrī, ortus sum (oritūrus), 166.
os-tendō, ere, -tendī, -tēnsum (-tentus), 155.

Pacīscor, ī, pactus sum, 165, 167, N. 2.
palleō, -ēre, -uī, *to be pale.*
pandō, ere, pandī, passum (pānsum), 160, 2.
pangō, ere { pepigī, 155, / panxī, 149, *b*, } pāctum.
parcō, ere, pepercī (parsī), parsūrus, 153.
pariō, ere, peperī, partum (paritūrus), 157.
partior, īrī, ītus, 166.
pāscō, ere, pāvī, pāstum, 140.
pate-facio, ere, -fēcī, -factum, 173, N. 2.
pateō, ēre, uī, *to be open.*
patior, ī, passus sum, 165.
paveō, ēre, pāvī, 159.
pectō, ere, pexī, pexum, 148.
pel-liciō, -licere, -lexī, (licuī), -lectum, 150, 1.

pellō, ere, pepulī, pulsum, 155.
pendeō, ēre, pependī, 152.
pendō, ere, pependī, pēnsum, 155.
per-cellō, ere, perculī, perculsum, 144.
percēnseō (CENSEŌ), ēre, -cēnsuī, -cēnsum, 135, I, *a*.
percitus (CIEŌ), 137.
per-dō, ere, -didī, -ditum, 169, 2, R. I; 151, I.
per-eō, īre, periī, itum, 169, 2, R. I.
per-ficiō, ere, -fēcī, -fectum, 160, 3.
per-fringō, ere, -frēgī, -frāctum, 160, 2.
pergō (REGO), ere, perrēxī, perrēctum, 147, 2.
per-petior (PATIOR), ī, perpessus sum, 165.
per-spiciō, ere, -spexī, -spectum, 150, I.
per-stō, -stāre, -stitī, 151, 2.
per-tineō (TENEŌ), ēre, uī, 135, I, *a*.
pessum-dō, -dare, -dedī, -datum, 151, I.
petō, ere, īvī (iī), ītum, 137, *c*.
piget, pigēre, piguit, pigitum est, *it irks*.
pingō, ere, pinxi, pictum, 149, *a*.
pīnsō, ere, uī (ī), pīnsitum (pīstum, pīnsum), 142, 3.
plangō, ere, planxī, planctum, 149, *b*.
plaudō, ere, plausī, plausum, 147, 2.
plectō, ere, (plexī), plexum, 148.
plector, ī, *to be punished*.
-pleō, 137, *b*.
plicō, āre, uī (āvī), itum (ātum), 142, 2.
pluō, ere, pluit, plūvit, 162.
polleō, ēre, *to be potent*.
polliceor, ērī, itus sum, 164.
pōnō, ere, posuī, positum, 139.
pōscō, ere, popōscī, 156.
pos-sideō (SEDEŌ), ere, -sēdī, -sessum, 159.
pos-sum, posse, potuī, 119.
potior, īrī, ītus sum, 166.
pōtō, āre, āvī, pōtum, pōtātum, 136, 4, *c*.
pōtus, 167, N. 1.
prae-cellō, ere, -celluī, 144.
prae-cinō, ere, -cinuī, 142, 3.
prae-currō, ere, -cucurrī, -cursum, 155.
prae-sideō (SEDEŌ), ēre, -sēdī, 159.
prae-sum, -esse, -fuī, 117.
prae-stō, -stāre, -stitī (-stātūrus), 151, 2.
prandeō, ēre, prandī, prānsum, 159.
prehendō, ere, prehendī, prehēnsum, 160, 2.
premō, ere, pressī, pressum, 147, 2.
prōd-igō (AGO), ere, -ēgī, 160, I.
prō-dō, ere, -didī, -ditum, 151, I.
pro-ficīscor, ī, profectus sum, 165.
pro-fiteor (FATEOR), ērī, -fessus sum, 164.
prōmō (EMO), ere, prōmpsī, prōmptum, 147, 2.
prō-sum, prōdesse, prōfuī, 118.
prō-tendō (TENDŌ), ere, -tendī, -tentum, tēnsum, 155.
psallō, ere, ī, 160, 2.
pudet, ēre, puduit, puditum est, *it shames*.
puerāscō, ere, *to become a boy*.
pungō, ere, pupugī, punctum, 155.
pūnior, īrī, ītus sum, 166.

Quaerō, ere, quaesīvī, quaesītum, 137, *c*.
quaesō, 175, 6.
quatiō, ere, (quassī), quassum, 147, 2.
queō, quīre, 170.
queror, querī, questus sum, 167.
quiēscō, ere, quiēvī, quiētum, 140.

Rādo, ere, rāsī, rāsum, 147, 2.
rapiō, ere, rapuī, raptum, 146.
rauciō, īre, rausī, rausum, 150, 2.
re-cēnseō (CENSEŌ), ēre, -cēnsuī, -cēnsum (recēnsītum), 135, I, *a*.
re-cidō, ere, reccidī, recāsum, 153.
recrūdēscō, ere, -crūduī, *to get raw again*.
re-cumbō, ere, -cubuī, 144.
red-arguō, ere, -arguī, 162.
red-dō, ere, -didī, -ditum, 151, I.
red-igō (AGO), ere, -ēgī, -actum, 160, I.
red-imō, -ēre, 160, I.
re-fellō (FALLŌ), ere, refellī, 155.
re-ferō, -ferre, -tulī, -lātum, 171.
rego, ere, rēxī, rēctum, 147, 2.
re-linquō, ere, -līquī, -lictum, 160, 2.
reminīscor, ī, *to recollect*.

renīdeō, ēre, *to glitter.*
reor, rērī, ratus sum, 164.
re-pellō, ere, reppulī, pulsum, 155.
re-periō, īre, repperī, repertum, 157, 161.
rēpō, ere, rēpsī, rēptum, 147, 2.
re-sipīscō, ere, -sipīvī (sipuī), 140.
re-sistō, ere, -stitī, -stitum, 154, 1.
re-spondeō, ere, -spondī, -spōnsum, 152.
re-stō, stāre, -stitī, 151, 2.
re-stinguō, ere, -stinxī, -stinctum, 149, *b.*
re-tineō (TENEŌ), ere, uī, -tentum, 135, 1, *a.*
re-vertor, ī, revertī, reversum, 160, 1; 167.
re-vīvīscō, ere, vīxī, vīctum, *to revive.*
rīdeō, ēre, rīsī, rīsum, 147, 1.
rigeō, ēre, uī, *to be stiff.*
rōdō, ere, rōsī, rōsum, 147, 2.
rubeō, ēre, ui, *to be red.*
rudō, ere, rudīvī, ītum, 137, *c.*
rumpō, ere, rūpī, ruptum, 160, 2.
ruō, ere, ruī, rutum (ruitūrus), 162.

Saepiō, īre, saepsī, saeptum, 150, 2.
saliō, īre, (saliī,) saluī, saltum, 142, 4.
sallō, ere, (sallī), salsum, 160, 2.
salvē, *def.*, 175, 4.
sanciō, īre, sānxī, sānctum, (sancītum), 150, 2.
sapiō, ere (sapīvī), sapuī, 141.
sarciō, īre, sarsī, sartum, 150, 2.
satis-dō, -dare, -dedi, -datum, 151, 1.
scabō, ere, scābī, *to scratch*, 160, 1.
scalpō, ere, scalpsī, scalptum, 147, 2.
scandō, ere, scandī, scānsum, 160, 2.
scateō, ēre, *to gush forth.*
scindō, ere, scidī, scissum, 160, 3.
scīscō, ere, scīvī, scītum, 140.
scrībō, ere, scrīpsī, scrīptum, 147, 2.
sculpō, ere, sculpsī, sculptum, 147, 2.
secō, āre, secuī, sectum, secātūrus, 142, 2.
sedeō, ēre, sēdī, sessum, 159.
sēligō (LEGO), ere, -lēgī, -lēctum, 160, 1.
sentiō, īre, sēnsī, sēnsum, 150, 2.
sepeliō, īre, īvī, sepultum, 137, *a.*
sequor, ī, secūtus sum, 165.
serō, ere, 142, 3.
serō, ere, sēvī, satum, 138.
serpō, ere, serpsī, serptum, 147, 2.
sīdō, ere, sīdī, 160, 1.
sileō, ēre, uī, *to be silent.*
sinō, ere, sīvī, situm, 139.
sistō, ēre, (stītī), statum, 154, 1.
sitiō, ire, ivi, *to thirst.*
soleō, ēre, solitus sum, 167.
solvō, ere, solvī, solūtum, 160, 1.
sonō, āre, sonuī, sonitum, sonātūrus, 142, 2.
sorbeō, ēre (sorp-sī), sorbuī, 142, 1.
sordeō, ēre, uī, *to be dirty.*
sortior, īrī, sortītus sum, 166.
spargō, ere, sparsī, sparsum, 147, 2.
spernō, ere, sprēvī, sprētum, 139.
-spiciō, 150, 1.
splendeō, ēre, uī, *to shine.*
spondeō, ēre, spopondī, spōnsum, 152.
spuō, ere, spuī, spūtum, 162.
squāleō, ēre, *to be rough, foul.*
statuō, ere, statuī, statūtum, 162.
sternō, ere, strāvī, strātum, 139.
sternuō, ere, sternuī, 162.
stertō, ere, stertuī, 142, 3.
-stinguō, ere, 149, *b.*
stō, stāre, stetī, stātum, 151, 2.
strepō, ere, strepuī, strepitum, 142, 3.
strīdeō, ēre (ere), strīdī, 159.
stringō, ere, strinxī, strictum, 149, *a.*
struō, ere, strūxī, strūctum, 147, 2.
studeō, ēre, uī, *to be zealous.*
stupeō, ēre, uī, *to be astounded.*
suādeō, ēre, suāsī, suāsum, 147, 1.
sub-dō, ere, -didī, -ditum, 151, 1.
sub-igō (AGO), ere, -ēgī, -āctum, 160, 1.
suc-cēdō (CĒDŌ), ere, -cēssī, -cēssum, 147.
suc-cendō, ere, -cendī, -cēnsum, 160, 2.
suc-cēnseō, ēre, uī, -cēnsum, 135, 1, *a.*
suc-currō, ere, -currī, -cursum, 155.
suēscō, ere, suēvī, suētum, 140.
suf-ferō, -ferre, sus-tinuī, 171, N. 2.
suf-ficiō (FACIŌ), ere, -fēcī, -fectum, 160, 3.

suf-fodiō, ere, -fōdī, -fossum, 160, 3.
sug-gerō, ere, -gessī, -gestum, 147, 2.
sūgō, ere, sūxī, sūctum, 147, 2.
sum, esse, fuī, 116.
sūmō (EMO), ere, sūmpsī, sūmptum, 147, 2.
suō, ere, suī, sūtum, 162.
superbiō, īre, *to be haughty*.
super-stō, -stāre, -stetī, 151, 2.
super-sum, -esse, -fuī, 117.
sup-pōnō, ere, -posuī, -positum, 139, A.
surgō (REGO), ere, surrēxī, surrēctum, 147, 2.
surripiō, ere, uī (surpuī), -reptum, 146.

Taedet, pertaesum est, *it tires*.
tangō, ere, tetigī, tāctum, 155.
tegō, ere, tēxī, tēctum, 147, 2.
temnō, ere, 149, *c*.
tendō, ere, tetendī, tēnsum (-tum), 155.
teneō, ēre, tenuī, (tentum), 135, 1, *a*.
tergeō, ēre, tersī, tersum, 147, 1.
terō, ere, trīvī, trītum, 137, *c*.
texō, ere, texuī, textum, 142, 3.
timeō, ēre, uī, *to fear*.
ting(u)ō, ere, tinxī, tinctum, 149, *b*.
tollō, ere (sustulī, sublātum), 155.
tondeō, ēre, totondī, tonsum, 152.
tonō, āre, uī, 142, 2.
torpeō, ēre, uī, *to be torpid*.
torqueō, ēre, torsī, tortum, 147, 1.
torreō, ēre, torruī, tōstum, 135, 1, *a*.
trā-dō, ere, -didī, -ditum, 151, 1.
traho, ere, trāxī, trāctum, 147, 2.
tremō, ere, uī, *to tremble*.
tribuō, ere, uī, tribūtum, 162.
trūdō, ere, trūsī, trūsum, 147, 2.
tueor, ērī (tuitus / tūtus) tūtātus sum, 164.
tumeō, ēre, uī, *to swell*.
tundō, ere, tutudī, tūnsum, tūsum, 155.
turgeō, ēre, tursī, 147, 1.

Ulcīscor, ī, ultus sum, 165.
ungō, ere, ūnxī, ūnctum 149, *b*.
urgeō, ēre, ursī, 147, 1.
ūrō, ere, ūssī, ūstum, 147, 2.
ūtor, ī, ūsus sum, 165.

Vādō, ere, 147, 2.
valē, 175, 4.
vehō, ere, vexī, vectum, 147, 2; 165.
vellō, ere, vellī (vulsī), vulsum, 160, 2.
vēn-dō, ere, -didī, -ditum, 151, 1; 169, 2, R. 1.
vēn-eō, īre, īvī (iī), 169, 2, R. 1.
veniō, īre, vēnī, ventum, 161.
vēnum-dō, -dare, -dedī, -datum, 151, 1.
vereor, ērī, veritus sum, 164.
verrō, ere, verrī, versum, 160, 1.
vertō, ere, vertī, versum, 160, 1.
vescor, ī, 165.
vesperāscō, ere, āvī, 140.
vetō, āre, vetuī, vetitum, 142, 2.
videō, ēre, vīdī, vīsum, 159.
vieō, ēre, ētum, *to plait*. *See* 137, *b*.
vigeō, ēre, uī, *to flourish*.
vinciō, īre, vinxī, vinctum, 150, 2.
vincō, ere, vīcī, victum, 160, 2.
vīsō, ere, vīsī, 160, 1.
vīvō, ere, vīxī, vīctum, 147, 2.
volō, velle, voluī, 142, 3; 174.
volvō, ere, volvī, volūtum, 160, 1.
vomō, ere, vomuī, vomitum, 142, 3.
voveō, ēre, vōvī, vōtum, 159.

GENERAL INDEX.

ABBREVIATIONS.—Abl., ablative; Abs., absolute; Acc., accusative; act., active; adj., adjective; adv., adverb; attrib., attributive, attribution; app., appositive, apposition; Comp., comparison, comparative; constr., construction; cop., copula, copulative; cpd., compound, compounded; Dat., dative; decl., declension; def., definite; dem., demonstrative; fem., feminine; Fut., future; Fut. Pf., future perfect; Gen., genitive; Ger., gerund, gerundive; Impf., imperfect; Impv., imperative; indef., indefinite; Indic., indicative; Inf., infinitive; interrog., interrogative; Loc., locative; masc., masculine; neg., negative; neut., neuter; Nom., nominative; obj., object; Part., partitive; part., participle; pass., passive; Pl., plural; poss., possessive, possession; pred., predicate; prep., preposition; pron., pronoun; rel., relative; Sg., singular; subj., subject; Subjv., subjunctive; subst., substantive; Sup., supine; vb., verb; Voc., vocative.

A—Sound of, 3; weakening of, 8,1; length of final, 707,1. See ab.

ab (ā)—In composition, 9,4; varies with ā as prep., 9,4; syntax of as prep., 417,1; position of, 413,R.1; Dat. after vbs. cpd. with, 347,R.5; gives Point of Reference, 335,N.; with Abl. takes place of second Acc., 339,N.2; with Abl. of Separation, 390; with Abl. of Point of View, ib.2,N.6; with Towns, 391,R.1; with Abl. of Origin, 395; with Abl. of Respect, 397, N.1; with Abl. of Agent, 401; to express Cause, 408,N.3; with Abl. Ger., 433.

abdicare-with se and Abl., 390, N.3.

abesse—with Acc. of Extent, or a and Abl., 335,R.2; with Dat., 349,R.4; with Abl. of Measure, 403,N.1; of Place, 390, N.3; tantum abest ut,—ut, 552,R.1.

abhinc—with Acc., 336, R.3. abhorrēre—with Abl. of Place, 390, N.3.

ability-adjs. of, with Inf., 423, N. 1,c.

abire—with Abl. of Place, 390, N.3.

ABLATIVE—defined, 23,6: 1st decl. Sg. in \$\bar{a}d, Pl. in \$\bar{e}is\$, 29, N.4; Pl. in \$\bar{a}bus\$, 29, R.4; 2d decl. Sg. in \$\bar{o}d\$, 33, N.3: Pl. in \$\bar{e}is\$, 33, N.5; 3d decl. Sg. in \$\bar{e}d\$, \$\bar{i}\$, \$\bar{e}\$, 37,4; mute stems with \$\bar{i}\$, 54: sporadic cases in \$\bar{i}\$, 54, N.2; vowel stems in \$\bar{i}\$, 57, R.2; adjs. used as substs. in \$\bar{i}\$, 57, R.2, N.; 4th decl. in ubus\$, 61, R.1; adjs. in \$\bar{d}\$, 75, N.6; adjs. of three endings in \$\bar{e}\$, 79, R.1; adjs. and parts. in \$\bar{i}\$ and \$\bar{e}\$, 82; adjs. in \$\bar{e}\$ and \$\bar{i}\$, and \$\bar{e}\$, an

83; Comp. of part., 89,R.1; forms advs., 91,2.

With act. vb. cannot be subj. of pass., 217.R.1; with vbs. involving comparison, 296, N.1; prepositional uses instead, ib. N.3; with pro of Disproportion, 298; for inner obj., 333,2, N.4: with abesse and distare, 335, R.2; of Point of Reference. ib. N.; with Acc. after vbs. of Giving and Putting, 348; with preps. instead of Part. Gen., 372.R.2. Scheme of Syntax 384; of Place where, 385: of Towns, 386: of Place whence, 390; with vbs. of Abstaining, 390,2; with Adjs., 390,3; of Towns, 391; preps. with Towns, ib. R.1; of Attendance, 392; of Time, 393; preps... 394; of Origin, 395; preps., ib. N.2; of Material, 396; of Respect, 397; with words of Eminence, ib. N.2; with Comp., 398, 296, and RR.1,2; of Manner, 399; of Quality, 400, and R.1; with cum of unnatural productions, ib. N.2; of Instrument, 401; of Agent, 314, and R.2, 401 and RR.1,2; with special vbs., 401. NN.1-7; of Standard, 402; of Difference, 403; of Price, 404; with vbs of Plenty and Want, 405; with opus and usus, 406: with ūtor, fruor, etc., 407; of Cause, 408 and NN.2-6; of Ger., 431; of Ger. with preps., 433; of Sup., 436.

ABLATIVE ABSOLUTE—concord with two subjs., 285, N.3; syntax of, 409,10; with Interrog., 469, N.; of part., 665, N.2.

abrumpere—with Abl. of Place, **390**,N.3.
absiste—with Inf. for Impv., **271**,2,N.2.
absolvere—with Abl. of Place, **390**,N.3.
absonus—with Abl., **359**,N.2.
Absorption of Correlative—**619**.
absque—**417**,2; with Subjv., **597**,N.
abstaining—vbs. of, with Abl., **390**,2.
abstinēre—with Abl. of Place, **390**,N.3.
abstract—relations expressed by Indic., **254**,R.1; substs. become concrete in Pl., **204**,N.5; formation of, **181**,2,*b*.
abundantia—**84**.
abundāre—with Gen., **383**,1,N.2.
abunde—*very*, **439**,N.3.
abūtī—with Abl., **407** and N.2,*a*.
āc—see **atque**; **āc sī** with Subjv. of Comparison, **602**; **āc sī**= **quasi**, *ib.* N.5.
accēdere—with Dat., *etc.*, **347**,R.2; with **quod**, **525**; with **ut**, **553**,4.
accent—in early Latin, **701**,R.2; in music, **729**; conflict with Ictus, **749**.
accentuation—**15**; effect of enclitics, *ib.* R.1; in cpds., *ib.* R.2; in Voc., *ib.* R.3; early, *ib.* N.
accidit—with Dat., **346**,R.2; sequence after, **513**,R.2; with **ut**, **553**,3.
accipere—with Inf., **527**,R.1.
accommodātus—with Dat. Ger., **429**,N.1.
accumbere—with Dat., *etc.*, **347**,R.2.
ACCUSATIVE—definition, **23**,4. 3d decl. **36**; in **im**, **37**,3; **54**,N.1; in **ēis**, **38**,3; of vowel stems, **57**,R.1 and 5; Pl. in **īs** and **ēs**, **57**, R.5; in Greek substs., **66**, NN. 3 and 4; of adjs. of three endings in **īs**, **ēis**, **79**,N.2; in **īs**, **83**,N.1; of Comp. in **īs**, **ēis**, **89**,R.2; forms advs., **91**,1.
Becomes subj. of pass., **216**; syntax of, **328–343**; general view, **328**, **329**; direct obj., **330**; with vbs. of Emotion, *ib.*R. and N.2; **333**,1,N.1; with verbal substs., **330**, N.3; with adjs. in **undus**, *ib.*N.4; with cpd. vbs., **331**. Inner obj., **332**, **333**; neut. pron and adj., **333**,1; Cognate, *ib.*2; Abl. instead, *ib.*2,N.4; with vbs. of Taste and Smell, *ib.*2,N.5; extension of Cognate idea, *ib.*2,NN.2 and 6. Double Acc., **333**, 1; of Extent, **334–336**; in Degree, **334**, in Space, **335**, in Time, **336**; with **abesse** and **distāre**, **335**,R.2; with **abhinc**, **336**, R.3; with **nātus**, *ib.*R.4; with adjs., *ib.* N.1; of Extent as subj. of pass., *ib.*N.3; of Local Object, **337**; prep. with Large Towns, *ib.* RR.1 and 2; **domum** and **in domum**, *ib.* R.3; force of **ad**, *ib.* R.4; with **ūsque**, *ib.*N.4; with verbal substs., *ib.* N.5; of Respect, **338**; with vbs. of Clothing, *etc.*, and passives, *ib.* N.2; Greek Acc. or Abl. instead, *ib.* N.1. Double Acc., **339–342**; with vbs. of Inquiring, *etc.*, **339**; special vbs., *ib.* RR., NN.; pass. form, *ib.* N.4; with vbs. of Naming, Making, *etc.*, **340**; pass. form, *ib.* R.1; End by **ad** or Dat., *ib.* R.2; one Acc. is cognate, **341** and N.2; one Acc. forms a phrase, **342**; as a general objective case, **343**; with Interjections, *ib.* 1; Acc. and Inf., *ib.* 2; and Dat. with vbs. of Giving and Putting, **348**; with preps. for Part. Gen., **372**,R.2; for Abl. of Standard, **403**,N.2; subj. of Inf., **203**,R.1; **420**; after impersonal Ger., **427**,N.2; of Ger., **430**; of Ger. with preps., **432**; of Sup., **435**; with Inf. as object clause, **526–535**; with Inf. as subj., **535**; with Inf. after vbs. of Emotion, **542**,R.; with Inf. in rel. clause, **635**; with **Inf.** in dependent comparative clause, **641**.
accusing—vbs. of, with Gen., **378**; with other constr., *ib.* RR.2 and 5.
acquiēscere—with Abl., **401**,N.6.
acquitting—vbs. of, with Gen., **378**; with other constr., *ib.* RR.2 and 3.
action, activity—suffixes for, **181**,2; **182**,1.
active voice—**112**,2; **213**; Inf. as pass., **532**,N.2; of something caused to be done, **219**; periphrastic, **247**.
ad—in composition, **9**,4; vbs. cpd. with, take Acc., **331**; with Towns and Countries, **337**,RR.1 and 4; with Acc. of End after vbs. of Taking, *etc.*, **340**,R.2; with Acc. for Dat., **345**,R.2; vbs. cpd. with, take Dat., **347**; *in the neighbourhood of*, **386**, R.2; *hence*, **403**,N.4,*e*; position of, **413**, R.1; as adv., **415**; as prep., **416**,1; with Acc. Ger., **429**,2; **428**,R.2; **432** and R.: after vbs. of Hindering, **432**,R.; with Ger. for Abl. Sup., **436**,N.3; **ad id quod**, **525**,2, N.2.
adaequē—with Abl., **296**,N.1, **398**,N.2.
adaptation—words of, with Dat. Ger., **429**,2.
addere—with **operam** and Dat. Ger., **429**, 1; with **quod**, **525**,1,N.1; with **ut**, **553**,4.
adding—vbs. of, with **quod**, **525**,1; list of, *ib.* N.1: with **ut**, *ib.* N.5; **553**,4.
adductus—with Abl. of Cause, **408**,N.2.
adeō—with **ut**, **552**.
adesse—with Dat., *etc.*, **347**,R.2.

adfatim—*very*, **439**,N.3.
adferre—with **ut**, **553**,1.
adhaerēscere—with Dat., *etc.*, **347**,R.2.
adhortārī—with **ut**, **546**,N.1.
adhūc—strengthens Comp., **301**; *as yet, still*, **478**,N.1.
adicere—with **quod**, **525**,1,N.1.
adigere—with **ut**, **553**,1.
adipīscī—with **ut**, **553**,1.
adīre—with Acc. or **ad**, **331**,R.3.
adiuvāre—with **ut**, **553**,1.
ADJECTIVE—**16**,**2**; and subst., *ib.* R.1,N.1; decl. of, **17**; defined, **72**; 1st and 2d decl., **73**; Gen. and Voc., **73**; stems in **ro**, **74**; with Nom. wanting, **74**,R.2; Pronominal, **76**; 3d decl., **77**; two endings, **78**; stems in **ri**, **78**,2; in **āli** and **āri**, **78**,R.; one ending, **80**: case peculiarities, **83**; abundantia, **84**; varying decl., **84**,2; defective and indeclinable, **85**; comparison of, **86**; correlative, **109**: formation of, **182**.
As subst., **204**,NN.1–4; agreement of pred., **211**; exceptions, *ib.* RR.; attrib. agrees in Gender, **286**; neut. with fem., *ib.* 3; concord of, **289**; with two subjs., **290**; position, **290**.N.2, **291**; meaning varies with position, *ib.* R.1; **676**; superlatives of Order and Sequence, **291**,1,R.2; numerals, **292–295**; comparatives, **296–301**; superlatives, **302**, **303**; of Inclination, Knowledge, *etc.*, in pred., **325**,R.6; verbal with Acc., **330**,N.3, neut. in Cognate Acc., **333**,1; of Extent in Degree, **334** and R.1; or Time, **336**,N.1; with Gen. of Quality, **365**,R.2; of 3d decl. as pred., **366**,R.2; with Abl. of Separation, **390**,3; with Abl. of Attendance, **392**,R.1; with Abl. of Quality, **400**; in Abl. Abs., **410**,NN.4,5; with Inf., **421**, N.1,*c*; with Inf. for Gen. of Ger., **428**,N.3; with Abl. Ger., **431**,N.1; with Abl. Sup., **436**,N.2; neut. with **ut**, **553**,4, and R.2.
adligāre—with **sē** and Gen., **378**,R.1.
admīrārī—with Inf., **533**,R.1.
admodum—*very*, **439**,N.3; with **quam** and Indic., **467**,N.; *yes*, **471**,1.
admonēre—with two Accs., **341**,N.2; with **ut**, **546**,N.1.
Adonic—measure, **789**, **792**.
adorīrī—with Inf., **423**,2.N.2.
adorning—vbs. of, with Abl., **401**,N.1.
adstringere—with **sē** and Gen., **378**,R.1.
adulēscēns—**437**,N.1.
advantage—vbs. of, with Dat., **346**.
ADVERB—defined, **16**,**5**, and R.3; discussion of, **91**, **92**; from Acc., **91**,1; from Abl., *ib.* 2; from Loc., *ib.* 3; uncertain, *ib.* 4; by terminations, **92**,1–5; syntactical and miscellaneous, **92**,6; comparison of, **93**; numeral, **98**; pron., **110**; with Dat., **359**, N.7; with Part. Gen., **372**,N.3; general use of, **439**; position of, **440**; for rel. with prep., **611**,R.1: position of, **677**.
adversārī—with Dat., **346**,R.2.
adversative—sentences, **483–491**; particles, **483**; **cum**, **580**,NN.1 and 2, **587**; **quī**, **634**.
adversus—gives obj. *toward which*, **359**, R.2; as adv., **415**; as prep., **416**,2.
advertere—**animum**, with Acc., **342**.
ae—pronunciation of, **4** and N.; weakening of, **8**,1.
aedēs—omitted, with Gen., **362**,R.3.
aequālis—with Gen. or Dat., **359**,R.1.
aequāre—with Dat., **346**,N.3.
aequum—with **est** instead of **sit**, **254**,R.1; **aequē** with Abl., **296**,N.1; **aequō** after Comp., **398**,N.1; with **atque**, **643**,N.3; **aequē—aequē**, **482**,3.
aes—decl. of, **47**,6.
aestimāre—with Gen., **379**; with Abl., **380**,N.1; with Abl. and **ex**, **402**,R.2.
aetās—in Abl. of Time, **393**,R.5; **id aetātis**, **336**,N.2.
aeternum—as adv., **336**,N.1.
afficere—with Abl. of Means, **401**,N.3.
affīnis—with Dat. or Acc., **359**,R.1; with Gen., **374**,N.2.
affīrmāre—with Inf., **527**,R.2.
age—with Pl., **211**,N.2; with Impv., **269**; **age vērō**, **487**,N.3; **id ago**, with **ut**, **546**,N.1.
agency—suffixes for, **181**,1.
agent—in Abl. with **ab**, **214**, **401**: in Abl., **214**,R.2; in Dat., **215**, **354**, **355**; and Instrument, **401**,R.1.
aggredī—with Inf., **423**,2,N.2.
āiō—**175**,1; supplied from **negō**, **447**,R.; introduces **Ō.R.**, **648**,R.2; with Inf., **527**, R.2.
ālāris—and **ālārius**, **84**,2.
Alcaic—measure, **791**, **799**.
Alcmanian—measure, **786**.
ali—forms indef. prons., **111**,1.
aliēnus—poss. of **alius**, **108**; with Gen. or Dat., **359**,R.1 and N.2.
aliquandō—aliquandō, **482**,N.1.
aliquantum—with **ante**, **403**,N.4.

aliquis and **aliquī**—107; with Pl. vrb., 211,N.2; syntax of, 314; with numerals, 314,R.2,*i*; for **quis** and **quī**, 107,N.1, and 315,N.1; with two negs., 315,N.1; **per aliquem stāre**, with **nē**, **quōminus**, 548,N.1.

alius—decl. of, 76, 108; reciprocal **alius alium**, 221,R.1; with Abl., 319; for **alter**, **cēterī**, *ib.* N.1; *besides*, *ib.* N.2; **alia** as Acc. of Respect, 338,2; **aliter** with Abl. of Measure, 403,N.3; **alius atque alius**, 477, N.9; **aliās—aliās**, 482, 1; **tum—aliās**, **aliās—plērumque**, **interdum—aliās**, *ib.* N.2; **aliō—aliō**, **alibi—alibi**, *ib.* 2; **aliter—aliter**, *ib.* 3; **aliter** strengthens **sīn**, 592; followed by **quam**, **nisi**, **praeter**, 643,N.4; with **atque**, 643,N.3.

allēc—decl. of, 68,12.

alphabet—1. Sounds of letters, *ib.* RR. 1-3; names of letters, *ib.* N.

alter—decl. of, 76, 108; for **secundus**, 96,5; **alter alterum**, reciprocal, 221,R. 1; and **alius**, 319.

alteruter—decl. of, 76, 108.

altitūdō—with Acc. of Extent, 335,R.1.

altus—with Acc. of Extent, 335,R.1.

amāre—122; **amābō**, with Impv., 269; **amāns**, 437,N.1; with Gen., 375,N.2.

amb—in composition, 9,4.

ambīre—conj. of, 169,2,R.1.

ambō—decl. of., 73,R.,95,108; and **uterque**, 292.

amīcus—with Gen. or Dat., 359,R.1.

amplius—with **quam** omitted, 296,R.4.

an—in disjunctive questions, 457,1; in phrases, *ib.* 2; strengthened by **ne**, *ib.* 1,N.2; as a simple interrog. particle, *ib.* 1,N.3; in second part of a disjunctive question, 458; **anne**, *ib.*; and **aut**, *ib.* N.4; **annōn** and **necne**, 459; for **num** or **ne** in indirect question, 460,1,N.1; *or* 497.

anacoluthon—697.

Anacreontic—measure, 819.

anacrusis—and anacrustic scheme, 739

anapaestic—foot, 734; rhythm, 736; varieties of, 777-782; substitutes for, 777.

anaphora—485,N.2; 636,N.4; 682.

angī—with Acc. and Inf., 533,R.1.

angiportus—decl. of, 68,5.

animadvertere—with Inf., 527,R.1.

animals—as instruments or agents, 214, R.2.

animus—with **ut**, 546,N.2; **animum advertere**, with Acc., 342; **animī** as Loc., 374,N.7; in **animō esse**, with Inf., 422, N.5.

Aniō—decl. of, 41,4.

annuere—with Dat., *etc.*, 347,R.2.

ante—in composition, 9,4; vbs. cpd. will take Acc. or Dat., 331, 347; with Abl. of Standard or Acc. of Extent, 403,N.4; position of, 413, R.1 and N.3; as adv., 415; as prep., 416,3; with Acc. Ger., 432 and N.1; with part., 437,N.2.

anteāquam—see **antequam**.

antecedent—action, 561-567; definite, 613; repetition of, 615; incorporation of, 616; indefinite, 621; def. or indef. with Indic. or Subjv., 631,1, and 2.

antecēdere—with Dat., *etc.*, 347,R.2.

antecellere—with Dat., *etc.*, 347,R.2; with Abl. of Respect, 397,N.2.

anteīre—with Dat., *etc.*, 347,R.2.

antepenult—11.

antequam—with Indic., 574-576; with Pr., 575; with Pf. and Fut. Pf., 576; with Subjv., 577.

anterior—87,8.

aorist—forms on **sō**, **sim**, 131,4,*b*.; definition, 224; Pure Pf. as Aor., 236,N.; Hist. Pf., 239; Plupf., 241,N.1; Pf. as Potential of Past, 258,N.2.

apodosis—589; omission of, 601; in comparative sentences, 602; in Indic. in Unreal Conditions, 597,R.3; after vrb. requiring Subjv., *ib.*R.5.

aposiopesis—691.

appārēre—as cop. vb., 206,N.1; with Nom. and Inf., 528,N.2; with **ut**, 553,4.

appellāre—with two Accs., 340; with two Noms., 206.

appointing—vbs. of, with Dat. of Ger., 429,2.

apposition—320; concord in, 321; exceptions, *ib.* RR.,NN.; Partitive, 322, 323; Restrictive, 322; Distributive, 323; whole and part, *ib.* N.2; to sentence, 324; predicate, 325; Gen. of, 361; to names of Towns, 386,R.1; to Loc., 411, R.3; pron. incorporated, 614, R.4; subst. incorporated, 616,2.

appropinquāre—with Dat., 346,R.2.

appurtenance—suffix of, 182,6.

aptus—constr., 552,R.2; with **quī** and Subjv., 631,1.

apud—416,4.

arbitrārī—with Inf., **527**,R.2.
arbitrātū—as Abl. of Cause, **408**,N.1.
arbor—decl. of, **45**,N.
arcēre—with Abl. of Separation, **390**,2,N.2.
Archilochian—measure, **788**, **800**.
arcus—decl. of, **68**,5.
ārdēre—with Inf., **423**,2,N.2; **ārdēns**, to express cause, **408**,N.2.
ārdor—with **ut**, **546**,N.2.
arguere—with Gen., **378**,R.1; with Inf., **528**,N.1.
Aristophanic—measure, **793**.
arrangement—of words, **671-683**; of clauses, **684-687**; grammatical or rhetorical, **672**; ascending and descending, **673**; of simple sentences, **674**; of interrog. sentences, **675**; of adj. and Gen., **676**; of advs., **677**; of preps., **678**; of particles, **679**; of attributes, **680**; of opposites, **681**; of pairs, **682**; anaphoric and chiastic, **682**; poetical, **683**; periods, **685**; historical and oratorical, **687**.
arrīdēre—with Dat., *etc.*, **347**,R.2.
artisan—suffixes for, **181**,3.
ās—decl. of, **48**,R.
Asclepiadean—measure, **802**, **803**.
asking—vbs. of, with two Accs., **339** and R.1,N.1; with Inf. or **ut**, **546** and R.3.
aspergere—with Dat. and Acc., or Acc. and Abl., **348**,R.1.
aspicere—with Inf., **527**,R.1; **aspectū**, **436**,N.1.
aspirates—**6**,2,B.
assentīrī—with Dat., **346**,R.2; **347**,R.2.
assequī—with **ut**, **553**,1.
-assere—as Inf. ending, **131**,4,*b*.4.
asseverations—in Subjv., **262**; in Fut. Indic., *ib.* N.; with **nisi**, **591**,*b*,2.
assidēre—with Dat., *etc.*, **347**,R.2.
assimilations—of vowels, **8**,4; of consonants, **9**,1,2,3; of preps., **9**,4; of Voc., **211**,R.3.
assuēfacere—with Abl. or Dat., **401**,N.2; with Inf., **423**,2,N.2.
assuēscere—with Abl. or Dat., **401**,N.2; with Inf., **423**,2,N.2.
astū—in Abl. of Manner, **399**,N.1.
asyndeton—after demonstrative, **307**, R.4; in coördination, **473**,N., **474**,N., **483**, N., **492**,N.
at—use of, **488** and NN.; **ast**, **488**,N.1.
atque—for **quam**, **296**,N.4; syntax of, **477** and notes; adds a third member, **481**,N.; with adjs. of Likeness, *etc.*, **643**; for **quam** after neg. Comp., **644**,N.2.
atquī—**489**; **atquīn**, *ib.* N.1.
attendance—Abl. of, **392**; with **cum**, *ib.* R.1; instrumental, *ib.* R.2.
attinet—with Inf., **422**,N.4; restrictions with, **627**,R.2.
attraction—in Gender, **211**,R.5; in mood, **508**,4, **629**; of vb. of Saying into Subjv., **541**,N.3, **585**,N.3, **630**,N.3; of Rel., **617**; inverse, **617**,N.2; of mood in general, **662**, **663**.
attributive—**288**; concord of adj., **289**; with two or more substs., **290**; position of, **291**; superlatives of Order and Sequence, **291**,1,R.2; pred., **325**; various peculiarities of, *ib.* RR.; omitted with cognate Acc., **333**,2,N.1; with Abl. of Time, **393**,R.5; omitted with Abl. of Manner, **399**,N.1; with Inf., **421**,N.2; with part., **437**,R.
au—pronunciation of, **4**; weakening of, **8**,1.
auctōrem—esse, with Dat., **346**,N.5; with Inf., **527**,R.2; with **ut**, **546**,N.1.
auctōritās—with **ut**, **546**,N.1; **auctōritāte** as Abl. of Cause, **408**,N.1.
audēre—with Inf., **423**,2,N.2.
audīre—like Gr. ἀκούειν, **206**,N.2; **audiēns**, with Dat., **346**,N.5; with **cum** and Subjv., **580**,R.2; with Inf. and part., **527**,R.1, and N.1; with rel. and Indic., **467**,N.; **audītū**, **436**,N.1.
auscultāre—with Dat., **346**,R.2.
aut—distinguished from **an**, **438**,N.4; use of, **493** and notes; **aut—aut** with Pl., **285**,N.1: subdivides a neg., **445**.
autem—position of, **413**,N.3, **484**,R.; syntax of, **484**; in lively questions, *ib.* N.1; strengthens **sed**, **485**,N.3, **592**.
auxiliārī—with Dat., **346**,R.2.
auxiliāris—and **auxiliārius**, **84**,2.
auxiliary—vbs. with Inf., **280**,1,*b*.
avēre—with Inf., **423**,2,N.2.
āversus—with Dat., **359**,R.5.

Baccar—**68**,12.
Bacchic—foot, **734**; measures, **811-814**.
balneum—**68**,3.
becoming—vbs. of, with two Noms., **206**.
beginning—vbs. of, with Inf., **423**, and N.2.
believing—vbs. of, with Acc. and Inf., **526** and **527**; with Nom., **528**.
bellāre—with Dat., **346**,N.6.

bellum—in Abl. of Time, **394**,R.; **bellī** as Loc., **411**,R.2.
belonging—suffixes for, **182**,5.
benevolus—compared, **87**,4.
beseeching—vbs. of, with **ut**, **546**.
bewaring—vbs. of, with **nē**, **548**.
bibere—with **dare**, **421**,N.1,*b*.
bidding—vbs. of, with Dat., **346**.
biiugus—and **biiugis**, **84**,1.
bimātris—**85**,1.
bīnī—for **duo**, **346**,R.2.
blandīrī—with Dat., **346**,R.2.
boards—with Dat. Ger., **429**,1.
bonus—comparison, **90**; **cuī bonō**, **356**, R.1; **bene**, as adv. of Degree, **439**,N.2, and 3.
books—omit **in** with Abl., **387**.
bōs—decl. of, **52**,7.
brachylogy—**689**.
breathings—**6**,2,A.
buying—vbs. of, with Gen. or Abl., **379**, **380**.

C—sound of, **1**,R.1; name of, **1**,N.
cadere—with Abl. of Separation, **390**,2,N.2.
cæsura—defined, **750**; varieties, **751**; masc. and fem., **752**; bucolic, **753**,R.2; in Iamb. Sen., **759**,N.2; in Iam. Trim. Cat., **761**,N.; in Iam. Trim. Claud., **762**, N.4; in Iam. Oct., **763**,N.*b*.; in Iam. Sept., **764**,N.2; in Troch. Sept., **770**,N.2; in Dac. Hex., **784**,N.2: in alcaic, **791**, **798**, **799**,N.1; in Glyconic, **795**; in Phalaecean, **796**,N.3; in Sapphic, **797**,N.2, **804**; in Archilochian, **800**,N.; in Asclepiadean, **802**,N.1.
calling—vbs. of, with two Accs., **340**; with two Noms., **206**.
calx—decl. of, **70**,D.
campī—as Loc., **411**,R.2.
cantica—defined, **747**; in early Latin, **824**; in later Latin, **825**.
capability—adjs. of, with Inf., **421**,N.1,*c*.
capacity—adjs. of, with Dat. Ger., **429**,2; suffixes for, **182**,2.
capī—with Gen. of Charge, **378**,R.1.
capital—decl. of, **78**,R.
caput—decl. of, **53**,8; **est** with Inf., **422**, N.2.
cardinal numbers—**94**; Gen. Pl. of, **95**, R.2; collective Sg. of, *ib.*; **duo** and **ambō**, **292**; with **singulī**, **295**; for Distributive, **295**,N.; position of, **676**,R.2.
carēre—with Abl., **405**; with Gen., **383**,1, N.2.
carō—decl. of, **41**,4; gender of, **43**,1.
Carthāginī—as Loc., **411**,R.1.
cārus—with Abl. of Price, **404**,N.2.
cases—defined, **23**; strong and weak, **rēctī** and **oblīquī**, **24**; case-forms, **25**; endings, **25**,2.
cassis—decl. of, **68**,12.
cāsū—as Abl. of Manner, **399**,N.1.
catalexis—**742**.
causā—with Gen., **373**; with poss. pron., *ib.* R.2; with Gen. Ger., **428**,R.2; **causa**, in phrases with **ut**, **546**,N.2; **causam vincere**, **333**,2,R.
CAUSAL SENTENCES—coördinate, **498**; particles, **498**; syntax of subordinate, **538**–**542**; general division, **538**, **539**; with **quod**, *etc.*, and Indic., **540**; with **quod**, *etc.*, and Subjv., **541**; with **quia**, *ib.* N.1; rejected reason, *ib.* N.2; with **quandōque**, *ib.* N.5; with vbs. of Emotion, **542**; **sī** for **quod**, *ib.* N.1; with **cum**, **580**,RR.1 and 2, **586**; with **tamquam**, *etc.*, **541**,N.4, **602**,N.4; relative, **634**; clauses in Ō.O., **655**.
causation—vbs. of, with part., **537**; with **ut**, **553**,1; pass. with **ut**, *ib.* 3.
causative verbs—formation of, **191**,4.
cause—Abl. of, **408**; various expressions for, *ib.* NN.; preventing, *ib.* N.4; external, *ib.* N.6; represented by part., **666**, **670**,2.
cavēre—with Subjv. for Impv., **271**,2; with Dat., **346**,N.2; constructions with, **548**,NN. 1 and 3.
ce—appended to **iste**, **104**,3,N.2; to **ille**, *ib.* N.3.
cēdere—with Dat., **346**,R.2; with Abl. of Separation, **390**,2,N.2.
cedo—defective, **175**,6.
cēlāre—with two Accs., or **dē**, **339** and R. 1 and 3,N.1.
celer—comparison of, **87**,1, and N.
cēnsēre—with Inf., **527**,R.2; with **ut**, **546**, N.1; **cēnseō**, *yes*, **471**,2.
centimanus—defective, **85**,2.
cernere—with Inf., **527**,R.1.
certāre—with Dat., **346**,N.6; **rem certāre**, **333**,2,R.
certus—strengthens **quīdam**, **313**,R.3; with Gen., **374**,N.9; **certē**, **certō**, *yes*, **471**,1; **certē**, strengthens **at**, **488**,N.2; **certius (quam)**, with Inf., **422**,N.3;

certum est, with Inf., 423,2,N.2; **certiōrem facere**, with Inf., 527,R.2.
cēssāre—with Inf., 423,2,N.2.
(**cēterus**)—Nom. masc. wanting, 74,R.2, 85,1; use of **cēterum**, 491: **cētera** used partitively, 291,R.2; **alius** instead, 319, N.1: as Acc. of Respect, 338,2.
charge—in Gen. with Judicial verbs, 378; with **nōmine**, *ib.* R.2; in Abl., *ib.* R.3.
chiasmus—682 and R.
choosing—vbs. of, with two Noms., 206; with two Accs., 340; End with Dat. or **ad**, *ib.* R.2; vbs. of, with Final Dat., 356,N.2.
choriambic—feet, 734; rhythms, 801.
cingī—with Acc., 338,N.2.
circā—position of, 413,R.1; as adv., 415; as prep., 416,5; with Acc. Ger., 432 and N.1.
circiter—as prep., 416,6.
circum—in composition, 9,4; vbs. cpd. with, take Acc., 331; never repeated, *ib.* R.2; as adv., 415; as prep., 416,5.
circumdare—with Dat. and Acc., or Acc. and Abl., 348,R.1.
circumfundere—with Acc. and Dat., or Acc. and Abl., 348,R.1.
circumspice—with direct question, 467, N.
circumstantial **cum**—585-588.
cis—as prep., 416,7.
citerior—87,2 and 7.
citius quam—constr. after, 644,R.3.
citrā—as adv., 415; as prep., 416,7.
cīvitās—concord of, in pred., 211,R.6.
clam—as adv., 415; as prep., 416,8.
clanculum—as prep., 416,8.
clīvus—decl. of, 67,2.
clothing—vbs. of, with Acc. of Respect, 338,N.2; with Abl. of Means, 401,N,1.
cluēre—with Nom. and Inf., 528,N.1.
coepī—175,5,*a*, and N.; with Inf., 423, N.3.
cōgere—with Inf., 423,2,N.2; with **ut**, 553, 2; *conclude*, with Inf., 546,R.1, 553,2,N.
cōgitāre—with Inf., 423,2,N.2.
cōgitātiō—in phrases with **ut**, 557,R.
Cognate Accusative—333,2; similar phrases, *ib.* R.; with second Acc., 341; with **prohibēre, iubēre**, *ib.* N.2.
cōgnātus—with Gen. or Dat., 359,R.1.
cōgnitiō—in phrases with **ut**, 557,R.
cōgnōmen esse—with Dat., 349,R.5.
cōgnōscere—with Inf., 527,R.1; **cōgnitū** as Sup., 436,N.1.
coincidence—constr. with, 513,N.3.
coīre—with Dat., 346,N.6.
colligere—with Inf., 527,R.2.
collocāre—with **in** and Abl., 385,R.1; with **in** and Acc., *ib.* N.2.
colus—decl. of, 61,N.5.
comitārī—with Dat., 346,N.2.
comitiīs—as Abl. of Time, 393,R.5.
commiserārī—with Acc., 377,N.2.
committere—with Acc. Ger., 430,N.1; with **ut**, 548.N.1.
commovēre—with **ut**, 553,2; **commōtus**, to express cause, 408,N.2.
commūne—as subst., 211,R.4: in phrases with **ut**, 557,R.; **commūnis**, with Gen. or Dat., 359,R.1.
comparative—in **ior**, 86; in **entior**, 87,4,5; lacking, 87,9; with **quam** or Abl., 296 and RR.; omission of **quam**, *ib.* R.4; age with **nātus**, *ib.* R.5; with **opīniōne**, *ib.* R.6; of Disproportion, 298; omission of **ut** after **quam**, *ib.* R.2; restriction of, 300; strengthened, 301; doubled, *ib.*; with Part. Gen., 372 and R.2; with Abl. of Respect, 398 and R.; with Abl. of Measure, 403,N.1; with Abl. Ger., 431,N. 2; with **quam quī**, 631,3.
COMPARATIVE SENTENCES—638-644; division of, 638; moods in, 639; vb. omitted in, 640; in dependent clauses, 641; correlatives in, 642; *the more—the more*, *ib.* R.2; with **atque**, 643; with **quam**, 644.
comparison—of adjectives, 86; peculiarities, 87; by **magis** and **māximē**, *ib.*6; by **plūs** and **plūrimum**, *ib.* 6,N.2; defective, 87,2,7,9: of participles, 88,89; of advs., 93; irregular, 90; standard of, omitted, 297; of qualities, 299; conditional sentences of, 602.
compelling—vbs. of, with **ut**, 553,2.
compensatory lengthening—9,6,*a*.
comperce—with Inf. for Impv., 271,2,N.2.
comperīre—with Gen., 378,R.1; with Inf., 527,R.1.
compēsce—with Inf. for Impv., 271,2, N.2.
complēre—with Gen., 383,1.
complexus—as a Present, 282,N.
compos—with Gen., 374,N.3.
composition—of words, 193-200; divisions, 193; of substs., 194-198; of vbs., 199, 200.

compounds—attrib., 197,1; dependent, *ib.* 2; poss., 198; quantity in, 715.

con—see **cum.**

cōnārī—with Inf., 423,2,N.2.

cōnātus—defective, 68,5.

concēdere—used personally in pass., 217, N.2; with Dat., 346,R.2; with Inf., 423,2, N.2; 532,N.1; with Acc. Ger., 430,N.1; with **ut,** 548,N.1.

conceiving—vbs. of, with obj. clause, 523.

concessive—Subjv., 264: **cum,** 580,NN.1 and 2, 587; **quī,** 634; part., 609,667,670,4.

CONCESSIVE SENTENCES—603-609; with **etsī,** *etc.*, 604; with **quamquam,** 605; with **quamvīs,** *etc.*, 606; with **licet,** 607; with **ut,** 608; representatives of, 609.

conclūdere—with Inf., 527,R.2.

concord—210; pred. with subj., 211; violations of, *ib.* RR.1-6,NN.1-3; of subj. and pred. multiplied, 285-287; of app., 321; neut. for persons, 323,N.2; of rel., 614.

concupiēns—with Gen., 375,N.2.

concurrere—with Dat., 346,N.6.

condecet—with Inf., 422,N.4.

condemning—vbs. of, with Gen., 378; with other constrs., *ib.* R.2; with Abl., *ib.* R.3; enforced destination, *ib.* R.4.

condiciō—in phrases with **ut,** 546,N.2.

condition—suffixes for, 181,8; indicated by a question, 453,N.3; represented by part., 667,670,4.

conditional **cum**—583.

CONDITIONAL SENTENCES—589-602; division of, 589; sign, 590; negatives, 591; two excluding, 592; equivalents of Protasis, 593; classification of, 594. LOGICAL, 595; in Ō.O., *ib.* R.1; with Subjv., *ib.* RR. 2,3; **sīve—sīve,** *ib.*R.4; **sīquidem,** *ib.*R. 5; **sī modo,** *ib.*R.6; phrases, *ib.*N.1; range of tenses, *ib.*N.2. IDEAL, 596; for unreal, *ib.*R.1; shift to unreal, *ib.*R.2; after **nōn possum,** *ib.* R.3; in Ō.O., *ib.* R.5. UNREAL, 597; Impf. of Past, *ib.* R.1; Indic. in Apodosis, *ib.* RR.2,3; in Ō.O., *ib.* R.4; after a vb. requiring Subjv., *ib.* R. 5; **absque,** *ib.*N.1. INCOMPLETE, 598-601; omission of sign, 598; of vb. of Prot., 599; of Prot., 600; of Apod., 601; of COMPARISON, 602; in Ō.O. general consideration, 656: Logical, 657; Ideal, 658; Unreal, 659: Pf. Inf. and **potuisse,** *ib.* N.

condūcit—with Dat., 346,R.2; with Gen., 379; with Acc. Ger., 430,N.1.

cōnficī—with Inf., 533,R.1; with **tu,** 553,3.

cōnfīdere—with Dat., 346,R.2 and N.2; with Abl., 401,N.6; with Inf., 527,R.2.

cōnfīrmāre—with Inf., 527,R.2.

congruere—with Dat., *etc.*, 347,R.2.

conjugation—defined, 17; systems of, 120; first, 122; second, 123; irregular second, 124; third, 125; third in **iō,** 126; fourth, 127; deponents, 128; periphrastic, 129; notes on; 130,131; change in, 136.

conjunction—defined, 16.7, and R.3.

cōniungere—with Dat. or **cum,** 359,N.3.

CONSECUTIVE SENTENCES—exceptional sequence in, 513; syntax of, 551-558; general division, 551; Pure, 552; **tantum abest ut,** *ib.* R.1; with **dīgnus,** *etc.*, *ib.* R.2; with idea of Design, *ib.* R.3; **ut nōn,** *without*, *ib.* R.4; Complementary, 553; vbs. of Effecting, 553; vbs. of Causation, *ib.* 1; of Compelling, *etc.*, *ib.* 2; Happening, *etc.*, *ib.* 3; impersonals, *ib.*4; vbs. of Hindering, 554-556; **quīn** with vbs. of Preventing, 555,1; with vbs. of Doubt, *ib.* 2; **quīn = ut nōn,** 556; **nōn dubitō quīn,** *ib.* RR.1,2; Explanatory **ut,** 557; Exclamatory question, 558; rel. sentences, 631; with def. antecedent, *ib.* 1; with indef. antecedent, *ib.* 2; with Comp., *ib.* 3; with adj., *ib.* 4; with **quīn,** 632; Indic. for Subjv., *ib.* 2,RR.1,2.

cōnsentāneum—with Inf., 422,N.3.

cōnsentīre—with Dat., *etc.*, 347,R.2.

cōnsequī—and **cōnsequēns,** with **ut,** 553, 1 and 4.

cōnsīdere—with **in** and Abl., 385,R.1.

cōnsilium—in Abl. of Cause, 408,N.1; in phrases, with Inf., 422,N.2, and 428,N.2; with **dare** and **ut,** 546,NN.1 and 2.

cōnsistere—with Abl. of Material, 396, N.1.

consonants—6; double, *ib.*3; sounds of, 7; phonetic variations in, 9; combinations of, 10,R.1.

cōnsors—with Gen., 374,N.2.

cōnspicārī—with Inf., 527,R.1.

cōnspicere—with Inf., 527,R.1.

cōnstāre—with Dat., *etc.*, 347,R.2; with Gen., 379; with Abl. of Material, 396,N. 1; with Nom. and Inf., 528,N.2.

cōnstituere—with **in** and Abl., 385,R.1; with Inf., 423,2,N.2; with **ut,** 546,N.1.

cōnstrūctiō—ad sēnsum, 211,R.1,N.3; ***praegnāns,*** 699.

cōnsuēscere—with Inf., 423,2,N.2; **cōnsuētus**, with Inf., 421,N.1,c.

cōnsuētūdō—in Abl. of Manner, 399,N.1; in phrases, with Inf., 422,N.2, or **ut**, 557, R.

cōnsulere—with two Accs., 339 and N.1; with Dat., 346,R.2 and N.2; **bonī cōnsulere**, 380,N.2.

contemporaneous action—538-573; in Extent, 569,570; in Limit, 571-573.

contendere—with Dat., 346,N.6; with Inf., 423,2,N.2; with **ut**, 546,N.1.

continērī—with Abl. of Material, 396,N.1; **contentus**, with Abl., 401,N.6.

contingit—with **ut**, 553,3; **contigit**, with Dat., 346,R.2; sequence after, 513, N.2; attraction of pred. after, 535,R.3.

continuance—vbs. of, with Inf., 423, and N.2.

contrā—position of, 413,R.1; as adv., 415; as prep., 416,9; with **atque**, 643,N.3.

contracting—vbs. of, with Acc. Ger., 430.

contraction—of shorts, 732.

contrārius—with Gen. or Dat., 359,R.1; with **atque**, 643,N.3.

contrasts—with **hīc—ille**, 307,RR.1,2; with **ipse**, 311,R.1; with **aliquis**, 314; **alter—alter**, *etc.*, 323.

convenīre—Indic. for Subjv., 254,R.1; with Dat., 346,N.2, 347,R.2.

convicting—vbs. of, with Gen., 378; other constr., *ib.* R.2.

coördination—defined, 472; without conjunction, 472,R.; syntax of, 473-503; copulative, 474-482; adversative, 483-491; disjunctive, 492-497; causal and illative, 498-503.

cōpia—with Inf., 428,N.2.

copula—with pred., 205; itself a pred., *ib.* N.; omitted, 209; agrees with pred., 211,R.1,EX.c.

copulative—vbs., 206; with Nom. and Inf., *ib.* R.3. Particles, 474; omitted, *ib.* N., 481. Sentences, 474-482; use of neg. to connect, 480.

cor—decl. of, 53,8; **cordī est**, with Inf., 422,N.5.

cōram—as adv., 415; as prep., 417,3.

cornus—decl. of, 68,5.

corpus—decl. of, 48.

correlatives—109-111; pronominal adjs., 109; advs., 110; cpds., 111; coördinating particles, as **tum—tum, aliās—aliās**, *etc.*, 482; of Rel., 618; absorption of, 619, 621; position of, 620; in comparative sentences, 642; omitted, 642,3.

correption—744.

cōs—defective, 70,D.

countries—in Acc., with prep., 337,R.1; without, *ib.* N.1; in Abl., 391,N.

crassitūdō—with Acc. of Extent, 335,R.1.

crassus—with Acc. of Extent, 335,R.1.

crāstinī—as Loc., 411,N.1.

creāre—with two Accs., 340; with two Noms., 206.

creation—vbs. of, with Inf., 280,1,b.

crēdere—personal in pass., 217,N.1; with Dat., 346,R.2; with Inf., 527,R.2; **crēditur**, with Inf., 528,R.2.

cretic—foot, 734; substitutions for, 806; rhythms, 806-810.

cruciārī—with Inf., 533,R.1.

cūius—as poss. pron., 106,N.4.

culpa—with Epexegetical Gen., 361,2.

cum—and **quom**, 7; in composition, 9,4; with subst. to form cpd. subj., 285,N.2; vbs. cpd. with take Acc., or Dat., 331, 347; with Abl. of Attendance, 392, and R.1; to indicate Time, 394,N.2; with Abl. of Manner, 399; with unnatural productions, 400,R.2; position of, 413,R.1; with Abl. Ger., 433; as prep., 417,4; with **eō** and **quod**, 525,2,N.2; (**prīmum**), *as soon as*, 561-563; Causal, 564,N.2; with Iterative action, 566, 567; with Subjv., *ib.* N.; derivation of, 578; general view of, 579; Temporal, 580; **fuit cum**, *ib.* R.1; **meminī cum**, *ib.* R.2; with Lapses of Time, *ib.* R.3; in early Latin, *ib.* N.1; Inverse, 581; Explicative, 582; Conditional, 583, 590,N.3; Iterative, 584; with Subjv., *ib.* R.; Circumstantial, 585-588; Historical, 585; Causal, 586; Concessive and Adversative, 587; **cum nōn** = *without*, *ib.* R.2; **cum—tum**, 588; mood, *ib.* 2; **cum interim**, with Inf., 635,N.2; with Indic. retained in Ō.O., 655,R.3.

-cumque—makes general relatives, 111,2.

cūncta—Acc. of Respect, 338,2; may omit **in** with Abl. of Place, 388.

cunctārī—with Inf., 423,2,N.2.

cupere—with Pf. Inf., 280,2.e,N.; with Dat., 346,R.2; **cupientī est**, 353,N.2; with Inf., 423,2,N.2; 538,N.4; **cupiēns**, with Gen., 375,N.2.

cupiditās—with **ut**, 546,N.2.

cupidus—with Gen., 374,N.5.

cupressus—decl. of, 68,5.

cūra—with **ut**, **546**,N.2; **cūrae est**, with Inf., **422**,N.5.

cūrāre—with Inf., **423**,2,N.2; with Acc. Ger., **430**,N,1; with part., **537**,N.2; with **ut**, **546**,N.1; **cūrā ut** for Impv., **271**,1, and 2,N.2.

curriculō—as Abl. of Manner, **399**,N.1.

Dactylic—foot, **734**; substitutions, **783**; rhythm, **736**; rhythms, **783-789**.

damnās—indeclinable, **85**,C.

daps—defective, **70**,D.

dare—Pf. **dedrot**, **131**,6; Pr. **danunt**, **133**,IV.,N.2; with **ad** or Dat., **345**,R.2; with Final Dat., **356**,R.2: **operam**, with Dat. Ger., **429**,N.1, or **ut**, **546**,N.1; with Acc. Ger., **430**,N.1; **nūptum**, *etc.*, **435**, N.1; with Pf. part., **537**,N.2; *permit*, with **ut**, **553**,2.

DATIVE—defined, **23**,3; 1st decl. in **āī**, **ā**, **ābus**, **ās**, **ēis**, **29**,NN.3,4; 3d decl. in **ēī**, **e**, **37**,2; 4th decl. in **ubus**, **uēī**, **ū**, **61**,R., and N.2; 5th decl., uncommon, **63**,R.1; in **ē**, **ī**, *ib.* N.2; in Greek substs., **66**,N.2; in adjs. in **āī**, **ā**, **ābus**, **īs** (for **iīs**), **75**, NN.2,6; in **ī** of pron. adjs., **76**,2; with act. vb. unchanged in pass., **217**, **346**, R.1; gives End with vbs. of Taking, *etc.*, **340**,R.2; with **ei** and **vae**, **343**,1,N.2; of Indirect Obj., **344**; with trans. vbs., **345**; with vbs. of Taking Away, *ib.* R.1; and **prō**, *ib.* R.2; with intrans. vbs., **346**; with cpd. vbs., **347**; with vbs. cpd. with **dē**, **ex**, **ab**, *ib.* R.5; and Acc. with vbs. of Giving and Putting, **348**; of Possessor, **349**; of Personal Interest, **350**; Ethical, **351**; of Reference, **352**, **353**; with participles, **353**; of Agent, **215**, **354**; Double, **356**; with substs., **357**; Local, **358**; with adjs., **359**; with cpds. of **dī**, **dis**, **390**,2,N.5; of Ger., **429**.

dē—with Abl. for second Acc., **339**,NN.2,3; vbs. cpd. with take Dat., **347**,R.5; with Abl. of Separation, **390**,1, and 2; to indicate Time, **394**,N.2; with Abl. of Origin, **395**,and N.2; with Abl. of Respect, **397**, N.1; with Abl. of Cause, **408**,N.3; position of, **413**,R.1; as prep., **416**.5; with Abl. Ger., **433**; with part., **437**,N.2; **dē eō quod**, **525**,2,N.2.

death—deponent vb. of as act. in Abl. Abs., **410**,N.1.

dēbēre—Indic. for Subjv., **254**, R.1; Impf. as tense of Disappointment, *ib.* R.2; with Pf. Inf., **280**,2,*b*, and N.3; with Inf., **423**,2,N.2.

decēre—with Pf. Inf., **280**,2,*b*,R.1; with Dat., **346**,N.3; with Abl. of Respect, **397** N.2.

dēcernere—with Inf., **423**,2,N.2, and **546**, R.1; with **ut**, **546**,N.1.

declension—defined, **17**; varieties of, **27**; rules for, **28**; 1st, **29**, **30**; 2d, **31-33**; stems in **-ro** and **-ero**, **32**; 3d, **35-60**; stems of, **35**; formation of Nom. Sg., **36**; liquid stems, **39-46**; sibilant, **47-49**; mute, **50-55**; vowel, **56-59**; 4th, **61**, **62**; 5th, **63**, **64**; vary between 5th and 3d, **63**,R.2; of Greek substs., **65**; adjs. of 1st and 2d, **73**; of pron. adjs., **76**; parts., **80**.

decōrus—with Abl., **397**,N.2.

decreeing—vbs. of, with Dat. Ger., **429**,2.

dēdecet—with Inf., **422**,N.4.

dēesse—with Dat., **349**.R.4.

dēferre—with Gen. of Charge, **378**,R.1.

dēfessus—with Inf., **421**,N.1,*c*.

dēficere—with Acc., **346**,N.3.

dēfīgere—with **in** and Abl., **385**,R.1.

degree—advs. of, modify other advs., **459**, N.2.

dēicere—with Abl., **390**,2,N.3.

dēlectārī—with Acc., **346**,N.3.

deliberative questions—**265**; Subjv. in Ō.O., **651**,R.2.

dēlīberātum est—with Inf., **423**,2,N.2.

dēlicium—decl. of, **68**,3.

dēligere—with two Accs., **340**; with two Noms., **206**.

demanding—vbs. of, with **ut**, **546**.

dēmergere—with **in** and Abl., **385**,R.1.

dēmīrārī—with Inf., **533**,R.1.

dēmōnstrāre—with Inf., **527**,R.2.

demonstratives—**104**; attracted in Gender, **211**,R.5, and N.3; syntax of, **305-307**; **hīc**, **305**; **iste**, **306**; **ille**, **307**; **hīc—ille**, *ib.* RR.1,2; advs. similarly used, *ib.* R.3; strengthened by **quidem**, *ib.* R.4; reflexive of, **521**,R.5; followed by **quod**, **525**,2; continue a rel. clause, **636** N.1; position of, **676**,R.1.

dēmovēre—with Abl., **390**,2,N.3.

denominative—**179**,2, and N.; Pf. of vbs., **134**,V.; formation of vbs., **192**.

dense growths—suffixes for, **181**,11.

dentals—**6**,1; suffixes with, **186**.

dēpellere—with Abl., **390**,2,N.3.

deponent—**113**; conjugation, **128**; list of, **163-166**; semi-, **167**; how used, **220**.

dēprecārī—with **nē, 548,N.1.**

dēprehendī—with Gen. of Charge, **378,** R.1.

depriving—vbs. of, with Abl., **405,**N.

derivative words—**179,**2.

descent—suffixes for, **182,11.**

dēsīderāre—with Inf., **423,**2,N.2.

desiderative verbs—formation of, **191,**3.

dēsinere—with Inf., **423,**2,NN.2,3.

desire—adjs. of, with Gen., **374** ; vbs. of, with Inf., **281,**c.; **423,**2,NN.2,4; sequence after, **515.**R.3 ; with Acc. and Inf., **532** ; with **ut**, *ib.* N.1-4 ; with part., **537,**N.1 ; with complementary Final clause, **546.**

dēsistere—with Abl., **390,**2,N.3.

dēspērāre—with Dat., **346,**R.2 ; with Inf., **527,**R.2.

determinative pronouns—**103** ; syntax of, **308.**

dēterrēre—with Inf., **423,**2,N.2 ; with **nē, 548,**N.1 ; with **quōminus, 549,**N.1.

dēturbāre—with Abl., **390,**2,N,3.

deus—decl. of, **33,**R.6.

dexter—decl. of, **74,**R.1 ; Comp. of, **87,**1, R.1 ; *ib.* 2 and 7,

diæresis—**5, 753.**

dialysis—**724.**

diastolé—**721.**

dica—defective, **70,**D.

dīcere—with two Noms. in pass., **206** ; omission of, **209,**N.5 ; **dīxerat** as Aor., **241,**N.1 ; **dīcat, dīxerit aliquis, 257,**2 ; with Acc. and Inf., **527,**R.1 ; with Nom. and Inf., **528,** and N.1 ; **dīcitur** and **dictum est,** *ib.* R.2 ; not confined to 3d person, *ib.* N.4 ; with **ut, 546,**N.1 ; **dīc,** with Indic. question, **467,**N.; **dictū,** in Sup., **436,**N.

[diciō]—defective, **70,**D.

diē—as Loc., **91,**3 ; as Abl. of Time, **393,** R.5 ; **diū,** *by day,* **91,**2.*f.*

difference—measure of, **403** ; vbs. of, with Abl., *ib.* N.1.

differre—with Dat., **346,**N.6.

difficile—comparison of, **87,**3 ; with **est** for Subjv., **254.**R.1; with Inf., **421,**N.1,*c.*

difficulty—adjs. of, with Abl. Sup., **436,**N.2.

diffīdere—with Dat., **346,**R.2, and N.2 ; not Abl., **401,**N.6.

dīgnārī—with Abl. of Respect, **397,**N.2.

dīgnus—with Gen., **374,**N.10 ; with Abl. of Respect, **397,**N.2 ; constr. after, **552,** R.2 ; **quī** or **ut,** with Subjv., **631,**1, and R.2.

dīluvium—heteroclite, **68,6.**

diminutive—suffixes for, **181,12, 182,12** ; vbs., **192,**2.

diphthongs—4 and N. ; length of, **14** ; quantity of, **705.**

dis—in composition, **9,**4.

disagreement—vbs. of, with Dat., **346,**N.6.

dīscere—pass. of **docēre, 339,**N.4 ; with Inf., **527,**R.1.

discrepāre—with Dat., **346,**N.6.

discruciārī—with Inf., **533,**R.1.

disgust—adjs. of, with Gen., **374.**

disinclination—adj. of, for advs., **325,**R.6.

disjunctive—particles, **492** ; sentences, **492-497** ; particles omitted, **492,**N. ; questions, **452** ; forms of, **458**; indirect, **460,**2.

displeasure—vbs. of, with Dat., **346** ; adjs. of, with Abl. Sup., **436,**N.2.

displicēre—with Dat., **346,**R.2 ; **displicet,** with Inf., **422,**N.4.

disproportion—by **quam prō, quī, ut,** *etc.*, **298** ; by positive, with preps.. *ib.* R.; omission of **ut** after **quam,** *ib.* N.2.

dispudet—with Gen., **377,**N.1 ; with Inf., **422,**N.4.

dissentīre—with Dat., **346,**N.6.

dissimilation—of Consonants, **9,5.**

dissimilis—Comp. of, **87,**3.

dissimulāre—with Inf., **527,**R.2.

distaedet—with Gen., **377,**N.1.

dīstāre—with Acc., or **ā** and Abl., **335,**R. 2 ; with Dat., **346,** N.6 ; with Abl. of Measure, **403,**N.1.

distributives—**97** ; with **plūrālia tantum,** *ib.* R.3 ; for cardinals, *ib.* N.1, **295,** N. ; syntax of, **295**; in apposition, **323.**

dīverbium—**747.**

dīves—Comp. of, **87,**10.

dīvīnam rem facere—with Abl. of Means, **401,**N.4.

docēre—with two Accs., or **dē, 339,** and R. 1; with **ab,** *ib.* R.2; **doctus,** *ib.* R.2, and N.4; **dīscere** as pass., *ib.* N.4 ; constr. after, **423,**N.6.

doing—vbs. of, take obj. clause, **523,** and **525,**1, and N.4.

dolēre—with Inf., **533,**R.1 ; **dolet,** with Dat., **346,**N.1 ; with Dat. and Inf., **533,** R.1.

dolō—as Abl. of Manner, **399,**N.1.

domus—decl., **61,**R.2, **68,**5; Acc. as Limit of Motion, **337**; Abl. of Separation, **390,** 2; **domī, 411,**R.2 ; with Gen. of poss. pron., **411,**R.4.

dōnāre—with Dat. and Acc., or Acc. and Abl., **348**,R.1.
dōnec—derivation, **568** and R.; of complete coextension, with Indic., **569**; *until*, with Indic., **571**; inverse, *ib.* N.6; with Subjv., **572**; to express subordination, *ib.* R.
dōnicum—**568**; range of, **571**,N.4.
dōnique—range of, **571**,N.4.
doubt—vbs. of, with **quīn**, **555**,2.
dropping—vbs. of, with **quod** clause, **525**, 1; with **ut**, *ib.* N.4.
dubitāre—**an**, **457**,2; with Inf., **423**,2,N. 2; **nōn dubitō**, with **quīn**, **555**,2,R.1; with Interrog., *ib.* R.2; with Inf., *ib.* R.3, and N.
dubium—with **an** and Subjv., **457**,2.
dūcere—with pred. Nom. or phrase, **206**, R.1; with Final Dat., **356**,R.2; with Gen. of Price, **379**; **pēnsī dūcere**, **380**,1,N.2; *deem*, with Acc. and Inf., **527**,R.2; *lead*, with **ut**, **553**,2.
dum—enclitic, with Impv., **269**; with Pr. Indic., **229**,R.; force of, **568**,R.; of complete coextension, **569**; of partial coextension, **570**; *until*, with Indic., **571**; with Subjv., **572**; to express subordination, *ib.* R.; *provided that*, **573**; with **modo**, *ib.*; with Pr. for participle, **570**,NN.1 and 2; causal, *ib.*; retained, with Indic. in Ō.O., **655**,R.3, **663**,1,N.1.
dummodo—*provided that*, **573**.
duo—decl. of, **73**,R., **95**, and **ambō, uterque**, **292**.
dūritia—heteroclite, **68**,2.
duty—vbs. of, with Inf., **423** and N.2.

E—sound of, **3**; weakening of, **8**,1; length of final, **707**,2; **ē** and **ex** in comp., **9**,4.
ease—adjs. of, with Abl. Sup., **436**,N.2.
ebur—decl. of, **44**,5.
ēcastor—strengthens **atque**, **477**,N.2.
ecce—with Acc. and Nom., **343**,1,N.2.
ecquis—**106** and N.5.
ecthlipsis—**719**,2.
edere—conjugation of, **172**,N.
ēdīcere—with Inf., **527**,R.2; with **ut**, **546**, N.1.
ēdūcere—with Abl., **390**,2.N.3.
effecting—vbs. of, have Final Sequence, **543**,R.1, and N.2; constr. of, **553**.
efferre—with Abl., **390**,2,N.3.
efficere—with Subjv. and **ut**, **553**,1 and 3; with Inf., **527**,R.2, **553**,2,N.
egēnus—Comp. of, **87**,5; with Gen. or Abl., **405**,N.3.
egēre—with Gen. or Acc., **383**,1, **405**,N.2.
ego—decl. of, **100**; Gen. Pl., **nostrum, nostrī**, **100**,R.2, **304**,2 and 3; poss. pron. instead, *ib.* 2,N.2; **nōs** in Ō.O., **660**,4.
ēgredī—with Abl., **390**,2,N.3.
ēgregiē—adv. of Degree, **439**,N.2.
ei—with Dat. in exclamations, **343**,1,N.2.
ēicere—with Abl., **390**,2,N.3.
ēlābī—with Abl., **390**,2,N.3.
Elegiambus—**821**.
elision—**719**,1; in Iam. Sen., **759**,N.3; in Dac. Hex., **784**,N.5; in Pent., **786**,N.2; in Sapphic, **797**,N.3; in Asclepiadean, **802**, N.2.
ellipsis—**688**; see Omission.
em—with Acc. of Exclamation, **343**,1, N.2.
emere—with Gen., **379**; **bene emere**, **380**, 2,R.
eminence—words of, with Abl., **397**,N.2.
ēmittere—with Abl., **390**,2,N.3.
emotion—vbs. of, with Acc., **330**,R. and N. 2, **333**,1, N.1; vbs. of, with Abl. of Cause, **408**; with Acc. and Inf., **533**; in Nom. of Part., **536**,N.2; Causal sentences after, **542** and R.; perplexing, with indirect question or **sī**, **542**,N.1.
emphasis—in arrangement, **672**,2,*a*.
ēn—in exclamations, **343**,1,N.2.
enallage—**693**.
enclitics—effect of, on pronunciation, **15**, R.1.
endeavour—vbs. of, with **ut**, **546**, 1.
ending—vbs. of, with Inf., **423**,2 and N.2.
endings—of cases, **26**,2. **27**.
endowing—vbs. of, with Abl. of Means, **401**,N.1.
enim—position of, **413**,N.3, **484**,R., **498**,N.1; *yes for*, **471**,R.; strengthens **sed**, **485**,N. 3, **498**; asseverative, **498**,N.2; combinations of, *ib.* N.6; after **quia**, *ib.* N.7.
enimvērō—strengthens **sed**, **485**,N.3.
ēnītī—with Inf., **423**,2,N.2.
enumerations—in Abl. without **in**, **387**.
epanorthosis—**484**,R 1.
epenthesis—of vowels, **8**,3; of consonants, **9**,7.
epicene substantives—**21**,3.
epulum—heteroclite, **68**,3.
ergā—use of, **416**,10; with Acc. Ger., **432** N.1.

ergō—with Gen., **373**; as adv., **399**,N.1; with Gen. Ger., **428**,R.2; usage of, **502** and N.1; position of, *ib.* N.2; combinations of, *ib.* N.3.

ēripere—with Abl., **390**,2,N.3.

ērudīre—with Abl. or **dē**, **339**,R.2 and N. 3; with **in** or Abl., **401**,N.1.

esse—conjugation of, **116**; early forms, *ib.* NN.; cpds., **117**; as copula, **205**; **esse prō, in numerō**, *etc.*, **206**,R.1; omitted, **209** and NN., **280**,2,*b*,R.2 and *c*; with Fut. part. to form periphrastic, **247**; cpd. tenses with **fuī**, *etc.*, *ib.* R.1; **forem** for **essem**, *ib.* N.1, **250**,N.2, **251**,N.2; with Pr. part., **247**,N.2; **futūrum esse ut**, **248**; other forms, *ib.* NN.; in **eō est ut**, **249**; with Pf. part., **250**; variations, *ib.* RR.,NN.; with Ger., **251**,1; with Final Dat., **356**,R.2; with Double Dat., *ib.* R.3; with Gen., **379**; with **in** and Acc., **385**,N.3; with Abl., **401**,N.7; with Gen. Ger., **428**,R.2; with Dat. Ger., **429**,1; **futūrus** as adj., **437**,N.; **esse quod**, **525**,1,N.2; **est**, *it is the case*, with **ut**, **553**,3; **fuit cum**, with Subjv., **580**, R.1; restrictions with, **627**,R.2; **sunt quī**, with Subjv., **631**,2.

esseda—heteroclite, **68**,1.

et—in numerals, **96**,4, **97**,4; **et—et**, with Pl., **285**,N.; usage of, **475**; = **et tamen**, *ib.* N.1; for **etiam**, *ib.* N.2, **482**,5,N.2; omitted, **481**,2,N. and 3; with adjs. of Likeness and Unlikeness, **643**,N.2.

etenim—use of, **498** and NN.

Ethical Dative—**351**.

etiam—strengthens comparative, **301**; syntax of, **478** and NN.; *yes*, **471**,1; and **quoque**, **479** R. and N.1; with **tum**, **478**, N.1; after **sed, vērum**, **482**,5, and N.1.

etiamsī—**603** and N.; syntax of, **604** and RR.

etsī—**603**; with Indic. or Subjv., **604**; *and yet*, *ib.* R.2; with part., **609**,N.1, **667**,N.; with adj. or adv., *ib.* N.2; with Inf., **635**, N.2.

ēvādere—with two Noms., **206**.

ēvenit—with Dat., **346**,R.2; with **ut**, **553**,3.

event—suffixes for, **181**,2.

ēvertere—with Abl., **390**,2,N.3.

ex—in comp., **9**,4; vbs. cpd. with, take Dat., **347**,R.5; with Abl. of Separation, **390**,1 and 2; with Towns, **391**,R.1; with Abl. of Origin, **395** and N.2; with Abl. of Material, **396**; with Abl. of Respect, **397**, N.1; with Abl. of Measure, **402**,R.2; with Abl. of Cause, **408**,N.3, **413**,R.1; use as prep., **417**,6; with Abl. Ger., **433**; **ex eō quod**, **525**,2,N.2.

exadversus—use of, **416**,2.

excēdere—with Abl., **390**,2,N.3.

excellere—with Dat., **347**,R.4; with Abl. of Respect, **397**,N.2; with Abl. of Measure, **403**,N.1.

exceptō—with **quod**, **525**,2,N.2.

exclamations—in Acc., **343**,1; in Gen., **383**,3; in Acc. and Inf., **534**; exclamatory questions, **558**.

exclūdere—with Abl., **390**,2,N.3.

excluding—vbs. of, with Abl., **390**,2.

exemplum—in phrases with **ut**, **546**,N.2.

exigere—with ordinal, **294**; with two Accs., **339** and N.1.

exīre—with Abl., **390**,2,N.3.

exīstimāre—with Gen., **379**; with **ex** and Abl., **402**,R.2; with Nom. and Inf., **528**, N.1; with Acc. and Inf., **527**,R.2.

exlēx—defective, **85**,2.

exōrāre—with **ut**, **553**,2.

exōrdīrī—with Inf., **423**,2,N.2.

expedit—with Dat., **346**,R.2.

expellere—with Abl., **390**,2,N.3.

expers—with Gen., **374**,N.2; with Abl., **390**,3,N.1.

expetere—with Pf. Inf. pass., **280**,2,*c*,N.

explēre—with Gen., **383**,1,N.2; **explēnunt**, **133**,IV.N.2.

explicative **cum**—**580**,NN.1,2, **582**.

expōnere—with **in** and Acc., **385**,N.2.

expōscere—with two Accs., **339** and N.1.

exprimere—with **ut**, **553**,1.

expūgnāre—with **ut**, **553**,1.

exsequiās—with **īre**, **333**,2,R.

exsistere—with Abl., **390**,2,N.3.

exsolvere—with Abl., **390**,2,N.3.

exspectāre—constr. of, **572**.

exspectātiōne—as Abl. of Respect, **398**, N.1.

exspēs—defective, **85**,2.

extent—in Degree, **334**; in Space, **335**; in Time, **336**; Acc. of, as subj. of pass., **336**,N.3.

exterior—Comp. of, **87**,2 and 7.

extorquēre—with **ut**, **553**,1.

extrā—as adv., **415**; as prep., **416**,11.

extrēmum—Comp. of, **87**,2; with masc. subj., **211**,R.4; with **ut**, **553**,4.

exturbāre—with Abl., **390**,2,N.3.

exuī—with Acc. of Respect, **338**,N.2; with Dat. and Acc., or Acc. and Abl., **348**,R.1.

facere—early Pf., **fēced**, **131**,6; omission of, **209**,N.5; **mīrum factum**, **209**,N.2; **fac (ut)** for Impv., **271**,1; **lūdōs** and second Acc., **342**; with pred. Gen., **366**, R.1; **nihil reliquī**, **369**,R.2; **quod facere possum**, **372**,N.3; with **reum** and Gen., **378**,R.1; with Gen. of Price, **379**; **bonī**, *ib.* 1,N.2; **(sacrum) facere**, with Abl., **401**,NN.4,7; **fīnem facere**, with Dat. Ger., **429**,N.1; *represent*, with Acc. and Inf., **527**,R.2; with Pf. part., **537**,N.2; with consecutive clause, **553**,1; with Inf., **553**,2,N.; **facere (faxō) ut** as periphrasis, *ib.* 1; **nōn possum (facere) quīn**, **556**; Sup. of, **436**,N.

facilis—comparison of, **87**,3; with Inf., **421**,N,1,*c*.

facinus—with **est** and Inf., **422**,N.2.

faex—decl. of, **52**,7, **70**,C.

fāgus—heteroclite, **68**,5.

falsus—without Comp., **87**,9; with **ut**, **553**,4.

fāma—with **est** and Inf., **527**,R,2.

fames—heteroclite, **68**,8.

fārī—conj. of, **175**,3, and N.

fās—**70**,B.; with Inf., **422**,N.2, **428**,N.2; with Abl. Sup., **436**,N.2.

fastening—vbs. of, with **ex, ab, dē**, **385**, R.2.

fāstīdiōsus—with Gen., **374**,N.5.

faterī—with Acc. and Inf., **527**,R.2.

fātum—with **est** and Inf., **422**,N.2, and **428**,N.2.

[**faux**]—decl. of, **52**,7.

favēre—with Dat., **346**,R.2.

fear—sequence after vbs. of, **515**,R.3; clauses of, and Final Clauses, **543**,R.3; syntax of clause of, **550**; Inf. or Indirect question after, *ib.* NN.4,5.

femur—decl. of, **44**.5, **68**,12.

ferē—position of, **677**,R.1.

ferīre—with **foedus**, **333**,2,R.

ferōx—with **est** and Inf., **533**,R.1.

ferre—conj. of, **171**; **lēgem** with **ut**, **546**,N.1; in phrases with **ut**, **553**,1 and 2.

fēstīnāre—with Inf., **423**,2,N.2.

fīcus—heteroclite, **68**,5.

fidem—habēre with Dat., **346**,N. 5.

fīdere—with Dat., **346**,R.2 and N.2; with Abl., **401**,N.6.

fierī—conjugation of, **173** and NN.; with two Noms., **206**, **304**,R.1; with Gen. of Price, **379**; with **ex** or **dē**, **396**,N.2; = *to be sacrificed*, with Abl., **401**,NN.5,7; with **ut**, **553**,3; **fierī potis est ut**, *ib.* N.

figure—Whole and Part, **323**,N.2; Figures of Syntax and Rhetoric, **688-700**; of Prosody, **718-728**.

fīlia—decl. of, **29**,R.4.

filling—vbs. of, with Abl., **405**.

fīlum—heterogeneous, **67**,2,*b*.

FINAL SENTENCES—with Interrogative particle, **470**; general view, **543**, **544**; Pure, **545**; **ut nē**, or **ut nōn**, *ib.* RR.1,2; Complementary, **546-549**; with vbs. of Will and Desire, **546**; Inf. instead, *ib.* R.1; with vbs. of Hindering, **547-549**; Subjv. without **ut**, *ib.* R.2; **ut nē**, *ib.* R,3; with Substantives, *ib.* N.2; Inf. instead, *ib.* N.3; **nē** with vbs. of Preventing, **548**; **quōminus**, **549**; with vbs. of Fear, **550**; eight circumlocutions for, **544**.R.2; sequence in, **512**.

final syllables—quantity of, **711-713**.

fine—in Gen. or Abl., **378**,R.3.

fīne(ī)—as prep., **417**,7.

fitness—adjs. of, with Dat., **359**; with Dat. Ger., **429**.

flāgitāre—with Abl. or **ā**, **339**,R.1, and N.1; with **ut**, **546**,NN.1,3.

flāgitium hominis—**369**,N.1, **361**,N.3.

flāmen—defective, **70**,D.

floccī—as Gen. of Price, **380**,1.

fluere—with Abl. of Means, **401**,N,5.

flūmen—with Gen. of App., **361**,N.1.

foedus—with **ferīre**, **333**,2,R.; in phrases with **ut**, **546**,N.2.

following—vbs. of, with **ut**, **553**,3.

foot—in Metre, **733**; names of, **734**; equality of, **740**; conflict of Word and Verse, **750**.

forās—**91**,1,*d*.

forbidding—vbs. of, with Dat., **346**; with **nē**, **548**.

forgetting—vbs. of, with Gen. or Acc., **376** and R.2.

FORMATION OF WORDS—**176-200**; simple words, **179-192**; primitives and derivatives, **179**; suffixes, **180**; formation of substs., **181**; of adjs., **182**; with suffixes, **183**. Suffixes in detail—vowels, **184**; gutturals, **185**; dentals, **186**; labials, **187**; *s*, **188**; liquids, **189**; formation of vbs., **190**; **verbālia**, **191**;

frequentatives or intensives, *ib.* 1; inchoatives, *ib.* 2; desideratives, *ib.* 3; causatives, *ib.* 4; meditatives, *ib.* 5; **dēnōminātīva**, 192; cpd. words, 193–200; substs., 191–198; vbs., 199, 200; see compounds.
formīdāre—with Inf. 423,2,N.2, and 533, R.1.
fōrsitan—457,2,N.
forte nisi—591,R.4, and N.3.
fortiter—*very*, 439,N.3.
forum—defective, 70,D.
fraude—as Abl. of Manner, 399,N.1.
fremere—with Acc. and Inf., 533,R.1.
frequēns—in pred. attribution, 325,R.6; with Abl., 405,N.3.
frequentative verbs—formation of, 191,1.
fretum—heteroclite, 68,5.
frētus—with Abl., 401,N.6.
friendliness—adjs. of, with Dat., 359.
frūgī—85,C.; Comp. of, 90.
fruī—with Abl., 407, and N.2,*b*; personal Ger., 427,N.5.
frūnīscī—with Abl., 407,N.2,*b*.
[**frūx**]—defective, 70,D.
fugere—with Inf. for Impv., 271,2,N.2; **fugit mē**, with Pr. Inf., 281,2,N.
fugitāns—with Gen., 375,N.2.
fulmentum—heteroclite, 68,3.
fulness—suffixes for, 182,10.
fulness—adjs. of, with Gen., 374; vbs. of, with Gen., 383,1.
function—suffixes for, 181,9; in Dat. Ger., 429.
fungī—with Abl., 406 and N.2,*c*; personal Ger., 427,N.5.
fūstis—heteroclite, 68,5.
FUTURE—112,3; formation of, 114,115; early forms, 130,3; part. in **ūrum** for fem., 211,N.1; definition of, 223; usage of, 243; of **volō** and **possum**, *ib.* R.2; as gnomic, *ib.* N.1; in Impv. sense, 243; periphrastic act., 247; Indic. for Deliberative Subjv., 254,N.2; part. act., 283; part. as subst., 437,N.1; part. as an adj., 438,N.; representation of in Ō. O., 514, 515; periphrastic in Unreal Cond., *ib.* R.1; Inf., 530; in rel. sentences, 622; syntax of part., 669, 670.
FUTURE PERFECT—112,3; formation of, 114,115; in **sō**, 131,4,*b*,1; defined, 223; syntax of, 244; as Fut., *ib.* R.1; with **nōlō, volō, possum**, *etc.*, *ib.* R.3; in both clauses, *ib.* R.4; independent use of, *ib.* N.1; periphrastic, with **habeō**, *ib.* N.2; as Impv., 245; Representation of, in Ō. O., 514,515; Pf. and Plupf. periphrastic in Unreal Condition, 515,R.1; in rel. sentences, 622.

Galliambic Verse—818.
gaudēre—with **sī**, 542,N.1; **gāvīsus** as Pr., 282,N.
gender—19; common, 21,1; epicene, *ib.* 3; **substantīva mōbilia**, *ib.* 2; of 1st Decl., 30; of 2d Decl., 34; of 3d Decl., 39, 43,46,49,55,58; of 4th Decl., 62; of 5th Decl., 64; concord in, 286; neut. Pl. with feminines, *ib.* 3.
GENITIVE—defined, 23,2; of 1st Decl. in **ās, āī, um**, 29,RR.,NN.; of 2d Decl. in **ī** (from stems in **io**), in **um**, in **ēī**, 33,RR., NN.; of 3d Decl. in **us, es**, 37,1; in **um, ium**, 38,2, 54, 57,R.3; of 4th Decl. in **os, is, ī, uum**, 61,N.1; of 5th Decl. in **ēs, ēī, ē**, 63,N.1; of Greek substs. in **ōn, eōn**, 65,R.1; **oes**, 66,N.1; of adjs., 73; in **ī, āī, aes, es, um**, 75,NN.; of pron. adjs. in **īus**, 76,1; of adjs. of three endings in **um, ium**, 79,R.2, 82, 83,N.2; of Comp. of part., 89,R.3; of Cardinals, 95,R.2; of Distributives, 97,R.1.
not subj. of pass., 217,R.1; with **mīlle**, 293 and N.; with Comp. for Abl., 296,N.2; **meī**, *etc.*, as objective, 304,2; **nostrum** as Part., *ib.*3; poss. pron. for Gen., 304,2,N. 2; in app. to poss. pron., 321,R.2; Part. Gen. for Part. App., 323,R.; with **nōmen est**, 349,R.6; general view, 360; translated by abstract subst., *ib.* R.2; Adnominal, Appositive, 361; Epexegetical, 361; Possessive, 362; **flāgitium hominis**, 361, N.1; Family, 362,N.1; Chorographic, *ib.* N.2; Subjective and Objective, 363; two with one subst., *ib.* R.2; 1st and 3d persons as possessive, 364; of Quality, 365; as Pred., 366; with **facere**, *ib.* R.1; **auctōris**, *ib.*; **generis**, 368,R.; with prepositional subst., 373; with adjs., 374 and NN.; with participles and verbals, 375; with vbs. of Memory, 376; with vbs. of Emotion, 377; with Judicial vbs., 378; with vbs. of Rating and Buying, 379,380; with **interest** and **rēfert**, 381; with vbs. of Fulness, 383,1; with vbs. of Separation, *ib.* 2; in Exclamations, *ib.* 3; pred. with Inf., 422,N.5; Ger., 428; with **esse, causā**, *etc.*, *ib.* R.

2; Ger. with Pl. subst., *ib.* N.1; Ger. with vb., *ib.* N.4; position of, **676** and NN.1,2.

genus—decl. of, **48**; **id genus**, **336**,N.2; with Epexegetical Gen.. **361**,**2**.

gerēns—with Gen., **375**,N.2.

GERUND and GERUNDIVE—**112**,5; formation of, **115**,3; early forms, **130**,8; Agent of, in Dat., **215**,2; with **esse** to form periphrasis, **251**; force of Gerundive, *ib.* N.1; syntax of, **425-433**; and Inf., **425**; and vb., **426**; Gerundive for Gerund, **427**; impersonal Gerundive, *ib.*N.2; from intrans. vbs., *ib.* N.4; Gen. of, **428**; Inf. instead, *ib.* N.2; depending on vb., *ib.* N.4; Dat. instead, *ib.*N.5; Dat. of, **429**; Acc. of, **430**; Abl. of, **431**; paralleled by part., *ib.* N.3; Acc. of, with preps., **432**; with **ad** after vbs. of Hindering, *ib.*R.1; Abl. of, with preps., **433**.

gestīre—with Inf., **423**,2,N.2, **533**,R.1.

gīgnere—(**genitus**), with Abl. of Origin, **395**,N.1.

giving—vbs. of, with Dat. and Acc., or Acc. and Abl., **348**; with Inf., **423**,N.1.*b*.; with Acc. Ger., **430**.

glōriārī—with Acc. and Inf., **527**,R.2.

glōriōsum—with **est** and Inf., **422**,N.3.

Glyconic verse—**795**.

gracilis—Comp. of, **87**,3.

grātiā—with Gen., **373**; with poss. pron., *ib.* R.2; with Gen. Ger., **428**,R.2; **grātiīs**, as Abl. of Manner, **399**,N.1.

grātificārī—with Dat., **346**,R.2.

grātulārī—with Dat., **346**,R.2.

gravārī—with Inf., **423**,2,N.2.

Greek substantives—decl. of, **65**; Greek Acc., **338**.

growth—vbs. of, in Abl. Abs., **410**,N.1.

guttural—vowels, **2**,1; consonants, **6**,1; suffixes with, **185**.

habēre—with two Noms. in pass., **206**; with Pf. part. to denote Maintenance of the Result, **238**,**241**,N.2, **244**,N.2; first Impv. wanting, **267**,R.; with two Accs., **340**,R.1; with **prō, locō, numerō,** and a second Acc., *ib.*; with Final Dat., **356**, R.2; with Gen. of Price, **379**; **pēnsī habēre**, *ib.* 1,N.2; with **in** and Acc., **385**,N.3; with Acc. Ger., **430**,N.1; **habeō dīcendum**, *ib.* N.2; *be able*, with Inf., **423**,2,N.2.

habit—vbs. of, with Inf., **423 and N.2.**

haerēre—with Dat., **346**,N.6.

hanging—vbs. of, with **ex, ab, dē, 385**,R.2.

happening—sequence after vbs. of, **513**, R.2; vbs. of, with **quod** clause, **525**,1; **ut** instead, *ib.* N.5; vbs. of, with consecutive clause, **553**,3.

hardening—in a verse, **723**.

haud—**441** and **443**, with NN.; **sciō an**, **457**,2.

(h)avēre—**175**,4.

helluārī—with Abl., **407**,N.**2**,*e*.

hendiadys—**698**.

heteroclites—**68**.

heterogeneous substantives—**67**.

heterologa—**69**,*c*.

hiatus—defined, **720**; in Iam. Oct., **763**, N.; in Anap. Oct., **778**,N.1; in Dact. Hex., **784**,NN.6,7; in Sapphic, **726**,N.

hīc—**104**, 1 and NN.; syntax of, **305**; contemptuous character of, **306**,N.; and **ille**, **307**,RR.1,2; strengthened by **quidem**, *ib.* R.4; two forms of, refer to different substs., *ib.* N.3; **hīc—illīc, hinc—hinc, hinc—inde, hinc—illinc, illinc — hinc, inde—hinc,** **482**,2; **hōc** with **ut**, **557**,R.; **hūius**, in Gen. of Price, **380**,1; with Abl. of Time, **393**,R.4; in Ō. O., **660**,3; **hinc** as coördinating conjunction, **503**.

hiems—decl. of, **40**; in Abl. of Time, **393**, R.5.

hindering—sequence after vbs. of, **543**, R.2 and N.2; vbs. of, with **nē**, **548**; with **quīn**, **554-556**; and vbs. of Preventing, **555**; and vbs. of Doubt, *ib.* 2.

Historical **cum**—**585** and NN.

HISTORICAL INFINITIVE—parallel with Impf., **254**,R.; syntax of, **647**; conjunctions with, *ib*, N.2.

HISTORICAL PERFECT—**224**; force of, **239**; and Pure Pf., **235**; and Impf., **231**, **240**; for Plupf., **239**,N.; as Potential of Past, **258**,N.2.

HISTORICAL PRESENT—**224** and **229**; with **dum**, **229**,N., **570**.

historical tenses—**225**.

hodiernus—in pred. Attrib., **325**,R.6.

homŏ—in early Latin, **42**,N.

honor—and **honōs**, **45**,N.

hope—constr. of, vbs. of, **423**,N.5; sequence after, vbs. of, **515**,R.3; vbs. of, with Acc. and Inf., **527**,R.4.

HORACE—Lyric Metres of, **826**.

horrēre—with Inf., **423**,2,N.2.
horrēscere—with Inf., **423**,2,N.2.
hortārī—with Inf., **423**,2,N.2; with **ut**, **546**,N.1; **hortātus**, as Pr., **282**,N.; **hortātū**, as Abl. of Cause, **408**,N.1.
humilis—Comp. of, **87**,3.
humus—in Abl. of Separation, **390**,2,N.4; **humī**, as Loc., **411**,R.2.
hypallagé—**693**.
hyperbaton—**696**.
hypotaxis—**472**.

I—and J., **1**,R.2; sound of, **3**; weakening of, **8**,1; effect of, on preceding vowel, **12**,R.2; I-class of vb. stems, **133**,VI.; length of final, **707**,4.
iam—with Pr. Indic., **230**; **iam diū**, **iam prīdem**, *ib.*; with Impf. Indic., **234**; **iam—iam**, **482**,1, and N.1; **iam vērō**, **487**,N.3; **iam dūdum**, with Impv., **269**.
Iambelegus verse—**820**.
Iambic—law, **716**, **717**; foot, **734**; rhythm, **736**; rhythms, **757-767**.
ictus—conflict of, with Accent, **749**.
IDEAL CONDITION—from present point of view, **596**,1; from past point of view, *ib.* 2; = Unreal, *ib.* R.1; shift to Unreal, *ib.* R.2; after **nōn possum**, *ib.* R.3; in Ō. O., *ib.* R.5, **658**.
Idem—decl. of, **103**,2, and NN.; syntax of, **310**; with **que**, **et**, **atque**, *ib.* R.1; *the same as*, with **quī**, **ut**, **atque**, **cum**, or Dat., **310**,R.3, **359**,N.6, **642**,R.1; not used with **is**, **310**,R.3; in pred. attrib., **325**,R.2.
idōneus—constrs. with, **552**,R.2; with **quī** and Subjv., **631**,1.
iecur—decl. of, **44**,5, **68**,12.
iēiūnus—with Gen., **374**,N.1.
igitur—position of, **484**,R.; usage of, **501**; with **ergō**, **502**,N.3; correl. of **sī**, **590**,N.1.
ignorance—adjs. of, in pred. app., **325**, R. 6; with Gen., **374**.
Ignōrāre—with Inf., **527**,R.1.
Ignōscere—with Dat., **346**,R.2.
ILLATIVE SENTENCES—**499**, **500**.
ille decl. of, **104**,3, and NN.; forms from **ollo**, *ib.* N.1; Syntax of, **307**; and **hīc**, *ib.* RR.1,2; **et ille**, *ib.* R.2; strengthened by **quidem**, *ib.* R.4; repeats a subst., *ib.* N.2; two forms with different antecedents, *ib.* N.3; refers to oblique case of **is**, *ib.* N.4; with Abl. of Time, **393**,R.4; **illinc—hinc**, **hinc—illinc**, **hīc—illīc**, **482**,2; **illud** with **ut**, **557**,R.; in Ō. O., **660**,2.
illūdere—with Dat., *etc.*, **347**,R.2.
illūstris—with Abl. of Respect, **397**,N.2.
imbēcillus—and **imbēcillis**, **84**,1.
imber—decl. of, **44**,2, **45**,R.1.
imberbis—and **imberbus**, **84**,2.
immāne—with **quantum** and Indic., **467**,N.
immēnsum—with **quantum** and Indic., **467**,N.
Immo—use of, **471**,*c*; scansion of, **717**,N.1.
Immolāre—with Abl. of Means, **401**,N.4.
immūnis—with Abl. of Sep., **390**,3,N.1.
impedīmentō—with **esse** and **nē**, **548**, N.1.
impedīre—with Inf., **423**,2,N.2; with **nē**, **548**,N.1; with **quōminus**, **549**,N.1.
impellere—with **ut**, **553**,2; **impulsus**, **impulsū**, of Cause, **408**, NN. 1 and 2.
impendiō—*very*, **439**,N.3.
impendēre—with Dat., *etc.*, **347**,R.2.
impēnsē—*very*, **439**,N.3.
imperāre—with Dat., **346**,R.2; with Inf., **423**,2,N.2, **532**,N.1; with **ut**, **546**,N.1.
IMPERATIVE—**112**,4; early forms, **130**,5; Subjv. for, **263**; answers deliberative question, **265**,N.; usage, **266-275**; First and Second, **267**; strengthening words, **269**; negative of, **270**; pronouns with, **267**,N.; concord with, **211**,N.2; periphrases of, **271**; representatives of, **272**; of Past, **272**,3; tenses of, **278**; for Protasis, **593**,4; in Subjv. with Ō. O., **652** and R.1.
IMPERFECT—**112**,3; early forms, **130**,2, force of, **223**, **231**; and Hist. Pf., **232**; of Endeavor, Disappointment, and Resistance to Pressure, **233**; a tense of Evolution, *ib.* N.1; overlapping, *ib.* N.2, **562**; of Awakening, *ib.* N.3; with **iam**, *etc.*, **234**; of opposition to Present, **254**,R.2; in Apodosis of Action begun, *ib.* R.3, **597**,R.2; as Potential of Past, **258**; in Wish, **260**; with **vellem**, *ib.* R.; Subjv. as Concessive, **264**; Subjv. as Impv. of Past, **272**,3; tense relations of Subjv., **277**; in Sequence, **510**,R.; in Coincidence, **513**,N.3; Subjv. as Principal Tense, **517**, R.2.
impersonal verbs—**208**,1 and 2; divine Agt. expressed, *ib.* 1,N.; vbs. of Saying, *etc.*, **208**,2,N 2, **528**; in Ger. constr., **427**, N.4; with **ut**, **553**,4.

impertīre—with Dat. and Acc., or Acc. and Abl., 348,R.1; **labōrem**, with Dat. Ger., 429,1.
impetrāre—with **ut**, 553,1.
implēre—with Gen., 383,1.
implōrāre—with **ut** only, 546,N.3.
impōnere—with **in** and Acc., 385,N.2.
impos—with Gen., 374,N.3.
imprimere—with **in** and Abl., 385,R.1.
imprūdēns—in pred. attrib., 325,R.6.
impulsū—as Abl. of Cause, 408,N.1.
in—in composition, 9,4; vbs. cpd. with take Acc. or Dat., 331, 347; with Countries and Towns, 337,R.1; with Acc. for Dat., 345,R.2; with app. to Towns, 386,R.1; with books, 387; *throughout*, 388,R.; with **recipere**, 389; with Abl. of Time, 394, R. and N.2; with Abl. of Cause, 408,N.3; position of, 413,R.1; as prep., 418,1; with Acc. Ger., 432, and N.1; with Abl. Ger., 433 and N.1; with part., 437,N.2; **in eō quod**, 525,2,N.2.
inānis—with Gen., 374,N.1.
incēdere—with Dat., *etc.*, 347,R.2.
īncendī—with **īrā** and Inf., 533,R.1; **incēnsus**, of Moving Cause, 408,N.2.
incertum—with **an** and Subjv., 457,2.
inchoative verbs—133,V., 191,2.
incidere—with Dat., *etc.*, 347,R.2.
incīdere—with **in** and Abl., 385,R.1.
incipere—with Inf., 423,2,N.2; with Ordinal, 294,N.
incitātus—of Moving Cause, 408,N.2.
inclination—suffixes for, 182,2.
inclination—adjs. of, in pred. attr., 325,R. 6; vbs. of, with Inf., 423 and N.2.
inclūdere—with **in** and Abl., 385,R. 1.
incommodāre—with Dat., 346,N.1.
incorporation—of antecedent, 616; **quā prūdentiā es**, 616,1,N.2; of correlative, 619.
incrēdibile—with Inf., 422,N.3; with **quantum** and Indic., 467,N.
increpāre—*charge*, with Gen., 378,R.1.
increpitāre—*charge*, with Gen., 378,R.1.
incubāre—with Dat., *etc.*, 347,R.2.
incumbere—with Dat., *etc.*, 347, R.2.
[**indāgo**]—defective, 70,D.
inde—as coördinating conj., 503; in contrast with **hinc**, 482,2.
indecōrus—and **indecoris**, 84,1.
indefinite pronouns—107; syntax of, 313-319; **quīdam**, 313; **aliquis**, 314; **quis**, 315; **quispiam**, 316; **quisquam** and **ūllus**, 317; **quisque**, 318; **alter** and **alius**, 319; rel. with Indic., 254,R.4, 625.
INDICATIVE—112,4; early forms of, 130,1-4; meaning of, 254; in Apodosis, 254,R.3; with indef. rel., *ib.* R.4; Pr. for Deliberative Subjv., *ib.* N.2; tense relations of, 276; neg. of, 257; in questions, 463, 464; after **nesciō quis**, *etc.*, 467,R.1; in Relative Sentences, *ib.* R.2; in Temporal Sentences, 560,1; to express Design, 630,N.2.
indigēre—with Gen., 383,1, 405,N.2.
indīgnārī—with Inf., 533,R.1; with **sī**, 542,N.1.
indīgnus—with Gen., 374,N.10; with **quī**, **ut**, or Inf., 552,R.2; with **quī** and Subjv., 631,1 and R.1.
indigus—with Abl. or Gen., 405,N.3.
induere—with Dat. and Acc., or Acc. and Abl., 348,R.1; **induī**, with Acc. of Respect, 338,N.2.
indulgēre—with Dat., 346,R.2 and N.2.
inermis—and **inermus**, 84,2.
inesse—with Dat., *etc.*, 347,R.2.
īnferior—87,2; with Dat., 296,N.3.
INFINITIVE—112,5; formation of, 115,3; early forms, 130,6; aor. in **-xe**, *etc.*, 131,4,*b*,4; Fut. in **assere**, *ib.*; act. for pass., 213,R.,*c.*; usage of, 279; as subst., 280; after **dēbeō**, *ib.* 2,*b*,N.3; after **decuit, oportuit**, *ib.* 2,*b*,R.1 and 2; as representative of Indic., 281; after **meminī**, *etc.*, *ib.* 2,N.; syntax of, 419-424; with Acc. as subj., 420; as subst., 421; traces of Locative nature, *ib.* N.1; as subj., 422; as obj., 423; **ut** instead, *ib.* N.4; as pred. with **esse**, 425; with preps., *ib.* N.; Fut. pass., 435,N.4; sequence after, 518; Acc. and Inf. after vbs. of Saying and Thinking, 527; part. instead, *ib.* N.1; tenses after these vbs., 529-531; after **posse, velle**, *ib.* N.3; after **spērāre**, *ib.* N.4; with vbs. of Will and Desire, 532; with vbs. of Emotion, 533; **ut** instead, 532,NN.3,4; in Exclamations, 534; and **quod**, *ib.*R.1; Acc. and Inf. as subj., 535; Acc. and Inf. after vbs. of Emotion, 542; with vbs. of Will and Desire, 546,N.3; with vbs. of Fear, 550,N.5; with **dīgnus**, *etc.*, 552,R.2; Acc. and Inf. in Relative Sentences, 635; after **potius**, *etc.*, 644,R.3, 646; in Ō. O., 650. See Hist. Inf.

īnfīnītum—with **est** instead of **sit, 254,** R.1; with **quantum** and Indic., **467,**N.
īnfitiās—70,A.; **īre, 333,**2,R.
inflection—17.
īnfrā—with Abl. of Measure, **403,**N.1; as adv., **415**; as prep., **416,**12.
īnfrēnus—and **īnfrēnis, 84,**1.
ingrātiīs—as Abl. of Manner, **399,**N.1.
ingeniī—as Loc., with adjs., **374,**N.7.
ingredī—with Inf., **423,**2,N.2.
inhaerēre—with Dat., *etc.*, **347,**R.2.
inhiāre—with Dat., *etc.*, **347,**R.2.
inicere manum—with Acc., **342.**
iniūriā—as Abl. of Manner, **399,**N.1.
innātus—with Dat., **347,**R.2.
Inner Object—Acc. of, **328, 330, 332**; Abl. instead, **333,**2,N.4; after vbs. of Taste and Smell, *ib.* 2,N.5.
inops—with Gen., **374,**N.1; with Abl., **405,**N.3.
inquam—**175,**2; **inquit,** impersonal, **208,** 2,N.2; in citing Ō. R., **648,**R.2; lacking forms supplied by **dīcere,** *ib.* R.3.
inquiring—vbs. of, with two Accs., **339,** and R.1,NN.1 and 2.
īnscrībere—with **in** and Abl., **385,**R.1.
īnsculpere—with **in** and Abl., **385,**R.1.
īnservīre—with Dat., **347,**R.2.
īnsīgnis—with Abl. of Respect, **397,**N.2; **īnsīgniter** as adv. of Degree, **439,**N.2.
īnsidiārī—with Dat., **346,**R.2.
īnsinuāre—with Dat., **347,**R.2.
īnsistere—with Dat., **347,**R.2.
īnstar—**70,**B.; with Gen., **373.**
īnstāre—with Dat., **347,**R.2; with Inf., **423,**2,N.2.
īnstruere—with **dē, 339,**N.3.
instrument—suffixes for, **181,**6; in Abl., **214, 401**; with **ab, 214,**R.2; Abl. of contrasted with Abl. of Attendance, **392,**R.2.
INSTRUMENTAL—case, **23,**N.
īnsuētus—with Gen., **374,**N.4.
integrum—with Inf., **422,**N.3.
intellegere—with Inf., **527,**R.1; **intellēctū** as Sup., **436,**N.
intendere—with Inf., **423,**2,N.2; **intentus,** with Abl., *etc.*, **359,**N.5.
intensive verbs—formation of, **191,**1.
inter—with reflexive to express reciprocal action, **221**; vbs. cpd. with, take Acc. or Dat., **331,347**; to designate Time, **394,**N.2; position of, **413,**R.1; as prep., **416,**13; with Acc. Ger., **432** and N.1; with part., **437,**N.2.
intercalāris—and **intercalārius, 84,**2.
intercēdere—with Dat., **347,**R.2; with **nē, 548,**N.1; with **quīn, 555,**1.
interclūdere—with Dat. and Acc., or Acc. and Abl., **348,**R.1; with Abl., **390,**2, N.3; with **nē, 548,**N.1; with **quīn, 555,**1.
intercurrere—with Dat., **347,**R.2.
interdīcere—with Abl., **390,**2,N.3; with **nē, 548,**N.1; with **quīn, 555,**1.
interdum—coördinates with **aliās, 482,** 1,N.1.
interesse—with Dat., **347,**R.2; **interest,** with Gen. and Abl., **381**; with Nom., *ib.* N.3; constr. of Object of Concern, **382,**1 and 2; constr. of Thing Involved, *ib.* 3; with **ut, 553,**4.
Interest—Dat. of Personal, **350.**
interior—**87,**2 and 8.
interjection—**16,**R.2; no syntax, **201,R.1.**
intermittere—with Inf., **423,**2,N.2.
interneciō—defective, **70,**B.
interpellāre—with **nē, 548,**N.1.
interpōnere—with **nē, 548,**N.1.
interrogāre—with two Accs., or **dē, 339,** R. 1 and N.1; with Indic., **467,**N.
interrogative pronouns — **106**; distinguished from rel., **467,**R.2; with part., **469**; in Final Sentence, **470**; doubling of, *ib.* R.
INTERROGATIVE SENTENCES — **450 - 470**; simple and cpd., **452**; particles in, **454-457**; moods in, **462-467**; Indic., **463,464**; Subjv., **465,466**; after vb. of Wonder, **542,**N.1; after vb. of Fear, **550,**N.4; for Protasis, **593,**4; in Ō. O., **651** and RR.
intervenīre—with Dat., **347,**R.2.
intrā—to designate Time, **394,**N.2; position of, **413,**R.1; as adv., **415**; as prep., **416,14.**
intransitive verbs—used impersonally, **208,**2; used transitively, **213,**R.*b*; construed as pass., **214,**R.1; with neut. subj. in pass., **217**; with personal Ger., **217,**R.2; with Pf. part. pass. used actively, **220,**N.1; Gerund of, used impersonally, **251,**2.
inūsitātum—with **ut, 553,**4.
invādere—with Dat., **347,**R.2.
invēnīrī—with Nom. and Inf., **528,**N.1; **inventū** in Sup., **436,**N.
inverse—**dōnec, 571,**N.6; **cum, 581**; attraction of rel., **617,**N.2.
invicem—to indicate reciprocality, **221** R.2.

invidēre—with personal pass., **217**,N.1; with Dat., **346**,R.2 and N.2; with Inf., **533**,R.1.
invidus—constr. of, **359**,N.5.
invītus—in pred. app., **325**,R.6; **invītō est**, **353**,N.2.
ioculō—as Abl. of Manner, **399**,N.1.
iocus—heterogeneous, **67**,2.
ionic—foot, **734**; rhythm, **736**; rhythms, **815-819**; substitutions for, **815**.
ipse—decl. of, **103**,3 and N.; **ipsus**, *ib.*N.2; syntax of, **311**; **et ipse**, *ib.* 1,R.2; emphasises reflexive, *ib.* 2; used indeclinably, *ib.* 2,N.; in Ō. O., **660**,5.
īrā—of Moving Cause, **408**,N.2; **incendor īrā** with Inf., **533**,R.1.
īrāscī—with Dat., **346**,R.2.
īre—**169**,2; omission of, **209**,N.5; with Dat., **358**,N.2; with Sup., **435**,N.1; with **īnfitiās**, *etc.*, **333**,2,R.
is—decl. of, **103**,1 and N.; strengthened by **quīdam**, **307**,R.4; taken up by **ille**, *ib.* N.4; two forms with different antecedent, *ib.* N.3; syntax of, **308**; = **tālis**, *ib.* R.1; with **et, atque, que**, *ib.* R.2; for reflexive, **309**,N.1; **id temporis, aetātis**, **336**,N.2; **eō** as coördinating conj., **503**; **ideō, idcircō**, *ib.*; with **quī** and Subjv., **631**,1; with **ut**, *ib.* R.1, **557**,R.; in Ō. O., **660**,2.
islands—in Local Acc., **337**; with **in**, *ib.* R.1 and N.3; prep. omitted with Large Islands, *ib.* N.1.
iste—decl. of, **104**,II. and NN.; syntax of, **306**; contemptuous character of, *ib.* N.; strengthened by **quidem**, **307**,R.4; in Ō. O., **660**,3.
ita—with **ut**, **482**,4; correlative of **sī**, **590**,N.1; *yes*, **471**,*a*,1.
Ītalicus Numerus—**756**.
itaque—usage of, **500**; position of, *ib.* R.; with **ergō**, **502**,N.3.
iter—decl. of, **44**,5.
iterative action—**566**, **567**; Subjv. in, *ib.* N.; with **cum**, **584**; in Relative Sentences, **623**.
Ithyphallic—verse, **774**.
iubēre—with two Accs., **341**,N.2; with Acc. and Dat., **346**,N.3; constr. after, **423**,N.6; with Acc. and Inf., **528** and N.1; with Inf., **423**,2,N.2, **532**,NN.1,2; with Subjv., **546**,R.2; **iūssū**, defective, **68**,5; **iūssū** as Abl. of Cause, **408**,N.1.
iūdicāre—with Inf., **423**,2,N.2.
[**iūger**]—decl. of, **68**,7.
iūnctus—with Dat., *etc.*, **359**,N.3.
iūs—with Inf., **422**,N.2, **428**,N.2; with **respondēre**, **333**,2,R.; in phrases with **ut**, **546**,N.2; **iūre**, **399**,N.1; **iūre** in Abl. of Respect, **397**.
iūstō—as Abl. of Respect, **398**,N.1.
iuvāre—with Acc., **346**,N.3.
iuvenis—Comp. of, **87**,9.
iūxtā—as adv., **415**; as prep., **416**,15.

Judgment—vbs. of, with Abl. of Standard, **402**.

K—sounds of, **1**,R.1; name of, *ib.* N.
knowledge—adjs. of, in pred. attrib., **325**, R.6; adjs. of, with Gen., **374**.

Labials—**6**,1; suffixes with, **187**.
labōrem—with **impertīre** and Dat. Ger., **429**,1.
labōrāre—with Inf., **423**,2,N.2; with **ut**, **546**,N.1.
lāc—decl. of, **53**,8; **68**,12.
laedere—with Acc., **346**,N.3.
laetārī—with Acc. and Inf., **533**,R.1.
lāmentārī—with Acc. and Inf., **533**,R.1.
largīrī—with **ut**, **553**,2.
later—defective, **70**,D.
lātitūdine—with Acc. of Extent, **335**,R.1.
lātus—with Acc. of Extent, **335**,R.1.
laurus—heteroclite, **68**,5.
leaving—vbs. of, with Acc. Ger., **430**.
lectus—heteroclite, **68**,5.
length—by nature, **12**,1, and R.; by position, *ib.* 2; representation of long vowels, *ib.* N.
lengthening—compensatory, **9**,6,*a*.
letters—tenses in, **252**; advs. in, *ib.*; dated from a place, **391**,R.3.
letting—vbs. of, with Acc. Ger., **430**.
levāre—with Abl., **390**,2,N.2.
lēx—in phrases with **ut**, **546**,NN.1 and 2; **lēge**, **397** and N.1, **399**,N.1.
līberālis—with Gen., **374**,N.1.
līberāre—with Abl., **390**,2,N.2.
-libet—added to rels., **111**,3; exact use of **libuerit**, **244**,R.3; **libēns**, in pred. attrib., **325**,R.6; with Dat., **346**,R.2.
licēre—exact use of Fut. Pf., **244**,R.3; with Dat., **346**,R.2; with Gen., **379**; **licet**, *although*, **603-607**; with **quamvīs**, *ib.* N. 2; with Indic., *ib.* N.3.
likeness—suffixes for, **182**,4.

likeness—adjs. of, with Dat., **349**; with **atque(āc)**, **643**.
linguals—6,1,N.
linter—decl. of, **44**,2, **45**,R.1.
liquids—**6**,2,A; 3d Decl. stems in, **39–46**; suffixes with, **189**.
litāre—with Abl. of Means, **401**,N.4.
litotes—**644**,N.1, 700.
lītterae—in phrases with **ut**, **546**,N.2.
living—vbs. of, with Abl., **401**,N.1.
Local Dative—**358**.
locality—suffixes for, **181**,5, **182**,9.
locāre—with Gen., 379; with **in** and Abl., **386**,R.1; with Acc. Gen., **430**.
LOCATIVE—**23**,N.; of 1st Decl., **29**,R.2; of 2d Decl., **33**,RR.3,5; 3d Decl., **37**,5; forms advs., **91**,3; syntax of, **411**; in 3d Decl., *ib.* R.1; other Locs., *ib.* R.2; app. to, in Abl., *ib.* R.3; **domī**, with poss. pron., *ib.* R.4.
locus—**67**,2; **in locō habēre**, **340**,R.1; Abl. without **in**, **385**,N.1.
logaœdic rhythms—**790–805**.
LOGICAL CONDITION—**595**; with Subjv. by Attraction, *ib.* R,2; with Ideal 2d Person, *ib.* R.3; **sīve—sīve**, *ib.* R.4; **sī quidem**, *ib.* R.5; **sī modo, vērō, tamen**, *ib.* R.6; tenses in, *ib.* N.2; in Ō. O., **657**, **595**, R.1.
longinquus—Comp. of, **87**,9.
longitūdine—with Acc. of Extent, **335**, R.1.
longum—with **est** for Subjv., **254**,R.1; **longē** strengthens Comp. or Superlative, **301**, **303**; with Acc., **335**,R.1.
loquī—with Acc. and Inf., **527**,R.2; with Indic. question, **467**,N.
lubīdō—in phrases with Inf., **422**,N.2.
lūdōs facere—with Acc., **342**.
lūgēre—with Inf., **533**,R.1.
lūx—**70**,D; in Abl. of Time, **393**,R.5.

M—final omitted, **27**,N.
macte—**85**,C, **325**,R.1.
maerēre—with Inf., **533**,R.1.
māgnificus—Comp. of, **87**,4.
māgnitūdine—with Acc. of Extent, **335**, R.1.
māgnus—comparison of, **90**; constr. with **māior**, **296**,R.5; **magis**, in comparison of Qualities, **299**; **māgnī**, as Gen. of Price, **380**,1; **māius**, with Inf., **422**,N.3; **māximī**, as Gen. of Price, **380**, 1; **nōn magis quam**, **644**,N.1.
making—vbs. of, with two Noms., **206**; with two Accs., **340**.
maledīcere—with Dat., **346**,R.2.
maledicus—Comp. of, **87**,4.
mālle—conj. of, **174** and N.3; **mālueram**, *could have preferred*, **254**,N.1; **mālim**, **māllem**, as Potential, **257**,2, **258**,N.1; in Unreal Wish, **261**,R.; with Abl., **296**, N.1; with Abl. of Measure, **403**,N.1; with Inf. or **ut**, **423**,2,N.2, **538** and N.3, **546**,N.1.
malus—comparison of, **90**; **male** as neg., **439**,N.2.
mānāre—with Abl. of Means, **401**,N.5.
mandāre—with **ut**, **546**,N.1.
manēre—as copulative vb., **206**,N.1; with Abl., **401**,N.6.
mānī—as Loc., **411**,N.1.
manifēstus—with Gen., **374**,N.2; with Inf., **421**,N.1,*c*.
Manner—Abl. of, **399** and NN.
manūs inicere—with Acc., **342**.
mare—in Abl. without **in**, **385**,N.1.
margarīta—heteroclite, **68**,1.
māteria—heteroclite, **68**,2.
Material—Abl. of, **396**; indicated by adj., *ib.*; suffixes for, **182**,4.
mātūrāre—with Inf., **423**,2,N.2.
mātūrus—Comp. of, **87**,1,R.2.
mātūtīnus—in pred. Attr., **325**,R.6.
Means—Abl. of, **401**, and RR.,NN.; suffixes for, **181**,6.
measure—vbs. of, take Abl., **402**.
Measure—Abl. of, **402**; of Difference, **403**; Abl. of, with vbs. involving Difference, *ib.* N.1; with **ante** and **post**, *ib.* N.4.
medērī—with Dat., **346**,R.2 and N.4.
medioximus—**87**,9,N.
meditārī—with Inf., **423**,2,N.2.
meditative verbs—formation, **191**,5.
medium—suffixes for, **182**,6.
medius—in pred. attrib., **325**,R.6; used partitively, **291**,R.2; Abl. used without **in**, **388**.
meminī—**175**,5,*b*; First Impv. wanting, **267**,R.; with Pr. Inf., **281**,2,N.; with Acc., **376**,R.2; with Inf., **423**,2,N.2, **527**,R.2; with **cum** and Indic., **580**,R.2.
memorātū—as Abl. Sup., **436**,N.
memoriā teneō—with Pr. Inf., **281**,2,N.
mendum—heteroclite, **68**,3.
mēns—in phrases with **ut**, **557**,R.; **in mentem venīre**, with Gen., **376**,R.3; **in mentem venīre**, with Inf., **422**,N.5.

meritus—Comp. of, **87**,9 ; **meritō** as Abl. of Manner, **399**,N.1.

-met—added to personal pron., **102**,N.2; to **ipse**, **103**,3,N.5.

metaplasts—**68**.

metathesis—of consonants, **9**,8.

metre—**730**; unit of, **731**.

metuere—with Dat., **346**,N.2 ; with **ut, nē**, or Inf., **550** and N.1 ; with Inf., **423**, 2.N.2.

metus—with Inf., **550**,N.5.

meus—**73**,R., **76** ; Voc. of, **100**,R.1: early forms of, *ib*.N.2; synizesis in, *ib*.N.3, **727**, N. ; **mea mihĭ**, **309**,N.2; **meī** with Gen. Ger., **428**,R.1; with **ut, 557**.R.

middle voice — **212**,R., **218** ; with Acc. of Respect, **338**,N.2.

mīlitia—in Abl. of Time, **393**,R.5; in Loc., **411**,R.2.

mīlle—a subst. in Pl., **95**,R.3 ; inscriptional forms of, *ib*.R.4; **mīlia**, with masc. vb., **211**,R.1,Ex.6 ; use of, in Sg. and Pl., **293** ; as subst. with Part. Gen., **293**,N.; **mīlia** for distributive, **295**,N.

minārī, minitārī—with Dat., **346**,R.2; with Inf., **527**,R.2.

minor—quam omitted with, **296**,R.4 ; with vbs. of Rating and Buying, **380**,1; **minōris, minimī**, as Gen. of Price, *ib*.; **minus**, *no*, **471**,*b*,1; **minimē**, *no*, *ib*.; **sīn minus, 592** ; **sī minus**, *ib*. R.; **nōn minus quam, 644**,N.1.

mīrārī—with Inf., **423**,2,N.2, **533**,R.1; with **quod, 542** ; with **sī**, *ib*. N.1.

mīrum—with **factum** and **nī, quantum, quīn**, **209**,N.2, **467**,N. ; with **quod, 542**; with **sī, 542**,N.1; with **nī**, *ib*. N.2 ; with Inf., **422**,N.3 ; with **quam** and Indic., **467**,N.; with **ut, 553**,4.

mīscēre—sē, with Dat., **346**,N.6; with Dat. and Acc., or Acc. and Abl., **348**,R.1.

miserārī—with Acc., **377**,N.2.

miserēre—with Gen., **377**,N.1 ; **miseret**, with Gen., **377**: **misereor**, with Gen., *ib*.; **miserēscō**, with Gen., *ib*. N.1.

mittere—mitte, with Inf. for Impv., **271**,2,N.2; with Inf., **422**,N.3; with **quod, 525**,1,N.1 ; followed by Impf. Indic. to give Design, **630**,N 2 ; **missū**, of Moving Cause, **408**,N.1.

mixed class of Verbs—**133**,vii.

moderārī—with Dat., **346**,R.2 and N.2.

modo—strengthens Impv., **269** ; **modo—modo**, **482**,1 ; contrasted with **tum, vicissim**, **482**,1,N.2 ; **nōn modo—sed etiam**, **482**,5 ; **nōn modo nōn, sed nē—quidem**, *ib*. R.1 ; *provided only*, **573** ; **modo nē**, *ib*. N.2.

mōlīrī—with Inf., **423**,2,N.2.

monēre—with Gen. or Acc., **376** and R.1; with Inf., **423**,2,N.2 ; with **ut, 546**,N.1.

mood—**112**,4, **253**; Indic., **254** ; Subjv., **255-265** ; Impv., **266-275** ; Inf., **279-281**; attraction of, **508**,4; in Temporal Clauses, **560** : in Relative Sentences, **624-635**; in Comparative Sentences, **639** ; in Ō. O., **650-652**.

morārī—with **nē, 548**, N. 1.

mōrigerārī—with Dat., **346**,R.2.

mōs—(**mōris**) with Inf., **422**,NN.2 and 5 ; with **ut, 557**,R.; **mōribus**, **399**,N.1.

motion—vb. of, with Inf., **421**,N.1,*a*; vb. of, with Sup., **435** ; vb. of, with Fut. part., **438**,N.; vb. of, with **quod, 525**,1,N.6; end of, conceived as Rest, **412**,R.1.

movēre—syncope in Pf., **131**,3; with Abl. of Separation, **390**,N.1 ; with **ut, 553**,2; **mōtus**, of Moving Cause, **408**,N.2.

Mulciber—heteroclite, **68**,4.

multāre—with Abl., **378**,R.3.

multitude — substs. of, with Pl., **211**,R.1, Ex.*a*.

multitūdō—with Pl. vb., **211**,R.1,Ex.*a*.

multum—for Abl. of Measure, **403**,N.2; *very*, **439**,N.3 ; **multō** with Comp., **301** ; with Superl., **303**.

mūnus—with Inf., **422**,N.2 ; with **ut, 546**, N.2.

mūtāre—with Abl., **404**,N.1.

mutes—**6**,2,B.

mūtuō—of reciprocal action, **221**,R.2.

myrtus—heteroclite, **68**,5.

Nam—usage of, **498** and NN.; position of, *ib*., N.1 ; asseverative, *ib*. N.2 ; *yes for*, **471**,R.

naming—vbs. of, with two Accs., **340**.

namque—**498**; position of, *ib*. N.1.

nārrāre—with Inf., **527**,R.2.

nasals—**6**,2 A.; nasal class of vbs., **133**,IV.

nāscī—with two Noms., **206** ; **nātus**, constr. of, **296**,R.5; with Acc., **336**,R.4; with Abl. of Origin, **395**,NN.1,3 ; **nātū** in Abl. Sup., **436**,N.

nātūra—in phrases with **ut, 557**,R.

naucum — defective, **70**,B.; **naucī**, as Gen. of Price, **380**,1.

nē—neg. of Opt. Subjv., **260**; of Impv.,

270; continued by **neque**, 260; by **nēve**, 270, 444,2; with Pf. Subjv., 270, R.2; syntax of, 441, 444; = **nōn**, 444,1, N.2; **nē—quidem**, *ib.* 1,N.2, 445,448,N.2, 482,5 and R.1; in Final Sentences, 543, 4; **ut nē**, 545,R.1; **quō nē**, *ib.*; parenthetical, *ib.* R.3; after vbs. of Hindering, 548; after vbs. of Fear, 550; **nē nōn**, *ib.* N.1; with **dum**, 573; as Concessive, 608.

ne—added to **hīc**, 104,1,N.3; to **iste**, *ib.* 2,N.3; to **ille**, 103,3,N.4; as interrogative, 454; asseverative, *ib.* N.2; added to interrogatives, *ib.* N.3; = **nōnne**, *ib.* N.5; added to **num**, 456,N.; strengthens **an**, 457,1,N.2; to introduce double questions, 458; **necne** or **annōn**, 459; to introduce second member of an indirect question, 460,2.

nearness—adjs. of, with Dat., 359.

nec = **nōn**, 442,N.3; see **neque.**

necessārium—with **ut**, 553,4.

necesse—85,C.; with **est** instead of Subjv., 254,R.1; with Inf., 538; with **ut** omitted, 538,R.2, 553,4,R.1; with pred. attracted, 538,R.3; with **ut**, 553,4; with **habeō** and Inf., 423,2,N.2.

necessity—adjs. of, with Inf., 421,N.1,*c*; expressed by Indic., 254,R.1, 255,R.

nēdum—482,5,R.2.

nefās—70,B.; with Inf., 428,N.2; with Abl. Sup., 436,N.2; with Inf., 422,N.2.

negāre—use of, 444,1,N.2; continued by **neque—neque**, 445,N.; = **dīcō nōn**, 447; with Inf., 527,R.2.

negative—of Potential, 257; of Opt., 260; of Impv., 270; **nōn** with Opt., 260; **nōn** with Impv., 270,R.1; **nōlī** with Inf., 270,R.2; advs., 441-449; **nōn**, 442; **haud**, 443; **nec** = **nōn**, 442,N.3; **nē**, 444; subdivision of, 445; combinations, 446; resolution of, *ib.* N.2; positive supplied from, 447,R.; position of, 448, 449; two, 449; **nec nōn** for **et**, *ib.* R.3; in Copulative Sentences, 480; in Final and Consecutive Sentences, 543,4.

negōtium—in phrases with **ut**, 546.N.2; with Inf., 422,N.5.

nēmŏ—decl. of, 70,D.; and **nūllus**, 108; with Pl. vb., 211,R.1,Ex.*a*; with Impv. Subjv., 270,N.; and **quisquam**, 317,2; as adj., *ib.*; **et nēmō**, *ib.* 2,N.1; strengthened by **ūnus**; = **nēquis**, 446, N.3.

nequam—85,C.; comparison of, 90.

neque—with Opt. Subjv. for **nē**, 260; adds Impv., 270,N.; **neque—neque** with Pl., 285,N.1; subdivides a general neg., or **negō**, 445 and N.1; **nec nōn**, 449,R.3; for **et nōn**, 480 and R.1; for **nec tamen**, *ib.* R.3; for **nē—quidem**, *ib.* N.1; compared with **nec**, *ib.* N.2; for **nōn**, *ib.* N. 4; for **nēve**, 543,N.3.

nequīre—conj. of, 170,*b*; **nequīnont**, 133,IV.N.2; with Inf., 423,2,N.2.

Nēriŏ—decl. of, 41,4.

nesciō—an, 457,2; **quis**, 467,R.1; **quōmodo**, *ib.* N.; with Inf., 423,2,N.2, 527,R.1.

neu, nēve—444,2; adds Final Clause, 543,4; **neque** instead, *ib.* N.3.

neuter—decl. of, 76, 108; **neutiquam**, 442,N.2.

neuter—adj. with masc. subj., 211,R.4; demonstrative when subst. is expected, *ib.* N.3; Sg. sums up Pl., *ib.*; Pl. pred. to two fems., 286,3; in app. to persons, 321,N.2; pron. and adj. in Cognate Acc., 333,1, 341,N.2; pron. and adj. with Part. Gen., 369; pron. and adj. not attracted to Ger., 427,N.3.

nēve—see **neu.**

nī—with **mīrum**, 209,N.2; range of, 591, N.2.

nihil—for **nūllus**, 108; with Impv. Subjv., 270,N.; neg. of **quisquam**, 317, 2; *no*, 471,*b*,1; **nihilī** as Gen. of Price, 380,1; for **nōn**, 442,N.2.

nihilōminus—490,R.

nimis—with **quam** and Indic., 467,N.

nimium—with **quantum**, 209,N.2, 467,N.; *very*, 439,N.3; **nimiō** as Abl. of Standard, 403,N.3.

nisi—with **quod**, 525,2,N.2, 591,*b*,R.3; with **ut**, 557,N.2, 591,*b*,R.4; and **sī nōn**, 591,*b*; *but, except*, *ib.* R.2; **sī**, *ib.*; **nisi forte**, **vērō**, *ib.* R.4; **nisi tamen**, *ib.* N.1; in asseverations, 591,*b*,2; with Inf., 635, N.2; with participle, 667,N.

nītī—with Abl., 401,N.6; with Inf., 423,2, N.2; with **ut**, 546,N.1.

nix—decl. of, 52,7.

no—how translated, 470,*b* and *c*.

nocēre—with Dat., 346.

nōlle—conj. of, 174; exact use of **nōluerit**, 244,R.3; **nōlim, nōllem**, as Potential, 257,2, 258; not in Unreal Wish, 261, R.; **nōlī**, with Inf. for Impv., 270 N.2, 271,2; **nōlim**, with Subjv. for Impv.,

271,2,N.2; with Pf. Inf. pass., 280,2,*c*.N.; **nōlēns**, in pred. app., 325,R.6; with Inf., 423,2,N.2; with **ut**, 546,N.1; with Inf. or **ut**, 538 and N.3.

nōmen—with **esse** and Dat., 349,R.5; with Appositional Gen., 361,1; with Gen. of Charge, 378,R.2.

nōminārī—with two Noms., 206.

NOMINATIVE—defined, 23,1; of 1st Decl., 29 and N.1; of 2d Decl., 31,33,N.4; of 3d Decl., 36,1 and 2, 38,1, 57,R.4; of Greek substantives, 66,N.4; of adjs., 75,N.4, 79, N.1; of Participles, 89,R.2; for Voc., 201, R.2; syntax of, 203; two Noms., 206; with Inf. after copulative vb., *ib.* R.3; for Voc. in app., 321,N.1; with **ō** and **ēn**, or **ecce**, 343,1,N.1; with Inf. by attraction, 527,N.2; after pass. vbs. of Saying and Thinking, 528; *nōminatīvus pendēns*, 627,N.2.

nōn—neg. of Potential, 257; neg. of Wish, 260; with Impv., 270,R.1; syntax of, 441, 442; with **ūllus** for **nūllus**, 446,N.2; **nōn possum nōn**, 449,R.1; **nec nōn** = **et**, *ib.* R.3; *no*, 471,*b*,1; **nōn modo—sed etiam**, 482,5 and N.1; **nōn modo—sed nē—quidem**, *ib.* R. 1; for **nē**, 573,N.2.

nōnne—syntax of, 455; with indirect question, 460,1,N.2; with rhetorical question, 464,R.

nōnnūllus—108.

nōscere—syncope in Pf., 131,3; **novī**, 175,5,*d*.

nostrī—with Gen. Ger., 428,R.1.

noun—defined, 16; inflection of, 17; and pronoun, 16,N.2.

nourishing—vbs. of, with Abl., 401,N.1.

novus—Comp. of, 87,9; with Inf., 422,N. 3; with **ut**, 553,4.

nox—decl. of, 53,8; with Abl. of Time, 393,R.5.

nūbere—with Dat., 346,R.2 and N.4.

nūdus—with Gen., 374,N,8.

nūllus—decl. of, 76,90; and **nēmō**, 108; with Impv. Subjv., 270,N.; and **ūllus**, 317,2; for **nōn**, *ib.* N.2.

num—456; with **ne** and **nam**, *ib.* N.; in indirect questions, 460,1,*a*; in rhetorical questions, 464,R.

number—Sg. and Pl., 22; Dual, *ib.* R. and 112,1; concord of, 285 and NN.; violation of Concord in app., 321,R.1; substs. of, with Gen., 368; definite numbers in Abl. of Time, 393,R.2.

numerals—cardinals, 94; ordinals, 95 and 294; cpd., 96; omission of **centēna mīlia**, *ib.* 6; insertion of **et**, *ib.* 5; fractions, *ib.* 7; signs, 96,ii.; distributives, 97 and 295; multiplicatives, 97; proportionals, 97; advs., 98; **duo, ambō, uterque**, 292; **mīlle**, 293; **singulī**, 295; distributives for cardinals, *ib.* N.; **aliquis** with, 314,R.2; **quisque** with, 318, 2; with Part. Gen., 370.

numerō—as adv., 399,N.1; **(in) numerō habēre**, 340,R.1.

nunc—strengthens **etiam**, 478,N.1; **nunc—nunc**, 482,1 and N.1.

nūntiāre—with Inf., 527,R.2; with Nom. and Inf., 528,N.1.

nūperum—defective, 85,1.

O—sound of, 3; weakening of, 8,1; as interjection, 201,R.2, 343,N.1; **ō sī** in Wishes, 261; length of final, 707,5.

ob—in composition, 9,4; vbs. cpd. with, take Acc. or Dat., 331,347; to give the Cause, 408,N.3; as prep., 416,16; with Acc. Ger., 428,R.2, 432 and N.1.

obesse—with Dat., 346,R.2, 347,R.2; with Inf., 422,N.4.

obicere—with Acc. Ger., 430,N.1.

object—direct, becomes subj. of pass., 216; indirect retained in pass., 217; direct, 330; inner, 330,332,333; outer, 338; indirect, 344; of Ger., 427,2; after Dat. Ger., 429,N.2; after Acc. Sup., 435, N.3; after Abl. Sup., 436.

OBJECT SENTENCES—523-537; with **quod**, 524,525; with Acc. and Inf., 526,527; with Nom. and Inf., 528; after vbs. of Will and Desire, 532; after vbs. of Emotion, 533; in exclamations, 534; as subj., 535; in part., 536, 537; in Ō. O., 655.

Objective Genitive—363; of pers. pron., 364,N.2.

obligāre—with **sē** and Gen. of Charge, 378,R.1.

obligation—expressed by Indic., 254,R.1, 255,R.

oboedīre—with Dat., 346,R.2.

obrēpere—with Dat., 347,R.2.

obsaturāre—with Gen., 383,1,N.2.

obsecrō—strengthens Impv., 269; without Inf., 546,N.3; with **ut**, 546,N.1.

obsequī—with Dat., 346,R.2.

obsistere—with Dat., 347,R.2; with **nē**, 548,N.1; with **quīn**, 555,1.

obstāre—with Dat., **347**,R.2; with **nē**, **548**,N.1; with **quīn**, **555**,1.
obstrepere—with Dat., **347**,R.2.
obtemperāre—with Dat., **346**,R.2.
obtēstor—with Inf., **546**,N.3.
obtingere—with Dat., **347**,R.2.
obtrectāre—with Dat., **346**,R.2 and N.2.
obvenīre—with Dat., **347**,R.2.
obversārī—with Dat., **347**,R.2.
occurrere—with Dat., **347**,R.2.
occursāre—with Dat., **347**,R.2.
ōcior—**87**,7.
ōdī—conjugation of, **175**,5,*c*; **odiō esse** as pass. of, *ib.* N.
office—suffixes for, **181**,10.
officere—with Dat., **346**,R.2.
officium—in phrases with Inf., **422**,N.2; with **ut**, **546**,N.2.
olle—for **ille**, **104**,3,N.1.
omission—of vowels, **8**,2, **701**,R.2,*a*; of consonants, **9**,6; of subj., **207**; of copula, **209**; of other vbs., *ib.* N.5; of **esse** in Pf. Inf. pass., **280**,2.*a*,R.2 and *c*; of conjunction, **474**,N., **481**,**483**,N., **492**,N.; of **nōn**, **482**,5,R.1; of vb. of Saying, **545**,R.3; of vb. with **sīn**, **592**,R.; of **sī**, **598**; of vb. of Protasis, **599**; of Protasis, **600**; of Apodosis, **601**; of vb. after **quasi** and **tamquam**, **602**,N.1; of vb. of comparative clause, **640**.
omittere—with **quod**, **525**,1,N.1; with Inf., **423**,2,N.2; **omitte**, with Inf. for Impv., **271**,2,N.2.
omitting—vbs. of, with **quod**, **555**,1; vbs. of, with Inf., **423**,2.
omnīnō—*yes*, **471**,*a*,1.
omnis—in Abl., without **in**, **388**; **omnia**, as Acc. of Respect, **338**,2.
onus—with Inf., **422**,N.2.
onustus—with Gen., **374**,N.1; with Abl., **405**,N.3.
operam—in phrases with Dat. Ger., **429**, 1 and N.1; with Inf., **422**,N.5; with **ut**, **546**,NN.1 and 2.
opīniō—in phrases with Inf., **527**,R.2; with **ut**, **557**,R.; **opīniōne** as Abl. of Respect, **398**,N.1.
opitulārī—with Dat., **346**,R.2.
oportet—Indic. for Subjv., **254**,R.1; with Pf. part. pass., **280**,2,*b*,R.2; with Inf. or Subjv., **535**,R.2; with **ut**, **553**,4,R.1.
oppidō—*very*, **439**,N.3; with **quantum**, **467**,N.
oppidum—has pred. adj. in agreement, **211**,R.6; requires prep., **337**,R.1.; with Epexegetical Gen., **336**,N.1; in app. to Town in Abl., **356**,R.1, **391**,R.1; in app. to Loc., **411**,R.3.
[**ops**]—defective, **70**,D.
optāre—with Inf., **423**,2,N.2; with **ut**, *ib.* N.4,**546**,N.1; **optātō**, as Abl. of Manner, **399**,N.1.
OPTATIVE SUBJUNCTIVE—**260–265**; in Wishes, **260**; particles with, **261**; in Asseverations, **262**; as Impv., **263**; as concessive, **264**; in Deliberative Questions, **265**.
optimum—with Inf., **422**,N.3.
opus—with Abl., **406**; with Gen., *ib.* N.3; with Nom., *ib.* N.4; with part., **437**,N.2; with Inf., **422**,N.2; with **ut**, **557**,R.; with Nom. and Inf., **528**,N.2.
ōrāre—with two Accs., **339** and N.1; with Inf., **546**,N.3; with **ut**, *ib.* N.1.
ŌRĀTIŌ OBLĪQUA—**508**,2; partial, *ib.*3, *ib.*4; sequence in, **516**; in Relative Sentences, **625**,R., **628**,R., **629**,R., **648**,**649**; comes in without notice, **649**,N.2; shift to, *ib.* N.3; moods in, **650–652**; interrogative in, **651**; Impv. in, **652**; tenses in, **653–655**; in Causal Sentences, **655**; Conditional Sentences in, **656–659**; Logical, **595**,R.1, **657**; Ideal, **596**,R.5 **658**; Unreal, **597**,R.4, **659**; pronouns in, **660**; by Attraction, **508**,4,**662**; partial, **508**,3,**663**; Representation, **654** and N.
orbus—with Abl., **405**,N.3.
order—adjs. of, in pred. attrib., **325**,R.6.
ordinals—**94**; early forms, **95**,N.5; **alter** for **secundus**, **96**,5; in dates, **294**; for cardinals, *ib.* and **336**,R.1; with **quisque**, *ib.* N.,**318**,2; position of, **676**,R.2.
ōrdine—as Abl. of Manner, **399**,N.1.
Origin—Abl. of, **395**; preps. with Abl. of, *ib.* NN.2 and 3; suffixes of, **182**,7.
orīrī—**166**,**169**,1; **ortus**, with Abl. of Origin, **395**,N.1.
oriundus—with Abl. of Origin, **395**,N.1.
ōs—*bone*, decl. of, **48**.R.; *mouth*, defective, **70**,D.
ostendere—with Acc. and Inf., **527**,R.2.
ostrea—heteroclite, **68**,1.
overlapping action—**562**,**571**,N.1.
oxymoron—**694**.

Paene—with Indic. in Apod. of Unreal Condition, **597**,R.3; position of, **677**,R.1.
paenitet—with Gen., **377**; with neut.

subj., *ib.* R.2; with Inf., **422**,N.4; with **quod**, **542**.
palam—as prep., **417**,8.
palatals—vowels, **2**; consonants, **6**,1,N.
palumbes—heteroclite, **68**,7.
pānis—heteroclite, **68**,12.
pār—with **est** instead of Subjv., **254**,R.1; with Gen. or Dat., **359**,R.1; with Dat. Ger., **429**,N.1.
parāre—with Inf., **423**,2,N.2; **parātus**, with Inf., **421**,N.1,*c*.
parataxis—**472**.
parcere—with Dat., **346**,R.2; **parce**, with Inf. for Impv., **271**,2,N.2.
parenthetical **ut** and **nē**—**545**,R.3.
pārēre—with Dat., **346**,R.2.
pariter—**pariter**, **482**,3.
pars—with Pl. vb., **211**,R.1,Ex.*a*; in Abl. without **in**, **385**,N.1; **tuam partem**, **334**,R.2.
Part Affected—in Acc., **338**,1.
partial obliquity—**508**,3, **663**.
particeps—with Gen., **374**,N.2.
participation—adjs. of, with Gen., **374**.
PARTICIPIAL SENTENCES—**664-670**; to express Time, **665**; Cause, **666**; Condition and Concession, **667**; relative clauses, **668**; Future similarly used, **669**,**670**.
PARTICIPLE—decl. of, **80**,**82**; Abl. of, **83**; Nom. and Acc. Pl. of, *ib.* N.1; comparison of, **88**,**89**; Abl. of Comp., *ib.* R.1; Nom. Pl. of, *ib.*R.2; Gen. Pl. of, *ib.* R.3; defined, **112**,5; formation of, **115**,3; early forms of, **130**,7; Pf. pass., **135**,I.; Fut. Act., *ib.* II.; Pf. pass. of Deponents as act., **167**,N.1; Pf. pass. of intrans. vbs. used as act., **220**,N.1; Pf. with **habeō** and **teneō**, **238**; Fut. periphrastic, **247**; Pr. periphrastic with **esse**, *ib.* N.2; Pf. with **fuī**, **250**; as adj., *ib.* N.2; as pred., **251**,N.1; usage of Pr. and Pf., **282**; usage of Fut. act., **283**; concord with two subjs. in Abl. Abs., **285**,N.3; Pr. with Gen., **375**; contrasted with adj., *ib.* N.1; Comp. of, with Gen., *ib.* N.2; of Birth with Abl., **395**; Pf. pass. with **opus** and **ūsus**, **406**; in Abl. Abs., **409**, **410**, and NN.; Pf. pass. parallel with Ger., **426**,N.2, **427**,N.1; as subst., **437**; Fut. as subst., *ib.* N.1; as adj., **438**; Fut. as adj., *ib.* N.1; parallel with rel. and Subjv., *ib.* R.; with interrog., **469**; sequence after, **518**; after vbs. of Perception, *etc.*, **527**,N.1, **536**; after vbs. of Causation, *etc.*, **537**; equiv. to **cum**, **585**, R.; for Prot., **593**,2; for Prot. in Comparative Sentence, **602**,N.3; Concessive, **609**; for rel., **637**.
particles—copulative, **474**; adversative, **483**; disjunctive, **492**; causal, **498**; illative, **499**; position of, **679**.
partitive apposition—**322**.
Partitive Genitive—**367-372**; with substs. of Quantity, *etc.*, **368**; with neut. Sg., **369**; with numerals, **370**; with pronouns, **371**; with comparatives and superlatives, **372**; preps. instead, *ib.* R.2; with **uterque**, **371**,R.1; extensions of, **372**, NN.: contrasted with Gen. of Characteristic, **369**,N.1.
parts of speech—**16**.
parvus—Comp. of, **90**; in Gen. of Price, **380**,1.
passive—voice, **112**,2; vbs. with two Noms., **206**; vb. agrees with pred., **211**, R.1, Ex. *b*; defined, **214**; Pf. with Dat. of Agent, **215**,1; as reflexive, **218**; of something endured, **219**; periphrastic forms of, **248-251**; with Acc. of Respect, **338**,N.2; impersonal, **346**,R.1.
patī—with **ut**, **553**,2; with Inf., *ib.*N.
patronymics—**182**,11.
paulō, **paulum**—with **ante** and **post**, **403**,N.4,*b*.
pause—in Verse, **742**.
pavēre—constr. of, **550** and N.1.
pāx—decl. of, **70**,D; in Abl. of Time, **393**, R.5, **394**,R.1.
pecūliāris—with Gen. or Dat., **359**,R.1.
pecus—heteroclite, **68**,12.
pellere—with Abl. of Separation, **390**, N.1.
pendēre—with Gen., **379**.
penes—position of, **413**,R.1; use of, as prep., **416**,17.
pentameter—elegiac, **785**; Pf. Inf. in, **280**, 2,*b*,N.2; position of words in, **683**.
penult—**11**.
penus—heteroclite, **68**,11.
per—vbs. cpd. with take Acc., **331**; with Acc. of Extent, **335**, **336**; to express Time Within Which, *ib.* R.2, **393**,R.1; *here and there in*, **385** R.3; for Abl. of Manner, **399**,N.1; with Person Through Whom, **401**; position of, **413**,R.1, and N. 2; use as prep., **416**,18.
perceiving—vbs. of, with Object Clause, **523**; with Acc. and Inf., **526**, **527**; with

Nom., 528; with part., 527,N.1, 536; Nom. after, 536,N.2.
percontārī—with two Accs., 339 and N.1.
perdius—defective, 85,2.
PERFECT—defined, 112,3: System, 114,2 and 3,*b*; formation of, 114, 115, 121,2; syncopated forms of, 131, 1-3; early forms of, 131,4; Stem, 134; part. pass., 135,I.; part. as subst., 167,N.1; pass. with Dat. of Agent, 215,1; part. used as act., 220,N.1; defined, 223; Historical, 225; Pure and Historical, 235; force of, 236; trans. by Eng. Pr., *ib.* R.; with Aor. force, *ib.*; Gnomic, *ib.* N.; for Fut. Pf., 237; part. with **habeō** and **teneō**, 238; pass. with **fuī**, 250; Subjv. as Potential, 257,2 and N.1; in wishes, 260; Subjv. as Impv., 263,2,*b*, 270,R.2; tense relations in Subjv., 277; Inf. as subj. or obj., 280,2; after **decuit**, *ib.* *a*, R.1; Emotional, *ib.*; after **oportuit**, *ib.* R.2; after **velle**, 280, 2,*b* and N.1; after **posse**, *ib.*; after **debeō**, *ib.* N.3; after vbs. of Will and Desire, 280,2,*c*; use of part., 282 and N.; part. as subj., 437,N.1; Sequence after, 511,RR.3,4; Subjv. in Final Sentences, 512,N.1; in Consecutive Sentences, 513 and NN.; Inf., 530; Inf. in Ō.O., 659,N.
perficere—with **ut**, 553,1.
pergere—with Inf., 423,2,N.2.
perhibēre—as copulative vb., 206, N.1; with Nom. and Inf., 528 and N.1.
period—Responsive and Apodotic, 685; forms distinguished by Nägelsbach, 686; Historical and Oratorical, 687.
periphrasis—for Impv., 271; for Fut. periphrastic, 515,R.2; for Fut., 531 and N.1; for Apod. in Unreal Condition, 597,R.5.
PERIPHRASTIC CONJUGATION—129; act., 247; pass., 251; with **fuī**, 247,R.1; with **forem**, *ib.* N.1; Pr. part. with **esse**, *ib.* N.2; with **futūrum esse ut**, 248; with **in eō est**, 249; with **posse**, **velle**, 248, R.; Pf. part. with **sum** and **fuī**, 250 and R.1; with **forem** for **essem**, *ib.* N.2; with Ger., 251; Fut. act., 283.
perīre—pass. of **perdere**, 169,2,R.1.
perītus—with Gen., 374,N.4.
permanēre—with two Noms., 206,N.1.
permittere—used personally in pass., 217,N.2; with Inf., 423,2,N.2, 532,N.1 553,2,N.; with **ut**, 553,2.
permitting—vbs. of, with Consecutive Clause, 553,2.
pernox—defective, 85,2.
perperum—defective, 85,1.
perpetuus—and **perpes**, 84,1; **perpetuum**, as adv. Acc., 336,N.1.
perquam—with Indic., 467,N.
persequēns—with Gen., 375,N.2.
persevērāre—with Inf., 423,2,N.2.
persons—in conjugation of vb., 112,1; concord of, 287; order of, *ib.* R.
personal endings—114.
personal pronouns—304; omitted, *ib.* 1; Gen. of, as objective, *ib.* 2, 364,N.2; poss. for, *ib.* 2,N.2; Gen. of, as Partitive, *ib.* 3; for poss., *ib.* 3,N.1; circumlocution for third personal pronoun, *ib.* 3,N.2.
perspicere—with Acc. and Inf., 527,R.1.
perstāre—with Inf., 423,2,N.2.
persuādēre—used personally in pass., 217,N.1; with Dat., 346,R.2, and NN.2,4; with Inf., 423,2,N.2, 527,R.2, 546,R.1; with **ut**, 546,N.1.
pertaesum est—with Gen., 377.
pessum—defective, 70,A; with **īre**, 435, N.1.
petere—with **ā** and Abl., 339,R.1 and N.1; with Acc. Ger., 430,N.1; with Inf., 423, 2,N.2; with **ut**, 546,N.1.
Phalaecean—verse, 796.
Pherecratean—verse, 794.
phonetic variations—in vowels, 8; in consonants, 9; in consonant stem-characteristic, 121,R.
piget—with Gen., 377; with subj., *ib.* R.2.
pilī—as Gen. of Price, 380,1.
pīnus—heteroclite, 68,5.
pius—Comp. of, 87,6,N.
place—*where*, in Abl., 385; with vbs. of Placing, *ib.* R.1; with Towns, 386; as Cause, Means, *etc.*, 389; with Books, *etc.*, 387; with **tōtus**, *etc.*, 388; in Loc., 411; *whence*, in Abl., 390, 391; with Towns, 391; of origin, 395,N.2; *whither*, in Acc., 337.
placēre—with Dat., 346,R.2; use of Fut. Pf., 244,R.3.
pleasure—vbs. of, with Dat., 346; adjs. of, with Abl. Sup., 436,N.2.
plēbs—decl. of, 63,N.1, 68,8.
plenty—vbs. of, with Abl., 405; adjs. of, with Gen. or Abl., *ib.* N. 3.

plēnus—with Gen., **374**,N.1; with Abl., **405**,N.3.
pleonasm—**692**.
plēraque—as Acc. of Respect, **338**,2.
pluere—with Abl. of Means, **401**,N.5.
PLUPERFECT—**112**,3; formation of, **114**, **115**; Aor. forms of, **131**,4,*b*,3; defined, **223**; force of, **241**; translated by Impf., *ib.* R.; used as Aor., *ib.* N.1; periphrastic, with **habeō**, *ib.* N.2; Subjv. as Potential of Past, **258**,N.2; in Wish, **260**; with **vellem**, **261**,R.; Subjv. as Concessive, *ib.* N.; Subjv. as Impv. of Past, **273**,3; tense force in Subjv., **277**; in Final Sentences, **512**,N.1; to express Resulting Condition, **563**,1; Indic. in Apod. of Unreal Condition, **597**,R.2.
plural—of abstracts, **204**,N.5; used for Sg., *ib.* NN.6,7; pred. with two subjs., **285**; neut. pred. to two fems., **286**,3.
plūs—**quam** omitted with, **296**,R.4; **plūris**, with vbs. of Rating and Buying, **380**,1; **plūrimum**, with **quantum**, **467**, N.; **plūrimī**, as Gen. of Price, **380**,1.
poēma—heteroclite, **68**,7.
pollēre—with Inf., **423**,2,N.2.
pollicērī—with Inf., **527**,R.2, **531**,N.4.
pollis—decl. of, **41**,4.
pondō—defective, **70**,A.
pōne—usage of, **416**,19.
pōnere—with **in** and Abl., **386**,R.1 and N. 2; *suppose*, with Inf., **527**,R.2.
pōscere—with two Accs., **339** and N.1; with **ā** and Abl., *ib.* R.1; with Inf. or **ut**, **546**, NN.1,3.
position—adjs. of, in pred. attrib., **325**,R. 6; of advs., **440**; of neg., **448** and NN.; of rel., **612**; of correlative clause, **620**; poetical peculiarities in, **683**.
positive—degree lacking, **87**,2,7,8, and 9; with prep. to express disproportion, **298**,R.; in comparing qualities, **299**; with **quam** after Comp., **299**,N.2; with Part. Gen., **372**,N.2; supplied from neg., **447**, R.
posse—conj. of, **119**; **potis** for **posse**, **209**, N.2; use of Fut. and Fut. Pf. of, **242**,R.2, **244**,R.3; needs no periphrasis, **248**,R.; Indic. for Subjv., **254**,R.1; Impf. Indic. of Disappointment, *ib.* R.2; with Pf. Inf. act., **280**,2,*b*, and N.1; with **quam**, *etc.*, to strengthen superlative, **303**; omitted, with **quam**, *ib.* R.1; with Inf., **423**,2,N.2; **nōn possum nōn**, **449**,R.1; in simple questions, **453**,N.1; for periphrastic, **513**,R.3, **531**,N.3 and 4; in Apod. of Unreal Condition, **597**,R.5,*c*; restrictions with, **627**,R.2; in Logical Condition, **657**,R.; in Unreal Condition in Ō.O., **659**,N.
Possession—Dat. of, **349**; compared with Gen., *ib.* R.2; of qualities, *ib.* R.3; Gen. of, **362**; in 1st and 2d person, *ib.* R.1; omission of governing word, *ib.* R.3.
possessive pronouns—**100**-**102**, **106**,N.4; usage of **suus**, **309**,4 and NN.; syntax of, **312**; intense use of, *ib.* R.1; for Gen. of personal pron., **304**,2,N.2; with Gen. in app., **321**,R.2; for 1st and 2d persons in Subjective Gen., **364**; as pred., **366**,R.3; with **interest** and **rēfert**, **381**; with **domī**, **411**,R.4; position of, **676**,R.1.
possibility—in Indic. rather than Subjv., **254**,R.1, **255**,R.
post—vbs. cpd. with, take Dat., **347**; with Abl. or Acc. of Measure, **403**,N.4; position of, **403**,N.4,*b*, **413**,R.1; omission of, with rel., **403**,N.4; as adv., **415**; as prep., **416**,20; with Pf. part. pass., **437**, N.2.
posteāquam—see **postquam**.
posterum—defective, **74**,R.2; Comp. of, **87**,2 and 7.
postquam—with Hist. Pf. or Pr., **561**; with Impf., **562**; with Plupf., **563**; range of tenses with, *ib.* NN.1-3; with Subjv., *ib.* N.4; Causal with Pr. and Pf., **564** and N.1; in Iterative action, **566**, **567**.
postrīdiē quam—**577**,N.5.
pōstulāre—with **ā** and Abl., **339**,R.1 and N.1; with Inf., **423**,2,N.2, **546**,N.3; with **ut**, *ib.* N.3.
potēns—with Gen., **374**,N.3.
POTENTIAL SUBJUNCTIVE—**257**-**259**; for Pr. and Fut., **257**; for Past, **258**; in questions, **259**; for Indic., **257**,N.3; not conditional, **257**,N.2, **600**,2; of Past coincides with Unreal of Present, **258**,N.2.
potīrī—with Abl., **407** and N.2,*d*; with personal Ger., **427**,N.5.
potis, e—**85**,C; **potior**, **87**,7; **potius** strengthens comparative, **301**; **potius quam**, with Subjv. or Inf., **577**,N.6, **631**, 3,R.2, **644**,R.3; see **posse**.
power—adjs. of, with Gen., **374**; vbs. of, with Inf., **423** and N.2; sequence after vb. of, **515**,R.3; in Indic. rather than Subjv., **254**,R.1, **255**,R.

prae—to express disproportion, **296**,N.3; vbs. cpd. with take Dat., **347**; gives Preventing Cause, **408**,N.4; as adv., **415**; as prep., **417**,9; **prae quod, 525**,2, N.2.

praecellere—with Abl. of Respect, **397**, N.2.

praecipere—with Inf., **423**,2,N.2; with **ut, 546**,N.1; used personally in pass., **217**,N.2; **praeceptum**, with **ut, 546**,N.2.

praecipitāre—with Abl., **390**,2,N.3.

praecipuum—with **ut, 557**,R.

praeesse—with Dat. Ger., **429**,1.

praeficere—with Dat. Ger., **429**,1.

praegestīre—with Inf., **423**,2,N.2.

(in) **praesentiā**—*for the present*, **394**,R.

praesidēre—with Dat., **347**,R.2.

praestāre—with Dat., **347**,R.2; with Abl. of Respect, **397**,N.2; with Abl. of Measure, **403**,N.1; with **ut, 553**,1.

praestōlārī—with Dat., **346**,N.2.

praeter—to express disproportion, **296**, N.3; vbs. cpd. with, take Acc., **331**; position of, **413**,N.3; use as prep., **416**,21; with Pf. part. pass., **437**,N.2; **id quod, quam quod, quod, 525**,2,N.2.

praeterīre—with **quod, 525**,1,N.1.

precārī—with **ut, 546**,N.1.

predicate—and copula, **205**; with copulative vbs., **206**; concord of, **211**; violation of concord of, *ib.* RR.1–6,NN.1–3; in Pl. with two subjs., **285**; in Pl. with **neque—neque**, *ib.* N.1; concord of, in Gender, **286**; in Person, **287**; Attribution, **325**; Apposition, *ib.* and R.6; with Abl. Abs., **410**,N.6; after Inf., **538**.

prepositions—assimilation of in composition, **9**,4; defined, **16**,6; repeated with cpd. vbs., **331**,RR.2,3; with Countries and Towns, **337**,RR.1–4; with **domum**, *ib.* R.3; omitted with Countries and Towns, **337**,NN.1–3; instead of Dat., **347**,R.1; omitted with vbs. and adjs. of Separation, **390**,2 and 3; with Abl. of Origin, **395**,NN.2,3; syntax of, **412–416**; origin of, **412**; position of, **413**,**678**; repetition and omission of, **414**; as advs., **415**; with Acc., **416**; with Abl., **417**; with Acc. and Abl., **418**; two with same case, **414**, R.4; improper, **412**,N.; with participles for abstract substantives, **437**,N.2.

PRESENT—**112**,3; System, **114**,3,*a*; rules for formation of, **121**,1; notes on System, **130**; formation of Stem, **133**; defined, **223**; Historical, **224**, **229**; Specific or Universal, **227**; Progressive, *ib.* N.1; of Endeavor, *ib.* N.2; of Resistance to Pressure, *ib.* N. 3; anticipates Fut., **228**; with **iam**, *etc.*, **230**; contrasted with Pf. to give Effect in VERGIL, *ib.* N.3; part. with **esse, 247**,N.2; Indic. for Deliberative Subjv., **254**,N.2; Subjv. as Potential, **287**,2; Subjv. in Wishes, **260**; Subjv. as Impv., **263**, **270**, R.2; Subjv. as Concessive, **264**; tense relations in Subjv., **277**; Inf. as subj. or obj., **280**, 1; Inf. after **meminī, 281**,2, N.; part., **282**; part. as subst., **437**,N.1; Hist. sequence after, **511**,R.1; Inf. after vbs. of Saying and Thinking, **530**; Inf. for Fut., **531**,NN.3 and 4.

preventing—vbs. of, with **nē, quōminus,** or **quīn, 548**, **549**, **555**,1.

previous condition—given by **ex** or **ab,** and Abl., **206**,R.2, **396**,N.2.

Priapean—verse, **805**.

Price—Gen. of, **379**; Abl. of, **404**.

prīdiēquam—usage of, **577**,N.5.

primitive words—**179**, 1.

prīmōris—defective, **85**,1.

prīmus—with **quisque, 318**,N,3; **prīmō, prīmum, 325**,R.7; in pred. attrib., **325**, R.6; used partitively, **291**; **prior, 87**,8.

principal parts—**120**.

principal tenses—**225**.

priusquam—with Indic., **574**, **576**; with Pr., **575**; with pure Pf., *ib.* N.1; with Pf. or Fut., **576**; **nōn priusquam = dum,** *ib.* R.; with Subjv., **577**; with **ut** or Inf., **644**,R.3.

prō—to express disproportion, **298**; with **habēre, 340**,R.1; with Nom. or Acc. in Exclamations, **343**,1,N.1; *for*, compared with Dat., **345**,R.2; position of, **413**,R.1; as prep., **417**,10; with Abl. Ger., **433**; **prō eō quod, 525**,2,N.2; **prō eō ut, 642**, R.4.

probāre—with Inf., **527**,R.2.

prōcreātus—with Abl. of Origin, **395**,N.1.

procul—with Abl. of Separation, **390**,3,N. 2; as prep., **417**,11.

prōdesse—conj. of, **118**; with Dat., **346**, R.2; with Inf., **422**,N.4.

prōdigus—with Gen., **374**,N.1.

profectō—strengthens **atque, 477**,N.2.

prōficere—with **ut, 553**,1.

profundus—never with Acc., **335**,R.1.

profūsus—with Gen., **374**,N. 1.
prōgnātus—with Abl. of Origin, **395**,N.1.
prohibēre—with two Accs., **341**,N.2 ; with Abl., **390**,2,N.3 ; with Inf., **423**.2,N.2 ; with **nē**, **548**, and N.1 ; with **quōminus**, **549**, and N.1 ; with Inf., **532**,N.1, **549**,N.1.
prohibiting—vbs. of, with Dat., **345**,R.1.
proinde—strengthens Impv., **269** ; as coördinating conj., **503** ; and **proin**, *ib.*
prolepsis—of subj. of leading clause, **468**.
promising—vbs. of, with Inf., **423**,N.5, **527**,R.4 ; **531**,N.4.
prōmittere—with Pr. Inf., **527**,R.2, **531**, N.4.
PRONOUNS—defined, **16**,3 ; compared with nouns, *ib.* N.2 ; decl. of, **17** ; Personal, **100-102** ; Determinative, **103** ; Demonstrative, **104** ; Relative, **105** ; Interrogative, **106** ; Indefinite, **107** ; Pronominal Adjectives, **108** ; Possessive, **100-102** ; omitted, **207** ; with Impv., **267**,N. ; syntax of, **304-319** ; Personal, **304** ; Demonstrative, **305-307** ; **hīc**, **305** ; **iste**, **306** ; **ille**, **307** ; Determinative **is**, **308** ; Reflexive, **309** ; **īdem**, **310** ; **ipse**, **311** ; Possessive, **312** ; Indefinite, **313-319** ; **quīdam**, **313** ; **aliquis**, **314** ; **quis**, **315** ; **quispiam**, **316** ; **quisquam** and **ūllus**, **317** ; **quisque**, **318** ; **alter** and **alius**, **319** ; with Part. Gen., **371** ; in Ō. O., **660**.
prōnūntiāre—used personally in pass., **217**,N.2.
prōnus—constr. of, **359**, N. 5.
prope—as adv., **415** ; as prep., **416**,22 ; position of, **678**,R.1 ; **propior** and **proximus**, **87**,8 ; with Acc. or **ab**, **359**,N.1.
properāre—with Inf., **423**,2,N.2.
prōpīnāre—with Acc. Ger., **430**,N.1.
propinquus—Comp. of, **87**,9.
prōpōnere—with Acc. Ger., **430**,N.1.
prōpositum—**est**, with Inf., **423**,2,N.2; with **ut**, **546**,N.2.
proprius—with Gen. or Dat., **359**,R.1 ; with **ut**, **557**,R.
propter—compared with Abl. of Cause, **408**,N.3 ; position of, **413**,R.1 ; as adv., **415**; as prep., **416**,23 ; with Acc. Ger., **432** and N.1.
propterеā—**503**.
prosody—**701-823**.
prōspicere—with Dat., **346**,R.2 ; with Inf., **527**,R.1 ; with **ut**, **546**,N.1.
prōstāre—with Gen. of Price, **379**.
protasis — defined, **589** ; equivalents of, **593** ; omission of vb. of, **599** ; total omission of, **600**.
protraction—**743**.
prōvidēre—with **ut**, **546**,N.1.
providing—vbs. of, with Abl., **401**,N.1.
prōvidus—Comp. of, **87**,5.
proximum—in phrases with **ut**, **557**,R.
prūdēns—in pred. attrib., **325**,R.6 ; with Gen., **374**,N.4.
-pte—added to personal pronouns, **102**,N. 3.
pudet—with Gen., **377** and R.1 ; with subj., *ib.* R.2.
puer—Voc. of, **33**,N.2.
pūgnāre—with Dat., **346**,N.6 ; with **ut**, **546**,N.1.
purpose—in Inf., **423**,N.1 ; in Dat. Ger., **429**,2; in Sup., **435**; in Fut. part., **438**,N. ; sequence in clauses of, **512** ; reflexive in clauses of, **521** ; rel. clauses of, **630** ; see Final Sentences.
pūrus—with Abl. of Sep., **390**,3,N.
putāre—with Gen. of Price, **379**; with two Noms. in pass., **206**: (**nōn**) **putāveram**, **254**,N.1 ; **puta**, **ut puta**, *for example*, **274**; with Inf., **527**,R.2.
putting—vbs. of, with Dat. and Acc., or Acc. and Abl., **348**.

Quā—quā, 482,3.
quaerere—with **ā**, **dē**, **ex**, **339**,R.1 ; with Inf., **423**,2,N.2 ; with Direct Question, **467**,N.
quaesō—**175**,6 ; with Impv., **269** ; without Inf., **546**,N.3.
quālis—in phrases instead of Comparative, **296**,N.3.
Quality—possession of, **349**,R.3 ; Gen. of, **365** and R.1 ; Gen. and Abl. of, *ib.* R.2, **400**,R.1 ; Gen. of, as pred., **366**; Abl. of, **400** ; personified quality as person, *ib.* R.2 ; Comparison of qualities, **299**.
quam—after comparatives, **296** and R.1 ; omission of, *ib.* R.4 ; preps. instead, *ib.* N.3 ; **atque** instead, *ib.* N.4 ; with **prō**, **ut**, **quī**, to express disproportion, **298** ; with positive for comparative, **299**,N.2 ; in comparison of qualities, **299**; with **potuit** and superlative, **303**; with **quī** and superlative, *ib.* R.2; **magis**, **nōn aliter**, **quam ut**, **557**,N.2 ; **quam sī**, with Subjv. of Comparison, **602** ; with **quī** or **ut** after comparatives, **631**,3 ; with **quam quī** and superlative, **642**,R.5;

after **alius** or **secus, 643,**N.4; with Comparative Sentences, **644**; with **potius, prius,** *etc.*, R.3.

quamdiū—**568**; with Indic., **569**; range of, *ib.* N.1.

quamlibet—**606.**

quamquam—**603** and N.; with Indic., **605**; with Subjv., *ib.* RR.1,2, and N; *and yet*, *ib.* R.3; with part., **609,**N.1, **667,**N.; with Inf., **635,**N.2.

quamvīs—**603** and N.; with Subjv., **606**; with Indic., *ib.* N.1; inflection of vb. of, *ib.* N.2; with **licet, 607,**N.2; with part., **609,**N.1, **667,**N.; with adj. or adv., **609,** N.2.

quandō—with Causal Indic., **540**; with Subjv., **541**; early use, **538,**N.3, **580,**N.3; conditional use, **590,**N.3.

quandōque—with causal clause, **541,**N.5; **quandōque—quandōque, 482,**1,N.1.

quantity—rules for, **702–706**; of final syllables, **707–713**; of polysyllables, **707–709**; of monosyllables, **710–713**; of stem syllables, **714**; of cpds., **715**; in early Latin, **716, 717.**

quantity—**12**; substs. of, with Gen., **368.**

quantum—with **mīrum, nimium,** *etc.*, **209,**N.2, **467,**N.; with **māximus** and **potuit** to strengthen superlative, **303**; **quantum quī,** with superlative, *ib.* R. 2; **quantī,** with vbs. of Rating and Buying, **380**; with advs. and Indic., **467,**N.

quantumvīs—**603** and N., **606.**

quasi—with subst., **439,**N.4; with Subjv. of Comparison, **602**; with Indic., *ib.* N.1; to apologize, *ib.*N.2; to give an Assumed Reason, *ib.* N.4, **666,**N.

quātenus—as a Causal particle, **538,**N.5.

quattuor—early forms of, **95,**N.3.

que—added to rels., **111,**2; syntax of, **476** and NN.; for **quoque, 479,**N.2; adds third member, **481,**N.

quemadmodum—**sīc, 482,**3,N.

querī—with Acc. and Inf., **533,**R.1.

questions—with Potential Subjv., **259**; deliberative, **265, 465**; passionate equiv. to command, **273, 453,**N.2; predicate and nominal, **451**; rhetorical, **265, 451,** R.2, **464, 466**; direct simple, **453–457**; equiv. to Condition, **453,**N.3; with **ne, 454**; with **nōnne, 455**; with **num, 456**; with **an, 457**; direct disjunctive, **458**; neg. of, **459**; particles in indirect, **460**; moods in, **462–467**; Indic. in, **463, 464**; Subjv. in, **465, 466**; indirect, **467**; genuine, **463**; disconnected, **467,**N.; exclamatory, **558.**

quī interrogative—**106** and R.

quī relative—**105** and NN.; with **quam** and Subjv. to express disproportion, **298**; after **dīgnus,** *etc.*, **552,**R.2; equiv. to **sī quis, 625,**2; explicative, **626**; strengthened by **ut, utpote, quīppe,** *ib.* N.1; **quod sciam, 627,**R.1; equiv. to **cum is, 626,**R., **633, 634**; equiv. to **ut is, 630, 631**; after comparatives with **quam, 631,**3; equiv. to adj., *ib.* 4; **sed quī, quī tamen, 636,**N.2; **quō quisque,** with comparative, **642,**R.2; see **quō** and **quā.**

quia—after vbs. of Doing and Happening, **525,**1,N.4; origin of and, correlatives with, **538,**NN.1,2; with Causal Indic., **540**; with Subjv., **541**; after vbs. of Emotion, **542,**R.; with Inf., **635,**N.2.

quīcumque—**105** and N.5; with Indic., **254,**4, **625.**

quīdam—**107,**2; syntax of, **313**; with **quasi, 319,**R.2; strengthened by **certus, ūnus, 313,**R.3.

quidem—with demonstrative pron., **307,** R.4; position of, **413,**N.3, **679**; *yes*, with **sānē, 471,**a.,1.

quīlibet—**107** and N.

quīn—with **mīrum, 209,**N.2; strengthens Impv., **269**; **nōn quīn** as Causal, **541,**N.2; force of, **547**; in Consecutive Sentences, **552,**3; with vbs. of Preventing, **555,**1; with vbs. of Doubt and Uncertainty, *ib.* 2; after **nōn dubitō,** *ib.* 2, R.1; equiv. to **ut nōn, 556**; after vbs. of Saying, *etc.*, **555,**2; in Relative Sentences of Character, **632** and R.; **facere nōn possum quīn, 556.**

quīppe—**498,**N.8; with **quī, 626,**N.1.

quīquī—**105** and N.4.

quīre—conjugation of, **170,***a*; with **Inf., 433,**2,N.2.

quis indefinite—and **quī, 107,**1; for **aliquis,** *ib.* R. and N.1; syntax of, **315**; **aliquis** instead, *ib.* N.1; familiar usage of, **317,**2,N.2.

quis interrogative—**106**; and **quī,** *ib.* R.; old forms of, *ib.* NN.1,2; **quī** in Wishes, **261**; for **uter, 300,**N.

quisnam—**106** and N.5.

quispiam—**107,**3, and N.1; syntax of, **316.**

quisquam—107,3, and N.2; syntax of, 317; strengthened by **ūnus**, *ib.* 1,N.1; negative of, *ib.* 2; as adj., *ib.* 1,N.3.

quisque—107,5, and N.; **quisquis** instead, 105,N.4; with Pl. vb., 211,R.1,Ex.*a*; with ordinal, 294,N., 318,2; syntax of, 318; with superlatives, *ib.* 2; with reflexives, *ib.* 3; attraction of, *ib.* N.2; **suum quisque**, *ib.* N.4; with **quō** and comparative, 642,R.2; **ut quisque**, with superlative, *ib.*

quisquis—105; as adj., *ib.* N.4; with Indic., 254,4, 625.

quīvīs—107,4 and N.

quō—as Causal conjunction, 541,N.2; **nōn quō** in Final Clauses, 545,2; **quōnē**, *ib.* R.1; **quō setius**, 549,N.4.

quoad—force of, 568; of complete coextension, 569; *until*, with Indic., 571; with Subjv., 572; *until*, with Subjv., *ib.* N.5.

quod—in Inner Obj., 333 1,N.1; introduces Object Sentences, 524; after vbs. of Adding and Dropping, 525,1: after demonstratives, *ib.* 2; and **ut**, *ib.* 1,N.5; **quid est quod**, *ib.* 1,N.2; after **verba sentiendī**, *ib.* N.7; after demonstratives, with preps., *ib.* 2,N.2; *as to the fact that*, with Subjv., *ib.* 2,N.3; with Subjv. in Ō. O., *ib.* 3; after vbs. of Motion, *ib.*1, N.6; gives Ground in Exclamations, 534, R.1; with Causal Sentence in Indic., 540; with Causal Sentence in Subjv., 541; after vbs. of Emotion, 542; with **dīceret**, *ib.* N.3; **nōn quod**, *ib.* N.2; **magis quod**, 541,N.2; correlatives of, 538,N.1; and **quia**, *ib.* N.2; **nisi quod**, 591,R.3; **quod sī**, 610,R.2.

quom—see **cum**.

quōminus—force of, 547; with vbs. of Preventing, *etc.*, 549; for **nē**, 548,N.2; and **quīn**, 549,N.3.

quōmodo—with Direct Question, 467,N.

quoniam—with Causal Indic., 540; with Subjv., 541; original force of, 538,N.3; early usage of, 580,N.3.

quoque—syntax of, 479; and **etiam**, 479, R. and N.1; **que** instead, *ib.* N.2; with **sed** and **vērum**, 482,5 and N.1.

Rating—vbs. of, with Gen. and Abl., 379, 380.

ratiō—in Abl. of Manner, 399,N.1; with **ut**, 546,N.2.

recēns—with Abl., 390,3,N.1.

recipere—with Abl. or **in**, 389.

reciprocal relations—given by **inter sē**, 221; by **alter alterum**, *etc.*, *ib.* R.1; by **invicem**, **mūtuō**, *etc.*, *ib.* R.2.

recitation of verses—754.

recordārī—with Pr. Inf., 281,2,N.; with Acc., 376,R.2.

rēctum—with Inf., 422,N.3.

recūsāre—with Inf., 423,2,N.2; with **nē**, 548,N.1; with **quōminus**, 549 and N.1; constr. with, 549,N.1.

red—in composition, 9,4, 715,R.3.

reddere—with Pf. part., 537,N.2; **reddī** and **fierī**, 206,N.1, 340,R.1.

reduplication—in Pr. stem, 133,II.; in Pf. stem, 134,III.; omitted in Pf. of cpd. vbs., *ib.*

Reference—Dat. of, 352.

rēfert—with Gen. and Abl., 381, 382; Nom. with, 381,N.3; origin of, *ib.* N.5; expression of Degree of Concern, 382,1 and 2; expression of Thing Involved, *ib.* 3.

refertus—with Gen., 374,N.1.

reflexive—218; passive used for, 218; approaches deponent, 218,R.; pronouns, 309; **is** retained instead of reflexive, *ib.* N.1; strengthened, *ib.* N.2; **suum quisque**, 318,N.3; with **ipse**, 311,2; with Acc. of Respect, 338,N.2; in subordinate clauses, 520-522; not in Consecutive Sentences, 521,R.1; refers to real subj., 309,2, 521,R.2; free use of, *ib.* R.3; Indic. Relative Sentences, *ib.* R.4; ambiguity in, *ib.* N.3; demonstrative instead of, *ib.* R.1,N.3.

reformīdāre—with Inf., 423,2,N.2.

refrāgārī—with Dat., 346,R.2.

refraining—vbs. of, with **quīn**, 555,1.

refusing—vbs. of, with **nē**, 548; with **quōminus**, 549; with Inf., 548,R.2; with **quīn**, 555,1.

Reiziānus Versus—822.

regiō—in Abl. without **in**, 385,N.1.

relation—suffixes for, 181,8.

relationship—suffixes for, 181,7,182,11.

relative pronouns—105; made indefinite, 111,1; or universal, *ib.* 2; in Inner Obj., 333,1,N.2; instead of app. with **rēfert**, 381,N.2; contrasted with interrogative, 467,R.2, 611,R.2; indefinite with Indic., 354,R.4; with Subjv., 567,N.; advs. instead, 611,R.1; continued by demonstrative, 636,N.1; repetition of, 615.

RELATIVE SENTENCES—**610-637**; for Protasis, **593**,1; general consideration of, **610**; how introduced, **611**; position of, **612**; antecedent in, **613**; concord in, **614** and RR.; **id quod**, *etc.*, in app. to a sentence, *ib.* R.2; incorporation of app., *ib.* R.4; repetition of antecedent, **615**; incorporation of antecedent, **616**; attraction of, **617**; correlative of, **618**; absorption of correlative, **619**; position of correlative, **620**; indefinite antecedent, **621**; tenses in, **622,623**; in Iterative action, **623**; moods in, **624-635**; indefinite and generic relatives with Indic., **254**,R.4, **625**,1; or Subjv., *ib.* R.; conditional, **625**,2; explanatory, **626**; Subjv. in explanatory, **627**; **quod sciam**, *etc.*, *ib.* R.1; restrictions with **esse, posse, attinet**, *ib.* R.2; with Subjv. by Partial Obliquity, **628**; with Subjv. by Attraction, **629**; Final, **630**; attraction of **dīceret**, *ib.* N.3; Consecutive, **631**; after definite antecedent, *ib.* 1; after indefinite antecedent, *ib.*2; after comparative, *ib.* 3; parallel to adj., *ib.* 4; with **quīn**, **632**; Causal, **633**; Concessive and Adversative, **634**; in Inf., **635**; combination of, **636**; participle instead, **637,668**; in Ō. O., **655** and RR.

relātū—as Sup., **436**,N.

relieving—vbs. of, with Abl., **390**,2.

relinquere—with Acc. Ger., **430**,N.1.

reliquum est—with **ut**, **553**,4.

reliquus—used partitively with Subst., **291**,R.2; **alius** for, **319**,N.1; **reliqua**, as Acc. of Respect, **338**,2.

remembering—vbs. of, with Gen., **376**; with Acc., *ib.* R. 2.

rēmex—defective, **70**, D.

reminding—vbs. of, with Gen., **376**; with Abl. or Acc., *ib.* RR.1,2.

removing—vbs. of, with Abl., **390**,2.

rendering—vbs. of, with Inf., **421**,N.1,*b*.

reperīrī—with Nom. and Inf., **528**,N.1.

repetition of relative, **615**.

replētus—with Gen., **374**,N.1.

repōnere—with **in** and Acc., **385**,N.2.

repōscere—with two Accs., **339** and N. 1,

representātiō—**654** and N., **656**,N.1.

representation—vbs. of, with Acc. and Inf., **526, 527**; with part., **527**,N.1, **536**.

reprimere—with **nē**, **548**,N.1.

repūgnāre—with Dat., **346**,R.2; with **nē**, **548**,N.1

requiēs—heteroclite, **68**,8.

requiring—vbs. of, with two Accs., **339** and R.1,N.1; with **ab**, *ib.* N.2.

rērī—part. of, with Pr. force, **282**,N.

rēs—for neut., **204**,N.4; construed like neut., **211**,N.2; with Appositional Gen., **361**,1; in phrases with Inf., **422**,N.2; **dīvīnam rem facere**, with Abl., **401**,N. 4; **rem certāre**, **333**,2,R.

resistere—with Dat., **346**,R.2; with **nē**, **548**,N.1; with **quīn**, **555**,1.

resisting—vbs. of, with Dat., **346**.

resolution—of long syllable, **732**.

resolving—vbs. of, with Inf., **423** and N.2; with **ut**, **546**.

Respect—Acc. of, **338**; with vbs. of Clothing, *etc.*, *ib.* N. 2; Abl. of, **397**; Abl. of, with comparatives, **398**; Abl. of, with words of Eminence or Superiority, **397**, N.2; preps. instead, *ib.* N.1.

respice—with Direct Question, **467**,N.

responde—with Direct Question, **467**,N.; **iūs respondēre**, **333**,2,R.

rest—conceived as end of Motion, **412**, R.2.

restat—with **ut**, **553**,4.

restrictions—in Relative Sentences, **627**, RR.1,2.

result—for Sentences of, see Consecutive Sentences.

rētē—heteroclite, **68**,12.

retinēre—with **nē**, **548**,N.1.

reus—with Gen., **374**,N.2; **378**,R.1.

rīdēre—with Acc. and Inf., **533**,R.1.

rhotacism—**47**.

rhythm—in arrangement, **627**,2 *b*: defined, **739**; ascending or descending, **735**; names of, **736**; classes of, **737**; rhythmical series, **738**; union of language with, **748**.

rōbur—decl. of, **44**,5, **45**,R.2.

rogāre—with two Accs., **339**,and N.1; with Acc. Ger., **430**,N.1; with **ut**, **546**,N.1; with Direct Question, **467**,N.; **rogātū**, of Moving Cause, **408**,N.1.; with Inf. or **ut**, **546**,N.3.

root—defined, **25**,1.N., **177**.

rudis—with Gen., **374**,N.4.

rūs—as limit of Motion, **337**; in Abl. of Separation, **390**,2; **rūrī** in Loc., **411**, R.2.

S—final omitted, **27**,N., **703**,R.3; **suffixes** with, **188**.

sacer—with Gen. or Dat., **359**,R.1; **sacrum facere,** with Abl., **401**,N.4.

sacrāmentō—as Abl. of Manner, **399**, N.1.

sacrificāre—with Abl., **401**,N.4.

sacrificing—vbs. of, with Abl., **401**,N.4.

saepe—as attrib. to subst., **439**,N.4.

saltem—strengthens **at, 488**,N.2.

salūtāris—has no superlative, **87**,9.

salvēre—conjugation of, **175**,4.

sānē—strengthens Impv., **269**; *very*, **439**, N.3; with concessive **nē, 608**; with **quam** and Indic,, **467**,N.; *yes*, **471**,*a*.

sanguĭs—decl. of, **41**,4.

sapiēns—as subst., **437**,N.1.

sapientia—in phrases with Inf., **422**,N.2; with **ut, 557**,R.

Sapphic—verse, **797, 804**.

satiās—heteroclite, **68**,8 and 12.

satis—*very*, **439**,N.3; attraction of pred. after **satius est, 535**,R.3.

saturāre—with Gen., **383**,1,N.2.

Saturnian—verse, **755**.

satus—with Abl. of Origin, **395**,N.1.

saying—vbs. of, with Object Clause, **523**; vbs. of, with **quod, 525**,1,N.7; vbs. of, with Acc. and Inf., **526,527**; vbs. of, with Nom. in pass., **528**; vbs. of, attracted into Subjv. after **quod, 541**,N.3; vbs. of, omitted, **545**,R.3; vbs. of, with **quīn, 555**,2.

scatēre—with Gen., **383**,1,N.2.

scazon—verse, **762**.

scientia—in phrases with **ut, 557**,R.

scīlicet—*yes*, **471**,*a*,2.

scīre—first Impv. wanting, **267**,R.; **sciēns** in pred. attrib., **325**,R.6; **quod sciam, quantum sciō, 627**,R.1; with Inf., **423**,2,N.2, **527**,R.1; followed by direct question, **467**,N.; **sciēns,** with Gen., **375**,N.2; **scītū** as Sup., **436**,N.

scrībere—with Acc. and Inf., **527**,R.2; with **ut, 546**,N,1.

season—adjs. of, in pred. attrib., **325**,R.6.

secondary words—see Derivatives.

secundum—as prep., **416**,24; **alter** for **secundus.**

secus—**70**,B; **sequius, 87**,8; strengthens **sīn, 594**; with **quam, 643**,N.4.

sēd—in composition, **9**,4, **715**,R.1.

sed—introduces contrast to demonstrative, **307**,R.4; with **etiam, quoque,** after **nōn modo, 482**,5 and N.1; with **nē—quidem,** *ib.* R.1; omitted, *ib.* N.2; with **et,** *ib.* N.2; syntax of, **485**; repeated, *ib.* N.2; strengthened, *ib.* N.3.

seeking—vbs. of, with Final Dat., **356**,N.2.

seeming—vbs. of, with two Noms., **206**.

semi-deponents—**167**.

semi-hiatus—**720**,R.1.

semi-vowels—**6**,2,A.

sempiternum—as adv. Acc., **336**,N.1.

senātus—decl. of, **61, 68**,5.

sending—vbs. of, with Acc. Ger., **430**.

senex—decl. of, **56**,5; Comp. of, **87**,9.

sentence—simple or cpd., **201**; syntax of simple, **202**,ff.; simplest form of, **202**; simple expanded, **284**,ff.; incomplete, **450–470**; coördination of, **473**; Copulative, **474–482**; Adversative, **483–491**; Disjunctive, **492–497**; Causal and Illative, **498–503**; Object, **523–537**; Causal, **538–542**; Final, **543–550**; Consecutive, **551–558**; Temporal, **559–588**; Conditional, **589–602**; Concessive, **603–609**; Relative, **610–637**; Abridged, **645–663**; Participial, **664–670**.

sententia—in phrases with **ut, 546**,N.2, **557**,R.

sentīre—with Acc. and Inf., **527**,R.2.

Separation—Gen. of, **374**,N.8, **383**,2; Abl of, **390**.

SEQUENCE OF TENSES—**509–519**; rule and modifications, **509**; general considerations, **510**; shift from primary to secondary sequence, **511**,R.2; in sentences of Design, **512**; in sentences of Result, **513**; in coincident sentences, *ib.* N.3; representation of Subjv. in, **514, 515**; in Ō. O., **516**; after other moods, **517**; after Inf. or part., **518**; original Subjvs. in, **519**; derangement of, *ib.* R.; in Comparative Sentences, **602**,R.1; after Hist. Pr., **511**, R.1; after Pure Pf., *ib.* R.3, **513**,R.1; after Hist. Pf., **511**,R.4; after **accidit,** *etc.*, *ib.* R.2; after vb. with future character, **515**,R.3.

sequester—heteroclite, **68**,4.

sequitur—with **ut, 553**,3.

sertum—heteroclite, **68**,3.

servīre—with Dat., **346**,R.2.

servus—omitted, **362**,N.1.

shortening—of penult, **701**,R.2,*b*; of vowels, **716, 717**.

showing—vbs. of, with two Noms., **206**; with two Accs., **340**; with Acc. and Inf., **526, 527**; with Nom. and Inf., **528**.

sī—with **ō** in Wishes, **261** and N.1; with-

out ō in Wishes, *ib.* N.1; **sīs, sōdēs, sultis**, with Impv., **269**; in Indirect Question after vbs. of Trial, **460,1,***b*; in Iterative action, **566, 567**; sign of Condition, **590** and N.1; **sīquidem**, *ib.* N.2, **595,**R.5; **sī nōn** and **nisi, 591; sīn, 592; sī modo, tamen, vērō, 595,**R.6; **sī forte**, *ib.* N.1; Concessive, **604,**R.1; with Inf., **635,**N.2.
sibilants—**6,2,**A; suffixes with, **188.**
sīc—coördinate with other particles, **482, 4,**N.; correlative of **sī, 590,**N.1.
sīcut—gives Assumed Reason, **602,**N.4.
sīgnificāre—with Inf., **527,**R.2.
sīgnum—in phrases with **ut, 546,**N.2.
silentiō—as Abl. of Manner, **399,**N.1.
similis—compared, **87,3**; with Gen. or Dat., **359,**R.1 and N.4.
simul—as prep., **417,12**; **simul—simul, 482,1** and N.1; Temporal, with **atque (āc)**, *as soon as*, **561-563**; Causal with Pr. and Pf., **564** and N.; with Fut. and Fut. Pf., **565** and N.
simulāre—with Inf., **527,**R.2.
sīn—use of, **592**; strengthened by **minus**, *etc.*, *ib.* R.
sine—position of, **413,**R.1; as prep., **417, 13**; with Abl. Ger., **433,**N.2.
sinere—with Inf., **423,**N.6, **553,2,**N.; with **ut, 532,**N.1, **553,2.**
singular—in collective sense for Pl., **204,** N.8; Voc. with Pl. vb., **211,**N.2; neut. sums up preceding Pl., *ib.* N.3; as a subj., combined with **cum** and another word, **285,**N.2.
singulāre—in phrases with Inf., **422,**N.3; in phrases with **ut, 553,4.**
singulus—with numerals, **295.**
sīquidem—**590,**N.2, **595,**R.5.
sinister—Comp. of, **87,1,**R.1.
sīs—strengthens Impv., **269.**
sistī—as copulative vb., **206,**N.1.
sīve—use of, **496**; **sīve—sīve**, *ib.* **2,595,** R.4; or *ib.* N.1; and **seu**, *ib.* N.3.
smell—vbs. of, with Inner Object, **333,2,** N.5.
socer—and **socerus, 32,1,**N.
sōdēs—strengthens Impv., **269.**
solēre—with Inf., **423,2**,N.2; **solitō**, as Abl. of Respect, **398,**N.1.
sollicitārī—with Acc. and Inf., **533,**R.1.
sōlus—decl. of., **76**; in pred. attrib., **325,** R.6; **nōn sōlum sed**, *etc.*, **482,5,** and R.1; with **quī** and Subjv., **631,1.**
solvere—with Abl., **390,2,**N.2.
somniāre—with Acc. and Inf., **527,**R.1.
sonants—**6,2,**B.
sortītō—as Abl. of Manner, **399,**N.1.
Sotadean—verse, **816.**
sound—vbs. of, with neut. Acc. of Inner Object, **333,2,**N.6.
Specification—Gen. of, **361.**
spectāre—with **ex** and Abl., **402,**R.2.
specus—heteroclite, **68,9.**
spērāre—with Inf., **527,**R.2; with Pr. Inf., **531,**N.4.
spēs—with **est** and Pr. Inf., **531,**N.4; in phrases with Inf., **527,**R.2; with **ut, 546,**N.2; in Abl. of Respect, **398,**N.1.
spīnter—defective, **70,**B.
sponte—defective, **70,**A.
Standard—Abl. of, **402, 403**; **ex** and Abl. instead of Abl., **402,**R.2; Abl. of, with **ante** or **post, 403,**N.4; Acc. of Extent for Abl., *ib.* N. 3; of comparison omitted, **297.**
stāre—with Gen. of Price, **379**; *to abide by* with Abl., **401,**N.6; *to persist in*, with Inf., **423,2,**N.2.
statuere—with **in** and Abl., **385,**R.1; with Inf., **423,2,**N.2; with **ut, 546,**N.1.
status—in phrases with **ut, 557,**R.
stem—**25,1, 132**; Present, **114,3,***a*, **133**; Perfect, **114,3,***b*, **134**; Supine, **114,3,***c*, **135**; Formation of Verb stem, **132-135**: varies between Conjugations, **136**; quantity of stem syllables, **714.**
stem-characteristic—**26, 120**; euphonic changes in, **121,**R.
stīllāre—with Abl., **401,**N.5.
studēre—with Dat., **346,**R.2; with Dat. Ger., **429,1** and N.1; with Inf., **423,2,**N. 2; with **ut, 546,**N.1.
studiōsus—with Gen., **374,**N.5.
stultitia—in phrases with Inf., **422,**N.2.
suādēre—with Dat., **346,**R.2, and N.2; with Inf., **423,2,**N.2; with **ut, 546,**N.1.
sub—in composition, **9,4**; vbs. cpd. with, take Acc. or Dat., **331, 347**; with **condiciōne**, *etc.*, **399,**N.3; usage of, as prep., **418,2.**
subesse—with Dat, **347,**R.2; **timōrem,** with Acc. and Inf., **533,**R.1.
subject—**201**; in Nom., **203**; in Acc. with Inf., *ib.* R.1; forms of, **204**; omitted, **207**; of impersonal vbs., **208,1,**N. and **2,**N.1; Multiplication of, **285,**ff.; Qualification of, **288,**ff.; prolepsis of subj. of

dependent clause, **468**; of Inf. omitted, **527**,R.3, **532**, R.2 and N.2; Acc. and Inf. as, **535**; attraction of pred. after Acc. and Inf., *ib.* R.3.
Subjective—Genitive, **363**, **364**; poss. pron. instead, **364**.
SUBJUNCTIVE—**112**,4; early forms of, **130**,4; Aorist forms of Pf. and Plupf., **131**,4,*b*, 2,3; Indic. for Deliberative, **254**,N.2; with generic relatives, *ib.* R.6,**625**,R.; force of, **255**; Indic. with vbs. of Possibility, *etc.*, *ib.*R.; Ideal and Unreal, **256**,1; Potential and Opt., *ib.* 2 Potential of Pr. and Fut., **257–259**; Potential for Indic., *ib.* N.3; Potential of Past, **258**; Potential of Past with **vellem**, *etc.*, *ib.* N.1; Opt., **260**; negs. of Opt., *ib.*, particles with Opt., **261**; Impf. for Unreal wish, *ib.* N.2; in Asseverations, **262**; as Impv., **263**, **267**, **270**, R., **272**; as concessive, **264** and N.; tense relations of, **277**; with **quam ut** or **quam quī** to express disproportion, **298**; in Deliberative or Rhetorical questions, **265**, **465**, **466**; in Indirect questions, **467**; after vb. with Fut. character, **515**, R.3; Original in dependence, **519**; with **quod**, *as to the fact that*, **525**,2,N.3; in Final and Consecutive Sentences, **543**, 4; with **ut** for Inf., **557**,N.1; in Temporal Clauses, **560**,2, **563**,NN.4,5; in Iterative action, **567**,N.; in Contemporaneous action, **572**, **573**; in Subsequent action, **577**; with **cum**, **585**, **588**; in Relative Sentences, **627**, **628**; by Attraction, **509**,4, **629**; after **potius**, **644**,R.3; in Ō. O., **650–652**.
sublīmis—in pred. attrib., **325**,R.6.
subolet—with Inf., **422**,N.4.
subordination—defined, **472**; syntax of Subordinate Clauses, **504**,ff.; division of, **505–507**; moods in, **508**; Sequence of Tenses in, **509–519**.
subsequent action—syntax of Sentences of, **574–577**; with Indic., **574–576**; with Subjv., **577**.
substantives—defined, **16**,1, and R.1,N.1; inflection of, **17**; division of, **18**; gender of, **19**, **20**; **mōbilia**, **21**,2; epicene, *ib.* 3; irregular, **67–71**; heterogeneous, **67**; heteroclites, **68**; metaplasts, *ib.*; defective, **69**; **singulāria tantum**, *ib.* A; **plūrālia tantum**, *ib.* B; heterologa, *ib.* C; formation of, **180**, **181**; without suffixes, **183**; adjs. and parts. used as, **204**,NN.; Pl. of abstracts, *ib.* NN.5,6; agreement of pred., **211** and RR.,NN.; with several adjs. in Sg., **290**, R.2; common surname in Pl., **290**, N.1; verbal with Acc., **330**,N.3, **337**,N.5; verbal with Dat., **356**,N.3, **357**, **358**,N.2; in Abl. Abs., **410**,N.5; with Dat. Ger., **428**,N.5; with Inf. for Gen. Ger., *ib.* N. 4; in phrases with Final Sentence, **546**, R.2; in phrases with Consecutive Sentence, **557** and R.
subter—vbs. cpd. with take Acc., **331**; as adv., **415**; as prep., **418**,2.
subvenīre—with Dat., **347**,R.2.
succēdere—with Dat., **347**,R.2.
succrēscere—with Dat., **347**,R.2.
succumbere—with Dat., **347**,R.2.
succurrere—with Dat., **347**,R.2.
sūdāre—with Abl. of Means, **401**,N.5.
sufferre—Pf. of, **171**,N.2.
suffixes—**180**; primary and secondary, *ib.* N.1; of substantives, **181**; of adjs., **182**; forming diminutives, **181**,12, **182**,12; in detail, **184–189**; with vowels, **184**; with gutturals, **185**; with dentals, **186**; with labials, **187**; with **s**, **188**; with liquids, **189**.
suffrāgārī—with Dat., **346**,R.2.
suī—decl. of, **102** and N.1; with **-met**, *ib.* N.2; with **-pte**, *ib.* N.3; circumlocution for Part. Gen., **304**,3,N.2; usage of, **309**, **520–522**; complement of Inf., **309**,3; **is** instead, *ib.* N.1; with **suus**, *ib.* N.2.
sultis—strengthens Impv., **269**.
sum—see **esse**.
summus—comparison of, **87**,2; used partitively, **291**,R.2.
supellēx—decl. of, **44**,5.
super—vbs. cpd. with, take Acc. or Dat., **331**, **347**; as adv., **415**; as prep., **418**,4; with Acc. Ger., **432**,N.1; with Abl. Ger., **433**; **id quod, quam quod**, **525**,2,N.2.
superāre—with Acc. of Respect, **397**,N.2.
superesse—with Dat., **347**,R.2.
superior—**87**,2 and 7.
superiority—vbs. of, with Acc. of Respect, **397**,N.2.
superlative—in **issimus**, **86**; in **rimus**, **87**,1; in **limus**, *ib.* 3; in **entissimus**, *ib.* 4 and 5; lacking, *ib.* 9; of parts., **89**; of advs., **93**; meaning of, varies with position, **291**,R.2,**302**; strengthened, **303**; with **quam, quantum, quī**, *ib.* R.2,**642**,

R.5; with **quisque, 318**,2; with Part. Gen., **372**; with preps., *ib.* R.2; with **ut, 642**,R.2.
supersedēre—with Abl., **390**,2,N.3.
superstes—with Gen. or Dat., **359**,R.1.
SUPINE—**112**,5; system, **114**,3,*c*; formation of, **115**,3, **121**,3; stem, **135**; in Abl. of Sep., **390**,3,N.3, **436**,N.4; in Abl. of Respect, **397**,1; with **opus, 406**,N.5; defined, **434**; Acc. of, **435**; Abl. of, **436**.
suppetiae—defective, **70**,B.
supplex—with Dat., **346**,N.5.
supplicāre—with Dat., **346**,R.2 and N.4.
suprā—with **quam** after a comparative, **296**, N.3; with Abl. of Measure, **403**,N.1; as adv., **415**; as prep., **416**,25.
surds—**6**,2,B.
surname—common, in Pl., **290**,N.1.
sūs—decl. of, **59**.
suscēnsēre—with Dat., **346**,R.2.
suscipere—with Acc. Ger., **430**,N.1.
sūspicārī—with Acc. and Inf., **527**,R.2.
sūspicere—with Acc. and Inf., **527**,R.1.
sūspīrāre—with Acc. and Inf., **533**,R.1.
sustinēre—with Inf., **423**,2,N.2.
suus (os)—**102**; syntax of, **309**; emphatic, *ib.* 2; with prep. phrases, *ib.* 4; **is** instead, *ib.* N.1; **suum quisque,** *ib.* N.3; **suō tempore,** *ib.* 4; with Gen. Ger., **428**,R.1; in dependent clauses, **521**; **suom** with **ut, 557**,R.
syllaba anceps—**741**.
syllables—division of, **10**; names for, **11**; open, **11**,R.; close, *ib.*; length of, **12**; common, **13**; quantity of final, **707-713**; of polysyllables, **707-709**; of monosyllables, **710-713**.
syllepsis—**690**.
synapheia—**728**.
syncope—**725-743**; in Pf. forms, **131**, ff.
synecdoche—**695**.
synizesis—**727**.
syntax—defined, **201**.
systole—**722**.

T—sound of, **7**; **t**-class of vbs., **133**,III.
tābes—heteroclite, **68**,8.
tābō—defective, **70**,A.
taedet—with Gen., **377**; with pronoun as subj., **377**, R.2.
taking—vbs. of, with two Accs., **340**; End For Which given by Dat. or **ad,** *ib.* R.2; vbs. of Taking Away, with Dat., **347**,R.5; with Acc. Ger., **430**.
tālāris—and **tālārius, 84**,2.
tālis—with **quī** or **ut** and Subjv., **631**,1 and R.1.
tam—with **quam, quantum, quī,** and superlative, **303**,R,2; with **quī** or **ut** and Subjv., **631**,1 and R.1.
tamen—introduces contrast, **307**,R.4; position of, **413**,N.3; with **sed, 485**,N.3; syntax of, **490**; with **at, 488**,N.2; emphasises adversative relation, **587**,R.1; with **tametsī, 604**,R.3.
tametsī—form, **603** and N.; usage, **604** and RR.
tamquam—with subst., **439**,N.4; with Subjv. of Comparison, **602**; with Indic., *ib.* N.1; to give an Assumed Reason, *ib.* N.4; with part., **666**,N.; **tamquam sī, 602**,N.4; coördinate with **sīc, 482**,3,N.
tantī—as Gen. of Price, **380**,1.
tantīdem—as Gen. of Price **380**,1.
tantus—with **quī** or **ut** and Subjv., **631**,1 and R.1; **tantī,** with vbs. of Rating and Buying, **380**; **tantī est,** *it is worth while, ib.* R.1; **tantum,** with **quam, quantum, quī,** and superlative, **303**,R.2; **tantum,** for Abl. of Measure, **413**,N.2; **nōn tantum sed,** *etc.*, **482**, 5; **tantum quod, 525**,2,N.2; **tantum abest ut, 552**,R.1.
taste—vbs. of, with Inner Obj., **333**,2,N.5.
teaching—vbs. of, with two Accs., **339** and NN.2,3.
temperāre—with Dat., **346**,R.2 and N.2; with **nē, 548**,N.1; **temperāns,** with Gen., **375**,N.2.
templum—omitted, **362**,R.3.
TEMPORAL SENTENCES—**559-588**; division of, **559**; moods in, **560**; Antecedent Action, **561-567**; Iterative Action, **566, 567**; Contemporaneous Action, **568-573**; Subsequent Action, **574-577**; with **cum, 578-588**; general view of, **579**; Temporal **cum, 580**; **cum inversum, 581**, Explicative **cum, 582**; Conditional **cum, 583**; Iterative **cum, 584**; Circumstantial **cum, 585-588**; Historical **cum, 585**; Causal **cum, 586**; Concessive **cum, 587**; **cum—tum, 588**; in Ō. O., **655**.
temptāre—with Inf., **423**,2,N.2.
tempus—with Inf. or Ger., **428**,N.2; **tempore** or **in tempore, 394**,R.; **id temporis, 336**,N.2; with Inf., **422**,N.2; **temperī, 411**,N.1.
tendency—suffixes for, **182**,3.

tendere manūs—with Dat., **358**,N.3.

tenēre—with Pf. part. to denote Maintenance of Result, **238**; **memoriā teneō**, with Pr. Inf., **281**,2,N.; (**sē**) with **nē**, **548**,N.1; with **quōminus**, **549**; with **quīn**, **555**,1; with **ut**, **553**,1; **tenērī**, with Gen. of Charge, **378**,R.1.

tenses—**112**,3; signs of, **114**,2; formation of, **114**, **115**, **121**; syntax of, **222-252**; definitions, **223**; of continuance, attainment, or completion, **224**; Pr., **227-230**; Impf., **231-234**; Pure Pf., **235-238**; Hist. Pf., **239**, **240**; Plupf., **241**; Fut., **242**, **243**; Fut. Pf., **244**, **245**; periphrastic, **246-251**; in Letters, **252**; of Indic., **276**; of Impv., **278**; Sequence of, **509**; in Final and Consecutive Sentences, **543**, 3; in Relative Sentences, **622**, **623**; in Ō. O., **653-655**; in Inf., **279**, **653**; of Subjv., **277**, **654**, **655**; *Repraesentātiō*, **654**,N.

tenus—position of, **413**,R.1; usage of, as prep., **417**,14.

terminations of cases—**27**.

terra—in Abl. without **in**, **386**,N.1; **terrae** as Loc., **411**,R.2.

tertium—est with **ut**, **553**,4.

tēstis est—with Acc. and Inf., **527**,R.2.

thematic class of verbs—**133**,I.

thickness—how expressed, **335**,R.1.

thinking—vbs. of, with two Noms., **206**; with Object Sentence and **quod**, **523**, **525**,1, N.7; with Inf., **527**; vbs. of, attracted into Subjv. after **quod**, **541**,N.3; vbs. of, with **quīn**, **555**,2.

threat—vbs. of, with Inf., **423**,N.5.

Tīburī—as Loc., **411**,R.1.

time—adjs. of, in pred. attrib., **325**,R.6; suffixes for, **182**,8; *when*, in Abl., **393**; *how long*, in Acc., **336**; *within which*, in Abl., **393**; with **per**, **336**, **393**,R.1; with **tōtus**, *ib.* R.2; *when = for which*, *ib.* R.3; with **hīc**, **ille**, *ib.* R.4; preps. for Abl., **394**; lapses of, with **cum**, **580**,R.3; given by part., **665**, **670**,1.

timēre—constr. of, **550** and N.1; with Inf., **423**,2,N.2.

timor—est, with Inf., **550**,N.5; **timōrem subesse**, with Inf., **533**,R.1.

titles—position of, **676**,R.4.

tmesis—**726**.

tōtus—decl. of, **76**; in pred. attrib., **325**, R.6; with Abl. of Place Where, **388**; with Time How Long, **393**,R.2.

towns—with Acc., **337**; in Abl. of Place Where, **386**; in Abl. of Place Whence, **391**; in Loc., **411**; with preps., **337**,N.3, **391**, R.1; with appositives, **337**,R.2, **386**,R.1, **391**,R.1, **411**,R.3.

trāctātū—as Sup., **436**,N.

trade—suffixes for, **181**,4.

trādere—with Acc. Ger., **430**,N.1; with Acc. and Inf., **527**,R.2.

tradesman—suffixes for, **181**,3.

training—vbs. of, with Abl., **401**,N.1.

trajection—**696**.

trāns—in composition, **9**,4; vbs. cpd. with take Acc., **331**; as prep., **416**,26.

transitive verb—defined, **213**; used intrans., *ib.* R.*a*.

transposition—of consonants, **9**,8.

trēs—decl. of, **95**.

trial—vbs. of, with **sī**, **460**,1,*b*; with implied protasis, **601**.

tribes—in Abl. of Origin, **395**,N.2.

tribuere—with **ut**, **553**,2.

tribūtum—heteroclite, **68**,5.

tricorporis—defective, **85**,1.

trīnī—**97**,R.3.

trītum—with Inf., **422**,N.3.

trochee—shortened by Iambic Law, **717**; trochaic foot, **734**; rhythm, **736**; rhythms, **768-776**.

tū—decl. of, **101** and N.1; synizesis in, *ib.* N.4; with **met** and **-pte**, **102**,NN.2,3; **vestrī** and **vestrum**, **304**,2 and 3, **364**,R.; poss. pron. for, **304**,2,N.2; **tuī**, **vestrī**, with Ger., **428**,R.1.

tuērī—with Acc. and Inf., **527**,R.1.

tum—with subst., **439**,N.4; with **etiam**, **478**,N.1; as coördinating particle, **482**,1 and N.1; **tum—tum**, **482**,1 and N.1; **cum—tum**, **588**; correlative of **sī**, **590**, N.1.

tuus (**os**)—**101** and N.3; **tuum** with **ut**, **557**,R; **tuī** with Gen. Ger., **428**,R.1.

U—length of Final—**707**,6.

ubi—*as soon as*, with Indic., **561-563**; Causal, with Indic., **564**,N.1.**565** and N.1; with Iterative action, **566**, **567**; with Subjv., **567**,N.; Conditional, **590**,N.3.

ūllus—decl. of, **76**; and **quisquam**, **107**, 3,N.2, **108**; syntax of, **317**.

ūls—**416**,27.

ulterior—**87**,8; **ultimus** in pred. attrib., **325**,R.6.

ultimate—defined, **11**.

ūltrā—with Abl. of Measure, **403**,N.1; position of, **413**,R.1; as adv., **415**; as prep., **416**,27.
uncertainty—vbs. of, with **quīn**, **555**,2.
understatement—definition of, **700**.
undertaking—vbs. of, with Acc. Ger., **430**.
ūnimanus—defective, 85,2.
unlikeness—adjs. of, with **atque (āc)**, **643**.
UNREAL CONDITION—**597**; with Impf. of opposition to Past, *ib.* R.1; with Indic. in Apod., *ib.* RR.2,3; in Ō. O., *ib.* R.4, **659**; Apod. in, after vb. requiring Subjv., **597**,R.5; with **absque**, *ib.* N.
ūnus—decl. of, **76**, **95**,N.1; Pl. with **plūrālia tantum**, **95**,R.1; as distributive, **97**,R.3; with superlative, **303**; with **quīdam**, **313**,R.3; with **quisquam**, **317**, 1,N.1; with **nēmŏ**, **nūllus**, **317**,2,N.3; in pred. attrib., **325**,R.6; with prep. for Part. Gen., **372**,R.2; with **quī** and Subjv., **631**,1.
ūnusquisque—107,5.
urbs—with name of Town, requires prep., **337**,R.2, **386**,R.1, **391**,R.1, **411**,R.3; with Appositional Gen., **361**,N.1.
urgērī—with Gen. of Charge, **378**,R.1.
urging—vbs. of, with **ut**, **546**.
ūsque—with Acc. of Motion Whither, **337**, N.4; usage of, as prep., **416**,28.
ūsus—with Abl., **406**; with other constr., *ib.*N.5; as pred., *ib.*; with Pf. part., **406**, **437**,N.2; in phrases with **ut**, **557**,R.; **ūsū venit**, with **ut**, **553**,3.
ut—in wishes, **261**; with **quam**, to express disproportion, **298**, **631**,3,R.1; omitted, **298**,R.2; with **potuit**, to strengthen superlative, **303**; **ut—ita**, **482**,4; after vbs. of Adding and Happening, **525**,1,N.5; in Final and Consecutive Sentences, **543**; **ut nōn**, *ib.* 4, **545**,R.2, **552**; parenthetical, *ib.* R.3; **ut nē**, **545**,R.1, **546**,R 3; after vbs. of Fear, **550** and N.1; to add restriction, **552**,R.3; after vb. of Causation, **553**,1; after vbs. of Compelling and Permitting, *ib.* 2; after vbs. of Happening, *ib.* 3; after impersonals, *ib.* 4; Explanatory, **557**; Exclamatory, **558**; with **magis quam**, **557**,N.2; **ut prīmum**, *as soon as*, with Indic., **561-563**; Causal, **564**,N.; with Iterative sentences, **566**, **567**; **nisi ut**, **557**,N.2, **591**,R.3; with **sī** and Subjv., **602**; with Subjv., to give an Assumed Reason, *ib.* N.4; Concessive, **608** and R.1; with **quī**, **626**,R.1; after comparatives, **631**,3,R.1; with **quisque** and superlative, **642**,R.2; **prō eō ut**, as Causal, *ib.* R.4; **ut quī**, with superlative, *ib.* R.5; introduces Ō. O. after vbs. of Will and Desire, **652**,R.1; with part. to give Assumed Reason, **666**,N.
ūter, *bag*—decl. of, **44**,2, **45**,R.1.
uter, *which*—decl. of, **76**, **106**; **quis** for, **300**,N.; **utrum** as interrogative particle, **458**; in Indirect Question, **460**,2,N. 3; **utrum**, *whether or no*, **459**,N.2.
uterlibet—108.
uterque—decl. of, **108**; with Pl. vb., **211**, R.1,Ex.*a*, **292**,R.; to express reciprocal action, **221**,R.1 and 2; force of, **292**; with Part. Gen., **371**,R.1.
uterum—heterogeneous, **32**,1,N.
utervīs—108.
ūtī—with Abl., **407** and N.2,*a*; other constrs. of, *ib.* N.3; with personal Ger., **427**, N.5.
utinam—in wishes, **261** and N. 1.
utpote—with **quī**, **626**,N.1.

V—and **u**, **1**,R,2; pronunciation of, **7**.
vacāre—with Dat., **346**,N.2; attraction of pred. after, **535**,R.3.
vacuus—with Gen., **374**,N.8.
vae—with Dat., **343**,1,N.1.
valdē—*very*, **439**,N.3; with **quam** and Indic., **467**,N.
valēre—with Inf., **423**,2,N.2; with **ut**, **553**,1.
validus—with Abl. or Gen., **405**,N.3.
vās—heteroclite, 68,7.
ve—usage of, **495**; **ve—ve**, *ib.* N.2.
vehementer—*very*, **439**,N.3.
vel—with superlative, **303**; usage of, **494**; **vel—vel**, *ib.* 2; *for example*, *ib.* N.1; *as well as*, *ib.* N.3.
velle—conjugation of, **174**; exact use of Fut. or Fut. Pf., **242**,N.2 and R.3; has no periphrasis, **248**,R., **531**,N.3; **velim**, **257**,2; **vellem**, as Potential, **258**,N. 1; **vellem**, as Unreal, **261**,R.; with Subjv. for Impv., **270**,N.2; with Pf. Inf. act., **280**,2,*b*, and N.1; with Pf. Inf. pass., **280**,2,*c*,N.; **volēns** in pred. attrib., **325**,R.6; **sibī velle**, **351**,N.2; **volentī est**, **353**,N.2; with Inf. or **ut**, **532**, and N.3, **546**, R.1; with Inf., **423**,2,N.2; with **ut**, **546**,N.1.

velut—with Subjv., **602**; with part. to give Assumed Reason, **666**,N.
velutsī—with Subjv., **602**.
vēnālis—with Abl., **404**,N.4.
vēndere—with Gen. of Price, **379**; **bene vēndere, 380**,2,R.
venīre—omitted, **209**,N.5; **venit mihĭ in mentem,** with Gen., **376**,R.3; with Sup., **435**,N.1; **ventūrus** as adj., **438**, N.; **in sūspīciōnem,** with Nom. and Inf., **528**,N.2; with Inf., **422**,N.5; **ūsū venit,** with **ut, 553**,3.
vēnīre—pass. of **vēndere, 169**,2,R.1; with Gen. of Price, **379**.
venter—decl. of, **44**,2, **45**,R.1.
verbals—defined, **179**,1; pred. agreement of, **211**; subst. with Acc., **330**,N.3, **337**, N.5; adj. with Acc., *ib.* N.4; in **bilis,** with Dat., **355**,N.; in **āx,** with Gen., **375**; formation of *verbālia*, **191**.
VERBS—defined, **16**,4; conjugation of, **17**; inflection of, **114**; deponents, **113**; personal endings, **114**; regular, **120**,ff.; classes of, **133**; Stem or Thematic class, **133**,I.; Reduplicated Class, *ib.* II.; T-class, *ib.* III.; Nasal class, *ib.* IV.; Inchoative class, *ib.* V.; **i**-class, *ib.* VI.; mixed class, *ib.* VII.; list of, **137-162**; Deponents, **163-166**; Semi-deponents, **167**; Irregular, **168-174**; Defective, **175**; formation of, **190-200**; division of, **190**; Verbalia, **191**; Denominative, **192**; composition of, **199, 200**; Impersonal, **208**; intrans. used personally, *ib.* 2; Concord of, **210, 211, 285-287**; trans. and intrans., **213**; trans. used as intrans., *ib.* R.*a*; intrans. used as trans., *ib.* R.*b*.
verbum—with Appositional Gen., **361,1**; in phrases with **ut, 546**,N.2.
verērī—constr. with, **550** and N.1; **veritus** as Pr., **282**,N.; with Inf., **423**,2,N.2, **533**,R.1.
vērīsimile—in phrases with Inf., **422**,N.3; in phrases with **ut, 553,4**.
vērō—position of, **413**,N.3; *yes*, **471**,*a*,1; with **atque, 477**,N.2; with **sed, 485**,N.3; syntax of, **487**; with **nisi, 591**,R.4; with **sīn, 592**.
verse—**745**; methods of combining, **746**; Italic, **755**; Saturnian, **756**; compound, **820, 823**.
versification—**729-823**; anacrustic scheme of, **739**.
versus—position of, **413**,R.1; usage as prep., **416**,29; *versus Italicus*—**755**.
vertere—with Final Dat., **356**,R.2.
vērum—introduces contrast to demonstrative, **307**,R.4; *yes*, **471**.*a*,1; with **etiam, 482**,5 and N.1; syntax of, **486**; with Inf., **422**,N.3; with **ut, 553,4**.
very—translations of, **439**,N.3.
vescī—with Abl., **407** and N.2,*e*; with personal Ger., **427**,N.5.
vesper—decl. of, **68**,10; in Abl. of Time, **393**,R.5; **vesperī**—**37**,5, **411**,N.1.
vester—**101** and N.3.
vetāre—with Acc., **346**,N.3; with Inf., **423**,2,NN.3 and 6, **532**,N.1 and 2.
vetus—decl. of, **82**,2; comp. of, **87**,1,R.2.
viā—as Abl. of Manner, **399**,N.1.
vicissim—gives reciprocal relation, **221**, R.2; as coördinating particle, **482**,1, N.2.
vidēre—with Acc. and Inf., **527**,R.2; with **ut, 546**,N.1; with **nē, 548**,N.1; with Direct Question, **467**,N.; with two Noms. in pass., **206**; **vidērī,** and **vidētur, 528**,R.2; **vidē,** with Subjv. for Impv., **271**,N.2, **548**, N.3; **vīderĭs,** as Impv., **245**,N.
vīlis—with Abl. of Price, **404**.N.2.
vincere—with Abl. of Respect, **397**,N.2; **causam, 333**,2,R.
violentus—and **violēns, 84**,1.
vīrus—defective, **70**,C.
vīs—**70**,D; with Pl. vb., **211**,R.1,Ex.*a*; **vī,** as Abl. of Manner, **399**,N.1.
-vīs—with relatives, **111**,3.
vitium—with Epexegetical Gen., **361**,2; with Inf., **422**,N.2; **vitiō** as Abl. of Manner, **399**,N.1.
vīvere—with Abl., **407**,N.2,*e*.
[**vix**]—**70**,D; **tuam vicem, 334**,R.2.
VOCATIVE—defined, **23**,5; in **ī, 33**,R.2; in adjs. of 1st and 2d Decl., **73**; no syntax of, **201**,R.1; Nom. instead, *ib.* R.2; in app., *ib.* R.3; in pred., **211**,R.3; Sg. with Pl. vb., *ib.* N.2; Nom. instead, **321**, N.1; in pred. app., **325**,R.1; with **ō** or **prō, 343**,1,N.1.
voice—**112**,2, **212**; act., **213**; pass., **214**; middle, **212**,N.
voluntās—in phrases with **ut, 546**,N.2; **voluntāte** as Abl. of Manner, **399**,N.1.
volup—indeclinable, **85**,C.
vōmer—decl. of, **45**,R.2.
vowels—**2**; sounds of, **3**; phonetic varia-

tions in, **8**; weakening of, *ib.* 1; omission of, *ib.* 2; epenthesis of, *ib.* 3; assimilation of, *ib.* 4; quantity of final, **707**; suffixes with, **184**.
vōx—with Appositional Gen., **361**,1.
vulgō—as Abl. of Manner, **399**,N.1.
vultus—heteroclite, **68**,5.

Want—vbs. of, with Abl., **405**; adjs. of, with Gen. and Abl., *ib.*N.3.
warning—vbs. of, with **ut**, **546**.
weakening of vowels—8,1, **701**,R.2.
weight—substs. of, with Gen., **369**.
will—vbs. of, with Inf., **280**,2,*c*, **423**,2, **532**; sequence after vbs. of, **515**,R.3; **ut** instead of Inf. after, **532**,N.1–4; with Final sentence, **546**; with Inf. instead, *ib.* R.1; with simple Subjv., *ib.* R.2.
wishes—in Subjv., **260**, **261**; apodosis omitted with, **601**.
without—translated by **ut nōn**, **552**,R.4; **quīn**, **556**; **cum nōn**, **587**,R.2.
wonder—constr. with vbs. of, **542**.N.1.
words—Formation of, **176–200**.

Y—1,R.3; length of final, **707**,3.
yes—trans. of, **471**,*a* and c.
yielding—vbs. of, with Dat., **346**.

Z—when introduced, **1**,R.3; sound of, *ib.* N.
zeugma—**690**.

SYNTAX OF INDIVIDUAL AUTHORS.

The syntactical usage of individual authors is treated as follows:

ACCIUS—**358**,N.1; **525**,1,N.1.
AFRANIUS—**498**,N.1.
APULEIUS—**336**.N.1; **365**,N.; **406**,N.3; **498**, N.1; **591**,N.3; **607**,N.3; **626**,N.1.

CAELIUS—**574**,N.
CAESAR—**208**,2,N.2; **209**,N.5; **228**,N.1; **239**, N.; **250**,N.1 and 2; **260**; **280**,2,*c*,N.; **285**, N.2; **286**,3,N.; **311**,1,R.2; **323**,N.1; **324**; **335**,N.; **336**,N.2; **337**,N.1; **341**,N.2; **349**,R.5; **354**,N.2; **356**,N.2 and 3; **358**,N.3; **359**,N.1; **369**,N.2; **372**,N.2 and 3; **374**,N.1 and 9; **375**,N.2; **381**,N.4; **386**,N.; **391**,N.; **395**,N.2; **401**,N.7; **407**,N.2,*d*; **410**,N.4; **413**,R.1; **415**; **416**,2,3,8,15,16,19,22, and 24; **418**,2; **422**, N.2; **423**,N.2 and 3; **427**,N.2; **429**,N.1; **432**, N.1; **435**,N.2; **436**,N.1; **443**,N.3; **458**,N.1; **460**,2,N.1 and 2; **467**,N.; **475**,N.3; **476**,N.5; **478**,N.2; **480**,N.2 and 3; **482**,3; **482**,5,R.2 and N.1; **496**,N.1; **503**; **512**,N.1; **513**,N.1 and 2; **525**,2,N.3; **527**,R.3; **528**,N.1; **538**, N.4; **541**,N.1 and 3; **542**,N.1; **545**,R.1; **549**,N. 1 and 2; **563**,N.2 and 3; **567**,N.; **569**,N.1; **571**,N.3; **591**,R.2 and N.2; **602**,N.5; **615**,N.; **616**,1,N.1; **626**,N.1; **627**,R.2; **636**,N.1; **644**, R.3: **647**,N.2; **650**,N.; **666**,N.
B. Hisp.—**407**,N.2,*d*; **416**,8.
B. Afr.—**407**,N.2,*d*; **417**,7.
CATO—**285**,N.2; **394**,3,N.1; **401**,N.7; **407**,N.2; **417**,7; **418**,4; **437**,N.2; **477**,N.5; **548**,N.3; **574**,N.
CATULLUS—**207**,N.; **236**,N.; **380**; **417**,3; **454**, N.2; **455**,N.; **458**,N.1; **477**,N.5; **480**,N.3; **546**,N.3; **567**,N; **644**,N.2.
CELSUS—**602**,N.4.
CICERO—**204**,N.7; **206**,N.1; **209**,N.3 and 5; **211**,R.4 and N.3; **214**,R.2; **228**,N.1; **239**, N.; **242**,R.3; **245**,N.; **250**,N.1 and 2; **252**, N.; **254**,R.6 and NN.1,2; **257**,N.1; **261**; **269**; **271**,2,N.2; **280**,2,*c*,N.; **285**, N.2; **293**,N.; **298**,N.1; **299**,N.1; **301**; **311**, 1,R.2; **318**,N.1; **319**,N.2; **323**,N.1; **324**; **336**,N.2; **337**,N.1,2, and 4; **341**,N.2; **343**,N.1; **346**,N.1 and 2; **347**,R.2; **349**,

R.5; **351**,N.1; **352**,N.; **354**,N.2; **356**,R.3 and N.3; **357**; **358**,N.3 and 5; **361**,N.1; **362**,N.1; **364**,N.1; **369**,N.2; **372**,N.2 and 3; **374**,N.1,2,4, and 5; **375**,N.2 and 3; **376**,R.1,2, and 3; **380**,1,N.1 and 4; **383**,N.1; **385**, N.1; **386**,N.; **390**,2,N.2 and 3; **391**,N.; **395**, N.1 and 2; **396**,N.1; **398**,N.1; **403**,N.4; **406**, N.5; **407**,N.2,*d*; **410**,N.4; **411**,R.1 and 2, and N.1; **413**,R.1; **416**.1,2,3,5,7,13,14,15, 16,19,24,25,28, and 29; **417**,1,N.3 and 14; **418**,4; **422**,N.2,3, and 5; **423**,N.2 and 3; **427**,N.2 and 5; **428**,R.2 and N.1; **429**,N.1; **432**,N.1; **435**,N.1; **436**,N.1; **438**,N.; **439**,N.2,3 and 4; **443**,N.3; **453**,N.1; **457**,1,N.1 and 2, 2 and N.; **458**,N.1; **459**,N.1; **460**,1, N.2; **467**,N.; **476**,N.5; **477**,N.4 and 5; **478**, N.2; 480,R.1 and N.3; **481**,N.; **482**,1,N.1 and 2, 2, 3, and 5, R.2 and N.1; **484**,N.1 and 2; **485**,N.1 and 2; **486**,N.; **488**,N.1 and 2; **489**,N.1; **491**.N.; **493**,N.1; **494**,N.1; **495**; **496**,N.1; **497**; **498**,N.3,4,6 and 8; **501**; **503**; **511**,R.4; **513**,R.1 and NN.1,2; **525**,1, N.1 and 4, 2,N.2 and 3; **527**,R.1 and 3, and N.2; **528**,N.1 and 2; **532**,N.1 and 3; **533**,R.1; **536**,N.1; **538**,N.4; **541**,N.1,2,3 and 5; **542**,R. and N.1; **543**,N.3; **548**,N.3; **549**, N.1,2 and 4; **550**,N.1,2 and 5; **553**,1; **555**, R.1; **563**,N.2,3,4 and 5; **567**,N.; **569**,N.1; **571**,N.2 and 3; **573**,N.2; **574**,N.; **576**,N.1; **577**,N.4 and 5; **580**,N.3; **590**,N.1; **591**,R.4 and N.2; **602**,N.5; **604**.R.2; **605**,N.; **606**,N. 1; **608**; **615**,N.; **616**,1,N.2, and 2, N.; **617**, N.1; **626**,N.1; **627**,R.1 and 2; **635**,N.1 and 2; **636**,N.1; **643**,N.4; **644**,R.3; **647**,N.2; **666**,N.; **677**,N.

COLUMELLA—**592**,N.

CORNIFICIUS—**439**,N.3; **500**,R.; **549**,N.4.

CURTIUS—**416**,16; **532**,N.1.

DICTYS—**545**,R.1.

ENNIUS—**411**,R.2; **476**,N.5.

FLORUS—**467**,N; **525**,2,N.2.

FRONTO—**525**,2,N.3.

GAIUS—**525**,2,N.3.

GELLIUS—**580**,N.3.

HIRTIUS—**423**,N.2: **532**,N.1.

HORACE—**211**,R.1, Ex.*a*,N.; **271**,2,N.2; **301**; **346**,N.2; **351**,N.1; **416**,5,17,19, and 21; **417**,8; **418**,4; **421**,N.1,*c*; **422**,N.4; **427**,N. 2; **439**,N.3; **454**,N.2; **457**,N.2; **458**,N.1 and 2; **460**,2,N.3; **477**,N.8; **480**,N.1; **482**, 3; **498**,N.1; **500**,R.; **525**,1,N.1, 2,N.2; **533**, R.1; **536**.N.1; **538**,N.5; **541**,N.5; **563**,N.3; **569**,N.1; **591**,R.2; **592**,N.; **616**,1,N.2; **644**, N.2.

JUVENAL—**602**,N.4; **605**,N.

LIVY—**204**,N.8; **209**,N.3; **211**,R.1,Ex.*a*,N.; **247**,N.1; **249**,N.; **250**,N.1 and 2; **285**, Ex. 3 and N.2; **293**,N.; **311**,1,R.2, 2,N.: **317**,N. 1; **319**,N.1; **323**,N.1; **335**,N.; **337**,N.4; **338**,N.1; **346**,N.2; **347**,R.2; **350**,1,N.; **351**, N.1; **353**,N.2; **356**,N.2; **359**,N.1 and 4; **363**,R.1; **366**,R.1; **371**,N.; **372**,N.1 and 4; **373**,R.1; **374**,N.2 and 3; **383**,N.1; **385**,N. 1; **390**,2,N.3; **391**,R.1 and N.; **395**,N.1; **399**,N.1 and 3; **401**,N.2 and 6; **403**,N.3; **406**,N.3; **410**,N.2,3, and 4; **411**,R.1 and N.1; **413**,N.1; **415**; **416**,2,7,15,16,22,23, 24, and 28; **417**,1,8,10,11, and 14; **418**,2, and 4; **423**,N.2; **427**,N.2; **429**,2 and N.1; **430**,N.1; **435**,N.2; **436**,N.1; **437**,N.2; **438**, N.; **439**,N.3 and 4; **442**,N.3; **443**,N.4; **457**,1,N.3; **458**,N.1; **460**,2,N.3; **467**,N.; **477**,N.4,5 and 9; **478**,N.1 and 2; **480**,N.3; **482**,1,N.1,2 and 5,R.2 and N.1; **497**; **498**, N.1,3, and 8; **502**,N.3; **503**; **513**,N.1 and 2; **525**,1,N.1 and 7 and 2,N.2; **532**,N.1; **536**,N.1; **541**,N. 2 and 5; **542**,R. and N.2; **543**,N.3; **545**,R.1; **549**,N.1; **550**,N.5; **555**, 2,N.; **557**,R. and N.2; **563**,N.2, 3, and 5: **567**,N.; **569**,N.1; **570**,N.4; **571**,N.6; **576**, N.2; **577**,N.3,4, and 5; **597**,R.5; **602**,N.5; **615**,N.; **616**,1,N.1 and 2, and 2,N.; **626**,N. 1; **635**,N.2; **636**,N.1; **644**,R.3; **651**,R.1; **666**,N.; **687**.

LUCAN—**254**,N.1; **458**,N.1.

LUCILIUS—**383**,1,N.2; **496**,N.1.

LUCRETIUS—**372**,N.2; **383**,1,N.2; **405**,N.3; **406**,N.6; **422**,N.4; **459**,N.1; **480**,N.2; **482**, 1,N.1; **496**,N.1; **500**,R.; **525**,1,N.1; **533**, R.1; **564**,N.1; **571**,N.4; **606**,N.1; **636**,N.1.

MARTIAL—**280**,2,*b*,N.1.

NAEVIUS—**533**,N.1.

NEPOS—**249**,N.; **250**,N.2; **356**,R.3; **408**,N.2, *c*; **416**,10; **513**,N.1; **536**,N.1; **555**,2,N.; **571**,N.4; **605**,N.; **606**,N.1; **687**.

OVID—**270**,N.; **280**,2,*b*,N.1; **349**,R.5; **364**, N.1; **401**,N.7; **411**,R.2; **416**,7; **417**,7; **427**, N.2; **494**,N.3; **525**,1,N.; **545**,R.1; **616**,N.2.

PETRONIUS—207,N.; 525,1,N.1.

PLAUTUS—206,N.1; 211,R.1, Ex.*a*,N.; 270, N.1; 330,N.3; 336,N.1; 347,R.2; 357,N; 358,N.1; 361,N.1; 374,N.1,2,3, and 5; 375,N.3; 383,1,N.2, and 3; 398,N.2; 406, N.6; 407,N.2; 411,R.1; 415; 416,6,7,16, 19,21, and 24; 417,7; 418,4; 422,N.2; 439,N.3; 454,N.2; 455,N.; 467,N.; 476,N. 3 and 5; 477,N. 1 and 6; 478,N.2; 487, N.1; 494,N.1 and 6; 496,N.1; 498,N.3; 502,N.3; 525,1,N.4 and 2,N.2; 533,R.1; 538,N.1 and 3; 541,N.1; 545,R.1; 546, N.3; 548,N.3; 549,N.2; 563,N.3; 569,N. 1; 571,N.5; 576,N.1; 577,N.5; 580,N.1 and 3; 597,N.; 602,N.5; 610,N.1; 615,N.; 626,N.1; 643,N.3; 677,N.

PLINY MAIOR—381,N.3; 398,N.2; 460,2,N.3; 467,N.; 482,2; 498,1,N.1; 592,N.

PLINY MINOR—209,N.5; 252,N.; 418,4; 460, 2,N.3; 538,N.5; 548,N.3; 602,N.4; 605,N.; 616,1,N.2.

POLLIO—410,N.3.

PROPERTIUS—406,N.3; 421,N.1,*c*; 457,1,N.2; 458,N.1; 480,N.2 and 3; 498,N.1.

QUADRIGARIUS—407,N.2,*b*.

QUINTILIAN—359,N.5; 406,N.3; 512,N.1; 525 2,N.2; 538,N.5; 602,N.4; 604,R.2; 627,R.1.

SALLUST—207,N.; 208,2,N.2; 247,N.1; 250, N.1; 280,2,*c*,N.: 285,N.2; 286,3,N.; 311,1, R.2; 323,N.1; 338,N.1; 347,R.2; 349,R.4; 353,N.2; 356,N.3; 359,N.1 and 5; 369,N. 2; 372,N.2 and 3; 374,N.1,3, and 8; 390, 3,N.1; 391,N.; 407,N.2,*d*; 410,N.1,2 and 4; 416,2,4,7,16,20 and 24; 417,7; 418,4; 423, N.2; 428,R.2; 435,N.2; 436,N.1; 437,N.2; 439,N.3; 460,2,N.1; 467,N.; 475,N.3; 476, N.5; 478,N.2; 480,N.3; 482,3 and 5,R.2 and N.1; 488,N.2; 491,N.; 496,N.1; 501; 503; 512,N.1; 513,N.1; 525,2,N.2; 532,N.1; 536, N.1; 538,N.1; 541,N. 2 and 3; 542,N.1; 545, R.1; 548,N.3; 563,N.2; 569,N.1; 591,R.2; 604,R.2; 616,1,N.1 and 2; 626,N.1; 636, N.1.

SENECA—374,N.3; 616,1,N.2; 635,N.2.

SENECA RHETOR—445,N.

SUETONIUS—349,R.5; 407,N.2,*c*; 416,22; 513,N.1; 542,R.; 546,N.3; 577,N.5; 602, N.4; 665,N.2.

TACITUS—208,2,N.2; 209,N.3; 211,R.1,Ex. *a*,N.; 254,N.1; 285,Ex.3 and N.2; 346,N. 3; 353,N.2; 354,N.2; 356,N.2; 359,N.5; 364, N.1; 372,N.2; 376,R.1; 390,3,N.1; 401,N.6 and 7; 407,N.2,*a*; 410,N.2 and 4; 411,N. 1; 416,10,16,23 and 24; 417,3 and 12; 423,N.3; 428,R.2 and N.4; 432,N.1; 437, N.2; 442, N.3; 443,N.4; 460,2,N.3; 475, N.1; 476,N.5; 477,N.4; 480,N.3; 482,2,3 and 5,N.1; 484,N.2; 493,N.2; 496,N.1; 497; 513,N.1; 525,1,N.7, and 2,N.2 and 3; 532,N.1; 538,N.5; 542,R. and N.1; 546, N.3; 563,N.2,3 and 5; 567,N.; 569,N.1; 571,N.1 and 3; 573,N.1; 575,N.2; 576,N. 1; 602,N.4; 604,R.2; 605,N.; 616,1,N.2; 635,N.2; 647,N.2; 666,N.; 687.

TERENCE—211,R.1,Ex.*a*,N.; 271,N.2; 285, N.2; 337,N.4; 358,N.1; 361,N.1; 383,1, N.2; 399,N.1; 407,N.2; 411,R.2; 415; 416, 1,8, and 28; 423,N.2; 428,R.2; 439,R.3; 454,N.2; 455,N.; 482,5,R.2; 487,N.1; 489, N.; 494,N.1; 496,N.1 and 2; 498,N.3; 502, N.3; 525,1,N.1; 533,R.1; 541,N.1; 545, R.1; 549,N.2; 569,N.1; 571,N.4; 574,N.; 576,N.1; 578,N.; 580,N.1 and 3; 597, N.; 610,N.1; 615,N.; 626,N.1; 644,N.2; 677,N.

TIBULLUS—455,N.: 457,1,N.2; 458,N.1: 498,N.1.

VALERIUS MAXIMUS—285,N.2; 432,N.1; 460,2,N.3; 538,N.5; 577,N.5.

VARRO—416,7,15, and 23; 422,N.4; 427,N. 2; 437,N.2; 449,R.3; 574,N.; 606,N.1.

VATINIUS—606,N.1.

VELLEIUS—209,N.5; 285,N.2; 349,R.5; 391, N.; 460,2,N.3; 513,N.2.

VERGIL—211,R.1,Ex.*a*,N.; 230,N.2; 269; 276,2,N.2; 301; 336,N.1; 346,N.2; 374, N.3; 383,1,N.2 and 3; 390,2,N.4; 411,R. 2; 417,3; 421,N.1,*c*; 422,N.4; 442,N.3; 443,N.1; 458,N.3; 477,N.5; 480,N.2; 482, 1,N.1 and 2; 485,N.3; 525,1,N.1; 542,N. 1; 546,N.3; 563,N.2; 591,R.2; 644,N.2.

VITRUVIUS—353,N.1; 386,N.; 416,5 and 25; 418,3; 439,N.3; 536,N.1; 549,N.2; 571, N.4.

THE HISTORIANS—209,N.5; 211,R.1,Ex.*b*; 214,R.2; 363,R.1; 391,N.; 484,N.2; 485, N.1; 487,N.1; 491; 501,N.; 567,N.; 628,R.

THE POETS—211,R.1,Ex.*a*,N. and R.4; 217, N.1 and 2; 230,N.2; 241,N.1; 261; 269; 270; 271,2,N.2; 280,2,*b* and N.2; 290,N. 2; 295,N.; 296,N.1,3, and 4; 321,N.1; 332, 2,N.2 and 3; 333,2,N.6; 336,N.3; 337,N.

1 and 2; 338,N.1 and 2; 346,N.6; 350,1,N.; 351,N.1; 352,N.; 354,N.2; 358; 361,N.1; 362,N.1; 373,R.1; 374,N.1,3,6,8, and 10; 375; 383,1,N.1; 385,N.1; 386,N.; 390,3,N.1 and 2; 391,N.; 394,3,N.1; 396,N.1 and 3; 397,N.2; 401,N.4 and 6: 404,N.1; 407,N.2,*e*; 413,R.1 and 3, and N.1; 416,14, and 20; 417,5,12, and 24; 418,3 and 4; 421,N.1; 427,N.5; 428,N.2 and 3; 435,N.1; 436,N.1 and 3; 437,N.1; 439,N.2; 440,R.; 446,N.2; 449,R.3; 454,N.3; 457,1,N.3; 460,2,N.2; 467,N.; 476,N.2,3, and 5; 477,N.4; 482,3; 488,N.1 and 2; 495,N.2; 496,N.1; 498,N.1 and 5; 502,N.1; 525,1,N.7; 527,N.2; 532,N.1 and 6; 535,R.3; 536,N.2; 538,N.5; 546,R.2 and N.3; 552,R.2; 591,N.2; 604,R.2; 617,N.2; 631,2,N.1; 683.

THE COMIC POETS—211,R.1,Ex.*a*,N.; 228,N.1; 242,N.2; 243; 244,N.1; 247,N.2; 263,2,N.; 267,N.; 269; 280,2,*c*.N.; 346,N.1; 351,N.1; 406,N.2; 416,4; 443,N.4; 453,N.1 and 2; 467,N.; 468,N.; 477,N.3; 553,1; 617,N.2.

LATER PROSE—211,R.1,Ex.*a*,N.; 217,N.1 and 2; 221,R.2; 269; 361,N.1; 372,N.3; 374,N.1 and 3; 375; 386,N.; 390,2,N.3; 404,N.1; 413,N.1; 415; 416, 20, 23, 25, and 27; 417,5; 427,N.5; 428,N.1, 2, and 3; 449,R.3; 460,1,*a*; 467,N.; 476,N.5; 477,N.4; 528,R.2 and N.4; 535,R.3; 538,N.5; 546,R.2; 555,2,N.; 569,N.1.

ANTECLASSICAL LATIN—211,N.1 and 2; 220,N.2; 221,R.2; 241,N.1; 248,N.1; 254,N.2; 257,N.1; 260; 261,N.2; 271,1,N.1 and 2, and 2,N.1 and 2; 272,3,N.; 280,2,*a*.R.2; 293,N.; 296,N.1; 301; 303; 309,N.2; 319,N.1; 330,N.2; 339,N.1; 341,N. 2; 346,N.2; 347,R.1; 350,1,N.; 373,R.1; 374,N.4; 375,N.2; 383,1,N.2; 385,N.2; 390,2,N.1; 390,N.3; 391,R.2 and N.; 395,N.2; 397,N.2; 399,N.1; 403,N.3; 407,N.2; 408,N.6; 410,N.1,4, and 5; 413,R.1; 416, 10, 12, 16, 23, 24, and 27; 417,2,9, and 10; 421,N.1; 422,N.2 and 4; 423, N.2 and 3; 427,N.2; 428,N.1; 429,N.1; 430,N.1; 432,N.1; 433,N.2; 436,N.1 and 4; 437,N.2; 439,N.3; 442,N.3; 443,N.1 and 4; 444,1,N.2; 454,N.1 and 5; 456,N.; 457,1,N.1,2, and 3, and 2,N.; 459,N.2; 475,N.1; 476,N.1,2, and 5; 479,N.1; 480,N.1; 482,1,N.1, and 5,N.1; 487,N.2; 488,N.1; 495,N.1; 498,N.5,6, and 7; 500; 503; 513,N.1; 525,1,N.2,6, and 7, and 2,N.2, and 3; 527,R.3; 528,N.1; 536,N.1; 537,N.2; 541,N.5; 542,R. and N.2; 546,N.3; 549,N.4; 550,N.1 and 2; 553,3,N.; 557,R.; 563,N.1,2, and 5; 564,N.1; 571,N.2,3, and 5; 574,N.; 576,N.1; 577,N.1; 580,N.3; 591,R.2 and N.2; 602,N.5; 614,N.; 617,N.1 and 2; 626,N1. and 2; 627,R.1; 634,N.; 636,N.1; 651,R.1.

CLASSICAL LATIN—220,N.1; 241,N.1; 260; 263,2,N.; 269; 270,N.; 282,N.; 285, Ex.3; 301; 303; 309,N.2; 318,N.2; 330,N.2; 339,N.1 and 4; 342; 343,N.1: 346,N.2; 347,R.1; 348,R.2; 356,R.2; 359,N.4; 363,N.; 374,N.1,2,3,4, 5, and 9; 381,N.1; 383,1; 385,R.1 and N.1,2, and 3; 390,2,N.1, and 2; 391,R.1; 393,R.5; 394,N.1; 398; 399,N.1; 401,N.2 and 6; 403,N.3 and 4; 407,N.2; 408,N.6; 410,N.1,2,5 and 6; 413,R.3; 416,9,12,16,23, and 29; 417,9 and 11; 421,N.1 and 2; 422,N.4; 423,N.4; 429,1 and 2; 430,N.1; 432,N.1; 437,1; 438,N.; 439,N.3; 442,N.3; 444,1,N.2; 449,R.3; 460,1,N.1, and 2, N.3; 467,N.; 475,N.2; 477,N.8: 479,N.1; 482,4,N.; 494,N.2 and 3; 498,N.3 and 4; 500,R.; 501,N.; 502,N.1; 503; 511,R.1; 525,1,N.1; 528,R.2, and N.1; 532,N.1,3, and 4; 535,R.3; 537,N.2; 538,N. 2 and 3; 541,N.1 and 2; 545,R.1; 546,N.3; 549,N.1; 556; 571,N.2; 602,N.1; 610,N.1; 631,3,R.1; 643,N.3; 644,R.3; 651,R.1.

POST-CLASSICAL LATIN—211,R.2; 239,N.; 241,N.2; 247,N.1; 251,N.2; 254,R.6, and N.2; 257,N.1; 271,2,N.2; 292,N.; 296,N.1 and 2; 298,N.1; 299,N.2; 301; 309,N.2; 319,N.1; 330,N.4; 333,2,N.6; 337,N.1 and 2; 338,N.2; 339,N.1 and 3; 346, N.2; 349,R.5; 355,N.; 356,R.3; 362,N.1 and 2; 366,R.2; 374,N.2 and 3; 378,R.4; 380,1,N.2; 390,3,N.1; 391,N.; 393,R.5; 397,N.2; 398,N.1: 399,N.2: 403,N.4; 405,N.3; 407,N.2; 408,N.6; 410,N.1,2,3, and 5; 411,R.1; 415; 416,7,10,12,14,16,17,18, and 22; 417,7; 418,4; 422,N.2,4, and 5; 423,N.2 and 3; 431,N.1 and 3; 432,N.1; 433; 435,N.1; 436,N.1; 437,N.1; 438,N.; 439,N.2 and 3; 479,N.1 and 2; 480,N.1; 482,1,N.1 and 2, 3,4,N., and 5,N.1 and 2; 494,N.2; 498,N.1,3,6, and 8; 503; 513, N.2; 525,1,N.7, and 2,N.2; 528,R.2; 532,N.1; 541,N.1; 543,N.3; 545,R.1; 546,N.3; 549,N.2; 553,2,N. and 4,R.2; 557,N.2; 563,N.4 and 5; 573,N.2; 576,N.2; 590,N.1; 595,R.6; 602,N.5; 605,N.; 606,N.1; 616,2,N.; 625,1,R. and 2,R.; 626,N.1; 669; 677,N.

PRINTED BY R. & R. CLARK, LTD., EDINBURGH

PREFACE TO THE BIBLIOGRAPHY

In keeping with Professor Gildersleeve's enthusiasm for advancing classical studies in America, this is, in large measure, an American bibliography: it is designed primarily, although not exclusively, for an American audience with the intention of acquainting the reader with the range of scholarship that has been produced on Latin grammar in English during the past century. The scores of articles, notes, and dissertations on morphology, syntax, and word order are more than adequate testimony to the considerable contribution of American classicists. Even a brief survey of the works included will display the familiar names of grammarians whose editions of school texts remain the standards against which subsequent editions must be measured.

A closer inspection of the entries will introduce those who are uninitiated in the more arcane aspects of Latin grammar to an important period in the classical tradition, a golden age of scholarship that concludes in the years immediately following the first world war. The chief Latin grammars in current use were all originally published by the year 1910, and were produced within the context of a far more widespread interest in grammatical issues, as attention to the dates of publication in the present bibliography will easily demonstrate. The pages of *Classical Review* or *American Journal of Philology* at the turn of the century reveal an age more inclined to esteem the study of grammar as a valuable endeavor, not as a fastidious preoccupation with the purely mechanical problems of language reserved for scholars inspired by a lesser *Numen.*

It is for those whose interest in Latin grammar goes beyond the mere introductory level of a typical school text that this bibliography has been compiled. The availability of journals and pedagogical utility have been the foremost aims in deciding which publications to include. Other than among general works, where the important and comprehensive volumes by European grammarians are listed, the preponderance of articles may be found in the major American and British periodicals. The schema followed for the most part has been that of J. Cousin, whose *Bibliographie de la Langue Latine* has been by far the most important source for scholarship in print between 1880 and 1948. Categories permitted within Cousin's more comprehensive undertaking have been subsumed under broader headings in view of the more focused objective of the present bibliography. Wherever possible, the omissions of years, journal numbers, or pages of works cited by Cousin have been remedied. It is my hope that both student and teacher alike may find this a convenient source of reference to accompany the more enduring achievement of Professors Gildersleeve and Lodge.

William E. Wycislo
University of Illinois at Chicago

SELECTED BIBLIOGRAPHY

General Works

Allen, B. M., and J. B. Greenough, *New Latin Grammar.* 1st ed., 1903; reprint, New Rochelle, New York: Aristide D. Caratzas Publisher, 1983.

Allen, W. S., "Some Observations on the Pronunciation of Latin." *Didaskalos* 1 (1963): 45-53.

———. *Vox Latina: A Guide to the Pronunciation of Classical Latin.* Cambridge: Cambridge University Press, 1965.

Badellino, O., *Sommario di Sintassi Latina.* Turin: Paravia, 1936.

Bassols De Clement, M., *Syntaxis Latina.* 2 vols., Madrid: Consejo super. de Investig. Cientif., 1956.

Bennett, C. E., *Syntax of Early Latin.* 2 vols. Boston: Allyn and Bacon, 1910.

———. *New Latin Grammar.* Boston: Allyn and Bacon, 1908; reprint, Wauconda, Illinois: Bolchazy-Carducci Publishers, 1994.

Blatt, F., *Précis de syntaxe latine.* Lyon: I. A. C., 1952.

Buck, C. D., *Comparative Grammar of Greek and Latin.* Chicago: University of Chicago Press, 1933.

Carstairs, A., "Paradigm Economy in Latin." In *Transactions of the Philological Society.* Oxford: Blackwell, 1984.

Coleman, R., "Greek Influence on Latin Syntax." In *Transactions of the Philological Society.* Oxford: Blackwell, 1975.

Colson, F. H., "The Analogist and Anomalist Controversy." *Classical Quarterly* 13 (1919): 24-36.

Cousin, J., *Évolution et structure de la langue latine.* Paris: Les Belles Lettres, 1944.

D'ooge, B. L., *Concise Latin Grammar.* Boston: Ginn and Company, 1921.

Draeger, A., *Historische Syntax der lateinischen Sprache.* 2 vols. Leipzig: Teubner, 1878-1881.

———. *Syntax und Stil des Tacitus.* Leipzig: Teubner, 1888.

Ernout, A., and F. Thomas, *Syntax latine.* Paris: Klincksieck, 1951.

Fraenkel, E., "Grammatisches und Syntaktisches." *Indogermanische Forschungen* 28 (1911): 219-251.

———. *Plautinisches im Plautus*. St. Andrews: St. Andrews University Publications, 1907.

Giuffrida, G., *Principi di sintassi latina. Concetto e funzione del modo*. Turin: Paravia, 1938.

Glover, R. F., *Notes on Latin*. Oxford: Blackwell, 1954.

Hale, W. G., and C. D. Buck, *A Latin Grammar*. 1st ed., 1903; reprint, University, Alabama: University of Alabama Press, 1985.

Hammond, M. *Latin. A Historical and Linguistic Handbook*. Cambridge, Massachusetts: Harvard University Press, 1976.

Johnston, Patricia A., *Traditio. An Introduction to the Latin Language and its Influence*. New York: Macmillan, 1988.

Juret, A. C., *Système de la syntaxe latine*. Paris: Les Belles Lettres, 1933.

Keiler, A. R., "Some Problems of Latin Deep Structure." *Classical Journal* 65 (1970): 208-213.

Kent, R. G., *The Forms of Latin: A Descriptive and Historical Morphology*. Baltimore: Linguistic Society of America, 1946.

King, J. E., and Cookson, C., *Introduction to the Comparative Grammar of Greek and Latin*. Oxford: Clarendon Press, 1890.

Knapp, C., "Studies in the Syntax of Early Latin." *American Journal of Philology* 35 (1914): 268-293.

———. "A Phase of the Development of Prose Writing among the Romans." *Classical Philology* 13 (1918): 138-154.

Kroll, W., *Die wissenschaftliche Syntax im lateinischen Unterricht*. Berlin: Weidmann, 1925.

Kühner, R., *Ausführliche Grammatik der lateinischen Sprache*. 2 vols., Hannover: Hahn, 1912.

Lakoff, R. T., "Studies in the Transformational Grammar of Latin." Ph.D. diss., Harvard University, 1967.

———. *Abstract Syntax and Latin Complementation*. Cambridge, Massachusetts: Massachusetts Institute of Technology Press, 1968.

Landgraf, G., H. Blase, A. Dittmar, and J. Golling, *Historische Grammatik der lateinischen Sprache*. Leipzig: Teubner, 1903.

Lebreton, J., *Étude sur la langue et la grammaire de Cicéron*. Paris: Hachette, 1901.

Lindsay, W. *A Short Historical Latin Grammar*. Oxford: Clarendon Press, 1915.

———. *The Latin Language. An Historical Account of Latin Sounds, Stems, and Flexions*. Oxford: Clarendon Press, 1894.

———. *Syntax of Plautus*. St. Andrews: St. Andrews University Publications, 1907.

Löfstedt, E., *Vermischte Studien zur lateinischen Sprachkunde und Syntax*. Lund: Gleerup. 1936.

Marouzeau, J., "Logique, psychologie et méchanisme dans la syntaxe latine." *Revue des Études Latines* 7 (1929): 75-85.

Matthews, P. H., "Word Classes in Latin." *Lingua* 17 (1967): 153-181.

McWhorter, A. W., "Notes on Latin Syntax." *Transactions of the American Philological Association* 45 (1914): 23.

———. "Methods in Syntactic Studies." *Transactions of the American Philological Association* 58 (1927): 26.

Meillet, A., and J. Vendryes, *Traité de grammaire comparée des langues classiques*. 2nd ed., Paris: Champion, 1948.

Morgan, E. P., *Principles and Methods in Latin Syntax*. New York: Scribners, 1901.

Morris, E. P., "A Science of Style." *Transactions of the American Philological Association* 46 (1915): 103-118.

Murry, J. M., *The Problem of Style*. London: Milford, 1922.

Nettleship, "The Historical Development of Classical Latin Prose." *Journal of Philology* 15 (1886): 35-36.

Nutting, H. C., "Thought Relation and Syntax." *University of California Publications in Classical Philology* 6: 271-288.

O'Brien, R. J., *A Descriptive Grammar of Ecclesiastical Latin based on Modern Structural Analysis*. Chicago: Loyola University Press, 1965.

Palmer, L. R., *The Latin Language*. London: Faber and Faber, 1954.

Panduis, D. G. J., "Is Latin an S O V Language?" *Indogermanische Forschungen* 89 (1984): 140-159.

Pepicello, W. J., "Noun Phrase Movement in Latin." Ph.D. diss., Brown University, 1974.

Pinkster, H., *Latin Linguistics and Linguistic Theory*. Amsterdam: Benjamins, 1983.

———. *Latin Syntax and Semantics*. London: Routledge, 1990.

Riemann, O., *Syntaxe latine*. 7th ed., rev. by A. Ernout, Paris: Klincksieck, 1927.

———. *Étude sur la Langue et la Grammaire de Tite Live*. Paris, Klincksieck, 1884.

Stoltz, F. and A. Debrunner, *Geschichte der lateinischen Sprache*. 3rd ed. Berlin: de Gruyter, 1953.

Sweet, W. E., *Latin: A Structural Approach*. Ann Arbor: University of Michigan Press, 1957.

Ward, R. L., "Evidence for the Pronunciation of Latin." *Classical Weekly* 55 (1962): 161-164; 273-275.

Woodcock, E. C., *A New Latin Syntax*. London: Methuen & Co., Ltd., 1959; reprint, Wauconda, Illinois, and Bristol, U. K.: Bolchazy-Carducci Publishers and Bristol Classical Press, 1985 and 1987.

———. "Grammarian's Dilemna: An Introduction to an Historical Account of Latin Syntax." *Proceedings of the Classical Association* 50 (1953): 20-21.

Morphology

Abbott, F. F., "Note on Latin Hybrids." *Classical Review* 5 (1891): 18.

Anderson, A. R., "*-Eis* in the Accusative Plural of the Latin Third Declension." *Transactions of the American Philological Association* 45 (1914): 129-141.

Arnold, W. T., "The Termination *-ensis*." *Classical Review* 3 (1889): 201.

Bagge, L. M., "The Early Numerals." *Classical Review* 19 (1905): 259-267.

Bauer, C. F., "The Latin Perfect Endings *-ere* and *-erunt*." Ph.D., diss., University of Pennsylvania, 1933.

Blake, F. R., "The Origin of Interrogative Pronouns." *Transactions of the American Philological Association* 67 (1936): 31.

Boesen, P. J., "Certain Noun Suffixes of the Latin Period." *Transactions of the American Philological Association* 63 (1932): 59.

Buck, C. D., "Notes on Latin Orthography." *Classical Review* 13 (1899): 116-119; 156-167.

Bury, J. B., "Latin Tenses in *-bo -bam*." *Classical Review* 3 (1889): 195 ff.

Chase, G. D., "Latin Verbs in *-cinor*." *Transactions of the American Philological Association* 32 (1901): 73.

Claflin, A. F., "The Nature of the Latin Passive in the Light of Recent Discoveries." *American Journal of Philology* 48 (1927): 157-175.

Darbishire, H. D., "Abnormal Derivations." *Classical Review* 6 (1892): 147-149.

Dilke, O. A. W., "Final *-e* in Lewis and Short." *Greece and Rome* 6 (1959): 212-213.

Exon, C., "Verbs in *-io* with Infinitives in *-ere*." *Hermathena* 27 (1901): 383-402.

———. "The Evolution of the Subjunctive Form." *Hermathena* 46 (1920): 1-25.

Fay, E. W., "Studies of Latin Words in *-cinio -cinia*." *Classical Review* 18 (1904): 304-307; 349-453; 461-463.

———. "Composition, not Suffixation." *American Journal of Philology* 21 (1910): 404-427.

———. "Declension Exponents and Case-Endings." *American Journal of Philology* 15 (1919): 416-422.

———. "Lucilius on *-i* and *-ei*." *American Journal of Philology* 33 (1912): 311-316.

———. "The Latin Passive in *-ier*." *Classical Review* 10 (1896): 183-184.

———. "The Origin of the Gerundive." *Transactions of the American Philological Association* 29 (1898): 5-30.

Giles, P., "The Origin of the Latin Pluperfect Subjunctive and Other Etymologies." *Transactions of the Cambridge Philological Society* 3: 126.

Gray, L. H., "The Personal Endings of the Present and Imperfect Active and Middle." *Language* 6 (1930): 229-252.

Gummere, J. F., "*Dic, Duc* and *Fac*." *Transactions of the American Philological Association* 69 (1938): 389-391.

Hall, T. A., "Classical Latin Noun Inflection." *Classical Philology* 41 (1946): 84-90.

Hamdi, Ibrahim M., "Concerning the Origin of the Perfect Terminations in Latin." *Athena* 80 (1985-1989): 241-249.

Hamp, E. P., "Final *-s* in Latin." *Classical Philology* 54 (1959): 165-172.

Hempl, G., "The Origin of Latin *-issimus*." *Transactions of the American Philological Association* 31 (1900): 30.

Hodgmann, A. W., "Adverbial Forms in Plautus." *Classical Review* 17 (1903): 296-303.

Horton-Smith, L. "Concluding Notes on the Origin of the Gerund and Gerundive." *American Journal of Philology* 18 (1897): 439-452.

———. "Concluding Notes on the Origin of the Gerund and Gerundive." *American Journal of Philology* 19 (1898): 413-419.

Householder, F. W., "A Descriptive Analysis of Latin Declension." *Word* 3 (1947): 48-58.

Kent, R. G., *The Forms of Latin: A Descriptive and Historical Morphology.* Baltimore: Waverly Press, 1946.

———. "Final *-ae* in Latin Case Forms." *Language* 1 (1925): 103-108.

Knight, C. M., "Contamination in Morphology." *Journal of Philology* 34 (1919): 152-160.

Lease, E. B., "Livy's Use of *-arunt, -erunt, -ere*." *American Journal of Philology* 24 (1903): 408-422.

———. "Contracted Forms of the Perfect in Livy." *Classical Review* 18 (1904): 27-36.

Lindsay, W. M., "The Dative Singular of the Fifth Declension in Latin." *Classical Review* 10 (1896): 424-427.

Linscott, H. F., *The Latin Third Declension.* Chicago: University of Chicago Press, 1896.

Martin, R. H., "*-ere* and *-erunt* in Tacitus." *Classical Review* 60 (1946): 17-19.

Matthews, P. H., *Inflectional Morphology. A Theoretical Study based on Aspects of Latin Verb Conjugation.* Cambridge: Cambridge University Press, 1972.

Mayor, J. E. B., "Adjectives in *-icius*." *Classical Review* 24 (1910): 145-146.

McCartney, E. S., "Makeshifts for the Passive of the Deponent Verbs in Latin." *Philological Quarterly* 5 (1926): 289-298.

Merrill, W. A., "On the Contracted Genitive in *-i* in Latin." *University of California Publications in Classical Philology* (1910): 57-79.

Metzger, F., "Latin *-idus* and *-udo*." *Language* 22 (1946): 194-199.

Miles, E. H., "The Passive Infinitive in Latin." *Classical Review* 5 (1891): 198-199.

Nichols, E., "Verbals in *-tor*, *-ax*; *-dus* and *-ns*." *American Journal of Philology* 40 (1919): 373-395.

Pedersen, W., "Suffixes, Determinatives and Words." *Language* 4 (1928): 7-17.

Petersen, W., "Latin Diminutive of Adjectives." *Classical Philology* 11 (1916): 426-451.

———. "Latin Diminutive of Adjectives." *Classical Philology* 12 (1917): 49-67.

———. "The Personal Endings of Middle Voice." *Language* 12 (1936): 157-174.

———. "The Latin Perfect Forms in *-isti* and *-istis*." *Classical Philology* 34 (1939): 22.

———. "The Latin *-ui* Perfect." *Language* 4 (1928): 191-199.

Postgate, J. P., "The Latin Future Infinitive in *-turum*." *Classical Review* 5 (1891): 301.

———. "The Latin Future Infinitive." *Classical Review* 18 (1904): 450-456.

Radford, R. S., "Use of the suffixes *-anus* and *-inus* in forming Possessive Adjectives from the Names of Persons." In *Studies in Honor of B. L. Gildersleeve*. Baltimore: Johns Hopkins Press, 1902.

Riedel, E., "Latin Verb Forms." *Classical Quarterly* 10 (1916): 165-168.

Steele, R. B., "Endings *-ere* and *-erunt* in Dactylic Hexameter." *American Journal of Philology* 32 (1911): 328-332.

———. "The Passive Periphrastic in Latin." *Transactions of the American Philological Association* 44 (1913): 1.

———. "The Nominative of the Perfect Participle of Deponent Verbs in Livy." *American Journal of Philology* 24 (1903): 441-447.

Sturtevant, E. H., "Analogy, the Vital Principle of Language." *Classical Weekly* 20 (1927): 93-97.

———. "*O*-Stem Adjectives from Declined Genitives." *Transactions of the American Philological Association* 71 (1940): 575-578.

———. "The Genitive and Dative Singular of the Latin Pronominal Declension." *Transactions of the American Philological Association* 45 (1914): 129-141.

Sullivan, J. B., "Final *-s* in Early Latin." Ph.D. diss., Yale University, 1970.

Wheeler, B. J., "Analogy and the Scope of its Application in Language." *Transactions of the American Philological Association* 17 (1886): 21-22.

Parts of Speech: Grammar and Syntax

Gender

Ashworth, W. D., "Animals and Birds: Some Peculiarities of Gender in Latin." *Bulletin of the Institute of Classical Studies* 3 (1956): 56-57.

Greene, J., "Notes on the Emphatic Neuter." *Classical Review* 18 (1904): 448-450.

Gummere, J. F., *The Neuter Plural in Vergil.* Philadelphia: Linguistic Society of America, 1934.

Hodgman, A. W., "On Variation of Gender in Plautus." *Proceedings of the American Philological Association* 32 (1901): 83-85.

Sturtevant, E. H., "Neuter Pronouns Referring to Words of Different Gender or Number." In *Studies in Honor of H. Collitz*. Baltimore: Johns Hopkins, 1930.

Wheeler, B. I., "The Origin of Grammatical Gender." *Proceedings of the American Philological Association* 30 (1899): 19.

———. "Grammatical Gender." *Classical Review* 3 (1889): 390-392.

Zenn, E., *The Neuter Plural in Latin Lyric Verse*. Baltimore: The Linguistic Society of America, 1948.

Number

Bell, A. J., "The Latin Dual and Poetic Diction." In *Studies in Numbers and Figures*. London: Oxford University Press, 1923.

Conway, R. S., "On the Use of *Ego* and *Nos* in Cicero's Letters." *Transactions of the Cambridge Philological Society* 5 (1899): 1-71.

Cunningham, M. P., "Some Poetic Uses of the Singular and Plural of Substantives in Latin." *Classical Philology* 44 (1949): 1-14.

Glenn, J. M., "The Neuter Plural in Iambic and Trochaic Verse." Ph.D. diss., University of Pennsylvania, 1938.

Hancock, E., "The Use of the Singular *Nos* by Horace." *Classical Quarterly* 19 (1925): 43-60.

Nutting, H. C., "*Nos* and *Noster* for *Ego* and *Meus*." *Classical Weekly* 10 (1917): 71.

Case (General)

Bennett, C. E., *Syntax of Early Latin II: The Cases*. Boston: Allyn and Bacon, 1914.

Bertocchi, A., "Subject Ellipsis and Case Agreement in Latin." In *Syntaxe Latin. Actes du II congrès international de linguistique latine*, ed. C. Touratier, *Aix-en-Provence: Univ. de Provence*, 1985.

Bolkestein, A. M., "Subject-to-Object Raising in Latin?" *Lingua* 48 (1979): 15-34.

———. "Discourse and Case Marking." In *Syntaxe Latin. Actes du II congrès international de linguistique latine*, ed. C. Touratier, *Aix-en-Provence: Univ. de Provence*, 1985.

Binkert, P. J., "Case and Propositional Construction in a Transformational Grammar of Classical Latin." Ph.D. diss., University of Michigan, 1970.

Blake, F. R., *A Semantic Analysis of Cases*. Philadelphia: The Linguistic Society of America, 1930.

Conlin, V. C., "A Transformational Model of Latin Case and Transivity." Ph.D. diss., University of Toronto, 1973.

Fink, R. I., "Persons in Nouns. Is the Vocative a Case?" *American Journal of Philology* 93 (1972): 61-68.

Howard, J. H., "Case Usage in Petronius' Satires." Ph.D. diss., Stanford University, 1895.

Knapp, C., "Studies in the Syntax of Early Latin." *American Journal of Philology* 35 (1914): 268-293.

Lehmann, C., "Latin Case Relations in Typological Perspective." In *Syntaxe Latin. Actes du II congrès international de linguistique latine*, ed. C. Touratier, *Aix-en-Provence*: *Univ. de Provence*, 1985.

Neville, K. P. R., *The Case-construction after the Comparative in Latin.* New York: Macmillan, 1901.

Magoffin, F. Van, "The Vocatives in Livy." *Proceedings of the American Philological Association* 57 (1926): 38.

Müller, C. F. W., *Syntax des Nominativs und Akkusativs im Lateinischen.* Leipzig: Teubner, 1908.

Panduis, D. G. J., "The Vocative is Outside the Sentence." *Studies in Language* 10 (1986): 443-447.

Variel, H., "The Position of the Vocative in the Latin Case System." *American Journal of Philology* 102 (1981): 438-447.

Accusative Case

Adams, J. N., Review of "Studies on the Latin Accusative Absolute," by Anne Helttula. In *Classical Review* 38 (1988): 300-303.

Allen, B. M., "The Accusative and Ablative of Degree or Difference." *Proceedings of the American Philological Association* 57 (1926): 36.

Brown, L. D., "A Study of the Case Construction of Words of Time." Ph.D. diss., Yale University, 1904.

Hahn, E. A., "The Origin of the Greek Accusative in Latin." *Transactions of the American Philological Association* 91 (1960): 221-238.

Flickinger, R. C., "The Accusative of Exclamation in Plautus and Terence." *American Journal of Philology* 29 (1908): 303-315.

———. "The Accusative of Exclamation in Epistolary Latin." *American Journal of Philology* 34 (1913): 276-299.

———. "The Accusative of Exclamation: Lucretius to Ovid." *Transactions of the American Philological Association* 48 (1918): 27-40.

Harrington, K. P., "The Purpose Accusative in Propertius." *Transactions of the American Philological Association* 27 (1897): 23-26.

Kirk, W. H. "The Accusative of Specification in Latin." *Classical Weekly* 13 (1919): 91-93; 98-101.

Maguire, R., "*Sub* with the Accusative of Time." *Hermathena* 9 (1883): 420-421.

Maraldi, M. "New Approaches to Accusative Subjects: Case Theory vs. Raising." In *Studies in Language Companion* 12. Amsterdam: Benjamins, 1983.

Nutting, H. C., "Tacitus Annales III 2.1: *Fungor* and the Accusative." *Classical Weekly* 23 (1930): 160 ff.

Steele, R. B., *Case Usage in Livy III: The Accusative*. Leipzig: Brockhaus, 1912.

Genitive Case

Bassett, E. L., "The Genitive Absolute in Latin." *Classical Philology* 40 (1945): 108-115.

Caples, M. C., "A New Study of the Genitive of Description and the Ablative of Description." Ph.D. diss., University of Toronto, 1938.

Devine, A. M., *The Latin Thematic Genitive Singular*. Oxford: Blackwell, 1970.

Edwards, G. V., "*Ingenium* in the Ablative of Quality and the Genitive of Quality." In *Studies in Honor of B. L. Gildersleeve*. Baltimore: Johns Hopkins Press, 1902.

Eyres, L. E., "*-orum, -ndorum*." *Didaskalos* 1 (1964): 90-95.

Hale, W. G., "The Genitive and Ablative of Description." *Proceedings of the American Philological Association* 31 (1900): 31.

Lang, G. J., "The Genitive of Value in Latin and Other Constructions with Verbs of Rating." Ph.D. diss., University of Chicago, 1920.

Nutting, H. C., "On the Adnominal Genitive in Latin." *University of California Publications in Classical Philology* 10 (1930): 245-308.

Petersen, W., "The Adnominal Genitive." *American Journal of Philology* 46 (1925): 128-160.

Pike, J. B., "The Genitive Case with *Curare*." *Classical Journal* 16 (1920): 49.

Politzer, R. L., "A Note on the Late Latin Genitive." *Philological Quarterly* 31 (1952): 417-423.

Steele, R. B., "The Genitive in Livy." *Proceedings of the American Philological Association* 40 (1909): 87.

———. *Case Usage in Livy I: The Genitive.* Leipzig: Brockhaus, 1910.

Stout, G. D., "A Note on the Constructions following *Milia.*" *Classical Journal* 16 (1920-1921): 366-367.

Dative Case

Dewing, H. R., "The Latin Indirect Object Governed by Verbs of Favoring, Helping, etc." *Transactions of the American Philological Association* 36 (1905): 63.

Fay, E. W., "On the Construction of *Facere (Sacrificare) quasi Donare.*" *Classical Philology* 5 (1910): 368.

———. "The Latin Dative: Nomenclature and Classification." *Classical Quarterly* 5 (1910): 185-195.

Green, A., *The Dative of Agency: A Chapter of Indo-European Case-Syntax.* New York: Columbia University Press, 1913.

Johnson, I. L., "A Study of the Dative of Purpose in Caesar." *Transactions of the American Philological Association* 62 (1932): 57.

Lease, E. B., "The Dative with Prepositional Compounds." *American Journal of Philology* 33 (1912): 285-300.

Miles, E. H., "Notes on the Dative of the Possessor." *Classical Review* 11 (1897): 142-143.

Nutting, H. C., "The Dative with Certain Compound Verbs." *Classical Journal* 16 (1920-1921): 368-369.

Petersen, W., "Syncretism in the Indo-European Dative." *American Journal of Philology* 39 (1918): 1-26.

Richardson, L. J. D., "The Dative of Agent in Horace's Odes." *Classical Review* 50 (1936): 118-120.

Souter, A., "The Predicative Dative Especially in Later Latin." *Archivum Latinitatis Medii Aevi* (1925): 191-194.

Steele, R. B., *Case Usage in Livy II: The Dative.* Leipzig: Brockhaus, 1911.

Stout, E., "The Constructions of *Invideo.*" *Classical Philology* 20 (1925): 145-154.

Ablative Case

Allen, B. M., "The Ablative of Impersonal Agent." *Classical Journal* 22 (1926): 50.

———. "The Sociative Ablatives." *Transactions of the American Philological Association* 51 (1929): 102-116.

———. "The Accusative and Ablative of Degree or Difference." *Transactions of the American Philological Association* 56 (1926): 36 ff.

Bennett, C. E., "The Ablative of Association." *Transactions of the American Philological Association* 36 (1905): 64-82.

Cressman, E. H., "The Genitive and Ablative of Description." *Classical Journal* 9 (1913): 122-127.

Hale, W. G., "The Genitive and Ablative of Description." *Transactions of the American Philological Association* 31 (1900): 138-162.

Heick, O. W., "The *Ab Urbe Condita* Construction in Latin." Ph.D. diss., University of Nebraska, 1936.

Knapp, C., "Is the Ablative Absolute Necessary?" *Classical Weekly* 17 (1923): 9-10.

Lease, E. B., "The Ablative Absolute Limited by Conjunctions." *American Journal of Philology* 49 (1928): 348-352.

Lees, M. E., "The Ablative Case in Vergil." *Classical Quarterly* 15 (1921): 183-185.

Nutting, H. C., "The Ablative as an Appositive." *Classical Philology* 15 (1920): 389-392.

———. "*Fretus* with the Ablative Case." *Classical Journal* 21 (1925): 222-223.

———. "On the Syntax of *Fretus*." *University of California Publications in Classical Philology* 8 (1927): 305-330.

———. "The *Utor Fruor* Group." *University of California Publications in Classical Philology* 10 (1928): 1-16; 17-36; 37-61; 63-149; 151-168.

———. "On the Syntax of *Usus Est*." *Classical Quarterly* 24 (1930): 74-77.

———. "On the Syntax of *Nitor*." *University of California Publications in Classical Philology* 10 (1928): 199-191.

———. "The Latin Ablative as an Objective Case." *University of California Publications in Classical Philology* 10 (1929): 193-202.

———. "The Ablative Absolute and the Stenographic Ablative." *University of California Publications in Classical Philology* 10 (1929): 203-217.

Panduis, D. G. J., "The Latin Ablative." *Classical Journal* 73 (1978): 323-335.

Rolfe, J. C., "The Preposition *Ab* in Horace." *Harvard Studies in Classical Philology* 12 (1901): 249-261.

———. "On the Construction *Sanus Ab*." *Classical Review* 13 (1899): 303-305.

———. "On the Construction *Sanus Ab*." *Classical Review* 14 (1900): 126-127.

Sloman, A., "Constructions in Connection with *Pondo*." *Classical Review* 16 (1902): 317-319.

Steele, R. B., "The Ablative Absolute in Livy." *American Journal of Philology* 23 (1902): 295-312.

———. *Case Usage in Livy IV: The Ablative*. Leipzig: Brockhaus, 1903.

———. "The Ablative Absolute in the Epistles of Cicero, Seneca, Pliny, and Fronto." *American Journal of Philology* 25 (1904): 315-327.

———. "The Ablative of the Efficient." *Classical Philology* 16 (1921): 354-361.

Weston, A. H., "The Ablative Absolute." *Classical Journal* 30 (1935): 298-299.

Witton, W. F., "Heresies IX: *Scriberis Vario*." *Greece and Rome* 3 (1956): 70-72.

Locative Case

Bonnet, M., "*Domi Habeo*." *Classical Review* 13 (1899): 35.

Linscott, F. H., "The Syncretism of the Locative and Instrumental in Latin." *Transactions of the American Philological Association* 28 (1897): 4-52.

———. "Certain Functions of the Locative." *Transactions of the American Philological Association* 29 (1898): 9-62.

Pronouns and Pronominal Phrases

Bailey, D. R., Shackleton, "On and Idiomatic Use of Possessive Pronouns in Latin." *Classical Review* 4 (1954): 8-9.

Bell, A. J., *The Latin Dual and Poetic Diction: Studies in Numbers and Figures*. London: Oxford University Press, 1923.

Charney, B. L., "Ellipsis of the Pronoun in Seneca." *Classical Philology* 39 (1944): 107-111.

Fay, E. W., "*Quis* for *Aliquis*." *Classical Review* 12 (1898): 296-299.

Hahn, E. A., "The Supposed Reflexive Pronoun in Latin." *Transactions of the American Philological Association* 94 (1963): 86-112.

———. "Relative and Antecedant." *Transactions of the American Philological Association* 95 (1964): 111-141.

Hamp, E. P., "Remnants of the Pronominal Genitive Singular -i." *American Journal of Philology* 103 (1982): 214-216.

Housman, A. E., "*Nihil* in Ovid." *Classical Review* 33 (1919): 56.

———. "*Nihil* in Ovid." *Classical Review* 34 (1920): 161.

Howard, C. L., "An Alleged Type of Relative Clause in Latin." *Glotta* 40 (1962): 307-315.

Ingersoll, J. W. B., "*Quod*: Its Use and Meaning Especially in Cicero." *Transactions of the American Philological Association* 30 (1899-1900): 30-35.

Johnson, Ruth A. L., "The Direct Object Pronoun as a Marker of Transivity in Latin." Ph.D. diss., University of California at Los Angeles, 1991.

Laidlaw, W. A., "The Demonstrative Pronoun in the Plays of Terence." *American Journal of Philology* 57 (1936): 395-415.

McCartney, E. S., "Greek and Latin Constructions in Implied Agreement." *Classical Philology* 14 (1919): 185-200.

Meader, C. L., *The Pronouns* Is, Hic, Iste, Ipse. New York: Macmillan, 1901.

———. *The Usage of* Idem, Ipse *and Words of Related Meaning*. New York: Macmillan, 1910.

Morris, E. P., "On the Sentence Question in Plautus and Terence." *American Journal of Philology* 10 (1889): 397-437.

———. "On the Sentence Question in Plautus and Terence." *American Journal of Philology*. 11 (1890): 10-55; 145-182.

Naylor, H. D., "On the so-called "Indeclinable or Absolute" use of *Ipse* and Allied Constructions." *Classical Review* 15 (1901): 314-317.

———. "Grammatical Notes, II: Relative Attraction in Livy." *Classical Review* 18 (1904): 206-207.

Oldfather, W. A., "The Objective Genitive in the Case of Pronouns in Cicero." *Philological Quarterly* 20 (1941): 608-609.

Phillimore, J. S., "Emphatic "*Ego*" in Latin." *Classical Philology* 17 (1922): 306-312.

Salmon, E. T., "Concerning *Hic and Ille*." *Classical Weekly* 28 (1934): 64.

Watt, W. S., "The Plural of *Aliquis*." *Glotta* 57 (1979): 254-259.

Woolsey, R. B., "*Quod*: Relative Pronoun and Conjunction." *American Journal of Philology* 74 (1953): 52-69.

Numbers

Howard, C. L., "*Quisque* with Ordinals." *Classical Quarterly* 52 (1958): 1-11.

Kent, R. G., "Latin *Mille* and Certain *Numeralia*." *Transactions of the American Philological Associaltion* 42 (1911): 68-89.

Nutting, H. C., "The Ordinal in Accusative Expression of Time." *Classical Weekly* 23 (1930): 120.

Postgate, J. P., "The So-called Distributives in Latin." *Classical Review* 21 (1907): 200-201.

Villiers, M. De, *The Numeral Words: Their Origin, Meaning, History, and Lesson*. London: Witherby, 1923.

Adjectives

Lease, E. B., "Notes on Latin Syntax." *American Journal of Philology* 30 (1909): 298-309.

Modini, P. F., "Non-identical Receiver of Permission and Doer of Permitted Act, with Special Reference to Latin and English. Or, Who is Permitted to become Consul." *Archivum Linguisticum* 11 (1980): 13-19.

Myers, A. L., "The Use of the Adjective as a Substantive in Horace." Ph.D. diss., University of Pennsylvania, 1919.

Poultney, J. W., "The Declension of Latin Compound Adjectives." *American Journal of Philology* 74 (1953): 367-382.

Risselada, R., "Coordination and Juxtaposition of Adjectives in the Latin N P." *Glotta* 62 (1984): 202-231.

Rolfe, J. C., "The Formation of Substantives from Latin Geographical Adjectives by Ellipsis." *Transactions of the American Philological Association* 31 (1900): 5-27.

Swan, F., *The Use of the Adjective as a Substantive in the* De Rerum Natura *of Lucretius*. New York: MacMillan, 1911.

Vaughn, A. G., "Latin Adjectives with Partitive Meaning in Republican Literature." Ph.D. diss., University of Pennsylvania, 1942.

Adverbs

Echols, E. C., "The *Quid* Greeting: The Latin Good-bye." *Classical Journal* 45 (1950): 188-190.

Frischer, B., "Inceptive *Quoque* and the Introduction *Medias in Res* in Classical and Early Medieval Latin Literature." *Glotta* 61 (1983): 236-251.

Hamp, E. P., "*Hic* and *Ibi* in Latin." *American Journal of Philology* 103 (1982): 99-101.

Heyde, K. Van Der, "*Plus, Minus, Amplius, Longius*." *Mnemosyne* 58: 121-133.

Pinkster, H., *On Latin Adverbs*. Amsterdam: North Holland Publication Company, 1974.

Rolfe, J. C., "*Prorsus*." *Transactions of the American Philological Association* (1920): 30-39.

Rose, H. J., "*Mox*." *Classical Quarterly* 21 (1927): 57-66.

Ruebel, J. S., "The Ablative as Adverb: Practical Linguistics and Practical Pedagogy." *Classical Journal* 92 (1996): 57-63.

Witt, E. De, "*Iamque adeo*." *Classical Journal* 34 (1939): 291-292.

Comparison

Heyde, E. Van Der, "*Plus, Minus, Amplius, Longius.*" *Mnemosyne* 58: 121-133.

McCartney, E, S., "A Striking Inconsistency in Word Usage." *Classical Weekly* 23 (1930): 80.

Neville, K. P. R., *The Case Construction after the Comparative in Latin.* Ithaca, New York: Cornell Studies 15, 1901.

Postgate, J. P., "On the use of *Unus* in Propertius." *Journal of Philology* 41 (1892): 66-68.

Prepositions

Bonfante, G., "The Prepositions of Latin and Greek." *Word* 6 (1950): 106-116.

———. "The Prepositions of Latin and Greek." *Word* 7 (1951): 250-252.

Cornwall, E. W., "*Per* Denoting the Manner in which Time is Spent." *Classical Review* 27 (1913): 230-231.

Egger, K., "*De Verbis cum Particulis Pro et Sub Coniunctis.*" *Latinitas* 6 (1958): 251-255.

Francis, E. D., "*Particularum Quarundam Varietas*: *Prae* and *Pro.*" *Yale Classical Studies* 23 (1973): 1-59.

Knapp, C., "Notes on the Prepositions in Gellius." *Transactions of the American Philological Association* 25 (1894): 5-34.

Marandin, G. E., "On the Meaning of *Ad* in *Ad Opis* and Similar Expressions." *Classical Review* 11 (1897): 111-112.

Oliver, A., *Observations on the Use of Certain Prepositions in Petronius with special reference to the Roman* Sermo Plebeius. London: Blades, East, and Blades, 1910.

Rolfe, J. C., "Some Uses of the Prepositions in Horace." *Proceedings of the American Philological Association* 31 (1900): 34.

Schwane, J. G., "The Latin Preposition *In* with Personal Object." Ph.D. diss., University of Illinois at Urbana-Champaign, 1973.

Waters, W. E., "The Uses of the Preposition *Cum* in Plautus." *Transactions of the American Philological Association* 33 (1902): 80.

Witt, N. W. De, "Semantic Notes to *Ob, Optimus, Optimates*." *Language* 13 (1937): 70-73.

Verbs (General)

Baldi, P., "Deponent and Middle in Latin." Ph.D. diss., University of Rochester New York, 1973.

Chandler, S. O., "Nature and Range of the Middle Voice in Vergil." *Transactions of the American Philological Association* 54 (1932): 60 ff.

Claflin, E. F., "The Nature of the Latin Passive in the light of Recent Discoveries." *American Journal of Philology* 48 (1927): 157-175.

Daube, D., "*Demolior* as a Passive." *Classical Quarterly* 44 (1950): 117-120.

Dilke, O. A. W., "Used Forms of Latin Inchoative Verbs." *Classical Quarterly* 17 (1967): 400-402.

Foley, J., "Prothesis in the Latin Verb *Sum*." *Language* 41 (1965): 59-64.

Gray, L. H., "Athematic Verbs Durative, Thematic Verbs Momentary." *Language* 9 (1933): 82-84.

Gummere, J. F., "*Mitto*: Let Go." *Classical Journal* 67 (1971): 59.

Kravar, M., "An Aspectual Relation in Latin." *Romanitas* 3 (1961): 293-309.

Mather, M. W., "*Quo modo iacendi verbi composita in praesentibus temporibus enuntiaverint antiqui et scripserint*." *Harvard Studies in Classical Philology* 6 (1895): 83-153.

McCartney, E. S., "Makeshifts for the Passive of Deponent Verbs in Latin." *Philological Quarterly* 5 (1926): 289-298.

Nyman, M. A., "Where does Latin *Sum* Come From?" *Language* 53 (1977): 39-60.

Panduis, D. G. J., "Gapping in Latin." *Classical Journal* 75 (1980): 229-241.

———. "Topic Shift and other Discourse Functions of Passives in Latin Narratives." *Glotta* 62 (1984): 232-240.

Pepicello, W. J., "Transivity and Flip in Latin." *Glossa* 9 (1975): 149-158.

Postgate, J. P., "The Use and Meaning of *Liceo* and *Liceor*." *Journal of Philology* 11 (1883): 332-335.

Rouse, W. H. D., "The Active Construction kept with Passive Verbs." *Classical Review* 29 (1915): 140.

Steele, R. B., "The Passive Periphrastic in Latin." *Transactions of the American Philological Association* 44 (1913): 5-19.

Wallace, Rex E. and Joseph, Brian D., "*Sum*. Further Thoughts." *Classical Philology* 84 (1989): 319-321.

Velton, H. V., "On the Origin of the Categories of Voice and Aspect." *Language* 7 (1931): 229-241.

Tense

DeWandel, N. C., "The Origins and Development of the Latin Present System." Ph.D. diss., Ohio State University, 1982.

Elmer, H. C., *Studies in Latin Moods and Tenses*. Ithaca, New York: Cornell Studies 4, 1898.

———. "The Distinction between the Latin Present and Perfect Tenses in Expressions of Contingent Futurity." *Transactions of the American Philological Association* 28 (1897): 37-41.

Emery, A. C., "Historical Present in Early Latin." Ph.D. diss., University of Maine, 1898.

Farron, S. G., "The Imperfect Indicative Tense in Latin Narrative," Ph.D. diss., Columbia University, 1973.

Hale, W. G., "Origin of the Distinction of Tenses in Latin Prohibitions." *Indogermanische Forschungen* 31 (1912): 272-275.

Jensen, P. J., "The Use of the Perfect in Classical Latin." *Classica and Mediaevalia* 2 (1939): 55-85.

Johnston, W., "Volitive Use of the Future Indicative." *Classical Weekly* 19 (1925-26): 193.

Kelly, D. H., "Tense in the Latin Independent Optative." *Glotta* 50 (1972): 121-125.

Laughton, E., "A Point of Tense-Sequence." *Greece and Rome* 17 (1948): 128-129.

McWhorter, A. M., "Is Future Subjunctive or is Subjunctive Future?" *Transactions of the American Philological Association* 50 (1933).

Muir, J. T., "*Oratio Obliqua*: Future Perfect Indicative in Conditional Clauses in Primary Sequence." *Classical Review* 44 (1930): 12 ff.

———. "The Sequence of Tenses in Latin." *American Journal of Philology* 7 (1886): 444-466.

Nutting, H. C., "The Imperfect Indicative as a *Praeteritum ex Futuro*." *American Journal of Philology* 43 (1922): 359-362.

———. "Contrary to Fact and Vague Future." *University of California Publications in Classical Philology* 8 (1926): 219-240.

———. "Futurity and the Verb *eo*." *Classical Journal* 18: 236-239.

———. "Modal Suggestion of the Latin Imperfect." *Classical Philology* 21 (1926): 81-82.

Pinkster, H. "The Development of Future Tense Auxiliaries in Latin." *Glotta* 63 (1985): 186-208.

Steele, R. B., "The Future Periphrastic in Latin." *Classical Philology* 8 (1913): 457-476.

Sturgis, J. W., "The Second Person Singular of the Latin Future Indicative as an Imperative." Ph.D. diss., University of Michigan, 1910.

Tyng, E. McJimsey, "An Attempt to explain Tense Usage in Cicero's Orations." *Proceedings of the American Philological Association* 47 (1916): 30.

Taylor, C. H., "A Comparative Scheme of the Moods and Tenses in Cicero's Translations from the Greek." Ph.D. diss., Johns Hopkins University, 1911.

Watson, E. W., "*Velle* as an Auxiliary." *Classical Review* 13 (1899): 183.

Wheeler, A. L., "The Uses of the Imperfect Indicative in Plautus and Terence." *Transactions of the American Philological Association* 30 (1899): 14-24.

———. "The Imperfect Indicative in Early Latin." *American Journal of Philology* 24 (1903): 163-191.

———. "The Syntax of the Imperfect Indicative in Early Latin." *Classical Philology* 1 (1906): 357-401.

Zieglschmid, A., "Concerning the Disappearance of the Simple Past in the Various Indoeuropean Languages." *Philological Quarterly* 9 (1930): 153-157.

Moods (General)

Brauenlich, A. F., "The Indicative Indirect Question in Latin." Ph.D. diss., University of Chicago, 1921.

Elmer, H. C., *Studies in Latin Moods and Tenses*. Ithaca, New York: Cornell Studies 6, 1898.

Frank, T., "Attraction of Mood in Early Latin." Ph.D. diss., University of Chicago, 1904.

Maquart, G. H., "The Simple Past Condition with Potential Indicative in the Apodosis." *Classical Philology* 4: 313-315.

Nutting, H. C., "Methods in the Study of the Modes." *Classical Review* 15 (1901): 420-422.

Postgate, J. P., "The 'Deliberative' Indicative." *Classical Review* 15 (1901): 451-452.

Sonnenschein, E. A., "The Indicative in Relative Clauses." *Classical Review* 32 (1918): 68-69.

Subjunctive Mood

Allen, B. M., "On Subjunctive Conditions." *Classical Journal.* 8 (1912): 621-622.

———. "Indirect Discourse and the Subjunctive of Attraction." *Classical Weekly* 15 (1921): 185-187.

Bennett, C. E., *Critique of Some Recent Subjunctive Theories*. Ithaca: Macmillan, 1898.

———. "Kroll on the Independent Latin Subjunctive." *Classical Philology* 12 (1917): 121-151.

———. "The Stipulative Subjunctive in Latin." *Transactions of the American Philological Association* 31 (1910): 223-250.

Carmody, W. M., *The Subjunctive in Tacitus*. Chicago: University of Chicago Press, 1926.

Clément, W. C., "Elmer's Treatment of the Prohibitive: A Rejoinder." *American Journal of Philology* 22 (1901): 86-97.

———. "Notes on the Latin Prohibitive." *Classical Review* 14 (1900): 55.

———. "Prohibitives in Silver Latin." *American Journal of Philology* 21 (1900): 154-170.

———. "Prohibitives in Terence." *Classical Review* 15 (1901): 157-159.

———. "The Force of Tenses in the Prohibitive: The Poets of the Silver Age." *Transactions of the American Philological Association* 30 (1899): 35-37.

———. "The Latin Prohibitive and Professor Elmer." *Classical Review* 16 (1902): 172-176.

———. "Two Notes on the Latin Subjunctive, I: The May-Have Perfect." *Classical Review* 14 (1900): 160-162.

———. "Two Notes on the Latin Subjunctive, II: The Negation with Expressions of the *Restitisses* Type." *Classical Review* 14 (1900): 222.

Durham, C. L., *The Subjunctive Substantive Clauses in Plautus, not including Indirect Questions*. Ithaca, New York: Cornell Studies in Classical Philology 8, 1906.

Elmer, H. C., "A Neglected Use of the Latin Subjunctive." *Classical Review* 12 (1898): 199-205.

———. "*Modus Potentialis*." *Proceedings of the American Philological Association* 32 (1901): 117-120.

———. "On the Subjunctive with *Forsitan*." *Transactions of the American Philological Association* 32 (1901): 205-217.

———. "The Supposed May-Potential Use of the Latin Subjunctive." *Transactions of the American Philological Association* 28 (1897): 16-19.

———. "Should the May-Potential Use of the Subjunctive Be Recognized in Latin?" *Classical Review* 14 (1900): 219-222.

———. "Is there still a Latin Potential: A Reply to Professor Hale." *Transactions of the American Philological Association* 32 (1901): 115-118.

———. "The Aorist Subjunctive in Latin." *Classical Review* 12 (1898): 100-104.

———. "Prohibitives in Silver Latin." *American Journal of Philology* 22 (1901): 80-87.

———. "Clément's Prohibitives in Terence." *Classical Review* 16 (1902): 107-110.

———. "A Last Word on the Prohibitive in Terence." *Classical Review* 16 (1902): 408-409.

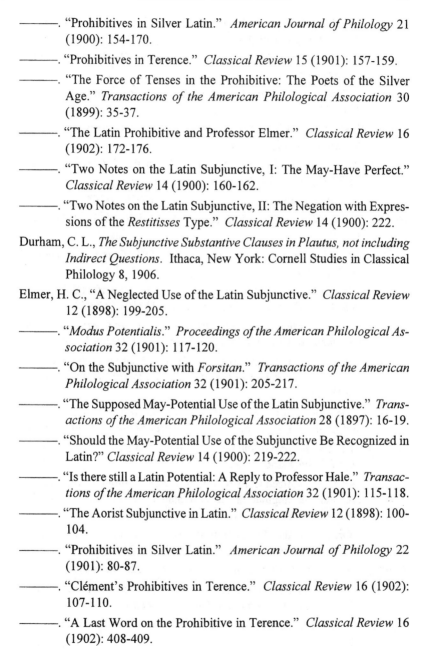

———. "The Latin Prohibitive." *Transactions of the American Philological Association* 24 (1893): 6.

———. "The Latin Prohibitive." *American Journal of Philology* 15 (1894): 133-154; 299-329.

Exon, C., "The Function of the Latin Subjunctive." *Hermathena* 43 (1922): 249-272.

Fowler, F. H., "The Latin Subjunctive of Determined Futurity." *Classical Weekly* 11 (1917): 161-164; 169-172.

———. "Latin Adjectival Clauses with the Subjunctive." *Classical Weekly* 12 (1918): 172-174.

———. "The Prospective." *Classical Review* 33 (1919): 97-99.

Geddes, W. D., "*Ne* Prohibitive in Cicero." *Classical Review* 14 (1900): 160-162.

———. "Subjunctive Tense after Prohibitive *Ne*." *Classical Review* 13 (1899): 22-32.

Goodrich, W. T., "On the Prospective Use of the Latin Imperfect Subjunctive in Relative Clauses." *Classical Review* 31 (1917): 83-86.

Hale, W. G., *The Anticipatory Subjunctive in Greek and Latin*. Chicago: University of Chicago Studies in Classical Philology 1, 1894.

———. "On the Latin Subjunctive and Greek Optative in Indirect Discourse." *Transactions of the American Philological Association* 26 (1895): 59.

———. "The Origin of the Subjunctive and Optative Conditions in Greek and Latin." *Harvard Studies in Classical Philology* (1901): 109 ff.

———. "The Prospective Subjunctive in Greek and Latin." *Classical Review* 8 (1894): 166.

———. "An Unrecognized Construction of the Latin Subjunctive: The Second Person Singular in General Statements of Fact." *Classical Philology* 1 (1906): 21-42.

———. "Origin of the Distinction of Tenses in Latin Prohibitions." *Indogermanische Forschungen* 31 (1912): 272-275.

Handford, S. A., *The Latin Subjunctive*. London: Methuen, 1947.

Harrington, K. P., "The Classification of Latin Conditional Sentences." *Transactions of the American Philological Association* 36 (1905): 41.

Inge, W. R., "The Prospective Subjunctive." *Classical Review* 7 (1893): 148-150.

James, A. J., *The Potential Subjunctive in Independent Sentences in Livy*. Northampton, Mass.: Smith College Classics 10, 1929.

Kirk, W. H., "Observations on the Indirect Volitive in Latin." *American Journal of Philology* 48 (1927): 111-121.

———. "On the Direct and the Indirect Volitive in Latin." *Classical Weekly* 17 (1923): 49 ff.

Kirkpatrick, F. A., "The Latin Aorist Subjunctive." *Classical Review* 4 (1890): 342-346; 398-399.

———. "The Latin Aorist Subjunctive." *Classical Review* 5 (1891): 67.

Lease, E. B., "Livy's Use of *Neque* and *Neve* with an Imperative or Subjunctive." *Classical Philology* 3 (1908): 302-316.

———. "*Neve* and *Neque* with the Imperative and Subjunctive." *American Journal of Philology* 34 (1913): 255-276; 416-437.

Lowrance, W. D., "The Uses of *Forem* and *Essem*." *Transactions of the American Philological Association* 53 (1931): 169-191.

Morse, C. J., "*Quid Do Ut (Ne)*: A Bargaining Construction in Juvenal and the Senecas." *Classical Review* 6 (1956): 196-198.

Nettleship, H., "On *Ne* Prohibitive with the Second Person of the Present Subjunctive in Classical Latin." *Journal of Philology* 5 (1890): 326.

Nutting, H. C., "Obligation as Expressed by the Subjunctive." *Classical Review* 13 (1899): 32-34.

———. "On the History of the Unreal Condition in Latin." *Classical Review* 15 (1901): 51-53.

———. "Subjunctive Conditions in Tacitus." *University of California Publications in Classical Philology* 7 (1923): 143-195.

———. "The Unreal Conditional Sentence in Plautus." *American Journal of Philology* 22 (1901): 297-316.

———. "The Unreal Conditional Sentence in Cicero." *American Journal of Philology* 28 (1907): 1-10; 153-178.

———. "The Use of *Forem* in Tacitus." *University of California Publications in Classical Philology* 7 (1923): 209-219.

O'Neill, H. P., "The Latin Subjunctive and its Problems." *Classical Bulletin* 9 (1932-1933): 44-46.

Paluszak, A. B., *The Subjunctive in the Letters of St. Augustine*. Washington: Catholic University of America, Patristic Studies 46, 1936.

Pease, E. W., "The Potential Subjunctive in Latin." *Proceedings of the American Philological Association* 31 (1900): 53.

Perkins, E. F., "The Expression of Customary Action or State in Early Latin." Ph.D. diss., University of Washington, 1904.

Price, C., "Commands and Prohibitions in Horace." *Transactions of the American Philological Association* 31 (1900): 60.

Sonnenschein, E. A., "Notes on Conditional Sentences in Latin." *Classical Review* 1 (1887): 124-128; 238-239.

———. "On the Latin Aorist Subjunctive." *Classical Review* 4 (1890): 398-399.

———. *The Unity of the Latin Subjunctive.* London: Murray, 1919.

———. "The Past Tenses of the Subjunctive in Expressions of Wish." *Classical Review* 25 (1911): 244-246.

———. "The Prospective Subjunctive." *Classical Review* 7 (1893): 7-11; 202-203.

———. "The Prospective in Subjunctive Clauses." *Classical Review* 32 (1918): 20-21.

———. "The Prospective in Subjunctive Clauses." *Classical Review* 33 (1919): 141-149.

Strong, E., "The Subjunctive of Obligation." *Classical Review* 13 (1899): 32.

Terrell, G., "The Apodosis of the Unreal Condition in *Oratio Obliqua* in Latin." *American Journal of Philology* 25 (1904): 59-73.

Witton, W. F., "Heresies: Don't Do It." *Greece and Rome* 3 (1934): 173-174.

Imperative Mood

Bergh, B., *On Passive Imperatives in Latin.* Stockholm: Almqvist and Wiksell, 1975.

Elmer, H. C., "Aorist Imperative in Latin." *Classical Review* 12 (1898).

Harrington, K. P., "A Neglected Use of the Latin Imperative." *Transactions of the American Philological Association* 26 (1895): 61-62.

Lease, E. B., "*I nunc* and *I* with Another Imperative." *American Journal of Philology* 19 (1898): 59-70.

McElwain, M. B., "The Imperative in Plautus." Ph.D. diss., Cornell University, 1910.

Granger, F. St., "The Influence of the Imperative on Latin Idiom." *Classical Review* 21 (1907): 47-51.

Infinitive Mood

Allen, B. M., "The Latin Present Infinitive." *Classical Journal* 19: 222-225.

Anderson, A. R., "Studies in the Exclamatory Infinitive." *Classical Philology* 9 (1914): 60-76.

Clément, W. K., "The Use of the Infinitive in Juvenal." *Proceedings of the American Philological Association* 33 (1902): 81.

———. "The Use of the Infinitive in Lucan, Valerius Flaccus, Statius, and Juvenal." *Transactions of the American Philological Association* 33 (1902): 71.

Coleman, R., "The Origin and Development of Latin *Habeo*+Infinitive." *Classical Quarterly* 21 (1971): 215-232.

———. "Further Observations on *Habeo*+Infinitive as an Exponent of Futurity." *Classical Quarterly* 26 (1976): 151-159.

———. "The Latin Future Passive Infinitive." *Glotta* 63 (1985): 208-212.

Fink, R. O., "Infinitives Don't Have Tenses." *Classical Journal* 48 (1952): 34-36.

Franck, T., "The Influence of the Infinitive upon Verbs Subordinated to it." *American Journal of Philology* 25 (1904): 428-446.

Fuglsang, P., "On the Latin Future Infinitive Passive and Related Expressions in Archaic and Classical Latin." *Classica and Mediaevalia* (1940): 236-252.

Hahn, E. A., "Genesis of the Infinitive with Subject-Accusative." *Transactions of the American Philological Association* 81 (1950): 117-129.

Howard, A., "On the Use of the Perfect Infinitive in Latin with the Office of the Present." *Harvard Studies in Classical Philology* 1 (1890): 111-138.

Kek, A. M., *Oportere, Debere, Convenire, Decere, Necesse esse, Opus esse, and Usus esse in Republican Latin.* Ithaca, New York: Cornell Studies, 1941.

Kirk, W. H., "On the Direct and Indirect Volitive in Latin." *Classical Weekly* 17 (1923): 49.

———. "Observations on the Indirect Volitive in Latin." *American Journal of Philology* 48 (1927): 111-121.

———. "Passive Verbs *Sentiendi et Dicendi* with the Declarative Infinitive." *Classical Philology* 31 (1936): 182-187.

Manning, R. C., "On the Omission of the Subject-Accusative of the Infinitive in Ovid." *Harvard Studies in Classical Philology* 4 (1893): 117-141.

Schlicher, J. J., "The Historical Infinitive I: Its Simple Form." *Classical Philology* 9 (1914): 279-294.

———. "The Historical Infinitive II: Its Literary Elaboration." *Classical Philology* 9 (1914): 374-394.

———. "The Historical Infinitive III: Imitation and Decline." *Classical Philology* 10 (1915): 54-74.

Thomas, F. W., "Some Remarks on the Accusative with the Infinitive." *Classical Review* 11 (1897): 373-382.

The Gerund and Gerundive

Hahn, E. A., "Was There a Nominative Gerund?" *Transactions of the American Philological Association* 96 (1965): 181-207.

Kirk, W. H., "The Syntax of the Gerund and the Gerundive." *Transactions of the American Philological Association* 64 (1942): 293-307.

Kooreman, Marion, "The Historical Development of the Ablative of the Gerund in Latin." In *Subordination and Other Topics in Latin: Proceedings of the Third Colloquium on Latin Linguistics in Bologna, Italy, April 1-5, 1985*, ed. by Gualtiero Calboli. Amsterdam: Benjamins, 1989.

MacKay, L. A., "A Syntactical Experiment of Sallust." *Classical Philology* 36 (1941): 280.

Maguinness, W. S., "The Gerundive as Future Participle Passive in the *Panegyrici Latini.*" *Classical Quarterly* 29 (1935): 45-47.

Norwood, G., *The Syntax of the Latin Gerund and Gerundive.* Toronto: Nelson, 1932.

Nutting, H. C., "The Ablative Gerund as a Present Participle." *Classical Journal* 22 (1926): 131-134.

Platner, S. B., "Notes on the Use of the Gerund and Gerundive in Plautus and Terence." *American Journal of Philology* 14 (1893): 483-490.

———. "Gerunds and Gerundives in Pliny's Letters." *American Journal of Philology* 9 (1888): 214-218.

———. "Gerunds and Gerundives in the Annals of Tacitus." *American Journal of Philology* 9 (1888): 464-473.

———. "Notes on the Use of Gerunds and Gerundives in Terence." *American Journal of Philology* 14 (1893): 483-490.

Steele, R. B., "The Gerund and Gerundive in Livy." *American Journal of Philology* 27 (1906): 280-305.

The Supine

Kroon, Caroline, "*Rarum Dictu.* The Latin Second Supine Construction." *Glotta* 67 (1989): 198-228.

Lydall, C. W. F., "*Misit Frumentatum.*" *Greece and Rome* 16 (1969): 169-171.

Naylor, H. D., "The Derivation of the Grammatical Term Supine." *Classical Review* 25 (1911): 206.

Steele, R. B., "Affirmative Final Clauses in the Latin Historians." *American Journal of Philology* 19 (1898): 255-284.

Participles

Adams, J. N., "The Substantival Present Participle in Latin." *Glotta* 51 (1973): 117-136.

Barret, J. Le Roy C., "Notes on the Latin Present Participle." *Proceedings of the American Philological Association* 40 (1909): 18.

Heick, O. W., "The *Ab Urbe Condita* Construction in Latin." Ph.D. diss., University of Nebraska, 1936.

Knight, C. M., "The -to-participle with the Accusative in Latin." *Classical Weekly* 13 (1919): 91-93; 98-101.

———. "The Time-meaning of the -to-participle in Vergil." *American Journal of Philology* 42 (1921): 260-264.

Lease, E. B., "The Use and Range of the Future Participle." *American Journal of Philology* (1919): 262-285.

Steele, R. B., "The Participial Usage in Cicero's Epistles." *American Journal of Philology* 39 (1913): 172-182.

———. "The Participle in Livy." *American Journal of Philology* 35 (1914): 163-178.

Sidey, T. E., "The Participle in Plautus, Petronius, and Apuleius." Ph.D. diss., University of Chicago, 1909.

Sentence: Structure and Syntax

Structure of the Sentence

Allen, B. M., "On the Omission of the Auxiliary *Esse*." *Classical Journal* 7 (1911-1912): 130-131.

Anderson, A. R., "The Unity of the Enclitic *-Ne-*." *Classical Philology* 9 (1914): 174-188.

Baxter, J. H., "Some Later Latin Usages: *An...aut* = *Utrum...an*." *Archivum Latinitatis Medii Aevi* (1932): 220-223.

Bloomfield, L., "Subject and Predicate." *Transactions of the American Philological Association* 47 (1916): 13-22.

Charney, B. L., "Ellipsis of the Verb in Seneca's *Epistulae Morales*." *Classical Philology* 38 (1943): 46-48.

Clément, W. C., "Two Notes on the Latin Subjunctive, II: The Negation *Non*." *Classical Review* 24 (1900): 162 ff.

Crittenden, A. R., "The Sentence Structure in Vergil." Ph.D. diss., University of Michigan, 1911.

Cunningham, M. P., "A Theory of the Latin Sentence." *Classical Philology* 60 (1965): 24-28.

Deane, J. P., "Deliberative Interrogations in Terence." *Transactions of the American Philological Association* 21 (1890): 38.

Egger, K., "*De Particulis Utique et Ubique.*" *Latinitas* 8 (1960): 39-42.

Exon. C., "Latin Questions of the Types *Quid Ago* and *Quid Agam.*" *Hermathena* 44 (1926): 17-29.

Fay, E. W., "The Impersonals of Emotion." *Classical Quarterly* 11 (1917): 88-93.

———. "Partial Obliquity in Questions of Retort." *Classical Review* 11 (1897): 344-345.

Fowler, F. N., "On Greek and Latin Negatives." *American Journal of Philology* 21 (1900): 443-445.

Frank, E., "Senses of the Particle *Dumtaxat.*" *Classical Bulletin* 36 (1960): 25-27.

Goebel, J., "On the Impersonal Verbs." *Transactions of the American Philological Association* 19 (1888): 20-33.

Granger, F., "The Influence of the Interjection on the Development of the Sentence." *Classical Review* 29 (1915): 12-18.

Greenough, J. B., "On Ellipsis in some Latin Constructions." *Harvard Studies in Classical Philology* 12 (1901): 1-7.

———. "Some Uses of *Neque, Nec* in Latin." *Harvard Studies in Classical Philology* 2 (1891): 129-148.

Hodgmann, A. V., "Latin Equivalents of Punctuation Marks." *Classical Journal* 19 (1923): 403-414.

Jones, F., "Subject, Topic, Given and Salient: Sentence Beginnings in Latin." *Proceedings of the Cambridge Philological Society* 37 (1991): 81-105.

Kelly, D. H., "Transformations in the Latin Nominal Phrase." *Classical Philology* 63 (1968): 46-52.

Kirk, W. H., "*Necdum.*" *American Journal of Philology* 24 (1903): 484.

———. "*Ne* and *Non.*" *American Journal of Philology* 44 (1923): 260-274.

Lease, E. B., "*Numne.*" *Classical Review* 11 (1897): 348-349.

———. "On the Use of *Neque* and *Nec* in Silver Latin." *Classical Review* 16 (1902): 212-214.

McCartney, E. S., "Greek and Latin Constructions of Implied Agreement." *Classical Philology* 14 (1919): 185-200.

———. "Psychological vs. Logical in Latin Syntax: Some Aspects of Synesis." *Classical Philology* 18 (1923): 289-293.

Meader, C. L., "Types of Sentence Structure in Latin Prose Writers." *Transactions of the American Philological Association* 36 (1905): 32-52.

———. "The Development of Copulative Verbs in the Indo-European Languages." *Transactions of the American Philological Association* 43 (1912): 173-200.

Meillet, A., *Remarques sur la Théorie de la Phrase.* Paris: Klincksieck, 1936.

Moore, F. G., "Studies in Tacitean Ellipsis: Descriptive Passages." *Transactions of the American Philological Association* 34 (1903): 5-26.

Morris, E. P. "*Malum* as an Interjection." *American Journal of Philology* 3 (1882): 208-211.

———. "On the Sentence Question in Plautus and Terence." *American Journal of Philology* 10 (1889): 397-437.

———. "On the Sentence Question in Plautus and Terence." *American Journal of Philology* 11 (1890): 16-55; 145-182.

Mulvany, C. M., "On the Enclitic *-Ne*." *Classical Review* 9 (1895): 15.

Murphy, P. R., "Variations on a Negative Pattern." *Classical Journal* 50 (1955): 253-254; 287.

———. "Archaiism and Colloquialism in the Use of a Latin Negative Pattern." *American Journal of Philology* 79 (1958): 44-51.

———. "The Origins and Survival of a Latin Negative Pattern." *American Journal of Philology* 77 (1956): 396-407.

Nichols, E. W., "Single Word versus Phrase." *American Journal of Philology* 42 (1922): 146-163.

Nutting, H. C., "The Indefinite First Singular." *American Journal of Philology* 45 (1924): 377-379.

———. "Note on the Indefinite Second Person Singular and Some Tendencies in Post-Augustan Latin." *University of California Publications in Classical Philology* 8: 241-249.

———. "On the Use of the Term Ellipsis." *American Journal of Philology* 51 (1930): 224-232.

———. "Prolepsis." *Classical Journal* 22 (1926): 51.

Pearce, T. E. V., "The Enclosing Word Order in the Latin Hexameter." *Classical Quarterly* 16 (1966): 140-171; 298-320.

Postgate, J. P., "On the Neuter Nominative, Some Impersonal Verbs, and Three Dramatic Quotations." *Classical Review* 18 (1904): 36-37.

Richmond, J. A., "*Atque* and *Neque* Again." *Glotta* 50 (1972): 96-97.

Solodow, J. B., *The Latin Particle Quidem*. Boulder, Colorado: American Philological Association, 1978.

Steele, R. B., "Some Phrases of Negation in Latin." *Classical Journal* 16 (1920): 1-25.

———. "The Formula *Non modo...sed etiam* and its Equivalents." *Illinois Wesleyan Magazine* (1896): 143-169.

———. "The Formula *Non modo...sed etiam* and its Equivalents." *Proceedings of the American Philological Association* 33 (1902): 65.

Walden, J. W., "*Nedum*." *Harvard Studies in Classical Philology* 2 (1891): 103-128.

Warren, M., "On the Enclitic -*Ne* in Early Latin." *American Journal of Philology* 2 (1881): 50-82.

Webster, T. B. L., "The Architecture of Sentences." In *Studies presented to M. K. Pope*. Manchester: Manchester University Press, 1939.

Whitelaw, R., "Interrogative Commands." *Classical Review* 16 (1902): 277.

Winbolt, E., "Exclamatory Questions with *"Ut"*." *Classical Review* 36 (1922): 114.

Sentence Connection

Barendt, P. O., "Ciceronian Use of *Nam* and *Enim*." *Classical Review* 16 (1902): 203 ff.

Baxter, J. H., "Some Later Latin Usages: *tam...quamque = et...et*." *Archivum Latinitatis Medii Aevi* (1932): 220-223.

Clement, W. K., "Postpositive *Etenim*." *American Journal of Philology* 7 (1886): 82.

———. "The Use of *Enim* in Plautus and Terence." *American Journal of Philology* 18 (1897): 402-416.

Coffin, H. C. "The Repeated Adversative Conjunction Again." *Classical Weekly* 15 (1922): 184.

Earle, R. H., "*Ita, Sic,* and *Tam* in the Prose Writers of the Ciceronian Period." *Transactions of the American Philological Association* 52 (1930): 43.

Elmer, H. C., "The Copulative Conjunctions *-que, et, atque* in the Inscriptions of the Republic, in Terence, and in Cato." *American Journal of Philology* 8 (1887): 292-328.

Fontenrose, J., "The Meaning and Use of *Sed enim*." *Transactions of the American Philological Association* 66 (1944): 168-195.

French, D., "Juncture in Classical Latin." Ph.D. diss., Princeton University, 1970.

Gillis, J. H., *The Coordinating Particles in Saints Hilary, Jerome, Ambrose, and Augustine.* Washington: Catholic University of America Press, 1938.

Housman, A. E., "*At tamen* and Ovid, Her. I, 2." *Classical Quarterly* 16 (1922): 88-92.

Kirk, W. H., "And an or." *American Journal of Philology* 42 (1921): 1-11.

———. "*De Quoque Adverbio*." *American Journal of Philology* 21 (1900): 303-309.

———. "*Etiam* in Plautus and Terence." *American Journal of Philology* 26 (1905): 26-42.

Knapp, C., "Comments on Dr. McCartney's Paper *About and Which*." *Classical Weekly* 26 (1933): 142-145.

———. "Notes on *Etiam* in Plautus." *Transactions of the American Philological Association* 41 (1910): 115-139.

Kroon, Caroline, "Causal Connectors in Latin. The Discourse Function of *Nam, Enim, Igitur,* and *Ergo*." In *Subordination and Other Topics in Latin: Proceedings of the Third Colloquium on Latin Linguistics in Bologna, Italy, April 1-5, 1985*, ed. by Gualtiero Calboli, 231-243. Amsterdam: Benjamins, 1989.

Lease, E. B., "Notes on Latin Syntax: *ne...quidem*." *American Journal of Philology* 30 (1909): 298-309.

———. "Notes on Quintilian: *Igitur*." *Classical Review* 13 (1899): 130.

———. "Notes on Latin Syntax: *Itaque*." *American Journal of Philology* 21 (1900): 452-456.

McCartney, E. S., "Latin Parallel to "and which" with no preceeding "which." *Classical Weekly* 26 (1933): 141-142.

Mendell, C. W., "Sentence Connection in Tacitus." Ph.D. diss., Yale University, 1911.

———. *Latin Sentence Connection.* New Haven: Yale University Press, 1917.

Nye, J., "Sentence Connection Illustrated Chiefly by Livy." Ph.D. diss., Yale University, 1912.

Poyser, G. H., "A Usage of *Nam*." *Classical Review* 66 (1952): 8-10.

Rebert, H. F., "The Origin and Meaning of Latin *"At"*." *Classical Philology* 24 (1929): 168-175.

Shipley, F. W., "Preferred and Avoided Combinations of the Enclitic *-que* in Cicero Considered in Relation to Questions of Accent and Prose Rhythm." *Classical Philology* 8 (1913): 23-47.

Sonnenschein, E. A., "*Tam...quam*." *Classical Review* 30 (1916): 158-159.

Spaeth, J. W., "Repeated Adversative Conjunctions." *Classical Weekly* 24 (1931): 103.

———. "More Repeated Adversative Conjunctions." *Classical Weekly* 21 (1928): 192 ff.

Spilman, M. M., *Cumulative Sentence Building in Latin Historical Narrative*. Berkeley: University of California Press, 1932.

Thompson, E. S., "*Quidem* in Augustan Verse." *Classical Review* 13 (1899): 395.

Tracy, H. L., "*Olim* as Particle." *Classical Weekly* 69 (1976): 431-433.

Weston, A. H., "On the Use of *Aut*." *Classical Journal* 29 (1933): 47-49.

Witt, N. W. De, "The Semantics of Latin Particles." *Classical Journal* 33 (1938): 450-456.

———. "*Abiit, Excessit, Evasit, Erupit*." *Classical Journal* 14 (1918): 331.

Subordination

Allen, B. M., "As to Cicero's Nodding." *Classical Weekly* 14 (1921): 87-88.

Andrews, M. "Caesar's Use of Tense Sequence in Indirect Speech." *Classical Review* 51 (1937): 114-116.

Brauenlich, A. F., "A Theory of the Origin of Hypotaxis." *Indogermanische Forschungen* 35 (1914): 237-244.

Coleman, R., "The Structure of Latin Complex Sentences." In *Studies in Language Companion Series* 12. Amsterdam: Benjamins, 1983.

Egger, C., "*De Recto Usu Vocis Ideo*." *Latinitas* 5 (1958): 306.

Elmore, J., "The Subjunctive in Restrictive *Qui* and *Quod* Clauses." *Classical Philology* 12 (1917): 253-258.

Fowler, S. "The Sequence of Tenses." *Classical Weekly* 4 (1911): 193.

Frank, T., "Attraction of Mood in Early Latin." Ph.D. diss., University of Chicago, 1905.

———. "The Semantics of Modal Constructions: *Nulla causa quin det.*" *Classical Philology* 3 (1908): 1-21.

Hahn, E. A., "The Development of Latin Subordinating Conjunctions." *Transactions of the American Philological Association* 62 (1940): 38.

Hale, W. G., "The Sequence of Tenses in Latin." *American Journal of Philology* 7 (1886): 446-466.

———. "The Sequence of Tenses in Latin." *American Journal of Philology* 8 (1887): 46-78.

———. "The Sequence of Tenses in Latin." *American Journal of Philology* 9 (1888): 158-178.

———. "Moods and Tenses in the Subjunctive Comparative Clauses." *American Journal of Philology* 13 (1892): 62-71.

Hamp, E. P., "Latin *Ut/Ne* and *Ut(...non).*" *Glotta* 60 (1982): 115-120.

Heffner, E. H., "The Sequence of Tenses in Plautus," Ph.D. diss., University of Pennsylvania, 1917.

Lease, E. B., "Concessive Particles in Martial." *Classical Review* 12 (1898): 30-31.

Petersen, W., "The Evidence of Early Latin on the Subjunctive in *Cum*-clauses." *Classical Philology* 19 (1931): 386-404.

Ross, D. J. Pennell, "The Order of Words in Latin Subordinate Clauses." Ph.D. diss., University of Michigan, 1987.

Sale, G. S., "On the Sequence of Tenses in Latin after a Principal Verb in the Perfect Absolute." *Classical Review* 3 (1889): 6-10.

Savundranayagam, A. P., and J. P. Postgate, "*Repraesentatio Temporum* in the *Oratio Obliqua* of Caesar." *Classical Review* 19 (1905): 207-213; 441-442.

Sonnenschein, E. A., "The Indicative in the Relative Clauses." *Classical Review* 32 (1918): 68-69.

Steele, R. B. "Some Forms of Complemental Statements in Livy." *Transactions of the American Philological Association* 33 (1902): 55-80.

———. "Affirmative Final Clauses in the Latin Historians." *American Journal of Philology* 19 (1898): 255-284.

Ting, A. M., "The Sequence of Tenses." *Classical Weekly* 30 (1936): 195.

Trayes, F. E. A., "Heresies IV: Sequence after the Pure Perfect in Latin." *Greece and Rome* 5 (1936): 98-102.

Walker, J., "The Sequence of Tenses in Latin: A Study based on Caesar's Gallic War." Ph.D. diss., University of Kansas, 1899.

Walker, A. T., "Sequence or Harmony of Tenses?" *Classical Journal* 10 (1914): 246-251.

Wright, R., Review of *Subordination and Other Topics in Latin*, ed. by Gualtiero Calboli. In *Studies in Language* 15 (1991): 227-233.

Oratio Recta and Oratio Obliqua

Allen, B. M., "Indirect Discourse and the Subjunctive of Attraction." *Classical Weekly* 15 (1922): 185-187.

Andrews, M., "The Function of Tense Variation in the Subjunctive Mood of *Oratio Obliqua*." *Classical Review* 65 (1951): 142-146.

Avery, M. M., *The Use of Direct Speech in Ovid's Metamorphoses*. Chicago: University of Chicago Library, 1837.

Fay, E. W., "Partial Obliquity in Questions of Retort." *Classical Review* 11 (1897): 344-345.

Gildersleeve, B. L., "Notes on the Evolution of the *Oratio Obliqua*." *American Journal of Philology* 27 (1906): 200-208.

Hahn, E. A., "On Direct and Indirect Discourse." *Classical Weekly* 22 (1929): 131-132.

———. "The Moods in Indirect Discourse in Latin." *Transactions of the American Philological Association* 83 (1952): 242-266.

Hale, W. G., "On the Latin Subjunctive and Greek Optative in Indirect Discourse." *Transactions of the American Philological Association* 26 (1895): 59.

Kirk, E. K., "Observations on the Indirect Volitive in Latin." *American Journal of Philology* 48 (1927): 111-121.

Muir, J. T., "*Oratio Obliqua*: Future Perfect Indicative in Conditional Clauses in Primary Sequence." *Classical Review* 44 (1930): 12.

Postgate, J. P., "*Repraesentatio Temporum* in the *Oratio Obliqua* of Caesar." *Classical Review* 19 (1905): 441-446.

Radford, R. S., "Modal and Temporal Signification." *Transactions of the American Philological Association* 23 (1892).

Salmon, E. T., "A Note on the Subordinate Clauses in *Oratio Obliqua*." *Classical Review* 45 (1931): 173.

Schleicher, J., "The Moods of Indirect Quotation." *American Journal of Philology* 26 (1905): 60-88.

Spicker, E., "On Direct Speech Introduced by a Conjunction." *American Journal of Philology* 5 (1884): 221-227.

Stephens, L. D., "Doings and Happenings. Why *Fore ut* + Subjunctive." *American Philological Association Abstracts* 18 (1988): 35.

———. "The Latin Construction *Fore/Futurum* (*esse*) *ut*(*i*). Syntactic, Semantic, Pragmatic, and Diachronic Considerations." *American Journal of Philology* 110 (1989): 595-627.

———. "The Development of *Fore/Futurum Ut* from Ovid to Festus: A Study in Semantic Change and its Basis in Discourse Situation." *American Journal of Philology* 111 (1990): 513-542.

Terrell, G., "The Apodosis of the Unreal Condition in the *Oratio Obliqua* in Latin." *American Journal of Philology* 25 (1904): 59-73.

Wales, M. L., "Another Look at the Latin Accusative and Infinitive." *Lingua* 56 (1982): 127-152.

Woodcock, E. C., "Rhetorical Questions in *Oratio Obliqua*." *Greece and Rome* 21 (1952): 37-42.

Questions

Adams, J. N., Review of "*L'Interrogation Indirecte en Latin*," by Colette Bodelot, in *Classical Review* 39 (1989): 405.

Bailey, D. R. Shackleton, "*Num* in Direct Questions: A Rule Restated." *Classical Quarterly* 47 (1952): 120-125.

Baxter, J. H., "Some Later Latin Usages: *An...aut* = *Utrum...an*." *Archivum Latinitatis Medii Aevi* (1932): 220-223.

Brauenlich, A. F., "The Confusion of the Indirect Question and the Relative Clause." *Classical Philology* 13 (1918): 60-74.

———. "The Indicative in the Indirect Question in Latin." Ph.D. diss., University of Chicago, 1921.

Deane, J. P., "Deliberative Interrogations in Terence." *Transactions of the American Philological Association* 21 (1890): 28.

Exon, C., "Latin Questions of the Types *Quid Ago* and *Quid Agam*." *Hermathena* 44 (1926): 17-29.

Handford, S. A., "Tense-Sequence in Indirect Questions." *Greece and Rome* 18 (1849): 138.

Murphy, Paul R., "On Questions Introduced by *Non* and *Nonne*." *Classical Journal* 86 (1990-1991): 226-232.

Stephens, L. D., "Indirect Questions in Old Latin." *Illinois Classical Studies* 10 (1986): 195-214.

Prohibitives

Ashmore, S. G., "On the So-called Prohibitive in Terence." *Proceedings of the American Philological Association* 32 (1901): 85.

Fowler, F. H., "Clauses of Willed Result." *Classical Philology* 15 (1920): 46-53.

Geddes, W. D., "The Sequence after *Ne* Prohibitive." *Classical Review* 12 (1898): 355-359.

Lease, E. B., "Livy's Use of *Neque* and *Neve* with an Imperative or Subjunctive." *Classical Philology* 3 (1908): 302-307.

Steele, R. B., Ut, Ne, Quin, *and* Quominus *in Livy*. Leipzig: Brockhaus, 1911.

Subordinate Relatives

Elerick, C., "Latin Relative Clause of Purpose. Lexical, Syntactic and Stylistic Determinants." In *Syntaxe Latin. Actes du II congrès international de linguistique latine*, ed. C. Touratier, *Aix-en-Provence: Univ. de Provence*, 1985.

Fowler, F. H., "The Origin of Latin *Qui*-Clauses." *Language* 7 (1931): 14-29.

McCartney, E. S., "Latin Parallel to "and which" with no preceeding "Which." *Classical Weekly* 26 (1933): 141-142.

Mendell, C. W., "The Anticipatory Element in Latin Sentence Connection." *Transactions of the American Philological Association* 43 (1912): 51.

Sonnenschein, E. A., "The Indicative in Relative Clauses." *Classical Review* 32 (1918): 68-69.

Steele, R. B., "Relative Temporal Statements in Latin." *American Journal of Philology* 31 (1910): 265-286.

Quod and Quia

Elmore, J. "The Subjunctive in the So-called Restrictive *Quod*-Clauses." *Transactions of the American Philological Association* 35 (1904): 55.

———. "The Subjunctive in Restrictive *Qui* and *Quod* Clauses." *Classical Philology* 12 (1917): 253-258.

Frank, T., "The Semantics of Modal Constructions: *Non habet quod det, nulla causast quin det*." *Classical Philology* 2 (1907): 163-187.

———. "The Semantics of Modal Constructions: *Non habet quod det, nulla causast quin det*." *Classical Philology* 3 (1908): 1-22.

Hale, W. G., "The Mode in the Phrase *Quod Sciam*, etc." *Proceedings of the American Philological Association* 22 (1891): 105.

Ingersoll, J. W. D., "*Quod*: Its Use and Meaning, especially in Cicero." *Proceedings of the American Philological Association* 30 (1900): 30-35.

Steele, R. B., "Causal Clauses in Livy." *American Journal of Philology* 27 (1906): 46-58.

Taylor, M. E., "The Development of the *Quod*-Clause." *Yale Classical Studies* 12 (1951): 227-249.

Quam, Antequam, Priusquam, Quamvis, etc.

Baker, W., "*Quandoquidem* or *Quandŏquidem*." *Classical Review* 17 (1903): 313-316.

Baxter, J. H., "Some Later Latin Usages: *Quoniam*." *Archivum Latinitatis Medii Aevi* (1932): 220-223.

Fowler, E. H., "The Origin of the *Quin* Clauses." *Classical Philology* 3 (1908): 408-428.

———. "The *Mirum-Quin* Sentences." *Classical Philology* 7 (1912): 355-357.

Hale, W. G., "Mode and Tense in the Subjunctive Comparative Clause in Latin." *American Journal of Philology* 13 (1892): 62-71.

———. *The Cum-Constructions: Their History and Functions.* Ithaca: Cornell University Studies in Classical Philology, 1887.

———. *The Cum-Constructions: Their History and Functions.* Ithaca: Cornell University Studies in Classical Philology, 1889.

Helm, N. W., "The Comparative Frequency of *Antequam* and *Priusquam*." *Classical Review* 14 (1900): 262-263.

Hullihen, W., "*Antequam* and *Priusquam* with Special Reference to the Historical Development of their Subjunctive Usage." Ph.D. diss., Johns Hopkins, 1903.

Kennedy, A. J., *On the Use of* Ne *in Horatius*. Cambridge: Cambridge Philological Society, 1883.

Kirk, W. H., "*Ne* and *Non*." *American Journal of Philology* 44 (1893): 260.

Knapp, C., "The *Cum*-Constructions Again." *Classical Weekly* 11 (1918): 168.

Lease, E. B., "Notes on Latin Syntax: the Use of *Antequam* and *Priusquam*." *American Journal of Philology* 30 (1909): 298-309.

———. "Concessive Particles in Martial." *Classical Review* 12 (1898): 30.

———. "Notes on Quintilian." *Classical Review* 13 (1899): 130.

Long, O. F., "On the Use of *Quotiens* and *Quotienscumque* in Different Periods of Latin." Ph.D. diss., Johns Hopkins University, 1901.

Mendell, C. W., "*Ut* Clauses." *American Journal of Philology* 46 (1925): 293-316.

———. "*Ut* Clauses." *American Journal of Philology* 47 (1926): 124-152.

Nisbet, R. G., "*Voluntas Fati* in Latin Syntax: Final *Ut*." *American Journal of Philology* 44 (1923): 27-43.

Nutting, H. C., Queries as to the *Cum*-Constructions." *University of California Publications in Classical Philology* 8 (1927): 289-303.

———. "Notes on the *Cum*-Constructions." *Classical Journal* 16 (1920): 26-33.

———. "Caesar's Use of Past Tenses in *Cum*-Clauses." *University of California Publications in Classical Philology* 5 (1918): 1-52.

———. "On the History of the *Cum*-Constructions." *American Journal of Philology* 54 (1933): 29-38.

———. "Circumstantial-Temporal *Cum*-Clauses." *Classical Weekly* 10 (1917): 16.

———. "Predicating Periods in Latin." *American Journal of Philology* 51 (1930): 57-61.

Owen, S. G., "On the Meaning of *Sicut*." *Classical Review* 12 (1898): 440-441.

Pascal, C., "*Credo ut*." *Hermathena* 55 (1929): 210-211.

Petersen, W., "The Evidence of Early Latin on the Subjunctive in *Cum*-Clauses." *Classical Philology* 26 (1931): 386-404.

Rolfe, J. C., "Some Temporal Expressions in Suetonius." *Classical Philology* 8 (1913): 1-13.

Rouse, W. H. D., "Indefinite *Quam* in Caesar." *Classical Review* 25 (1911): 74-75.

Schlicher, J. J., "The Temporal *Cum*-Clauses and Their Rivals." *Classical Philology* 4 (1909): 256-275.

———. "The Subjunctive in Consecutive Clauses." *Classical Philology* 2 (1907): 79-81.

Sonnenschein, E. A., "Interrogative Commands: A New Theory of Prohibitives in light of *Quin* with Moods of Command." *Classical Review* 16 (1903): 105-169.

Steele, R. B., "Relative Temporal Statements in Latin." *American Journal of Philology* 31 (1910): 265-286.

———. Ut, Ne, *and* Quominus *in Livy*. Leipzig: Brockhaus, 1911.

Trehern, E. M., "Heresies IV: *Ubi* Temporal?" *Greece and Rome* 13 (1944): 81-82.

Wild, H. D., "Notes on the Historical Syntax of *Quamvis*." *American Journal of Philology* 17 (1896): 347-352.

Conditional Sentences

Elden, W. S., "Notes on the Conditional Sentence in Horace." *Proceedings of the American Philological Association* 33 (1901): 93.

Greenough, J., "Some Features of the Contrary to Fact Construction." *Harvard Studies in Classical Philology* 7 (1896): 13-20.

Horton-Smith, R., *The Theory of the Conditional Sentence in Greek and Latin.* London: MacMillan, 1894.

Lodge, G., "On the Theory of the Unreal Condition in Latin." In *Studies in Honor of B. L. Gildersleeve.* Baltimore: Johns Hopkins, 1902.

Mugler, F., "Concerning the Usage and Evolution of the Conditional Sentence." *Glotta* 58 (1980): 119-132.

Nutting, H. C., *The Latin Conditional Sentence.* Berkeley: University of California Press, 1925.

———. "Notes on Cicero's Use of the Imperfect and Pluperfect Subjunctive in *Si*-Clauses." *American Journal of Philology* 21 (1900): 260-273.

———. "The Order of the Conditional Thought." *American Journal of Philology* 24 (1903): 25-39; 149-163; 278-303.

———. "Notes on the Correlatives of *Si*." *Transactions of the American Philological Association* 37 (1906): 49.

———. "Some Theories on Subjunctive Protasis with Indicative Apodosis." *Classical Review* 17 (1903): 449-456.

———. "The Substantive *Si*-Clause." *Classical Philology* 3 (1908): 178-183.

———. "The *Si*-Clause in Substantive Use." *University of California Publications in Classical Philology* 8 (1926): 129-142.

———. "Cicero's Conditional Clauses of Comparison." *University of California Publications in Classical Philology* 5 (1922): 183-251.

———. "The Form *Si sit...erit*." *University of California Publications in Classical Philology* 8 (1926): 187 ff.

———. "Elliptic Conditional Sentences." *Classical Weekly* 14 (1921): 94.

Oliver, A., "*Ni*-Clauses in Vergil." *Transactions of the American Philological Association* 38 (1907): 40.

Pope, M., "*Quid si non*: An Idiom in Latin." *Phoenix* 36 (1982): 53-70.

Ritchie, M. H., "A Study of Conditional and Temporal Clauses in Pliny the Younger." Ph.D. diss., University of Pennsylvania, 1902.

Roby, H. J., "The Conditional Sentence in Latin." *Classical Review* 1 (1887): 197.

Sonnenschein, E. A., "Notes on Conditional Sentences in Latin." *Classical Review* 1 (1887): 124-128; 238-239.

Steele, R. B., *Conditional Statements in Livy*. Leipzig: Brockhaus, 1910.

———. "Analysis and Interpretation of Conditional Statements." *Classical Journal* 13 (1917): 354-363.

Witton, W. F., "Heresies 5: *Si quid habeam*." *Greece and Rome* 6 (1936): 46-48.

Dum, Donec, Quoad

Hahn, E. A., "The *Dum* Proviso Clause." *Transactions of the American Philological Association* 57 (1935): 199-207.

Knapp, C., "Catullus 62: 39-58." *Transactions of the American Philological Association* 27 (1897): 25-27.

Lease, E. B., "Notes on Quintilian." *Classical Review* 13 (1899): 130.

Wightman, A. R., "*De Dum Donec Quoad Coniunctionum Usu apud Ciceronem, Caesarem, Tacitum, Plinium Minorem, Suetonium*." Ph.D. diss., Harvard University, 1909.

Word Order

Adams, J. N., "A Type of Hyperbaton in Latin Prose." *Proceedings of the Cambridge Philological Society* 17 (1971): 1-16.

———. "A Typological Approach to Latin Word Order." *Indogermanische Forschungen* 81 (1976): 70-99.

Brink, K. O., "A Forgotten Figure of Style in Tacitus." *Classical Review* 30 (1944): 43-45.

Bryant, A. A., "Some Plautine Words and Word Groups." *Harvard Studies in Classical Philology* 9 (1898): 121-125.

Butler, N. M., "On the Postpositive *"Et"* in Propertius." *American Journal of Philology* 6 (1885): 349-350.

Conway, R. S., "On the Interweaving of Words with Pairs of Parallel Phrases." *Classical Review* 14 (1900): 357-360.

Cunningham, M. P., "Latin Word Order: The Status *Quaestionis*." *Yearbook of the American Philosophical Association* (1954): 360-370.

Greenberg, N. A., "Word Juncture in Latin Prose and Poetry." *Transactions of the American Philological Association* 121 (1991): 297-333.

Hahn, E. A., "Vestiges of Partitive Apposition in Latin Syntax." *Transactions of the American Philological Association* 84 (1953): 92-123.

Hempl, G., "The Psychological Basis of Word Order." *Proceedings of the American Philological Association* 31 (1900): 30.

Hodgmann, A. W., "Word Grouping in Vergil." *Classical Weekly* 14 (1920): 193-195.

Ingraham, A., "Word Order in Lucan." *Transactions of the American Philological Association* 22 (1891): 10.

Hutchins, L., "The Place of Demonstrative Adjectives in Plautus and Terence." Ph.D. diss., University of Chicago, 1935.

Jong, J. R. De, "Word Order within Latin Noun Phrases." In *Studies in Language Companion Series* 12. Amsterdam: Benjamins, 1983.

Keep, W. L., "The Separation of the Attributive Adjective from its Substantive in Plautus." *University of California Publications in Classical Philology* 2 (1911): 151-164.

Kellog, G. D., "Cross-suggestion: A Form of Tacitean Brachylogy.

Lateiner, Donald, "Mimetic Syntax: Metaphor from Word Order, especially in Ovid." *American Journal of Philology* 111 (1990): 204-237.

Meader, C. L., "Notes on the Order of Words in Latin." *Proceedings of the American Philological Association* 34 (1903): 31.

Menk, E. A., "The Position of the Possessive Pronouns in Cicero's Orations." Ph.D. diss., University of Iowa, 1925.

Naylor, H. D., *Horace, Odes and Epodes: A Study in Poetic Word Order*. Cambridge: Cambridge University Press, 1922.

Naylor, H. D., "Quintilian on Latin Word Order." *Classical Review* 37 (1923): 156.

Hutting, H. C., "Hysteron Proteron." *Classical Journal* 11 (1915): 298-301.

Ostafin, D. M., "Studies in Latin Word Order. A Transformational Approach." Ph.D. diss., University of Connecticut, 1986.

Palmer, W. H., "The Use of Anaphora in the Amplification of a General Truth." *Transactions of the American Philological Association* 45 (1914): 1.

———. "Anaphora: Its Origin and Use." *Washington University Studies* 5 (1917): 51.

Panduis, D. G. J., "The Communicative Perspective in Latin Word Order." Ph.D. diss., University of Michigan, 1981.

———. "Archaic and Contemporary Speech: Word Order in the Formula *Deum Virtute* in Plautus." *Indogermanische Forschungen* 89 (1984): 26-28.

Postgate, C. P., "On Trajection of Words or Hyperbaton." *Classical Review* 30 (1916): 143-146.

Prescott, H. W., "Some Phases of the Relation of Thought to Verse in Plautus." *University of California Publications in Classical Philology* (1907): 205-262.

———. "Studies in the Grouping of Nouns in Plautus." *Classical Philology* 4 (1909): 1-25.

———. "The Position of Deferred Nouns and Adjectives in Epic and Dramatic Verse." *Classical Philology* 7 (1912): 35-58.

Roberts, W. Rhys., "A Point of Greek and Latin Word Order." *Classical Review* 26 (1912): 177-179.

Sadler, J. D., "Latin Paranomasia." *Classical Journal* 78 (1982): 138-141.

Schwegler, A., "Predicate Negation and Word-Order Change: A Problem of Multiple Causation." *Lingua* 61 (1983): 297-334.

Smiley, E. F., "A Study in Latin Word Order." *Classical Journal* 8 (1913): 364-365.

Steele, R. B., "Anaphora and Chiasmus in Livy." *Transactions of the American Philological Association* 32 (1901): 154-186.

———. "Chiasmus in Sallust, Caesar, Tacitus, and Justinus." Ph.D. diss., Johns Hopkins University, 1892.

———. "Chiasmus in the Epistles of Cicero, Seneca, Pliny, and Fronto." In *Studies in Honor of B. L. Gildersleeve*. Baltimore: Johns Hopkins, 1902.

Ulman, B. L., "Latin Word Order." *Classical Journal* 14 (1919): 404-417.

Walker, A. T., "Some Facts of Latin Word Order." *Classical Journal* 13 (1918): 644-657.

Warner, R., "Word Order in Old Latin: Copulative Phrases." *Orbis* 29 (1980): 251-263.

Whitsel, L. A., "Studies in the Grouping of Words in Roman Comedy." Ph.D., diss., University of Wisconsin, 1932.

Young, A. M., "Schematized Word Order in Vergil." *Classical Journal* 27 (1932): 515.

———. "Pictorial Arrangement of Words in Vergil." *Transactions of the American Philological Association* 64 (1933): 51-52.